THE CAMBRIDGE HISTORY OF
THE AGE OF ATLANTIC REVOLUTIONS

*

VOLUME II

France, Europe, and Haiti

Volume II delves into the revolutions of France, Europe, and Haiti, with particular focus on the French Revolution and the changes it wrought. The demarcation between property and power, and the changes in family life, religious practices, and socioeconomic relations are explored, as well as the preoccupation with violence and terror, both of which were conspicuous aspects of the revolutions. Simultaneous movements in England, Germany, Hungary, Ireland, Italy, and Poland–Lithuania are also discussed. The volume ends with the Haitian Revolution and its impact on neighboring countries, revealing how the revolution was comprised of several smaller revolutions, and how, once the independent black State of Haiti was established, an effort was made to fulfill the promises of freedom and equality.

WIM KLOOSTER is Professor and the Robert H. and Virginia N. Scotland Endowed Chair in History and International Relations at Clark University. He is the (co-)author and (co-)editor of twelve books. His monograph *The Dutch Moment: War, Trade, and Settlement in the Seventeenth-Century Atlantic World* won the Biennial Book Award of the Forum on Early-Modern Empires and Global Interactions and the Hendricks Award of the New Netherland Institute.

THE CAMBRIDGE HISTORY OF
THE AGE OF ATLANTIC REVOLUTIONS

Edited by
WIM KLOOSTER

In three volumes, *The Cambridge History of the Age of Atlantic Revolutions* brings together experts on all corners of the Atlantic World who reveal the age in all its complexity. The Age of Atlantic Revolutions formed the transition from an era marked by monarchical rule, privileges, and colonialism to an age that stood out for republican rule, legal equality, and the sovereignty of American nations. The seventy-one chapters included reflect the latest trends and discussions on this transformative part of history, not only highlighting the causes, key events, and consequences of the revolutions, but also stressing political experimentation, contingency, and the survival of colonial institutions. The volumes also examine the attempts of enslaved and indigenous people, and free people of color, to change their plight, offering a much-needed revision to R. R. Palmer's first synthesis of this era sixty years ago.

The Cambridge History of the Age of Atlantic Revolutions, Volume I: The Enlightenment and the British Colonies
EDITED BY WIM KLOOSTER

The Cambridge History of the Age of Atlantic Revolutions, Volume II: France, Europe, and Haiti
EDITED BY WIM KLOOSTER

The Cambridge History of the Age of Atlantic Revolutions, Volume III: The Iberian Empires
EDITED BY WIM KLOOSTER

THE CAMBRIDGE HISTORY OF
THE AGE OF ATLANTIC REVOLUTIONS

*

VOLUME II

France, Europe, and Haiti

WIM KLOOSTER
Clark University, Massachusetts

Shaftesbury Road, Cambridge CB2 8EA, United Kingdom

One Liberty Plaza, 20th Floor, New York, NY 10006, USA

477 Williamstown Road, Port Melbourne, VIC 3207, Australia

314–321, 3rd Floor, Plot 3, Splendor Forum, Jasola District Centre, New Delhi – 110025, India

103 Penang Road, #05-06/07, Visioncrest Commercial, Singapore 238467

Cambridge University Press is part of Cambridge University Press & Assessment, a department of the University of Cambridge.

We share the University's mission to contribute to society through the pursuit of education, learning and research at the highest international levels of excellence.

www.cambridge.org
Information on this title: www.cambridge.org/9781108475983

DOI: 10.1017/9781108599405

© Cambridge University Press & Assessment 2023

This publication is in copyright. Subject to statutory exception and to the provisions of relevant collective licensing agreements, no reproduction of any part may take place without the written permission of Cambridge University Press & Assessment.

First published 2023

Printed in the United Kingdom by TJ Books Limited, Padstow, Cornwall

A catalogue record for this publication is available from the British Library.

Library of Congress Cataloging-in-Publication Data
NAMES: Klooster, Wim, editor.
TITLE: The Cambridge history of the age of Atlantic revolutions / Wim Klooster.
DESCRIPTION: Cambridge, United Kingdom ; New York : Cambridge University Press, 2023. | Includes bibliographical references and index.
IDENTIFIERS: LCCN 2022058499 (print) | LCCN 2022058500 (ebook) | ISBN 9781108476034 (v. 1 ; hardback) | ISBN 9781108469432 (v. 1 ; paperback) | ISBN 9781108475983 (v. 2 ; hardback) | ISBN 9781108469326 (v. 2 ; paperback) | ISBN 9781108599405 (v. 2 ; eub) | ISBN 9781108475969 (v. 3 ; hardback) | ISBN 9781108469319 (v. 3 ; paperback) | ISBN 9781108598248 (v. 3 ; epub) | ISBN 9781108567671 (v. 1 ; epub)
SUBJECTS: LCSH: Revolutions–History–18th century. | Social change–History–18th century. | Revolutions–History–19th century. | Social change–History–19th century. | History, Modern–18th century. | History, Modern–19th century.
CLASSIFICATION: LCC D308 .C36 2023 (print) | LCC D308 (ebook) | DDC 940.2/7–dc23/eng/20221207
LC record available at https://lccn.loc.gov/2022058499
LC ebook record available at https://lccn.loc.gov/2022058500

ISBN – 3 Volume Set 9781108567817 Hardback
ISBN – Volume I 9781108476034 Hardback
ISBN – Volume II 9781108475983 Hardback
ISBN – Volume III 9781108475969 Hardback

Cambridge University Press & Assessment has no responsibility for the persistence or accuracy of URLs for external or third-party internet websites referred to in this publication and does not guarantee that any content on such websites is, or will remain, accurate or appropriate.

Contents

List of Figures ix
List of Maps xi
List of Contributors to Volume II xii
Preface xiii

Introduction 1
WIM KLOOSTER

PART I
FRANCE

1 · Overview of the French Revolution 53
DAVID ANDRESS

2 · Abolishing Feudalism 78
RAFE BLAUFARB

3 · The Countryside 100
NOELLE PLACK

4 · The Revolution and the Atlantic: The Society of the Friends of the Blacks 118
ERICA JOHNSON EDWARDS

5 · Tracking the French Revolution in the United States: Popular Sovereignty, Representation, Absolutism, and Democracy 143
MATTHEW RAINBOW HALE

6 · The French Revolution and Spanish America   172
CLÉMENT THIBAUD

7 · Violence and the French Revolution   195
HOWARD G. BROWN

8 · Jacobins and Terror in the French Revolution   225
MARISA LINTON

9 · The Directory, Thermidor, and the Transformation of the Revolution   247
PHILIPPE BOURDIN

10 · Rethinking Gender, Sexuality, and the French Revolution   272
JENNIFER NGAIRE HEUER

PART II
WESTERN, CENTRAL, AND EASTERN EUROPE

11 · Switzerland: Local Agency and French Intervention: The Helvetic Republic   303
MARC H. LERNER

12 · Revolution at Geneva: Genevans in Revolution   329
RICHARD WHATMORE

13 · The Modernity of the Dutch Revolution: Ideas, Action, Permeation   349
JORIS ODDENS

14 · The United States of Belgium   375
JANET POLASKY

15 · Revolution in England? Abolitionism   396
SEYMOUR DRESCHER

16 · The Irish Rebellion of 1798   421
THOMAS BARTLETT

17 · Italy: Revolution and Counterrevolution (1789–1799)   443
JOHN A. DAVIS

18 · Germany and the French Revolution   467
MICHAEL ROWE

19 · Reform and Resistance: Hungary and the Habsburg Monarchy, 1780–1795   490
ORSOLYA SZAKÁLY

20 · Poland–Lithuania in the Age of Atlantic Revolutions: Dilemmas of Liberty   514
RICHARD BUTTERWICK

21 · Transnational Perspectives: The French Revolution, the Sister Republics, and the United States   540
ANNIE JOURDAN

PART III
HAITI

22 · Overview of the Haitian Revolution   563
ROBERT D. TABER

23 · Saint-Domingue on the Eve of the Revolution   588
JOHN GARRIGUS

24 · The Haitian Revolutions   614
BERNARD GAINOT

25 · Toussaint Louverture, the Cultivator System, and Haiti's Independence (1798–1804)   637
PHILIPPE GIRARD

26 · Establishing a New Nation: Haiti after Independence, 1804–1843   663
ERIN ZAVITZ

27 · Aspirations and Actions of Free People of Color across the Caribbean   689
JESSICA PIERRE-LOUIS

Contents

28 · The Unruly Caribbean: Reverberations of Saint-Domingue's Rebellions on the Caribbean Coast of New Granada and Venezuela, 1790–1800 715
CRISTINA SORIANO

29 · The Impact of the Haitian Revolution on the United States 739
ASHLI WHITE

Index 761

Figures

4.1	Jacques-Pierre Brissot.	119
7.1	The taking of the Tuileries Palace.	205
7.2	Execution of Robespierre and his men.	211
9.1	Allegorical figure representing Justice during the Directory.	250
9.2	Democracy, represented by the statue, embattled during the Directory.	255
13.1	The Committee of the Confederacy. Print, possibly by James Gillray, after David Hess. Satirical representation of the discord between the seven provinces during the first year of the Batavian Revolution (1795), which did not look so different from the situation in the old-regime Dutch Republic.	357
13.2	Grim festivities in Rotterdam. Print by Reinier Vinkeles after Jacobus Buys. Depiction of a riotous procession of Orangist shipwrights, led by a figure dressed as a Harlequin, on 8 March 1783, the birthday of Stadtholder William V.	365
14.1	The Brabant Lion sweeping the Grand Place in Brussels clean of soldiers during the Brabant Revolution.	390
16.1	Chaotic scenes at the rebel camp at Vinegar Hill (1798).	431
18.1	The siege of Mainz (1793).	483
19.1	Emperor Joseph II.	491
19.2	The coronation of Leopold II.	508
20.1	Tadeusz Kościuszko.	515
22.1	Fighting in the hills.	576
22.2	French reprisals.	583
25.1	Louverture's constitution.	648
26.1	Parade ground at Sans-Souci.	676
26.2	Cap-Haïtien.	685
27.1	Marius-Pierre Le Masurier, *Famille métisse*. Mixed-race family in Martinique, 1775.	691

27.2 Nicolas André Monsiau, The National Convention abolishes slavery in the French colonies, 1794.   704
27.3 G. Thompson, The British capture of Martinique in 1809.   709
29.1 Pillaging of Cap Français, 1793.   749

Maps

1.1   A map of France in 1789.   63
6.1   Revolts in the Caribbean, 1794–1799.   194
7.1   Military threats to France, 1792–1794.   208
16.1 Army barracks in eighteenth-century Ireland.   427
18.1 The Holy Roman Empire.   468
24.1 The Haitian Revolution, 1791–1793.   620
25.1 Saint-Domingue in 1791.   641
28.1 The Caribbean in the 1790s.   719

Contributors to Volume 11

David Andress
Thomas Bartlett
Rafe Blaufarb
Philippe Bourdin
Howard G. Brown
Richard Butterwick
John A. Davis
Seymour Drescher
Erica Johnson Edwards
Bernard Gainot
John Garrigus
Philippe Girard
Matthew Rainbow Hale
Jennifer Ngaire Heuer
Annie Jourdan
Marc H. Lerner
Marisa Linton
Joris Oddens
Jessica Pierre-Louis
Noelle Plack
Janet Polasky
Michael Rowe
Cristina Soriano
Orsolya Szakály
Robert D. Taber
Clément Thibaud
Richard Whatmore
Ashli White
Erin Zavitz

Preface

I thank Debbie Gershenowitz and Cecelia Cancellaro at Cambridge University Press for the smooth and pleasant collaboration. I would also like to express my gratitude to the three scholars who made up an advisory board that assisted me in choosing the contributors: Rafe Blaufarb, Ben Weider Eminent Scholar in Napoleonic Studies at Florida State University, Patrick Griffin, Madden-Hennebry Professor of History at the University of Notre Dame, and Gabriel Paquette, Professor of History at the Johns Hopkins University. All three have also written a chapter in this book.

About a dozen of the chapters were first presented at the workshop "Black Men and Women in the Age of Revolutions" in January 2020. I thank Yale University for providing an excellent venue for the workshop and Mark Peterson for making arrangements.

Some contributors contracted Covid-19, whereas others were affected by lockdowns. I thank them all for their perseverance. Although a number of invited authors reneged on their contractual promise to write a chapter far into the project, I am confident that the age of Atlantic revolutions has been covered sufficiently in the pages that follow.

Wim Klooster

Introduction

WIM KLOOSTER

Sixty years ago, R. R. Palmer published his two-volume *Age of the Democratic Revolution*, in which he described a "revolution of Western Civilization," that, he argued, had occurred in the years between 1760 and 1800. These decades, Palmer went on, saw numerous agitations, upheavals, and conspiracies on either side of the Atlantic, that arose out of specific or universal conditions, not simply as the result of the French Revolution. What Palmer outlined was what we now call the Age of (Atlantic) Revolutions, a theme that has been and continues to be the inspiration for high-quality publications, in part because this period in history supposedly laid the foundations for the countries shaped in the aftermath of these revolutions, and in part because of the need to explain the unusual political activity and social upheaval on display in this era. Virtually absent from the countless monographs, articles, and edited volumes is an overview of this important period in Atlantic history. Many specialists work within their own subfield, writing and conducting research on, for example, the American Revolution without closely following the newest trends in scholarship on the revolutions in France or Latin America. The aim of this book is to bring together current scholarship for the first reference work dedicated to the age of revolutions. Jointly, the chapters that make up this book will reveal the era in all its complexity. They will reflect the latest trends, discussing more than simply the causes, key events, and consequences of the revolutions by stressing political experimentation, contingency, and the survival of old regime practices and institutions. The time is ripe for analyzing these matters in a way that does justice to both the local nature of the revolts and their much wider Atlantic context.

Most scholars of the Age of Revolutions no longer share Palmer's geographic and temporal frameworks. They include the quarter-century (or more) after 1800 and look beyond western Europe and the United States to Haiti and Latin America. No general agreement exists, however, on the exact start and end dates, nor on its confinement to the Atlantic world. The periodization advocated by C. A. Bayly, who has made a case for the timeframe 1760–1840, is about the same as that adopted in this *Cambridge History of the Age of Atlantic Revolutions*.[1] Like any time limits, these are somewhat arbitrary. One could push the outer boundary to 1848. By that year of revolution, however, so many new factors and forces had emerged on the various national political scenes – including full-fledged liberalism and nationalism, and capitalism's working class – that there is more reason to see them as elements of a new era.

Although the geographic scope of these three volumes is vast, it has been my choice not to include all instances of rebellion, but to focus on coherence. What ties the numerous rebellious movements on either side of the Atlantic basin together in the half-century between the shots fired at Lexington and Concord (1775) and the Spanish loss at the siege of Callao, Peru in 1826 is more than just the, often violent, transitions from old to new regimes. The common glue is what marked these transitions: the questioning of time-honored institutions in the name of liberty; the invention and spread of a politics of contestation at local and national levels; the unprecedented experimentation with new forms of democracy; the abolition of numerous forms of legal inequality; and last but not least the aspiration to universal rights. These were processes in which plebeians, elites, and members of middling groups all participated. These phenomena were not experienced wherever in the world riots and rebellions broke out. They were largely absent, for example, from the Ottoman empire, although it was in great turmoil during the age of revolutions, especially in the years 1806–1808, when two sultans were deposed and thousands of people killed.[2]

What the age of revolutions brought was hope for fundamental change, a scarce good in the early modern world. Any criticism of authorities had previously been forbidden and heavily punished. It was only during periods of unrest that peasants in Europe could express their dissatisfaction without fear of reprisal. In such times, there are also glimpses of the hidden transcript of enslaved men and women throughout the Americas, which reflected the

---

[1] C. A. Bayly, *The Birth of the Modern World, 1780–1914: Global Connections and Comparisons* (Oxford: Oxford University Press, 2004); C. A. Bayly, "The Age of Revolutions in Global Context: An Afterword," in David Armitage and Sanjay Subrahmanyam, eds., *The Age of Revolutions in Global Context, c. 1760–1840* (Houndmills: Palgrave Macmillan, 2010), 209–17: 217.

[2] Ali Yaycioglu, *Partners of the Empire: The Crisis of the Ottoman Order in the Age of Revolutions* (Stanford: Stanford University Press, 2016), 158.

awakening of their hopes.³ A historian of the Russian Revolution has written that "revolutions disrupt assumptions that the future can only appear along the straight tracks where the present seems to be heading, and so challenge how we understand time and history ... Utopia is this open disruption of the now, for the sake of possibility, not a closed map of the future. It is the leap not yet the landing."⁴ This leap was made time and again by the oppressed. On the eve of the French and Haitian Revolutions, writes **John Garrigus** (Volume II, Chapter 23), many enslaved residents of Saint-Domingue "believed change was possible, whether that came through applying new laws or actively confronting the master class." For the 1790s, no fewer than forty-seven slave revolts and conspiracies have been documented for the Greater Caribbean, a number much larger than ever before or afterwards. Similarly, the years 1789–1802 saw 150 mutinies on single ships and half a dozen fleet-wide mutinies in the British, French, and Dutch navies, which meant that between 67,000 and 100,000 mobilized men were involved in at least one mutiny.⁵

Hope in the American Revolution often took the form of millennial expectations, which were so intense "during the early years of the revolutionary war that numerous patriots foresaw the final destruction of Antichrist and the establishment of the Kingdom of God within the immediate future." One revolutionary on Long Island saw the millennium as "the happy period when tyranny, oppression, and wretchedness shall be banished from the earth; when universal love and liberty, peace and righteousness, shall prevail."⁶ The French Revolution aroused hope, both at home and abroad, that tended to be secular in nature. After arriving in France in 1792 as the United States' Minister Plenipotentiary, Gouverneur Morris wrote in a letter that he was delighted to find "on this Side of the Atlantic a strong resemblance to what I left on the other – a Nation which exists in Hopes, Prospects, and Expectations. The reverence for ancient Establishments gone, existing Forms shaken to the very Foundation, and a new Order of Things about

---

³ Martin Merki-Vollenwyder, *Unruhige Untertanen: Die Rebellion der Luzerner Bauern im Zweiten Villmergerkrieg (1712)* (Luzern: Rex Verlag, 1995), 121–2; James C. Scott, *Domination and the Arts of Resistance: Hidden Transcripts* (New Haven: Yale University Press, 1990).
⁴ Mark D. Steinberg, *The Russian Revolution 1905–1921* (Oxford: Oxford University Press, 2017), 292–3.
⁵ David Geggus, "Slave Rebellion during the Age of Revolution," in Wim Klooster and Gert Oostindie, eds., *Curaçao in the Age of Revolutions, 1795–1800* (Leiden: KITLV Press, 2011), 23–56: 41–3; Nyklas Frykman, *The Bloody Flag: Mutiny in the Age of Atlantic Revolution* (Oakland: University of California Press, 2020), 10.
⁶ Ruth H. Bloch, *Visionary Republic: Millennial Themes in American Thought, 1756–1800* (Cambridge: Cambridge University Press, 1985), 79, 81.

to take Place in which even to the very names, all former Institutions will be disregarded."⁷ The imagined new order caused tremendous optimism on the part of enthusiasts for the French Revolution. Norwegian-born Henrik Steffens recalled in his memoirs that when he was sixteen and living with his family in Copenhagen, his father came home one day, deeply impressed by the French Revolution, and told his three sons: "Children, you are to be envied, what a happy time lies ahead of you! If you don't succeed in gaining a free independent position, you have yourselves to blame. All restrictive conditions of status, of poverty will disappear, the least will begin the same struggle with the most powerful, with the same weapons, on the same ground. If only I were young like you!"⁸ Steffens experienced the time that followed as not simply a French but a European revolution that was planted in millions of hearts: "The first moment of excitement in history ... has something pure, even sacred, that must never be forgotten. A boundless hope took hold of me, my whole future, it seemed to me, was planted in a fresh, new soil ... From then on my whole existence had taken on a new direction ..."⁹

Rights

If revolutionaries were guided by ideas emanating from the Enlightenment, did the Enlightenment produce the revolutions? No, answers **Johnson Kent Wright** (Volume 1, Chapter 2), at least not in the case of France. "Had 'enlightened' criticism of the Bourbon monarchy been sufficient to have launched the Revolution, it ought to have occurred some two decades earlier than it did." And yet, Wright adds, the French Enlightenment was essential to the way the revolution unfolded. Likewise, enlightened ideas helped steer the revolutions in the Ibero-American world, but, as **Brian Hamnett** argues (Volume 1, Chapter 3), the Enlightenment did not lead inevitably or automatically to support for revolution. In New Spain, for example, the outbreak of insurrection in 1810 divided its proponents into hostile camps.

Rights were an essential element of the sometimes baffling transformations that took place during the age of Atlantic revolutions. Rights used to

---

⁷ Cited in Philipp Ziesche, "Exporting American Revolutions: Gouverneur Morris, Thomas Jefferson, and the National Struggle for Universal Rights in Revolutionary France," *Journal of the Early Republic* 26:3 (2006), 419–47: 426.
⁸ Henrich Steffens, *Was ich erlebte: Aus der Erinnerung niedergeschrieben* (Breslau: Josef Mar und Kompanie, 1840), vol. 1, 362–3.
⁹ Steffens, *Was ich erlebte*, 364–5.

be privileges, granted to someone for the common good. Every male had rights commensurate with his station in life, which thereby confirmed the hierarchical organization of society. They were accompanied by obligations that forced the rights' holders to use their powers for the common good. The new notion that gradually took shape – and remained unfinished – was that humans' own moral power allowed them to stake their claims and relate their own rights to those of others. Rights transcended all structures of authority and were thus common to humankind. Human equality now trumped any differences in rank, nationality, or culture.[10] The US Declaration of Independence – the first revolutionary document to invoke rights – echoed this new idea by positing the existence of a supreme law against which positive law could be measured and, if needed, changed.[11] The French Declaration of the Rights of Man and Citizen served the same function, for which it was criticized by supporters of liberalism as metaphysical.

Once formulated, these catalogs of rights could inspire groups who had not been among the intended beneficiaries to claim parity. Just like Black people could argue that their humanity sufficed to negate their status as slaves, some women pressed for their equal rights. The authors of two Belgian pamphlets, who predicted that the current tide of revolutions would bring an end to "seventeen centuries of masculine abuse," called for a national assembly, half of whose members were to be women. If their demand was ignored by the nation's leaders, women would withdraw from society.[12] Adversaries of such rights, however, used the same language of natural rights to oppose these demands. Woman's nature, male French revolutionaries argued, made her unfit to exercise political power.[13]

The invocation of a higher law coexisted in the age of revolutions with the continued emphasis on ancient positive rights by men and women challenging the social order. In many places across the Atlantic world, as **Stephen**

---

[10] Knud Haakonssen, "From Natural Law to the Rights of Man: A European Perspective on American Debates," in Michael J. Lacy and Knud Haakonssen, eds., *A Culture of Rights: The Bill of Rights in Philosophy, Politics, and Law – 1791 and 1991* (Cambridge: Cambridge University Press, 1991), 19–61: 21, 32, 35–6; Simon Middleton, *From Privileges to Rights: Work and Politics in Colonial New York* (Philadelphia: University of Pennsylvania Press, 2006), 5–6.

[11] Andrew J. Reck, "Natural Law in American Revolutionary Thought," *The Review of Metaphysics* 30:4 (1977), 686–714: 712.

[12] Janet L. Polasky, "Women in Revolutionary Belgium: From Stone Throwers to Hearth Tenders," *History Workshop* 21 (1986), 87–104: 93.

[13] Annelien de Dijn, *Freedom: An Unruly History* (Cambridge, MA: Harvard University Press, 2020), 226.

Conway argues in Volume I, Chapter 11, "the events associated with Palmer's 'democratic revolution' began as a conservative reaction to the reforming endeavors of rulers, not as a grassroots desire to extend popular participation." Ireland's Protestants, he shows, were looking backwards "in seeking to reclaim their autonomy." "Most of them were not interested in a democratic transformation of Ireland." **Janet Polasky** (Volume II, Chapter 14) writes that one of the groups challenging Austrian rule in Belgium "wanted to restore the medieval constitutions and reestablish the rule of the three Estates. Instead of natural rights, they referred to 'the eternal rights of man,' meaning something quite different from the enlightenment ideal. Instead of the 'rights of the People,' they referred to the privileges of the 'nation belge.'" In the (Swiss) Helvetic Republic, a document presented to the authorities of Zurich in 1794 that has been labeled the *Stäfner Memorial* demanded both the restoration of old privileges and a constitution that defended individual human rights.[14]

The introduction of rights was no straightforward process, as can be illustrated by the uncertain status of the right to profess one's religious belief. The tone was set by the Virginia Declaration of Rights, which stipulated that "all men are equally entitled to the free exercise of religion, according to the dictates of conscience."[15] Although it has been argued that religious freedom was achievable in Protestant places such as Virginia where tolerance had already been practiced, its adoption was usually a matter of controversy. In Pennsylvania's constitutional debate of 1776, one side – made up of Protestants – opposed religious leniency, which they feared would put them at the mercy of the alien creeds of Islam, Catholicism, and Judaism. Likewise, although Massachusetts' constitution may have guaranteed the exercise of religion in private, it contained an injunction to the legislature to support Protestant teachers.[16] Nor was such intolerance the exclusive domain of elite politicians in the age of revolutions. A series of Catholic relief bills proposed

---

[14] Urte Weeber, "New Wine in Old Wineskins: Republicanism in the Helvetic Republic," in Joris Oddens, Mart Rutjes, and Erik Jacobs, eds., *The Political Culture of the Sister Republics, 1794–1806: France, the Netherlands, Switzerland, and Italy* (Amsterdam: Amsterdam University Press, 2015), 57–64: 62.

[15] Daniel L. Dreisbach, "George Mason's Pursuit of Religious Liberty in Revolutionary Virginia," *The Virginia Magazine of History and Biography* 108:1 (2000), 5–44: 16.

[16] Charles D. Russell, "Islam as a Danger to Republican Virtue: Broadening Religious Liberty in Revolutionary Pennsylvania," *Pennsylvania History: A Journal of Mid-Atlantic Studies* 76:3 (2009), 250–75: 251; Eduardo Posada-Carbó, "Spanish America and US constitutionalism in the Age of Revolution," in Gabriel Paquette and Gonzalo M. Quintero Saravia, eds., *Spain and the American Revolution: New Approaches and Perspectives* (London: Routledge, 2020), 210–23: 217.

by the British government threw into sharp relief the existence of a popular Protestantism that defined itself in opposition to French Catholicism and eventually led to the Gordon Riots (London, 1780).[17]

The antipluralist tendency was, however, stronger in the Catholic world, even in France, where the Catholic faith lost its status as state religion and where Protestants and Jews were emancipated. Political culture proved hard to change.[18] And so it could happen that a small town in Alsace decided in 1794 that the Jews had to shave their beards, and could no longer carry their Decalogues in public or show any other signs of their religion.[19] It was not different in the colonies. When the planters of Saint-Domingue sought protection from the British king in 1793, proposing some articles of government, they insisted on the exclusivity of the Catholic religion.[20] Soon, of course, French revolutionary intolerance went beyond the insistence on Catholicism, when the adoption of the Civil Constitution of the Clergy led to discrimination against the millions of people who clung to the old Church.

The influential constitution of Cádiz stated unambiguously that the religion of the Spanish nation was and would always be the only true Roman Catholic one. When the legislators gathered in Cádiz voted for press freedom in 1810, they followed it up by setting up boards of censorship that would make sure that published works did not threaten religion. Three years later, they went one step further by decreeing the death penalty for anyone suggesting the implementation of a policy of tolerance vis-à-vis non-Catholics.[21] At the same time, as **Roberto Breña** notes (Volume III, Chapter 3), the constitution "tried to control what up to that moment was an almost exclusive role of the Church in public education, publishing, and public discourse." Javier Fernández Sebastián has convincingly argued that "the overwhelming preponderance of Catholicism in the Hispanic world explains how difficult it was to conceive of religion and politics as separate spheres, and the correlative difficulty of regarding 'religion' as an abstract category of a general nature, capable of embracing several 'religions,' in the

---

[17] Brad A. Jones, "'In Favour of Popery': Patriotism, Protestantism, and the Gordon Riots in the Revolutionary British Atlantic," *Journal of British Studies* 52:1 (2013), 79–102.
[18] Bronislaw Baczko, *Politiques de la Révolution française* (Paris: Gallimard, 2008), 62–3.
[19] Claude Muller, "Religion et Révolution en Alsace," *Annales historiques de la Révolution française* 337 (2004), 63–83: 76.
[20] J. Marino Incháustegui, ed., *Documentos para estudio: Marco de la época y problemas del Tratado de Basilea de 1795, en la parte española de Santo Domingo* (Buenos Aires: Academia Dominicana de la Historia, 1957), 640.
[21] Juan Pablo Domínguez, "Intolerancia religiosa en las Cortes de Cádiz," *Hispania* 77:255 (2017), 155–83: 164, 178.

plural." Since Catholicism was the foundation of the nation's identity, tolerance meant "disunion, illegitimacy, even civil war."[22] This sentiment was shared by the priests of central Switzerland when the constitution of the Helvetic Republic was promulgated, which meant that irreligiosity and heresy were no longer punishable.[23]

Residents of the Catholic world would not have viewed religious exclusivity as a form of inequality. As members of the Christian community, every individual enjoyed an equal status by virtue of their baptism. Their ties were governed by brotherly love. At least, that was the case in theory. In practice, it remained an ideal, pursued by Hidalgo and other priests involved in the Mexican uprising of 1810. The early Church fathers rather than Enlightenment *philosophes* were the inspiration for Hidalgo, who stated that his goal was to build a society in which all were recognized as equal children of God.[24] Likewise, the 1797 republican conspiracy in Venezuela, writes **Cristina Soriano** in Volume II, Chapter 28, "argued in favor of social harmony between whites, *pardos*, Indians, and blacks, because all these racial groups were seen as 'brothers in Christ.'"

Not all Catholic leaders were bent on continuing the exclusivity of their religion. Some sought to introduce a measure of tolerance. The difference between tolerance and religious freedom was expressed by the "Jews, settled in France" in a petition to the National Assembly a few months after the Declaration of the Rights of Man and Citizen had been adopted. "The word tolerance," they wrote, "which after so many centuries and so many *intolerant acts* seemed to be a word of humanity and reason, no longer suits a country that wishes to establish its rights on the eternal basis of justice .... To tolerate, indeed, is to suffer what one would have the right to prohibit." Under the new conditions, the dominant religion had no right to prohibit another religion from humbly placing itself by its side.[25] But religious inequality was not to vanish, while tolerance – that typically early modern phenomenon – was still a viable option in Europe and the Americas. The

---

[22] Javier Fernández Sebastián, "Toleration and Freedom of Expression in the Hispanic World between Enlightenment and Liberalism," *Past & Present* no. 211 (May 2011), 159–97: 162–3, 186, 188.

[23] Eric Godel, "La Constitution scandaleuse. La population de Suisse centrale face à la République helvétique," in Andreas Würgler, ed., *Grenzen des Zumutbaren: Erfahrungen mit der französischen Okkupation und der Helvetischen Republik (1798–1803)* (Basel: Schwabe Verlag, 2011), 29–44: 32.

[24] Laura Ibarra García, "El concepto de igualdad en México (1810–1824)," *Relaciones* 145 (2016), 279–314: 287.

[25] "Pétition des juifs établis en France, adressée à l'Assemblée Nationale," 28 January 1790, in *Adresses, mémoires et pétitions des juifs 1789–1794* (Paris: EDHIS, 1968), 17–18.

Polish constitution, writes **Richard Butterwick** (Volume II, Chapter 20), began "with a stirring preamble and an article maintaining the prohibition against 'apostasy' from the Roman Catholic 'dominant and national religion,' while assuring freedom of worship and the protection of government to all creeds." Similarly, the Organic Law that saw the light in Pernambuco, Brazil in 1817 said that the state religion was Roman Catholicism, while the other Christian sects of any denomination were tolerated.[26] In early independent Colombia, a campaign for religious toleration failed to achieve its goal. Foreigners could still not hold Protestant services in public in spite of sustained criticism of the Catholic clergy, which was held responsible for blocking new ideas.[27] The most radical constitution adopted in a Catholic country was that issued by Jean-Jacques Dessalines in 1805. While Toussaint Louverture's constitution of 1801 had declared Catholicism the official state religion, that of Dessalines (although short-lived) introduced religious tolerance.[28]

Sovereignty and Public Opinion

Many historians have assumed that a form of self-government was already in place in Britain's North American colonies. These are considered to have thrived in a long era of "salutary neglect." When that era ended in the aftermath of the Seven Years' War, a revolution became thinkable. In Volume I, Chapter 6, **Holly Brewer** shows that "salutary neglect" was largely a myth: "The political, legal and economic situations in the colonies were constantly negotiated in a struggle for power that was occurring not only on the level of empire but in England itself ... To the degree that such 'salutary neglect' existed ... it was part of this negotiation and struggle over the meaning and terms of power. While some could escape the power of empire in the short term, it was constantly tugging at their sleeves. One could take up land in the 'wilderness,' for example, ... but the only way one owned it was by getting a legal title – and that demanded negotiation with all the ligaments of colonial authority, from surveyor and courts to secretary of

---

[26] Leonardo Morais de Araújo Pinheiro, "Análise da Lei Orgânica da Revolução pernambucana de 1817 à luz dos direitos fundamentais," *Revista Brasileira de História do Direito* 4:2 (2018), 114–34: 130.

[27] David Bushnell, *The Santander Regime in Gran Colombia* (Westport, CN: Greenwood Press, 1970 [1954]), 210, 215.

[28] Lorelle D. Semley, "To Live and Die, Free and French: Toussaint Louverture's 1801 Constitution and the Original Challenge of Black Citizenship," *Radical History Review* 115 (2013), 65–90: 78.

the colony. How one could develop it, and what one could grow, how one could pass it on, were often regulated by laws that might emerge in the colonies but were subject to Royal veto. Other regulations were imposed directly by imperial authorities."

Revolutions are always a struggle for sovereignty. Despite the widely shared support for popular sovereignty, opinions were divided on the people's postrevolutionary political role. A prominent monarchist member of France's National Assembly opined that while all powers emanated from the people, their well-being depended on leaving the exercise of these powers to the king to prevent the chaos of anarchy.[29] In continental British America, **Max Edling** remarks (Volume 1, Chapter 17), the ideology of the American Revolution "introduced a nebulous concept of popular sovereignty, which somehow existed both at state and at national level." "Several of the new constitutions incorporated Congress's declaration of independence in whole or in part, thus illustrating how legitimate authority was based on popular sovereignty simultaneously expressed at national and local level." In Spanish America, it was unclear whether self-rule extended to a town's immediate vicinity or whether administrative centers could claim to govern vast areas. The assumption of sovereignty in Spanish America implied a return to nature. As Clément Thibaud has explained, that meant not a return to a Hobbesian world of lone individuals but *pueblos*, peoples in the sense of free communities. If indeed the *pueblo* was the repository of sovereignty, opinions differed on the *pueblo*'s identity, at least in New Granada. Was it the town, the province, or all of New Granada?[30] Federalists in many parts of the Atlantic world, often inspired by the United States and opposed to the horrors to which centralism had allegedly given rise in Jacobin Paris, usually found support outside traditional political centers. To legitimize the dispersion of political power, Dutch federalists used the climate argument – according to which each land had its own character and was therefore entitled to its own legislation – to plead for separate laws for each of the seven small provinces. Another argument was that the distance between the population and its rulers was much smaller on

---

[29] His name was Jean-Joseph Mounier. Nicolai von Eggers, "Popular Sovereignty, Republicanism, and the Political Logic of the Struggles of the French Revolution" (Ph.D. dissertation, University of Aarhus, 2016), 216.
[30] Clément Thibaud, "Des républiques en armes à la République armée. Guerre révolutionnaire, fédéralisme et centralisme au Venezuela et en Nouvelle-Grenade, 1808–1830," *Annales historiques de la Révolution française* no. 348 (2011), 57–86: 63; Isabel Restrepo Mejía, "La soberanía del 'pueblo' durante la época de la independencia, 1810–1815," *Historia Crítica* 29 (2005), 101–23: 102–5.

a provincial level. Such democratic reasoning had its limits, though, because the federalists' emphasis on the preservation of provincial laws and customs was at odds with the new egalitarian spirit.[31]

Penetrating everywhere, that new spirit changed the nature of political debates, which were no longer confined to elite venues. **Javier Fernández Sebastián** points out in Volume III, Chapter 12 that the "increase in the pace of publication of newspapers and readers' insatiable demand for news rapidly accelerated the circulation of new concepts and multiplied the uses, often contradictory, of basic political terminology." To succeed in achieving political goals, the mobilization of public opinion became indispensable, as in the Dutch Republic, where Patriot newspapers were not just sold widely but also carried many readers' letters, showcasing public opinion.[32] Public opinion, which rebels constantly invoked, came to be seen as an enlightened court with universal authority.[33] In order to expose the French king to this new "court" and remove him from the royal court in Versailles, plebeians forced Louis XVI to settle in Paris, where he would be surrounded by "the people." In Venezuela, conversely, several representatives proposed to move the seat of Congress away from Caracas and avoid the crushing weight of the capital's public opinion. Their adversaries opined that at least in Caracas, some Enlightenment may be found. One of them argued: "Public opinion is not power, but the sum of all opinions that cannot be formed without knowledge. And could it be that they exist among shepherds, farmers or peasants, who don't even know the name of those who govern them? Public opinion, in matters of government, resides only in the big cities and not in the villages and shacks, especially in America, where the previous government has always kept under a black veil even the inhabitants of the capital city."[34] And even in the big cities, only a small group of men were zealots for liberty, Genevan native Étienne Dumont noted when he arrived in Paris on the eve

---

[31] Peter A. J. van den Berg, *Codificatie en staatsvorming: De politieke en politiek-theoretische achtergronden van de codificatie van het privaatrecht in Pruisen, de Donaumonarchie, Frankrijk en Nederland, 1450–1811* (Groningen: Wolters-Noordhoff, 1996), 306, 307, 314, 319.

[32] Nicolaas van Sas, "The Patriot Revolution: New Perspectives," in Margaret C. Jacob and Wijnand W. Mijnhardt, eds., *The Dutch Republic in the Eighteenth Century: Decline, Enlightenment, and Revolution* (Ithaca, NY: Cornell University Press, 1992), 91–120: 102–3.

[33] Keith Michael Baker, *Inventing the French Revolution: Essays on French Political Culture in the Eighteenth Century* (Cambridge: Cambridge University Press, 1990), 186, 193–6.

[34] Véronique Hébrard, "Opinion publique et représentation dans le Congrès Constituant Vénézuélien (1810–1812)," *Annales historiques de la Révolution française* no. 365 (2011), 153–75: 162 (quote), 167, 170–1.

of the revolution: "There are in the immense population of this metropolis about fifteen or twenty thousand persons, who consider the meeting of the Estates-General as a matter of the utmost importance, and who anxiously watch all the measures of the court; these men, being to be found everywhere, in coffee-houses, at the theatres, in private companies, and in public places, may be said to form the public opinion."[35] That most delegates at the Estates-General and National Assembly would have agreed with Dumont is suggested by the highly centralized polity they set up. **David Andress** argues in Volume II, Chapter 1 that the revolutionaries expected only obedience from locally elected leaders, did not introduce intermediary bodies outside Paris, and opted not to set up institutional checks on the legislature.

To focus single-mindedly on the politically active members of a society would obscure the politicization on a vast scale – inside and outside France – of ordinary people, who appropriated the official rhetoric that was expressed in official documents and proclamations, and employed it when they thought it useful.[36] A new democratic culture emerged in the countries neighboring France, characterized by newspapers, pamphlets, societies, republican catechisms, and civic feasts which featured freedom trees and Phrygian hats.[37] In Italy, writes **John A. Davis** (Volume II, Chapter 17), "freedom of the press, official and unofficial newspapers, pamphlets and broadsheets offered unprecedented platforms for public debate, while the newly created consultative and executive committees, public assemblies, the drafting of constitutions, the debates on the procedures and formalities of government, the organization of plebiscites and formalized civic and public ceremonies gave opportunities to experience active citizenship, as did the political clubs and societies."

Essential to the process of cultivating peoples bound together by horizontal ties of citizenship and shared visions of revolutionary transformation, writes Michael Kwass, was material culture "as legislators, producers, and

---

[35] Richard Whatmore, "Étienne Dumont, the British Constitution, and the French Revolution," *The Historical Journal* 50:1 (2007), 23–47: 32.

[36] Jean-Luc Chappey, "Révolution, régénération, civilisation. Enjeux culturels des dynamiques politiques," in Jean-Luc Chappey, Bernard Gainot, Guillaume Mazeau, Frédéric Régent, and Pierre Serna, eds., *Pour quoi faire la Révolution* (Marseille: Agone, 2012), 115–48; Maxime Kaci, *Dans le tourbillon de la Révolution: Mots d'ordre et engagements collectifs aux frontières septentrionales (1791–1793)* (Rennes: Presses universitaires de Rennes, 2016), 288; Eugenia Molina, "Politización y relaciones sociales en Mendoza (Argentina) durante la década revolucionaria (1810–1820). Conflictos y consensos en la configuración de un nuevo orden," *Boletín Americanista* 58 (2008), 251–71: 253.

[37] Annie Jourdan, *La Révolution, une exception française?* (Paris: Flammarion, 2004), 271–2.

consumers imbued everyday objects with revolutionary meaning. More than merely reflecting political ideas and aspirations, material objects mediated their very expression ..."[38] In one rural part of the Dutch Republic in the 1780s, all sorts of everyday objects demonstrated one's allegiance on both sides of the political divide: crockery, pottery, drinking utensils, sugar-casters, cookie boards, scent bottles, and tobacco and snuff boxes.[39] Just as cultural objects were invested with a revolutionary meaning, cultural *practices* underwent a transformation. They served, argues **Nathan Perl-Rosenthal** (Volume I, Chapter 4), as vehicles for new political ideas and practices. These cultural practices, such as letter-writing, were not in themselves revolutionary, and could be used by the revolutions' opponents, but in the hands of revolutionaries they were given new forms.

Politicization was not by definition, or at least not exclusively, ideological. **Joris Oddens** contends in Volume II, Chapter 13 that "in some rural areas [of the Dutch Republic] passions ran high, but what was at stake seems to have been a long-running tribal conflict rather than an ideological divide dating to the revolutionary era itself: rival factions in a village sided with the Patriots or with the Orangists, but more particularly *against* each other, or the entire population of one village sympathized with one camp because the people of a neighboring town politically or economically dwarfing them supported the other." This phenomenon existed everywhere. Preexisting disputes or grievances often conditioned the choice for revolution or status quo. If a large town in Spanish America embraced revolution, nearby smaller towns seeking greater autonomy would remain faithful to the old regime. Similarly, the feuding Anglicans and Presbyterians ended up on opposing sides in the American Revolution in good part to avoid each other. Yet another example can be found in Africa. Shortly after Brazil declared its independence, the elite of Benguela (Angola) used the crisis of the Portuguese empire to try to break away from its subordination to Luanda, join Brazil, and become a province attached to Rio de Janeiro. **Roquinaldo Ferreira** reveals in Volume III, Chapter 22 that this was no surprise move. Benguela and Rio were linked through the transatlantic slave trade, the Benguela elite sent its sons to study in Brazil, and it had regularly imported foodstuffs from Brazil in time of need.

---

[38] Michael Kwass, *Consumer Revolution, 1650–1800* (Cambridge: Cambridge University Press, 2022), 198.
[39] Jouke Nijman, "Politieke cultuur en volkscultuur in de Patriottentijd," *Groniek* 30 (1997), 417–31: 425, 426.

Rhetoric was, of course, also largely strategic. No fewer than 227 towns in France petitioning the National Assembly to reassign lawcourts and other institutions to them adopted egalitarian language.[40] Similarly, in German cities, writes **Michael Rowe** (Volume II, Chapter 18), "demands that had previously been couched in the familiar language of historic rights and privileges now included references to the universal liberties triumphant in France." Elsewhere, old and new regime values mixed, as in the case of a free merchant of color from Guayaquil who petitioned the Cortes of Cádiz in 1820 for both citizenship and recognition as an *hidalgo*.[41] And in the hinterland of the Swiss canton of Zurich, the language of reform was combined with an insistence on inalienable rights. This pragmatic republicanism, writes **Marc H. Lerner** (Volume II, Chapter 11), was typical of Switzerland in the age of revolutions.

The defenders of the status quo responded to revolutionary activity in various ways, appealing to the public themselves in person or in writing, or simply muzzling the press, as the viceroy of New Spain did in Mexico City, an act he defended by alleging that press freedom had led to an "extraordinary number of seditious and insulting publications."[42] Nor were the revolutionaries, once in the saddle themselves, content with an alternative opinion being expressed. During the American Revolutionary War, Patriots bullied printers into retracting contentious statements. In other instances, they seized and destroyed the entire print run of pamphlets they considered dangerous. In addition to book burnings, there were monetary rewards for the capture of certain pamphleteers. Amid such escalating levels of violence, Loyalists found it increasingly hard to make their voices heard.[43]

Not everyone engaged in political contestation. Many peasants and urban workers were indifferent to the revolutions as long as they could maintain such a stance. Farmers in Chile were only gradually drawn into the political conflict as they were mobilized on either side of the divide through ties of clientage. Indifference could also give way to outright opposition to the state,

---

[40] Wim Klooster, *Revolutions in the Atlantic World: A Comparative History*, new edition (New York: New York University Press, 2018), 173–4; Ted W. Margadant, *Urban Rivalries in the French Revolution* (Princeton: Princeton University Press, 1992), 157.

[41] Federica Morelli, *Free People of Color in the Spanish Atlantic: Race and Citizenship, 1780–1850* (New York: Routledge, 2020), 127–8.

[42] Juan Ortiz Escamilla, *Calleja: Guerra, botín y fortuna* (Xalapa: Universidad Veracruzana; Zamora: El Colegio de Michoacán, 2017), 112.

[43] Holger Hoock, *Scars of Independence: America's Violent Birth* (New York: Crown Publishers, 2017), 38–9. See also Harry M. Ward, *The War for Independence and the Transformation of American Society* (London: Routledge, 1999), 59–65.

as it did in the Dutch province of Friesland, where those who were largely interested in issues that were of their immediate concern such as food prices or high taxes ended up turning their back on the Batavian Republic when the electorate was forced to sign a declaration signaling their resistance to any form of rule by stadtholders, aristocrats, or autocrats.[44]

Democracy

Most thinkers and activists conceived of freedom as the ability to live under laws that the inhabitants of a country made themselves.[45] The revolutionaries agreed that the regimes they built had to be supported by some form of popular control over the government. Only a political system that reflected the people's voice – which was often, but certainly not always, called democracy – could supplant aristocratic or monarchical rule. That voice was to be expressed through representation, which was inseparable from suffrage.[46]

Who constituted the people? At least a section of the adult population, and usually – in line with classical republicanism – those who had taken up arms to defend the revolution. The 1826 constitution of Bolivia said that Bolivians included "those who fought for liberty in Junín or Ayacucho," the sites of two battles that had doomed the Spanish empire in South America.[47] Similarly, the French constitution of 1795 singled out "veterans of one or more campaigns for the establishment of the Republic" as citizens who did not have to qualify financially in order to cast their vote.[48] The earlier French constitution of 1791, which was never implemented, had even granted suffrage to every adult male, a decision replicated only in

---

[44] Igor Goicovic Donoso, "De la indiferencia a la resistencia: Los sectores populares y la Guerra de Independencia en el norte de Chile (1817–1823)," *Revista de Indias* 74:260 (2014), 129–60: 136; Jacques Kuiper, *Een revolutie ontrafeld: Politiek in Friesland 1795–1798* (Franeker: Van Wijnen, 2002), 517.

[45] De Dijn, *Freedom*, 177–8.

[46] Minchul Kim, "Pierre-Antoine Antonelle and Representative Democracy in the French Revolution," *History of European Ideas* 44:3 (2018), 344–69: 351. Earlier forms of representation were now abandoned. Cf. Joaquim Albareda and Manuel Herrero Sánchez, eds., *Political Representation in the Ancien Régime* (London: Routledge, 2019).

[47] Constitution of Bolivia, 22 November 1826, in J. R. Gutiérrez, ed., *Las constituciones políticas que ha tenido la República Boliviana (1826–1868)* (Santiago: Imprenta de "El Independiente," 1869), 4–5.

[48] Andrew Jainchill, "The Constitution of the Year III and the Persistence of Classical Republicanism," *French Historical Studies* 26:3 (2003), 399–435: 418.

Paraguay (1813).⁴⁹ Some constitutions extended voting rights not to every male, but the vast majority of men. That of Cádiz (1812) enabled many inhabitants in the Spanish empire to cast their vote. In Mexico City, for example, 93 percent of the adult male population was enfranchised. Likewise, the Brazilian constitution of 1824 incorporated in the electorate vast numbers of small urban and rural proprietors as well as tenant farmers and sharecroppers, although it did not give the vote to journeymen and free men who lived from piecework or who were not regularly employed.⁵⁰ Formal exclusion did not necessarily mean the inability to take part in the election process. In both France and Spain, communities were represented by well-known individuals, who received the vote after days of deliberation, during which anybody could chime in. Commoners who could not vote were still believed to be *virtually* represented through their public demonstrations of support or rejection of elected candidates.⁵¹ North American Patriots, of course, scoffed at the notion of virtual representation. During the crisis that preceded the American Revolution, Britain's insistence that Americans were represented in Parliament despite their inability to vote had alienated numerous Americans from the metropole.

In most parts of the Atlantic world, representative democracy was introduced sooner or later, but without citizens resigning themselves to the reduced role that would later become the norm, when their input became largely limited to the periodic casting of votes. Many North Americans left little leeway to the delegates, whom they saw as "mere agents or tools of the people" who could give binding directions "whenever they please to give them."⁵² During the Cortes of Cádiz, Spanish newspapers as well as politicians invoked the demand that the people control their representatives very closely, reserving for themselves the last say in expressing the general will.⁵³

---

[49] Richard Allan White, *Paraguay's Autonomous Revolution, 1810–1840* (Albuquerque: University of New Mexico Press, 1978), 56.

[50] Jaime E. Rodríguez O., *The Independence of Spanish America* (Cambridge: Cambridge University Press, 1998), 105; Cecília Helena de Salles Oliveira, "Contribuição ao estudo do Poder Moderador," in Cecília Helena de Salles Oliveira, Vera Lúcia Nagib Bittencourt, and Wilma Peres Costa, eds., *Soberania e conflito: Configurações do Estado Nacional no Brasil do século XIX* (São Paulo: Editora Hucitec, 2010), 185–235: 214.

[51] Jean-Clément Martin, *Nouvelle histoire de la Révolution française* (Paris: Perrin, 2012), 208; François-Xavier Guerra, "The Spanish-American Tradition of Representation and Its European Roots," *Journal of Latin American Studies* 26:1 (1994), 1–35: 7.

[52] Gordon S. Wood, *The Creation of the American Republic, 1776–1787* (Charlotte: The University of North Carolina Press, 1969), 371.

[53] Javier Fernández Sebastián, "Democracia," in Javier Fernández Sebastián and Juan Francisco Fuentes, eds., *Diccionario político y social del siglo XIX español* (Madrid: Alianza Editorial, 2002), 216–228: 218.

Militant Parisians known as Enragés, who were wrongly portrayed at the time as forming a movement, considered direct democracy the only option for their city. They agreed with Rousseau that sovereignty could not be delegated. The people should have the right to sanction the laws and if there were to be delegates, they must be revocable at will.[54] A form of direct democracy was actually established in one city 400 kilometers to the north. In 1796, voters in Amsterdam received the right to send proposals to the municipal government. If two-thirds of the electorate backed a proposal, it would be binding.[55]

The man who crucially intervened in the French Revolution on more than one occasion, the Abbé Sieyès, disagreed with the view that delegates should be kept on a leash by the voters. He summarized the legislative process as follows: "The members of a representative assembly ... gather in order to balance their opinions, to modify them, to purify some through others, and to extract finally from the *lumières* of all, a majority opinion, that is to say, the common will which makes the law. The mixing of individual wills, the kind of fermentation that they undergo in this operation, are necessary to produce the result that is desired. It is therefore essential that opinions should be able to concert, to yield, in a word to modify one another, for without this there is no longer a deliberative assembly but simply a *rendez-vous of couriers*, ready to depart after having delivered their dispatches."[56]

Sieyès did not simply favor representative democracy; he also introduced the distinction between active and passive citizens that was adopted in France. Fulfilling income or property requirements, the first group was allowed more extensive participation in political life. Sieyès' distinction was soon copied in other new regimes. By virtue of Brazil's 1824 constitution, for example, citizens were all males of age at least twenty-five years who lived on their own and did not work as domestic servants. They also had "a yearly net income above a hundred thousand reis derived from real estate property, industry, trade, or employment." These men could vote in the parochial assemblies, which chose the provincial electors. Electors, however, could

---

[54] Albert Soboul, "Audience des Lumières. Classes populaires et Rousseauisme sous la Révolution," *Annales historiques de la Révolution française* 34:170 (1962), 421–38: 425.

[55] Thomas Poell, "The Democratic Paradox: Dutch Revolutionary Struggles over Democratisation and Centralisation (1780–1813)" (Ph.D. dissertation, University of Utrecht, 2007), 91.

[56] Murray Forsyth, *Reason and Revolution: The Political Thought of the Abbé Sieyes* (Leicester: Leicester University Press; New York: Holmes & Meier Publishers, 1987), 134.

only be members of the active citizenry, made up of all men with an income of at least 200,000 reis, who had not been freed from slavery.[57]

Underlying this division was a difference between the people as conceptualized by Enlightenment thinkers and the actual population. The abstract people were a source of legitimacy, whereas the real people were deemed ignorant and superstitious by the elites.[58] The natural representatives of the people, d'Holbach and Diderot had taught, were those who were the best informed and educated.[59] Where revolutionaries succeeded in toppling a regime, they commonly began the process of enlightening the vast mass of the population. Delegates presented themselves as moral guides in a society that allegedly had become corrupt, which meant that it would take time for civilization to become rooted. The moral decay that he accused Spain of bringing to its colonies at the same time made Simón Bolívar oppose the establishment of a genuine democracy. The people, he maintained, were simply not ready yet for a political role. He was not alone. Six days before the storming of the Bastille, one deputy of the Third Estate wrote that the revolution – a term he presciently used – should be postponed by ten years, allowing the people to educate themselves.[60] To the Italian intellectual Vincenzio Russo, representative democracy was a temporary stage that should last as long as popular education was needed. Once that goal had been achieved, direct democracy could be introduced.[61]

Thomas Paine asserted, on the other hand, that the educational effect of representative democracy would be immediate. "[T]he case is," he wrote, "that the representative system diffuses such a body of knowledge throughout a nation, on the subject of government, as to explode ignorance and preclude imposition ... Those who are not in the representation, know as much of the nature of business as those who are. An affectation of

---

[57] Márcia Regina Berbel and Rafael de Bivar Marquese, "The Absence of Race: Slavery, Citizenship, and Pro-slavery Ideology in the Cortes of Lisbon and the Rio de Janeiro Constituent Assembly (1821–4)," *Social History* 32:4 (2007), 415–433: 416, 425.

[58] Valérie Sottocasa, *Les brigands et la Révolution: Violences politiques et criminalité dans le Midi (1789–1802)* (Ceyzérieu: Champ Vallon, 2016), 363.

[59] Jonathan Israel, *A Revolution of the Mind: Radical Enlightenment and the Intellectual Origins of Modern Democracy* (Princeton: Princeton University Press, 2010), 66.

[60] Adrien Duquesnoy, *Un révolutionnaire malgré lui: Journal mai–octobre 1789*, ed. Guillaume Mazeau (Paris: Mercure de France, 2016), 137. See for the changing meaning of the term "revolution" in those days: Keith Michael Baker, "Enlightenment Idioms, Old Regime Discourses, and Revolutionary Improvisation," in Thomas E. Kaiser and Dale K. Van Kley, eds., *From Deficit to Deluge: The Origins of the French Revolution* (Stanford: Stanford University Press, 2011), 165–97: 191–6.

[61] Luciano Guerci, *"Mente, cuore, coraggio, virtù repubblicane": Educare il popolo nell'Italia in rivoluzione (1796–1799)* (Turin: Tirrenia Stampatori, 1992), 112–13.

mysterious importance would there be scouted. Nations can have no secrets; and the secrets of courts, like those of individuals, are always their defects. In the representative system, the reason for everything must publicly appear. Every man is a proprietor in government and considers it a necessary part of his business to understand."[62] Although Jacobins embraced it, this conviction was not widely shared. While they may have hoped for a rapid enlightenment of the masses, most revolutionary regimes adopted constitutions that included a literacy requirement. This was necessary, explained French lawmaker Boissy d'Anglas, because a man "is only truly independent when he does not need anyone to enlighten him about his duties and to convey his ideas."[63] The leaders of the new Spanish American republics shared the Enlightenment ideal of popular education, many of them embracing the system of mutual education invented by the Englishman Joseph Lancaster. In that way, writes **Karen Racine** (Volume III, Chapter 15), large numbers of people could become literate in a short amount of time. The goal of education, however, was to train not participatory citizens, but moral subjects who were economically useful.

Even so, urban crowds made up of literate and illiterate residents alike often performed an important legitimizing function for revolutionary elites. Leaders of Central American revolts, writes **Timothy Hawkins** (Volume III, Chapter 6), "relied on the energy of subaltern groups, in particular the urban masses, to advance their causes. In not a few cases, these uprisings arose from popular demands for redress of traditional grievances, which suggests a disconnect between the priorities of the leadership and the protesters." Some of the watershed moments in the age of revolutions saw the intervention of vociferous crowds that had been invited to show up. One such occasion was the popular response in Bogotá to the refusal of the viceroy of New Granada to form a junta that would be the local government. The crowd's anti-Spanish demonstrations on 20 July 1810 forced the viceroy to change his mind. Agents working for the rebel elite had used various methods to urge the plebeians to make their way to certain downtown sites, where they energized them. These agents were scribes and other middle-rank local officials who mingled with working men and were known to the elite because of their positions.[64]

---

[62] Thomas Paine, *The Rights of Man for the Benefit of All Mankind* (Philadelphia: D. Webster, 1797), 31.
[63] Jainchill, "The Constitution of the Year III," 421.
[64] Manuel Pareja Ortiz, "El 'pueblo' bogotano en la revolución del 20 de julio de 1810," *Anuario de Estudios Americanos* 71:1 (2014), 281–311: 283–4, 287, 291.

When crowds were not manipulated but operated autonomously, they instilled fear in the elites. **Anthony McFarlane** writes in Volume I, Chapter 18 that elites in Quito and Arequipa (both in the viceroyalty of Peru) backed local revolts against Spanish policies until they "took fright at plebeian mobilization and rallied to defend the established order," terrified of a breakdown in social discipline.[65] John Adams feared that new claims would arise. "Women will demand a Vote. Lads from 12 to 21 will think their Rights not enough attended to, and every Man, who has not a Farthing, will demand an equal Voice with any other in all Acts of State. It tends to confound and destroy all Distinctions, and prostate all Ranks, to one common Levell."[66] Although such arguments were usually self-serving, they also expressed a sense of reality, as **Howard Brown** argues in Volume II, Chapter 7: "Actually implementing democratic ideals meant dismantling existing structures of authority and risked unleashing less appealing impulses across all social strata. Too often, notions of liberty, equality, reason, and progress acted as bellows on the glowing coals of resentment and jealousy."

Pursuing their own agendas, peasants and urban plebeians nonetheless achieved many of their loftier goals. In France, **Noelle Plack** (Volume II, Chapter 3) notes, "for four years the peasantry rose in waves of protest and insurrection which ultimately forced legislators in Paris to abolish once and for all the feudal regime. These actions should not be underestimated as it has been argued that without them, peasants in France would most likely have been responsible for feudal dues until at least the middle of the nineteenth century." She adds that "[t]ax revolt, in the form of petition, riot, resistance, and noncompliance was far more prevalent in the French Revolution than many historians realize. Popular refusal to pay taxes was as important an aspect to bringing down the *ancien régime* as subsistence riots and attacks on seigneurial chateaux." The balance sheet looked different in Brazil, where the struggles of the popular classes ended in defeat. A dozen years into the construction of the new independent polity, the goal of most legislators was to obtain more local autonomy and an increased federalization of the provinces instead of more social participation in politics. The social structure was consequently left largely untouched, which set off riots

---

[65] See, for Buenos Aires, Gabriel di Meglio, "Un nuevo actor para un nuevo escenario. La participación política de la plebe urbana de Buenos Aires en la década de la revolución (1810–1820)," *Boletín del Instituto Argentina y Americana "Dr. Emilio Ravignani,"* 3rd series, 24 (2001), 7–43: 32–3.

[66] Cited in Joan Hoff, *Law, Gender, and Injustice: A Legal History of U.S. Women* (New York: New York University Press, 1991), 62.

and revolts of those whose demands did not find an expression on the parliamentary level.⁶⁷ Their defeat, however, writes **Hendrik Kraay** (Volume III, Chapter 20), does not mean "that these struggles were unimportant; rather, they were what made independence such an uncertain and contingent process and these years such a dynamic period in Brazilian history." **Gabriel Paquette** (Volume III, Chapter 16) adds that by contrast with preceding years, the decades after Brazilian independence "were characterized by tempestuous relations between the capital and the provinces, between urban and rural areas, between landed proprietors and their subalterns, between masters and slaves." At independence, "the destruction of the Old Regime was incomplete, perhaps not even yet under way."

Women

Women's contributions to revolutions and counterrevolutions have often gone unheralded. In France and Spanish America, more than a few examples have been found of women who actually took part in the armed struggles, sometimes disguised as men.⁶⁸ More frequently, their role was that of noncombatants, as **Ami Pflugrad-Jakisch** mentions in Volume I, Chapter 14. During the American Revolution, thousands of poor women "followed both the British and the continental armies as cooks, washerwomen, seamstresses, nurses, scavengers, and sexual partners." American women were also active on the political front, engaged in boycotts of British goods or in spinning bees, producing cloth to substitute for British manufactures. In numerous ways, women shared the plight of men. Loyalist women in South Carolina, for instance, were "verbally abused, imprisoned, and threatened with bodily harm even when they had not taken an active role in opposing the rebel cause." Those women who did help the British armies

---

⁶⁷ Andréa Slemian, "Os canais de representação política nos primórdios do Império: Apontamentos para um estudo da relação entre Estado e sociedade no Brasil (c. 1822–1834)," *Locus: Revista de história* 13:1 (2007), 34–51: 49–51.

⁶⁸ Claude Guillon, "Pauline Léon, une républicaine révolutionnaire," *Annales historiques de la Révolution française* 344 (2008), 147–59: 150–1; Christine Peyrard, *Les Jacobins de l'Ouest: Sociabilité révolutionnaire et formes de politisation dans le Maine et la Basse-Normandie (1789–1799)* (Paris: Publications de la Sorbonne, 1996), 231; Evelyn Cherpak, "The Participation of Women in the Independence Movement in Gran Colombia, 1780–1830," in Asunción Lavrin, ed., *Latin American Women* (Westport, CN: Greenwood Press, 1978), 219–34: 221–2; Alberto Baena Zapatero, "Las mujeres ante la independencia de México," in Izaskun Álvarez Cuartero and Julio Sánchez Gómez, eds., *Visiones e revisiones de la Independencia Americana: Subalternidad e independencias* (Salamanca: Ediciones Universidad de Salamanca, 2012), 115–35: 121.

also suffered physical abuse.[69] When their husbands fled, Loyalist women often stayed behind and, as one historian has argued, "seized this moment to exert a new form of independence. War shook up the existing social order and provided women with a brief moment to act independently of existing gender restrictions."[70]

Shortly after the French commissioners put a de facto end to slavery in Saint-Domingue, women in the southern part of the colony who benefited from emancipation contested the new labor regime under which they had to toil. Along with their male counterparts, the women protested the regulations that the same commissioners introduced in an attempt to keep the plantation economy afloat. On more than a few occasions, only women expressed their displeasure by refusing to work or working less than was expected from them.[71]

The small group of revolutionaries who championed women's rights in Europe, writes **Jennifer Ngaire Heuer** in Volume II, Chapter 10, "were often politically marginal, or only intermittently engaged with the issue," adding that Olympe de Gouges and Mary Wollstonecraft are probably better known today than they were in their own time. Gerrit Paape, a rare male activist for women's rights, still remains virtually unknown to this day. This prolific Dutch writer sketched the outlines of a Batavian Republic 200 years in the future, in which women were educated and had the same rights as men. Their inborn intelligence and their ingenuity were no longer "smothered in kitchen smoke." As Batavian citizens, they helped build a better world.[72]

In France, the revolution did entail a number of new rights for women, which Heuer sums up as follows: "Women acquired a decree of legal autonomy, were able to sign contracts and enter in justice in their own names, marry without parental authorization once they reached the age of majority, divorce their husbands, and inherit equally with their brothers." Women actively campaigned for equal rights within the family, presenting equality in petitions as a natural right. But they also invoked a moral

---

[69] Jim Piecuch, *Three Peoples, One King: Loyalists, Indians, and Slaves in the American Revolutionary South, 1775–1782* (Columbia, SC: University of South Carolina Press, 2008), 61.

[70] Kimberly Nath, "Left Behind: Loyalist Women in Philadelphia during the American Revolution," in Barbara B. Oberg, *Women in the American Revolution: Gender, Politics, and the Domestic World* (Charlottesville: University of Virginia Press, 2019), 211–28: 223.

[71] Judith Kafka, "Action, Reaction and Interaction: Slave Women in Resistance in the South of Saint Domingue, 1793–94," *Slavery and Abolition* 18:2 (1997), 48–72.

[72] Gerrit Paape, *De Bataafsche Republiek, zo als zij behoord te zijn, en zo als zij weezen kan: Of revolutionaire droom in 1798: Wegens toekomstige gebeurtenissen tot 1998* (Nijmegen: Vantilt, 1998 [1798]), 77–9.

language to question the traditional gender hierarchy in the family.[73] Bringing up changes in gender roles was still anathema around the Atlantic world. In the early American republic, both men and women saw women's discussion of their natural rights as dangerous because they feared that women would give up their domestic tasks.[74]

Politicians and intellectuals in the Iberian world took every effort to exclude women from public affairs. Those who thought otherwise were ignored. **Nuno Gonçalo Monteiro** (Volume III, Chapter 17) mentions that Portugal's parliament did not even vote on the proposal by one deputy to at least allow the mothers of six legitimate children to take part in elections. **Mónica Ricketts** contends in Volume III, Chapter 13 that in Spanish America "much like in France after the Revolution, women's participation in war and politics was seen as a sign of disorder and anarchy, for it was believed that their passions made them prone to corruption." If women were to remain aloof from politics, some politicians expressed their desire to see women educated. However, the goals of education did not differ from colonial days. Women were to be prepared for marriage, motherhood, and domestic skills.[75] One could argue that women in the Americas were not as a rule excluded from political rights due to sexual discrimination, but because, just like two other categories that were excluded – children and domestic servants – they belonged to the family as a political unit. As such, they were presumed to share the interests of the male members of their households.[76] In British North America, **Jessica Choppin Roney** explains (Volume I, Chapter 8), citizenship denoted the performance of duties for the benefit of the community, especially military protection. Since women were viewed as incapable of performing such duties, they could not be citizens and their "political personhood was subsumed under that of the male head of her household."

Economic Equality

If inequality of birth was a major target for revolutionaries, that cannot be said for inequality of property. **Lloyd Kramer** (Volume I, Chapter 20) cites

---

[73] Suzanne Desan, "'War between Brothers and Sisters': Inheritance Law and Gender Politics in Revolutionary France," *French Historical Studies* 20:4 (1997), 597–634: 624–6.
[74] Rosemarie Zagarri, "The Rights of Man and Woman in Post-Revolutionary America," *The William and Mary Quarterly* 55:2 (1998), 203–30: 217.
[75] Cherpak, "Participation of Women," 230.
[76] Anne Verjus, *Le cens de la famille: Les femmes et le vote, 1789–1848* (Paris: Bellin, 2002), 19–22.

the French Marquis de Chastellux, who became concerned during his travels in the early American republic about the political consequences of unequal wealth. He "identified a socioeconomic threat that could soon weaken or even destroy the institutional structures of republican equality." Although economic considerations were conspicuously absent from most political debates and writings in the age of revolutions, there was no lack of thinkers who proposed considerable economic reforms. In his *Agrarian Justice*, Thomas Paine cried out: "The present state of civilization is as odious as it is unjust ... [I]t is necessary that a revolution should be made in it. The contrast of affluence and wretchedness continually meeting and offending the eye, is like dead and living bodies chained together."[77] Charity, which had been the traditional response to poverty, would no longer do. The French revolutionaries made a serious effort to provide poor relief, as shown by fifty-six decrees enacted within just a year by the Legislative Assembly that targeted this issue.[78] Besides, the Convention adopted a maximum limit on the prices of a wide array of staples.

In *Du contrat social*, Rousseau had already warned of the dangers of economic inequality. "As for wealth," he wrote, "no citizen should be so rich that he can buy another, and none so poor that he is compelled to sell himself." When that happens, those who are less advantaged may be forced to follow the will of someone else rather than their own. In other words, dependence will lead to a loss of freedom.[79] The idea that equality must extend to the economic realm was articulated by a special deputy to the French National Assembly from a town in Auvergne: "In the division of benefits, poverty alone has rights, and wealth must be repulsed; legislators must remove all the means that can produce extreme wealth and extreme poverty. Equality must be the goal of all their institutions and all their laws, because from equality alone is born happiness, which is the purpose of all societies."[80] Why was it, one French author asked, that one person received more land than his fellow men? Since their needs are the same, why would enjoyment be different? Such a law can only derive from force. Another one

---

[77] Thomas Paine, *The Complete Writings of Thomas Paine*, ed. Philip S. Foner (New York: Citadel Press, 1969), vol. 1, 617.
[78] Alan Forrest, *The French Revolution and the Poor* (New York: St. Martin's Press, 1981), 23.
[79] Frederick Neuhouser, "Rousseau's Critique of Economic Inequality," *Philosophy & Public Affairs* 41:3 (2013), 193–225: 197.
[80] Margadant, *Urban Rivalries*, 164–5.

agreed. The common good had become a source of pillage.⁸¹ Such sentiments were not limited to France. Around the same time, a schoolteacher in Delaware named Robert Coram stressed economic equality by arguing that God had given the earth in common to all and for the benefit of everybody. Each person was therefore born with the natural right to enough land to survive.⁸²

The question was how to achieve such equality. The naïve idea, adhered to by some North American politicians, that equal opportunity was the panacea did not find support among small farmers and marginal artisans in the early American republic.⁸³ Was a leveling of property a good idea? Jacob Green, a Presbyterian minister and advocate of the American Revolution, welcomed an equality of estate and property, but believed it could not be expected. Georg Forster, the prominent German revolutionary, admired the American constitution, which, he wrote, allowed for only one aristocracy, namely that of wealth. That, however, could not be removed without implementing an impracticable Spartan community. The French militant politician Jacques-Nicolas Billaud-Varenne agreed that, especially in a large country, the "balance of fortunes" could not be just and immobile.⁸⁴ The French Jacobins nonetheless did consider imposing a limit on the accumulation of property in response to a demand by the *sans-culottes*, but failed to take that step when push came to shove.⁸⁵

Some authors living in parts of Germany unaffected by revolutionary turmoil, where practical changes were out of the question, proposed radical solutions. Since every person had the same right to the earth's goods, private property had to be abolished, argued Carl Wilhelm Frölich. It militates

---

⁸¹ Antoine de Cournand, *De la propriété, ou la cause du pauvre: Plaidée au tribunal de la raison, de la justice et de la vérité* (Paris, 1791), 5; Pierre Dolivier, *Essai sur la justice primitive, pour servir de principe générateur au seul ordre social qui peut assurer à l'homme tous ses droits et tous ses moyens de bonheur* (Paris, 1793), 15.

⁸² Seth Cotlar, "Radical Conceptions of Property Rights and Economic Equality in the Early American Republic: The Trans-Atlantic Dimension," *Explorations in Early American Culture* 4 (2000), 191–219: 193.

⁸³ Ruth Bogin, "Petitioning and the New Moral Economy of Post-Revolutionary America," *The William and Mary Quarterly* 45:3 (1988), 391–425: 392.

⁸⁴ S. Scott Rohrer, *Jacob Green's Revolution: Radical Religion and Reform in a Revolutionary Age* (University Park: Pennsylvania State University Press, 2014), 203. Georg Forster to Therese Forster, Arras, 21 August 1793, in Klaus-Georg Popp, ed., *Georg Forsters Werke: Sämtliche Schriften, Tagebücher, Briefe: Briefe 1792 bis 1794 und Nachträge* (Berlin: Akademie-Verlag, 1989), 425. Citoyen Billaud-Varenne, *Les élémens du républicanisme: Première partie* (Paris, 1793), 57.

⁸⁵ Massimiliano Tomba, "1793: The Neglected Legacy of Insurgent Universality," *History of the Present: A Journal of Critical History* 5:2 (2015), 109–36: 120.

against the fulfillment of the needs of everyone. For his part, the philanthropist Heinrich Ziegenhagen proposed the organization of small-scale agricultural colonies based on communal property in which children of the poor and the rich would be raised together to become sociable beings.[86] These plans had in common with contemporary radical French proposals that they did not reflect the rapidly changing economies of western Europe. Far from taking into account the reality of industrialization, they revered subsistence agriculture and idealized peasant simplicity.[87] If these were lone voices, a popular belief in genuine economic equality did take root in Italy. Various authors took up their pens to address the population and convince them that their ideas were mistaken and that they had to content themselves with equality before the law. Economic differences were the logical consequence of differences in natural abilities.[88]

Nor were the rural dwellers insisting on economic change in New York and Virginia looking for equalization of property. Confronted with unfair taxes and economic constraints, they simply tried to end their status as tenants and become part of a reformed society based on landownership. Revolutionary elites did not meet such demands but they made land available in the western parts of their states, thereby easing tensions.[89] In the Río de la Plata, José Artigas organized an agrarian reform, as **Gabriel di Meglio** writes (Volume III, Chapter 9). He distributed vast rural properties from the enemies of the revolution among free blacks, free *zambos*, Indians, and poor creoles. The independence war in northern Spanish America had no comparable outcome. Simón Bolívar's land policy was more concerned with preserving the support of the *caudillos* – the warlords who controlled regional supplies and soldiers – than with offering hope to the rural poor. The caudillos could thus form a new landowning elite who benefited from confiscated property and public land.[90]

---

[86] Helmut Reinalter, *Die Französische Revolution und Mitteleuropa: Erscheinungsformen und Wirkungen des Jakobinismus. Seine Gesellschaftstheorien und politischen Vorstellungen* (Frankfurt am Main: Suhrkamp, 1988), 126–8.

[87] R. B. Rose, "The 'Red Scare' of the 1790s: The French Revolution and the 'Agrarian Law,'" *Past & Present* no. 103 (1984), 113–30: 125. Inside and outside France, these values retained their strength into the nineteenth century. Cf. Giorgio La Rosa, "La représentation dans la pensée politique d'un jacobin italien. Luigi Angeloni (1759–1842)," in *Le concept de représentation dans la pensée politique* (Aix-en-Provence: Presses universitaires d'Aix-Marseille, 2003), 313–20.

[88] Guerci, *Mente, cuore, coraggio, virtù repubblicane*, 131–9.

[89] Thomas J. Humphrey, "Conflicting Independence: Land Tenancy and the American Revolution," *Journal of the Early Republic* 28:2 (2008), 159–82: 174, 182.

[90] John Lynch, "Bolívar and the Caudillos," *Hispanic American Historical Review* 63:1 (1983), 3–35: 25.

Introduction

If equalizing property may have ultimately been unachievable anywhere, the French Revolution did accomplish a comprehensive transformation of property. In Volume II, Chapter 2, **Rafe Blaufarb** explains what the famous abolition of feudalism entailed. In 1789–1790, the French revolutionaries did away with the old system of property and replaced it with an entirely new one. "Feudalism," Blaufarb writes, was "not a special form of property-holding specific to the nobility, but rather *the system* of real estate itself, a system whose essence was to produce a hierarchy of multiple claims to single parcels of land." By blurring public power and private property, feudalism blocked the establishment of national sovereignty. Feudalism was replaced by the national domain, which became the repository of confiscated ecclesiastical properties and properties that had belonged to the royal domain. The sale of these *biens nationaux* was a long, drawn-out process that benefited numerous groups in French society, including, as **Philippe Bourdin** mentions in Volume II, Chapter 9, "the *petite bourgeoisie* (innkeepers, butchers, and merchants, whose numbers were increasing), the stockjobbers who sometimes acted as intermediaries for families of the old nobility, and the state creditors." However, a law of 1796 that forbade the sale of *biens nationaux* in small lots shut the door to the small and medium-sized peasantry, which had fervently hoped to acquire more land since the start of the revolution.[91]

Violence

Revolutions are not straightforward affairs. The search for freedom never leads directly to emancipation, but brings about a crisis in which the revolutionaries are presented with different solutions.[92] The initial claims to autonomy in Spanish America following the king's resignation in Bayonne, writes **Stefan Rinke** (Volume III, Chapter 1), "were not hard revolutionary ruptures, but rather events in which the elites cautiously groped their way into unknown territory and gradually expanded their own ideas and demands." Independence was not yet on the horizon. Revolutions could gain momentum when many plebeians suddenly stopped resigning themselves to the old hierarchical civic order and became aware of the potential power of the joint

---

[91] Bernard Bodinier and Éric Teyssier, *L'événement le plus important de la Révolution: La vente des biens nationaux (1789–1867) en France et dans les territoires annexés* (Paris: Société des Études Robespierristes, 2000), 383–98.

[92] Federica Morelli, "Guerras, libertad y ciudadanía. Los afro-descendientes de Esmeraldas en la independencia," *Revista de Indias* 76 (2016), 83–108: 84.

efforts of like-minded people. That was a nightmare scenario for the champions of the status quo. When the Haitian revolution broke out, one planter believed his class might need to kill half of the enslaved workforce to stop the "epidemic" and replace those killed with new imports from Africa.[93]

While polarization was deadly in Saint-Domingue, the middle ground was also lost sooner or later in other revolutionary theaters. In Mexico, any reluctance to support one side was seen as a sign of sympathy for the other.[94] Similarly, Patriot authorities in North America summoned, secured, or confined anyone suspected of being "unfriendly to the rights of America."[95] After the end of the revolutionary war, John Jay explained to Peter Van Schaack that the latter had been mistaken to try to maintain his neutrality: "No man can serve two masters: either Britain was right and America was wrong; or America was right and Britain was wrong. They who thought Britain right were bound to support her; and America had a just claim to the services of those who approved her cause. Hence it became our duty to take one side or the other."[96] **Liam Riordan** (Volume I, Chapter 13) cites Massachusetts Governor Thomas Hutchinson, who wrote in 1776 that "under the present free government in America, no man may, by writing or speaking, contradict any part of this Declaration, without being deemed an enemy to his country, and exposed to the rage and fury of the populace."

One of the features of the revolutions was the amount of violence that accompanied them. In Ireland, **Thomas Bartlett** writes (Volume II, Chapter 16), "the extreme violence witnessed during the 1798 rebellion, and during the run-up to it, bears comparison to that perpetrated in the Vendée, and later in Spain during the Peninsular War. As in these theaters, irregular combatants were simply not recognized as legitimate fighters and therefore the normal ethical constraints on soldiers' conduct could be ignored." In Mexico, another historian has suggested, the rebellion created "a political space for the emergence of violent men of little principle and

---

[93] Philippe Girard, *Toussaint Louverture: A Revolutionary Life* (New York: Basic Books, 2016), 125.
[94] Timo Schaefer, "Soldiers and Civilians: The War of Independence in Oaxaca, 1814–1815," *Mexican Studies/Estudios Mexicanos*, 29:1 (2013), 149–74: 168. As exemplary punishment, at least in Oaxaca, both sides also tended to set fire to villages. Ibid., 172.
[95] Christopher F. Minty, "'Of One Hart and One Mind': Local Institutions and Allegiance during the American Revolution," *Early American Studies: An Interdisciplinary Journal* 15:1 (2017), 99–132: 115.
[96] T. H. Breen, *The Will of the People: The Revolutionary Birth of America* (Cambridge, MA: The Belknap Press of Harvard University Press, 2019), 146.

large ambition."⁹⁷ During Hidalgo's revolt and the following counterinsurgency, thousands of people were executed. **Juan Ortiz Escamilla** writes in Volume III, Chapter 5 that the military dictatorship set up by the royalists in Mexico, which lasted six years, "was a period characterized by assassinations, plundering, arbitrary executions, exemplary punishments, the burning of villages, and the raping of women." In other parts of Spanish America, the death toll was initially relatively small, but as **Ernesto Bassi** tells us (Volume III, Chapter 8), northern South America was where the low-intensity confrontation first mutated into violent warfare under the banner of "war to the death." Bassi adds that in the same region, the Spanish recapture of most of South America was launched and took its most violent form. Chile and Upper Peru also registered a large mortality. A census held in La Paz in 1824 after hostilities had ceased revealed a very small number of men between ages fifteen and twenty-five.⁹⁸ Even by then, the end to violence was not in sight in Spanish America. **Juan Luis Ossa Santa Cruz** argues in Volume III, Chapter 7 that "the following decades witnessed countless armed conflicts, transforming violence into a daily and legitimate political practice that, with ups and downs, lasted for the rest of the century."

Was the French Revolution notoriously violent or has the violence unleashed in France been exaggerated? **Marisa Linton** writes (Volume II, Chapter 8): "The received opinion is that the French Revolution was unique in its time in its recourse to political violence. Yet comparisons with the death toll in the English Civil Wars (that stretched throughout the British Isles) and 'revolutions' of the seventeenth century, with the American Revolution, and with the suppression of the revolt in Ireland in 1798, suggest that it would be more accurate to see revolutionary violence in the context of wider factors such as fear, repression, and the degree of retaliation, rather than as the consequence of a specific ideology unique to the French Revolution." Revolutionary Saint-Domingue offers another example of widespread violence, and certainly not only on the part of enslaved insurgents. White residents, as **Bernard Gainot** shows (Volume II, Chapter 24), engaged in lynching and mutiny. These so-called "patriots" were driven by a violent rejection of equal rights.

---

⁹⁷ Eric Van Young, *The Other Rebellion: Popular Violence, Ideology, and the Mexican Struggle for Independence, 1810–1821* (Stanford: Stanford University Press, 2001), 196.
⁹⁸ Karen Racine, "Death, Destiny, and the Daily Chores: Everyday Life in Spanish America during the Wars of Independence, 1808–1826," in Pedro Santoni, ed., *Civilians in Wartime Latin America: From the Wars of Independence to the Central American Civil Wars* (Westport, CN: Greenwood Press, 2008), 31–53: 36.

The American Revolution was indeed remarkably violent as well. The British Army left in its wake landscapes that were so affected that it seemed they had been hit by a tornado or earthquake. "Rape," writes one historian, "was endemic within the British Army."[99] Areas that could not be held by either side were pillaged relentlessly, such as, for example, Westchester County, just north of New York: "From 1775 through 1782, the county became a no man's land whose four thousand families enjoyed neither personal security nor freedom from plunder. Contending armies, militias, and partisan bands took farm surpluses and left families with too little to last through winter. They raided friend and foe alike to pilfer personal property, steal livestock, burn barns and houses, and cut trees and fences for firewood. Soldiers and criminal gangs looted what armies and militias left behind."[100] Violence was also of central importance on the Patriot side, studied by **Wayne Lee** in Volume 1, Chapter 12. He notes that "the American revolution and the accompanying war included a wide set of categories of political violence, all of which occurred within the same overall clash of wills." And in most cases, those categories were also *stages*. Lee distinguishes between violence that was "intimidative and catalytic," "regular and logistical," and "retaliatory."

Violence was not the monopoly of warring armies. In revolutionary Pennsylvania, acts of violence were often committed by those frustrated about the lack of decisive action on the part of politicians whose rhetoric they shared. Such violence required the revolutionary elites to take the rebels' grievances seriously.[101] The peasant revolts across early revolutionary France were part of a similar dynamics with massive consequences, since they helped bring about the end of "feudalism." In France, violence away from the battlefield continued in the years to come. Howard Brown has explained that "the Revolution not only destroyed the institutional constraints on popular violence, it eroded many of the cultural ones as well. This included the diminished role of the clergy in community life, the decline in deference accorded social status, the disruption in patronage patterns, and the reduced primacy of the local community."[102] There was a transatlantic continuity in

---

[99] Hoock, *Scars of Independence: America's Violent Birth*, 131, 170 (quote).
[100] Allan Kulikoff, "Revolutionary Violence and the Origins of American Democracy," *The Journal of the Historical Society* II:2 (Spring 2002), 229–60: 236.
[101] Kenneth Owen, "Violence and the Limits of the Political Community in Revolutionary Pennsylvania," in Patrick Griffin, Robert G. Ingram, Peter S. Onuf, and Brian Schoen, eds., *Between Sovereignty and Anarchy* (Charlottesville: University of Virginia Press, 2015), 165–86: 180–1.
[102] Howard G. Brown, *Ending the French Revolution: Violence, Justice, and Repression from the Terror to Napoleon* (Charlottesville: University of Virginia Press, 2006), 50.

Introduction

French violence, as one historian has argued. It was no coincidence that the French campaign in Saint-Domingue of 1802–1803 resembled that in the Vendée in its goal to exterminate the enemy. Contemporaries already referred to the "colonial Vendée" as they laid (at least partial) blame for both on the British enemy. As if to confirm this connection, the Directory appointed as its agent in Saint-Domingue one of the generals who had "pacified" the Vendée.[103]

Royalism

The Vendée's opposition to the revolution was symbolized from the start by white cockades worn in public, which gave expression to the rebels' adherence to royalism. Yet royalism did not necessarily denote a progressive or conservative ideology. Neither the revolutionaries in the Americas nor those in France started out as republicans. Only when King George did not live up to the expectation of orators and writers to reclaim the royal privileges that his predecessors had lost did a republican solution become a possibility in North America. It was at that juncture that Thomas Paine's *Common Sense* came out, condemning the "royal brute of Britain."[104] Monarchist members of the French Assembly favored the revolution, but more as a set of early achievements than as a seemingly endless movement. They hoped to entrust the king with sovereign powers, assisted by a bicameral parliament that would provide counsel. After this constitutional project was rejected, they tried to maintain a centrist position between revolution and counterrevolution.[105] **Caroline Winterer** (Volume I, Chapter 1) stresses that during their revolution, North Americans were impressed by Europe's enlightened despots, who mixed monarchical rule with Enlightenment. And **Matthew Rainbow Hale** (Volume II, Chapter 5) notes that there was an intimate relationship between monarchy and democracy that proved to be resilient. What exerted a particularly powerful force in the 1790s on both sides of the North Atlantic was the allure, derived from monarchies, of indivisible sovereignty.

---

[103] Malick Ghachem, "The Colonial Vendée," in David Patrick Geggus and Norman Fiering, eds., *The World of the Haitian Revolution* (Bloomington: Indiana University Press, 2009), 156–76.
[104] Eric Nelson, *The Royalist Revolution: Monarchy and the American Founding* (Cambridge, MA: The Belknap Press of Harvard University Press, 2014), 33, 57–8, 63.
[105] Pascal Simonetti, "Les monarchiens. La Révolution à contretemps," in Jean Tulard, ed., *La contre-révolution: Origines, histoire, postérité* (Paris: Perrin, 1990), 62–84.

Nor were the political elites of Spanish America who assumed sovereignty after the forced abdication of Fernando VII in Bayonne natural republicans. Their intention was not to repudiate the monarchy, but to redefine it in a constitutional framework that was dictated locally and not in Cádiz. Before they embarked on independentist projects, the elites aimed to consolidate governmental rule and maintain the basic laws in a Hispanic structure.[106] Individuals and groups across the Atlantic world, then, continued to display allegiance to their hereditary rulers, from whom they sought protection and the concession of privileges.[107] Slaves in New Granada often understood the republican fight for independence as an attempt of their owners to limit the authority of the king. At the same time, they tried to have their defense of the king's power expressed in the form of individual or collective advantages.[108] Many enslaved freedom fighters in Saint-Domingue also supported a distant European king, carrying royalist banners and proclaiming that they wanted to restore Louis XVI to his throne after they had heard about his arrest.[109] Other rebels sided with Spain, in part because, as **Robert D. Taber** writes in Volume II, Chapter 22, "Spain also offered a king, a potent symbol of good government." Monarchism survived the revolution in Saint-Domingue and was alive and well in independent Haiti. Dessalines was crowned Emperor Jean-Jacques I, while Henry Christophe later led the kingdom of Haiti as King Henry I. And even the republic that Alexandre Pétion established, in which universal male suffrage was introduced, was "an oligarchy with a democratic veneer," writes **Erin Zavitz** (Volume II, Chapter 26).

In Latin America, too, monarchism remained a viable option after independence. One reason, as **Gabriel di Meglio** contends in Volume III, Chapter 9, was the Congress of Vienna's condemnation of governments created by revolution. That influenced the debate in Buenos Aires about postrevolutionary rule, in which some fancied a constitutional king, who could maintain order and put an end to local turmoil. In Brazil, the outcome of the independence process was an imperial state. Besides, writes **Jurandir**

---

[106] José M. Portillo Valdés, *Crisis atlántica: Autonomía e independencia en la crisis de la monarquía hispana* (Madrid: Fundación Carolina, Marcial Pons, 2006), 147–53.

[107] Hannah Weiss Muller, "Bonds of Belonging: Subjecthood and the British Empire," *Journal of British Studies* 53:1 (2014), 29–58: 57–8.

[108] Marcela Echeverri, *Indian and Slave Royalists in the Age of Revolution: Reform, Revolution, and Royalism in the Northern Andes, 1780–1825* (New York: Cambridge University Press, 2017), 60.

[109] Jeremy D. Popkin, *You Are All Free: The Haitian Revolution and the Abolition of Slavery* (New York: Cambridge University Press, 2010), 94, 104, 129–30.

Malerba in Volume III, Chapter 18, regent prince Dom João, who had moved the Portuguese court to Rio de Janeiro, played an important role in the independence process: "willingly or not, by coopting the Brazilian upper classes through his patriarchal and enticing policy, the sovereign helped decisively define the profile of the new elite that was formed in Brazil during the thirteen years he spent in Rio de Janeiro." When the unpopular first emperor, Dom Pedro, suddenly abdicated in 1831, a fresh opportunity was presented to radical leaders of the liberal opposition, writes **Jeffrey Needell** in Volume III, Chapter 19. The parliamentary leadership, however, "interwoven with the families and interests of the elite," balked. Instead, they chose, again, to support the vision of a constitutional monarchy that they had been trying to force upon Dom Pedro since 1823. Faced with radical republicanism, with its associated, clear threat of socioeconomic and national destabilization, they chose, again, the hope of constitutional, balanced partnership with a "unifying, charismatic national leader." Dom Pedro II thus started his reign as the new emperor.

Monarchical leadership also marked the start of Mexican independence. Cultivating close ties with the local elites, Agustín de Iturbide worked out the Plan of Iguala, which declared "the absolute independence of this kingdom," but also extended an invitation to Fernando VII or one of his family members to govern New Spain.[110] After the Spanish government declined, Iturbide assumed command and, supported by the Mexican elite, was enthroned as Emperor Agustín I. José de San Martín also strongly favored organizing independent states as monarchies, while even the committed republican Simón Bolívar had begun to flirt with monarchism by 1825. A British diplomat quoted him as saying in a private conversation: "Of all Countries South America is perhaps the least fitted for Republican Governments. What does its population consist of but Indians and Negros who are more ignorant than the vile race of Spaniards we are just emancipated from. A country represented and governed by such people must go to ruin." It would, however, take a while, he believed, for the inhabitants of the former Spanish colonies to embrace the notion of a new king.[111] Bolívar was not the only one during his presidency of Colombia to advocate a constitutional monarchy. A French agent wrote that the clergy, the army, and the common

---

[110] Jaime E. Rodríguez O., *"We Are Now the True Spaniards": Sovereignty, Revolution, Independence, and the Emergence of the Federal Republic of Mexico, 1808–1824* (Stanford: Stanford University Press, 2012), 253–63.

[111] Harold Temperley, *The Foreign Policy of Canning 1822–1827: England, the Neo-Holy Alliance, and the New World*, 2nd edition (London: Frank Cass & Co., 1966), 557–8.

people all favored that option. Some wanted Bolívar himself to be crowned, while others debated his possible succession, if he died, by a foreign prince.[112]

On the whole, royalists belonged to the counterrevolutionary camp, those desirous to maintain the status quo or pursue their goals without overthrowing the government. In Central America, people across the social spectrum steadfastly clung to Spain during the 1810s, when in all other parts of Spanish America people began to aspire to independence. **Timothy Hawkins** (Volume III, Chapter 6) notes that this was "despite exposure to the widespread political ideas of this revolutionary age and the kind of persistent internal grievances that united to spark and fuel independence movements in other colonies. Combined with a colonial administration single-minded in its dedication to root out dissent, this broad consensus helped marginalize and suffocate the few substantive challenges to the colonial order that did arise during this decade." More generally, writes **Marcela Echeverri** in Volume III, Chapter 10, "even within a position of loyalty, all subjects in the Atlantic empires embraced and produced radical lasting change."

In British America, royalists did not automatically adopt certain views. The only matter on which Loyalists agreed was the need to defend royal rule.[113] Royalist disunion in Spain during that country's constitutional triennium (1820–1823) even led to confrontations between different royalist factions, as **Juan Luis Simal** tells us in Volume III, Chapter 4. The constitutional monarchy was challenged by ultraroyalists, who engaged in guerrilla activities with the support of a rural population that resented taxes, conscription, and recent socioeconomic changes.

Loyalists in North America included members of ethnic and religious minorities who perceived the Crown as "a buffer against the tyranny of the majority."[114] Likewise, Indians in Spanish and Portuguese America sought to uphold the time-honored colonial pact, on account of which they paid royal tribute, and thus contributed to Crown income, in exchange for assuring themselves of the possession of their lands and the preservation of their way

---

[112] C. Parra-Pérez, *La monarquía en la Gran Colombia* (Madrid: Ediciones Cultura Hispánica, 1957), 95, 105, 129, 323.

[113] Maya Jasanoff, *Liberty's Exiles: American Loyalists in the Revolutionary World* (New York: Vintage Books, 2012), 189.

[114] David J. Fowler, "'Loyalty Is Now Bleeding in New Jersey': Motivations and Mentalities of the Disaffected," in Joseph S. Tiedemann, Eugene R. Fingerhut, and Robert W. Venables, eds., *The Other Loyalists: Ordinary People, Royalism, and the Revolution in the Middle Colonies, 1763–1787* (Albany: State University of New York Press, 2009), 45–77: 50.

of organizing their community.[115] Indian tributaries in the Spanish colonies had different demands than their caciques, who were exempt from tribute payments, and enjoyed the privilege to ride horseback and use arms. One feature of Túpac Amaru's revolt in Peru was the rift in many communities between caciques, who remained loyal to the Spanish Crown, and their tributaries, who supported the uprising.[116] The end of the colonial pact could be devastating. In Argentina, **Gabriel di Meglio** explains in Volume III, Chapter 9, "the end of tribute and juridical inequality meant that those villages no longer had rights to their common land, which they had used to pay the tribute, nor to maintain their ethnic leaders, who were in charge of the tribute. Thus, many villages lost their lands, which were sold out." Even the term "Indian" was being erased. The liberal Mexican politician José María Luis Mora proposed to the Congress of his country to do away with that term, since "the Indians should not continue existing" as a social group subject to special legislation. Nonetheless, the term was used throughout the 1820s, although at times the indigenous population was labeled "the so-called Indians."[117]

To the degree that the age of revolutions challenged royal authority, contemporary movements in Africa have been described by some historians as parallel. John Thornton has advanced the argument that Kongo's political system contained an absolutist concept that bestowed all power on the king. In the eighteenth century, absolutism was challenged by a movement (mislabeled "republican" by Thornton) that stressed the need for popular consent to royal rule.[118] Even more forcefully, Paul Lovejoy has made a case for the great significance of jihad in west Africa, especially in the central Bilād al-

---

[115] María Luisa Soux, "Rebelión, guerrilla y tributo: Los indios en Charcas durante el proceso de independencia," *Anuario de Estudios Americanos* 68:2 (2011), 455–82: 458; Mariana Albuquerque Dantas, "Os indios 'fanáticos realistas absolutos' e a figura do monarca português: Disputas políticas, recrutamento e defesa de terras na Confederação do Equador," *Clio* 33:2 (2015), 49–73: 50, 56.

[116] Alexandra Sevilla Naranjo, "'Al mejor servicio del rey.' Indígenas realistas en la contrarrevolución quiteña, 1809–1814," *Procesos. Revista ecuatoriana de historia* no. 43 (2016), 93–118: 111; David T. Garrett, "'His Majesty's Most Loyal Vassals': The Indian Nobility and Túpac Amaru," *Hispanic American Historical Review* 84:4 (2004), 575–617: 597. Caciques in New Spain did not collect tribute, nor did they enjoy the same social standing as their counterparts in the viceroyalty of Peru: Aaron Pollack, "Hacia una historia social del tributo de indios y castas en Hispanoamérica. Notas en torno a su creación, desarrollo y abolición," *Historia Mexicana* 66:1 (2016), 65–160: 71.

[117] Laura Ibarra García, "El concepto de igualdad en México (1810–1824)," *Relaciones* 145 (2016), 279–314: 306.

[118] John K. Thornton, "'I Am the Subject of the King of Congo': African Political Ideology and the Haitian Revolution," *Journal of World History* 4:2 (1993), 181–214: 187.

Sūdān (south of the Sahara) between 1804–1808 and 1817. In response to the despotic rule of warlords, Islamic governments "based on religious leadership and consensus among Muslim officials" were established. How revolutionary west African jihad actually was remains to be seen. What is clear is that the universalist strain of the revolutions in Europe and the Americas was absent. Debates about slavery focused on the illegitimacy of enslaving Muslims, while ending slavery for non-Muslims never came up.[119] In other words, Islamic west Africans had arrived at the point that Christian Europeans had reached in the late Middle Ages, when they ended slavery, but only among their own.

Counterrevolution and Banditry

Ideologies that challenged the revolutions were not exhausted by royalism. Revolts that were directed against revolutions, such as that in the Vendée, had in common their communal character; rural dominance; the importance of religious sentiments; their spontaneous nature; and the opposition to the politics of progress defended by the state that jeopardized the beliefs, structures, and functioning of traditional rural societies.[120] Across Europe and even in Spanish America, the fear of French influence and its ability to dramatically change traditional societies was enormous. Typical is the judgment of the Spanish Inquisition in late 1789 when it forbade the printing of materials that referred to the events in France: these works were produced by a new race of philosophers, who were men with a corrupted spirit. By posing as defenders of liberty, they actually plotted against it and destroyed the political and social order.[121] Spain's Secretary of State, the count of Floridablanca, did all he could stop the flow of information arriving from France. In Volume III, Chapter 2, **Emily Berquist Soule** writes that he "placed more Spanish troops on the border with France in order to deter unsanctioned crossings of people and goods. He implemented a policy of strict censorship designed to keep out all news of the events in France;

---

[119] Paul E. Lovejoy, *Jihād in West Africa during the Age of Revolutions* (Athens, OH: Ohio University Press, 2016), 90, 245–6.
[120] Jean-Pierre Poussou, "Les autres 'Vendées,' jalons pour une thématique des 'Vendées,'" in Yves-Marie Bercé, ed., *Les autres Vendées: Actes du colloque international sur les contre-révolutions paysannes au XIXe siècle* (La Roche-sur-Yon: Éditions du Centre vendéen de recherches historiques, 2013), 299, 304.
[121] Gonzalo Anes Álvarez de Castrillón, "España y la Revolución francesa," in Almudena Cavestany, ed., *Revolución, contrarrevolución e Independencia: La Revolución francesa, España y América* (Madrid: Turner Publicaciones, 1989), 17–39: 20.

forbidding French newspapers, and even employing Inquisition officials to inspect mail coming across the Pyrenees."

British American Loyalists, writes **Trevor Burnard** (Volume I, Chapter 9), "especially those of higher social status, feared that the wild ideas of liberty thrown about by revolutionaries would have a leveling tendency and by promoting lawless anarchy" were harming the empire. Anarchy was projected onto the new republican regimes because of their commitment to democracy. Revolutionaries tended to believe that only republics, ruled as they were by laws and not the royal will, could resist the tendency of men to pursue only their own, personal interest.[122] Counterrevolutionaries rejected the way in which these laws took effect. The large mass of people, asserted a priest from Guayaquil in the viceroyalty of Peru, cannot judge for themselves their own interests unless they put themselves in the hands of a single individual. A Dutch thinker who supported the antirevolutionary Orangists wrote in the same vein that the "people" was incapable of acting by itself. Since they were dependent on a few among them, democracy was in practice always a struggle between various groups of demagogues.[123] The quest of revolutionaries to erect a new society was chimerical in the eyes of their opponents, who rejected the fictitious state of nature. The natural, transcendent order established by God could not be changed.[124]

While prominent rebels and conservatives created the script for each revolution, the vast mass of people involved in the revolutions were motivated by their own individual or group goals, as the abovementioned motives of peasants, slaves, and Indians make clear. In northern South America, **Ernesto Bassi** argues in Volume III, Chapter 8, "support from the *pardos* [the light-skinned free people of color] was highly contingent and depended on the fact that they tended to see political independence or continued allegiance to Spain not as an end in itself but as a means to achieving a more

---

[122] Anthony Pagden, *Spanish Imperialism and the Political Imagination: Studies in European and Spanish-American Social and Political Theory 1513–1830* (New Haven: Yale University Press, 1990), 136.

[123] Victor Samuel Rivera, "José Ignacio Moreno. Un teólogo peruano. Entre Montesquieu y Joseph de Maistre," *Araucaria. Revista Iberoamericana de Filosofía, Política y Humanidades* 15:29 (2013), 223–41: 238. Wyger R. E. Velema, "Elie Luzac and Two Dutch Revolutions: The Evolution of Orangist Political Thought," in Margaret C. Jacob and Wijnand W. Mijnhardt, eds., *The Dutch Republic in the Eighteenth Century: Decline, Enlightenment, and Revolution* (Ithaca, NY: Cornell University Press, 1992), 123–46: 138.

[124] Serge Bianchi, *Des révoltes aux révolutions: Europe, Russie, Amérique (1770–1802). Essai d'interprétation* (Rennes: Presses universitaires de Rennes, 2004), 447.

important aim: legal equality. The same assertion is valid for slaves, although in their case the goal was to secure freedom."

Principle often combined with opportunism to persuade people to join or oppose the revolution. **Liam Riordan** writes in Volume 1, Chapter 13: "The complex web of circumstance and opportunity that informs allegiance in times of uncertain change and military mobilization is necessarily shaped by perceptions of self-interest." In Mexico, Hidalgo's rebellion "encouraged certain marginalized and semi-marginalized Mexicans to employ violence in order to adjust deeply held grievances against the regime, provincial administrators, and members of the propertied classes who had long enjoyed the benefits of power, and it presented to many others an opportunity to get rich-quick, or at least to stake out for themselves a place in any new society."[125] These men engaged in guerrilla warfare, as **Juan Ortiz Escamilla** explains. Violent raids on towns and habitual looting of haciendas were their trademarks. Their leaders, often locally born, saw to the distribution of booty and captured livestock among their supporters. Italy's bandits engaged in robbery and armed revolt as a form of revenge against a society that had marginalized them. They found common cause in attacking the privileged classes, fighting government bureaucracy, as well as the French invaders. Those invaders' insults of personal or family honor convinced many a peasant to take up arms.[126] Besides, peer pressure and a search for adventure must have played a role as well.[127]

The distinction between rebellion/counterrebellion and banditry was often blurred, either because ordinary bandits sided with the royalists or the patriots, or – particularly in countries in which Napoleon's armies lived off the land and introduced mass conscription – because banditry doubled as resistance, but also because guerrillas on both sides often engaged in crimes that had no political dimension. At the same time, authorities were eager to label counterrevolutionary attacks as brigandage since that served to discredit the enemy's political demands. In France, the term "brigand," which had initially both caused aversion and won admiration among the members of the National Assembly, was increasingly defined negatively in the course of the Revolution, especially after the start of the war in the Vendée. In their

---

[125] Christon I. Archer, "Banditry and Revolution in New Spain, 1790–1821," *Bibliotheca Americana* 1:2 (1982), 58–89: 59, 88.
[126] Massimo Viglione, *Le insorgenze: Rivoluzione & Controrivoluzione in Italia, 1792–1815* (Milan: Edizioni Ares, 1999), 96–7; Michael Broers, *Napoleon's Other War: Bandits, Rebels, and Their Pursuers in the Age of Revolutions* (Oxford: Peter Lang, 2010), 110.
[127] Van Young, *The Other Rebellion*, 105–6.

subsequent fight against insurgents in countries occupied by France, lawyers and gendarmes ceased to distinguish between bandits and guerrilla fighters.[128]

Bandits – with or without a political agenda – used the breakdown of law and order that was the result of revolution. Chilean banditry, for example, was encouraged by the anarchy of the civil war between republicans and royalists, as many poor people were displaced or otherwise affected.[129] In northern South America, the disruption of the colonial state and colonial institutions opened the door to the caudillos, military leaders who drew to them the *llaneros*. These plainsmen lived by plunder and lacked any political objectives. They followed "the first caudillo who offers them booty taken from anyone with property. This is how Boves and other bandits of the same kind have been able to recruit hordes of these people, who live by vagrancy, robbery, and assassination."[130] Such bandits may have been able to fill the political vacuum left by the disappearance of the old government, but in turn they prevented a new civilian government from taking hold. The Thirteen Colonies in North America fell prey to banditry – which included the stealing of slaves – that was hardly political in nature. As historian Holger Hoock observes, by 1780, "large swaths of the American lower South presented a scary scene – a virtually permanent little war of raiding and plundering between Patriot and Loyalist militias, prisoner abuse, even outright murder. In addition, armed gangs unaffiliated with any real military units operated in the semi-lawless wasteland between the lines."[131] Many of the smaller bands "operated independently, though often in the guise of serving one side or the other."[132] Nor can the Maroons who refused to remain on their plantations during the Haitian Revolution and retreated into the interior be categorized as counterrevolutionaries. As **Philippe Girard** writes (Volume II, Chapter 25), the Maroons distrusted all elite actions vying for control of Saint-Domingue, opposing "whichever side was dominant to preserve their freedom and autonomy."

---

[128] Sottocasa, *Les brigands et la Révolution*, 60, 146, 289; Broers, *Napoleon's Other War*, 55, 102–3.
[129] Leonardo León, "Montoneras Populares durante la gestación de la República, Chile: 1810–1820," *Anuario de Estudios Americanos* 68:2 (2011), 483–510: 487–8, 492.
[130] John Lynch, "Bolívar and the Caudillos," *Hispanic American Historical Review* 63:1 (1983), 3–35: 5.
[131] Hoock, *Scars of Independence*, 309.
[132] Matthew P. Spooner, "Origins of the Old South: Revolution, Slavery, and Changes in Southern Society, 1776–1800" (Ph.D. dissertation, Columbia University, 2015), 62.

Ideology, then, was just one of many factors motivating individuals. On both sides of the American Revolution, desertion was rampant. One historian has written, "A steady stream of Loyalists deserted, as they were converted to the American cause, discouraged because of limitations placed on looting, disheartened by the ever-lengthening conflict, enticed by the colonial lifestyle, or simply out of boredom." Patriots also deserted, "many of them for the same reasons as the Loyalists, because of uncertainty of the rightness of their cause, because the changing seasons meant they were needed for work on their farms, or because the war was not the adventure or sure meal ticket they had thought it would be."[133] If many men changed their minds, others avoided choosing sides as long as possible. Their lack of affiliation did not mean indifference. Instead, their personal or group goals might or might not align with the two main adversaries. Tenants in the northern Hudson Valley whose goal was to own the land on which they worked put off a choice for either side in the war until they could no longer avoid it. For their part, indigenous groups in Upper Peru often withdrew to their communities and only did the absolute minimum to satisfy patriots and royalists, waiting to see which side was gaining the upper hand.[134]

Nor did enslaved men and women in the Thirteen Colonies automatically take side with one of the two main sides. **James Sidbury** contends (Volume 1, Chapter 15) that "the Revolutionary War offered Blacks in North America many potential opportunities, but none that were reliable, so it is unsurprising that different people living in different places pursued different strategies." Still, 20,000 of them actually ran to the British armies during the course of the war, attracted by vague promises of freedom; 8,000 to 10,000 of them survived and managed to leave the United States, as Sidbury writes, "to live the rest of their lives as free people."

International Dimensions

Textbook accounts of revolutions tend to obscure their strong international dimension. The American Revolution, for example, cannot be understood without acknowledging the role of the French colonies of Martinique and

---

[133] Anne Pfaelzer de Ortiz, "German Redemptioners of the Lower Sort: Apolitical Soldiers in the American Revolution?," *Journal of American Studies* 33:2 (1999), 267–306: 290.

[134] Thomas J. Humphrey, *Land and Liberty: Hudson Valley Riots in the Age of Revolution* (DeKalb: Northern Illinois University Press, 2004), 93; Soux, "Rebelión, guerrilla y tributo," 458.

Saint-Domingue and the Dutch island of St. Eustatius, as **Wim Klooster** stresses in Volume I, Chapter 19. As for Spain's role, **Gonzalo M. Quintero Saravia** argues in Volume I, Chapter 10, that when its government joined the French war effort against Britain in 1778, it "not only tipped the balance of the conflict, giving France and Spain numerical superiority both at land and at sea, but also profoundly changed the general strategy of the war ... This clear superiority opened up new theaters in this now truly global war, spreading British resources thin. Britain would be forced to abandon a purely American perspective of the conflict and adopt a more global view of the war ..." France's support for the American Revolution was accompanied in the same years by its defeat, alongside Bern and Savoy, of Geneva, where an insurrection had taken place against the magistrates. Geneva was unfortunate, writes **Richard Whatmore** (Volume II, Chapter 12), that in 1782 the strength of France was at a peak unparalleled since the 1680s. French invasions of foreign countries may have stopped during the early stages of the French Revolution, but the fear of an international conspiracy aimed at defeating the revolution helped forge a parliamentary majority in Paris in favor of war in 1792. From then on, warfare was a permanent feature of French life until the Battle of Waterloo, conquest of neighboring territories doubling or masquerading as liberation.[135]

The Spanish American independence movements were even more borderless than those in Europe. Troops from Buenos Aires were deployed not only in battles against Spanish forces in Chile and Upper Peru, but also outside the viceroyalty of the Río de la Plata in Peru. Similarly, natives of New Granada were instrumental in ending the Spanish regime in Peru. In addition, the independence movement in Spanish America was entangled with that in Brazil, as **João Paulo Pimenta** shows in Volume III, Chapter 21. One element of this braided history was the repeated Portuguese and later Brazilian interventions in the Banda Oriental, starting in 1811, which were predicated on fear of the successive revolutionary governments in Buenos Aires. These military incursions ended only with the creation of Uruguay in 1828.

International connections were not just military in nature. What gave the revolutionary age coherence was the spread of ideas and ideals, inspiring both enthusiasm and aversion. Pimenta notes that through "newspapers, as well as diplomatic reports, official and private correspondence, and the

---

[135] T. C. W. Blanning, *The Origins of the French Revolutionary Wars* (London: Longman, 1986).

circulation of people, rumors, and news, Spanish America became increasingly familiar in Brazil, arousing interest, fears, and expectations, and provoking reactions." All around the Atlantic world, the North American Declaration of Independence and the constitutions spawned by the new nation and its component states became powerful documents in the hands of rebels in other locales.[136] The French Declaration of the Rights of Man and Citizen and the French constitutions of the first revolutionary years served the same purpose. In Hungary, **Orsolya Szakály** writes in Volume II, Chapter 19, the radical Society of Liberty and Equality "called for a democratic republic of equal citizens in Hungary with references to the French Revolution." Political awareness in several Spanish colonies was also stimulated by the French Revolution. In Volume II, Chapter 6, **Clément Thibaud** shows that members of Spanish American elites could derive inspiration from the French Declaration as much as slaves and free people of color, as they both did during the French revolutionary decade and the Spanish imperial crisis after 1808. No explicit reference could be made to the French example, but, writes Thibaud, "between 1811 and 1813, all constitutional projects in Spanish America included a section on the Rights of Man and of the Citizen." The French model did not arrive alone, mingling with that of the Haitian Revolution to form a potent mixture of revolutionary ideas, slogans, and practices. In the 1790s, **Cristina Soriano** writes (Volume II, Chapter 28), the new revolutionary language "that arrived on the coast of the Spanish Main challenged the already tense relations that existed among different socioracial groups. The majority of the white population interpreted this revolutionary narrative as a violent torrent that sought to destroy their political system and social order, while many free and enslaved people of African descent saw this as their opportunity to achieve social justice and emancipation from the system of slavery, or to at least renegotiate their labor conditions and political roles." One free man of color in Spanish Louisiana expressed his admiration for French rule in Saint-Domingue, where, he said, men like himself enjoyed civil equality. "We can speak openly, like any white person and hold the same rank as they." It is unjust that we don't enjoy equality in Louisiana. Anticipating a line from Martin Luther King's famous speech, he added: "Only their method of thinking – not color – should differentiate men."[137]

---

[136] George Athan Billias, *American Constitutionalism Heard Round the World, 1776–1789: A Global Perspective* (New York: New York University Press, 2009).

[137] Kimberly Hanger, "Conflicting Loyalties: The French Revolution and Free People of Color in Spanish New Orleans," *Louisiana History* 34:1 (1993), 5–33: 26.

Among German radicals, debates revolved around the French catalog of rights, which they saw as the foundation for social order. The French example still resonated internationally when, in France itself, Thermidor set in and principles of natural law were no longer considered the foundation of liberty but denounced as an arsenal for anarchists and levelers which had produced the Terror.[138] The international impact of the ideas spawned by both the French Revolution and the American Revolution, as well as those associated with the Enlightenment, has often been presented as ideological absorption. It was, however, not the force of these ideas themselves that enabled them to spread to certain locales. As one historian has argued, ideas can make history only when they successfully process reality and offer ways out of a social impasse. Crises make those seeking solutions look for appropriate intellectual and political instruments.[139] And once a revolutionary situation is unfolding, creative energies are unleashed that produce new ideas and ideals.[140]

As had happened under the influence of the Revolution in France, a surge of politicization also occurred under the influence of the constitution of Cádiz of 1812, at least in the Iberian world. **Jane Landers** writes in Volume III, Chapter 11 that this constitution "reversed long-promulgated racial prohibitions and decreed that 'Spaniards of African origin' should be helped to study sciences and have access to an ecclesiastical career." The new constitution, Landers continues, was read in plazas across the Atlantic, to enthusiastic crowds that included free and enslaved Blacks. After the constitution reached Cuba, a series of slave revolts swept through the island, as hope born of debates in the Cortes and British Parliament helped launch rumors about abolition decrees authored by authorities as diverse as the king of Spain, the Spanish Cortes, the king of England, the king of Haiti, and the king of Kongo. Those debates did not create such beliefs but activated the often deep-felt conviction of Black men and women of the illegality of their enslavement. News from afar was not necessary to trigger such ideas, as suggested by the impact of the constitution of Antioquia (New Granada), which was saturated with the metaphor of liberty, on a group of slaves who

---

[138] Yannick Bosc, *La terreur des droits de l'homme: Le républicanisme de Thomas Paine et le moment thermidorien* (Paris: Éditions Kimé, 2016); Günther Birtsch, "Naturrecht und Menschenrechte. Zur vernunftrechtlichen Argumentation deutscher Jakobiner," in Otto Dann and Diethelm Klippel, eds., *Naturrecht – Spätaufklärung – Revolution* (Hamburg: Felix Meiner Verlag, 1995), 111–20: 119–20.

[139] Peter Blickle, *Von der Leibeigenschaft zu den Menschenrechten: Eine Geschichte der Freiheit in Deutschland* (Munich: Verlag C. H. Beck, 2006), 15.

[140] Kristin Ross, *Communal Luxury: The Political Imaginary of the Paris Commune* (London: Verso, 2015), 6–7.

claimed to represent more than 10,000 fellow bondspeople. Convinced of the existence of a liberating decree, they approached the tribunal of justice in Medellín, only to be arrested.[141]

The movement to abolish slavery was one that transgressed boundaries. In Volume II, Chapter 4, **Erica Johnson Edwards** shows that the French Society of the Friends of the Blacks and its successor organization, the Society of the Friends of the Blacks and the Colonies, enjoyed membership from both sides of the Channel and both sides of the Atlantic. In another sense, abolitionism also extended across international borders. As **Seymour Drescher** details in Volume II, Chapter 15, Great Britain sent a large fleet to Algiers, which succeeded in liberating many enslaved Europeans, victims of the Barbary corsairs, took great pains to stimulate international condemnation of the transatlantic slave trade, and made recognition of the new Latin American countries dependent on a commitment to abolish the slave trade. News about the termination of slavery in foreign lands was not always a welcome boon for abolitionists. Abolition in Saint-Domingue in 1793, sanctioned by the French Convention the following year, made antislavery activists both in Great Britain and in the United States lose ground in their struggle. **Ashli White** demonstrates in Volume II, Chapter 29 that those bent on upholding slavery in the United States spread the fiction that Black people in Saint-Domingue were fighting a war of revenge against their former masters after they had been set free thanks to false philanthropists.

The Haitian Revolution also proved to be a major source of inspiration among those living in bondage in the New World's many slave societies, while the French Revolution found resonance among both whites and nonwhites. That was in part due to the initiatives of Victor Hugues, France's most senior representative in the years 1794–1798, whose revolutionary troops were composed largely of former slaves. This massive force, **Jessica Pierre-Louis** tells us in Volume II, Chapter 27, "forced the British to recruit and emancipate more enslaved conscripted soldiers to cope with the increase in French troops. Thus, general French freedom also generated, albeit to a lesser extent, emancipation in the British colonies."

Separating the reception of the closely intertwined French and Haitian revolutions is not easy. In Brazil, **Alejandro Gómez** asserts (Volume III, Chapter 14),

---

[141] María Eugenia Chaves, "Esclavos, libertades y república: Tesis sobre la polisemia de la libertad en la primera república antioqueña," *Estudios Interdisciplinarios de América Latina* 22:1 (2011), 81–104: 87–9. Cf. Wim Klooster, "Slave Revolts, Royal Justice, and a Ubiquitous Rumor in the Age of Revolutions," *The William and Mary Quarterly* 71:3 (2014), 401–24.

both the revolution in Saint-Domingue and the support of revolutionary activity by the French colonial regime in Guadeloupe affected the city of Salvador, where conspirators in 1798 criticized the "monarchical yoke" and praised the "freedom, equality, and fraternity" of the French.[142] The impact of these two revolutions on the Americas was dissimilar, David Geggus has argued: "If the French Revolution proclaimed the ideals of liberty and equality, the Haitian Revolution demonstrated to colonized peoples that they could be won by force of arms. Plantation societies built on bondage, prejudice, and inequality were peculiarly vulnerable to the ideology of revolutionary France, but the dramatic example of self-liberation offered by Saint-Domingue's transformation into Haiti brought the message much closer to home."[143]

In Spanish America, writes **Clément Thibaud** (Volume II, Chapter 6), the legacy of the French or Haitian revolutions was not explicitly invoked, but hiding in plain sight. Revolutionaries had a thorough grasp of what the French assemblies had accomplished and adopted several institutions that had originated in France. It would also be impossible to imagine the revolutionaries' acceptance of racial equality without the shadow of the Haitian Revolution.[144] And then there was the Haitian republic, a vivid reminder of the successful revolution, which officially maintained its neutrality, but provided crucial support to rebels in Caribbean South America. **Ernesto Bassi** writes (Volume III, Chapter 8) that the obvious sympathies for the Spanish American revolutions of Alexandre Pétion (the president of one of Haiti's two polities at the time) led to the characterization of his republic by Spanish officials as "the receptacle of all the adventurers."

Like the Haitian Revolution, that of France was particularly influential in its own hemisphere. In nearby Switzerland, for example, both intellectuals and peasants who had suffered under the remnants of feudalism responded enthusiastically in the first months after the storming of the Bastille, while in rural areas in western Germany peasants refused to pay tithes or perform the *corvée*, the unpaid labor owed to their lords.[145] Usually, however, the

---

[142] See also Luiz Geraldo Silva, "El impacto de la revolución de Saint-Domingue y los afrodescendientes libres de Brasil. Esclavitud, libertad, configuración social y perspectiva atlántica (1780–1825)," *Historia* 49:1 (2016), 209–33.

[143] Geggus, "Slave Rebellion," 27–8.

[144] David Geggus, "The Sounds and Echoes of Freedom: The Impact of the Haitian Revolution on Latin America," in Darién J. Davis, ed., *Beyond Slavery: The Multilayered Legacy of Africans in Latin America and the Caribbean* (Lanham, MD: Rowman & Littlefield, 2007), 19–36: 25.

[145] Marc H. Lerner, *A Laboratory of Liberty: The Transformation of Political Culture in Republican Switzerland, 1750–1848* (Leiden: Brill, 2012), 79; T. C. W. Blanning,

revolution's supporters were small in number and to be found among radical city-dwellers, who often pinned all their hopes on a French invasion. Joseph Schlemmer, a German lawyer, wrote in 1792: "The happiness of half the world depends on the luck or misfortune of French arms. For if they win, the subject can hope for equity and justice, for better laws to protect him. If they lose, the most terrible slavery in monarchical states is inevitable."[146] The French, indeed, brought freedom, introducing various degrees of rural emancipation in Belgium, the Helvetic Republic, several parts of northern and western Germany, and the Grand Duchy of Warsaw. These French policies also led to preemptive emancipation in German states that were not invaded.[147]

Despite the changes wrought, bitterness and opposition eventually prevailed in the areas subdued by French arms. In Volume II, Chapter 21, **Annie Jourdan** writes: "In view of the political, economic, and social consequences, the so-called sister republics were a flagrant failure. Their alliance with the French republic brought them continuous disorder, increased taxation, military violence and depredations, and infinite abuses of power." Italian territories were particularly badly affected. In Milan, the French provoked outrage by billeting soldiers in private homes, establishing a National Guard for which all able-bodied men between sixteen and fifty-five were recruited, and eliminating religious festivals and sacred wall paintings on public buildings.[148] Apart from strong local cultural and religious traditions, the French invaders were confronted with deep-rooted judicial cultures which challenged their uniformist impulse.[149] Sooner or later, although not universally, the French presence descended into boundless military violence, which inspired counterviolence.[150] **John A. Davis** (Volume II, Chapter 17) nuances this picture. Even brutal features of the French presence, he writes,

---

Reform and Revolution in Mainz 1743–1803 (Cambridge: Cambridge University Press, 1974), 306.

[146] Jörg Schweigard, Aufklärung und Revolutionsbegeisterung: Die katholischen Universitäten in Mainz, Heidelberg und Würzburg im Zeitalter der Französischen Revolution (1789–1792/ 3–1803) (Frankfurt am Main: Peter Lang, 2000), 155.

[147] John Markoff, "Violence, Emancipation, and Democracy: The Countryside and the French Revolution," The American Historical Review 100:2 (1995), 360–86: 383.

[148] Laura Gagliardi, "Il volto della Rivoluzione: Milano di fronte all'invasione francese (1796–1799)," in Cecilia Nubola and Andreas Würgler, eds., Ballare con nemico? Reazioni all'espansione francese in Europa tra entusiasmo e resistenza (1792–1815) (Bologna: Società editrice il Mulino; Berlin: Duncker & Humblot, 2010), 23–34.

[149] Luigi Lacchè, "L'Europe et la révolution du droit: Brèves réflexions," Annales historiques de la Révolution française no. 328 (2002), 153–69: 162.

[150] Jean-Clément Martin, Violence et révolution: Essai sur la naissance d'un mythe national (Paris: Éditions du Seuil, 2006), 289–91.

"were not sufficient to reduce the republican experiments of 1796–1799 to a mere narrative of military oppression. The attraction of the promised new republican order had been evident when in April 1796 Bonaparte was greeted enthusiastically in Milan as a liberator. Republican sympathizers and political exiles from Naples, Rome, and Piedmont flocked to the city where political clubs and associations were founded, and newspapers and journals were launched." The response was similar in other parts of the Italian peninsula. Besides, Davis argues, the popular anger that did erupt in 1799 – on a scale vaster than the insurrection in the Vendée – "was in many respects a continuation of insurrections and unrest that had been evident throughout the peninsula from much earlier, but existing discontents had been exacerbated by the impact of the revolution, the military occupation, and the new republics."

In some countries, the fear of a French invasion caused officials to stoke fear about the baneful presence of imaginary Frenchmen. In Saxony and Austria, French agents were accused of stirring up the population or preparing a coup d'état.[151] Nowhere, though, was the fear of French emissaries so great as in Spanish America in the first years after Fernando VII and Carlos IV surrendered to Napoleon in 1808. A tremendous amount of bureaucratic energy was spent on detecting unknown travelers and checking the countless reports about their alleged activities.[152] In reality, Napoleon did send some agents to Spanish American shores, but they remained harmless.

By the time Napoleon seized power, France rarely served as a beacon of hope anymore, at least in Europe.[153] In the eyes of numerous commentators, who now looked to Great Britain for inspiration, the French Revolution had failed, and its supporters were simply terrorists and anarchists.[154] If books by

---

[151] Jirko Krauß, *Ländlicher Alltag und Konflikt in der späten Frühen Neuzeit: Lebenswelt erzgebirgischer Rittergutsdörfer im Spiegel der kursächsischen Bauernunruhen 1790* (Frankfurt am Main: Peter Lang, 2012), 411; Helmut Reinalter, "Gegen die 'Tollwuth der Aufklärungsbarbarei': Leopold Alois Hoffmann und der frühe Konservatismus in Österreich," in Christoph Weiß, ed., *Von "Obscuranten" und "Eudämonisten": Gegenaufklärerische, konservative und antirevolutionäre Publizisten im späten 18. Jahrhundert* (St. Ingbert: Röhrig Universitätsverlag, 1997), 221–44: 227–8.

[152] Timothy Hawkins, *A Great Fear: Luís de Onís and the Shadow War against Napoleon in Spanish America, 1808–1812* (Tuscaloosa: The University of Alabama Press, 2019).

[153] By contrast, liberals and conservatives at the Cortes of Cádiz tried to learn lessons from the early stages of the French Revolution. José M. Portillo, "El poder constituyente en el primer constitucionalismo hispano," *Jahrbuch für Geschichte Lateinamerikas* 55 (2018), 1–26. In addition, as seen above, radicals in the Spanish colonies continued to be inspired by French revolutionary thought and practice.

[154] Richard Whatmore, *Terrorists, Anarchists, and Republicans: The Genevans and the Irish in Time of Revolution* (Princeton: Princeton University Press, 2019), 349–50.

Voltaire, Rousseau, and Raynal had always been banned in the Catholic world, publications associated with the revolution in France were seen by moral guardians of monarchical regimes as equally impious, seditious, or obscene. It was not even necessarily a book's content that was judged – authorship by a disreputable person sufficed for a work to be condemned. Censors in Brazil in the 1810s prohibited the sale of the innocent-sounding *Liberty of the Seas* because its author, the former Jacobin Bertrand Barère, had been "one of the most bloodthirsty associates of the monster Robespierre." And although the *philosophe* Gabriel Bonnot de Mably had died in 1785, his works were blacklisted because his doctrines of equality and liberty were found to have contributed much to the French Revolution.[155]

Whereas anti-French feelings abated, anti-Spanish sentiment in Spanish America grew after 1808, as the fight between patriots and royalists intensified. In Buenos Aires, a series of repressive measures against the *peninsulares* commenced with the May revolution of 1810, although persecution was limited to those who openly rejected the new regime. It became much more comprehensive after the discovery of an antigovernment conspiracy with Spanish ringleaders.[156] At the tail end of the independence process, there was also a reckoning for Spanish natives in both Peru and Mexico. Their massive expulsion caused so much ill-will on the part of the Spanish government that it embarked on an unsuccessful reconquest of Mexico in 1829–1830.[157] Like in other former colonies, Brazil also initiated measures against natives of the former metropole. **Hendrik Kraay** (Volume III, Chapter 20) asserts that these policies were not simply aimed at eliminating an enemy ethnicity. Anti-Portuguese rhetoric and violence were also about political choices and local power struggles. Besides, "expelling Portuguese-born office holders also conveniently opened up spaces in the civil and military bureaucracy for Brazilian patriots."

The French themselves, meanwhile, were not above excluding foreigners, who were seen by the Jacobins as treacherous enemies of the revolution. Months after the outbreak of war with Britain, all British nationals were arrested, and their property was confiscated. Englishmen soon stood accused

---

[155] Lúcia Maria B. P. das Neves and Tânia Maria T. B. da C. Ferreira, "O medo dos 'abomináveis princípios franceses': A censura dos livros nos inícios do século XIX no Brasil," *Acervo* 4:1 (1989), 113–19: 116.

[156] Mariana Alicia Pérez, "¡Viva España y Mueran los Patricios! La conspiración de Álzaga de 1812," *Americanía. Revista de Estudios Latinoamericanos* special issue (May 2015), 21–55.

[157] Harold Dana Sims, *The Expulsion of Mexico's Spaniards, 1821–1836* (Pittsburgh: University of Pittsburgh Press, 1990).

of "lese humanity." War to the death was consequently declared on them.[158] Such policies stood in stark contrast to the universalism the revolutionaries had professed in the first years of the revolution. As late as January 1793, *Le Moniteur Universel*, the government's official newspaper, had invoked "the bonds of universal fraternity which the French have extended to all peoples and on which they stake their lives."[159] Universalism did not disappear once France's armies began to cross the country's boundaries, although its adherents were now usually to be found elsewhere. In his *A Letter to the People of Ireland* (1796), Irishman Thomas Russell connected the plight of those countrymen of his who had been impressed by the Royal Navy not only to the oppression of Catholics in Ireland but also to that of enslaved Africans. Impressment, after all, enabled Britain to wage wars that aimed at continuing the Atlantic slave trade.[160] Russell thus tapped into the remarkable popular success of Britain's abolitionist movement. **Seymour Drescher** writes (Volume II, Chapter 15): "Unlike its counterparts in France and America it endured for half a century as a national social movement. Its participants were initially aroused by what they deemed violations of the 'principle of humanity.' Their intended beneficiaries were not their own fellow Britons nor even residents of their own colonies. They differed from the enslaved in race, color, religion, or culture."

If imperialism did not raise its head in France until a few years into the revolution, the American Revolution was more blatantly imperialist from the very start. In Volume I, Chapter 16, **Colin Calloway** contends that "the Revolution was also, quite simply, a war over Indian land. Speculators like George Washington had worked long and hard to get their hands on the best western lands; western settlers sought to rid lands of Indian neighbors, and Congress and the individual states needed land to fulfill the bounties and warrants they issued in lieu of pay during the war." Those Indian neighbors paid the price for westward expansion. Calloway relates that the Cherokees sued for peace after a genocidal campaign had been waged against them. At the peace treaties they signed, they lost more than 5 million acres. The indigenous plight throws into relief the apparent contradiction discerned by **Patrick Griffin**

---

[158] The rebels in the Vendée, who were officially excluded from the nation – not humanity – were treated the same way: Sophie Wahnich, *L'impossible citoyen: L'étranger dans le discours de la Révolution française* (Paris: Éditions Albin Michel, 2010), 11, 359.

[159] Rachel Rogers, "The Society of the Friends of the Rights of Man, 1792–94: British and Irish Radical Conjunctions in Republican Paris," *La Révolution française* (2016), 1–26: 6, http://lrf.revues.org/1629.

[160] Anthony Di Lorenzo and John Donoghue, "Abolition and Republicanism over the Transatlantic Long Term, 1640–1800," *La Révolution française* (2016), 14, 48–9, http://lrf.revues.org/1690.

(Volume 1, Chapter 7). The creoles of British North America, he writes, were "a people of paradox: anti-imperial when it came to the metropole and imperial when it came to dominance at home." Westward expansion continued after the peace treaty with Britain was signed in 1783, but, as **Mark Peterson** notes (Volume 1, Chapter 5), the Confederation Congress (the body that initially governed the new republic) was ill-equipped to manage claims on western lands. It was in part to solve this problem that a constitutional convention was convened that ended up creating a new form of national government.

The Realm of Freedom

Some revolutionaries, even those who stood to benefit more than others, had always doubted the possibility of introducing a new order.[161] The German "Jacobin" Joseph Görres believed in a four-stage development that had begun with the transition from barbarism to society, which was followed by that from a despotic to a representative regime. Next, a pure democracy would arise that would eventually give way to the period of "anarchy," during which people no longer needed a government. This progression took time, however. To move from the second stage to the third, as the French revolutionaries had tried to accomplish by introducing the constitution of 1791, did not make sense. That constitution came thousands of years too early. A long process of popular education was first required.[162]

Still, the upheaval of the late eighteenth and early nineteenth centuries created new regimes that often bore no resemblance to the old ones. These regimes made a start, however incomplete and reversible, and more in some places than others, with the emancipation of the many men and women who previously had been voiceless. And yet the belief, generated by the revolutions around the Atlantic world, in an imminent entry into the realm of freedom was proven to be misplaced. In the course of the revolutions, goals that had been embraced in the early stages mutated into ideological phrases that lacked urgency.[163] What gained currency was, once again, the idea that change would come only gradually. For most residents of the Atlantic world, true liberty would have to wait until a distant future.

---

[161] Domenico Losurdo, "Vincenzo Cuoco, la révolution napolitaine de 1799 et l'étude comparée des révolutions," *Revue Historique* 281:1 (1989), 133–57: 151.
[162] Joseph Görres, "Mein Glaubensbekenntnis (Juni/Juli 1798)," in Axel Kuhn, ed., *Linksrheinische deutsche Jakobiner: Aufrufe, Reden, Protokolle. Briefe und Schriften 1794–1801* (Stuttgart: J. B. Metzler, 1978), 240–50: 242–3.
[163] Stefan Greif, "Das Diskontinuierliche als Kontinuum. Aufklärung und Aufklärungskritik im Werk Georg Forsters," *Georg-Forster-Studien* 15 (2010), 77–93: 87.

PART I

★

FRANCE

I

Overview of the French Revolution

DAVID ANDRESS

The identity of France in the eighteenth century, as a kingdom held together by the character of its monarchy, hinged on a narrative of kingship constructed in the previous century. Louis XIV, completing the work of his father's great cardinal-ministers, made a claim of absolutist power both ideologically coherent and effectively irresistible. Louis XV's reign, almost as lengthy as his great-grandfather's, preserved that heritage intact, and Louis XVI, callow as he was in many ways, was as certain of his own right to untrammeled political initiative as any of his ancestors. The great political problem of the eighteenth century was that, after 1715, it was repeatedly made clear that other powerful people in the kingdom had never accepted the absolutist narrative, and alternative stories of the character of France increasingly flourished, with decisive political effect. The roots of revolutionary change were wide and deep, and ran to the heart of the "Old Regime" itself.

The fragility of what Louis XIV had built at Versailles was shown almost immediately after his death, when the Regent duc d'Orléans and the judges of France's highest court, the *Parlement* of Paris, did a deal to overturn the old king's will, giving Orléans more power. The judges in return got back the power, which Louis XIV had stripped from them, to "remonstrate" against royal edicts before registering them in their statute-books. By confining remonstrance to a gesture after registration, the old king had nullified its ability to hinder the royal will, but now, and right down to the Revolution, the *parlementaires* in Paris and a dozen other regional centers would be able to haggle over the implications of any royal act. For these judges, the claims of absolutism were simply a giant mistake, a misunderstanding of the reality of an unshakeable ancient constitution, to which any new piece of legislation or taxation must conform, and of which they were the unimpeachable guardians. The demonstrable fact that different provinces operated by entirely different codes of law, and that historically grounded inconsistency was the general rule of internal administration, gave their position additional weight.[1]

Around this basic clash, the whole course of eighteenth-century French public policy played out. Imperial ambitions, religious persecutions, and the swelling tide of publication and discussion that subsequently became "the Enlightenment" all found their place on this battlefield, where ultimately all the forces of Old-Regime society and culture came close to annihilating each other. The context for all this internal conflict was the reality of dynastic and imperial war that dominated the middle decades of the new century.

France was the most populous state of western Europe, and under Louis XIV had become a military juggernaut, repeatedly expanding its boundaries, and fighting a widespread alliance of other powers to a stalemate in the final years of his reign, albeit at a ruinous fiscal and human cost the king did not choose to see. Although the Regency and the ministries of Louis XV's early adulthood kept France out of major conflicts, and thus stabilized the finances, there was ultimately little hesitation in rejoining the round of European dynastic struggles when potential advantage presented itself. The War of the Polish Succession in the early 1730s thus brought France effective control of the Duchy of Lorraine, but the War of the Austrian Succession that dominated the 1740s saw no such clear-cut gains, as unsuccessful campaigns spread from central Europe to the furthest extent of European settlement in North America, and from the Caribbean to India. France dramatically changed sides in the politics of Europe in 1756, a "Diplomatic Revolution" that aligned it, traumatically for some, with the ancestral Austrian foe. The Seven Years' War that began at that point was, in global terms, a continuation of conflict with the British Empire which had never entirely ceased in the intervening years, and which had ramped up significantly since 1754.[2]

Renewed war ended in 1763 with the near-miraculous survival of Frederick the Great's Prussia, and hence the catastrophic failure of the "Diplomatic Revolution" on the Continent, made far worse for France by a virtual clean sweep of British victories in North America and India. Although France held onto the economic powerhouse of its Caribbean slave colonies, it had to surrender an empire that had stretched, nominally at least, the length of the Mississippi Valley and across the Great Lakes into Quebec, and which

---

[1] Colin Jones, *The Great Nation: France from Louis XIV to Napoleon* (London: Allen Lane, 2002), Chapters 1 and 2.
[2] Miranda Spieler, "France and the Atlantic World," in Peter McPhee, ed., *A Companion to the French Revolution* (Oxford: Blackwell, 2013), 57–72.

on the other side of the world had offered the prospect of military and economic dominance of southern India. This geopolitical disaster – and the enormous cost of it in temporary taxation and borrowing – was the foundational crisis of the long slide to revolutionary collapse.

For the following seven years, the aging Louis XV and his ministers struggled to get the *parlementaires* to accept changes in governmental practice that would facilitate paying down the crown's debts and securing longer-term stability in taxation. Both sides dredged up again and again their core positions, royal power assuming that, eventually, the threat of temporary exile would cow the judges as it had before, but the judges finding growing confidence through public support and a new articulation of the idea that the rights they defended were those of "the nation." In March 1766, facing growing *parlementaire* pretensions to be a national network, rather than separate instruments of his will, the king confronted them physically, using a speech to the Paris *parlement* given in his presence to deliver a "scourging" that resounded in public opinion at home and abroad:

> It is as if they forgot that my courts derive their existence and their authority from me alone, and that the discharge of that authority, which they exercise in my name only, always remains with me and can never be employed against me. Independent and undivided legislative power belongs to me alone ... Public order in its entirety emanates from me, and the rights and interests of the nation, for which some dare to create a separate body from the monarch, are necessarily united with my rights and interests and rest only in my hands.[3]

Yet such thundering had little effect. The king, working through his minister Maupeou, eventually at the end of 1770 did what absolutist doctrine said he had always had the power to do, and demanded obedience; when in early 1771 it was not forthcoming, recalcitrant judges were arrested, and the *parlements* replaced with more compliant institutions.

Reaction to the "Maupeou coup" demonstrated the wider cultural shifts that had been taking place through the middle years of the century. Although the king and his ministers held firm to their decisions, they did so through a howling storm of public outrage.[4] None of this yet had any institutional traction to touch them directly, but it illuminated the extent to which

---

[3] Text: https://revolution.chnm.org/d/236, see also Mike Rapport, *Rebel Cities: Paris, London and New York in the Age of Revolution* (London: Little, Brown, 2017), Chapter 3.
[4] Durand Echeverria, *The Maupeou Revolution: A Study in the History of Libertarianism; France, 1770–1774* (Baton Rouge: Louisiana State University Press, 1985).

"enlightened" culture had become far more than just genteel discussion about abstract philosophy. The French never spoke of "the Enlightenment," a later coinage from German, using rather the metaphor of "lights," *lumières*, to describe both individual and collective new wisdom and its spread. Similarly, the famous *salons* in which the social and intellectual elites met to chew over the affairs of the day and the novelties of culture were unknown by that term until the end of the century. The circles of sociability that the word later described were nonetheless real, although the most serious-minded of the female hostesses (and their male guests) were in a decided minority amidst a wider throng of wealthy people with time to talk.[5]

The value of salon culture in promoting, sponsoring, and patronizing a wave of rationalizing and reformist ideas should not be underestimated, but the tensions and contradictions of its context were also significant. Darlings of the salons like Denis Diderot continued to risk arrest if they actually published some of their more daring ideas, and kept many of their challenging texts in circulation only in manuscript among friends, or entirely secret until after their deaths. Jean-Jacques Rousseau, like Diderot plucked from social obscurity by the salon-going elite for his talents, gave vent in print to misogynistic declamations against the very same kinds of "unnatural" female social and intellectual engagement practiced by many of his greatest fans. This helped to produce an increasingly hostile cultural backlash against female scholarship, notably from nonelite men who, in an era of rising prosperity for the middling classes, formed their own single-sex cultural associations rejecting the "rule" of hostesses.[6]

Misogyny also reigned in a wider world of print. The official realm of approved, censored publication lived in constant battle with two different, but connected, illicit realms. In one, significant publishing enterprises based outside the borders of France, often in Protestant jurisdictions unconcerned with assisting in papist censorship, bypassed official controls by smuggling texts to networks of otherwise-licit booksellers. Much of their trade was relatively innocuous, but from the middle of the eighteenth century it also included a stream of materials that blended the sexually explicit (and often

---

[5] Antoine Lilti, *The World of the Salons: Sociability and Worldliness in Eighteenth-Century Paris* (New York: Oxford University Press, 2015).

[6] Dena Goodman, *The Republic of Letters: A Cultural History of the French Enlightenment* (Ithaca, NY: Cornell University Press, 1994), Chapters 3 and 6; Haydn T. Mason, *The Darnton Debate: Books and Revolution in the Eighteenth Century* (Oxford: Voltaire Foundation, 1998).

sexually abusive) with the socially and intellectually critical. The fact of a well-established market for such materials helped sustain the second, more flagrantly illegal, publishing realm. Marginalized aspiring writers in the capital were easy prey for networks of illicit printers and pamphleteers, who readily turned society gossip and political disputes into the raw materials of defamatory printed matter – quite often working at the behest of parties to such disputes. Libel was an arms-race with no concept of mutually assured destruction.[7]

Just such obscene charges swirled around all the principals of the "Maupeou coup," and while prudence restrained direct attacks on the monarch until his death in 1774, thereafter there were few limits to the descriptions of depravity his court was charged with. With supreme irony, such corrosive condemnations circulated at the same moment that Louis XVI, a young man with clear sympathies for reform and for the voice of "public opinion," was being urged in the name of *lumières* and the nation both to radically open up the mechanisms of government and to restore the *parlements* and their historic rights. With further brutal irony, complying with the public wish for the latter helped to assure that his genuine effort to promote widespread structural reform through his minister Turgot was brought to a chaotic collapse within two years of his accession.[8]

Overcoming obscene gossip about the inadequacies of his own sexuality and the profligacy of his queen's favors, Louis XVI made himself popular by openly embracing the cause of American independence in renewed war from 1778 – and more popular still by largely deferring the cost into the future through new loans. French elite enthusiasm to reverse the battlefield verdict of 1763 was matched by their infatuation with the republican virtues of the rebellious colonists. Those who inhabited the pinnacle of a grossly unjust hierarchical society gave as little thought to the meaningful implications of this for their own lives as they had for decades to the destabilizing potential of other enlightened enthusiasms.[9]

As very expensive victory over Britain in 1783 failed to translate into major territorial gains, or significant economic advantage, other burdens from the

---

[7] Simon Burrows, *A King's Ransom: The Life of Charles Théveneau de Morande, Blackmailer, Scandalmonger, and Master-Spy* (London and New York: Continuum, 2010); Simon Burrows, *The French Book Trade in Enlightenment Europe II: Enlightenment Bestsellers* (London: Bloomsbury Academic, 2018).
[8] John Hardman, *The Life of Louis XVI* (New Haven: Yale University Press, 2016).
[9] Dena Goodman and Thomas E. Kaiser, eds., *Marie Antoinette: Writings on the Body of a Queen* (London: Routledge, 2003); Sarah Maza, "The Cultural Origins of the French Revolution," in McPhee, *Companion to the French Revolution*, 42–56.

past began to press urgently on the French body politic. The monarchy was still, as it had been doing since the days of Henri IV, generating income by selling public offices to the wealthy as private property that conveyed privileged legal and fiscal status – up to and including personal and heritable nobility. The wider social desirability of privilege and status was reflected in a lively market for seigneurial rights – paper claims of lordship that brought real entitlements to payments and services from peasant communities, and helped purchasers up the ladder toward "living nobly." The increasing value (and cost) of these as a capitalist investment was racking up tensions in the countryside, as lords and their agents sought to maximize revenues, and peasants used royal courts to challenge abusive impositions. In these ways and others, revenues of the swelling economy that might have alleviated the state's difficulties were locked away behind barriers of privilege. Meanwhile the farming out of indirect taxation, on easily identifiable goods and activities, produced endemic low-level conflict between the mass of the population and the paramilitary agents of the tax-farmers, empowered to go where they liked in pursuit of revenue.[10]

It is in the intractable existence of such collisions that the political and cultural history of the coming of revolution meets its social history. While many administrators and intellectuals had bemoaned a falling population across the century, it had in fact been rising, by perhaps as much as a third since Louis XIV's day. Soaring global trade, centered on a near-explosive growth in slave-grown produce, had swollen the port cities, while villages across many regions counteracted growing pressure on land by diversifying into cottage industry. The French economy had been growing more complex, more "modern," and as a consequence more fragile, as rising numbers of people depended on increasingly elaborate networks of production, trade, and movement to survive.[11]

Economic fragility struck hard in the second half of the 1780s. The costs of war were still unrelieved, and the new United States failed to offer the massive trading boost its ally had expected. Misplaced optimism in government led to a trade treaty with Britain in 1786 that opened French markets to

---

[10] William Doyle, *Venality: The Sale of Offices in Eighteenth-Century France* (Oxford: Clarendon Press, 1996)

[11] Lauren R. Clay, "The Bourgeoisie, Capitalism and the Origins of the French Revolution," in David Andress, ed., *The Oxford Handbook of the French Revolution* (Oxford: Oxford University Press, 2015), 21–39; Jean-Pierre Jessenne, "The Social and Economic Crisis in France at the End of the *Ancien Régime*," in McPhee, *Companion to the French Revolution*, 24–41.

competition at prices its manufacturers could not match, spreading unemployment in many proto-industrial districts. Harvests in these years grew erratic, and by 1788 catastrophic. If large numbers of those who prospered from trade – directly, or indirectly as men of the law – still sent their new wealth to find safe haven in rural land and seigneurial rights, wider patterns of change were shifting to expose the jarring contradictions of such conduct.

Louis XVI's postwar finance minister Calonne, pursuing a twin-track policy of boosting confidence with grandiose spending plans and haggling once again with the *parlements* for a reformed tax settlement, succeeded by 1786 only in reaching the realization that full-blown structural reform was needed to see off real state bankruptcy. Launching into increasingly desperate efforts to avoid that outcome demonstrated perhaps the most ironic influence of the Enlightenment on the coming Revolution. It was the growing conviction amongst scholars and publicists that acts of state bankruptcy – a common phenomenon in early-modern monarchies – represented an intolerably despotic approach to governance, that colored the combined determination of almost all parties that such an event was out of the question.[12]

To avoid bankruptcy required reform, but in 1787 Calonne's efforts to persuade a handpicked national Assembly of Notables of that simple conclusion foundered disastrously. The Notables, for myriad personal and sectional reasons, rejected every aspect of Calonne's diagnosis. His own confidence-boosting spending plans were held against him, and made to look criminally irresponsible, and were perhaps even the short-term cause of a crisis he was exploiting to promote the same old changes that had been rejected in the 1760s and 1770s. Calonne fell from office, replaced by Brienne, a former vigorous opponent of the reforms – which did not help his own subsequent efforts to propel them forward. Out of the Notables' meetings, and continuing into further wrangling with the *parlements*, an antidespotic alliance was forged between conservative elites and the "enlightened" reading public, increasingly convinced that the protection of France's historic constitution and the furtherance of a more inclusive "national" political settlement went hand-in-hand.[13]

---

[12] Michael Sonenscher, *Before the Deluge: Public Debt, Inequality, and the Intellectual Origins of the French Revolution* (Princeton: Princeton University Press, 2007).

[13] Vivian R. Gruder, *The Notables and the Nation: The Political Schooling of the French, 1787–1788* (Cambridge, MA: Harvard University Press, 2008).

The marker of this unspoken alliance was the claim – supposedly first articulated by the marquis de Lafayette, patriot-hero of the American War – that a "truly national representation" was needed, and this meant the revival of the historical Estates-General, a consultative body of medieval origin that had not met since 1614. Through further months of chaotic confrontation, including an abortive attempt in May 1788 to abolish the *parlements* outright (met with popular protest and a collapse in state credit), the need for the Estates-General became a truism in the public mind. Brienne fell from office in late August, to be replaced with Jacques Necker, regarded as a popular hero, and a financial wizard, for steering the finances during the American War. His administration now placed all its hopes in an Estates-General meeting the following year, which abruptly brought into focus the question of what that actually meant.[14]

In September 1788 the antidespotic alliance shattered irreparably. The Paris *parlement* declared that the Estates-General should, self-evidently, meet as it had last done – in "the forms of 1614" – and thus as three separate (and separately voting) chambers for the three historic Estates: Catholic clergy in the First, fully authenticated nobles in the Second, and everyone else, 98 percent or more of the population, in the Third. What would soon be denounced as the "privileged orders" would thus be able to outvote the Third by two to one. The huge majority of the reading, thinking public outside the clergy and nobility were forced to confront in the coming months the fact that most of those inside those two groups really did insist on remaining elevated above them, in the new, more consultative monarchy they had seemed to be forging together.

Aided by the (possibly strategic) relaxation of censorship on publication about the Estates-General's composition, a flood of pamphlets denounced the privileged orders toward the end of 1788. The minority amongst the privileged who stood out for thorough-going reform, some of whom grouped in Paris in the soon-notorious "Society of Thirty," became as vociferous as any. Amongst them was the clergyman Emmanuel Sieyès, who in January 1789 published the 200-page "pamphlet" *What Is the Third Estate?*, lambasting the privileged as little more than a tumor on the body-politic. A whole new chapter of public division and antagonism was opened up, as the country prepared for the practicalities of an unprecedented national election.

---

[14] Annie Jourdan, "Tumultuous Contexts and Radical Ideas (1783–89): The 'Pre-Revolution' in a Transnational Perspective," in Andress, *Oxford Handbook*, 92–108.

Deputies for the Estates-General were chosen in a process that reached down to every town neighborhood, guild association, and village community. Householders, largely but not exclusively male, gathered in early 1789 both to delegate some of their number upwards to the final 300 district-court constituencies that chose deputies and to write down their communal grievances. These *cahiers de doléances*, the time-honored textual basis of the gathering, reflected the notion of kingship as a judge and righter of wrongs. What they produced in 1789 was the spectacle of a country set on articulating the injustice of practically every element of its public life.[15]

Many urban documents, and notably those compiled and condensed for final transmission to the Estates-General, proposed a reordering of state administration and politics on representative grounds far beyond anything imagined in official reforms. Many even amongst the nobility and clergy agreed that fiscal privileges, at least, should be removed for the public good. From the towns and villages, on top of sometimes-blistering attacks on the injustices of royal taxation, came variously respectful, pleading, bitter, angry, and occasionally desperate statements about the iniquity of seigneurial rights and the abuses of the church tithe. Elite contemporaries, unable to gain an overview of the vast amounts of complaint recorded, found the widespread unrest that broke out in the spring of 1789 almost inexplicable, but historians' investigations have shown that the entire country was primed to throw off the yoke of multiple abuses that, once voiced, had become intolerable.[16]

Thus, from the bottom up, revolution came to France. At Versailles, a fundamentally divided body of men gathered for the Estates-General. Noble representation was dominated by the "old" nobility for whom their status in itself was an indelible component of their identity, clearly threatened by Third-Estate pretentions. Before and after the opening of the Estates-General in early May, reports of rural unrest, the repossession of crops delivered up as seigneurial dues and clerical tithes, and the outright pillage of other stocks flowed around the nation. After that opening, left to organize themselves by Necker and the king, the Estates deputies could not even agree whether to constitute themselves as one body, or three. Fears of some decisive coup against the national movement were everywhere.

[15] Pierre-Yves Beaurepaire, "The View from Below: The 1789 *cahiers de doléances*," in Andress, *Oxford Handbook*, 149–63.
[16] Gilbert Shapiro and John Markoff, *Revolutionary Demands: A Content Analysis of the Cahiers de Doléances of 1789* (Stanford: Stanford University Press, 1998).

In June, with prices of basic foodstuffs rising to dangerous levels, widely believed to be provoked by an aristocratic "famine plot" to subjugate a hungry nation, the political landscape shifted. The Third Estate deputies and their noble and clerical sympathizers dubbed themselves, on Sieyès' suggestion, the National Assembly, and days later, in an atmosphere of panic fear at the prospect of dissolution, swore to give France a new constitution. Belated royal efforts to seek reforms that now seemed pitiful half-measures fell flat, and by the start of July, voices in the royal family that had been calling for a hard line since late 1788 rose again. Louis XVI, still essentially well-meaning but vulnerable to claims that his prerogatives were under attack, heeded his brothers and other relatives who demanded tough action. Growing numbers of troops were summoned to encircle the capital, and on 11 July Necker was dismissed in the first phase of a planned slow strangulation of the National Assembly. Amidst nationwide turmoil, with almost no hesitation, Paris rose up, shattering these plans. The king's own brother, Artois, fled into exile, as did the leader of the "Ministry of the Hundred Hours" that had briefly replaced Necker. Louis was forced to capitulate to an Assembly that, only hours before, had feared its own destruction.[17]

Principles and Politics

The revolution of 1789 was born under the sign of deadly treason, and would never shake off the mark of its origin. It was widely and inaccurately asserted that the Bastille's governor, de Launey, butchered and decapitated by a crowd on 14 July, deserved his fate because he had opened the gates to the crowd and then opened fire on them. The city's royally appointed mayor, de Flesselles, perished similarly, having supposedly tried to palm off a crowd demanding weapons with some empty chests. The blundering coup attempt of early July cemented the perceived reality of the otherwise mythical "famine plot," which led directly to the brutal lynching of two senior officials, Foulon and Berthier, at the hands of Parisian crowds a week after the Bastille fell.

Narratives of betrayal rapidly spread beyond the Parisian streets. Almost simultaneously with these lynchings, the first edition of the *French Patriot* newspaper carried a scaremongering tale of citizens blown sky-high by a

---

[17] Robert H. Blackman, *1789: The French Revolution Begins* (Cambridge: Cambridge University Press, 2019).

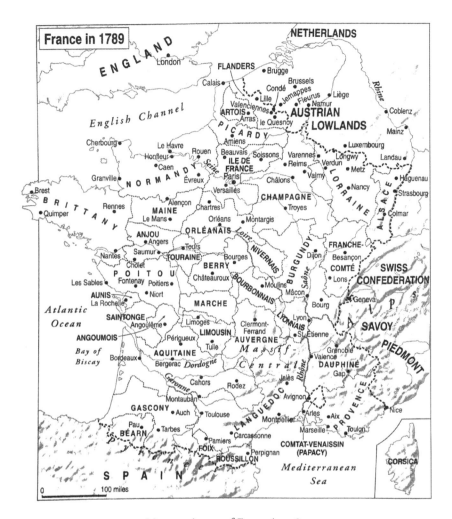

Map 1.1 A map of France in 1789.

treacherous seigneur. Across swathes of the countryside, the prospect of inevitable aristocratic revenge in the rumored form of harvest-burning brigand bands produced a "Great Fear" of community mobilization. News of these deeply disturbing, though ultimately short-lived, movements reached Versailles in waves, prompting further alarm in the National Assembly that simultaneous disturbances must have been coordinated by their enemies. Out of this complex stew of fear at betrayal and loss of control emerged the idea of regaining the initiative by a renunciation of the privileges that so many *cahiers* had denounced. Propelled by a radical minority, the bulk of the Assembly joined on the "Night of 4 August" in an event they would identify as the "abolition of feudalism," which they persuaded themselves was ecstatic.[18]

In its first months of power, the Assembly staked out positions that would determine much of what followed. Although the late-August Declaration of the Rights of Man seemed to address individuals, much of it was in fact devoted to folding such people into a highly centralized and unitary vision of a sovereign nation. The revolutionaries empowered future legislators – and implicitly themselves – with many of the attributes of an absolutist sovereign, while at the same time awkwardly squeezing their actual monarch (who still believed himself absolute) into a limited chief-executive role. They made a commitment to giving localities, down to the individual village, responsible elected leaders, but in practice expected only obedience from them. There was no question of "intermediary bodies" outside the capital, any more than there was of a revising chamber or other privileged check on the "general will" that, according to the Declaration, produced laws.[19]

Reconciling such principles with the realities of politics proved persistently impossible. The renewed activism of popular crowds that resulted in the transfer of the royal family to Paris in the "October Days" ratcheted up tension with the crown. It also fueled "moderate" suspicions that radicalism was itself a plot by the king's cousin Orléans to seize the throne. The high-handed appropriation of Church assets the following month furthered the logic of the end of privilege, while offering a route out of the state's fiscal crisis. However, it marked the start of a slippery slope toward a choice between submission and rebellion for all who did not agree that secular authorities could demand obedience from the Church hierarchy. In the following years the Assembly moved to double down on its individualist logic by banning anything that resembled a trade union, while also insisting that the end of "feudalism" still meant that peasants had to hand over their onerous dues to the wealthy owners of seigneurial rights, or buy them out for the absurd sum of twenty years' payments. The suppression of violent

---

[18] Michael P. Fitzsimmons, *The Night the Old Regime Ended: August 4, 1789, and the French Revolution* (University Park: Pennsylvania State University Press, 2003).

[19] Barry M. Shapiro, *Traumatic Politics: The Deputies and the King in the Early French Revolution* (University Park: Pennsylvania State University Press, 2009).

protest against doctrinaire efforts to "liberalize" the markets for basic food-grains, which recurred annually, and sometimes spread into wider denunciations of economic disruption, showed yet another dimension of the revolutionary elite's detachment from genuinely popular concerns.[20]

While such policies were pushed through, often with little or no substantive debate, the revolutionary political class continued to understand itself as under siege. Those plotters who had fled abroad in July 1789 had been joined thereafter by a steady trickle of new *émigrés*, a cohort of "counterrevolution" both vocal and visible, and generally assumed, with some good reason, to be intertwined with internal networks of similarly intransigent opposition, dedicated to the destruction of the Revolution. The aristocratic counterrevolution – signified not least by the positions of a good quarter of the National Assembly's members, some of whom fought duels against leading patriots – provided the context for understanding all revolutionary politics as crisis. In that crisis, the "good citizens" were perpetually pitted against not just the overt counterrevolution, but also the abiding fear that any discord strengthened the risk of collapse – and the second-order fear that such discord was stoked precisely to achieve that end.[21]

As something akin to a political spectrum developed over the Revolution's first years, differences were defined less by positive policy positions than by views over who was a genuine patriotic leader and who a dangerous agitator. Ultracentrist *monarchiens* had been pushed out of politics by attacks from both sides by the end of 1789. Royalist publications heaped scorn on the whole project of revolution. Partisans of strong authority rallied around the Marquis de Lafayette, an unimpeachable patriot, but also, at the head of the Parisian National Guard, a sworn foe of radical agitation. *Fayettistes* saw such agitation as the work of despicable "factious" and "seditious" people, and a front for the supposed continuing ambitions of the duc d'Orléans to seize the throne. The swirling contentious landscape of the new uncensored revolutionary press was made more turbulent by the fact that these and other factions did subsidize publications (much as they had before 1789), in which

---

[20] Barry M. Shapiro, *Revolutionary Justice in Paris, 1789–1790* (Cambridge: Cambridge University Press, 1993); John Markoff, *The Abolition of Feudalism: Peasants, Lords and Legislators in the French Revolution* (University Park: Pennsylvania State University Press, 1996); Noelle Plack, "Challenges in the Countryside, 1790–92," in Andress, *Oxford Handbook*, 346–61.

[21] Kirsty Carpenter, "Emigration in Politics and Imagination," in Andress, *Oxford Handbook*, 330–45; Timothy Tackett, *Becoming a Revolutionary: The Deputies of the French National Assembly and the Emergence of a Revolutionary Culture (1789–1790)* (Princeton: Princeton University Press, 1996).

their infighting and constant reinterpretation of minor incidents fueled a paranoia that other authors – Jean-Paul Marat for example – needed no financial incentive to share. The other side of the charge of sedition was the radical belief that – again, with little reference to specific policy choices – those leading the Assembly and the politics of the capital were navigating toward a compromise with counterrevolution that would usher in repression and resubjugation.[22]

The printed dimension of politics pullulated – several hundred mostly short-lived titles, of every political shade, fought for Parisian (and hence national) market share in 1789–1791 – and the politics of personal correspondence and verbal exchange was little less fervid. Deputies within the Assembly had wasted little time in marking out sharp divisions amongst themselves, which were thereafter constantly reinforced by their own exchanges with constituents, and from the end of 1789 by the foundation of what became the Jacobin Club. Its name, which initially merely gestured toward the previous tenants of a monastic building, became the label for a whole ideology of radical patriotic partisanship. At the same time, it was constantly asserted as part of that ideology that Jacobins were merely the "good citizens" on whom the Revolution depended. The Paris club, initially reserved for Assembly deputies, but soon attracting other activist members, and a regular public audience, spawned first dozens and by 1791 several hundred provincial imitators. Revolutionary political engagement became a form of sociability, although most clubs followed the Rousseauist line of excluding formal female participation. Within Paris, some more radical Jacobins took the lead in forming a club with lower subscriptions, the Cordeliers, which itself in early 1791 spawned a clutch of explicitly "popular" societies, all loudly, though somewhat formlessly, radical in outlook.[23]

The ideological possibilities of Jacobin participation may have contributed to the decline of large-scale electoral participation. As the numbers of clubs steadily rose, so the percentage of "active citizens" taking part in repeated rounds of time-consuming voting for wave after wave of newly created offices drifted downwards. The two processes would ironically coincide to

---

[22] David Andress, *Massacre at the Champ de Mars: Popular Dissent and Political Culture in the French Revolution* (Woodbridge: Boydell Press, 2000).

[23] Charles Walton, "Clubs, Parties, Factions," in Andress, *Oxford Handbook*, 362–81; Isser Woloch, "A Revolution in Political Culture," in McPhee, *Companion to the French Revolution*, 437–53.

leave only the committed activist minority engaged with public office, while both Jacobin ideology and the rules of elections (no declared candidates, the ability to nominate any individual with your vote) insisted that those involved were merely patriots seeking the best outcome for the nation. Within this politics of nonpolitics, the corollary was that opposing the patriotic line was not dissent, but treason. Deputies had implicitly endorsed this when they transformed the old crime of *lèse-majesté* into the new one of *lèse-nation*, and eagerly debated how it was to be punished.[24]

The difficulty was that revolutionary politics in practice continued to create divisions where ideology preached there should be only unity. In its takeover of financial responsibility for the Catholic Church, the National Assembly's majority took the view that it was entitled thereafter to remodel ecclesiastical institutions for greater efficiency. This had been done successfully in other enlightened states, but not by rulers perceived, as the Revolution was, as the enemy of sanctified institutions. From the closing down of "surplus" convents in early 1790, what were supposed to be administrative measures generated ideological resistance. The intrusion of sectarian fears about Protestant influence brought real violence to southern cities in the following months. Revolutionary doubling-down, inserting the clergy into effectively secular structures of electoral control in June 1790, was met with increasingly disruptive resistance. The attempt to set a hard limit, demanding in January 1791 a loyalty-oath from all beneficed clergy, produced only mass refusal by half of all priests, and violent protest across the nation. "Fanaticism" became a charge to add to "aristocracy" and "counter-revolution" to explain all opposition, and to justify harsh measures to eliminate it.[25]

The immediate repercussions of the clerical oath had barely died away before the whole Revolution was thrown into doubt by the king's attempted escape on the night of 20 June 1791. While the royal couple swiftly discovered that France outside Paris did not nurture the feelings for them they had fondly believed, the leadership of the National Assembly was forced to confront the monarch's clearly expressed unwillingness to be a constitutional figurehead. They did so by smothering the evidence of his dissent, proclaiming that he had been kidnapped by the aristocratic counterrevolution, and

---

[24] Charles Walton, *Policing Public Opinion in the French Revolution: The Culture of Calumny and the Problem of Free Speech* (Oxford: Oxford University Press, 2009).

[25] Edward J. Woell, "The Origins and Outcomes of Religious Schism. 1790–99," in McPhee, *Companion to the French Revolution*, 145–60.

desperately conducting a secret negotiation with the recaptured royal couple to preserve the appearance of agreement.

The Paris Jacobins split over the public consequences of this strategy, with the more centrist wing (including most of the deputy-members) joining Fayettists in a new "Feuillant" club (like the Jacobins, named for its monastic home), while radicals regrouped in the aftermath of an explosive public clash in Paris. Crowds gathered on 17 July on the Champ de Mars to petition for a referendum on Louis' constitutional fate were attacked by National Guard militia under martial-law provisions, and in the belief that radical protesters were being egged on by counterrevolutionary *provocateurs*. The Constitution of 1791 was thus finally enacted in the aftermath of fatal conflict between self-defined patriots, and under the shadow of proscriptions (albeit ones lifted immediately by general amnesty). Radicals had been given decisive proof, to their own minds, that their moderate opponents were in league with the counterrevolution. That the king perjured himself as he accepted his new role (and later wept at his fate in doing so), was only one of the challenges France faced.[26]

The progression of French revolutionary history from the founding of its new constitution, through war, Republic, and Terror to the post-Thermidorian aftermath of corruption and division, is often seen as the central story of the decade. In essence, however, much of it amounted to the playing-out with variations of the political attitudes and approaches already clearly evident by 1791, in situations of greater peril and with consequently more heightened effects, both rhetorical and real. Little new entered the political equation, even if events now proceeded with more memorably colorful language, and the ramping up of violence by orders of magnitude.

The dread of the counterrevolution was the lever by which a grouping of radical Jacobins in the new Legislative Assembly, associated with the journalist and activist Jacques-Pierre Brissot, and thus inevitably labeled "Brissotins," seized the political agenda. Proposing measures which provoked the king into using his veto barely two months into the new system, thereafter the Brissotins advocated with increasing force and intransigence for a war to remove the *émigré* threat from France's eastern frontiers. With internal politics deadlocked, a lunge to war started to appeal across almost the whole political spectrum. Brissotin radicals saw it as a chance for uncomplicated

---

[26] Munro Price, *The Road from Versailles: Louis XVI, Marie Antoinette, and the Fall of the French Monarchy* (New York: St. Martin's Press, 2002).

patriotic triumph; Feuillants and Fayettists, still entrenched in government, as a route to restore social discipline against radical hotheads; the royal family, incomprehensibly, as a route to restored absolute power through defeat and destruction of the whole Revolution.[27]

Only a small minority of radicals, Maximilien Robespierre among them, opposed war, and they did so precisely because they saw it as a plot to lure an unprepared nation into destruction – yet another in the long line of treasons since the commandant of the Bastille had supposedly opened the fortress gates, only to open fire on the patriots with cannon. When Brissotin allies entered government, taking up ministerial posts explicitly quarantined from the national representatives as potentially corrupting in nature, they gave sustenance to well-established tropes of revolutionary paranoia. When war against Austria came in April 1792, bringing early defeats, the terror of real betrayal, and by the summer the addition of Prussia as a further potent foe, the constitutional structure shattered.

Lafayette tried to launch a military coup against Jacobinism in June, but was allowed to return to his army command unhindered. The Assembly seized executive authority from the king in early July, yet hesitated over any move to formal deposition. *Émigrés* threatened devastation to Paris if the king was touched. Radicals, convinced that the isolated and helpless monarch was somehow actively directing French defeat, used control of Parisian local government to launch their own coup on 10 August. A new radical-patriotic identity as *sans-culottes* – an invented label of highly contentious significance – was cemented in blood, as hundreds were killed in a pointless clash with the royal Swiss Guards, after the king had already surrendered himself to the Assembly.[28]

The following year was dominated – through the declaration of a republic, the trial and execution of the king, the widening of the war to every frontier and colony, and the desperate steps to create structures able to fight that war – by the unremitting fratricidal hatred between the original "Brissotins" and their sympathizers on one side, soon relabeled "Girondins," and the alliance of Parisian *sans-culottes* and other more radical "Montagnard" politicians on the other. This played out both within the National Convention elected in September 1792 to constitute a new republican order and across

---

[27] Leigh Ann Whaley, *Radicals: Politics and Republicanism in the French Revolution* (Stroud: Sutton Publishing, 2000).
[28] David Andress, "Politics and Insurrection: The *Sans-culottes*, the 'Popular Movement' and the People of Paris," in Andress, *Oxford Handbook*, 401–17.

the wider field of politics. A remarkable facet of the Revolution's history is how antagonists on both sides repeatedly leveled charges of the most treasonous conduct against their opponents, then managed to press on with parliamentary business for weeks or months until the next explosion was reached. Girondins inherited the Feuillant mantle of pragmatic politicians who saw their more radical opponents as deranged and ignorant at best, and prospective looters of a collapsed polity at worst. *Sans-culottes* stood where the Brissotins once had, and condemned those close to power as selfish profiteers who slid at every moment closer to open counterrevolution. Parliamentary and press argument raged over which factions were "true" or "false" friends of the people, while the *sans-culottes* short-circuited the question by declaring quite simply that they were the people, and that the National Guard putsch which finally expelled the Girondin leadership from the Convention in early June 1793 was the people's will.[29]

Revolutionary leaderships preached the imperative of national unity – and increasing national mobilization – while fomenting divisions that increasingly became immediately murderous. Conscription decreed to fight the expanded war had set the spark to a tinder of religious and cultural alienation in the west, producing an overtly counterrevolutionary peasant army in the Vendée that amateurish National Guard forces struggled to contain. As this weakness helped drive local massacres and panicky division at the center, so the antagonisms there spread back out, with Paris-backed radical factions in Lyon, Marseille, and elsewhere condemned by locals as ignorant disorganizers and shameless looters. Explosive revolt in such major cities fed back into the purging demands of the *sans-culottes*, and ensured that, when Girondin leaders fled the capital, a ready-made civil war erupted around them.

This was the context for the consolidation of what is conventionally called "the Terror." An escalation of ruthless measures of national emergency, to contain revolt while building an unprecedented million-man army to fight the external war, it produced an equally unprecedented vision of a nation rebuilt from the bottom up by patriotic energies. Later partisans could find within it ammunition to denounce radical republicanism as a satanic project of indiscriminate slaughter, or to laud it as a new vision of justice, clawed free at dreadful cost from reactionary foes. It was also a process in which, driven by the same paranoid fears and demands for unconditional unity that

---

[29] Marisa Linton, "Friends, Enemies and the Role of the Individual," in McPhee, *Companion to the French Revolution*, 263–77; Paul R. Hanson, "From Faction to Revolt," in Andress, *Oxford Handbook*, 436–52.

had been in place since 1789, the leadership of the Republic steadily cut deeper and deeper into its own collective body, obsessionally seeking to grub out the imaginary counterrevolutionary roots of all dissent and misconduct. Emblematic of this is the process whereby, as military victories seemed to bring no relief from the purgative demands of Robespierre and those around him, hardened survivors of previous political battles turned in fear of their own lives on him as a scapegoat for the whole process, and defamed him as an aspiring counterrevolutionary monarch.[30]

In some accounts, particularly those within the twentieth-century Marxist tradition, the fall of Robespierre and his closest allies in the so-called "Thermidorian Reaction" of July 1794 marked the effective end of the French Revolution, because a regime that was not moving forward on a path of greater social radicalization could not be "revolutionary" any more. There are many reasons for thinking such an easy division untenable. Thermidor itself was an event largely organized by those who had been active collaborators in the "Terrorist" project. While politics over the following year swung emphatically toward a relaxation that liberated very many "suspects" from the propertied classes, others detained for their dangerously ultraradical sympathies also benefited. The Thermidorians certainly were callously doctrinaire in their removal of price controls at the end of 1794, exacerbating what would almost certainly have been a famine winter anyway, but the operation of those controls had been so riddled with corruption and malfeasance that crowds had cursed them as they jeered Robespierre to the guillotine. The politics of 1795 and after did brutally scapegoat an entire class of more plebeian local activists as "terrorists," but the politics of early 1794 had already closed down the institutions of the *sans-culottes'* movement as dangerously disruptive. Parisian crowds in the spring of 1795 did invade the legislature demanding "Bread and the Constitution of 1793," but the architects of the Terror had refused to implement that totemically "democratic" document, proclaiming the people untrustworthy until their Jacobin masters had won the war for them.[31]

The wider truth that emerged from politics in the later 1790s was that the nature of the conflicts in the first half of the decade had shattered the persistent assumption of those years that a widely based body of "good

---

[30] Dan Edelstein, "What Was the Terror?," in Andress, *Oxford Handbook*, 453–70; Marisa Linton, "Terror and Politics," in Andress, *Oxford Handbook*, 471–86.
[31] Laura Mason, "Thermidor and the Myth of Rupture," in Andress, *Oxford Handbook*, 521–37.

citizens" could rally to an effective form of government. When the National Convention finalized its second constitution in late summer 1795, it compromised the liberal balance of powers the document embodied by insisting that two-thirds of the new national representatives should be existing Convention members. Imposing this settlement provoked a "royalist" rising from conservative Parisian neighborhoods, duly suppressed with military force, and marked the "Directorial" regime from its start as alienated from the electoral legitimacy that revolutionaries since 1789 had declared essential – even if they had often honored such a claim only in the breach.

Victims and Survivors

The French Revolution was an extraordinary outburst of cultural innovation and political liberation. From the streets of Paris to the most remote villages, the events of 1789 stirred the sense that individuals could be, and were, free, in a quite new way. Reckless expressions of this sentiment from too far down the social ladder still tended to get squashed quite effectively by the local partisans of good order and decency, while even prosperous peasant property-owners had to embark on several years of resistant struggle before their feudal burdens were actually erased in 1793. But the general sentiment that people – men and women, and occasionally even children – could speak up and speak out was an undammable river that flowed on even through those moments, like the spring and summer of 1794, when such behavior carried a significant risk of arrest, or worse. One of the most remarkable things about the records of police spies who lurked in Parisian crowds during the Terror is the volume and variety of things they found to report. Between the wooden expressions of loyalty and the paranoia of subversion, there still emerges time and again the echo of a people uncowed, critical, often alarmed but always engaged.[32]

Although the printed expression of political disagreement was steadily ground down between 1792 and 1794, and remained a site of sharp and frequently censorious contestation under the Directory, the wider landscape of publication flourished more continuously. The world of unregulated pamphleteering became so extensive as to be a labyrinth for unwary

---

[32] Jill Maciak Walshaw, *A Show of Hands for the Republic: Opinion, Information, and Repression in Eighteenth-Century Rural France* (Woodbridge: Boydell Press, 2014).

researchers, in which it is possible to find almost any view expressed. Every crank in France had the freedom to express themselves at length if they could pay a printer, and almost all of them, it seems, could. But beyond this, new freedoms produced more noteworthy consequences. It became, for example, far more likely that female authors would receive publication than under the Old Regime. The Revolution's atmosphere of radical change also stimulated stylistic and substantive innovations in literature, from protofeminist accounts of activism to proto-science-fictional speculations on automata, including one which invoked the name "Frankenstein" from an older German text, three decades before Mary Shelley.[33]

The French revolutionary stage, with allowances for periodic excesses of censorship, came alive in bold new ways as playwrights, actors and audiences wrestled to make new uses of the potential of drama to enlighten and stimulate society. As millions lived through years of trouble, thousands, at least, invested their time, effort and imagination in the idea that there might be new ways of making sense of new times. Nor should it be forgotten that real personal freedom took leaps forward in other ways. Divorce, from 1792, became a route to escape from unhappy or abusive marriages taken by thousands, the majority women, until snatched away a decade later. More generally, the Revolution transformed the legal basis of the family from one of dominance and subordination to a meeting of (near-)equals, even if some provisions around illegitimacy seemed to shield men from responsibilities older morals had insisted upon.[34]

In wider terms, revolutionary freedom often formed an unpalatable stew. Revoking all forms of feudal rights and subordination turned out to create knotty legal problems, as old-regime custom had inserted almost-nominal reference to such relationships in routine leases, loan agreements, and even bills of sale. Liberating private property often entangled it in years of unforeseen disputation. In parallel vein, the beliefs revolutionaries shared around the *assignat* paper currency, not least that its perceived value (or lack thereof) was a matter of political rather than economic confidence, led them into policy choices that created both

---

[33] Carla Hesse, *The Other Enlightenment: How French Women Became Modern* (Princeton: Princeton University Press, 2001); Julia V. Douthwaite, *The Frankenstein of 1790 and Other Lost Chapters from Revolutionary France* (Chicago: University of Chicago Press, 2012).

[34] Susan Maslan, *Revolutionary Acts: Theater, Democracy, and the French Revolution* (Baltimore: Johns Hopkins University Press, 2005); Susanne Desan, *The Family on Trial in Revolutionary France* (Berkeley: University of California Press, 2004).

misery for the common people and exploitative opportunities for augmenting the estates of the wealthy.[35]

In all the realms of policy that touched on real poverty, intensifying doctrinaire hostility to the religious personnel who tended the sick, crippled, or orphaned, or distributed charity to the old or the dispossessed, burned down structures of relief with little more than periodic expressions of good intentions offered as replacement. Similarly, bold plans for general schemes of education, again displacing the clerical role, were cheered to the rafters, but went unfunded and undelivered. With endemic unrelieved poverty came beggary, despair, and the fear and reality of banditry – sometimes aligned with continuing ideological battles, sometimes mere murderous rampage.[36]

Directorial politics, in its own way, was a project of making sense of the new reality. In practical terms this would ultimately mean pragmatic decisions to reintroduce things like excise taxes that had been execrated in 1789 – and indeed to embark on a partial state bankruptcy, the very thing whose shadow had sparked the revolutionary process. In political terms the Directory reeked of hypocrisy. From the two-thirds decree onwards, the conduct of public life conspicuously failed to match up to the promise of the constitution. The animosities of previous years drove voters across the nation toward the formation of "Jacobin" and "Royalist" groupings – far too diverse to be called parties, but both antagonistic to the control of the self-selected political survivors in Paris (as well as, of course, to each other). Once regular annual elections were initiated in 1797, the government showed its determination to remain in control by blatantly refusing to seat dozens or hundreds of elected figures in the national legislature, and purging local results to secure compliant administrators. But before simply condemning this, the political and social reality of many areas of France needs to be acknowledged.[37]

France in the later 1790s was a society of victims and survivors. Hundreds of thousands had good reason to feel they had been unjustly persecuted under the Terror by people who still lived among them – and tens of thousands denounced as "terrorists" since 1794 were also learning what such persecution felt like, and who to blame for it. The discourse of ideological conflict and suffering was also a language with many self-centered uses.

---

[35] Rafe Blaufarb, *The Great Demarcation: The French Revolution and the Invention of Modern Property* (Oxford: Oxford University Press, 2016); Rebecca L. Spang, *Stuff and Money in the Time of the French Revolution* (Cambridge, MA: Harvard University Press, 2015).
[36] Alan Forrest, *The French Revolution and the Poor* (Oxford: Blackwell, 1981).
[37] Howard G. Brown, *Ending the French Revolution: Violence, Justice, and Repression from the Terror to Napoleon* (Charlottesville: University of Virginia Press, 2006).

Survivorhood could also mean having tacked with the prevailing political winds, and remaining ruthlessly determined to hold onto power in one's particular village, town, or locality. It could equally mean continuing to prosecute vendettas that went back to individual and familial grievances long predating 1789, and in which revolutionary politics might be little more than a stage-setting for grimly small-scale epics of revenge. Directorial political manipulation worked against these trends as much as it cynically safeguarded the power of the elite.[38]

Understanding the final years of the revolutionary decade is a delicate balance between confronting the self-interested and exclusionary nature of Directorial politics and questioning whether any alternatives, given the ingrained strife of previous years, could have been better. Directorial policy initiatives did much to reconstruct an educational and scientific landscape that had been relentlessly pummeled by revolutionary hostility to the former privileged corporations of old-regime intellectual life, and latterly to any suggestion that there might be merit in anything other than a chaotic individualist free-for-all in the marketplace of ideas (an attitude which, carried over into the realms of production, had resulted in a catastrophic slump in the quality of French goods in the middle years of the decade). To justify reforming an intellectual elite in the new Institut national, Directorial thinkers increasingly articulated what they saw as a positively elitist understanding of cultural and scientific endeavor. Yes, the argument went, the people in general formed a republican citizenry, but they were not all sufficiently advanced along the road of understanding, and it was vital that those who were should be supported by the state to continue their own development freely, while the remainder were gently but firmly led toward a *future* capacity for political engagement.[39]

Such guidance went hand-in-hand with the wider elaboration of what has been called a "security state," where an increasingly militarized approach to suppressing the worst excesses of criminal disorder was accepted by local stakeholders as a satisfactory substitute for their own democratic autonomy. These trends found a sharp echo in the decision to project France's newly asserted status as the "Great Nation" into the conquest of Egypt under

---

[38] Ronen Steinberg, *The Afterlives of the Terror: Facing the Legacies of Mass Violence in Postrevolutionary France* (Ithaca, NY: Cornell University Press, 2019); D. M. G. Sutherland, *Murder in Aubagne: Lynching, Law, and Justice during the French Revolution* (Cambridge: Cambridge University Press, 2009).

[39] Jean-Luc Chappey, "The New Elites: Questions about Political, Social and Cultural Reconstruction after the Terror," in Andress, *Oxford Handbook*, 556–72.

General Bonaparte. Strategically justified as a stepping-stone to attacking British India, and revenge for the global defeat of 1763, the expedition birthed its own Institut d'Egypte, with dozens of French scholars devoted to reclaiming through scientific expertise the knowledge of Egyptian antiquity buried under centuries of Muslim "ignorance." This line was maintained through Bonaparte's subsequent atrocity-stained campaigning in the Holy Land, and the eventual defeat and evacuation of the French presence. Ironic testament to its potency lay in the forlorn grouping of republican sympathizers, natives of various corners of the Ottoman domains, who left with the French, hoping for support to extend republican principles across the Levant.[40]

A further ironic impact of Directorial politics was felt on the other side of the world, where a complex stew of colonial revolt and multipolar war had steadily thickened ever since white settlers and planters had rejected the racially egalitarian implications of 1789. Metropolitan fears of the loss of an economic powerhouse had encouraged a pandering approach to white alarm, but had not been able to stop different groups of whites escalating political violence, especially in Saint-Domingue, attacking the nonwhite free population, and creating the conditions for massive slave rebellion in August 1791. Radicalizing politics on the ground and in Paris had eventually led to first a local and then a general declaration of the end of slavery (by February 1794), but its global effects were patchy (Indian Ocean colonies simply refused to implement it) and confused in the Caribbean by a multipolar conflict between slave rebels, "official" French forces, local whites, and British and Spanish armies. Nonetheless, the later 1790s (until the discreditable Napoleonic restoration of slavery) were the only period in which official French policy was to support unqualified freedom for people of all races. Evidence suggests that, in at least some of the scattered military and insurgent campaigns across the Lesser Antilles, a vision of a free multiethnic republic was what some people were indeed fighting for.[41]

Events in the later 1790s in the Levant and the Caribbean testify to the remarkable power of the idealistic narratives generated by the French Revolution. They are not the only such narratives, of course: counterrevolutionary belief in the wickedness of proceedings has also left a clear legacy,

---

[40] Ian Coller, "The Revolutionary Mediterranean," in McPhee, *Companion to the French Revolution*, 419–34.

[41] Paul Friedland, "Every Island Is Not Haiti: The French Revolution in the Windward Islands," in David A. Bell and Yair Mintzker, eds., *Rethinking the Age of Revolutions: France and the Birth of the Modern World* (Oxford: Oxford University Press, 2018), 41–79.

while suppression of antirepublican revolt in the Vendée in 1793–1794 produced a potent legend of Catholic martyrdom, more recently escalated to forceful, if highly contestable, claims about genocide. There are views and analyses of the 1790s available to suit any political position one might care to imagine. Like many of the great "events" of history, much of what we understand about the French Revolution is the outcome of a persistent duel between the hunt for new evidence and the human desire for myth-making, and is unlikely to ever be anything else.[42]

---

[42] Pascal Dupuy, "The Revolution in History, Commemoration, and Memory," in McPhee, *Companion to the French Revolution*, 486–501.

2

Abolishing Feudalism

RAFE BLAUFARB

This chapter examines the constitutional ramifications of the French Revolution's transformation of the old regime of property. This process is generally termed the abolition of feudalism. But this fails to capture the breadth of the transformation. While the revolutionaries certainly abolished feudal property relations, they also eliminated or altered nonfeudal property forms. By the end of 1790, they had remade the entire system of property. Another problem with characterizing the revolution in property as merely feudal abolition is that it ignores the creative, even utopian thrust of the transformation. Having destroyed the existing property system, the revolutionaries replaced it with a new one based on radically different principles. Their ultimate goal was to refashion the concept of property itself – and with it, the fundamental concepts through which to articulate the New Regime.

The history of the abolition of feudalism has been approached mainly from an economic perspective. This reflects the concerns of the twentieth-century academics, mainly French, who long dominated the field.[1] Their

---

[1] Anatoli Ado, *Paysans en Révolution: Terre, pouvoir, et jacquerie, 1789–1794* (Paris: SER, 1996); Alphonse Aulard, *La Révolution française et le régime féodal* (Paris: Alcan, 1919); Robert Bautruche, *Une société en lutte contre le régime féodal: L'Alleu en Bordelais et en Bazadais du XIe au XVIIIe siècles* (Rodez: P. Carrère, 1947); Jean Boutier, *Campagnes en émoi: Révoltes et révolution en Bas-Limousin, 1789–1800* (Treignac: Les Monédières, 1987); Jean-Jacques Clère, *Les paysans de la Haute-Marne et la Révolution française* (Paris: CTHS, 1988); Anthony Crubaugh, *Balancing the Scales of Justice: Local Courts and Rural Society in Southwest France, 1750–1800* (University Park: Pennsylvania State University Press, 2001); Philippe Goujard, *L'abolition de la "féodalité" dans le pays de Bray (1789–1793)* (Paris: Bibliothèque nationale, 1979); Jean-Pierre Jessenne, *Pouvoir au village et révolution: Artois, 1760–1848* (Lille: Presses universitaires de Lille, 1987); P. M. Jones, *Politics and Rural Society in the Southern Massif Central, c. 1750–1850* (Cambridge: Cambridge University Press, 1985); Georges Lefebvre, *Les paysans du Nord pendant la Révolution française* (Lille: Marquant, 1924); Georges Lefebvre, *Questions agraires au temps de la terreur* (Paris: CTHS, 1989); Guy Lemarchand, *Paysans et seigneurs en Europe: Une histoire comparé* (Rennes: Presses universitaires de Rennes, 2011); John Markoff, *The Abolition of Feudalism: Peasants, Lords, and Legislators in the French Revolution* (University Park: Pennsylvania State University Press, 1996); Philippe Sagnac and Pierre Caron, *Les*

studies start from the premise that 1789 was a bourgeois revolution that replaced feudal economic relations with capitalist ones. They furthermore assume that the economic interests of their social class drove the men behind feudal abolition. These studies do not investigate what the revolutionaries themselves believed they were doing and thus foreclose the possibility that feudal abolition had additional – or even different – aims than economic transformation.

What did the revolutionaries mean by "feudalism"? Some understood it as a retrograde economic system that was stifling productivity. These men, including Pierre Samuel Dupont de Nemours, identified with the physiocratic movement that had long advocated a more rational system of landownership.[2] Although many shared these concerns, most seem to have been more concerned with the constitutional ramifications of feudalism. This is clear from the term they often used to discuss it, "feudal government." For them, feudalism was a constitutional form characterized by the blurring of public power and private property. They believed this confusion had arisen historically in Western Europe from two institutions: the private ownership of public function and the hierarchical linkage of parcels of land into chains of superiority and subordination. The weakness of kings and greed of powerful lords in the centuries following the Roman Empire's collapse combined to produce the classic expression of patrimonialized public power, the fief-*seigneurie* complex. In France, the situation was compounded by a uniquely Gallic institution – the venality of judicial and administrative office. Presiding over it all was the Crown, whose simultaneous claims to absolute sovereignty and universal proprietary lordship incarnated the confusion of private property and public power.

This confusion was so integral to the Old Regime that one jurist described it as "the key to our public law."[3] Some applauded it, notably Montesquieu,

---

comités des droits féodaux et de législation et l'abolition du régime seigneurial, 1789–1793 (Geneva: Megariotis Reprints, [1907]); Albert Soboul, *Les campagnes montpelliéraines à la fin de l'Ancien Régime: Propriété et cultures d'après les compoix* (Paris: Presses universitaires de France, 1958); Albert Soboul, *Problèmes paysans de la Révolution (1789–1848)* (Paris: François Maspero, 1976). A key exception, which exhaustively covers the legal dimension of the revolutionary abolition of feudalism, is Marcel Garaud, *La Révolution et la propriété foncière* (Paris: Sirey, 1958).

[2] Elizabeth Fox-Genovese, *The Origins of Physiocracy: Economic Revolution and Social Order in Eighteenth-Century France* (Ithaca, NY: Cornell University Press, 1977); Liana Vardi, *The Physiocrats and the World of the Enlightenment* (Cambridge: Cambridge University Press, 2012).

[3] Lefebvre de la Planche, *Mémoires sur les matières domaniales, ou traité du domaine* (Paris: Desaint et Saillant, 1764), vol. I, xliiii.

who saw it as essential to the privileged intermediate bodies that balanced state–society relations.[4] Most, however, denounced the blurring of property and power. The royal historiographer, Jacob-Nicolas Moreau, bemoaned seigneurial usurpation of royal authority, denounced their conversion of the "power of government" into the "power of property," and urged the nation to reassert "their essential difference."[5] From a different ideological perspective, the Jansenist member of the Paris *parlement*, the Abbé Mey, also underlined the "total difference between public power and domain or property."[6] The debate over feudalism was not primarily economic, but rather a constitutional clash over the proper relationship between property and power.

The Atlantic revolutionary generation understood this and grasped what was at stake. For Thomas Paine, monarchy had to be destroyed in order to end the private ownership of public sovereignty. "All hereditary government is in its nature tyranny," he wrote in *The Rights of Man* (1791). "An hereditary crown or an hereditary throne, or by what other fanciful name such things may be called, have no other significant explanation than that mankind are hereditable property. To inherit a government is to inherit the people as if they were flocks and herds."[7] In response, Edmund Burke argued in his *Reflections on the Revolution in France* (1790) that it was precisely the proprietary nature of government that guaranteed the people's liberties. These he understood not as universal rights, but as a type of property. They were "an entailed inheritance derived to us from our forefathers, and to be transmitted to our posterity." Our "advantages," he continued, "are locked fast as in a sort of family settlement; grasped as in a kind of mortmain forever." "We hold, we transmit our government and our privileges in the same manner in which we enjoy and transmit our property."[8] Paine and Burke both recognized that the confusion of property and power was the organizing principle of the existing European order and that its fate depended on whether or not that confusion would continue.

---

[4] Charles-Louis de Secondat, Baron de Montesquieu, "L'esprit des lois," in Daniel Oster, ed., *Montesquieu: Œuvres complètes* (Paris: Éditions du Seuil, 1964), 535, 555.

[5] Jacob-Nicolas Moreau, *Leçons de morale, de politique, et de droit public, puisées dans l'histoire de notre monarchie* (Versailles: Imprimerie du département des affaires étrangères, 1773), 81, 179.

[6] Claude Mey, *Maximes du droit public François*, 2 vols., 2nd edition (Amsterdam: Marc-Michel Rey, 1775), vol. I, 41–43.

[7] Edmund Burke and Thomas Paine, *Reflections on the Revolution in France/The Rights of Man* (Garden City, NY: Anchor Books, 1973), 407.

[8] Ibid., 45.

On the night of 4 August 1789, the French revolutionaries drew a sharp line between property and power.[9] Preparing the way for the reforms to follow, this was the Revolution's fundamental act. On that night, the National Assembly proclaimed the abolition of the *seigneurie*, venal office, all forms of hierarchical landholding (both feudal and nonfeudal), and privilege, and dramatically curtailed the Church's political existence – some of the principal institutional manifestations of the confusion of property and power. The shorthand phrase "abolition of feudalism" captures neither the magnitude nor the underlying logic of these changes. A more evocative term is the "Great Demarcation," for it simultaneously alludes to the conceptual blurring of the wide-ranging abolitions it sought to dispel and the distinction between private property and public power at the heart of the New Regime.[10]

The Great Demarcation of the Night of 4 August 1789 simultaneously reassembled the fragments of patrimonialized public power as undivided sovereignty and created private property by eliminating all trace of jurisdiction, formal dependence, and shared ownership from real estate. Without these acts, there could have been no national sovereignty, for public power would have remained dispersed among many private hands. Nor could there have been electoral democracy, for public offices would have remained the property of families, disposed of by hereditary succession or private sale. The Great Demarcation thus laid the foundations on which the New Regime – and political modernity – would rest. To see in the Night of 4 August 1789 only the "abolition of feudalism" and, worse, view it in primarily economic terms is to overlook its greater significance. The true legacy of the Night was the legal imposition of the conceptual grid that would structure modern political and social systems and sharpen the binaries that define the modern way of seeing: the political and the social, state and society, sovereignty and ownership, public and private.

The Night of 4 August

The decree that issued from the Night of 4 August 1789 opens by declaring that the "feudal regime is abolished in its entirety." At that time, much of

---

[9] On the Night of 4 August, see Michael P. Fitzsimmons, *The Night the Old Regime Ended: August 4, 1789 and the French Revolution* (University Park: Pennsylvania State University Press, 2003); Jean-Pierre Hirsch, *La Nuit du 4 août* (Paris: Gallimard/Julliard, 1978); Patrick Kessel, *La Nuit du 4 août 1789* (Paris: Arthaud, 1969).

[10] Rafe Blaufarb, *The Great Demarcation: The French Revolution and the Invention of Modern Property* (New York: Oxford University Press, 2016).

France was in the grip of peasant unrest, the Great Fear.[11] Many historians have consequently seen the decree as an attempt by worried deputies to pacify the peasantry by concessions. That the Great Fear caused the deputies deep anxiety is clear. However, to conclude that the Night of 4 August was merely "the product of a specific political and economic conjuncture in a socially explosive context," devoid of any "conscious political program," elides the question of the ideas, assumptions, and aspirations that informed the deputies' response to the crisis.[12] Even responses to the most pressing crises are necessarily conditioned by culture and belief of some kind. There are many possible ways the deputies of the National Assembly could have reacted to the Great Fear. (In fact, the National Assembly adopted strong repressive measures to accompany the abolitions.) Our challenge is to understand why they responded with the particular slate of abolitions they chose – many of which had nothing to do with peasant grievances. The deputies did not act in an intellectual void, but rather within a climate of ideas.

The key to understanding those ideas is the legal background of a large proportion of the deputies. As lawyers steeped in the foundational texts of their profession – those of Dumoulin, Bodin, Loyseau, and others – they were familiar with the critique of the private ownership of public power that these jurists had progressively elaborated. Under Dumoulin's well-known dictum, "fief and *seigneurie* have nothing in common" (that is, the landed and jurisdictional elements of lordship, while usually found together, were essentially different), these jurists had condemned seigneurial justice as a usurpation of royal sovereignty and envisioned more independent forms of property as an alternative to the existing feudal hierarchies. The efforts of allodial provinces to defend the free status of their lands from royal claims to universal overlordship reinforced the jurists' critique of the imbrication of property and power.[13] Against the royal claims, the advocates of allodiality not only upheld the ideal of free property, but also attacked the Crown's proprietary character. One of the leading allodialists, Pierre de Caseneuve,

---

[11] The classic work is Georges Lefebvre, *La Grande Peur de 1789* (Paris: Armand Collin, 1932).

[12] Silvia Marzagalli, "Economics and Demographic Developments," in David Andress, ed., *The Oxford Handbook of the French Revolution* (Oxford: Oxford University Press, 2015), 3–20: 13.

[13] Thomas Kaiser, "Property, Sovereignty, the Declaration of the Rights of Man, and the Tradition of French Jurisprudence," in Dale Van Kley, ed., *The French Idea of Freedom: The Old Regime and the Declaration of Rights of 1789* (Stanford: Stanford University Press, 1994), 300–39.

argued that free property actually augmented the Crown's brilliance.[14] As sovereign, the king was "unique," but as feudal overlord, he was just one among many. Sharing the same quality as "so many lords," he warned, "took something away" from the grandeur of sovereignty that was the king's alone. "Like the Sun, whose light is all the more beautiful when alone and no stars share its splendor," a purely sovereign king could be "the grandest, most potent, and triumphant prince to wear a Crown." In the final decades of the Old Regime, the critique of the confusion of property and power drew support from an unexpected quarter – physiocracy. Despite the physiocrats' insistence that the king should be the universal "coproprietor" of the kingdom, a position some interpreted as a call for an even more proprietary conception of sovereignty, their deeper impact was to develop a new way of speaking about property. Their works eschew terms like venal office, fief, and *seigneurie* – terms that accurately reflected the imbrication of property and power that actually existed in the real world. Instead, they spoke only abstractly – of "land," "property," and "proprietors." The physiocrats' terminology linguistically erased the confusion of property and power, naturalized the notion of property, and lent it a purely material character.[15] All these critiques of the confusion of property and power informed not only the deputies' approach to the issue of "feudalism," but also their vision for the New Regime.

This emerges clearly from the abolitions they first proclaimed on the Night of 4 August and decreed over the course of the next week. Two of the decree's articles, Articles 4 and 7, abolished seigneurial justice and venal office. It testifies to the extent to which the deputies had absorbed the jurists' denunciations of both of these institutions that they abolished them without debate and, in the case of seigneurial justice, without indemnifying the lords. It is also telling that both measures would be extremely disruptive and expensive – and this at a time of unprecedented financial crisis. Since seigneurial justice formed the first rung of the kingdom's judicial system, its abolition required the creation of an entirely new, nationwide network of lower courts. And as it was through the sale of venal office that the higher levels of the magistracy were filled, the elimination of that institution meant that the rest of the judicial system would need to be rebuilt as well.

---

[14] Pierre de Caseneuve, *Instructions pour le franc-alleu de la province de Languedoc* (Toulouse: J. Boute, 1640), 68–70.
[15] For an example, see Pierre-Paul Le Mercier de la Rivière, *L'Ordre naturel et essentiel des sociétés politiques* (London: Jean Nourse, 1767).

Moreover, since the deputies were committed to reimbursing the owners of venal offices, their abolition substantially increased the national debt. It ultimately cost the nation 800 million French pounds, increasing the debt by 50 percent.[16] The men of 1789 were willing to pay virtually any price to end private ownership of public power.

Four other articles – Articles 1, 2, 3, and 6 – sought to transform hierarchical property-holding into a new regime of free, independent, and legally equal ownership. Article 1's declaration, "the feudal regime is abolished in its entirety," expressed this forcefully – perhaps too forcefully for some lords, since many peasants took it literally and acted on it immediately. The following two articles complemented this by ending the seigneurial hunting and pigeon-breeding prerogatives. These articles were more than just attacks on the lords and concessions to the peasantry. Many commoners owned fiefs, as did trade guilds and municipalities. In fact, the largest single owner of fiefs in 1789 was the Church, whose lordships covered much of urban France. Feudalism was thus not a special form of property-holding specific to the nobility, but rather *the system* of real estate itself, a system whose essence was to produce a hierarchy of multiple claims to single parcels of land. In abolishing "the feudal regime in its entirety," the deputies were taking aim at this system in general, rather than at the nobility in particular.

This becomes clear from Article 6, which abolished formally *nonfeudal* perpetual ground rents. Before 1789, some proprietary hierarchies were generated by the alienation of parcels of land in exchange for perpetual ground rents. The parties involved in these arrangements were frequently commoners, and the properties involved were just as frequently nonfeudal. By outlawing these kinds of alienations and the perpetual rents they spawned, the deputies showed their determination to abolish proprietary hierarchy in all its forms, nonfeudal and feudal alike. For the deputies, only property owned fully and independently could provide the necessary basis for political freedom and, thus, citizenship. The Abbé Sieyès was one of many revolutionaries to state this plainly. "Legitimate property guarantees independence," he wrote. "Those who depend on the property of others are

---

[16] David D. Bien, "Property in Office under the Ancien Régime: The Case of the Stockbrokers," in John Brewer and Susan Staves, eds., *Conceptions of Property in Early Modern Europe: Consumption and Culture in the 17th and 18th Centuries* (London: Routledge, 1996), 132. See also William Doyle, *Venality: The Sale of Offices in 18th Century France* (Oxford: Clarendon Press, 1996), 288–309.

slaves."[17] Whether feudal or nonfeudal, hierarchical tenure was incompatible with this understanding of political liberty. Often overlooked, Article 6 is the key to understanding the Revolution's new regime of property and its importance to the new political order.

A third set of articles – Articles 9, 10, 11, and 15 – abolished particularistic privileges such as provincial liberties, noble tax exemption, and the nobility's exclusive right to enter certain professions. Although these privileges were not technically property, for they could not be bought and sold, they functioned like personal property in public power. Giving individuals special rights, prerogatives, functions, and exemptions, privileges had similar practical effects to *seigneuries* and venal office. Like those institutions, privilege fragmented sovereignty by scattering and privatizing public power. It therefore had to be abolished to delineate a sphere of unitary sovereignty distinct from private property.

The final set of articles – Articles 5, 8, 12, 13, and 14 – curtailed the financial autonomy of the Catholic Church, paving the way for its elimination as an independent political body. It was well-understood that this heralded the expropriation of the Church and sale of its properties, a measure many hoped would save the nation's finances. But more than fiscal considerations were involved in the transformation of the Church from a corporate state-within-the-state into a public organization of salaried professionals. This is because the Church possessed sweeping political powers and functions, such as education, charity, health care, and overseeing the civil status of the kingdom's inhabitants. Under these conditions, the continued existence of the Church was incompatible with undivided national sovereignty and the demarcation of power from property. As a property-holding corporation with public powers, it posed the same threat to the new order as feudal lords and venal office-holders, albeit on a much larger scale. By stripping it of the tithe and other sources of revenue, the decree's ecclesiastical articles went far toward destroying the Church's financial independence and corporate personhood.

Expropriating the Church, Creating the National Domain

Yet, as long as the Church kept its landed properties, which included many feudal and nonfeudal rents, it would necessarily retain a corporate existence. This is because those properties would require an executive board to manage

---

[17] J. Madival and E. Laurent, et al., eds., *Archives parlementaires de 1787 à 1860* (Paris: Dupont/CNRS, 1867–2000) (henceforth *AP*), vol. VII, 503.

them. It thus came as no surprise when a deputy proposed on 10 October 1789 that the nation take over the Church's property. The idea of using the Church's wealth to solve the nation's fiscal crisis had been in the air for several years; familiar financial arguments for and against expropriation were rehashed in the opening stages of the National Assembly's debate on the motion. But discussion soon shifted to constitutional terrain as the deputies began to consider the questions of whether the new regime could countenance independent political bodies within it and what, if any, property rights such bodies could have. The debate proved to be one of the most consequential of the entire Revolution. In deciding the question of the property rights of the corporation, it also decided the question of those of the nation.

Were the property rights of corporate bodies of the same nature (and thus imprescriptible) as those of individuals? This was an issue familiar to most deputies. In 1757, Anne-Robert-Joseph Turgot had published an article on religious endowments in the celebrated *Encyclopédie* in which he had argued that corporate property rights were fundamentally different and less absolute than those of individuals.[18] The advocates of expropriating the Church generally based their position on Turgot's distinction, to which they frequently referred in the debate. But the defenders of ecclesiastical property, most of whom were members of the clergy, invoked weighty authorities of their own. Perhaps the most surprising was Jean-Jacques Rousseau. Citing the Genevan philosopher's famous works *Émile* and the *Social Contract*, they attacked the Turgotian distinction by arguing that all property, whether corporate or individual, arose from the same source – society and the laws it established. "The right of property," one claimed, was a "civil right, founded on law, maintained by law." Whether exercised by an individual or a corporation, the right itself was the same. It followed that if the nation could expropriate a corporation, it could "just as well and for the same reasons" take the property of a citizen.[19] To deprive the Church of its possessions would thus threaten all property rights and place the belongings of every citizen at the mercy of the state.

It was tempting for the advocates of expropriation to respond to this argument by reinforcing Turgot's distinction with Locke's notion that individual property was a natural right antedating the formation of societies.

---

[18] Anne-Robert-Joseph Turgot, "Fondation," in Denis Diderot and Jean-Rond d'Alembert, eds., *Encyclopédie, ou dictionnaire raisonné des sciences, des arts, et des métiers* (Paris: n.p., 1751–1772), vol. VII, 72–5.
[19] *AP*, vol. IX, 416–18.

Some indeed did, but this was not the approach that ultimately won the day. Instead of going down the path of natural law, expropriation's most powerful voice, Count Mirabeau, instead accepted battle on the Rousseauian ground his enemies had chosen.[20] Yes, he admitted, there was no such thing as a natural property right anterior to the formation of society. Instead, as the defenders of Church property had claimed, property rights were a "civil effect" – for individuals and corporations alike. This did not mean, however, that their respective property rights were identical. Those of individuals arose instantaneously with the formation of the social contract itself. For the individual, therefore, property right was "coexistent" with society and needed "no distinct laws to ensure" it, for it was integral to the "social pact" itself. This was not the case with corporations. Given that they were "established only after the formation of society," they could have "no right coexistent with it." Their property rights were thus "the work of the legislature and the law" alone. And what the law could bestow, the law could take away. The National Assembly could thus strip the property of corporations quite easily, but could do so to individuals only at the cost of the social contract itself.

Reassuring the deputies that individual property would remain secure even as the properties of the Church were confiscated, this theory of property rights carried the day. On 2 November 1789, the deputies voted to place the ecclesiastical properties at the disposition of the nation. Although it would be nearly a year before sales began, the seizure of Church property raised an immediate question: what did the nationalization say about the property rights of the nation itself? The prospect that the nation might take over ecclesiastical property had already prompted discussion about the possible existence of a "national domain," for, as one deputy observed, the nation's property "must reside somewhere."[21] But its existence had never been formally declared, nor had its capacities and content been defined. And more problematically, its relationship to the still-extant royal domain had yet to be worked out. In fits and starts over the course of the next year, the deputies would find answers to these questions as they gave shape to a new institution, the national domain. This was vitally important, for it was only in marking out the limits of national property rights that they delineated the realm of private property. With this, the Great Demarcation between property and power would be complete.

---

[20] *AP*, vol. IX, 641–5.   [21] *AP*, vol. IX, 491.

The deputies had to decide the question of national property rights when they considered what to do with the royal domain. The royal domain consisted of a multitude of "properties," from things that would soon be redefined as sovereign powers, such as the right of taxation and other public functions, to physical and nonphysical properties both feudal and nonfeudal. The most imposing of these, at least in theory, was the Crown's claim to royal universal lordship over the entire kingdom. Yet, the king's ability to dispose of his domain was constrained by legal restrictions stipulated in the Edict of Moulins (1566) and the Edict on Reunion (1607).[22] These required that the prince cede all of his personal properties into the royal domain upon accession to the throne, that princely appanages also revert to the domain when an appanage-holder became king or died without male issue, and that the king could not alienate any part of the domain. Taken together, these three rules strove to foster a seamless unity of interest between the ruler and the State. By depriving the king of his right to private property, they sought to prevent him from having a personal, pecuniary interest potentially at odds with that of the kingdom as a whole.

Domanial inalienability offered both promise and peril to the revolutionaries, as they considered how to construct a national domain. Promise because inalienability gave the nation a legal mechanism to recover illegal alienations and usurpations. Peril because it threatened to extend the state's reach beyond illegal alienations to encompass all private property. Given that centuries of jurisprudence, history, and royal propaganda held that all property in France originated in royal land grants, the possibility of a nationwide property inquisition was not far-fetched – not least because kings had periodically engaged in such machinations. The principle of domanial inalienability would loom with particular menace over the recently nationalized ecclesiastical properties. Would citizens dare to buy these properties if the principle of inalienability persisted, casting doubt on the nation's right to sell them? The deputies realized that they had to formulate a new theory of the national domain capable of preserving the benefits of inalienability while allowing the nation to sell off the properties it had expropriated.

---

[22] Robert Descimon, "Les Fonctions de la métaphore du mariage politique du roi et de la république, France, XVe–XVIIIe siècles," *Annales ESC* 47:6 (1992), 1127–47; Robert Descimon, "L'Union au domaine royal et le principe d'inaliénabilité. La construction d'une loi fondamentale aux XVIe et XVIIe siècle," *Droits* 1:22 (1995), 79–90; and François Olivier-Martin, "La réunion de la Basse-Navarre à la couronne de France," *Anuario de historia de derecho español* 9 (1932), 249–89.

Their solution was to make the nation the historical origin of the royal domain. The established histories, which described how Frankish kings had created the first "private" properties by making grants from their domain, were wrong. Instead, the domain had originally belonged to the nation, which had lent it to the Crown to help defray the cost of government. But the kings had always been just "simple administrators," never true owners of the domain.[23] It had never ceased to belong, in its entirety, to the nation. Enshrined by the National Assembly's decree of 8 November 1790, this reinterpretation nationalized the royal domain and provided a rationale for retaining both alienability and inalienability. Since the domain belonged to the nation, it could alienate all or part of it as it saw fit. This provided a legal basis for the sale of the confiscated ecclesiastical and royal-domanial properties, reassuring prospective buyers that their purchases would be secure. At the same time, national ownership of the domain meant that alienations made in the past without the nation's consent (all of them) were illegal and could be revoked.

This national rationale for inalienability was potentially quite problematic. Historians and jurists had agreed that most property in France had originated in royal grants of fiefs. "Casting one's eyes on the origin of the monarchy," admitted one of the deputies in charge of drafting the new domanial legislation, "we discover that very many private properties were successively dismembered from the public domain."[24] As domanial alienations made by the Crown without national consent, they were now subject to revocation and reabsorption into the national domain. The implication of this was startling: if something were not done to limit the nation's right to revoke these nonconsensual concessions, then there would remain no legitimate private property in France. The deputies recoiled from the prospect of a state that could invoke the new theory of domanial inalienability to expropriate private individuals. To prevent this, they decided to establish a line of demarcation between the realm of illegally alienated properties that the national domain should recover and the realm of legitimate private property that would be sacrosanct. To draw this line, they fell back on the Edict of Moulins, which had enshrined inalienability as a constitutional principle. Properties acquired before 1566, the year of its promulgation, were declared forever immune from domanial investigation. They would form the initial content of the sphere of private property. Those acquired after 1566 were

---

[23] *AP*, vol. x, 50.   [24] *AP*, vol. xx, 319.

classified as national. They were to be recovered and sold, together with the ecclesiastical and royal properties that had already been confiscated. The distinction between private and public property would thus have a chronological dimension.

With the passage of the domanial legislation of November 1790, the nation made ready to alienate itself back to fiscal health. The sale of nationalized properties would have an added, political-economic benefit. By converting the large estates of conservative public institutions like the Church and Crown into smaller, individually managed private holdings, the operation would increase the nation's economic productivity. But in addition to these material benefits, the sale of the national properties would play an essential role in the constitutional transformation of France. Deploying the powerful mechanisms of inalienability and alienability, the national domain would sweep up public properties and convert them by sale into private ones. Nothing truly national would escape its maw; ultimately, all would be digested and then disgorged back into society as individual property. In the end, having transformed all "political" and corporate goods into private property, the national domain would stand empty of all but those things – like roads, rivers, and market squares – that were truly public because insusceptible of private ownership. The national domain was thus a critical part of the machinery to realize the Great Demarcation. Through its workings, the state would rid itself of the proprietary character it had inherited from the monarchy by converting the "political" properties of the Old Regime into purely "social" private ones.

Feudal Abolition in Practice

With the passage into law of the abolitions of 4 August 1789 and the domanial reforms of November 1790, the revolutionaries completed their blueprint for a Great Demarcation between property and power. By abolishing *seigneuries*, venal offices, and privilege, they had ended private ownership of public power. By abolishing hierarchical property-holding in all its forms, they had replaced the tenurial chains of superiority and dependence with "absolute" property ownership that in principle was free, undivided, and juridically equal. By preparing the way for the expropriation of political bodies, first and foremost the Church, they had prohibited state-like public entities from owning property and enjoying legal personality. These measures delineated a social sphere of property in which owners would be individuals and the things they owned would generally be physical rather than incorporeal. However, this transformation left a major problem unsolved: the confusion of property and power at the heart of sovereignty itself, in the royal domain. The domanial reforms of 1790 dispelled this confusion and made the state purely sovereign by expropriating the royal domain and selling its contents to individual citizens. In the end, all of the Crown's former properties, along with those of the Church and other political bodies, would be transferred from the political sphere to society and thus transformed into true private property. Once these operations had been completed, the French polity would consist of a property-owning society of individual citizens, on one side, and a purely sovereign state, on the other. This fundamental demarcation between a private sphere of individual property and a public sphere of political power would provide the constitutional matrix for the New Regime and provide the basis for all of the Revolution's key reforms, such as equal rights and voting. But putting the Great Demarcation into practice was no simple matter.

The revolutionaries' first challenge was to design a method for carrying out their promise to abolish hierarchical property holding. It had been an easy decision for them to abolish jurisdictional lordships – the *seigneuries* – without compensation; the jurists and historians had long ago established that these institutions were nothing but violent usurpations. But feudal dues were another matter. The men of 1789 were nothing if not respectful of property, and they believed that most feudal dues had been established contractually, as the price tenants had agreed to pay their lords for their parcels of land. If these dues were abolished outright, the tenants would have acquired their lands for nothing, while the lords would have lost both land and rent. Uncompensated feudal abolition, the deputies concluded, amounted to unjust expropriation. They thus decided to create a system of redemption, which would allow tenants to buy out the feudal dues imposed on their land. The system was based on the notion that tenant parcels were actually loans of landed capital made by lords in exchange for interest payments – the feudal dues. Since the usual rate of interest in France at the time was 5 percent, the revolutionaries worked backward to fix the repurchase value of the feudal due at twenty times its annual amount. If the dues were stipulated in kind, however, the repurchase rate was set at twenty-five times the annual amount – a premium because such dues were protected against inflation. Finally, the redemption rate of the occasional, but heavy, dues collected when a tenant's property was sold were calculated by a complex formula based on a number of shifting, interrelated variables such as average frequency of sales and average price of land. These repurchase mechanisms went into effect in mid-1790.[25]

The system was coherent, but it proved politically disastrous. The peasants, who had rejoiced in the revolutionaries' proclamation that "the feudal regime is abolished in its entirety" were not pleased to learn, several months later, that they actually had to pay – and pay heavily – to free themselves from their feudal burdens. Many, probably the vast majority, simply stopped paying their dues. Most were able to do this with impunity because of the instability, weakness, and occasional complicity of the new, elected governing institutions. When local authorities attempted to force payment, their efforts could provoke violent resistance. Large parts of rural France were swept by full-scale jacqueries.[26] To be sure, not all peasants resorted to violence and some may have even been willing to comply with the new legislation. But the repurchase rates were simply too high for all but the wealthiest to afford. A few provinces, notably Anjou and Poitou, displayed relatively high levels of peasant participation in the repurchase system – but only compared with the prevailing noncompliance of the rest of rural France.[27] Most of the countryside refused – whether willfully or because of financial incapacity – to participate in the compensated abolition of feudal dues.

This is why most historians have concluded that repurchase was a categorical failure. But the system of hierarchical landholding did not only concern the countryside; as the kingdom's system of real estate, it characterized property-holding in urban France as well. Most cities fell under the lordship of bishops or powerful abbots, and those areas that did not were usually held from the royal domain under feudal conditions. By November 1790, all of the dues generated by these urban lordships had become national properties thanks to the expropriation of the Church and royal domain – and were promptly (and awkwardly) renamed "formerly feudal national dues." A significant portion of the urban population, from nobles and high magistrates to lawyers, doctors, and merchants, had the financial wherewithal and the will to avail themselves of the repurchase system to emancipate their properties from these national dues. Even people of more modest social

---

[25] For a useful short survey of the Revolution's feudal legislation, see Jean-Jacques Clère, "L'abolition des droits féodaux en France," *Cahiers d'histoire. Revue d'histoire critique* 94–5 (2005), 135–57.
[26] See note 1, particularly the works of Ado and Markoff.
[27] Jean-Noël Luc, *Paysans et droits féodaux en Charente-Inférieure pendant la Révolution française* (Paris: CHRF, 1984).

background, such as established artisans and market-gardeners, could occasionally do so as well. As a result, French cities saw a markedly greater rate of repurchase than the countryside.[28] From mid-1790 until mid-1793, there were 407 instances of redemption in Aix-en-Provence (a city of about 20,000), 744 in Marseille (France's principal Mediterranean port), and 307 in Tours (a mid-sized town in western France).[29] While these figures do not indicate unqualified acceptance by the cities of the Revolution's program of compensated feudal abolition, they do show that part of the urban population felt confident enough in the benefits, legitimacy, and durability of the Revolution to bet financially on its survival. Thus, while the view from the countryside reveals a dismal landscape indeed, marked by the near-total refusal of peasants not merely to participate in the repurchase system but even to continue paying their nonredeemed dues, the urban perspective offers a more mixed picture. In French towns and cities, well-to-do inhabitants availed themselves of the repurchase system to free their holdings from national lordship.

Urban participation alone was not enough to save the Revolution's program of compensated feudal abolition. By early 1792, pressure was building to relax the strict regulations established by the original legislation. Peasant resistance continued unabated, and, as international tension grew over the winter of 1791–1792, prowar deputies realized that something needed to be done to consolidate the support of the rural population – which would soon be summoned to fill the ranks of the revolutionary armies. Accordingly, from June through August 1792, a number of changes were approved that made it much easier for people to free themselves from feudal dues. The key change was to reverse the burden of proof for establishing the validity of a feudal due (from tenant to lord). The original abolition legislation had pronounced all dues legitimate unless proven otherwise; now lords would have to furnish documentary evidence – in the form of the initial feudal lease – to prove that a contested due had been created contractually in exchange for a piece of real estate. As this was impossible for most lords to do, peasants could now free their lands at no cost simply by making a formal repurchase demand and forcing the lords to admit that they did not possess the required original titles. Thousands of peasants now rushed to take part in the repurchase

---

[28] The sole work to address the urban dimension of feudal abolition is André Ferradou, *Le rachat des droits féodaux dans la Gironde, 1790–1793* (Paris: Sirey, 1958).

[29] For Aix and Marseille, see Archives départementales des Bouches-du-Rhône, 1 Q 1025, 1027, and 1095. For Tours, see Archives départementales du Rhône, 1 Q 43–45 and 48.

system. But as radical as this shift proved to be in practice, it still countenanced the possibility that a feudal due might be legitimate and, thus, that a contractual, noncoercive feudalism could potentially exist.

This potential was canceled on 17 July 1793, when the National Convention ruled that all feudal arrangements were necessarily coercive and could never possess the element of volition required to make a contract legitimate. Henceforth all real estate contracts with any trace of feudal language would be annulled without compensation and publicly burned. The measure was supposed to close the feudal question, but it instead opened a new phase in the history of feudal abolition. Many nonfeudal rents – those established by a nonlord for a concession of land that had already been dismembered from a fief and had thus lost its noble character – were stipulated in contracts laced with feudal terminology. Indeed, given that feudal hierarchical tenure had served as the model for all real estate arrangements before 1789, it would have been exceedingly hard to find an untainted title. Opponents of the Convention's radical approach to feudal abolition, together with proprietors who simply wanted to preserve their nonfeudal rents, seized upon this linguistic ambiguity to argue that one needed to examine the substance and context of a given rent, rather than its superficial wording, to determine its true nature. The battle lines were drawn, pitting contextualists against textualists in successive legislatures and the judiciary. The contextualists finally won in 1838 when the national appeals court ruled that language alone was not enough to judge the character of a rent.

Emptying the National Domain

The emptying of the national domain through the sale of ecclesiastical, royal, and other confiscated properties was also a tortuous process. It took hundreds of laws and seventy-five years (until 1867) until the last nationalized property was sold.[30] The problems encountered along the way, however, were purely economic and political; they did not raise any fundamental questions about the constitutional principles of the new regime. But there were two types of national properties that did: *engagements* and nationalized feudal dues. Straddling the line between public and private property, *engagements* were revocable grants of property made by kings to individuals in exchange for large capital sums. The king could take back these grants at will

---

[30] Eric Bodinier and Eric Teyssier, *L'Événement le plus important de la Révolution: La vente des biens nationaux* (Paris: CTHS, 2000).

and reunite them to the royal domain by reimbursing the original capital. But this rarely happened because the monarchy was chronically short of money and depended upon *engagements* and other forms of disguised borrowing, to finance the government.[31] By threatening the holders of *engagements* with reimbursement and expropriation unless they added new capital to their original investment, the Crown could keep wringing money out of them. The families of *engagistes* (the holders of these grants) invariably paid and thus retained their possessions for decades and centuries. By 1789 most considered their holdings veritable patrimonial property.

The domanial law of November 1790 shattered this illusion. It declared that all *engagements* made after 1566 were not private property, that they would be recovered by the national domain, and that they would then be sold just like other national properties. On three occasions – in 1791, 1792, and 1794 – the *engagistes* were ordered to declare their holdings and prepare to relinquish them. However, these efforts to reclaim the *engagements* came to naught because the new regime was just as impecunious as the old and could not afford the cost of reimbursement. A fourth attempt to liquidate the *engagements* succeeded in 1797 when the legislature changed tack and abandoned its attempt to recover the grants for the national domain. Instead, it borrowed a page from the old regime and demanded that all *engagistes* pay a final supplement of 25 percent of the value of their original capital. Those who complied would receive full property title to their grant; those who did not would receive reimbursement in 5 percent government scrip and see their possession confiscated by the national domain. The law was practical and could have worked, but it lacked mechanisms for enforcement. *Engagistes* soon realized that they could keep government agents away simply by offering to pay the 25 percent supplement and then stalling indefinitely. This strategy, together with bureaucratic inertia and the financial administration's prioritization of more promising sources of revenue, ensured that the problem of *engagements* persisted well into the nineteenth century.

Even more problematic than the *engagements* were the dues and rents that the nation acquired by nationalizing the properties of the Church and royal domain. They consisted in the feudal and nonfeudal rents owed to ecclesiastical lords, as well as the dues owed to the domain by fiefs held directly from the Crown. These "formerly feudal national dues" were successively renamed "incorporeal national dues" and then "national rents." This flight

---

[31] David D. Bien, "Les offices, les corps et le crédit de l'Etat. L'utilisation des privilèges sous l'Ancien Régime," *Annales ESC* 43:2 (1988), 379–404.

toward increasingly bland nomenclature suggests the discomfort these properties caused the revolutionaries. For in taking them over, the nation had made itself a lord. Yet, the awkwardness this caused was outweighed by the financial resource the national rents represented. One estimate placed their total capital value at 500 million *livres*.[32] The rents were thus a highly problematic, but financially irresistible resource for the cash-strapped nation. They were, judged one of their critics, "a cure worse than the disease itself."[33]

The shifting legislation on the national rents reflected not only the ebb and flow of the revolutionaries' discomfort with them, but also the changing laws on feudal abolition. From the start, the National Assembly was determined to use them to raise revenue. The only disagreements concerned how this was to be done – whether through leasing out the right to collect them to private entrepreneurs, collecting them directly through local or national authorities, realizing their capital value through the general feudal repurchase system, or selling them to individuals in the same manner as other national properties. The last of these practices was quickly ended, however, when complaints reached the deputies that "companies" of speculators were purchasing the national dues in mass and would "reproduce the feudal regime ... in a more hideous and repressive form" than before.[34] The practice of leasing out the national rents also soon disappeared because peasant resistance to their payment made their collection all but impossible and, by 1793, the emission of paper money and rising inflation made doing so unprofitable. And not long after this, the government suspended the repurchase of national rents because, thanks to the prevailing inflation, those subject to them could liberate themselves with depreciated paper. The failure of these attempts to capitalize the national rents meant that the National Convention had one reason fewer for pause when it abolished all feudally tainted contracts in July 1793. For, although this measure annihilated a great mass of nationalized feudal dues, the vast financial resources they had appeared to promise in 1789 had proven illusory.

This changed dramatically in 1796, when the Directory withdrew all paper money from circulation. This meant that the state could now demand payment from repurchasers in badly needed silver. This consideration not

---

[32] *Aperçu estimatif de la valeur capitale des droits incorporels-casuels nationaux, par M. Belle, vice-président du comité de l'ordinaire des finances* (Paris: Imprimerie nationale, 1792).
[33] M. Boudin, *Nouvelles réflexions sur le rachat des droits féodaux* (Paris: Dessene, 1790), 16.
[34] AP, vol. XXIII, 763.

only led it to revive the collection and repurchase of the rents, but also spurred attempts to relax the National Convention's uncompromising approach to feudal abolition. Repealing the law of 17 July 1793, advocates of relaxation argued, would increase the mass of national rents at the nation's disposition. The move to loosen the antifeudal legislation grew even stronger under Napoleon, as his victories brought fresh feudal dues (from the lands he conquered) under French control.[35] In 1811, the emperor established a commission to devise a policy on the application of feudal abolition in the conquered territories to spare these resources from destruction. The two commissioners, who had been critics of the radical 1793 abolition, went further. They proposed not only implementing the original, 1790 legislation in the newly annexed territories, but also reactivating that legislation in the French core.[36] But the annihilation of Napoleon's armies in Russia the following year scuttled these plans. Nonetheless, a number of apparently feudal national rents remained inscribed on the registers of French financial administrators and continued to be collected and repurchased well into the nineteenth century. Whether we consider the tortuous abolition of the hierarchical model of property or the slow exit of property from the national domain, the implementation of the Great Demarcation was a contested, contingent process that ultimately proved less total than the utopian vision that inspired it.

Conclusion

In his article on the Jewish question, Karl Marx described the transformation the French Revolution had wrought.

> What was the character of the old society? It can be characterized in one word: *feudalism*. The old civil society had a *directly political* character, i.e. the elements of civil life such as property, family and the mode and manner of work were elevated in the form of seignory and guild to the level of elements of political life ...
>
> The political revolution which overthrew this rule ... inevitably destroyed all the [social] estates, corporations, guilds and privileges which expressed the separation of the people from its community. The political revolution thereby *abolished* the *political character of civil society* ... It

---

[35] Geneviève Massa-Gille, "Les rentes foncières sous le Consulat et Empire," *Bibliothèque de l'Ecole des Chartes* 133:2 (July–December 1975), 247–337.
[36] *Rapport et projet de décret sur le mode d'application des lois françaises concernant l'abolition de la féodalité aux départements nouvellement réunis à l'Empire* (Paris: n.p., 1811).

unleashed the political spirit which had, as it were, been dissolved, dissected and dispersed in the various cul-de-sacs of feudal society; it gathered together this spirit from its state of dispersion, liberated it from the adulteration of civil life and constituted it as the sphere of the community, the *universal* concern of the people ideally independent of those *particular* elements of civil life . . .

But the perfection of the idealism of the state was at the same time the perfection of the materialism of civil society. The shaking-off of the political yoke was at the same time the shaking-off of the bonds which had held in check the egoistic spirit of civil society. Political emancipation was at the same time the emancipation of civil society from politics . . .

The *constitution* of the *political state* and the dissolution of civil society into independent *individuals* . . . are achieved in *one and the same act*.[37]

This was the Great Demarcation – the conceptual distinction between state and society the revolutionaries sought to achieve by disentangling the idea of property from that of public power. Yet, while Marx was right about what the Revolution had done, he was somewhat off the mark when he described who had done it. The Great Demarcation was the work not of a self-conscious economic class, the bourgeoisie, but rather of a compact group of lawyer-revolutionaries who shared a common professional milieu, education, ideas, and aspirations. They seem to have been in control of the concepts they had acquired from their professional culture and used them purposefully to achieve their goals. They were doing more than serving as conduits for discourse and reacting to immediate crises. They were consciously pursuing a program. Of course, they had to do so in the face of multiple challenges – political opposition, social upheaval, war, and fiscal chaos. But they kept their eyes on their goal, weathered the storms of the Revolution, and ultimately achieved what they had set out to accomplish. By recognizing that a core of revolutionary jurist-legislators successfully pursued a conscious vision of change with deep intellectual roots in their profession, we can restore the missing element of volition – and thus meaning – to our understanding of the French Revolution. Understood as the Great Demarcation, the Revolution was the moment when Europeans began a deliberate effort to break fundamentally with their old constitutional order.

The conceptual distinction between property and power initiated a cascade of further binaries – the social and the political, state and society, public and private – that structure the social sciences and, more generally, modern

---

[37] Cited in François Furet, ed., *Marx and the French Revolution*, trans. Deborah Kan Furet (Chicago: University of Chicago Press, 1988), 113–14.

ways of seeing the world. But the absolute separation between these various spheres was never, and could never, be realized. Like all utopian projects, the attempts of the revolutionaries and their successors to implement the Great Demarcation were incomplete and ambiguous. Most obviously, it soon became clear that property, and wealth in all its forms, could indirectly produce political power. So, even if the rich are no longer able to buy public offices, functions, and privileges directly, they can obtain the same powers and benefits by deploying their wealth in the political process. The separation between property and power thus proved illusory in practice. Rather than creating a new reality, the Great Demarcation established a new set of norms through which we make sense out of our world.

3
The Countryside

NOELLE PLACK

Given the diversity of the French countryside on the eve of the Revolution, it might seem impossible to write a history of the collective experience of those who lived there. How was *La France profonde*, or the deep culture of rural village life, impacted by the tremendous changes wrought by the revolutionary decade? Which aspects of daily life were most fundamentally altered by the new social, political, fiscal and cultural landscape? And how did the attempt to destroy the established practices of social hierarchy, authority, and religious belief play out in rural areas? This chapter will attempt to capture the multifaceted, complex, and sometimes contradictory experiences of the people living in the villages and small market towns of the French countryside. It will explore these transformations through three distinct lenses: rural conditions in 1789, peasant resistance and revolt, and the extraordinary shift in sociocultural norms and behaviors by 1799. The people who lived in the countryside are often referred to as "peasants." The French word *paysan*, meaning people of the land (*pays*), is usually employed to refer to the country-dwellers, who worked the land and, because of their close links to native soil, shared a common lifestyle and outlook. It is often said that these people played an important role in the French Revolution. Yet it is difficult to unpack *the* role the peasantry played as they operated in various ways at different times: as active agents, pushing the Revolution forward; as docile, aloof witnesses far from the capital; and sometimes as hostile adversaries, openly engaging in counterrevolutionary acts. Indeed, historians have argued about the peasantry's role in the origins, course, and impact of the French Revolution for generations.[1] What is clear, however, is that the revolutionary decade was fraught with tension, negotiation, and compromise

---

[1] In the first instance, see Peter M. Jones, *The Peasantry in the French Revolution* (Cambridge: Cambridge University Press, 1988); Peter McPhee, *Living the French Revolution* (Basingstoke: Palgrave Macmillan, 2006).

in many arenas. Throughout the 1790s legislators in Paris worked to devise policies that tried to bridge the considerable hopes and expectations of 1789 with practical, and often harsh, realities. Indeed, the relationship between revolutionaries in the capital and the mass of country dwellers was sometimes one of dialectical confrontation with each side pushing the other toward more radical and egalitarian reforms. Whilst it is impossible to fully recapture *the* role the peasantry played in the French Revolution, it is without doubt that the people who inhabited villages and small market towns in the 1790s were forever changed by what occurred and that many of them helped to make the world around them anew.

Rural France in 1789

While there are no accurate census statistics for eighteenth-century France, demographic historians have estimated that approximately 28 million people lived there in the 1780s. The inhabitants were spread across the kingdom, with at least 22 million living in the countryside and the rest living in urban areas. The French use 2,000 people as the measure of the urban threshold; this meant that roughly 2 in 10 people lived in such a town or *bourg*. The rest inhabited the 38,000 rural communities or parishes with an average of 600 residents.[2] Larger villages and smaller towns were important centers for microregions, where weekly, monthly, or annual market-fairs brought together local people for collective rituals and exchange of commodities. The patchwork of these microregions also knitted together a vast ethnic and linguistic diversity where various groups were incorporated into France. While French was the official language of the Crown and Church, in reality only a minority of subjects used a language that Louis XVI would have understood. French was used by those involved in administration, commerce, or the professions, but by and large the majority of those living in the countryside spoke *patois*. This was a pejorative term deriving from *patte*, meaning an animal's paw. Local languages took the form of variants of French, *langue d'oïl*, in the northern half of the kingdom, and variations of Occitan, or *langue d'oc*, in the southern Midi. On top of these local dialects were non-French- and non-*patois*-speaking populations: Basque and Catalan along the Pyrenees, Flemish and German in the northeast and Celtic or

---

[2] All population figures from Jacques Dupâquier, *Histoire de la Population Française de 1789 à 1914*, 3 vols. (Paris: Presses universitaires de France, 1988), vol. III.

Breton in the northwest, with pockets of Italian in the southeast and on Corsica.

Alongside this linguistic diversity was great geographic and administrative variance. The fertile agricultural plains and gentle rolling hills of the northern Paris basin are punctuated by the vast mountain ranges of the Massif Central in the center, the Pyrenees in the southwest, and the Alps in the east. The country is traversed by four main rivers, the Loire, the Seine, the Rhine, and the Rhône, and has 2,900 km of coastline with major ports on both the Atlantic (Nantes, Bordeaux) and the Mediterranean (Marseilles). The eighteenth-century communication and road network was often slow and uncertain, but significant improvements to roads had been made after 1765, meaning that no city in France was more than ten days' travel from the capital. The development of navigable waterways, including manmade canals, connected communities and facilitated trade. On the eve of the Revolution, river and canal routes measured approximately 8,000 km, while roads (paved, gravel, or dirt) totaled around 27,000 km. France's total land mass of 550,000 km^2 was divided into fifty-eight provinces or *pays*. These were grouped into thirty-three *généralités* for administrative and fiscal purposes; they varied in size and autonomy, and the powers that the king's *intendants* could exercise in them differed considerably. Perhaps two-thirds of the kingdom had been reduced to the status of *pays d'élection*, where officials, answerable only to the Crown, gathered taxes on the king's behalf. The other third of the country, the *pays d'états*, consisted of several large provinces (Brittany, Languedoc, Burgundy) and a number of smaller entities, which had retained the right to consent to royal taxation through representative bodies known as Estates; they claimed a wider range of independence than the *pays d'élection*.

For much of its history and well into the nineteenth century, no western European civilization was more profoundly rural than that of France. This civilization was characterized by both regional diversity and various agricultural systems. A simple and widely observed contrast is between the large grain-growing, open field provinces of the north and the smaller polyculture system of the Mediterranean south. Yet these prototypes do not account for the many similarities. To be sure, most peasants practiced subsistence agriculture, meaning that the household tried to produce as much as possible for its needs. Three out of four people were peasants on the eve of the Revolution, but there were a number of internal ranks within this group. The majority of peasants, about 55 percent, were owners of small plots who had to supplement their income by renting, sharecropping, or wage labor.

Above this group were wealthy and independent landowners (*laboureurs* or *fermiers*), who were the most powerful peasants in their respective communities. At the bottom of the peasant hierarchy were the landless poor (*journaliers* or *travailleurs de terre*), who made up around 30 percent of the rural population; they were hired as day laborers or domestic servants and although humble, usually had a simple cottage with a kitchen garden. Beyond the village center, with its various houses and gardens, were the cultivated lands, subject to the twin constraints of heavy seigneurial dues and strong communal controls or collective rights. The best known of these were the right of common grazing of animals after the harvest on arable land (*vaine pâture*) and the vast tracks of communal land that were never cultivated. The rights of gleaning and grazing were precious to poorer members of rural society and were intensely contested during the Revolutionary decade. Nonetheless, the three elements of farming – gardens, cultivated land, and communal property – showed marked variations from region to region, as did the emphasis of crops grown. Cereals were central everywhere, but wheat was often mixed with rye, barley, millet, and oats; peas, beans, and corn were also cultivated either in fields or in gardens. In the Midi, fruit, olive, and nut trees were added along with vines. Indeed, the prevalence of viticulture and its importance to the entire economy should not be underestimated. However, while the agricultural sector was booming for most of the eighteenth century, there was a distinct decline in production from the 1770s, which led to rising prices for foodstuffs in the following decade. Hence, the years before the revolution were marked by inflation and sharp price fluctuations for grain, meat, and wine. A disastrous harvest in 1788 unleased a full-blown subsistence crisis.

What did foster unity were the formal structures of the Catholic Church and traditional forms of popular culture. The sacraments marked each phase of a person's life, and church festivals and the weekly ritual of mass were intrinsic to rural life where the vast majority of the population attended church regularly. Catholicism, the faith of 97 percent of the population, was strongest in the west and Brittany, the north and east, the southern Massif Central, the Pyrenees, and the Basque country, and less so in the center, the Paris Basin, and the southeast. Yet in all areas the parish church was the village's link with the outside world, with the priest relaying news and translating official documents into the local dialect. There existed, however, a widening gap between elite and official Church culture and the mass of the peasantry, who were often seen as ignorant and superstitious. Indeed, many priests saw it as their mission to wage an undying war against popular customs and beliefs. "Let us regard ourselves," a Breton priest wrote to a colleague in 1731, "as if we were in China or in Turkey, even though we are in the middle of Christianity, where one sees practically naught but pagans."[3] To be sure, beneath a veneer of external religious conformity lay a very hybridized belief system, which mixed animism, magic, and elements of Christian doctrine. An overt example of this was the universal tendency to believe that there was no such thing as simple misfortune; when things went wrong there was always a malevolent cause. Wicked spirits (working with or without the devil) or a wayward glance of a neighbor (the evil eye) were believed to have caused freak hailstones to destroy crops, animal diseases, or stillborn births. Above all, however, religious practice provided a framework through which rural households and by extension whole villages and parishes could affirm their collective identity. Nowhere was this on display more forcefully than on feast days celebrating religious patron saints or traditional points in the harvest cycle when dancing, singing, eating, and drinking mixed vernacular and religious practices. Depending on the region, the great period of Carnival could begin as early as Christmas and climax on Shrove Tuesday and Ash Wednesday. These celebrations which "turned the world upside down" were crucial to hierarchical society as all rules, inhibitions, restrictions, and regulations were temporarily suspended. Poverty, restraint, ranks, and privileges were momentarily replaced with egalitarianism, communal autonomy, and popular justice. Some of these temporary inversions and ideals became more permanent after 1789.

The importance of privileges, or special legal rights accorded to particular groups, sustained the culture of hierarchy and inequality so characteristic of the *ancien régime*. A Latin word, meaning private laws, privileges before 1789 referred to legal entitlements. In theory everyone had privileges, but in practice members of the first (clergy) and second (nobility) estates had the most lucrative privileges, which accorded them much social status and power. For those living in the countryside, the nobility's privileges and rights were manifested as seigneurial authority which impinged upon and permeated daily life. While the village chateaux with their coat of arms and weathervane symbolically conveyed seigneurial power, few lords resided there permanently by the late eighteenth century. Instead, seigneurial privilege was chiefly expressed through fiscal extraction and judicial repression. In theory the relationship between seigneurs and peasants was based on

---

[3] Quoted in Roger Chartier, *The Cultural Origins of the French Revolution* (Durham, NC: Duke University Press, 1991), 104.

reciprocity, with lords providing protection, security, and assistance in times of crisis in return for regular payments of dues in cash or kind. Many of these privileges were fiscally beneficial and reminded lord and peasant alike of the other's position. This hierarchy was reinforced by rights of symbolic deference, such as a noble's right to carry a sword in public or his front bench in the parish church. Harvest dues, however, were the most profitable for seigneurs and the most burdensome to peasants. Known as the *champart*, *censive*, or *tasque* depending on the region, these dues were a percentage of the cereal or vine harvest ranging from as little as 4 percent in Beauvaisis to a substantial 33 percent in the Limousin. In addition, lords also had other significant privileges or "rights" known as *banalités*. These were monopolies over the village bread oven, grape and olive presses, and grain mill as well as the right to charge a fee for property transfers and even marriages. The exclusive right to hunt, fish, and keep rabbits and pigeons along with the *corvée*, unpaid labor by the community on the lord's land, rounded out seigneurial privileges. Peasant income was also tapped by the Church in the form of the *tithe* and by the state through both direct and indirect taxation. The *taille*, along with the *capitation* and the *vingtième*, represented the main taxes on land, while the taxes on salt (*gabelle*), tobacco (*tabac*), and alcohol (*aides*) were the most hated and contested indirect levies.[4] In all, these three pillars of power and privilege – the nobility, the Church, and the state – extracted "surplus" from the peasantry. This ranged from as little as 14 percent of what a peasant household produced in Brittany to as much as 40 percent in the Massif Central.[5]

In January 1789, against a backdrop of political uncertainty, fiscal emergency and subsistence crisis, the monarchy called upon its subjects to draw up lists of grievances (*cahiers de doléances*) and appoint delegates to represent their communities at the upcoming Estates General. All male adult taxpayers aged over twenty-five years gathered in special meetings to discuss the most pressing issues facing their parishes. Although these documents must be approached with caution as they were often influenced by model *cahiers*

---

[4] The *taille* was a personal direct tax on land that was attached to nonnoble individuals, while the *capitation* and *vingtième* were universal direct taxes imposed on all royal subjects regardless of privilege status. See Michael Kwass, *Privilege and the Politics of Taxation in Eighteenth Century France* (Cambridge: Cambridge University Press, 2000); Gail Bossenga, *The Politics of Privilege: Old Regime and Revolution in Lille* (New York: Cambridge University Press, 1991).
[5] See Jones, *The Peasantry*, Chapter 2; Donald Sutherland, *The Chouans: The Social Origins of Popular Counter-Revolution in Upper Brittany, 1770–1796* (Oxford: Clarendon Press, 1982).

from larger cities and towns, and because they were most likely written by the more affluent members of the community (sometimes with pressure from a local seigneur or priest), they are still an invaluable resource for the historian as they contain the hopes, fears, and concerns of rural France. Asking people to reflect on the structures of power and privilege which dominated their lives was unprecedented, and the resulting 40,000 parish *cahiers* are an extraordinary documentation of mass politicization and social friction. John Markoff and Gilbert Shapiro have investigated a sample of 748 parish *cahiers*, and their findings provide a statistical analysis of the peasantry's grievances on the eve of the Revolution.[6] First and foremost, the most common complaint was the theme of surplus extraction from the state (in the form of taxation), from seigneurs (in the form of dues, produce, or labor), or from the Church (in the form of the *tithe* or the *dîme*). Indeed, the claims on peasant income make up almost one-half of all peasant grievances. However, peasants also made distinctions among their various burdens, with calls to reform the tax system, but to abolish most seigneurial rights. This discovery is significant as there were many contemporaries as well as modern-day historians who claimed that the peasantry lacked any revolutionary cognizance or intellectual capacity to grasp the different powers impinging upon them. The great *Encyclopédie* of Diderot and d'Alembert echoed these sentiments, when in reference to peasants, it commented that "many (educated) people see little difference between this class of men and the animals they use to farm."[7] Yet the peasantry's discernment between calls to reform some extractions and abolish others demonstrates that they had a quite sophisticated understanding of the hierarchies that encroached upon them. Even though there was intense anger over the distribution and weight of taxation, villagers agreed that they paid for valued services, while seigneurial dues were a burden that offered little in return. In general, there was a tone of optimism in the *cahiers*, with words like "patrie," "nation," and "citizen" signaling the hope for a regenerated kingdom and public realm. The demands made in these grievance lists presupposed the radical transformation of the social and political sphere which unfolded in 1789 and beyond.

---

[6] Gilbert Shapiro and John Markoff, *Revolutionary Demands: A Content Analysis of the Cahiers de Doléances of 1789* (Stanford: Stanford University Press, 1998).

[7] François Quesnay, "Fermiers," in *Encyclopédie ou Dictionnaire raisonné des sciences, des arts et des métiers*, vol. VI (Paris: Briasson, David l'aîné, Le Breton, Durand, 1756), 528–40.

Peasant Revolt

The eighteenth-century French countryside was the scene of much resistance and rebellion. Indeed, the number of revolts rose as the century progressed. Historians have calculated that in the years 1720–1788 there were no fewer than 4,400 "troubles" in the countryside, some three-quarters of them occurring after 1765. About 39 percent of all documented cases of rebellion were antifiscal in nature, followed by subsistence riots (18 percent), attacks on police, military, or judicial institutions (14 percent), and antiseigneurial uprisings (5 percent).[8] All of these rebellions represented opportunistic and defensive communal rejections of external threats. Many of them contained traditional forms of collective violence and a culture of retribution, that is, threatened or real physical damage to persons or property, carried out by a group of individuals whose efforts were coordinated, either by improvising on the spot, or through prior planning. These instances also contained a distinctly vindictive aspect which sought to humiliate and punish the abuse of power by authorities or social superiors. For example, in antifiscal uprisings, tax collectors would be ceremoniously stripped naked, hands bound, and marched through the town square, degraded, and dishonored as if they were common criminals. Bread rioters would seize stocks and sell them at a "just price" (*taxation populaire*) instead of the inflated and rapacious amounts charged in times of shortage. These acts tapped into a shared language of protest which everyone understood. However, all of this resistance and revolt, no matter how highly choreographed, took place within a system that people assumed would never end. The calling of the Estates General and the drawing up of the *cahiers* served as a massive *prise de conscience* as people began behaving and voicing attitudes that challenged the structures of their world in unprecedented and even unimaginable ways. To be sure, the substance of the grievances and the forms in which they were expressed echoed the past, but the idea which emerged in 1789 that the social system could be altered was revolutionary.

From December 1788 through to March 1790 an old-style subsistence crisis combined with a new-style political crisis to produce a series of rural insurrections which engulfed the kingdom. A pressing and immediate cause was the harsh winter of 1788–1789 when much of the country

---

[8] Guy Lemarchand, "Troubles populaires au XVIIIe siècle et conscience de classe. Une préface à la Révolution française," *Annales historique de la Révolution française* 279 (1990), 32–48; Jean Nicholas, *La Rébellion française: Mouvements populaires et conscience sociale 1661–1789* (Paris: Gallimard, 2008).

was snowbound and subject to exceptional frosts. Under an icy blanket, grain harvests perished, grape vines froze, and in the Midi chestnut and olive orchards were destroyed. Virtually every region of France was touched to some degree by insubordinate action or collective violence, but historians have identified eight main epicenters: Franche-Comté, Dauphiné, Provence, Hainaut and Cambrésis, Lower Normandy, Mâconnais, Alsace, and the southwest. Throughout the spring of 1789 many of these insurrections merged traditional subsistence revolts with newer antifeudal antagonisms. These actions only intensified when news of the events of 11–14 July in Paris reached the countryside. Beginning on 20 July, in six or seven flashpoints waves of fear, panic, and revolt took hold. Angry rumors, fearful speculations, and imagined sightings of "brigands" or agents of vengeful seigneurs sparked off the events of late July and early August which are known as "the Great Fear."[9] Peasants armed themselves with knives, scythes, pitchforks, and axes for defense against malfeasant outsiders and to secure scarce food supplies. They attacked grain convoys and raided monastic storehouses, but very quickly turned their attention to attacking seigneurial chateaux and defacing or destroying symbols of feudal power. These incursions comprised traditional forms of protest like seizing food and drink, but also contained new actions such as the ceremonious burning of manorial rolls or registers and publicly humiliating lords or their agents. Some rural communities believed that they were carrying out the king's will in refusing to pay feudal dues as they had written down these desires in their *cahiers*, while others claimed a new authorization for disobedience. In Montmartin, to the northeast of Paris, over 300 inhabitants broke into the chateau of Mme. the Marquise de Longaunay and stole the titles of rents and dues, while also demolishing her dovecotes. They left a receipt for the theft signed "The Nation."[10] Actions like these clearly indicate a rural awareness that the entire social system was crumbling. They also represent a new thinking about power. The privileges of the past were now openly confronted, and country dwellers implicitly claimed that any new social and political relationships would be negotiated.

---

[9] The classic account is Georges Lefebvre, *The Great Fear of 1789: Rural Panic in Revolutionary France* (New York: Vintage Books, 1973); see also Clay Ramsay, *The Ideology of the Great Fear: The Soissonnais in 1789* (Baltimore: The Johns Hopkins University Press, 1992).

[10] A. de Lestapis, "Sur la révolte agraire dans le Bocage normand," *Annales historiques de la Révolution française* 27:139 (1955), 161–72: 161–2.

The events of the summer of 1789 had significant and direct consequences in the National Assembly. Led by liberal nobles, the deputies passed a decree (4–11 August 1789) which essentially abolished the feudal regime as exclusive hunting rights, seigneurial courts, the tithe, tax exemptions, civil distinctions, venal offices, perpetual rights, and harvest dues were all eradicated. However, many of these reforms required further legislation before they could be put into effect because of the pervasive intertwining of property and power that characterized the *ancien régime*. Thus, when collectors of seigneurial dues and the tithe tried to extract these payments in the autumn of 1789 they were met with foot-dragging, quibbling, passive resistance, or outright revolt throughout the rest of 1789 and all of 1790 and 1791. While legislators tried to distinguish between "real rights" and "personal obligations" by adopting the law of 15–28 March 1790 and set the rates for buying out the former on 3–9 May 1790, the peasantry *en bloc* rejected the idea of indemnification of seigneurial dues. Indeed, there is very little evidence that redemption payments were ever made. In essence, the revolutionaries were attempting to destroy what they called "feudal government," which was based on the twin pillars of privately owned public power and hierarchical landholding. This radical, forward-looking transformation of all forms of tenure into independent, individual private property ordered the new nation and paved the way for a constitution based on citizenship and elective government.[11]

Yet peasant unrest did not abate in the years that followed, and during the spring and summer of 1792, insurrection spread across the countryside on a scale not seen since the summer of 1789. There were anxieties and tensions around food supplies and the escalation of the war with France's enemies, but these revolts signified an accumulation of impatience, irritation, and frustration with the direction of the Revolution thus far. For many, the hopes and desires of a complete and total abolition of the feudal regime had not been met. Violent outbursts culminated in the *guerre aux châteaux* in the Centre and Midi, where hundreds of seigneurial estates were ransacked by armed inhabitants. The crisis of the summer of 1792 served as a major turning point in the Revolution as it forced legislators to pass laws that satisfied the common people of France, both urban and rural. The law of

---

[11] See Rafe Blaufarb's Chapter 2 in this volume and Rafe Blaufarb, *The Great Demarcation: The French Revolution and the Invention of Modern Property* (New York: Oxford University Press, 2016). See also M. Fitzsimmons, *The Night the Old Regime Ended: August 4, 1789 and the French Revolution* (University Park: Pennsylvania State University Press, 2001).

25 August 1792 had major consequences for the seigneurial regime, proclaiming that all feudal dues were abolished without indemnity, except in cases where the *ci-devant* (former) seigneur could produce an original title. This law effectively ended antifeudal protests in the countryside as former lords rarely had possession of actual title deeds, either because they had been destroyed in 1789 or because they had never existed in the first place. A final law of 17 July 1793 abolished all feudal rights and dues, even if the former lord could produce a title, and also ordered all remaining titles to be ceremoniously burned in village squares. These open, public, and legally sanctioned acts were very important to many peasant communities because such actions had previously always been defined as *jacquerie* (peasant revolt).[12] Regardless of whether the titles were actually set alight, for four years the peasantry rose in waves of protest and insurrection which ultimately forced legislators in Paris to abolish once and for all the feudal regime. These actions should not be underestimated as it has been argued that without them, peasants in France would most likely have been responsible for feudal dues until at least the middle of the nineteenth century.

Taxes were at the heart of the French Revolution. In many ways the popular struggle against the tax system was similar to the battle against seigneurs as protests and insurrection combined to bring down one of the most hated aspects of the *ancien régime*. Which taxes were most problematic? Indirect taxes on consumer goods were the target of much popular fury because many people felt that the money went not to the state, but into the coffers of the corrupt tax farming institution which collected them, La Ferme Générale.

There were widespread tax revolts in the spring and summer of 1789, but the challenge for deputies in the National Assembly was to engineer a new system without losing revenue in the intervening time. This meant that the old taxes would remain in place for the rest of 1789 and all of 1790 until the new fiscal system could begin in 1791. This situation seriously tested the goodwill of the majority of ordinary people, who believed, or chose to believe, that the Revolution had brought an end to state taxation as parish *cahiers* had been filled with requests to lighten their tax burdens. Tax revolt, in the form of petition, riot, resistance, and noncompliance was far more prevalent in the French Revolution than many historians realize. Popular refusal to pay taxes was as important an aspect to bringing down the *ancien*

---

[12] Anatoli Ado, *Paysans en Révolution: Terre, pouvoir et jacquerie 1789–1794* (Paris: Société des Études Robespierristes, 1996).

régime as subsistence riots and attacks on seigneurial chateaux.¹³ These events, however, often go underresearched, perhaps because tax revolts do not fit within the classic interpretative frameworks of French Revolutionary historiography as they cannot solely be described as antifeudal, anticapitalist or antistate. Nevertheless, there were widespread tax revolts in the first few years of the Revolution that touched most parts of France; the challenge is to find some meaningful way to analyze and interpret them.

The salt tax (*gabelle*) and taxes on alcoholic beverages (*aides*) were the focus of most of the revolts from 1789–1791. There were widespread rebellions and attacks on customs barriers in cities and towns in the first months of the Revolution, including the destruction of forty out of fifty-four toll houses on the newly built customs wall ringing Paris from 11–14 July 1789. The National Assembly tried to reestablish collection of indirect taxes with the decree of 23–27 September 1789, but opposition to these extractions continued and intensified after the principle of equality of taxation without distinction was enshrined in October. Resistance to taxes on consumer goods continued and had serious implications for the nation's revenue. The General Tax Farm collected over 18.7 million *livres* in indirect taxes during the first third of 1790, but that figure dropped to 8.6 million for the final trimester of that year. The salt tax was the first to come under legislative attack when the National Assembly abolished the *gabelle* with the decree of 21–22 March 1790, along with taxes on leather, iron, oils, and soap. Once this detested levy had been rescinded, the focus of revolt moved to the equally reviled tax on alcoholic beverages. Disturbances were reported throughout the country, with inhabitants in Touraine and Berry ready "to exterminate" tax agents or anyone who supported the collection of the *aides*. What was different about the revolt against taxes on wine in the context of 1790–1791 was that people were beginning to employ the ideals of liberty and equality in their struggle against these extractions.¹⁴ Wine was one of the most heavily taxed commodities in the eighteenth century, its price effectively tripling when all of the levies were applied. For many people, these taxes were immoral because of their regressive nature as the poor were hit harder than the rich and as such did not belong in a nation inhabited by free and equal citizens. This determined resistance had a dramatic effect as the *aides* as well as the hated

---

[13] R. B. Rose, "Tax Revolt and Popular Organization in Picardy 1789–1791," *Past & Present* 43:1 (1969), 92–108.
[14] Noelle Plack, "Drinking and Rebelling: Wine, Taxes and Popular Agency in Revolutionary Paris, 1789–1791," *French Historical Studies* 39:3 (2016), 599–622.

municipal excise duties (*octrois*) were abolished on 17–19 February 1791. When these laws came into effect on 1 May 1791, there were prolonged and exuberant celebrations along the customs wall in Paris and across the country to commemorate the ending of taxes on wine, meat, and tobacco. For many ordinary people, making items of daily consumption affordable was a way of ensuring that the ideals of liberty and equality became tangible and real. Throughout most of the 1790s these products were sold without excises, until Napoleon brought back taxes on wine, tobacco, and salt in 1804.

Impact on Daily Life

What impact did these changes have on the daily lives of ordinary people? For some historians the revolutionary decade altered very little for the masses and was "a magnificent irrelevance" as their world remained one of unremitting poverty, uncertainly, violence, and despair. Others have claimed that the French Revolution was largely an urban affair and left a legacy of perhaps even greater misery for the poor.[15] However, these essentially pessimistic assessments seem out of step with the actual transformations that took place up and down the new nation. Indeed, no adult living through the 1790s was left with any doubt that they had witnessed something entirely unknown and that society was fundamentally transformed. One of the most profound changes was the shift from being a subject inhabiting a kingdom with privileges to a citizen living in a nation with rights. The concepts of citizenship and sovereignty became deeply ingrained and were vivified in a political culture in which elections, political societies and clubs, debates, and discourse played an important part in the lives of many. Central to this "apprenticeship in democracy" was the fact that public officials drew their legitimacy from the new act of voting rather than appointment and that these servants of the people were accountable to them rather than the monarch. Up to 6 million adult males were enfranchised by 1793 and participated in elections on an unprecedented scale. Turnout varied according to how important and relevant issues were to local concerns. It was consistently high in rural communities in the Revolution's early years, with participation rates at 50 percent for the Estates-General in 1789 and up to 75 percent for

---

[15] The phrase "a magnificent irrelevance" is from Richard Cobb, *Reactions to the French Revolution* (Oxford: Oxford University Press, 1972), 125; see also Donald Sutherland, *The French Revolution and Empire: The Quest for Civic Order* (Oxford: Wiley-Blackwell, 2003), 387.

the first municipal elections in 1790 in certain areas.¹⁶ Running parallel to the new responsibility of voting was the corresponding principle of equal rights. From now on all citizens, whatever their social background, were to be judged according to a single uniform law code, and administered, taxed, and regulated in the same way thanks to the August decrees of 1789 and the Declaration of the Rights of Man and Citizen. These transformations from a hierarchy of privileges and appointment to a body politic of equal citizens were at the heart of why the French Revolution is often seen as the birth of modern democracy.

The Revolutionary decade also fundamentally changed the administrative map of France. The eighty-three new departments (there are ninety-six today) were the cornerstone of a system based on rationality and efficiency rather than privilege and precedent. Even their names, drawn from local rivers, mountains, and topographical features, ensured national unity. Every department, district, canton, and commune had identical structures of power, responsibilities, and personnel. An improved national postal service ensured the reliable delivery of packets of revolutionary decrees and official announcements to even the most remote parts of the country. The new bureaucrats, some 6,000 by 1793, were accompanied by 1.2 million elected officials, including local councilors, justices of the peace, and officers in the National Guard. They not only ensured that everyone experienced the nation's laws in the same way, but also oversaw the implementation of a national system of decimal weights, measures, and currency. This rationalization of the complexities of the *ancien régime* system meant that producers and manufacturers could trade more efficiently and effectively. Commerce was bolstered further by the abolition of customs duties and lowering of transaction costs. All of these developments in the 1790s put the principles of free trade within a national market on solid foundations. With the impediments to commerce so bluntly criticized in the *cahiers* lifted, producers, manufacturers, and merchants could commit themselves to capitalist practices fostered by the Revolution. Even though external trade was seriously hindered by a decade of war and instability, internal demand had not collapsed as disastrously as might have been feared. The call for new consumer products reached the countryside. Cotton clothing, in addition to wool and linen, hats, shoes, and boots alongside watches, ribbons, glasses,

---

¹⁶ Malcolm Crook, *Elections in the French Revolution: An Apprenticeship in Democracy, 1789–1799* (New York: Cambridge University Press, 1996); Melvin Edelstein, *The French Revolution and the Birth of Electoral Democracy* (Farnham: Ashgate, 2014).

and glazed earthenware became sundry items in many peasant households. Even the range of foodstuffs consumed expanded, especially if we consider what constituted items of "necessity" in the General Maximum of 1793. A cornucopia of fresh and salted meats, oils, wines, brandies and beer, fish and anchovies, legumes, honey, almonds, figs, apricots, coffees, sugars, and tobaccos were all listed as essentials of daily consumption. The realm of popular tastes, expectations, and desires was transformed as the "consumer revolution" of the late eighteenth century slowly seeped into the countryside in the aftermath of 1789.[17]

The fact that the majority of country dwellers were better fed, clothed, and housed in the 1790s translated into longer life expectancies. Linked to numerous changes in agricultural and socioeconomic relations (discussed below), people were living longer. From the 1780s to the 1820s women's life expectancy increased from 28.1 to 39.3 years and that for men from 27.5 to 38.3 years. This was partly due to higher wages for agricultural workers – people's purchasing power increased by up to 20 percent from 1790 to 1810 – and to growth in food production. In addition, despite wartime losses, the entire population of France increased by 1.3 million over the revolutionary decade and by 2.5 million in 1789–1814. This was coupled, however, with an overall decline in birth rate, one of the clearest consequences of the Revolution for daily life. Nationally the decrease was from 38.8 live births per 1,000 in 1789 to 32.9 in 1804, with a reduction of 22.6 percent in female fecundity from 1789 to 1824. This may have been due to the collapse of clerical authority over birth control or increased awareness of the fertility cycle, abortion, or other methods of family limitation. This shift can also be understood as a reaction by rural people against one of the Revolution's greatest changes to family life: egalitarian inheritance. By abolishing the centuries-old practice of primogeniture and mandating equal inheritance between all children, regardless of sex, birth order, or legitimacy, legislators antagonized traditional agrarian and familial practices. Partible inheritance certainly challenged paternal authority, but it also threatened the entire agricultural system by subdividing peasant holdings to an untenable degree.

[17] See Daniel Roche, *A History of Everyday Things: The Birth of Consumption in France, 1600–1800* (Cambridge: Cambridge University Press, 2000); Cissie Fairchilds, "The Production and Marketing of Populuxe Goods in Eighteenth Century Paris," in John Brewer and Roy Porter, eds., *Consumption and the World of Goods* (London: Routledge, 1993), 228–48; Colin Jones and Rebecca Spang, "*Sans-culottes*, sans café, sans tabac: Shifting realms of necessity and luxury in eighteenth century France," in Maxine Berg and Helen Clifford, eds., *Consumers and Luxury: Consumer Culture in Europe, 1650–1850* (Manchester: Manchester University Press, 1999), 37–62.

Various tactics and strategies were developed to undermine the law in the interests of the long-term survival of the household. Younger siblings were forced to give land to older sons or sell at seriously undervalued rates, or junior offspring would receive their entitlements by installments without interest. However, these attempts were sometimes challenged in local courts as daughters and younger sons sought legislative and judicial protection to defend their new rights and protect their legacies. The impact of equal inheritance was tempered by the Civil Code of 1804, which permitted parents to dispose of a portion of their estates as they wished, usually favoring an elder son. Yet in Normandy, the Midi, and other customary law areas, the legal standing of women was improved by the new inheritance practices enshrined in the laws of 1791 and 1793–1794.[18]

In terms of religion, the Revolution played a key part in irrevocably moving faith from the public to the private sphere, and the Catholic Church lost much power, prestige, and authority during the 1790s and the Napoleonic Empire. Some 3,000 clerics died in violent circumstances, with at least 920 clergy publicly executed for counterrevolutionary activities. In addition, the Church's extensive property was seized and sold by the State, and it lost the lucrative right to collect the tithe, worth 130 million *livres*, in 1790. The Civil Constitution of the Clergy also restructured the Gallican Church to an unprecedented degree. Priests were elected by the laity and their salaries paid by the State; the internal boundaries where they were stationed were also rationalized and reorganized. The total number of bishoprics was reduced from 136 to 83, one for every new department. Several hundred parish churches, many in outlying hamlets, were closed in this restructuring. This caused significant anger and resentment in many rural communities as the physical environment of the church, with its yard and cemetery, was central not only to spiritual, but also to temporal life. Around 25 percent of all clergy, between 30,000 and 40,000, emigrated over the course of the revolution, leaving some regions almost entirely devoid of any religious official. Never again would there be as many clergy for parishioners; before 1789, there was one priest for every 480 people, but that number had fallen to one for every 750 people by 1850. The near-universal practice of churchgoing ended during the Revolution, especially for young men who had experienced life in the army away from the influence

---

[18] Suzanne Desan, *The Family on Trial in Revolutionary France* (Berkeley: University of California Press, 2004); Margaret Darrow, *Revolution in the House: Family, Class and Inheritance in Southern France, 1775–1825* (Princeton: Princeton University Press, 1989).

and authority of the Church. But the revolutionaries found it extremely difficult to replace the deeply engrained rituals of belief, practice, and structure that Catholicism offered.[19] Revolutionary political culture could never fill that gap for many, and the tensions between the two caused much of the violence in the countryside during the 1790s. In contrast, for France's Protestant and Jewish minorities, the Revolution brought legal emancipation, civil equality, and the freedom to worship.

One of the most significant and enduring social changes for the countryside was the abolition of feudalism and access to land. The ending of seigneurial dominance and the shift in the nobility's relationship to land represented a sea change in rural areas across France. A minority of peasants enlarged their land holdings either through the sale of *biens nationaux* or the acquisition of common land.[20] Although the results varied tremendously according to region, it is estimated that the peasantry added around 1.5 million hectares of land, or around 3 percent of the total surface area, to its ownership through the sale of Church and *émigré* land. According to the law of 10 June 1793, all of the members of a village community, regardless of age or sex, provided they were over twenty-one years of age, were allowed to equally share out their communal lands, if a majority voted for such an action. The results of this decree are difficult to quantify, but it seems that it was implemented with some success in the departments north of Paris, the northeast, and the Midi. Many of the new plots were planted in cereal crops to increase subsistence, or in the south with grape vines for sale in the expanding wine market.[21] As a result of these changes to land tenure, the ranks of the smallholding peasantry were bolstered; landownership reinforced citizenship. And it was these very landowners who benefited the most from the abolition of seigneurial dues as they no longer owed the lord a portion of their harvest. The rates of seigneurial extraction, as we have seen,

---

[19] Nigel Aston, *Religion and Revolution in France, 1780–1804* (Washington, DC: Catholic University of America Press, 2000); Timothy Tackett, *Religion, Revolution and Regional Culture in Eighteenth Century France: The Ecclesiastical Oath of 1791* (Princeton: Princeton University Press, 1986).

[20] See Bernard Bodinier and Éric Teyssier, *L'événement le plus important de la Révolution: La vente des biens nationaux en France et dans les territoires annexés, 1789–1867* (Paris: Société des Études Robespierristes, 2000); Nadine Vivier, *Propriété collective et identité communale: Les biens communaux en France, 1750–1914* (Paris: Publications de la Sorbonne, 1998).

[21] Noelle Plack, *Common Land, Wine and the French Revolution: Rural Society and Economy in Southern France, c. 1789–1820* (Farnham: Ashgate, 2009); Peter McPhee, *Revolution and the Environment in Southern France: Peasants, Lords, and Murder in Corbières, 1780–1830* (Oxford: Oxford University Press, 1999).

varied, but it was on average about one-quarter of all produce in many regions outside the west of France. These extra foodstuffs were consumed by a better-fed population. For tenants and sharecroppers, dominant in Brittany for example, the material benefits were more limited; perhaps this explains why it was in areas of the west that the counterrevolution took hold. Everyone, however, regardless of their status as proprietors, profited from the ending of seigneurial tolls, compulsory labor, hunting and fishing rights, and the lord's monopoly over bread ovens, mills, and olive and wine presses. Peasants across France also gained from the liquidation of seigneurial justice in which cases were tried by judges appointed and paid by the lord. The new civil justice system with its elected justices of the peace was fairer, quicker, and less expensive, and ensured equal treatment under the law.[22]

There were, of course, more profound, nontangible benefits from the abolition of feudalism. The innumerable affronts to human dignity embodied in the peasant–lord relationship were eliminated. Symbolic deference and "honorific rights" were abolished as the revolutionaries sought to destroy the nobility as an idea that resulted from "a long habit of respect and the spirit of chivalry." Former nobles certainly did maintain much social eminence into the nineteenth century, but it was henceforth based on economic, not legal, power and privilege. The transformation of the mental universe that the eradication of social deference caused should not be underestimated as it was a clear manifestation of the idea of equality. The psychological markers which gave meaning to people about who they were and what they might become had dramatically altered. The everyday labors of the majority in the countryside remained much the same in that they were manual, repetitive, and exhausting, but the extraordinary shifts in cultural and social behaviors lasted beyond the 1790s. While the Napoleonic Empire brought much war, hardship, and suffering, the fundamental changes wrought by the Revolution endured. Some of these changes were economic, for example more commercialized production in the cereal plains north of Paris and the wine-producing regions of the Midi, while others were broadly linked to the abolition of privilege and the call to participate in civic life. The idea of equality before the law, secularization, and sovereignty of the people became forever embedded in French life. These very real and powerful conceptual shifts were the most profound legacy of 1789.

---

[22] Anthony Crubaugh, *Balancing the Scales of Justice: Local Courts and Rural Society in Southern France, 1750–1800* (University Park: Pennsylvania State University Press, 2001).

4

The Revolution and the Atlantic: The Society of the Friends of the Blacks

ERICA JOHNSON EDWARDS

French involvement in the North Atlantic movement to end the slave trade and slavery predates the French Revolution by several decades. Anthony Benezet (1713–1784) was a Frenchmen, a Quaker, and a naturalized British subject living in the Pennsylvania colony who founded the African Free School[1] in Philadelphia in the summer of 1770 and became the first president of the Society for Relief of Free Negroes Unlawfully Held in Bondage in 1775. During his life, he influenced other American Quaker abolitionists, such as Benjamin Franklin and Benjamin Rush, as well as British abolitionists like Granville Sharp and Thomas Clarkson and the French philanthropists Jacques-Pierre Brissot de Warville and Abbé Henri Grégoire. (The French did not use the term *abolitionniste* during the French and Haitian Revolutions. The term did not emerge until the 1820s and 1830s. During the revolutions, the French used *philantrope* or *philanthrope* to identify those seeking the abolition of the slave trade and slavery, as well as equality for free people of color.[2]) Benezet earned the respect of those while he lived and inspired those who came after his death in 1784. He was born French, lived British, and died American, and his ideas made an undeniably significant impact on those opposed to the slave trade and slavery within the Atlantic World.[3]

Building upon the work of Benezet before him, Brissot (Figure 4.1) founded the Society of the Friends of the Blacks in Paris in early 1788. Although primarily operational in Paris, the society was very much an Atlantic organization. Since the 1970s, scholars have focused on this

---

[1] Nancy Slocum Hornick, "Anthony Benezet and the Africans' School: Toward a Theory of Full Equality," *The Pennsylvania Magazine of History and Biography* 99:4 (October 1975), 399–421; William C. Kashatus, III, "A Reappraisal of Anthony Benezet's Activities in Educational Reform, 1754–1784," *Quaker History* 78:1 (Spring 1989), 24–36.
[2] For visual representations of these trends from 1750 to 1850, see Google Ngram.
[3] Maurice Jackson, *Let This Voice Be Heard: Anthony Benezet, Father of Atlantic Abolitionism* (Philadelphia: University of Pennsylvania Press, 2010).

Figure 4.1 Jacques-Pierre Brissot. Getty Images.

philanthropic organization as the primary driver of France's first – and "failed" – abolitionist[4] movement. Through superficial examinations of the efforts of the Friends of the Blacks, scholars have categorized the French movement as based solely in the printed word and engagement through revolutionary assemblies. Taken in isolation from other Atlantic philanthropic activity, the movement appears diminutive, sporadic, and

---

[4] For the dominant interpretation of the French movement, see for example Ruth F. Necheles, *The Abbé Grégoire, 1787–1831: The Odyssey of an Egalitarian* (Westport, CN: Greenwood Publishing, 1971); Edward Derbyshire Seeber, *Anti-Slavery Opinion in France during the Second Half of the Eighteenth Century* (New York: B. Franklin, 1971); Daniel P. Resnick, "The Société des Amis des Noirs and the Abolition of Slavery," *French Historical Studies* 7:4 (Autumn 1972), 558–69; Ann Julia Cooper, *Slavery and the French Revolutionists (1788–1805)* (Lewiston: The Edwin Mellon Press, 1988); Lawrence C. Jennings, *French Anti-Slavery: The Movement for the Abolition of Slavery in France, 1802–1848* (New York: Cambridge University Press, 2002).

ineffectual. Yet, France granted rights to free people of color and abolished slavery – lasting from 1794 to 1802 – before England, the United States, and other countries deeply entangled in the Atlantic struggle over the status of peoples of African descent. Further, few studies include the revival of the organization as the Society of the Friends of the Blacks and the Colonies in 1797.[5] The French movement was not a failure; it was part of a longer process of abolition. Both iterations of the society sought to create an international coalition, making them much more Atlantic organizations than just French. While neither the first nor the second version of the society brought about a permanent end to slavery in the French Caribbean – something achieved only in 1848 – both advocated for peoples of African descent during the French Revolution, laying the groundwork for the later success of the nineteenth-century abolitionists.

Brissot's interest in slavery and the slave trade developed while he was in England. He found inspiration for the founding, the goals, and even the name of the Friends of the Blacks in encounters with the Religious Society of Friends, or Quakers. As early as 1761, Quakers began to exclude enslavers from membership, and Quakers in London put together a twenty-three-member antislavery committee in 1783. While writing on British political affairs for the *Courier de l'Europe*, he first traveled to London in 1779. While there and on subsequent trips, he made contacts. After leaving this position, Brissot and his wife returned to London in 1782. He intended to establish a philosophical club called the Lycée de Londres, but ultimately failed. However, he met several Quakers, including Robert Pigott, James Phillips, and Mary Capper, a friend of Brissot's wife. He also met William Murray, First Earl of Mansfield, the judge known for his 1772 decision in the *Somerset v. Stewart* case, which established that enslaved persons who were on English soil – outside of it, England's colonies – became free.[6] Upon his return to France in 1784, the authorities imprisoned Brissot in the Bastille for inflammatory pamphlets he had published. Lord Mansfield was among the many who petitioned for Brissot's release. He maintained correspondence with

---

[5] One exception is Marcel Dorigny and Bernard Gainot, *La Société des Amis des Noirs, 1788–1799: Contribution à l'histoire de l'abolition de l'esclavage* (Paris: Éditions UNESCO, 1998).

[6] For more on the Somerset case, see for example William M. Wiecekt, "Somerset: Lord Mansfield and the Legitimacy of Slavery in the Anglo-American World," *University of Chicago Law Review* 42:1 (1974), 86–146; James Oldham, "New Light on Mansfield and Slavery," *Journal of British Studies* 27:1 (1988); William R. Cotter, "The Somerset Case and the Abolition of Slavery in England," *History* 79 (1994), 31–56.

those he met in England as he founded the Gallo-American Society and the Friends of the Blacks.[7]

Gallo-American Origins

The Gallo-American Society was the precursor to the Friends of the Blacks. In January 1787, Brissot, Nicolas Bergasse, Étienne Clavière, and Michel-Guillaume-Saint-Jean de Crèvecœur founded the Gallo-American Society in hopes of strengthening commercial relations between France and the United States following the American Revolutionary Wars. The two countries had some tensions over the American failure to compensate French forces that fought on their side against England as well as the United States' overall debt. Clavière, a Swiss banker living in France, attempted to work on possible solutions to these issues with Thomas Jefferson, Minister to France from May 1785 to September 1789. Despite the economic strains on relations between France and the United States, the Gallo-American Society propagated a romanticized idea of the newly formed American republic. This idealized vision of the United States included the potential to end the slave trade and slavery before any European country.

For the first four months of 1787, the society met almost every week in the Chancellerie d'Orléans in the Palais Royal. Louis-Philippe-Joseph duc d'Orléans was Louis XVI's cousin.[8] It is likely the duke supported the Gallo-American Society even though he was not a member, since it met at his residence and because of his relationship with Brissot. Félicité Dupont, Brissot's wife, served as undergoverness for the duke's family, and he became the duke's secretary. Brissot also served as the Gallo-American Society's secretary, while other members rotated as moderators of its meetings. They discussed a variety of topics from trade, correspondence, and the Assembly of Notables to morality, philanthropy, and slavery. For example, to begin the second meeting, Brissot reported having corresponded with James

---

[7] For more on Brissot and Quakers, see Leonore Loft, "Quakers, Brissot and Eighteenth-Century Abolitionists," *The Journal of the Friends Historical Society* 55:8 (1989), 277–89; Marie-Jeanne Rossignol, "Jacques-Pierre Brissot and the Fate of Atlantic Antislavery during the Age of Revolutionary Wars," in Richard Bessel, Nicholas Guyatt, and Jane Rendall, eds., *War, Empire and Slavery, 1770–1830* (Basingstoke: Palgrave Macmillan, 2010), 139–52; Bryan Banks, "Real and Imaginary Friends in Revolutionary France: Quakers, Political Culture, and the Atlantic World," *Eighteenth-Century Studies* 50:4 (Summer 2017), 361–79.

[8] George Armstrong Kelly, "The Machine of the Duc D'Orléans and the New Politics," *The Journal of Modern History* 51:4 (December 1979), 667–784.

Phillips, a Quaker in London. Phillips expressed frustration about the society's focus on commercial relations between France and the United States without including England. Therefore, the members debated the appropriateness of the organization's name and its goals. They decided to expand the nature of the organization to have a more universal focus. They concluded with the society's prospectus. In it, the members opened with a reference to France's assistance in the American Revolutionary Wars, as well as the possibility of signing of a Franco-American commercial treaty, perhaps similar to the one signed by the English and French in 1786.

On 23 February, they drafted regulations for the society. They determined that France and the United States should each have twenty-four members, but they agreed the number of foreign members would be unlimited. They amended the fourteen original articles of the regulations in following meetings. For instance, on 28 February, they adopted an article regarding visits by corresponding members. During the meeting on 6 March, Brissot presented examples of letters he sent to Jefferson and Gilbert du Motier, marquis de Lafayette – neither of which joined – presenting the society's prospectus. The members decided they needed to translate the prospectus into English, especially since they intended to present it to the US Congress. They revealed that an Englishman, M. Meekle had attended the meetings and would provide the translation. The involvement of Meekle and the unlimited number of foreign members suggest the importance of the English in this organization supposed to connect France and the United States. This international element was also present with both iterations of the Friends of the Blacks.

The members of the Gallo-American Society were part of what Robert Darnton calls an "American colony" in Paris. Often meeting at the Palais Royal or the home of Guillaume Kornmann, the group formed around Jefferson. Darnton has written about what he termed the "Kornmann group." Many members of the Gallo-American Society participated in this group, including Bergasse, Brissot, and Clavière. They embraced mesmerism, a theory based on the ability to manipulate magnetic fluids within humans in order to alleviate ailments.[9] The leading members were Kornmann's friends, Lafayette and François-Jean de Beauvoir, marquis de

---

[9] For more on the Kornmann group, see Robert Darnton, "Trends in Radical Propaganda on the Eve of the French Revolution (1782–1788)" (Ph.D. dissertation, Oxford University, 1964), 1–55 and *Mesmerism and the End of the Enlightenment in France* (New York: Schocken Books, 1968).

Chastellux (veterans of France's expeditionary force during the American War of Independence), Marie-Jean-Antoine-Nicolas de Caritat, marquis de Condorcet and François Alexandre Frédéric, duc de la Rochefoucauld-Liancourt. Some of these Americanophiles met in the home of Elisabeth Françoise Sophie Lalive de Bellegrade, comtesse d'Houdetot, who regularly exchanged letters with Jefferson and Benjamin Franklin. Jefferson maintained correspondence with most of the American colony throughout the 1780s. The group also provided support for publications. For example, Lafayette helped Philip Mazzei, an Italian settler in North America and supporter of the American Revolution, publish his four-volume *Recherches historiques et politiques sur les États-Unis de l'Amérique septentrionale*. In addition, Chastellux wrote *Voyages de M. le Marquis de Chastellux dans l'Amérique septentrionale*, an account of his travels in North America. Apparently, Jefferson preferred these two accounts, because they were less romanticized than those of the Gallo-American Society.

Three of the founding members of the Gallo-American Society contributed to the organization's goals through publications that differed from those of Mazzei and Chastellux. Their works portrayed the United States in an overly positive light while challenging French ideas about slavery. Brissot wrote his *Examen critique des Voyages dans l'Amérique* in direct response to Chastellux's account, rebuking him for his views on slavery and claims of African racial inferiority. Crèvecœur based his 1787 edition of *Lettres d'un cultivateur américain* on the more than twenty years following the Seven Years' War that he spent farming in what became the United States and his time as French consul in New York from 1783 to 1785. He also approvingly cited Abbé Guillaume Thomas François Raynal's multivolume *Histoire des deux Indes*.[10] The new edition included a list of over 100 products from the United States he thought would interest French readers. Crèvecœur also countered French critics of slavery in the United States, detailing the harsh realities of enslavement in the French colonies. Further, he claimed the enlightened American republic was in the best position to abolish slavery. The third book written by founding members of the Gallo-American Society was Brissot and Clavière's coauthored *De la France et des États-Unis*. In preparation, Brissot had borrowed a copy of Jefferson's *Notes on Virginia*. As was customary at the time, Jefferson reviewed parts of the manuscript as

[10] For more on Crèvecœur and Raynal, see Christopher Iannini, "'The Itinerant Man': Crèvecoeur's Caribbean, Raynal's Revolution, and the Fate of Atlantic Cosmopolitanism," *The William and Mary Quarterly* 61:2 (2004), 201–34.

the American Minister to France. Similarly to the other two publications, the book emphasized the model the United States served for Europe, especially France, with respect to morality and politics. In this regard, they championed the American federal government and asserted a decline in slavery in the United States. In discussing economics, the authors proposed the United States remain agrarian, buying manufactured goods from France.

In the last meeting of the Gallo-American Society, on 3 April 1787, there was no indication in the minutes of the members' intention to dismantle the society. In fact, Brissot mentioned the organization's plan to meet in the winter in a letter he wrote in June 1787. On that day in April, Brissot announced the return of Crèvecœur to the United States and explained how Crèvecœur would distribute the prospectus and regulations there. He also indicated that one of the two important goals of the members was henceforth the abolition of slavery, looking to the Quakers as an example.[11] At the time, Bergasse,[12] Brissot, and Clavière were embroiled in significant controversies likely preventing them from meeting, because they found themselves facing legal battles or were driven into hiding. Brissot went to England briefly, just as Thomas Clarkson, Granville Sharp, James Phillips, and William Wilberforce were founding the London Committee for Effecting the Abolition of the Slave Trade. In his *Mémoires*, Brissot stated that he and Clavière had been made members. Upon his return to France, the Gallo-American Society did not meet again. Nonetheless, in its short existence, the organization had been an ambitious Atlantic organization, with a cosmopolitan membership and associations, focused on applying enlightened universal ideas to better life in

---

[11] For more on the Gallo-American Society, see J.-P. Brissot, *Mémoires et Documents relatifs aux XVIIIe and XIXe siècles*, ed. Claude Perroud (Paris: Librairie Alphonse Picard et Fils, 1912), 106–44; Eloise Ellery, "Brissot de Warville: A Study in the History of the French Revolution" (Ph.D. dissertation, Cornell University, 1915), 59–80; L. A. Vigneras, "La Société Gallo-Américaine de 1787," *Bulletin de l'Institut de Washington* no. 2 (December 1952), 59–84; Darnton, "Trends in Radical Propaganda," 131–70; Andrew Moore, "The American Farmer as French Diplomat: J. Hector St. John de Crèvecoeur in New York after 1783," *Journal of the Western Society for French History* 39 (2011), 133–43; Bette W. Oliver, *Jacques Pierre Brissot in America and France, 1788–1793* (Lanham, MD: Lexington Books, 2016), 10–12.

[12] In 1787 alone, Bergasse published at least nine documents related to what historians call the "Kornmann affair." He published half a dozen more in 1788 and 1789. For more on this, see Sarah Maza, *Private Lives and Public Affairs: The Causes Célèbres of Prerevolutionary France* (Berkeley: University of California Press, 1995), 295–311; Virginia Yvernault, "An Adulterous Woman in Public Opinion: The Kornmann Affair; Gender, Culture and Politics on the Eve of the French Revolution," *Dix-Huitième Siècle* no. 48 (2016), 481–97.

France, the United States, and England through commercial, moral, and political relationships.[13]

The Society of the Friends of the Blacks

The Friends of the Blacks followed the Gallo-American Society in February 1788. Brissot and Clavière joined ten other men in founding the Friends of the Blacks at No. 3 rue Française in Paris. Honoré-Gabriel Riqueti, comte de Mirabeau, another member and one of the main protagonists during the early French Revolution, published Brissot's speech from the first meeting in his journal, the *Analyse des papiers anglais*. Despite the society's interest in and connections with British and American abolitionists and organizations, the Friends of the Blacks remained centered in Paris without any chapters in other parts of France. One month after the founding, the *Journal de Paris* printed a lengthy editorial about the Friends of the Blacks explaining how the society sought to end the slave trade and slavery. Intriguingly, none of the founders had personally witnessed the slave trade or slavery or had had any encounters with peoples of African descent on either side of the Atlantic, and many members were connected to the slave trade or slavery themselves.

Soon after founding the Friends of the Blacks, Brissot traveled to the United States from June to December 1788 to investigate possible French immigration to North America, the United States' newly founded government, and the institution of slavery there. Some people in France were drawn to the availability of land and republican form of government in the United States, and members of the Friends of the Blacks hoped the young republic might be the first nation to end slavery. Before his departure, Brissot spoke about Benezet's work on the slave trade at a meeting of the Friends of the Blacks on 13 March. Clavière and two other bankers financed Brissot's trip, requiring him to report on the American debt and possible American lands to purchase and meet with American financiers. Even though not all subsidized his voyage, many members of the "American colony" in Paris were interested in his trip and findings. Brissot fulfilled his obligations to those who funded his trip by commenting on his encounters with merchants and giving advice to anyone from France hoping to immigrate to the United States. He encouraged them to learn English and relocate as families with

---

[13] For more on Anglo-French-American joint strategies, see J. R. Oldfield, *Transatlantic Abolitionism: An International History* (Cambridge: Cambridge University Press, 2013), 68–99.

some knowledge of farming. In regard to slavery, he noted his presence in August at a meeting of the Society for Promoting the Manumission of Slaves[14] in New York City, where he received honorary membership. Further, he wrote about abolitionists in Philadelphia, visiting Blacks in a prison, and meeting Black children in a school Benezet founded. He emphasized the role of the Frenchman in the American Quaker antislavery movement. Brissot later published his account of his time in the United States, including numerous letters between Clavière and him, as *Nouveau Voyage dans les États-Unis de l'Amérique Septentrionale*.[15]

Although the Friends of the Blacks started in 1788, the society did not formalize its regulations until 1789 after Brissot returned from the United States. Condorcet drafted the society's constitution. A sixteen-page preamble to the regulations detailed the motives for founding it, described the horrors of slavery, and made reference to the English and American Quakers and abolitionists. The rules were thorough, with eight chapters and sixty-seven articles. The third chapter discussed the society's general assembly that met each Tuesday. The members elected the three officers – a president, secretary, and treasurer – as outlined in Chapters 4–6. The president was salaried and could hire a clerk. Clavière was the first president, chosen unanimously by the founding members, and Brissot became the second president. According to Chapter 7, there was also a committee of twenty-one members, including the officers, each serving three-year terms. The committee prepared agendas for the meetings, notified members of the agenda before meetings, and translated documents.

Even though the second chapter of the regulations for the Friends of the Blacks established membership unrestricted by numbers and gender, the extant lists reveal some limitations. Foremost, the organization required considerable dues that prevented some from joining. Some sources suggest Abbé Henri Grégoire could not afford the dues, but the members chose to make him an honorary member. However, the dues did not deter everyone, as the society had well over 100 documented members. There was overlap in the memberships of the Gallo-American Society, the American colony in

---

[14] For more on Society for Promoting the Manumission of Slaves in New York City, see Paul J. Polgar, "'To Raise Them to an Equal Participation': Early National Abolitionism, Gradual Emancipation, and the Promise of African American Citizenship," *Journal of the Early Republic* 31:2 (Summer 2011), 229–58; Leslie M. Harris, *In the Shadow of Slavery: African Americans in New York City, 1626–1863* (Chicago: University of Chicago Press, 2004), 48–71.

[15] Olivier, *Brissot in America and France*, 15–48; Jackson, *Let This Voice Be Heard*, 174–6.

Paris, and the Friends of the Blacks. Crèvecœur was a corresponding member, since he was no longer in France. Kornmann, Lafayette, and Rochefoucauld joined the Friends of the Blacks. Jefferson did not join, but his secretary William Short did. Mazzei was a foreign member. Beyond these overlaps, there were other well-known French Revolutionaries who joined, such as Abbé Emmanuel Joseph Sieyès, Jérôme Pétion de Villeneuve, and Louis-Sébastien Mercier.[16] The Friends of the Blacks had five female members. The wives of Clavière, Lafayette, and Rochefoucauld were members; two other women joined without any apparent connection to a male member: Madame la Marquise de Baussans and Madame Poivre. Scholars have located only two membership lists, one from 1789 and the other from 1790, yet the society remained active until 1793, so it is likely more members joined. Further, Gary Kates has argued that the Friends of the Blacks merged with the Confederation of the Friends of the Truth by the summer of 1791.[17] Albert Soboul described the Confederation as "a mixture of revolutionary political club, the Masonic Lodge, and a literary salon."[18] The merger of the two organizations could account for confusion related to membership of certain people in the Friends of the Blacks, such as men of color and other French Revolutionary figures.

The activities of the Friends of the Blacks did not go unchallenged. In July 1788, Louis-Marthe, marquis de Gouy d'Arsy formed a group called the Colonial Committee to counter the efforts of the Friends of the Blacks. During the fall of 1788, the group met over twenty times with hopes for colonial representation in France as well as to defend slavery. The members decided to hire skilled writers to draft pamphlets on their behalf. Jacques-Vincent Delacroix authored *Vœu patriotique d'un Américain sur la prochaine assemblée des États-généraux* for the Colonial Committee. Gouy d'Arsy also tried to have Mirabeau write pamphlets for the group as well. While he considered it because he needed the money, he chose not to after a member suggested Mirabeau would need to purchase a plantation and enslave peoples of African descent. While Delacroix's pamphlet did not mention

---

[16] Mercier's membership is controversial. He was critical of the organization in his publications, but he did attend at least one meeting and was listed as a member. For more, see Laure Marcellesi, "Louis-Sébastien Mercier: Prophet, Abolitionist, Colonialist," *Studies in Eighteenth-Century Culture*, 40 (2011), 247–73.

[17] Claude Perroud, "La Société française des Amis des Noirs," *La Révolution française* 69 (1916), 122–47; Gary Kates, *The Cercle Social, the Girondins, and the French Revolution* (Princeton: Princeton University Press, 1985).

[18] *Dictionnaire historique de la Révolution française* (Paris: Presses universitaires de France, 1989), 196.

slavery, Pierre-Victor Malouet urged the Colonial Committee to publish one openly defending the institution. He believed it was necessary to put forth a rebuttal of Condorcet's *Réflexions sur l'esclavage des nègres* from August 1788. In it, Condorcet proposed gradual emancipation to take place over a seventy-year period, but the *Journal de Paris* portrayed it as much more radical. The group encouraged Malouet to wait with such a pamphlet until after the Estates General met. He ignored them and published *Mémoire sur l'esclavage des nègres*, which sparked a debate within the *Journal de Paris* in April 1789, the month before the convening of the Estates General.

The Friends of the Blacks and the Colonial Committee both lobbied across France for the inclusion of their ideas in the various *cahiers de doléances* to be presented at the Estates General. Around fifty of the surviving *cahiers* included the issue of slavery, proving the success of the Friends of the Blacks in influencing public opinion. For instance, the Third Estate in Versailles, Chateau-Thierry, Amiens, Mont-de-Marsan, Reims, Charolais, Thimerais, and Coutances all mentioned opposition to the slave trade and/or slavery. Further, the nobility in Mantes and Aval and the clergy in Mantes, Metz, and Saumur expressed similar sentiments in their *cahiers*. On the other hand, the Colonial Committee was less successful, as only about half as many *cahiers* supported their interests. Yet, the *cahiers* from the major port cities of Nantes, Bordeaux, Le Havre, La Rochelle, Saint-Malo, and Marseille remained deliberately silent on the issues of the slave trade and slavery.[19] Once the representatives met in May and reviewed the *cahiers*, the Friends of the Blacks and the Colonial Committee had to defend their positions in the press and the Estates General.

Mirabeau was an invaluable member of the Friends of the Blacks, as he provided a venue to publish their ideas and prepared for action in the National Assembly, which replaced the Estates General after June 1789. Under the absolute monarchy of Louis XVI, the press was heavily censored, so the Friends of the Blacks were initially unable to create their own journal. However, Mirabeau had begun to publish the *Analyse des papiers anglais* in November 1787. Mirabeau's paper was an ideal unofficial organ for the Friends of the Blacks. The society used it to educate the French public through translations of English works related to ending the slave trade and

---

[19] For more on the Friends of the Blacks, the Colonial Committee, and the *cahiers de doléances*, see Jeremy D. Popkin, "Saint-Domingue, Slavery, and the Origins of the French Revolution," in Thomas E. Kaiser and Dale K. Van Kley, eds., *From Deficit to Deluge: The Origins of the French Revolution* (Stanford: Stanford University Press, 2011), 223–36.

slavery, as well as reports on their meeting minutes, correspondence, and activities. Later, the organization also relied upon Condorcet's *Chronique de Paris* and Brissot's *Le patriote français*. In addition, Mirabeau emerged as a parliamentary spokesperson for the society during the debates over colonial representation in June and July of 1789. He argued that white deputies from Saint-Domingue could not represent the colony's population of African descent. In over 20 letters – nearly 200 pages – between August 1789 and March 1790, Mirabeau corresponded with the British abolitionist Thomas Clarkson, who was in Paris to assist the Friends of the Blacks. Clarkson fed Mirabeau facts about the slave trade, and the two men discussed the changing attitudes toward France's colonies in the National Assembly. Clarkson may have even helped Mirabeau draft a speech calling for the abolition of the slave trade.[20]

Some of the Friends of the Blacks believed colonization in Africa could bring about the end of the slave trade. They drafted plans for new colonies in Africa, similar to the British colony of Sierra Leone that had been established in 1787,[21] after ending the slave trade and introducing gradual emancipation. When speaking before the Jacobin Club in Paris, Mirabeau emphasized the ability of Africa's rich soil to produce numerous crops, including tobacco, rice, indigo, cotton, and sugar. He also explained how merchants could trade goods without the barbarity of trading enslaved peoples. François Xavier Lanthenas published a pamphlet in 1790 echoing Mirabeau's claims about the soil, calling out Saint-Louis slave trader Dominique Lamiral for claiming the opposite as a justification for the slave trade. Lanthenas suggested establishing free colonies where African peoples could have rights and economic prosperity. He even went as far as to state that Africans were morally equal to whites, rejecting a racial hierarchy of peoples.[22] In his account of his

---

[20] For more on Mirabeau and the Friends of the Blacks, see Françoise Thésée, "Autour de Société des Amis des Noirs: Clarkson, Mirabeau et l'abolition de la traite (août 1789–mars 1790)," *Présence africaine* no. 125 (1983), 3–82; Marcel Dorigny, "Mirabeau and the Société des Amis des Noirs: Which Way to Abolish Slavery," in Marcel Dorigny, ed., *The Abolitions of Slavery: From L. F. Sonthonax to Victor Schoelcher, 1793, 1794, 1848* (Paris: UNESCO, 2003), 121–32; Popkin, "Saint-Domingue, Slavery, and the Origins of the French Revolution," 238–47.

[21] M. B. Abasiattai, "The Search for Independence: New World Blacks in Sierra Leone and Liberia, 1787–1847," *Journal of Black Studies* 23:1 (1992), 107–16 and Stephen J. Braidwood, *Black Poor and White Philanthropists: London's Blacks and the Foundation of the Sierra Leone Settlement, 1786–1791* (Liverpool: Liverpool University Press, 1994).

[22] For more on these African colonization projects, see Marcel Dorigny, "La Société des Amis des Noirs et les projets de colonisation en Afrique," *Annales historiques de la révolution française*, nos. 293–4 (1993), 421–9.

travels in the United States, Brissot suggested "retransportation" of those enslaved in the United States to Africa after freeing them. He believed enslavement had rendered Africans unequal to whites, but education could elevate them to equality. If education was not an option, Brissot claimed relocating them to Africa was an alternative solution.[23] The Friends of the Blacks wanted to end the slave trade and eventually slavery, but not all members saw Africans as equal to whites, and most could only envision Africans as laborers in European colonies.

Like Condorcet, other members of the Friends of the Blacks also advocated for gradual emancipation. Even before the founding of the society, Lafayette experimented with gradual emancipation in French Guiana in 1785. He purchased a plantation called "La Belle Gabrielle" and around seventy enslaved people, forbidding their resale. Under the management of Henri de Richeprey, the enslaved worked on the plantation growing cloves and cinnamon for a wage and received religious instruction and an education. Lafayette proudly wrote to his American friend George Washington about his experiment. Around the same time, Charles-Eugène-Gabriel, maréchal de Castries, the Minister of the Marine, sent orders to emancipate all the monarchy's enslaved people to the commissioner in French Guiana, Daniel Lescallier, another future member of the Friends of the Blacks. While Lescallier did not carry out de Castries' instructions, Lafayette manumitted his enslaved people in 1789. As he became more involved in revolutionary activities in France, Adrienne de Noailles, marquise de Lafayette, his wife and a member of the Friends of the Blacks, began to administer the plantation, corresponding with the manager. Leaders of the French revolutionary government seized Lafayette's property, including the plantation, after he fled France in August 1792, and the colonial administrators resold the enslaved from the plantation.[24] Although Lafayette's efforts in Guiana did not inspire France to end slavery in its empire, it demonstrates the variety of efforts of the Friends of the Blacks beyond the press and parliament.

Early in the French Revolution, the focus of questions related to peoples of African descent shifted from the slave trade to the status of free people of

---

[23] Rossignol, "Brissot and the Fate of Atlantic Antislavery," 148–9.
[24] For more on French Guiana, see Daniel Lescallier, *Notions sur la culture des terres basses dans la Guiane et sur la cessation de l'esclavage dans ces contrées* (Paris: F. Buisson, 1798); Laurent Dubois, *A Colony of Citizens: Revolution and Slave Emancipation in the French Caribbean* (Chapel Hill: University of North Carolina Press Books, 2004), 324–5; Malick Ghachem, *The Old Regime and the Haitian Revolution* (Cambridge: Cambridge University Press, 2012), 229–30.

color. In mid-1789, there were wealthy freed colored men, such as Vincent Ogé and Julien Raimond, lobbying for their rights in Paris.[25] These men shopped around their ideas about their rights within Paris's revolutionary climate. Near Angoulême, Raimond notarized a claim that he officially represented free people of color in Saint-Domingue. In response, *maréchal de camp* Louis Charles de Rohan-Chabot, comte Jarnac volunteered to bring the case of free people of color before the Estates General and legally secure the rights of mixed-blood people who could prove legitimacy for two generations. According to Gabriel Debien, Jarnac was disliked by much of the nobility because of his ego. He desired to "play the liberal" in the lead up to the Estates General, and he had investments in Saint-Domingue. However, Jarnac was not successful in advocating for men of color.[26] In addition, Raimond and Ogé presented before the Correspondent Society for the French colonists, or the Club Massiac, the principal opponents of the Friends of the Blacks. Primarily an alliance between colonial planters and merchants in France, the Club Massiac worked to maintain the slave trade, slavery, and the racial hierarchies that guaranteed their continuity in the French Atlantic. It had chapters in Bayonne, Dunkerque, Lorient, Rouen, Bordeaux, La Rochelle, and Nantes.[27] On 26 August, the same day the National Assembly passed the Declaration of Rights of Man and Citizen, Raimond appeared before the Club Massiac. He hoped the members would receive him as a fellow planter with an interest in protecting slavery. On 7 September, the Club Massiac received Ogé, who sought membership in the organization and to present them with a plan he had crafted. He explained his desire to preserve his property as much as they did, and he warned of a

---

[25] For more on Ogé and Raimond, see John D. Garrigus, "Opportunist or Patriot? Julien Raimond (1744–1801) and the Haitian Revolution," *Slavery and Abolition* 28:1 (April 2007), 1–21 and "Vincent Ogé Jeune (1757–91): Social Class and Free Colored Mobilization on the Eve of the Haitian Revolution," *The Americas* 68:1 (July 2011), 33–62. See also Chapter 24 by Bernard Gainot and Chapter 23 by John Garrigus in this volume.

[26] For more on Raimond's relationship with the comte Jarnac, see John D. Garrigus, *Before Haiti: Race and Citizenship in French Saint-Domingue* (New York: Palgrave Macmillan, 2006), 236, 356 n. 18; Gabriel Debien, "Gens de couleur libre et colons de Saint-Domingue devant la Constituante (1789–mars 1790)," *Revue d'histoire de l'Amérique française* 4: 2 (1950), 224.

[27] For more on the Club Massiac, see Lucien Leclerc, "La politique et l'influence du club de l'hôtel Massiac," *Annales historiques de la Révolution française* 14 (1937), 342–63; Gabriel Debien, *Les Colons de Saint-Domingue et la Révolution: Essai sur le club Massiac (août 1789–août 1792)* (Paris: A. Colin, 1953); Déborah Liébart, "Un groupe de pression contre-révolutionnaire: Le club Massiac sous la constituante," *Révolution française* no. 354 (October–December 2008), 29–50.

coming slave revolt. The Club Massiac did not extend membership to either man, so they sought support elsewhere.

Although the Club Massiac dismissed Ogé and Raimond's proposals, a Parisian barrister and secretary for the Commune of Paris, Étienne Louis Hector de Joly, was more receptive. Just days after appearing before the Club Massiac, Raimond met with de Joly, who had already begun to gather free men of color to draft a *cahier de doléances* to submit to the National Assembly. Ogé joined them after his visit to the Club Massiac. The group continued to increase in numbers, with nearly eighty members in November 1789, and they came to call themselves the American Colonists. The members chose de Joly, Raimond, and Ogé as their deputies to the National Assembly. There were tensions among the members over the status of free Blacks and people of mixed ancestry. Nonetheless, they released their petition in late September. The articles explained the division of colonial populations into free and enslaved, arguing that men of mixed ancestry specifically deserved equal rights to free whites. They claimed the Declaration of Rights of Man and Citizen made men of color aware of the existing inequalities, implying that the National Assembly, which authored the document, was responsible for bringing it to their attention and rectifying the situation. Therefore, they demanded the National Assembly make a declaration to that end, and insisted on the election and admittance of deputies of color in local assemblies in the colonies and the National Assembly. When appearing before the National Assembly's Credentials Committee, Raimond met Abbé Grégoire. Although the committee accepted the free colored representatives, Grégoire was unable to present its report to the National Assembly, of which he was a member, over continuous shouting. Nevertheless, the men of color inspired Grégoire to take an interest in colonial affairs and join the Friends of the Blacks in December 1789.

Although it is not known whether de Joly was a member of the Friends of the Blacks,[28] he and the American Colonists actively associated with and influenced the society. In October, Lafayette invited members of the American Colonists to dine in his home, when he was hosting Clarkson. Finally, on 24 November, the Friends of the Blacks received Raimond and

---

[28] De Joly was not listed in either available membership roster. For discussions of his memoires and involvement with the Friends of the Blacks, see Jacques Godechot, "Mémoires de Etienne-Louis-Hector Dejoly," *Annales historiques de la Révolution française* no. 104 (October–December 1946), 289–382; Gabriel Debien, "Gens de couleur libres et colons de Saint-Domingue devant la Constituante (1789–mars 1790)," *Revue d'histoire de l'Amérique française* 4:2 (1950), 211–32.

Ogé. With Clarkson present, the members voted in the meeting to support the American Colonists, and the Friends of the Blacks soon shifted their efforts from ending the slave trade to securing rights for free men of color. In February 1790, de Joly presented a group of twenty to thirty men of color to the Commune of Paris,[29] hoping its representatives in the National Assembly would advocate for the rights of free people of color. Brissot, member of the Commune's constitutional committee, also addressed its General Assembly. He spoke about the need to abolish the slave trade and accused the white planters of working against the men of color. Members of the Club Massiac were also present and denied Brissot's claims. Further, they cautioned the Commune on attempting to influence the colonial regime across the Atlantic Ocean. In the end, the Commune rejected de Joly and Brissot's requests, a victory for the Club Massiac.[30] However, neither side gave up, taking the issue to the National Assembly.

In early March 1790, the National Assembly created a twelve-member Committee on the Colonies to handle the questions of colonial representation and voting rights. Although they pushed for its formation, no members of the Friends of the Blacks were on the Committee. However, they hoped the Committee would decide in favor of the free people of color. The Committee split its interests between French commerce and colonial agriculture. Six of the Committee members owned property in the colonies, and two were lawyers in French cities with chapters of the Club Massiac. Antoine Pierre Joseph Barnave, one of the leading orators during the early stages of the Revolution, served as the Committee's secretary. Raimond and de Joly both spoke to Barnave and the Committee, suggesting specific wording to guarantee the inclusion of men of color. On 28 March, the Committee issued voting instructions for the colonies, but it remained vague about voting rights for men of color. When the instructions came before the National Assembly for discussion, Grégoire requested clarification in regard to men of color, but the colonial deputies pushed for the discussion to close. While the committee members likely expected the colonial assemblies to admit men of color, white colonists interpreted the instructions to exclude them.[31] After the Committee issued its instructions, the de Joly group dissolved.

---

[29] For more on the importance of Paris's municipal government, see Kates, *The Cercle Social*, 15–37.
[30] For more on de Joly, see J. Godechot, "Dejoly et les Gens de Couleur Libres," *Annales historiques de la Révolution française* 23:121 (1951), 48–61.
[31] Valerie Quinney, "Decisions on Slavery, the Slave-Trade and Civil Rights for Negroes in the Early French Revolution," *The Journal of Negro History* 55:2 (April 1970), 117–30

In the midst of the debates in pamphlets, newspapers, and assemblies in Paris, Ogé had decided to return to Saint-Domingue, but he was unable to do so until the middle of October 1790. While he was in France, free men of color had already begun to protest the injustices they faced in the colony, especially being denied the right to vote. Ogé had sent numerous letters to Saint-Domingue after the Committee on the Colonies issued its instructions. He had to travel from Paris to London to Charleston and finally to Le Cap to get home. When in London, he briefly met with Clarkson, who gave him some money. Once he was back in the colony, Ogé met with Jean-Baptiste Chavanne at the home of Charles Guillaume Castaing, both free men of color. They then went to Chavanne's plantation in Grande-Rivière, where other men of color joined them. They wrote to the colonial governor and provincial assembly on 21 and 28 October. In response to what the white officials perceived as an aggressive tone, troops went to Grande-Rivière to confront Ogé, Chavanne, and approximately 300 other men of color. After a brief armed conflict, the troops retreated, and the men of color fled to the mountains separating the French and Spanish halves of the island. When they attempted to seek refuge in Santo Domingo, the Spanish authorities extradited the colored men, who faced interrogations, execution, and corpse mutilation.

News of Ogé's death had a strong impact on the fight over rights for men of color in France. The Friends of the Blacks allied with the Confederation of the Friends of the Truth in continuing to advocate for men of color. Brissot and Condorcet were members of both organizations, and Clavière and Raimond wrote for the Confederation's press, the Cercle Social. The Friends of the Blacks took their campaign for free men of color to Jacobin Clubs across France. Raimond joined a Jacobin Club, and he denounced Ogé's tactics, insisting men of color needed to work with the legislature to secure their rights. Clavière wrote a pamphlet addressed to the National Assembly that the society disseminated to municipal governments throughout the country. Mirabeau had died in April, so Grégoire spoke on behalf of the cause when it came before the National Assembly in May 1791. This time, the National Assembly issued a law explicitly granting rights to free people of color who owned property and whose parents had been born free. Violence broke out in Saint-Domingue between whites and free coloreds in the following months. In August, the enslaved in the north revolted. By

and "The Problem of Civil Rights for Free Men of Color in the Early French Revolution," *French Historical Studies* 7:4 (Autumn 1972), 544–57.

September, the National Assembly repealed the May decree and sent civil commissioners to restore order in Saint-Domingue.

The Legislative Assembly replaced the National Assembly under France's new constitution, and newly elected legislator Brissot assumed the parliamentary fight for the rights of free people of color. He sought to portray people of color as the best defense against the rebelling enslaved population in Saint-Domingue. Around this time, Felicité Léger Sonthonax joined the Jacobin Club of which Brissot and his supporters were members. Although he did not join the Friends of the Blacks, Sonthonax shared Brissot's antislavery opinions and was politically active in the same circles.[32] On 4 April 1792, the Legislative Assembly voted to extend rights to all free men of color. In June, the Assembly sent new civil commissioners to deliver the law and continue to try to quell the slave uprising. Sonthonax and Étienne Polverel, another Brissotin, were selected as two of the civil commissioners. Soon after their arrival, the second civil commission dissolved the all-white Colonial Assembly and replaced it with a racially integrated Intermediary Commission. In December 1792, Sonthonax wrote to Brissot, and Raimond wrote to Sonthonax. By the summer of the next year, the civil commissioners' advocacy for free men of color shifted to abolishing slavery. Sonthonax and Polverel declared general emancipation in Saint-Domingue's three provinces in August, September, and October of 1793.[33]

After Sonthonax and Polverel declared general emancipation, peoples of all colors in Saint-Domingue voted for deputies to deliver the decrees to France. They selected two blacks, Jean-Baptiste Mars Belley and Joseph Georges Boisson, two men of color, Jean Baptiste Mills and Réchin, and two whites, Louis Pierre Dufay and Pierre Nicolas Garnot. Three of the deputies, Dufay, Mills, and Belley, arrived in Paris in January 1794, only to encounter adversity before getting the opportunity to appear before the National Convention, which had replaced the Legislative Assembly in September 1792. An opposing faction in the Convention led by Pierre François Page and Augustin-Jean Brulley, previously elected Saint-Dominguan deputies, attempted to prevent them from presenting on behalf of emancipation. Days after arriving in France, police officers acting on the authority of the Committee of General Security arrested and interrogated the

---

[32] For more on the connections between Sonthonax and Brissot, see Marcel Dorigny, "Sonthonax et Brissot. Le cheminement d'une filiation politique assumée," *Revue française d'histoire d'outre-mer* 84:316 (1997), 29–40.

[33] See also Bernard Gainot's Chapter 24 in this volume.

three deputies. From prison, the deputies wrote to the Convention, and the Committee of Public Safety intervened to have them released. Maximilien Robespierre, a member of the Friends of the Blacks, was also a member of the Committee of Public Safety at the time. When the tricolored deputation was able to present itself to the Convention in February 1794, their appearance started a debate on emancipation. Dufay made a lengthy speech explaining how he had seen racial differences disappear in revolutionary Saint-Domingue. In the end, the Convention decreed abolition in all of France's colonies. However, the tribulations endured by the deputies were evidence of the continued need for philanthropists to take actions to safeguard the tenuous abolition of slavery achieved in the French Atlantic.

In France, the Friends of the Blacks came to an end with a shift in the revolutionary government. In 1793, the main opposition to the Brissotins, the Montagnards, arrested Clavière, Raimond, and Brissot. Robespierre led the offensive against Brissot and other Girondins. He accused Brissot of being a paid spy for the English and an enemy of the revolution. While they were jailed, Grégoire managed to get subsidies for slave traders abolished before the Convention suppressed all societies. Without a stronghold in the Convention or the Friends of the Blacks to advocate for them, Brissot was executed by guillotine on 31 October, and Clavière committed suicide in December. They likely heard about the emancipation decrees from Saint-Domingue from their prison cells. In June 1794, the Convention, under the influence of Page and Brulley, recalled Sonthonax and Polverel to answer for their actions in Saint-Domingue. Polverel died in France in 1795 prior to exoneration of the charges against them.[34] Raimond was released in late 1794, but he was not exonerated until the next year. With Brissot, Clavière, and Polverel dead, Raimond and Sonthonax would carry on their campaigns in the second half of the 1790s.

In accordance with the Constitution of 1795, Saint-Dominguans elected deputies to the Legislative Corps in 1796. Owing to the British occupation of parts of the colony since 1793 (as well as of Martinique and Guadeloupe), the deputies would represent only select geographic regions. To participate in the elections, the Constitution of 1795 required voters to pay a poll tax, preventing most of the formerly enslaved from participation. Despite these

---

[34] A member of the Cercle Social and a deputy to the Convention, Jean-Philippe Garran de Coulon wrote a nine-volume report on the case against Sonthonax and Polverel. See *Débats entre les accusateurs et les accusés, dans l'affaire des colonies*, 9 vols. (Paris: Imprimerie Nationale, 1795).

limitations, eligible Saint-Dominguans elected the whites Sonthonax, Étienne Laveaux, and Martin-Noël Brothier and the men of color Louis-François Boisrond, Pierre Thomany, and Jean-François Pétiniaud. In the spring of 1797, the colonial citizenry elected additional deputies for the Legislative Corps, according to the law of 15 February 1797, which increased Saint-Domingue's representation to thirteen deputies. To supplement the deputies elected in 1796, electors chose as their representatives the whites Claude Pierre Joseph Leborgne de Boigne and Guillaume-Henri Vergniaud; the blacks Étienne Victor Mentor, Jean Louis Annecy, and Pierre Antoine; and the men of color Jacques Tonnelier and Antoine Chanlatte.

After the newly elected representatives arrived in Paris in the fall of 1797, they met opposition directed at the entire deputation. The Constitution of 1795 integrated the colonies into the nation, making them equally subject to French laws and the Constitution. However, the Clichyens, a group of moderate republicans and constitutional royalists, which had become the majority in the parliament, opposed the colonial policies of 1795, attracting proslavery Saint-Dominguan émigrés.[35] In the spring of 1797, a five-person commission, with two confirmed Clichyens, investigated the validity of the Saint-Dominguan elections of 1796, and ultimately recommended nullifying the results. They deemed the elections unconstitutional, and they did not regard the formerly enslaved as citizens equal to white Europeans. They grossly exaggerated the illiteracy rates of the Saint-Dominguan population, assuming that the formerly enslaved, people of color, and even white creoles could not read, and, therefore, could not participate in electoral politics. The commission also emphasized the inability of citizens from the west and south to participate in the elections, because of the British occupation. A law in March 1797 officially nullified the elections of 1796. However, French domestic politics resurrected the chances of Saint-Dominguans to be represented in the French legislature. By purging many Clichyens from the Legislative Corps in Paris, the 18 Fructidor Coup shaped politics in a way that favored Saint-Domingue's elections. Seeing this opposition, the Saint-Dominguan representatives elected in 1796 petitioned the Legislative Corps to reinvestigate the previously nullified elections. A new commission formed and determined that the nullification of the elections of 1796 had been unconstitutional and part of a conspiracy to push France and its colonies apart. Therefore, the

---

[35] Bernard Gainot, "The Constitutionalization of General Freedom under the Directory," in Marcel Dorigny, ed., *The Abolitions of Slavery: From L. F. Sonthonax to Victor Schoelcher, 1793, 1794, 1848* (Paris: UNESCO, 2003), 180–96.

commission recommended that the legislature deem the elections valid and admit the multiracial colonial deputation.[36] The Legislative Corps finally adopted the recommendation of the commission on 16 June 1798.

The Society of the Friends of the Blacks and Colonies

During the months between the initial investigation of the elections and the final decision of the Legislative Corps, Saint-Domingue's delegation engaged in Atlantic politics through the Society of the Friends of the Blacks and the Colonies, a revised form of the Friends of the Blacks from 1788. The society had four goals: abolish slavery; enlighten the colonists; advance agriculture, industry, and commerce in the colonies; and establish new colonies. Whereas members of the first Friends of the Blacks saw colonization as a way to end the slave trade, members of the Friends of the Blacks and Colonies believed new colonies would be a way to compete with the English, who were also launching new colonization efforts. The society frequently published their ideas in the *Décade philosophique*, coedited by Jean-Baptiste Say, an economist and member of the society. The organization was vigorous in its short existence, meeting every two weeks for almost two years, with members of all colors taking part in the organization, discussions, and actions of the institution.[37]

Although the renewed organization incorporated eleven of the members from the earlier Friends of the Blacks, the Friends of the Blacks and the Colonies included white, Black, and mixed-race members, as well as representatives from Saint-Domingue, Guadeloupe, Martinique, Cayenne, England, Italy, and the Dutch Batavian Republic. Other affiliates ranged from former French Minister of War Joseph Servan de Gerbey, English poetess Helen Maria Williams, and French economist Jean-Baptiste Say to the Guadeloupean notary Louis Elias Dupuch, the colored planter Louis-François Boisrond from Saint-Domingue, and the formerly enslaved Jean Louis Annecy. Dufay, Belley, and Boisson, members of the first deputation sent to France by the second civil commission, also participated in the society. The second society had a president, a treasurer, two secretaries,

---

[36] Auguste Kuscinski, *Les députés au corps législative, conseil des cinq-cents, conseil des anciens, de l'an IV à l'an VII* (Paris: Société de l'histoire de la révolution française, 1905), 178–9.

[37] For more on the Society of the Friends of the Blacks and the Colonies, see Alyssa Goldstein Sepinwall, *The Abbé Grégoire and the French Revolution: The Making of Modern Universalism* (Berkeley: University of California Press, 2005), 149–55.

and an archivist chosen by a majority of the members. Membership was open to both sexes, and the dues were much lower than for the first organization. The only limit on membership was the exclusion of anyone directly or indirectly involved in the slave trade.

Saint-Dominguans were not the majority in the Friends of the Blacks and Colonies, but they were a constant, spirited, and vital presence in the organization. Five of the Saint-Dominguan deputies attended the first meeting of the society on 30 November 1797. Accompanied by Thomany, Tonnelier, Leborgne, and Petiniaud, Laveaux encouraged all the deputies to join the society. In January 1798, Saint-Dominguan representation increased with the attendance of Boisrond, Mentor, Annecy, Pierre Antoine, Boisson, and free Black proprietor Jean-Louis Larose, as well as former civil commissioner Saint-Léger. The next month, Sonthonax began to attend the society's meetings, eventually serving as the President of the society in February 1799. In these first meetings, the members discussed possibilities for agriculture and public instruction in the French colonies, institutions in colonial society of which Sonthonax had had direct experience during his service on the second and third civil commissions. Thomany served as organization President, and Mentor was the Secretary in late 1798. In January 1799, the Friends of the Blacks and Colonies admitted Jean-Baptiste Deville, a free Black elected to represent Saint-Domingue in 1798. Another free black, the abovementioned Belley, who joined the society the month before, presented his fellow representative from the Convention, Dufay, for membership in February 1799. In all, eleven of the thirteen Saint-Dominguan deputies elected in fall 1796 and spring 1797 were members or attended the meetings of the revived philanthropic organization from November 1797 through March 1799.[38]

The Friends of the Blacks and the Colonies was more Atlantic in its membership as well as its activities, as its members worked within and alongside French officials sent to Saint-Domingue to fulfill the society's goals. The Directory, which replaced the Convention, sent a third civil commission to Saint-Domingue in 1796. Sonthonax and Raimond were members of the new commission. Sonthonax made a proclamation specific to education of the children of the formerly enslaved in June 1796. He explained that education

---

[38] For more on the Friends of the Blacks and Colonies, see Bernard Gainot, "La société des Amis des Noirs et des colonies, 1796–1799," in Marcel Dorigny and Bernard Gainot, eds., *La Société des Amis des Noirs, 1788–1799: Contribution à l'histoire de l'abolition de l'esclavage* (Paris: UNESCO, 1998).

was the only way to maintain emancipation. After Sonthonax's initial proclamation in June 1796, Julien Raimond, who had been appointed as a member of the third civil commission, took responsibility for the development and supervision of colonial public schools. In the summer of 1796, Alexandre-Benjamin Giroud, a mining engineer who accompanied the third commission, wrote to the Minister of the Marine on the status and development of education in Saint-Domingue. He was seeking texts. He referenced a conversation he had had with Grégoire before leaving France. Grégoire spoke of an abundance of books in the "depots of the Republic" that could be reserved to create a colonial public library. The commissioners chose to open new schools through the North Province, and in early 1797, Raimond reported that over 1,600 students were attending the northern schools. Giroud and Raimond formed the Free Society of Sciences, Arts, and Humanities. Both were members of the National Institute of Sciences and Arts founded in 1795 in Paris, and, consequently, organized the new society on that model. Giroud wrote to the Institute in Paris about the successes of Raimond's schools and the importance of education in linking Saint-Domingue and France. These men worked in Saint-Domingue to enlighten the colonists.

While on a mission in the United States from December 1796 to March 1797, Giroud established connections with the abolitionist society in Philadelphia. In his relations with the Pennsylvania Society for the Abolition of Slavery,[39] Giroud referred to himself as a representative of the Society of the Friends of the Blacks and the Colonies in Paris – though he was not listed as a member and it would not meet until November 1797. He explained how the revived society acknowledged that efforts to end the slave trade, slavery, and racial inequality began with abolitionists in Pennsylvania. Therefore, they thought it wise to reestablish and continue correspondence with the society in Philadelphia. Grégoire also actively corresponded with the abolitionists in Philadelphia. Their communication with the American society reveals a complex Atlantic abolitionist network, connecting France

---

[39] For more on the Pennsylvania Abolition Society, see for example Dee E. Andrews, "Reconsidering the First Emancipation: Evidence from the Pennsylvania Abolition Society Correspondence, 1785–1810," *Pennsylvania History: A Journal of Mid-Atlantic Studies* 64 (1997), 230–49; Richard S. Newman, "The Pennsylvania Abolition Society: Restoring a Group to Glory," *Pennsylvania Legacies* 5:2 (2005), 6–10; Margaret Hope Bacon, "The Pennsylvania Abolition Society's Mission for Black Education," *Pennsylvania Legacies* 5:2 (2005), 21–6; Beverly Tomek, "Seeking 'An Immutable Pledge from the Slave holding States': the Pennsylvania Abolition Society and Black Resettlement," *Pennsylvania History: A Journal of Mid-Atlantic Studies*, 75 (2008), 26–53; Jackson, *Let This Voice Be Heard*.

and Saint-Domingue, as well as France and the United States, suggesting continuity in the interconnectedness of abolitionist and philanthropic societies from the 1780s into the late 1790s.

The Friends of the Blacks and the Colonies came to an end with a change in the revolutionary government much like the first iteration of the society. One of its last acts was a ceremony to commemorate the abolition of slavery on 4 February 1799. However, the next month Charles-Bernard Wadström, a member of both iterations of the organization, died – symbolically marking the end of the society's life – and the Friends of the Blacks and the Colonies stopped meeting. It is unclear why, but the Minister of the Marine, Marc-Antoine Bourdon Vatry opened an inquiry into its end in August 1799, concluding that his predecessors were responsible and likely under the influence of the members of the Directory. Napoleon Bonaparte came to power in November, proclaiming in December that the colonies would be governed by particular laws. In 1802, Bonaparte sent an expedition to the French Caribbean to regain control of Saint-Domingue and reinstitute slavery there and in Guadeloupe, Guiana, and Martinique. Forces in Saint-Domingue repelled the expedition, and Haiti declared its independence in 1804. Haitians achieved what American and British abolitionists and French philanthropists could not until decades later.

An Atlantic movement to end the slave trade and slavery grew and evolved through the Age of Revolutions. Although members of the eighteenth-century French and British societies collaborated a great deal, they differed in their overall goals. The British abolitionists believed that if they abolished the slave trade, the institution of slavery would naturally come to an end with time. In contrast, the French philanthropists saw abolishing the slave trade as one part of their program, and after bringing about the end of the trade, they intended to pursue the abolition of slavery as well. During the French Revolution, the Convention abolished slavery in 1794 without officially addressing the slave trade. While the deputies likely assumed they did not need to outlaw the trade since slavery was no longer legal, it left an opening for Haitian Revolutionary leader Toussaint Louverture to continue forcefully bringing African laborers to Saint-Domingue.[40] Enslaved Africans still experienced the brutality of the slave

---

[40] See Title 6, Article 17 of the Constitution of the French Colony of Saint-Domingue from 1801, in Laurent Dubois and John Garrigus, eds., *Slave Revolution in the Caribbean, 1789–1804: A Brief History with Documents* (New York: Palgrave Macmillan, 2006), 167–70.

trade, and although they were technically freed upon arrival in the colony, they had to engage in regimented labor. For this reason, Louverture's nephew led a rebellion against him in 1801. The Atlantic movement was not successful in ending the slave trade or slavery in the eighteenth century, but it roused opposition through groups like the Club Massiac, raised awareness in society through publications, and introduced the issues in parliaments. This effort laid the groundwork for the successes, discussed in several other chapters in this and the other volumes in the *Cambridge History of the Age of Atlantic Revolutions*, of nineteenth-century abolitionists in ending the slave trade and slavery in the broader Atlantic World.

5

Tracking the French Revolution in the United States: Popular Sovereignty, Representation, Absolutism, and Democracy

MATTHEW RAINBOW HALE

To a degree that will likely surprise, developments in the new American republic tracked successive phases of the French Revolution. Both in France and in the United States, the ascendance in the late 1780s and early 1790s of a version of constitutional popular sovereignty oriented around disembodied representation laid the foundation for the abrupt invention of an alternative, absolutist understanding of "the people's" authority in 1792–1793. Known as democracy, that absolutist conception simultaneously energized and destabilized each polity by demanding embodied, iconic formulations of "the people." The resultant political muddle in the second half of the 1790s partially obscured institutional innovations critical to the turn-of-the-century reconciliation of disembodied representation and democratic absolutism. With Napoleon's rise to power and the election of Thomas Jefferson to the presidency, democratic absolutism flourished, achieving a degree of legitimacy scarcely imaginable only a few years before. The stability that ensued was greater in the United States than in France, yet assessments casually contrasting American constitutional steadiness with French irregularity preempt recognition of noteworthy Franco-American analogues. Indeed, Jeffersonian political culture and its Jacksonian successor mirrored Napoleonic dynamics in ways that compel reconsideration of democracy itself.

The author thanks the members of Lawrence Peskin's writing group and the participants in an October 2019 Western Society for French History panel session, especially Philipp Ziesche, Micah Alpaugh, and Michelle Orihel, for providing feedback on incomplete, early drafts of this chapter. For constructive criticism of a full draft, the author thanks Wim Klooster, Todd Estes, Bradley Hale, Christine Heyrman, and Max Matherne.

The analogous relationship between developments in France and the United States in the 1790s and early nineteenth century was the consequence of two distinct, albeit interrelated, phenomena. For starters, it demonstrated the diffusionary dynamics of the French Revolution, as the circulation of ideas, people, and goods forced Americans to come to terms with events originating in Paris and other Atlantic-world locales. Diffusionary forces would not have registered so powerfully, however, if residents of the United States had not been prepared for them. In that regard, Brendan McConville's observation that "British America and Bourbon France" were "two of the most monarchical societies in the Atlantic world" and "[t]heir political cultures more alike, particularly in their visualization, than we have been comfortable admitting" is helpful in that it invites an interpretive sketch of how absolutism helped structure American engagement with the French Revolution.[1] Developments in the United States tracked closely to successive French revolutionary phases, in other words, because absolutist principles, habits, and hopes continued to animate large numbers of people long after the adoption of the Constitution.[2]

The Late 1780s and Early 1790s (c. 1787–1791)

In response to comparable financial and governance crises, genteel French and American reformers in the late 1780s and early 1790s created new, national institutions that sought to regulate popular influence on public affairs even as they championed an innovative version of constitutional popular sovereignty. Central to that novel rendition of popular sovereignty was disembodied representation, the idea that elected delegates stood in for

---

[1] Brendan McConville, *The King's Three Faces: The Rise and Fall of Royal America, 1688–1776* (Chapel Hill: University of North Carolina Press, 2005), 139.

[2] There are five caveats, however. (1) Framing the "long" American 1790s in terms of French revolutionary periodization does not mean that stark differences between what happened in the United States and France are unimportant; full understanding of these two nations' histories in this time period must account for numerous, obvious, profound dissimilarities. (2) Any brief attempt to analyze parallels between what happened in France and the United States in the 1790s and early nineteenth century will necessarily flatten out or omit certain complexities. (3) The chronological phases designated in this chapter should be understood flexibly, as partially overlapping rather than as entirely distinct stages. (4) Prodemocracy individuals in France and the United States did not experience false consciousness; their invention of an absolutist version of popular sovereignty complemented rather than belied their rejection of monarchy. (5) Additional evidence for American developments in the mid-1790s will be shared by the author in future work.

rather than reconstituted the nation. Although reformers enjoyed substantive support as they drafted constitutions, and although they bolstered that support by using newfound national institutions to address pressing problems and undermine privilege, discontent emerged. That dissatisfaction revolved partly around a desire for greater access to central government, and partly around an aspiration for more enchanting expressions of popular sovereignty. In neither France nor the United States did these two aspects merge and realize their potential in the late 1780s and early 1790s. Even so, the establishment of constitutional popular sovereignty heightened expectation. Only by taking seriously the sense of disconnect produced in these years by unfulfilled expectation can we understand the explosive developments that followed in the mid-1790s.

In France, Paul Friedland has shown, the National Assembly's formation and early career crystallized the displacement of medieval theology-derived, embodied re-presentation of the *corpus mysticum* (mystical body) by Enlightenment-derived, disembodied representation. Instead of "claim[ing] to *be* the French nation" as the Estates General or the absolute monarch had done, "the National Assembly merely claimed to speak on the nation's behalf."[3] The shift from numinous re-presentation to spiritually detached representation enhanced the status of "public opinion," the "general will," and the "nation," but the abstract nature of those concepts rendered them instruments of mystification. Those who held power were less likely to scrupulously ascertain constituent opinion than to claim it as justification for specific agendas. Common voters were empowered to empower gentlemen. Elections invigorated citizen-electors rather than citizen-rulers. The unalienable sovereignty of the "nation" – a phrase often used interchangeably with "the people" – assumed centrality, yet how exactly the masses could formulate and implement their collective will remained obscure, if not elusive. In short, constitutional creativity in the name of "the people" not only partially sidelined sizeable numbers of actual people, but also institutionalized a nonmaterial, obfuscatory version of popular sovereignty.

Something analogous occurred in the United States, as leading federalists' late 1780s assertion of an expansive "people" cloaked their elitism. In response to the intertwined problems of state governments' (supposed)

---

[3] Paul Friedland, *Political Actors: Representative Bodies and Theatricality in the Age of the French Revolution* (Ithaca, NY: Cornell University Press, 2002), 6.

irresponsibility and the American union's shortcomings, a cohort of gentlemen reformers constructed a framework of government, the Constitution, that both placed states in an explicitly subordinate position relative to new national institutions and attempted to regulate popular involvement in those institutions. Encountering severe criticism, federalists extended the populist logic of American constitutional theory, deploying revolutionary notions of "the people" against those who believed state legislatures and nonelites were being shunted aside. As in France, the elaboration of popular sovereignty notions resulted in the "disembodiment of government," as "the people" ceased being a divinely ordained social body animating a particular branch of government and instead came to operate as a religiously neutral supervisor distributing power from without. Popular government via disembodied representation necessarily rested on abstraction, such that "the people" seemed to function in many instances as a mere legitimating symbol. Symbolization in turn implied a degree of marginalization, in the sense that "the people's" most dynamic role was constitutional and electoral authorization rather than constant involvement in governance. That federalists yearning for rule by "the better sort" pioneered one of the most capacious versions of popular sovereignty in the American revolutionary era was therefore logical as well as paradoxical.[4]

Highlighting late-1780s mystifications of "the people" does not mean constitutional innovators in France and the United States were thoroughgoing cynical manipulators of public opinion. Most sincerely believed they were acting in the best interests of the majority and the ideal of republican self-government. Equally importantly, genteel French and American reformers in the late 1780s and early 1790s enjoyed substantial support, not only because their call for state ratifying conventions and/or new elections instantiated popular sovereignty, but also because the new, national institutions they created utilized that sovereignty to address pressing problems in ways that roughly accorded with the values of numerous citizens. The National Assembly raised needed funds by expropriating and selling Catholic Church land; abolished feudalism and noble titles; and composed the Declaration of the Rights of Man and of the Citizen. Congress and President George Washington's administration worked together, albeit sometimes discordantly, to assume states'

---

[4] Gordon S. Wood, *The Creation of the American Republic, 1776–1787* (New York: W. W. Norton & Company, 1972 [1967]), 383–9.

American Revolutionary War debts and thus alleviate average families' tax burden; establish the federal government's financial standing in the international sphere; and pass a Bill of Rights. Forceful employment of representative institutions and constitutionalism in 1789–1791 was not victimless; it came at the expense of privilege. In France, the monarchy was no longer absolutist, while nobles, the Catholic Church, assorted guilds, venal officeholders, and various municipalities and provinces had beneficial legal exemptions and conferment stripped away. In the United States, states as corporate bodies – and by implication, certain cohorts of local elites – endowed with longstanding, exclusive authority in matters such as taxation, and longstanding, partial authority in matters such as foreign policy, commercial affairs, and western expansion now competed with or were often overshadowed by a strong central government. The reformers who created a version of constitutional popular sovereignty oriented around disembodied representation were thus not disingenuous interlopers disconnected from the masses; their claim to speak and act in the name of "the people" rested on a plausible, easily identifiable foundation.

Even so, the elitist, abstract nature of constitutional popular sovereignty occasioned dissatisfaction. One strain of that dissatisfaction was manifested as criticism of insufficient popular influence on central government. In France, newspapers and political clubs originally formed in support of the new regime increasingly challenged it, with specific resentments stemming from the voter-disenfranchising category of "passive citizenship," the prohibitive *marc d'argent* (the 50 *livres* demanded of future legislative deputies), the impermanence of local assemblies, and the National Assembly's refusal to allow popular ratification of the Constitution of 1791.[5] In the United States, inchoate opposition activists, many of them one-time foes of the Constitution's ratification, fought against Treasury Secretary Alexander Hamilton's fiscal–military program in part because they believed it would create a "monied interest" removed from everyday citizens; broached the

---

[5] Timothy Tackett, *The Coming of the Terror in the French Revolution* (Cambridge, MA: Harvard University Press, 2015), 85; Jeremy D. Popkin, *A New World Begins: The History of the French Revolution* (New York: Basic Books, 2019), 186–7; Malcolm Crook, "The New Regime: Political Institutions and Democratic Practices under the Constitutional Monarchy, 1789–1791," in David Andress, ed., *The Oxford Handbook of the French Revolution* (Oxford: Oxford University Press, 2015), 221, 223–4, 228–30; Jeremy D. Popkin, *Revolutionary News: The Press in France, 1789–1799* (Durham, NC: Duke University Press, 1990), 181.

idea of a political party (and associated clubs) oriented around popular sovereignty; contended that district (rather than at-large) elections, states' rights, and explicit limits on the federal government's authority over taxation, the militia, and national elections were necessary for robust representation; and started a newspaper dedicated to spreading their views and pressuring the national government.[6] Taken together, these French and American critiques, in 1789–1791, of popular government through disembodied representation conveyed an emergent perception that government in the name of "the people" was not necessarily government of the people.

Dissatisfaction with constitutional reformers' late 1780s–early 1790s version of popular sovereignty also materialized as persistent or refashioned royalism. In France, the king remained a widely revered figure despite mounting evidence that he was not fully on board with – and in fact, disloyal to – the French Revolution. In the United States, the cult of George Washington took on more elaborate royalist overtones after his inauguration as the first president.[7] That many French and American citizens enthusiastically celebrated, respectively, Louis XVI and Washington indicates that (neo)monarchical sovereignty remained as emotionally satisfying as, if not more so than, its constitutional popular sovereignty counterpart. Whereas the tepidly religious (and sometimes openly anticlerical) institutionalism at the heart of disembodied representation stunted visceral identification with the regimes taking root in 1789, (neo)royalist ritualism invited it by providing an embodied exemplar of national glory. Newfound French and American constitutional popular sovereignty in that sense stood on somewhat shaky ground; unless political forms equal to early modern absolutism in iconic (rather than symbolic) power were assimilated to the new regimes, popular disgruntlement had the potential to metamorphose into something more dynamic.[8] Louis XVI and Washington's popularity in the late 1780s and early 1790s thus did more than suggest that old, monarchical habits die hard; it also

---

[6] Lance Banning, *The Jeffersonian Persuasion: Evolution of a Party Ideology* (Ithaca, NY: Cornell University Press, 1980), 158–64; Saul Cornell, *The Other Founders: Anti-Federalism and the Dissenting Tradition in America, 1788–1828* (Chapel Hill: University of North Carolina Press, 1999), 147–94; Jeffrey L. Pasley, *The Tyranny of the Printers: Newspaper Politics in the Early American Republic* (Charlottesville: University of Virginia Press, 2002), 68–70.

[7] Simon Newman, *Parades and the Politics of the Street: Festive Culture in the Early American Republic* (Philadelphia: University of Pennsylvania Press, 1997), 44–82.

[8] Whereas a symbol alludes to an absent entity, an icon is a perfect, alternative rendering of that entity; whereas a symbol evokes the power of an absent entity, an icon channels it.

revealed profound shortcomings in the charismatic capacity of popular government through disembodied representation.[9]

Whether expressed as criticism of insufficient popular influence on central government or as (neo)royalism, dissatisfaction with disembodied representation stemmed from unfulfilled, heightened expectation. More specifically, the disjuncture between the constitutional apotheosis of popular sovereignty and the transmutation of "the people" into a desacralized abstraction geared toward enlightened reformers engendered widespread experience of disconnect; enthusiasm for "the people" as the sole source of authority produced anxiety regarding the fact that the version of popular sovereignty being institutionalized at that moment did not feel as authentic, compelling, or exalted as it should. Individuals excited by the apparent triumph of popular sovereignty found disappointing constitutional barriers to average citizens' access to national government. Individuals hopeful that the newly ascendant, sovereign national "people" would animate the body politic as majestically as Old Regime kings and queens had done found unsatisfactory the "disembodiment of government."

In both instances, the desire was for more tangible participation of "the people" in its sovereignty. By demanding the enlargement of popular influence on national government, various groups served noticed that they expected "the people" to infuse, on a day-to-day basis, the exercise of supreme authority. By lauding King Louis XVI and President Washington, numerous persons demonstrated that they hoped for an embodied projection of sovereignty so enthralling that it would enable each person to experience the transcendence associated with "the people's" ascendance to rulership. Discontentment with popular government via disembodied representation thus assumed distinct practical and mystical modes; a desire to assert "the people's" unceasing presence in national government coexisted with a desire to intuit and propagate cosmic order through "the people's" magisterial political presence.

These twin desires for popular presence did not carry as much sway as they might have between 1789 and 1791, in large part because they were not conjoined. In both countries, criticism of disembodied representation was either largely incompatible or insufficiently interwoven with absolutist folkways to unloose from populaces long conditioned to monarchy the complete force of popular sovereignty. Entanglement with popular sovereignty's

---

[9] David A. Bell, *Men on Horseback: The Power of Charisma in the Age of Revolution* (New York: Farrar, Straus and Giroux, 2020).

critics, meanwhile, made (neo)royalism unacceptable to increasing numbers of people. The full potential of dissatisfaction with republican constitutionalism and representation accordingly remained latent. Until practical attempts to insert "the people" into national government merged with some iconic rendering of political absolutism, they would struggle to develop the requisite momentum for additional dramatic change. Until spiritual yearnings for an embodied projection of sovereign authority shed their (neo)royalism, they would alienate important constituencies and appear out of step with republican self-government trends. Dissatisfaction with popular government through disembodied representation in that sense constituted a necessary precondition for, but not a sufficient stimulus to, widespread populist insurgency because it was internally at odds, because the political alchemy for fusing its two distinct modes had not yet materialized.

The Mid-1790s (c. 1792–1795)

The republicanized, militarized French Revolution served as that alchemy, and the particular way it fused the distinct strands of discontentment with the "disembodiment of government" underscored the disconnect occasioned by the constitutional apotheosis of "the people." More specifically, preexisting longing for a more tangible version of popular sovereignty primed numerous French and American citizens to experience the events surrounding the fall of the Bourbon dynasty and the onslaught of French revolutionary war in epiphanic terms. Experiences of cognitive discovery helped produce the creativity, bravado, and enthrallment necessary for the abrupt concoction of a version of the sovereign "people" that was simultaneously antimonarchical and absolutist. The attempts in 1792–1795 to exert popular presence in French and American affairs reflected "the people's" yearning to know itself as sovereign through self-aggrandizing projections of embodied, iconic authority *and* through dispossessive, rapturous submission to those projections. Agents *and* objects of sovereignty, proponents of a version of selfhood oriented toward autonomy *and* mystical absorption, "the people" discovered the fullness of its supreme authority in a sudden, unforgettably vivid manner.

Integral to the "people's" experience with its supremacy between 1792 and 1795 was the escalation of popular sovereignty ideology and the proliferation of self-consciously democratic rhetoric.[10] The latter development rendered

[10] David Andress, "Representing the Sovereign People in the Terror," in Máire F. Cross and David Williams, eds., *The French Experience from Republic to Monarchy, 1792–1824:*

Aristotelian political theory virtually obsolete and exposed the ambiguities of republicanism by simultaneously complementing and inflaming it.[11] Perhaps more importantly, the spread of democratic terminology implicitly challenged the legitimacy of popular sovereignty through disembodied representation. The invention of democracy in Revolutionary France rested less on electoral processes and constitutional structure than on longing for embodiment of the sovereign "people" and distaste for intervening assemblies.[12] The sudden surge in 1793–1795 in American mentions of the word "democracy" and its cognates was likewise less concerned with formal theories of "the people's" precise role in government than visceral displays of the coincidence of sovereignty and "the people."[13] Indeed, in tandem with the establishment of scores of Democratic-Republican Societies, various Americans' flamboyant declarations that they were "democrats" functioned as imperious attempts to render popular authority immediate and material rather than mediated and abstract.

The flowering of French and American democratic rhetoric hence reflected an absolutist affinity for self-magnifying, performative assertions of embodied sovereignty. Less negations of the idea of representation *per se* than demands that representatives faithfully enact their subordinate position, such assertions demonstrated the self-reverential obsession with distinction at the heart of democratic self-invention. The "people," a February 1793 Philadelphia newspaper author explained in a barefaced reapplication of absolutist theory, "are ... the centre of the system towards whom every body ought to gravitate[;] they are the fountain of power, and the representatives ... are but emanations from them."[14]

If "the people's" sovereign authority revolved around self-reverence and distinction, its everyday identity was relational and belligerent; the "democratic" body politic in France and the United States defined itself through conflict with those it labeled "aristocrats." Eminently suited to class warfare,

---

New Dawns in Politics, Knowledge and Culture (London: Palgrave Publishers, 2000), 30; Tackett, *Coming of the Terror*, 150, 161, 229.

[11] Matthew Rainbow Hale, "Regenerating the World: The French Revolution, Civic Festivals, and the Forging of Modern American Democracy, 1793–1795," *Journal of American History* 103 (2017), 896–8; Matthew Rainbow Hale, "Defining Democracy, Challenging 'Democrats,'" https://ageofrevolutions.com/2018/07/16/defining-democracy-challenging-democrats.

[12] François Furet, *Interpreting the French Revolution* (Cambridge: Cambridge University Press, 1981 [1978]), 24–31; Pierre Rosanvallon, "The History of the Word 'Democracy' in France," *Journal of Democracy* 6:4 (1995), 140–54.

[13] Hale, "Regenerating the World," 896–9.

[14] *General Advertiser* (Philadelphia), 18 February 1793.

the terms "democrat" and "aristocrat" were nonetheless not so much reliable indicators of a person's socioeconomic or legal condition as the declaiming "democrat's" perspective.[15] "Democrat" and "aristocrat" were partisan, moralistic phrases; they rendered anyone who supported the French Revolution good and those who opposed it evil. Partisan moralism encompassed assorted religious impulses, and pro-French Revolution citizens on both sides of the Atlantic compared themselves to Jesus and his disciples.[16] In conjunction with the contemporaneous fascination with Greco-Roman civilization, identification with Christianity's founders disclosed a primitivist streak, a desire to return to pure beginnings, experience rebirth, and dwell in a millennial or "mythic present."[17] Of equal consequence, it revealed an inclination to impute to the sovereign democratic "people" a sacramental essence reminiscent of monarchy. The goodness of the democratic body politic thus differed from that of the refurbished eighteenth-century aristocracy because it was not primarily a matter of achieved character, patriotism, or piety.[18] Rather, it stemmed from an idealized reflection of the divine, a type of innate, messianic perfection through which individuals could realize their full selves and community salvation.

The "democrat"-versus-"aristocrat" opposition superseded the older monarchy-versus-aristocracy struggle for legitimacy and popular support in a way that portended trouble for both monarchy and aristocracy. With the democratic community displacing monarchy as the moral center and primary embodiment of the nation in the battle against aristocratic usurpation, (neo)monarchy suddenly stood out for its identity with, rather than opposition to, aristocracy; it was henceforth impossible to defend any sort of hierarchical, hereditary privilege without coming across as an enemy of "the people." At the same time, "the people's" arrogation of sovereignty enabled its advocates to draw upon absolutist concepts and practices without significant risk of being associated with monarchy. Through their invention

---

[15] Patrice Higonnet, "'Aristocrate,' 'Aristocratie': Language and Politics in the French Revolution," in Sandry Petrey, ed., *The French Revolution, 1789–1989: Two Hundred Years of Rethinking* (Lubbock: Texas Tech University Press, 1989), 51.

[16] Albert Soboul, *Understanding the French Revolution* (New York: International Publishers, 1988), 131–44; *Boston Gazette*, 5 August 1793.

[17] Lynn Hunt, *Politics, Class, and Culture in the French Revolution* (Berkeley: University of California Press, 1984), 27.

[18] Jay M. Smith, *Nobility Reimagined: The Patriotic Nation in Eighteenth-Century France* (Ithaca, NY: Cornell University Press, 2005); Craig Bruce Smith, *American Honor: The Creation of the Nation's Ideals during the Revolutionary Era* (Chapel Hill: University of North Carolina Press, 2018); R. R. Palmer, *Twelve Who Ruled: The Year of the Terror in the French Revolution* (New York: Atheneum, 1965 [1941]), 33, 277.

of the "democrat"-versus-"aristocrat" schematic, the democratic community had its absolutist cake and ate it too.

The democratic community's ability to weaponize antimonarchical, absolutist politics shone forth through the Herculean image. That icon's French revolutionary appeal stemmed from its monarchy-derived invocation of monumental force, unity of action, precognitive virtue, and transparency of representation.[19] Pro-French Revolution Americans similarly employed Hercules to brandish the idea that "the people-at-large were the enactors as well as the source of popular sovereignty," to warn that "they possessed not only a peculiar might and courage, but also a ferocious, unwieldy attachment to their rights."[20] That warning was directed toward avowed opponents of the French Revolution *and* duly elected officials who did not readily yield to popular sovereignty. No matter their origin, encroachments – even perceived potential encroachments – upon "the people's" authority could not be tolerated. Democratic sovereignty, like its monarchical forerunner, was stridently circumscribing; its integrity depended on monitorial jealousness and wrathful interventions on behalf of exclusivity. Precisely because it depicted the democratic "people" as the opposite of genteel representatives, as virile, earthy, and unpredictable, as capable of and perhaps even eager to commit, in the manner of Old Regime princes, fear-inducing deeds in the name of undivided, plenary authority, the Herculean image resonated.

Popular affinity for absolutist versions of awesome justice also yielded a democratic cult of the guillotine in France and the United States. In both nations, numerous pro-French Revolution individuals exulted in the guillotine's prodigious efficiency; used pet names to domesticate its haunting work; employed religious language to sacralize it as an instrument of democratic rebirth; and were seduced by its theatricality and imagined association with feminine sexuality.[21] Various French revolutionaries and American Francophiles embraced this executionary object because their

---

[19] Hunt, *Politics, Class, and Culture*, 87–119.

[20] Matthew Rainbow Hale, "American Hercules: Militant Sovereignty and Violence in the Democratic-Republican Imagination, 1793–1795," in Patrick Griffin, Robert G. Ingram, Peter S. Onuf, and Brian Schoen, eds., *Between Sovereignty and Anarchy: The Politics of Violence in the American Revolutionary Era* (Charlottesville: University of Virginia Press, 2015), 247.

[21] Paul Friedland, *Seeing Justice Done: The Age of Spectacular Capital Punishment in France* (New York: Oxford University Press, 2012), 239–65; Daniel Arasse, *The Guillotine and the Terror* (London: Penguin Press, 1989 [1987]); Regina Janes, *Losing Our Heads: Beheadings in Literature and Culture* (New York: New York University Press, 2005), 67–96.

historical experiences with monarchy caused them to view terror as a necessary attribute of strong rulership.[22] Indeed, even though National Assembly delegate Joseph-Ignace Guillotin intended the lethal instrument named after him to be a contribution to humanitarianism and equality before the law, certain pro-French Revolution cohorts on both sides of the Atlantic repurposed it as a charismatic icon of "the people's" ruthless supremacy. A preexisting, vernacular hunger for absolutist experiences of sovereign terribleness thus led numerous French and American citizens to endorse not only employment of the guillotine to do actual violence to thousands, but also cooptation of its image to do metaphorical violence to the genteel altruism undergirding disembodied representation.

Displays of military power were the ultimate form of commanding obedience through terribleness in the early modern era, and many in France and the United States viewed the French revolutionary wars as an opportunity to prove that republics were the equals, if not the superiors, of polities governed by kings and queens. Only by waging war as effectively as monarchs did could democrats establish the legitimacy of their newfound regimes; only by projecting power in such a way as to make resistance futile and humiliating could democratic authority acquire an absolutist aura of grandeur and givenness.

Enthusiasm for French revolutionary warfare was also predicated on millennial dreams of a purgative war to end all wars. Those dreams imparted to martial culture an apocalyptic dynamic, and noncombatants as well as soldiers and sailors often developed a romantic attachment to a putatively exceptional, all-or-nothing political crusade.[23] That attachment yielded images of "the people in arms" because the newfound democratic nation hungered to perceive itself as an embodied icon rather than as an abstract symbol.[24] French revolutionary warfare in that sense functioned as a form of worship enabling its supporters to achieve individual and national exaltation through self-abnegation.[25] By giving themselves over to military combat, republican citizens helped "the people" realize itself as divine, glorious, and elevated, as worthy of sacrifice, veneration, and enthronement.

---

[22] Ronald Schechter, *A Genealogy of the Terror in Eighteenth-Century France* (Chicago: Chicago University Press, 2018), 38–57.

[23] David A. Bell, *The First Total War: Napoleon's Europe and the Birth of Warfare as We Know It* (Boston: Houghton Mifflin Harcourt, 2008); Hale, "American Hercules."

[24] John A. Lynn, "French Opinion and the Military Resurrection of the Pike," *Military Affairs* 41 (1977), 1–7.

[25] Hale, "American Hercules," 249–50.

The democratic community's longing for a captivating, praiseworthy projection of its sovereignty appeared as well in festive ritualism. In France and the United States, supporters of the French Revolution in the mid-1790s engaged in antimonarchical, antiaristocratic iconoclasm, mockery, and intimidation; enacted the sacramentality of "the people's" supremacy through civic ceremonies redolent with religious imagery; and participated in fraternal rites establishing equality as the new regime's central "doctrine" to which everyone must subscribe or acquiesce. In conjunction, these expressions of festive ritualism served as political confessionalization mechanisms, as forges of stereotyped identities reminiscent of those produced during the (Counter-) Reformation. By insisting on a political order grounded on "the people's" embodied precedence, the harshly galvanizing force of egalitarian creedalism, and immanent and transcendent experience for true democratic believers, various French and American citizens endeavored, in effect, to reformulate for a new era the *corpus mysticum*. Dubbed by contemporaries "regeneration," an apt term given its dual association with bodily vigor and spiritual renewal, that endeavor evinced a desire to reassert, in the face of enlightened constitutionalism and new, national institutions, the vital role of local communities' traditional rituals in the organization of society. Only by hearkening to and refashioning the absolute monarch's festive, confessional, and disciplinary work could the democratic "people" be satisfied with its sovereignty.

The alternately effervescent and alarmed overtones of the democratic insurgencies in France and the United States in the mid-1790s demonstrated how invigorating the antimonarchical, absolutist version of popular sovereignty could be. Actors in and spectators of their collective melodrama of sacred revolutionary authority, large numbers of people lived as they had never had lived before, so much so that time itself seemed to accelerate and/or slow down.[26] Precisely because the democratic "people's" experience in 1792–1795 with its preeminence was so heartfelt, it successfully established an absolutist version of popular sovereignty as a potential alternative to, alter ego of, or muse for popular governance through disembodied representation. The

---

[26] David Andress, "Living the Revolutionary Melodrama: Robespierre's Sensibility and the Construction of Political Commitment in the French Revolution," *Representations* 114 (2011), 103–28; David Andress, "Jacobinism as Heroic Narrative: Understanding the Terror as the Experience of Melodrama," https://h-france.net/rude/vol5/andress5; Lynn Hunt, "The World We Have Gained: The Future of the French Revolution," *American Historical Review* 108:1 (2003), 1–19; Matthew Rainbow Hale, "On Their Tiptoes: Political Time and Newspapers during the Advent of the Radicalized French Revolution, circa 1792–1793," *Journal of the Early Republic* 29 (2009), 191–218.

authentic conviction at the heart of French and American democratic insurgencies guaranteed that various individuals and communities' embodied performances of their recently ascertained self-understanding were truthful and therefore extraordinarily compelling. The phenomenological integrity of that self-understanding imparted to absolutist popular sovereignty a staying power that belied its highly improvisational, gestural character. In the same way Old Regime kings and queens rendered themselves glorious through lightning-like acts of ineffable imperiousness, the mid-1790s democratic "people" made itself a touchstone for modern political culture by precipitously willing into existence an antimonarchical, absolutist iteration of its sovereignty.

The Mid- to Late 1790s (c. 1794–1800)

That the democratic "people" in France and the United States succeeded in establishing an antimonarchical, absolutist version of popular sovereignty as a potential alternative to, alter ego of, or muse for disembodied representation was not immediately apparent. In fact, during the mid- to late 1790s it appeared in many respects that attempts to enact an embodied, iconic version of "the people's" supremacy had been defeated. At the center of that apparent defeat was the strategic retreat of some pro-French Revolution individuals, especially those of genteel status, from what they considered excessive fervor. Taking advantage of this retreat, conservatives sought to exact revenge and crush democracy.

In spite of conservative attacks, militant democrats elaborated upon or refashioned the antimonarchical, absolutist version of popular sovereignty. Deepened polarization created space for centrist initiatives by genuine moderates as well as by opportunists seeking to use ideas of neutrality to assert power or avoid condemnation. The neutral center broached by moderates and opportunists had little chance of prevailing in either France or the United States; its appearance as a putative option reflected the disordered environment wrought by the transatlantic democratic awakening that erupted in 1792–1793. Both polities were characterized in the second half of the 1790s by volatility, cross-cutting trends, and a search for order, by a struggle to reconcile popular sovereignty through disembodied representation and its democratic, absolutist counterpart.[27]

---

[27] Laura Mason, "The Thermidorian Reaction," in Peter McPhee, ed., *A Companion to the French Revolution* (Oxford: Blackwell, 2013), 323; Matthew Rainbow Hale, "'Many Who Wandered in Darkness': The Contest over American Nationality, 1795–1798," *Early American Studies*, 1 (2003), 127–75.

Notwithstanding its muddled political character, the mid- to late 1790s witnessed seminal developments relating to the grounding of democracy. The French iteration of this grounding elevated military and bureaucratic structures, while the American accentuated voluntaristic organization. Both addressed practical problems undercutting or hindering the enactment of "the people's" supremacy. The years that at first glance seemed to mark the collapse of the absolutist version of popular sovereignty were crucial to its reconciliation with disembodied representation at the turn of the century.

Signs that French and American democracy was embattled, if not damaged, were plentiful in the mid- to late 1790s. In France, the overthrow and execution of Robespierre and more than 100 of his closest associates on 9–11 Thermidor (27–29 July 1794) set the stage for the closure of those political clubs that had remained active during the Terror; show trials of scapegoated terrorists; use of the military to crush the Germinal and Prairial uprisings in spring 1795; passage of the 1795 Constitution, with its intricate checks and balances, stricter property-holding requirements for voter eligibility, and the stipulation that two-thirds of the First-Councils membership be drawn from its own ranks; criminalization of support for the 1793 Constitution and a purge of various Jacobin officials in 1796; and the repression of the Conspiracy of Equals in 1796–1797. A similarly noteworthy series of setbacks rocked the democratic movement in the United States. In the summer and fall of 1793, Citizen Genet and his brand of pro-French Revolution diplomacy were disgraced. One year later, the Whiskey Rebellion dissipated on its own even before President Washington and his 12,950-man army marched west in late September–early October 1794 and put it down for good. A month after that display of federal power, Washington's characterization of Democratic-Republican Societies as Whiskey Rebellion fomenters both prompted the House of Representatives to debate formal censure of political clubs and helped propel the speedy demise of most of those societies. Massive street demonstrations and Democratic-Republican maneuvering failed to prevent, in 1795 and 1796, respectively, presidential endorsement and Congressional funding of Jay's Treaty. In April 1798, finally, the XYZ Affair badly embarrassed Federalists' opponents, accelerating the ongoing recession of popular Francophilia.

As a result of these assorted political defeats, a degree of demoralization set in among democrats on both sides of the Atlantic. That demoralization shaped the Germinal, Prairial, and Jay Treaty uprisings and their aftermaths. Germinal protesters failed to extort significant concessions from Convention members in part because they were unarmed, while Prairial marchers were apparently unwilling to use the arms they carried. Although Germinal and Prairial demonstrators chanted demands for food, they stayed clear of previously common terroristic threats.[28] As for Jay Treaty protesters, their simultaneously angry and mournful gatherings evinced a bitter foreboding that the high-water mark for the absolutist version of popular sovereignty had passed. American democrats' inability to sustain nationwide protests in the wake of President Washington's approval on 18 August 1795 of Jay's Treaty in that sense represented not so much a dawning realization of the merits of Anglo-American comity as a reluctant accession to ill portent. That Boston was one of the few locales to experience street demonstrations following Washington's endorsement, and that those demonstrations, unlike the vast majority of earlier anti-Jay Treaty activities, devolved into violent riots, is telling.[29] Those disorders revealed how the sense of frustration afflicting large portions of the American democratic community combined with the particular strain of living in a Federalist stronghold to induce some Massachusetts residents to perceive the catharsis available in mob behavior as a reasonable tradeoff for the bad publicity such behavior generated.

In France and the United States, then, willingness to employ street insurgency as a means of achieving absolutist goals was waning. It would be decades before Paris would see democratic demonstrations as large as the 1795 Germinal and Prairial ones, and the same was true for American cities and the size of anti-Jay Treaty assemblies.

Integral to the struggles plaguing the transatlantic democratic movement in the mid- to late 1790s were pro-French Revolution individuals disappointed, unnerved, or threatened by certain aspects of absolutist popular sovereignty. Virtually all of the antidemocratic French events from Robespierre's overthrow to the Conspiracy of Equals' repression were instigated by officials intimately involved in the terroristic democratic movement of 1792–1794. Various pro-French Revolution persons in the United States were likewise crucial to democratic retreat from aspects of absolutist popular sovereignty in the mid- to late 1790s. Secretary of State Thomas Jefferson and Congressman James Madison encouraged Genet until he became a political liability, at which point they took steps to distance their cause. Genteel Francophiles' deescalation efforts in mid-August 1794 played a pivotal role

---

[28] D. M. G. Sutherland, *The French Revolution and Empire: The Quest for a Civic Order* (Malden, MA: Blackwell Publishing, 2003), 254–5.

[29] Anson Morse, *The Federalist Party in Massachusetts to the Year 1800* (Miami: HardPress Publishing, 2016 [1909]), 154–5.

in stunting the Whiskey Rebellion's violent potential, while the subsequent militia mobilization of various mid-Atlantic Democratic-Republican Society members helped Washington command such an awe-inspiring anti-Whiskey army.[30] Opponents of the Federalist administration had enough votes in the House of Representatives to prevent Jay Treaty funding in early 1796, but moderates in their coalition shied away. Also shying away were most Democratic-Republican Societies, which in the face of Washington's denunciation and Federalist pressure cut back their activities or disbanded altogether in 1795–1796. Culminating this entire wave of strategic retreats, a number of Democratic-Republicans responded to events surrounding the XYZ Affair by publicly renouncing their earlier zeal for the French Revolution.[31]

Seizing the opportunity provided by genteel transatlantic democrats' mid- to late 1790s partial pullback, conservatives resentful of earlier treatment and contemptuous of absolutist popular sovereignty sought revenge. The French iteration of this phenomenon came to be known as the "White Terror" and produced approximately 2,000 deaths and the imprisonment and harassment of tens of thousands more. Much less severe, the American conservative quest for revenge nevertheless encompassed instances of violence, intimidation, and harrying. Disappointed there was no rebel army waiting for them in western Pennsylvania, gung ho anti-Whiskey soldiers attempted to lynch pro-French Revolution moderate Hugh Henry Brackenridge and indiscriminately imprisoned and/or assaulted witnesses, suspects, and bystanders, with at least three deaths resulting.[32] Two additional waves of antidemocratic, vengeful persecution were unloosed by the XYZ Affair and Fries's Rebellion. Particularly noteworthy in these two waves were the attacks on Democratic-Republicans by informal bands of young men and recently organized Federalist military units, both of which unwittingly resembled the "gilded youth" of Paris and young anti-Jacobins in southern France.[33]

---

[30] Thomas Slaughter, *The Whiskey Rebellion: Frontier Epilogue to the American Revolution* (New York: Oxford University Press, 1986), 183; Jeffrey A. Pasley, "Whiskey Chaser: Democracy and Violence in the Debate over the Democratic-Republican Societies and the Whiskey Rebellion," in Griffin et al., *Between Sovereignty and Anarchy*, 208–11.

[31] Jasper M. Trautsch, *The Genesis of America: US Foreign Policy and the Formation of National Identity, 1793–1815* (Cambridge: Cambridge University Press, 2018), 140–2.

[32] Slaughter, *Whiskey Rebellion*, 205.

[33] Albrecht Koschnik, *"Let a Common Interest Bind Us Together": Associations, Partisanship, and Culture in Philadelphia, 1775–1840* (Charlottesville: University of Virginia Press, 2007), 113–30; Colin Lucas, "Themes in Southern Violence after 9 Thermidor," in Gwynne Lewis and Colin Lucas, eds., *Beyond the Terror: Essays in French Regional and Social History, 1794–1815* (Cambridge: Cambridge University Press, 1983), 169; François

At the same time they engaged in bloodthirsty revenge, French and American conservatives sought to use constitutional means to seize or assert power. In France, a coalition of reactionary royalists and antidemocratic constitutionalists styled themselves "friends of order" and acted in ways that approximated a political party. So well did this coalition perform in the elections of spring 1797 that an alarmed cohort of Directory officials engineered the Fructidor coup d'état and implemented renewed repression of right-wing foes. Federalists in the United States also styled themselves "friends of order" and went against their instincts by engaging in innovative electioneering.[34] American conservatives utilized their electoral successes in the mid- to late 1790s to pursue anti-French diplomatic policies and opponent suppression, with recent work showing that use of the 1798 Alien and Sedition Acts to silence, intimidate, and punish opponents was more extensive than had previously been known.[35] That Federalists had the chance to follow through on electoral success while their antidemocratic French counterparts did not should not obscure the fact that in the mid- to late 1790s both groups dreamed of political dominance and were willing to accommodate themselves to electioneering in order to realize their dreams.

Despite conservative actions, militant democrats in France and the United States elaborated upon or reworked the absolutist version of popular sovereignty. Gracchus Babeuf's flamboyant call, in the months surrounding the establishment of the Directory in November 1795, for the abolition of private property was paralleled by the 1796–1797 publication in the United States of various works, including Thomas Paine's *Agrarian Justice*, focused on socioeconomic inequality.[36] Babeuf and Paine were animated in part by millennialism and theology; their egalitarianism was as much a product of early modern prophetic traditions as of modern, materialistic concerns.[37] In the minds of democrats such as Babeuf and Paine, the ascendance of "the people"

Gendron, *The Gilded Youth of Thermidor* (Toronto: McGill-Queens University Press, 1993).

[34] Todd Estes, "Shaping the Politics of Public Opinion: Federalists and the Jay Treaty Debate," *Journal of the Early Republic* 20:3 (2000), 393–422.

[35] Wendell Bird, *Criminal Dissent: Prosecutions under the Alien and Sedition Acts of 1798* (Cambridge, MA: Harvard University Press, 2020).

[36] Seth Cotlar, *Tom Paine's America: The Rise and Fall of Transatlantic Radicalism in the Early Republic* (Charlottesville: University of Virginia Press, 2011), 150.

[37] Alain Maillard, Claude Mazauric, and Eric Walter, eds., *Présence de Babeuf: Lumières, révolution, communisme* (Paris: Publications de la Sorbonne, 1994); Jack Fruchtman, Jr., *Thomas Paine and the Religion of Nature* (Baltimore: Johns Hopkins University Press, 1993); J. C. D. Clark, *Thomas Paine: Britain, America, and France in the Age of Enlightenment and Revolution* (Oxford: Oxford University Press, 2018), 349–55.

to sovereignty paved the way for a cosmic order so thoroughly regenerated that egalitarian ideas were directed toward not only interpersonal etiquette and legal status, but also economic welfare.

Another set of militant democrats eschewed strident challenges to private property in favor of partisan actions designed to shape public discourse and (re)acquire power. In France, assorted neo-Jacobins repositioned themselves as a loyal opposition and then jumped at the opportunities afforded by the Fructidor (September 1797) and Prairial (June 1799) coups d'état to reestablish clubs and newspapers through which they could educate, advocate, and electioneer. In the United States, the Democratic Society of New York and a few other political clubs bravely maintained their existence after Washington's denunciation, while the years 1797 and 1798 witnessed what has been called a "second wave of Jeffersonian societies" and the founding of numerous branches of the American Society of United Irishmen.[38]

To be sure, militant democrats constituted a minority of French and American citizens attracted to an absolutist version of popular sovereignty. But their stridency and publicity skills intensified polarization and thus enabled them to make an impact disproportionate to their numbers.

Aggravated polarization created space for centrist rhetoric and initiatives, and into that space ventured genuine moderates as well as opportunists hoping to use the notion of a temperate middle to advance their particular political agendas. The French Directory's condemnation of both "royalists" and "anarchists" paralleled Federalists' "neither Britons nor Frenchmen, but Americans" phrase.[39] Some individuals sought to translate centrist language into action. In France, various officials advocated for concessions to moderate conservative opponents as a way to broaden support for the Directorial regime. In the United States, president-elect John Adams reached out to Thomas Jefferson and James Madison in the early months of 1797 in the hopes that a bipartisan leadership team could generate the gravitas and public backing necessary to succeed the inimitable Washington.[40]

Virtually all of the centrist political initiatives of the mid- to late 1790s failed. Spurning a conciliatory approach, a triumvirate of French Directory

---

[38] Philip S. Foner, ed., *The Democratic-Republican Societies, 1790–1800: A Documentary Sourcebook of Constitutions, Declarations, Addresses, Resolutions, and Toasts* (Westport, CN: Greenwood Press, 1976), 38; David A. Wilson, *United Irishmen, United States: Immigrant Radicals in the Early Republic* (Ithaca, NY: Cornell University Press, 1998), 43.

[39] Mason, "Thermidorian Reaction," 323; Hale, "Many Who Wandered in Darkness," 134.

[40] Joseph Ellis, *Founding Brothers: The Revolutionary Generation* (New York: Alfred A. Knopf, 2001), 179–85.

members voted, in July 1797, to remove ministers and delegates most open to compromise with conservatives. Heeding confidant Madison's advice, Jefferson spurned Adams' offer of collaboration, while Madison declined to serve as minister to France in the new administration. Earlier strategic retreats notwithstanding, the vast majority of French and American democrats determined to triumph over rather than find common ground with their partisan opponents. Centrism did not and could not constitute a foundation for political stability.

In fact, the instability was so severe in the mid- to late 1790s that extraordinary constitutional as well as blatantly extraconstitutional rhetoric and challenges surfaced both in France and in the United States. Events in the former are well-known and include democratic and royalist conspiracies, constitutional revisions and manipulations, and multiple coups d'état. Less well-known because less consequential in the end, American occurrences nevertheless entailed calls for constitutional revision along the lines of the French Directory; ethically bankrupt, last-minute proposals to change state electoral processes in order to benefit one side; fierce intrigue surrounding both the 1800 electoral college vote and the thirty-six post-electoral-college House of Representatives votes in February 1801; militia preparedness orders by two Democratic-Republican governors; frequent talk of civil war; and decades-long, retrospective discussion of the need to abolish, amend, or find alternatives to the presidency and presidential elections.[41]

Regime upheaval in the United States was more likely, in other words, than many realize. Exceptionalist paeans to Americans' penchant for compromise, constitutional genius, and distaste for political violence are thus not only unconvincing, but also misleading. Developments in the United States in the second half of the 1790s were impelled by some of the same political dynamics that drove happenings in Thermidorean and Directorial France. That the United States survived the 1790s without constitutional breakdown while France did not is more an indication that analogous transatlantic forces played out somewhat differently in distinct national contexts than evidence

---

[41] Marcus Daniel, *Scandal and Civility: Journalism and the Birth of American Democracy* (New York: Oxford University Press, 2009), 141–2; Joanne B. Freeman, "A Qualified Revolution? The Presidential Election of 1800," in Francis D. Cogliano, *A Companion to Thomas Jefferson* (Oxford: Wiley-Blackwell, 2011), 145–63; Thomas N. Baker, "'An Attack Well Directed': Aaron Burr Intrigues for the Presidency," *Journal of the Early Republic* 31 (2011), 553–98; James E. Lewis, Jr., "'What Is to Become of Our Government?': The Revolutionary Potential of the Election of 1800," in James Horn, Jan Ellen Lewis, and Peter S. Onuf, eds., *The Revolution of 1800: Democracy, Race, and the New Republic* (Charlottesville: University of Virginia Press, 2002), 3–29.

that the former was preternaturally resistant to breakdown. Poles on the same political spectrum rather than isolated points in utterly disconnected grids, the French and American polities of the mid- to late 1790s were characterized by strikingly similar struggles for stability.

Unsettling as those struggles were, they proved critical to the reconciliation of popular sovereignty through disembodied representation and its absolutist counterpart. In France, issues stemming from war and internal security predominated, necessitating a reconciliation revolving around administrative efficiency and executive power. The expansion of the French revolutionary military crusade in the half-decade after Robespierre's fall helped put to rest the politics of the Terror by providing a continuous rallying point for those drawn to a majestic projection of "the people's" sovereignty. The establishment of internal military courts and commissions, meanwhile, helped quell persistent counterrevolutionary resistance, vicious tit-for-tat violence, and an unprecedented crime wave. Both the escalation of foreign war and the introduction of internal judicial structures, moreover, instantiated democratic egalitarianism by opening up government careers to ambitious individuals excluded during the Old Regime.[42]

Because American conservatives had controlled the presidency since the first federal elections in 1788, and because issues stemming from war and internal unrest were less pressing than in France, the inchoate rapprochement in the United States between the two available versions of popular sovereignty inclined toward electoral success rather than military operations and executive control. The major occurrence, in that regard, was the invention, cooptation, or accelerated elaboration of various voluntary institutions conducive to voter mobilization. Historians have identified the creation of the Manhattan Company, the politicization of the Tammany Society, the takeover of Freemasonry, the establishment of scores of newspapers, the formation of young men's militia units, and the maturation of a national partisan organization as developments pivotal to democratic victory in the election of 1800. The last item on that list held particular significance because, in conjunction with Jefferson's burgeoning populist persona, the Democratic-Republican Party served both as an instrument to acquire power *and* as the locus of "the people's" iconic sovereignty. The rapid rise of professional campaigners and unabashedly partisan newspaper printers in

---

[42] Howard G. Brown, *Ending the French Revolution: Violence, Justice, and Repression from the Terror to Napoleon* (Charlottesville: University of Virginia Press, 2006).

the late 1790s, meanwhile, mirrored the growth of military and bureaucratic culture in France in that it instantiated democratic egalitarianism.[43]

On both sides of the Atlantic, therefore, the second half of the 1790s functioned as a temporal incubator of crucial developments in the accommodation of absolutist democracy to popular sovereignty through disembodied representation. Compared with what transpired between 1792 and 1795, the developments of the mid- to late 1790s were unflamboyant. Yet a dearth of flash was the point. Pragmatic rather than utopian, the actions of various democrats in the second half of the 1790s bridged the gap between the two available versions of popular sovereignty. The reconciliation of popular authority through disembodied representation and its absolutist counterpart in turn allowed French and American democracy to develop in all their inspirational, distressing glory.

The Early Nineteenth Century (c. 1799–1820s)

Many scholars will balk at the idea that Napoleonic France and the Jeffersonian republic are comparable vis-à-vis democracy. But if democracy is defined in terms of embodied, iconic projections of the sovereign "people's" supremacy rather than in terms of liberty-promoting norms or participatory politics, then the similarities between what happened in France and the United States on either side of the Atlantic come into view. Those similarities reflected analogous absolutist folkways even as they clarified the aforementioned political poles. Only by considering those poles in the context of practices and principles derived from monarchy can we formulate a richer understanding of democracy.

Napoleon and Jefferson were central players in the forging of modern democracy, and despite obvious differences, those two leaders and their regimes expressed similar absolutist impulses. Both Napoleon and Jefferson cultivated an intimate relationship with "the people" that channeled the

---

[43] Brian Phillips Murphy, "'A Very Convenient Instrument': The Manhattan Company, Aaron Burr, and the Election of 1800," *The William and Mary Quarterly* 65:2 (2008), 233–66; John L. Brooke, "Ancient Lodges and Self-Created Societies: Voluntary Associations and the Public Sphere in the Early Republic," in Ronald Hoffman and Peter J. Albert, eds., *Launching the "Extended Republic": The Federalist Era* (Charlottesville: University of Virginia Press, 1996), 273–377; Pasley, *The Tyranny of the Printers*, 132–228; Jeffrey A. Pasley, "'A Journeyman, Either in Law or Politics': John Beckley and the Social Origins of Political Campaigning," *Journal of the Early Republic* 16 (1996), 531–69; Albrecht Koschnik, "Let a Common Interest," 130–48; Noble E. Cunningham, Jr., *The Jeffersonian Republicans: The Formation of Party Organization, 1789–1801* (Chapel Hill: University of North Carolina Press, 1957).

longstanding popular yearning for an embodied, iconic projection of sovereignty. That yearning simultaneously generated an egalitarian emphasis on citizen sovereigns, on the twinned concepts of equality before the law and patriarchal empowerment. Patriarchal rule complemented Napoleonic and Jeffersonian efforts to reinstate or buttress slavery and to domesticate colonial subjects. Another group targeted for domestication by Napoleon and Jefferson's regimes was internal dissenters, and both Napoleon and Jefferson tactfully balanced, à la numerous early modern regents, acts of repression or marginalization and gestures of mercy and reconciliation.

The resemblances between Napoleonic France and the Jeffersonian American republic were therefore numerous and substantive. Poles on the same spectrum, the former can be characterized as a republican-tinged authoritarian regime, the latter as an authoritarian-tinged republic. Both projected authority through imperious assertions of "the people's" sovereignty. Both were democratic and absolutist.

At the heart of French and American political culture in the early nineteenth century was Napoleon and Jefferson's ability to embody "the people" in an absolutist manner. Bonaparte assumed the trappings of monarchy not because he disdained the French republic, but rather because he claimed to represent the sovereign democratic "people" more fully than formally elected officials.[44] The Sage of Monticello likewise prided himself on his identity with "'the people' whom he represented, who were the source of his authority and subject of his dreams."[45]

That the absolutist imperatives helping to animate these two democratic executives resonated with large numbers of people is indisputable. Napoleon's allies inflated his vote totals, but the plebiscites held during his rule nevertheless registered strong support.[46] Jefferson followed up his narrow 1800 presidential victory with a resounding 1804 triumph, which in turn laid the basis for electoral wins by fellow Virginians and dynastic successors James Madison (1808 and 1812) and James Monroe (1816 and 1820).

Popular support for Napoleon and Jefferson encompassed cultish veneration as well as plebiscitary and electoral approval. In the same way

---

[44] Steven Englund, *Napoleon: A Political Life* (Cambridge, MA: Harvard University Press, 2004), 247–51.
[45] Annette Gordon-Reed and Peter S. Onuf, *"Most Blessed of the Patriarchs": Thomas Jefferson and the Empire of the Imagination* (New York: W. W. Norton & Company, 2016), 40.
[46] Malcolm Crook, "The Uses of Democracy: Elections and Plebiscites in Napoleonic France," in Cross and Williams, eds., *French Experience*, 58.

numerous French citizens considered Bonaparte a Christ-like redeemer, "more a divinity than a man," so Democratic-Republicans in the United States extolled the third president as a "savior" and "deliverer" comparable to Jesus, and as their "guardian" and "protector."[47] Bolstering these democratic redeemer dynamics, artists created an array of laudatory visual images and objects.[48] To be sure, depictions of Napoleon and Jefferson differed greatly, with the former usually emphasizing grandiose military or imperial action and the latter restrained, enlightened statesmanship. Yet in their encouragement of popular adoration, they similarly disclosed an absolutist affinity for embodied, iconic projections of "the people."

Acutely conscious of their roles as exemplars of "the people's" sovereignty, Napoleon and Jefferson carefully crafted their egalitarian personas. Napoleon famously encouraged the informal *tu* form of address and reveled in the "little corporal" nickname bestowed on him by adoring soldiers. Jefferson made a point of shaping a presidential etiquette that contrasted with Washington's, replacing courtly levees with pell-mell dinners and on occasion astonishing foreign ministers and Federalists by wearing a casual robe to receive visitors. Both the Corsican general and the third American president thus cultivated an aura of familiarity; they balanced their iconicity with an informality that solicited feelings of closeness.

Those solicitations were heeded, and monarchy-evoking expressions of love for Napoleon and Jefferson abounded. It is impossible to "love too much our leader," wrote one Parisian of Napoleon in 1804, while a Trenton, New Jersey newspaper printed a series of statements beginning, "*I love Mr. Jefferson*, because . . ."[49] The prominence of *love* in expressions of approval for Napoleon and Jefferson makes clear that "the people" were animated as

---

[47] Bell, *Men on Horseback*, 129; Frank Paul Bowman, *French Romanticism: Intertextual and Interdisciplinary Readings* (Baltimore: Johns Hopkins University Press, 1990), 34–60; Philip G. Dwyer, "Napoleon Bonaparte as Hero and Savior: Image, Rhetoric and Behaviour in the Construction of a Legend," *French History* 18 (2004), 379–403; Robert M. S. McDonald, *Confounding Father: Thomas Jefferson's Image in His Own Time* (Charlottesville: University of Virginia Press, 2016), 115–18; "Enclosure: St. George Tucker's Ode to Thomas Jefferson, 20 October, 1809," https://founders.archives.gov/documents/Jefferson/03-01-02-0486-0002.

[48] Robert B. Holtman, *Napoleonic Propaganda* (Baton Rouge: Louisiana State University Press, 1950), 162; Wayne Hanley, *The Genesis of Napoleonic Propaganda* (New York: Columbia University Press, 2005), Chapters 4 and 5; McDonald, *Confounding Father*, 117–19.

[49] Philip G. Dwyer and Peter McPhee, eds., *The French Revolution and Napoleon: A Sourcebook* (London: Routledge, 2002), 154; Jeffrey L. Pasley, "Politics and the Misadventures of Thomas Jefferson's Modern Reputation: A Review Essay," *Journal of Southern History* 72:4 (2006), 876.

much by a yearning for intense experiences with iconic rulership as by rational endorsement of particular political policies. Democracy in its Napoleonic and Jeffersonian forms thus not only implicitly challenged the symbolic abstractions of popular sovereignty through disembodied representation; it also encouraged absolutist emotional ties and assigned them a constitutive role in the political order.[50] Effervescent though they were, the emotions prompted by Bonaparte and the Sage of Monticello offered a tangible, relatively sustainable way for "the people" to partake in its sovereignty.

The "people's" involvement in its sovereignty was not confined to the emotional realm, and Napoleon and Jefferson's regimes fostered a political environment oriented toward male citizen sovereigns equal before the law. The Napoleonic Code affirmed the French Revolution's abolition of privilege and feudalism at the same time that it empowered adult men to rule over wives and children.[51] Jeffersonians similarly held that male citizens were unquestionable authorities within their households as long as they obeyed laws enacted by "the people's" representatives.[52] Far from accidental, the parallels between Napoleonic and Jeffersonian conceptions of proper familial dynamics reflected the transmutation of monarchical absolutism's king-as-father-of-the-nation and father-as-king-of-the-household ideology into democracy's empowerment of citizen patriarchs.

Given the expansiveness of monarchical patriarchalism, such that servants and the enslaved were not infrequently considered part of the master's "family," it is unsurprising that democratic empowerment of male citizen sovereigns coincided with Napoleonic and Jeffersonian efforts to reestablish or bolster the institution of slavery. Soon after his ascent to power, Bonaparte unsuccessfully attempted to subjugate newly freed Saint-Dominguans and successfully reinstated chattel slavery and plantation labor in Martinique, Guadeloupe, and Guiana. Jefferson took steps to isolate Haiti and facilitated the expansion of slavery in the United States by authorizing the Louisiana Purchase. Equally importantly, the third president presided over a Democratic-Republican organization so intent on ensuring "the people's" supremacy through electoral domination of Anglophilic "aristocrats" that

---

[50] Philip G. Dwyer, "Napoleon and the Foundation of Empire," *The Historical Journal* 53:2 (2010), 354; Peter S. Onuf, *The Mind of Thomas Jefferson* (Charlottesville: University of Virginia Press, 2007), 115–18.

[51] Suzanne Desan, *The Family on Trial in Revolutionary France* (Berkeley: University of California Press, 2004).

[52] Gordon-Reed and Onuf, *"Most Blessed of the Patriarchs."*

numerous of its northern members sublimated or relinquished their antislavery beliefs, thus paving the way for Southern, slaveholding dominance of the party.[53] Democratic absolutism was not, of course, the sole factor shaping Napoleonic and Jeffersonian support for slavery. But its patriarchal dimension increased the likelihood that citizen sovereignty would embrace or accommodate itself to masters' absolute authority over enslaved "family" members.[54]

Democratic patriarchalism also informed Bonapartist and Jeffersonian efforts to domesticate colonial subjects. Familial rhetoric was integral to Napoleonic imperialism, and numerous officials and conquered groups employed the term "father" when describing Bonaparte.[55] The patriarchal element of the Empire was also embraced by the emperor himself, who sought to unify far-flung regions by drawing from early modern dynastic practices and placing close relatives in charge. Jefferson, meanwhile, addressed Native American leaders as "children" or "brothers" and referred to the heterogeneous peoples of the recently purchased Louisiana Territory as "new fellow citizens" who "are as yet as incapable of self-government as children."[56] As that paradoxical characterization of Louisianans makes clear, democratic patriarchalism simultaneously promised and undercut popular sovereignty for colonized populations. The Napoleonic and Jeffersonian regimes' commitment to self-determination ironically obligated them to reserve the right to decide when exactly an alien or subjugated group was ready to self-determine; the authority to enact citizen sovereignty was such an extraordinary privilege that failing to exclude those deemed not yet worthy of democratic supremacy would dishonor the "people."

Jealous concern for the integrity of democratic sovereignty also informed the Bonapartist and Jeffersonian administrations' approach to internal dissent. In keeping with monarchical precedents, both administrations purged,

---

[53] Padraig Riley, *Slavery and the Democratic Conscience: Political Life in Jeffersonian America* (Philadelphia: University of Pennsylvania Press, 2016).

[54] Joseph la Hausse de Lalouvière, "Enslavement, Family Law and Patriarchy in Revolutionary French Guiana," Paper for the Economic and Social History of the Early Modern World Seminar, Institute of Historical Research, 19 February 2021.

[55] Ronald Schechter, *Obstinate Jews: Representations of Jews in France, 1715–1815* (Berkeley: University of California Press, 2003), 213–15; Owen Connelly, *Napoleon's Satellite Kingdoms* (New York: The Free Press, 1965), 19; Dwyer, "Napoleon and the Foundation of Empire," 356.

[56] Peter S. Onuf, "'We Shall All Be Americans': Thomas Jefferson and the Indians," *Indiana Magazine of History* 95:2 (1999), 103–41; Philipp Ziesche, *Cosmopolitan Patriots: Americans in Paris in the Age of Revolution* (Charlottesville: University of Virginia Press, 2010), 160.

marginalized, or suppressed domestic opposition at the same time that they offered leniency and integration.

Napoleon's crackdown on Jacobin diehards and royalists is well-known and included press censorship, scrutiny of the mail, the construction and activation of an effective network of informants and spies, and imprisonment and execution. Perhaps less well known is that Bonaparte reversed some of the most severe measures of the Directory; opted for banishment rather than imprisonment and/or execution for some of those who committed treason or viciously criticized him in print; and bolstered the 1801 Concordat – the Franco-Papal pact that reduced tension by affirming both the Catholic Church's subordination to the state and its role as the majority religion – by allowing émigrés from the Revolution to return to France.[57]

Jefferson's regime is justifiably known as relatively liberal in relation to political opposition and religious freedom. The worst fears of Federalists – dechristianization and an American Reign of Terror – never materialized because those types of programs were never considered by those in power. Along the same lines, the "we are all republicans, we are all federalists" rhetorical olive branch extended by the third president in his March 1801 First Inaugural Address was immediately heralded and helped lay the foundation not only for most partisan dissenters' accession to Jeffersonian presidential authority, but also for the conversion of a few Federalists to the Democratic-Republican party.[58] Yet as Peter S. Onuf has explained, the "we are all republicans, we are all federalists" phrase was less evidence of an expansive commitment to civil liberties than a marker of an exclusionary Democratic-Republican party intent on absorbing wayward children.[59] As for Federalists who refused to be absorbed, Jefferson and his supporters evinced an inclination to suppress them or render them virtually powerless. Democratic-Republican endeavors in that regard included the establishment of the United States Military Academy partly for the purpose of shunting aside Federalist officers and recruiting loyal Jeffersonian ones; politically motivated removals from federal office; private calls to prosecute "seditious" opposition printers; passage of laws disenfranchising Blacks (and in New

---

[57] David A. Bell, *Napoleon: A Concise Biography* (New York: Oxford University Press, 2015), 53.
[58] Freeman, "A Qualified Revolution," 157–8; Robert R. Thompson, "John Quincy Adams, Apostate: From 'Outrageous Federalist' to 'Republican Exile,' 1801–1809," *Journal of the Early Republic*, 11 (1991), 161–83.
[59] Peter S. Onuf, *Jefferson's Empire: The Language of American Nationhood* (Charlottesville: University of Virginia Press, 2000), 105–8.

Jersey, property-owning women) in large part because they tended to vote against democratic politicians; and impeachments of some Federalist judges.[60]

Jefferson and many of his followers thus shared with Napoleon's regime an inability to conceptualize the legitimacy of political opposition. Democratic absolutism precluded pluralism because indivisibility was a central trait of the "people's" sovereignty, such that one of the primary tasks of the chief executive and his agents was to avenge the "majesty of the people" whenever challenged. Suppression or marginalization of dissenters was in that sense an inescapable by-product of democracy's advent. By punishing or relegating to insignificance those who transgressed the "people's" honor, Napoleonic and Jeffersonian enthusiasts helped constitute "the people" as supreme, as worthy of distinction enforcement.

In various ways, then, the Napoleonic and Jeffersonian regimes resembled each other. Franco-American resemblances in the early nineteenth century did not stem either from a common history or from pervasive French imperial influence. Rather, they derived from longstanding, parallel absolutist impulses that found new, democratic life after coming to terms with disembodied representation.

The Jeffersonian settlement was undoubtedly more stable than the Napoleonic one, in large part because the latter was so utterly dependent on war and a single personality. Napoleon's defeats and downfalls of 1814–1815 yielded the return of royalty and frequent swings between republicanism and monarchism. While the United States continues to operate under the Constitution that received a major boost simply by surviving the crisis of 1800–1801, France failed, until the twentieth century, to resolve fully the tension between popular authority via disembodied representation and its democratic counterpart.

Even so, perfunctory depictions of American stability and French instability obscure important convergences. Spared regime change as well as warfare

---

[60] Theodore J. Crackel, *Mr. Jefferson's Army: Political and Social Reform of the Military Establishment, 1801–1809* (New York: New York University Press, 1987); Carl E. Prince, "The Passing of the Aristocracy: Jefferson's Removal of the Federalists, 1801–1805," *Journal of American History* 57 (1970), 563–75; Leonard W. Levy, *Jefferson and Civil Liberties: The Darker Side* (Chicago: Ivan R. Dee, 1989 [1963]); Alexander Keyssar, *The Right to Vote: The Contested History of Democracy in the United States* (New York: Basic Books, 2000), 56; Alan Taylor, *American Revolutions: A Continental History, 1750–1804* (New York: W. W. Norton & Company, 2016), 455; Richard Ellis, *The Jeffersonian Crisis: Courts and Politics in the Young Republic* (New York: W. W. Norton & Company, 1971).

on the scale of Austerlitz, many residents of the early United States nevertheless found Napoleonic military conflict and political culture enthralling. That enthrallment played a role in the coming of the War of 1812 as well as in subsequent American martial engagements with various Native American groups, internal regional foes, and foreign nations. Equally importantly, it animated and reflected the rise of both the American leader, Andrew Jackson, most similar to Napoleon and the Jacksonian iteration of the Jeffersonian partisan organization birthed in the 1790s. In the person and democratic party of the authoritarian, Bonaparte-idolizing Tennessee general, the United States fulfilled its absolutist destiny.[61]

[61] Matthew Rainbow Hale, "For the Love of Glory: Napoleonic Imperatives in the Early American Republic," in Nicole Eustace and Fredrika J. Teute, eds., *Warring for America: Cultural Contests for America in the Era of 1812* (Chapel Hill: University of North Carolina Press, 2017), 205–49.

6

The French Revolution and Spanish America

CLÉMENT THIBAUD

Introduction

For the nations that emerged from the disintegration of the Spanish Empire, the relationship between the French Revolution and their respective independence movements raises key questions of historical memory. This connection can be traced back to the origins of these states, which, during the period of their emancipation in the 1820s, stretched from modern-day Oregon to the tip of Chile. Indeed, Napoleon's invasion of Portugal and Spain (1807–1808) triggered a sequence of unpredictable events that paved the way for the liberation of this continent. France's aggression was seen at the time, beyond military conquest, as a symptom of its revolution, the mantle of which Napoleon had, willingly or not, taken up. Nineteenth-century Latin American historians and writers were convinced that the "Great Revolution" was the decisive factor in the birth of ten new South American republics between 1810 and 1825. Whether they were for or against, these authors did not doubt the link between their nations' independence and the ideological shock and surge in popular sovereignty produced by the Declaration of 1789.[1] Until the First World War, France continued to represent a political and cultural "second homeland," a rallying point both for the Spanish American elites and for a significant part of the nascent workers' movement.[2] Accordingly, the bicentenary of the French Revolution was cause for numerous exhibitions and publications that emphasized the significance of 1789 in Latin America.[3]

---

[1] José María Samper, *Ensayo sobre las revoluciones políticas y la condicion social de las repúblicas colombianas (hispano-americanas)* (Paris: Thunot, 1861), 139.

[2] Nicola Miller, *In the Shadow of the State: Intellectuals and the Quest for National Identity in Twentieth-Century Spanish America* (London: Verso, 1999).

[3] François-Xavier Guerra and Maria Victoria Lopez-Cordon, *La Révolution française, la Péninsule ibérique et l'Amérique latine* (Paris: BDIC, 1989); Solange Alberro, Alicia

Today, this evidence has crumbled. During the 1990s, the creation of the Spanish American nations was completely rethought, driven by François-Xavier Guerra and Jaime Rodríguez O.[4] The effects of the 1808 crisis and the influence of the Cortes of Cádiz (1810–1814) placed the Spanish American revolutions within a wider context of *Hispanic* revolutions, in which Spain played a key role. Today, the rupture between Madrid and the Americas is considered from an *imperial* rather than a *transatlantic* perspective. The "Gaditan shift" has displaced the view of the French Revolution as both trigger and model for the Hispanic independence movements, a leading light for the new republics. Today, there is little impetus to revisit the relationship between the French Revolution – to which we might add the Haitian Revolution and the events in the French Caribbean of the 1790s – and the liberation of Spanish America.

From another, more methodological point of view, political history has matured in its conceptions of revolutionary trajectories, with more nuanced approaches in regard to their center and periphery, dismissing notions of model or influence and their associated metaphors ("contagion," "winds of change"). These trends in global history have thus challenged the diffusionist perspective of a "North Atlantic" revolution that gradually spread south. Today, Saint-Domingue and Haitian independence are considered more relevant than the French Revolution in examining the link between the revolutions in the region,[5] because of the centrality of the shared colonial experience in the extended context of the construction of the first European empires.[6]

Thus, this historiographical evolution undid the French Revolution's role in Spanish American emancipation in two ways: by exposing the teleological link between the two events, and by underlining the French Caribbean's significance in the process. This allows us to rethink the Franco-Hispanic link and, by extension, the Atlantic revolutionary cycle, by reformulating two

---

Hernández Chávez, and Elías Trabulse, eds., *La revolución francesa en México* (Mexico City: El Colegio de México, 1993).

[4] François-Xavier Guerra, *Modernidad e independencies: Ensayos sobre las revoluciones hispánicas* (Madrid: MAPFRE, 1992); Jaime E. Rodríguez O., *The Independence of Spanish America* (New York: Cambridge University Press, 1998).

[5] María Dolores González Ripoll, Consuelo Naranjo, Ada Ferrer, Gloria García Rodríguez, and Josef Opatrný, *El rumor de Haití en Cuba: Temor, raza y rebeldía, 1789–1844* (Madrid: CSIC, 2005); Alejandro E. Gómez Pernía, *Le spectre de la révolution noire: L'impact de la révolution haïtienne dans le monde atlantique, 1790–1886* (Rennes: Presses universitaires de Rennes, 2013).

[6] Jeremy Adelman, "An Age of Imperial Revolutions," *The American Historical Review* 113:2 (2008), 319–40.

classic questions. First, we should reevaluate the revolutions in France and Saint-Domingue in terms of their impact on Spanish American events, rather than direct causation. Second, we should analyze how events in France – that is, the empire as a whole – were appropriated by independence actors; to paraphrase Jean-Joseph Mounier, it was not the influence of French principles that triggered the Spanish American revolutions, but rather the latter that created this influence.[7]

Our analysis is structured around two contrasting propositions. First, neither the French Revolution, nor the (similar yet separate) Haitian Revolution, *caused* the liberation of Spanish America. Second, it is equally impossible to limit the explanation for these phenomena to the effects of the Cádiz Constitution, without considering cultural movements and underground politicization processes related to earlier revolutions, including, to a certain extent, those of France and the French Caribbean. A shared imperial and colonial dimension encouraged forms of identification among the Spanish Crown's American territories. This perspective requires us to step back and review Franco-Hispanic political relations, and so subdue the notion of an inevitable march toward independence, or an unstoppable "tide" from a Francophone center to a passive Hispanic periphery, through a comparative history of the French and Spanish American revolutions, analyzing the circulation of people and ideas as well as disconnections and rejections. Such a perspective is based on a polycentric view of these circulations, which favors local sources on the ground over emissary communications, and on the idea that the revolutionary experience was forged from multiple centers. We will also look beyond a traditional history of ideas to explore social mediations of ideology, such as political or religious organizations, clubs, associations, etc.[8] We will look closely at the chronology of events, with its upswings of support and opposition. The aim is to deconstruct the monolith of the French Revolution as nineteenth-century liberals conceived it, to distinguish its various phases, from radical, moderate, and conservative to reactionary – if we include the first Consul's decision in 1802 to reestablish the pre-1789 colonial situation. Finally, we must distinguish between the different phases of the Hispanic revolutions: some radical periods drew on

---

[7] Jean-Joseph Mounier, *De l'influence attribuée aux philosophes, aux francs-maçons et aux illuminés sur la révolution de France* (Paris: Ponthieu, 1822), 108.

[8] François-Xavier Guerra and Annick Lempérière, eds., *Los espacios públicos en Iberoamérica: Ambigüedades y problemas, siglos XVIII y XIX* (Mexico City: FCE, 1998); Pablo Piccato, "Public Sphere in Latin America: A Map of the Historiography," *Social History* 35:2 (2010), 165–92.

the Haitian precedent; others favored the moderation of the French Directory, or even the conservatism of the Consulate or the Empire; while most of Spanish America remained royalist and rejected these forms outright. This complex situation was also reflected in society, given the diversity of local contexts and configurations of identity.

The Basis for an Entangled History of Empires and Revolutions

During their independence struggles, revolutionary leaders, including Bolívar in Venezuela, San Martín in Río de la Plata, O'Higgins in Chile, and Morelos in Mexico, sought to frame their actions in the context of the great political transformations of the western hemisphere, from the Thirteen Colonies to 1789 and the unprecedented political legacy it left in France, the Caribbean, and Europe. Inheriting the diverse experiences that had shaken the British and French empires, the Spanish American revolutions were eventually triggered by Spain's crushing defeat by Napoleonic forces, and the abdication of the monarchy in favor of the emperor at Bayonne, then his brother Joseph in May 1808. Although independence remained the project of a small minority in Spanish America, patriots established strong links in their political imagination with the revolutions in France and Saint-Domingue. Let us start by outlining the context of this formative alignment.

The first cause appears self-evident: the invasion of Spain by "Robespierre on horseback" (this expression was used in counterrevolutionary circles after 1814, before eventually being borrowed by Germaine de Staël and the Coppet group) cast a spotlight on France and the events occurring there over the previous twenty years. Yet there are earlier, medium-term factors to consider. The French language, widely spoken among Hispanic elites, was a gateway to a pantheon of ideas: ecclesiastical history, literature, and science rubbed shoulders with Enlightenment thinkers (as we think of them now), such as Montesquieu, Rousseau, and Raynal,[9] despite constraints on the distribution of printed material. The Holy Office, the royal censor, and the "judge of the library" (a post established in 1785) prohibited most Enlightenment texts, particularly those in French and reputed to attack religion. These institutions were not always effective, and a royal order (of 22 May 1795) was required to ensure necessary precautions against the

---

[9] Gabriel Entin, ed., *Rousseau en Iberoamérica: Del reformismo borbónico a las revoluciones de independencia* (Mexico City: UNAM, 2017).

"detestable and pernicious maxims of misunderstood liberty"[10] and curb the spread of "seditious writings." As such, the public sphere remained limited to a few small circles, although negative reactions to the expulsion of the Jesuits had provided it with a thin foundation in New Spain as early as 1767.[11] Compared with the Thirteen Colonies, there were few newspapers, limited to large urban centres like Mexico City, Bogotá, Lima, or Buenos Aires, with only a few thousand copies in circulation at most. (Sales – not necessarily numbers of active readers – were *Diario de México*, 7 November 1811: 7,000 copies; *El Mercurio peruano* (1790) of Lima: 517 subscribers; *Papel periódico de la Nueva Granada* (1791–1796): 144 subscribers.) Active readership was more or less restricted to the great ruling families. Literacy levels among the popular classes were generally very low, although increasing by the end of the colonial era.[12] And there were natural obstacles too: materials were carried over vast distances on muleback, for example between Buenos Aires and modern-day Sucre, while termites (*comején*) flourished in Cartagena's tropical climate.[13]

Within these constraints, informal social groups gathered in large cities to discuss new ideas. A far cry from the salons of Europe, these were relaxed, friendly affairs, *tertulias*. Cafés became a common sight, while the *pulpero*, a grocer-cum-tavern, was a hub for popular political activities. In the various institutions established during the enlightened reforms of Carlos III and Carlos IV, such as trade consulates or law academies, the landed, commercial, and mining elites gathered to read the works of the Enlightenment. Practical men, dreaming of colonial reform,[14] found themselves exposed to physiocracy, the French and Scottish economists like Quesnay, Turgot, and

---

[10] Lucienne Domergue, *La censure des livres en Espagne à la fin de l'ancien régime* (Madrid: Casa de Velázquez, 1996), 37; Richard Herr, *España y la revolución del siglo XVIII* (Madrid: Aguilar, 1990), 210ff.

[11] Gabriel Torres Puga, *Opinión pública y censura en Nueva España: Indicios de un silencio imposible (1767–1794)* (Mexico City: El Colegio de México, 2010).

[12] Cristina Soriano, *Tides of Revolution: Information and Political Mobilization in Venezuela, 1789–1810* (Albuquerque: New Mexico University Press, 2018), 170.

[13] Renán Silva, *Los ilustrados de Nueva Granada, 1760–1808: Genealogía de una comunidad de interpretación* (Medellín: Banco de la República, EAFIT, 2002), 270–2.

[14] Gabriel B. Paquette, *Enlightenment, Governance and Reform in Spain and Its Empire 1759–1808* (Basingstoke: Palgrave Macmillan, 2008). On fiscal reform, see John Fisher, *Imperial "Free trade" and the Hispanic Economy* (Cambridge: Cambridge University Press, 1981); Arnaud Bartolomei, "L'impact des indépendances américaines sur le commerce de Cadix dans la première moitié du XIXe siècle," in Xavier Huetz de Lemps and Jean-Philippe Luis, eds., *Sortir du labyrinthe: Études d'histoire contemporaine de l'Espagne* (Madrid: Casa de Velázquez, 2012), 241–74.

Smith, Neapolitans like Filangieri, Genovesi, and Galiani,[15] and even the rich voices of reform coming out of Spain such as those of Ward, Gálvez, Campomanes, and Jovellanos.[16] Many future revolutionaries were members of these institutions established after the Seven Years' War, including Manuel Belgrano from the Río de la Plata, who was a proponent of physiocracy. The discussions among them in no way envisaged secession from Spain, but rather a return to past greatness and better representation of creole interests in Madrid.

Here, we find one of the main reasons for the relative ease with which the French Revolution's cultural references spread in Spanish America from the 1790s: the two monarchies faced the same problems, which were related to the economic, military, and religious reforms introduced in these imperial states after their common defeat by the British in the Seven Years' War. Reform had been a key concern of the Spanish monarchy since the accession of the Bourbons, backed by unambiguous reports about its political and economic limitations compared with its British and French rivals.[17] Many elites found inspiration in the writings of the Enlightenment. Carlos III's far-reaching reforms had sought to adapt the Empire's administrative, economic, and military frameworks to the constraints imposed by inter-imperial rivalries. One guiding principle proposed by "enlightened" ministers was the shift from a "conquering empire" to a commercial *emporium*. Once coequal kingdoms within the Spanish Crown, the Indies would be reduced to the status of colonies. Many creoles criticized these initiatives, which saw them reduced to mere subjects of the empire, seeking instead a monarchy of equal European, American, and Asian parts.[18] This discontent also spread to popular, indigenous, and mestizo groups, with opposition to fiscal reforms triggering revolts in Cuzco, La Paz, and New Granada.[19] This broad spectrum of political expectations, which varied according to region and social

---

[15] Geneviève Verdo, Federica Morelli, and Elodie Richard, eds., *Entre Nápoles y América: Ilustración y cultura jurídica en el mundo hispánico (siglos XVIII y XIX)* (Medellín: La Carreta Editores, IFEA, 2012).

[16] Jesús Astigarraga and Javier Usoz, eds., *L'économie politique et la sphère publique dans le débat des Lumières* (Madrid: Casa de Velázquez, 2013).

[17] Bernardo Ward, *Proyecto económico: En que se proponen varias providencias, dirigidas a promover los intereses de España con los medios y fondos necesarios para su planificación* (Madrid: D. Joachin Ibarra, 1779).

[18] Francisco Ortega, "Ni nación ni parte integral. 'Colonia,' de vocablo a concepto en el siglo XVIII iberoamericano," *Prismas* 15:1 (2011), 11–29.

[19] On the links between these rebellions and the independence movements, see Brian R. Hamnett, *The End of Iberian Rule on the American Continent, 1770–1830* (Cambridge: Cambridge University Press, 2017), Chapter 2.

group, determined how the radical changes wrought by the French Revolution and Haitian independence were later received.

Other factors pertaining to dynastic, diplomatic, and economic history serve to explain specific aspects of the Franco-Spanish link. France had enjoyed durable commercial ties with Spanish America since the seventeenth century, with a strong presence of its merchants in the port of Cádiz, the commercial gateway to the Americas.[20] With the accession of Louis XIV's grandson, Philip of Anjou, to the Spanish throne, the two monarchies found themselves allied against common enemies. During the eighteenth century, three Family Compacts served to consolidate this alliance, the last being sealed during the American Revolution. Yet the French monarchy played an ambiguous game with Spain, seeking to subsume the latter into its foreign policy to form a united front against British dominance. As such, Spain's colonies were viewed with envy from across the Pyrenees, which was still the case during the French Revolution, when the Girondin Jacques-Pierre Brissot dreamed of seizing Spanish America,[21] while Napoleon, with his invasion of Spain, resumed his nation's old conquering ambitions, which had previously been hampered by British vigilance.

On a larger geographic scale, the potential for mutual exchange, whether violent or peaceful, was increased by the war, and then the alliance, between the two empires. Spanish policy toward revolutionary France evolved, changing from muted opposition to armed conflict, then alliance under Godoy, before descending into warfare once more from 1808. The 1793–1795 War of the Convention involved significant mobilization of Spanish American elites, who were called on to contribute to a ruinous conflict. Navies, line regiments, and militias saw action around the Gulf of Mexico and beyond. Spain, for reasons more strategic than abolitionist, supported the insurgents in Saint-Domingue, going so far as to recruit them into its armies.[22] Yet, the French Wars were inextricably imperial and ideological in nature, a twenty-year struggle between two irreconcilable world views that fanned the flames of politicization. Thus, the French governor of Guadeloupe, Victor Hugues, invoked the "arms of liberty" to

---

[20] Arnaud Bartolomei, *Les marchands français de Cadix et la crise de la Carrera de Indias (1778–1828)* (Madrid: Casa de Velázquez, 2017).

[21] Marcel Dorigny, "Brissot et Miranda en 1792, ou comment révolutionner l'Amérique espagnole?," in M. Dorigny and M.-J. Rossignol, eds., *La France et les Amériques au temps de Jefferson et de Miranda* (Paris: Société des Études Robespierristes, 2001), 93–105.

[22] Jorge Victoria Ojeda, *Tendencias monárquicas en la revolución haitiana: El negro Juan Francisco Petecou bajo las banderas francesa y española* (Mexico City: Siglo XXI, 2005).

destabilize both British and Spanish territories in the Caribbean: liberty for slaves, equality for free people of color, self-rule for the elites. His fleets of privateers, using Spanish American ports as a foothold, were a great strain on British trade in the region. The presence of French crews in allied ports embodied the shifting state of the world, as Alexander von Humboldt observed in the port of Cumaná in 1800:

> The arrival of so great a number of military Frenchmen, and the manifestation of political and religious opinions, that were not altogether conformable to those by which mother-countries think to confirm their authority, excited a singular agitation in the population of Cumaná. In the streets the mulattoes crowded round the agent of the Directory, whose dress was rich and theatrical ... men with a white skin inquired also with indiscreet curiosity ... concerning the degree of influence granted by the republic to the planters in the government of Guadeloupe ...[23]

It was no coincidence that, after 1810, the first patriot ships of Mexico, Río de la Plata, and New Granada were made up of Franco-Caribbean officers, corsairs, and sailors who had lived through the greatest moments of the French and Haitian revolutions.[24]

The numerous changes in sovereignty in the region after the Seven Years' War created a network of exiles and refugees across the empires. Following the British conquest of Grenada in 1762, Trinidad and eastern Venezuela were authorized to accommodate French migrants. As Spanish minister Floridablanca encouraged an "enlightened" project that involved francophone colonization, contingents of political refugees from the French Caribbean settled in Trinidad later during the Revolution, their presence facilitating the distribution and translation of information.[25] The uprising in Saint-Domingue, civil war between royalists and patriots in the French Caribbean, and the fall of Santo Domingo to Toussaint Louverture saw many French and Spanish exiles flee to Cuba, Puerto Rico, New Spain, New Granada, and Venezuela. Ceded

[23] Alexandre de Humboldt, *Voyage aux régions équinoxiales du nouveau continent* (Paris: J. Smith, 1825), vol. IX, 46.
[24] Johanna von Grafenstein, *Nueva España en el Circuncaribe, 1779–1808: Revolución, competencia imperial y vínculos intercoloniales* (Mexico City: UNAM, 1997); Nicolas Terrien, *Des patriotes sans patrie: Histoire des corsaires insurgés de l'Amérique espagnole* (Mordelles: Les Perséides, 2015); Edgardo Pérez Morales, *No Limits to Their Sway: Cartagena's Privateers and the Masterless Caribbean in the Age of Revolutions* (Nashville: Vanderbilt University Press, 2018).
[25] Frédéric Spillemaeker, "Quand les cocardes étaient marronnes: La Trinité espagnole en révolution," *Monde(s)* 2 (2017), 221–37; Nikolaus Böttcher, "Neptune's Trident: Trinidad, 1776–1840. From Colonial Backyard to Crown Colony," *Jahrbuch für Geschichte Lateinamerikas* 44:1 (2007), 157–85.

to Spain after the Seven Years' War, then restored to France at the Treaty of Amiens in 1801, Louisiana eventually became home to many of them.[26] During the Revolution and after the Restoration, thousands of political exiles, often of French origin, together with migrants from Béarn and the French Basque Country (in Buenos Aires and Montevideo for example), helped spread revolutionary – or counterrevolutionary – experiences, symbols, and ideas throughout the Spanish-speaking world. Yet French-speaking minorities were not the only vectors for revolutionary politicization. The transition of Curaçao to the Batavian Republic, sister republic to France, was marked by civil conflicts between stadtholderians and patriots. In this context, the island produced and received many republican texts that then found their way to the Venezuelan mainland a short distance away.

These facts highlight a key aspect of Franco-Hispanic interactions: the centrality of the Caribbean as a space of political mediation and cultural movement as well as new ideas and actions. This transimperial hub, with its tangled sovereignties, represented the main gateway for revolutionary experiences entering the Americas.[27] But, crucially, the region also demonstrated how a revolution could transform a colonial empire. For Spanish America, the Haitian Revolution – inseparable, yet distinct from its French counterpart – adapted revolutionary repertoires of liberty and equality to specific elements of its colonial reality such as slavery, a fact that shaped the impact of French events on these Spanish colonies.

The Rights of Man in Spanish America

From the start, the French Revolution earned the discreet condemnation of monarchical and ecclesiastical authorities, who preferred not to draw attention to the event with overt criticism,[28] yet remained vigilant for any signs of approval among the population, particularly in New Spain. Surveillance decreased in 1794–1795, before increasing again after 1796.[29] Floridablanca

---

[26] Alain Yacou, "L'expulsion des Français de Saint-Domingue réfugiés dans la région orientale de l'île de Cuba (1808–1810)," *Cahiers du monde hispanique et luso-brésilien* 39 (1982), 49–64.

[27] This is emphasized by Michael Zeuske, "The French Revolution in Spanish America," in Alan Forrest and Matthias Middell, eds., *The Routledge Companion to the French Revolution in World History* (London: Routledge, 2015), 91–110.

[28] Carlos Herrejón Peredo, "La Revolución francesa en sermones y otros testimonios, 1791–1793," in Alberro et al., eds., *La revolución francesa en México*, 97–110: 98.

[29] Cristina Gómez Alvarez and Guillermo Tovar de Teresa, *Censura y revolución: Libros prohibidos por la Inquisición de México (1790–1819)* (Mexico City: Trama Editorial, 2009), 41.

sought to establish strict control over news from France, even prohibiting, in February 1791, the publication of all periodicals except the *Diario de Madrid* and two official journals. The religious and royal propaganda machine during this period failed to stifle a rising wave of counter-information that attested to the great interest in French events. Following the execution of Louis XVI, a close relative of the Spanish monarch, anxiety among the Spanish American authorities turned to fear, inaction to political containment. This act was particularly abhorrent to moderate Spaniards: a parricidal nation building a republic on the corpse of a king related to their own. The guillotine anchored itself in the popular imagination, an all-encompassing symbol of revolutionary excess, according to the *Gaceta de Lima* at least.[30] The revolution had clearly become a threat to the core principles of monarchy and religion. A few weeks after the king's execution, war with France gave hope of a just retribution brought by Spain, once more the instrument of Divine Providence. Paradoxically, however, the conflict served to spread awareness of the revolution. Across the Spanish Empire, subjects were asked to contribute to the Royal Treasury (*donativos*) to finance the war. This campaign was led by the Church, which called on the clergy, from the highest bishops to the lowliest clerics, to rally the faithful to the cause. Meanwhile, municipal authorities ensured that the *bandos* were published everywhere, down to the most isolated Andean villages. The lists of donors included the names of great local families, citing the amount given in service of king and country. Fiery sermons against the sacrilegious enemy were read out from pulpits by priests from New Spain to Peru. The fledgling press enthusiastically printed – often well-informed – articles on the Réveillon riots (bloody riots in Paris in April 1789 that are considered the first great popular insurrection during the French Revolution), the queen's execution, the *sans-culottes*, and Robespierre.

While the general spirit of the time appeared to reflect the profession of royalist faith, other signs point to discordant voices surreptitiously challenging the validity of the war against France and its revolution. The most obvious sign of dissent took the form of anonymous graffiti under cover of darkness. On 24 August 1794, the anniversary of the Declaration of the Rights of Man, seditious statements were scrawled in one of Mexico City's busiest streets, claiming, among other follies, that: "there are none more astute than the French ... No matter what the Law may do, it can never stifle the inspired cries of Nature." In New Spain, alongside a few exalted

---

[30] Claudia Rosas Lauro, *Del trono a la guillotina: El impacto de la Revolución Francesa en el Perú (1789–1808)* (Lima: PUCP, 2013), 45ff.

Frenchmen such as Jean Durrey or the Montpellier doctor Maurel,[31] the Mexico City seminary became a center for the spread of new ideas; some of its students were reported and arrested for reading the *Encyclopédistes*. Above all, the Revolution interested proponents of the Enlightenment and monarchical reform.[32] Faced with this threat, the viceroy, the Marquis de Branciforte, sought the expulsion of all French individuals to limit the "contagion," as the authorities had begun to call it.

Despite the rejection of the revolution's "monstrosities," it is also important to understand how the event aroused interest beyond the elites. For obvious reasons, there is little documentary evidence as to the sources of such interest, leading us to extrapolate from cases where it is apparent. We limit ourselves to two examples that showcase very different socioracial identities: free people of color and slaves from the Venezuelan coast, and Antonio Nariño, a member of the Bogotá elite.

The first case relates to the arrival in Venezuela, in September 1793, of a large contingent of "republican" prisoners, captured in Saint-Domingue by Spanish forces. Sources describe them as slaves, mulattoes, and whites, though it is unclear in which proportion.[33] The 1,500 captives represented a significant group for a small port like La Guaira that had around 2,000 inhabitants at most. Such was the fear they instilled that Venezuela's Captain-General called an extraordinary meeting of the civil, military, and religious authorities in response to their presence. They discussed the notable effect of these prisoners of war and their revolutionary symbols on the free and enslaved blacks and people of color, speaking openly and freely as they did with their jailers and other locals. Inaccurate translations and word of mouth must have played a significant part in spreading rumor, the crucial politicizing vector in illiterate or semiliterate societies.[34] The colonial authorities drew up a list of the *alteraciones* caused by the "prisoners of La Guaira [who] demonstrate a continual disregard for all limits of modesty, blaspheming against all things sacred, cursing our government, claiming at all times to be Free Men." Two local slaves were said to have mentioned their imminent freedom, "like those of Saint-Domingue," while kneading bread. The blacks

---

[31] Liliana Schifter, Patricia Aceves, and Patrice Bret, "L'inquisition face aux Lumières et à la révolution française en Nouvelle-Espagne. Le dossier et le procès d'Esteban Morel (1781–1795)," *Annales historiques de la Révolution française* 365 (2011), 103–27.

[32] Frédérique Langue, "Les Français en Nouvelle-Espagne à la fin du XVIIIe siècle. Médiateurs de la révolution ou nouveaux créoles?," *Caravelle* 54 (1990), 37–60: 47–8.

[33] Archivo General de Simancas (AGS), SGU, t. 7159, doc. 3-17, f. 1v.

[34] Soriano, *Tides of Revolution*, 80, on rumor, citing Ranajit Guha, *Elementary Aspects of Peasant Insurgency in Colonial India* (Durham, NC: Duke University Press, 1999), 251.

of the Aragua valleys reportedly used "obscure expressions, alluding to the same fantasies of equality and liberty that the prisoners were professing." One "free black or mulatto woman" allegedly told her mistress that "there was no more difference between them than color, and that in all other things they were the same."[35] Naturally, these words belonged to an older local history, whereby, through various actions, free people of color demanded their place in the Republic of Spaniards. But it is not an exaggeration to see here a turning point, precipitated by the presence of the Saint-Domingue prisoners. No longer did one wait on the grace of kings or masters; now was the time to demand the same freedom and equality that nature had afforded all men.

The other significant event that shook New Granada was the first printed translation of the 1789 Declaration of the Rights of Man and of the Citizen, striking at the heart of the Bogotá elite, since the main actor, Antonio Nariño, had been the city's *alcalde*, a provincial judge and tithe collector. He also belonged to three literary societies or *tertulias*, two of them secret. He was responsible for translating the Declaration. This reflects the colonies' "advance" on Spain, such was the importance of questions of liberty and equality in America. This event took place in 1794 at the same time as anonymous lampoons criticizing the viceroy's government were going up in Bogotá, Cartagena, Tunja, Quito, and Cuenca.[36] These disruptions to public order led to three separate trials, and Nariño was arrested alongside several other prominent individuals in the city. It was no longer just slaves and free people of color being affected by the "foul ideas" coming out of France; so too were the elite families on whom the local government depended.[37] Readership was ruthlessly suppressed, with those accused imprisoned or exiled after a patient, meticulous judicial process that rooted out the least sign of political contamination. Nariño's trial thus marks a shift in Madrid's political containment strategy designed to prevent the spread of the French contagion. It was no longer enough to demand silence; what mattered now was to counter the threat with strict surveillance and a show of repression.

On reading the papers from Nariño's trial, several things become clear, no doubt applicable to Spanish America as a whole. Nariño was no radical.

---

[35] AGS, SGU, t. 7202, 2 (8), fol. 1–2, *Junta de las autoridades* de Caracas, 2 November 1793.
[36] Georges Lomné, "1794, ou l'année de la 'sourde rumeur', la faillite de l'absolutisme éclairé dans la vice-royauté de Nouvelle-Grenade," *Annales historiques de la Révolution française* 365 (2011), 9–29.
[37] Juana M. Marín, *Gente decente: La élite rectora de la capital, 1797–1803* (Bogotá: ICANH, 2008).

Although he possessed a few illicit texts, including Baron d'Holbach's *Éthocratie*, his aim was to reform the Spanish Empire rather than undermine it. During the trial, he argued that modern natural law, of which the 1789 Declaration was but one expression, existed in Spanish jurisprudence.[38] Indeed, the recognition of "natural rights" in the civil code functioned as a remedy against political and commercial "despotism." While his analysis could have been perceived as highly revolutionary, in reality, Nariño advocated a reforming ambition in line with changes previously introduced by the last Spanish Bourbons. In the spirit of the creoles who invoked them, the Rights of Man gave weight to the implicit demand for a constitutionalized monarchy (a recurrent demand in Spain since the 1780s).[39] As such, Nariño and Bogotá's intellectual elite were less admirers of the French Revolution than prominent individuals seeking solutions to what they saw as the growing disparities between the American and European parts of the monarchy, and to Spanish "decadence." It should be noted, however, that Nariño, sent to Spain in captivity, successfully escaped to France and Britain, returning later to his native land armed with copies of the *Social Contract* and the French Constitution of the Year III, with a view to rousing his people.[40]

The examples of La Guaira and Bogotá demonstrate how the symbols of the French Revolution were reappropriated by various actors according to their respective interests and cultures, enough to worry the colonial authorities. Time and again, we see the Rights of Man invoked to justify comparisons with events in France, in a number of different ways, though always in rejection of the inequality between metropole and colonies. Free people of color in La Guaira demanded equality for themselves and liberty for slaves. Antonio Nariño, as a member of the elite, emulating the "Freeborn Englishmen" of the Thirteen Colonies or the whites of Saint-Domingue, sought to constitutionalize his province of New Granada, demonstrated by his desire to translate the 1789 Declaration to guarantee the rights of his homeland within the Spanish Nation, that is, the monarchy as a whole. This nascent politicization explains why some regions (New Granada, Venezuela) pursued autonomy early on, then later independence, while others (New Spain, Peru) remained loyal to the king. This also cemented the bridge of ideas between the Spanish American world and transatlantic revolutionary processes.

---

[38] *Archivo Nariño* (Bogotá: Presidencia de la República, 1990), vol. II, 11ff.
[39] José María Portillo, *Revolución de nación. Orígenes de la cultura constitucional en España, 1780-1812* (Madrid: CEPC, 2000).
[40] *Archivo Nariño*, vol. II, 162.

Conspiracies, *"negros franceses,"* and *"papeles sediciosos"*

The 1795 Peace of Basel between republican France and the Spanish Crown heralded a reversal of alliances in which Madrid would join the French Directory in its war against "the Englishman." This unnatural yoke, sought by Charles IV's prime minister Godoy, strengthened concerns about revolutionary contagion while encouraging a broad spectrum of seditious events influenced by France and Saint-Domingue, some minor, some more seriously disruptive. The categories defined by colonial authorities are revealing of the scale of the threat perceived, particularly under the Directory. They sought out *papeles sediciosos* (seditious texts) and feared *negros franceses* (French Blacks) sewing *conspiraciones* and *alteraciones*. The prevailing siege mentality was only reinforced by the victorious slave revolt in Saint-Domingue and the abolition of slavery there in 1793–1794.

In terms of "seditious texts," a handwritten translation of an antimonarchical pamphlet by Robespierre, published in France in December 1793 and seized in Caracas in April 1794 from pardo militias, had not troubled the authorities.[41] This changed after Antonio Nariño's trial, as demonstrated by the Gual and España conspiracy, notable for its unambiguous connection with the texts of the Montagnard Convention. So called in Venezuelan historiography, it refers to the network of conspirators who sought to change the form of government in Spain. Foiled in 1797, it remains significant as one of the few republican movements against the Spanish Crown, all the more threatening in a region witnessing a sudden and unprecedented number of kingless states: from 1796, Curaçao and the other Dutch islands were part of the Batavian Republic; US merchant ships began to dock after trade was opened to neutral powers in 1797; the Republic of Haiti was pronounced in the south of Hispaniola in 1804. The affair began in Caracas on 11 July 1797 when Manuel Montesinos y Rico, a wealthy Catalan merchant and *hacendado*, tried to convince mulatto militiaman Juan José Chirinos to rouse the pardo battalion against the government. Frightened, Chirinos reported him. Among the plotters' papers, officials discovered plans to arm the citizens and establish provisional local-level governing juntas. Some documents called for an end to slavery, indigenous tribute, racial classes, the colonial pact, and monopolies, and the creation of a "free and independent

---

[41] "Capitan general de Caracas sobre introducción de papel sedicioso," Archivo General de Indias (AGI), Estado, t. 65, 20, fol. 9.

Republic,"⁴² including translations, albeit uncited, from the revolutionary texts of the Montagnard Convention. Victor Hugues, the administrator of Guadeloupe, authorized one fleeing conspirator, Picornell, to print a booklet entitled *Derechos del Hombre*⁴³ containing an American Carmagnole (the Carmagnole was a French revolutionary song that was born when the monarchy fell on 10 August 1792) and a translation of the French Declaration of the Rights of Man of 1793.

Authorities grew alarmed as the true extent of the conspiracy became apparent in the course of the hearings. The plot involved more than 100 individuals from La Guaira, Caracas, and beyond, of all social and racial backgrounds. A list from 8 August 1797 contained the names of 113 suspects and 35 pardons, comprising public officials, military officers, and merchants, and 16 pardos, mostly noncommissioned officers and soldiers in the militias. The whole social spectrum was represented, including a large proportion of free people of color,⁴⁴ as well as certain Spanish "state criminals" (*reos de estado*) who had been deported to La Guaira for their own plot to establish a constitutional monarchy, foiled in Madrid on 3 February 1795. The Venezuelan conspiracy went much further, however, envisaging a republican regime with neither slavery nor racial discrimination. Here too, the colonies showed themselves more radical than those in Spain. The backlash was fierce: around eighty severe sentences, including seven death sentences.⁴⁵

For the authorities, the proliferation of *alteraciones* was also associated with the underground activities of *negros franceses* across the Caribbean. In May 1795, three months before the slave uprising on Curaçao, undoubtedly inspired by Saint-Domingue, the Coro rebellion occurred, involving Caquetío Indians, free people of color, and slaves. Primarily in reaction to economic factors, the rebellion reportedly sought a "French Law," though it is unclear whether this claim was factual or intended to discredit it. In fact, the link to revolutionary France was not so far-fetched, since there had been two sightings of French corsairs in the year leading up to the uprising. Framed in a "culture of expectation" (Julius S. Scott), abolition rumors had traversed the region after Spain's adoption of the *Código negro* in 1789. Put down with the help of Indian and pardo militias, the rebellion stood as a

---

[42] Caracas, 23 March 1798, AGI, Estado t. 70, 25 (1), fol. 1.
[43] Anne Pérotin-Dumon, "Révolutionnaires français et royalistes espagnols dans les Antilles," *Revue française d'histoire d'outre-mer* 76:282 (1989), 125–58.
[44] Francisco J. Yánez, *Compendio de la historia de Venezuela: Desde su descubrimiento y conquista hasta que se declaró estado independiente* (Caracas: A. Damiron, 1840), 127–34.
[45] 11 June 1799, AGI, *Estado* 59, 6 (16), fol. 1v.

warning in the region that marked a shift from the succession of slave revolts in the new global, abolitionist zeitgeist.[46] Indeed, at the other end of the Captaincy General that same year, Trinidad faced its own troubles. The French connection was more immediate here, with many French-speaking landowners and slaves. With close ties to Martinique, Guadeloupe, and the French-speaking populations on Tobago and Saint Lucia, Trinidad witnessed clashes between royalists and republicans. On 7 and 8 May 1796, while a French ship was anchoring in Port of Spain, slaves and free people of color rose in arms in the context of a brawl between French and British navy crews. In Santo Domingo, so close to the uprising of Saint-Domingue, an attempted rebellion was thwarted in Samaná Bay in November 1795, while the Boca de Nigua hacienda was set alight in a revolt by almost 200 slaves in October 1796.[47] On Cuba, French Blacks were accused of inciting an uprising at the Cuatro Compañeros hacienda near Puerto Príncipe de Cuba (Camagüey), where many Saint-Domingue landowners had fled. These *alteraciones* were not limited to the Caribbean: several months earlier, on 13 April 1795, Santiago Antonini, a Buenos Aires artisan originally from Piedmont, had been arrested and tortured for a "conspiracy" against the Viceroyalty. Over a long investigation, the authorities interrogated dozens of suspects, among them several artisans of French origin, including one Barbarin. With a looming economic crisis, these free laborers were deemed susceptible to revolutionary values, and this clandestine movement became known as the "French Conspiracy." Some slaves and free blacks were accused of taking part, although those questioned claimed complete ignorance of the Saint-Domingue revolt.[48] A few years later, in April 1799, Cartagena de Indias witnessed disturbances incited by "French slaves" and local ones as part of a "conspiracy." Where these rebels came from is not clear, but it was common to sell off the most virulent agitators in the French Caribbean into foreign colonies, which may explain the presence of these "French slaves" in a New Granada port, where they set fire to a large

---

[46] Frédéric Spillemaeker, "La révolte de Coro: Les catégories bouleversées à l'ère des révolutions (Venezuela, 1795)," *Nuevo Mundo Mundos Nuevos* [Online], Debates, online since 19 February 2019 at http://journals.openedition.org/nuevomundo/75193. See also Ramón Aizpurua, "La insurrección de los negros de la Serranía de Coro de 1795: Una revisión necesaria," *Boletin de la Academia Nacional de la Historia* 283 (1988), 705–23.

[47] Graham T. Nessler, *An Islandwide Struggle for Freedom: Revolution, Emancipation, and Reenslavement in Hispaniola, 1789–1809* (Chapel Hill: University of North Carolina Press, 2016), 62–3.

[48] Lyman L. Johnson, *Workshop of Revolution: Plebeian Buenos Aires and the Atlantic World, 1776–1810* (Durham, NC: Duke University Press, 2011), Chapter 5.

property. The same year, in Maracaibo, the crews of two Saint-Domingue privateering vessels were accused of inciting rebellion among the local pardos. In this age of revolutions, the authorities feared that these Black corsairs might combine their struggle with the rebelling Indians in the neighboring region of La Guajira.[49]

Since the bicentenary, Spanish American historiography has examined these forms of political mobilization with a persistently recurring question framed in the European context of the *ancien régime*: should these events be seen as traditional protest or revolutionary conditioning? On the one hand, there is a long list of fiscal revolts, in the name of the good king and against bad government, with local and limited goals; on the other, there were movements for institutional reform, such as the abolition of slavery, in the name of general principles. Until the 1980s, in the context of Spanish America, all political actions with a proven link to the French Revolution were placed in the latter category, and the rest in the former. Since then, historians have found very few slave revolts with an immediate, visible link to Saint-Domingue, abolition in 1794, or indeed the French Revolution.[50] Thus, these movements must have been of the traditional type. Yet we should also look beyond the dichotomy of revolt and revolution to view these events, for example, as a cluster of near-simultaneous uprisings centred around the Caribbean slave system:[51] the Jamaican and Saint Vincent Maroons,[52] Julien Fédon's French-speaking slaves on Grenada, and the great slave rebellion on Curaçao. The immediate factors behind this concurrence of events, their possible interconnections, and their intrinsic nature are of less significance than the wave of politicization that the proliferation of these experiences unleashed across the region, and the correlation ascribed to them by the authorities and maturing public opinion. Indeed, many contemporary commentators grouped these events in the same frame of reference – the Franco-British war and its ideological derivations. In this way, starting in the 1790s, a constellation of homegrown insurrections unwittingly served to

---

[49] "El virrey de Santafé da parte de la noticia que le ha comunicado el Gobernador de Cartagena," AGI, Estado, 52, no. 81, fol. 1r.

[50] David P. Geggus, "Slave Rebellion during the Age of Revolutions," in Wim Klooster and Gert Oostindie, eds., *Curaçao in the Age of Revolutions, 1795–1800* (Leiden: KITLV Press, 2011), 23–56.

[51] David P. Geggus, "The French and Haitian Revolutions, and Resistance to Slavery in the Americas: An Overview," *Outre-Mers. Revue d'histoire* 76:282 (1989), 107–24; David Barry Gaspar and David Geggus, eds., *A Turbulent Time: The French Revolution and the Greater Caribbean* (Bloomington: Indiana University Press, 1997).

[52] Michael Craton, *Testing the Chains: Resistance to Slavery in the British West Indies* (Ithaca, NY: Cornell University Press, 2009), 180–94.

undermine the Spanish colonial order, by fueling a growing sphere of political counterpublic: secret, not always subversive, but separate from official propaganda channels.[53]

Palimpsests of the French and Haitian Revolutions in Spanish America

In addressing the links between the French Revolution and Spanish America, we must also invert the terms of the relationship to understand how the patriots cited this event as a precedent at the start of their own movements. Indeed, by 1808, the Spanish monarchy was crumbling under the Napoleonic invasion. Some parts of its American empire claimed autonomy before declaring independence: Venezuela and New Granada, 1811–1813; Río de la Plata, 1816; Chile, 1818; and what remained, between 1821 and 1825. Could it be mere coincidence that the areas most impacted by the Franco-Hispanic revolutionary movements of the 1790s were the first to declare complete separation from Spain?

Two key phases mark the road to independence in the region: the first is constitutional, liberal, and monarchical, linking the Spanish American territories to the Cádiz Revolution in Spain. The 1812 constitution transformed the monarchy into a vast global empire of equal parts, its people citizens (except for descendants of Africans), in response to longstanding creole demands. After this first major upheaval came a second phase, during which certain territories drew inspiration from the Spanish Cortes while simultaneously severing ties. While this move toward republicanism was not directly influenced by the French Revolution, it did rest on two related processes. First, the longstanding debate among creole elites on monarchical reform, fueled by examples drawn into underground counterpublic discourses from the French and Caribbean revolutions. Next, the popular uprisings, often involving groups of African descent, seeking equality before the law and political participation, as seen in republican France and Saint-Domingue. These movements were often strained, yet they established these predominantly mixed-race groups as key political stakeholders. These observations invite us to reconsider the indirect role of the French and Caribbean revolutions in the independence process, as well as the significance of Spain's

---

[53] On the concept of "counterpublic," see Alexander Kluge and Oskar Negt, *Public Sphere and Experience: Toward an Analysis of the Bourgeois and Proletarian Public Sphere* (New York: Verso, 2016).

monarchical crisis and the successful appropriation of these references by local movements. More than imitation of ideas, models, and symbols, what matters here are the endogenous processes used by Spanish American patriots to invent their revolutions (and loyalists their counterrevolutions), taking this earlier political experiment and molding it to their own interests and culture.

The first point to address in this regard is the alleged Jacobinism of certain creole revolutionaries, like Francisco de Miranda. If there was one person who truly embodied the "influence" of the French Revolution, it was this former General of the French Republic, one of the Convention's military chiefs.[54] Born in Caracas in 1750, he was one of few creoles who believed in emancipation prior to 1808. "Colombia," his independentist project, consisted in the creation of a vast free state comprising all of Spain's American possessions, overseen by two "Incas" and a legislature. In 1806, he sailed from New York for Venezuela with two armed ships, stopping on Haiti to take on crews.[55] He failed twice in his attempts, but returned to Caracas in 1810 and briefly became the leader of the first Venezuelan Republic two years later. He and the Sociedad Patriótica of Caracas were labeled Jacobins, but this description does not make sense.[56] Miranda hated Jacobins as he had been imprisoned in France in July 1793 during the fall of the Brissotins. In the second issue of *El Patriota de Venezuela*, the Sociedad's republican newspaper, a translation appeared of a short pamphlet condemning Robespierre and the Montagnard Convention that the "Universal American" had published in Paris in 1795.[57] As a revolutionary he was, like many patriots, more in tune with the moderation that marked the Directory than with Montagnard radicalism. Meanwhile, in Buenos Aires, *de facto* independent from 1810, the revolution was marked by tension between Saavedra's moderates and Mariano Moreno's radicals. Yet was the latter a Jacobin, as has been claimed? Moreno did indeed advocate certain extreme positions, though quite

---

[54] Karen Racine, *Francisco de Miranda, a Transatlantic Life in the Age of Revolution* (Wilmington: SR Books, 2003). See also Caracciolo Parra Pérez, *Miranda et la Révolution française* (Paris: J. Dumoulin, 1925).
[55] Clément Thibaud, "'Coupé têtes, brûlé cazes'. Peurs et désirs d'Haïti dans l'Amérique de Bolívar," *Annales. Histoire, Sciences Sociales* 58:2 (2003), 305–31.
[56] See Carole Leal Curiel, "Tensiones republicanas: De patriotas, aristócratas y demócratas. El club de la Sociedad Patriótica de Caracas," in Guillermo Palacios, ed., *Los caminos de la democracia en América Latina: Revisión y balance de la Nueva Historia Política, s. XIX* (Mexico City: El Colegio de México, 2005), 231–64.
[57] Francisco de Miranda, "Sobre la situación actual de Francia," *El Patriota de Venezuela* 2 (1811).

different ones from those made famous by the French club.⁵⁸ His religious views led him, for example, to omit the parts on civic religion from his translation of *The Social Contract*, no doubt due to Rousseau's critique of Christianity. Generally, Jacobinism, in terms of political radicalism drawing support from popular groups, and characterized by anticlerical (even anti-Catholic) and antifederal policies, had little to no presence in Spanish America due to a combination of religious, cultural, and political factors that made it impossible for it to gain a foothold. Even the conspiracy of Gual and España, which was accompanied by the translation of the texts of the Montagnard Convention, was not of this nature. The appropriation of earlier revolutionary experiences manifested itself in local cultural configurations, based on rich, longstanding intellectual traditions and sociopolitical practices supported by a certain conception of natural law compatible with Catholicism, to be preserved at all costs after independence.⁵⁹

The other point to consider is natural law, the basis of the Rights of Man, but which also drew on an older intellectual tradition dating back to Golden Age Spanish neoscholasticism. Faced with the same liberal ideas that later triumphed in Cádiz, the notion was used to justify self-government in the Americas. In Cádiz, the monarchy's representative institutions had reduced the clout of the colonies by adopting two distinct systems to appoint deputies at home and across the Atlantic.⁶⁰ This injustice shocked the creole populations, who demanded parity with "European Spain," seeing in its colonial implications an affront to their dignity. In response to this insult, several provinces, including New Granada, Venezuela, Río de la Plata, and to a lesser extent Chile,⁶¹ implicitly referred to the corpus of the Rights of Man, through which they could claim a basis of legitimacy at least equal to the monarchy's sacred and customary authority. Viewed as an explication of the rules that God has laid out in nature, compatible with traditional scholastic teachings, these natural rights were contrasted with the liberal measures of Cádiz. Between 1811 and 1813, all constitutional projects in Spanish America

---

⁵⁸ Noemí Goldman, *Mariano Moreno: De reformista a insurgente* (Buenos Aires: Edhasa, 2016).
⁵⁹ See José Carlos Chiaramonte, *Fundamentos intelectuales y políticos de las independencias: Notas para una nueva historia intelectual de Iberoamérica* (Buenos Aires: Teseo, 2010).
⁶⁰ See Roberto Breña's Chapter 3 in Volume III of this book; Manuel Chust, *La cuestión nacional americana en las Cortes de Cádiz (1810–1814)* (Valencia: Centro Francisco Tomás y Valiente, 1999); Marie-Laure Rieu-Millán, *Los diputados americanos en las Cortes de Cádiz: Igualdad o independencia* (Madrid: CSIC, 1990).
⁶¹ Cristián Gazmuri Riveros, "Libros e ideas políticas francesas en la gestación de la Independencia de Chile," *Caravelle* 54 (1990), 179–207.

included a section on the Rights of Man and of the Citizen. Naturally, this appropriation of the terms of the French Revolution was never expressed as such. Yet these texts were often literal translations of articles from the three French Declarations of 1789, 1793, and 1795, as well as the charters of North American states like Massachusetts.[62]

These translations marked a resurgence of forms of underground politicization, dating back to 1790, specific to the counterpublics of the rights of man. Despite this, the legacy of the French or Haitian revolutions, in their classical phases (1789–1799; 1791–1804), was never invoked. It was common practice, however, for publishers to translate from French great Enlightenment or revolutionary writers (who were not necessarily French) and insert them into official texts, articles, and books. Hiding in plain sight, the terms of the French Revolution served as palimpsests underlying Spanish American revolutionary prose. There was no other option, since the French and Haitian revolutions, as syntagma, evoked impiety and violent radicalism, popular power and the violent inversion of social hierarchies. Yet close textual analysis reveals a thorough understanding of the constitutional work of the French assemblies, particularly during the Directory and the Consulate, which had sought to reconcile revolution and social order, while briefly extending political parity to the overseas departments. Institutions like electoral colleges, inspired by the French Constitution of the Year III, were adapted and substantially restructured; councils of state mirrored similar bodies under the Consulate. This emulation was most common in institution building, although the preservation of older judicial structures limited the revolutionary scope of such innovations in the young republics.[63]

Regarding the circulation of ideas, the Franco-Hispanic link had far-reaching intellectual effects that lasted until the First World War. There has been much historiographical emphasis on the influence of French ideas in Spanish America, but without seeing this connection in the context of a complex (though heavily one-sided) debate over the course of a century between politicians, publicists, and writers (exiled or otherwise) on both continents. This connection also concerned overlapping social and political

---

[62] Clément Thibaud, *Libérer le Nouveau Monde: La création des premières républiques hispaniques (Colombie et Venezuela, 1780–1821)* (Bécherel: Les Perséides, 2017), Chapter 4.

[63] Antonio Annino and Marcela Ternavasio, eds., *El laboratorio constitucional iberoamericano: 1807/1808–1830* (Madrid: Iberoamericana-Estudios AHILA, 2012). See also Carlos Garriga and Marta Lorente Sariñena, *Cádiz, 1812: La Constitución jurisdiccional* (Madrid: CEPC, 2007); Natalia Sobrevilla Perea and Scott Eastman, eds., *The Rise of Constitutional Government in the Iberian Atlantic World: The Impact of the Cádiz Constitution of 1812* (Tuscaloosa: The University of Alabama Press, 2015).

issues in the postrevolutionary context, with two key problems providing common ground in this transatlantic debate. First, in a revolution based on civil equality and liberty necessitating a clean break with the old world, how should one deal with its legacies, from the crushing weight of the Church to slavery and *limpieza de sangre*? Second, how could one end the revolution while ensuring the preservation of its fundamental assets: constitutional reform over institutional stability? One can see how the political science of reconciling revolutionary ideas with imperial structures occupied the Spanish American elites, particularly ideologues like Destutt de Tracy, Volney, and Daunou, or other republican-leaning liberals like Benjamin Constant or Madame de Staël.[64] Thanks to doctrinaire liberals and the positivism of Auguste Comte, this fascination continued throughout the century, while Spanish American conservatives celebrated *la hispanidad* in response to what they deemed superficial *afrancesamiento*.

It should be noted that significant opposition to the French and Haitian revolutions came from the images spread by religious and royal propaganda: a time of madness and chaos, when the most sacred principles of the human and divine orders were being turned on their head. These "monstrous revolutions" had plunged the world into confusion, a metaphysical drama to which the Catholic monarchy represented the virtuous foil. The guillotine, furious revolutionary masses, the persecution of the Catholic religion and its clergy, the execution of the king and queen, the imprisonment of the pope, Black generals, massacres of whites: the radical phases of these revolutions faced lasting condemnation that endured beyond the Spanish American wars of independence twenty years later. Thus, the French and Haitian revolutions, in the strictest sense, could not have triggered the Spanish American liberation movements directly, nor even provided a model. It was Spain's military defeat and the establishment of a constitutional monarchy at Cádiz that ushered in an era of Hispanic revolutions.[65] However, these upheavals were part of a broader imperial revolution, with a Caribbean epicenter, as shown by the overlap of the republican and abolitionist revolutionary periods in France and Saint-Domingue with the proliferation of slave revolts and conspiracies in the region between 1794 and 1799 (Map 6.1). The 1802 Bonapartist Restoration marked a definitive end to this chapter, which

[64] Carlos Altamirano and Jorge Myers, eds., *Historia de los intelectuales en América Latina* (Buenos Aires: Katz Editores, 2008), 184–204.
[65] François-Xavier Guerra, ed., *Revoluciones hispánicas: Independencias americanas y liberalismo español* (Madrid: Editorial Complutense, 1995).

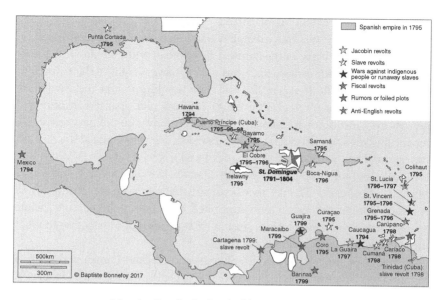

Map 6.1 Revolts in the Caribbean, 1794–1799.

had sought to mend, at least on paper, colonial disparities between the mainland and overseas.

The "seduction" of the Rights of Man, invoked against both Old World "absolutism" (the terms in quotation marks are those of the actors) and the "liberalism" of the Spanish revolution, is without doubt one of the clearest links between Spanish America and the French and Haitian revolutions. From this emerged a process of identification and translation embraced by a broad spectrum of regional actors. Starting in the 1790s, this Franco-Hispanic link was an underground driver of politicization, making it possible to align patterns of discontent within a horizon of expectation. Fresh conceptions of liberty and equality, law and representation, civic virtue and participation did indeed open the door for slaves and creoles, mestizos and Indians, to voice their specific demands within a wider system, so affording them unprecedented weight. It was here that the symbolic effects of counter-publicity were most successful, expectations over the 1808 crisis and the Cádiz Constitution highest, and the ensuing disappointment strongest, driving these territories sooner rather than later toward autonomy and independence. Thus, the role of the French Revolution in the course of the Spanish American independence movements should be considered less consequential than later events in Spain. All the more reason for the latter not to be forgotten.

7

Violence and the French Revolution

HOWARD G. BROWN

By the middle of the twentieth century, a fairly broad scholarly consensus had developed about the role of violence in the French Revolution. It emphasized antiseigneurialism in the countryside and the activism of artisans and shopkeepers in cities and towns. It also treated the crescendo of state-authorized violence in 1793–1794 as a flawed but necessary response to the pressures of foreign war and domestic rebellion. Challenges to this scholarly consensus first emerged in debates about class antagonism as the primary cause of the French Revolution. The new neoliberal "revisionists" emphasized an acute sclerosis that prevented the monarchy from managing its responsibilities and the social elite from adapting to the cultural currents of the Enlightenment. Shifting the focus to politics and ideas, packaged together as political culture, also changed interpretations of the more extreme forms of violence perpetrated in the mid-1790s. From this perspective, the so-called "reign of terror" became the almost inevitable result of the ideology of liberty and equality articulated in 1789, especially when viewed through the lens of Rousseau. Revolutionary language and practice fused into an intense politics of exclusion and elimination, one that Jacobins extended beyond nobles and priests. First they decried political opponents, even if former allies, as enemies of the people, then declared them outside the law. Furthermore, interpretations of this ilk suggested a genealogy for totalitarianism in the twentieth century.[1]

Scholars who seek to avoid either Jacobin-influenced apologetics or anachronistic ideological affiliations often prefer to explore the cultural patterns

---

[1] Given the voluminous literature on which this chapter rests, references have been reduced to a minimum and revolutionary violence committed outside France has necessarily been left to other chapters in this volume. On the mid-century orthodoxy, see Georges Lefebvre, *The French Revolution*, 2 vols. (New York: Columbia University Press, 1962–1964 [1951–1957]); Albert Soboul, *The French Revolution, 1787–1799* (London: Verso, 1974 [1958]); on the revisionist challenge, see François Furet, *Interpreting the French Revolution* (Cambridge: Cambridge University Press, 1981 [1978]).

and internal logics that shaped various forms of violence. Such alternative perspectives have enabled a more thorough assessment of the violence generated in opposition to revolutionary changes and impositions. Popular resistance to conscription, taxation, or the creation of a Constitutional Church is seen as antirevolutionary, rather than overtly counterrevolutionary.[2] Historians of violence during the Revolution have also used the methods of cultural anthropology to analyze the rituals of popular violence, notably the spectacular forms that advanced the revolutionary cause, in order to discern the motives of plebian perpetrators.[3] Ultimately, the severe dislocations and polarizing factionalism of the early 1790s inspired years of endemic violence in which personal, political, and criminal motives became exceptionally difficult to disentangle.

Violence is a defining characteristic of revolution as a *mode* of historical change. Adopting dates for the start and end of revolutions, that is, labeling a particular period as revolutionary, depends on taking note of patterns of violence. This is not the same as claiming that violence was the driving force of the French Revolution.[4] Violence is a factor, not an actor, in history. The revolutionary mode of change could not be ended simply by adopting a new constitution and proclaiming the revolution over, as was attempted three times – in 1791, 1795, and 1799 – without success. Instead, popular violence that helped to end absolutism and promote social justice led to state-authorized terror on an unprecedented scale, much of it operated with little control from above. This fueled continuing cycles of violence at the local, regional, and national levels that could be contained only by expanding and depoliticizing the repressive powers of the state. Anticlericalism, mass emigration, foreign war, economic chaos, parlous policing, and partisan judges all prolonged political uncertainty and endemic violence. These challenges provoked a growing liberal authoritarianism after 1797. Efforts to ensconce the republic and contain violence at the same time, notably by militarizing domestic repression and suppressing democracy, paved the road to a security

---

[2] Richard Cobb, *Reactions to the French Revolution* (Oxford: Oxford University Press, 1972), 8–16; Colin Lucas, "Résistances populaires à la révolution dans le Sud-Est," in Jean Nicholas, ed., *Mouvements populaires et conscience sociale XVIe–XIXe siècles* (Paris: Maloine, 1985), 473–85.

[3] For example, Antoine de Baecque, *Glory and Terror: Seven Deaths under the French Revolution* (New York: Routledge, 2002 [1997]).

[4] Contrast with Simon Schama, *Citizens: A Chronicle of the French Revolution* (New York: Alfred A. Knopf, 1989); Patrice Gueniffey, *La politique de la Terreur: Essai sur la violence révolutionnaire, 1789–1794* (Paris: Fayard, 2000).

state and a personal dictatorship. Thus, the French Revolution finally ended with the Life Consulate of 1802.

Early Revolution, 1788–1792

A variety of urban revolts and demonstrations in the years 1788–1789 intensified the monarchy's political crisis and encouraged the most aggressive reformers to condone popular violence. The monarchy's effort to remain absolute through a drastic reorganization of the judiciary in 1788 triggered huge demonstrations in various cities that housed *parlements*, notably Grenoble, Rennes, and Pau. The army had long been used as an auxiliary to urban police, but in these cases various units proved reluctant to fire on crowds. That permitted extensive pillaging and a triumph for both the magistrates and bourgeois radicals. In contrast, the Réveillon riot in Paris ended on 28 April 1789 when French Guards opened fire on the huge crowd, killing and wounding hundreds, while sustaining almost 100 casualties themselves. The extent of popular protest around the country inspired a turn toward the summary justice of constabulary courts. Oddly, however, this did little to increase judicial repression before 14 July 1789. Delayed trials and light sentences reflected concerns about a public backlash. Above all, the urban violence of 1788–1789 illustrated the risks that royal officials ran if they either deployed military force against unruly crowds or waited for courts to take action.[5]

These critical factors determined the events of 14 July 1789. A growing army presence around the capital, combined with the dismissal of Jacques Necker, a political folk hero, sparked an urban panic. Angry at high prices, crowds destroyed most of the city's customs barriers, all while French Guards stood aside. In a desperate effort to defend their city against deliberate starvation or a military occupation, Parisians rushed to arm themselves. After seizing thousands of muskets and a few cannon from the Invalides, a huge crowd surged to the Bastille in search of more weapons and munitions. The attack became a shockingly bloody affair. After first killing at least 100 attackers and wounding some 70 others, the governor of the Bastille, the Marquis de Launay, contemplated blowing up the fortress. However, unwilling to inflict massive damage on the surrounding neighborhood, he

---

[5] Jacques Godechot, *The Taking of the Bastille, July 14th 1789* (New York: Scribner, 1970 [1965]), 146–8; Ted Margadant, "Summary Justice and the Crisis of the Old Regime in 1789," *Historical Reflections/Réflexions historiques* 29 (2003), 495–528. However, judicial repression increased markedly in the second half of 1789.

agreed to surrender instead. De Launay quickly paid the price of his prudence, as did Jacques de Flesselles, effectively the mayor of Paris. Rioters ruthlessly beheaded both men in front of the Hôtel de Ville, long the site of royal executions. The crowd then paraded the two heads around on pikes, thereby mimicking the Europe-wide practice of publicly displaying traitors' heads after executions. These improvised rituals were integral to the violence as a form of popular justice.[6]

The urban violence of 1788–1789 led royal officials to fear using military force in decisive acts of bloody repression. Thus, ministerial hopes of using the army to retake control of the capital evaporated when unit commanders expressed doubts about whether their soldiers would obey orders to fire on civilians. The public murder of two royal officials terrified deputies in the fledgling National Assembly.[7] However, when the king combined a withdrawal of force with a conciliatory trip to Paris, the more assertive deputies of the Third Estate realized that the violence of 12–14 July had greatly strengthened their hand. Rather than being seen as a frightening collapse of law and order, therefore, events in Paris became the triumph of a courageous people over the forces of despotism, symbolized by the Bastille itself.

That progressive deputies could see benefits in even the most gruesome forms of popular violence soon became obvious. A week after the fall of the Bastille, Parisian mobs lynched and decapitated two more top Parisian officials. Cutting out the heart of one and stuffing grass into the mouth of the other, then parading the ensemble around on pikes, embodied the perceived barbarism of the lowest orders. Nonetheless, in response to shocked condemnations from fellow deputies, one of the emerging leaders of the Third Estate, Antoine Barnave, posed the rhetorical question: "So, the blood that was just shed, was it so pure?" Instantly famous and forever regrettable, Barnave's comment reveals the circumstantial ethics of revolutionaries who justified popular violence without imagining the longer-term consequences of doing so. And yet, it would be surprising if politicians who had only just begun to see themselves as revolutionaries could have envisioned the extraordinarily bloody events to come.

Thus, to describe the trajectory of violence from 1789 to 1793 as fulfilling an ideological program is too reductionist and leaves no room for historical

---

[6] Colin Lucas, "The Crowd and Politics between the Ancien Régime and the French Revolution," *Journal of Modern History* 60:3 (1988), 421–57.

[7] Barry M. Shapiro, *Traumatic Politics: Deputies and the King in the Early French Revolution* (University Park, PA: Penn State University Press, 2009).

contingency. In contrast, historians who emphasize the dire circumstances facing the republic in 1793 tend to ignore the extent to which revolutionary leaders capitalized on outbursts of popular violence well before then. Furthermore, historians who seek an alternative approach argue that the early revolutionaries failed to create both theoretical and practical means to contain popular violence.[8] This was extremely difficult to do while simultaneously removing most of the basic underpinnings of the social and political order. Containing violence while also dismantling the *ancien régime* would have required considerable political consensus, which was highly elusive in a National Assembly whose members had been elected on the basis of antiquated distinctions between clergy, nobility, and commoners. It would also have required a ruler with the will and the skill to adapt to a new source of political legitimacy. Louis XVI was not that kind of ruler. That many revolutionaries thought that he could be coopted – including Barnave as late as 1792 – helps to explain why they also believed that they could both condone and contain popular violence in 1789.

The urban unrest of 1788–1789 was matched by widespread rural strife. The poor harvest of 1788 had provoked extensive rioting over grain prices even before the Estates General met in May 1789. Many rioters invoked notions of a moral economy, or just prices. Moreover, most local authorities proved reluctant to engage in serious repression at a time when the kingdom bubbled and fizzed with political concerns. During the early summer of 1789, peasant attacks on seigneurial lords (both secular and religious) spread to several widely disparate regions. These localized acts of hostility focused on securing relief from various dues, obligations, and past debts, as well as cultural features of seigneurial privilege such as church pews, weathervanes, and dovecotes. Though utterly distinct in their motivations, attacks on market centers and grain shipments seemed to blend with antiseigneurial violence to create a generalized threat to law and order. This stoked fears of repression. Rural communities had long believed in a "famine plot" whereby authorities would cut off the supply of grain in order to starve recalcitrant peasants into submission. This was supplemented by fears of an "aristocratic plot" in which seigneurs would strike back at peasant opposition by arming the many vagabonds and sturdy beggars that swarmed the countryside.

---

[8] Colin Lucas, "Revolutionary Violence, the People and the Terror," in Keith Michael Baker, ed. *The French Revolution and the Creation of Modern Political Culture*, vol. IV: *The Terror* (Oxford: Pergamon, 1994), 57–79.

Peasant unrest reached a crescendo in late July and early August. As news of the fall of the Bastille radiated from Paris, communities around the country reacted with jubilation and alarm. The resulting "Great Fear," an almost kingdom-wide panic, was inspired by fears of hired brigands or foreign troops devastating the land and its agricultural output. Towns and villages scrambled to find weapons and organize themselves in defense of their communities and the ripening harvest. In the meantime, peasants also attacked scores of chateaux in parts of central and eastern France. Remarkably, however, the waves of panic and antiseigneurial violence in July and August 1789 led to only three murders. Nonetheless, extensive destruction, whether of feudal documents, seigneurial gibbets, granaries, wine cellars, or entire chateaux, intimidated most seigneurs and prevented any coordinated action with the monarchy. As a result, many nobles simply signed away their families' feudal rights.[9]

The National Assembly responded to this widespread unrest with a sweeping legislative assault on seigneurial dues and privileges on the night of 4 August 1789. Although the resulting decrees proclaimed an end to feudalism in France, the details remained devilish for several years to come. The complexity and uncertainty that beset the process helped to justify later regional outbreaks of antinoble violence in the countryside. These were especially intense in the first few months of 1790 and again in the summer of 1792. The obvious need to maintain order, combined with deep mistrust of the royal army, led to the formation of new local militias that soon peppered the country. Although dominated by bourgeois revolutionaries, these National Guard units sometimes acted in concert with rural rioters. In the relatively urbanized Rhône Valley, for example, a wave of antinobilism in 1792 saw large crowds of peasants aided and abetted by national guardsmen carry out assaults that pulled down towers and destroyed archives in over 100 castles and manor houses. Such regional waves did not lead to a kingdom-wide peasant movement; however, they did help to justify the increasingly radical policies of successive legislatures that eventually ended seigneurialism, largely without compensation, by 1793. In other words, national elections did more to end feudalism in France than did regionalized rioting.[10]

---

[9] Clay Ramsay, *The Ideology of the Great Fear: The Soissonais in 1789* (Baltimore: Johns Hopkins University Press, 1992).

[10] John Markoff, *The Abolition of Feudalism: Peasants, Lords, and Legislators in the French Revolution* (University Park, PA: Penn State University Press, 1996) presents the relationship as an extended dialogue.

Elections to the Legislative Assembly in September 1791 and to the National Convention in September 1792 reflected larger trends in violence around the country. Subsistence issues often provided a catalyst for politicized violence, most famously in the women's march to Versailles on 5–6 October 1789. Having trudged twenty kilometers in the rain in order to force government action on soaring bread prices, the riotous crowd, accompanied by Lafayette's National Guard from Paris, gave revolutionary leaders the perfect opportunity to force Louis XVI to accept and promulgate both the August decrees that ended "the feudal regime" and the Declaration of the Rights of Man and Citizen. Few events in the French Revolution better encapsulate the opportunistic response of revolutionary leaders to crowd violence. The royal family moved to the political hothouse of Paris. The price was memorably gory, but acceptably modest: the heads of two palace guards promenaded alongside the royal carriage. The National Assembly followed some days later. The profound consequences of the "October Days" in diminished royal authority and increased revolutionary militancy left lingering suspicions that the women's march had been politically orchestrated.

Although 1790 is often taken to be the peaceful year of the French Revolution, it was not without notable unrest. This included sporadic anti-seigneurial violence in more remote rural regions and a steady erosion of military discipline highlighted by a massive mutiny at Nancy. More importantly, burgeoning counterrevolutionary movements provoked violent outbursts in the south thanks to sectarian tensions that went back to the religious wars of the sixteenth century. The Revolution offered Protestants unprecedented pathways to local power. Resentful Catholics across the Midi became more staunchly royalist in response. Clashes often arose over the local National Guard, an increasingly important source of power. Such tensions provoked an outburst of violence at Montauban in May, then again at Nîmes in June. In both cases, mobilizing regional units of national guardsmen ended the Catholic aggression. The so-called "brawl at Nîmes" left 300 dead, almost all of them Catholics openly massacred in the streets. In response, the Cévennes mountains came alive with mass peasant gatherings numbering in the tens of thousands, all led by local nobles and priests determined to keep the Revolution at bay.[11] These overt manifestations of

---

[11] Valérie Sottocasa, *Mémoires affrontées: Protestants et catholiques face à la Révolution dans les montagnes de Languedoc* (Rennes: Presses universitaires de Rennes, 2004).

counterrevolution fueled a growing patriotic paranoia about royalist plots to restore the *ancien régime*.

Resistance to the Revolution from Catholics was greatly increased by the National Assembly's inept restructuring of the Catholic Church in France. After creating an entirely new ecclesiastical map of dioceses and parishes, lawmakers responded to pockets of predictable resistance by imposing an oath of allegiance on all clerics. This forced all active priests to come out publicly for or against the Revolution. Many priests faced an agonizing decision, made more difficult by parishioners determined to cajole or even coerce them into making the "right" choice. Although regional reactions varied greatly, by late 1790, half of all clerics had refused to support the new order. Wherever these "refractory" or "nonjuring" clergy remained active, whether publicly or secretly, resistance to the Revolution acquired a figurehead if not actual leader. The anticlericalism of bourgeois patriots, whose urban bases of power allowed them to dominate the new administrative structures, fueled an intense hostility to peasant religiosity. Seeing religion as a potential basis for political subversion, revolutionaries often used the National Guard to install "constitutional" priests in rural communities, notably in Brittany and other parts of western France. Priests who took the oath and thereby gained posts saw themselves as "patriot priests," whereas hostile villagers treated them as "intruders" to be ostracized, intimidated, even eliminated. Thus, the extent to which the oath crystalized opposition to the Revolution would be hard to overstate. Defense of traditional Catholicism and refractory priests gave violent counterrevolution a popular base that sustained it for a full decade thereafter.[12]

Conflict over refractory priests helped to provoke the most important event of 1791, the royal family's failed attempt to flee Paris and negotiate the nature of the new regime from a position of strength on the northeastern frontier. Louis' capture and ignominious return from Varennes crippled his credibility as the keystone of a constitutional monarchy. Gathering signatures for republican sounding petitions led on 17 July 1791 to a massacre on the Champ de Mars in which the National Guard, under Lafayette's direct command, killed at least fifty petitioners and wounded many times more. At first, this bloody repression bolstered the forces of law and order. Leading radicals like Marat and Danton disappeared from the capital. The Jacobin Club became a rump of democratic purists led by Robespierre. Deputies

---

[12] Roger Dupuy, *De la Révolution à la chouannerie* (Paris: Flammarion, 1988); D. M. G. Sutherland, *France 1789–1815: Revolution and Counterrevolution* (London: Fontana, 1985).

from the moderate Feuillant Club persuaded the king to accept a constitution, which took effect on 1 October 1791. In support of its claim that this ended the Revolution, the Assembly promulgated a sweeping amnesty for acts of rebellion and revolution since 1788. The amnesty released thousands of activists and agitators back into their communities. Beneficiaries ranged from peasants who had pillaged chateaux to republican radicals determined to bring down the monarchy.

The amnesty of 1791 became even more generous, and thus more subversive of a return to order, when the Legislative Assembly extended it to include a large-scale massacre at Avignon. The papal enclave had been annexed to France in September 1791. A month later, the killing of a patriot in the cathedral prompted his allies to round up sixty opponents. Led by "Head-Chopper" Jourdan, patriots slaughtered the prisoners, women included, and tossed their bodies into the latrines of the Papal Palace's Glacière Tower. Despite a government inquiry that revealed the full horror of the massacre, the Legislative Assembly later voted to apply the amnesty to the perpetrators on the grounds that the violence that accompanied the unification of Avignon with France was a product of revolution, even though the Glacière masssacre had occurred a month after both the annexation and the amnesty. The logic was clear: violence is inherent in revolution, therefore, ending a revolution requires forgiving the once illegal violence that accompanied it.[13]

This failure to distinguish between acceptable and unacceptable violence in the course of revolution appeared repeatedly throughout 1792. Revolutionary officials in the provinces never quite knew when lawmakers in Paris would endorse or repudiate efforts to uphold the law. A notorious incident of this sort happened on 3 March 1792 at Étampes, an important grain market south of Paris. There a mass of country dwellers overwhelmed the town's defensive forces and murdered the mayor and businessman, Jacques Guillaume Simonneau, in the marketplace. His offense: deploying force to maintain an open commerce in grain, rather than setting lower prices. The Legislative Assembly made Simonneau a national martyr, a hero who died resisting a "counterrevolutionary conspiracy" to undermine the new order. Radicals in the clubs and neighborhood assemblies of Paris took a different view. They painted the riot as a justified popular action and

---

[13] Mary Ashburn Miller, *A Natural History of Revolution: Violence and Nature in the French Revolutionary Imaginary, 1789–1794* (Ithaca, NY: Cornell University Press, 2011), 44–55.

Simonneau as a symbol of "aristocrats" who ignored the people's hardships and denied them the right of subsistence. This view complemented the interpretation they had put on the repression of a large mutiny by the garrison at Nancy in the summer of 1790. Subduing the mutineers had led to over 200 casualties and so the leaders were harshly punished: 23 executions and 111 sentences of hard labor or imprisonment. Despite many local celebrations of the return to order, Jacobins in Paris protested the punishments and eventually had the mutineers exonerated. When the released soldier-convicts arrived in Paris, militants greeted them with a massive "Festival of Liberty" on 15 April 1792. The moderate Feuillant Club responded seven weeks later with a "Festival of the Law" to honor Simonneau. Holding rival festivals that either celebrated violent opposition to authority or lionized those who died defending the law illustrates just how polarized attitudes had become. Extending the amnesty of 1791 both to the mutineers of Nancy and to the murderers of Avignon did not bode well for the near future. Once the war against Austria and Prussia – proclaimed on 20 March 1792 – turned sour, increased political radicalism spawned even greater waves of violence.

The Republican Revolution, 1792–1795

The overthrow of the monarchy on 10 August 1792 brought a "second revolution" that proved far bloodier than that of 1789. The foreign war had been inspired by ambitious politicians determined to flush out aristocratic conspirators at court and elsewhere. Rather than uniting revolutionaries, the war divided moderates in the Legislative Assembly from radicals in the clubs and neighborhood assemblies of Paris (known as "sections"). Left-wing lawmakers, led by Brissot, hoped to use the demands of foreign war and fear of popular insurrection to coerce the king into returning them to government. Their earlier dismissal had inspired well-armed Parisians to invade the Tuileries Palace on 20 June. The day had ended peacefully, however, thanks to the dignified actions of Louis himself. The king stubbornly refused to reinstate the "patriot" ministers while their allies declined to prosecute the intruders, who might well prove to be crucial in a future show of force. A month later, the Assembly proclaimed the "fatherland in danger." This jolted local officials at all levels into aggressive mobilization efforts. With the Assembly paralyzed by partisan infighting, little-known leaders of the nascent *sans-culottes* movement organized another assault on the Tuileries Palace. More famous figures, such as Pétion, Danton, and

Violence and the French Revolution

Figure 7.1 The taking of the Tuileries Palace. Courtesy of the Bibliothèque Nationale.

Robespierre, feared a debacle followed by ruthless repression and so avoided conspicuous involvement.[14]

When the Assembly refused to suspend the king, militants from the sections of Paris took matters into their own hands. They seized the city government and immediately launched an assault on the Tuileries Palace on the morning of 10 August (Figure 7.1). The insurgents, led by militia units from Marseille and Brest, and assisted by defections amongst the defenders, easily occupied the palace grounds. The Swiss Guards, lacking clear orders because the king had already fled to the Assembly, opened fire on the insurgents and managed to clear the courtyards. A ferocious second assault by over 10,000 attackers, many in National Guard uniforms and equipped with cannons and horses, overwhelmed the defenders and seized the palace. By nightfall, 600 Swiss Guards, loyal aristocrats, and palace servants lay dead. Though some died in battle, most were simply slaughtered, many by ordinary Parisians armed with pikes, hatchets, and carving knives. Contemporaries, including Captain Buonaparte, as Bonaparte was then known, shuddered at the savage mutilation of corpses and the

[14] Marcel Reinhard, *La chute de la royauté* (Paris: Gallimard, 1969).

parading of heads and body parts as trophies. These gruesome emblems of popular justice highlight the retributive element of the postsurrender massacre. The assailants had suffered over 100 killed and many more wounded, mostly in the first phase, which they considered an ambush. Participants burnished the political purity of their intentions by also killing a dozen looters. Although presented as a "popular uprising" and an act of "popular sovereignty," the events of 10 August 1792 were really a coup d'état followed by a people's massacre. The triumph of the Insurrectionary Commune compelled the Assembly to suspend the king and announce its own replacement by a new National Convention based on universal manhood suffrage. The *journée* was both the bloodiest and the most decisive of the French Revolution.

The overthrow of the monarchy in the name of "popular sovereignty" reflected the growing power of an explicitly revolutionary ideology to inspire and justify popular violence. Traditional justifications based on the moral economy and defense of the community did not disappear; rather, they were supplemented with lofty ideals from the Enlightenment. Classical antiquity and the fledgling United States offered the learned elite distant, largely idealized, examples of democracy and republicanism. Actually implementing democratic ideals meant dismantling existing structures of authority and risked unleashing less appealing impulses across all social strata. Too often, notions of liberty, equality, reason, and progress acted as bellows on the glowing coals of social resentment and personal jealousy. Fear that the gains of the Revolution might be reversed fit easily with outsized hopes for greater social leveling and individual opportunity. The resulting mix of traditional moral, newly democratic, and frankly utopian impulses created the heady cocktail of "popular sovereignty." Crowds that imbibed such strong drink felt fully justified in committing violence, making it a form of revolutionary discourse in its own right.

The summer of 1792 saw a major escalation in brutal forms of popular violence. Even before 10 August 1792, the lynching of perceived enemies of the Revolution had begun to proliferate, notably in the cities and towns of the Rhône Valley. The victims included numerous clerics, factional rivals, even elected officials. Crowds preferred major streets or squares. Several patterns prevailed: hanging from lampposts, beating or stabbing to death (rather than victims being shot), mistreating corpses in order to humiliate and intimidate. Moreover, local authorities largely failed to prevent the factional violence or to punish perpetrators. Dozens of lynchings, together with armed expeditions from Marseille and Toulon, helped Jacobins to gain power throughout the region.[15] Thus, acts of "popular justice" proved a vital means to secure "popular sovereignty" in practical terms.

The impulse to strike down enemies of the Revolution, especially refractory priests and recalcitrant nobles, gained enormously from the fear of foreign invasion (Map 7.1). Nowhere was this more obvious than in Paris. The formation of armies led by emigrant nobles gave substance to the wild-eyed fear of aristocratic treason, especially after Lafayette tried, unsuccessfully, to turn his Northern Army against Paris. A fortnight later, the fall of two fortresses on the northern frontier precipitated a series of prison massacres. The bloodletting began on 2 September, spread to nine prisons over five days, and left at least 1,100 dead. The killing was neither spontaneous nor haphazard. Rather, militants operating under the auspices of the Insurrectionary Commune's Surveillance Committee improvised "popular tribunals" that freed as many prisoners as they killed. The victims included 240 priests, scores of aristocrats (male and female), Swiss Guards, and many common criminals. Most were hacked to death, though a few suffered the ritual mutilation famously inflicted on the Princesse de Lamballe. All of Paris knew what was happening and yet politicians did nothing to stop the carnage. Many were paralyzed by fear; others saw opportunity. Elections to the National Convention began even before the killing ended. The results: a triumph in Paris for Jacobin candidates who later blocked efforts to prosecute the *septembriseurs*.

News of the prison massacres at Paris spawned a wave of massacres in the provinces, many involving beheadings and gruesome mutilations. At Versailles, an organized mob ambushed a convoy of royalist prisoners, beat some unrecognizable, and left forty-four corpses, some headless and badly mangled. Perpetrators included members of the military escort. Vigilantes then broke into local prisons and butchered at least twenty-seven more, including common criminals. In fact, within a few weeks, 32 departments had experienced 75 distinct events involving 244 murders.[16] Angry threats and postmortem displays reflected a widespread determination to intimidate opponents. In short, aggressive, vengeful acts against select members of the social elite became integral to the democratic radicalism of 1792. The extreme savagery of these actions revealed a widespread collapse of state authority, which allowed the populace to enact its own, extravagant forms of

---

[15] D. M. G. Sutherland, *Murder in Aubagne: Lynching, Law, and Justice during the French Revolution* (New York: Cambridge University Press, 2009).
[16] Frédéric Bluche, *Septembre 1792: Logiques d'un massacre* (Paris: Robert Laffont, 1986).

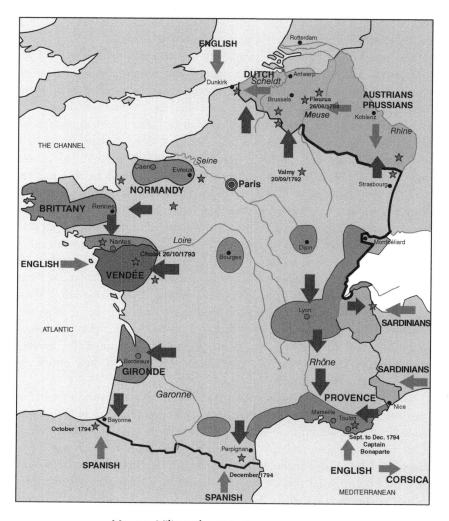

Map 7.1 Military threats to France, 1792–1794.

retributive justice. Popular justice could neither be delayed nor be denied. Political demagoguery, especially evident in revolutionary newspapers, fostered conspiracy theories and incited violence. As a result, the discourse of popular sovereignty lost some luster in the frenzied gore of urban massacres.

The surge in popular violence during the summer of 1792 abated considerably in the autumn. The bourgeois politicians elected in September

1792 largely agreed on exiling refractory priests, prosecuting emigrants, pursuing an aggressive war, and repressing food riots, notably in the grain belt. However, these policies further stoked rural opposition. Inside the Convention, the Jacobins split between those who wanted to punish *septembriseurs* (Girondins) and those who justified them (Montagnards). The Girondins accused the Montagnards of promoting popular violence and trying to impose Parisian radicalism on the rest of France.

The trial, conviction, and execution of Louis XVI on 21 January 1793 further polarized the Convention and the country. Louis' death did not, however, provoke any immediate surge in counterrevolutionary violence in the provinces. That came when the Convention tried to draft 300,000 men to fight the growing anti-French First Coalition. Anticonscription riots erupted all over the country. Local officials managed to repress most of these quite quickly; however, in western areas south of the Loire River, a botched military response allowed all of the previous grievances against the Revolution, especially the religious settlement, disappointments over fiscal relief, and bullying from the towns, to turn into a widespread rebellion by the end of March 1793. The initial uprising brought a series of atrocious massacres in which several hundred people, including many officials, were murdered for their allegiance to the Revolution. Repeated batch killings, notably at Machecoul, became a rallying cry for republican revenge.[17]

Just as the *Vendée militaire* erupted in western France, the French invasion of the Austrian Netherlands suddenly collapsed. General Dumouriez negotiated a truce in order to turn his army against the radicals in Paris. When his army refused to follow, Dumouriez defected to the Austrians. The combination of civil war, military defeat, and blatant treason inspired the Convention to reach for more aggressive means of repression, including using military commissions to judge rebels, creating a special Revolutionary Tribunal, and forming a Committee of Public Safety to oversee the Executive Council. Having drummed up the war, the Girondins were blamed for Dumouriez' defeat and treason. By late May, Parisian extremists based in section assemblies and the Cordeliers Club dominated the Paris Commune, the Ministry of War, and the National Guard. They loudly denounced the Girondins as traitors. On 2 June, thousands of national guardsmen surrounded the Convention and coerced it into expelling twenty-nine Girondins. Thereafter, the Montagnards took the helm, with the violence-

---

[17] Jean-Clément Martin, *La Guerre de Vendée, 1793–1800* (Paris: Points, 2014).

prone *sans-culottes* as dangerously exigent allies. Above all, developments in the spring of 1793 further politicized the war effort, making political discord a form of treason. Yesterday's revolutionary allies became today's counter-revolutionaries with supposed ties to foreign powers.

The expulsion of the Girondins on 2 June 1793 inspired the so-called "Federalist Revolt" that summer. The second city of France, Lyon, had already burst into open conflict a few days earlier with the overthrow of the fiery demagogue Chalier and his acolytes. This became the centerpiece in a general movement to defeat Jacobin extremists and reverse the events of 2 June. Although this so-called "federalism" appeared in many cities, only Caen, Bordeaux, Marseille, Toulon, and Lyon organized against the Convention. This opened "federalism" to the charge of being counterrevolutionary, even though most adherents supported the revolution and could legitimately claim to be enacting "popular sovereignty." However, once confronted with real military force, Caen, Bordeaux, and even Marseille, quickly capitulated. In contrast, it took sizeable armies and prolonged sieges to defeat the resistance at Lyon and Toulon. By then, republican resistors had admitted royalists to their ranks. Toulon even treasonously allowed an English fleet to occupy its vital naval port.

The Convention's response to the Federalist Revolt opened the door and crossed the threshold into the "reign of terror." Historians who emphasize the dire circumstances of 1793 to explain the Terror tend to ignore the origins of the circumstances. The Jacobins chose to follow Robespierre in allying with the pseudoproletarian *sans-culottes* movement. This left them dependent on the Parisian "party of violence" (later dubbed Hébertistes) that controlled the War Ministry, the Paris Commune, and the National Guard. When these extremists mobilized the sections for another show of force on 4–5 September 1793, they demanded that the Convention adopt "terror" as a national policy. Though it was never made law, having "terror on the daily agenda" soon became a common slogan.[18] Months later, when deputies began to question the need for continuing severity, Robespierre famously defended terror as a necessary complement to civic virtue in times of revolution.

Following the overthrow of Robespierre on 9 Thermidor Year II (27 July 1794; Figure 7.2), his successors, known as Thermidorians, constructed an image of the Revolutionary Government of 1793–1794 as an historically

---

[18] Annie Jourdan, *Nouvelle histoire de la Révolution française* (Paris: Flammarion, 2018), 198–211.

Figure 7.2 Execution of Robespierre and his men. Courtesy of the Bibliothèque Nationale.

unprecedented "reign of terror." Their narrative did not lack evidence. The Convention had resorted to draconian policies and exceptional institutions in response to the manifold crises of 1793. This included authorizing local watch committees to lock up political "suspects" and hold them without trial, which was applied to at least 70,000 citizens. If actually put on trial, such suspects were likely to face a "revolutionary" (i.e. exceptional and expedited) judicial process adopted by a regular criminal court or an improvised tribunal. Imposing price ceilings, known as the General Maximum, on basic essentials from bread to leather was intended to ensure supplies for France's cities and armies, but it also turned all market-based noncompliance into counterrevolution. The formation of a sizeable "Revolutionary Army" at Paris, and the proliferation of smaller ones around the country, provided militants with a means to coerce hoarders, round up opponents, and impose dechristianization. (These notorious "moustaches" mixed armed bullying with frequent thievery and so were disbanded in the spring of 1794.)[19] The Committee of Public Safety gradually took charge of steering France through the wartime emergency, implementing mass conscription after late August 1793. Meanwhile, the Committee of General Security mastered the growing apparatus of repression. Representatives on mission, watch committees, revolutionary tribunals, civilian agents, and army generals all became responsible to the two committees, thus making it easy to exaggerate the Jacobin dictatorship as a ubiquitous "system of terror."

Such an image lacks the local perspective, however. The guillotine was a rare sight outside major cities: almost half the departments had fewer than a dozen executions. Repression was concentrated in the west, the south, along the frontiers, and at Paris. Moreover, rather than operating repression from the center, the Convention often found itself authorizing local action that the two great committees sought to contain and canalize. In many places, the so-called "Terror" was experienced as the triumph of a minority of militants, the Jacobins, over their rivals thanks to support from outside the local community. Individuals mattered as much as policy. Draconian laws against émigrés and refractory priests were very unevenly enforced. Proclaiming categories of people "outside the law" – the ultimate proscription – led to mixed results: only 60 percent of the 22,000 individuals judged as "outlaws" were actually condemned to death. In short, local judges determined their fate more than the law or the government ever intended.[20] Laxity and creativity matched excesses of zealotry. Nonetheless, numerous examples of extreme repression shaped by local reprisals and the settling of scores tarnished the Revolutionary Government for all time.

Repression reached its peak both in the south and in the west in the winter of 1793–1794. After a prolonged bombardment helped to end the siege of Lyon, extremists in Paris insisted on exemplary punishment. Therefore, new representatives replaced special tribunals (already responsible for 200 executions) with a "revolutionary commission" that condemned 1,673 individuals, half of them members of the social elite, over the winter. Of these, 268 were shot in batches by cannons loaded with grapeshot in order to "imprint terror

---

[19] Richard Cobb, *The People's Armies* (New Haven: Yale University Press, 1987 [1961]).
[20] Éric de Mari, *La mise hors de la loi sous la Révolution française (19 mars 1793 – An III)* (Paris: LGDJ, 2015).

without inciting pity."[21] The siege and recapture of Toulon in late December led to another major massacre. Rather than hold hearings, local Jacobins simply culled the population left behind once the English fleet departed, then summarily shot 700 or more supposed royalists.[22] Similar mass shootings were part of the repression of the *Vendée militaire*, especially following republican victories over the "Catholic and Royal Army" at Le Mans and Savenay in December. Until then, the prolonged success of the Vendéans had been largely due to three factors: effective use of the local population and local terrain; poorly trained and undisciplined republican forces; and fierce rivalries among politicians and generals. Both sides perpetrated atrocities against civilians, executed prisoners, and suffered horribly from malnutrition and disease. Republican mopping-up operations included the mass slaughter of combatants and noncombatants alike. The sheer volume of prisoners led to appalling responses. Not only were thousands executed in the aftermath of republican victories, but also over 5,000 prisoners (including hundreds of women) were summarily shot in batches large and small, most of them anonymously. Dozens of military commissions also played their part, sometimes condemning scores of people a day, including whole villages. The Bignon Commission alone shot 2,620 "brigands" at Nantes. Others operated more judiciously, though rarely for long.[23]

Dangerous overcrowding in prisons led to the most notorious atrocities of the period, a series of mass drownings (*noyades*) in the Loire River. Although carried out secretly, evidence remains of at least seven *noyades* that dispatched several thousand prisoners over two months. They began with the drowning of ninety priests, then expanded to a broad range of men, women, and children. The local *sans-culottes* militia, the Marat Company, took charge of stripping prisoners to their undershirts, tying them together, herding them onto skiffs and barges, then sinking the boats in the river, all at night. But darkness could not muffle desperate screams or hide floating corpses. Moreover, representatives on missions such as Carrier and Francastel reported on these "vertical executions" and "patriotic baptisms." "The

---

[21] William Edmonds, *Jacobinism and the Revolt of Lyon, 1789–1793* (Oxford: Oxford University Press, 1990).

[22] Malcolm Crook, *Toulon in War and Revolution* (Manchester: Manchester University Press, 1991), 126–57.

[23] Brunot Hervé, "Noyades, fusilades, exécutions: Les mises à mort des brigands entre justice et massacres en Loire-Inférieure en l'an II," *La Révolution française. Cahiers de l'Institut de la Révolution française* 2011 (no. 3), https://journals.openedition.org/lrf/209.

Vendée will be depopulated, but the republic will be avenged and tranquil," they assured the government.[24]

Despite the crushing defeats and mass killings of December–January, pockets of resistance remained. In response, and with tacit approval from his civilian overlords, General Turreau marched a dozen military columns across the region with orders to slaughter anyone and burn everything in their paths. Commanders of these "infernal columns" proudly reported on the mass murder and widespread carnage that left over 11,000 dead in three months.[25] On the one hand, describing this as a genocide is an abuse of language; on the other, describing the region as "brutalized," rather than "terrorized," in order to separate the Vendée from the Terror is also misleading.[26] Already in the summer of 1793, the Committee of Public Safety had explicitly made crushing the Vendée the key to the republic's survival both at home and abroad. The Revolutionary Government adopted a rhetoric of terror and extermination to compensate for its political weakness and to avoid succumbing to rabid extremists who practiced what they preached. Thus, spectacular violence was used to terrorize opponents and coopt rivals, at least until they too could be mastered.

The Revolutionary Tribunal in Paris exemplifies the changing nature of repression. From March to October 1793, it pronounced only ninety-two death sentences (26 percent). Complaints from the *sans-culottes* led the Convention to double its capacity and hasten proceedings, which produced 1,167 condemnations to death (58 percent) over seven months. This phase included the political show trials of the Girondins, Hébertists, and Dantonists alike. Liquidating the leaders of these *republican* factions revealed just how elastic the concept of "counterrevolution" had become. By May 1794, the tribunal was judging several hundred defendants a week, often condemning to death men and women exclusively on the basis of their status and functions during the *ancien régime*. This included scores of magistrates, generals, clerics, courtiers, and tax farmers. A third phase, dubbed the Great Terror, lasted from mid-June to the end of July 1794. By this time, the government had shut down revolutionary justice in the provinces, except at Orange. In order to clear the

---

[24] Alain Gérard, *"Par principe d'humanité . . .": La Terreur et la Vendée* (Paris: Fayard, 1999), 297.
[25] Anne Rolland-Boulestreau, *Les colonnes infernales: Violences et guerre civile en Vendée militaire (1794–1795)* (Paris: Fayard, 2015).
[26] Reynald Sécher, *A French Genocide: The Vendée* (Notre Dame, IN: Notre Dame University Press, 2003 [1986]); Jean-Clément Martin, *La Terreur: Vérités et légendes* (Paris: Perrin, 2017), esp. 144.

backlog of 8,000 prisoners in the over-stuffed prisons of Paris, the draconian law of 22 Prairial eliminated defense lawyers, witnesses, and punishments other than death. Sending people before the tribunal in batches produced 1,366 executions (80 percent) in seven weeks. The spectacle of such relentless killing helped to provoke the overthrow of Robespierre. Thereafter, restoring basic procedures and requiring jurors to decide on "criminal intent" produced only forty-six executions (5 percent) over six months. A final reorganization of the Revolutionary Tribunal lasted from February to May 1795. All but one of the seventeen death sentences during this period (15 percent) were pronounced against former members of the Revolutionary Tribunal itself.[27] The Thermidorians had vowed to replace "terror" with "justice" and, despite other failings, here they largely kept their word.

The Revolutionary Tribunal retains a special place in the history of political justice. It was not, however, uniquely terrible. Some seventy other institutions of expedited justice, including military commissions, popular tribunals, and regular courts using "revolutionary" procedures, operated during Year II. Some of these bodies adhered to a few basic judicial procedures, but most were more political than judicial in nature. Acquittal rates can be very misleading because the logic of "terror" ensured that the condemned included a large number of people who posed no threat to the government. Altogether, almost 17,000 individuals were formally condemned to death between March 1793 and July 1794. About half of them were condemned and shot – not guillotined – by military commissions devoid of jurisprudence. Approximately 20,000 others, mostly unrecorded as individuals, were summarily executed or died in prison.[28] Though modest compared with many later revolutions, such numbers take on greater meaning in the context of a society built on face-to-face communities, not masses or classes.

Many of the excesses of Year II (1793–1794) became nationally known only during the course of Year III (1794–1795). Thermidorian politicians and journalists used these revelations to put "horror on the daily agenda." Combining sentimentalist pathos with frequent exaggeration – hundreds of thousands if not millions killed – fostered a national reckoning with the Jacobins, increasingly dubbed "terrorists" and "drinkers of blood."[29] The

---

[27] Antoine Boulant, *Le Tribunal révolutionnaire: Punir les ennemis du peuple* (Paris: Perrin, 2018).
[28] Donald Greer, *The Incidence of the Terror* (Cambridge, MA: Harvard University Press, 1934).
[29] Bronislaw Baczko, *Ending the Terror: The French Revolution after Robespierre* (Cambridge: Cambridge University Press, 1994 [1989]); Howard G. Brown, *Mass Violence and the*

republic's military victories, notably in June 1794, and the execution of 104 Robespierrists without trial in late July dramatically altered the political landscape. These events led inexorably to replacing representatives on mission, releasing tens of thousands of prisoners, closing the Jacobin Club, and systematically purging provincial administrations. After the Convention reinstated the surviving Girondin deputies in early 1795, rectifying the wrongs of Year II became a top priority. Nullifying all verdicts rendered by "revolutionary" procedures helped to restore property and rehabilitate reputations. However, such a sweeping decree essentially criminalized anyone who had participated in the machinery of repression in Year II. Efforts to prosecute the "perpetrators" were fraught with legal challenges. Where did implementing revolutionary laws end and personal responsibility begin? Unable to formulate some form of transitional justice, the regime's authority declined rapidly, once again opening the door to popular violence.[30]

In the spring of 1795, the republic was whip-sawed by violence from the left and the right. Mounting economic distress provoked disturbances across northern France and exacerbated shortages in Paris. A huge largely unarmed crowd invaded the Convention on 1 April demanding lower bread prices. Supplies did not improve and so, on 20 May, another huge crowd, led by women and supported by armed *sans-culottes*, again invaded the Convention. In addition to bread, they demanded a return to Jacobin government. Killing a deputy and promenading his head into the chamber was followed the next day by a large show of force, including cannons, organized by militants from the poorer sections. No fighting ensued, however. Moderates used the reprieve to mount a cautious military response. The regular army occupied and disarmed the eastern Faubourg Saint-Antoine with little bloodshed. The arrest of 1,200 militants from across the city ended the *sans-culottes* movement once and for all. A military commission condemned leading insurgents to death, including six Montagnard deputies. Involving the army in policing operations and using military justice against political rebellion pointed the way to the future.

In the southeast, anti-Jacobinism inspired a wave of vigilante violence. The region had been torn apart by the Federalist Revolt and the brutal repression that followed. The Convention's efforts to rectify the injustices of Year II

Self: From the French Wars of Religion to the Paris Commune (Ithaca, NY: Cornell University Press, 2019), 113–60.

[30] Howard G. Brown, "Robespierre's Tail: The Possibilities of Justice after Thermidor," *Canadian Journal of History* 95 (2010), 503–35.

included arresting many former Jacobin officials. Others were simply dismissed, disarmed, and required to return to their home towns, possibly to face intense, even deadly, hostility. Anti-Jacobin activists took the opportunity to punish these "terrorists" for subjugating local communities. The resulting popular violence bore gruesome similarities to the vigilantism of 1792, including public lynching and prison massacres. The murder of former officials and revolutionary militants began in late 1794. Demagogic rhetoric from reactionary journalists and politicians incited ever greater reprisals. The first major massacres took place – almost inevitably – at Lyon. Convinced that arrested "terrorists" would be acquitted at trial, vigilantes slaughtered at least seventy "mathevons" (local Jacobins) detained in three different prisons. Local officials claimed to be paralyzed by the enormous crowds that shielded the killers. Smaller massacres took place at a half dozen other cities in the southeast. Counterterrorists struck twice at Tarascon, first throwing twenty-five prisoners from the top of the medieval castle, then, a month later, killing twenty-three more and setting a fire in their cells. The largest prison massacre happened on 5 June at Marseille. The dead numbered over 100, many captured after Jacobins from Toulon mounted a punitive military expedition against Marseille a few weeks earlier. (A military commission condemned another fifty-two to death, many more than in Paris at the same time.) In total, mob attacks and reprisal killings led to some 2,000 deaths in the region, making republican talk of "royalist" murder gangs enduringly credible. Efforts to prosecute the perpetrators were desultory at best: at Aubagne, the site of fourteen political murders in six weeks, it took until 1801. Too many local officials presented the killings as possibly regrettable, but certainly not preventable, acts of popular justice. In contrast to 1792, the vigilantism of 1795 replaced ritualized humiliation postmortem with elements of community purification using fire (burning corpses) or water (dumping them in rivers). Talk of popular sovereignty also disappeared, replaced by the language of vendetta that befitted killings in which perpetrators and victims knew one another personally. The ideology of community became especially obvious when hundreds of townsfolk celebrated the murder of a "terrorist" by dancing a farandole through the streets.[31]

---

[31] Colin Lucas, "Themes in Southern Violence after Thermidor," in Gwynne Lewis and Colin Lucas, eds., *Beyond the Terror: Essays in French Regional and Social History, 1789–1815* (Cambridge: Cambridge University Press, 1983), 152–94; Sutherland, *Murder in Aubagne*; Bronislaw Baczko, *Politiques de la Révolution française* (Paris: Folio histoire, 2008), 210–36.

As popular violence flared in Paris and the southeast, rebellion in western France also roared back to life. Peace treaties negotiated with rebel leaders in early 1795 proved to be mere truces. In late June, the British Navy landed a large force of French émigrés, refugees from Toulon, and former prisoners of war at Quiberon Bay (Brittany), where they planned to join with local *chouans* (royalist rebels). The republican army swiftly crushed the invasion, taking over 6,000 prisoners in the process. General Hoche only partly succeeded in sparing them from the full rigors of the law. Over the next six months, 21 military commissions condemned and shot 750 émigrés, half of them former nobles; 2,850 others were acquitted as unwilling participants, but then enrolled in the republican army. (Another 3,000 *chouans* captured in the operation received only modest fines.)[32] Thus, the Thermidorian Convention continued the use of martial justice against rebels, but with far less haste and far more discretion.

The Search for Stability, 1795–1802

The Convention sought to end the French Revolution by implementing a new constitution. After three harrowing years, however, the republic had become widely unpopular. When the Convention insisted that two-thirds of deputies in the new bicameral legislature must come from the Convention itself, the now deeply anti-Jacobin sections of Paris reacted with outrage. The majority of sections, agitated by a disastrous economy and the recent rehabilitation of *sans-culottes*, organized a well-armed insurrection. The Convention's forces included 5,000 regular troops, given added fighting spirit by 1,500 rearmed militants. General Bonaparte's ruthless use of grapeshot helped to end several hours of intense street fighting. Each side suffered some 200 casualties, making it the second bloodiest *journée* in Paris after 10 August 1792. The insurrection of 13 Vendémiaire Year IV (3 October 1795) was more anti-Jacobin than proroyalist.[33] Its failure ended the Paris sections' ability to coerce the government. Henceforth, the army became a vital instrument to preserve and even impose the constitutional republic, known as the Directory (1795–1799).

The Directorial regime faced extraordinary challenges when it began in November 1795. Not least, the prevailing economy of violence posed a

---

[32] Jean-Louis Debauve, *La justice révolutionnaire dans le Morbihan* (Paris: self-published, 1965); Robert Garnier, *Lazare Hoche, ou l'honneur des armes* (Paris: Payot, 1986), 216–44.

[33] Baczko, *Politiques*, 272–311; Loris Chavanette, *Quatre-vingt-quinze: La Terreur en procès* (Paris: CNRS, 2017), 271–85.

serious threat to the social and political order. Hyperinflation, economic chaos, soaring debt, woeful social welfare, politicized judges, and inadequate police meant widespread misery and record criminality. Collective action prompted by economic hardship increasingly deteriorated from communicative violence based on the moral economy to a broadly solipsistic violence that eschewed any legitimizing rituals. The epidemic of highway robbery, house-breaking, and banditry in the late 1790s constituted France's worst crime wave of modern times. Moreover, efforts to stabilize the polity and restore law and order confronted four countervailing forces: conspiratorial royalism, resurgent Catholicism, fervent Jacobinism, and foreign war. Ending the French Revolution required a regime that combined administrative efficacy with political legitimacy. Protracted civil strife delayed this outcome until 1802.[34]

The Constitution of 1795 proved a serious obstacle to restoring law and order. An admirable emphasis on elected officials, including judges, hampered the government's ability to overcome resistance and the extremes of local factionalism. Annual elections also fostered political strife and undermined continuity. The Executive Directory often found its hands tied when trying to impose the republican order on a deeply disaffected populace. Local officials routinely declined to enforce laws against refractory priests, returned émigrés, and draft dodgers, even though all three were important sources of antirepublican resistance, if not outright royalist counterrevolution. The legacy of 1793–1794 further complicated matters. On its final day, the Convention issued a sweeping amnesty for "all acts related to the revolution." This nullified all arrests and prosecutions related to the repression of Year II, thereby ending any effort to distinguish between "patriots" inspired by "an excess of zeal for liberty" and would-be "terrorists" who deserved criminal punishment. Henceforth, political rivals caricatured one another as "anarchists" who threatened the social order or "quality folk" who favored property and prosperity over liberty and equality. The new regime confronted avatars of political violence from both sides, be it Babeuf and the radical "conspiracy of equals" or Brottier and the royalist "Agence de Paris."

The Constitution was initially not applied to western France, where the Vendée civil war had flared up and spread. Despite the disastrous Quiberon invasion, royalist leaders managed to organize several small peasant armies

---

[34] Howard G. Brown, *Ending the French Revolution: Violence, Justice, and Repression from the Terror to Napoleon* (Charlottesville: University of Virginia Press, 2006), 23–65. Most of the remaining paragraphs are based on this book.

to combat republican forces. In response, General Hoche imposed a military dictatorship across ten departments. More troops, better discipline, and increased tolerance, especially of religious worship, steadily eroded support for the rebels. The relentless pursuit, capture, and execution of key leaders, such as Stofflet and Charette, along with an amnesty for rebels who surrendered their weapons, divided leaders and demoralized followers. Furthermore, seizing livestock, taking hostages, and cutting off grain supplies forced towns and villages to unite in self-interest against the rebels in their midst. Whether called pacification or subjugation, the Directory ended the military dictatorship in the region on 30 July 1796. This officially ended the *Vendée militaire*, three years of civil war that killed 200,000 people: 170,000 inhabitants (combatants and noncombatants combined – a fifth of whom supported the revolution) and 30,000 republican soldiers.[35] Most died of disease and deprivation; nonetheless, the myriad battles and massacres indicate how Luciferian the struggle had been.

Ending the civil war did not end civil strife. On the contrary, the original conflict spread north of the Loire River, mutating into widespread guerrilla warfare. This *chouannerie* differed from the *Vendée militaire* more in style than in substance: small bands instead of peasant armies; local raids rather than regional domination; sowing terror more than waging war. *Chouans* fought for an idealized local community, but rarely mobilized whole communities. They attacked purchasers of national land, robbed stage coaches, killed constitutional priests, kidnapped for ransom, and ambushed army units. The movement enjoyed local support due to the ongoing brutality and marauding of republican soldiers. Grand strategists at the Bourbon Pretender's court in exile failed to appreciate the extreme localism of *chouannerie* and so sent émigré nobles to take charge of various bands, which usually alienated seasoned leaders. Moreover, the rebels' misdeeds in their own localities, including threats, looting, and extortion, made them appear more mercenary than idealistic.[36]

The coup d'état of 18 Fructidor Year V (4 September 1797) precipitated the regime into liberal authoritarianism as a means to ensconce the republic.[37] The bloodless coup purged the conservative opposition in the legislature on the grounds that it was the handmaid of an Anglo-royalist conspiracy

---

[35] Jacques Hussenet, *"Détruisez la Vendée!"* (La Roche-sur-Yon: Centre vendéen de recherches historiques, 2007).

[36] Maurice Hutt, *Chouannerie and the Counter-Revolution: Puisaye, the Princes and the British Government in the 1790s*, 2 vols. (Cambridge: Cambridge University Press, 1983).

[37] On "liberal authoritarianism," see Brown, *Ending the French Revolution*, 236, 358.

known as the Grand Plan. The coup included reviving harsh measures against émigrés and refractory priests. Over the next two years, ad hoc military commissions judged over 1,000 individuals for emigration, condemning 279 of them to death, many of them active leaders in violent counterrevolution. The so-called "Second Directory" also prioritized deporting priests, purging the rural constabulary, and republicanizing the courts. These measures were justified by a major surge in antirepublican violence over the summer of 1797, especially across the south. *Chouannerie* also persisted in western France. Chronically short of troops due to the ongoing foreign war, the Directory resorted to more sinister forms of counterinsurgency. The resulting "dirty war" included midnight raids on suspect farms, soldiers disguised as *chouans*, paid informants, detention without trial, prisoners killed while "trying to escape," military sweeps of rural regions, and hostage taking. These practices were no more brutal than those of the *chouans* themselves, but they clearly violated the punctilious code of police and judicial conduct adopted on the eve of the Directory.

High levels of provincial violence prompted the Directory to expand the army's role in policing and punishment. Declaring towns under a "state of siege," which transferred all police powers to the local army commander, became an increasingly common response to collective violence, resistance to authority, and attacks on the forces of order. By late 1799, at least 220 communities had been placed under a "state of siege." These ranged from major cities (Lyon, Marseille, Toulon, Nice, Geneva, Antwerp, Ghent) to scores of rural cantons in areas of open rebellion. In January 1798, the regime began using regular military courts to judge civilians charged with house-breaking or highway robbery. The law aimed to combat the scourge of brigandage that afflicted much of France. Targets ranged from classic bandits to diehard *chouans*. Whereas military commissions continued to judge rebels captured with arms in hand, adding military courts to the arsenal of repression prevented brigand bands from intimidating judges and paralyzing juries. Notably, regular military courts pronounced at least 280 death sentences in response to the "Peasants' War" of late 1798 in annexed Belgium. Endemic violence in the countryside, whether politically motivated or not, badly eroded the regime's legitimacy, whereas aggressive efforts to restore law and order met with general approval.

Just as provincial violence seemed to be abating, the War of the Second Coalition (1798–1802) renewed the civil strife. The Directory's mass recruitment effort again sparked widespread resistance. Draft-dodgers swelled the ranks of brigand bands and royalist rebels alike. Moreover, transferring regular troops away from domestic policing duties to the frontiers allowed the bubbling cauldron of discontent to boil over. To bolster the coalition's military efforts, royalists organized peasant revolts both in the south and in the west. Aggressive conscription prematurely triggered a planned uprising on 6 August 1799 in the countryside around Toulouse. Although royalist-led rebels seized a large swath around the city, hastily mobilized National Guard columns fragmented and defeated them piecemeal. Despite the capture of some 5,000 prisoners over three weeks, military courts executed only 15 of them. Reconciliation quickly replaced repression.[38]

In the west, *chouannerie* took heart from foreign coalition victories and fuel from the Jacobin "law of hostages" adopted in July. A well-funded plan, implemented by émigré nobles carrying brevets from the Pretender, created the most militarized form of guerrilla warfare yet. The Count of Bourmont even seized Le Mans for three days in mid-October, the greatest single triumph in the history of *chouannerie*. Despite their possession of uniforms, weapons, cavalry, and cannons, the rebels lacked enough manpower to take, let alone hold, other urban centers. Mobilizing national guardsmen from fifteen departments and transferring back regular troops gave the Directory the upper hand even before Bonaparte's seizure of power. (Even so, the widespread internal unrest of 1799 helped to justify the coup d'état of 18 Brumaire.) General Hédouville obtained a cessation of hostilities, but when negotiations dragged out, First Consul Bonaparte ordered a return to Hoche's earlier methods. This included reopening churches and amnesties in exchange for weapons, offset by regional military dictatorship, widespread use of the "state of siege," shooting all rebels seized with arms, letting the army supply itself in cash and kind, and brutally disarming the populace. Before long, rebel commanders began to surrender (Frotté, in Normandy) or flee (Cadoudal, in Brittany). The civil war officially ended (again) on 21 April 1800. All the same, assaults, holdups, and farmhouse invasions remained alarmingly common. Though they acted more like brigands, latter-day *chouans* remained die-hard royalists. As a result, the Consulate continued many of the counterinsurgency techniques developed under the Directory.

The Consulate's first innovation in repression came from exceptional military commissions. Politicized brigandage, bolstered by traditions of vendetta and antistatism, had become especially intractable in the southeast. By 1800, so-called *barbets* dominated the foothills of the Alps; murder gangs and

[38] Howard G. Brown, "Revolt and Repression in the Midi Toulousain (1799)," *French History* 19 (2005), 234–61.

highway robbers plagued the Rhone Valley; and the "Vendée cévenole" raged in eastern Languedoc, where mounted royalists led their rustic, but well-armed, followers. In one incident, 150 outlaws sacked Les Vans (Ardèche), looted the town coffers, burned official records, and stole 500 muskets. The four itinerant military commissions received most of their "prey" from flying columns of troops that showed scant regard for legality due to the sheer violence of the resistance. Over 400 individuals were tried in upland towns from Rodez to Digne and coastal cities from Montpellier to Toulon. Firing squads were often set up near the site of the original crimes in order both to intimidate and to reassure. Another three military commissions operated in western France. There, some 1,200 *chouans* were arrested, 250 condemned to death, and 150 killed "while resisting arrest" during the winter of 1800–1801.

The Consulate's use of "booted justice" proved difficult to control. However, when the government proposed "special tribunals" as a more regulated alternative, liberal lawmakers balked on the grounds that they lacked juries and appeals. An attempt to blow up Bonaparte on 24 December 1800, which killed or injured dozens of bystanders, changed the climate. Over the next two years, one-third of the departments of France acquired Special Tribunals in order to combat violent crime in the countryside (1801 saw several gendarmes attacked or killed every day). Special Tribunals, with their civilian prosecutors and official defense attorneys, marked a major improvement over revolutionary tribunals, military commissions, or regular military courts. Nonetheless, they raised national penal rates to extraordinary levels: roughly 800 executions and 3,000 terms of hard labor per annum (four times the rate of the tumultuous 1780s!).[39]

Liberal authoritarianism helped to end the French Revolution and paved the road to personal dictatorship. The early Consulate combined militarized policing, better regulated exceptional justice, the deportation of extreme radicals, and magistrates appointed by the government. This enhanced apparatus of repression proved increasingly effective because the Consulate also addressed root causes of prolonged civil strife. Almost all elections ceased in 1799, churches began reopening in 1800, émigrés returned legally in 1801, peace with victory took hold in 1801–1802, and a Concordat with the papacy settled religious disputes in 1802. Whereas some areas had experienced the worst violence of the French Revolution during the years

---

[39] Brown, *Ending the French Revolution*, 329–30.

1799–1800, the new regime's mastery of provincial violence became increasingly clear in 1801–1802. Cracking down on revolutionary factionalism played its part. On the one hand, little more than a brawl between soldiers and Jacobins brought more military and judicial repression to the Mediterranean town of Sète in spring 1802 than the monarchy's combined responses to the famous popular uprisings at Grenoble, Pau, and Rennes in 1788–1789. On the other, the criminal justice system abandoned protracted partisan prosecutions from the Second Directory, while also punishing the known perpetrators of anti-Jacobin murders from 1795–1797. The link between "popular justice" and "popular sovereignty" – so important in the violence of 1792 and the turn to policies of terror in 1793 – had been replaced in 1795 by a constitutional democracy. Rather than consolidating a representative democracy, however, efforts to end civil strife and endemic violence generated a security state.[40] The new security state, reified by the Life Consulate for Napoleon Bonaparte in August 1802, derived its legitimacy from providing law and order in lieu of participatory democracy. Not all violence in the French Revolution was revolutionary violence. But ending the violence provoked by the Revolution ensured that Hobbes triumphed over Rousseau.

---

[40] On the "security state," see Brown, *Ending the French Revolution*, 343–4.

8
Jacobins and Terror in the French Revolution

MARISA LINTON

Introduction

The French Revolutionary terror was a shattering political and social event. It raised difficult questions about the nature of transformative politics, questions that are still passionately debated today. Possibly the most controversial question of all is this: how could a revolution that began as an idealistic and humanitarian project, with the goal of establishing liberty, equality, fraternity, and "the rights of man," descend, step by step, into violence? The French Revolutionary terror continues to haunt our imaginations, above all through the image of that murderous invention, the guillotine. Ironically, it is this instrument of death – not the Declaration of the Rights of Man – that has served as the indelible emblem of the Revolution. Ask anyone, outside a narrow circle of specialists, what they think of when they hear the words *French Revolution* and almost invariably the first thing that comes to mind is the guillotine. In the minds of many observers, the terms "revolution" and "terror" are virtually synonymous.

Despite the fame, or rather, notoriety, of the French revolutionary terror, there are many fallacies and misconceptions about its nature. One of the most persistent is that it was created by Maximilien Robespierre, who personally masterminded a "Reign of Terror." People who know relatively little about the French Revolution will confidently state that *the Terror* was invented and led by Robespierre. If they know a little more they may call it the "Jacobin Terror," after the political group of whom Robespierre was a leading member.

The reality was much more complex. Recent historiography has moved away from the idea that the Jacobins instituted a "system of terror," showing instead that what is commonly known as *the Terror* (with a capital T) was in reality much more an ad hoc and improvised, even at points chaotic, response to events than a coherent ideological "terror system." When we look at the gradual evolution of terror, a much more contingent picture emerges, one in which events and emotional responses did as much as – or indeed more than – ideology to drive violence.

Historians have been posing some new questions, and posing older questions in different ways. The questions begin with basic nomenclature: what should we call it, "terror" or the Terror? And how does that capital "T" affect the way we conceptualize the subject? Did terror stem from an ideology, an ideology already present in 1789, or an ideology specific to the Jacobins? Did terror grow out of escalating circumstances, above all the war with the foreign powers? Can we agree on a chronology of terror? When and how did it begin? And when and how did it end? What was the relationship between terror and justice? To what extent was terror a rhetoric, a form of words, a threat to intimidate enemies? What about the experiences of individuals? Who were the principal victims? How far was terror something to which revolutionaries themselves – including the nation's elected representatives – were subject, and how did their consciousness of the danger in which they stood affect their choices and their actions?

We might start by giving a preliminary definition of *the Terror*. Even that is difficult, for there were many forms of violence, conflict, intimidation, and coercion between 1792 and 1799, deployed by groups with different political agendas. When historians speak of *the Terror* what they usually mean is a body of legislation passed by the National Convention between 1793 and 1794 (the specific dates are, as we will see, open to debate) and the human consequences of the implementation of those laws. This was a legalized terror, a policy of government.[1]

In the past it was often argued that *the Terror* was an inevitable consequence of prerevolutionary political ideologies, adopted by the Jacobins to justify the recourse to terror. Chief amongst these ideologies is said to have been Rousseau's concept of the "general will."[2] An alternative ideology that

---

[1] A growing body of work is building the case for a rethinking of the French revolutionary terror. For the most comprehensive statement so far of this case, see Michel Biard and Marisa Linton, *Terreur! La Révolution française face à ses démons* (Paris: Armand Colin, 2020). Much of the recent work on this subject is discussed in some key articles in the H-France Salon on "Rethinking the French Revolutionary Terror," with contributions by Marisa Linton, Michel Biard, Carla Hesse, Mette Harder, and Ronen Steinberg, *H-France Salon* 11:16 (2019), https://h-france.net/h-france-salon-volume-11-2019/?fbclid=IwAR3XFqIyAt-7sOK7lTo_zebC4AoeJpFebg72iHE3oo6D9TSLXygptTLJ9xM.

[2] The argument that Rousseau's concept of the "general will" was the principal ideology driving *the Terror* has been made many times, notably by François Furet, "Terreur," in François Furet and Mona Ozouf, eds., *Dictionnaire critique de la Révolution française*

has more recently been identified with *the Terror* is that of the concept of "natural right."³ Against this "terror out of ideology" argument is the "terror out of circumstances" argument. This is the idea that *the Terror* was a regrettable necessity, that came about as a result of circumstances – that is, that terror developed in response to war and foreign invasion.⁴

Recent work has been looking at the origins of terror rather differently. Historians have been looking more closely at contingent events. In a move away from overarching explanations of *the Terror* based on ideology, class, or a "system of terror," historians have been investigating the web of connections between politics, ideology, tactical strategies, emotions, and the role of individuals. This recent historiography gives due weight to the role of circumstances, especially external and internal military conflict, but is much more ready to acknowledge how terror, once instituted, took on a dynamic of its own, and was not just a cause-and-effect response to war.

A growing number of historians has been exploring the emotional dimensions of the Revolution, especially the relationship between emotion and terror.⁵ Terror had an emotional dynamic as well as an intellectual one: it took place in the hearts and stomachs of those who participated in it, as well as in their heads. Emotions continue to draw the attention of historians, particularly the relationship between political ideas, rhetoric, and emotions.

(Paris: Flammarion, 1988); Keith Michael Baker, *Inventing the French Revolution* (Cambridge: Cambridge University Press, 1990).

[3] On the relationship of the ideology of "natural right" to *the Terror*, see Dan Edelstein, *The Terror of Natural Right: Republicanism, the Cult of Nature, and the French Revolution* (Chicago: University of Chicago Press, 2009).

[4] The vast historiography on *the Terror* is too extensive to list here, though readers can consult the bibliography of works in English and French, listed in Biard and Linton, *Terreur*. In addition to other works mentioned in this chapter, Hugh Gough, *The Terror in the French Revolution*, 2nd edition (Houndmills: Palgrave, 2010) provides a clear summary of the debates, especially the ideology versus circumstances arguments. For an incisive narrative of events, see David Andress, *The Terror: Civil War in the French Revolution* (London: Little, Brown, 2005).

[5] Two recent studies that trace the role of emotions in the genesis of terror are Timothy Tackett, *The Coming of the Terror in the French Revolution* (Cambridge, MA: Harvard University Press, 2015); and, on the emotional and ideological reasons that led the revolutionaries to choose a terror that rebounded strongly upon themselves, Marisa Linton, *Choosing Terror: Virtue, Friendship and Authenticity in the French Revolution* (Oxford: Oxford University Press, 2013). See, too, Biard and Linton, *Terreur*, Chapter 3, "Le poids des peurs et des émotions." For an overview of this historiography, see Jack R. Censer, "Historians Revisit the Terror – Again," *The Journal of Social History*, 48:2 (2014), 383–403. The relationship between emotions and terror is also addressed by Sophie Wahnich, *La liberté ou la mort, essai sur la Terreur et le terrorisme* (Paris: La Fabrique, 2003).

The fear of conspiracy and its accompanying rhetoric, which permeated all social levels, and which intensified at moments of crisis, is a case in point.[6] There is much that we can learn from looking at emotions in the revolutionary context. Yet the study of emotions in the context of revolutionary politics is fraught with problems. One of these is source material: namely the difficulty of finding sources, together with problems of how to interpret them.[7] Another challenge is how much we can directly attribute to the emotions of participants. To see revolutionaries solely in terms of their emotional responses would be reductive and would deny them the agency that they undoubtedly had. Emotions should not be studied in isolation from contexts and ideologies, strategic thinking, and a myriad of other elements that constituted the experience of revolutionaries.

Consequently, a more complex picture of the politics of terror has begun to emerge. This chapter will examine the dynamics around the emergence, incidence, and nature of the revolutionary terror, and look at the motives of the people who are credited with implementing a policy of terror. It will seek to throw light on three interconnected questions. First, who were the Jacobins, and what united them, and what disunited them? Second, what was the policy of terror and how and why did it develop? Third, what was the role of emotions in the political decision-making that led to the adoption of terror? Finally, it will consider how our answers to these questions may affect our historiographical interpretations of the revolutionary terror.

Turning Points

The origins of the Jacobins lay in the Breton Club, which was founded shortly after the outbreak of the Revolution in 1789 by deputies to the new National Assembly. It became a focus for the "patriots" (at that time a term for radicals who supported the Revolution). The membership of the Club rapidly expanded, and it moved into the premises of a former Jacobin monastery in the rue St. Honoré in Paris. Here it took the name "Society of the Friends of the Constitution," but soon became known as the Jacobin Club. Over time a network of affiliated clubs sprang up throughout France.

---

[6] Peter R. Campbell, Thomas E. Kaiser, and Marisa Linton, eds., *Conspiracy in the French Revolution* (Manchester: Manchester University Press, 2007).

[7] On problems of source material for the study of revolutionary emotions, see Marisa Linton, "The Power of Emotions: New Light on the *Conventionnels* and the Process of the Terror," *H-France Salon* 11:1 (2019), https://h-france.net/h-france-salon-volume-11-2019/#1101.

At its height there were as many as 1,544 provincial Jacobin clubs. These clubs maintained connections through correspondence with the mother club in Paris through the circulation of pamphlets and speeches. The Jacobins acted as a debating club and political pressure group rather than as a formal political party. The revolutionaries were opposed to the idea of political parties, thinking that parties would be used to promote particular interests rather than the "good of all." Membership of the Jacobins came mostly from the middle and professional classes. Up until June 1791, however, the leaders of the Jacobins came disproportionately from the ranks of the social elite of the *ancien régime*. In those early years the Jacobin Club was dominated by relative moderates such as Barnave, Duport, and Lameth.

Insofar as Jacobinism contained elements of a shared set of political views, it was founded on the optimistic belief that mankind was basically good, and that human society could be made better in the here and now, rather than in an afterlife. Jacobins believed in open and transparent politics. In theory at least, they were radical democrats, supporting popular sovereignty. Their conception of politics was a moral as well as a democratic one: they believed that it was the responsibility of politicians to consider only the public good, that is, to be politically virtuous. Political leaders should reject financial corruption and refuse to profit personally from their public office. Jacobins were politically rather than socially egalitarian, though they were opposed to extremes of wealth or poverty. Their social ideal was that of a republic of small producers, peopled by landed peasants and independent artisans.

Many of these ideas were not exclusive to men who attended meetings of the Jacobin Club, rather they were part of the common currency amongst the "patriots" of 1789. There was also the very real and growing problem of political authenticity. How could observers be sure that men who purported to espouse the principles of liberty, equality, and fraternity were genuine in their beliefs? Might they not be motivated, at least in part, by expediency? Could radical words be a cloak for personal ambition? Over time this problem of the authenticity of revolutionary leaders would come to the forefront of revolutionary politics.

Within the Jacobin Club itself there were significant divergencies that widened over time. On the radical left of the Jacobins were several men who also served as deputies in the National Assembly. These men started out in close alignment with Barnave and the other "natural leaders" of the Jacobins, but gradually came to suspect them of being motivated more by personal ambition to achieve ministerial posts and political influence than by genuine commitment to popular sovereignty. One man who was a radical from the outset was Maximilien Robespierre, a lawyer from Arras. Like the other radical Jacobins, he supported equality of rights, regardless of wealth or poverty, and religious toleration for France's religious minorities, and was opposed to slavery. He was also opposed to the death penalty. In May 1791 he attempted, without success, to secure the abolition of capital punishment under the new constitution. He deplored the death penalty as a barbaric, brutal, and unjust punishment.

> I come to ask ... legislators ... to erase from the code of the French the blood laws that command judicial murders, and that their morals and their new constitution reject. I want to prove to them: that the death penalty is essentially unjust and, that it isn't the most repressive of penalties and that it multiplies crimes more than it prevents them.[8]

It is hard, at this point, to see Robespierre and his fellow radicals as men who would one day become advocates of terror. They themselves could not have anticipated it. What then changed? To address that question, we need to pinpoint a sequence of turning points that, step by step, transformed the face of politics.

One such turning point occurred less than a month after Robespierre's abortive attempt to get the death penalty abolished: this was the attempted flight of Louis XVI in June 1791. Louis was intercepted at Varennes, on his way to the Austrian frontier, and brought back to Paris, where crowds met him in ominous silence. The flight of Louis XVI was a fateful step on the road to a new political crisis and a second revolution. For how could the system of constitutional monarchy be maintained when the constitutional monarch had so clearly and drastically repudiated it? Up until that moment the great majority of people, including Robespierre and most of the radicals, were committed to retaining the monarchy and working with the king. The flight of the king was seen as a betrayal: almost overnight loyalty to the monarch began to fall away.[9] The behavior of the king was a slap in the face for more moderate revolutionaries. It led to a split in the Jacobin Club. The moderates, already at loggerheads with the radicals, left to form a new club, the Feuillants.

---

[8] Speech against the death penalty, 30 May 1791, Maximilien Robespierre, Œuvres de Maximilien Robespierre, ed. Marc Bouloiseau, Albert Soboul et al., 12 vols. (Paris: Société des Études Robespierristes, 1910–2007), vol. VII, 432–46.

[9] By far the best study of the king's flight to Varennes and its traumatic impact, is Timothy Tackett, When the King Took Flight (Cambridge, MA: Harvard University Press, 2004).

In late 1791 the Jacobin Club came under the sway of one of the most radical Jacobins, Jacques-Pierre Brissot. He and a loose group of his friends and allies (who became known as the Brissotins, later as the Girondins) argued that the best way to deal with the aggressive rhetoric of Austria and other foreign powers against the Revolution was to declare preemptive war on them. Brissot knew that a war could bring the French monarchy out into the open to side with the invaders against the Revolution: in fact, he was counting on it. It was a reckless strategy, based on the optimistic assumption that France would be militarily victorious and that invaded peoples would welcome French invaders bringing "a crusade for liberty." Robespierre and Brissot had been part of the same radical group, with amicable relations. But now Robespierre opposed the war strategy, warning of the cataclysmic potential that might be unleashed, and Brissot's group attacked Robespierre as unpatriotic and intimated that he was secretly in the pay of the monarchy. It was the warmongers, portraying themselves as the true "patriots," who won the debate. In April 1792, war was declared amidst excited scenes in the Assembly.[10] For a time Robespierre was relatively isolated in his opposition. But soon another split began in the Jacobin Club, this time over the war; it grew larger over suspicions that Brissotin ministers had "sold out." Divisions widened to become an insuperable gulf, and eventually Brissot and the members of his group were either expelled from, or voluntarily left, the Jacobins.

Contrary to the Brissotins' expectations, the war went very badly for France. The intense crisis it sparked lasted to the summer of 1794, and it was against this chaotic, relentless, and dangerous backdrop that the recourse to terror needs to be understood. One of the first consequences of the war was that on 10 August 1792 a second revolution took place. Louis XVI was deposed and imprisoned. The following month fears that Paris could be overrun by the invading armies in league with counterrevolutionary conspirators sparked a notorious event known as the September Massacres. Groups of *sans-culottes* (Paris militants from the lower orders) entered the city's prisons and murdered about 1,200 people as a "precautionary measure," whilst revolutionary leaders, Jacobins and Girondins alike, stood by making no attempt to intervene, moved both by fear and by their conviction that most of those killed were genuine conspirators against the Revolution.[11]

---

[10] On the path to war, see Linton, *Choosing Terror*, Chapter 4.

[11] On the fears roused by rumors of conspiracy, and the extent to which these emotions were an inciting factor in the massacres, see Timothy Tackett, "Rumor and Revolution: The Case of the September Massacres," *French History and Civilisation* 4

Though there was no recurrence of the massacres in revolutionary Paris, the events of September 1792 cast a long shadow.

A new representative body was set up, the National Convention, voted for under a franchise that was, at least in principle, democratic, but which gave no voice to supporters of the monarchy, in a country that was now deeply divided. On 22 September 1792 France was declared a republic. Initially and for many months to come the Brissotin/Girondin group dominated the Convention. They were opposed by a faction of Jacobin deputies (also known as the Montagnards), amongst whom sat Robespierre, Georges Danton, Camille Desmoulins, Louis-Antoine Saint-Just, Jean-Paul Marat, and many others.[12] Under pressure from the *sans-culottes*, the deposed king was put on trial by the Convention. The trial, conviction, and execution of the king, an act of regicide inconceivable just two years earlier, took place against a rising tide of anger at a monarch who had betrayed the Revolution, and rejected the trust and loyalty that his people had placed in him. Radical revolutionaries felt nothing but indifference and contempt for their former king. Choudieu, a Jacobin deputy from Angers, spoke for many: "What's it to us? We always wanted him; he never wanted us."[13]

The king's trial became a further moment on the path that led to terror. Robespierre's political views had evolved. He argued that, whilst he stood by his earlier opposition to the death penalty in normal circumstances, the struggle to establish the Republic amidst war and counterrevolution took place under circumstances that were *not* normal. The highest law was that of "public security":

> Yes, the penalty of death generally is a crime, and for that reason alone, according to the indestructible principles of nature, it can be justified only in cases when it is necessary for the safety of individuals or the social body. . . .
>
> It is with regret that I pronounce this fatal truth. But Louis must die so that the *patrie* can live.[14]

(2011), 54–64, https://h-france.net/rude/wp-content/uploads/2017/08/TackettVol4.pdf.

[12] Identifying "Girondin," "Jacobin," and "Montagnard" deputies is far from a simple matter and has been intensely debated by historians. For a recent assessment, see Biard and Linton, *Terreur*, Chapter 6, "Les luttes politiques au sein de la Convention, un moteur de la 'terreur.'"

[13] Cited in Peter McPhee, *Liberty or Death: The French Revolution* (New Haven: Yale University Press, 2016), 173.

[14] On the judgment of Louis XVI, 3 December 1792, see Robespierre, *Œuvres*, vol. IX, 129–30.

This view was not limited to Robespierre or to the Jacobin deputies. Though the declaration of war had done so much to bring about the overthrow of the monarchy, a majority of the Girondins (though by no means all) would have spared the king's life if they could. But the argument of "public security" carried weight throughout the Convention, amongst men who had no links to the Jacobin Club. No fewer than 361 of the 721 deputies present voted for immediate execution. Others voted for death, but with various stays of execution, but there was an overall majority for putting the king to death without delay. The king was executed on 21 January 1793, the first political victim of the guillotine. His death would set an ominous precedent, though the rate of executions in Paris was slow at first; only in the autumn of that year did the numbers begin to rise alarmingly.

The spring of 1793 saw a renewal of crisis. General Dumouriez, then commander in chief on the northern front, having lost the battle of Neerwinden, struck a pact with the Austrians, and attempted to lead his soldiers to overthrow the Convention, sending the population of the city into turmoil. Only the loyalty of the soldiers to the Republic prevented Dumouriez from succeeding in his attempts. Like Lafayette – who had attempted a similar coup – Dumouriez defected to the Austrians. The treason of General Dumouriez was followed by further military reversals. Mass conscription aimed at recruiting soldiers to fight in the conflict sparked off a revolt in the western department of the Vendée, which escalated into a full-scale civil war against the Republic.

It was against this backdrop that a succession of measures began to be taken. Chief amongst these measures was the law of 19 March 1793 which provided for the execution of rebels in arms. Anyone captured with weapons in their hands, engaging in "counterrevolutionary revolt," was to be sent before a military commission within twenty-four hours and, if convicted, executed. There was no jury; and no appeal was permitted. The law was harsh, but it was a wartime law, and not out of step with much of the treatment handed out to fighters in civil war conflicts in the eighteenth century. Jean-Jacques Régis de Cambacérès, who presented the law, acknowledged its severity, but reminded the deputies that the "pressure of circumstances almost always dictates decisions."[15] This single piece of legislation

---

[15] Cited by Annie Jourdan, *Nouvelle histoire de la Révolution* (Paris: Flammarion, 2018), 177. On this law, see Eric De Mari, *La mise hors de la loi sous la Révolution française (19 mars 1793 – an III): Une étude juridictionnelle et institutionnelle* (Paris: LDGJ, 2015).

was responsible for the majority of executions following a trial during the crisis years of 1793 and 1794.

That month also saw the setting up of a Revolutionary Tribunal in Paris to hear cases of counterrevolution. Part of the rationale for establishing this tribunal was to avoid any repetition of the kind of street violence that had taken place during the September Massacres when, driven by fear, panic, and suspicion, people had taken matters into their own hands. That is, suspects should have a right to a trial to establish guilt or innocence. As the Jacobin leader Danton put it: "Let us be terrible in order to stop the people from being so."[16]

In the wake of the panic that followed the news of the treason of Dumouriez, the Convention passed a further law that removed the inviolability of deputies. Henceforth, deputies could be subject to arrest on the basis of their opinions and, like other suspects, could be indicted and sent before the Revolutionary Tribunal.

All of these measures, which initiated the process of setting up a legalized form of terror, were voted for by the Convention as a whole, whilst the Girondins were still an important voice in the Convention, and before the ascendancy of the Jacobin deputies. Amidst mutual fear, suspicion, and bitter mutual recriminations, the factional conflict between Girondins and Jacobins escalated.[17] The Girondin deputies were tainted by their close association with Dumouriez, and their loyalty to him was a key factor in their overthrow and arrest two months later.

At the start of June 1793 tens of thousands of Parisians surrounded the Convention, demanding and finally obtaining the expulsion and arrest of the Girondin deputies. This was the moment that brought the Jacobins to power. Beyond Paris, however, there was growing opposition to the Jacobins and to the radicalism of the *sans-culottes*. The deputies of the Convention had difficulties in enforcing their will on a population that was often recalcitrant. Ironically, that relative weakness of the Convention was one of the reasons why it pursued a hardline policy, in order to push through measures that were relatively unpopular.

Expectations were high that the Jacobin-led government would prove more effective than the Girondins, both at winning the war and at sustaining

---

[16] Danton addresses the National Convention on the establishment of the Revolutionary Tribunal, 10 March 1793, in Georges Danton, *Discours de Danton*, ed. André Fribourg (Paris: Librairie Édouard Cornély, 1910), 291.

[17] On the factional struggle between Girondins and Montagnards, see Linton, *Choosing Terror*, Chapters 4–6.

the Republic, by putting strong measures in place. Throughout the summer *sans-culottes* put intense pressure on the Convention to take steps both to ensure food supplies for the urban poor and to crack down on counter-revolutionaries.[18] On 4 and 5 September large numbers of *sans-culottes* demonstrated before the Convention, demanding that it make "terror the order of the day."

What did that demand mean? And what did the revolutionaries understand by the word "terror"? The revolutionaries did not invent the term.[19] It was in widespread use long before the Revolution, and, ironically, it had largely positive connotations, often used to denote the righteous power of God, or the authority and justice of the king.[20] It was linked particularly to the concepts of royal justice and of terror dealt out by God (particularly the God of the Old Testament), both of which were seen as salutary. The revolutionaries of 1793 had rejected royal authority, and many of them had little time for the doctrines of the Catholic Church in which most had been raised. But they kept the idea of terror as salutary, terror as harsh justice in extreme circumstances, terror that would keep the *patrie* (fatherland) safe, by terrifying the *patrie*'s enemies. The duty to preserve the *patrie* was the most important law of all. In the words of Cicero: *Salus populi suprema lex esto*.

Yet there were dangers in going down this path, as the deputies were aware, even as they followed it. Contrary to the assumption often encountered in older history books, the Convention stopped short of decreeing "terror the order of the day," either on that day or on any other.[21]

Two committees were at the forefront of revolutionary government during Year II. The first was the Committee of General Security, with responsibility for arrests, the prisons, and the police. The second was the

---

[18] Though the Parisian crowds resorted to actual violence much less often than is commonly assumed, the threat of violence constituted a significant dimension of the political pressure that they exerted. See Micah Alpaugh, *Non-violence and the French Revolution: Political Demonstrations in Paris, 1787–1795* (Cambridge: Cambridge University Press, 2014).

[19] By contrast, the words "terrorism" and "terrorist" were coined in the second half of 1794, after the fall of Robespierre, as part of a retrospective invention by the Thermidorians of the concept of a system or reign of terror.

[20] On the linguistic origins of the concept of "terror," see Ronald Schechter, *A Genealogy of Terror in Eighteenth-Century France* (Chicago: University of Chicago Press, 2018); Biard and Linton, *Terreur*, Chapter 2.

[21] Biard and Linton, *Terreur*, 26–30. See also Jean-Clément Martin, *Violence et révolution: Essais sur la naissance d'un mythe national* (Paris: Éditions du Seuil, 2006), 186–93; Annie Jourdan, "La journée du 5 septembre 1793. La terreur a-t-elle été a l'ordre du jour?," in Michel Biard and Hervé Leuwers, eds., *Visages de la terreur: L'exception politique de l'an II* (Paris: Armand Colin, 2014), 45–60.

Committee of Public Safety, with still greater powers, both military and civilian, for the conduct of the war and for organizing support and supplies for the soldiers, but also for the wider remit of ensuring "public security." The Committee was made up of twelve men, subject to reelection each month by the deputies of the Convention. Several of the most prominent Jacobins became members of this Committee: including two of the Revolution's foremost theorists, Saint-Just and Robespierre. Jacobin deputies dominated but did not control revolutionary government. Non-Jacobins, such as Lazare Carnot and Bertrand Barère, also sat on the Committee and shared collectively in the decisions to set up a terror policy. A further committee, the Legislative Committee, was responsible for drawing up laws such as the decree of 19 March and the Law of Suspects, and was led by men like Cambacérès and Philippe-Antoine Merlin de Douai, who were not habitués of the Jacobins and were careful to keep out of factional politics.[22]

The Committee of Public Safety acquired growing powers over the course of Year II, but its proposals for new legislation continued to require the backing of the Convention. While Robespierre exerted a powerful influence in the Jacobin Club and in the Convention, he was one of twelve in the Committee. The men of the Committee of Public Safety worked long and exhausting hours, spurred on by their dedication, their fervor, and by the desperate nature of the crisis. Whilst the Committee of Public Safety presented a united front to the Convention, within its ranks there were growing tensions and rivalries, though these were kept discreet until the explosion of July 1794.

Under pressure from *sans-culottes*, the Convention instituted the Law of Suspects (which authorized the arrest of tens of thousands of people whose loyalty to the Revolution was seen as "suspect"), the Maximum (the principal law regulating food prices), and the creation of an *armée révolutionnaire* (a *sans-culotte* militia empowered to go through the countryside requisitioning supplies and hunting down counterrevolutionaries).

The succeeding months marked the apogee of the terror policy. Two further key pieces of legislation followed. On 10 October it was decreed that the government should be "revolutionary until the peace." That is, the government would be accorded exceptional powers to manage the circumstances arising from the military crisis. The "Jacobin constitution," written the previous June, the most egalitarian and libertarian that the world had yet seen, was set aside and not put into effect (after the fall of the Jacobins the

---

[22] On the Legislative Committee, see Jourdan, *Nouvelle histoire de la Révolution*, 176–7, 203.

following year it would be repealed, so it was never enacted). On 4 December (14 Frimaire, Year II in the new revolutionary calendar), further decrees set out terms for the organization of "revolutionary government." The laws that enabled the recourse to terror were shaped gradually by many hands, a collective choice on the part of the deputies of the Convention, in an attempt to control a politically unstable situation amidst the panic engendered by war and civil war.

The Convention responded to the crisis of war and the fear of further military betrayals by organizing a system whereby deputies of the Convention were sent out in pairs as civilian representatives (*en mission*) embedded with the armies, to aid military efforts, ensure the maintenance of recruits and supplies, and to keep a watchful eye on the officers. Fearful of further betrayals, the deputies used terror tactics to control and eliminate generals whose ambitions, loyalty, and competence were suspect. They took no chances, especially with officers who had served during the *ancien régime*. Between April 1793 and January 1794, fifty-eight generals were dismissed from their posts; some were imprisoned, and several indicted, condemned, and executed.[23]

Terror was also used to strike at revolutionary officials and functionaries who were tainted by corruption. Institutionalized venality had been an integral part of the *ancien régime*. From the outset of the Revolution, the revolutionaries had tried to break the hold of the privileged orders on money-making posts and positions. By 1790 the Revolution itself had become a career path with well over half a million new posts created (some, though by no means all, remunerated). The setting up of the Republic, along with mobilization to support the war, opened up additional possibilities for the unscrupulous to enrich themselves at the public expense. Competition to secure lucrative contracts to supply the growing needs of the armies was an additional problem. Not all the deputies *en mission* were men of integrity. In the eyes of a man like Robespierre, establishing a "republic of virtue" was in large part about rooting out financial corruption in the Republic's own officials.[24]

Nor were revolutionary leaders themselves immune from terror. In most cases the Revolutionary Tribunal made efforts to establish the guilt or innocence of the people who appeared before it. Almost half the people who came before the Tribunal were acquitted, though after the Loi Prairial

---

[23] See Guillaume Mazeau, "La 'Terreur', laboratoire de la modernité," in Jean-Luc Chappey, Bernard Gainot, Guillaume Mazeau, Frédéric Régent, and Pierre Serna, eds., *Pour quoi faire la Révolution* (Marseille: Agone, 2012), 88.

[24] On terror used against functionaries and officials, see Linton, *Choosing Terror*, Chapter 7.

that figure declined considerably. But the treatment accorded to the most active revolutionaries, above all members of the Convention, was different. Ironically, they were treated more harshly than ordinary citizens. As the former deputy Antoine-Claire Thibaudeau later recalled: "The terror was more deadly towards the friends of liberty than towards its enemies."[25]

There was an expectation that revolutionary politicians should act as "men of virtue," that is, that they should put the public interest before their personal interests and ambitions.[26] During the early years of the Revolution a politician who was seen to be corrupt and personally ambitious was castigated in the clubs and the revolutionary press, and could face disgrace. At the height of the Revolution, the risks involved increased exponentially, as revolutionaries attacked one another's integrity and hidden motives. Successive laws stripped away the immunity of deputies. They could be arrested, indicted, and brought before the Revolutionary Tribunal. Terror thus rebounded on the revolutionary leaders in a particularly ruthless form of terror, which I have termed the "politicians' terror"; that is, the terror that revolutionary activists directed against one another. This form of terror was both a body of laws to which the deputies were subject and an emotion that affected their choices.[27]

A series of factions was identified, sent before the Tribunal, convicted in what amounted to show trials, and executed. First of these were the Girondins. In scenes that shocked witnesses, they were convicted en masse of being traitors to the very Revolution to which they had dedicated their lives and their efforts. They were followed by the Hébertists, the Dantonists, and – executed without any form of trial beyond identification before the Tribunal – the Robespierrists. The trials of the factions were atypical of the usual procedures of the Revolutionary Tribunal: there was little or no effort to establish guilt or innocence – only to secure convictions. None of the deputies brought before the Tribunal during Year II escaped the death sentence. The former deputy Marc-Antoine Baudot later stated in his memoirs that eighty-six deputies of the Convention died violent deaths, most under the guillotine, a few by their own hand.[28] Almost a third of the

---

[25] A. C. Thibaudeau, *Mémoires sur la Convention et le Directoire*, 2 vols. (Paris: Baudouin, 1824), vol. 1, 50.

[26] This argument is developed more fully in Linton, *Choosing Terror*. On emotions and the "politicians' terror," see also Linton, "The Power of Emotions."

[27] On the politicians' terror, see Linton, *Choosing Terror*, esp. 227–31.

[28] Marc-Antoine Baudot, *Notes historiques sur la Convention nationale, l'Empire et l'exil des votants* (Paris: D. Jouaust, 1893), 202–4.

Convention's deputies suffered imprisonment at some point during the life of the Convention.[29] Whilst executions of deputies decreased after the fall of Robespierre, they did not cease, whilst the numbers of arrests increased – figures that call into question the traditional chronology of *the Terror* as ending with the death of Robespierre.

The most notorious piece of terror legislation, the Loi Prairial, was decreed by the Convention on 10 June 1794 (22 Prairial). It inaugurated a traumatic period known as the "great terror," which lasted for seven weeks over the summer of 1794. About a half of the total number of people executed in Paris under the authority of the Revolutionary Tribunal met their deaths during those seven weeks. Though the law was sponsored by Robespierre, it was implemented by other leading revolutionaries on the committees, whilst Robespierre, possibly on the verge of some form of breakdown, ceased for several critical weeks to attend meetings of the Committee of Public Safety. The bloodletting unleashed by the Loi Prairial was partly an attempt to centralize and expedite the procedures of government. At the same time as the death sentences dealt out by the Paris Revolutionary Tribunal increased, most of the other revolutionary tribunals (the tribunal at Orange was a notable exception) were closed down.[30]

In the crisis of 1793–1794, Robespierre, once an opponent of the death penalty, had become, like many other revolutionaries, an advocate of terror. Unlike most deputies, who were more pragmatic in their support for terror, Robespierre sought to give terror a – deeply problematic – moral justification, arguing that it must be wielded by men motivated only by virtue, that is, dedication to the public good.[31] He remained deeply uneasy at the militarization of the Revolution. Robespierre, Saint-Just, and other Jacobins

---

[29] On the extent of arrest of deputies and the ways in which continual political "purging" undermined the regime's stability, see the pioneering work of Mette Harder, "A Second Terror – The Purges of French Revolutionary Legislators after Thermidor," in Laura Mason, ed., "Forum on Thermidor and the French Revolution," *French Historical Studies* special issue, part 1, 38:1 (2015), 33–60; Mette Harder, "'Elle n'a pas même épargné ses membres!' Les épurations de la Convention nationale entre 1793 et 1795," *Annales historiques de la Révolution française* 381:3 (2015), 77–105.

[30] On the Loi Prairial, see Annie Jourdan, "Les journées de Prairial an II: Le tournant de la Révolution?," *La Révolution française* 10 (2016), https://journals.openedition.org/lrf/1591; Biard and Linton, *Terreur*, Chapter 7.

[31] For an analysis of Robespierre's connection between "virtue" and "terror," see Marisa Linton, "Commentary on Maximilien Robespierre, *On the Principles of Political Morality* (1794)", in Rachel Hammersley, ed., *Textual Moments in the History of Revolutionary Thought* (London: Bloomsbury Academic Press, 2015).

shared the concern that the rapid increase in militarization was undermining the authority of the civil revolutionary state, by putting an unprecedented amount of power into the hands of generals. They pointed at historical figures such as Julius Caesar and Oliver Cromwell, who had used their ascendancy over their armies to seize personal power, toppling republican or revolutionary regimes.

On 26 June 1794 the French armies won a major victory at Fleurus, which ended the danger of invasion. If terror had indeed been necessary as a weapon of war, that argument could no longer hold. On 26 July (8 Thermidor) Robespierre spoke to the Convention in his own name, rather than on behalf of the Committee of Public Safety, in an ill-judged speech in which he denounced several of his fellow Jacobin deputies for excesses of terror, without naming any of them. This fateful step on his part precipitated fears of a new purge, and that night a coup was finalized by several Jacobins, both inside and outside the Committees, determined to act first to bring down Robespierre and anyone aligned with him. The execution of Robespierre and 107 of his associates on 10–12 Thermidor was part of the ongoing factional struggle within the Convention. The men who destroyed Robespierre were not planning to end the policy of terror, or to dissolve the Committee of Public Safety: rather their intention was to continue with this policy under new management. But the crisis of Thermidor began a process of reaction away from terror policy. Fear of new purges led the new leaders to repeal the Loi Prairial and limit the powers of the Committee of Public Safety. Slowly the laws enabling terror began to be dismantled: the Maximum was repealed, and the Jacobin Club was closed, though the Revolutionary Tribunal continued to operate until the end of May 1795. Over the ensuing months prisoners began to be released, many of them traumatized; a number were determined on revenge. The ascendancy of the Jacobins might be over, yet terror and violence continued, much of it retributive and directed against Jacobins. Robespierre was retrospectively stigmatized as having been the mastermind behind a regime of terror in which, in reality, many revolutionaries had been deeply involved.

Robespierre had argued against fighting an expansionist war. But war did not end with his death and the fall of the Jacobin government. Instead, the revolutionary wars changed track from defensive to expansionist. Military success became about exploiting the resources of other countries, and shoring up the survival of successive political regimes: the Thermidorian Convention, the Directory, the Consulate, and the

Empire. Untold millions would die in military conflicts that would last almost continuously until 1815.[32]

The Myth of Systemic Terror

What can this – admittedly brief – account tell us about the nature of the revolutionary terror and its recent historiography? As we have seen, the term "terror" was not invented by the French revolutionaries. The concept of terror would change its meaning during the course of the Revolution, in ways that the revolutionaries could not have envisaged. Nevertheless, until after the fall of Robespierre the idea that political terror was in some sense salutary, that is, that it could be the means to secure the "public good" and prevent the overturning of the Revolution, was maintained by the revolutionary leaders, including many who would live to repudiate the experience of terror and subsequently seek to disassociate themselves from choices they had made at the time of crisis.

The implementation of terror was a gradually escalating process, which developed against the backdrop of a series of military crises, external and internal, accompanied by some very high-profile betrayals.[33] Laws enabling terror were envisaged as a form of justice, albeit a harsh wartime justice. Brutal though these laws were, they were seen by the revolutionary government as conforming to principles and forms of justice in a way that the unregulated interventions of the crowd did not. In part the policy of terror – using coercion, state-sanctioned violence, and harsh justice – came about as a consequence of the comparative weakness and unpopularity of the revolutionary government. The revolutionary leaders used terror and coercion, along with a *rhetoric* of terror, to strike fear and intimidate enemies both internal and external.

The laws on terror were seen by the men who devised them as a necessary means of ensuring military victory, supplying the armies and urban centers, above all Paris, and trying to ensure that monarchists and counterrevolutionaries would be too fearful and intimidated to pose a substantial threat to

---

[32] On the figures for deaths of soldiers and civilians, French and non-French, in the revolutionary and Napoleonic wars, see Carla Hesse "Terror and the Revolutionary Tribunals," and Marisa Linton, "Rethinking the French Revolutionary Terror: Introduction," both in *H-France Salon*, "Rethinking the French Revolutionary Terror."
[33] Tim Tackett makes a strong case for March 1793 as a key moment in this process: Tackett, *The Coming of the Terror*.

the Republic. Yet the laws on terror had additional purposes. Contrary to what one might assume, a substantial part of the revolutionary terror was devoted to ensuring the good conduct of the Republic's own people. The revolutionary government was a civilian institution that was proactive in curbing the power of military leaders and ensuring that army officers remained loyal and effective. Terror was also used to control officials and government functionaries. Amongst functionaries and public servants were the deputies themselves. Most disturbingly, revolutionary leaders used terror in an effort to destroy rival political factions, within the Convention and the Paris Commune, a practice that did much to destabilize revolutionary government.

The incidence of terror in the period 1793–1794 varied greatly. Some areas were greatly affected, especially those towns or regions where there were armed uprisings against the Convention, and where reprisals were exacted. Areas close to frontiers where there was fighting against the invading forces saw significant numbers of casualties. At the same time, extensive parts of the country away from the frontiers and other centers of conflict witnessed few executions and very little violence. It has been estimated that between 40,000 and 50,000 deaths can be attributed directly or indirectly to the laws on terror, of which 2,639 were people condemned by the Revolutionary Tribunal in Paris.[34] These numbers were dwarfed by the scale of deaths on both sides in the brutal civil war in the Vendée and neighboring departments.[35]

The received opinion is that the French Revolution was unique in its time in its recourse to political violence. Yet comparisons with the death toll in the English Civil Wars (that stretched throughout the British Isles) and "revolutions" of the seventeenth century, with the American Revolution, and with the suppression of the revolt in Ireland in 1798, suggest that it would be more accurate to see revolutionary violence in the context of wider factors such as fear, repression, and the degree of retaliation, rather than as the consequence of a specific ideology unique to the French Revolution.[36]

---

[34] For the most recent assessment of the distribution of deaths, see the maps in Biard and Linton, *Terreur*, Chapter 8, "Quels bilans?"

[35] On the civil war in the Vendée, the most authoritative study is that by Jean-Clément Martin, *La Vendée et la France* (Paris: Éditions du Seuil, 1987).

[36] For a revisionist view of violence in the American Revolution, see Holger Hoock, *Scars of Independence: America's Violent Birth* (New York: Crown Publishing, 2017). See too the figures that call into question the French Revolution as a period of "exceptional violence" in Hesse, "Terror and the Revolutionary Tribunals."

The revolutionary government was one of "exception," that is, a crisis government for exceptional circumstances. Its aims and parameters were set out in a decree of 10 October 1793, which temporarily set aside the egalitarian and libertarian constitution of June 1793, and stated that "the government of France shall be revolutionary until the peace" – the closest that the revolutionary government came to formulating a coherent policy, a wartime policy that encompassed the recourse to necessary means, including terror, to maintain the revolutionary government.

The meaning of terror was problematic for the revolutionary leaders themselves. Over the course of Year II, they returned to this difficult subject, asserting that their intention was to implement a form of justice in the extreme circumstances of war and counterrevolution against the Revolution's enemies, rather than to terrorize a population. The so-called policy of "terror" pursued by the Convention emerged in large part from a position of relative weakness in the context of external war, civil war, and large-scale unrest. It was seen by those who perpetrated it as a temporary form of justice, albeit harsh justice, necessitated by war and revolutionary crisis. The Revolutionary Tribunal and the guillotine were designed as examples of spectacular violence, to show the strength of the revolutionary government, and intimidate counterrevolutionary opponents. Nor should we mistake the rhetoric of terror for the reality. The rhetoric of terror was sweeping and absolute, designed to be intimidating to enemies both external and internal, promising complete and salutary terror to annihilate opponents. Paradoxically, the rhetoric of salutary terror was a weapon of empowerment for the revolutionaries, designed to make them feel stronger and safer. The reality was often very different, however, and many perished through the very terror that they had themselves supported.

Amongst historians there has been a new recognition of the need to explore the emotional dimensions of revolutionary politics. We are no longer content to limit ourselves to political questions, to ask about ideologies, tactics, and events. We want to know how revolutionary politics *felt* to the people who were there. We are more ready to acknowledge that revolutionary activists were complex, as complex as we are ourselves; people who felt as well as thought; who initiated and reacted; who were subject to intense and conflicting pressures; who worked at fever-pitch whilst often stressed and exhausted; who pursued strategies; who changed their minds and contradicted themselves; who had deep-seated convictions, but who found themselves obliged to improvise and make rapid decisions, some of which were inspired, many of which were questionable; in short, who were three-dimensional human beings, and need to be understood as such by their historians.

Revolutions are profoundly emotional events, both for the people who take part and for people who oppose them. The revolutionaries themselves were well aware of the effect of uncontrolled emotions in revolutionary politics. They often referred to these emotions as "the passions" and tended to interpret them in a negative light, as feelings that overrode reason. Amongst such passions, one should include patriotic fervor, altruism and concern for the well-being of others, friendship, and intense loyalty, along with more negative emotions such as ambition, suspicion, hatred, and fear.

Alongside interest in the emotions is a new concern about agency and the lived experienced of the Revolution. Historians are exploring how the experience of revolution shaped and changed revolutionaries' attitudes and ideas.[37] This emphasis on revolutionaries as formed by their lived experiences helps us to get behind the myths – many of which originated after Thermidor, or during the early nineteenth century, and have become ossified over time – and see the lives of revolutionary activists not as fixed or inevitable, but as open-ended, contingent, and subject to improvisation. This willingness on the part of historians to look beyond the myths and to see the lives of some of the Revolution's best-known figures afresh has resulted in some notable new biographies, particularly of Robespierre.[38] The public and private personas of revolutionary activists, and how they consciously shaped their identities, deployed their rhetoric, even consciously presented how and where they ate, and how and where they lived, in order to project the requisite image of "men of virtue," is a subject which is helping us to understand more about the complex relationship between *ancien régime* political "corruption" and revolutionary "virtue," and the forging of new political identities.[39]

Much of the traditional narrative of *the Terror*, especially the idea of *the Terror* as a coherent "system," is in large part a myth, invented after the fall of

---

[37] Varieties of revolutionary experience are explored in David Andress, ed., *Experiencing the French Revolution* (Oxford: Voltaire Foundation, University of Oxford, 2013).

[38] There have been several excellent studies of Robespierre in recent years, notably Peter McPhee, *Robespierre: A Revolutionary Life* (New Haven: Yale University Press, 2012); Hervé Leuwers, *Robespierre* (Paris: Fayard, 2014); Jean-Clément Martin, *Robespierre: La fabrication d'un monstre* (Paris: Perrin, 2016).

[39] Marisa Linton and Mette Harder, "'Come and Dine': Deputies and the Dangers of Conspicuous Consumption in French Revolutionary Politics, 1789–95," *European History Quarterly* 45:4 (2015), 615–37; Marisa Linton, "The Man of Virtue: The Role of Antiquity in the Political Trajectory of L. A. Saint-Just," *French History* 24:3 (2010), 393–419.

Robespierre.⁴⁰ The fabrication of the narrative of a systematic policy of terror masterminded by Robespierre and imposed on an unwilling Convention began immediately after his execution by the men who overthrew him, the Thermidorians. Whilst Robespierre bears his share of responsibility for the deaths of Year II, the charge that he was a dictator was fabricated to scapegoat him for the entire legacy of the revolutionary terror.⁴¹

Increasingly, historians have been pointing out the difficulties in speaking of a "system of terror" or even of *the Terror*.⁴² To use the term *the Terror* implies that there was a unified system of terror, with a coherent and consistent policy. The term is problematic because we are now much more aware that the context in which revolutionaries deployed terror was far more chaotic, improvised, and less coherent than the Thermidorian narrative had led us to believe. The term *the Terror* has been used to denote a chronological period – usually said to be from September 1793 to the end of July 1794, with the implication, whether intended or not, that everything within those dates was about *the Terror*, and nothing outside those dates qualifies as terror. It is a neat term, and simple to write, and many historians – including myself – have used it as a convenient shorthand. But in many ways, it is inaccurate and misleading.

For all those reasons, there is a strong case for historians of the Revolution to establish some new common ground in how they conceptualize the revolutionary terror. It is time, we suggest, to stop calling it *the Terror*, because the term implies a systematic coherence that did not actually exist. It would be better and more accurate to talk about "terror," or "recourse to terror," or, if we must, "the terror" (without a capital).⁴³

---

⁴⁰ Carla Hesse gives an illuminating analysis of the "myths" of the French revolutionary terror in Hesse, "Terror and the Revolutionary Tribunals."

⁴¹ Along with the recent biographies of Robespierre cited above, note 38, see the study by Marc Belissa and Yannick Bosc, *Robespierre: La fabrication d'un mythe* (Paris: Ellipses, 2013).

⁴² Amongst these works, see Biard and Linton, *Terreur*; Michel Biard, "Réflexions autour de 'la Terreur,'" in *H-France Salon* 11:1 (2019), https://h-france.net/h-france-salon-volume-11-2019/#1101; Jourdan, *Nouvelle histoire de la Révolution*; Martin, *La Terreur*; Jean-Clément Martin, *Les échos de la Terreur: Vérités d'un mensonge d'État, 1794–2001* (Paris: Belin, 2018); Jean-Clément Martin, *La Terreur: Part maudite de la Révolution* (Paris: Gallimard, 2010).

⁴³ For extended versions of the arguments for changing the nomenclature of terror, see Biard and Linton, *Terreur*; Michel Biard, "Remplacer *la Terreur* par la 'terreur' pour mieux comprendre l'une et l'autre?," in "Rethinking the French Revolutionary Terror," *H-France Salon* 11:16 (2019), https://h-france.net/h-france-salon-volume-11-2019/?fbclid=IwAR3XFqIyAt-7sOK7lT0_zebC4AoeJpFebg72iHE3006D9TSLXygptTLJ9xM.

To speak of "terror," rather than *the Terror*, is not to seek to minimize the violence, or to excuse it, but rather to avoid an overly schematic reification of that violence, as though it were part of an organized system, rather than an improvised, ad hoc, and often chaotic response to events. Violence there was aplenty, though this violence was far from uniform. Nor did trauma and violence end with the fall of Robespierre, far from it.[44] By referring to a French revolutionary terror, rather than *the Terror*, we are better able to avoid the tendency to reify the events of 1793–1794 as though they were of a different order from other forms of political and state violence that took place either before or subsequently. The term "the Reign of Terror" is still more problematic, because it carries the implication that an individual or group or individuals – usually understood to be Robespierre and the men who died with him – were imposing a rule through terror on a bravely resistant Convention.

Finally, we might ask how our understanding of the French Revolutionary terror is affected by our own experience of contemporary politics. Anyone who has seen the sudden political destabilization of the United States, Britain, and much of Europe in the last few years is likely to respond with recognition to hearing that the French revolutionary terror was a much more ad hoc, improvised, and even chaotic response to circumstances than the old narrative of Robespierre's "Reign of Terror." Contemporary audiences can readily appreciate that emotions count for a great deal in politics, not only on the streets but also in the "corridors of power." We can see the power of emotions drive politics every day on our TVs and on the Internet. Why would we think that the emotional experience of the French Revolution would have been any less intense?

---

[44] On trauma and the aftermath of the crisis of 1793–1794, see Ronen Steinberg, *The Afterlives of the Terror: Facing the Legacies of Mass Violence in Postrevolutionary France* (Ithaca, NY: Cornell University Press, 2019); and, for a longer-term perspective on violence and trauma in French history, see Howard G. Brown, *Mass Violence and the Self: From the French Wars of Religion to the Paris Commune* (Ithaca, NY: Cornell University Press, 2018).

9

The Directory, Thermidor, and the Transformation of the Revolution

PHILIPPE BOURDIN

The Directory has long suffered from a dark image. Perhaps a "Bourgeois Republic,"[1] and certainly much more conservative than reactionary, the Directory firmly established civic and political order in order to put an end to grassroots upheavals. It had to deal with the political wounds of the Republican camp, born of federalism and the Terror. It was necessary to reinstate the perpetrators and the victims in the government and the legislature. But the ideological debates carried on by a host of efficient newspapers remained intense. Royalist offensives led to election success in Year V and an ensuing coup d'état. The Republican camp then regained a taste for action, initiating important reforms in the cultural, economic, and administrative fields. The domestic context was marked, however, by impoverishment, the rapid financial gain of the few, and inflation. These were the main consequences of the wars carried out in Europe and the difficult construction of the Sister Republics. The relationship between civil powers and military authorities was debated more than ever.[2]

The Constitution of Year III

The Thermidorians – the members of the Convention who were responsible for Robespierre's downfall and subsequently came to power – adopted in August 1795 a new constitution conceived by a politically very moderate commission (the Commission of Eleven).[3] One of its members, Boissy

---

[1] Denis Woronoff, *La République bourgeoise* (Paris: Éditions du Seuil, 1972).
[2] Georges Lefebvre, *La France sous le Directoire (1795–1799)* (Paris: Éditions sociales, 1977); Philippe Bourdin, ed., *La République directoriale*, 2 vols. (Clermont-Ferrand: Presses universitaires Blaise-Pascal; Paris: Société des Études Robespierristes, 1997); Martin Lyons, *France under the Directory* (Cambridge: Cambridge University Press, 1975).
[3] Michel Vovelle, ed., *Le Tournant de l'an III: Réaction et terreur blanche dans la France révolutionnaire* (Paris: CTHS, 1997); Roger Dupuy and Marcel Morabito, eds., *1795: Pour*

d'Anglas, summed up the project as follows: "You must guarantee the property of the wealthy. Civil equality is all that a reasonable man can demand ... Absolute equality is a chimera ... We must be ruled by the best ... A country ruled by the owners is part of the social order, one where the non-owners govern is in the state of nature."[4]

The Constitutional Act is long (377 articles) and very precise, contrary to its predecessors,[5] and preceded by a declaration of rights and duties. It omits the assertion of equality of 1789 ("men are born and remain free and equal in rights"), which seemed to be tantamount to rebellion. Individual freedom is reduced to that of expression and thought, and to do "what does not harm others." The submission to laws, state agents, and military needs, and the injunction to be a "good father, good son, good husband," are affirmed as duties. The rights to education, assistance, work, and insurgency are forgotten, and the prohibition of slavery is maintained. Land ownership is conceived as the source of society. Drawing lessons from recent history, legislators offered the right to vote only to landowners who were at least twenty-one years of age and paid taxes equal to what they earned in at least three days of working or had taken part in several army campaigns. Foreigners who had lived in France for seven years, were wealthy landowners and paid taxes, or were married to a French woman, could acquire citizenship.

While a referendum could be held, it could only pertain to constitutional issues. The regime was essentially representative, based on two-tier elections by secret ballot. The primary assemblies elected the justices of the peace and the assessors, the cantonal and municipal administrations, and the second-round voters. The latter must be more than twenty-five years old and possess a property or an income equivalent to at least 150 working days. These second-round voters comprised the electoral assemblies, which elected the members of the legislature, the civil and criminal courts, the Court of Cassation, the High Court of Justice, and the departmental administrations. To break with the Convention's omnipotence, the legislature was divided for

---

une République sans Révolution (Rennes: Presses universitaires de Rennes, 1996); Antonio de Francesco, Il governo senza testa (Naples: Morano, 1992).

[4] Report of Boissy d'Anglas on the constitutional project, 5 Messidor Year III (23 June 1795), in Gérard Conac and Jean-Pierre Machelon, eds., La Constitution de l'an III: Boissy d'Anglas et la naissance du libéralisme constitutionnel (Paris: Presses universitaires de France, 1999).

[5] Jacques Godechot, Les institutions de la France sous la Révolution et l'Empire (Paris: Presses universitaires de France, 1951); Marcel Morabito and Daniel Bourmaud, Histoire constitutionnelle et politique de la France (1789–1848) (Paris: Monchrestien, 1996).

the first time into two chambers, the Council of Five Hundred (which had the right of legislative initiative and voted on bills) and the Council of Ancients (which approved or rejected draft bills, and proposed any constitutional revisions). These assemblies were elected for three years, and one-third of the members were renewed each year. No standing committee was allowed. Protected by immunity, the representatives had a workload that was incompatible with any public service.

The executive, a collective body to avoid any dictatorial drift, was entrusted to the five-member Directory, which was elected for five years by the legislature (Figure 9.1). One of the five positions was renewed every year and was not filled again for another five years. The directors were obliged to be at work at the Palais du Luxembourg almost all the time. In return, great honors were conferred on them and they were protected by a Praetorian Guard. They could be brought, however, before the High Court of Justice, just like the deputies. They directed diplomacy, the army, and public service, and were assisted by executive commissioners working alongside the various elected governing bodies. These commissioners, many of them former Convention members, played a major role in monitoring and facilitating local political, economic, and social life. They would sometimes face much more moderate elected officials than themselves or, when confronted with armed or violent opposition, were forced to direct a state of siege necessary for the return to civil peace in the west and the Rhone Valley.

Nothing was foreseen in the Constitution in the event of a conflict between the executive and the legislature, nor in the event of exceptional circumstances such as war, even though it was a constant factor in this period. From its inception, the Constitution seemed to be built on exceptional laws. In fact, two decrees of Fructidor, Year III specified that two-thirds of the representatives should be chosen from among the former Convention members. Legislators thus ensured continuity in the Revolution and in their careers. They proved above all their permanent obsession with the future and disorder. A referendum was held by universal suffrage on the constitutional text, and on the two decrees. It generated a low turnout (just over 1.1 million voters) and led to many proposed amendments – from the left on the two-tier voting system, the composition of the executive, and the salaries of the elected; from the right on national property and freedom of worship. In the end, there was an overwhelming majority of yes votes for the Constitution, but the decrees were rejected in Paris and its region.

Royalists organized a violent campaign against the deputies that had just been elected as well as against those who kept their seats, who were accused

Figure 9.1 Allegorical figure representing Justice during the Directory. Getty Images.

of filling their pockets. The campaign paved the way for the Parisian insurrection of the 13 Vendémiaire, Year IV, which was suppressed by the army. The influence of the army continued to grow. Essential to political power, it also became tied up with the judicial system by controlling military committees charged with dispensing extraordinary criminal justice against the insurgents of Camp Grenelle in September 1796 – see below – and those in the Vendée, and against "brigandage" starting in January 1798. It enforced the state of siege that had been imposed on Marseille since Year II.

An Intense Political Life

However, as soon as it was established, the new regime sought a middle ground, removed from the Terror of Year II, whose black legend was carefully maintained, and even farther from the White Terror practiced in the Bouches-du-Rhône. There, armed groups of royalists hunted down republicans and constitutional priests, beating and killing them. Their main targets were the old Jacobins, those who had served the Terror in Year II, many of whom were massacred in their jail cells in May 1795. The quest for moderation cost many officials their position. In Year IV, twelve departments lost their governing body, dismissed in whole or in part. In more than 10,000 rural towns, these imposed changes caused a shortage of educated and qualified candidates. They also demotivated even the most committed. For at least a year, the political system was disrupted by strikes by elected officials and voters, resignations, and "Chouans" or royalist intimidations.[6]

These facts should not conceal an essential innovation: a democratic system was established through the elections held annually in the month of Germinal.[7] A whole election ceremonial was put in place, including

---

[6] Jacques Bernet, Jean-Pierre Jessenne, and Hervé Leuwers, eds., *Du Directoire au Consulat: Le lien politique local dans la Grande Nation* (Lille: CRHENO, 1999); Philippe Bourdin, *Le Puy-de-Dôme sous le Directoire: Vie politique et esprit public* (Clermont-Ferrand: Académie des sciences, belles-lettres et arts, 1991); Pierre Clémendot, *Le département de la Meurthe à l'époque du Directoire* (Raon-l'Étape: Fetzer, 1966); Jean-René Suratteau, *Le département du Mont-Terrible sous le régime du Directoire* (Besançon: Université de Besançon, 1965); Marcel Reinhard, *Le département de la Sarthe sous le régime directorial* (Saint-Brieuc: Les Presses bretonnes, 1936); Jean Brelot, *La vie politique en Côte-d'Or sous le Directoire* (Dijon: Rebourseau, 1932).

[7] Serge Aberdam, Serge Bianchi, Robert Demeude et al., *Voter, élire pendant la Révolution française (1789–1799): Guide pour la recherche* (Paris: CTHS, 1999); Patrice Gueniffey, *Le nombre et la raison: La Révolution française et les élections* (Paris: École des Hautes Études en Sciences Sociales, 1993); Melvin Edelstein, *La Révolution française et la naissance de la démocratie électorale* (Rennes: Presses universitaires de Rennes, 2013); Malcolm Crook,

regulations for assemblies and long appeals by those who claimed the right to vote – voter lists depended on the goodwill of local authorities, who interpreted the requirements in different ways. Elections took place for the polling stations to appoint a president, a secretary, and assessors, and collective oaths were sworn to uphold basic values. Rules were laid down, such as the need to deposit the ballot paper in a box. Schools, public squares, and town halls which had become temples to celebrate the decadary cult (the *fêtes décadaires* celebrated every *décadi*, the day of rest in the ten-day week of the Republican calendar) were suddenly civically sacralized. Individual preferences were not always expressed on the ballots because one could be led astray by the writings of cultured people, votes could be bought, and some were constrained by ties to superiors, but fraud – if it existed – was far from common.

Although election campaigns were officially forbidden, speeches, songs, banquets, street fights, and uproar anticipated and accompanied the casting of votes. From one year to the next, partisan strategies led to divisions within the primary and electoral assemblies. The executive power took advantage of these divisions at the time of the validation or rejection of the local and national results, organizing a coup d'état on 18 Fructidor, Year V against the victorious royalists, and two electoral power grabs, one on 22 Floréal, Year VI (11 May 1798) against the neo-Jacobins who had achieved electoral success, and another one on 30 Prairial, Year VII (18 June 1799) to their profit.[8]

On the whole, electoral turnout revealed a very marked disenchantment of the peasantry from Year VII onwards, but the large cities were also experiencing spectacular collapses: turnout rarely exceeded half of the electorate, and was rarely even over 20 percent in many rural areas. The causes were numerous, including dislocation of old rural communities, resistance to religious and military laws, disappointment about social reforms and the sale of *biens nationaux* (the property of the Church and the émigrés which had been nationalized and sold by the state to private individuals), the fact that proportionally fewer elected officials represented rural France, and the cumbersome and lengthy election ritual. The reluctance of the new political class to accept election as an open method of selecting the political elite also explains why, in Year VI, the government did not hesitate to overturn the

---

Elections in the French Revolution: An Apprenticeship in Democracy, 1789–1799 (Cambridge: Cambridge University Press, 1996).

[8] Albert Meynier, *Les coups d'État du Directoire* (Paris: Presses universitaires de France, 1928); Jean-René Suratteau, *Les élections de l'an VI et le "coup d'État" du 22 Floréal (11 mai 1798)* (Paris: Les Belles-Lettres, 1971).

results and promote certain candidates. In the summer of 1799, the development of an Electoral Code made it possible to take a decisive step toward the recognition of pluralism: if it reaffirmed the rule of the majority, and considered above all the protection of the rights of the minority.

Nevertheless, there were obstacles to the development of public debate. The constitution of Year III prohibited any association "contrary to public order," a ban upheld by the police. Political societies were targeted in particular. Nevertheless, former Jacobins soon found themselves in Toulouse meeting in the Club des Patriotes, which corresponded with the capital and the rest of the province; in Angers, they joined the Society of Literature and Games, affiliated with its Nantes counterpart; in Sète, in the Cercle Patriotique; and in Montpellier, Toulon, Metz, and other towns they also found ways to organize themselves. In Paris, numerous neo-Jacobins regrouped joined the Panthéon club, led by Lebois, a former supporter of Marat, and Drouet, whose fame reached back to the arrest of Louis XVI in Varennes.[9] This "Gathering of the Friends of the Republic" (the bourgeois, the military, and some workers) had a membership of up to 2,000 when it closed its doors in February 1796. Commenting on the press and publishing *La vérité au peuple*, the attendees discussed the high cost of living, the refractory priests, the emigrants, the Chouans, and the persecution of pardoned patriots. They soon organized a more radical opposition to the regime, notably under the leadership of Gracchus Babeuf, an avid reader of Enlightenment texts, and editor of the *Tribun du Peuple*. He gathered around him and his newspaper former *sans-culottes*, merchants, former members of the National Guard, and independent craftsmen, but also members of the liberal professions and administrative employees. They were to provide a revolutionary vanguard defending a program that proposed a new community organization and did not exclude the notion of "agrarian law," which stressed the need to partition landholdings for the benefit of individual families. Landownership was the order of the day, as in March 1796 the Directory abolished the sale of *biens nationaux* in small lots, requiring a down payment equivalent to half of the total price, and thereby again excluding small and medium-sized peasantry.

This "Conspiracy of Equals" illustrated the new way in which the democratic opposition responded to the Directory, employing a secretive mode of

---

[9] Bernard Gainot, *1799, un nouveau jacobinisme?* (Paris: CTHS, 2001); Isser Woloch, *Jacobin Legacy: The Democratic Movement under the Directory* (Princeton: Princeton University Press, 1970); *Annales historiques de la Révolution française* special issue, no. 308 (1997).

operating. For Babeuf, its principal designer, only a revolutionary vanguard, organized and clandestine, was likely to make a popular revolution triumph. He gathered around himself a heterogeneous group of spokesmen, made up of former militants of the Jacobin club and sections of Year II, Hébertists, and Robespierrists. The originality of the movement was also due to the presence of foreign "patriots" like Filippo Buonarroti: they gave it a scope that went beyond the borders of France. Opposition to the Directory's economic liberalism and the narrowing of political freedoms "cemented" this hard core. With 590 subscribers, the *Tribun du peuple* first reached the Parisian population, as did the eventual conspiracy, but another 238 readers lived in the departments, particularly in the Var, Pas-de-Calais, and the north. In March 1796, as official repression measures grew stronger, Babeuf and his associates, who claimed to be able to rely on 17,000 militants, developed an insurrectionary structure called the "Secret Public Salvation Directory." This was a pyramidal and hierarchical organization of agents, not all of whom shared the same level of information about the "concerted purpose." Their task was to control the planned popular uprising. Once that uprising had succeeded, according to Babeuf, a transitional stage would be necessary before the realization of the ideal society, during which power would be vested in a secret leadership. Immediate measures would be introduced to please the people such as lodging the poor in the houses of the rich and free distribution of bread and food. Disseminated through intense propaganda (in the form of pamphlets and songs), the conspirators' agenda went beyond the ideas that had first been proposed by "Exagérés" and "Hébertists." (The Exagérés had been very influential among the Parisian *sans-culottes* in 1792–1793. They were in favor of the arrest of the king and supported the death penalty for hoarders, speculators, the émigrés, and all their political enemies.) Economic measures would include the nationalization of commerce, the abolition of money and inheritance, the obligation to work (devoid of any profit motive and limited to a part of the day), the planning of agricultural production, and equal consumption for all. In the political sphere, Babeuf and his men favored direct democracy, limiting the executive power to economic issues. But the ideological divisions of the conspirators, especially over the collectivization of lands, and the militants' lack of experience in clandestine action weakened a movement that the authorities would quickly annihilate with the assistance of some who betrayed the cause. In April 1796, a law introduced the death penalty for defending the Constitution of 1793 and calling for the Directory to be dissolved. Babeuf and his friends were arrested on 21 Floréal, Year IV (16 May 1796). An attempt to stir up an army regiment

Figure 9.2 Democracy, represented by the statue, embattled during the Directory. Getty Images.

at Grenelle, on 23 and 24 Fructidor, Year IV (9 and 10 September 1796), by former Jacobins and residents of the Parisian suburbs of Saint-Antoine and Saint-Marcel failed and backfired, leading to military trials and executions. This affair put an end to the Babouvistes' adventure, although those loyal to Babeuf were only a minority among these rebels. The Babouvistes' trial had the effect of enabling the broad dissemination of the egalitarian and democratic ideals which had inspired the leaders of the revolutionary movements of the early nineteenth century (Figure 9.2). Babeuf, however, was sentenced to death and guillotined on 8 Prairial, Year V (27 May 1797).[10]

---

[10] Bernard Gainot and Pierre Serna, eds., *Secret et République (1795–1840)* (Clermont-Ferrand: Presses universitaires Blaise-Pascal, 2004); Claude Mazauric, *Babeuf et la Conspiration pour l'égalité* (Paris: Éditions sociales, 1962); Jean Bruhat, *Gracchus Babeuf et les Égaux ou Le premier parti communiste agissant* (Paris: Perrin, 1978); Robert Legrand, *Babeuf et ses compagnons de route* (Paris: Société des Études Robespierristes, 1981); Jean-Marc Schiappa, *Gracchus Babeuf pour le bonheur commun* (Paris: Spartacus, 2015); Alain Maillard, *Présence de Babeuf: Lumières, révolution, communisme* (Paris: Publications de la Sorbonne, 1994).

The difficulty of the neo-Jacobins to make themselves heard in the aftermath of the failed conspiracy left room for a while for the moderates and royalists of the Clichy club,[11] who could count on the support of like-minded newspapers.[12] The royalist victory in the Year V elections gave the Clichy club its moment of glory. The coup d'état of 18 Fructidor, however, sounded the death knell for supportive journalists, many of whom were deported to the island of Oléron off the French west coast. The desire for monarchical restoration was then kept alive by the Philanthropic Institute, which was organized in provincial networks (Societies of Friends of the Order, Coterie des fils légitimes, Enfants du soleil, and Compagnies de Jésus ou de Jéhu). They would never succeed in carrying out the plan of total insurrection dreamed of since 1793.

The danger momentarily removed by the coup of 18 Fructidor incited a part of the Left to a historical reversal: since they could not refer approvingly to the Constitution of Year I without falling foul of the law, they defended henceforth, in the name of safeguarding the Republic, the Constitution of Year III. They adjusted to the fluctuating goodwill of the Directory (repressive in Year V, encouraging from Fructidor, Year V to Floréal, Year VI) to strengthen clandestinely or openly a network of constitutional circles throughout the territory. But there was no reason to believe in a peaceful republic. In 1799, rumors of a conspiracy were everywhere. In Paris, some former leaders of the Terror kept discreet ties to each other while claiming to have withdrawn to the private sphere. Journalist Rigomer Bazin prophesied a "popular conspiracy" that would put an end to all others.

Cultural Mobilization

The press asserted the preeminence of political questions and was concerned about the rebirth of royalism and impoverishment. Official newspapers such as *Le Rédacteur* and the *Journal des Défenseurs de la Patrie* emphasized military

---

[11] Jacques Godechot, *La contre-révolution (1789–1804)* (Paris: Presses universitaires de France, 1961); Jean-Clément Martin, *Contre-Révolution, Révolution et Nation en France, 1789–1799* (Paris: Éditions du Seuil, 1998); J.-C. Martin, ed., *La Contre-Révolution en Europe: Réalités politiques et sociales, résonances culturelles et idéologiques* (Rennes: Presses universitaires de Rennes, 2001).

[12] Hugh Gough, *The Newspaper Press in the French Revolution* (London: Routledge, 1988); Lawrence Stoll, "The Bureau Politique and the Management of the Popular Press: A Study of the Second Directory's Attempt to Develop Directorial Ideology and Manipulate the Newspapers" (Ph.D. dissertation, University of Wisconsin, 1975).

and financial matters. But *La Décade philosophique* placed reason guided by the sciences, particularly biology and physics, at the heart of its project. Its editors (Cabanis and Destutt de Tracy) not only intended to uproot the tree of knowledge and impose new standards of science (analysis, observation, etc.), but also aimed to "change man" by inventing the moral and political sciences.[13]

The Directory applied the Republican calendar and established festivals with a social and moral design, devoted, for example, to Agriculture, Youth, Old Men, and Spouses. It preferred 9 Thermidor, which recalled the defeat of Robespierre, to 31 May, the anniversary of the fall of the Girondins. The official festive dates were expanded to include the glory of the army by celebrating military entries into the conquered cities and organizing funeral marches for great generals. But few engaged in civic worship: temples dedicated to the day of rest in the ten-day week were deserted, references to antiquity could not be understood by all, and municipalities did not always have the means or the desire to respect the calendar. Those who were most hostile to the regime allowed the renaissance of feasts of the past. While the Catholic Church was struggling to reorganize itself, still fractured between refractory and constitutional clergy, the government continued to seek worship in conformity with the Republic. Theophilanthropy, conceived by the bookseller Chemin and Valentin Haüy and active between January 1797 and the summer of 1798, was intended to be a reasonable religion, reconciling the various Churches.[14] It proposed to honor the Supreme Being and to restore morality to families and society. This religion was highly syncretic, borrowing elements from Catholic, Protestant, Masonic, and civic rituals. This worship, organized locally by Moral Steering Committees and intended more for education than for God, promoted open-air public practices and readings of ancient philosophers and the Koran. Theophilanthropy enjoyed a brief Parisian success in circles of both workers and bourgeois, and spread to some fifteen departmental capitals due to the support of constitutional circles.

---

[13] Yves Citton and Lise Dumasy, eds., *Le moment idéologique: Littérature et sciences de l'homme* (Paris: ENS Éditions, 2013); Joanna Kitchin, *Un journal philosophique: La Décade (1794–1807)* (Paris: Minard, 1965); Philippe Bourdin, "Les fantômes de l'Opéra ou les abandons du Directoire," *Annales historiques de la révolution française* no. 379 (2015), 109–29.

[14] Albert Mathiez, *La Théophilanthropie et le culte décadaire, 1796–1801: Essai sur l'histoire religieuse de la Révolution* (Paris: F. Alcan, 1904).

The Directory put much of its hope in public education, but resources were not made available.[15] The Daunou Law of 3 Brumaire, Year IV (30 October 1795) reorganized primary schools. However, it left instruction of the youngest children to mothers, and primary schools at the whim of the local authorities. It limited them to one per canton, and parents had to pay the teachers according to a departmental scale. The cantonal authorities, however, had the power to exempt a quarter of the pupils from school on the grounds of poverty, to the detriment of the teacher. This type of payment, applied during a school year that lasted no more than six months, impoverished the teachers considerably. It often forced them to take on another job or made them abandon their vocation. It was difficult to recruit them, and their level often fell short of expectations. Private initiatives would continue to be permitted, and these would become as much of a resource for rural communities concerned with maintaining control of their schools as for the former religious institutions, and for those who were second-rank scholars or had recently learned how to read and write, who cut the price of their services. Compulsory school curricula were reduced to a minimum, and the policy of unifying the nation through language was abandoned in favor of regional idioms, which were recognized as "auxiliary vehicles" of education. The opponents of the Directory were able to use the school against the Republic, reintroducing the use of catechism, and initiating the Catholic reconquest of minds. Republican schoolmasters were forced to make concessions to reconcile families. For example, they made the days of rest coincide with religious feasts and field work to combat the low attendance of rural classes. The need for public education of girls was recognized, but it was understood that their curriculum should allow them to be trained in manual work. The general results were far from exemplary, even if the government, especially after Year VI, encouraged the writing of republican textbooks, censoring others. In Year VII, the government itself published the *Republican Manual*, which was an annotated compilation of the main laws.

Innovation was more present in the establishment of a central school in each department.[16] This new type of secondary education, which would exist

---

[15] René Grevet, *L'avènement de l'école contemporaine en France (1789–1835)* (Lille: Presses universitaires du Septentrion, 2001); Isser Woloch, "La République directoriale et l'enseignement primaire," in Michel Vovelle, ed., *Révolution et République: L'exception française* (Paris: Kimé, 1994), 312–23.

[16] Robert Palmer, "The Central Schools of the First French Republic: A Statistical Survey," *Historical Reflections* 7 (1980), 223–47; Dominique Julia, ed., *Atlas de la Révolution française*, vol. II: *L'enseignement (1760–1815)* (Paris: École des Hautes Études

until 1802, was characterized by broad disciplinary ambitions and by autonomous courses without an imposed order, duration, or specialization. The teachings were based on experimentation and observation. Mathematics, physics, experimental chemistry, natural history, logic, analysis of sensations and ideas, political economy, legislation, philosophical history of peoples, hygiene, arts and crafts, grammar, literature, the humanities, ancient languages, modern languages, drawing, agriculture, and commerce were offered to students. In Year VII, in their finest hour, central schools brought together between 10,000 and 15,000 students – sons of administrators, lawmen, traders, doctors and surgeons, and to a much lesser degree craftsmen and laborers, who lived in the main cities. Scholarships existed, however, especially for the offspring of the most valiant defenders of the homeland ... or its orphans. Attendance was three to four times lower than that of the former colleges, a drop-out that once again benefited the private sector.

This belief in the essential benefits of education was of less use for the arts. As Director La Revellière-Lépeaux and Minister François de Neufchâteau reflected on the best possible use of music for propaganda purposes, the Directory rallied the musicians: they fully adhered to the festival calendar and saw the creation of the Conservatory as a normalization of their situation.[17] The lack of financial means, on the other hand, limited investment in monumental art, despite the annually returning concern to develop squares and avenues of Paris in celebration of victorious armies. Only the palaces and gardens of the Ancients and the Five Hundred attracted the necessary lavish expenses. Circles of militant artists, such as the Portique républicain, did not cease, however, to emphasize the need for a theater by and for the people, art that upheld the Republic's values and symbols, and music that borrowed popular tunes, in order to build a lasting foundation for the revolutionary enterprise.[18]

en Sciences Sociales, 1987); Marie-Madeleine Compère, "Les professeurs de la république. Rupture et continuité dans le personnel enseignant des écoles centrales," *Annales historiques de la révolution française* no. 243 (1981), 39–60; Catherine Mérot, "La fréquentation des écoles centrales: Un aspect de l'enseignement secondaire pendant la Révolution," *Bibliothèque de l'École des Chartres* 145 (1987), 407–26.

[17] Jean-Louis Jam, "Pédagogie musicale et idéologie: Un plan d'éducation musicale durant la Révolution," in Jean-Rémy Julien and Jean Mongrédien, eds., *Le Tambour et la harpe: Œuvres, pratiques et manifestations musicales sous la Révolution, 1788–1800* (Paris: Du May, 1991), 37–48.

[18] Jean-Luc Chappey, "Le Portique républicain et les enjeux de la mobilisation des arts autour de brumaire an VIII," in Philippe Bourdin and Gérard Loubinoux, eds., *Les arts*

Financial Strangulation and Social Aspirations

These political and cultural projects were constrained by a disastrous economic situation, characterized by the continuous depreciation of the assignat and galloping inflation, which left the salaries of the civil servants lagging behind, and worsened the situation of a floating proletariat enlarged by unemployment.[19] (Established in 1789, *assignats* were paper money whose value was based on that of the *biens nationaux*. When Church property was partitioned, those who wanted to acquire a share of it would receive an assignat, which they could eventually exchange for land, with a promised 5 percent annual premium. But the proprietors' money did not end up in the state's coffers as quickly as expected, while the state kept printing assignats. Their value collapsed, leading to a crisis of confidence.) Remarkably, the government paid the directors, ministers, and deputies in wheat! Requisitions were poorly enforced and forced loans from the wealthy were poorly distributed and misperceived. The state coffers were insufficiently filled by the war indemnity paid by the Dutch and the sale of Belgian *biens nationaux*. In February 1796 the Treasury gave up printing assignats and replaced them with "territorial mandates," whose value was also based on the *biens nationaux*. They, too, depreciated very quickly. A cash injection was sorely lacking, which made the authorities highly dependent on the credits granted by suppliers and the contributions demanded by the generals in the conquered territories. From March 1796, the only currency was the so-called "Germinal franc," worth a pound and three deniers.

But deputies mastered economic policies and the economic vocabulary, which allowed them to develop an impressive set of organic laws after 18 Fructidor. The legislators reduced the debt by means of a real bankruptcy, called the "two-thirds" (the debt was discharged by two-thirds in a distribution of bonds to creditors, valid for the purchase of *biens nationaux*). They reorganized the collection of four taxes: the land tax, the tax on moveable property, patents, and the tax on doors and windows. The success was mixed: if back taxes were gradually paid up, collection agencies nevertheless lacked the means to ensure the full payment of taxes, and collectors were not all competent and honest. Indirect taxes were extended. They were levied on canal navigation, customs, hunting, fishing, registration of deeds, mortgages, letter-post service, tobacco,

---

de la scène et la Révolution française (Clermont-Ferrand: Presses universitaires Blaise-Pascal, Musée de la Révolution française, 2004), 487–508.

[19] François Hincker, *La Révolution française et l'économie: Décollage ou catastrophe?* (Paris: Nathan, 1989); François Crouzet, *La Grande inflation: La monnaie en France de Louis XVI à Napoléon* (Paris: Fayard, 1993).

gold and silver marks, newspapers, playing cards, manuscript paper, and posters. At the end of Year V, barriers were even restored to the roads, reviving a hateful memory, provoking many demonstrations and fires, and leading especially to fraud. In Year VII, subsidies from Paris in turn made up for local municipal budget deficits. It was necessary, above all, to rely on war contributions: the occupied countries (Switzerland, the Italian republics) contributed more than a quarter of the annual budget of France. Conversely, military defeats and evacuations of territories (Italy in 1799) permanently affected its balance and necessitated, if only to pay with great delay the servants of the state, a new forced loan of 100 million francs, with the threat of confiscating any fortune based on speculation. A syndicate of bankers agreed to grant an advance on the expected revenues, but the wealthy in general, without confidence in the future of the regime, preferred to hide their money and desert the towns.

The obsession with the economy also led to much regulatory activity,[20] applied, among other things, to the salaries of officials whose employment was not guaranteed and intended to reverse the decline in purchasing power. The authorities played with bonuses, pensions, and gratuities, but this did not prevent strikes and threats of collective resignations in the provinces. Ministerial practice, however, called for rational management of the state, based on economic liberalism regarding agriculture and industry. During his tenure at the Interior Ministry, François de Neufchâteau, one of the most active proponents of the physiocratic school of thought, regulated departmental bookkeeping, methodically charted the population, established statistics on agriculture, and introduced a plan for inland navigation. Philippe-Victoire Lévêque de Vilmorin and Antoine-Augustin Parmentier assisted him in those tasks by encouraging agriculture societies, competitive events, and the diffusion of knowledge, if only by editing the *Feuille du cultivateur*.

Meanwhile, national exhibitions, official festivals, and the Conservatoire des Arts et Métiers, founded in 1796, exalted French genius and industrial production. Above all, they attempted to prove that the country could manage without English goods in times of blockade. The captains of industry, however few, received encouragement from the state, for there was also the desire to affirm that the government had regained control of affairs at the end of a troubled period.[21]

---

[20] Guy Lemarchand, *L'économie en France de 1770 à 1830* (Paris: Armand Colin, 2008).
[21] Gérard Gayot and Jean-Pierre Hirsch, eds., *La Révolution française et le développement du capitalisme* (Lille: Revue du Nord, 1989); Jean-Luc Chappey, "Sciences et politique en Révolution (1792–1802)," in Serge Bianchi and Philippe Bourdin, eds., *Révoltes et révolutions de 1773 à 1802* (Paris: Éditions du Temps, 2004), 251–76; Patrice Bret,

Many laws were also introduced that related to mortgages and the sale of *biens nationaux* (in Years IV, V, and VII).[22] These now concerned the properties of emigrants, and royal or communal estates. Among the acquirers, the great bourgeoisie was less present than in 1791–1792: it was concerned about the political situation, had less liquidity, and retreated in the face of any claims that returning nobles may have made. This discretion benefited the *petite bourgeoisie* (innkeepers, butchers, and merchants, whose numbers were increasing), the stockjobbers who sometimes acted as intermediaries for families of the old nobility, and the state creditors. The peasants, lacking the resources to invest in farms or estates sold in one piece, were at best satisfied with the plots of the presbyteries (the residences of parish priests). These sales were mainly a speculator's game. Speculators took advantage of the decline in paper money and lived out their golden age through their association with army supplier companies in the north, the Haute-Garonne and elsewhere. The Directory also reviewed a series of previous laws concerning the division of communal property, land leases, and in particular the redemption of perpetual leases, which resulted in numerous lawsuits.

The Directory remained confronted with social problems that it did not resolve. Deprived of the men who were mobilized for war, the countryside faced the high price of labor and the growth of fallow land. Although the harvests of 1797 and 1798 were good, they led to a fall in prices, which accentuated a deflation that was due to the scarcity of money, which greatly dissatisfied the rural bourgeoisie.[23] Several social movements defended the standard of living, favored, among others, by the active clandestineness of the former guilds despite their prohibition promulgated in 1791. Suppressed, and subject to legislation enacted in Fructidor, Year IV, which involved penalties to be shared by the managers and their employees in case of protest, strikes nonetheless took place: in Paris, the employees of the assignat factories went on strike in Year IV, and the carpenters in Year VI. In that year, unemployment was all the more severe because soldiers returned from the front. The small renters, deprived of dividends, were forced into ruin; the war-wounded

L'État, l'armée, la science: L'invention de la recherche publique en France (1763–1830) (Rennes: Presses universitaires de Rennes, 2002).

[22] Bernard Bodinier and Éric Teyssier, *L'événement le plus important de la Révolution: La vente des biens nationaux* (Paris: CTHS and Société des Études Robespierristes, 2000).

[23] Jean-Pierre Jessenne, ed., *Vers un ordre bourgeois? Révolution française et changement social* (Rennes: Presses universitaires de Rennes, 2007); Sarah Maza, *The Myth of the French Bourgeoisie: An Essay on the Social Imaginary (1750–1850)* (Cambridge, MA: Harvard University Press, 2003).

waited in vain for their pensions; the increase in rents and the revision of leases overwhelmed the poorest, both in town and in the countryside. These difficult years were also marked by excess mortality: in Year IV, there was a surplus of 10,000 deaths compared with births in the Seine department. In spite of the official distribution of flour, bread, and rice, measures to organize a genuine aid policy did not ensue, hence the reactivation of charitable offices inherited from the Old Regime. Those left behind by the Republic swelled the ranks of beggars. Some, a minority, joined gangs of professional brigands.[24]

Misery was all the more unbearable in light of the garish successes of the unworthy few. The *nouveaux riches*, clients of the gambling and prostitution houses which multiplied in Paris, liked to gamble on currency. Parisian money lenders could offer annual interest at over 90 percent! By lobbying among the representatives, the suppliers to the armies benefited from the system.[25] They negotiated equally skilfully for equipment, horses, weapons, and food as they did for drafts for the government's accounts, the sale of crown diamonds, and the financing of shipments. These money lenders then raised taxes abroad, helping themselves, plundering if needed, and obtaining immense *biens nationaux* in the conquered countries.

All made lavish carelessness a way of life. It was shared through the provocations in word and dress of the Incroyables and the Muscadins, who claimed to bury the Terror forever.[26] Entertainment enlivened dozens of places on a daily basis in Paris. The wealthy were under the spell of the frenzy of dance. Artists of the Opéra, such as Abraham or Vestris, whose finances faltered, popularized the gavotte; the waltz, imported from Germany, competed with the contredanse, a trend that extended to the provinces. Costume and the décor of private homes, with a certain taste for portraiture, were also a way of self-placement on the social and political scene.[27] Despite the sarcasm, a "Directory-style," above all neoclassical, was

---

[24] Robert Allen, *Les tribunaux criminels sous la Révolution et l'Empire (1792–1811)* (Rennes: Presses universitaires de Rennes, 2005); Valérie Sottocasa, ed., *Les Brigands: Criminalité et protestation politique (1750–1850)* (Rennes: Presses universitaires de Rennes, 2013); Valérie Sottocasa, *Les brigands et la Révolution: Violences politiques et criminalité dans le Midi (1789–1802)* (Seyssel: Champ Vallon, 2016).

[25] Jacques Godechot, *Les commissaires aux armées sous le Directoire*, 2 vols. (Paris: Presses universitaires de France, 1941).

[26] François Gendron, *La jeunesse dorée: Épisodes de la Révolution française* (Quebec: Presses de l'Université du Québec, 1979); Musée Carnavalet, *Au temps des merveilleuses: La société parisienne sous le Directoire et le Consulat* (Paris: Éditions Paris-Musées, 2005).

[27] Musée des Beaux-Arts de Lyon, *Juliette Récamier, muse et mécène* (Paris: Hazan, 2009); Musée Galliera, *Modes et Révolutions* (Paris: Éditions Paris-Musées, 1989).

established. The business oligarchy redesigned rich houses on the Rue de la Chaussée d'Antin or in the Saint-Lazare district. The private mansions of the high-society Tallien, Beauharnais, and Récamier ladies revealed the particular taste of these rich, ambitious, and powerful seducers, who displayed wigs that varied according to the time of day, the finesse and transparency of their long, skilfully pleated dresses, precious Indian shawls and stoles, and finely crafted cameos. These objects freely reinterpreted a claimed passion for the Antique. The decorations, wallpapers, and furniture were also inspired by models seen in Pompei. They used clean lines, symmetry, architectural elements, and noble materials such as marble and mahogany. They favored winged lions, sphinxes, and griffons.

"Great Nation" Diplomacy

The war was therefore very different depending on whether one made up the advance party or the rearguard. It was, however, one of the constant features of the regime; indeed, it circumscribed the financial state and, therefore, the political stability of the regime. Internally, the conflict resulted in the Vendée and Chouan uprisings, and in territories soon being controlled by General Lazar Hoche's troops. Externally, hostilities spread during the military campaign of Italy, where Bonaparte distinguished himself in 1796, as did Joubert and Championnet in 1798–1799; they also spread in the Swiss campaign in 1798. The war got bogged down in the German countryside (where Jourdan and Moreau were defeated in 1796), in the failure of landings in Ireland (December 1796 and August 1798), and in the Egyptian expedition, which began in the spring of 1798 and, after several victories, ended in a military disaster. And it all started again in 1799: while the royalists caused unrest in the region of Toulouse, defeats piled up in Switzerland and Italy, until the victories of Brune in September in Holland and Masséna in Switzerland.

These military episodes were accompanied by intense and permanent diplomatic activity.[28] Many followed on from each other and were briefly

---

[28] Virginie Martin, "In Search of the 'Glorious Peace': Republican Diplomats at War, 1792–1799," in Antonino de Francesco, Judith Miller, and Pierre Serna, eds., *Republics at War, 1776–1840: Revolutions, Conflicts, and Geopolitics in Europe and the Atlantic World* (London: Palgrave Macmillan, 2013), 46–64; Virginie Martin, "Du modèle à la pratique ou des pratiques aux modèles: La diplomatie républicaine du Directoire," in Pierre Serna, ed., *Républiques-sœurs: Le Directoire et la Révolution atlantique* (Rennes: Presses universitaires de Rennes, 2009), 87–100.

halted by an armistice or ended by a treaty – sometimes after long negotiations. The congress of Rastadt, which was to settle the fate of the German possessions of France, thus lasted from November 1797 to the spring of 1799, interrupted on 28 April because of the assassination of two of the three French plenipotentiaries by Austrian hussars. This crime was exploited by the Directory: it aroused a strong patriotic drive in France. Diplomacy was not limited to the European continent: after signing a trade deal with Great Britain, John Adams' United States put an end to the Franco-American alliance of 1778 and wanted to expel French "Jacobins" from its territory. In March 1797, this led to maritime skirmishes between the two states, through privateers. In August of the same year, Toussaint Louverture dismissed the commissioner of the republic Sonthonax, affirming Saint-Domingue's autonomy.

The Egyptian adventure obviously occupies a unique position in this context.[29] Expedition plans had existed since the 1770s. Diplomatic relations with the Ottoman Empire had been renewed in 1792 and from 1794 to 1797, during the rule of the new Sultan Selim III (1789–1807). He refused, however, the role of diversion that the French revolutionaries hoped for by waging war against Russia and Austria. Franco-Ottoman relations were broken off after the Treaty of Campo Formio (17 October 1797), in view of Bonaparte's interest in the Balkans and then the occupation of Egypt. If the Directory, by sending the general across the seas, wished to move him away from the French political terrain, it was understood at the same time that the occupation of Egypt by Europeans was intended to reintroduce the progress that the ancient civilization once represented. One hundred and sixty scientists and engineers accompanied the 35,000 men of the army of the Orient in 1798. As soon as Cairo was conquered, an "Institute for the Sciences and the Arts" was founded for them there. It became part of the network of the Republic of Letters. This intellectual ambition would suffer, however, from the vagaries of the military situation, the resistance of the population, and the material conditions of the discovered objects. Expeditions and scientific missions piled up in the Nile Delta, the desert, and Upper Egypt, reflected in cartography, geography, hydrography, the natural sciences, archaeology in Gîza or Lûqsor, and ethnology – sciences that were brought together in the

[29] Henri Laurens, *L'expédition d'Égypte (1798–1801)* (Paris: Éditions du Seuil, 1997); Patrice Bret, *L'Égypte au temps de l'expédition de Bonaparte (1798–1801)* (Paris: Hachette, 1998); Juan Cole, *Bonaparte et la République française d'Égypte* (Paris: La Découverte, 2007); Ian Coller, *Une France arabe: Histoire des débuts de la diversité (1798–1831)* (Paris: Alma, 2014).

Description of Egypt. This book conveyed a civilizing utopia by reinventing a perfectly harmonious ancient Egypt, obedient to enlightened princes and an enlightened military, and marked by a religion whose temples declared the power of the deities. The discourse on Egypt's "regeneration" borrowed much from the concept of civilization as laid out by Condorcet in his *Esquisse d'un tableau historique des progrès de l'esprit humain*. A philosophical school called the Ideologues believed it was possible to have a colonization radically different from that in the Americas, which would bring relief to the peoples of the east, integrate them, and ultimately unite Europe with Asia. Bonaparte, a fighter and founder of new institutions, seemed to them to bring together these ideals.

Beyond the military operations that filled the gazettes, the scientific and cultural work continued to be praised in the columns of *La Décade philosophique*. Bonaparte's indigenous policy, with the struggle against the oppression of the Mamluks, the establishment of diwans, his recurring speeches to the Egyptian notables on Arab culture in the time of the caliphs, the pompous participation of the French in the rites of the country, the sumptuous revolutionary celebrations presented to the Egyptians as symbols of the alliance of the two peoples, the great scientific and technical performances deployed by the members of the Institute in front of the Egyptian notables, all made sense in this context. But this importation of the Enlightenment did not always meet with great success. It was true that Coutelle and Conté built windmills, optical telegraphs, sheets, and sword blades, but the Egyptians remained unconvinced of the prowess of chemists and the painstaking tests of balloonists. Incomprehension and mistrust between the peoples persisted, compounded by the brutality and rigors of the occupation, given that the day-to-day management of the territory was essentially under the control of the military machine. The Egyptian elite, interested in the library and printing house of the Institute, to which none of its members were invited, were satisfied with the teachings of the Koran, which seemed to them superior to the ideology of French progress. The occupants were seen as dirty, drunken, and debauched successors of the Crusaders. Few indigenous people, such as the Copt Ya'qûb and Sheikh Hassan al'Attâr, came to share the spirit of the Enlightenment. And on the French side, there were few who took a benevolent view of the Egyptians, such as the singer Villoteau, who discovered the originality of Egyptian music, and made the Egyptians aware of it.

Vis-à-vis the rest of Europe, French public officials and generals used a discourse reminiscent of that of the Constituents. Until the establishment of the Consulate, they presented the Revolution as a liberating force. They revealed a Republic proud of the victory of its armies, convinced of the strength and correctness of its principles, which believed it played a historical role in the development of freedom, civilization, and the sovereignty of peoples. The perceived exceptional character of the French Revolution was reflected in the expression "la Grande Nation," adopted by Bonaparte before the peace of Campo Formio, and reinforced by the military successes of the autumn of 1799.[30] This belief in French excellence was symbolically reflected in the attraction of the republic to the arts and sciences, of which Paris would be the capital. It provided legitimization for the plundering of Egyptian heritage, and then the Italian tribute payments in the form of masterpiece paintings, ancient statues, and manuscripts pursuant to the treaties of 1796 signed with the dukes of Modena and Parma and the Holy See.[31] This loot was paraded as trophies as soon as the items arrived in the French capital. Artists such as David, Girodet, and Soufflot opposed their entry without success.

From November 1795, it was Jean-François Reubell who directed foreign policy. He imposed a policy of annexations. The Dutch Republic, proclaimed on 3 February with the support of the Northern Army, was the first to suffer the consequences. The Treaty of The Hague of 16 May 1795 awarded the "Grande Nation" 100 million guilders, the right to leave behind an occupying force of 25,000 men, an offensive and defensive alliance, and territories (Maastricht, Venlo, and Dutch Flanders, the middle course of the Meuse) that offered the possibility of an extension to the Rhine. For the Dutch Patriots, the crucial element was undoubtedly the recognition of their republic, but they suffered soon from their divisions. After the refusal of a compromise text by the voters (August 1797), a constitution ensuring the unity of the republic was adopted by referendum. The obligation on voters to swear an oath of hatred of the stadtholder, federalism, and the aristocracy

---

[30] Jacques Godechot, *La Grande nation* (Paris: Aubier, 1983); Michel Vovelle, *Les Républiques-sœurs sous le regard de la Grande Nation (1795–1803): De l'Italie aux portes de l'Empire ottoman, l'impact du modèle républicain français* (Paris: L'Harmattan, 2000); Pierre Serna, ed., *Républiques sœurs: Le Directoire et la Révolution atlantique* (Rennes: Presses universitaires de Rennes, 2009); Hervé Leuwers, ed., *Du Directoire au Consulat: L'intégration des citoyens dans la Grande Nation* (Lille: CRHENO, 2000).

[31] Michael Broers, *Napoleonic Imperialism and the Savoyard Monarchy, 1773–1821: State Building in Piedmont* (Lewiston: Edwin Mellen Press, 1997); Michael Broers, *The Napoleonic Empire in Italy, 1796–1814: Cultural Imperialism in a European Context?* (Basingstoke: Palgrave Macmillan, 2005); Gilles Bertrand and Pierre Serna, eds., *La République en voyage (1770–1830)* (Rennes: Presses universitaires de Rennes, 2013).

dissuaded a significant number from voting (April 1798).[32] France intervened in Switzerland in January 1798, following the uprising of the canton of Vaud against the aristocratic government of Bern. With the support of French Commissioner Lecarlier, the patriots proclaimed the Swiss Republic on 21 April. For France, which signed a peace with Austria at Campo Formio, that development enabled it to gain control over the most direct route to Milan. In addition to the contributions required of the Swiss, it allowed the confiscation of the "treasures" of five aristocratic cantons (Bern, Zurich, Solothurn, Freiburg, and Lucerne).

In the meantime, Bonaparte took advantage of his Italian successes of the spring of 1796 to promote the establishment of Sister Republics in the north of the peninsula, acting without the authorization of the Directory.[33] The first was the Cisalpine, heir of the Cispadane Republic (Bologna, Modena, Reggio, Ferrara), which was created in October 1796. This was extended and transformed eight months later after Austria's renunciation of Lombardy, according to the preliminaries of Leoben (April 1797), and then through the cession of territories taken from Venice at the Treaty of Campo Formio. A second creation, in Genoa, followed a patriotic insurrection in May 1797. Bonaparte registered the birth of the Ligurian Republic, which was accepted by the Directory, which needed the support of the victorious general to organize the coup d'état of the 18 Fructidor. In the Papal States and the kingdom of Naples, republics were created later. In January 1798, the Directory decided that General Louis Alexandre Berthier would intervene militarily in Rome after the death of General Duphot, who had intervened during a riot the previous month. The French presence enabled the patriots to proclaim the Roman Republic (15 February 1798). In response to an offensive by the armies of Naples against this new republic (November 1798), General Championnet took over the holy city before occupying the south of Italy and approving the creation of a republic by the Neapolitan patriots on 26 January 1799: the Parthenopian Republic.

The birth of these Sister Republics did not correspond to any preconceived plan. In the autumn of 1797, France also absorbed the territory of the Cisrhenian Republic within its own boundaries. It understood, above all, the military and financial importance of this buffer zone, which also corresponded to the theory of "natural boundaries" (imposed by mountains or

---

[32] See Chapter 13 by Joris Oddens in this volume.
[33] Gilles Candela, *L'Armée d'Italie: Des missionnaires armés à la naissance de la guerre napoléonienne* (Rennes: Presses universitaires de Rennes, 2011).

rivers). The French political and social model was thus exported to foreign lands: declarations of rights, constitutions partly drafted by French legislators, equality before the law, abolition of tithes and feudalism, confiscation of ecclesiastical property and sale of national property, reform of justice, abrogation of corporations, and even tricolor flags, as witnessed in infinite variation from one state to another. For this model had to be adapted everywhere to the identities and diversity born of history: in Rome, the elected republicans called themselves consuls, senators were tribunes, judges were praetors, and magistrates aediles; in Naples, once a Hellenic colony, some preferred to call themselves archontes or ephors.

The expression of radical ideas was fairly easy, depending on the autonomy of foreign patriots and also on the political context. The constitutions recognized the right to work and public relief, and established a quasi-universal suffrage; that of the Neapolitan Republic proclaimed the right to education, subsistence, and resistance to oppression. While freedom of worship was acquired in the former United Provinces, traditional lands of tolerance, the Italian revolutions were generally more respectful of traditions – in the Roman republic, neither divorce nor secularization of civil status was introduced. (Secularizing the civil status means that the registration of births, deaths, and marriages, and the celebration of matrimonial unions is done by civil, not religious, authorities.) The presence of patriots would be essential to rule the new territories, but it was not necessary everywhere. The armistice signed with the king of Piedmont–Sardinia (Cherasco, 28 April 1796) abandoned the Italian patriots who took advantage of the French offensive to proclaim the republic in Piedmont; the Venetian patriots would likewise be left to their fate after Venice was awarded to Austria by the Treaty of Campo Formio. When the French troops invaded Tuscany in March 1799, the Directory refused to support the local patriots in their plan to establish a Sister Republic. Italy would, however, be the most ambitious experiment, since the idea was launched to proclaim its long-term unity under a French protectorate. This plan was drawn up in November 1798 by men in the entourage of General Joubert, including French Jacobins, such as Marc-Antoine Jullien and Jean Bassal, and Italian patriots, such as Carlo Lauberg.

The Sister Republics saw much political experimentation, which deeply marked the countries concerned. The structure, however, was fragile. The uprisings against the occupying forces were permanent (at Pavia in 1796, at Verona and Rome in 1797, in the "Belgian Vendée" in autumn 1798, in the Swiss cantons of Schwyz, Valais, and Nidwald in 1798, and in Graubünden and Nidwald in 1799 against conscription). The social base of the Sister Republics was too weak. In both Italy and Belgium, elections for public officials were eventually replaced by appointments. Political instability reigned, in accordance with the vagaries of war, and coups d'état in France, which were prolonged by coups d'état in the Sister Republics. The Dutch, Cisalpine, and Swiss patriots, who were too moderate, were excluded from their governments after 18 Fructidor; the most radical ones were excluded in the United Provinces and in the Cisalpine Republic after 22 Floréal. The state of war and the French military presence in friendly territories led to requisitions and financial contributions that were not accepted by the people. All these factors could hardly facilitate the establishment of the new regimes and removed many patriots from France. In much of Italy, the War of the Second Coalition put an end to these experiences, and not without extreme violence in Tuscany and Naples, where the "Viva Maria" and the Sanfedists of Cardinal Ruffo, respectively, were rife.

The war, and the political uncertainties of the regime, favored the rise of generals. They had been indispensable to the Directory on several occasions. On 13 Vendémiaire, Year IV (5 October 1795), the soldiers commanded by Barras and Bonaparte repressed a royalist insurrection in Paris. Bonaparte, who had become the Chief General of the Army of the Interior, was ordered on 9 Ventôse, Year IV (28 February 1796) to close the neo-Jacobin Club called the Panthéon. The events of 18 Fructidor would not have taken place without his pressure and help. "Is there no longer a republican in France? If you need strength, call the armies!," he then wrote to the Directory, urging the various units of the Italian army to express themselves in the same way. Next, Pierre Augereau, his right-hand man, occupied Paris militarily, and ordered the arrest of Director François Barthélémy, the royalist generals Jean-Charles Pichegru and Amédée Willot, and royalist deputies and journalists. France's foreign policy was established partly in Bonaparte's tent. At the head of his "armed missionaries," Bonaparte gave Italy a shining example of his independence from the politicians in Paris, freeing himself from the guardianship of civilian commissioners in diplomatic, financial, and political matters, and building a special relationship with his soldiers. Long before 18 Brumaire, for some of the staff, a coup d'état was lurking. In fact, of the twelve coups that took place in France and in the Sister Republics, six benefited from the assistance of French generals. For more than one polity, the coup d'état became an acceptable remedy to defend its institutions and republic. In view of the need to stabilize and end the revolution, a possible dictatorship was increasingly discussed in 1798–1799. After Sieyès, a supporter of Bonaparte, became a member of the Directory in May 1799, a constitutional revision was debated. Between June and November 1799, newspapers that claimed to be "conservatively moderate" and pretended to defend the constitution of Year III gradually helped introduce the notion that there was a general crisis. It gave rise to a fear that could not be justified by the actual political, economic, and social situation, and promoted a "black legend" of the Directory. Gradually, the need arose for a providential appeal to a "savior." Back from Egypt, where he had failed, Bonaparte achieved popular success throughout his journey from Fréjus to Paris in October 1799. Still playing with the fear of a "Jacobin" plot, the general prepared the coup d'état of 18 and 19 Brumaire, which, contrary to legend, met strong resistance, particularly within the Council of Five Hundred. Bonaparte's success was assured only by the intervention of the army on 19 Brumaire.[34] Everything thus ended with the paradox emphasized by Tocqueville: a regime imagined by its creators as a republic without revolution ended in a revolution without republic.

[34] Jean-Pierre Jessenne, ed., *Du Directoire au Consulat: Brumaire dans l'histoire du lien politique et de l'État-nation* (Lille: CRHENO, 2001); Jean-Paul Bertaud, *Bonaparte prend le pouvoir* (Brussels: Éditions Complexe, 1987).

10

Rethinking Gender, Sexuality, and the French Revolution

JENNIFER NGAIRE HEUER

The French Revolution was a sexual revolution. Not, perhaps, in the way the term is often associated with "free love" of the late 1960s. But the Revolution repeatedly challenged ideas of what it meant to be masculine or feminine and what rights or duties were associated with those identities. It also fundamentally transformed the family and changed the legal status of forms of sexual behavior. At the same time, popular understandings of gender and sexuality shaped how revolutionaries approached everything from political rights to policing, education to nationality, military recruitment to community festivals.

This chapter concentrates on two major themes regarding the centrality of gender and sexuality in the French Revolution. We begin with women's citizenship. Historians first reflected on the Revolution's impact on gender by debating how, and how much, women claimed rights, acted as citizens, or were distanced from political life. This remains a lively field of inquiry. Here we bring together recent research from different domains, including on both revolutionary and counterrevolutionary women and on both metropolitan France and the Caribbean. We reassess key turning points in empowering or disenfranchising women, and use these moments to explore how the tumultuous events of the time affected gender relations and citizenship.

The second section turns more directly to sexuality. Historians in the late 1980s and 1990s innovatively explored links between sexuality and power in eighteenth-century France, especially ways in which sexually charged imagery could be used to attack prominent figures.[1] The field has since expanded dramatically. We look here not only at lascivious gossip about

---

My thanks to Meghan Roberts, Alyssa Sepinwall, Laura Talamante, and Mónica Ricketts for their comments.

[1] Especially Lynn Hunt, ed., *Eroticism and the Body Politic* (Baltimore: Johns Hopkins University Press, 1991).

nobles and royals, but also at changes in the forms of behavior revolutionaries treated as legally or socially acceptable, from transformations in marriage and the recognition of children born out of wedlock to the decriminalization of prostitution and male homosexuality. Doing so reveals just how much the revolutionary personal was political – to borrow a phrase from 1960s activists. It also reveals new challenges for thinking about both historical sources and the motors of historical change.

Citizenship in the Feminine?

Many debates among historians about gender and the French Revolution have focused on women's citizenship. For some, the story is inspirational: women demanded rights and acted politically in ways that would have been inconceivable earlier. Their examples would encourage later champions of women's rights in France and around the world. There are dramatic examples of women's political action, like the October Days March on Versailles in 1789. Women joined revolutionary armies to defend the beleaguered nation. Individual women became the face of revolutionary or counterrevolutionary action, like Charlotte Corday, who assassinated the radical journalist Marat.[2] New languages of rights also provided many less famous women with tools for asserting their causes.[3] A few people explicitly championed women's rights, like the Marquis de Condorcet, who advocated for citizenship in 1790, Olympe de Gouges, who famously rewrote the Declaration of the Rights of Man as the Rights of Woman, and the Girondin Pierre Guyomar and Montagnard Gilbert Romme who, though politically opposed to one another, both argued for women's suffrage in 1793.

For others, the story of women's citizenship is one of political exclusion, or, as Anne Verjus has reframed it, noninclusion, less a deliberate rejection of women as a class than an inability to imagine them as political actors outside of patriarchal households.[4] Those revolutionaries who did champion women's rights were often politically marginal, or only intermittently

---

[2] Guillaume Mazeau, *Le bain de l'histoire: Charlotte Corday et l'attentat contre Marat* (Seyssel: Champ Vallon, 2009).

[3] For some examples, see Darline Gay Levy, Harriet Branson Applewhite, and Mary Durham Johnson, eds., *Women in Revolutionary Paris, 1789–1795* (Urbana: University of Illinois Press, 1980).

[4] Anne Verjus, *Le cens de la famille: Les femmes et le vote 1789–1848* (Paris: Belin, 2002); Anne Verjus, *Le bon mari: Une histoire politique des hommes et des femmes à l'époque révolutionnaire* (Paris: Fayard, 2010).

engaged. Condorcet, for example, called for women's rights in 1790, but did not mention them in his 1793 project for a constitution. Women in France did not get the right to vote until 1944, and first exercised that right only in 1945. The limits on women's political rights are striking given the experiences of other groups. The National Assembly recognized male Protestants and Jews, who had been excluded from citizenship under the Old Regime, as full citizens, and enfranchised free men of color. (After enslaved people revolted in the Caribbean, France abolished slavery in its empire and recognized them as full citizens, although Napoleon would try to reimpose slavery.) Women not only lacked suffrage; revolutionary leaders also shut down women's clubs in 1793, and two years later, forbade women from participating in any political assembly.

Yet assessing the Revolution as good or bad for women, as opportunity or exclusion, misses the complexities of citizenship in the period. It also misses how different kinds of rights and obligations affected each other. Women, for example, acquired a decree of legal autonomy, including being able to sign contracts and pursue legal matters in their own names, marry without parental authorization, divorce their husbands, and inherit equally with brothers. As Joan Scott has argued, the apparent paradox of recognizing women as civil agents and excluding them from formal politics can be seen to have engendered feminism.[5]

More generally, thinking about gender requires broadening our definition of citizenship beyond suffrage. It requires considering ways in which women acted as citizens or were understood to be citizens, even when they were excluded from the direct exercise of political rights. It requires relating forms of citizenship for both men and women. It also means considering degrees of citizenship or thinking about citizenships in the plural.[6] Finally, it means viewing citizenship not as fixed, but as a moving target, and considering how and why it changed across the Revolution.

Rousseau's Shadow?

For many scholars, the story begins in the eighteenth century. In a line of argument popularized in the late 1980s, several historians have claimed that the Revolution continued a long-term process of relegating women to the

---

[5] Joan Scott, *Only Paradoxes to Offer: French Feminists and the Rights of Man* (Cambridge, MA: Harvard University Press, 1996), 19–20.

[6] Guillaume Mazeau and Clyde Plumauzille, "Penser avec le genre: Trouble dans la citoyenneté révolutionnaire," *La révolution française* (2015), http://lrf.revues.org/1458.

domestic realm even as politics became more democratic – even, perhaps, precisely because politics became more democratic.[7] For those who support this interpretation, Jean-Jacques Rousseau's shadow looms large. The eighteenth-century *philosophe* and subsequent favorite of many revolutionaries promoted an image of an ideal woman who was subservient and modest. In *Émile*, his influential treatise on creating and educating citizens, he infamously claimed that "woman was specifically made to please man."

Yet Rousseau did not simply denigrate women; he also offered new models of civic virtue. Readers could also read his novels and treatises in different ways. He often equated women with mothers, despite abandoning his own children at the gates of an orphanage. Combined with new ideas about education and self-expression, Rousseau's vision of motherhood could actually appear empowering. Several historians have recently insisted on liberating aspects of his views. Jennifer Popiel argues that while Rousseau's ideals anchored women in domestic life, they also encouraged new forms of civic participation for both men and women. In Annie Smart's reading of Rousseau and his supporters, mothers were similarly critical for creating an egalitarian society; they generated the bonds of love that underpinned a virtuous state.[8]

Revolutionaries also did not necessarily follow Rousseau's injunctions or respond to them consistently. Alyssa Sepinwall has shown that while historians often see Jacobins' disparagement of women's intellectual abilities as a continuation of Old Regime prejudices, such attitudes could represent a *retreat* from their prerevolutionary positions. Most notably, Maximilien Robespierre, often seen as instituting Rousseauian ideas of virtue in 1793–1794, argued forcefully for admitting women to royal academies in 1787.[9] While Rousseau's model of gender roles was not the only one to shape the Revolution, it is a useful reminder that revolutionary thinking about gender included not only constraints, but also surprising possibilities for imagining feminine courage, intellect, and engagement.[10]

---

[7] Joan Landes' interpretation has been particularly influential. See Joan Landes, *Women and the Public Sphere in the Age of the French Revolution* (Ithaca, NY: Cornell University Press, 1988).

[8] Jennifer J. Popiel, *Rousseau's Daughters: Domesticity, Education, and Autonomy in Modern France* (Durham, NH: University of New Hampshire Press, 2008); Annie Smart, *Citoyennes: Women and the Ideal of Citizenship in Eighteenth-Century France* (Newark: University of Delaware Press, 2012).

[9] Alyssa Sepinwall, "Robespierre, Old Regime Feminist? Gender, the Late Eighteenth Century and the French Revolution, Revisited," *Journal of Modern History* 82:1 (2010), 1–29.

[10] On alternatives, see Suzanne Desan, *The Family on Trial in Revolutionary France* (Berkeley: University of California Press, 2004).

Acting and Speaking as Citizens in the Early Revolution?

If long-term developments shaped how men and women viewed citizenship, the Revolution still can appear a dramatic break. Some women self-consciously claimed rights starting in 1789. Other factors that encouraged political roles for women were unanticipated and evolved over the course of the Revolution. As William Sewell has noted, the word *citoyenne* was not created to enfranchise women. It appeared because *citoyen* or citizen was meant to be a replacement for titles like Monsieur; it thus required a feminine counterpart. But it also legitimated women's claims to be members of the sovereign.[11]

Politicization took many forms. Women led specific actions, most famously, the October Days March of 1789. Some attended local political assemblies, like Parisian *sections* (neighborhood-based organizations created in 1790); others attended meetings of the National Assembly. Starting in 1791, Jacobin women formed at least sixty political clubs across France.[12] Women were not part of many institutions of formal political power, but they participated in demonstrations, festivals, and other public events. They also used politicized language and expressed political opinions in everything from petitions to public declarations, works of art to choices in clothing.

Women could be profoundly influenced by Revolutionary discourses and experiences even if they talked about those influences only privately.[13] Both those hopeful and those concerned about changes to women's citizenship also often focused on effects on private life. Legislators began to empower women and children with civic rights, while reducing men's – especially fathers' – control over their families. In August 1790, the Constituent Assembly abolished *lettres de cachet* (which had made it possible for fathers to imprison wayward family members without a trial), and replaced them with family tribunals, which granted mothers equal rights in supervising their children. The National Assembly abolished primogeniture in 1790, then

---

[11] William Sewell, "Le citoyen/la citoyenne: Activity, Passivity, and the Revolutionary Concept of Citizenship," in Colin Lucas, ed., *The French Revolution and the Creation of Modern Political Culture* (Oxford: Pergamon Press, 1987), 105–23.

[12] Suzanne Desan, "'Constitutional Amazons': Jacobin Women's Clubs in the French Revolution," in Bryant Ragan and Elizabeth Williams, eds., *Recreating Authority in Revolutionary France* (New Brunswick: Rutgers University Press, 1992), 11–35.

[13] Lindsay A. H. Parker, *Writing the Revolution: A French Woman's History in Letters* (Oxford: Oxford University Press, 2013).

decreed in April 1791 that intestate legacies had to be divided equally among children regardless of sex or birth order.[14]

In September 1792, the Assembly legalized divorce. The reasons for this decision are themselves controversial. Activists denounced indissoluble marriage as despotism, trapping women in unhappy unions. Members of the *Cercle social*, for example, actively campaigned for divorce, along with changes to property law.[15] Some historians have seen the legalization of divorce as a feminist victory. But it can also be seen as a consequence of a new emphasis on contract law. If, as the 1791 Constitution established, marriage was a contract, not a sacrament, then it, like other contracts, should be dissolvable. Looking at the consequences of the decree shows that whether or not divorce was intended to benefit women, it helped them more than men, and they were more likely to use it.[16]

More generally, women's politicization was not always in the name of women's rights. In considering what the Revolution meant for women, historians have often generalized from the experiences of particular groups: militant *sans-culotte* women, women writers, or elite figures of the court. But these people had very different interactions with the state, dependent not only on their gender, but also on their class and social position, race, and region.

Even when women acted in explicitly political ways, they did not always do so as women, or at least, not only as women. One of the more famous women of the period, Madame (Marie-Jeanne "Manon") Roland, was a leading figure among the Girondins. Her salon served as a political gathering site; she exercised particular influence after her husband Jean-Marie became Minister of the Interior in 1792, and would be guillotined for her political associations a year later. But she did not champion women's rights per se.[17] Similarly, looking at the *Dames des Halles*, the Parisian market women responsible for provisioning the city with basic food supplies, Katie Jarvis rejects the idea that gender was the most salient criterion for their political

---

[14] Jennifer Ngaire Heuer, *The Family and the Nation: Gender and Citizenship in Revolutionary France* (Ithaca, NY: Cornell University Press, 2005).

[15] Gary Kates, "The Powers of Husband and Wife Must Be Equal and Separate: The Cercle Social and the Rights of Women, 1790–91," in Harriet Applewhite and Darline G. Levy, eds., *Women and Politics in the Age of Democratic Revolution* (Ann Arbor: University of Michigan Press, 1990), 221–33.

[16] Desan, *Family on Trial*.

[17] Sian Reynolds, *Marriage and Revolution: Monsieur and Madame Roland* (Oxford: Oxford University Press, 2012).

actions. The *Dames* actively shaped policy on currency, business licenses, and price limits. They justified their activities and claimed the status of citizens by touting their public utility and economic centrality.[18]

The Expulsion of Women from the Military

Some women acted as citizens in a particularly visible way: by taking up arms. The archives reveal traces of over 100. Women had been part of Old Regime troops in multiple ways, including as laundresses and *vivandières* (women who provisioned the troops with basic foodstuffs), and as soldiers' companions, prostitutes, and camp followers. Women who joined the ranks after 1789 filled these roles, but also sometimes became soldiers themselves, either openly, or disguised as men. It is challenging for historians to untangle their motives, which encompassed financial need, desire for adventure, and romantic or familial connections. Their presence in the military could prove the depth of revolutionary patriotism: all citizens were ready to defend their nation in its time of need. At the same time, women-soldiers' appearance as "virtual men" profoundly unsettled gendered hierarchies.

On 30 April 1793, the National Convention expelled "useless" women from the armies, leaving only a few laundresses and *vivandières*. This decree is one of the first measures explicitly excluding women from citizenship. A few days earlier, the deputy Pierre Guyomar had insisted that women be allowed to vote in primary assemblies, demanding that women either be considered citizens, or identified as slaves and called wives or daughters of citizens, but not citizens themselves. In a speech on 29 April, Jean-Denis Lanjuinais responded that women's physical condition, destiny, and employment precluded most from political rights and duties; as a political term, "citizen" should not encompass women.[19] While legislators did not refer to these exchanges when expelling women from the troops the following day, it seems likely that the view of women as incapable of political rights made them appear unfit to be part of the military defending those rights.

Yet other factors were also at play, which historians have usually overlooked. In March 1793, the government overturned a prohibition that banned soldiers from marrying without special permission from their

---

[18] Katie Jarvis, *Politics in the Marketplace: Work, Gender, and Citizenship in Revolutionary France* (Oxford: Oxford University Press, 2019).
[19] *Archives Parlementaires*, vol. LXIII, 561–4.

superiors.[20] The new law reflected changes to marriage: since 1789, marriage had been secularized, divorce legalized, and new limits placed on parental ability to control their children's choice of partner. The March 1793 decision also reflected changes to the military, as volunteers – including married men – joined the ranks and as revolutionaries overturned traditional military order. In such circumstances, it seemed logical that soldiers, like other citizens, should marry as they chose.

While our evidence comes from disgruntled authorities who likely exaggerated for their own purposes, permitting soldiers' marriages seems to have dramatically increased the number of women in the troops. One official complained to the Minister of Foreign Affairs that sixty women might accompany eighty gendarmes, and that wagons were so filled with women, cradles, and children that there was no room for the injured. Another wrote to the Minister of War on 17 April, deriding women as "mouths that are infinitely expensive for the Republic," who destroyed soldiers' morale. He concluded that if women were allowed to remain in the military, "our soldiers will finish by being good for nothing."[21] Such complaints combined practical concerns about military logistics with worries about venereal disease and moral judgements about the presence of women.

The expulsion of women from the military thus reflected debates over women's place in the nation. But it also corresponded to unexpected changes in *men*'s citizenship. Permitting military marriage and treating soldiers as family men actually created a new legal separation between domestic and military space, between the realm of family and that of military and political action.

Economic Controls, Tricolored Cockades, and Women's Political Clubs

Women sometimes remained in the troops after they were officially expelled, and were even heralded for their service – though usually after they had stopped fighting. Women also continued to act politically in 1793. Some played an important role in the confrontations between the Girondins and the Montagnards on 31 May and 2 June 1793, including guarding the

---

[20] Jennifer Ngaire Heuer, "Celibacy, Courage, and Hungry Wives: Debating Military Marriage and Citizenship in Pre-revolutionary France," *European History Quarterly* 46:4 (2016), 648–67.

[21] Thomas Cardoza, *Intrepid Women: Cantinières and Vivandières of the French Army* (Bloomington: Indiana University Press, 2010), 49.

doors of the Convention and refusing to let deputies leave.²² Others participated in local electoral assemblies in summer 1793. Unintended factors may have made it easier for them to do so. Serge Aberdam has called attention to a 10 June 1793 law on *biens communaux*, rights to pasture animals on town commons or gather wood from the forest. These rights applied "without distinction of fortune or sex" to those registered as tax-paying heads of household. The law, which emphasized the social position over sexual differences, coincided with public debates over a new Constitution of 1793. The timing may have opened the way for wider practices of suffrage.²³ Women proclaimed their adhesion to the Constitution alongside men, although the *procès-verbaux* sent to the National Convention rarely mentioned their involvement.²⁴

In July 1793, Charlotte Corday assassinated Jean-Paul Marat, hoping to stop the radical journalist from inciting violence. Her act actually helped consolidate Paris-based Jacobin power. It also fed a "Federalist" movement, centered around four provincial cities – Caen (Corday's home), Bordeaux, Lyon, and Marseille – which rose up against Paris-based authorities to defend competing visions of revolution. Historians have only recently begun to look closely at women's participation in these movements.²⁵ Laura Talamante has especially uncovered gendered dynamics in one Federalist city: Marseille. Women were visible across urban political spaces, including revolutionary clubs, section meetings, streets, courtrooms, and prisons.²⁶ They had joined the crowds that helped push democratization in 1789 and 1790. They also participated in coalition building, using familial, social, and economic networks to influence revolutionary culture and

---

[22] Noah Shusterman, "All of His Power Lies in the Distaff: Robespierre, Women, and the French Revolution," *Past and Present* 223 (2014), 129–60.

[23] Serge Aberdam, "L'élargissement du droit de vote entre 1792 et 1795 au travers du dénombrement du Comité de division et des votes populaires sur les Constitutions de 1793 et 1795" (Ph.D. dissertation, Université de Paris 1 Panthéon-Sorbonne, Paris, 2001), 766–70.

[24] Dominique Godineau, "Femmes en citoyenneté: Pratique et politique," *Annales historiques de la révolution française* 300:2 (1995), 197–207; Desan, "Constitutional Amazons," 24.

[25] Nicolas Soulas, "Le 'fédéralisme' au féminin. La crise politique de l'été 1793 au prisme des rapports de genre en révolution," *Provence historique* 265 (2019), 37–53.

[26] Laura Talamante, "Political Divisions, Gender and Politics: The Case of Revolutionary Marseille," *French History* 31:1 (2017), 63–84; Laura Talamante, "Mapping Women's Everyday Lives in Revolutionary Marseille," in Mette Harder and Jennifer Ngaire Heuer, eds., *Life in Revolutionary France* (London: Bloomsbury, 2020), 51–80. See also Jacques Guilhaumou, "Conduites politiques de Marseillaises pendant la révolution française," *Provence historique* 186 (1996), 471–89.

practices. This continued in 1793. Both Jacobins and Federalists in Marseille identified women's political power as potentially transgressive and placed it within gendered frameworks of power and political expectations. These frameworks, however, allowed for flexibility depending on the political context within which women acted.

One of these frameworks for women to express political views ended nationally in fall 1793. On 30 October 1793, the National Convention decreed that "clubs and popular societies of women, under whatever denomination, are forbidden." Even more than the expulsion of women from the military, this decree has been associated with their exclusion from citizenship. The deputy André Amar's speech to the National Convention reveals this logic explicitly. He asked, "should women exercise political rights and get mixed up in the affairs of government?" and "should women gather together in political associations?" For Amar, the answer to both questions was clearly no: women lacked the knowledge, objectivity, and commitment for public affairs. He also insisted that motherhood was more important and incompatible with participating in government.[27]

Amar's speech echoed older views that women lacked intellectual rigor, and should behave first and foremost as mothers. Historians who stress the importance of Rousseauian ideals present the closing of political clubs as completing a long-term process of excluding women from democracy. Joan Landes influentially proclaimed that "by 1793 women were banned from active *and* passive participation in the political sphere."[28] But seeing this decision simply as a culmination of engrained prejudices or as inherent to forms of democracy leaves aside the factors that prompted it. The decision was sparked by a conflict between two groups: the *Dames des Halles* and the Society of Revolutionary Republican Women, a club formed in May 1793 and aligned with the radical *sans-culottes* known as the *enragés*. The Society demanded that all women wear the tricolor cockade. Some commentators saw this as a first step to greater claims to feminine militancy. The deputy Fabre d'Églantine thus complained on 29 October 1793 that women would not stop with adopting the cockade or the red cap of liberty, but would "soon demand a belt with pistols."[29]

---

[27] "Discussion of Women's Political Clubs and Their Suppression, 29–30 October 1793," *Liberty, Equality, Fraternity: Exploring the French Revolution*, https://revolution.chnm.org/items/show/556.
[28] Landes, *Women and the Public Sphere*, 147.
[29] *Archives Parlementaires*, vol. LXXVIII, 21.

If the two groups clashed over the symbols of citizenship, they also had different political affiliations and modes of political organizing.[30] Their conflicts were actually precipitated by struggles over market regulation. A month earlier, the National Convention had passed the General Maximum, sweeping price controls on basic foodstuffs. The Society supported such measures to secure food for wage-laborers, but market women found their livelihood endangered, especially as laws initially did not distinguish between retail and wholesale prices. The Dames and the Society thus confronted each other in the streets of Paris over France's economic choices, perhaps even more than over women's rights or obligations.[31]

It was also not until after Fabre d'Églantine raised the possibility of investigating all "revolutionary clubs" that one woman asked "for the abolition of all special women's clubs." As Katie Jarvis notes, the Society was the only women's club in the capital; closing it deflected attention from women's participation in mixed-sex clubs. But the petitioner's impromptu request has also become a turning point in the narrative of women's citizenship.

Following the decree, women were expelled from other politicized spaces. Two weeks later, the Paris Commune barred women from its sessions. Jacobin women's clubs elsewhere closed, although the Paris-inspired decree was not the only factor behind their shuttering. Many provincial Jacobin women's clubs had faced ridicule, as accusations of female irrationality were combined with aspersions about the morality of the women involved; the Parisian decree resonated with local prejudices and conflicts.[32]

As political clubs served as one of the key tools for revolutionary organizing, closing clubs shut women out of a critical site of revolutionary politics. The decree was an important moment in defining women's citizenship and their relationships with the Revolution, but it was neither an inevitable development nor a complete turning point.

Viragos, Victims, and the "Terror"

Scholarship on gender and citizenship sometimes stops with the closing of political clubs. But the French Revolution is also intrinsically associated with the months between September 1793 and Robespierre's fall from power on

---

[30] Olwen Hufton, *Women and the Limits of Citizenship in the French Revolution* (Toronto: University of Toronto Press, 1992), 28.
[31] Katie Jarvis, "The Cost of Female Citizenship: How Price Controls Gendered Democracy in Revolutionary France," *French Historical Studies* 41:4 (2018), 647–80; Jarvis, *Politics in the Marketplace*.
[32] Desan, "Constitutional Amazons."

9 Thermidor (27 July 1794), usually referred to as the "Terror." Contemporary caricaturists represented the Jacobin Republic that oversaw the Terror as a deranged, bloodthirsty woman. Subsequent literature reinforced such associations. Indeed, the most infamous woman associated with the Terror may be fictional: Madame Lafarge, knitting obsessively at the foot of the guillotine. (The character in Charles Dickens' 1859 *Tale of Two Cities* reflects the tendency of nineteenth-century writers to identify working-class women with violence.)[33] But historians' focus on women's rights has often overshadowed questions both of how much women were actually responsible for the Terror and of the extent to which they were themselves judged guilty of political crimes.

While no woman had a position of power within the Jacobin government, women participated in the Terror. Some called for repressive measures and denounced people they believed to be enemies.[34] Such denunciation built on women's traditional roles of observing local communities and enforcing social norms. As the Terror progressed, the process of accusing and judging counterrevolutionary crime increasingly became the realm of men. A decree of 21 March 1793 charged surveillance committees with compiling lists of foreigners; the September 1793 Law of Suspects extended their powers. Women could not usually be members, but could present denunciations and testify. As the committees gained power, judging revolution became more masculine.[35] Women instead appeared more often as witnesses of punishment, and may have constituted a majority of those at the foot of the gallows. Dominique Godineau speculates that women came to witness executions precisely because they were increasingly excluded from other forms of political, judicial, and military participation.[36]

In writing a Declaration of Rights of Woman and Citizen, Olympe de Gouges argued that if women faced the scaffold – the possibility of death for

---

[33] Dominique Godineau, "Femmes et violence dans l'espace politique révolutionnaire," *Historical Reflections* 29:3 (2003), 559–76.
[34] Jacques Guilhaumou and Martine Lapied, "Les femmes actrices ou victimes de la Terreur," in Michel Biard, ed., *Les politiques de la Terreur, 1793–1794* (Rennes: Presses universitaires de Rennes, 2008), 171–82.
[35] Guilhaumou and Lapied, "Les femmes actrices"; Julie Johnson, "The 'Fury': The Case of an Activist Woman of Lyon in 1792–1793," *Lilith: A Feminist History Journal* 25 (2019), 63–75; Martine Lapied, "Parole publique des femmes et conflictualité pendant la révolution dans le sud-est de la France," *Annales historiques de la révolution française* 344 (2006), 47–62.
[36] Dominique Godineau, "Masculine and Feminine Political Practice during the French Revolution, 1793 – Year III," in Applewhite and Levy, eds., *Women and Politics in the Age of Democratic Revolution*, 61–81.

political crimes – they should be able to "mount the rostrum," that is, speak politically. De Gouges herself faced the scaffold: she was executed in November 1793, in part because of her associations with the Girondins and the queen, who had herself been dramatically executed two weeks earlier. Pierre Gaspard Chaumette, president of the Paris Commune, denounced de Gouges' transgression of gender roles and her desire to "mount the rostrum." He labeled her "the first woman to start women's political clubs, who abandoned the cares of her home to meddle in the affairs of the Republic" and rejoiced that her "head fell under the avenging blade of the law." In denouncing de Gouges' involvement with clubs, Chaumette associated her with the Society of Republican Revolutionary Women, although her Girondin politics were antithetical to it.[37]

The Paris Revolutionary Tribunal condemned 2,684 people to death between April 1793 and July 1794, 387 of whom were women. A higher proportion of accused women than men were nobles. While aristocratic women were less likely than men to have left the country, they may also have appeared as enemies because of both their gender and their social position.[38] But like most male victims of the Terror, women were arrested and executed, at least in theory, for what they had done, not just who they were. They were accused of specific crimes rather than simply transgressing gender roles. Their crimes were not always the same as those of men; they were more likely to be accused of religious offenses and crimes like emigration or correspondence with the enemy.[39] But these were still political acts for which they could be required to "mount the scaffold."

Holding women personally responsible for political crimes challenged their status within the family. At the same time, their legal dependence within the household provided ways for women to absolve themselves of political responsibility. A woman accused of emigration, for example, might claim that she had been forced to leave the country by her husband, rather than by her own volition – or that she had used the new institution of divorce to separate herself from her husband's acts. Both representatives of the state and ordinary men and women usually resolved conflicts between family and nation by emphasizing the civic obligations of dependents over their legal subordination within the family. In the later years of the Revolution, this

---

[37] Smart, *Citoyennes*, 144.
[38] Stephanie A. Brown, "Women on Trial: The Revolutionary Tribunal and Gender" (Ph. D. dissertation, Stanford University, 1996), 53.
[39] Brown, "Women on Trial," 86.

situation would be reversed, as authorities began to subordinate national bonds to familial ones.[40]

Staking Citizenship after Thermidor

This reversal, however, was slow and complicated. Women actually remained politically engaged after Robespierre's fall from power on 9 Thermidor. They mobilized especially to protest food shortages. But militant women also continued to claim to embody popular sovereignty, particularly during crowd actions.[41] Paradoxically, women were most recognized as citizens during insurrections, when the people attempted to reclaim rights that women, as women, did not enjoy.[42] In Prairial Year III (May 1795), women spearheaded an invasion of the National Assembly and demanded "bread and the constitution of 1793," the constitution associated with the radical revolution. The uprising failed; in its wake, the government forbade women from entering political tribunals or participating in any political assembly, while those attending public gatherings of more than five women risked arrest. The decree, instituted by an increasingly conservative regime, followed the Jacobin ban on women's political clubs, but came from those seeking to oppose any return to Jacobin order.

Conservatives also mobilized around family. As Suzanne Desan has shown, petitioners besieged the legislature seeking both to challenge specific laws and to institute a more patriarchal order.[43] While they did not immediately overturn most changes to family law, legislators did develop the conceptual foundations for the misogynistic Napoleonic Code. Uncovering their attitudes and actions suggests that the cult of nineteenth-century domesticity emerged not, or at least not simply, from revolutionary republicanism, but rather from the reactionary dynamics of the late 1790s and early Napoleonic period.

But even as the government curtailed much of the legal and political power of women, they did not disappear from the public eye. As Christine Adams has demonstrated, some women, like Madame de Tallien, partially returned to Old Regime forms of political power in the later 1790s, using their beauty and intimate connections to further their agendas.[44] Étienne Gosse's 1799 play *Political Women* mocked a woman who "claimed to govern

---

[40] Heuer, *The Family and the Nation*.
[41] Godineau, "Masculine and Feminine Political Practice."
[42] Godineau, "Femmes en citoyenneté."   [43] Desan, *Family on Trial*.
[44] Christine Adams, "'Venus of the Capitol': Madame Tallien and the Politics of Beauty under the Directory," *French Historical Studies* 37:4 (2014), 599–629.

the cabinets of Europe" and concluded that women should use their sewing needles, not pens.[45] Women did not govern the cabinets of late eighteenth-century Europe, at least not of France. This did not mean they were silent. Carla Hesse has actually documented an increase in women's authorship both during and immediately *after* the Revolution.[46] The subjects women wrote about could be limited, but they did not set down their pens.

If Robespierre's fall from power on 9 Thermidor has come to be seen as the end of "Terror," France also struggled with the legacies of mass violence for years. Women, especially widows, sought restitution. They sought to clear victims' names and to reclaim property seized when their relatives were executed by revolutionary tribunals. Ronen Steinberg argues that dealing with legacies of Terror actually opened up new space for women as political actors: "The violence of Year II was by and large a masculine affair, but the struggle for redress was very much the domain of women."[47]

Indeed, the experiences of the Revolution, combined with prolonged war – in which men could be away from home for years – often increased women's interactions with the state. Women negotiated government bureaucracy in myriad situations throughout the late 1790s and early 1800s. These included not just those seeking redress after the Terror, but also family members pleading for husbands' or sons' release from military service and relatives seeking to discover what had happened to those missing in action; people asking for exceptions to restrictions on marriage law; individuals seeking work or pensions; and "refugees" from the colonies hoping for financial support in France. Their interactions built on established models of supplication, and, for the illiterate or semiliterate, were shaped by professional writers. But the combined effects of revolution and war did bring women into repeated and novel contact with the state, long after they had been kept from participating politically in that state.

Counterrevolution, Counter-Citizenship, Counter-Narratives?

If these accounts of women in the Revolution focus on those who fought for change, women also opposed the new order. Doing so often brought them, like prorevolutionary women, into the public in new ways. Yet counterrevolutionary women and their contemporaries often understood their

---

[45] Étienne Gosse, *Les Femmes politiques* (Paris, 1799).
[46] Carla Hesse, *The Other Enlightenment: How French Women Became Modern* (Princeton: Princeton University Press, 2001).
[47] Ronen Steinberg, *The Afterlives of the Terror: Facing the Legacies of Mass Violence in Post-Revolutionary France* (Ithaca, NY: Cornell University Press, 2019), 88.

activities not as republican citizenship, but rather as a response to revolutionary threat.

In both eighteenth-century and modern accounts, religion often looms large. Religious action could be combined with revolutionary ideas of liberty and popular sovereignty.[48] But it was particularly associated with feminine opposition to the Revolution. The Civil Constitution of the Clergy, instituted on 12 July 1790, required priests to take an oath of loyalty to the revolutionary state; those who refused to do so were forbidden to perform mass or religious sacraments. Women's Jacobin clubs mobilized in part to defend the Civil Constitution, but conservative women protected "nonjuror" priests, and defended religious spaces and symbols.[49] They mocked new forms of religion promoted during the Revolution, like the Festival of the Supreme Being. After the Thermidorian government reauthorized limited forms of public worship in February 1795, women were often at the forefront of rebuilding the Church. Historians have identified this with a feminization of religion in the wake of the Revolution.[50]

Like assessing the reasons that led women-soldiers to enlist in republican armies, assessing how, and how much, counterrevolutionary women were motivated by religion can be challenging. Certainly, women participated in religious riots and may have seen their participation in more religious terms than men.[51] But the interests of different groups also converged to make women appear particularly inspired by religious devotion or swayed by priests. Most of our sources on religious resistance to the revolution come from officials who saw peasant women as superstitious. It was useful for men arrested for religiously based uprisings to blame their wives for fanaticism – and for arrested women to play upon belief in their supposed irrationality in hopes of being treated more leniently. For nineteenth-century conservatives, stories of religious women as victims of brutality dramatized the horror of the revolution.[52]

---

[48] Suzanne Desan, "The Role of Women in Religious Riots during the French Revolution," *Eighteenth-Century Studies* 22:3 (1989), 451–68.
[49] On Jacobin clubs, see Desan, "Constitutional Amazons," on nonjuror priests, Hufton, *Women and the Limits of Citizenship*; Solenn Mabo, "Des Bretonnes en résistance: Genre, religion, et contestation politique," *La révolution française. Cahiers de l'histoire de la révolution française* (2020), https://journals.openedition.org/lrf/4306#ftn3.
[50] Hufton, *Women and the Limits of Citizenship*, 122, 124.
[51] Timothy Tackett, "Women and Men in Counterrevolution: The Sommières Riot of 1791," *Journal of Modern History* 59:4 (1987), 680–704.
[52] Hufton, *Women and the Limits of Citizenship*; Mabo, "Des Bretonnes"; Martine Lapied, "La fanatique contre-révolutionnaire: Réalité ou représentations," in Luc Capdevila, Sophie Cassagnes, Martine Cocaud et al., eds., *Le genre face aux mutations: Masculin et*

Civil war also deeply affected women as well as men. In some cases, war forced women to take a side whether or not they intended to become politically involved.[53] Vendean armies were often accompanied by women, children, and the elderly, some of whom fled before the advance of republicans. A few women fought with counterrevolutionary troops. These women were not affected by the expulsion of women from revolutionary armies, but, like their counterparts on the republican side, their presence in the ranks challenged gendered order. When the Bourbon monarchy claimed power in 1814/1815, authorities sought to minimize women's roles – contending that none could have earned military honors – while still heralding a few as heroines. One of the most famous, Renée Bordereau, known as the Angevin, had allegedly killed twenty men. When she published her memoirs in 1814, critics both heralded her authenticity and royalism and sought to downplay her violence.

The View from the Caribbean

Before leaving the question of women's citizenship, we need to shift focus, to the Caribbean. Revolution did not just take place on the territory of modern-day France. It shook the world, especially the Caribbean, where prerevolutionary France claimed its most valuable colonies. The relationships between the French and Haitian Revolutions are complex; slave revolt and the eventual independence of the former colony were not, or not exclusively, by-products of revolution in the European continent, nor can the complex dynamics of upheaval and civil war throughout the Caribbean be mapped directly onto metropolitan struggles.

Yet while other chapters in this collection look more directly at the Caribbean, considering it here shows how much questions of gender were entangled with both metropolitan and colonial experiences and connections between the two. Some connections were self-conscious. French supporters of women's rights compared the bonds of marriage to slavery to justify divorce; a few also directly opposed slavery or championed rights for free people of color. Condorcet, for example, was a founding member of the Society of the Friends of the Blacks, while de Gouges criticized slavery in her plays. Other connections were less intentional. For example, slave revolt

---

féminin, du Moyen Age à nos jours (Rennes: Presses universitaires de Rennes, 2003), 255–64.
[53] Jean-Clément Martin, "Femmes et guerre civile, l'exemple de la Vendée, 1793–1796," *Clio: Femmes, Genre, Histoire* 5 (1997), https://doi.org/10.4000/clio.410.

increased the price of sugar in France; it thus indirectly helped spark women's protests over the costs of food in Paris and Lyon.

Looking at the Caribbean also pushes us to rethink the stakes and chronology of women's citizenship. It is harder for historians to find information about women, especially women of color, involved in the Haitian Revolution and elsewhere in the French Caribbean than it is to find similar information for metropolitan France. Enslavers deliberately kept people illiterate, and women were particularly unlikely to be able to read and write; much of what we know about their lives thus comes from others' accounts. The desires of slave-holding empires to deny the radicality of the Haitian Revolution led to active "silencing" of enslaved people's agency and the erasure of their stories from archives – a silencing compounded by the physical destruction of archival records with war and natural disaster.[54] Recent attempts to reclaim figures as national heroines have since called attention to a few women's stories, but also sometimes mythologized their lives.[55]

Yet Caribbean women were active participants in both revolution and war. Those whose names we know include Cécile Fatiman, the Vodou priestess who played a critical role in the ceremony at Bwa Kayiman (Bois Caïman) which sparked slave rebellion in Haiti in 1791; spies, like Henriette Saint Marc, and soldiers like Suzanne (or Sanité) Bélair, a mixed-race woman who became a sergeant and then lieutenant in Toussaint Louverture's army.[56] Women like Bélair had different motivations for taking up arms than their counterparts in the metropole. They were more concerned with fighting against the brutality of slavery and white supremacy than with calling for women's rights or defending the endangered French nation. The relative fluidity of their roles in the troops and the timing of their engagement contrasts with those of women in continental Europe.[57] Armed women were part of the slave revolt that began in August 1791, around the same time as women began to call for the right to bear arms in the metropole. But if women were officially expelled from continental French armies in April

---

[54] Michel-Rolph Trouillot, *Silencing the Past: Power and the Production of History* (Boston: Beacon Press, 1995).

[55] These dynamics are revealed by Nicole Willson, "Unmaking the Tricolore: Catherine Flon, Material Testimony, and Occluded Narratives of Female-Led Resistance in Haiti and the Haitian *Dyaspora*," *Slavery & Abolition* 41:1 (2020), 131–48.

[56] Philippe Girard, "Rebelles with a Cause: Women in the Haitian War of Independence, 1802–04," *Gender & History* 21:1 (2009), 60–85.

[57] Elizabeth Colwill, "Gender, Slavery, War and Violence in and beyond the Age of Revolutions," in Karen Hagemann, Stefan Dudink, and Sonya O. Rose, eds., *The Oxford Handbook of Gender, War, and the Western World since 1600* (Oxford: Oxford University Press, 2020).

1793, armed Caribbean women became most prominent in the early Napoleonic era. They actively resisted General Leclerc's expedition when it landed in Haiti in December 1801, and opposed Napoleon's plans to reinstitute slavery in the Caribbean. Marie-Jeanne Lamartinière, for example, defended a Haitian fort besieged by French soldiers in March 1802. Similarly, Solitude, a mixed-race woman who would later become a national heroine in Guadeloupe, fought against Napoleon's attempts to reimpose slavery in Guadeloupe. Captured while pregnant, she was allowed to live until she gave birth.[58]

As in the metropole, however, armed women were rare in the Caribbean. Enslaved men could achieve emancipation by joining the Republican army before 1793; taking up arms subsequently provided an alternative to plantation labor. Arms-bearing rarely served the same purposes for women. Mimi Sheller has argued further that because Haiti was under constant threat of invasion after it claimed independence, the country promoted an armed male citizenry. Since women were generally excluded from the military, they were also excluded from many forms of citizenship.[59]

Formerly enslaved women who succeeded in claiming freedom during and after the Revolution usually did so by other means, including marriage. While women in the metropole used the rhetoric of slavery to denounce a woman's subservience to her husband, marriage to a free – or freed – man could enable an enslaved woman to establish her own emancipation and that of her children. Marriage, however, did not guarantee that freedom would last. Women sometimes bore free children only to mourn their reenslavement, as when French forces restored the slave regime in Guadeloupe and elsewhere, or when the vagaries of war, civil war, and revolution forced them to travel to places where slavery persisted. Both men and women could show remarkable determination in trying to defend their own freedom and that of their family across the transatlantic world, determination which was fed by revolution but outlasted and resonated beyond it.[60]

---

[58] Laurent Dubois, "Gendered Freedom: Citoyennes and War in the Revolutionary Caribbean," in Karen Hagemann, Gisela Mettele, and Jane Rendall, eds., *Gender, War, and Politics: Transatlantic Perspectives, 1775–1830* (New York: Palgrave Macmillan, 2010), 59–70: 67.

[59] Mimi Sheller, "Sword-Bearing Citizens: Militarism and Manhood in Nineteenth-Century Haiti," *Plantation Society in the Americas* 4:2–3 (1997), 233–78.

[60] Colwill, "Gender, Slavery, War, and Violence"; Rebecca Scott and Jean M. Hébrard, *Freedom Papers: An Atlantic Odyssey in the Age of Emancipation* (Cambridge, MA: Harvard University Press, 2012).

Rethinking Citizenship, Causality, and Chronology

Looking across the French Revolution reveals both the centrality and the complexity of women's citizenship. A few people dramatically claimed rights for women; others acted as citizens, but foregrounded political, economic, or religious identities. Possibilities for women to act as citizens – or requirements that they do so – narrowed over the course of the Revolution, but did not completely disappear. How we interpret these developments as historians has real stakes both for understanding the French Revolution and for learning its lessons: do we emphasize long-term developments or specific turning points? Deliberate demands for rights or active misogyny, ingrained assumptions or unexpected developments? Changes in civil and private life or participation in political institutions? The decisions of the Jacobin Republic or counterrevolutionary reactions?

Moving beyond the most familiar account of women in the Revolution – a Paris-based account of demands for women's political rights and exclusion from political power at the hands of a Jacobin government – shows us that there was not one single decisive event or trajectory. Without underestimating either the boldness and creativity of individuals or the power of entrenched misogyny, we can see surprising contingencies and unplanned consequences. Looking across the 1790s reveals myriad sites of contestation, even after women were officially excluded from the institutions of political citizenship. Considering the Caribbean shifts our chronology still further: critical turning points in the stories of women's citizenship include not just the March on Versailles or the exclusion of women from the army and political clubs, executions of prominent figures or even changing laws on religious worship, but also repeated struggles for freedom.

Policing and Sexuality

The Revolution did not only reshape women's citizenship, it also transformed sexuality. Indeed, invoking and policing sexuality were closely tied to political struggles throughout the Revolution. Looking more closely at sexuality allows us to think further about the challenges of historical sources, from the uses of salacious materials to silences surrounding key legislative decisions. It reveals how different sources can give us very different views of sexual and gender relations. It also pushes us to consider different motors of historical change.

Sexual Scandal and Political Struggles

The dynamics of censorship in the Old Regime had meant that pornography and politically subversive tracts often circulated together. Salacious stories discredited the monarchy, from attacks on royal mistresses to prerevolutionary mockery of Louis XVI's impotence during the first seven childless years of his marriage.[61] Tales of aristocratic debauchery and scandal similarly linked sexual and political disorder. These threatened state power, though Simon Burrows has recently argued that libels were often intended to blackmail the government into paying for silence rather than to stir up popular discontent.[62]

The most infamous accusations of sexual misconduct concerned Marie-Antoinette.[63] These intensified in the last years of the Old Regime, especially during the 1785 "Diamond Necklace Affair," when a con-woman pretended to be the queen as part of a crime intended to defraud the crown jewelers; the fallout from the affair tarnished Marie-Antoinette. Accusations against the queen became increasingly important during the Revolution itself. If Louis XVI's trial focused on his actions and identity as king, the queen's trial invoked her purported lesbianism and incest with her son. Such claims served both to undermine her personally and to attack women's political power generally.[64]

While historians usually associate such sexualized imagery with republican attacks on the elites of the Old Regime, counterrevolutionaries used similar imagery to discredit their rivals. Suzanne Desan has recently shown how much the conservative press attacked the revolutionary leader Théroigne de Méricourt. Méricourt appeared an ideal candidate for ridicule as a foreigner and a single woman with a sexually ambiguous past and an outspoken passion for revolutionary politics.[65] Even when such attacks originated in a particular ideological context, they resonated more broadly and quickly became entrenched as "facts."

Sexualized insults could also promote competing models of masculinity and femininity. The accusation of "enormous effeminacy" in one Corsican

---

[61] Lynn Hunt, *The Family Romance of the French Revolution* (Berkeley: University of California Press, 1992).
[62] Simon Burrows, "The Character Assassination of Marie-Antoinette: Defamation in the Age of the French Revolution," in Sergei A. Samoilenko, Martijn Icks, Jennifer Keohane, and Eric Shiraev, eds., *The Routledge Handbook of Character Assassination and Reputation Management* (New York: Routledge, 2019), 186–208.
[63] Hunt, *Family Romance*.
[64] Dena Goodman and Thomas Kaiser, eds., *Marie-Antoinette: Writings on the Body of a Queen* (New York: Routledge, 2003).
[65] Suzanne Desan, "Théroigne de Méricourt: Gender and International Politics in Revolutionary Europe," *Journal of Modern History* 92 (2020), 274–310.

struggle was associated not with homosexuality, but with calumny, masculine weakness, and social pretention; it opposed austere virtue to aristocratic refinement.[66] For women of the popular classes, displaying one's buttocks was a traditional form of protest. Some revolutionaries used the strategy to mock opponents, like a Jacobin domestic servant in Lyon who showed her derrière to bourgeois neighbors in July 1793.[67] Those angry with the revolution sometimes adopted the same strategy, as when the entire female audience at a celebration of the Supreme Being arose, turned their backs to the altar of liberty, and exposed their bare butts to the revolutionary deity.[68] At the same time, publicly undressing and beating other women was a form of humiliation. In April 1791, the *Dames des Halles* dragged counterrevolutionary nuns into the streets, exposed their butts, and hit them with brooms.[69] In the most famous such episode, militant Jacobin women spanked Méricourt in May 1793, presumably for her connections to the Girondins.[70]

Sexualized images could also play more positive roles. Joan Landes has argued controversially that artists depicted the revolutionary nation as a desirable female body. Such imagery eroticized patriotism and bound male subjects to the nation-state.[71] Other historians have emphasized how often the "mother-country" of France was represented as a literal mother. Such representations established the republican nation as above its citizens and encouraged equality among citizen-children, even as they reinforced the role of real women as mothers.[72]

Recasting Marriage

If sexually charged images served to castigate authority or reinforce national bonds, revolutionaries also changed people's lived experiences of sexuality, perhaps most centrally by challenging the nature and legal power of

---

[66] Antoine Franzini, *Haine et Politique en Corse: L'affrontement de deux hommes au temps de la révolution française, 1780–1800* (Ajaccio: Alain Piazolla, 2013).
[67] Johnson, "The 'Fury.'" [68] Hufton, *Women and the Limits of Citizenship*.
[69] Katie Jarvis, "'Patriotic Discipline': Cloistered Behinds, Public Judgment, and Female Violence in Revolutionary Paris," in Nimisha Barton and Richard Hopkins, eds., *Practiced Citizenship: Women, Gender, and the State in Modern France* (Lincoln: University of Nebraska Press, 2019), 19–50.
[70] Dominique Godineau emphasizes that such violence was between women. Godineau, "Femmes et violence," 563.
[71] Joan Landes, *Visualizing the Nation: Gender, Representation, and Revolution in Eighteenth-Century France* (Ithaca, NY: Cornell University Press, 2001).
[72] Anne Verjus and Jennifer Heuer, "Les mères de la patrie révolutionnaire: Entre représentation et incarnation du politique, 1792–1801," *Les Cahiers de la maison de la recherche en sciences humaines* 45 (2006), 259–70.

marriage. Some eighteenth-century couples, especially in the popular classes, had formed socially sanctioned bonds outside of wedlock, and young men boasted of their sexual adventures.[73] At the other end of the social spectrum, nobles were associated with libertinage, at least in the pages of novels like Choderlos de Laclos's 1782 *Dangerous Liaisons*. Yet in principle, sexual relations were supposed to be contained within marital relationships that could be ended only with the death of a partner.

Revolutionaries changed that. When the National Assembly legalized divorce in September 1792 on a remarkably equal basis, it effectively challenged the idea that sexuality and love had to be tied to permanent bonds. Legislators also transformed the status of children born out of wedlock, removing the legal stigma that had been attached to them, and, in November 1793, granted such children full inheritance rights.

These changes were not intended to undermine marriage. Revolutionaries sought to reform marriage, not abolish it; indeed, one justification for divorce was that it would allow couples to form happier unions and have more children. Remaining single and childless could appear selfish and even counterrevolutionary. This particularly applied to clergy. Catholic doctrine had required priests and nuns to remain celibate; as revolutionaries closed monasteries and nunneries, they encouraged or even forced people to marry to prove their devotion to the revolutionary nation.[74]

Marriage could also serve as a means of state control. This was especially true in the Caribbean. Both French republican leaders and Haitian authorities sought to promote marriage among formerly enslaved peoples to undergird a gendered division of work in coercive labor regimes.[75] The constitution Toussaint Louverture created for the French colony of Saint-Domingue in 1801 enshrined marriage and decreed that divorce would not take place there. In contrast, divorce remained legal in Napoleonic France, although

---

[73] Arlette Farge, *La vie fragile: Violence, pouvoirs et solidarités à Paris au XVIIIe siècle* (Paris: Hachette, 1986).

[74] Anne Verjus, Claire Cage, Jennifer Heuer, Andrea Mansker, and Meghan Roberts, "Regards croisés sur le mariage à l'époque révolutionnaire et impériale," *Annales historiques de la révolution française* 398 (2017), 144–71; Claire Cage, "'Celibacy Is a Social Crime': The Politics of Clerical Marriage, 1793–1797," *French Historical Studies* 36:4 (2013), 601–28.

[75] Elizabeth Colwill, "Fêtes de l'hymen, fêtes de la liberté: Matrimony, Emancipation, and the Creation of New Men," in David Geggus and Norman Fiering, eds., *The World of the Haitian Revolution* (Bloomington: Indiana University Press, 2009), 125–55; Elizabeth Colwill, "Freedwomen's Familial Politics: Marriage, War and Rites of Registry in Post-emancipation Saint-Domingue," in Hagemann et al., eds., *Gender, War and Politics*, 71–89.

the Civil Code made it more restrictive; the Catholic Restoration monarchy would ultimately ban it in France in 1816, fifteen years after Haiti. (Divorce was relegalized in France in 1884.)

Revolution and its aftermath also affected interracial relationships. While slavery did not officially exist in France itself, emancipation theoretically made it easier to imagine more egalitarian and legal interracial relationships. Conversely, the 1802 reinstitutionalization of slavery under Napoleon led to a ban on marriage between Blacks and whites in the metropole. This reintroduced prerevolutionary restrictions, following a renewed ban on the travel of Blacks and people of color from the colonies into the metropole. Yet officials now applied that restriction only to those deemed Blacks "properly speaking." People regarded as mixed-race were allowed to marry whites; the ban as a whole would be quietly rescinded in 1819.[76]

More generally, changes to family law did not always have the consequences their creators anticipated. Rumors that the National Convention had decreed equality between illegitimate and legitimate children helped spark a revolt in Guadeloupe, in 1793, where the decree promised to change relations between whites and free people of color. As Suzanne Desan has noted, new inheritance law in metropolitan France paradoxically did more to harm illegitimate children than to help them. It stipulated that to inherit, children had to be recognized by their fathers, with recognition proven only by a father's written word or evidence of "continuous" care. Such emphasis on the voluntary acceptance of paternity undercut women's ability to press paternity suits and provide for children born out of wedlock.[77]

Decriminalizing "Sodomy" and Prostitution

Revolutionaries also changed sexual practices and relations through decriminalization. One of the most important changes affected what we now think of as LGBTQ+ relations. There were no formal laws against lesbianism in the Old Regime, but sodomy – a multivalent term associated with male homosexuality – was deemed a crime against both god and natural law. The last two French men executed for the alleged crime were hanged in 1750. Revolutionaries effectively legalized sodomy by leaving it off the list of crimes in a major new legal code in 1791, while instituting the principle that individuals could be condemned only for crimes named in law. The

---

[76] Jennifer Heuer, "The One-Drop Rule in Reverse? Interracial Marriages in Napoleonic and Restoration France," *Law and History* 27:3 (2009), 515–48.
[77] Desan, *Family on Trial*.

Napoleonic regime revised the code in 1810 and reinstated some prerevolutionary laws, but did not recriminalize sodomy.[78]

There is no record of the decision to remove sodomy from the code or the debates that led to this decision. As Bryant Ragan has observed, while human rights discourse was central to much of the revolution, it was irrelevant in this case; legislators simply did not conceive of LGBTQ+ people as a discriminated-against group. Instead, the decision may have been an unforeseen consequence of secularization, combined with new ideas of personal autonomy.[79] Decriminalization did not equate to legalization or even tolerance; authorities increasingly treated sodomy as something that could be ignored in private, but prevented in public.

Legislators also decriminalized prostitution in October 1791. As with sodomy, prostitution was legalized simply by omitting it from the new penal code. Here too there seems to have been no political or legislative debate, so we can only guess at the motives behind the change. Clyde Plumauzille has characterized it as a "paradoxical decriminalization"; prostitution became legal, but prostitutes were discriminated against in new ways.[80]

Indeed, Revolutionaries increasingly decried prostitution after 1791. Doing so stigmatized militant *sans-culotte* women; it also reflected fears of the effects of venereal disease on the army and a general rhetoric of sexual and political corruption. In October 1793, a decree put into place new controls without formally recriminalizing prostitution. That decree would disappear after the Terror, but the idea of prostitution as a social, medical, and moral danger continued. At the same time, legalization led to a state-controlled system of brothels, registration, and medical inspections in the nineteenth century.

The Motors of Change

If Revolutionaries actively deployed sexualized images to attack public figures and changed legislation regulating sexual behaviors, the revolution

---

[78] Bryant T. Ragan, "Same-Sex Sexual Relations and the French Revolution: The Decriminalization of Sodomy in 1791," in Sean Brady and Mark Seymour, eds., *From Sodomy Laws to Same-Sex Marriage: International Perspectives since 1789* (London: Bloomsbury, 2019), 13–30.

[79] Michael D. Sibalis, "The Regulation of Male Homosexuality in Revolutionary and Napoleonic France, 1789–1815," in Jeffrey Merrick and Bryant T. Ragan, eds., *Homosexuality in Modern France* (Oxford: Oxford University Press, 1996), 80–101; Ragan, "Same-Sex Sexual Relations."

[80] Clyde Plumauzille, *Prostitution et Révolution: Les femmes publiques dans la cité républicaine (1789–1804)* (Paris: Champ Vallon, 2016).

also changed sexuality in less direct ways. Most notably, two decades of almost constant warfare profoundly reshaped gender roles and expressions of sexuality. It could do so in unexpected ways. Perhaps the most surprising case is that of Romaine-la-Prophétesse, a free black coffee farmer in Haiti who dressed in women's clothes and claimed that the Virgin Mary was his godmother. In 1791–1792, Romaine amassed a large following of insurgents who briefly conquered the two main cities of southern Haiti.[81]

In metropolitan France, the Revolution made military service an obligation for citizens. Revolutionaries instituted mass conscription as an emergency measure with the *levée en masse* in August 1793, then as a permanent institution in 1798. While many men initially anticipated fighting only for a season or a campaign, they often remained in the troops for years.[82] Prolonged separations, combined with new views of martial masculinity, transformed relationships between men and their families, friends, and romantic or sexual interests. How we understand the effects of those changes, however, depends in part on the sources we examine. Plays produced for civilian audiences, ditties for soldiers on the march, internal military regulations, medical treatises, military memoirs, and postrevolutionary pamphlets can all give us very different views of the effects of war. In different materials, revolutionary soldiers appear as cultural heroes embodying new forms of virtue and entitled to romantic reward, as swashbucklers trained to conquer on the battlefield and in the bedroom, or as violent, debauched, or weakened veterans.

Considering disparate forms of evidence together also helps us reconcile competing interpretations of how military service changed sexuality from the revolutionary era to the Napoleonic era. Michael Hughes has contended that Napoleonic military culture promoted aggressive heterosexuality, as sex as a reward replaced a puritanical stance of the revolutionary army.[83] Conversely, Brian Joseph Martin has argued that military fraternity evolved into an unprecedented sense of camaraderie and homoerotic desire among

---

[81] Terry Rey, *The Priest and the Prophetess: Abbé Ouvière, Romaine Rivière, and the Revolutionary Atlantic World* (Oxford: Oxford University Press, 2017).

[82] Jennifer Ngaire Heuer, "Citizenship, the French Revolution, and the Limits of Martial Masculinity," in Rachel Fuchs and Anne Epstein, eds., *Gender and Citizenship in Historical and Transnational Perspective* (Basingstoke: Palgrave Macmillan, 2016), 19–38.

[83] Michael J. Hughes, *Forging Napoleon's Grande Armée: Motivation, Military Culture, and Masculinity in the French Army, 1800–1808* (New York: New York University Press, 2012).

Napoleonic soldiers.[84] Such apparently contradictory developments reflect different accounts of warfare, even as they both reveal potential long-term effects of mass mobilization and the prolonged separation of civilians and combatants.

Finally, changing medical ideas of "natural" differences between men and women both preceded the Revolution and helped shape understandings of sexuality as it developed. In one particularly influential interpretation, Thomas Laqueur contended that a "one-sex" model – in which women's anatomy was understood as an inversion of men's – was replaced by a "two-sex" model over the eighteenth century. Among other things, seeing women's anatomy as different than men's implied that women did not need to experience orgasm during sex in order to become pregnant.

Historians have since challenged Laqueur's framing, arguing that the two models coexisted rather than followed one another.[85] Whether or not we can identify a clear-cut shift, doctors in the late eighteenth century did emphasize distinctive aspects of women's physiology. They provided "scientific" evidence that women's physical characteristics made them well suited for motherhood and ill-suited for intellectual pursuits. They sometimes explicitly connected medical judgements to social ones; one prominent doctor, Pierre Cabanis, argued that careers for women would undermine family and civil society, while his colleague Moreau de la Sarthe depicted female temperaments as pathological.[86] How much causal weight we place on these judgements, however, depends on our views of what matters in history. Did medical developments shape political ones, did political imperatives mobilize medical ones, or were they intertwined?

Scientists and medical personnel also became particularly fascinated by Black bodies, especially women's bodies. The most famous case is Sara Baartman, the "Venus Hottentot." In 1810, two men brought the Khoikhoi woman from South Africa to England and France. They forced her to display herself in various public forums, treating her body as a sexual curiosity because of her large buttocks and supposed apron over her genitals.[87]

---

[84] Brian Joseph Martin, *Napoleonic Friendship: Military Fraternity, Intimacy, and Sexuality in Nineteenth-Century France* (Durham, NH: University Press of New England, 2011).
[85] Thomas Laqueur, *Making Sex: Body and Gender from the Greeks to Freud* (Cambridge, MA: Harvard University Press, 1992).
[86] Hunt, *Family Romance*, 156–8.
[87] Robin Mitchell, *Vénus Noire: Black Women and Colonial Fantasies in Nineteenth-Century France* (Athens, GA: University of Georgia Press, 2020); Clifton Crais and Pamela Scully, *Sara Baartman and the Hottentot Venus: A Ghost Story and a Biography* (Princeton: Princeton University Press, 2009).

French and British authorities subjected her to scrutiny and abuse even after her death. The naturalist Georges Cuvier dissected her body in 1815; her brain, skeleton, and genitalia were held in the Museum of Man in Paris until 2002, when she was reburied in South Africa. Such forms of sexual and racial "science" seeking to prove that women's bodies and those of people of color were fundamentally different from the bodies of white male Europeans helped justify misogyny and renewed slavery and colonialism.

Conclusion

The French Revolution was, indeed, a sexual revolution. Gender and sexuality appear everywhere, from demands for rights to racy caricatures of royalty, from divorce laws to the policing of sodomy, from military regulations to medical treatises. The revolution both fostered and limited new forms of gendered citizenship, transformed the legal basis of family and sexuality, and reshaped how people understood and experienced their relationships.

Yet if looking at the Revolution illuminates changes to citizenship and sexuality, looking at gender and sexuality during the Revolution also illuminates critical dynamics of historical change. Assessing gendered forms of citizenship and thinking about sexuality requires us to wrestle with chronology and causality, to decide how much weight we want to put on specific decisions or unanticipated consequences, and to read past the contradictions and silences in our sources. Ultimately, thinking about gender and sexuality in the Revolution reflects how we understand revolution itself.

PART II

★

WESTERN, CENTRAL, AND
EASTERN EUROPE

11

Switzerland: Local Agency and French Intervention: The Helvetic Republic

MARC H. LERNER

French General Philippe-Romain Ménard of the Army of Italy declared to the people of the Pays de Vaud that the French armies had arrived in order to liberate the "Vaudois people" from "the enemies of liberty" and "your despots."[1] These French troops crossed the Swiss borders on 25–28 January 1798 at the instigation of Swiss patriots in Lausanne, the capital of the Pays de Vaud, and helped to establish the short-lived Lemanic Republic. The Old Swiss *Eidgenossenschaft* (Confederation) did not dissolve until March, and the Helvetic Republic was not officially declared until 12 April 1798, but with the entry of a French army, the Old Regime ended in the Swiss Republics. The French invasion resulted from the French Directory's geopolitical calculations and local, Swiss patriot agitation for French help against the oligarchs of the Old Regime.

Reforms undertaken by the ruling Swiss cantons of the Old Confederation dismantled some of the privileged structures of the Old Regime even before a new constitution went into effect, showing the agency of local, Swiss elites in setting up the new republic. The 1798 constitution of the Helvetic Republic, originally drafted by Peter Ochs of Basel, introduced a "one and unitary Republic." The constitution demanded that the form of government for the Helvetic Republic always remain a "representative democracy," a structure that included "the natural, inalienable rights of man."[2] The

---

[1] Proclamation of General Ménard, 26 January 1798, in Danièle Tosato-Rigo and Silvio Corsini with the collaboration of Valérie Berthoud and Nathalie Manteau, eds., *Bon peuple vaudois, écoute tes vrais amis!: Discours, proclamations et pamphlets diffusés dans le Pays de Vaud au temps de la révolution (décembre 1797–avril 1798)* (Lausanne: Revue historique vaudoise and Bibliothèque historique vaudoise, 1999), document 43, p. 143; also found in Johannes Strickler, ed., *Actensammlung aus der Zeit der Helvetischen Republik [ASHR]*, vol. 1 (Bern: Stämpfli'sche Buchdruckerei, 1886), 172, with date of 28 January 1798.

[2] "Constitution de la République helvétique/Verfassung der helvetischen Republik," 12 April 1798, Articles 2, 5, in Alfred Kölz, ed., *Quellenbuch zur neueren schweizerischen*

constitution brought legally binding conceptions of modern individual rights into Swiss spaces. These rights included freedom of the press, opinion, and settlement as well as equality among cantons, lifting up the previously subject territories.[3] The Old Confederation had been dominated by the thirteen full member cantons, which ruled over the other areas without full sovereign rights. The elimination of cantonal frontiers and subject territories, such as the Pays de Vaud or Aargau, as well as the rejection of hereditary powers, social rank, and honors, demonstrates the new regime's demolition of the Old Swiss Confederation, which had managed to adopt, evolve, and survive in varying forms for centuries.[4]

French intervention undeniably played a fundamental role in the creation of the Helvetic Republic. In the first place, the constitution, which was adopted as the Constitution of the Helvetic Republic, was based on that of the French Directory. The Directory in Paris instructed General Brune, Ménard's successor, to implement and promulgate the draft constitution written by Ochs, a patrician member of Basel's governing class. This intervention by the French Directory happened even though much of the Swiss political elite, including Ochs himself, had moved on to a different proposal put forth by the Basel National Assembly, which would have preserved many more elements of the decentralized confederal structure of the Old Confederation.[5]

Although the Helvetic constitution implemented protections for a slew of individual rights, the Helvetic Republic was not a full-fledged creation of a modern Swiss state. Throughout its five-year existence there was significant opposition and resistance to the unitary structure of the new Swiss state and the perception of a "Paris" constitution.[6] Four coups and a Napoleonic intervention later, the Helvetic Republic was replaced in 1803 by the Napoleonic Act of Mediation. Napoleon cast blame for the failures of the

---

Verfassungsgeschichte, vol. 1: Vom Ende der Alten Eidgenossenschaft bis 1848 (Bern: Stämpfli, 1992), 126.

[3] "Constitution de la République helvétique," esp. Articles 1–14, 126ff.

[4] For more on the Old Eidgenossenschaft see Andreas Würgler, "'The League of Discordant Members' or How the Old Swiss Confederation Operated and How It Managed to Survive for So Long," in André Holenstein, Thomas Maissen, and Maarten Prak, eds., The Republican Alternative: The Netherlands and Switzerland Compared (Amsterdam: Amsterdam University Press, 2008); Hans Conrad Peyer, Verfassungsgeschichte der alten Schweiz (Zurich: Schulthess, 1980).

[5] Entwurf der helvetischen Staatsverfassung von der National-Versammlung des Cantons Basel (Zurich: Wilhelm Haas, 1798).

[6] See, for example, Christian Simon, ed., Widerstand und Proteste zur Zeit der Helvetik/ Résistance et contestations à l'époque de l'Helvétique (Basel: Schwab, 1998).

Helvetic Republic on the Swiss, but at the same time the Mediation regime restored political stability to the region for over a decade by embracing elements of a decentralized Swiss Confederation and ensuring the continued flow of soldiers to Napoleonic armies.[7]

The tension between reformers seeking a more unitary Swiss state, on the one hand, and traditional Swiss confederalists, on the other, remained at least until 1848 and the creation of the Swiss Federal state. Despite the claims of the confederalists, the Helvetic Revolution was a part of Swiss development that should not be dismissed as purely foreign invention.[8] The way in which the Helvetic Republic was formed demonstrates that Swiss actors were willing participants in the Atlantic Age of Revolutions and simultaneously were swept up by transnational events beyond their control. Importantly, the Helvetic Republic is a means to understanding different paths through the Age of Revolutions.

There should not be one model for understanding an overall conception of the Atlantic Age of Revolutions. The path to, and the formation of, the Helvetic Republic demonstrates another revolutionary path – a simplistic notion of French lust for territory does not fully explain an international process. Native patriots had agency and played a role in the destruction of the Old Regime in the Swiss Confederation, the creation of the Helvetic Republic, and the introduction of a revolutionary political culture.

The Helvetic Revolution occurred in the context of a wider framework of the Atlantic Revolutions. Although perhaps triggered by financial distress,[9] these revolutions were political events. In the Swiss case the fight over political authority existed within a wider, international political framework. As Richard Whatmore has demonstrated, the Swiss arena, including Geneva, had already been politically destabilized by the Anglo-French imperial

---

[7] *Acte de médiation fair par le premier Consul de la République française, entre les partis qui divisent la Suisse*, excerpts in Kölz, ed., *Quellenbuch*, vol. 1, 159–88. For the supply of troops and financial subsidies, see Chapter 20, "Acte fédéral/Bundesverfassung," Article 2 of the *Acte de médiation*, in Kölz, ed., *Quellenbuch*, vol. 1, 175–6. For a further guarantee of 8,000 soldiers see *Traité d'alliance défensive entre la République française et la Suisse*, 27 September 1803, Articles 3–4, in Kölz, ed., *Quellenbuch*, vol. 1, 189. For casting blame, see Heinrich Zschokke, *The History of the Invasion of Switzerland by the French and the Destruction of the Democratic Republics of Schwitz, Uri, and Unterwalden*, trans. J. B. Briatte (London: J. Taylor for T. N. Longman and O. Rees, 1803), 353 in supplement.

[8] See Andreas Würgler, "Grenzen des Zumutbaren? Revolution und Okkupation als Erfarhrung und Erinnerung," in Andreas Würgler, ed., *Grenzen des Zumutbaren: Erfahrungen mit der französischen Okkupation und der Helvetischen Republik (1798–1803)* (Basel: Schwab, 2011), 9–10.

[9] Jeremy Adelman, "An Age of Imperial Revolution," *The American Historical Review* 113:2 (2008), 319–40.

competition.[10] This destabilization allowed longer-term discussions about the nature of political authority to explode into actual contestation of the ruling elites. We can see this in the Geneva described by Whatmore and the Patriot movement in the Dutch Republic, as well as in subject territories in Switzerland such as Stäfa in the Zurich hinterland, the Pays de Vaud subject to Canton Bern, or the Landschaft March in Canton Schwyz. The explosion of the French Revolution and the movement of French troops certainly impacted the actions of Swiss or other patriot actors, but patriot agency shaped how each revolution took advantage of the opportunity for reform wrought by a wider Atlantic destabilization.

Part of the wider framework of the Revolutionary Age is the key role played by those who were excluded from the *ancien régime* political processes demanding to be included in the Old Regime. When that inclusion failed, there was even greater support for revolution. In the Swiss Confederation and elsewhere there was often a relationship between reform and revolution. Reformers had long argued to expand the body politic beyond an oligarchic elite in Swiss cities. In the pursuit of these reforms and the recognition of rights, Swiss patriots were willing to use any potential tool to achieve these ends, including, after 1789, the use of the rhetoric of the French Revolution and the implicit threat of violence.

Long-Term Debates

The Swiss considered themselves free long before the Helvetic Republic. Political actors in the old Swiss Confederation had been debating concepts of (Swiss) freedom, individual and collective liberty and liberties since the late seventeenth century, long before 1798 or even 1789.[11] This conception of liberty was not universal, but rather applied to all full members of the

---

[10] Richard Whatmore, Chapter 12 in this volume; Richard Whatmore, *Against War and Empire: Geneva, Britain, and France in the Eighteenth Century* (New Haven: Yale University Press, 2012); Richard Whatmore, *Terrorists, Anarchists, and Republicans: The Genevans and the Irish in Time of Revolution* (Princeton: Princeton University Press, 2019).

[11] For an overview of these discussions in Swiss circles, see Michael Böhler, Etienne Hofmann, Peter H. Reill, and Simone Zurbuchen, eds., *Republikanische Tugend: Ausbildung eines Schweizer Nationalbewusstseins und Erziehung eines neuen Bürgers* (Geneva: Slatkine, 2000); Michael Kempe and Thomas Maissen, *Die Collegia der Insulaner, Vertraulichen und Wohlgesinnten in Zürich, 1679–1709: Die ersten deutschsprachigen Aufklärungsgesellschaften zwischen Naturwissenschaften, Bibelkritik, Geschichte und Politik* (Zurich: NZZ, 2002); Béla Kapossy, *Iselin contra Rousseau: Sociable Patriotism and the History of Mankind* (Basel: Schwabe, 2006).

community, namely male citizens who had inherited or bought membership in the political community. The traditional sense of republican Swiss liberty was understood as having been earned. Into the eighteenth century, patriot leaders used the same definition, they just argued that a wider circle had earned those rights; Swiss liberty remained earned, either through military service or through contribution to the cantonal community. Rather than individual rights, traditional Swiss liberty focused on collective self-rule.

A pragmatic conception of republicanism informed the Swiss discussions. It is a mistake to think causally about either natural law or Enlightenment discussions directly instigating political revolution. Conceptions of natural rights were used to claim equality at the origins of society, but did not function as the fundamental basis of a rights-based political culture until after the revolutions began.[12] Intellectual debate helped to create a framework in which public opinion could open up a wider understanding of popular sovereignty and challenge oligarchic or patrician regimes in the Swiss cantons, but the Swiss discussions were fundamentally reformist. Classical republican and natural law strains of thought featured in the Swiss Enlightenment discussions about the nature of Swiss liberty, but the pragmatic Enlightened strain dominated. Economic patriotic societies – improvement societies, which sought to emphasize the love of country, prosperity, and rational economic reforms – were developed from the 1760s into the 1790s.[13] Only when pragmatic republicans were shut out of the Old Regime was there more momentum for upending the Old Regime.

The intertwining of reformist and revolutionary attempts to challenge the Old Regime is evidenced by the events in Stäfa in 1794–1795. Stäfa, a lake town in the Zurich hinterland, was subject to the rule of the city of Zurich. In 1794 several members of the educated elite of the area produced an effective protest document. This Stäfa Memorial is a great example of the interaction of reformist and revolutionary ideals.[14] It was authored by Heinrich

---

[12] Jack Censer, *Debating Modern Revolution: The Evolution of Revolutionary Ideas* (London: Bloomsbury, 2016), 9–12, 15.

[13] Ulrich Im Hof and François de Capitani, *Die Helvetische Gesellschaft: Spätaufklärung und Vorrevolution in der Schweiz*, 2 vols. (Frauenfeld and Stuttgart: Verlag Huber, 1983); Kapossy, *Iselin contra Rousseau*; Holger Böning, *Der Traum von Freiheit und Gleichheit: Helvetische Revolution und Republik (1798–1803) – Die Schweiz auf dem Weg zur bürgerlichen Demokratie* (Zurich: Orell Füssli, 1998), 46.

[14] I refer to to the version available in [Heinrich Nehracher], "Das Stäfner Memorial von 1794," in Christoph Mörgeli, ed., *Memorial and Stäfner Handel, 1794/1795* (Stäfa: Gemeinde, Lesegesellschaft, 1995). For more see Marc H. Lerner, *A Laboratory of Liberty: The Transformation of Political Culture in Republican Switzerland, 1750–1848* (Leiden: Brill, 2012), 84ff.

Nehracher, organized by Johann Caspar Pfenninger, and supported by other members of the Stäfa branch of the Lesegesellschaft am See, a local reading society modeled after the pragmatic learned societies of the European Enlightenment. Through this society rural elites had access to a wide variety of reading materials and European newspapers.

This Stäfa Memorial challenged the cantonal social, political, and economic structure. Moreover, it challenged the status quo simultaneously in multiple ways. On one level the Memorial demanded inclusion into the Zurich Old Regime: the residents of the hinterland deserved the same rights as the citizens of the city of Zurich. On the other hand, the introductory section of the document also demanded the inalienable rights of man and later the authors explicitly used the threat of French Revolutionary events to demand change.[15] The same document mixed rhetorical claims, republican discourses, and the languages of reform and inalienable rights. Most likely, the authors sought improvement in their daily lives and were willing to use any rhetorical device to forward their cause. This pragmatic republicanism was typical of the Swiss case during the Atlantic Age of Revolutions.

The authors begin the Memorial with a traditional claim of Swiss *Freiheit*: "From free Fathers, we are free sons."[16] This claim of inherited freedom fits with the common practice in traditional Swiss protest repertoire to refer back to fairly earned or granted historical rights. The entire Stäfa conflict of 1794–1795, in fact, fits into the framework of a long history of Swiss urban–rural divide and social conflicts.[17]

The main thrust of the Memorial consists of a long middle section that includes six complaints, which were demands to reform the Old Regime. It was not radical revolutionary claim making, but rather relied on a strategy of pointing to historical precedence and previously ensured rights. In this case, the authors claimed that missing documents from 1489 demonstrated the necessity of inclusion of rural residents in the political structure of the city of Zurich. The authors demanded the end of the last remnants of serfdom, the

---

[15] [Nehracher], "Das Stäfner Memorial," 127, 138.
[16] [Nehracher], "Das Stäfner Memorial," 127.
[17] Rolf Graber, *Demokratie und Revolten: Die Entstehung der direkten Demokratie in der Schweiz* (Zurich: Chronos, 2017), 11–13, 54–5, 72; Rolf Graber, "Von Memorialhandel zu den Stäfner Volksunruhen: Landbürgertum und plebejische Bewegung," in Helmuth Holzhey and Simone Zurbuchen, eds., *Alte Löcher – neue Blicke, Zürich im 18. Jahrhundert* (Zurich: Chronos, 1997), 85; Lerner, *Laboratory of Liberty*, 87; see also Barbara Weinmann, *Eine andere Bürgergesellschaft: Klassischer Republikanismus und Kommunalismus im Kanton Zürich im späten 18. Und 19. Jahrhundert* (Göttingen: Vandenhoeck & Ruprecht, 2002), 118.

end of limitations on choice of profession for rural residents, the end of limitations on possibilities for field of study, abolishing the restrictions on joining the militia, changing the use of privilege as the basis of the tax system, and expanding the city's constitution to apply to the hinterland and its residents.[18] The protestors claimed to be seeking to restore the restricted freedoms that should have been inherited from their ancestors. They wanted the right to join the militia and spill blood for the community, a classically republican path to full membership in the community. In short, the petitioners sought to join the Old Regime, not to undermine it. The very word *memorial* suggests a desire to remember former rights now in disuse rather than create a new regime.[19]

However, the protestors in Stäfa also made reference to a natural rights-style argument through the demand for *Menschenrechte*. The last of the seven main demands – a guarantee of the inalienable rights of man – implies support for the perceived revolutionary principle of natural rights. Reminiscent of The Declaration of the Rights of Man and the Citizen, the authors wrote, "each has equal claim on both the free use of his talent and skill as on the security of his person and property."[20] However, this was not a fully developed radical program, but rather radical language layered on top of the traditional reformist complaints that make up the rest of the demands of the Memorial. Throughout the revolutionary Atlantic, natural rights were used in conjunction with conceptions of historical rights or republicanism to build new regimes. There were mixed discourses in France, the Netherlands, and the United States, as well as Zurich.[21] Since the Declaration of Independence in the American colonies and since revolution broke out in France and the National Assembly passed the Declaration of the Rights of

---

[18] General complaints (*allgemeine Klage*) in [Nehracher], "Das Stäfner Memorial," 128–33.
[19] Weinmann, *Eine andere Bürgergesellschaft*, 118.
[20] [Nehracher], "Das Stäfner Memorial," 137.
[21] David Armitage, *The Declaration of Independence: A Global History* (Cambridge, MA: Harvard University Press, 2007), 18; Keith Michael Baker and Dan Edelstein, eds., *Scripting Revolution: A Historical Approach to the Comparative Study of Revolutions* (Stanford: Stanford University Press, 2015), 3–4, 10; Dale Van Kley, ed., *The French Idea of Freedom: The Old Regime and the Declaration of Rights of 1789* (Stanford: Stanford University Press, 1994), 23–7, 75–87, 156, 190. See also Janet Polasky, *Revolutions without Borders: The Call to Liberty in the Atlantic World* (New Haven: Yale University Press, 2015); Jonathan Gienapp, *The Second Creation: Fixing the American Constitution in the Founding Era* (Cambridge, MA: Harvard University Press, 2018), esp. 24, 33, 354–5, n. 23; Katherine Aaslestad, *Place and Politics: Local Identity, Civic Culture, and German Nationalism in North Germany during the Revolutionary Era* (Leiden: Brill, 2005); Simon Schama, *Patriots and Liberators: Revolution in the Netherlands, 1780–1813* (New York: Alfred A. Knopf, 1977).

Man and Citizen, the idea of individual rights derived from an intellectual theory of natural rights had been used by revolutionaries across the Atlantic World to further promote their goals of constructing a new political reality. By referring to the events in France, the voice of the people, and general prosperity in the sense of the common good, the supporters of the Memorial in the countryside of Zurich made a transnational republican critique of Zurich's political structure.[22] The protestors were aware of wider events and their ability to act within the same framework.

The authors of the Stäfa Memorial sought to challenge the leaders of Old Regime Zurich through the mixed vocabulary and languages, including both traditional claims of Swiss *Freiheit* and the radical claims of the "inalienable rights of man."[23] Mentioning the inalienable rights of man and simultaneously referring to events in France in 1794 directed attention to the violence of the Terror and the radical republic. In this way, the petitioners implied a threat of violence on top of their traditional demands for greater liberty within the preexisting structure of the Swiss republics. The petitioners told the city government of Zurich that equalizing the rights of the rural and urban residents would guarantee peace and harmony within the Zurich state and between Zurich and France.[24] What was left unsaid is what the petitioners would undertake if their freedom were not "restored." When the authors promise peace, harmony, and the admiration of the French nation in return for equality between city and hinterland, it is no reach to see the threat of violence in the face of inaction by the city government. If the reforms were not introduced, there is a suggestion of an increased willingness to topple the regime that the authors of the Memorial had just recognized in the text as the best form of government.[25]

The leaders of the Zurich city government certainly perceived the document as threatening and cracked down on the movement with arrests and sentences of exile and prison.[26] Once the government of the city of Zurich had rejected the call for the expansion of the Zurich constitution to include the male residents of the hinterland, the subjects of the countryside turned toward a more radical language of universal natural rights, fulfilling the assumptions of the Zurich government. In 1795, a broad popular uprising was crushed by troops from Zurich.[27]

---

[22] [Nehracher], "Das Stäfner Memorial," 127, 131, 135, 137–8.
[23] [Nehracher], "Das Stäfner Memorial," 127–8.
[24] [Nehracher], "Das Stäfner Memorial," 138.
[25] [Nehracher], "Das Stäfner Memorial," 128.   [26] Graber, *Demokratie und Revolten*, 30.
[27] Wolfgang von Wartburg, *Zürich und die französische Revolution: Die Auseinandersetzung einer patriarchalischen Gesellschaft mit den ideellen und politischen Einwirkungen der*

Despite the defeat of the uprising, we should look at the Stäfa Memorial as a constitutional document in much the same way that we see the Declaration of the Rights of Man and Citizen, the Declaration of Independence, or the *Leiden Draft* from the Dutch Patriot Revolt. The mixed discourses or hybrid republicanism were deliberately crafted as a pragmatic revolutionary strategy. The Memorial addresses questions of fundamental law and inalienable rights. The defeat of the 1795 rural uprising does not diminish the importance of the rights-based or historical claims from 1794. The elite-driven Memorial, the popular rural uprising, and the response by the traditional government of Zurich were all part of the process of ending the Old Swiss Confederation.[28] When the Old Regime refused to reform, there was more willingness to topple the regime. This pattern happened in the hinterland of Zurich before the French invasion of 1798, and this strategy was also used in the Pays de Vaud, which helped precipitate the French invasion.

Looking to France

After the events of 1789 in France, inhabitants of the Swiss Republics signaled a variety of different forms of support for the revolutionary movement in France. The educated Swiss elite, aware of the international ramifications, were engaged in a public debate about the nature of liberty. Some Swiss supporters of revolutionary France insisted that France was only now properly honoring liberty as did the Swiss. Johann Caspar Lavater, for example, congratulated the French for becoming as free as the Swiss. Others, such as Swiss emigrants in Paris had formed a Club Helvétique, in order to show support for new ideas and import some of these French revolutionary ideas and pamphlets to the Swiss Confederation.[29] In 1790 Fréderic-César de La Harpe, under the pen name Philanthropus, had published in *The London Chronicle* a full call for a revolution in the Pays de Vaud, and in 1797 Basel patrician Peter Ochs declared himself free for a few hours because he had

---

französischen Revolution (Basel: Helbing & Lichtenhahn, 1956), 216–19, 245ff; Graber, "Vom Memorialhandel zu den Stäfner Volksunruhen," 86–92.

[28] See Lerner, *Laboratory of Liberty*, 92; Graber, "Vom Memorialhandel zu den Stäfner Volksunruhen," 94.

[29] Holger Böning, *Revolution in der Schweiz: Das Ende der Alten Eidgenossenschaft, Die Helvetische Republik, 1798–1803* (Frankfurt am Main: Peter Lang, 1985), 58–9; Ariane Méautis, *Le Club Helvétique de Paris (1790–1791) et la diffusion des idées révolutionnaires en Suisse* (Neuchâtel: La Baconnière, 1969); Holger Böning, *Der Traum von Freiheit und Gleichheit*, 63–4.

simply crossed the border into France, rejecting traditional Swiss notions of liberty.[30]

Ochs and La Harpe were part of a small group of elite Swiss patriots active in Enlightenment learned societies who were working for political change in Switzerland in order to dismantle the Old Confederation and to usher in a new regime based on individual rights and revolutionary liberty. These Swiss patriots often simultaneously argued for a restoration of ancient Swiss liberties and a new conception of individual liberty. By the time of the Helvetic Revolution there were at least three schools of Swiss liberty, two of which routinely mixed rhetorical discourses of liberty in pragmatic ways: those who argued that the Old Eidgenossenschaft guaranteed Swiss liberty best, those who sought to reform the Swiss Republic within its own institutions, and those, such as La Harpe, who were convinced that revolution was the only remaining path forward.

Fréderic-César de La Harpe (1754–1838) was a native of the Pays de Vaud who sought autonomy for the French-speaking region from its Bernese overlords. La Harpe was the main pamphleteer behind the Vaudois argument for a complete political separation with Canton Bern and eventually a new Swiss system. He saw the only path to this status as opening up the entire Swiss Confederation, which included overthrowing the old, outdated structure.[31] Only a few members of the Vaudoise political elite sought to completely overthrow Bern rule before the French invasion even began; most joined after the entry of the French troops.[32]

By 1798 La Harpe had been seeking independence from Bern for the Pays de Vaud under French protection with a wide variety of arguments encompassing mixed discourses about the nature of liberty and political rights. In 1796–1797 in his *Essai sur la constitution du Pays de Vaud*, he argued for the

---

[30] Andreas Würgler, "Gemeinderevolution-Fiktiv: 'États' und 'villes et communautés' in Frédéric-César Laharpes Bericht über die noch nicht geschehene Revolution in der Waadt (1790)," in Heinrich R. Schmidt, André Holenstein, and Andreas Würgler, eds., *Gemeinde, Reformation und Widerstand: Festschrift für Peter Blickle zum 60. Geburtstag* (Tübingen: Bibliotheca academica Verlag, 1998). Peter Ochs to Frédéric-César de la Harpe, 22 Vendémiaire Year VI (13 October 1797), in Jean Charles Biaudet and Marie-Claude Jequier, eds., *Correspondance de Frédéric-César de la Harpe sous la République Helvétique*, vol. I: *Le révolutionnaire 16 mai 1796–4 Mars 1798* (Neuchâtel: Baconnière, 1982), 179–80.

[31] Antoine Rochat, "Frédéric-César de la Harpe," in *Historisches Lexikon der Schweiz*, 27 August 2020, https://hls-dhs-dss.ch/de/articles/015222/2020-08-27.

[32] Danièle Tosato-Rigo and François Flouck, "La révolution vaudoise: Choix ou nécessité," in François Flouck, Patrick-R. Monbaron, Marianne Stubenvoll, and Danièle Tosato-Rigo, eds., *De l'Ours à la Cocarde: Régime bernois et révolution en Pays de Vaud (1536–1798)* (Lausanne: Payot, 1998), 37, 40.

Pays de Vaud to be fully included in Swiss liberty, implying freedom from Canton Bern. He used arguments based on historical precedent, constructing a narrative of freedom denied since a sixteenth century treaty, social contract thought, and natural law.[33]

Once there was no movement on the part of Bern's governing patriciate, La Harpe started contacting the French Directory in 1797.[34] This path accelerated in the wake of the Fructidor coup d'état of 4 September 1797, a key political turning point for French foreign policy. The new Directory moved toward a policy of foreign intervention to create satellite republics and reshape governments to form a buffer for France.[35] Immediately after news of the coup reached La Harpe, he agitated for French intervention in Switzerland, claiming it was in the interests of the French Republic to intervene.[36]

La Harpe wrote directly to Philippe Antoine Merlin de Douai, a former member of the Committee of Public Safety and one of the newly appointed members of the French Executive Directory after Fructidor. La Harpe recommended that Merlin de Douai and the French Directory call for a meeting of the ancient Estates of the Pays de Vaud. "This freely elected assembly of the true representatives of the Vaudois people" would authorize the proclamation of Vaudois independence and the formal solicitation of French protection.[37] La Harpe demanded that France impose its defense of the rights of the people of the Pays de Vaud based on the 1564 Treaty of Lausanne. In the same breath, La Harpe referenced the violation of the "social pact" by the oligarchs of Bern and Fribourg.[38] In addition to invoking historical privileges granted by treaties, La Harpe also used the universalist rhetoric of Revolutionary rights and the social contract.

---

[33] Fréderic-César de La Harpe, *Essai sur la constitution du Pays de Vaud*, 2 vols. (1796-1797); Fréderic-César de La Harpe, *Énumération des principaux griefs du peuple Vaudois, à la charge des olygarchies de Berne et de Fribourg* (1797); Marc Lerner, "The Helvetic Republic: An Ambivalent Reception of French Revolutionary Liberty," *French History* 18 (2004), 56-7.

[34] Lerner, "Helvetic Republic," 57. He wrote to Foreign Minister Delacroix as early as 8 September 1796. See Biaudet and Jequier, *Correspondance*, vol. 1, 95-6.

[35] Böning, *Der Traum von Freiheit und Gleichheit*, 96.

[36] La Harpe to Merlin de Douai, 11 September 1797, in Biaudet and Jequier, *Correspondance*, vol. 1, 168-75. This correspondence was later published as Fréderic-César de La Harpe, *Des intérêts de la République française considérés relativement aux olygarchies de Berne et de Fribourg* (Paris: Batilliot, 1797).

[37] La Harpe to Merlin de Douai, 11 September 1797, in *Correspondance*, vol. 1, 171; La Harpe, *Des intérêts de la République française*, 24-5.

[38] La Harpe to Merlin de Douai, 11 September 1797, in Biaudet and Jequier, *Correspondance*, vol. 1, 171; La Harpe, *Des intérêts de la République française*, 24-5.

Through this tactical shift to directly contacting the French Directory, La Harpe recognized the prevailing political winds and requested French intervention. By referencing both a historically based conception of liberty and the social contract, La Harpe's argument was that Bern had usurped the legitimate authority of the Pays de Vaud and that this usurpation threatened the safety and legitimacy of the French Republic. He further claimed that the oligarchic City and Republic of Bern would never fully support the Revolution. In fact, La Harpe pointed out that the Bernese patricians had only recognized the French Republic in 1796, that they had supported the counterrevolutionary *émigré* army, and that the patricians of Bern have "overtly been ... the accomplices of conspirators ... [who] menaced the Directory in Paris."[39]

La Harpe made the argument that intervention in the Pays de Vaud was also in the interest of the larger strategic agenda of the French Directory and French Republic. La Harpe claimed that the Bernese leaders opposed the French out of fear of French Revolutionary influence in Switzerland. La Harpe thus appealed to the French conception of their revolution as the cradle of European liberty and conqueror of despotism.[40] La Harpe actively tried to bring France into the Swiss arena; this was not simply a case of a great power manipulating events for its own benefit.

At first the French were willing to engage only indirectly, which let the Swiss patriot minority pursue its own agenda. However, by October 1797, La Harpe had effectively lobbied for a change in policy through articles, letters, and pamphlets; he convinced the Directory to consider direct action against the oligarchs of Bern. La Harpe's communication with Jean-François Reubell, another member of the Directory, implicated the leadership of Bern as enemies of France and the Revolution.[41] These attacks on Bern were also published as articles in *L'Ami des Lois*, the semi-official newspaper of the French Directory, starting in October 1797.[42] By the fall of 1797 there was a

---

[39] La Harpe to Reubell, 31 October 1787, in Biaudet and Jequier, *Correspondance*, vol. 1, 187–95; La Harpe, *Énumération des principaux griefs*, 5–6.
[40] See the speech of the Duke Mathieu de Montmorency in the National Assembly, 1 August 1789, and the speeches of Pierre Victor Malouet reprinted and translated in Lynn Hunt, ed., *The French Revolution and Human Rights: A Brief Documentary History* (New York: Bedford St. Martin's, 1996), 73–6 and Jean-Nicolas Desmeuniers, 3 August 1789, quoted in Dale Van Kley, "Religion and the Age of 'Patriot' Reform," *Journal of Modern History* 80:2 (2008), 252–95: 294.
[41] La Harpe to Reubell, 31 October 1797, in Biaudet and Jequier, *Correspondance*, vol. 1, 186–95.
[42] Biaudet and Jequier, *Correspondance*, vol. 1, 17–18. *L'Ami des Lois* was one of several official papers of the Directory. The articles in *L'Ami des Lois* written by La Harpe were

clear shift in French policy, very possibly encouraged and initiated by La Harpe's preparatory work and Napoleon Bonaparte's travels through Switzerland, when he made promises of protection in front of enthusiastic crowds.[43]

Initially, La Harpe did not ask for armed intervention to defeat the Bernese enemies, but it is clear that La Harpe thought that the Swiss patriots needed French help to reform the Old Regime. On the one hand, local patriots initiated reform efforts, but, on the other hand, patriot action was clearly not enough of a force to quickly topple the Old Regime. La Harpe had to convince his fellow citizens of the Pays de Vaud that autonomy or independence from Bern would be an improvement over the status quo.

There were multiple views on how best to serve the Pays de Vaud. In the published version of his letter to Merlin de Douai, La Harpe explicitly told his fellow citizens of the Pays de Vaud the idea that they could be "a free people" and should "aspire to become an *independent republic*."[44] Not everybody agreed with La Harpe, who resided in Paris at the time, that foreign interference and Vaudois independence were appropriate paths. Henri Monod and the author of an anonymous pamphlet directed at the citizens of the Pays de Vaud both warned of the dangers of French intervention and the possibility, if not likelihood, that the Pays de Vaud would be annexed by France and caught up in a European war.[45]

La Harpe tried to increase the pressure by writing directly to the communes of the Pays de Vaud, initiating a petition campaign, and publishing a pamphlet (that he also sent to French General Brune), in which he urged the citizens of the Pays de Vaud to reject Bernese lordship and "claim the protection of the French Republic."[46] In these December documents La Harpe declared that "the Pays de Vaud must never become a department

---

published on 27 October 1797, 31 October 1797, 10 November 1797, 12 November 1797, 19 November 1797, 23 November 1797, and 15/20 January 1798. Biaudet and Jequier, *Correspondance*, vol. 1, 489–90. La Harpe also published a list of Vaudois grievances. Biaudet and Jequier date the publication of La Harpe, *Énumération des principaux griefs* as late November or early December 1797.

[43] Böning, *Der Traum von Freiheit und Gleichheit*, 107.
[44] La Harpe, *Des intérêts de la République française*, 5 (emphasis original).
[45] For example, Henri Monod to La Harpe, 22/24 October 1797, in Biaudet and Jequier, *Correspondance*, vol. 1, 182; Anon., *Étrennes d'un Habitant du Pays-de-Vaud à ses Concitoyens* (Paris, 1798).
[46] La Harpe to the communes of the Pays de Vaud, 10 December 1797, in Biaudet and Jequier, *Correspondance*, vol. 1, 267–8; [Fréderic-César de La Harpe], *Aux habitants du Pays de Vaud, esclaves des oligarques de Fribourg et de Berne*, in Tosato-Rigo et al., eds., *Bon peuple vaudois*, 4. For more on the petition campaign, see Danièle Tosato-Rigo, "La continuité par la révolution? L'exemple du canton du Léman," in Daniel Schläppi, ed.,

of France,"[47] and that the citizens of the Pays de Vaud, the "slaves of the Oligarchs of Fribourg and Bern," had to make an immediate choice in favor of "eternal servitude ... or liberty and independence."[48]

La Harpe told Merlin de Douai that he sought to destroy the entire oligarchic regime of the Old Swiss Confederation, not just secure the autonomy of the Pays de Vaud.[49] In doing so, La Harpe aligned himself and his cause of Vaudois liberty with French Revolutionary rhetoric and a French republican worldview. La Harpe consciously used French terminology, highlighting French self-interest, both ideological (concepts of liberty and antifeudalism) and practical (the threat of émigrés and the Austrians). Interestingly, he continued to encourage citizens of the Pays de Vaud to reclaim ancient historical privileges and simultaneously based his demands on natural rights and on the voice of the people as expressed through petitions.[50]

In late December, the patrician class of Bern struck back through its own published declarations, demonstrating the effectiveness of La Harpe's campaign and the fear of French intervention. In the face of French troop movements, the Chancellery of Bern published a decree on 22 December 1797, accusing La Harpe and others of sedition and conspiring against the Republic of Bern. Furthermore, Bern promised to defend the entirety of Canton Bern, including its subject territories, and specifically to defend its liberty, "acquired at the price of the blood of our fathers."[51] As the Bern government promised to fight, members of the Bern elite such as Karl Ludwig von Haller sought to dismantle La Harpe's argument and claims of historical rights and precedent. Like La Harpe, these defenders of the status quo used elements of natural law and social contract theory in denying the legitimacy of the Vaudois claims, demonstrating the variety of republican political thought within the Swiss Confederation.[52]

Umbruch und Beständigkeit: Kontinuitäten in der Helvetischen Revolution von 1798 (Basel: Schwabe, 2009).

[47] [La Harpe], *Aux habitants du Pays de Vaud*, 6.
[48] [La Harpe], *Aux habitants du Pays de Vaud*; La Harpe to the communes of the Pays de Vaud, 10 December 1797, in Biaudet and Jequier, *Correspondance*, vol. 1, 267–8.
[49] La Harpe to Merlin de Douai, early December 1797, in Biaudet and Jequier, *Correspondance*, vol. 1, 246.
[50] [La Harpe], *Aux habitants du Pays de Vaud*, 4.
[51] LL. EE., "À leurs sujets vaudois," 22 December 1797, in Tosato-Rigo et al., eds., *Bon peuple vaudois*, 15–16.
[52] For example, [K]arl Ludwig von Haller, *Exposé historique des faits concernants la Neutralité de la Suisse envers la France* (n.p., 1797); Nicolas-Frederic de Mulinen, *Recherches Historiques sur les Anciennes Assemblées des États du Pays-de-Vaud* (Bern, 1797).

Unsurprisingly, La Harpe and his French allies rejected these arguments and governmental threats of violence. By late December, the French Directory signaled its acceptance of La Harpe's arguments about the historical rights of the Pays de Vaud and ancient treaties. The Directory made clear its intention to reclaim France's rights to mediate the affairs of the Pays de Vaud. Signed by Paul Barras and Louis Marie Révellière-Lépeaux, the President and Secretary General of the French Directory, respectively, this decree threatened to hold the members of the governments of Bern and Fribourg "personally responsible" for any act against the individual security and property of the inhabitants of the Pays de Vaud.[53]

Once the French Directory had committed itself to this guarantee of the security of the subject inhabitants of Canton Bern, the situation escalated. The government of Bern had already recognized the increased danger of troops on the border and called for an emergency session of the Swiss Federal Diet in December. In the immediate aftermath of the news of the French decree of 8 Nivôse, on 5 January, Bern also demanded that the subject inhabitants of the cities and communes of the Pays de Vaud renew their oaths of loyalty to the City and Republic of Bern and the "almost 300-year-old constitution," which leaders of Bern claimed had served the Pays de Vaud well.[54]

The oath of loyalty to Bern, however, satisfied nobody. This was an attempt to reaffirm the loyalty of the Vaudois elites, but Bernese official actions pushed the wider population of the Pays de Vaud to greater support for La Harpe and his radical solutions. The demand to reissue the oath led to contesting the ceremonial oath itself. By demanding a loyalty oath, the leaders of Bern gave permission to more Vaudois residents to question their loyalty and opened up the wider question of reevaluating the relationship between Bern and the Pays de Vaud. In fact, the discussion of the oath further spread the news of the French decree.[55] Once again, as the Old Regime closed off opportunities for political reform, patriots sought more radical options.

---

[53] "Arrêté du Directoire du 8 Nivôse," 28 December 1798, in Tosato-Rigo et al., eds., *Bon peuple vaudois*, 17.
[54] "Nous l'Avoyer, Petit et Grand Conseils de la Ville et République de Berne, savoir faisons," document 8 in Tosato-Rigo et al., eds., *Bon peuple vaudois*, 40–1. For the text of the oath, see document 15, "Serment proposé le 10 janvier 1798 par le Seigneur Député de Berne aux bataillons de Lucens et Payerne, et refusé," in Tosato-Rigo et al., eds., *Bon peuple vaudois*, 56.
[55] Danièle Tosato-Rigo, "On jure fidélité à leurs Excellences," in Tosato-Rigo et al., eds., *Bon peuple vaudois*, 37–9.

Tensions continued to mount as pro-Bern publications warned of societal collapse,[56] but the pro-independence movement continued to gain support. The representative body in Lausanne, the Council of 200, pushed the petition campaign in favor of the Vaudois Estates on 8 January and established an executive committee on 9 January.[57] Radical patriot petitioners in the Pays de Vaud organized a *Comité de reunion* to advocate for the meeting of the ancient estates and restoration of ancient privileges. These committees supported independence from Bern rather than moderate reform of the Bern–Pays de Vaud relationship.[58] On 23 January, General Ménard basically issued a call to revolution, proclaiming that "The French Republic offers you its protection, its help. The executive Directory orders me to employ all means to render you free."[59]

The revolution in the Pays de Vaud immediately followed this French promise to intervene. On 24 January, the local representatives of the Bern government were overthrown, even though the moderate provisional assembly refused to declare the independence of Pays de Vaud. Liberty trees were planted and representatives of the *Comité de réunion* flew a banner with "République Lémanique" inscribed on one side and "Liberté – Egalité" on the other.[60] On the next night, that of 25 January 1798, the French crossed the border, delivering an ultimatum to the Bernese troops. General Ménard used the resulting small skirmish in which two French soldiers were shot to justify marching across the borders on 28 January at the head of 11,000 troops.[61]

The Bern government was unable to successfully mount a campaign to defeat what it labeled a mere "insurrection" in the Pays de Vaud.[62] In early

---

[56] Proclamation of Bern to Vaud, 12 January 1798, in Tosato-Rigo et al., eds., *Bon peuple vaudois*, 80–81; Anon., *Aux Habitants des Villes du Pays-de-Vaud* (n.p., 1798), 2.

[57] Tosato-Rigo, "On jure fidélité à leurs Excellences," 38–9. See document 12, "Très chers Concitoyens et Compatriotes, Votre Magistrat a vu avec peine l'agitation croissante que des écrits répandus parmi vous ont fait naître ...," in Tosato-Rigo et al., eds., *Bon peuple vaudois*, 49–51.

[58] Le Comité de réunion to La Harpe, 16 January 1798, in Biaudet and Jequier, *Correspondance*, vol. I, 339–40.

[59] Decree of General Ménard, 23 January 1798, in Tosato-Rigo et al., eds., *Bon peuple vaudois*, 117; Jean-Charles Biaudet, "Henri Monod et la Révolution vaudoise de 1798," *Revue historique vaudoise* 81 (1973), 89–155: 104.

[60] Danièle Tosato-Rigo, "L'Indépendance," in Tosato-Rigo et al., eds., *Bon peuple vaudois*, 115.

[61] "Proclamation" of the Provisional Assembly [24 January 1798], in Tosato-Rigo et al., eds., *Bon peuple vaudois*, 132; Tosato-Rigo, "L'Indépendance," 116; Danièle Tosato-Rigo, "La France intervient," in Tosato-Rigo et al., eds., *Bon peuple vaudois*, 141–2; Böning, *Der Traum von Freiheit und Gleichheit*, 111; Lerner, *Laboratory of Liberty*, 114.

[62] ASHR, vol. I, 160–1.

February 1798 the Pays de Vaud voted to accept the Helvetic Constitution, which had not yet even been finalized. Nonetheless, with this decision, the citizens of the Pays de Vaud became the first Swiss citizens to live under a constitutional republic founded on the principles of liberty and equality.[63] The success of a Helvetic Revolution depended on whether other patriotic Swiss political actors would follow.

Patriot Action

In the aftermath of the French invasion, the future structure of the Swiss Confederation was unsettled. The French army had not yet targeted the city of Bern itself in order to topple the entire Swiss regime. However, Swiss actors had already begun to take revolutionary steps, some even before the entrance of French troops. In early January, Peter Ochs wrote a draft constitution based on that of the French Directory, and a National Assembly formed in Basel, which eventually proposed yet another new constitution for the Swiss. Furthermore, many of the thirteen ruling cantons of the Old Confederation instituted their own reforms, increasingly welcoming inhabitants of subject territories into their citizenry and bodies politic. The eventual presence of French troops in the Pays de Vaud probably had a coercive effect, but these fundamental political changes were made according to traditional cantonal norms and responded to ongoing Swiss debates and repertoires of action. Both local agency and French intervention created the Helvetic Republic, which was a full participant in the Age of Atlantic Revolutions.

Popular uprisings in the Valais, Fribourg, Solothurn, Luzern, and Basel followed the revolution in the Pays de Vaud. But in other areas Swiss political actors had reformed the status quo on their own.[64] In Basel, elites changed the structure of its government, giving equal rights to the rural population and disowning the privileges of the city. The Basel patriciate made plans to discuss a new constitution by forming a National Assembly that produced a constitutional draft for a regenerated Swiss state.[65]

---

[63] Tosato-Rigo, "La continuité par la révolution?," 46. See also Danièle Tosato-Rigo, "Février 1798, le premier 'vote' des Vaudois," in François Flouck et al., eds., *De l'Ours à la Cocarde*, 367–80.
[64] See Lerner, *Laboratory of Liberty*, 115–17; Böning, *Der Traum von Freiheit und Gleichheit*, Chapter 5; Zschokke, *Invasion of Switzerland*, 117–19.
[65] Böning, *Der Traum von Freiheit und Gleichheit*, 99–105.

An argument can be made that Canton Basel was in many ways the site of the initiation of the Helvetic Revolution.[66] The Basel example of a bloodless revolution from above that implemented ideas of liberty and equality was exactly what Peter Ochs sought when he wrote in early January a provisional constitution for a new Swiss Confederation.[67] In Ochs' section on fundamental principles in the constitutional draft, he declared that the "Helvetic republic is one and indivisible," and asserted the end of subject territories and cantonal boundaries, which cut to the core of Swiss identity as a Confederation.[68] Overall, the draft constitution, written in Paris while Ochs was on a diplomatic mission for Basel, was based on the constitution of the French Directory, with a list of fundamental principles such as "citizens comprise the sovereign," "the natural liberty of man is inalienable," and "the liberty of conscience is unlimited." This constitution also protected the liberty of the press and eliminated hereditary powers and ranks.[69] Furthermore, Ochs replicated the French governmental structures, creating an executive Directory of five Directors, two legislative bodies, a Council of Ancients, and a Grand Council of 240 members. Like in Paris, the larger body proposed laws and the Council of Ancients could approve or reject resolutions.[70]

Importantly, however, Ochs' first sentence explicitly states that the constitution was provisional. He essentially demanded a public referendum on any permanent constitution that was meant to establish a representative regime. Ochs insisted that the first act of a new national legislative body would be to lay before the electorate the question of whether to convene a constituent assembly.[71] This demand was removed from the provisional version by the French before General Brune imposed Ochs' basic framework in the spring.[72]

Beyond Ochs' individual action of proposing a draft constitution, the Basel elite also acted collectively in January. The patrician-led government of the City of Basel seemed to take its cue from the French as well. In an action compared by contemporaries to the activities of the French National Assembly on the night of 4 August 1789, the government voluntarily renounced its power and granted equal rights to the rural, formally subject,

---

[66] Böning, *Der Traum von Freiheit und Gleichheit*, 99.
[67] Peter Ochs, "Plan d'une Constitution provisoire pour la République Helvétique ou Suisse," in Kölz, *Quellenbuch*, vol. 1, 113–25.
[68] Article 1 of Ochs, "Plan d'une Constitution provisoire," 113.
[69] Articles 2 and 6–9 of Ochs, "Plan d'une Constitution provisoire."
[70] Articles 33, 35, and 42–3 of Ochs, "Plan d'une Constitution provisoire."
[71] Avant-propos in Ochs, "Plan d'une Constitution provisoire," 113.
[72] "Constitution de la République helvétique," 126ff.

population of the canton. The change in Basel started with urban patriots reaching out to rural inhabitants of the canton and including them in celebrations and political discussions. Pressure continued with rural protests against the remaining feudal remnants such as ground rents and the Old Regime's privileging of the inhabitants of the city.[73] In Basel, unlike in Stäfa and Zurich in 1794–1795, the rural and urban agitators worked increasingly together to expand rural participation in cantonal sovereignty, though rural protestors lost patience with the lack of speedy progress.

The government was pushed by the patriot citizens of the city and countryside of Canton Basel. On 11 and 13 January, rural protesters demanded that representatives of the legislative bodies of Basel support equality among urban and rural inhabitants, as well as liberty, equality, a constitution, and the rights of man.[74] These demands were reemphasized on 15 and 17 January by residents in Liestal, the largest community of Basel-Land, who erected a liberty tree as well as a black, red, and white tricolor flag at City Hall. On 19 January 1798, representatives of the rural militia marched into the city of Basel for a public oath taking. In this oath, which was published along with an image of the mythical three original confederates swearing the founding oath of the Swiss Confederation, citizen members of the militia in Basel declared their desire first and foremost to remain Swiss. However, in addition to a guarantee of order and property, these oath takers explicitly declared that "freedom and equality [are] citizen rights."[75] The juxtaposition of these two points is interesting, prioritizing the explicit declaration of remaining Swiss and stating that freedom and equality were Swiss rights. This oath echoed the 11 and 13 January demands of rural representatives to the legislative bodies of Basel.[76] It is unclear whether these citizens were consciously coopting revolutionary rhetoric and claiming new rights or were claiming that these rights of *Freyheit* and equality were traditional Swiss rights. I suggest that the vagueness was intentional. Supporters who argued for a restoration of ancient rights and those who

---

[73] Böning, *Der Traum von Freiheit und Gleichheit*, 100–1.
[74] Böning, *Der Traum von Freiheit und Gleichheit*, 101–2. See especially the four demands of 13 January 1798 from Liestal.
[75] "Militärischer Eid, geleistet von den bewafneten Stadt- und Landbürgern des freyen Cantons Basel den 19 January 1798," Zentral Bibliothek Zürich Wv306.10.
[76] Böning, *Der Traum von Freiheit und Gleichheit*, 101–2. For more on the revolution in Basel, see Christian Simon, "Die Basler Revolution," in Museum der Kulturen Basel, Karikatur & Cartoon Museum Basel, Basler Papiermühle, and Peter Ochs Gesellschaft, eds., *Basel 1798: Vive la République hélvetique* (Basel: Christoph-Merian-Verlag, 1998), 13–60.

argued for inalienable rights could both embrace the mixed discourse and rally support for the unifying decisions of the Basel citizenry and assembly.

It was following these actions that the mayor and members of the legislative bodies resigned, allowing the demands of the rural population for equality to be accepted on 20 January 1798. By 6 February, a provisional "National Assembly" had formed to discuss the structure of the new order. When Ochs returned from Paris, this Basler "National Assembly" started its constitutional debate, which produced a second proposal for the Helvetic Constitution.

Before the twin March events of the publication of this proposed "Basel constitution" and the military defeat of the City and Republic of Bern, other cantons continued to act on their own without direct involvement of French troops.[77] The Canton of Zurich finally returned "ancient" liberties to the rural population and, after French troops had crossed the border of the Pays de Vaud, the Zurich government acknowledged the reform demands of the Stäfa affair. The cantonal government issued a general amnesty for the Stäfa protestors. Johann Caspar Pfenninger, one of those pardoned, led further demands for reform. In February, the Zurich government declared the equality of rights among residents of the city and its hinterland. All of this happened before the French army occupied the city in April 1798.

Furthermore, in late January, the government of Canton Luzern allowed for popular representation and at the beginning of February, Schaffhausen granted equal rights to all citizens and invoked a constitutional convention. In Toggenburg and St. Gallen the secular and clerical authorities abdicated power, whereas Thurgau, one of the collective subject territories of the ruling cantons of the Old Confederation, declared independence. All of these cantonal actions were in addition to the aforementioned popular uprisings elsewhere.[78]

Inner Switzerland

Inner Switzerland provides another case study of self-reform between the invasion of the Pays de Vaud and the French imposition of a new constitution for the Helvetic Republic. Letters from localities to General Brune and the protocols of the extraordinary *Landsgemeinden* in Schwyz show a fascinating story of Swiss reform actions and negotiation with the French.

---

[77] Würgler, *Grenzen des Zumutbaren*, 12–13; Lerner, *Laboratory of Liberty*, 115–16.
[78] Lerner, *Laboratory of Liberty*, 115.

Canton Schwyz, for which the country was named and which was one of the original three mythological founding members of the Confederation, was one of the Alpine cantons that claimed to be purely democratic. Its governing system was based on the sovereign *Landsgemeinde*, the popular assembly of all full citizens of the commune, which met each May under the open sky since time immemorial, according to local beliefs. However, only male full members of the village of Schwyz, in the central district of the Canton, were eligible to be citizens and participants in the *Landsgemeinde*. Periodically residents of subject territories, such as the *Landschaft* (district of) March, had attempted to claim that they too had inherited rights to participate in the sovereign assembly, but the central district kept control over the *Landsgemeinde*. After the outbreak of the French Revolution, the district of March had made several attempts to restore what residents saw as their ancient rights and privileges, including sending representatives to Schwyz to demand autonomy.[79]

Similar to the residents of Stäfa in Canton Zurich, residents of the district of March in Canton Schwyz made no progress toward equality with the sovereign unit of the canton until French armies entered the Pays de Vaud. On 1 February, the Schwyz sovereign *Landsgemeinde* declared its intention to send military aid to Bern. This opened the possibility of subject inhabitants acting politically in defense of what they saw as their long-lost legitimate privileges. On 11 February, the residents of March mimicked the forms of the central district and held a district *Landsgemeinde*. At this meeting, which took place without the approval of Central Schwyz, the members of this district popular assembly declared that their condition for putting soldiers in the field to fight for "freedom, fatherland and holy religion" was the liberation of the countryside of Schwyz.[80]

Faced with the threat of invasion, a shortage of soldiers, and the potential collapse of the constitutional framework of the canton, Schwyz conceded the debate to its own subject territories, though the concession was not particularly graceful. The Schwyz *Landsgemeinde* met for an extraordinary meeting the next week, on 18 February, and declared the inhabitants of the subject

---

[79] Regula Hegner, "Geschichte der March unter schwyzerischen Oberhoheit," *Mitteilungen des Historischen Vereins des Kantons Schwyz [MHVS]* 50 (1953), 1–238: 70; Lukas Vogel, "'Die Herren sind alle Schelmen': Politische, soziale und religiöse Hintergründe des Schwyzer Widerstandes gegen die Helvetik," *MHVS* 90 (1998), 169–78: 171; Benjamin Adler, *Die Entstehung der direkten Demokratie: Das Beispiel der Landsgemeinde Schwyz, 1789–1866* (Zurich: NZZ, 2006), 46.

[80] Adler, *Die Entstehung der direkten Demokratie*, 64–5.

districts of the Canton to be free, except for the inhabitants of district March. It was not until 10 March that another extraordinary *Landsgemeinde* of Canton Schwyz declared the same equality of rights for the upstart subject territory.[81] After these rights had finally been granted, the residents of district March declared they would "fight and struggle until the last drop of blood for our holy religion, freedom, and fatherland."[82] Indeed, throughout the Swiss republics, after they had been granted equal rights, many groups of Old Regime subjects were similarly willing to fight alongside their former rulers against the French and never demanded the full destruction of the Old Regime.[83] What remains unknown is whether this was a missed opportunity for the status quo powers across the Atlantic Revolutionary world: would wider acceptance of citizens into the Old Regime have blunted the revolutionary dynamic?

In many ways, the Schwyz *Landsgemeinde* was no different from the governments of other cantons which instituted reforms during the period of uncertainty between the initial invasion of January and the April promulgation of the Helvetic Constitution. Saving the cantonal structural framework was well worth extending privileges to those who had never before participated in cantonal decision-making, especially for the full members of Canton Schwyz, who understood their cantonal framework to be directly granted by God. In post-Napoleonic Europe, Schwyzer defenders of the Old Regime claimed that the actions taken in February and March 1798 had not been voluntary and were therefore illegal and forced upon legitimate governments by the invading French armies.[84] Those who thus attempted to reassert the authority of the central district to the exclusion of formerly

---

[81] Protocol of extraordinary *Landsgemeinde*, 18 February 1798 and Protocol of extraordinary *Landsgemeinde*, 10 March 1798, reconstructed and edited by Josef Wiget, in Josef Wiget, ed., "Die letzten Landsgemeinden des alten Standes Schwyz: Die Landsgemeindeprotokolle vom 26. April 1795 bis 4. Mai 1798," *MHVS* 89 (1997), 40–6.

[82] Hegner, "Geschichte der March," 83; Vogel, "Die Herren sind alle Schelmen," 171, 174; Adler, *Die Entstehung der direkten Demokratie*, 67–9.

[83] For the examples of former subjects in Ticino, Luzern, the Berner Oberland, and Graubunden allying with their former lords, see Thomas Maissen, "Bedrohte Souveränität: Schweizer Städte um 1800," in Peter Blickle and Andreas Schmauder, eds., *Die Mediatisierung der oberschwäbischen Reichstädte im europäischen Kontext* (Epfendorf: Bibliotheca academica Verlag, 2003), 212–14.

[84] For example, [Friedrich Schärer], *Replik auf die Antwort gegen die Schrift: Urkundliche Beleuchtung der bernischen Reclamationen* (n.p., 1814), 9–11, 33–5; Anon., *Réplique à la réponse faite à la brochure, intitulée: Dans quel jour paroit Berne, etc. Etc. De juillet 1814* (n. p., 1814), 29–33; [Kanzlei des altgefreiten Landes Schwyz], *Rückblick auf ein Memorial der neuen Landleute des altgefreiten Landes Schwyz an die alten Landleute desselben* ([Schwyz], 1830), 10–15.

subject inhabitants fundamentally claimed that the reforms of 1798 were exclusively implemented by France and its armies, ignoring local Swiss agency.

Certainly, the status quo was preferred by the leadership of cantons such as Schwyz, but in reality the members of the Old Regime preferred enacting political reforms themselves, through local Swiss mechanisms, rather than having reform forced upon them by France. After the French defeat of Bern in early March, Canton Schwyz and other localities became explicitly concerned about French intervention in their own territories and political structure. During the 10 March extraordinary *Landsgemeinde*, the residents of Schwyz assured the French that "a purely democratic government such as ours could never be dangerous to the French Constitution."[85] Additionally, the inner Alpine cantons began to collectively lobby the French General Brune to retain elements of the decentralized Swiss Eidgenossenschaft. The five "democratic cantons" of Uri, Schwyz, Unterwalden, Zug, and Glarus wrote to Brune on 16 March 1798 that "none among us can believe that it is in the intentions or the principles of the French government to disturb the small democratic cantons in the exercise of liberty . . ." and that their political organization "has consecrated as its principles, in all their purity, the rights of man and the sovereignty of the people; it is therefore in perfect consonance with that adopted by the French Republic."[86] The citizens of Appenzell followed up this claim with their own statement that "from us the great nation [France] took the first sparks of that sacred fire, kindled by our ancestors whose valor struck the first blows against the tyrants of Europe!" The authors of this statement to Brune claimed their localities had honored the "Rights of Man" for over 300 years, implying that France had only just discovered these ideas and should leave the Swiss Republics alone.[87]

Amazingly, these democratic areas of Switzerland and those areas that supported the constitutional draft that emerged from the Basel National Assembly were to some degree successful in their lobbying of Brune to retain elements of the old system. At first, General Brune assured the inhabitants of Canton Schwyz, Luzern, and Unterwalden that the French

---

[85] Protocol of extraordinary Schwyz *Landsgemeinde*, 10 March 1798, in Wiget, "Die letzten Landsgemeinden," 45.
[86] Uri Schwyz, Unterwalden, Zug, and Glarus to General Brune, 16 March 1798 quoted in Zschokke, *Invasion of Switzerland*, 197–201. See also *ASHR*, vol. 1, 495–6.
[87] "Memorial of the People of Appenzell, St. Gall, Toggenburg, Rheinthal, and Sargans to the Executive Directory of the French Republic" [5 April 1798], quoted in Zschokke, *Invasion of Switzerland*, 224–7; *ASHR*, vol. 1, 605–7.

army had been drawn into Switzerland "through the *provocations* of the oligarchs of Bern," and the French army did not intend to march into the democratic territory.[88] Brune further suggested the division of the Old Swiss Eidgenossenschaft into three parts: the Rhodanic Republic for the French- and Italian-speaking areas, governed by the Basel Constitution; the Helvetic Republic for the midlands, ruled by the "Paris Constitution" drafted by Ochs; and Tellgau for the central, democratic cantons, which would be allowed to maintain their own system.[89] Brune went so far as to proclaim the "République Rhodanique" on 16 March 1798, even though he had already been informed by the French Directory that a centralized state fit French interests best.[90]

One day before, on 15 March 1798, the Basel National Assembly had published its draft for a national constitution. The Basel constitution declared the Helvetic Republic to be a single state, abolished subject territories and guaranteed inalienable rights such as "natural freedom," freedom of conscience, freedom of the press, and property rights. At the same time, this constitutional draft gave more sovereignty to the cantons than the original Ochs draft and actually maintained direct democracy in some areas.[91] This constitution gained tremendous popularity as eleven cantons held votes in support of the Basel draft.[92] The depth of Swiss ambivalence toward the French-style constitution was so great that even supporters of a Helvetic Revolution preferred the Basel draft, as was evidenced by the fact that Peter Ochs presided over the creation of the Basel constitutional draft.

Even in framing the constitution of the Helvetic Republic, a so-called satellite republic of the French republic, Swiss patriot agency mattered. Not only did the notable elite rally behind the Basel proposal, but some patriot actors such as La Harpe and Ochs continued to lobby the French Directory and General Brune in order to maintain the territorial integrity of the Swiss Confederation rather than dividing Switzerland into three separate republics

---

[88] Letter from Brune to the inhabitants of Canton Schwyz, 16 March 1798, in *ASHR*, vol 1, 512. See also General Brune to Canton Luzern and General Brune to Obwalden 10 March 1798 in *ASHR*, vol. 1, 500–1; Zschokke, *Invasion of Switzerland*, 196–7, 202.

[89] Brune to the Directory, 17 March 1798, in *ASHR*, vol. 1, 514–15.

[90] Proclamation de la République Rhodanique par le Général Brune, 16 March 1798, in Tosato-Rigo et al., eds., *Bon peuple vaudois*, 263; *ASHR*, vol. 1, 496. For further communication between Brune and the Directory, see also *ASHR*, vol. 1, 502–9.

[91] *Entwurf der helvetischen Staatsverfassung*.

[92] Rufer, *La Suisse et la Révolution française*, 75–6. Aargau, Baden, Bern, Luzern, the Bernese Oberland, Obwalden, Schaffhausen, Solothurn, Thurgau, and Zurich all accepted the Basel project. Rufer argues that Fribourg and the Pays de Vaud would have approved as well.

as Brune had suggested. With the French Directory in Paris dictating a unitary republic to Brune and with La Harpe and others demanding a unified Switzerland, Brune was able to frame his 22 March 1798 declaration of the Helvetic Republic "one and indivisible" as supportive of the popular will.[93]

Conclusion

On 12 April 1798, the constitution of the Helvetic Republic was promulgated, and a new unitary state was enforced by French arms. The need for French military enforcement continued throughout most of the lifespan of the Helvetic Republic.[94] This constitution was an edited version of Ochs' initial draft; it included essentially the same list of fundamental rights, ended the cantonal system and subject territories, and created a five-person Directory and two national legislative bodies.[95] However, Merlin de Douai struck out the passage from Ochs' draft requiring a popular vote to enact the constitution.[96]

The Helvetic Republic did not last long, nor was it popular among Swiss inhabitants. The fact that its government was overturned four times in its five-year existence and that there was nearly continuous armed resistance to the new unitary state demonstrates its unpopularity. However, the Helvetic Revolution introduced fundamental rights to the Swiss political arena and was a product of Swiss political action in addition to French military support.

Too often Swiss historians have dismissed the short-lived Helvetic experiment as a foreign graft onto the Swiss political body.[97] This fits with the view of many European historians, who have presented the formation of the Helvetic Republic and other satellite republics as a mere outgrowth and spillover from the events in France. However, if we put the Swiss debates into a broader chronological context and the French Revolution into a broader transnational context, we can better understand the origins and

---

[93] Brune, General in Chief, to the Citizens of all the Cantons, 22 March 1798, *ASHR*, 1: 528–29; translation in Zschokke, *Invasion of Switzerland*, 205–6.

[94] For more on Swiss resistance to the introduction of the Helvetic Constitution, see Simon, ed., *Widerstand und Proteste*; Lerner, *Laboratory of Liberty*, 122–30; Böning, *Der Traum von Freiheit und Gleichheit*, 252–68.

[95] Ochs, "Plan d'une Constitution provisoire," 113–25; "Constitution de la République helvétique," 126–52.

[96] Andreas Fankhauser, "Philippe Antoine Merlin de Douai," *Historisches Lexikon der Schweiz*, 30 October 2007, https://hls-dhs-dss.ch/de/articles/046096/2007-10-30; Ochs, "Plan d'une Constitution provisoire," 113.

[97] Würgler, *Grenzen des Zumutbaren*, 9–10 also discusses this overcompensation in a nationalist historiography.

formation of the Helvetic Republic as part and parcel of the revolutionary period, rather than a mere reflection of events elsewhere.

In order to fully understand the legacy of the Helvetic Republic, we have to think about balancing this broader context with its short-lived existence. This requires a balance between native political action and armed French intervention, between continuity and rupture, with traditional Swiss conceptions of liberty, as well as new ideas in disguised frameworks that spoke to traditionalists.[98] These tensions existed within the Swiss revolutionary period and the wider Age of Atlantic Revolutions.

[98] Würgler, *Grenzen des Zumutbaren*, 12.

12

Revolution at Geneva: Genevans in Revolution

RICHARD WHATMORE

Explaining Political Turbulence at Geneva

The topsy-turvy and complicated revolutionary politics of the late eighteenth century is nowhere better illustrated than in the history of Geneva. In the enlightenment era the independent republic acquired a notoriety it had last experienced in the evangelizing decades following Calvin's conversion of the city to Protestantism in 1536. Protestant sons came from everywhere to be educated at the famous Genevan Academy. Thomas Jefferson called the Academy one of the eyes of Europe (the other was the University of Edinburgh).[1] Prominent nobles and wealthy visitors streamed into the city, especially during Grand Tours. Illustrious Genevans distinguished themselves in the fields of theology, natural philosophy, literature, and politics. Although it was often lauded as a haven of peace and justice, where magistrates were revered and the people contented, as in the portrait provided by Rousseau in the preface of 1755 to his *Discours sur l'origine et les fondements de l'inégalité parmi les hommes* (*Discourse on the Origins and Foundation of Inequality among Men*), domestic politics at Geneva were increasingly troubled. Through the seventeenth century Geneva had famously avoided embroilment in the wars of religion. Yet in the eighteenth century, intermittent rebellion erupted in 1707, the 1730s, and the 1760s. This led to speculation about whether the Protestant Rome would meet its end through civil war. Alternatively, one of its rapacious and imperially minded neighbors, the monarchies of France or Savoy, might devour the republic. There was a natural element to such speculation. If Geneva did cease to exist, it would follow so many of the continent's lesser states into oblivion.

---

[1] Jefferson to Wilson Cary Nicholas, 23 November 1794, in B. Oberg and J. Jefferson Looney, eds., *The Papers of Thomas Jefferson Digital Edition* (Charlottesville: University of Virginia Press, 2008).

Geneva was in theory a popular state, popular because sovereignty lay with the General Council of all citizens and bourgeois. The General Council met at least once a year, to give consent to new laws and to appoint magistrates. As Jean Bodin had written in his *Six livres de la république* (1576), although sovereignty lay with citizens and bourgeois, the two leading ranks of the republic, the government of Geneva was aristocratic.[2] Matters of day-to-day rule were left to the Council of Twenty-Five, which included the chief-magistrates who determined matters of immediate concern, and a Council of Two Hundred. These three councils were supposed to balance one another to maintain liberty.[3] From the first decade of the eighteenth century onwards, however, the claim was made that both executive councils, the Twenty-Five and the Two Hundred, contained far too many members of the same prominent families. The accusation was leveled that these families had become a noble class serving themselves rather than magistrates serving the public good. Pierre Fatio, a lawyer who made this claim in 1707, was executed for treason.[4] By the 1730s unrest within Geneva arose from a widespread belief that the ruling magistrates had turned themselves into a corrupt oligarchy, organizing the tax system for their own benefit, relying upon indirect taxes that hit the poor rather than the rich. In addition, members of the executive councils from eminent families were increasingly investing their own profits, and the revenues of the Genevan state, in the French national debt, thereby making Geneva more dependent upon France. Making huge sums as *rentiers*, many members of the magisterial class purchased grand properties beyond the city walls and erected town houses, away from the artisans of the lower town, on the hill within the city.[5] In the 1730s many of the artisans initiated civil unrest, being worried at the erosion of both independence and Calvinist mores.[6] Popular rioting occurred between 1734 and 1737. In the end peace was restored only through the involvement of mediators from France and from Bern and Zurich, the two

---

[2] Jean Bodin, *Les six livres de la république de J. Bodin Angevin: À Monseigneur du Faur, Seigneur de Pibrac, Conseiller du Roy en son Conseil privé* (Paris: Jacques du Puis, 1576), 267–8.

[3] Henri Fazy, *Les Constitutions de la République de Genève* (Geneva: H. Georg, 1890).

[4] André Corbaz, *Pierre Fatio, précurseur et martyr de la démocratie genevoise, 1669–1707* (Geneva: Atar, 1923).

[5] J. B. G. Galiffe, *D'un siècle à l'autre: Correspondances inédites entre gens connus et inconnus du XVIIIe et du XIXe siècle*, 2 vols. (Geneva: Sandoz, 1877), vol. I, 113–32.

[6] Helena Rosenblatt, *Rousseau and Geneva: From the First Discourse to the Social Contract, 1749–1762* (Cambridge: Cambridge University Press, 1997).

Swiss cantons allied to Geneva. Civil violence flared up once more in the 1760s. In the early 1780s it led to revolution.

In studying Geneva, and indeed the period as whole, we have to be careful to avoid mistakes in the historiography arising from attractively simple explanations deriving from overgeneralization. We also have to make sure that the present is not read into the past. It is an error to believe there was an ever-growing republican or liberal tradition of political argument which came to fruition at the close of the eighteenth century. No one called themselves a liberal in the eighteenth century; liberalism is a nineteenth-century philosophy. Furthermore, rather than being in rude health, republicanism was a doctrine in crisis. Republics were accepted as being small states. Survival was therefore never certain. Since the Renaissance, small states had forever risked invasion by a larger military power, faced civil war fomented by a Caesar figure or a demagogue, had to be concerned about economic collapse, and feared especially the growth of luxury and corruption, sapping the *virtù* (manliness) that the republic relied upon to defend itself. Such factors explained the collapse of the republics of Pisa in 1399, Novgorod in 1478, Florence in 1537, and Sienna in 1555. The republics that survived into the eighteenth century were the United Provinces, the only new republic to have established itself in the early modern era, Venice, Genoa, Lucca, the Grisons, San Marino, Switzerland, Geneva, and Ragusa.

Prospects for survival were further complicated by the development of commerce. The initiation of reason of state politics geared to the pursuit of commerce was charted by David Hume to the second half of the seventeenth century, as France, the Dutch Republic, and England battled to generate revenues by creating new markets for their goods through empire or by competing for the markets of rival states.[7] Revenues were required to maintain a state at a time when the costs of warfare had risen exponentially during what is now termed the military revolution.[8] The capacity of states to borrow on the basis of anticipated future national revenues was equally transformative. One of the consequences was that small republics could no longer rely upon the manliness of their troops. The gargantuan armies of the major monarchies would always be able to overwhelm them. Adam Smith

---

[7] David Hume, "Of Civil Liberty," in David Hume, *Essays: Moral, Political, and Literary*, ed. Eugene F. Miller, revised edition (Indianapolis: Liberty Fund, 1987), 88.

[8] Michael Roberts, *The Military Revolution, 1560–1660: An Inaugural Lecture Delivered before the Queen's University of Belfast* (Belfast: Queen's University, 1956); Geoffrey Parker, *The Military Revolution: Military Innovation and the Rise of the West, 1500–1800* (Cambridge: Cambridge University Press, 1996).

summarized dominant perceptions in his *Lectures on Jurisprudence* in 1763, "Monarchies are the prevailing government; they set the fashion and give the tone to the custom of all the others."[9] Such was the gulf in military resources between republics and commercial monarchies that the French statesman René-Louis de Voyer de Paulmy, the marquis d'Argenson, argued in the 1740s that the only remaining survival strategy for republics and small states was to beg the powerful to allow them to survive. Republics were so weak that "friendship with great states is most certain to sustain them."[10] The existence of a republican and small-state crisis in the eighteenth century does more than anything else to explain the history of Geneva during the age of revolutions.

Revolution at Geneva from 1782

The revolutionary era for Genevans commenced in 1782 with the people rising up against the sitting magistrates in April. The magistrates, confident of the support of France, refused to yield to demands for a constitution more directly founded upon the sovereignty of citizens and bourgeois. Although tired of the political stalemate, the reformist party did not seek revolution. It was forced to take control of the state, however, after mass demonstrations against the magistrates turned violent on the night of 4–5 April. Geneva was then divided into districts, each of which elected a representative, who in turn formed an executive committee that pushed through numerous reforms. Appeals were made by the new government to all of the powers of Europe to accept the outcome of the revolution. France refused to accept the situation immediately, although Geneva was peaceful in the aftermath of the revolution, and despite the fact that the new government was supported by the populace.

Crucial in the French decision was the fact that Geneva's rejected magistrates were far closer to the French court than they were to their fellow citizens. Heavily invested in the French economy, the rich magistrates from eminent families felt that they had secured Geneva's future by allowing France to control the republic's politics in return for facilitating the economic links between the two states and in return for protection from other

---

[9] Adam Smith, *Lectures on Jurisprudence*, eds. R. L. Meek, D. D. Raphael, and P. G. Stein (Indianapolis: Liberty Fund, 1982), 97 (14 March 1763).

[10] René-Louis de Voyer, Marquis d'Argenson, *Mémoires et journal inédit*, ed. Marquis d'Argenson, 5 vols. (Paris: Jannet, 1857–1858), vol. v, 299–300.

powerful monarchies, such as Savoy; Savoy had renounced its claim to sovereignty over Geneva only in 1752 and was seen by Genevans to be their greatest enemy. Pressure was applied by France upon Bern to condemn events at Geneva. In violation of existing treaties and in order to underscore the grave offence committed by Genevans in removing their magistrates, France also brought Savoy into the group of nations that claimed an interest in Genevan affairs. By June 12,000 troops were on the march from France, Bern, and Savoy. Only Zurich – the other major canton closely allied to Geneva – refused to be involved in the invasion. Britain, weakened by the war in North America, rejected requests for succor.[11] The French invaders included some regiments recently returned from North America. In North America they were deemed liberators, but in Europe they were perceived as the agents of despotic France.

The French-led army put an end to the revolution at the beginning of July. Massacre was averted because the leaders of the revolution chose to run away rather than turn themselves into republican martyrs. The people of Geneva were now under martial law and experiencing a foreign military presence; the unpopular restored magistrates were more than ever akin to a foreign aristocracy. In these conditions a substantial number of Genevans decided to abandon their city on the grounds that it was no longer free and had been turned into an illegitimate polity maintained by tyrants. The would-be migrants were invited to form new communities across Europe. Many of the monarchs who had condemned the revolution of 1782 were nevertheless welcoming of the revolutionaries themselves on the grounds that their skills in watchmaking and in commerce would contribute to the economic health of any state. An attempt was made to move the republic *in toto* to Ireland, then a kingdom subject to the British Crown rather than a component part of what became the United Kingdom. The view of the exiled Genevans was that republicanism in the modern world required protection from willing monarchical superpowers, in this case Britain.[12] The Irish experiment collapsed, however, because of a lack of support from the powerful Protestant Ascendency, the landowning class who ruled Ireland. From the perspective

---

[11] "British and Foreign History," in Andrew Kippis, ed., *The New Annual Register, or, General Repository of History, Politics, and Literature for the Year 1782* (London; G. Robinson, 1783), 63–4.

[12] Jennifer Powell-McNutt and Richard Whatmore, "The Attempts to Transfer the Genevan Academy to Ireland and to America, 1782–1795," *The Historical Journal* 56:2 (2013), 345–68.

of the former Genevan revolutionaries, they had once again been stymied by aristocrats wielding illegitimate authority.

A few years after the Irish experiment collapsed, revolutionary Genevans found their world unexpectedly transformed. France had always been accepted as the major bulwark against republican constitutional reform, being ever more involved in the day-to-day politics of numerous small states and unwilling to countenance more popular structures of government anywhere across the continent. In a very short time aspirations for greater liberty were suddenly supported by France after the outbreak of revolution at Paris. In the 1790s Geneva itself then followed France into popular ardor for liberty and French-style revolution, a process that brought with it civil instability, ending only when the republic lost any vestige of independence by being annexed by France in 1798.

Having traveled across Europe and battled for liberty over such a long time span, Genevan republicans who survived tended toward skepticism about grand revolutionary narratives. For figures such as the lawyer Jacques-Antoine Du Roveray, one of the leaders of the revolution of 1782, the lessons were salutary. True republicanism was a doctrine in decline, threatened by the logic of international commercial competition which saw large states lust for markets and drive out the weak.[13] Republican revolution might be successful in particular circumstances, such as in the new United States of America, where the geopolitical circumstances were unique. It could not succeed in the small states of Europe. It was unlikely to succeed either globally or in large states such as France, where manners, as Jean-Jacques Rousseau had always aggressively proclaimed, were more corrupt than anywhere else.[14] This was why Du Roveray ended up a spy for the British in the 1790s, dedicating his life to war against revolution in France just as he had dedicated it to revolution at Geneva. In short, many Genevans remained wary of the assertions being made about the transformative effect of revolutions. Many of them remained wedded to the older Machiavellian republican tradition in which political change depended upon *mœurs* or manners, the public and private cultures of a polity. From such a standpoint, revolutions would only ever be successful when the political culture accorded with the aspirational politics. If this were not the case, revolutions would result in

---

[13] Jacques-Antoine Du Roveray, *An Appeal to Justice and True Liberty: Or, an Accurate Statement of the Proceedings of the French towards the Republic of Geneva* (London: Debrett, 1793).

[14] Jean-Jacques Rousseau, *Émile, ou De l'éducation*, 2 vols. (Amsterdam: Marc Michel Rey, 1762), Book III, vol. II, 68.

replicating the society they were seeking to replace. Education had to precede revolution. This chapter summarizes what happened in 1782 and why the failed revolution placed Genevans at the forefront of subsequent political turbulence across the continent, with men such as the pastor Étienne Dumont and Du Roveray writing speeches for Gabriel-Honoré Riqueti de Mirabeau, and their friend Étienne Clavière serving as the last finance minister of Louis XVI and the first of the first French Republic.[15] Genevans were notable in North America too, with figures such as Albert Gallatin serving as United States Secretary of the Treasury between 1801 and 1814. Exodus from revolution has oftentimes been successful.

Rousseau and Geneva

It is still sometimes said that ideas about republican reform and revolution at Geneva need to be read off the works that inspired them, those of Jean-Jacques Rousseau. Rousseau was unquestionably the best-known Genevan of the century. The son of a watchmaker, Rousseau had left the city during his teenage years, abjured Calvinism and embraced Catholicism. After a peripatetic existence, he dedicated the *Discours sur l'origine et les fondements de l'inégalité parmi les hommes* to the city in 1755, fulsomely praising the magistrates as the ideal rulers of a state. The Consistory of pastors responded by forgiving Rousseau's years of heresy, and his privileges as a citizen were restored. Rousseau had earlier, in the *Discours sur les sciences et les arts* (*Discourse on the Sciences and Arts*) of 1750 that made him famous, provided the first intimations of what became his infamous religion of the heart, based on the claim that humans were naturally good but had been corrupted by the development of society and the dangerous standard-bearers of societal progress, namely science, politics, and trade. Rousseau had nevertheless contributed to contemporary science in agreeing to write articles for his friend Diderot's *Encyclopédie*. Rousseau only became the arch-opponent of his *philosophe* associates as a result of a dispute about the nature of Geneva.

There can be no doubt that Rousseau's history and writings were intertwined with the city of his birth and that he contributed to the unrest it experienced. It is an error, however, to presume that the Genevan republicans were Rousseauists or acting in accordance with his views. Indeed, the broader claim, associated with the work of Robert Darnton, that "gutter

---

[15] Jean Bénétruy, *L'atelier de Mirabeau: Quatre proscrits genevois dans la tourmente révolutionnaire* (Paris: J. A. et J. Picard, 1962).

Rousseaus" or the denizens of grub street in different European cities were laying the foundations for revolution is altogether false because it neglects the very precise reform strategies that were being enunciated by the hack journalists and others. In most instances they were well aware of the nature of Rousseau's philosophy and the complicated maneuvers that would be necessary to turn it revolutionary. In the case of the Genevan republicans, they rejected Rousseau's advice that for a tiny weak republic peace was more important than liberty.[16] Rousseau was used by the rebels, just as he was abused by their enemies.

An article by the mathematician Jean d'Alembert, Diderot's fellow *Encyclopédie* editor, was the cause of Rousseau's involvement in the politics of the republic. At the instigation of his mentor Voltaire, then living on Geneva's border with France, d'Alembert composed an article on Geneva that appeared in the seventh volume of the *Encyclopédie* in 1757. D'Alembert's article described Geneva as the archetypal city of enlightenment. According to d'Alembert, old intolerances and prejudices were being abandoned. Commerce and luxury were flourishing. Geneva had no external enemies, having recently signed a treaty of peace with Savoy and being protected by France and the Swiss cantons. The citizens enjoyed their lives, were united, and were increasingly civilized. Evidence came from the fact that once-bigoted Calvinist pastors had become Socinians. They no longer believed in the Trinity, in original sin, or in predestination. Rather, in d'Alembert's view, the pastors had become advocates of a rational religion of social progress, emphasizing forgiveness, open-mindedness, and cosmopolitanism. What the Genevans needed, in d'Alembert's opinion, was to foster enlightened culture still further by establishing a theater. Such an establishment had always been forbidden within the city. Theaters were, from a Calvinist perspective, frivolous, disreputable, and corrupting. The sumptuary laws that governed social behavior within Geneva forbade public singing, display, and entertainment. Theaters represented a culture turning against Calvinism. Signs that traditional sumptuary laws were no longer being respected provided proof of enlightenment. D'Alembert anticipated this in his article, fully aware that Voltaire could readily inundate the city with his plays. Indeed, Voltaire was putting on plays at Les Délices, his

---

[16] Richard Whatmore, "'A Lover of Peace More Than Liberty.' The Genevan Response to Rousseau's Politics," in Avi Lifshitz, ed., *Engaging with Rousseau: Reception and Interpretation from the Eighteenth Century to the Present* (Cambridge: Cambridge University Press, 2016), 1–16.

Genevan residence between 1755 and 1760; he also established his own theater at the village of Ferney, just over the French border.

The response of the Genevans to the article "Genève" was vitriolic. Rousseau defended the reputation of the pastors and of the city in his *Lettre à d'Alembert sur les spectacles (Letter to d'Alembert on the Theatre)* of 1758. The pamphlet argued that a theater at Geneva would poison social relationships and corrupt morals. A theater would be especially dangerous for maternal women, upon whose virtues every stable society depended.[17] Furthermore, a theater would waste the money of the poor and give people false ideas about life and morality. Above all, it would introduce into republican Geneva a value system that was inspired by France: the love of luxury and libertinism, the superiority of the rich and the noble, and the foolishness of a life of dedication to the public good when compared with a life devoted to the pursuit of pleasure. Rousseau presented the theater as a dire threat to the Genevan republican tradition of virtue and right reason, which he believed could be traced historically to the lessons of two of the great republics of old, Sparta and Rome.

Rousseau intended his pamphlet to be read as an attack upon the *philosophe* movement. He saw Voltaire's and d'Alembert's schemes for promoting what they called civilization in apocalyptic terms. The *philosophes* were in fact suffocating the established liberties of the free states of Europe, and especially the independent republics, by turning them French. Philosophic culture was hegemonic and all-encompassing, imperialist in the sense that it rejected as inferior and in need of replacement traditional cultures, such as Genevan Calvinism. As such, *philosophe* notions of civilization dovetailed with more dangerous forces that were abroad. Rousseau believed that western Europe was about to enter a new dark age because commerce and luxury were rampant. These forces made men weak and prevented women from being good wives and mothers. Yet the aristocracies and the wealthy classes of western Europe were addicted to commerce, and the luxury that accompanied it, because it offered a form of happiness based on the immediate satisfaction of individual desires. Trade-obsessed European governments were altogether addicted, because commerce generated tax revenues, and promised future revenues that allowed states to borrow money, which in

---

[17] Jean-Jacques Rousseau, *J. J. Rousseau Citoyen de Genève, À Mr. D'Alembert, de l'Académie Françoise, de l'Académie Royale des Sciences de Paris, de celle de Prusse, de la Société Royale de Londres, de l'Académie Royale des Belles-Lettres de Suède, & de l'Institut de Bologne sur son Article Genève: Dans le VIIme. Volume de l'Encyclopédie, et Particulièrement, sur le projet d'établir un Théâtre de Comédie en cette Ville* (Amsterdam: Marc Michel Rey, 1758).

turn paid for vast mercenary armies to fight wars and exercise control over the poor and the industrious. Rousseau did not believe the commercial monarchies of Europe could last, because their lust for commerce and capacity for war would ultimately bankrupt them. France and Britain were expected to be the first to fall. Barbarian invaders from the east would once more rule a Europe in which rotten empires had destroyed themselves from within by embracing a moral system that made them ultimately incapable of self-defense. The continent was "approaching conditions of crisis and a century of revolutions."[18]

From Rousseau to the *représentants*

With Geneva a minor cog in the wheel of international commerce and with domestic reform without violence seemingly a real option within the city, Rousseau did not expect that his pamphlet would foment rebellion or revolution. On its publication, he received adulatory comments from numerous magistrates and pastors who, whatever their view of the necessity of intertwining French and Genevan politics, were concerned about the French threat to Calvinist mores.[19] It was happenstance that the renewal of disputes concerning the levying of taxes upon the industrious by increasingly wealthy magistrates coincided with the publication of Rousseau's letter to d'Alembert. Rousseau found himself the inadvertent figurehead of the movement opposed to the existing magistrates. This movement within Geneva identified itself as that of the *représentants* in the 1750s.

Being a *représentant* did not mean being a representative in a contemporary sense. Rather, they were the "representationers," those who identified injustice and took proposals for reform to the executive Council of Twenty-Five. As such, the movement was at first in no sense revolutionary. Radical upheaval, except in theology, was associated with disaster rather than success. The lesson of the previous century and indeed of the classical past was that popular rebellion ultimately led to civil war and the rise of Caesar figures who would create a tyranny worse than any experienced hitherto. The whole purpose of enlightenment was to prevent religious extremism from ruining societies. Maintaining enlightenment, the real peace between civil and

---

[18] Rousseau, *Émile*, Book III, vol. II, 54: "Nous approchons de l'état de crise et du siècle des revolutions ... Je tiens pour impossible que les grandes Monarchies de l'Europe aient encore long-temps à durer."

[19] Richard Whatmore, "Rousseau and the *représentants*: The Politics of the *Lettres écrites de la montagne*," *Modern Intellectual History* 3 (2006), 1–29.

religious authorities that marked the eighteenth century, was to be achieved through moderation and reform rather than revolution. Revolution was the stuff of fanatics and enthusiasts, people so committed to a transformative cause that they themselves would end up justifying atrocity and injustice. Projectors, those who promised a world made virtuous by violence or the taking control of institutions by force in order to alter society at its foundations, were to be avoided at all costs. There was no notion among the *représentants* of following such courses of action, which were associated with the extremist groups of the Reformation. As the leading *représentant* Clavière wrote to the Alpine artist Marc-Théodore Bourrit in 1782, the outbreak of revolution would likely bring disaster because it would paint the moderate reform movement in exactly the wrong colors. Clavière even worried that revolution would be initiated by the magistrates, because it was more likely to confirm their rule through French intervention.[20]

The *représentants'* solution to the problems of the city was the reassertion of the popular element of the constitution, the General Council, which would meet more regularly and be more assertive in the exercise of its sovereignty, especially by means of the direct scrutiny of the magistrates. Rousseau did not support such proposals, having little faith in assemblies of citizens, but his works from the attack upon d'Alembert onwards painted the magistrates as would-be tyrants who were more loyal to France than to the Genevan republic or to Calvinism. This was why his sensationally popular novel *Émile*, the story of the education of an individual uncorrupted by society, and the *Contrat social (Social Contract)*, both published in 1762, were condemned first in France and then at Geneva for threatening the foundations of government and religion. An arrest warrant was issued at Geneva should Rousseau return to the city; he had by this time fled to Yverdon-les-Bains in Bernese territory. The Genevan *représentants* argued that the legal process was improper because the General Council had condemned neither Rousseau's person nor his books. The Genevan magistrates were carrying out a French-inspired vendetta against a Genevan citizen whose liberties they ought to have been defending. French "enlightenment" was revealing its true colors and Rousseau himself became the focus of the *représentants'* cause by arguing that the way he had been treated was in violation of existing law.

---

[20] Clavière to Théodore Bourrit, 4 February 1782 and 15 February 1782, in Édouard Chapuisat, "Étienne Clavière," in *Figures et choses d'autrefois* (Paris: Éditions G. Crès & Cie.; Geneva: Éditions Georg et Cie., 1920), 30–6.

The magistrate Jean-Robert Tronchin, whose rich family had especially close connections with France, defended the actions of the government of Geneva with regard to Rousseau. In his *Lettres écrites de la campagne* (*Letters from the Country*) of 1763, Tronchin identified the *représentants* as radical democrats, so extreme that they would ruin the state. Entirely incorrectly, Rousseau, himself labeled an arch-anarchist and subverter of authority, was called the chief of the *représentants*. Rousseau defended himself and the *représentants* in his *Lettres écrites de la montagne* (*Letters from the Mountain*) that appeared in December 1764. Tronchin and his ilk were attacked as tyrants and were themselves portrayed as radical innovators crushing domestic traditions of Calvinism and republicanism. At the same time Rousseau rejected the reform strategy of the *représentants* in his *Lettres*. He repeated his long-held view that popular assemblies running countries would result in ruin because an assembled populace was likely to be unstable and irrational. Furthermore, changing the constitution was mad because it would never be accepted at Paris. Geneva could never defend itself militarily against France. Rousseau's work upset the radicals at Geneva. It angered the magistrates much more. Voltaire was able to get a form of revenge for Rousseau's attack on d'Alembert when he anonymously published a pamphlet, *Sentiment des citoyens*, at Geneva in 1765, which revealed to the world that Rousseau, the great advocate of education, had abandoned his own five children on the steps of the foundling hospital at Paris.

French-led mediators restored peace yet again in 1767, and a treaty was signed between magistrates and the *représentants* in 1768. It did not last. A new generation took over the leadership of the *représentants*. Such figures as Clavière, Du Roveray, and his fellow lawyer François d'Ivernois felt that the French domination of Geneva had to be combated more directly. Magistrates from traditional families had to be replaced by new blood because they could no longer be trusted. They had turned themselves into Frenchmen rather than Genevans in their political allegiances. They were focused upon making money for themselves and enjoying luxury rather than on serving the republic. Removing aristocracy within the city was to be accomplished by direct elections, the assumption being that the small and educated populace would be able to reject candidates who would not follow the public good. Equally, a plan was put forward for Geneva to no longer depend upon revenues generated from investments in the French national debt. A moral reformation was expected to accompany political reform as luxury and selfishness, the values of aristocracy, were removed from public culture. The goal was a highly educated community of industrious citizens, all of whom enjoyed moderate wealth. Excessive inequality was now identified as the root cause of many of Geneva's problems over the previous century and the key to the level of political turbulence.[21]

The Events of 1782

The strategy of the new generation of *représentants* was at first to convince the French foreign minister Charles Gravier, comte de Vergennes, that France would benefit from having as its neighbor a commercially powerful free and popular republic. Neither the French nor other powers from which support was sought were willing to accept an alternative to the rule of the existing magistrates. This made the outbreak of revolution an especially fraught affair when it came, not least because the *représentants* did not want it.

On 18 March 1782, the *représentants* demanded the confirmation of a law passed on 10 February 1781 which gave greater civil and political rights to inhabitants at Geneva called *natifs*, the majority of the population and the group below the rank of bourgeois. The resulting written representation submitted to the magistrates, and published for all to read, asserted that France was taking control of the republic and that the sovereignty of the General Council had been abrogated, itself in violation of the peace agreement established in 1768. The divisions of the republic were to be healed gradually, not least by new forms of civic education.[22] The representation ended with thirty-five pages of documentation underlining the evidence for the sovereignty of the General Council, including, facetiously, Jean-Robert Tronchin's *Lettres écrites de la campagne*. The Council of Twenty-Five refused to ratify the edict on 7 April 1782. On the evening of 7 April crowds began to gather in the streets demanding the removal of the magistrates.

Représentant and *natif* leaders, including Du Roveray and Jean-Pierre Marat, the brother of Jean-Paul Marat, for the *natifs*, then met at the house of the lawyer Jacques Grenus. Avoiding revolution, which was the plan of the leaders, proved impossible by the following day when the numbers of

---

[21] Richard Whatmore, *Against War and Empire: Geneva, Britain, and France in the Eighteenth Century* (New Haven: Yale University Press, 2012).

[22] Anon., *Très-humble et très-respectueuse représentation des citoyens et bourgeois représentans, dans laquelle on réfute la partie de la Déclaration des Négatifs du 29ᶜ 8bre 1781, qui traite de la Prise d'Armes & de l'Edit du mois de février 1781. Suivie de Notes essentielles sur la Souveraineté du Conseil Général. Remise aux Seigneurs Sindics et à Monsieur le Procureur Général, par la Généralité des Citoyens et Bourgeois Représentans, le 18 mars 1782* (Geneva: n.p., 1782), 14, 38–9, 44, 50.

people on the streets were growing, with arms in evidence. Magistrates were harassed, and a crowd formed outside the house of French *résident* Jean-Baptiste Castelnau. As rumors went around that the magistrates were going to use force against the populace and crush the demonstrations, a cry "Aux armes!" went up and the gates of the city were taken by the people.[23] Thirty-five deaths were later reported, although the actual figure was undoubtedly smaller. The *représentants* took control of the institutions of the state in order to prevent further disorder. By 10 April Castelnau was fleeing to Paris. A new General Council appointed further committees to choose new magistrates. Some former magistrates were taken hostage. On 12 April, a committee of security (*comité de sûreté*) was created, with eleven members under the former magistrate and member of the Council of Two Hundred Julien Dentand.[24] The supporter of the former magistrates Perrinet Des Franches wrote that "total anarchy reigns in our city," the "factious" had become the masters, and were violating "the rights of nations [droit des nations]." His correspondent stated that "the spirit of conspiracy against authority is the spirit of this century."[25]

An appeal was made by the new government to the former magistrates for support, promising national unity and moderation in the process of creating a new constitution. At the same time, the *représentants* asserted that they were willing to perish "as free men and virtuous citizens," should providence so will it.[26] Bern and Zurich rejected the new government as factious and illegitimate. Vergennes "returned unopened the dispatches of the new Senate."[27] Frederick the Great of Prussia wrote to the Bernese giving his support for intervention to restore "the ancient form of government."

---

[23] Édouard Chapuisat, *La prise d'armes de 1782 à Genève* (Geneva: A. Jullien, 1932), 18, 22, 24, 30–1.

[24] Marc Neuenschwander, "Carrière et convictions," in Marc Neuenschwander, Bernard Lescaze, and Gabriel Mützenberg, *Un Genevois méconnu: Julien Dentand (1736–1817)*, special issue consisting of three studies, *Bulletin de la Société d'Histoire et d'Archéologie de Genève* 16:2 (1977), 137–61.

[25] Saconay to Perrinet Des Franches, 12 April 1782 and the reply of 19 April 1782, in Hippolyte Aubert, "Les troubles de Genève en 1781 et 1782. Extrait des papiers de Perrinet Des Franches conservés aux Archives Nationales de France," *Bulletin de la Société d'Histoire et d'Archéologie de Genève* 3 (1913), 435–6.

[26] Anon., *Très-humble et très-respectueuse déclaration*, 7–11.

[27] Anon., *Traduction d'une Lettre du Louable Canon de Berne, adressée aux Seigneurs Syndics* [10 May 1782] (Geneva: n.p., 1782); William Coxe, *Travels in Switzerland: And in the country of the Grisons: In a series of letters to William Melmoth, Esq. from William Coxe*, 3 vols. (London: T. Cadell, 1791), vol. II, 362–3; Jean Roget to Samuel Romilly, 27 April 1782, in François-Frédéric Roget, ed., *Les affaires de Genève, 1780–1783: Lettres de Jean Roget, 1753–1783: Ministre de l'Église de Genève* (Geneva: Éditions Georg et Cie., 1911), 195–6.

Neither Joseph II nor the Dutch were interested in Geneva.[28] Vergennes wrote to the cantons that all parties were seeking the restoration of "tranquillity by restoring legitimate government."[29] Clavière was the person deemed the most unruly and significant leader of the *représentants* and most deserving of reprisals.[30]

Geneva was a pawn in an international power game, the problem being that in 1782 the strength of France was at a peak unparalleled since the 1680s. Using the pretense that the legitimate magistrates were requesting the military intervention of France, Vergennes stated that he was forced to act upon their demand. Vergennes cited a letter of 28 September 1781 to the magistrates. This stated that while the *Règlement* or domestic peace treaty of 1738 had given twenty-five years of prosperity, that of 1768 had intensified unrest at Geneva. The reason, according to Vergennes, was obvious. After 1768 France had been less involved in the government of the republic.[31] Whilst this was nonsense, clear justifications for intervention had been formulated and the decision taken to act upon them. The government of Bern was reputed soon to be chasing Genevans supportive of the revolution from its territories. That the lead of France was accepted by the most important canton was highly significant.[32] Attempts by the pastors of Geneva's Consistory to persuade Bern to defend the *représentants* came to nothing.[33]

Jean Roget, a pastor observing Geneva from Lausanne, expressed concern that Geneva would be turned into an oppressive monarchy supported by a corrupt aristocracy in the fashion of Denmark's recent history. After all, he informed his nephew the English lawyer Samuel Romilly, the French minister Vergennes had fomented revolution in Sweden in 1771, resulting in absolutist government.[34] The *représentants* presented themselves as defenders

---

[28] Albin Thourel, *Histoire de Genève: Depuis son origine jusqu'à nos jours, suivie de la vie des hommes illustres qui y ont pris naissance*, 3 vols. (Geneva: Collin et Cie., 1833), vol. III, 288–9.
[29] Charles Gravier, comte de Vergennes, *Lettre de S. E. M. le comte de Vergennes à S. E. M. l'Ambassadeur de France à Soleure* [2 May] (Versailles: n.p., 1782).
[30] Bénétruy, *L'Atelier de Mirabeau*, 26.
[31] Charles Gravier, comte de Vergennes, *Lettres de son excellence Mr le Comte de Vergennes, ministre des affaires étrangers aux sindics et conseil* [15 April] (Geneva, 1782), 1–6.
[32] Jean Roget to Samuel Romilly, 27 April 1782, Catherine Roget to Samuel Romilly, 4 May 1782, in Roget, ed., *Les Affaires de Genève*, 202, 207.
[33] Jennifer Powell McNutt, *Calvin Meets Voltaire: The Clergy of Geneva in the Age of Enlightenment, 1685–1798* (Farnham: Ashgate, 2013).
[34] Jean Roget to Samuel Romilly, 17 April 1782, 18 May 1782, in Roget, *Les affaires de Genève*, 192–4, 219.

of the historic constitution that maintained the liberty of the republic. The French were working together with an aristocratic fifth column within the city that was hell-bent upon creating a republic founded upon a noble class, similar to Venice or Bern. The marker of the plot and its strength was the growth of luxury.[35] The magisterial party naturally itself claimed that it was the true defender of liberty and the ancient constitution. In accordance with this self-presentation, they termed themselves *constitutionnaires* or *négatifs*, the latter signifying opposition to representations made to the General Council. The counterclaim of the *représentants* was that commerce and industry would decline if the current magistrates remained in power. Broadening the civic base to include the *natifs* made sense because increasing their civic status would help to combat the corrupt magistrates and at the same time foster economic progress.[36]

By the third week of April 1782 there could be no doubt that Geneva was going to be invaded by a French-led coalition. Work was initiated by every inhabitant supportive of the new government, including women and children, to repair the walls.[37] The young and patriotic Henri-Albert Gosse wrote to his French friend and future Girondin Jean-Marie Roland de la Platière that "the true patriots among the men, women and children are resolved to defend their liberty to the last drop of their blood."[38] Politics was discussed in *cercles* that met constantly, creating a real sense of cohesion. Every leader undertook guard duty. Clavière asserted that by means of such collective labor a true form of equality was being created within the city.[39] Death was proclaimed to be a price worth paying for self-defense in the name of liberty. Large amounts of gunpowder were carried into certain magistrates' houses and into the Cathedral of Saint Peter. Pastor Isaac Salomon Anspach asked his fellow citizens to "embrace our oppressors – but let it be the embrace of Samson, to crush them in the last ruins and ashes of our temples." The world was no longer safe for independent republics.

---

[35] Jacob Vernes, *Catéchisme destiné particulièrement à l'usage des jeunes-gens* (Geneva: Du Villard, 1781), 112–13; Maria-Cristina Pitassi, "Le catéchisme de Jacob Vernes ou comment enseigner aux fidèles un 'christianisme sage et raisonnable,'" *Dix-huitième siècle* 34 (2002), 213–23.

[36] Anon., *Précis historique de la dernière révolution de Genève: Et en particulier de la Réforme que le Souverain de cette République a faite dans les Conseils Administrateurs* (Geneva: n.p., 1782), 3.

[37] Chapuisat, *La prise d'armes de 1782 à Genève*, 49.

[38] Henri-Albert Gosse to Jean-Marie Roland de la Platière, 16 March 1782, in Danielle Plan, *Un Génevois d'autrefois: Henri-Albert Gosse (1753–1816). D'après des lettres et des documents inédits* (Paris: Librairie Fischbacher, 1909), 123.

[39] Chapuisat, "Étienne Clavière," 45–6.

Protestants ought to fight to the last, revealing the true state of politics and pulling back the veil of aristocratic dominion and French ambition.

The invading forces, led by the marquis de Jaucourt, arrived at the gates on 29 June and immediately prepared for an assault after bombardment. The inhabitants were granted two days to surrender. All of the *cercles* gathered on the night of 30 June, and the initial resolutions were to stand and fight. Early on 1 July, however, the leading *représentants* voted narrowly to abandon Geneva. One argument was that defeat was not worth the destruction of one of Europe's greatest cities and the massacre of its people by fire. Another was that, given that resistance was not going to have a positive outcome, old Geneva had to be abandoned to its fate and plans made for new and free Genevas in other places. Almost all of the leading *représentants* then fled by boat to neighboring Neuchâtel, then governed by Prussia. From the perspective of the magistrates, who were quickly restored to their prerevolutionary offices, Geneva had been rescued "from anarchy and oppression," a democratic plot to take control of the city and delude its people.[40]

On 21 November 1782 what became known as the "Édit noir" was passed, removing the right of the General Council to remove magistrates annually from the Council of Twenty-Five and elect half of the members of the Council of Two Hundred. These two councils now ran the state, each determining the membership of the other. All *cercles*, militia, and the bearing of arms were prohibited.[41] Every citizen had to declare an oath supportive of the new constitution. Madame Roland de la Platière, visiting the city in the mid-1780s, wrote that Geneva was now a French town governed by a noble class. She accepted that the revolution had been doomed from the first, because democracy was not compatible with republican austerity. Indeed, the love of luxury and the corruption of manners explained the events of 1782.[42]

Genevan Legacies

Every *représentant* who fled the city rather than fighting and dying was accused of cowardice and castigated by former friends.[43] At the same time,

---

[40] Anon., *Lettre des très illustres & très excellens Seigneurs les Ministres Plénipotentiares de leurs Majestés très Chrétienne & Sarde & de la République de Berne, aux Magnifiques Seigneurs les Syndics & Conseil de la République de Genève* [21 November 1782] (Geneva: n.p., 1782).

[41] Coxe, *Travels in Switzerland*, vol. II, 380–3.

[42] Jeanne-Marie Phlippon, Madame Roland, "Voyage en Suisse," in *Œuvres de M. J. PH. Roland, femme de l'ex-Ministre de l'Intérieur*, 3 vols. (Paris: Bidault, 1800), vol. III, 290–1.

[43] Jean Roget to Samuel Romilly, 18 February 1783 and Catherine Roget to Samuel Romilly, 4 September 1782, in Roget, *Lettres de Jean Roget*, 262–3, 297–301; François

the movement was deemed to continue to exist and an assumption was made that the leadership of the *représentants* remained as it had been before the invasion. One reason for the forgiveness expressed toward the migrant leaders of the *représentants* was that they had allowed the city to survive rather than be set alight and destroyed. Another was the iniquities of the returning magistrates, their facile acceptance of their subjection to France, and the abandonment of Calvinism that this entailed. A final reason was that the *représentants* argued that they had been planning all along for a future Geneva in another place since the presence of France, as Rousseau had recognized, meant that revolutionary politics at Geneva would always come to a bad end. Once the possibility of moving Genevans was mooted, offers were delivered to the *représentants* requesting that they establish new Genevas in the form of trading communities of watchmakers. These came from the Elector Palatine, the prince of Baden-Dourlach, the landgrave of Hesse-Hombourg, the Dutch Republic, and the grand-duchy of Tuscany.[44] The Holy Roman Emperor Joseph II granted numerous families the privilege of residing in Brussels. Other *représentants* founded a community at Constance.[45]

The most commented upon and eagerly anticipated New Geneva was unquestionably outside Waterford in the south of Ireland. This project was given the enormous sum of £50,000 toward the building of a new city and to facilitate the emigration, through the support of the then British Prime Minister William Petty, Lord Shelburne. Geneva's magistrates and the French court worried that the old city would collapse because of the attractiveness of the new settlement. Several of the *représentants*, including Clavière, d'Ivernois, and Du Roveray, became Irish subjects of the British Crown, swearing fealty to George III at Dublin in 1783. As many as 100 families arrived at Waterford. Hopes were soon dashed, however, as Shelburne fell from power, condemned in Parliament for making peace with France and the new republic in North America. Subsequent Prime Ministers, Lord North and William Pitt, governing in an era of acute political crisis, refused to give the kind of support Shelburne had given. Ireland was also a country in turmoil, facing the kinds of division experienced at Geneva, derived from excessive inequality and an economic downturn consequent upon the loss of trade with North America.

---

d'Ivernois, *Tableau historique et politique des deux dernières révolutions de Genève*, 2 vols. (London: n.p., 1789), vol. II, 138.

[44] Thourel, *Histoire de Genève*, vol. III, 332.   [45] Coxe, *Travels in Switzerland*, vol. II, 384.

Neglect at the ministerial level meant that in Ireland Protestant politicians in charge of the funds granted by the government either took money for themselves or refused to help Genevan families directly. Genevans who had moved to Ireland traveled elsewhere, especially to Constance or Brussels. The sense of failure among the *représentants* was acute. They had left Geneva in the hope of creating a new world but found the problems of Geneva replicated in Ireland. The crisis of the small states was not easily avoided. Maintaining small states' cultures was extraordinarily difficult in conditions of global commerce and monarchies battling for supremacy through the pursuit of empire and markets. Clavière took the failure especially hard. He blamed a cabal of self-interested aristocrats, bankers, and merchants. Drawing upon the language of Adam Smith's *Wealth of Nations*, Clavière condemned the mercantile system which he saw to be turning Genevan magistrates into French nobles and Irish landowners into tyrants. The lust for gain among the contemporary leaders of society was particularly deadly for the small states. When he moved to Paris in the mid-1780s, Clavière, through the stable of writers he employed, including Jacques-Pierre Brissot and Mirabeau, launched assault after assault upon the evils of aristocrat-dominated trade.

The buildings of New Geneva that were erected and then abandoned were purchased by the army and turned into New Geneva Barracks. Troops were housed there for short or long periods, moving to different parts of the empire and also ready to deal with unrest within Ireland. When the United Irishmen rebelled against British rule in 1798, unrest was acute in neighboring Wexford, and New Geneva Barracks was turned into a prison. The bitter irony was that a planned haven for exiled republicans became a jail for Irish republicans a decade later. New Geneva prison was infamous for the rotten conditions within and for the brutality of the guards. It was a place where republicans were executed. Stories of the horrors passed into folklore, turned into a ballad by Caroll Malone (the pseudonym of the poet William B. McBurney) in 1845 and mentioned in James Joyce's *Ulysses* (1922).[46]

Revolutions rarely maintain the much-vaunted unanimity, sense of injustice, and purpose that tend to characterize such movements at their outset. The Genevan *représentants* are illustrative in this respect. Leaders who had been tied together through decades of struggle within the republic came to diverse conclusions about contemporary politics once they abandoned the

---

[46] Richard Whatmore, *Terrorists, Anarchists, and Republicans: The Genevans and the Irish in Time of Revolution* (Princeton: Princeton University Press, 2019).

city. Despite dedicating his life to reform and using his large fortune to foster the projects he believed in, Clavière was the most unfortunate of all the *représentants*. Having been castigated as a coward for running away in 1782, Clavière, as a Girondin minister under Jean-Marie Roland by 1792, was attacked for seeking vengeance on his magisterial enemies, who accused him of demanding the annexation of Geneva by revolutionary France when troops once more arrived at the city gates in October 1782. Clavière was deemed an arch-hypocrite and turncoat, favoring the termination of the independence of the republic that he had formerly done all he could to maintain. This was a harsh verdict in the midst of a revolution, but Clavière's reputation has never recovered in Geneva. He committed suicide in prison, having been arrested during the Terror in 1793.

While Clavière moved to Paris by the mid-1790s, his fellow *représentants* and close friends, Du Roveray and d'Ivernois, remained in Britain. Unlike Clavière, neither had any faith in France, despite the outbreak of revolution at Paris. They remained Rousseauists in their pessimistic assessment of the French capacity for reform. What changed was their detestation of revolution as a political tactic. These Genevan revolutionaries turned agents of the British state, laboring against the French Revolution in every way they could. Du Roveray became a spy working across Switzerland in the early 1790s. D'Ivernois was knighted Sir Francis d'Ivernois in 1796 for counterrevolutionary activity serving Britain. It is always important when studying the eighteenth century to recall Montesquieu's dictum that what works in politics in one theater will not necessarily work in another. Revolution could be tried at Geneva. This did not mean it would work or ought to be supported in France or elsewhere. The age of revolutions was full of fractures, with political stances complicated by the legacy of small-state failure and the inability of revolutionaries to establish stable states.

13

The Modernity of the Dutch Revolution: Ideas, Action, Permeation

JORIS ODDENS

How modern was the Dutch Revolution? This chapter revisits that classic question, taking stock of recent literature. "Modern" is defined as constituting a rupture with the old regime of the Dutch Republic. The "Dutch Revolution" is used as a shorthand for the revolutionary phase in the history of the Netherlands that stretched from the beginning of the "Patriot Revolt" (1780–1787) to the end of the "Batavian Revolution" (1796–1801).[1] My question can thus be reformulated as follows: to what extent did the Patriot Revolt of the 1780s and the Batavian Revolution of the 1790s break with the old regime? In recent decades diverse responses to this question have found their advocates: the Patriot Revolt was modern;[2] the Batavian Revolution was modern;[3] the modernity of the Dutch Revolution did not preclude continuity;[4] or the Dutch revolutionary movement was largely irrelevant for the road to modernity.[5] Intellectual, political, cultural, social, and economic historians have highlighted different aspects of the revolution

---

[1] Previous studies to have treated the various phases as one revolution (sometimes with different periodizations) are Simon Schama, *Patriots and Liberators: Revolution in the Netherlands, 1780–1813* (London: Collins, 1977); Joost Rosendaal, *De Nederlandse Revolutie: Vrijheid, volk en vaderland, 1783–1799* (Nijmegen: Vantilt, 2005); Joris Oddens, "De Nederlandse revolutie in dorp en stad. Lokale geschiedschrijving over de Patriots–Bataafse tijd, 1875 tot heden," *Tijdschrift voor Geschiedenis* 130:4 (2017), 565–91.

[2] N. C. F. van Sas, *De metamorfose van Nederland: Van oude orde naar moderniteit, 1750–1900* (Amsterdam: Amsterdam University Press, 2004), 175–253.

[3] Maarten Prak, "Burghers into Citizens: Urban and National Citizenship in the Netherlands during the Revolutionary Era (c. 1800)," *Theory and Society* 26:4 (1997), 403–20; Frans Grijzenhout, Niek van Sas, and Wyger Velema, eds., *Het Bataafse experiment: Politiek en cultuur rond 1800* (Nijmegen: Vantilt, 2013).

[4] Judith Pollmann and Henk te Velde, "New State, New Citizens? Political Change and Civic Continuities in the Low Countries, 1780–1830," *BMGN – Low Countries Historical Review* 133:3 (2018), 4–23.

[5] Paul Brusse and Wijnand Mijnhardt, *Towards a New Template for Dutch History: De-urbanization and the Balance between City and Countryside* (Zwolle: Waanders, 2011), 67–93.

and reached opposing conclusions. This chapter aims to offer a synthesis that takes in these various perspectives.

The Dutch Revolution: A Very Short History

When in 1780 war broke out between the Dutch Republic and Great Britain, this was to many Dutch citizens the last straw that added to existing discontent about economic decline and political degeneration. The prime targets of their indignation were William V, prince of Orange-Nassau and stadtholder of the United Provinces, and his chief advisor, the duke of Brunswick. These citizens, who started calling themselves "Patriots," considered William a pawn of his cousin George III. They were also dissatisfied with the political system that had been created when his predecessor William IV had assumed office in 1747. Since its de facto independence in the sixteenth century, power structures in the Dutch Republic had primarily been organized from the bottom up. City governments had much autonomy. Together with the nobility, they constituted the Provincial States. Sovereignty was believed to reside in these collegial bodies, so the Dutch Republic was really a confederation of seven smaller republics.

In the middle of the eighteenth century, the office of stadtholder had been made hereditary. The stadtholder had obtained a crucial say in the appointment of political officeholders at the local government level. This enabled him to exert great influence on the decision-making process.[6] Traditionally the stadtholders were military commanders of the various provincial armies. The combination of these prerogatives had transformed the stadtholderate into a quasi-monarchical office. William V also behaved like a monarch, and to his supporters, who believed that the House of Orange-Nassau had God-given power to rule, he was nothing short of a monarch.[7] The stadtholderian system favored a political class of patricians, the regents (*regenten*), who strove to maintain the status quo. The system was also supported by part of the intellectual elite, who defended it on ideological grounds.[8] The "Patriot movement" that emerged in the early 1780s attacked the

---

[6] A. J. C. M. Gabriëls, *De heren als dienaren en de dienaar als heer: Het stadhouderlijke stelsel in de tweede helft van de achttiende eeuw* (The Hague: Stichting Hollandse Historische Reeks, 1990).

[7] Donald Haks, "Oranje in veelvoud. De aanhang van de Prins van Oranje, 1747–1780," in Henk te Velde and Donald Haks, eds., *Oranje onder: Populair orangisme van Willem van Oranje tot nu* (Amsterdam: Prometheus Bert Bakker, 2014), 69–89.

[8] W. R. E. Velema, *Enlightenment and Conservatism in the Dutch Republic: The Political Thought of Elie Luzac (1721–1796)* (Assen: Van Gorcum, 1993).

stadtholder, his courtiers, the regent class, and the "Orangist" ideology. Other grievances were shared by specific groups within the movement. These could, for instance, be economic – merchants believed existing policies harmed commerce and trade – or local.

In 1784 the Dutch signed a peace with Great Britain and the much-hated Brunswick resigned, but the conflict between the Patriots and the Orangists (*prinsgezinden*) hardened. As this happened, cracks started to appear in the Patriot movement, which had been a marriage of convenience. These cracks developed into a schism between "Patriot Regents," members of the regent class who wanted to curtail the powers of the stadtholder in order to regain civic autonomy, and "ordinary" Patriots, who demanded more fundamental reforms of the political system. In various cities the second group forced local governments to introduce new local constitutions (*regeringsreglementen*) based on the principle of representative democracy, which disregarded the stadtholder's privileges. For the time being, the confederative structure of the Dutch Republic was not called into question. The Patriots did experiment with supralocal governance by organizing several provincial assemblies and even a national assembly of civic militias.

When the stadtholder, at the request of the Orangist States of Gelderland, intervened with military force in the rebellious Patriot towns of Hattem and Elburg, the Patriot States of Holland responded by suspending William V as military commander of the troops on their payroll. This conflict escalated into open civil war between the troops still under the command of the stadtholder and a Patriot army mostly composed of volunteers dispatched by the many civic militias. The armed conflict was won by the stadtholder due to the intervention of the king of Prussia, his brother-in-law, against whose forces the Patriots did not stand a chance. Thus, the Patriot Revolt ended in 1787.

The Patriot movement went underground in the Dutch Republic and continued abroad in exile, where many Patriots had gone in fear of legal repercussions or popular justice.[9] Most of them ended up in France, where in 1789 the French Revolution broke out. Despite having sprung from very different seeds, the Dutch and French revolutionary movements found considerable common ground.[10] After extensive lobbying by leading

---

[9] Joost Rosendaal, *Bataven! Nederlandse vluchtelingen in Frankrijk, 1787–1795* (Nijmegen: Vantilt, 2003).

[10] Annie Jourdan, *La Révolution batave entre la France et l'Amérique, 1795–1806* (Rennes: Presses universitaires de Rennes, 2015).

Patriots, they formed a military alliance when France declared war on the stadtholder, who in response joined the First Coalition. After several failed attempts, an army of French and Dutch Patriot troops succeeded in invading the Dutch Republic in early 1795. As a result, the weakened stadtholderian system imploded, and the prince of Orange-Nassau fled to England. Until the end of the century, Orangism was to remain outlawed.

The Patriots founded a new republic, which they called the "Batavian Republic," a name inspired by the legendary Germanic tribe of the Batavians.[11] The French right of conquest was bought off. The French kept a close eye on their new ally, but for the time being they mostly refrained from intervening in Dutch internal politics.[12] The new Batavian political establishment was made up of leading figures from the Patriot movement of the 1780s but also a younger generation of revolutionaries.[13] The democratic experiment of the Patriot era was continued and expanded. Representative government was now introduced everywhere at the local – both in towns and in the countryside – as well as the provincial and national levels of government.

With their common enemies gone, internal disagreement in the Patriot movement immediately surfaced. Four topics dominated the public debate: the extent to which repressive actions should be taken against supporters of the old regime; the question whether the confederative Dutch Republic should be transformed into a unitary state; the desired degree of political participation; and the degree to which the Batavian Republic should comply with the demands of its French ally. About these and many other questions, discussions continued throughout the Batavian Revolution (and in most cases also long after that). Some issues were settled already at an early stage. In 1795 Holland issued a declaration of rights that stipulated equality before the law for members of all religious denominations; the other provinces followed Holland's example. This granted Catholics and dissenters access to politics. A year later this equality was also extended to Jews.

In March 1796 the National Assembly (Nationale Vergadering), a much smaller version of the French National Assembly, replaced the States General

---

[11] E. O. G. Haitsma Mulier, "De Bataafse mythe opnieuw bekeken," *Bijdragen en Mededelingen betreffende de Geschiedenis der Nederlanden* 111:3 (1996), 344–76.

[12] Raymond Kubben, *Regeneration and Hegemony: Franco-Batavian Relations in the Revolutionary Era, 1795–1803* (Leiden: Nijhoff, 2011).

[13] A. M. Elias and P. C. Schölvinck, *Volksrepresentanten en wetgevers: De politieke elite in de Bataafs–Franse tijd, 1796–1810* (Amsterdam: Van Soeren, 1991); P. Brood, P. Nieuwland, and L. Zoodsma, *Homines novi: De eerste volksvertegenwoordigers van 1795* (Amsterdam: Schiphouwer en Brinkman, 1994).

in The Hague. It was intended as a temporary assembly with legislative, executive, and constituent powers. While the provinces held on to their sovereign status, the National Assembly succeeded in becoming the most important political arena.[14] The discord in the Patriot movement culminated during the assembly's sessions. After endless debates, the assembly did vote in favor of a draft constitution produced by some of its members, but when the people were left to judge this draft in a referendum, an overwhelming majority rejected it. It took two parliamentary coups to overcome the stalemate this created. The first coup in January 1798 was staged by a radical minority of the National Assembly with the support of the French envoy and generals of the French–Batavian army. After having purged the parliament of their fiercest opponents, the radicals nullified the sovereign status of the provinces and drafted a new constitution in which the principle of unitarism prevailed. This constitution was ratified by the people in a new plebiscite, but only after the primary assemblies where citizens voted had been purged as well. The political purges and other repressive measures caused whatever political support the radical regime had to crumble rapidly.[15] A new coup followed five months after the first, this time staged by remorseful radicals and more moderate revolutionaries, and supported by a different faction within the French government. The new regime maintained the constitution and called for elections for the new, constitutional Representative Body (Vertegenwoordigend Lichaam), a bicameral legislature. A five-man Executive Government (Uitvoerend Bewind) was modeled on the French Directory.

Contrary to what the Patriots had hoped, the establishment of a constitutional regime did not end discord. Different factions continued to passionately oppose each other in the Representative Body. The constitution had decided on a number of crucial issues, but whatever decisions had been taken still needed to be implemented. In the perception of many Patriots, too little progress was made because of the complex legislative procedures prescribed by the constitution.[16] In 1799 the nation was briefly united in defending the country against an Anglo-Russian attack – as an ally of France, the Batavian

---

[14] Joris Oddens, *Pioniers in schaduwbeeld: Het eerste parlement van Nederland, 1796–1798* (Nijmegen: Vantilt, 2012).
[15] Niek van Sas, *Bataafse Terreur: De betekenis van 1798* (Nijmegen: Vantilt, 2011).
[16] Joris Oddens, "Zoeken naar eendracht. Parlementaire vertegenwoordiging in Nederland tot 1815," in Remieg Aerts, Carla van Baalen, Joris Oddens, Diederik Smit, and Henk te Velde, eds., *In dit Huis: Twee eeuwen Tweede Kamer* (Amsterdam: Boom, 2015), 253–77.

Republic continued to be at war with the anti-French coalitions – but when this danger had passed, calls for a new constitution grew stronger.

A majority of the Representative Body opposed such a step, but the parliament was set aside by three members of the Executive Government, who staged a new coup in 1801. For the third time the coup was executed with the support of the French, who were increasingly unhappy about their ally not fulfilling its financial and military obligations. A new constitution largely reversed the introduction of representative democracy, and partly annulled the establishment of the unitary state. From that moment on, France intervened more pervasively in Dutch politics. The constitution of 1801 concluded the revolutionary phase of the Batavian–French period in the history of the Netherlands. This doesn't mean that the reform agenda that originated in the Dutch Revolution was entirely abandoned. Many reformist ideas were adopted, further developed, and implemented under the subsequent regimes of the Batavian Commonwealth (1801–1806), the kingdom of Holland (1806–1810), the incorporation into the French Empire (1810–1813), and the enlightened autocracy of King William I of Orange (after 1813).

Revolutionary Ideas in Theory and Practice

The Patriot movement was deeply rooted in the political thought of the Dutch Republic, but the Patriots also found inspiration in their own age of Atlantic Revolutions. The history of the Dutch Republic is a history of conflicts between the *prinsgezinden* (supporters of a powerful stadtholder) and the *staatsgezinden* (supporters of autonomous cities and sovereign provinces). The Patriot regents of the 1780s were the direct intellectual heirs of the latter party. Their ideology amounted to keeping the stadtholder on a short leash. The demands of the radical wing of the movement went much further.

The ideology of the radical Patriots started to mature in cities such as Leiden and Utrecht in the center of the Dutch Republic. The cities of Deventer and Zwolle in the eastern province of Overijssel also became hotbeds of Patriot radicalism. In Deventer a scholar named Simon de Vries was a central figure in a network that also included future leading revolutionaries such as Joan Derk van der Capellen, Rutger Jan Schimmelpenninck, and Herman Daendels. De Vries had an important library, including many works in English from the British Commonwealthmen tradition. As early as the 1770s, Van der Capellen translated works of Andrew Fletcher and Richard Price into Dutch; later he would also translate Joseph Priestley. These works would prove of crucial importance in the Patriot movement.[17] Their influence was more decisive than that of the French *philosophes*.

In his *Discourse of Government with Relation to Militias* (1697), Andrew Fletcher had argued that civic militias could prevent monarchs from suppressing their own people. He advocated civic militias in which citizens were trained in civic virtues. The idea of civic militias was by no means new in the Dutch Republic; it was even one of its founding principles. The Union of Utrecht, which was entered into by the Northern-Netherlandish provinces against Spanish rule in 1579 and cherished as an unofficial constitution of the Dutch Republic, had prescribed that most adult male urban citizens had to be members of a civic guard. By the end of the eighteenth century the old civic guards still existed, but they had become weak institutions, not least because local governments had considered them a potential threat to their authority. In his pamphlet *Aan het volk van Nederland* (*To the People of the Netherlands*, 1781), which caused a great stir everywhere in the Republic, Van der Capellen called for a revitalization of the old ideal of citizen-soldiers.

Van der Capellen's translations of Price became the go-to texts of the early years of the Patriot era. In his *Observations on the Nature of Civil Liberty*, Price combined the Lockean notion of the inalienability of the sovereignty of the people with the classical republican interpretation of civil liberty, which entailed that a people could be truly free only when it was permanently and actively involved in politics. Price wanted to achieve this by making the existing British representative system more democratic. Nevertheless, his ideal form of government remained a type of mixed government, in which the monarchical and aristocratic elements would continue to have a place. Though the political system of the Dutch Republic was very different, Van der Capellen had a similar interpretation of the Dutch situation. He believed that the Dutch system had once come close to its ideal state, but had since then drifted far from that.[18]

Van der Capellen identified the aristocratic element with the landed nobility to which he himself belonged. In his view, the urban regents were supposed to represent the democratic element, which they could do only if

---

[17] S. R. E. Klein, *Patriots republikanisme: Politieke cultuur in Nederland (1766–1787)* (Amsterdam: Amsterdam University Press, 1995), 78–82.
[18] Wyger R. E. Velema, "Generous Republican Sentiments: The Political Thought of Joan Derk van der Capellen tot den Pol," in Arthur Weststeijn, ed., *A Marble Revolutionary: The Dutch Patriot Joan Derk van der Capellen and His Monument* (Rome: Palombi, 2011), 39–65.

they were elected and held to account by the people. According to Van der Capellen, the regents currently behaved as if they formed the aristocratic element. The stadtholder, while representing in Van der Capellen's view the monarchical element of the mixed constitution, had far exceeded the limits of his legitimate authority. He therefore wanted to restrict the power of the regents and the stadtholder to restore the balance in the mixed constitution.

A constitutional restoration was also advocated in the two most important political creeds of the Patriot movement, *Grondwettige herstelling* (*Constitutional Restoration*, 1784–1786) and the text best known as the *Leids Ontwerp* (*Leiden Draft*, 1785), both written by multiple authors. Historians disagree regarding whether the Patriots at the time of publication of these texts, after Van der Capellen's untimely death, still believed that they were restoring a situation that had really existed in the past.[19] What is clear is that the system of representative democracy they wanted to introduce at the local level of government was entirely new, because until then the underlying notions of popular sovereignty and political representation had had a different meaning in the political theory of the Dutch Republic.[20] The urge to disguise democratic reform as constitutional restoration disappeared after the suppression of the Patriot Revolt. Thomas Paine's *Rights of Man* (1791–1792) played a decisive role in this development: the Dutch translation was at the top of the reading lists of the underground Patriot movement. According to Paine, the only acceptable form of government was based on the principle of electoral representation. He rejected all hereditary government as well as all forms of mixed government.

During the restoration years, (the political thought of) the French Revolution also became a point of reference. Perhaps the most profound rupture with the Dutch intellectual tradition was that many Patriots started to believe that the doctrine of "unity and indivisibility," which the French revolutionaries had inherited from their old-regime predecessors, would also

---

[19] Stephan Klein and Joost Rosendaal, "Democratie in context. Nieuwe perspectieven op het Leids Ontwerp (1785)," *Documentatieblad Werkgroep Achttiende Eeuw* 26:1 (1994), 77–100; Maarten Prak, "Citizen Radicalism and Democracy in the Dutch Republic: The Patriot Movement of the 1780s," *Theory and Society* 20:1 (1991), 73–102; W. R. E. Velema, *Republicans: Essays on Eighteenth-Century Dutch Political Thought* (Leiden: Brill, 2007), 186–8.

[20] E. H. Kossmann, "Popular Sovereignty at the Beginning of the Dutch Ancien Regime," *Low Countries History Yearbook* (1981), 1–28; Martin van Gelderen, *The Political Thought of the Dutch Revolt, 1555–1590* (Cambridge: Cambridge University Press, 2002), 199–207.

The Modernity of the Dutch Revolution

Figure 13.1 The Committee of the Confederacy. Print, possibly by James Gillray, after David Hess. Satirical representation of the discord between the seven provinces during the first year of the Batavian Revolution (1795), which did not look so different from the situation in the old-regime Dutch Republic. Collection Rijksmuseum Amsterdam, BI-B-FM-096-17. Courtesy of Rijksmuseum.

have to become the leading doctrine in the Dutch Republic, and that the Dutch confederacy would have to be transformed into a unitary state. Many other Patriots did not share this goal. For them the essence of the Union of Utrecht, which was intended as a union between sovereign states, should remain intact (Figure 13.1).

What was true for the ideal state type was equally true for many other items on the reform agenda: the Patriots deeply disagreed among themselves about how profound the rupture with the old regime would have to be. With respect to the 1780s, Rousseau's skepticism about the adequacy of electoral representation resonated more, both among "federalists," who longed for the old system of representation with a binding mandate, and among democratic radicals, who demanded that the people not only be able to cast their vote, but be given the power to initiate binding referendums in between elections. For the time being, however, a majority remained of the opinion of the leading moderate Schimmelpenninck, who had already in the

Patriot era rejected this aspect of Rousseau's thinking and expressed his confidence in representative democracy.[21]

For Roman Catholics, Jews, and Protestant dissenters such as Remonstrants and Mennonites, the Batavian Revolution was an emancipatory moment.[22] Secular Patriots wanted to confine religion to the private domain and ban any display of religion in the public sphere. Non-Dutch Reformed citizens as well as Dutch Reformed activists wanted the state to stop paying the salaries of Dutch Reformed clerics and to distribute church properties more evenly. Their efforts were undermined by a Dutch Reformed majority that was reluctant to give up the privileged status of its Church.[23] In parliament many deputies advocated a long transitional period. Antipapism and antisemitism continued to pervade Dutch society.[24]

Many Patriots at the central level of government wished to do away with the corporatism and particularism of the old regime, but this was easier said than done. The guilds remained a driving force of the Patriot movement in the early 1780s. Leading Patriots, such as Van der Capellen, had already considered the guilds an outdated institution at the time, but they had also realized that they could not do without their grassroots support. In the Batavian Republic the guilds fought for their survival, as did the local poor-relief institutions of the various churches – here the different denominations were in agreement.[25] The guild system was abolished in the 1798 constitution, which also stipulated the nationalization of the poor-relief system, but in the first case implementation would take many years and in the second it

---

[21] Mart Rutjes, *Door gelijkheid gegrepen: Democratie, burgerschap en staat in Nederland, 1795–1801* (Nijmegen: Vantilt, 2012), 45–6.

[22] H. J. M. van der Heijden, *De dageraad van de emancipatie der katholieken: De Nederlandsche katholieken en de staatkundige verwikkelingen uit het laatste kwart van de achttiende eeuw* (Zundert: Vorsselmans, 1947); Simon Vuyk, *De verdraagzame gemeente van vrije Christenen: Remonstranten op de bres voor de Bataafse Republiek (1780–1800)* (Amsterdam: De Bataafsche Leeuw, 1995); R. G. Fuks-Mansfield, "Verlichting en emancipatie omstreeks 1750–1814," in J. C. H. Blom, Rena Fuks-Mansfield, Ivo Schöffer et al., eds., *Geschiedenis van de Joden in Nederland* (Amsterdam: Balans, 1995), 177–203.

[23] W. H. den Ouden, *Kerk onder patriottenbewind: Kerkelijke financiën en de Bataafse Republiek, 1795–1801* (Zoetermeer: Boekencentrum, 1994).

[24] R. G. Fuks-Mansfeld, "Kezen en smousen in 1787. De moeizame verhouding tussen patriotten en Joden in Amsterdam," in Th. S. M. van der Zee, J. G. M. M. Rosendaal, and P. G. B. Thissen, eds., *1787: De Nederlandse revolutie?* (Amsterdam: De Bataafsche Leeuw, 1988), 134–45; Edwina Hagen, *"Een meer of min doodlyken haat": Antipapisme en cultureel natiebesef in Nederland rond 1800* (Nijmegen: Vantilt, 2008).

[25] C. Wiskerke, *De afschaffing der gilden in Nederland* (Amsterdam: H. J. Paris, 1938); P. A. B. Melief, *De strijd om de armenzorg in Nederland, 1795–1854* (Groningen: J. B. Wolters, 1954).

was never executed. Attempts to centralize and standardize institutions such as the tax system proved equally challenging. By contrast, the languid East Indies Company was nationalized. Other national institutions, such as the National Library (the later Royal Library) and the National Art Gallery (the later Rijksmuseum) were founded in the Batavian era.[26]

There were also domains in which neither the Patriot Revolt nor the Batavian Revolution made major changes. The Patriots referred to 1795 as "the first year of Batavian liberty," but unlike the French did not introduce a new calendar. The judiciary and the education system were not fundamentally reformed.[27] Within the Batavian political elite there was almost unanimous consensus about the continued exclusion of women from the formal sphere of politics, although this did not prevent women from participating in informal ways.[28] In theory many revolutionaries supported the abolition of slavery and the slave trade, but in practice they did absolutely nothing to achieve it.[29]

A final issue that needs addressing here is the Dutch revolutionary generation's attitudes toward the classics. The political thought of the early Patriot era was deeply classically republican, as the belief in armed citizens and mixed government demonstrates. As the idea of representative democracy was being put into practice, ancient political theory became less directly applicable to the situation the revolutionaries found themselves in. Even so, the classical republican emphasis on the need for civic virtue to protect the republic against the ever-present danger of moral degeneration remained a

---

[26] Jan Postma, *Alexander Gogel (1765–1821): Grondlegger van de Nederlandse staat* (Hilversum: Verloren, 2017); G. J. Schutte, *De Nederlandse patriotten en de koloniën: Een onderzoek naar hun denkbeelden en optreden, 1770–1800* (Groningen: Tjeenk Willink, 1974); Ellinoor Bergvelt, *Pantheon der Gouden Eeuw: Van Nationale Konst-Gallerij tot Rijksmuseum van Schilderijen (1798–1896)* (Zwolle: Waanders, 1998); N. C. F. van Sas, "Barbarisme of beschaving. Rondom de stichting van een Nationale Bibliotheek in 1798," *Jaarboek voor Nederlandse Boekgeschiedenis* 4 (1997), 57–74.

[27] M. W. van Boven, *De rechterlijke instellingen ter discussie: De geschiedenis van de wetgeving op de rechterlijke organisatie in de periode 1795–1811* (Nijmegen: Gerard Noodt Instituut, 1990), 276–7; Martijn van der Burg, *Nederland onder Franse invloed: Culturele overdracht en staatsvorming in de napoleontische tijd, 1799–1813* (Amsterdam: De Bataafsche Leeuw, 2009), 149–52.

[28] Miriam Everard, "In en om de (Nieuwe) Bataafsche Vrouwe Courant. Het aandeel van vrouwen in een revolutionaire politieke cultuur," *Mededelingen van de Stichting Jacob Campo Weyerman* 24 (2001), 67–80; Elisa Hendriks and Joris Oddens, "Bataafse vrouwen, politieke rechten en het digitaliseringsproject Revolutionaire Petities: Twee onbekende verzoekschriften uit het jaar 1799," *Holland* 52:1 (2020), 11–19.

[29] Pepijn Brandon, "Shrewd Sirens of Humanity: The Changing Shape of Pro-slavery Arguments in the Netherlands (1789–1814)," *Almanack* 14 (2016), 3–24.

crucial frame of reference in the Batavian Republic.[30] In a broader, cultural sense classical antiquity continued to be a source of inspiration and a vehicle for social distinction for those with a classical education, who could be found in all camps during the revolutionary era.[31] Stoic philosophy provided solace to the victims of the revolution, even if, as a model of emotional conduct, it encountered competition from the eighteenth-century cult of sensibility.[32]

The Repertoire of Contention

What was the contentious repertoire of the Dutch Revolution? In a general sense the revolution's tools and actions were not radically different from those of the old regime, but they developed more rapidly during the revolutionary era, both with respect to the "normal" period that preceded it and with respect to earlier moments of political crisis. The developments can be summarized under the headings of politicization, professionalization, and scaling-up. Changes and innovations did not remain confined to the revolutionary camp: in many cases, counterrevolutionary forces saw no option but to copy the strategy of their adversaries.

Much of the action of the Dutch Revolution came in the guise of, or was produced by, voluntary associations. In the second half of the eighteenth century, cultural societies flourished in the Dutch Republic as they did elsewhere. In the 1770s, future Patriots continually came across each other in literary societies and Masonic lodges.[33] Initially they frequented these associations together with those who would later side with the Orangists. Prerevolutionary sociability, then, did not necessarily function as a

---

[30] Jan Rotmans, "Enlightened Pessimism: Republican Decline in Dutch Revolutionary Thought, 1780–1800" (Ph.D. dissertation, University of Amsterdam, 2020), 174–85.

[31] W. R. E. Velema, "Conversations with the Classics: Ancient Political Virtue and Two Modern Revolutions," *Early American Studies* 10:2 (2012), 415–38; Mart Rutjes, "'Niet geheel applicabel op deze tijd'. De Klassieke Oudheid in het politieke discours van de Bataafse Republiek, 1795–1801," in Alexander J. P. Raat, Wyger R. E. Velema, and Claudette Baar-De Weerd, eds., *De Oudheid in de Achttiende Eeuw* (Utrecht: Werkgroep 18e Eeuw, 2012), 75–86; Amber Oomen-Delhaye, *De Amsterdamse schouwburg als politiek strijdtoneel: Theater, opinievorming en de (r)evolutie van Romeinse helden (1780–1801)* (Hilversum: Verloren, 2019).

[32] Joris Oddens, "Emotional Self-Fashioning in the Age of Revolution: Stoicism and Sensibility as Models of Emotional Conduct," in Marc H. Lerner and Alexander Mikaberidze, eds., *Selected Papers of the Consortium on the Revolutionary Era 2014* (Shreveport: Louisiana State University Press, 2018), 1–20.

[33] Marleen de Vries, *Beschaven! Letterkundige genootschappen in Nederland, 1750–1800* (Nijmegen: Vantilt, 2002); Joost Rosendaal, "Vrijmetselarij en Revolutie," in Joost Rosendaal and Anton van de Sande, eds., *'Een stille leerschool van deugd en goede zeden': Vrijmetselarij in Nederland in de 18ᵉ en 19ᵉ eeuw* (Hilversum: Verloren, 1995), 63–84.

democratic laboratory. The associations were indeed meeting places, but in this they were not unique. In Leiden, for instance, future Patriot leaders such as Pieter Vreede and François Adriaan van der Kemp were members of the same cultural societies, but they also belonged to the same commercial, religious, and family networks.

After 1780 latent tensions within associations politicized and escalated into open conflicts. As a result, many associations became Patriot- or Orangist-only organizations. The topics that were discussed also became more political. Existing supralocal networks that had developed because citizens were (honorary) members of societies in multiple cities could now be put to political use. A new type of association emerged around 1783: throughout the Dutch Republic, voluntary civic militias were founded both in cities and in the countryside. These societies were partly modeled on (an idealized image of) the old civic guards, but the Patriots were also inspired by enlightened military ideas.[34]

In establishing new militias, local Patriots answered the repeated calls of periodicals such as *De Post van den Neder-Rhijn* (*The Nether-Rhine Mail*, 1781–1787) and *De Politieke Kruyer* (*The Political Porter*, 1782–1787).[35] These thoroughly political periodicals were a new phenomenon. The format was similar to that of the spectatorial genre, which enjoyed great popularity in the eighteenth-century Dutch Republic. Spectators had offered mild and sometimes more biting social critique, but unlike the political periodicals had not openly attacked the authorities.[36] Another popular genre in the revolutionary era was the satirical periodical, which also used genre conventions familiar to the reader to convey more political messages.[37] Besides these periodical formats, newspapers prospered as well: traditionally outlets for foreign news, they now became strongly partisan media that commented on national events and voiced the opinions of either the Patriot or the Orangist camp.

---

[34] Frans Grijzenhout, *Feesten voor het Vaderland: Patriotse en Bataafse feesten 1780–1806* (Zwolle: Waanders, 1989), 56–7; Olaf van Nimwegen, *De Nederlandse burgeroorlog, 1748–1815* (Amsterdam: Prometheus, 2017), 94–109; Renée Vulto, "Singing Communities: Politics of Feeling in Songs of the Dutch Revolutionary Period (1780–1815)" (Ph.D. dissertation, Ghent University, 2022), 53–102.

[35] P. J. H. M. Theeuwen, *Pieter 't Hoen en "De post van den Neder-Rhijn" (1781–1787): Een bijdrage tot de kennis van de Nederlandse geschiedenis in het laatste kwart van de achttiende eeuw* (Hilversum: Verloren, 2002); Pieter van Wissing, ed., *Stookschriften: Pers en politiek tussen 1780 en 1800* (Nijmegen: Vantilt, 2008).

[36] P. J. Buijnsters, *Spectatoriale geschriften* (Utrecht: HES, 1991).

[37] Ivo Nieuwenhuis, *Onder het mom van satire. Laster, spot en ironie in Nederland, 1780–1800* (Hilversum: Verloren, 2014).

The combination of partisanship and periodicity offered new opportunities. Before the Patriot era the pamphlet had been the favored medium for political ends. Pamphlets continued to appear in the revolutionary era, and incidentally played a decisive role in the public debate, but the periodical surfaced as the dominant genre. Even more than pamphlet series, periodicals enabled the Patriots to repeat their key message over and over again. Periodicals were also a business model, so numerous hacks entered this market. Against the many Patriot periodicals, there was a smaller number of Orangist ones, some of which received financial support from the circles of the stadtholder.[38]

After the suppression of the Patriot movement, political periodicals were banned. In their stead new spectators were founded. During the restoration years, the Patriots writing these spectators operated at the edge of what was still tolerated. Most of the cultural societies continued to exist but outwardly returned to their core business. Below the surface they continued to be Patriot meeting places. In Amsterdam members of the cultural society Doctrina et Amicitia created a secret revolutionary committee that became the nerve center of the underground Patriot movement. The committee took the initiative for the founding of a network of reading societies, where citizens read and discussed the work of Paine and the highly influential *Verhandeling over de vrage: In welken zin kunnen de menschen gezegd worden gelyk te zyn?* (*Treatise on the Question: In What Sense Can People Be Said to Be Equal?*, 1793) by the Dutch lawyer Pieter Paulus.

When the Patriots got their chance to overthrow the stadtholderian regime in early 1795, they relied on this infrastructure of societies and revolutionary committees. It also laid the foundations for the dense network of political associations that was to characterize the Batavian Republic. The political sociability of the Batavian era was a multilevel phenomenon. At the urban level, the reading societies were transformed into political clubs. The larger cities witnessed the creation of neighborhood assemblies that built on older structures of neighborhood autonomy. In Amsterdam, neighborhoods sent delegates to a Central Assembly of Neighborhood Assemblies. Similarly, and following the example of the Patriot era, delegates of local political clubs met in provincial and national central assemblies.[39] The Batavian authorities

---

[38] P. W. van Wissing, *In louche gezelschap: Leven en werk van broodschrijver Philippus Verbrugge (1750–1806)* (Hilversum: Verloren, 2018).

[39] R. E. de Bruin, "Democratie in Utrecht 1795–1798," *Tijdschrift voor Geschiedenis* 92 (1979), 377–90; Pepijn Brandon and Karwan Fatah-Black, "'The Supreme Power of the People': Local Autonomy and Radical Democracy in the Batavian Revolution

were suspicious of such initiatives, which they considered a challenge to their authority. At the same time, leading revolutionaries considered political sociability a prerequisite of a free republican state and used it to mobilize support.[40] In 1797, when the moderate and radical camps in the National Assembly campaigned for and against the constitutional draft at issue in the referendum, they relied on rival networks of political clubs for the dissemination of their views.[41]

When the Patriots rose to power in 1795, the political periodicals returned. Titles such as *De Republikein* (*The Republican*, 1795–1797), *De Democraten* (*The Democrats*, 1796–1798), and *De politieke blixem* (*The Political Lightning*, 1797–1798) were written by well-informed authors in high circles, but they constituted the tip of the iceberg of the countless spectatorial, satirical, and newspaper-like periodicals that appeared in the Batavian Republic with a local, regional, and often also national distribution.[42] A new and influential periodical was the *Dagverhaal*, which strove to give a verbatim account of the national parliament's sessions.

From the moment of their emergence in the early 1780s, political sociability and the political press formed a trinity with political petitioning. In the Dutch Republic petitioning had always been a popular form of action, but during the revolutionary era it transformed in important ways. As long as their demand for representative democracy had not been met, the Patriots believed that petitioning was as close as one could get to exercising popular sovereignty. The Patriots thus had a more inclusive attitude toward petitioning than the old-regime elites on all sides of the political spectrum, who had concurred that the political instrument of petitioning should be used with moderation and preferably only by the more distinguished members of a community. Patriots employed the instrument with greater frequency and their language was less deferential. They also started collecting more signatures than had been deemed appropriate under the old regime. Their

---

(1795–1798)," *Atlantic Studies* 13:3 (2016), 370–88; Peter Altena, *Gerrit Paape (1752–1803): Levens en werken* (Nijmegen: Vantilt, 2012), 454–84.

[40] René Koekkoek, *The Citizenship Experiment: Contesting the Limits of Civic Equality and Participation in the Age of Revolutions* (Leiden: Brill, 2019), 219–27.

[41] H. de Lange, "De Gemeenebestgezinde burgersocieteit te Den Haag, 1797–1798," *Jaarboek geschiedkundige vereniging Die Haghe* 1 (1970), 42–81; Thomas Poell, "The Democratic Paradox: Dutch Revolutionary Struggles over Democratisation and Centralisation (1780–1813)" (Ph.D. dissertation, Utrecht University, 2007), 91–6.

[42] Erik Jacobs, "Hartslag van een Revolutie. Pers en politiek in de Bataafse Republiek (1795–1802)" (Ph.D. dissertation, University of Amsterdam, 2020).

subscriptional efforts were facilitated through circulation of petitions in political clubs and publicization of petition drives in periodicals.[43]

While local petitions remained the bread and butter of petitionary practices during the Patriot era, political petitions to provincial and national authorities were on the rise. An important precedent was created in 1782, when John Adams and some of his Patriot associates in Leiden launched a petition campaign intended to get Adams recognized as the official American envoy to the Dutch Republic, which would amount to recognizing the United States as an independent state. Local Patriots – including many merchants seeing trade opportunities – submitted petitions to their local governments, but also directly to the Provincial States and the States General. This trend culminated in the Batavian era, when the national parliament became the most important recipient of petitions, even if the issues addressed by these petitions continued to be local in many cases. Petitions concerned with provincial or national issues were often drawn up in the ranks of radical political clubs, but the petitions that got most signatures came from opponents of the revolutionary reforms.[44]

The contentious repertoire discussed so far includes actions that were overwhelmingly initiated and regulated by a revolutionary elite that founded political clubs, wrote and published pamphlets and periodicals, drew up petitions, and canvassed for signatures; a much larger part of the population frequented clubs, read political texts, and signed petitions. In addition to this activity, the Dutch Revolution witnessed much action that seems to have been less orchestrated: local, collective action of a ritualistic or charivariesque nature, which for those involved carried a deeper symbolic meaning. Such action usually resulted from a conviction that the authorities had fallen short in preserving the moral order of the local community, which in the eyes of members of this community justified taking the law into their own hands. Their behavior therefore mirrored that of the established authorities, sometimes by mocking them in parades or street theater, often by challenging their monopoly on authority and violence. Mobbing, extortion of money or goods (popular taxation), targeted attacks against the symbols of the opposing party (such as the tombs of members of the House of Orange-Nassau or the liberty trees of the Patriots), and plundering formed part of this

---

[43] Joris Oddens, "The Greatest Right of Them All: The Debate on the Right to Petition in the Netherlands from the Dutch Republic to the Kingdom (c. 1750–1830)," *European History Quarterly* 47:4 (2017), 634–56.

[44] Joris Oddens, "Verzoekschriften aan het Bataafse parlement. Een terreinverkenning," *Jaarboek Parlementaire Geschiedenis* 19 (2017), 19–30.

The Modernity of the Dutch Revolution

Figure 13.2 Grim festivities in Rotterdam. Print by Reinier Vinkeles after Jacobus Buys. Depiction of a riotous procession of Orangist shipwrights, led by a figure dressed as a Harlequin, on 8 March 1783, the birthday of Stadtholder William V. Collection Rijksmuseum Amsterdam, RP-P-OB-64.135. Courtesy of Rijksmuseum.

repertoire. Incidents were more likely to happen on public holidays, such as the Feast of Saint Nicholas (as in The Hague in 1782) or the birthday of the stadtholder (as in Rotterdam in 1783) (Figure 13.2).[45]

Historians have usually paid less attention to this type of contention because it is firmly rooted in a tradition of early modern popular culture and awkwardly fits the narrative that considers the age of revolutions the cradle of modernity. The reality is, however, that we find such action

[45] E. H. A. H. Palmen, "Oranjebitter. De smalle gemeente van Rotterdam in de partijstrijd tussen de patriotten en de orangisten," *Rotterdams Jaarboekje*, 10th series, 2 (1994), 243–93; Jouke Nijman, "Politieke cultuur en volkscultuur in de patriottentijd," *Groniek* 30:137 (1996–1997), 417–31.

throughout the Dutch Revolution and on both sides of the revolutionary spectrum. Around 1787, for instance, there were many instances of plundering on both the Patriot and the Orangist sides. In May a Patriot crowd in Amsterdam plundered, on the island of Kattenburg, various pubs where Orangist shipwrights gathered. These actions provoked reactions when in the autumn of 1787 Orangists got the upper hand. In Amsterdam, the Orangist shipwrights responded with large-scale plundering of houses of well-to-do Patriots. They also organized festivities, including large processions, to celebrate the stadtholderian restoration.[46]

In the first year of the Batavian Revolution, an armed group of Patriots in Rotterdam showed up at inns that were frequented by Orangists and the houses of innkeepers who worked at these places. They left a trail of destruction and carried along with them as trophies Orangist symbols.[47] The Batavian period also witnessed outbursts of Orangist collective action. In 1797 the countryside of northeast Friesland, which had a tradition of popular unrest, witnessed the so-called "revolt of Kollum" (*Kollumer oproer*).[48] An inhabitant of this village who hindered the registration for conscription in a civic guard was arrested. That night thousands of armed Frisians attacked Kollum and surrounding villages. The anger of the crowd was directed at specific members of the community. In Kollum their main target was a local Patriot leader. Rioters physically abused him and his family and plundered his house and possessions. As it turned out, the rage of the crowd was partly inspired by the moral conduct of this local Patriot. He apparently mistreated his domestics, including a maid who was the daughter of the leader of the attackers. As well as being politically motivated, the attack also had the characteristics of a traditional charivari against immoral behavior. Similar ambiguity can often be witnessed: local grievances with prerevolutionary origins got tied up with new antagonisms created by ideological differences of opinion.[49]

---

[46] I. J. van Manen and K. Vermeulen, "Het lagere volk van Amsterdam in de strijd tussen patriotten en oranjegezinden 1780–1800 II," *Tijdschrift voor Sociale Geschiedenis* 31 (1981), 3–43: 25–7.

[47] R. A. D. Renting, "Orangisten en Orangisme te Rotterdam na de Bataafse Republiek II," *Rotterdamsch Jaarboekje*, 7th series, 3 (1965), 195–221: 199–200.

[48] Jacques Kuiper, *Een revolutie ontrafeld: Politiek in Friesland 1795–1798* (Franeker: Uitgeverij Van Wijnen, 2002), 256–98.

[49] M. M. Romme, "Charivari en patriottisme. Een nieuw perspectief," in G. Rooijakkers, A. van der Veen, and H. de Wit, eds., *Voor "Brabants Vryheyd": Patriotten in Staats-Brabant* (Den Bosch: Stichting Brabantse Regionale Geschiedbeoefening 1988), 105–21.

A Total Revolution?

Throughout its existence, the Dutch Republic had a power structure that included elements also present in other states, but in its totality was unique in the world. This lack of older and contemporary models allowed different state actors to all have their own interpretation of the balance of power. In the seventeenth century the locus of sovereignty had remained contested. Since the early eighteenth century, the dominant doctrine had been that it resided with the Provincial States, but what this meant in practice varied from province to province. Civic republicanism continued to loom large: urban regents still considered the cities over which they ruled autonomous city republics of sorts, even if, since the middle of the eighteenth century, the stadtholder could strategically intervene in local politics using his powers of appointment.

The local government in the cities was oligarchic, but in the countryside it tended toward absolutism. Ownership of noble titles and estates was hereditary; the same was true for the seminoble seigneurial titles and seigneuries (*heerlijkheden*), but they were tradable as well. The individuals and (in the case of the seigneuries) corporations that owned these titles and lands were minisovereigns. So were the owners of the so-called "free seigneuries," which were located within the territory of the Dutch Republic, but did not belong to it. Many of these microstates had over the years come into the possession of the prince of Orange-Nassau, who was, for instance, Lord of IJsselstein, duke of Culemborg, and count of Buren. The fact that the stadtholder derived his status as a sovereign lord not only from his foreign titles and possessions strengthened his position of power within the Dutch Republic. The domains of the stadtholder were governed by stewards and by a domain council (*Domeinraad*) in The Hague. Similarly, the States General governed the Generality Lands (*Generaliteitslanden*), including the large region of States-Brabant. This means that the States General, the Provincial States, the prince of Orange, the lesser nobles, and the seigneurial lords (often urban citizens or city governments) all imagined themselves to be sovereigns in the eighteenth-century Dutch Republic.

Government was often collegial, from guild boards and minor offices in the city government to the States General. Even if power was formally vested equally in each of the members of a collegial body, there were in practice great power imbalances, caused by traditions of precedence and seniority or by differences in economic strength. Notorious conflicts of power existed between Amsterdam and the other cities in the States of

Holland and between Holland and most other provinces in the States General, but such rivalry could be found everywhere in the Dutch Republic and at all levels of government. Besides, many parts of the Dutch Republic lacked formal representation at the supralocal level. This was the case for the Generality Lands and for the region (*landschap*) of Drenthe, but there were also many cities that were denied representation in the Provincial States. Noble estates were theoretically represented if their owners had a seat in the provincial knighthoods (*ridderschappen*), the colleges of nobles that constituted, together with the cities, the Provincial States. The seigneuries, which made up the lion's share of the countryside, were not represented at the provincial level at all. The free seigneuries weren't either, but they at least reserved the right to ignore laws issued by provincial authorities, allowing them a special status that brought them considerable benefit, but irritated the provinces surrounding them.

The Dutch Revolution was to become a revolution against this system in all its aspects. Joan Derk van der Capellen, who as a baron had a seat in Overijssel's knighthood, used this position in the late 1770s to give a voice to inhabitants of the Overijssel countryside who stood up against the so-called *drostendiensten* (seigneurial labor): nobles who held the office of steward (*drost*) claimed to have the right to constrain farmers to work for them for two days a year. The knighthood punished Van der Capellen for his activism by suspending him as a member. The matter became national news because of a series of pamphlets that Van der Capellen published together with the Leiden-based Mennonite minister François Adriaan van der Kemp. Later this collaboration would result in the publication and wide distribution of *To the People of the Netherlands*. During Van der Capellen's lifetime, his authorship of this pamphlet was known only to his immediate circle, but because of his endeavors in Overijssel, he was nevertheless widely recognized as a hero of the early Patriot movement.[50]

The seigneurial labor controversy also revived an old conflict about the relative weight of the votes of the cities and the knighthood in the States of Overijssel. Both of these issues were at the top of the agenda of the local Patriots in various Overijssel cities in the early 1780s. In Deventer and Zwolle these Patriots created "citizen committees" (*burgercommissies*) that were probably inspired by the local committees of the American Revolution. After the mid-1780s, when these issues were settled and Van der Capellen

---

[50] M. de Jong, *Johan Derk van der Capellen: Staatkundig levensbeeld uit de wordingstijd van de moderne demokratie in Nederland* (Groningen: J. B. Wolters, 1922).

had died, the committees focused more on reforming the local government structure. In 1785 both citizen committees filed petitions to their respective city governments, signed by a large part of the citizenry. They requested an end to the stadtholder's right of nomination and wanted to leave the appointment of new members of the city government to the Common Council (*Gezworen gemeente*), an old representative institution typical of the eastern provinces. The members of the Common Council would have to be elected by the citizenry rather than coopted by the Council itself. The petitioners, in short, advocated a form of representative democracy.[51]

The example of Overijssel shows that discontents about power structures at different levels – the remnants of the feudal system in the countryside, the disproportionate power of the nobility in the Provincial States, the urban oligarchy, and the privileges of the stadtholder – could get entangled with one another, and individual Patriots could become champions of multiple causes. The example also shows that the Patriot movement was not a monolithic bloc. In Zwolle, for instance, the city government sided with the citizen committee as long as this had the city's interests in the Provincial States at heart. However, when the committee wanted to change the local constitution, citizens and regents found themselves on opposing sides. When we shift our perspective to the smaller cities of Overijssel, such as Ootmarsum, Almelo, Oldenzaal, or Hardenberg, we find that in each of these cities the local Patriot movement was differently composed and had slightly different aims.[52]

The Patriot movement was not received with equal enthusiasm everywhere in the Dutch Republic. All of the provinces had their Patriot strongholds and their Orangist refuges, as well as localities where the population was relatively indifferent to the revolution.[53] In some rural areas passions ran high, but what was at stake seems to have been a long-running tribal conflict rather than an ideological divide dating to the revolutionary era itself: rival factions in a village sided with the Patriots or with the Orangists, but more particularly *against* each other, or the entire population of one

---

[51] W. Ph. Te Brake, *Regents and Rebels: The Revolutionary World of an Eighteenth-Century Dutch City* (Cambridge, MA: Blackwell, 1989).
[52] M. A. M. Franken and R. M. Kemperink, eds., "Herstel, hervorming of behoud? Tien Overijsselse steden in de Patriottentijd, 1780–1787," special issue *Overijsselse Historische Bijdragen* 99 (1984).
[53] G. J. Schutte, *Een Hollandse dorpssamenleving in de late achttiende eeuw: De banne Graft 1770–1810* (Franeker: Van Wijnen, 1989); S. W. Verstegen, *Gegoede ingezetenen: Jonkers en geërfden op de Veluwe tijdens Ancien Régime, Revolutie en Restauratie (1650–1830)* (Zutphen: Walburg Pers, 1990).

village sympathized with one camp because the people of a neighboring town politically or economically dwarfing them supported the other.[54] Elsewhere the conflict between Patriots and Orangists was primarily experienced as a religious conflict. Orthodox Calvinists in the countryside of Zeeland, in the strip of land now known as the Dutch Bible Belt, saw the Patriot movement as a violation of the God-given social order and therefore as an attack on the Dutch Reformed religion itself, and responded by engaging in mass-scale plundering after 1787.[55] In the 1790s, the overwhelmingly Roman Catholic region of States-Brabant witnessed a wave of religiously inspired symbolic violence by Catholic Patriots. In many villages these Patriots plundered the local churches, which were in use by a Protestant minority. With desacralization rites, they demonstrated their resentment against the Calvinist ruling elite.[56]

In the Batavian Republic, the existing power structure was turned on its head right from the start. At the urban level the oligarchic governments were replaced by new provisional administrations. This local regime change cannot be understood without taking into account the older Dutch tradition of *wetsverzettingen* (literally, replacements of the law), local regime changes which had been imposed by the stadtholder during the political crisis years 1618, 1672, and 1748. While these earlier regime changes had been top-down affairs, the new Batavian establishment did not shy away from steering things in the right direction either. In villages and towns with a Patriot majority, it was left to the locals to elect a new government by acclamation, but communities that were not prone to revolutionize themselves were forced to do so under threat of political or military intervention. The free seigneuries were incorporated into the provincial structure against the will of the population.[57] Thus, Orangist communities ended up with Patriot governments without popular support. Later local elections were organized, and the

---

[54] Tom Nieuwenhuis, "Keeshonden en Prinsmannen. Durgerdam, Ransdorp en Holisloot: Drie waterlandse dorpen in de Patriottentijd en de Bataafs–Franse tijd" (Ph.D. dissertation, University of Amsterdam, 1986); Joost Rosendaal, *Tot nut van Nederland: Polarisatie en revolutie in een grensgebied, 1783–1787* (Nijmegen: Vantilt, 2012).

[55] P. T. van Rooden, "De plunderingen op Schouwen en te Zierikzee, 1786–1788," *Archief van het Koninklijk Zeeuwsch Genootschap der Wetenschappen* (1983), 173–99.

[56] J. G. M. M. Rosendaal and A. W. F. M. van de Sande, eds., *Dansen rond de vrijheidsboom: Revolutionaire cultuur in Brabant en de Franse invasie van 1793* (Den Bosch: Stichting Brabantse Regionale Geschiedbeoefening, 1993), 276–7.

[57] A. P. van Schilfgaarde, "De incorporatie van het graafschap Buren 1795–1814," *Bijdragen en Mededeelingen* 38 (1935), 249–75; A. J. van Weel, *De incorporatie van Culemborg in de Bataafse Republiek* (Zutphen: Walburg Pers, 1977).

provisional governments were replaced by established ones. If supporters of the old regime were prepared to serve in office under the new central government, it was not always easy for the Patriots to keep them from doing so if they were democratically elected by an overwhelmingly Orangist local population.

In early 1795 the revolutionized cities sent delegates to the provincial capitals, where the Provincial States were replaced by assemblies calling themselves Provisional Representatives of the People (*Provisionele Representanten van het Volk*). After elections had been held at the provincial level as well, they changed their name to Provincial Administration (*Provinciaal Bestuur*). In these provincial assemblies, both cities without provincial representation under the old regime and countryside districts were now represented. Voting no longer happened by city but by head. The provincial assemblies in turn sent delegates to the States General. For the time being, this institution continued to exist, and the principle of one province, one vote was maintained. Patriots in States-Brabant and Drenthe formed their own assemblies that immediately started lobbying to get their regions recognized as new provinces.[58]

Their emancipatory efforts were rewarded when the States General made way for a democratically elected National Assembly to which Brabant and Drenthe could send deputies on an equal footing (according to population size) with the seven provinces that had been represented in the States General. The establishment of the National Assembly meant the introduction of representative government at the national level. This had been a wish of the unitarist wing of the Patriot movement, but it was only one battle won in the struggle for the unitary state. In most provinces besides Holland as well as in the powerful Holland city of Amsterdam, many citizens feared loss of political autonomy and influence. Moreover, it would be to the disadvantage of most provinces if the provincial debts were amalgamated, as the debts of Holland were sky high (which was caused, the Hollanders claimed, by military expenditure employed to defend the Republic as a whole).[59]

---

[58] A. R. M. Mommers, *Brabant van Generaliteitsland tot gewest: Bestuursinrichting en gezagsuitoefening in en over de landen en steden van Staats-Brabant en Bataafs-Brabant, 14 september 1629–1 maart 1796*, 2 vols. (Utrecht: Dekker & Van de Vegt, 1953); J. Spoelman, "Van landschap tot gewest (Drenthe in de patriottentijd)," *Nieuwe Drentse Volksalmanak* 84 (1967), 1–57.

[59] L. S. Godefroi, "De eerste fase van de financiële unificatie van Nederland (1796–1801)" (Ph.D. dissertation, Erasmus University Rotterdam, 1986); J. M. F. Fritschy, *De patriotten en de financiën van de Bataafse Republiek: Hollands krediet en de smalle marges voor een nieuw beleid (1795–1801)* (The Hague: Stichting Hollandse Historische Reeks, 1988).

In the National Assembly, deputies on the federalist spectrum of the Patriot movement continued to advocate provincial sovereignty whenever they got the chance. Even after the radical regime of 1798 had formally subordinated the provinces to the central government, they persisted in their rhetoric of provincial identity and autonomy. In an ultimate attempt to break this particularistic spirit, the provinces were replaced by departments with different names and different borders. This proved not to be a magic bullet either: the departmental reorganization was reversed in 1801.[60]

As it was more top-down and more systematic, the Batavian Revolution had a wider impact than the Patriot Revolt; every inhabitant of the republic was exposed to its effects, at least to some degree. Yet there remained large differences in responsiveness: reforms such as granting citizenship to Jews, ending the privileged status of the Dutch Reformed Church, or abolishing the guilds were supported by a majority of the enlightened elite in the National Assembly, but not by society at large. As in the Patriot era, revolutionary enthusiasm varied greatly from place to place, and historically determined animosities within and between towns and villages continued to loom large.

Conclusion

How profoundly would someone living in the Netherlands around 1800 perceive the world around them to have changed with respect to two decades earlier? In 1799, when he wrote the introduction to his adaptation of an early work by Benjamin Constant, Jacob Hahn observed that many once-enthusiastic citizens had grown disillusioned with the Dutch Revolution. According to Hahn, a leading member of the National Assembly in the first years of the Batavian Republic, they had expected more immediate results, but how, he asked, "was it possible to plow, sow, mow, and harvest all at once?"[61] Three years later, Cornelis Sorgdrager, a Mennonite lay preacher who lived on the small island of Ameland, one of the remotest places in the

---

[60] H. A. Kamphuis, *Stad en Lande tijdens de Bataafse Republiek: Bestuurlijke en gerechtelijke verhoudingen in Groningen, 1795–1807* (Assen: Van Gorcum, 2005); Joke Roelevink, "Van provisioneel bestuur tot constitutionele tekentafel. Gewestelijke herindeling van Holland in de Bataafs-Franse tijd," in F. W. Lantink and J. Temmink, eds., *Holland: Geschiedenis en archieven van provincie(s) en gewest* (Hilversum: Verloren, 2014), 37–53.

[61] Quoted in Joris Oddens and Mart Rutjes, "Scenario voor een voltooide revolutie. Jacob Hahns bewerking van Benjamin Constants *Des réactions politiques* (1799)," in Frans Grijzenhout and Peter Raedts, eds., *Deze lange eeuw: Metamorfosen van het vaderland 1780–1950: Opstellen voor Niek van Sas* (Amsterdam: Prometheus Bert Bakker, 2015), 51–64: 56.

country, wrote an entry in his diary. For Sorgdrager, like most of his fellow islanders a staunch Orangist, the revolution had been an utterly traumatizing experience, but now he felt to his great relief that "everything slowly seems to be returning to the old ways of government."[62] The insider Hahn and the outsider Sorgdrager both saw a revolution that had not (yet) produced irreversible results. For Hahn the revolution had been only a beginning, and more work was needed to reap its benefits. Sorgdrager, who wrote after the counterrevolution of 1801, hoped that the revolution had been a temporary aberration.

Looking at the Dutch Revolution from a historical distance, we cannot but conclude that it had a deep and lasting impact on the political life of the Dutch Republic. This was certainly the case for Catholics, Jews, Brabanders, and rural dwellers, among other groups, because they were accepted, for the first time since Dutch independence, as full citizens. More generally, the higher degree of political participation and the introduction of public access to government entirely changed the dynamics of citizen–ruler interactions. A large proportion of the population took part in primary assemblies to vote for referendums and elections, frequented political clubs, and engaged with the decision-making process in other ways. These novelties were not there to stay. After 1800, they would be viewed with suspicion for decades to come. Yet, their memory could not be banned from people's minds.

That said, there were also many inhabitants of the Dutch Republic who largely remained outside the political domain. This could be because they were actively excluded, as was the case for Orangists, women, and those living in the colonies, but it could also be the result of a self-imposed stance of noninvolvement. Just over a third of the citizens eligible to vote in the plebiscites about the constitutional drafts of 1797 and 1798 effectively voted. This means two-thirds did not.[63] Between 1796 and 1801, the Batavian legislative assemblies received on average 3,000 petitions per year. No representative institution in the history of the Netherlands has ever received more, but relatively few of these petitions were submitted by large collectives who addressed political issues, suggesting that the majority of the population never signed a political petition to the parliament. Many Dutch Reformed inhabitants probably signed only once, after they had been told to

---

[62] Quoted in Joris Oddens, "The Experience of State Formation: Chronicling and Petitioning on the Dutch Island of Ameland (c. 1780–1815)," *National Identities* 22:1 (2020), 1–22: 11.

[63] Jos de Jong, *Democratie in kinderschoenen: Twee referenda over de eerste Nederlandse grondwet, 1797–1798* (Nijmegen: Vantilt, 2018).

do so from the pulpit, resulting in the largest petition by far of the revolutionary era. Its approximately 215,000 signatories threatened to reject the constitutional draft if the privileged status of their Church was violated. It remains difficult to say what the Dutch Revolution meant to this thus far understudied silent majority. Perhaps they understood it as a sign that the end of times was near.[64] Compared with such an event, any worldly revolution was, of course, small beer.

---

[64] R. H. Kielman, "In het laatste der dagen. Eindtijdverwachting in Nederland op de drempel van de moderne tijd (1790–1880)" (Ph.D. dissertation, Leiden University, 2017).

14
The United States of Belgium

JANET POLASKY

The "Army of the Moon" routed Austrian troops and chased them from Brussels across the border of the Austrian Netherlands to Luxembourg. Women on the rooftops showered the fleeing soldiers with paving stones, and men fired from their windows. The Austrians were so surprised by the strength of this ragtag army that they speculated it had to be otherworldly. By noon on 12 December 1789, they were forced to admit the facts. "The bourgeois and volunteers are masters of the city," they were forced to report back to Vienna.[1] All of Europe was stunned. How had the militia raised from peasants and artisans throughout the Belgian provinces defeated the professional armies mustered by the Austrians?

One of the leaders of the Brabant Revolution, the Brussels lawyer Henri van der Noot, and his mistress, Jeanne de Bellem, having declared the independence of the Belgian provinces from Austrian rule, processed triumphantly into the new capital of the United States of Belgium. With city buildings illuminated to celebrate their victory, Van der Noot was crowned with laurel and heralded as "the Belgian Washington."[2] Van der Noot and his deputy, a canon from Antwerp, Pierre van Eupen, explained the victory as a miracle. Like the Israelites thousands of years earlier, they argued, God had led the Belgians, His chosen people, to victory. "God visibly blessed an enterprise whose purpose was to avenge religion and laws," Van der Noot proclaimed in his letter to the assembled delegates of the United Estates of Belgium.[3] The Belgians were the most loyal Catholics left in a Europe ravaged by Enlightenment skepticism.

---

[1] 12 December 1789, IV DD B blau 50a (17), Haus-Hof und Staatsarchiv, Vienna. See also "Relation exacte de la prise de Bruxelles par ses habitans" (Brussels, 1789), Varia Belgica, M-7, Maurits Sabbebibliotheek, Katholieke Universiteit Leuven, Louvain, Belgium.
[2] *Esprit des Gazettes* 20 (25 December 1789), 511; *Journal de Bruxelles* 1 (8 January 1790), 56.
[3] C. F. François and Henri van der Noot, "Lettre au Congrès" (5 March 1790), in L. P. Gachard, *Documens politiques et diplomatiques sur la Révolution belge de 1790* (Brussels: H. Rémy, 1834), 204.

Catholicism was the basis of the governing of the Belgian provinces, in 1787 as it had been for centuries. The leaders of the three Estates of the central Brabant provinces, for example, explained the endurance of their medieval constitution, the Joyeuse Entrée, as a demonstration that it had been divinely inspired. For centuries, the Belgians had kept their faith, and honored the clergy as the first of the three Estates. In their struggle with the Austrians, a revolutionary Abbé told them, "You have just served as the instruments enlisted by God to punish the ungodly desecration and persecution of our Holy Religion . . . Yes! I repeat, it is the God of Armed Might who called on you to carry out His designs, who filled your enemies with terror and gave strength to a small number of sheep to drive away a large number of wolves driven by rage and wrath."[4]

There was another explanation for the victorious Brabant Revolution. It was offered by the general recruited to lead the revolutionary armies, Jean-André van der Mersch, and by the revolutionary leaders who had armed and drilled the Belgian troops, and led them into battle. The quest for liberty, defined as the exercise of their natural rights and their traditional privileges, had led the Belgians to throw off the yoke of the Austrian rulers. Beginning with the visit of the newly crowned emperor, Joseph II, to the Belgian provinces in 1781, the Belgians had fought to defend their sovereignty from Austrian tyranny.

Enlightened Inspiration

Joseph II inherited the Austrian Netherlands from his mother, the beloved Maria Theresa.[5] The editor of the *Journal générale d'Europe* hailed Joseph as a revolutionary who would enlighten the backward Belgian provinces.[6] His subjects in the Belgian provinces contested that designation. As their opposition to his reforms developed, they claimed the heritage of the Enlightenment for themselves. They were fighting for their natural rights, for their sovereignty as a free people.

---

[4] "Godefroi, par la grace de Dieu, Abbé de Tongerloo, Supérieur Spirituel des troupes belgiques etc. À tous ses Aumoniers, Officiers, Lieutenants etc." (Brussels), in *Révolution belge*, vol. VI, pamphlet 2, Bibliothèque Royale/Koninklijke Bibliotheek, Brussels.

[5] On Joseph II, see Derek Beales, *Joseph II, vol. II: Against the World, 1780–1790* (Cambridge: Cambridge University Press, 2009); Timothy Blanning, *Joseph II* (London: Longman, 1994); Walter Davis, *Joseph II: An Imperial Reformer for the Austrian Netherlands* (The Hague: Nijhoff, 1974); Jan Roegiers, "De Nederlandse Kerkpolitiek van Jozef II: Verlicht of despotisch?," *Documentatieblad Werkgroep Achttiende Eeuw*, 49 (February 1981), 39–50.

[6] *Journal générale d'Europe* 341 (3 January 1786), 23.

The United States of Belgium

The Belgian provinces had been ruled by the Austrian Habsburgs since 1713, and before that by the Spanish. The Austrian emperor reigned in the ten provinces as duke of Brabant, Luxembourg, Gelderland, and Limbourg, count of Flanders, West Flanders, Namur, and Hainaut, and lord of Mechelen and Tournai according to the terms of the medieval provincial constitutions. The constitutions provided protection for the provinces that in turn voted the emperor his taxes twice a year, in March and October. The government institutions varied by province. The provincial judicial councils retained the power to petition the sovereign to protest his decisions. The membership of the representative Estates also differed from province to province. An advisor to both Maria Theresa and her son Joseph II explained, "Governed according to their own laws, assured of the control of their property and their personal liberty, paying only moderate taxes that they impose on themselves, the Belgians enjoy the precious gifts of a free constitution."[7] That constitution assured them the protection of a powerful empire and established the Estates as a check to guard their rights against transgressions. Even though the Belgian national anthem recalls "centuries of slavery," in the eighteenth century, that was not the way that most Belgians would have seen foreign rule, until Joseph II ascended the throne.

The new emperor visited the Belgian provinces in the summer of 1781, the first sovereign to travel to Brussels since Philip II's visit in 1559. He apparently did not heed his mother's advice. She had warned him that Belgian customs differed significantly from what he knew, but the Austrian Netherlands as "the only happy country ... that has given us so many resources" should not be troubled. While attached to "their old, even ridiculous prejudices, they are obedient and contribute more than our German lands that are irritated and unhappy."[8]

The Belgian provinces were one of the most prosperous and urban territories in Europe. Trade flourished, as did industry. After steam engines were introduced to pump water from the mines, coal mining took off, as did the metal industries in the southern provinces. Chambers of commerce were established in Bruges and Ghent, and a commercial academy opened in Ghent. Nobles invested in cotton manufacturing and sugar refining in Antwerp, and linen production spread throughout the Flemish countryside.

---

[7] Wenzel Anton von Kaunitz, cited by Théodore Juste, *Histoire des États Généraux des Pays Bas, 1465–1790* (Brussels: Bruylant-Christophe, 1864), vol. I, 122.

[8] Maria Theresa to Joseph II, 22 July 1789, in Alfred Ritter von Arneth, ed., *Briefe der Kaiserin Maria Theresia an ihre Kinder und Freunde* (Vienna: Braumüller, 1881), vol. I, 3.

Visitors noted the intensive agriculture on smallholdings. The Austrian Netherlands had the highest population density of Europe. All the ingredients for an industrial revolution were to be found there by the end of the eighteenth century.

Joseph visited sawmills and factories, and inspected army garrisons, hospitals, and schools, instead of attending formal receptions. In Antwerp, instead of staying at the Prinsenhof Palace, he found rooms at the Hôtel du Grand Laboureur. He left Brussels, disguised under a large overcoat, before the new governors-general of the Austrian Netherlands, namely his sister Marie Christine and her husband Albert, could receive him. He refused to kneel on the customary velvet cushion to watch the traditional procession of the Holy Blood in Bruges and ordered clothes painted on Van Eyck's triptych of Adam and Eve hanging in St. Baaf's Cathedral in Ghent.

Resistance to the Austrian emperor rallied from many quarters, beginning in the Catholic Church.[9] He attempted to rein in the authority of the Catholic Church by issuing a Patent of Toleration, by declaring nine religious

---

[9] For the history of the Brabant Revolution, see Pierre Delsaerdt and Jan Roegiers, *Brabant in Revolutie, 1787–1801* (Leuven: Centrale Bibliotheek KU Leuven, 1988); Luc Dhondt, "La cabale des misérables de 1790. La révolte des campagnes flamandes contre la Révolution des notables en Belgique (1789–1790)," *Études sur le XVIIIe Siècle* 7 (1980), 107–34; Luc Dhondt, "De conservatieve Brabantse Omwenteling van 1789 en het proces van revolutie en contrarevolutie in de Zuidelijke Nederlanden tussen 1780 en 1830," *Tijdschrift voor Geschiedenis* 102 (1989), 411–50; Jane Judge, *The United States of Belgium: The Story of the First Belgian Revolution* (Leuven: Leuven University Press, 2018); Théodore Juste, *La Révolution Brabançonne* (Brussels: Lebègue et Cie., 1884); Johannes Koll, *Die belgische Nation: Patriotismus und Nationalbewusstsein in den Südlichen Niederlanden im späten 18. Jahrhundert* (Münster: Waxmann, 2003); Johannes Koll, ed., *Nationale Bewegungen in Belgien: Ein historischer Überblick* (Münster, Waxmann, 2005); Eric Mielands, "De publieke opinie ten tijde van de Brabantse Omwenteling. Een comparatief onderzoek tussen Brabant en Vlaanderen," *Belgisch Tijdschrift voor Nieuwste Geschiedenis/Revue belge d'histoire contemporaine* 26:1–2 (1996), 5–32; Henri Pirenne and Jérôme Vercruysse, *Les États Belgiques Unis: Histoire de la révolution belge de 1789–1790* (Paris: Duculot, 1992); Janet Polasky, "Traditionalists, Democrats and Jacobins in Revolutionary Belgium, 1787–1793," *Journal of Modern History* 41:2 (1984), 227–64; Janet Polasky, *Revolution in Brussels, 1787–1793* (Brussels: Académie royale de Belgique, 1986); Suzanne Tassier, *Les démocrates belges de 1789: Étude sur le Vonckisme dans la révolution brabançonne* (Brussels: Marcel Hayez, 1930); Yvan vanden Berghe, *Jacobijnen en traditionalisten: De reacties van de Bruggelingen in de revolutietijd (1780–1794)* (Brussels: Pro Civitate, 1972); Geert van den Bossche, *Enlightened Innovation and the Ancient Constitution: The Intellectual Justifications of Revolution in Brabant (1787–1890)* (Brussels: Koninklijke Vlaamse Academie van België voor Wetenschappen en Kunsten, 2001); Hugo van de Voorde, Pierre Delsaerdt, Louis Preneel, Karel Veraghtert, and Mark D'Hoker, *Bastille, Boerenkrijg, en Tricolore: De Franse Revolutie in de Zuidelijke Nederlanden* (Leuven: Davidsfonds, 1989); Stijn van Rossem, *Revolutie op de koperplaat: Repertorium van prenten tijdens de Brabantse Omwenteling (1787–1792)* (Leuven: Peeters, 2014).

orders "useless," by inventorying the "excessive" church treasures, by refusing to fill church vacancies, and by building his own General Seminary to be staffed not with Jesuits, but with his handpicked Jansenists. The respected editor of the *Journal historique et litéraire*, an ex-Jesuit, the Abbé François Xavier de Feller, warned that the new seminary would introduce the subversive ideas "of this perverse century that is so corrupted by crimes."[10] A flurry of pamphlets came to the defense of Belgian Catholicism as the most faithful branch of the church, now under attack from Austrian infidels and skeptics. The pamphleteers vowed to restore the "primitive rights of the people."[11]

Next, Joseph's administrative and judicial reforms that threatened to take authority away from traditional provincial judicial institutions and centralize them in Vienna brought out the lawyers. The Conseil de Justice and the Estates of the central province of Brabant charged in a treatise, written by their counsel, Henri van der Noot, that the proposed judicial reorganization violated Belgian sovereignty. The emperor had usurped authority not given him under the terms of the Joyeuse Entrée. In the *Mémoire*, Van der Noot reminded Joseph II that, as duke, he had entered into a contractual relationship with the Estates, the rightful representatives of the people. The Estates of Namur also cited their "constitutional Pact" with the emperor, who had sworn to protect their constitution.[12] The Flemish Estates did not condemn the emperor's reforms themselves, but objected to his method of imposing them in violation of their constitution.

Not all of the judiciary and its lawyers were invested simply in defending their traditional privileges. Thirty lawyers signed a petition to the Estates arguing that sovereigns either governed according to the terms of a constitution or they reigned by conquest. Joseph ignored the limits imposed on his authority by the constitution, and therefore, according to its terms, had

---

[10] "Documents pour la Révolution brabançonne," Mss. RII 3255, Bibliothèque Royale/ Koninklijke Bibliotheek, Brussels.

[11] "Mémoire des États," 17 July 1789, États Belgiques Unis 186, Archives générales du Royaume/Algemeen Rijksarchief, Brussels. Among the several histories of the Estates and the movement led by Van der Noot, see Janet Polasky, "Providential History in Belgium at the end of the Eighteenth Century," *Revue belge de philologie et d'histoire* 54 (1977), 416–24; Jan Roegiers, "Un janséniste devant la Révolution," in F. Stevens and E. Van den Auweele, eds., *Houd voet bij stuk: Xenia jurishistoriae G. van Dievoet oblata* (Leuven: Katholieke Universiteit Leuven, Faculteit der Rechtsgeleerdheid, 1990), 75–103; Jan Roegiers, "P. S. Van Eupen (1744–1804): Van ultramontaan tot revolutionair," in P. Lenders, *Het einde van het Ancien Régime in België: Colloquium van zaterdag 3 december 1988 te Brussel/La fin de l'ancien régime en belgique: Colloque du samedi 3 décembre 1988 à Bruxelles* (Kortrijk: UGA, 1991), 263–328.

[12] "Représentation des États de Namur à Leurs Altesses Royales, à Bruxelles" (May 1787), cited by Judge, *The United States of Belgium*, 87.

broken his contract. "When the Sovereign, in defiance of his Oath & of the Rights of man, infringes on the Rights of the People, his Sovereign Authority should be suspended until he resolves his infractions, & if he does not, it falls to the Representatives of the People, intervening according to the Law, to declare his authority suspended in conformity with what he swore in his oath in the Joyeuse Entrée."[13] Sovereign authority would thereby flow to the Estates.

Hailed by foreign journalists as an enlightened reformer, Joseph was attacked within the Belgian provinces as an arbitrary tyrant. One of Joseph's strongest supporters when he ascended the throne, the lawyer Charles Lambert d'Outrepont, posited that the Belgians had long been a free people. The Joyeuse Entrée clearly delineated the rights and mutual contractual obligations of the Belgian people and their sovereign. Under its provisions, the provinces had flourished for centuries. He asked whether the emperor, alone, could decide what was in the best interest of the people, concluding that Joseph was treating the Belgians as slaves in imposing reforms.[14] Pamphleteers in what became known as "the little Brabant revolution" compared him to the Spanish monarch Philip II, against whom the Dutch had fought for their independence in the sixteenth century. Like Joseph's supporters, they cited the *philosophes*, especially Rousseau.

A number of pamphleteers cast the Belgian people as the enlightened ones fighting for liberty. They freely cited Enlightenment philosophers, especially Voltaire, Mably, Montesquieu, and Rousseau, predicting that the Belgians would write new laws for their society to promote their common interests and to protect their natural rights.[15] The Belgians, they added, were echoing the Americans, fighting to protect their constitutional rule against a foreign ruler who did not understand the interests of his distant subjects. Joseph II resembled George III, they argued, and their Joyeuse Entrée was not so different from the Magna Carta. D'Outrepont was convinced, "Never has an enlightened people better understood the dignity of man and the value of civil liberty. Almost everywhere we can see the continuous struggle between

---

[13] "Avis signé par trente Avocats du Brabant au Conseil souverain," 19 May 1787, in *Révolution belge* 61, Bibliothèque Royale/Koninklijke Bibliotheek, Brussels.

[14] Charles Lambert d'Outrepont, "Considérations sur la Constitution des Duchés de Brabant et Limbourg" (23 May 1787), *Révolution belge* 35, pamphlet 13, Bibliothèque Royale/Koninklijke Bibliotheek, Brussels.

[15] Peter Illing, "Montesquieu's Shadow: Debating Reform in the Austrian Netherlands," *History of European Ideas* 35:3 (2009), 330–6.

a throne secured by force, & liberty supported by the voice of nature & the authority of law."[16] In a short poem, Van der Noot's mistress, Jeanne de Bellem, urged the readers of her pamphlet: "Belgian People/ Tyrannical Court/ Do just like the Americans."[17]

Revolutionary War

Facing increased resistance from the Estates and from the people who took to the streets in a number of cities, the Austrian governors-general, Maria Christine and Albert, capitulated, promising to withdraw all of Joseph's edicts that contradicted the constitution. They had been complaining to Joseph about his reforms and his refusal to yield to Belgian objections. The emperor was supposed to rely on them for governance of the Belgian provinces, but he kept ignoring his sister, as he had his mother. Furious, Joseph called the governors-general back to Vienna. Rumors spread through the provinces that Joseph would increase their taxes and institute military conscription. Neither concessions nor threats tamped down the escalating insurrection in the Belgian provinces.

Van der Noot called an emergency meeting of the heads of the "nine Nations" – the Brussels guilds – and of the five Serments – the middle-class guard groups – and a few "notables." The assembled leaders called on the bourgeoisie to take up arms. Austrians reporting to the emperor noted an increase in unrest in Brussels in response, especially in cafes and taverns.

In January 1788, angered by the growing Belgian resistance, Joseph sent General Alton, who had recently suppressed resistance in Hungary, to Brussels.[18] Alton ordered the Brabant Conseil d'État to publish the emperor's edicts or face cannon fire. A crowd gathered in the Grand Place awaiting the Conseil's response and heckling the assembled Austrian troops. Soldiers fired into the crowd, killing several people. Alton commended his troops and basked in victory when the Conseil relented, publishing the edicts in question. Alton disbanded the civilian guard, ordered the Austrian soldiers to remain in place, and banned incendiary journals. The Belgians would be treated as a conquered people and enlightenment would be imposed from above.

---

[16] D'Outrepont, "Considérations sur la Constitution."
[17] Jeanne de Bellem, "Préliminaires de la Révolution 1787–1789," États Belgiques Unis 1, Archives générales du Royaume/Algemeen Rijksarchief, Brussels.
[18] See Chapter 19 by Orsolya Szakály in this volume.

Joseph turned his attention to another center of resistance, the medieval Louvain University where students and faculty had blocked every effort at reform. The faculties of law, philosophy, and medicine were to be transferred to Brussels, where they would be under the supervision of the Austrian governors. Ignoring the explicit ban on their assembly, the Brussels guilds, the so-called Nations, gathered and addressed a petition to the Brabant Estates. They maintained that the university, as a Brabant institution, was subject to the Estates, not the emperor. The Third Estate accepted the petition and accordingly refused to vote the emperor his taxes, while the first two Estates buckled under the pressure. The Third Estate had veto power. Wined and dined by the Austrians, who promised concessions, the Third Estate finally relented, and again, after a confrontation, the emperor received his tax monies from the Austrian Netherlands.

Acting on the reports of his spies, Joseph ordered seditious pamphlets publicly burned on a bonfire in the Grand Place in July. He issued arrest warrants for the suspected authors and for the known leaders of the insurrectionary movement. While Van der Noot fled to London, the Austrians imprisoned Jeanne de Bellem, the author of many of the pamphlets, as well as Jean Joseph Saegermans, a haberdasher and leader of the Nations, and Henri Goffin, a lawyer. Even without their leaders, the insurgency continued to grow.

In November 1788, the provincial Estates assembled for their twice-yearly debate about the emperor's taxes. The emperor had vacillated between threats and overtures to his Belgian subjects. The Brabant Third Estate appealed to the first two Estates to stand firm in their defense of their constitution. De Bellem wrote to Van der Noot, still in exile, that the first two Estates, "although they have eyes, ears, and mouths, see nothing, hear nothing, and say nothing."[19] Van der Noot chided them for their cowardice. Were they afraid of a popular resistance movement?

One arose anyway. After the Third Estates of the provinces of Brabant and the Hainaut voted to refuse the emperor his taxes in November 1788, while Namur and Luxembourg acquiesced to the Austrians' demands, Flanders, led by the city of Ghent, boldly refused to grant its taxes until the emperor stopped abusing its constitution. In January 1789, the emperor sent troops into the center of Brussels, and, under Alton's command, they fired into the crowds, killing several demonstrators. Fearful, the Brabant Third Estate

---

[19] Jeanne de Bellem, Goethals 210, Bibliothèque Royale/Koninklijke Bibliotheek, Brussels.

capitulated. News filtered down from the second-floor meeting rooms to the crowds assembled in the Grand Place below. That night, someone posted a "death notice" announcing: "The legitimate heirs of Liberty, of the Privileges & of the valor of the Belgians, announced the death of their Grandmother, the Joyeuse Entrée, as well as its ancestor the Brabant Constitution, both cruelly assassinated, Monday 26 January 1789."[20]

Joseph pressed his advantage and ordered seminary students to attend the opening of the new Séminaire générale in Louvain to be presided over by the Archbishop of Mechelen, one of its earliest opponents. His probing questions during the opening session infuriated the emperor. Joseph announced his plans to change the membership of the Third Estate, with the promise that blood would be shed if necessary, moved more troops into Brussels, and ordered the Estates to vote him a permanent tax subsidy, as well as to sanction the establishment of a new judicial order and the weakening of the Conseil de Brabant. Troops were stationed just outside the doors of the Estates meeting. When the Third Estate refused to go along with this imposition and publish his edicts, Joseph announced that he would henceforth rule the provinces himself and that their medieval constitutions were no longer in force. He effectively ended centuries of representative government in the Belgian provinces. He also closed the door to legal remonstrance.

Having named himself minister plenipotentiary of the Estates, Van der Noot requested military assistance from the Triple Alliance – the Dutch, English, and Prussian governments – to launch a military campaign against the Austrians. They did not take the presumptuous Belgian envoy seriously, even as he suggested that the Austrians were taking money from the Belgians to launch attacks on the neighboring powers. What would they do if they were victorious, the Dutch asked Van der Noot. Even his offer to crown the second son of the Prince of Orange the Belgian ruler if they won their independence did not move the neighboring powers. William Pitt refused to meet with him in England, and Van der Noot returned to the Netherlands, taking up residence in Breda near the border with the Austrian Netherlands.[21]

---

[20] "Billet mortuaire," 26 January 1789, Écrits politiques du XVIIIe siècle 60, 367, Archives générales du Royaume/Algemeen Rijksarchief, Brussels.

[21] For more on the diplomatic relations with Prussia, England, and the Netherlands, see L. P. van de Spiegel, *Résume des négociations qui accompagneront la révolution des Pays Bas autrichiens* (Amsterdam: J. Müller, 1841); Henri van der Noot, "Réflexions sur les troubles des Pays Bas autrichiens," Manuscrits divers, 2519, Archives générales du

The odds seemed to be stacked against the Belgian struggle for independence. It appeared rather ridiculous. "The idea of five Prussian regiments commanded by lawyer Van der Noot should make Your Majesty laugh," the Austrian Minister Plenipotentiary advised the emperor. "They talk about 60,000 men as if so many soldiers will arise from the earth and then go dine at the cabaret, because they have made no preparations, collected no ammunition or provisions."[22] He did not know about the other prong of popular resistance activity that was gathering strength.

In the spring of 1789, a coterie of lawyers, financiers, merchants, and a few nobles, increasingly frustrated by the halting nature of the Estates' resistance against the Austrians, organized a secret revolutionary committee, Pro Aris et Focis (For Hearth and Home). Charter members included the lawyers Jan Vonck, Jan Baptist Verlooy, J. J. Torfs, and Jacques Dominique 't Kint, the wine wholesalers Antoine d'Aubremez and J. B. Weemaels, and the city engineer Claude Fisco.[23] Impressed by the resilience and persistence of their compatriots' growing protests, Pro Aris et Focis appealed to their fellows "of whatever rank or condition" to join a revolution.[24] In founding Pro Aris et Focis, Jan Baptist Verlooy, suggested, "Three million Belgians are groaning in slavery... and among them we can find at least seven thousand angry men who will fight by our side."[25] They did. Men signed up and reported, with weapons, for drills. Austrian soldiers were also convinced to desert. They also swore themselves and new recruits to secrecy to protect themselves from Austrian spies. They would together mount a resistance against the Austrians.

Royaume/Koninklijk Archief, Brussels; Johannes Hubertus Post, *De Driebond van 1788 en de Brabantse Revolution* (Bergen op Zoom: Drukkerij van Gebr. Juten, 1961).

[22] Trauttmansdorff, 14 and 15 August 1789, in Hans Schlitter, ed., *Geheime Correspondenz Josefs II mit seinem Minister Trauttmansdorff* (Vienna: Holzhausen, 1902), 349, 352.

[23] Biographies of the leaders of the so-called Belgian democrats are more numerous than studies of Van der Noot's cadre. See Jean Bouchary, "Les manieurs d'argent sous la Révolution française: Le banquier Édouard de Walckiers," *Annales historiques de la Révolution française* 15 (1938), 133–55; Jan C. A. de Clerck, *Jean-François Vonck: Juriste et chef démocrate de la Révolution Belgique (1743–1792)* (Brussels: Hayez, 1992); Suzanne Tassier, *Figures révolutionnaires* (Brussels: La Renaissance du Livre, 1942); Vanden Berghe, *Jacobijnen en traditionalisten*; Jan van den Broeck, *J. B. C. Verlooy, vooruitstrevend jurist en politicus uit de 18de eeuw, 1746–1797* (Antwerp: Standaard, 1980).

[24] Charles Terlinden, ed., "Les souvenirs d'un Vonckiste. Les aventures de J. B. Vanderlinden ou détails circonstanciés sur la Révolution de Brabant," *Bulletin de la Commission royale d'Histoire* 96 (1932), 101–254: 118–19. See also Mss. 19648, p. 124, Bibliothèque Royale/Koninklijke Bibliotheek, Brussels.

[25] J. B. C. Verlooy, cited by Suzanne Tassier, *Figures révolutionnaires* (Brussels: La Renaissance du Livre, 1942), 90.

Pro Aris et Focis did not question the intent of Joseph's reforms but challenged his imposition of new institutions and laws without consulting the Belgian people. Their constitution provided legal means for implementing change. The emperor had refused to abide by the terms of their constitution. Like George III and Louis XVI, Joseph II had trampled on the natural and civil rights of his subjects.[26] Following the example of the Americans and now the French, the Belgian people should banish the tyrant and reclaim the sovereignty that rightfully belonged to them. Significantly, they added, unlike the French, who had had to establish constitutional rule from the ground up, the Belgians had but to reestablish theirs. "We are positioned one hundred times better than the French to regain our liberty because we have a fixed & permanent Constitution, something that is still in doubt in France," they asserted.[27]

Pamphlets appeared throughout the Belgian provinces, as if out of nowhere, Austrian spies complained to the emperor. Cafes were filled with men and women talking about the fall of the Bastille. The Austrians should be worried about the growing unrest, journalists suggested, because it was the Belgians who had set the example for the French in their 1787 resistance. Joseph confided to his sister his worries about the most prosperous of his territories. "French drunkenness comes from champagne that is quick but light and dissipates easily, while that of the Brabançons comes from beer that is tenacious."[28]

Jan Vonck, one of the leaders of Pro Aris et Focis, approached colonel Van der Mersch, who had distinguished himself in the Austrian army, but retired to the Flemish village of Dadizeele, about leading their troops. At the end of August 1789, together with other members of Pro Aris et Focis, Vonck discussed revolutionary strategy with Van der Mersch, who had come to the meeting disguised as a hunter, for nine hours. To convince Van der Mersch, Vonck liberally cited from Rousseau about common purpose. Agreed on the urgency of their cause, they concluded that what they needed was a safe place outside Austrian reach to train the forces they were raising.

---

[26] "Antiochus Erboren ofte het gedrag der Nederlanders gerechtveerdigt door het recht van God, van den natuer, van de volkeren, ende van de borgelyke wetten" (1789), *Révolution belge* 5, pamphlet 19, Bibliothèque Royale/Koninklijke Bibliotheek, Brussels.

[27] "Trompette anti-autrichienne," *Révolution belge* 102, pamphlet 20, Bibliothèque Royale/Koninklijke Bibliotheek, Brussels.

[28] Joseph II to Marie Christine, as cited by Frans van Kalken, *Histoire de Belgique* (Brussels: J. Lebegue & Cie., 1924), 165. On the governors-general, see Eliane van Impe, *Marie-Christine van Oostenrijk, Gouvernante-Generaal van de Zuidelijke Nederlanden 1781–1789; 1790–1792* (Heule: UGA, 1979).

They found that in Hasselt on the territory of Liège, as offered by the mayor of Liège.

The two groups leading the Belgian resistance, Pro Aris et Focis and the Breda Committee, were well aware of each other's existence, but continued to work separately. Nevertheless, there was substantial overlap, with artisans especially going back and forth between them. Saegermans, a haberdasher from Van der Noot's inner circle, accompanied Weemaels and the notary De Coster of Pro Aris et Focis, leading a contingent of aspiring soldiers from Brussels to Liège to buy guns and ammunition. Other members of the Breda Committee joined Vonck and Verlooy and their friends at the salon run by the comtesse d'Yves and in cafes. Comtesse Anne Thérèse Philippine d'Yves, a prolific and insightful pamphleteer herself, gathered an informal salon in the Brussels house she shared with her mother.[29] When the Austrians arrested a number of revolutionary leaders, the mayor of Brussels warned her to be discreet. She arranged confidential meetings to bring together members of the Estates with the leaders of Pro Aris et Focis.

Young men eager to volunteer for the military resistance traveled to Breda, not having learned of the training grounds in Liège. Van der Noot and the Estates were the more public leaders of the resistance. Van der Noot turned them away. Whether there was actual hostility between the two committees remains a matter of debate. Clearly, there were differences in their revolutionary goals, if not their actual grievances against the Austrians. The men gathered around Van der Noot in Breda wanted to restore the medieval constitutions and reestablish the rule of the three Estates. Instead of natural rights, they referred to "the eternal rights of man," meaning something quite different from the enlightenment ideal. Instead of the "rights of the People," they referred to the privileges of the "nation belge," as if it were an organic entity that owed its unrivaled prosperity to "privileges ... liberty ... and the constitution that they have enjoyed for several centuries."[30] The membership of the two groups differed, the Breda Committee being made up of men and women from privileged positions, whereas Pro Aris et Focis was led by educated and wealthy men outside of the governing circles. Whether these differences proved decisive, or were limited to

---

[29] Janet Polasky, "Women in Revolutionary Belgium: From Stone Throwers to Hearth Tenders," *History Workshop* 21 (Spring 1986), 87–104.

[30] Pierre van Eupen to De Rode, États Belgiques Unis 189, Archives générales du Royaume/Rijksarchief, Brussels.

personalities, they diverged in their visions of the battles to come, one negotiating for diplomatic support and the other organizing a militia.

By September 1789, the Austrians had realized that an insurgent army was training. In the countryside, they seized pamphlets calling the peasants to revolution, giving them images of a pitchfork-armed battalion led by monks. Brigades of volunteers were in fact assembling in guild halls and cafes.

The Austrians wrested permission from the mayor of Liège to invade and to surround the Belgian forces in Hasselt. The mayor, however, had time to warn the Belgian troops, who scattered into the countryside. The Austrians arrived, but found no one, dubbing the phantom Belgian army "the Army of the Moon." The leaders of the insurgent army regrouped in Brussels, only to be betrayed by a spy. The Austrians surprised a gathering of three members, seized their stash of pamphlets, and arrested the supposed leaders of Pro Aris et Focis. Although they caught a Swiss tutor, Philippe Secrétan, who implicated his employer, the duchesse d'Ursel, the real leaders escaped and made their way to Breda.

The Austrians attempted unsuccessfully to stem the steady flow of men across the Dutch border. They posted spies in cafes along the route posing as recruiters, put the Estates under surveillance and required lawyers to return to Brussels to register in person if they wanted to continue to practice. The Austrians were more worried about foreign assistance to the Belgians than about pitchfork-wielding peasants.

Van der Noot had continued to negotiate for support from the Dutch, the Prussians, and the English. He did not think that the Belgians alone could defeat the Austrian armies. His diplomacy come to naught, so Van der Noot and the leaders of the First Estate called on God to come to their aid. Van der Noot reminded the Breda committee that their struggle was God's own cause, because they were defending the Catholic religion. "The same God" who had parted seas for the Israelites would save the Belgians from "Thieves, Robbers, Murderers, Sacrilegious Zealots, and Blasphemers, who have been dispatched to torment us by their master, Joseph."[31] He would not allow skeptics and atheists to overcome his most faithful people. Special masses every Thursday were dedicated to the Sacrament of Miracles.

On 24 October 1789, the feast day of the Archangel Raphael, the Belgians declared war on their Austrian rulers. By then, under the direction of Van der

---

[31] "Storm-klok ofte Rechtveerdigen Roep om Hulp," *Révolution belge* 114, pamphlet 10, Bibliothèque Royale/Koninklijke Bibliotheek, Brussels.

Mersch, the army drilling near Breda was ready for battle. Citizens throughout the provinces were also ready to rise up in support of the army. Although Van der Noot had wanted to wait until spring, the leaders of Pro Aris et Focis convinced him that their best chance was to catch the Austrians unprepared. They would continue to guide the military strategy together with the general they had recruited. Van der Noot dispatched deputations to the Triple Alliance and to the French to elicit support.

The Breda committee issued a "Manifeste du Peuple Brabançon," modeled on the American Declaration of Independence among other documents, declaring their independence. The emperor's right to rule derived from constitutions that defined the mutual obligations of the sovereign and the people with whom he had contracted. Joseph had violated the terms of that ancient contract. Borrowing directly from the baron d'Holbach whose "Annotata hors la politique natur" Van der Noot had carefully read and annotated, the preamble recognized the general will of the people as a preexisting claim to rights. The emperor's authority depended on the consent of the people. Therefore, the committee declared "Emperor Joseph II, duc de Brabant etc. ipso jure fallen from his sovereignty."[32]

The army marched out of Breda to meet the Austrian army stationed in Flanders. The first battle in Turnhout on 27 October drew in villagers, reinforcing the Belgian army sniping from the windows of their homes and attacking from the shelter of small streets. Women reportedly joined the fray, heaving paving stones from roofs onto the Austrian troops below. Under heavy bombardment from Belgian soldiers and civilians alike, the Austrian army fled in disarray, leaving behind their heavy guns. They had expected a ragged band of peasants.

On the march toward Brussels, however, no villagers materialized to reinforce the Belgian army. Without their support, Van der Mersch paused and decided to return and stage a second attack in Flanders. Troops were loaded into boats bound for Sint-Niklaas, where they arrived on 7 November. Marching toward Ghent, they attracted new recruits, though they remained short on arms and ammunition. Efforts to raise funds in Brussels were unsuccessful, so they spontaneously raided Austrian tax collectors' offices.

---

[32] "Manifeste du Peuple Brabançon," *Révolution belge* 72, pamphlet 12, Bibliothèque Royale/Koninklijke Bibliotheek, Brussels. See also Jerome Vercruysse, "L'indépendance américaine et la Révolution brabançonne," *Revue belge de philologie et d'histoire* 54 (1976), 1098–1108; Jerome Vercruysse, "Van der Noot, Holbach, et le Manifeste du Peuple Brabançon," *Revue belge de philologie et d'histoire* 46 (1968), 1222–7.

Van der Noot warned that such disrespect for property would lead to mob insurrection, perhaps, he feared, as in France. In Ghent, once again supported by the citizens, the patriot army defeated the Austrians. Significantly, that victory gave them control of one of the key fortresses in Belgium.

Van der Mersch trained the next round of new recruits and led them into battle in the Hainaut province. As the 2,000 Belgian soldiers entered the city of Mons to confront the Austrians in battle, townspeople built barricades from paving stones, giving the Belgians another unexpected victory. Three times, victory was achieved within city walls and depended on the guerrilla tactics of the local citizens. The Belgian general praised "the nascent Republic where every Citizen is a Soldier," but he worried that their undertrained and poorly equipped forces would be overpowered in open warfare.[33] Over the objections of Van der Noot, who had never trusted such irregular warfare, he proposed a ten-day armistice to the Austrians, to give the exhausted Belgians a chance to regroup.

The Austrians seized the opportunity to negotiate, offering concessions to the Belgians, such as freeing all political prisoners, closing the Séminaire général, and reinstating provincial privileges, if the Belgians would recognize Joseph II as their lawful sovereign. While the Triple Alliance reconsidered its stance toward the Belgians now that they had proved their courage, the Belgians decided they could proceed without foreign assistance or intervention. Village committees set up by Pro Aris et Focis were effectively governing, and the revolutionary committee was coordinating at a national level. It had become clear that neither an emperor nor Estates were necessary in order to govern.

In a month of battle, the Belgians had coalesced as a new nation. A pamphleteer explained in "Mercure Flandrico-Latino-Gallico-Belgique" that although the Belgians were governed by Estates divided over ten separate provinces and spoke three different languages, "which might seem to others a ridiculous crazy quilt, for the BELGIANS, it is simply an amusing and useful set of variations."[34] Theirs had developed into a national and a popular revolution, even if it had not started that way.

Two days before the end of the armistice, on 8 December 1789, men and women in Brussels launched their own offensive against the Austrian troops

---

[33] Van der Mersch, cited by Emmanuel J. Dinne, *Mémoire historique et pièces justificatives pour M. Vander Mersch* (Lille: Jacquez, 1791), vol. I, 246.

[34] "Mercure Flandrico-Latino-Gallico-Belgique," *Révolution belge* 19, Bibliothèque Royale / Koninklijke Bibliotheek, Brussels.

Figure 14.1 The Brabant Lion sweeping the Grand Place in Brussels clean of soldiers during the Brabant Revolution. Courtesy of the Rijksmuseum.

quartered in their city (Figure 14.1). They did not wait for the army that was officially observing the armistice. Two days later a solemn mass was celebrated in the central Brussels Cathedral of St. Gudule. People left donning cockades and shouting "Long live the patriots." The next morning, armed volunteers clashed with soldiers, and the battle began again. Again, civilians joined the fray, firing from the windows of their houses and dropping paving stones from the roofs.

By 12 December, the Austrian army was in retreat, leaving the Belgians masters of the city of Brussels. Although the French minister explained: "The insurrection of Brussels ... was the result of a long-suppressed hatred and fermentation," the rest of Europe was stunned by the victory of the Belgian rebels over the Austrian army.[35] They had become accustomed to guerrilla tactics in the American Revolution, but had not expected it in the Belgian provinces, known for their quiescence.

---

[35] Gravière to Montmorin, 13 December 1789, in Eugène Hubert, *Correspondance des Ministres de France accrédités à Bruxelles de 1780 à 1790*, 2 vols. (Brussels: Commission Royale d'Histoire, 1920), vol. II, 199; Extrait d'une lettre de Bruxelles, 11 December 1789, Staatskanzlei IV DD V 49/50a (16), Haus-, Hof- und Staatsarchiv, Vienna.

In the Age of Atlantic Revolution

Historians routinely echo contemporary journalists in dismissing the Brabant Revolution as a short-lived and backward-looking affair. Their interpretation poses a difficult question framed by the Belgian historian Jan Craeybeckx, who asked how such a conservative revolution could prevail in the most prosperous and industrially advanced region of continental Europe.[36] That question assumes that the Brabant Revolution was a conservative revolution that Van der Noot, supported by clerics and peasants, directed without dissent.

Within weeks of his triumphal reentry into Brussels, Van der Noot, together with his second in command, Pierre Van Eupen, assembled delegates from the Estates of nine of the ten Belgian provinces. On 7 January 1790, they signed a treaty of union as the foundation of the new United States of Belgium. The Estates would assume the sovereignty previously held by the Austrian emperor.

One pamphleteer asked rhetorically whether the Estates would follow the example of neighboring France now that Belgium had secured its independence in a revolution. "Could Christian people be better represented than by their Bishops? Could the people of the countryside be better represented than by the lords who treat their subjects as good masters & fathers would, who know their interests & see in these interests their own?" a pamphleteer answered, in the spirit of the earliest Belgian resistance.[37] The Belgians shared interests, another spokesman added. "Everyone here lives in the midst

---

[36] Jan Craeybeckx, "De Brabantse Omwenteling: Een conservatieve Opstand in een achterlijk land?," *Tijdschrift voor Geschiedenis* 80:3 (1967), 303–30. On the Belgian economy in the eighteenth century see, among others, Roger de Peuter, *Brussel in de achttiende eeuw: Sociaal-economische structuren en ontwikkelingen in een regionale hoofdstad* (Brussels: VUB Press, 1999); Pierre Lebrun, Marinette Bruwier, Jan Dhondt, and Georges Hansotte, *Essai sur la révolution industrielle en Belgique, 1770–1847* (Brussels: Palais des Académies, 1979); Catharina Lis and Hugo Soly, "Entrepreneurs, corporations et autorités publiques au Brabant et en Flandre à la fin de l'Ancien Régime," *Revue du Nord*, 76 (1994), 725–44; Janet Polasky, "Revolution, Industrialization and the Brussels Commercial Bourgeoisie, 1780–1793," *Belgisch Tijdschrift voor Nieuwste Geschiedenis/Revue belge d'histoire contemporaine* 11:1–2 (1980), 205–35; C. Vandenbroeck, *Hoe rijk was arm Vlaanderen? Vlaanderen in de 18de eeuw, 1746–1797* (Bruges: Van de Wiele, 1995).

[37] "Réflexions d'un belge patriote ou comparison respective de la Révolution de France avec celle du Brabant" (London, 1790), in *Révolution belge* 9, Bibliothèque Royale/Koninklijke Bibliotheek, Brussels; "Le Curé, le bailli et le berger du village," *Révolution belge* 3, pamphlet 4, Bibliothèque Royale/Koninklijke Bibliotheek, Brussels.

of prosperity. The planter, the artisan, the nobility, all form one big family attached to the Estates."[38] The Estates proceeded to reopen canals for trade, establish a customs union, and restore religious orders declared obsolete by the Austrians. Meeting alongside the Estates General, a Congress convened three times a week. Neither body had any intention of changing the provincial constitutions that they dubbed "democratic Constitutions tempered by a reasonable aristocracy" and written by God.[39]

Vonck and the other leaders of Pro Aris et Focis protested this usurpation of the people's newly won sovereignty. The men and women who had risen up to defeat the Austrians had not delegated the emperor's sovereignty back to the Estates. Excluded from the government, they formed a new committee, the Patriotic Society (Société Patriotique), to discuss their national interests. In a barrage of new pamphlets, these former leaders of Pro Aris et Focis charged that the Estates were but a remnant of feudal society which no longer represented the diverse interests of the people. Vonck proposed doubling the Third Estate to give commoners a voice equal to the first two privileged estates. Rather than looking to the past for their models of a new society, they suggested, the Belgians should adapt the examples of other eighteenth-century revolutionaries. "It will be a duty of our representatives to know and study the different constitutions," one member advised, adding the proviso that every nation would of course be different.[40] More radical suggestions included a national assembly. Some members demanded that the Belgians call a constitutional convention, suggesting that the Belgians had returned to the state of nature with their revolution. In any case, they should not follow the Estates, which had grabbed power for the privileged orders.

The ruling coalition had already started to break apart on its own. Provinces complained that the deputies of the central Brabant province were too dominant, and that although the presidency of the Congress rotated weekly, Van der Noot and Van Eupen seemed unwilling to cede control. The first two Estates sensed disgruntlement among the Third Estate, and they demanded that the Third Estate swear an oath and agree to maintain secrecy

---

[38] George Talker, "Quelques réflexions politocopratiques ou adieux à Bruxelles," Acquisitions récentes 4/13, Archives générales du Royaume/Algemeen Rijksarchief, Brussels.

[39] "Aen de Negen Natien der Stad Brussel" (28 February 1790), Écrits politiques 57, 316–19, Archives générales du Royaume/Algemeen Rijksarchief, Brussels.

[40] "Coup d'œil sur les principaux points d'une constitution à adopter dans la république belgique," in Varia 343, Abdij Bornem, Bornem.

in its deliberations, not reporting out to the guilds as it had always done. The Third Estate refused and instead insisted that all three Estates deliberate together, one of the key French demands, and that the Third be doubled. That was just what the French Abbé Sieyès had proposed, Van der Noot objected.

One place where the opposing factions continued to meet each other was in the home of the comtesse d'Yves. A pamphlet dedicated to her reminded the comtesse that her leadership in the revolution derived from a "centuries-old heritage."[41] The author proceeded to list page after page of examples of women who had contributed to the Belgian nation. "The Belgians, the first free people, have maintained their liberty throughout the centuries because women no less than men have worked continuously to guard it," the author, "the friend of women," concluded.[42] She had a unique ability to bring together the increasingly polarized factions.

Although the Patriotic Society made comparisons and considered models from the American Revolution, Van der Noot and other leaders of the Estates disparaged them as the "French party" and spread rumors that they were plotting to invite French revolutionaries to invade the Belgian provinces. The members of the Society acknowledged their differences from the French, who were routinely caricatured as godless equalizers. Instead, they pointed to the Americans as a "people who know the price of liberty with all their being, and who have conserved from their old constitutions that they cherish only what is compatible with democracy."[43] In numerous pamphlets destined for a wide audience, they proposed provisions from the American Declaration of Independence and various state constitutions that emphasized individual liberty.

The leaders of the Society, including members of two of the oldest noble families, the duc d'Arenberg and the duc d'Ursel, invited the volunteers of the militia stationed in Brussels to join their circle. The nobles staged elegant balls and invited the artisans and shopkeepers to dinners in taverns. Their ally, the banker Edouard Walckiers, proposed that all of the militia volunteers swear an oath recognizing that sovereignty resided in the people.

---

[41] *Précis historique sur les anciennes Belges en faveur et pour l'émulation des modernes, avec les preuves du droit qu'ont les femmes d'entrer aux États, de commander les armées, de traiter des affaires publiques et d'être consultées sur toutes les résolutions à prendre*, Bibliothèque 813/2, Archives de la Ville de Bruxelles, Brussel Stadsarchief, Brussels.

[42] *Précis historique sur les anciennes Belges*.

[43] Gérard Poringo, "Les Représentans légitimes du peuple," Brochures 1790, vol. II, Université libre de Bruxelles, Brussels.

Worried by their slipping allegiance, Van der Noot countered by summoning the volunteers to the City Hall on the Brussels Grand Place on 9 February. The battle over the volunteers continued for a month, and in the end, they swore an oath to the people in the presence of Van der Noot. They recognized the duc d'Ursel as their leader.

Dissension was also rife in the army, which had been virtually abandoned wherever it happened to be in December when victory was declared. It had never really been the Estates' army, but had been led by Pro Aris et Focis. Other nations had not recognized the independent Belgian nation; they had yet to be convinced this new conglomerate nation would endure. Upon the death of Joseph II, his brother Leopold, who succeeded him, launched a campaign to win back the Belgians. He promised no new taxes would be collected without the approval of the Estates and that all revenue collected would be spent in the provinces. He also promised to abide by the terms of the Belgian constitution.

The Estates responded to the threats that loomed inside and outside their new nation by gathering thousands of signatures on a petition condemning the troublemakers, who, they charged, wanted to dismantle the constitutions and suppress the Catholic religion. The Patriotic Society reacted with its own petition drive demanding that the Estates call a national assembly to establish a government concerned with the common good. In contrast to the thousands from the countryside who signed the Estates' petition, only forty signed this one. The Estates exploited it as the opening volley of "civil war."[44] They incited bands of shopkeepers and artisans, who were already roaming the streets of Brussels, to pillage the houses of the leaders of the Society and to threaten to hang them from lampposts. News of the unrest reached as far as the pope, who urged the clergy to restore calm, and also perhaps Austrian rule.

Van der Mersch, who approached the Estates to make the army's case for better pay and living conditions, was arrested and transported to the fortress at Antwerp. The pamphlet war intensified. Vigilante justice ruled Brussels; the leaders of the Patriotic Society fled. Vonck followed the comte de la Marck across the border to Lille, where they formed a new political society, Pro Patria, to publish a new round of pamphlets calling for liberty, popular sovereignty, and the expansion of representations in the Estates. Another group coalesced in Flanders, where Van der Mersch had been transferred.

---

[44] "Relation exacte de ce qui s'est passé à Bruxelles les journées de 16 & 17 mars," Brochures 1790, vol. II, Université libre de Bruxelles, Brussels.

The Flemish Estates were markedly more democratic. Attempted popular uprisings throughout the provinces fizzled out. Vonck and Verlooy worked on compromises with Van Eupen, but it all came to naught in May 1790. The Estates whipped up support in the countryside, summoning peasants to the cities to fight for the Belgian nation and the Catholic Church. God would deliver them from the sacrilegious democrats, just as He had led them to victory over the Austrians, they were promised.

In July 1790, at the Congress of Reichenbach, Leopold called for an armistice with the Turks and for a settlement of the Belgian question. The Triple Alliance agreed to a return of the Belgian provinces to Austrian rule. "Over several months, our poor country finds ten enemies for everyone who wishes us well," a member of the Belgian Estates lamented.[45] The Brussels guilds protested that they were an independent nation, not just a piece of territory to be exchanged among European powers. And yet, the Belgians had no viable army. Now that the Austrians' Turkish campaign was over, the Austrians could attack at full strength. The Estates offered a compromise settlement with the Austrians, proposing Leopold's second son as a hereditary grand duke of the independent nation of Belgium. Leopold rejected that, and on 24 November, Austrian troops invaded Belgium. After the first volley, the Belgian troops, such as they were, retreated.

The general who had replaced General Van der Mersch had neither recruited nor drilled new soldiers for his army. All that was left after the Estates imprisoned their general and ignored his pleas for provisioning the troops was a straggling band of peasants. It looked like what the Austrians had expected to find a year earlier when they confronted the Belgian troops. The strategists who had led the so-called Army of the Moon to victory had long since taken shelter in France, chased away by the mobs mobilized by the Estates. Their explanation of the Belgian triumph in the autumn of 1789, that the Belgian people had risen up in revolt against a distant, overreaching sovereign who had trampled on their constitution, was obviously the correct one, not the religious messianism of the Estates.

The Estates met once more. This time it was to discuss the best escape routes from Brussels. Even the Estates seem to have abandoned their faith in the divine mission of the Belgians. The Austrians marched into Brussels on 3 December 1790. There was no government to sign a surrender. They had all fled north to the Netherlands.

---

[45] P. Hearn to J. Saegermans, 21 August 1790, États Belgiques Unis 206, Archives générales du Royaume/Algemeen Rijksarchief, Brussels.

15

Revolution in England? Abolitionism

SEYMOUR DRESCHER

The editor of this collection included a question mark in his invitation to address this subject. Given the historiography of the "Age of Revolutions" this is quite appropriate. R. R. Palmer's seminal *Age of the Democratic Revolution* made no reference whatsoever to any variant of abolitionism. His one reference to a British *levée en masse* referred only to the counter-revolutionary mobilizations through which Britain's ruling classes made themselves safe from democratization for another half-century. David Armitage's Foreword to the reprinting of Palmer's work pointedly emphasizes the plethora of assaults on race and slavery in that era that were absent from Palmer's account, exemplified above all by the Haitian Revolution. Armitage's own coedited collective volume on *The Age of Revolutions* gives readers a far broader temporal and global perspective to the struggle against slavery. A whole chapter is devoted to the Haitian Revolution and its Caribbean reverberations. The fate of slave systems in the Americas and France is more briefly presented. But, apart from scattered mentions of the dates and main protagonists, the abolition of the British slave trade and colonial slavery receives very short shrift. The volume contains only one essay on the abolition of slavery in the Caribbean.[1]

Why should this be so? The plain and simple reason appears to be the inability to think of British abolition as a revolutionary process when Britain experienced neither revolution nor foreign conquest by revolutionaries in the "Age of Revolution." No other European nation got through that era so lightly. One alternative is to claim that British abolition was the result of protorevolutionary events – and the *threat* of revolution. Britain's oligarchs

---

I would like to express my appreciation to Wim Klooster and Erica Johnson Edwards for their comments on this chapter.

[1] David Geggus, "The Caribbean in the Age of Revolution," in David Armitage and Sanjay Subrahmanyam, eds., *The Age of Revolutions in Global Context, c. 1760–1840* (New York: Palgrave Macmillan, 2010), 83–100.

finessed potential revolutionary crises by redirecting potential opposition to "reforms" farther away from home. In *The Problem of Slavery in the Age of Revolution*, David Brion Davis similarly portrayed British abolition of the slave trade as a hegemonic diversion from the ills of the emergent economic revolution potentially threatening capitalist industrialization. In other words, abolitionist leaders were consciously or unconsciously displacing potential violence toward industrialists and capitalists at home by shifting resentment to slave owners. Overseas motives are displaced by hegemonic elites.[2] Davis subsequently revised this evaluation.[3]

My point of departure is different. There is also another historical perspective that pays due attention to the long British assault on the transatlantic slave trade and slavery that coincided with the Age of Revolution. First, British abolitionism was, in global historical perspective, a major assault on conditions long considered to be an inevitable and perennial part of the human condition. It is quite true that reductions or abolitions of the slave trade and slavery often occurred as unanticipated by-products of wars and colonial revolutions for independence from imperial powers. Even Britain fell into this pattern before the abolition of the British slave trade. During the American Revolutionary War, pre-abolitionist Britain freed runaway slaves of supporters of the Revolution, but the British also casually shipped thousands of slaves of American Loyalists to their West Indian colonies. The British government itself continued to purchase and recruit slaves from Africa in order to defend and extend its own colonial slave systems. The British government also continued to purchase, nominally liberate, and induct Africans for military service.[4]

---

[2] On abolitionism as a millennial moral revolution, see David Brion Davis, *The Problem of Slavery in Western Culture* (Ithaca, NY: Cornell University Press, 1966); Olivier Grenouilleau, *La Révolution Abolitionniste* (Paris: Gallimard, 2017). On British abolition as a defensive reaction by political elites, see Robin Blackburn, *The Overthrow of Colonial Slavery, 1776–1848* (London: Verso, 1988), 312–13. In David Brion Davis' *The Problem of Slavery in the Age of Revolution, 1770–1823* (Ithaca, NY: Cornell University Press, 1975) abolitionist elites provided a diversionary psychological function.

[3] See David Brion Davis, *Inhuman Bondage: The Rise and Fall of Slavery in the New World* (New York: Oxford University Press, 2006), 238–49.

[4] For estimates of the number of slaves and freed blacks transported from the United States to other British dominions, see Maya Jasanoff, *Liberty's Exiles: American Loyalists in the Revolutionary World* (New York: Alfred A. Knopf, 2011), 355; Cassandra Pybus, "Jefferson's Faulty Math: The Question of Slave Defection in the American Revolution," *The William and Mary Quarterly* 62:2 (2005), 243–64; Roger Norman Buckley, *Slaves in Red Coats: The British West India Regiments, 1795–1815* (New Haven: Yale University Press, 1979).

However, even while British liberations continued to be linked to pragmatic war-induced calculations, a new form of antislavery was emerging within British society, which became the abolitionist movement. Unlike its counterparts in France and America it endured for half a century as a national social movement. Its participants were initially aroused by what they deemed violations of the "principle of humanity." Their intended beneficiaries were not their own fellow Britons, or even residents of their own colonies. They differed from the enslaved in race, color, religion, or culture.[5] Over the course of fifty years, abolitionism remained a fairweather movement, employing measures of nonviolent mass agitation to achieve their evolving aims. Abolitionism was a civil society movement born at a moment of extraordinary peace and prosperity in Britain. The movement receded in moments of severe internal crisis or external threat.[6] It was not formed in search of creating a new social or political order. It was a major egalitarian intervention, creating what some historical social scientists regard as a pioneer of the modern social movement.[7] John Markoff, another historical sociologist of modern democratization, chooses antislavery as the first example of its historical development.[8] British abolitionism showed itself to be a remarkably enduring social formation, reacting creatively to a sequence of political, social, and military opportunities and crises endured by the nation and its empire between the 1780s and 1830s.[9]

---

[5] The novelty of this undertaking is emphasized by Adam Hochschild, *Bury the Chains: Prophets and Rebels in the Fight to Free an Empire's Slaves* (Boston: Houghton Mifflin, 2005), 5–7.

[6] On the political environment that enabled the emergence of abolitionism in 1788, see Seymour Drescher, "The Shocking Birth of British Abolitionism," *Slavery and Abolition* 33:4 (2012), 571–93; Seymour Drescher, *Capitalism and Antislavery: British Mobilization in Comparative Perspective* (New York: Oxford University Press, 1987), Chapter 3. On its intellectual and religious origins, see Christopher Leslie Brown, *Moral Capital: Foundations of British Abolitionism* (Chapel Hill: University of North Carolina Press, 2006), esp. 188–220.

[7] Charles Tilly, *Popular Contention in Great Britain, 1758–1834* (Cambridge, MA: Harvard University Press, 1995); Charles Tilly and Sidney Tarrow, *Contentious Politics*, 2nd edition (New York: Oxford University Press, 2015); Sidney Tarrow, *Power in Movement: Social Movements and Contentious Politics*, 2nd edition (New York: Cambridge University Press, 2011).

[8] John Markoff, *Waves of Democracy: Social Movements and Political Change* (Boulder: Paradigm Press, 2015).

[9] To identify periods of general insecurity and reduced governmental tolerance of public agitation I have relied on two major studies of the period: E. P. Thompson, *The Making of the English Working Class* (New York: Pantheon, 1964); Tilly, *Popular Contention in Great Britain*, Appendix II, 419–22. For the most detailed study of each stage of the movement's operations, see Mark Jones, "The Mobilization of Public Opinion against the Slave Trade and Slavery: Popular Abolitionism in National and Regional Politics, 1787–1838" (D.Phil. dissertation, University of York, 1998).

The First Wave – 1787–1792

In 1787 a small group of abolitionists met in London to form a Society for Effecting the Abolition of the Slave Trade. They viewed themselves as part of a cosmopolitan transatlantic coalition, with counterparts in the United States and France. Within five years of its formation, the London Society was clearly the only one of the three that had succeeded in forming a mass national movement and in having persuaded at least one branch of its legislature to formally resolve to abolish the nation's slave trade. At that same moment across the Atlantic, proslavery forces in the United States had already ensured that their new nation's federal constitution could not pass such legislation against the slave trade for at least twenty years. Nor could the national US government alter the legal status of slavery in any state. The first US Congress emphatically reaffirmed that constitutional provision. The slave trade to North America then rose to record annual heights before the abolition of its transatlantic slave trade to the United States in 1808.

Across the Channel, in France, the London Society's counterpart (the Société des Amis des Noirs) had failed to have any mention of slavery or the slave trade included in the foundational documents of France's revolutionary government, the Declaration of the Rights of Man and Citizen (1789).[10] It contained no reference to slavery or the slave trade. There was no mention of the slave trade or slavery in either of France's first two national constitutions, in 1791 and 1793. Nor did abolitionists in either of those two countries manage to create a national social movement.[11]

The trajectory of abolitionism in Britain was quite different. Within seven months of the formation of a London Society for the Abolition of the Slave Trade, the city of Manchester launched a petition campaign for abolition, publishing its own text in other newspapers and inviting others to join. A hundred other petitions reached Parliament, half of the total number of petitions submitted to the legislature. The petitions were enthusiastically

---

[10] For this movement, see Erica Johnson Edwards' Chapter 4 in this volume.
[11] For accounts of British, French, and American abolitionism which emphasize the international aspects of their particular approaches to abolitionist mobilization, see, inter alia, J. R. Oldfield, *Transatlantic Abolitionism in the Age of the Revolution: An International History of Anti-slavery, 1787–1820* (Cambridge: Cambridge University Press, 2013); Micah Alpaugh, "The British Origins of the French Jacobins: Radical Sociability and the Development of Political Club Networks," *European History Quarterly Review* 44:4 (2014), 593–619; Jeremy Popkin, *You Are All Free: The Haitian Revolution and the Abolition of Slavery* (New York: Cambridge University Press, 2010).

welcomed by both the prime minister and the leader of the opposition as registering the opinion of the nation.

Given the magnitude of the economic and colonial interests at risk in such a significant proposal, the question was subjected to a vast administrative collection of information and years of parliamentary hearings from both supporters and opponents of abolition. Over the next three years, abolitionists mobilized witnesses from ships' captains and medical officers to seamen to convey the realities of the African markets and the slave ships, the conditions of the middle passage, and the harsh fate of its survivors. Nevertheless, in 1791, a wary House of Commons rejected abolition as a measure that might endanger a major source of British colonial prosperity.

The abolitionists immediately intensified their appeal for an even greater display of nationwide popular support. The response surpassed the expectations of the organizers. The second drive of 1791–1792 quintupled the performance of 1788, with 519 petitions bearing nearly 400,000 signatures sent to Parliament. As Thomas Clarkson advised, parliamentary abolitionists acted to maximize the impact of their presentation. The signatures were submitted to the House of Commons in clusters in order to ensure that the effect of surges from all parts of the country did not go unnoticed. The national press soon began to note the numbers arriving each week, along with a running tabulation of their cumulative number. Even more effective was the presentation of the petitions. As was the general rule, Members of the House of Commons would read the text of each petition aloud as the day's first order of business, so that each community's opinion could be heard by the nation's representatives. Newspapers took special note of the unprecedented amount of time consumed at each session before any of the day's scheduled business could begin. Sympathetic Members of the House could also point to the mounting pile of sheepskins accumulating on the table as visual evidence of the "voice of the people" and the "opinion of the nation."[12]

Outside Parliament, abolitionists developed a very different form of national presence. A separate campaign, neither initiated nor directed by the London Society, demonstrated the commitment of a large segment of the

---

[12] On the early developments of the British Abolitionist Society, see Brown, *Moral Capital*, Chapter 7; Jones, "The Mobilization of Public Opinion," 55–71; Seymour Drescher, *Pathways from Slavery: British and Colonial Mobilizations in Comparative Perspective* (London: Routledge, 2018), Chapter 2; J. R. Oldfield, *Popular Politics and British Antislavery: The Mobilization of Public Opinion against the Slave Trade, 1787–1807* (Manchester: Manchester University Press, 1995).

population who were excluded from petitioning. By custom, petitioning was ordinarily restricted to adult males. The new form of mobilization was launched in order to permit women to take part in the movement through abstention from the purchase of slave-grown sugar. Parliament had rejected the previous motion to abolish the slave trade, and propaganda for abstention was presented as an implicit rebuke by the women of Britain to the legislators who had rejected the previous Bill. At the height of the campaign, abolitionists claimed the participation of 300,000 families in the boycott movement.

The distinctiveness of British women's mobilization was underscored in part by the appearance of their published poems and pamphlets, in classified advertisements, and in news reports of their appearance as speakers in debates on the morality and humanity of the slave trade. Their behavior could also be contrasted with that of women in Revolutionary Paris. There, women were angrily rioting for cheap sugar in the wake of the shortage of supply occasioned by the Saint-Domingue slave revolution. Nor did the male radicals at the Jacobin Club, who deliberated on these events at length, mention the movement across the Channel.[13]

The impact of the popular mobilization became clear in the parliamentary debate. Speaker after speaker supporting abolition evoked public opinion and the need to attend to "the will of the nation." Reversing its vote of 1791, the packed House of Commons overwhelmingly resolved, one year later, to abolish the slave trade. A follow-up debate targeted 1796 as the date for enforcement in order to allow merchants and planters time to prepare for legislated implementation.

Outside Parliament, anti-abolitionists did not remain inactive. They had already begun to link British abolitionists to the more violent course of the French Revolution and the slave uprising in Saint-Domingue. They emphasized the French National Assembly's offer of honorary citizenship to William Wilberforce and Thomas Clarkson. British abolitionists, however, bolstered by their successes, confidently took the charges in their stride. The activities of their counterparts in France, they replied, whatever their political

---

[13] On the sugar boycott, see Clare Midgely, "Slave Sugar Boycotts, Female Activism and the Domestic Base of British Antislavery Culture," *Slavery and Abolition* 17:3 (1996), 137–62. For a different response in revolutionary France, see Seymour Drescher, "Women's Mobilization in the Era of Slave Emancipation: Some Anglo-French Comparisons," in Kathryn Kish Sklar and James Brewer Stewart, eds., *Women's Rights and Transatlantic Antislavery in the Era of Emancipation* (New Haven: Yale University Press, 2007), 98–120.

affiliations, were welcome to the extent that they favored abolition of the slave trade. Even the Amis des Noirs had not extended their abolitionism to the point of opposing their government's dispatch of troops to suppress the Saint-Domingue uprising.

Both before and after the vote on British abolition, in 1792, British and French abolitionists regarded each other as being on the same cutting edge of justice in opposition to the slave trade. Immediately after Parliament targeted a date to abolish the slave trade, Earl Stanhope published a letter to the marquis de Condorcet, expressing the hope that the French National Assembly would now follow the British example. Stanhope concluded: "We approach the glorious moment when philosophy and reason make justice triumph everywhere, and when the rights of men overthrow all abuses and all tyrannies." Condorcet's published reply to Stanhope was even more exuberant: "Every year, every day, will be marked by the destruction of a prejudice – at least one of the chains of humankind will fall." Condorcet's colleague, Jean-Jacques Brissot, added a postscript to Condorcet's reply with particular praise for the petitions that had swept away the arguments of the slaveowners.[14]

Quiescence 1793–1804

Within a year of its major victory, the prospects for abolitionism were transformed. France launched revolutionary warfare against much of western Europe early in 1792. By the end of that year the surge of British political radicalism that had emerged in tandem with abolitionism was being subjected to a conservative countermobilization reinforced by government surveillance. France's declaration of war against Britain early in 1793, and its decree of colonial slave emancipation a year later, made even more credible the association of abolitionism with foreign revolutionary threats to both Britain's political order and its overseas colonies. The threats materialized when French revolutionaries in the Caribbean recruited newly liberated French slaves to launch attacks on British possessions in the eastern Antilles and thwarted Britain's campaign to conquer Saint-Domingue.[15] At

---

[14] *The Diary* (London), 16 April 1792. Jacques-Pierre Brissot, Condorcet's fellow abolitionist and Jacobin, made special reference to Britain's 519 petitions for abolition. Nor was "Rights of Man" discourse confined to France. See, for example, Durham's petition entitled "Abolition of a Trade to the Coast of Africa for Slaves," Durham, 29 February 1792, Durham City Records, Box 55, file 7, 107.

[15] For developments in the Caribbean, see David Geggus, *Slavery, War, and Revolution: The British Occupation of Saint Domingue, 1793–1798* (New York: Oxford University Press,

home, the British government vigorously sought to suppress both reform gatherings and radical writings as subversive of the political order.[16]

In this context chances for conversion of the Commons Resolution of 1792 into a legislative act rapidly diminished. Wilberforce's annual parliamentary motions, premised on the Resolution, were argued before diminished numbers of MPs. The House of Lords deliberately drew out its own hearings from year to year and finally abandoned even a pretense of a serious investigation. By the mid-1790s popular reform mobilizations were at a standstill. The ebb and flow of British fortunes both in Europe and the Caribbean remained the rationale for endless postponement. Uncertain times were simply not moments for risky experiments. After 1794 even the London Society ceased to hold its meetings. Toward the end of the decade, Wilberforce himself abandoned his annual motions, awaiting a more favorable turn of events. Without any outcry from Parliament or British civil society, the British government began to purchase slaves in Africa, simultaneously liberating them and subjecting them to extended periods of military service. As Roger Anstey concludes, the decade after 1793 was a barren and sterile one for abolitionists.[17]

Even during that decade, however, Parliament never rescinded its Resolution of 1792. Wilberforce and other sympathetic MPs chose to consider that lack of revocation as evidence that the parliamentary pledge remained intact during these years of stalemate. For their part, successive British governments recognized abolition as suspended, at least pending a return to peace. During negotiations with France at the turn of the century, its new ruler, Napoleon Bonaparte, was asked whether he would consider mutual withdrawal from the slave trade. The proposal was dismissed, but British abolitionist MPs later invoked it against allowing the slave trade to be extended to areas conquered by the British during the course of the war.[18]

Although French initiatives in the Eastern Caribbean had added a substantive threat to British colonies, Britain's failure in Saint-Domingue actually became a new source of security in the western Caribbean. When the Black general Toussaint Louverture emerged as the de facto ruler of the colony, he

---

1982); Laurent Dubois, *A Colony of Citizens: Revolution and Slave Emancipation in the French Caribbean, 1787–1804* (Chapel Hill: University of North Carolina Press, 2004).
[16] Thompson, *Making of the English Working Class*, Chapter 5; Oldfield, *Transatlantic Abolitionism*, Chapter 4.
[17] On African slave recruitment, see Buckley, *Slaves in Red Coats*, Chapters 2–4.
[18] Roger Anstey, *The Atlantic Slave Trade and British Abolition, 1760–1818* (Atlantic Highlands: Humanities Press, 1975), Chapter 3.

effectively prevented France's reassertion of full control of the colony. Seeking British trade and support, he sabotaged a French venture against Jamaica by secretly notifying the British governor of the identity of the French agent charged with provoking the uprising.

Toussaint's strategic aim, to revive Saint-Domingue's economy by forced labor, also led him to request the governor of Jamaica to allow British slave traders to bring cargoes from Africa to Saint-Domingue. His successors, Jean-Jacques Dessalines and Henri Christophe, repeated Toussaint's request. Haiti proved to be no threat to Britain or its Caribbean slaver system thereafter. When a British government finally began a two-pronged strategy to abolish the slave trade in 1806, Haiti was rather identified as one of the economic rivals to the British colonies as an importer of Africans when Parliament moved to abolish the British Foreign Slave Trade in 1806.[19]

The passage of the British Slave Trade Abolition Act the following year again came in the wake of a conjuncture quite favorable to Britain's external and internal security. Napoleon's mobilization of 200,000 French troops on the Channel opposite England in 1804 elicited a massive mobilization of Britain's civilian home guard. Although it was never put to the test in battle, the successful mobilization boosted the government's confidence in the loyalty of its population.[20]

In 1805 Napoleon's redeployment of the Channel army for continental combat, combined with Nelson's decisive victory at Trafalgar, guaranteed the security both of the metropolis and of the overseas colonies. The combination of Napoleon's restoration of French slavery in 1802, his catastrophic defeat in Saint-Domingue in 1803, and his refusal to negotiate a joint abolition of slavery in peace negotiations with Britain in 1806 ensured that abolitionism could no longer be identified as a weapon of Britain's "mortal enemy." The public arena once again became more accessible to popular

---

[19] On the negotiations of Toussaint Louverture and Dessalines with the British for the delivery of Africans from British slavers, see Philippe Girard, *Toussaint Louverture: A Revolutionary Life* (New York: Basic Books, 2016), Chapters 15–16; Philippe Girard, "Jean-Jacques Dessalines and the Atlantic System: A Reappraisal," *The William and Mary Quarterly* 69:3 (2012), 549–82. On the government's assessment of Haiti's status as a potential importer, see "Motion to end the British 'foreign' slave trade, House of Commons, 31 March 1806," *The Times*, 1 April 1806; Seymour Drescher, "Public Opinion and Parliament in the Abolition of the British Slave Trade," in Stephen Farrel, Melanie Unwin, and James Walvin, eds., *The British Slave Trade: Abolition, Parliament and People* (Edinburgh: Edinburgh University Press, 2007), 42–65.

[20] On the significance of the successful civilian volunteer mobilization in boosting the government's confidence in popular loyalty to the regime, see Linda Colley, *Britons: Forging the Nation, 1707–1837* (New Haven: Yale University Press, 2009), 285–319.

expression in favor of reform. In 1807 abolition of the slave trade was one of the principal beneficiaries of this conjuncture. There was no repetition of mass nationwide petitioning, but abolitionists did benefit from the reopened opportunity to express themselves in elections to Parliament and managed to generate one more critical popular petition from Manchester in favor of abolition.[21]

As was quite evident in the decisive final debates over British abolition of the slave trade in 1807, the absence of slave violence in the British colonies and the persistence of popular sentiment in the metropolis were made evident both by its supporters and by its opponents. Introducing the Bill in the Commons, Lord Howick made a special point of the absence of major slave uprisings thus far in the British colonies in an age of massive revolutions. Opening the debate in the Commons, he noted "that there were never so few insurrections" in the British Caribbean as there had been during the two decades in which abolition was being discussed in Parliament.

The first speaker for the opposition likewise began by bemoaning the state of metropolitan opinion as his worst problem. He was facing, he lamented, not only his honorable colleagues' arguments but innumerable sources of "public clamor" from the church, the theater, and the press, all teeming with news of colonial abuses, especially at "election campaigns," where pledges were actually extracted from candidates "in every manufacturing town of the kingdom."[22] Abolition was overwhelmingly approved by Parliament in 1807, and by a far greater majority than the Resolution of 1792 had achieved.

The Second Wave

With overwhelming dominance at sea, Britain after 1807 was in a position to pursue belligerent slavers and to close ports of conquered colonies to all slavers without exception. Victory in Europe in 1814 further allowed the British government to require slave trade abolition as the price of returning the conquered colonies of Sweden, Denmark, and the Netherlands. Toward indebted allies like Spain and Portugal, relief from British war loan debts could be used as bait for at least partial restriction of their slave trades.

---

[21] Seymour Drescher, "Whose Abolition? Popular Pressure and the Ending of the British Slave Trade," *Past and Present*, 143:1 (1994), 136–66. For further evidence of popular pressure on candidates for Parliament, see Peter F. Dixon, "The Politics of Emancipation: The Movement for the Abolition of Slavery in the British West Indies, 1807–1833" (D.Phil. dissertation, Oxford, 1971), 113–31.

[22] *Hansard's Parliamentary Debates*, VIII (December 1806–March 1807), 23 February 1807.

As a major power, however, France had to be approached in more conciliatory fashion. Up to the final moments of his rule in 1814, Napoleon refused to allow any negotiations about abolition. Even in his final negotiation with the allies in 1814, Napoleon's negotiator dismissed Britain's suggestion for negotiations on the subject by asking: "Do you think we are Denmark?"[23] A few months later, Louis XVIII, owing his throne to the victorious allies, was reluctant, but more accommodating. Arguing that British planters had been given ample notice to adjust to abolition in 1792, he held out for a similar five-year period to allow France to replenish its colonial slave population. The British foreign minister agreed, and returned to London with that proviso incorporated into the Anglo-French treaty of peace. The cheers that initially greeted his entrance into Parliament vanished as he read the treaty. Wilberforce denounced the reopening of the French slave trade as the death warrant for a multitude of innocents in Africa.[24]

Considering the urgency of a popular response, the London Society dispatched letters to more than 2,000 correspondents. Within four days London itself submitted a petition with more than 30,000 signatures demanding further diplomatic talks with France and further action at the upcoming European peace conference in Vienna. The whole nation massively answered the call.[25] The 1,368 petitions bearing 2 million names that reached Parliament amounted to nothing less than a national consensus. This petition drive may have attracted the largest share of the population that ever signed an abolitionist petition between 1788 and 1838.

British abolition of the slave trade was now transformed into a major national project with global implications. Britain took the lead in pressing for international condemnation of the slave trade and further negotiated treaties for enforcing its termination. It introduced a range of activities; economic, diplomatic, and even violent ones, during two more generations to come. Just two years after the petition of 1814, a large British fleet, accompanied by a smaller Dutch auxiliary, was dispatched to North Africa to demand the liberation of enslaved Europeans in Algiers. The resulting encounter cost the British 128 dead and 690 wounded, almost twice the number of casualties

---

[23] See Paul Michael Kielstra, *The Politics of Slave Trade Suppression in Britain and France, 1814–1848: Diplomacy, Morality and Economics* (London: Macmillan, 2000), Chapter 2; Blackburn, *The Overthrow of Colonial Slavery*, 316–24.
[24] *Hansard's Parliamentary Debates* 27 (1813–1814), cols. 1078–9.
[25] Kielstra, *The Politics of Slave Trade Suppression*, 29–32; Jones, "The Mobilization of Public Opinion," 119–27.

suffered at Trafalgar. As a result, 3,000 Europeans were liberated, only 18 being British subjects.[26]

Equally illustrative of Britain's commitment was its relationship with the new Haitian nation. One of the principal reasons for France's insistence on the revival of its slave trade was its plans for recovering Haiti. The nation's former colonial masters, assembled in Paris, boldly envisioned the restoration of their plantations. They went so far as to publish the number and gender of new Africans they would need to acquire. The British press reported these detailed accounts as yet another justification for their twenty-year struggle against French tyranny. They particularly welcomed one aspect of Haiti's own response to the French effort to resume sovereignty over the Caribbean nation. Alexandre Pétion, president of the southern half of Haiti, greeted the French proposal with a vow of absolute defiance in a speech to his national assembly. The British press printed Pétion's final sentence with particular glee: "The Republic," Pétion said, "expects that everyone will do his duty." What newspaper in Britain could fail to note this new twist to Admiral Nelson's final orders to his seamen at the Battle of Trafalgar? (Nelson's own words had been, "England expects that every man will do his duty.") The court of northern Haiti's royal ruler, Henry Christophe, could hardly fail to deliver its own tribute to Britain's triumph over their mutual enemy. The new nation's elite toasted the "victorious King George" who had conquered the enemies of Britain and "saved liberty."[27]

The northern kingdom's praises for Britain were no momentary gesture. For the remainder of his reign, Christophe looked to British abolitionists to furnish him with diplomatic connections to Europe, with none other than Thomas Clarkson acting as his unofficial representative to sympathetic sovereigns abroad. The king also looked to England to establish the foundations of his ambitious plans for an educational system in the new nation. The British government also found it advantageous to incorporate Haiti into its burgeoning diplomatic network of international treaties against the slave trade. Toward the end of his reign, Christophe negotiated a new agreement with a visiting British admiral. Under its terms, Haiti was to become one of many designated havens for enslaved Africans rescued by the British navy ("recaptives") from the transatlantic slave trade. Haiti, still seeking labor

[26] Oded Löuenkeim, "Do Ourselves Credit and Render a Lasting Service to Mankind: British Prestige and Humanitarianism and the Barbary Pirates," *International Studies Quarterly* 47 (2002), 23–48.

[27] For the texts of the speeches in Haiti, see *The Times* (London), 2 February 1815 and 30 October 1816.

recruits to revive its economic system, engaged to pay 45 dollars for each recaptive landed on the island.[28]

In this postwar afterglow Haiti continued to be regarded as unthreatening to the British slave colonies. The British metropolitan press had no difficulty in emphasizing the long-term significance of Haiti's dramatic transformation from a colony of slaves into an independent nation of free citizens who had triumphed over the one-time master of most of Europe. That story was cited as evidence against theories of African inferiority.

Leading British abolitionists never had a moment of more sustained interaction against the slave trade with a Haitian ruler. Sympathetic abolitionists were more embarrassed by episodes of upheaval or brutality within Haiti itself. During this brief period of attention in the late 1810s, British abolitionism was itself confined to a small group of London activists. When popular antislavery revived in the mid-1820s, Haiti's economic and demographic performance was one of many similar "experiments" in free labor that concerned both abolitionists and their opponents.[29]

Haitian rulers were not alone in seeking British support at a critical moment in their ongoing struggle for national independence. In Spanish America's revolutionary wars, British volunteers probably constituted the largest contingent of overseas foreigners fighting with Bolívar's armies. The British also made recognition of the Iberian-American states depend upon their committing themselves to abolish the slave trade. On both sides of the Atlantic British negotiators were pioneers in the internationalization of slave trade abolition.[30]

Britain also made sorties within Africa. British officers, acting as agents of their government, negotiated an accord with the ruler of the Jihad state of Sokoto for the abolition of sales of slaves to Europeans. While rulers might agree to abstain from selling slaves to Christians, they were deeply engaged in acquiring slaves to consolidate and expand their own states on the basis of enslaved non-Muslims. Cursory negotiations were also begun with rulers in

---

[28] On Christophe's negotiations with British admiral Home Popham, see, inter alia, *The Times*, 14 November 1820; *Providence Patriot* (Rhode Island), 5 July 1820.

[29] Karen Racine, "Britannia's Bold Brother: British Cultural Influence in Haiti during the Reign of Henry Christophe, 1811–1820," *Journal of Caribbean History* 33:1–2 (1999), 25–45.

[30] On Spanish America, see Matthew Brown, *Adventuring through Spanish Colonies: Simón Bolívar, Foreign Mercenaries and the Birth of New Nations* (Liverpool: Liverpool University Press, 2006); Fabian Klose, "The Entanglement of Civil Society in Action," in Fabian Klose, ed., *The Emergence of Humanitarian Intervention: Ideas and Practice from the Nineteenth Century to the Present* (Cambridge: Cambridge University Press, 2016), 91–120.

the Indian Ocean and East Africa. Under British auspices the globalization of the movement against slave trading was under way.[31] After British slave emancipation, American slaveholders feared that any outbreak of Anglo-American hostilities might induce the British to dispatch their black Caribbean military forces to the mainland, where they could quickly initiate a massive slave uprising.[32]

In Europe itself, the British government began a long process of inducing other governments to take action against the slave trade. At the Congress of Vienna in 1815 the "great powers" were induced to add a final, extra-European, article to the peace treaty. It declared the trade contrary to civilization and vaguely pledged governments to abandon it. Everywhere, as David Eltis observes, "the major distinguishing factor of the international antislave-trade system was that it was always centered on only one country. No country in the world in this era signed a treaty containing antislave provisions to which Britain was not also a party."[33]

Toward Emancipation

While the British government continued to engage in diplomatic and naval activity in pursuit of suppression of the slave trade, popular abolitionist activity within Britain almost came to a halt in the seven years following the momentous mobilization in 1814 and the victorious ending of the Napoleonic menace at Waterloo. Once again Britain entered a period of

---

[31] In the Eastern Hemisphere the British government authorized explorers, merchants, and naval officers to initiate negotiations with rulers in Africa and the Indian Ocean world. Initially, revolutionary Haiti posed the greatest danger to Cuban slavery. See Ada Ferrer, *Freedom's Mirror: Cuba and Haiti in the Age of Revolution* (New York: Cambridge University Press, 2014). Thereafter the main threat was British abolitionism. See Jonathan Curry-Machado, "How Cuba Burned with the Ghosts of British Slavery: Race, Abolition, and the Escalera," *Slavery and Abolition* 25:1 (2004), 79–93; Robert L. Paquette, *Sugar Is Made with Blood: The Conspiracy of La Escalera and the Conflict of Empire over Slavery in Cuba* (Middletown: Wesleyan University Press, 1988); Christopher Schmidt-Nowara, *Empire and Slavery: Spain and Puerto Rico, 1833–1874* (Pittsburgh: University of Pittsburgh Press, 1999). On British abolitionist initiatives against the slave trade and slavery in the Afro-Eurasian world, see Bernard K. Freamon, *Possessed by the Right Hand: The Problem of Slavery in Islamic and Muslim Culture* (Leiden: Brill, 2019), Chapter 7; Ehud Toledano, *Slavery and Abolition in the Ottoman Middle East* (Seattle: University of Washington Press, 1998), Chapters 4 and 5.

[32] See Rosalyn Narayan, "Creating Insurrections in the Heart of Our Country: The Fear of British West India Regiments in the Southern US, 1839–1860," *Slavery and Abolition* 39:3 (2018), 497–517.

[33] David Eltis, *Economic Growth and the Ending of the Atlantic Slave Trade* (New York: Oxford University Press, 1987), 90.

economic depression, radical political mobilization, and state repression. The iconic abolitionist medallion of the kneeling African slave crying "Am I not a man and a brother?" now reappeared as the image of a cringing Manchester worker, being trampled down by an "old Waterloo man" in the "Peterloo Massacre" of 1819. Overseas, the year after Waterloo was marked by the first major British colonial slave uprising in four decades at Barbados.[34] Parliamentarian abolitionists remained on the defensive and civil society hardly stirred.

The assessment of working-class attitudes toward abolitionists and Blacks before slave emancipation remains an important and unsettled question.[35] Concerning the "diversion" theses mentioned above, Jones concludes that historians have been unable to find evidence to show that abolitionists attacked slavery in order to divert attention away from domestic ills. He concludes that abolitionists were not only cognizant of the "wage" slavery argument, but also attempted to pursue remedies for both problems.[36]

Even as a more prosperous period reappeared in the early 1820s and the government became more open to reform, abolitionists were cautious about beginning popular agitation for changing the status of colonial slaves in preparation for full emancipation.[37] In question now was the fate of slaves who were actually the productive wealth and property of fellow British subjects created under British laws. Some abolitionists suggested strategies of economic legislation that would pressure slave owners into accepting emancipation.

There were also other suggestions for ameliorating patterns of slave labor and discipline as preliminary steps toward emancipation. A good deal of organizational energy was also spent on strengthening the regional organization and on strengthening abolitionism in the provinces. This involved creating more structured organizational networks of local societies that would educate members of their own communities about the conditions of slavery and create new means of communication able to coordinate the

---

[34] On the impact of the Barbados slave revolt, see Gelien Matthews, *Caribbean Slave Revolts and the British Abolitionist Movement* (Baton Rouge: Louisiana State University Press, 2006), 49–76.

[35] See Ryan Hanley, "Slavery and the Birth of Working Class Racism in England, 1814–1833," *Transactions of the Royal Historical Society* 26 (2016), 103–23; Seymour Drescher, "Cart Whip and Billy Roller: Antislavery and Reform Symbolism in Industrializing Britain," *Journal of Social History* 15:1 (1981), 3–24.

[36] Jones, "The Mobilization of Public Opinion," 208.

[37] David Brion Davis, *Slavery and Human Progress* (New York: Oxford University Press, 1984), 168–91.

bringing to bear of national pressure on the central government. At some point abolitionists also sought to tap into existing civil society associations that might be induced to support abolitionist initiatives. Religious denominations were a prime target, given their language of commitment to moral action.

The largest single target for abolitionist recruitment was the cohort of the British population that included half the adult population in the nation – its women. Women had long since demonstrated deep commitment to abolition, whether as individual writers and debaters, as canvassers in elections, or as abstainers from slave-produced commodities. Women would revive the abstention movement of the first wave and intrude forcefully into the discussion of alternative strategies of both gradual and immediate paths to emancipation. Women also began to form their own regional branches of the movement. By the end of the 1820s, they helped break through the barriers against female signatures for emancipation. In 1833 women constituted a third of the 1.3 million individuals who signed the national petition in favor of immediate emancipation.

They also used their breakthrough to enhance the impact of their mass intrusion into Parliamentary petitioning. Four decades after their predecessors in 1792, they timed and dramatized their submission of a petition in order to have maximum effect upon both the public and the MPs. On the eve of the crucial debates on emancipation in 1833, they delivered "a huge featherbed" of a single petition bearing the names of 187,000 women. Drawn up to the doors of Parliament, it required four sturdy MPs to haul it through the doors, accompanied by the cheers and laughter of the recipients.[38]

Finally, in the mid-1820s abolitionists discovered a less anticipated new cohort of supporters. These did more to present themselves to their metropolitan supporters as fellow abolitionists than the latter had yet imagined. They did this in the course of two British colonial slave uprisings of a new kind, in Demerara in 1823 and Jamaica in 1831. Both uprisings occurred in the wake of long metropolitan mobilizations, demanding further steps toward emancipation. In both cases the slave leaders were closely connected with colonial Baptist chapels, and in Jamaica with Methodist ones. The Demerara uprising clearly demonstrated that the leaders did not seek to

---

[38] Clare Midgley, *Women against Slavery: The British Campaigns, 1780–1870* (London: Routledge, 1992), 62–9. See also Linda Colley, *Britons: Forging the Nation* (New Haven: Yale University Press, 1992), 273–81.

overthrow British authority. When plantations were occupied by insurgent slaves there was no repetition of the atrocities of the Haitian uprising. Significantly, only 3 whites died in the entire Demerara uprising, compared with 250 slaves. Above all, the insurgent leaders attempted to impose collective self-discipline among their own participants and then in negotiation with British authorities. Their demands included time off to attend Sunday services. Above all, they wanted immediate clarification about the British government's ameliorative ordinances, whose content had been concealed from them. At the final confrontation, the revolt's leaders handed the British commanding officer a document signed by their captive masters and managers testifying to their good treatment.

The outstanding result of the revolt was its reception by British abolitionists as a very British contention. Hundreds of petitions were sent to Parliament by dissenting organizations against the brutality of the colonial repression. No prior uprising had ever induced such a metropolitan mobilization. The slaves identified themselves as being British subjects within the empire – not remote, uncivilized aliens, in language, behavior, or religious aspiration. They were no longer just fellow men and brothers, but now fellow Christians and fellow British workers, although subjected to special constraints, cruelties, and vulnerabilities unlike their fellow British subjects.[39]

The Jamaica slave uprising in 1831, the largest in the history of British colonization, followed a similar pattern. Leaders of the rebellion proclaimed a refusal to work any longer without wages. A large number of plantations were burned but, again, casualties among planters were kept to a minimum. This time abolitionists in Britain went on the offensive immediately, making the uprising itself a rationale for emancipation. The symbolic linkage between unnaturally constrained fellow subjects and vengeful masters was to be even more evident in the suppression of the uprising, adding fuel to the metropolitan movement toward immediate emancipation. Its very name, the "Baptist War," showed how deeply the slave uprisings had been entwined with Christian symbolism, and positioned the slaves themselves as equal if not superior to the morally isolated and brutal masters.[40]

---

[39] Emilia Viotti da Costa, *Crowns of Glory, Tears of Blood: The Demerara Slave Rebellion of 1823* (New York: Oxford University Press, 1997), Chapter 21; Michael Craton, *Testing the Chain: Resistance to Slavery in the British West Indies* (Ithaca, NY: Cornell University Press, 1982); Matthews, *Caribbean Slave Revolts*.

[40] Mary Turner, *Slaves and Missionaries: The Disintegration of Jamaican Slave Society, 1787–1834* (Urbana: University of Illinois Press, 1982).

The Jamaica revolt itself was sandwiched between major abolitionist manifestations in the metropole petitions calling for the immediate emancipation of the slaves. Once again, the petition became the most imposing element of the agitation. Both in 1830–1831 and in 1833 the more than 5,000 abolitionist petitions delivered to the House of Commons on each occasion were more than 10 times as many as it received in 1792. Because of the exponential expansion of petitioning, Parliament could no longer allow the reading of each submission. Instead, a special committee was charged with the task of summarizing central demands, numbers, and collective identities of adherents. The printed summaries of particular groups collectively signing documents often enable us to estimate the relative number of petitioners by gender, religion, and occupation. In the petition of 1833, we conclude that members of the working classes, dissenting religious groups, and women played a significant role in the process.

The petitions themselves, however, only hint at the enormous organizational structure that lay behind them. The three years of this final push for emancipation embodied significant additions to the methods of mobilization. A new organization, the Agency Committee, continually pressed the London leadership to make more urgent and uncompromising demands on the government. The country was also kept in a state of agitation by a cohort of well-honed lecturers and public debates between abolitionists and spokesmen for the West Indian opposition. The provinces organized delegations to Cabinet ministers, keeping them aware of the intense sentiment of the country at large. Provincial delegations also attended meetings of the Antislavery Society in London. Public activity appears to have been more continuously engaged than in previous mobilizations.[41] Abolitionists both competed and combined with popular mobilizations aimed at ending religious barriers for Catholics in Ireland and nonconformists in Britain.

One may note the limitations on the power of abolitionists to force consideration and frame the terms of abolition. In 1831 and 1832, abolitionists had to yield primacy of importance to the political and constitutional crisis of domestic political reform within Britain. Ministers did assure them that the question of slave emancipation would closely follow the success of political reform.

Only when the reform of Parliament was resolved in the spring of 1832 was the antislavery movement free to capture the full attention of the

---

[41] Drescher, *Capitalism and Antislavery*, Chapter 7; Jones, "The Mobilization of Public Opinion," 241–81.

administration. Throughout the country demands for pledges of support for immediate emancipation were successfully solicited. The Agency Committee simultaneously sponsored nationwide lecturers and debate. Local affiliate organization societies more than quadrupled. The legacy of the Jamaica uprising positively interacted with the rising tide of agitation in the metropole. The campaign harvested a huge majority of electoral pledges. In the wake of another mass petition early in 1833, the government felt sufficiently pressed to bring a plan to Parliament and to hammer out passage of emancipation after four long months of debate.

The final act again demonstrated the limits of even this massive popular mobilization. A provision for a period of "apprenticeship" – compulsory unpaid labor – clearly did not conform to abolitionist expectations for complete as well as immediate emancipation. The leading abolitionist MP Fowell Buxton desperately warned that such a provision might provoke another insurrection – to no avail. The government minister countered by threatening that without some period of transition the government would withdraw its own support. Fearing that postponement might turn into another lost opportunity, the majority of parliamentary abolitionists yielded to the principle of apprenticeship, or fought only for halving its duration. The government also raised the compensation to a payment of 20 million pounds to the slave owners. This had long been demanded by West Indian spokesmen in and outside Parliament. The abolitionist compromise on both major points was bitterly noted by the radical press as a reason why small public gatherings called in support of the final legislation were labeled "hole-in-the-corner" affairs, heaping unanticipated burdens both on the colonial slaves and on the metropolitan poor of Britain. It foreshadowed difficulties to come.

After Emancipation

Emancipation Day on 1 August 1834 passed without major disturbances in the Caribbean colonies. The event was not only reassuring to British abolitionists but inspiring to those elsewhere. It offered an alternative to the earlier deadly and destructive French and Spanish American paths to slave liberation. Overseas, abolitionists in the United States and France could now offer British emancipation as a revolutionary moment with the possibility of repetition in their own country. William Lloyd Garrison hailed "the instantaneous transformation of almost a million chattels into rational and immortal beings" as a "miracle of the age." Frederick Douglass, celebrating the anniversary of British Emancipation in the wake of the French Revolution of 1848, declared, "We have discovered in the progress of the anti-slavery movement that England's passage to freedom is not through rivers of blood ... [as is] bloody revolution in France ..." For sixty years the rulers of England had resisted taking action until "the popular torrent swept it along."[42]

In France a new French Society for the Abolition of Slavery formed within months of the implementation of British slave emancipation. Yet a decade later not a single proposal for emancipation had even been debated in the French national legislature. In 1843 Alexis de Tocqueville, a member of the French Society for the Abolition of Slavery, sought to assuage the fear of a nation that had gone through more than half a century of revolution and wars. He asked his countrymen to look across the Channel at a neighboring nation that had engaged in a sixty-year revolution which culminated in a great social transformation, without the trauma of death and destruction endured by France and its own colonies. On the day of emancipation, he wrote, 800,000 slaves had been summoned from social death to life. Moreover, he observed, this was the "achievement of the people and not its rulers." On the day of emancipation and during the whole decade to follow, the former slaves, he noted, had not caused "a tenth of the disorders of 'civilized nations of Europe' – of France for example. If you pore over the histories of all peoples, I doubt that you will find anything more extraordinary or more beautiful."

Meanwhile, after the passage of the Emancipation Act, in 1833 British abolitionists still had another hurdle to overcome – the termination of apprenticeship in the West Indies before its prescribed termination date of 1840. The familiar sequence of activity and agitation was revived: exploratory investigations of continuing abuses of power, national gatherings in London by provincial delegates of the movement, and a call for yet another round of petitions. Some innovations were made possible by unforeseen events. The death of William IV in 1837 allowed the women of Britain not only to sign petitions but also to send a massively signed women's address to another woman – the new heir to the throne. They appealed directly to young Victoria not to begin her reign shadowed by the residue of slavery within her dominions.

---

[42] For the quotations, see Seymour Drescher, *Abolition: A History of Slavery and Antislavery* (New York, Cambridge University Press, 2009), 265–6. For the impact of emancipation on the French Antislavery Society, see Lawrence C. Jennings, *French Reaction to British Slave Emancipation* (Baton Rouge: Louisiana State University Press, 1988).

In 1838 the final battles over apprenticeship were fought out not as great debates in a packed House of Commons, but in sparsely attended sessions with marginal outcomes. The real victory came through relentless popular demonstrations, indicating that the pressure from without would not cease until, as one Member promised, the House itself was filled with petitions to the walls. Finally, a weary government at home declared to its colonial governors in the Caribbean that further resistance was futile. By the fifth anniversary of the Emancipation Act, on 1 August 1838, every colonial assembly had proclaimed the end of apprenticeship. This time Parliament itself had been bypassed by a mass mobilization in Britain and nonviolent agitation in the colonies.[43] In Ireland, 70,000 women added their names to this petition drive, and those who delivered that petition were invited to an audience with the new queen.[44]

For some triumphant abolitionists, however, their work had only begun. A newly formed British and Foreign Antislavery Society now adopted the goal of ending slavery and the slave trade throughout the world in the "name of outraged humanity and the Rights of Man."[45] The Society now called upon Britain's East India Company to enact the end of the enslavement of millions under its jurisdiction. Even while awaiting the outcome of that issue, abolitionists successfully, if only briefly, induced the British government to call a halt to another form of servitude – indentured migration from India to Britain's Caribbean colonies and Mauritius in the Indian Ocean.

At this peak of global abolitionist ambitions, Britain was naturally charged by other slave-holding nations of using antislavery as a means to gain economic or geopolitical global domination. United States Southerners accused the British of forming an Anglo-Haitian alliance in order to block the United States' westward expansion, and denounced Britain for offering to recognize the independence of Texas from Mexico in exchange for prohibiting further slave imports. Britain was already offering refuge to American slaves who escaped to Canada or the West Indies. Anti-abolitionists in France likewise attacked Britain for having ended its slave system in the Americas as a means of shifting the center of tropical agriculture to Britain's vaster empire in India.

---

[43] Jones, "The Mobilization of Public Opinion," 282–9.
[44] Nini Roberts, *Ireland, Slavery and Anti-Slavery, 1612–1865* (London: Palgrave Macmillan, 2007).
[45] Howard Temperley, *British Antislavery 1833–1870* (London: Longman, 1972), 23.

The reverberations of the waves of the 1830s can also be observed in the burst of British governmental activity against the slave trade. Diplomatically, the British negotiated more bilateral treaties for the abolition of the slave trade in the decade following slave emancipation than during any such period before or after in the history of the transatlantic slave trade. An enlarged naval force was authorized to enforce the newly negotiated treaties to search for and seize slaves on foreign ships. Under British abolitionist pressure, the government launched an expedition into Africa in order to create model "free labor" farms and to demonstrate the superiority of free labor over slave labor. The British government pressured foreign governments to enact their own laws outlawing the slave trade in Africa, Asia, and the Caribbean. Within Britain itself, an international World Antislavery conference was held in London in 1840 to survey the extent and magnitude of slavery in areas of the world which might be susceptible to antislavery initiatives.[46]

From Movement to Lobby

However, a series of changes was occurring in Britain that quickly altered the fortunes of British abolitionism. Overseas, the end of apprenticeship produced a sharp shortfall in the production of British colonial sugar. In order to ease the passage from slavery to "free labor," the government had also acted to protect West Indian sugar from foreign competition. They also legislated an increase in the customs charged on colonial sugar imports. Domestic consumers would have to bear the cost of the loan that funded the masters' compensation. The consequent rise in sugar prices disproportionately affected Britain's poorest consumers.

Far more serious than the bitterness of radicals and working-class consumers was a far more consequential economic development in the nation at large. Britain entered into one of its deepest crises in the nineteenth century – retrospectively called "the hungry forties." As if this were not enough, the abolitionist leadership added insult to injury. Having unreservedly embraced the principle that free labor would match or exceed the cost of slave labor, they were unable to demonstrate that the new labor system could match its predecessor either in price or in volume of production. The *Anti-slavery*

---

[46] Howard Temperley, *White Dreams, Black Africa: The Antislavery Expedition to the River Niger, 1841–1842* (New Haven: Yale University Press, 1991); Eltis, *Economic Growth*, 99, Table 4. On India, see Andrea Major, *Slavery, Abolitionism and Empire in India* (Liverpool: Liverpool University Press, 2012), 172–84.

Reporter presented a glowing new picture of life in the Caribbean, emphasizing the enormous increase in consumption, comfort, and prosperity of the newly freed slaves.[47]

The inevitable comparison between metropolitan misery and colonial comfort was soon evident. Instead of triumphant celebratory gatherings, abolitionists' meetings were disrupted by crowds demanding that projects for both charity and justice should now begin at home. New social movements, above all Chartism and the Anti-Corn Law League, denounced abolitionist indifference to unemployment and hunger at home. Racial overtones, always present in some radical and anti-abolitionist writings, became more frequent at meetings, and angry voices shouted that they would surely be treated better if their own skins were black. The Chartists explicitly identified the abolitionists as both competitors and tactical models: "The same power that broke the chains of slavery can rescue the children of Britain ... The same zeal as animated the country in 1833 is required now, and the same will follow."[48]

Rival mass organizations did far more than stalk antislavery gatherings. They enthusiastically adopted the tools that had served abolitionists so well for fifty years: mass organization, mass propaganda, and mass petitioning. Their publications brimmed with outrage at the indifference of the wealthy and powerful to their fellow British subjects and citizens. They began to match or exceed abolitionism's old record harvests of signatures. The Chartists spectacularly replicated the abolitionist women's presentation of their giant emancipation petition of 1833. The Chartists' monster petition was so huge that the doors of Parliament actually had to be removed so that their document could be brought into the House of Commons.[49]

The rapid descent of the abolitionist movement may be seen in the changing perspective of the *Times* of London. In the Spring of 1841, the *Times* sensed that a decade of Whig domination in Parliament was coming to an end. Its defeat was secured, said the *Times*, by the abolitionists – "the central embodiment of an almost unanimous feeling" throughout the country. Its supporters might be "a promiscuous enrollment of Churchmen, Dissenters, Jews, Quakers, Papists, Conservatives, Whigs, Radicals of all

---

[47] "Results of Emancipation," in *Anti-slavery Reporter*, 4 November 1840, 275; Temperley, *British Antislavery*, 148–52.
[48] *Northern Star*, 28 May 1842.
[49] Drescher, *Pathways from Slavery*, 261–99. On abolitionist Chartists, see Betty Fladeland, "Our Cause Being One and the Same: Abolitionists and Chartism," in James Walvin, ed., *Slavery and British Society, 1776–1846* (London: Macmillan, 1982), 69–99.

sects in religion and of all parties in politics." They might not be constituted in one formal organization, but they held the balance of power in the tenure of the government. Three years later abolitionists had become to the *Times* a "monomaniac Committee," the hobby of dukes, Quakers, and "presumptuous" presidents of the female civilization of African society – a condescending comment on the women's excessive fervor.[50] Abolitionists in the colonies were also disillusioned. Catherine Hall has traced the widening division between slaves and former slaves from 1842.[51]

The abolitionists had simply lost their mass voice. They sought, in 1841 and 1842, to launch a new popular mobilization to pressure the East Indian Company into legislating immediate and complete slave emancipation in their dominions. There was no national response whatsoever. The East India Company's Act V on slavery, in 1843, simply specified that Indian courts would not recognize demands for service on the grounds of enslavement. The doors were left open for demands for service on grounds of contractual or religious obligation. That did not go much further than Lord Mansfield's Somerset decision seventy years earlier. In India compulsory service would continue well into the twentieth century. Britain remained nationally pledged to end slavery, but henceforth by degrees, and allowing ample room for a slow and gradual process. The abolitionists adapted to their new role as a respected but far less overbearing civil association.[52]

The Abolitionist Revolution in Larger Perspective

As it adjusted to its new status, abolitionism became a partner in the advocacy of a nuanced hierarchy of compulsory labor, acting as an organization primed to intervene in cases of abuse within overseas labor systems. Britain sustained its leading role in the advocacy of international initiatives against the slave trade and slavery and its reputation as an antislavery nation. Residues of the slave trade in Africa and Asia or brutal atrocities in systems of forced labor could be occasions for exposure. The old abolitionist rhetoric, of course, could also now serve non-Britons against Britain and other forms of

---

[50] *Times* editorials: 12 and 15 May 1841; 8 October 1841; 18 November 1842; 15 May 1843; 24 June 1843; 31 October 1843.
[51] Catherine Hall, *Civilising Subjects: Colony and Metropole in the English Imagination, 1830–1867* (Chicago: Chicago University Press, 2002), Chapters 2 and 6.
[52] Susan Zimmerman, "The Long-Term Trajectory of Anti-slavery in International Politics," in Marcel van der Linden, ed., *Humanitarian Intervention and Changing Labor Relations* (Leiden: Brill, 2011), 435–98.

abusive inequality, even within the boundaries of the British empire. The outstanding examples of imperial civil society mobilizations inspired by abolitionism took place in South Africa and India. Gandhi's long battle at the beginning of the twentieth century against unequal treatment and status for Indians in South Africa and his campaign for the abolition of indentured migration from India consciously deployed nonviolent civil disobedience and mass petitioning inspired by the prior example of nonviolent mass abolitionism to bring the system to an end in 1917.[53] In a careful assessment of the impact of British antislavery, David Geggus concludes that, "whether measured in absolute or relative terms, British abolitionism contributed as much as the Caribbean revolutions to freeing slaves and reducing its slave populations." British abolitionism was also "arguably more significant in contributing to the demise of American slavery than the Haitian Revolution." Moreover, in the world beyond the Caribbean, British abolitionism certainly did far more to secure the suppression of the transoceanic slave trades than did that of any other nation, both during and long after the Age of Revolution.[54] Geggus elsewhere also concludes that, while the Haitian revolution was "the most transformative of the Atlantic revolutions," it was ambiguous in its overall impact on subsequent revolutions.[55] If the abolitionist revolution did not terminate slavery or even preclude a subsequent revival of coercion, it did produce both international condemnation and a global diminution of all of its forms.[56]

---

[53] See Richard Huzzey, *Freedom Burning: Anti-slavery and Empire in Victorian Britain* (Ithaca, NY: Cornell University Press, 2012); Drescher, *Pathways from Slavery*, 261–99.

[54] See Geggus, "The Caribbean in the Age of Revolution," 84–5; Eltis, *Economic Growth*, Parts III–V.

[55] David Geggus, "The Haitian Revolution in Atlantic Perspective," in Nicholas Canny and Philip D. Morgan, eds., *The Oxford Handbook of the Atlantic World c. 1450–1820* (Oxford: Oxford University Press, 2012), 533–45; David Geggus, "Slavery and the Haitian Revolution," in David Eltis, Stanley L. Engerman, Seymour Drescher, and David Richardson, eds., *The Cambridge World History of Slavery*, vol. IV: *AD 1804–AD 2016* (Cambridge: Cambridge University Press, 2017).

[56] David Eltis, Stanley L. Engerman, Seymour Drescher, and David Richardson, "Introduction," in Eltis et al., *The Cambridge World History of Slavery*, vol. IV, 3–19; B. W. Higman, "Demographic Trends," in Eltis et al., *The Cambridge World History of Slavery*, vol. IV, 20–48; Kevin Bales, "Contemporary Coercive Labor Practices – Slavery Today," in Eltis et al., *The Cambridge World History of Slavery*, vol. IV, 655–78. For further long-term global reverberations of British antislavery, see also David Brion Davis, *Inhuman Bondage: The Rise and Fall of New World Slavery* (Oxford: Oxford University Press, 2006); Drescher, *Abolition*; James Walvin, *Freedom: The Overthrowing of the Slave Empires* (London: Robinson, 2019). For a truly comprehensive assessment of the rise and success of British antislavery as a world-changing accomplishment in its boldness, see David Richardson, *Principles and Agents: The British Slave Trade and Its Abolition* (New Haven: Yale University Press, 2022).

16

The Irish Rebellion of 1798

THOMAS BARTLETT

Politicization

In the present great era of Reform when unjust governments are falling in every quarter of Europe ...[1]
That stupendous event, the Revolution in France ...[2]
Appear! Appear! Fair Freedom
And set the captive Negro free.[3]
Come let us dance, let us dance
Happy, happy days have appear'd at last.[4]
America, and virtuous France
Did break the chains of slavery
They set a pattern to mankind
To know their rights and to be free.[5]
I believe in the Irish Union, in the supreme majesty of the people, in the equality of man, in the lawfulness of insurrection and of resistance to oppression.[6]
The United Irishmen, before they adopted a secret revolutionary system, walked in the footsteps of the Americans in '74.[7]

---

[1] *The Declarations ... of the Societies of United Englishmen*, in *Report of the Committee of Secrecy of the House of Commons of Great Britain* (Dublin: J. Miliken, 1799), 75.

[2] Theobald Wolfe Tone, cited in T. W. Moody, R. B. McDowell, and C. J. Woods, eds., *The Writings of Theobald Wolfe Tone* (Oxford: Oxford University Press, 2001), vol. II, 122 (hereafter Tone, *Writings*).

[3] *Paddy's Resource: Being a Select Collection of Original and Modern Patriotic Songs, Toasts and Entertainments* (Belfast: n.p. [*The Northern Star*?], 1795), 27.

[4] *Paddy's Resource*, 34.   [5] *Paddy's Resource*, 79.

[6] *The Union Doctrine or Poor Man's Catechism* (Dublin?: n.p., n.d. c. 1797), 3, copy in the National Archives of Ireland, Rebellion Papers 620/43/1 (hereafter NAI RP). The "Irish Union" was another term for the United Irishmen.

[7] John Daly Burk, *History of the Late War in Ireland* (Philadelphia: Francis and Robert Bailey, 1799), iii. Burk (1772?–1808) was expelled from Trinity College Dublin for blasphemy, and in 1796 fled to the United States to avoid arrest for subversion.

What really happened in Ireland in 1798? These quotations – and there are any number of similar ones – supply one answer. Just as the American Revolution had destabilized the political system in the Atlantic world, for it was the first time any European dependency had successfully broken free from the mother country in pursuit of self-government,[8] so too the French Revolution – or, as both admirers and critics preferred to style it, the Revolution in France, meaning a universal upheaval – further shook the existing order. Through its watchwords of liberty, equality, and fraternity, and its example of successful insurrection by the "people," the revolution swiftly sparked disturbances elsewhere in Europe, then helped ignite a slave rebellion in Saint-Domingue, and ultimately provided that essential stimulus to rebellion in Ireland in the form of the promise of a French invasion force. Since the 1660s at least, Irish Protestants had feared that a French incursion and a French-sponsored uprising were highly likely to occur in Ireland.[9]

We may date the birth of the republican project that was to engulf Ireland during the 1790s to the setting up of the Society of United Irishmen in Belfast in October 1791. In that month a group of mostly middle-class Presbyterian and Church of Ireland reformers – Samuel Neilson, Samuel McTier, Thomas Russell, and Theobald Wolfe Tone among them, enthused by the revolution in France and inspired by the principles that appeared to underlie it – came together to found a society dedicated to seeking reform of the Irish parliament in order to make it more representative. "With a parliament thus reformed," they declared with breathtaking confidence, "everything is easy; without it, nothing can be done."[10] The Irish parliament essentially represented landowners, and those without landed estates, namely Presbyterians, probably a majority of the Protestant community, were mostly excluded, while Catholics, at least 75 percent of the entire population of the island, were entirely excluded. The British and Irish authorities, however, were distinctly unimpressed with the stated objective of the society, and immediately dismissed its stated aim as a mere cover for revolutionary change. The real goal of the United Irishmen, they claimed, was nothing less than an Irish republic, separate and distinct from Britain, and with Ireland placed firmly in the orbit of revolutionary France. In point of fact, at least one of those behind

---

[8] David Armitage, "The American Revolution in an Atlantic Perspective," in Nicholas Canny and Philip Morgan, eds., *The Oxford History of the Atlantic World, 1450–1850* (Oxford: Oxford University Press, 2011), 516–32: 516.
[9] See James Kelly, "'Disappointing the Boundless Ambitions of France': Irish Protestants and the Fear of Invasion, 1661–1815," *Studia Hibernica*, no. 37 (2011), 27–105.
[10] Burk, *History of the Late War*, 20.

the society, Theobald Wolfe Tone, had already set out his political creed in a letter to his friend Thomas Russell, in which he declared that "the bane of Irish prosperity is the influence of England" and maintained that "separation [from Britain] would be a regeneration of this country." For reasons of prudence, however, he had shared his opinions only with a few trusted friends.[11] In any case, whatever Tone's views, British officials and some of their Irish counterparts had long been accustomed to discerning a separatist desire behind any hint of Irish assertiveness. Thus the innocuous political squabbles in the Irish parliament in the 1750s had been viewed as a potential threat to the Anglo-Irish connection, while the Volunteers, a military formation independent of government that had sprung up to defend Ireland during the American War of Independence, were viewed from the beginning with the utmost suspicion. When that armed body, having apparently won legislative independence for the Irish parliament, turned its attention to parliamentary reform in the early 1780s, it seemed that these suspicions were well grounded. Those in favor of parliamentary reform, announced the chief governor, the admittedly excitable duke of Richmond, "drink the French king on their knees and their declared purpose is a separation from England and the establishment of the Roman Catholic religion."[12] In short, metropolitan anxiety about political developments in Ireland, while undoubtedly heightened by the experience of the American Revolution, had long predated both it and the French Revolution.

The United Irishmen hoped to realize their objective of parliamentary reform largely by employing the same methods the Volunteers had used to achieve legislative independence in 1782. They would, of course, seek to revive the Volunteers – as a body they had been quite dormant since the mid-1780s – and then they would call a convention to draw up proposals for parliamentary reform. They would then propagate their cause through publications – newspapers, pamphlets, even ballads – the objective being to politicize the masses and make "every man a citizen." In addition – and this was new, even revolutionary – they would seek to enlist the support of the Catholics of Ireland in their campaign. Hitherto, it had been a largely unchallenged axiom that Irish Catholics, the overwhelming mass of the people of Ireland, must never be entrusted with political rights, however limited. Irish Catholics were viewed by their Protestant fellow countrymen

---

[11] Tone, *Writings*, vol. I, 104–6.
[12] Quoted in Thomas Bartlett, *The Fall and Rise of the Irish Nation: The Catholic Question, 1690–1830* (Dublin: Gill and Macmillan, 1992), 110.

as quietly biding their time to avenge their defeat in the wars of the seventeenth century and thus to recover their forfeited estates. Hence, opening the constitution to them could not be other than utter folly. For reformers the problem here was plain enough: if Catholics were excluded from the proposed reforms, then the drive for reform, lacking numbers, would lose impetus and fail. On the other hand, if Catholics were included, then the reform movement would inevitably split, and the quest for reform would be easily seen off. How could this conundrum be resolved? This is where events in France, and Theobald Wolfe Tone's interpretation of them for an Irish Protestant audience, came in.

In his pamphlet *An Argument on Behalf of the Catholics of Ireland* (Dublin, 1791), Tone dissected with forensic brilliance the reasons for earlier reform failures, drew appropriate lessons from the French Revolution, and concluded that parliamentary reform in Ireland could be achieved only through the unity of Catholics, Protestants, and Dissenters. To those who feared the admission of Irish Catholics to the body politic, Tone pointed to the example of France, where Catholics had apparently led the revolutionary charge and embraced the new order. If French Catholics, previously seen as the most faithful of the Church's children, could act as citizens, even elect Protestants to the National Assembly in Paris, then surely it stood to reason that Irish Catholics could be trusted to promote liberty too. Dazzled by admiration for the great events afoot in revolutionary France – monarchy brought to heel, a republic soon to be installed, an imminent separation of church and state, a ringing Declaration of the Rights of Man, and, not least, the Catholic Church in France apparently prostrate – Tone and his friends were supremely confident that reform in Ireland would be theirs for the taking.[13]

It need hardly be said that all this political activity in Belfast and elsewhere, notably in Britain itself, with new clubs being set up, strident demands for reform voiced, and events in France openly applauded – was viewed with growing hostility by officials in Ireland and especially by the British government headed by William Pitt. It was evident that monarchical government everywhere would face an unprecedented challenge, one made explicit by Edmund Burke's excoriation of the French Revolution, in his words "the great overbearing master-calamity of our time."[14] Moreover, as if to reinforce these fears, word emerged in November 1792 of a dinner held in

---

[13] Tone, *Writings*, vol. I, 108–27.
[14] R. B. McDowell, ed., *The Writings and Speeches of Edmund Burke, vol. IX: Part I: The Revolutionary War 1794–1797; Part II: Ireland* (Oxford: Oxford University Press, 1991), 4.

Paris, at White's Hotel, to celebrate the French victory at Valmy over the Prussians. Those attending numbered around 100 and were later dubbed the "British club," though there were many other nationalities present as well. The dinner was presided over by Thomas Paine, the most famous radical of his day, and author most recently of a trenchant reply to Burke. In an atmosphere of exuberant, intoxicating conviviality, the diners proposed to convey an address to the French National Convention congratulating it on its work, and celebrating the revolution. The address was duly presented some ten days later and was received with great enthusiasm by the Convention: significantly, of the fifty who signed it, no fewer than sixteen were Irish, including Lord Edward FitzGerald and John and Henry Sheares (all three destined to die violently in the summer of 1798), along with some who had served in the Irish regiments in French service, and some who were seminarians at the Irish College in Paris.[15]

The implications of this dinner and the subsequent address were unmistakable, for a pattern had now emerged of transnational radicalism or republicanism, stemming directly from France, a country whose revolution, as Pitt put it, "had shaken Europe itself to its foundations" and was deeply inimical to British interests.[16] United Irish radical reformers in Dublin and Belfast, and Irish and British republicans in London and Paris, were making common cause. The issues at the heart of the Burke–Paine pamphlet war of 1790 would surely soon lead to a real war between Britain and France, while the French revolutionary decree offering succor to nations aspiring to be free must have set alarm bells ringing in Britain and Ireland. True, the French republic had publicly turned its back on the secret diplomacy of the *ancien régime*, but that could not mean that the revolutionaries had renounced the time-honored maxim of French military strategists: to attack England, one must go through Ireland. Pitt made much of this offer of support from the French for those yearning to be liberated in his speech justifying war with France.[17]

Pitt moved swiftly. It was widely accepted in British government circles that "the mistake of America" had been to delay in taking decisive action, and

---

[15] Mathieu Ferradou, "Histoire d'un 'festin patriotique' à l'Hôtel White (18 novembre 1792): Les Irlandais patriotes à Paris, 1789–1795," *Annales Historiques de la Révolution Française*, no. 382 (December 2015), 123–43.
[16] Pitt's speech of 12 February 1793 in W. S. Hathaway, *The Speeches of the Right Honourable William Pitt*, 4 vols. (London: Longman, Hurst, Rees and Orme, 1806), vol. II, 116.
[17] Ibid., 117.

this was not going to happen with Ireland.[18] In quick order, substantial Catholic Relief Bills – permitting Catholics to join the armed forces of the crown and offering them the vote in the counties on the same terms as Irish Protestants – were put through a largely hostile Irish parliament. These concessions were intended to keep Irish Catholics far removed from a Presbyterian–Protestant alliance. Then, conventions that claimed a representative function were outlawed, and the editors of the United Irish newspaper, *The Northern Star*, were prosecuted. More menacingly, the army was permitted to openly intimidate known radicals. Thus General Richard Whyte, the commanding officer in Belfast in March 1793, reckoning his situation "pretty similar to my late friend Gen. Gage at Boston ... daily threatened by the malcontents with a Bunker's Hill or a Lexington," thought to get his retaliation in first and turned his soldiers loose on the radicals of that town. Some of the United Irishmen had dared to exhibit pictures of the revolutionary heroes the comte de Mirabeau and Benjamin Franklin, and a fiddler had apparently provoked the soldiers by continuing to play "a rascally, outlandish, disloyal tune," *Ça ira*. *Ça ira (It'll Be Fine)* was a well-known French revolutionary song, and the term had been much uttered by Benjamin Franklin during his time as ambassador in France. Many windows, and heads, were broken before Whyte's "charming boys" were called off. (The locations of their barracks are shown in Map 16.1.) It was a foretaste of the military mayhem that would ensue later in the decade.[19]

A year later, in May 1794, on the grounds of clear evidence of its treasonable collusion with the French, the Society of United Irishmen was proscribed. Its members, or at least some of them, promptly went underground to make plans for an insurrection in Ireland to coincide with the arrival of a substantial French invasion force.[20] Key parts of their plan included swearing in new members – by 1797 they were boasting that they had some 400,000 sworn adherents – and suborning soldiers so that in the event of a French landing large numbers of the crown forces could be expected to desert to the invaders. They also made overtures to the Defenders, a rural secret society, which was at that time creating havoc in

---

[18] See Camden to Pitt, 29 May 1798, TNA Chatham Mss. 30/8/326/303.
[19] Gen. Whyte to E. Cooke, 8 April 1793, The National Archives London, Home Office papers (hereafter TNA HO) 100/46/59-60; Whyte to Hobart, 29 March 1793, TNA HO 100/43/152-4.
[20] I have drawn on Nancy J. Curtin, *The United Irishmen: Popular Politics in Ulster and Dublin, 1791–1798* (Oxford: Clarendon Press, 1994) in this short account of the United Irishmen.

The Irish Rebellion of 1798

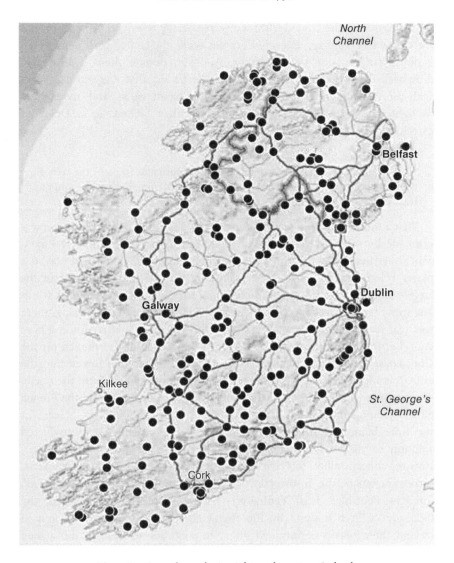

Map 16.1 Army barracks in eighteenth-century Ireland.

south Ulster, north Leinster, and north Connacht. In theory, an alliance between the United Irishmen and the Defenders should have been impossible, for the Defenders appeared to be everything that the United Irishmen were not. The Defenders were rural, the United Irishmen were, mostly, urban; the Defenders were generally characterized as "poor, ignorant labouring men," the United Irishmen were socially removed from them; and the Defenders were aggressively Catholic, while the United Irishmen offered a nonsectarian vision of the future. And yet, despite these considerable drawbacks the United Irishmen were persuaded that they could work with the Defenders, moderate their anti-Protestant views, and invite them to fight alongside the French if and when they landed. As a Defender catechism had it:

> Where did you get your commands from?
> First from Orleans castle we first got our commands to plant the tree of liberty in the Irish lands: the French Defenders will uphold the cause and the Irish Defenders will pull down the British laws.[21]

That a French invasion was no idle pipe dream of the United Irishmen was dramatically revealed by the arrival of a French war fleet in Bantry Bay in southwest Ireland in December 1796. Theobald Wolfe Tone had played a major role in encouraging the French Directory to undertake one of the largest amphibious landings of the revolutionary war, and, while high winds and mountainous seas would prevent the soldiers from disembarking, there was real fear in Dublin and London that the French would return at a later date. During the emergency provoked by the arrival of the French off the Cork coast, the Lord Lieutenant, Lord Camden , had been forced into the embarrassing admission that he dared not withdraw soldiers from the northern province of Ulster lest an insurgency take place there, should the French effect a landing in the south of Ireland. With the danger now over, at least for the time being, the Irish government chose repression as its preferred solution to the massive threat posed by those "partners in revolution," Irish republicans allied to French Jacobins.[22] In quick succession, new laws, some draconian (the Insurrection Act), were introduced and new armed forces – Fencibles, Irish Yeomanry – were mobilized. In addition, the blockade of French ports by the Royal Navy was tightened up, and in Ireland there was a determined effort to root out sedition in the armed forces of the crown. After a series of courts martial in 1797 some twenty soldiers were executed, and scores of others were flogged and sent to serve abroad for life. Most notably, the army was encouraged to go beyond what the letter of the law permitted. Initially Ulster was to be dragooned, but soon

---

[21] Thomas Bartlett, ed., "Select Documents xxxviii: Defenders and Defenderism in 1795," *Irish Historical Studies*, 24:95 (1985), 373–94: 389.
[22] The classic account of this "alliance" is Marianne Elliott, *Partners in Revolution: The United Irishmen and France* (New Haven: Yale University Press, 1982).

all Ireland was held to be enemy territory. If the French did return, they would not find a United Irish organization or a native insurgent army to welcome them ashore. The model for this counterinsurgency campaign was to be the French efforts to crush counterrevolutionary insurrection in west France. "I look upon Ulster to be a La Vendée and [believe]," wrote General Thomas Knox, "that it will not be brought into subjection but by the same means adopted by the French Republicans in power – namely spreading devastation through the most disaffected parts."[23] Accordingly, throughout 1797 and on into 1798 the United Irish organization that had been for years relentlessly swearing in members and drilling them in a military fashion came under ruthless attack in Ulster and elsewhere. Numerous arrests were made, with house-burnings, flogging, torture, and shootings all routinely carried out by the military in an attempt to ensure that, should the French return, there would be little or no support for them in Ireland.

In its determination to destroy the United Irish movement in Ulster, the authorities did not shy away from playing the sectarian card. Sectarian rioting and feuding had been an endemic feature in east and mid-Ulster during the 1790s, when the Catholic Defenders clashed with the Protestant Peep of Day Boys, a violently loyalist grouping widely accepted as forerunners of the Orange Order (formed in 1795). In general, Dublin Castle had not taken sides in these disturbances and had instead urged local magistrates to deal even-handedly with those culprits who appeared before them in court. From mid-decade on, however, it was evident to Camden and his advisors that a more partisan policy was required, one that involved "arming the Protestants who can be depended on." Thus the newly formed and strongly Protestant Orange Order received official countenance, and in late 1796 a Yeomanry force was embodied. The Yeomen were designed to be deployed in their local areas to pursue wrongdoers and subversives so that regular soldiers could be freed up for service elsewhere, or to confront the French, should they land. But the formation of the Yeomanry was also meant to give confidence to those Protestants who were hostile to the United Irish conspiracy, who were fuming at the apparent lack of robust action against its leaders and were fearful at what appeared to be the inexorable rise of the Irish Catholics. Armed with new laws and new forces, and well-briefed on the progress of the United Irish plans through the efforts of a large number of informers, Dublin Castle through 1797 and 1798 turned the tide against the

---

[23] Knox to duke of Abercorn, 21 March 1797, Public Record Office of Northern Ireland (hereafter PRONI) T2541/1B3/6/10.

United Irishmen and their rural allies. In March 1798, on the basis of information received, almost the entire Dublin directory of the United Irish leadership was arrested; in May, a key leader of the planned insurrection, Lord Edward FitzGerald, was shot and captured. He died from his wounds in early June, and shortly afterwards, his designated successors, John and Henry Sheares, were arrested and tried, convicted, and executed in July 1798.

By that date, a full-scale insurrection had broken out, not, as had been anticipated, in Dublin city, but in the counties around the capital, and especially in Wexford, where an initial rebel victory at Oulart (27 May) had electrified the southeast and had drawn thousands into the movement. After a number of victories, however, the insurgents, almost all Catholic, though often with Protestant leaders, found themselves hemmed in by the crown forces and were finally routed at Vinegar Hill, outside Enniscorthy, county Wexford on 21 June 1798 (Figure 16.1). Meanwhile, on 6 June, a smaller rising had taken place in county Antrim and then, a week later, in county Down. Deprived of an initial victory, however, these rebels, mostly Presbyterian, though with some Catholics in their ranks, had easily been scattered. A landing by a small French force under General Jean Humbert at Killala, county Mayo on 22 August 1798 could do nothing to alter that overall verdict of total rebel failure, and the year ended with a long series of trials, courts martial, executions, and banishments. Altogether around 20,000 rebels died (Alexander Marsden, an undersecretary in Dublin Castle, offered this figure, and suggested that the loss of so many rebels would be to the country's advantage)[24] – the true figure will never be known – and with them around 600 soldiers. A further casualty was to be the Irish Parliament: on learning that rebellion had broken out in Ireland, William Pitt determined that this offered the perfect opportunity to push through a long-desired Anglo-Irish legislative union, duly accomplished in 1800.

The rebellion had only been a few days old when an alarmed Camden described the mood among his advisors.

> Savage cruelties, party and religious prejudice has literally made the Protestant part of the country mad. The army partake of the fury. It is scarcely possible to restrain the violence of my own immediate friends and advisers within justifiable bounds. They are prepared for extirpation and any appearance of lenity on the part of government raises a flame that runs like wildfire through the street and over the country.[25]

---

[24] Marsden to Unidentified, 4 August 1798, NAI Rebellion Papers 620/3/51/17a.
[25] TNA Camden to Pitt, 29 May 1798, Pitt Papers, 30/8/326/302.

The Irish Rebellion of 1798

Figure 16.1 Chaotic scenes at the rebel camp at Vinegar Hill (1798). Courtesy of the British Library.

Camden's fears of a bloodbath were fully justified, as reports of massacres of prisoners and grisly sectarian atrocities poured into the Castle (among them 350 rebels intent on surrender slaughtered by General Sir James Duff on the Curragh of Kildare, and over 100 Protestants burned alive at Scullabogue, county Wexford). Camden was replaced as lord lieutenant in June 1798 by Lord Cornwallis, a veteran of the American war, and he too tried to restrain crown forces, as he complained, from regarding every man in "a brown coat" as a rebel to be put to death,[26] but with as little success as his predecessor: he was soon wringing his hands over the "numberless murders committed by our people," such crimes reminding him of those committed by American loyalists.

The extreme violence witnessed during the 1798 rebellion, and during the run-up to it, bears comparison with that perpetrated in the Vendée, and later in Spain during the Peninsular War. As in these theaters, irregular combatants were simply not recognized as legitimate fighters, and therefore the

[26] Cornwallis to Portland, 28 June 1798, TNA HO 100/77/200-1.

normal ethical constraints on soldiers' conduct could be ignored. Thus General Humbert and his French soldiers, on their surrender at Ballinamuck, county Longford, were granted the status of enemy combatants and were well-treated, some might say fêted in their captivity. In marked contrast, their Irish auxiliaries, around 2,000 strong, were immediately set upon by crown forces, with scores more executed on the road back to Killala, a distance of around 140 kilometers, and with many more killings when that undefended town was taken by storm.[27]

"The brotherhood of affection is over: rancour and animosity to an incredible degree have succeeded it."[28] So a correspondent of the earl of Charlemont, sometime commander of the Volunteers, described the atmosphere in the north of Ireland in the aftermath of the rebellion of 1798. The United Irish project, one directly stemming from the examples of America and France and the Enlightenment principles that underpinned them, had apparently perished in the bloody rebellion in the summer of 1798. Frustrated in their hopes of peaceful reform, the United Irishmen had been reluctant rebels, goaded into action by military excesses, and they had understandably, but naïvely, relied too much on French assistance. In the end, disunited Irishmen had triumphed over United Irishmen.

Sectarianism

It is a Jacobinical conspiracy throughout the kingdom, pursuing its object chiefly with Popish instruments.[29]

The whole is what I long foresaw, a popish conspiracy.[30]

At Wexford there has so far back as 36 years to my knowledge existed a violent Protestant and Catholic party.[31]

They felt themselves under the necessity of proving that they are the direct descendants of the very people who committed the same barbarities in 1641.[32]

---

[27] For the aftermath of the surrender at Ballinamuck, see Joshua Kemmis to Thomas Kemmis, 25 September 1798, in NAI Fraser/2/89.

[28] Edward Hudson to Lord Charlemont, 18 July 1798, in Historical Manuscripts Commission (hereafter HMC), *Charlemont Mss.*, vol. II, 327.

[29] Lord Castlereagh to William Wickham, 12 June 1798, in Marquis of Londonderry, ed., *Memoirs and Correspondence of Viscount Castlereagh*, 4 vols. (London: Henry Colburn, 1850), vol. I, 219–20.

[30] John Foster, Speaker of the Irish parliament, to Lord Sheffield, 5 June 1798, in PRONI T3465.89.

[31] Lady Louisa Conolly to Lord Richmond, 18 June 1798, PRONI T3048/B/27.

[32] Thomas Bond to Archbishop of Cashel, 21 July 1798, PRONI T3719/C32/101.

> Ní ó dhúchas fuair Luther nó aon neach dá spór
> A bhfuil de cúirteanna úrgeal' ó Luimneach go Bóinn
> Tiocfaidh sciúirse ar na búir seo le Gaelaibh i ngleo
> Is ní bhíonn dúiche nó dún acu in Éirinn níos mó.
> (It wasn't from their fathers that Luther and his breed
> got all the bright new dwellings from Limerick to the Boyne;
> These boors will surely be whipped by the Gaels in battle
> And they'll never again have house, home nor habitation in Ireland)[33]
> The spearmen used to take pleasure in piercing the victims through and with exaltation licking their bloody spears.[34]
> Oh Dear! What a sad, sad thing is a civil war.[35]
> It is much to be lamented that the Irish Roman Catholics in general, have, for two hundred years, manifested a marked hostility against the Protestant empire, which all of the rebellions kindled on the score of religion, or in which its influence chiefly predominated, unquestionably prove.[36]

What really happened in Ireland in 1798? These quotations, and there are any number of similar ones, suggest other answers that very many contemporaries were prepared to embrace. The United Irish leaders may have been possessed of "a vision of a non-sectarian, democratic and inclusive politics" and they certainly believed that they were embarked on a noble enterprise to bring freedom and equality to their fellow citizens. As well, it is evident that they viewed their efforts in Ireland as but a part of an extended plan to promote republicanism in the Atlantic world. Those who opposed their entire project, however, were not at all persuaded.[37]

As noted above, from the beginning, the United Irishmen's initial campaign for parliamentary reform was denounced as subversive of the existing order, then as treasonous when France and Britain went to war, and finally as essentially a rerun of the seventeenth-century conflicts of 1641 and 1688.

---

[33] Anon., 1790s, quoted in Vincent Morley, *The Popular Mind in Eighteenth Century Ireland* (Cork: Cork University Press, 2017), 256 (my, somewhat free, translation). "Limerick" is a reference to the final surrender of the Jacobite forces in Ireland in 1691, while "the Boyne" refers to the battle in 1690, north of Dublin, where the forces of James II were defeated by those led by William III.

[34] Information of Richard Grundy, 23 June 1798, TNA HO 100/81/215.

[35] Lady Louisa Conolly to Lord George Lennox, 10 September 1798, in Historical Manuscripts Commission, *Report on the Manuscripts of Earl Bathurst* (London: His Majesty's Stationery Office, 1923), 716.

[36] Sir Richard Musgrave, *Memoirs of the Different Rebellions in Ireland*, 3rd edition (Dublin: Robert Marchbank, 1802), author's preface, xx. Musgrave began his account of the 1798 rebellion in 1152.

[37] Kevin Whelan, "Reinterpreting the 1798 Rebellion in County Wexford," in Dáire Keogh and Nicholas Furlong, eds., *The Mighty Wave: Aspects of the 1798 Rebellion in Wexford* (Dublin: Four Courts Press, 1996), 9–36: 9.

"This plan of reform," wrote Camden, "is really only a popular question under which to shelter the treason they [United Irishmen] are plotting and executing."[38] On occasion the blame for the mayhem of the 1790s was laid not on the French Revolution, but at the door of "British party." "How many times has Ireland been fought for already," wrote undersecretary Edward Cooke, "and were not the last two rebellions of 1641 and '88 the consequences of British party? Was not America severed from England by British party? Did not British party take up the principle of Irish independence?"[39] In a similar vein, the Irish lord chancellor, Lord Clare, claimed that the Catholic Irish had "a rooted and hereditary hatred of the British name and nation" and that "the people of England will learn, I fear too late, the consequences of tampering with this giddy country. They [successive British governments] have been making experiments in Ireland since the year 1782."[40] John Foster, speaker of the Irish House of Commons, concurred: "Your cabinet," he told a correspondent based in England, "in its policy of interfering in our internal concerns for the papists, began this business,"[41] while a son-in-law of the Archbishop of Cashel remarked triumphantly that "what I have been in vain prophecying [sic] for some years, namely that we must fight once more for Ireland, has happened in my days."[42] It was axiomatic, claimed the largely absentee chief secretary, Thomas Pelham, that "nothing short of the establishment of the Catholic religion will satisfy those of that persuasion and as the property of the country is in the hands of the Protestants such an event can never take place without a civil war."[43]

Property, or the recovery of estates forfeited in the seventeenth century, figured prominently in contemporary analyses of the rebellion, while Enlightenment ideals or French principles were scarcely mentioned. One witness claimed that "the intention of rebellion was signalled years ago" by the publication of a map "in which the whole kingdom was divided, not by the names of the counties only but by the names of the old proprietors such as O'Tool's country, the Burns country etc."[44] Another declared that "the present is a contest of the poor against the rich and of the Irishman against the British government," adding, "the loyalty of any Irishman who is unconnected with

[38] Camden to Duke of Portland, 9 March 1798; TNA HO 100/69/132–8.
[39] Cooke to Auckland, c. 14 August 1798, PRONI T3229/34.
[40] Clare to Camden, 28 August 1796, PRONI CT2627/4/199; Clare to Mornington, 20 April 1797, PRONI T3287/5/1.
[41] Foster to Sheffield, 5 June 1798, PRONI T3465/89.
[42] Lord Mendip to Archbishop of Cashel, 14 June 1798, PRONI T3719/C32/82.
[43] Pelham to Portland, 29 September 1797, TNA HO 100/70/146–9.
[44] Unidentified to Archbishop of Cashel, [24?] May 1798, PRONI T3719/C32/62.

property is artificial."⁴⁵ From Granard, county Longford, the Reverend Alexander Montgomery wrote to William Pitt giving him the benefit of his insight into the Catholic mind: "No lapse of time can extinguish the leading principle of popery, the extermination of heretics, particularly in a country where they allege these heretics have usurped their ancient possessions."⁴⁶

Particularly gratifying for the Irish authorities were the comments reportedly made by the French commanders about their Irish allies. Much was made of their confirmation of the Castle's view of the rebels as variously "drunkards, robbers, cannibals" and barbarians, religious fanatics, and savages.⁴⁷ "The French officers," wrote chief secretary Lord Castlereagh, "express'd the utmost contempt and abhorrence of their Irish auxiliaries [who were] so unmanageable as to prove really an encumbrance."⁴⁸ Even the United Irishman Bartholomew Teeling, who had accompanied the French to Killala, allegedly told Cooke "the country people were very ill-behaved, came in, got arms and clothes and ran away and that their sole object was plunder."⁴⁹ There were gleeful reports that the French, veterans of the Italian and Vendéan campaigns, and certainly no friends to the Catholic Church, were variously shocked and amused at the Irish who flocked to them offering to fight for "France and the Blessed Virgin."⁵⁰

Destabilization

What happened in Wexford or Antrim, Kildare or Armagh cannot be separated from what was happening elsewhere in the Atlantic world at this stage.⁵¹

The republican disaffection of the 1790s was, despite some superficial indications to the contrary, a direct continuation of the Jacobite disaffection that had prevailed among the Irish-speaking community since the 1690s.⁵²

---

⁴⁵ Thomas Knox to Pelham, 14 May 1797, British Library, Pelham papers, MS 33104/59.
⁴⁶ Alex. Montgomery to Pitt, 24 January 1795, TNA Pitt papers 30/8/328/365–8.
⁴⁷ Shannon to Henry Boyle, 10 September 1798, PRONI Shannon Papers 2707/A3/3/114.
⁴⁸ Castlereagh to Wickham, 10 September 1798, TNA HO 100/78/324.
⁴⁹ Cooke to Wickham, 11 September 1798, in Charles Derek Ross, ed., *Correspondence of Marquis Cornwallis*, 3 vols. (London: J. Murray, 1859), vol. II, 402.
⁵⁰ Harman Murtagh "General Humbert's Futile Campaign," in Thomas Bartlett, David Dickson, Dáire Keogh, and Kevin Whelan, eds., *1798: A Bicentenary Perspective* (Dublin: Four Courts Press, 2005), 174–87: 180. See also the French officers' accounts conveniently collected in Pierre Joannon, ed., *La descente des Français en Irlande, 1798* (Paris: La Vouivre, 1998), where they reveal their contempt for their Irish allies.
⁵¹ Whelan, "Reinterpreting the 1798 Rebellion," 11.
⁵² Morley, *The Popular Mind*, 242–3.

> Complex economic, military and ideological connections ... linked the world crises of the revolutionary and Napoleonic ages.[53]
>
> Atlantic civilisation was swept in the last few decades of the eighteenth century by a single revolutionary movement which manifested itself in different ways and with varying success in different countries, yet in all of them showed similar objectives and principles. ... These years are in fact the Age of the Democratic Revolution.[54]

What really happened in Ireland in the summer of 1798? There are at least three contexts in which to view the Irish Rebellion of 1798. The first, as some of these quotations suggest, is the Atlantic context. And here we might begin, not with the American Revolution, as has been traditional, but with the impact of the stunning victory of British arms in the Seven Years' War (1756–1763). Triumph in this far-flung conflict resulted in the acquisition of the whole of Canada, most of India, and a clutch of West Indian islands to boot. By the war's end, a British Empire had emerged that shook the global order, destabilized the Atlantic world, and excited thoughts of emulation and/or revenge in other countries. The so-called voyages of discovery to the Pacific undertaken by Captain James Cook between 1768 and 1779 further unbalanced the world order. These explorations in the Pacific Ocean certainly resulted in winning for Britain the "possession of convenient situations" – as Cook had been commanded to do – but they also caused many a youthful pulse to race with the dream, or expectation, of foreign booty, title, and fame.[55] For this was an era when young men who were not well-born – and there were many more of them in the western world than before – had little to look forward to by way of an exciting or rewarding career. Godechot regarded "la poussée démographique" that occurred in the late eighteenth-century Atlantic world as fundamental to the "Age of the Atlantic Revolution."[56] We may note that the future Irish revolutionary Theobald Wolfe Tone's first entry into public life was to propose establishing British military colonies in the South Seas from which raids could be launched against Spanish possessions in that region. In all, Tone put forward three rather different justifications in the detailed plans he sent to Pitt's government in the late 1780s: the earliest one stated that plunder would be the object, the

---

[53] C. A. Bayly, *The Birth of the Modern World* (Oxford: Blackwell, 2004), 86.
[54] R. R. Palmer, quoted by Brendan Simms, "Continental Analogies of 1798," in Bartlett et al., eds., *1798: A Bicentennial Perspective*, 577–95: 578–9.
[55] For the impact of Cook's voyages, see Tone, *Writings*, vol. I, 10–16.
[56] Jacques Godechot, *Les Révolutions, 1770–1799* (Paris: Presses universitaires de France, 1963), 85.

second one promised to liberate the colonies and make them independent, and the final one, sensationally, made the freedom of the slaves its objective. Successive British ministers dismissed Tone's schemes, and Tone, still seeking to escape that "nameless obscurity" which seemed to be his destiny, within a few years would attempt to persuade the French revolutionary government to dispatch an expedition to Ireland with himself holding a command position.[57] On board a French invasion fleet destined for Ireland in 1796, Tone recalled how his plans to attack Spanish possessions in the New World had been rejected. "In my anger I made something like a vow that if ever I had an opportunity I would make Mr Pitt sorry [for ignoring them]."[58]

The acquisition of a new empire posed huge challenges, both fiscal and military, for Britain. As is well known, paying for the new empire would rapidly lead Britain into acrimonious disputes with her colonies in North America, which ultimately would result in revolution and independence. Less well known, however, is that Britain's demand for soldiers to police the empire led Britain to radically reconsider its traditional policy of firmly excluding all Irish Catholics from the armed forces of the crown. And this policy shift, on its own, had the capacity to shake the Irish political structure.

Since the seventeenth century Irish Catholics had not been permitted to serve in the British army or Royal Navy, and strict instructions that only Protestants, and British Protestants at that, could be enlisted were constantly being issued. True, some Irish Catholics were always nonetheless recruited, for the manpower needs of the individual regiment might often take priority over government bans, but such recruitment had to be done covertly and without fanfare. What was an identifiable trickle in the 1760s, however, had become a stream in the 1780s and then a torrent from the 1790s on, with over 150,000 Irish enlisted in the British army and some 25,000 in the Royal Navy during the Revolutionary and Napoleonic wars. Irish Catholic numbers were central to Britain's prosecution of these wars, not just in that graveyard of armies, the West Indies,[59] but also in India, where war was carried on by the East India Company, and in continental Europe. The importance of Irish recruits in the European theater is revealed by Home Office minister Lord Sidmouth's remark that "it was the supply of troops derived from Ireland that turn'd the scale on the 18th of June at Waterloo."[60]

---

[57] Tone, *Writings*, vol. I, 10–87. [58] Tone, *Writings*, vol. II, 279.
[59] See Roger Norman Buckley, *The British Army in the West Indies: Society and the Military in the Revolutionary Age* (Gainesville: University Press of Florida, 1998).
[60] Sidmouth to Whitmouth, 24 June 1815, TNA HO 100/184/204.

The urgent need for Irish recruits to garrison Britain's new empire, and to fight Britain's wars after 1760, sparked the emergence of the Catholic Question in Irish politics from the 1760s on and had the effect of destabilization by undermining the exclusive regime that had survived since the seventeenth century. Just as Catholic numbers were vital for the manpower needs of the British army, so too these numbers themselves appeared to constitute a compelling argument against permanent exclusion. The American and French Revolutions further shook the governing establishment in Ireland. Middle-class Irish Protestants guardedly welcomed the American Revolution, but held back from a wholehearted embrace, for the thorny problem of Irish Catholic intentions remained unresolved. William Drennan, a founder of the United Irish Society, admitted that he had grave doubts that Irish Catholics, the large majority in Ireland, would ever have that *capaces libertatis* that would allow them to act as citizens rather than as revanchist sectarians bent on extirpating "heretics." Events in France from 1789 on, however, appeared to remove those anxieties, and Theobald Wolfe Tone's arguments were both eloquent and persuasive on this score.

Irish Presbyterians, too, were similarly enthused by events in France, but they drew rather different lessons from them. The end of the French monarchy, the fall of the Catholic Church in France, and the establishment of a republic had profound biblical significance for Irish Presbyterians, even auguring the Second Coming of Christ. At the very least, shorn of French support, universal Catholicism was clearly doomed to wither into insignificance, or so they thought. Moreover, sacred prophecies from the Book of Revelations might come to pass and millennial beliefs were surely about to be vindicated. As a historian of Irish Dissent puts it, "Presbyterian radicalism was suffused with theological learning, biblical imagery and religious conviction."[61] Emboldened by the belief that "History" was on the march, Irish Presbyterians – not all, but very many of them – resolved to confront the Church of Ireland state in Ireland and seek by force of arms to establish a republic. This is what ultimately led them to the "turn out" – as they styled the rebellion in Antrim and Down in the summer of 1798. ("Rebellion" was very rarely used in counties Antrim and Down to describe the events of the summer of 1798: preferred terms were "the turn out," "the hurry," "the hurries," "the ruction," or even "the Troubles.")[62]

---

[61] Ian McBride, *Scripture Politics: Ulster Presbyterianism and Irish Radicalism in the Late Eighteenth Century* (Oxford: Clarendon Press, 1998), 4.

[62] Guy Beiner, *Forgetful Remembrance: Social Forgetting and Vernacular Historiography of a Rebellion in Ulster* (Oxford: Oxford University Press, 2018), 40.

For Irish Catholics, the lessons of the American and especially the French Revolutions were all rather different again. Catholic writers urging the repeal of the exclusionary Penal Laws from the 1760s on made much play with the peaceful conduct of Catholics in the decades since the 1690s – for example, there had been little stir among them at the time of the 1715 and 1745 Jacobite rebellions in Scotland. By the 1760s, Catholic apologists such as Charles O'Connor and John Curry could claim that Irish Catholic allegiance to the Stuart or Jacobite cause was all but gone. True, "red-hot" Protestants such as Sir Richard Musgrave and various Protestant bishops dismissed Catholic quiescence as evidence of loyalty to the Hanoverian dynasty and to the Protestant establishment. They would instead point to the widespread peasant insurgencies that punctuated the middle and later decades of the eighteenth century as proof of undying Catholic disaffection. And they would have frequent recourse to the accepted narrative of the 1641 Rebellion that revealed that Irish Catholics were always cruel, wholly untrustworthy, being bound by their religion to murder Protestants, should opportunity offer, and constantly harboring thoughts of the recovery of their forfeited lands.

Research into the vernacular prose and poetry in the Irish language of the late eighteenth century – and it must be remembered that the Catholic masses were overwhelmingly Irish-speaking – confirms that there was indeed a covert but highly significant popular attachment to the Jacobite cause right into the 1790s. Moreover, this affection for the Jacobites was completely resistant to hard reality – by every measure, the Jacobite cause was definitely lost by the 1760s – but this was not accepted by the Catholic underclass. In fact, a continued adherence to Jacobitism among the Irish-speaking community had the effect of preparing them for the promise of domestic upheaval, even regime change, aided by military assistance from abroad. As Vincent Morley has written, in the 1790s, "so far as the Catholic masses were concerned, their embrace of republicanism involved little more than a change of political nomenclature." Jacobite would seamlessly become Jacobin.[63]

From the foregoing, it is evident that we need to distinguish between leaders and followers, between planning and execution. What the Presbyterian leaders of the United Irishmen in Ulster, Henry Joy McCracken, William Steele Dickson, and the Simms brothers among them, aspired to, and what the Church of Ireland leaders elsewhere anticipated, was

---

[63] Morley, *The Popular Mind*, 243. See also B. Ó Buachalla, "From Jacobite to Jacobin," in Bartlett et al., eds., *1798: A Bicentenary Perspective*, 75–96.

far removed from what their followers – the alleged 400,000 sworn members of the Union, overwhelmingly Catholic but with many Presbyterians among them – anticipated. And it was understandable that when the peasants of Mayo witnessed the small French force under Humbert coming ashore at Killala, they immediately interpreted this "invasion" as the fulfillment of that Jacobite prophetic literature in which they had been schooled.

These conflicting contexts, I think, explain the chaotic nature of the rebellion of 1798 in Ireland. Contrary to what had been planned, there was no rising in Dublin, for the city was flooded with troops and the United Irish leadership had been seized. Instead, rebellion – swiftly repressed – had broken out in a circle of counties around the capital and then further south in Wexford, hitherto seen by Dublin Castle as a peaceful county in which the United Irishmen had made few inroads. In fact, the United Irishmen had successfully infiltrated Wexford – it was Dublin Castle's intelligence on the United Irishmen's progress that was defective here – while the rebels' early victory at Oulart against the North Cork Militia brought out thousands more supporters.

What motivated these Wexford rebels? Their being predominantly Irish-speaking cannot mean that they were ignorant of events in France or in the wider world, or that we can ignore politicization as a factor in their mobilization. Lord Westmorland commented that among the Defenders there was an "expectation of change [and] a general belief that the French were the friends of the poor," but he was puzzled as to how "such people in such uncultivated places could be made acquainted with these ideas."[64] Sermons by Catholic priests denouncing the Revolution and all its works would surely have proved informative for the congregation, while newspaper coverage of events in France would also have found an eager and receptive audience. Years later, Miles Byrne, a former United Irishman, recalled "the happy days when we used to read at the Chapel the newspapers giving an account of his [Napoleon Bonaparte's] brilliant campaigns from 1795 down to the peace of Campo Formio."[65] And yet, though Micheál Óg Ó Longáin, a Cork poet, was well informed concerning Bonaparte's deeds in Italy, in his sequence of poems on the 1798 Rebellion in Wexford the "language of earlier religious and colonial conflicts" was predominant.[66] On the other hand, when Miles

---

[64] Westmorland to Dundas, 8 June 1793, TNA HO 100/57/336-42.
[65] Cited in Thomas Bartlett, "Miles Byrne: United Irishman, Irish Exile and *Beau Sabreur*," in Keogh and Furlong, eds., *The Mighty Wave*, 118-38: 119.
[66] Tom Dunne, *Rebellions: Memoir, Memory and 1798* (Dublin: Lilliput Press, 2004), 156-7.

Byrne, a United Irishman in Wexford in 1798 and later an officer in the French army, came to list his military career for pension purposes in 1835, he dated his French service from the moment he was sworn in as a United Irishman in January 1797, and in his memoirs, published in the 1860s, he dismissed claims that the Wexford rebels were motivated by sectarianism or that the rebel army was simply a mob out for plunder.[67]

What motivated the rebels of counties Antrim and Down in 1798? They were mostly Presbyterian, though with Catholics in their ranks, and it is tempting to ascribe lofty ideals to them, and to see their "turn out" as a principled assault on the Protestant Ascendancy in order to put an end to monarchical government in Ireland and to establish a republic. (As a result of the upheavals of the sixteenth and seventeenth centuries, Irish Protestants, though only constituting around one-quarter of the Irish population, monopolized all political power, occupied almost all government offices, commanded all military commissions, and owned most of the land of Ireland, a situation generally referred to as the "Protestant Ascendancy.") Certainly, the rebels' narrative of their battles at Saintfield and Ballynahinch stressed their commitment to the ideals of the American and French Revolutions – as well as their determination to exact revenge on Crown forces that over the previous two years had been severely harrying them. Would they have seen the Wexford rebels or those in Mayo as engaged in a common struggle – as partners in revolution – with them? It is unlikely. The socially elevated *leaders* of the rebels in the southeast and the west would easily have fitted in with those in Ulster, but with the rank and file – Catholic, Irish-speaking, and filled with memories of conquest and colonization – there would surely have been little common ground.[68]

In short, the origins of the 1798 rebellion in Ireland can be traced in the first instance to that great destabilization in the Atlantic world provoked by British victories in the Seven Years' War, and the consequent acquisition of a worldwide empire. This impacted directly on Ireland in that the quest for recruits to garrison this empire led to the reversal of a decades-old exclusion of Irish Catholics from the armed forces of Britain. In its turn, this policy turnaround triggered a continual political crisis in Ireland that was further sharpened by the American rupture and the attendant whiff of British vulnerability. Lastly, the French Revolution sent out mixed but powerful

---

[67] Bartlett, "Miles Byrne," 126.
[68] See Beiner, *Forgetful Rembrance*, for a full analysis of the memory of the 1798 Rebellion in Ulster.

messages. Its Jacobin promise of liberty and equality found an eager audience in Ireland (and elsewhere) among those who were educated but marginalized, and among those who viewed the success of French arms as a vindication of the Revolution's principles. Among some Irish Presbyterians the incredible events in France were viewed as a preliminary to the downfall of the Anti-Christ and as a prelude to the Second Coming. For others, events in France offered an opportunity to rerun the American Revolution in an Irish context. As for Irish Catholics, the French Revolution's message was also clear: the Jacobite moment had finally come, and with deliverance from abroad assured, recovery, restoration, and revenge were surely now at hand. These mixed, sometimes contradictory, strands led inexorably to armed rebellion in 1798, and largely explain its chaotic nature.

17
Italy: Revolution and Counterrevolution (1789–1799)

JOHN A. DAVIS

Introduction: The French Revolution and Italy's "Passive Revolution"?

Vincenzo Cuoco's *Historical Essay on the Neapolitan Republic* was the earliest and most influential account of the impact of the French Revolution on Italy. It was published in Milan in the summer of 1801 immediately after the fall of the Italian republics that had been founded following the French invasion of the peninsula in 1796. The author had served in the Neapolitan Republic that was founded in January 1799, but before the republic fell five months later, he had escaped to Marseille. After the triumphant return of Bonaparte's armies to northern Italy in the spring of 1800, Cuoco made his way to Milan, the capital of the reconstituted Italian Republic.

Cuoco's *Essay* was published at a moment when hopes were still high that France's new First Consul would reconstitute the republican order in Italy. Milan had become a refuge of the survivors of the earlier republics, and Cuoco's essay was written to warn fellow republicans against repeating the errors that he believed had caused them to fail. The greatest of these had been the Italian republicans' reliance on ideas adopted uncritically from France that had no roots in Italian political culture or traditions, making their revolutions no more than "passive" imitations of the French Revolution. That was why the republicans had failed to communicate their political aims to the people, a fault compounded by their social background. Drawn overwhelmingly from the educated, propertied, and professional classes and the clergy, the republicans were ill-equipped to communicate with the masses or to understand the brute ignorance and superstition that lay behind the popular counterrevolutionary insurrections that in 1799 had turned Italy into a second Vendée. To be successful, Cuoco concluded, the republicans must first learn to communicate and to find ways of demonstrating that the revolution was for, and not against, the people.[1]

These conclusions echoed the experiences of many fellow republicans and proved very influential. Nineteenth-century Italian liberals took Cuoco's observations to identify the Italian republicans of 1796–1799 as "Jacobins" and looked on the French Revolution as one more chapter of foreign occupation that interrupted more moderate and indigenous processes of change that had been in progress since the eighteenth century. Democrats were also wary of the French revolutionary tradition, and while Giuseppe Mazzini embraced the wider political ideals of the Declaration of the Rights of Man and the French Revolution, he rejected Jacobin egalitarianism as materialist and divisive.[2] For Catholic historians, by contrast, the French Revolution was the product of a rationalist and secularist Enlightenment that was the root cause of all the subsequent misfortunes of Catholic Europe, the Papacy, and Italy. However, they hailed the counterrevolutionary insurrections of 1796–1799 as expressions of popular loyalty to the legitimate rulers and their faith, whereas for a later generation of Italian nationalists the insurrections signaled the first stirrings of a popular sense of Italian identity that contrasted with the effete cosmopolitanism of the intellectual elites who had championed an alien, un-Christian, and hence un-Italian Revolution.[3]

Denigration of the French Revolution and the Italian republics of 1796–1799 reached its peak in the fascist decades, but in the highly charged public debates on the origins of fascism that followed the fall of Mussolini's regime Vincenzo Cuoco's "passive revolution" found an unexpected new lease of life. This was thanks to Antonio Gramsci, the former communist leader and prominent antifascist martyr who devoted his arduous incarceration in fascist jails to the weaving of earlier democratic and republican critiques into a Marxist alternative to the triumphant portrayal of Italy's achievement of national unity and independence – the *Risorgimento* – by liberal and nationalist historians.

---

[1] See Vincenzo Cuoco, *Historical Essay on the Neapolitan Revolution of 1799*, ed. Bruce Haddock and Filippo Sabetti (Toronto: Toronto University Press, 2014); Vincenzo Cuoco, *Saggio storico sulla rivoluzione napolitana*, ed. Pasquale Villani (Bari: Laterza, 1976); Antonino De Francesco, *Vicenzo Cuoco: Una vita politica* (Bari: Laterza, 1997); Antonino De Francesco, *Rivoluzioni e costituzioni: Saggi sul democratismo politico nell'Italia napoleonica 1796–1821* (Naples: ESI, 1996).

[2] Franco della Peruta, *I Democratici e la Rivoluzione italiana: Dibattiti ideali e contrasti politici all'indomani dell'1848* (Milan: Feltrinelli, 1958); Nadia Urbinati, "Mazzini and the Making of Republican ideology," *Journal of Modern Italian Studies* 17:2 (2012), 183–204.

[3] Carlo Capra, *Gli italiani prima dell'Italia: Un lungo Settecento dalla fine della Controriforma a Napoleone* (Rome: Carocci, 2014), 331–7.

Gramsci not only returned to Cuoco's *Essay* but also adopted his "passive revolution" as the premise of his own interpretation, and in the process turned the original meaning of the term on its head. Whereas Cuoco had blamed the republicans for trying to follow the French Jacobins too closely, Gramsci blamed them for not imitating the Jacobins closely enough, and went on to argue that the errors of the Italian Jacobins of 1796–1799 had been repeated by the Risorgimento democrats half a century later. Their failure to adopt a democratic program capable of mobilizing popular discontent had replicated Cuoco's "passive revolution" on a broader scale, and was the reason that Italy had not experienced a modern bourgeois revolution in the nineteenth century and hence the cause of the subsequent weakness of Italian parliamentary democracy when confronted by Mussolini's fascism after the First World War.[4]

In the ideologically charged climate after the Second World War, Gramsci's posthumously published *Prison Notebooks* gave the French Revolution a privileged place in determining the course of Italian history, but as Cold War concerns faded, the ideological and teleological premises of Gramsci's scantly documented interpretation became evident. The portrayals of the French Revolution and the Italian republics are now of interest primarily as illustrations of ideological constructs, while the determinist structure of Gramsci's analysis greatly exaggerated the roles of Italian democrats such as the Tuscan follower of Gracchus Babeuf, Filippo Buonarroti, and failed to take account of the wide range of political views held by those who supported the revolution in France.

Nor has the idea that republican ideals were simply imported from France and the French Revolution stood the test of time well, and there is now abundant evidence that the ideas that the Italian republicans attempted to put into practice between 1796 and 1799 had deep roots in prerevolutionary Italian political culture. In the words of Gian Luca Fruci, "French ideas interacted with existing Italian ideas to provide a fervor of interest in democratization and its implications perhaps to a greater extent than anywhere else in Europe, including France itself."[5]

These more recent interpretations reflect a radical change in historical perspectives, in which the revolution in France has been set against the broader canvas of the democratic revolutions and the Enlightenment.

---

[4] John A Davis, ed., *Gramsci and Italy's Passive Revolution* (Oxford: Routledge, 2014 [1979]).
[5] Gian Luca Fruci, "Democracy in Italy: From Enlightenment Republicanism to Plebiscitary Monarchy," in Joanna Innes and Mark Philp, eds., *Re-imagining Democracy in the Mediterranean, 1780–1860* (Oxford: Oxford University Press, 2018), 25–50.

Building on, but moving well beyond, the transatlantic frame of the earlier studies of R. R. Palmer and Jacques Godechot, the Enlightenment and the democratic revolutions have provided meeting points for historians of ideas, culture, politics, institutions, and economies that have demonstrated the essentially international and transnational character of that intense moment of intellectual and cultural interaction that historians now call the Republic of Letters. Ideas and projects traveled freely between the European states and nations, and backwards and forwards across the Atlantic. Ideas were not only constantly on the move, but also continually being revised and redefined in the light of local circumstances and traditions.[6]

Italian historians have played leading roles in pioneering these new approaches, and the monumental studies of Franco Venturi, for example, critically reshaped understanding of the cosmopolitan character of the Enlightenment debates in ways that have profoundly influenced subsequent discussion. The prominence of Italian historians in these debates reflects the importance and originality of the contributions of Italian thinkers and writers to the prerevolutionary Republic of Letters. Hence the Italian states offer a fertile ground not only for understanding the impact of the French Revolution in transnational contexts, but also for addressing the new questions these contexts pose: was there a single Enlightenment or many; a single democratic revolution or many?[7]

Italy before the Revolution: Enlightenment, Reform, and the Crisis of the *Ancien Régime*

Debates on the best ways to promote good government acquired prominence in the second half of the eighteenth century because the *ancien régime*

---

[6] Capra, *Gli italiani prima dell'Italia*; Anna Maria Rao, "Enlightenment and Reform," in John A. Marino, ed., *Early Modern Italy* (Oxford: Oxford University Press, 2002), 229–52; Anna Maria Rao, "Republicanism in Italy from the Enlightenment to the Early Risorgimento," *Journal of Modern Italian Studies* 17:2 (2012), 149–67; De Francesco, *Rivoluzioni e costituzioni*; R. R. Palmer, *The Age of the Democratic Revolution: A Political History of Europe 1760–1800* (Princeton: Princeton University Press, 2014 [1959/1964]; Annie Jourdan, review of David Armitage and Sanjay Subrahmanyam, eds., *The Age of Revolution in Global Context* (London: Palgrave, 2009), *Annales Historiques de la Révolution Française* no. 373 (2013), 208–24; Jacques Godechot, *Les Révolutions, 1770–1799* (Paris: Presses universitaires de France, 1963); Allan Panofsky, "The One and the Many: The Two Revolution Question and the 'Consumer-Commercial' Atlantic from 1789 to the Present," in Manuela Albertone and Antonino De Francesco, eds., *Rethinking the Atlantic World: Europe and America in the Age of the Atlantic Revolution* (Houndmills: Palgrave Macmillan, 2009), 18–35.

[7] Panofsky, "The One and the Many"; John Robertson, *The Case for the Enlightenment: Scotland and Naples 1680–1760* (Cambridge: Cambridge University Press, 2005).

rulers were everywhere facing very similar challenges. As R. R. Palmer rightly understood, the underlying causes and consequences of the crisis of the *ancien régime* were similar. To overcome the fiscal and financial constraints imposed by the political and institutional structures of the *ancien régime*, the rulers adopted absolutist strategies that brought them into conflict with the nobility, the Church, and the privileged corporations. But the scale of those conflicts was exacerbated by irreversible economic changes that were undermining the fabric of the European *ancien régime* and, by the closing decades of the century, were provoking rural and urban unrest throughout Europe.[8]

The Italian states were no exception. On the eve of the revolution in France, Italy consisted of a mosaic of principalities, duchies, kingdoms, and ancient republics that reflected centuries of foreign intervention and occupation. The new balance of European power that followed the wars of dynastic succession in the early eighteenth century had brought significant political changes, the most important being the decline of Spanish power and the ascendancy of the Austrian Habsburgs. The acquisition of the former Spanish Duchy of Lombardy made the Habsburgs the dominant power in northern Italy. Their power expanded when in 1737 the last Medici ruler of the Grand Duchy of Tuscany was succeeded by Duke Francis Stephen of Lorraine, the consort of the Austrian empress Maria Theresa. The reign of his son and future Austrian emperor, Peter Leopold, in Tuscany would be one of the high points of European enlightened absolutism.

To the east, Venice and its hinterland were still part of the ancient Republic of St. Mark. To the northwest lay the multiple territories of the former dukes of Savoy – Piedmont, Nice, Aosta, and Savoy – who became kings following the acquisition of the island and kingdom of Sardinia in 1720. This was Italy's most independent dynastic state and, since it formed a geographic buffer separating Bourbon France and Habsburg Austria, its territorial integrity was repeatedly guaranteed by the European powers. By contrast, the rulers of the small principalities to the south of the river Po, the duchies of Modena and Reggio ruled by the d'Este family and the Bourbon dukes of Parma, Piacenza, and Guastalla, were clients of the principal dynastic powers. Then came the temporal dominions of the Pope, the second largest of the Italian states that was ruled as a secular kingdom by the Pope-kings and their cardinals. To the south lay the oldest and largest of the Italian

---

[8] See David Armitage, "Foreword," in Palmer, *The Age of the Democratic Revolution*, xv–xxii.

monarchies, the kingdoms of Naples and Sicily that after 300 years of Spanish rule had in 1734 become independent dynastic monarchies ruled by the eldest son of the king of Spain, Charles of Bourbon.

Within the *ancien régime* structure of devolved power sharing with the nobility, the Church, and autonomous corporations, the Italian rulers, just like their counterparts elsewhere in Europe, looked to increase their power and revenues. That meant creating new bureaucracies, increasing the productivity of agriculture, trade, and manufactures, and, for the rulers of the larger states, building modern armies and navies. In addition, dynastic pretentions demanded conspicuous expenditure on magnificent new palaces, hunting lodges, theaters, and lavish courts. All of this required massive increases in their revenues, and the strategies they adopted to that end followed well-established templates and were often directed by seasoned administrators who moved freely from one princely court to another.

As in many other European states, the wealth and extensive jurisdictions exercised by the papacy, the secular clergy, and the religious orders seemed initially to be easy targets. Indeed, the measures taken in Habsburg Lombardy, Tuscany, Naples, and Sicily to reduce the power and privileges of the papacy and the wealth of certain religious orders attracted strong support even from sections of the clergy. But when it came to reducing the power of privileged corporate bodies and the feudal nobility, the absolutist initiatives proved to be more divisive. That was to be expected in the Bourbon kingdoms of Naples and Sicily, where feudal institutions and power were greater than in any other part of western Europe, but absolutist strategies proved to be no less contentious in the other Italian states.[9]

These initiatives created new openings for public debate, however, and the rulers turned to the world of learning and professional expertise for support. Any reference to "public opinion" in the eighteenth century must take account of the limits imposed by illiteracy, the remoteness of large sections of the population, and ever-present censorship, but within these constrictions new opportunities were opening up. Eminent thinkers were recruited to administrative positions, and the princes looked to the *philosophes* to legitimize their initiatives. Italy's political fragmentation encouraged the development of numerous intellectual hubs, and in Milan, Florence, Turin, Naples, and Palermo new ideas and projects were eagerly debated in the context of models drawn from ancient Greece and Rome, and ideas

---

[9] See Capra, *Gli italiani prima dell'Italia*.

ranging from Machiavelli and the traditions of the early modern Italian city-states to the more recent political theories of English and French luminaries such as Hobbes, Locke, and Montesquieu and the works of the political economists were vigorously debated.[10]

Italians made major contributions to these international debates. The Neapolitan economist Antonio Genovesi, for whom the first Chair in Political Economy in Europe was founded at the University of Naples in 1754, the Milanese economist and penal reformer Cesare Beccaria, who recommended the abolition of capital punishment, and the Neapolitan jurist and philosopher Gaetano Filangieri, whose seven-volume *Scienza della Legislazione* (published between 1780 and 1791) is considered to be one of the major achievements of the Enlightenment were only the most notable of the Italians whose work was read throughout Europe and across the Atlantic. In 1783, for example, Benjamin Franklin invited Filangieri to comment on a draft of the new American constitution, to which the Neapolitan jurist responded. Filangieri subsequently referred to the American experiment in federal democracy in his own writings, and his followers did so too. Italians traveled widely, even to the United States, where the Florentine merchant and patriot Filippo Mazzei developed personal contact with leaders of the American Revolution, while accounts of the American Revolution began to appear in Italy.[11]

Even in its new American guise, however, republicanism posed problems for Italians. The surviving republics of Venice and Genoa embodied anachronistic oligarchic and aristocratic features, whereas the medieval city republics were synonymous with the weakness and internal divisions that left Italy exposed for centuries to foreign invasion and occupation. For many southerners, conquest by Republican Rome had destroyed the independent pre-Roman indigenous southern communities.

In the words of one of Italy's leading scholars, instead of the "republican tradition," it is better "to speak of republican ideals, ideas, themes, and influences than of a single, monolithic republican tradition," which explains why Italians were more inclined to look at the American Revolution not as a model, but as an incentive for "grafting republican virtue on monarchy."[12] But although these debates were taking place in many different Italian

---

[10] Rao, "Republicanism in Italy"; Eugenio Biagini, "Citizenship and Religion in the Italian Constitutions, 1796–1849," *History of European Ideas* 37 (2011), 211–17.
[11] Fruci, "Democracy in Italy," 28–9.
[12] Rao, "Republicanism in Italy"; De Francesco, *Rivoluzioni e costituzioni*.

centers, they were not limited to a narrow group of thinkers and administrators. Following the example of the Austrian Habsburgs, the absolutist rulers actively sought a broader base for their reforms, for which freemasonry was the chosen instrument. By the 1780s, freemasonry was actively being promoted in all the Italian states except the Papal Dominions, and even in remote provincial centers the lodges provided opportunities for members of the professions, landowners, and the clergy to debate the reform projects.[13]

In Italy, as elsewhere in Europe, the era of absolutist reform proved to be a golden age in appearance only, and the partnership between the princes and the philosophers was short-lived. By the mid-1780s the Habsburg rulers in Lombardy had alienated not only the nobility, but also many former supporters, including the economist, philosopher, and writer Pietro Verri, one of the most influential of the Milanese intellectuals who had served in the reform administrations of Emperor Joseph II.[14] In Tuscany reform projects, including the widely admired Tuscan Penal Code based on Beccaria's principles, were suspended amidst growing popular unrest. Rising food prices and unemployment were the immediate cause, and hence in Habsburg Lombardy and Tuscany controls on food prices were reintroduced in the late 1780s. In Piedmont the authorities were also alarmed by the impact of new commercial agricultural leases on the rural poor.[15] But throughout Italy unprecedented rates of demographic growth were exerting new pressures on resources, bringing unemployment to rural areas and swelling migration to the towns, exacerbating conflicts over access to land and the exercise of customary and collective rights that led to often violent conflicts both within and between neighboring communities.[16]

Absolutist policies frequently became targets of popular anger. In Tuscany, Peter Leopold's support for the Jansenist-inspired religious reforms promoted by the Bishop of Pistoia became a major focus of popular riots and demonstrations, while the suppression of religious orders and the sales of Church and communal lands were a cause of popular unrest throughout the

---

[13] Giuseppe Giarrizzo, *Massoneria e illuminismo nell'Europa del Settecento* (Venice: Donzelli, 1994); Patrick Chorley, *Oil, Silk and Enlightenment: Economic Problems in Eighteenth Century Naples* (Naples: Istituto per gli Studi Filosofici, 1965).
[14] Carlo Capra, "The Rise of Liberal Constitutionalism in Italy; Pietro Verri and the French Revolution," *Journal of Modern Italian Studies* 17:5 (2012), 516–26.
[15] Alessandra Contini, "Istituzioni e politica nell'età delle Riforme," in E. Fasano Garini, G. Petralia, and P. Pezzino, eds., *Storia della Toscana*, vol II: *Dal Settecento a oggi* (Bari: Laterza, 2004), 3–19.
[16] Capra, *Gli italiani prima dell'Italia*, 295–302.

Italian states. The reasons were well illustrated by the Bourbon government's response to the earthquake that devastated Calabria and parts of eastern Sicily in 1783. In what was in many respects a model Enlightenment project, the lands and goods of the Calabrian religious houses were expropriated to fund the recovery. But when the properties were sold, most lands ended up with wealthy landowners, leaving the former peasant tenants dispossessed and destitute.

Absolutist initiatives unintentionally inflamed existing conflicts in other ways, too. In the south, for example, crown agents encouraged local communities to bring lawsuits against neighboring lay and ecclesiastical feudatories, but the courts were already overwhelmed with cases, some stretching back over centuries, and could offer no solutions. Hence, while the actions of the Crown agents brought the rhetoric of the campaign against feudalism to even remote rural communities, they raised expectations that could not be met in ways that heightened existing conflicts.[17]

Well before the start of the revolution in France, there were alarming signs of political and social discontents in all the Italian states. To make matters worse, the absolutist initiatives had failed in their key objectives. Everywhere the finances of the Italian rulers were on the point of collapse, and it only took the preparation for war once relations with revolutionary France deteriorated after 1792 to precipitate their military, political, and financial collapse.

The French Revolution and Italy

Initially the Italian rulers greeted the 1789 revolution in Paris as an opportunity rather than a threat, while many of the reformers were hopeful that the events in France would revive the reform project and open the door to constitutional government at home. But those expectations did not outlive the arrest of Louis XVI and Marie Antoinette in August 1792 and the declaration of the Republic in September.

Relations with France quickly deteriorated. When Naples refused to receive the representative of the new French Republic in December, Admiral Latouche Tréville made a threatening show of arms off the Bay of Naples after French troops had occupied Nice and Savoy. Following the

---

[17] Contini, "Istituzioni e politica nell'età delle Riforme"; Capra, *Gli italiani prima dell'Italia*; John A. Davis, *Naples and Napoleon: Southern Italy and the European Revolutions 1780–1860* (Oxford: Oxford University Press, 2006), 54–70.

execution of Louis XVI in January 1793 and the outbreak of war between France and Austria, the Italian rulers came under strong pressure to join the alliance against France. Most prevaricated, but, even before the execution of her sister, Marie Antoinette, in October, Maria Carolina of Naples had become the outspoken voice of counterrevolution in Italy, and in July Naples secretly joined Austria and Britain in the First Coalition.

The Mediterranean was the theater of operations. The French held Nice and Savoy, but their attempts to occupy Sardinia were repulsed by the British Navy, which also supported Pasquale Paoli's revolt in Corsica. When in August the Allies tried to exploit a royalist uprising in Toulon to destroy the French Mediterranean fleet, the Neapolitan government agreed to join the expedition. Its failure marked a turning point: Spain withdrew from the coalition, Pasquale Paoli's rebellion in Corsica collapsed, and the attempts to dislodge the French from Nice and Savoy were unsuccessful. Meanwhile, the interruption of Mediterranean trade caused food prices to soar, and provoked popular protests throughout Italy. Tensions were heightened when republican conspiracies were discovered in Naples and Palermo in March, in Turin in May, and then in the papal city of Bologna in November.

By the autumn of 1795, France had regained control of the Mediterranean, and following the peace treaties with Prussia, the Netherlands, and Spain, the new government, the Directory, was free to expand the war. The principal objective was the Rhineland, but as a diversion Admiral Hoche was sent to raise an insurrection in Ireland and another army was to invade northern Italy to force the Austrians to split their forces on two fronts. But the scale and scope of the Italian campaign was changed by Napoleon Bonaparte's remarkable string of victories.[18]

After defeating the Piedmontese forces, Bonaparte crossed the river Po at Lodi on 10 May and five days later entered Milan. Verona, the papal cities of Bologna and Ferrara, and the duchies of Modena and Reggio fell in quick succession, and punitive armistices were imposed on the Papal and Neapolitan governments. Piedmont ceded Nice and Savoy to France, but during the summer there were republican insurrections in many Piedmontese towns. Meanwhile, a Provisional General Administration was established in Milan, and in October Bonaparte convened representatives of

[18] For overviews, see Alexander Grab, "From the French Revolution to Napoleon," in John A. Davis, ed., *Italy in the Nineteenth Century* (Oxford: Oxford University Press, 2000), 25–50; Michael Broers, *Napoleon: Soldier of Destiny* (London: Faber & Faber, 2014); Phillip Dwyer, *Napoleon: The Path to Power, 1769–1799* (London: Bloomsbury, 2008).

the former d'Este duchies and the Papal Legation cities of Bologna and Ferrara in Modena. In December the Cispadane Republic, the first Italian "sister" republic, was proclaimed at Reggio.[19]

In February 1797 the Austrians gave up the key fortress of Mantua, then in May Venice was occupied, and the last doge of the ancient Republic of St. Mark was deposed. Venice itself was plundered, and some of its most famed artworks, including the Roman bronze horses of St. Mark, were carried off to Paris. In the meantime, the political reorganization of the "liberated" territories was completed when on 19 June the Cisalpine Republic was proclaimed. With Milan as its capital, the republic incorporated the former Duchy of Lombardy, the former Cispadane Republic, the former Venetian territories sited to the east of the river Mincio, and parts of the Valtellina. The Cisalpine Republic, the largest and most important of the Italian sister republics, was given a modified version of the French Constitution of Year III (1795). It was divided into twenty departments, with representative assemblies that were never convened, and Bonaparte personally nominated the members of the two governing chambers.

In June, the creation of the Ligurian Republic brought the port of Genoa under French control. After a brief visit to Paris to take a critical role in thwarting a planned monarchist coup (18 Fructidor Year V; 4 September 1797), Bonaparte returned to Italy in September and, without consulting the Directory, negotiated the Peace of Campo Formio (17 October 1797). France acquired Lombardy and Belgium from Austria, which in return acquired Venice and the Venetian territories east of the Mincio river.

With northern Italy and the Adriatic coast now firmly under French control, in the spring of 1798 Napoleon returned to France to take command of the expedition to Egypt, but in his absence the French occupation of the Italian states continued. As punishment for the accidental killing of a French general, in January 1798 the Directory ordered Marshal Berthier to occupy Rome. In February a Republic was proclaimed, and Pope Pius VI fled to Tuscany, but was captured and taken in captivity to France, where he died a year later at Valence.

The final chapter in the Italian republican experiment followed Nelson's destruction of the French fleet at Aboukir Bay on 1 August 1798. King Ferdinand of Naples now came under strong pressure from Vienna, London, and St. Petersburg (the Tsar had joined the new coalition) to take

---

[19] Biagini, "Citizenship and Religion in the Italian Constitutions," 212; Capra, *Gli italiani prima dell'Italia*.

the offensive, which he did in November, to drive the much smaller French forces from Rome. But when the French counterattacked, the Neapolitan army was routed and the king fled, pausing in Naples only long enough to collect his family, courtiers, and the cash in the state treasury before Nelson's warships carried them to safety in Palermo on 22 December. Commanded now by General Jean-Antoine-Étienne Championnet, the French forces crossed the Neapolitan frontier in January, provoking violent divisions within the capital, which, with nearly half a million inhabitants, was the largest city in Italy. On 21 January a pro-French faction proclaimed a republic, and the following day Championnet entered the city, but it was only after three days of fierce popular resistance that a republican government was installed.

The proclamation of the Neapolitan Republic in January 1799 was the high point of the republican moment in Italy. Many of the provincial towns on the southern mainland declared support, although, across the narrow Straits of Messina, Sicily remained under the control of the Bourbons and the British navy. In December, the king of Piedmont had surrendered to the French and gone into exile in Sardinia, and shortly afterwards French forces occupied Lucca and Tuscany. But the republican ascendancy was to be brief. In April, Russian and Austrian forces launched a spring offensive in the Po valley that forced the French armies to withdraw, leaving the Italian republics to their fate.

"Sister" or "Vassal" Republics?

The political make-up of the Italian states during the "Republican Triennium" was mixed. Piedmont and Tuscany were occupied briefly by the French, but no republics were established. The Directory recognized first the Cispadane Republic, then its successor the Cisalpine Republic, the Ligurian Republic, and the Roman Republic as "sister" republics, but not the Neapolitan Republic. Yet, although the autonomies of the "sister" republics were always limited and subsequently further restricted, recent studies challenge the older description of the Italian republics as "vassal" rather than "sister" republics.[20]

---

[20] For an older view, see Adolfo Omodeo, *L'età del Risorgimento italiano* (Naples: ESI, 1954), 163–7; for a more recent interpretation, see Pierre Serna, "Introduction: War and Republic. Dangerous Liaisons," in Pierre Serna, Antonino De Francesco, and Judith A. Miller, eds., *Republics at War, 1776–1840: Revolutions, Conflicts and Geo-politics in Europe and the Atlantic World* (Houndmills: Palgrave Macmillan, 2013), 1–17; Pierre

For the Directory, the Italian campaign was primarily a "financial operation," and French advances in Italy were constantly accompanied by systematic requisitioning of goods, crops, and livestock, extortionate levies, and unprecedented seizures of precious artworks. The scale of the plunder was a major cause of popular revolt and horrified many who had initially welcomed the French armies.[21] But even these brutal features of the French presence were not sufficient to reduce the republican experiments of 1796–1799 to a mere narrative of military oppression. The attraction of the promised new republican order had been evident when in April 1796 Bonaparte was greeted enthusiastically in Milan as a liberator. Republican sympathizers and political exiles from Naples, Rome, and Piedmont flocked to the city, where political clubs and associations were founded and newspapers and journals were launched. Reactions were similar in the cities of the Cispadane Republic and would be repeated in Naples in 1799.

The debates on what form the Italian republics should take now began. The rapidity of the collapse of the Italian rulers had made republicanism the only practical alternative to monarchy, and the constitution drafted for the Cispadane Republic by the pro-French patriots in Bologna in December 1796 looked to restore local autonomies (in this case of a former city state) with the more general rights of freedom, equality, security, and property for its citizens that drew both on the French Constitution of Year III (1795) and on the long tradition of Italian Enlightenment debates.[22]

The Italian patriots were generally agreed that the transformative innovation of the French Revolution was constitutional government, but that still left ample room for debate, as was revealed in the responses to the famous competition launched in Milan in the spring of 1797 for proposals on "What Form of Representative Government Is Best Suited to Bring Happiness to Italy?" The competition attracted over fifty submissions, and the author of the winning entry, Melchiorre Gioia, proposed in modified form the system of representative government set out in the French Constitution of Year III (1795). Gioia also proposed the creation of a single Italian Republic, following the French model. That won support from many leading patriots, while others favored a federalist solution, although they were divided between champions of direct democracy and of the representative system of the

---

Serna, "War and Citizenship. Central Italy, 1798–1799," in Serna et al., eds., *Republics at War*, 211–21.

[21] Grab, "From the French Revolution to Napoleon," 27.
[22] Biagini, "Citizenship and Religion in the Italian Constitutions," 25; Rao, "Republicanism in Italy."

Constitution of Year III. These debates were comprehensively surveyed in Giuseppe Compagnoni's *Elementi di diritto costituzionale democratico*, the first European treatise on constitutional law, published in Venice in the autumn of 1797, but despite their differences the Italian patriots were agreed on the fundamental importance of constitutional government.[23]

When it came to religious policies, the republicans were at pains to avoid offending religious sensibilities or the clergy, amongst whom the new republican order found supporters ranging from bishops to humble priests. Not surprisingly, the clergy were eagerly recruited to celebrate the planting of the Liberty Trees and to sing *Te Deums* to legitimize the new republics. By contrast, debates on religious freedom were limited, and an attempt to remove a clause on the preservation of the Roman Catholic religion and the exclusion of non-Catholics from office in Bologna in 1796, for example, was unsuccessful. When the Genoese Republic adopted freedom of religion, it was met with fierce popular protests.[24]

Nor did the politics of the Italian patriots reflect neat sociological divisions. Moderates and radicals all came from similar backgrounds: the propertied and educated classes, the nobility, the clergy, the military, the professions (notably lawyers), and the world of science, the arts, and learning. Women were active in republican politics, as were a handful of craftsmen, but the patriots were well aware that they did not represent either the urban or the rural masses. The Lombard writer and reformer Pietro Verri was a great admirer of the French constitutional experiment in 1789, but in a letter to his brother he expressed the fear that in Italy the main obstacle would be the reactions of the plebs.[25] He was not alone, and his fellow patriots went to great lengths to win popular support for the objectives of their revolution. Everywhere great efforts were made to make contact with the people and inform them of the aims of the republican project. As the Neapolitan patriot Mario Pagano insisted, it was a matter not just of communication but of education, the prerequisite of active citizenship without which no form of popular government could function. Since the reach of the printed word was limited, the patriots became inventive in developing new ways of

---

[23] Salvo Mastellone, "Linguaggio politico e giacobinismo italiano," in Eluggero Pii, ed., *Idee e parole nel giacobinismo italiano* (Florence: CET, 1990), 1–12; Fruci, "Democracy in Italy," 32; see also Antonino De Francesco, "Ideologie e movimenti politici," in Giovanni Sabattucci and Vittorio Vidotto, eds., *Storia d'Italia* (Bari: Laterza, 1994), vol. 1, 229–336: 236–8.

[24] Biagini, "Citizenship and Religion in the Italian Constitutions," 213; Rao, "Republicanism in Italy."

[25] Capra, "The Rise of Liberal Constitutionalism," 517.

"instructing the People." Eleonora Fonseca Pimentel, a poet, writer, and prominent figure in prerevolution Neapolitan culture who became editor of the Neapolitan *Republican Monitor,* proved to be especially innovative in the use of dialect songs and street theater to reach and educate the people. Everywhere catechisms were produced and distributed to explain republican ideals for popular audiences and underline the connections between "republicanism," "good government," "citizenship," and the need for education.[26]

Citizens of the *ancien régime* were familiar with the daily succession of symbolic demonstrations and processions, which republicans adapted to their own ends. But as well as festivities to commemorate the planting of the Liberty Tree and significant public events, revolutionary adaptations of older practices served to publicize the Revolution and its aims. This was something to which French military commanders attached great importance, as the English traveler Mariana Starke discovered in October 1792 when she arrived by chance in Nice on the day before it was occupied. The French forces entered the city at dawn, marching in an orderly column of 10,000 soldiers, headed by "women carrying battle-axes, an Olive branch, and the National colours crowned with a cap of Liberty," and Starke recorded that after this display the commander addressed the assembled citizens, "promising mercy and protection."[27] Despite their otherwise meager resources, in 1796 Bonaparte's invading forces were extremely well-provisioned with an arsenal of commemorative medals, fly-sheets, posters, maps, and printed images to publicize their "liberating" mission and to promote the figure of its heroic young general.[28]

The politicization of everyday life during the "revolutionary triennium" went beyond propaganda and display, however. Freedom of the press, official and unofficial newspapers, pamphlets, and broadsheets offered unprecedented platforms for public debate, while the newly created consultative and executive committees, public assemblies, the drafting of constitutions, the debates on the procedures and formalities of government, the organization of plebiscites, and formalized civic and public ceremonies gave opportunities to experience active citizenship, as did the political clubs and

---

[26] See Eleonora Fonseca Pimentel, *From Arcadia to Revolution: The Neapolitan Monitor and Other Writings,* ed. Verina Jones (Toronto: Iter Press, 2019); Luciano Guerci, *Istruire nelle verità repubblicane: La letteratura politica per il popolo nell'Italia in rivoluzione (1796–9)* (Bologna: Il Mulino, 1999); Rao, "Republicanism in Italy"; De Francesco, "Ideologie e movimenti politici," 239–41.

[27] Mariana Starke, *Letters from Italy between the Years 1792 and 1798* (London: R. Phillips, 1800), 37.

[28] Dwyer, *Napoleon.*

societies. The Italian republicans who had fled to France after 1794 had played an important role in establishing clubs on the French model and prior to the French invasion. Christophe Saliceti, Bonaparte's Corsican former patron and ally who would be the logistical mastermind of the 1796 campaign, had created extensive networks of secret republican societies in Piedmont and Liguria.[29]

The French reopened the masonic lodges that had been closed down by the Italian rulers after 1792, but quickly became suspicious of the rapidly proliferating Italian clubs and societies. The closure of one of the most prominent, the Milan Society for Public Education, made the ambiguous political objectives of the French invasion very evident.[30] By 1796 the Jacobin moment of the revolution in France was over, and the participation of the Tuscan democrat Filippo Buonarroti in Gracchus Babeuf's Jacobin Conspiracy of Equals meant that the Italian exiles who accompanied the French armies were under close surveillance as suspected "anarchists," and Jacobin sympathizers were carefully excluded from office in the Italian republics.[31]

But the question still remained: was Italy a theater for democratization or simply for republican expansionism? On this the French remained deeply divided. When the Commissars Jullien and Bassault strongly supported the Italian patriots in Milan, they were recalled by the Directory. Likewise, General Championnet, who staunchly believed that republicanization was the best means to retain support on the peninsula, where France's military resources were thin and overextended, was recalled to Paris in February 1799 for supporting the Neapolitan radicals.[32]

These conflicts grew rather than declined as time passed, and growing numbers of Italian patriots were alienated by the Directory's flagrant and repeated disregard of Italian interests. The Venetian poet and soldier Ugo Foscolo spoke for many Italian republicans when he expressed his horror at how the Treaty of Campo Formio had taken no account of Italian aspirations, describing the cession of the Veneto to Austria as both a betrayal of the

---

[29] See Starke, *Letters from Italy*, 111–12.
[30] De Francesco, "Ideologie e movimenti politici," 239–40.
[31] Anna Maria Rao, *Esuli: L'emigrazione politica italiana in Francia (1792–1802)* (Naples: Guida, 1992); Florencia Peyrou and Juan Luis Simal, "Exile, Secret Societies and the Emergence of an International Democratic Culture," in Innes and Philp, eds., *Reimagining Democracy in the Mediterranean*, 205–30.
[32] De Francesco, "Ideologie e movimenti politici," 237; Serna, "Introduction," 10.

revolution and a "sacrifice of our fatherland."[33] These resentments were deepened by the Directory's incessant demands for taxes and tributes, the seizures of artworks and bullion, and the repeated curtailments of the limited autonomies of the sister republics. The Franco-Italian republican partnership was at best an uneasy one.

Counterrevolution

In 1799 the Italian republics collapsed. The Austro-Russian spring offensive in northern Italy exposed the dangerously extended lines of communication of the French forces, whose hasty withdrawal left the Italian sister republics defenseless against the legitimist rulers and their allies. But throughout the peninsula their fall was accompanied by popular counterrevolutionary insurrections that outstripped even the Vendée in their scale and violence.

In the Veneto, Lombardy and Piedmont, popular risings preceded the advance of the Austrians, and peasant bands raised by the Austrian irregular Branda de Lucioni took vengeance on communities held guilty of failing to resist the invaders. In Tuscany the urban and rural poor who rallied to the cry of *Viva Maria!* committed terrible acts of violence as they marched from Arezzo to Siena and Florence. Popular risings spread rapidly through the neighboring Papal State as the French withdrew, but none of these rivaled the southern Army of the Holy Faith (*Santa Fede*) in scale or notoriety. After landing with a few followers in Calabria in February 1799, Cardinal Fabrizio Ruffo's appeal for a crusade against the republic in Naples proved unexpectedly successful. The towns that had declared for the republic in the southern provinces either joined the royalists or were overwhelmed. On 13 June Ruffo's Sanfedists entered Naples, triggering a second popular insurrection that overwhelmed the patriots and their families in a bloodbath of revenge.[34]

However, neither Vincenzo Cuoco's image of the counterrevolution as the product of the ignorance and superstition of the masses nor the contrasting portrayals of the insurgents as patriots and defenders of the faith are

---

[33] Eugenio Biagini, "Liberty, Class and Nation-Building. Ugo Foscolo's 'English' Constitutional Thought 1816–1827," *European Journal of Political Theory* 5:1 (2005), 34–49: 34; Capra, *Gli italiani prima dell'Italia*, 327–31.

[34] Capra, *Gli italiani prima dell'Italia*, 327–31; Gabriele Turi, *Viva Maria: Riforme, rivoluzione e insorgenze in Toscana (1790–1799)* (Florence and Bologna: Il Mulino 1999 [1969]); Anna Mario Rao, ed., *Folle contrarivoluzionarie: Le insorgenze popolari nell'Italia rivoluzionaria e napoleonica* (Rome: Carocci, 1999); Gaetano Cingari, *Giacobini e Sanfedisti in Calabria nel 1790* (Reggio Calabria: Casa del libro, 1978 [1957]); Davis, *Naples and Napoleon*, 107–26.

convincing. The popular anger that erupted in 1799 was in many respects a continuation of insurrections and unrest that had been evident throughout the peninsula much earlier, but existing discontents had been exacerbated by the impact of the revolution, the military occupation, and the new republics.

At first the Italian rulers had been the primary targets of popular unrest, and in her account of events in Nice in October 1792, for example, Mariana Starke noted that the scale of discontent with Piedmontese rule in Savoy and Nice was the main reason that the government had not attempted to resist the French occupation. Two years later, when food shortages and rising prices were causing popular protests to spread across Italy, Starke commented again that the rulers feared that popular unrest was directed against them, not the revolution, and she noted "the rapid growth of Democratic opinion throughout Italy."[35]

After 1796 the extreme brutality of the French responses to popular protest, together with indiscriminate requisitioning and other impositions, gave the popular revolts an increasingly anti-French and antirepublican imprint. But even horrifying reprisals like those inflicted after the Veronese "Easter Revolt" ("Le Pasque Veronesi") in April 1797 did not stop the popular insurrections that during the summer spread from the Alpine valleys to the Romagna and the Marche. More followed the founding of the Ligurian Republic and the French occupation of Rome in February 1798.

Failure to address popular discontents also caused popular anger to target the republics. In the south, for example, the promise of reform and especially the abolition of feudalism divided the feudal landowners (many of whom supported abolition), but mobilized resistance amongst the numerous groups whose livelihoods were dependent on the feudal order. And while republican officers quickly came to demand new taxes and contributions, the republics were slow in implementing reforms. In Naples the critical law abolishing feudalism was not finally approved until 26 April, and as the Neapolitan diarist Carlo de Nicola caustically commented: "they should have done this sooner." By then the southern provinces were already in the hands of the counterrevolution, and the law abolishing feudalism would never be implemented.[36]

Numerous forces were at work to shape and direct these insurrections, and when Mariana Starke commented in July 1796 that "a new and

---

[35] Starke, *Letters from Italy*, 49.
[36] Ibid; Carlo de Nicola, *Diario Napoletano, 1798–1825*, ed. R. De Lorenzo, 3 vols. (Naples: Regina Editore, 1999).

formidable Enemy shrouded in Religion's mantle and brandishing a Crucifix in one hand and a dagger in the other was now threatening to impact the rapid tide of Victory," this was more than a standard expression of Anglo-Protestant prejudice.[37] From 1789, pamphlets denouncing and lampooning the political objectives of the revolution in France had been proliferating in Rome, while voices in the Roman Curia had from much earlier been calling for the organization of popular crusades to combat the secularist and rationalist reforms promoted by the absolutist princes.[38]

The opportunity came when the Italian rulers abandoned their reform projects. On the day that the Neapolitan government closed down the masonic lodges, the Cardinal Archbishop of Naples was instructed to organize popular devotional associations to combat the "libertine ideas" of the revolutionaries. Just days before the discovery of the Jacobin conspiracy in Naples in 1794, the two royalist clubs had been founded in Naples, followed by others in Salerno and the Cilento. Following the French invasion in 1796, in Rome the former Jesuit priest Francesco Gusti appealed for the Church to adopt new forms of religious practice to mobilize popular mass resistance.

It is unclear how effective these attempts to direct and discipline popular unrest were in practice, however. The *Viva Maria!* insurrection originated in parts of Tuscany untouched by the brief French occupation, and its targets were traditional figures such as Jewish merchants suspected of hoarding. In Lombardy the followers of Branda de Lucioni were similarly ill-disciplined, and like its Tuscan counterpart the Sanfedist crusade in the south began far from the northern frontiers and was never in contact with any French invader. By Cardinal Ruffo's own account, the image of a mass revolt inspired by popular loyalty to the Church and the monarchy was largely a myth. He claimed that his followers were motivated by local rivalries and the desire for plunder, and he had forced them to adopt the insignia of the *Santa Fede* in an attempt to impose legitimacy and discipline. Its success ultimately derived in large part from the professional military commanders recruited by Ruffo, the Albanian troops provided by the Ottoman emperor, and, not least, Nelson's fleet that blockaded the capital to enable Ruffo and his followers to enter the city in June.[39]

---

[37] Starke, *Letters from Italy*, 75.
[38] Eluggero Pii, "La polemica contro la democrazia," in Pii, ed., *Idee e parole nel giacobinismo italiano*, 207–29; Mario Tosti, "Force of Arms, Force of Opinions. Counter-revolution in the Papal State 1790–1799," in Serna et al., eds., *Republics at War*, 224–40; Massimo Cattaneo, "L'opposizione popolare al giacobinismo a Roma e nello stato pontificio," in Rao, *Folle contrarivoluzionarie*, 255–90.
[39] Davis, *Naples and Napoleon*, 90–3.

Legacies

The republican experiments of 1796–1799 provided supporters of the Revolution in France with ample opportunities to consider the forms of government best suited to Italy and Italians, and the debates that followed revealed continuities with the decades before the revolution. As Eugenio Biagini has argued, "in a sense the republican gospel of the 1790s instead of being simply 'imported' into Italy from France was more a coming home after an extensive *grand tour* in Western Europe and North America."[40]

Those debates continued after the collapse of the Republics, but in ways that were deeply influenced by the intense and often contradictory experiences of the republican episode. Among these, the counterrevolution weighed heavily. The popular violence that had accompanied the collapse of the republics continued long after the French withdrew. No less bloody were the reprisals taken by the restored rulers that took their most savage and systematic form in Naples. More than 8,000 individuals were accused of treason, and of those who had played major or minor roles in the republic, 1,800 went to the scaffold. The victims included members of the leading noble families and even Eleonora Fonseca Pimentel, the editor of *Il Monitore Napoletano* (*The Neapolitan Monitor*), while in the provinces the persecution of former republicans continued uncontrolled for much longer. For the Neapolitan diarist Carlo de Nicola the "royalist Terror" was a "third anarchy," following the revolution and the Sanfedist counterrevolution.[41]

Fears inspired by the popular counterrevolutionary fury of 1799 weighed heavily on successive generations of Italian political activists, yet despite the rural unrest and revolts that were a constant and often violent backdrop to the politics of the Risorgimento the popular counterrevolutionary movements of 1799 would never be repeated. In Italy the French Revolution did not leave a popular counterrevolutionary tradition comparable to Spanish Carlism.[42]

Yet even if in Italy popular counterrevolution proved to be the dog that did not bark, Vincenzo Cuoco's 1801 *Essay* vividly captured both the deep impressions it had made and the awareness of the social chasms that had

---

[40] Biagini, "Citizenship and Religion in the Italian Constitutions," 212; Capra, *Gli italiani prima dell'Italia*, 401–11.
[41] Rao, *Esuli*, 243; Capra, *Gli italiani prima dell'Italia*, 329–32.
[42] Jordi Canal, *El Carlismo: Dos siglos de contrarrevolución en España* (Madrid: Alianza Editorial, 2000); Pedro Rugula, "Institutional War, National War, Civil War," in Serna et al., eds., *Republics at War*, 211–21.

been revealed. The republics had exposed the existence of two Italian nations, on the one hand, the educated and affluent classes, on the other, the urban and rural masses, separated by a cultural abyss. In phrasing these responses Cuoco was the first to place the Italian republican project in the context of the "people" and the "nation," and to conclude that without social unity there could be no progressive reform and that henceforth public education was the indispensable premise for progress.[43]

Cuoco's conclusions echoed the experiences of many other Italian republicans. After the fall of the republics, many had headed for France just like he did, and in Chambéry the executive committee of the Cisalpine Republic was set up as a government in exile. But when the republicans returned to northern Italy after Napoleon's victories in the spring of 1800, they found a changed political climate. When, for example, the Lombard republican Teodoro Lechi, who had recruited some 300 officers and nearly 4,000 men from the exiles to form an Italian Legion, returned to Milan in June 1800, the Legion was immediately disbanded.[44]

The absence of even the pretense of autonomy when Napoleon reconstituted the former Cisalpine Republic, first as the Italian Republic (1801) and then as the kingdom of Italy (1805), increased the disillusionment of former republicans, but many rallied to the new order even after the transition to empire. In April 1805, for example, Vincenzo Cuoco published an article welcoming the political change in France and the transformation of the Italian Republic into the kingdom of Italy. A constitutional monarchy, he argued, was "the only proper form of government for a large population that is surrounded by other powerful populations ... the change in government that has taken place in France is necessary for the French people, but also for the Italian."[45]

Many of the Italian republicans of 1796–1799 saw the new Napoleonic order as an opportunity to implement the reforms that had been debated during the republican experiment and earlier. Although in 1799 the Italian legitimist rulers had been briefly restored, the *ancien régime* was beyond repair, and during the Napoleonic regnum the Italian states would be remodeled as centralized bureaucratic autocracies. Feudalism, where it still existed, was abolished, public finances were restored, and the sovereign

---

[43] Cuoco, *Saggio storico sulla rivoluzione napolitana*, 218–19; Mastellone, "Linguaggio politico e giacobinismo italiano," 1–12; Capra, *Gli italiani prima dell'Italia*, 332–7.
[44] Katia Visconti, "A Patriotic School. The Raising of the Italian Legion in France 1799–1800," in Serna et al., eds., *Republics at War*, 149–64; Rao, *Esuli*.
[45] Mastellone, "Linguaggio politico e giacobinismo italiano," 11.

debts of the former rulers were liquidated and refloated through the sales of church, former Crown, and feudal lands. But while the political determination and the institutional templates came with the French administrators, their inspiration reached back to the absolutist projects of the eighteenth century.

Italian administrators played key roles in the reorganization of the Italian states, but institutional restructuring only highlighted the absence of the political reforms promised by the Revolution. That deficit was especially evident in the repeated failures to implement the advisory assemblies and constitutions promised by the Napoleonic rulers, and opposition took the form of demands for representative government. But since the freedom of assembly and of the press that had been enjoyed briefly during the republics was never restored after 1800, the secret societies became the only vehicle for political opposition. The political societies and clubs were a legacy of the republican years, but their revolutionary credentials caused the French authorities to ban them, although, like their absolutist predecessors, they enthusiastically promoted freemasonry. But as opposition to Napoleonic autocracy and imperialism escalated after 1811, the masonic lodges were closed, only to reemerge in the form of secret societies.[46]

Their political objective, however, was no longer republican democracy, but constitutional government. This political parabola reflected the experiences of a generation that had come of age with the revolution in France, the republics of 1796–1799, and the Napoleonic sequel, a political itinerary that was captured with unusual clarity in the reflections of another former republican democrat, Guglielmo Pepe.

From a Calabrian family with a long tradition of military service, Pepe was the youngest of twenty-two brothers, many of whom, like him, became professional soldiers. When the republic was proclaimed in Naples in January 1799, he was a sixteen-year-old cadet at the Nunziatella military academy and immediately declared his support. He was subsequently imprisoned, but escaped to France and later returned to Naples to serve in the armies of the Napoleonic kings of Naples, first the emperor's brother Joseph Bonaparte and then his brother-in-law Joachim Murat.[47]

---

[46] Davis, *Naples and Napoleon*, 248–9, 296–9.
[47] On Pepe, see Silvio de Majo, "Guglielmo Pepe," in Raffaele Romanelli, ed., *Dizionario biografico degli Italiani*, vol. LXXXII (Rome: Treccani, 2015); Maurizio Isabella, *Risorgimento in Exile: Italian Émigrés and the Liberal International in the Post-Napoleonic Era* (Oxford: Oxford University Press, 2009).

Like the Venetian poet Ugo Foscolo and the Milanese Lechi brothers, Pepe and his brothers embodied the republican ideal of military valor once personified by the young Napoleon Bonaparte. But Pepe's role model was the marquis de La Fayette, the figure who best linked the American and the French revolutions, and, like many of the Italians who had served in Napoleon's armies, Pepe became deeply opposed to the Napoleonic autocracy and the subordination of the Italian states to Bonaparte's imperial and dynastic designs. Returning to Naples, he joined the generals who tried unsuccessfully to persuade Murat to concede a constitution.

After the Bourbon Restoration in 1815, he was furloughed but subsequently reinstated to high rank. But by now he had established close contacts with the secret Carbonarist lodges, with whose support he led the first phase of the revolution of June 1820 that forced King Ferdinand of Naples to adopt the constitution of Cádiz of 1812. The revolution in Naples ended when an Austrian army invaded in March 1821. Before he escaped, Pepe commanded the unsuccessful attempt to resist. Condemned to death *in absentia*, Pepe traveled to Madrid and Lisbon before finding sanctuary in London, where in 1824 he published his lengthy reflections "on the recent revolutions in southern Europe, in South America and the more recent movement for Greek independence."[48]

The aim was to set these revolutions in the context of a revolutionary tradition that Pepe traced back to the American War of Independence. Of these revolutions, Pepe singled out the French Revolution as "the truest," because it alone had completely overthrown the *ancien régime*, the monarchy, and the Church. But the French Revolution had failed where the American Revolution had succeeded, because its leaders had lost control of the people. That was the consequence of its egalitarian aims, which deviated from what was for Pepe the core of the revolutionary tradition: not democracy, but liberty and representative government.[49]

Pepe's critique of the French Revolution illustrated the reasons why the leaders of the liberal revolutions of 1820 in Spain, Portugal, Naples, and Piedmont had adopted the Spanish Constitution of 1812. The constitution had originally been drafted by the Cortes of Cádiz in 1812 to rally Spaniards during the war against Napoleon, but had been abolished at the Restoration.

---

[48] Guglielmo Pepe, "The Non-establishment of Liberty in Spain, Naples, Portugal and Piedmont, to Which Is Added Comparison between the Successful Revolutions in North America, the Partly Successful One in France and That Which Is Now the Object of Greece ...," *The Pamphleteer* 46 (1824), 221–75.

[49] Ibid.

It was restored in 1820, following a liberal military *pronunciamiento* in Seville. The attraction of the 1812 Spanish Constitution for liberals throughout southern Europe in 1820 was that it combined demands for constitutional government with the opposition to imperial ambitions that had taken shape during the Napoleonic decades and had been accentuated by the powers accorded to France, Austria, and Great Britain under the terms of the Vienna settlement.[50]

In making the demands for liberty and representative government the driving force of the revolutionary tradition that stretched back to the American War of Independence, Guglielmo Pepe's reflections accurately captured the political program of the recent liberal revolutions, while illustrating how contemporaries reconfigured the French Revolution to fit their own political itineraries. Shorn of its erroneous egalitarian goals, the revolution in France featured a milestone in an ongoing revolutionary itinerary that led directly to the liberal revolutions in southern Europe and the struggles for Greek independence that had just begun when Pepe was writing.[51]

Opposition to imperialism gave the liberal revolutions in southern Europe a sense of common purpose with the anticolonial revolutions in Spanish and Portuguese America, but that liberal internationalism was less visible when Italy experienced the next major revolutionary upheavals in 1848 (in which the aging Guglielmo Pepe made his last stand). By then liberals were everywhere being challenged again by democrats, and representations of the French Revolution had to be remodeled once again.

---

[50] See Richard Stites, *The Four Horsemen: Riding to Liberty in Post-Napoleonic Europe* (Oxford: Clarendon Press, 2014); John A. Davis, "The Spanish Constitution of 1812 and the Mediterranean Revolutions (1820–25)," *Bulletin for Spanish and Portuguese Historical Studies* 37:2 (2012), Article 7.

[51] James Miller, "Modernizing the Mediterranean; The Liberal Thread," *Contemporanea* 23:1 (2020), 133–58; Maurizio Isabella, "Nationality before Liberty? Risorgimento Political Thought in Transnational Context," *Journal of Modern Italian Studies* 17:5 (2012), 507–15; John Robertson, "Pietro Verri: Between Enlightenment and Risorgimento," *Journal of Modern Italian Studies* 17:5 (2012), 527–31; Rao, "Republicanism in Italy," 160–7.

18

Germany and the French Revolution

MICHAEL ROWE

Most Germans lived within the Holy Roman Empire in 1789. This polity was located in the center of Europe, bounded by France and the Low Countries in the west, Poland and Hungary in the east, Denmark to the north, and Switzerland to the south (Map 18.1). Its roots extended back to the tenth century.[1] Though sometimes styled Holy Roman Empire of the German Nation (Heiliges Römisches Reich deutscher Nation), it was not a nation-state: Samuel von Pufendorf famously described it as "an Irregular Body, and like some mis-shapen Monster."[2] The Empire was essentially a loose confederation whose members were bound by laws and agreements that had accumulated over the centuries. It proved so durable not least because it stood at the heart of the European state system, into which it was interwoven through a dense mesh of treaties and dynastic networks.[3] Key imperial institutions included the parliament (Reichstag), the two imperial courts (Reichskammergericht and Reichshofrat), and the elective emperorship monopolized (with one brief exception) by Austria's Habsburg dynasty.

The Empire was divided into just under 300 territorial entities, whose rulers were represented in the Reichstag. The eight most significant princes

---

[1] For a recent overview of the Empire's long history, see Peter H. Wilson, *The Holy Roman Empire: A Thousand Years of Europe's History* (London: Allen Lane, 2016); R. J. W. Evans, Michael Schaich, and Peter H. Wilson, eds., *The Holy Roman Empire, 1495–1806* (Oxford: Oxford University Press, 2011). The most recent research on the early modern Empire focuses especially on its rituals and symbols, as reflected in the essays published in Jason Philip Coy, Benjamin Marschke, and David Warren Sabean, eds., *The Holy Roman Empire Reconsidered* (New York: Berghahn Books, 2013); and more fully in Barbara Stollberg-Rilinger, *The Emperor's Old Clothes: Constitutional History and the Symbolic Language of the Holy Roman Empire* (New York: Berghahn Books, 2015).
[2] Samuel Pufendorf, *The Present State of Germany, or, An Account of the Extent, Rise, Form, Wealth, Strength, Weaknesses and Interests of That Empire* (London, 1690), 152.
[3] For the Empire's centrality to the wider European states system, see R. J. W. Evans and Peter H. Wilson, eds., *The Holy Roman Empire, 1495–1806: A European Perspective* (Leiden: Brill, 2012).

Map 18.1 The Holy Roman Empire.

Germany and the French Revolution

Map 18.1 (cont.)

were the "electors," whose title reflected their right to elect the emperor. Three of the eight were prelates (the archbishop-electors of Cologne, Mainz, and Trier), whilst the five secular electors were the heads of the most important German dynasties: the Habsburgs, who apart from monopolizing the imperial office also ruled Austria, the Hohenzollerns of Prussia, the Wittelsbachs of Bavaria, the Wettins of Saxony, and the Guelphs of Hanover. Some of these dynasties also governed substantial territories outside the Empire. The Habsburgs ruled parts of north Italy and Hungary, and the Hohenzollerns a large part of western Poland. From 1714 onwards, the Guelphs were also kings of Great Britain, and as such resided in London, from where they managed their Hanoverian affairs via the German Chancellery based in St. James' Palace.[4]

Immediately beneath the eight electorates came 235 principalities (of which 77 were ecclesiastical) and 51 independent city states, known as free imperial cities.[5] Some of these cities were substantial: Hamburg's population numbered approximately 100,000 at the time of the French Revolution, making it the third-largest city after Vienna and Berlin, which were respectively the seats of the Habsburg and Hohenzollern courts. The majority of the imperial cities were no more than glorified walled villages, concentrated especially in southwestern Germany. Their best days were behind them, in most cases. Enclosed by medieval fortifications and dominated by guilds jealous of their privileges, they spent much of the eighteenth century rotting into picturesque decay rather than sharing in the economic developments of the wider Atlantic world.[6] Far more vibrant, certainly culturally and intellectually, were Germany's so-called "court cities" (*Residenzstädte*) that served as the capitals of the larger principalities. As noted, Berlin and Vienna were the largest, and were cultural and economic hubs as well as political centers of European importance. Smaller versions included Dresden, Munich, Mainz, Bonn, and Würzburg. In addition to the electorates, the secular and ecclesiastical principalities, and the imperial cities, came the landed estates of the approximately 400 families of Free Imperial Knights. Collectively, these estates may have amounted to no more than 200 square miles containing 400,000 inhabitants. The Free Imperial Knights were not represented in the

---

[4] Nick Harding, *Hanover and the British Empire, 1700–1837* (Woodbridge: Boydell Press, 2007).
[5] Karl Zeumer, ed., *Quellensammlung zur Geschichte der deutschen Reichsverfassung in Mittelalter und Neuzeit* (Tübingen: J. C. B. Mohr, 1913), 552–5.
[6] Mack Walker, *German Home Towns: Community, State, and General Estate, 1648–1871* (Ithaca, NY: Cornell University Press, 1971).

Reichstag, but were nonetheless directly (or "immediately," to use the correct terminology) subordinate to the emperor, which legally made them just as "sovereign" as the greater princes.[7]

Not all Germans lived within the Empire, and not all of the Empire's inhabitants spoke German. Substantial communities of German speakers lived in eastern Europe, notably in Transylvania and other parts of Hungary, and in the Russian Empire, to which they had been encouraged to migrate by the German-born tsarina, Catherine the Great. At the same time, large numbers of Germans also migrated westwards across the Atlantic. About 100,000 Germans or their descendants constituted just under 10 percent of the population of the newly founded United States, many of them living in Pennsylvania, where they made up a third of the state's citizenry.[8] The southwest of Germany, including notably the region of Swabia, was especially productive of migrants on account of the scarcity of land there, made worse by a general population increase across the eighteenth century. On the other hand, those within the Empire who were not native speakers of German included the Czechs of Bohemia and the Flemish and French populations of the Austrian Netherlands and of the prince-bishopric of Liège (together covering roughly the territory of modern Belgium).

The preceding paragraphs, though essentially summaries and simplifications, nonetheless convey the complexity of the Holy Roman Empire, which baffled even contemporaries. Easier to follow are the geopolitics of the Empire, which were dominated by the rivalry of the two largest states, Austria and Prussia. "Austria" and "Prussia," it should be understood, are simply convenient shorthand that both contemporaries and modern historians use to refer to the composite states governed respectively by the Habsburg and Hohenzollern dynasties. They too, like the wider Holy Roman Empire to which they partially belonged, were agglomerations of provinces, some of them detached, stretching across northern (in the case of Prussia) and southern (in the case of Austria) Germany. Austria and Prussia together were home to approximately half of the Empire's 25 million inhabitants. The other half of the Empire's population was scattered across the numerous other, smaller, territories referred to previously. For them, the adage common in the modern United States that "all politics is local" was

---

[7] William D. Godsey, *Nobles and Nation in Central Europe: Free Imperial Knights in the Age of Revolution, 1750–1850* (New York: Cambridge University Press, 2004), 8.

[8] For early German emigration to North America, see Aaron Spencer Fogleman, *Hopeful Journeys: German Immigration, Settlement, and Political Culture in Colonial America, 1717–1775* (Philadelphia: University of Pennsylvania Press, 1996).

especially pertinent: their rulers were not remote figures, as is the case in large states, but persons one might realistically encounter on a frequent basis. What this could mean in practice is illustrated in the school reforms instituted by the prince-bishop of Würzburg in the late eighteenth century. His efforts did not stop at issuing orders to subordinates that reforms should be carried through, but involved the prince personally visiting schools, sitting in on classes, and interviewing teachers and pupils to insure his policy was implemented as he intended.[9] Arguably, this combination of extreme localism and direct "hands-on" involvement by the head of government helped immunize large parts of Germany against revolution, not least because rulers of smaller territories were more responsive to crises like harvest failures that were common in the unsettled climatic conditions of the 1780s, and took preemptive measures to counter grievances before they got out of hand.

Legalism as well as localism shaped Germany's eighteenth-century political culture. The Holy Roman Empire was above all a legal order that bound together its members. It was the function of the courts, both at the territorial and at the imperial level, to preserve this order. The two imperial courts, which in this period were based in Vienna and Wetzlar, stood at the apex of the juridical pyramid. Long dismissed as glacial in terms of the speed with which they decided cases, more recent scholarship has assessed their role more positively.[10] They appear to have been surprisingly accessible, including to marginalized groups such as Germany's Jewish communities. Their reluctance to arrive at decisive final rulings in favor of one plaintiff or the other can be seen positively as an attempt to arrive at consensus and compromise. In the Empire, disputes which in other countries might have resulted in riots or vendettas instead supplied the contents of legal depositions. The advantage of this was that Germany, by the standards of the age, cannot be seen as having been especially violent or lawless. The disadvantage, though, was that it was incredibly hard to reform anything across the Empire as a whole. Imperial structures were geared to upholding the law. What was lacking were mechanisms to make new laws in response to a changing world. This deficiency was most obvious when it came to economic and commercial policy, which was managed by the individual states, if

---

[9] John Christopher Doney, "The Catholic Enlightenment and Popular Education in the Prince-Bishopric of Würzburg, 1765–95," *Central European History* 21 (1988), 3–30.

[10] Michael Rowe, "The Political Culture of the Holy Roman Empire on the Eve of Its Destruction," in Alan Forrest and Peter H. Wilson, eds., *The Bee and the Eagle: Napoleonic France and the End of the Holy Roman Empire, 1806* (Basingstoke: Palgrave Macmillan, 2008), 42–64.

at all, and not at the level of the Empire. The Empire did not possess a uniform system of weights and measures, a single currency, a common external tariff, or a single internal market. There was no unified economic or commercial policy. There were no imperial trading companies analogous to the East India companies of Britain, France, and the Netherlands. There was no mechanism for managing trade along rivers like the Rhine that flowed through multiple states. Instead, states arbitrarily levied tolls on vessels and failed to cooperate in preserving the navigability of the river by keeping it clear of obstacles and maintaining the tow paths. These and other similar deficiencies retarded economic development until the appearance in the nineteenth century of institutions such as the German Customs Union (Zollverein).[11]

The imperial courts acted as an effective break on princely power, especially in the smaller German states. In the larger ones, the emperor had conceded what was known as the *privilegium de non appellando*, which limited or precluded completely the ability of people to appeal to the imperial courts over the heads of their princes. Nonetheless, the greater princes prided themselves on building up their own territorial court system to a high standard. Most, though by no means all, German rulers in the late eighteenth century cared about their public image, which was subject to scrutiny by an expanding press and an increasingly literate and judgmental public. Interestingly, this public, like the newspaper press that sustained it, operated at an all-German level. A professional and impartial judicial system became a requirement for any self-respecting German state in the course of the eighteenth century, no less essential than a progressive university, court theater, and public opera house. Rulers like Prussia's King Frederick the Great (1740–1786) and Austria's Emperor Joseph II (1780–1790) gained public acclaim not least for their interventions to insure that even the humblest of their subjects gained justice against their social superiors. Frederick's spectacular involvement in 1779 in the so-called Miller Arnold affair, when he intervened in favor of one of his poorer subjects seeking justice, was an especially effective publicity stunt that burnished the king's reputation internationally as a benevolent ruler of all his people. Joseph of Austria followed suit in the 1780s, passing decrees that tightened state supervision of local

---

[11] For the impediments to navigation on the Rhine under the Old Regime, and their removal during the period of French rule, see Robert Mark Spaulding, "Revolutionary France and the Transformation of the Rhine," *Central European History* 44 (2011), 203–26.

courts previously dominated by noble landlords, and pushing through a sentencing policy that was more lenient for the poor on the grounds that the rich should know better.[12]

Not all German rulers earned or deserved a reputation as paragons of enlightenment. Those located at the despotic end of the spectrum included Karl Eugen, Duke of Württemberg (1737–1793). His achievements did in all fairness include the foundation of what would become the state library of Württemberg, in Stuttgart. Less commendably, he responded to criticism of his style of governance with arbitrary arrest and imprisonment. His high-profile victims included one of Germany's most eminent jurists, Johann Jakob Moser, and the journalist Christian Friedrich Daniel Schubart, the latter imprisoned on account of his having ridiculed the duke's mistress and criticized the sale of Württemberg soldiers to the British for service in the American Revolutionary War. The writer Friedrich Schiller, who was forced to flee Württemberg in 1782, may well have had Duke Karl Eugen in mind in his portrayal of King Philip II of Spain in the historical drama *Don Carlos*, which he completed in exile a few years later. Nonetheless, even within Württemberg there were limits to what a ruler could do. As was the case in many other German states, so in Württemberg the prince shared power with "representatives of the land" (*Landschaft*), whose cooperation was typically required for the approval of taxes. The composition and political weight of representative bodies varied from state to state, and within the larger states, from province to province. Despite the best efforts of Karl Eugen, they remained peculiarly formidable in Württemberg, to the extent that the British opposition leader Charles James Fox lauded the duchy as the only constitutional state in Europe apart from England! Württemberg's dukes, like Germany's other princes whether great or small, operated under a series of constraints, both at the level of the Empire and within their states.[13] This limited their freedom of maneuver, whether to persecute opponents, mobilize resources for war, or institute enlightened reform.

No one was more infuriated by these restraints than the greatest ruler of all, the Holy Roman Emperor and ruler of Austria, Joseph II. His reign coincided with the outbreak of the French Revolution, which concerned him personally as the queen of France, Marie Antoinette, was his sister. Despite

[12] For the Miller Arnold affair, see T. C. W. Blanning, *Frederick the Great: King of Prussia* (London: Allen Lane, 2015), 395. For Joseph II's reforms, see Derek Beales, *Joseph II*, 2 vols. (Cambridge: Cambridge University Press, 1987–2009).

[13] Wolfgang Mährle, ed., *Aufgeklärte Herrschaft im Konflikt: Herzog Carl Eugen von Württemberg 1728–1793* (Stuttgart: Kohlhammer, 2017).

this, Joseph was initially not ideologically opposed to the Revolution, which was hardly surprising, given that he was himself a radical reformer: from his perspective, the French were simply catching up. Joseph's reforms, which got going in earnest following the death in 1780 of his mother, Maria Theresa, covered a wide area of policy. What held them together was their aim of creating a direct relationship between the state and its subjects, at the expense of elite groups and institutions like the nobility and Church that had previously stood between such a relationship. This imperative was most obvious in Joseph's reforms directed at the peasantry, whose status varied across his dominions. In Austria's core territories, their freedoms were relatively extensive, but in Bohemia the peasants subsisted in a state of serfdom. Joseph's decree of 1 November 1781 (the so-called Emancipation Patent) extended rights to Bohemia's peasants: they now no longer needed their landlord's permission to leave the estate, to buy or sell land, to marry, or to enter into a new trade.[14]

In improving the lot of the peasantry Joseph undermined the social preeminence of the nobility. His reforms also undermined the integrity of the Catholic Church, to which the majority of his subjects belonged. Joseph saw himself as a devout Catholic, but he objected to what he regarded as encroachments by the Church into the temporal domain. He sought to increase state supervision over the Catholic Church in Austria at the expense of the Pope's capacity to intervene from Rome. Joseph forbade the Pope from communicating directly with the Austrian bishops: his letters and instructions first needed to be cleared by the government in Vienna. Joseph also targeted Austria's monasteries, which were quite numerous. In particular, the emperor disapproved of those run by contemplative orders, because he found "useless" a life given over to religious reflection as opposed to practical activity like teaching or nursing. During the 1780s Joseph dissolved just over half of all the abbeys within the core Austrian provinces, and more still in his outlying dominions. The money saved was used to improve the salaries of ordinary parish priests, and to enhance the pastoral care for his Catholic subjects at the local level through the construction of new churches and realignment of parochial boundaries. Joseph also unilaterally redrew diocesan boundaries to make them conform with the external borders of his dominions, and furthermore he interfered with clerical education, increasing the proportion of time seminaries spent on practical subjects at the

[14] Charles Ingrao, *The Habsburg Monarchy 1618–1815* (Cambridge: Cambridge University Press, 1994), 201.

expense of theology. Joseph expected parish priests to function as development workers as well as being saviors of souls. Protestant clerics were similarly enlisted in northern Germany.[15]

Joseph, though Holy Roman Emperor, had no authority to extend his reforms beyond Austria. However, he was nonetheless inspirational for many Catholic Germans who, over the course of the eighteenth century, had begun to feel that they were falling behind their Protestant competitors. (The best estimate is that just under 60 percent of the Empire's population was Catholic, and about 40 percent Protestant, with the Jewish population representing approximately 1% of the total.)[16] Prussian and British military success at the expense of Austria and France in the Seven Years' War only encouraged this sense of inferiority. This sentiment helped inspire a distinctive Catholic Enlightenment in western and southern Germany, led by reform-minded archbishop electors such as Maximilian Francis of Cologne (Joseph II's youngest brother), Friedrich Karl Joseph von Erthal of Mainz, and his younger brother Franz Ludwig von Erthal, who was prince-bishop of Würzburg and Bamberg. Their reforms focused especially on the improvement of public education, at primary, secondary, and tertiary level.[17] Amongst the beneficiaries of these reforms were radical intellectuals like Mathias Metternich and Georg Forster, both affiliated to the University of Mainz. Many ordinary Catholics, in contrast, were less impressed by the reforms initiated by their princes. In particular, they took offense at efforts by the authorities to dismantle or at least diminish various "unenlightened" religious practices, such as pilgrimages and holidays, and to simplify the liturgy along lines that many regarded as heretical. The extension of tolerance to Protestants and Jews, following the example of Joseph II, was generally unpopular. So was the dissolution of monasteries to finance schools, which the authorities could fill only by punishing parents who refused to send their children to them. Ultimately, the Catholic Enlightenment, like the German Enlightenment more generally, remained an elitist rather than a popular project.

---

[15] Anthony J. La Vopa, *Grace, Talent, and Merit: Poor Students, Clerical Careers, and Professional Ideology in Eighteenth-Century Germany* (Cambridge: Cambridge University Press, 1988).

[16] Peter Claus Hartman, "Bevölkerungszahlen und Konfessionsverhältnisse des Heiligen Römischen Reiches deutscher Nation und der Reichskreise am Ende des 18. Jahrhunderts," *Zeitschrift für Historische Forschung* 22 (1995), 345–69.

[17] T. C. W. Blanning, *Reform and Revolution in Mainz, 1743–1803* (Cambridge: Cambridge University Press, 1974).

Catholic Germany may have been rushing down the path of reform in the 1780s, but there were signs of a reversal in Prussia, which before then had been seen as the trailblazer. This reversal came with the death of Frederick the Great in 1786, and the accession of his nephew Frederick William II (r. 1786–1797). The fact that a simple change of ruler could create such a massive impact in cultural policy reflects the dependence of the "German Enlightenment," whether Protestant or Catholic, on the state. Prussia's new king thought that public teaching that undermined belief in the literal truth of the Bible encouraged disorder. In response, he issued the Religion Edict of 9 July 1788 directed against such teaching. When this provoked public criticism, he approved the Censorship Edict of 19 December 1788, which curbed freedom of expression. These measures were mitigated by the Holy Roman Empire's territorial fragmentation: writers and publishers determined to circumvent the legislation simply moved to neighboring states where Prussian laws had no force. For example, the enlightened publisher Friedrich Nicolai transferred production of his periodical *Allgemeine deutsche Bibliothek* to the independent city state of Hamburg. The monthly *Berlinische Monatsschrift* decamped to Jena, which was located in the duchy of Saxe-Weimar, a model enlightened state where Johann Wolfgang von Goethe served as a senior official.[18]

That radical writers and publishers could circumvent censorship in Germany by simply moving a relatively short distance illustrates the advantages, insofar as freedom of speech is concerned, of the extreme territorial fragmentation of the Holy Roman Empire. However, what was good for freedom of speech was disadvantageous for confronting a common external enemy.[19] The outbreak of the French Revolution in July 1789 did little to encourage the formation of a united stance between the German states. Instead, the old geopolitical and dynastic rivalries between the princes persisted, trumping ideological considerations. As already noted, the most important rivalry was that between the two largest states, Austria and Prussia. At the time of the storming of the Bastille, it appeared that the two were sliding toward yet another war, which, had it broken out, would have been their fourth in fifty years. The reasons for this latest breakdown lay with the so-called Eastern Question, which was about the future of the

---

[18] Brigitte Meier, *Friedrich Wilhelm II. König von Preußen, 1744–1797: Ein Leben zwischen Rokoko und Revolution* (Regensburg: F. Pustet, 2007).

[19] Peter H. Wilson, *German Armies: War and German Politics, 1648–1806* (London: UCL Press, 1998).

Ottoman Empire. Austria, along with Russia, had been waging war against the Ottomans since 1787. This war, initially fought mainly in the Balkans, then spread to the Baltic when Sweden declared war on Russia in June 1788, triggering a Danish offensive against Sweden in September. Britain and Prussia then threatened to intervene on the Swedish side, forcing the Danes out of the war in July 1789.[20]

For Austria, the Ottoman War proved something of a disaster. The campaign in the Balkans turned into one of attrition that bore fruit only in October 1789 when a massive Austrian field army, numbering over 120,000 troops, forced the surrender of the Ottoman garrison in Belgrade. However, the deployment of the bulk of Austrian forces against the Ottomans left the Habsburgs exposed elsewhere. Joseph II's radical reforms had alienated opinion, especially in those parts of his dominions that traditionally enjoyed a great measure of autonomy. These included notably the Austrian Netherlands and Hungary. In the Austrian Netherlands, opposition to Joseph finally spilled over into open revolt, which broke out in earnest in October 1789. In Hungary, meanwhile, nobles plotted to overthrow Habsburg rule, possibly with Prussian help. On 31 January 1790, Prussia signed an offensive alliance with the Ottoman Empire, and proceeded with the buildup of its forces on its borders with Austria and Russia. War appeared imminent. Then, three weeks later, Emperor Joseph II died, and was succeeded by his younger brother Leopold II (r. 1790–1792).

Leopold had previously ruled Tuscany, a dependency of the Habsburgs, before becoming emperor. In Tuscany, Leopold gained a reputation as a model enlightened ruler, pushing through a whole raft of progressive measures, including the abolition of capital punishment. However, unlike his brother Joseph, Leopold was also an astute politician, and he employed his skills to rapidly extricate Austria from the mess his brother had left it in. On the international front, he moved quickly to improve relations with Prussia, which was achieved with the Convention of Reichenbach concluded on 27 July 1790. This was done on the basis of Leopold agreeing to terminate the war against the Ottomans on the basis of the *status quo ante bellum*, finalized in the Austro-Ottoman Treaty of Sistova (4 August 1791). Prussia for its part agreed to end its support for Belgian rebels and Hungarian plotters, and this allowed Leopold to reestablish Habsburg authority domestically. Reichenbach ended a fifty-year period of Austro-Prussian hostility and

---

[20] Paul W. Schroeder, *The Transformation of European Politics 1763–1848* (Oxford: Clarendon Press, 1994), 56–61.

opened up a new phase characterized by a greater degree of cooperation in German affairs that would endure, on and off, until 1850.

The French Revolution was a factor in encouraging Austro-Prussian rapprochement. However, the immediate impact of the Revolution was felt more in the western part of the Holy Roman Empire than in Austria or Prussia. The Rhineland was geographically closer, and a complicated mesh of overlapping jurisdictions, enclaves, and exclaves insured that it would not be insulated from the political convulsions overcoming France. In the southern part of the region, known as the Palatinate, rural disturbances broke out in the summer of 1789 following the arrival of news of the French Revolution. Peasants in the duchy of Pfalz-Zweibrücken had for some time been dissatisfied with their lot, which hardly improved under the rule of Duke Karl II August (r. 1775–1795). The duke was in line to inherit Bavaria, and he sought to assert his dynastic pretensions through the maintenance of a lavish court. Unfortunately, the burden of this representational extravaganza was more than his subjects could bear. Hunting, which formed a component of traditional court culture, imposed particularly high costs on the peasantry. The situation in France, and especially neighboring Alsace, where a wave of riots swept the countryside in July and August 1789, emboldened peasants in the duchy, who now asserted themselves more vigorously. Matters reached a head in September, in the town of Bergzabern, which housed the local administration and hence supplied an obvious target to the peasants from the surrounding area, who proceeded to storm its town hall. They were appeased only when the authorities set up a special commission to hear their complaints, which centered especially on the issue of access to forests, which the duke had restricted in order to preserve game for the hunt.[21]

Further north, the French Revolution had a greater effect on urban politics, including in the imperial city of Aachen. Again, the Revolution itself did not initiate the conflict, which was of a type that had a fairly long history, but rather changed the language used by the participants. Demands that had previously been couched in the familiar language of historic rights and privileges now included references to the universal liberties triumphant in France. In Aachen, two opposing factions had been jockeying for power for years, both of them corrupting ostensibly republican institutions for their

---

[21] Erich Schunk, "Forstunruhen im Herzogtum Pfalz-Zweibrücken zu Beginn der Französischen Revolution 1789–1792/93," *Geschichte und Gesellschaft* 12, special issue "Soziale Unruhen in Deutschland während der Französischen Revolution" (1988), 45–66.

own advantage. In 1787, the conflict threatened to descend into violent disorder, to the extent of provoking an imperial ruling that allowed neighboring states to deploy troops in the city to restore peace whilst a special commission convened to draft an "improved constitution for the free imperial city of Aachen." This commission was chaired by the Prussian official Christian Wilhelm von Dohm, who is better known as the author of *Über die bürgerliche Verbesserung der Juden*, an important contribution to the debate then raging in Germany over Jewish emancipation. Von Dohm's commission completed its work in 1790, adopting something of a middle path between revolution and reaction in its proposal to democratize old civic institutions.[22]

Other parts of Germany, including ones further to the east, also witnessed conflict at this time. Saxony experienced a serious peasant revolt in 1790, which was inspired, at least according to government reports, by the spread of news from France. There were even rumors at the time of French emissaries spreading propaganda, though in reality there is little evidence for such activity. Peasants in Saxony were aware of dramatic reforms to the rural order occurring in neighboring states even without the activities of emissaries. They, or rather the legally trained village advocates who spoke on their behalf, referred to the French Revolution and the "Rights of Man," and also to Joseph II's progressive reforms in neighboring Bohemia. Beyond Saxony and the Rhineland, threats to proceed according to the "French manner," references to the "Rights of Man," and the appearance of tricolor cockades became a feature of otherwise traditional conflicts from 1789 onwards. But beyond this, Germany remained largely unreceptive to the French Revolution in its first years.[23]

The French Revolution's substantial and lasting impact on Germany came only with the outbreak of the so-called French Revolutionary Wars in 1792. These would run until the Treaty of Lunéville in 1801, before morphing into the Napoleonic Wars that ended only in 1815. This generation of large-scale conflict transformed Germany. The relationship between France and Habsburg Austria was central to the outbreak of these wars. Franco-Habsburg rivalry had shaped European affairs for a quarter of a millennium before being interrupted, temporarily as it turned out, by the so-called "Diplomatic Revolution" of 1756. In that year, Austria and France concluded

---

[22] Horst Carl, "Die Aachener Mäkelei 1786–1793: Konfliktmechanismen in der Endphase des Alten Reiches," *Zeitschrift des Aachener Geschichtsvereins* 92 (1985), 103–88.
[23] Siegfried Hoyer, "Die Ideen der Französischen Revolution und der kursächsische Bauernaufstand 1790," *Neues Archiv für sächsische Geschichte* 65 (1994), 61–76.

an alliance in order to better confront the rising powers Prussia and Britain. This immediately triggered the Seven Years' War that proved a disaster for France. The new alliance became controversial on the French side, where opponents argued – not without reason – that it benefited only Austria. This fed into an increasingly vocal and public Austrophobia, of which Queen Marie Antoinette became the lightning rod. This sentiment strengthened following the outbreak of the Revolution, when radicals suspected the "Austrian bitch," as she became known, of conspiring with her Habsburg relatives to restore the absolute monarchy. French domestic politics thereby became intertwined with the politics of the Holy Roman Empire, and through a series of crises led to the outbreak of war in April 1792. Revolutionary policy makers in France hoped to restrict the war to Austria, but rapprochement between the two German powers meant that Prussia was also immediately drawn into what historians know as the First Coalition.[24]

Initially, Prussian and Austrian forces gained the advantage in the conflict, before suffering reversals at Valmy (20 September 1792) and Jemappes (6 November 1792). It was now the turn of the armies of the French Republic, as it had become, to go on the offensive. This they did, occupying the Austrian Netherlands and a substantial swathe of the Rhineland by the end of the year. In the Rhineland, the French created a satellite state known as the Republic of Mainz, which some historians have claimed to be the first modern democratic German state.[25] This short-lived polity (it lasted from March to July 1793) was dominated by radical staff and students of the University of Mainz, and is associated especially with Georg Forster, who was already famous on account of his participation in James Cook's second voyage of exploration. Forster, along with the other so-called "German Jacobins," received support from the local French military commander in Mainz, who sought their collaboration in managing the occupation. The French government, for its part, assumed that ordinary Rhinelanders would welcome the expulsion of the Old Regime, an assumption encouraged by people like Forster. It hoped to exploit this sentiment to win democratic legitimacy for the occupation. To this end, Paris dispatched civilian

---

[24] T. C. W. Blanning, *The Origins of the French Revolutionary Wars* (London: Longman, 1986).
[25] The historiography on the Republic of Mainz is substantial, not least because it figured as a bone of ideological contention between the two German states during the Cold War. For an older historiographical review, see T. C. W. Blanning, "German Jacobins and the French Revolution," *The Historical Journal* 23 (1980), 985–1002. For Georg Forster, see Ludwig Uhlig, "Antinomien der Politik: Georg Forsters Weg zur Revolution," *Historische Zeitschrift*, 274 (2002), 329–65.

commissioners to Mainz with the task of organizing elections there. Crucially, only those willing to swear a revolutionary oath were admitted to the polls, which meant the results were in effect a foregone conclusion. The elections produced the Rhenish-German National Convention, and it was this body that in March 1793 declared Mainz to be an independent state founded upon the principles of liberty and equality. It then immediately sought Mainz's separation from the Holy Roman Empire and incorporation into the French Republic. In the meantime, a resurgence of Austrian and Prussian military fortunes, which was well under way already at the beginning of 1793, made it unlikely that this move would have any practical consequences: April saw the beginning of the siege of the city of Mainz by Coalition forces (Figure 18.1), and this ended with the capitulation of the French garrison on 23 July. Those "Jacobins" who failed to leave with the French army were arrested, in some cases after having been mishandled by the populace, who could now vent retrospectively their opposition to the occupation.

The experience of Mainz justified Maximilien Robespierre's observation, made before the occupation, that no one likes armed missionaries. The limited capacity of eighteenth-century military logistics meant that all armies depended in large measure upon local resources for sustenance. Occupation by any army in this period was onerous for the civilian population, but occupation by the French revolutionary army was particularly burdensome. For a start, the revolutionary army was especially large, as it needed to be to make up for its qualitative inferiority. A larger army meant a greater demand for billeting, food, forage, and other supplies, which needed to be sourced locally. Second, the revolutionary army was less disciplined than its opponents: much of the officer corps had emigrated, and those who remained or had risen through the ranks were reluctant to impose severe punishments for fear of being denounced as royalists. The consequence was that soldiers had less to fear when committing outrages against the civilian population. Finally, the army was enthused with an anticlerical spirit, which manifested itself in the desecration of churches. This greatly offended the sensibilities of Germans, who did not share the hostility to organized religion common amongst their French neighbors. Ordinary people overwhelmingly detested the French occupation, and this detestation then extended to the so-called German Jacobins who for ideological reasons had collaborated with the French.[26]

---

[26] Michael Rowe, *From Reich to State: The Rhineland in the Revolutionary Age, 1780–1830* (New York and Cambridge: Cambridge University Press, 2003), 48–83.

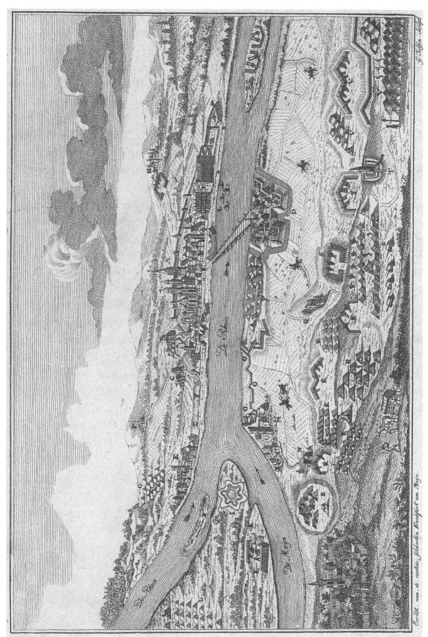

Figure 18.1 The siege of Mainz (1793). BTEU/RKMLGE/Alamy.

The surrender of Mainz to coalition forces in July 1793 marked the end of a phase in the French Revolutionary Wars. Pressured on all fronts, the French Republic responded with mass mobilization (the *levée en masse*, 23 August 1793), and proceeded over the following year to raise an army numbering perhaps 800,000 men. French forces then surged forward again, reoccupying Belgium and most of the Rhineland by the end of 1794, before conquering the Dutch Republic the following year. The French resurgence of 1794 and 1795 in part caused Prussia to abandon the First Coalition and to sign a neutrality agreement (Treaty of Basel, 5 April 1795) with the French Republic. The details of the agreement did much to undermine the integrity of the Holy Roman Empire, and indeed can be seen as the start of the process that ended with its formal dissolution in 1806. Prussia secretly agreed to recognize French rule on the left bank of the Rhine in return for compensation on the right bank. This set in motion a process whereby Germany's extreme territorial fragmentation into approximately 300 "states" would be simplified, resulting at the end of the process in a structure of just over 30 states, some of which survive as constituent *Länder* of today's Federal Republic. The winners in this process were the larger secular states, including Bavaria, Baden, and Württemberg. The main losers were the church states, which were abolished, the imperial cities, which lost their independence, and the hundreds of imperial nobles whose estates were "mediatized" (made subordinate to princely authority). The long-term implications of this territorial consolidation process set in motion in 1795 were profound, not least when it came to the development of a German national identity in the nineteenth century.

A second important consequence of the Treaty of Basel was to neutralize northern Germany to the east of the Rhine. This made a mockery of any notion of imperial unity against the French, but was good news for the northern economy. Northern Germany, and especially its major commercial ports such as Bremen and Hamburg, benefited from the displacement of trade from belligerent states. Hamburg, as already noted, Germany's third-largest city after Vienna and Berlin, had already benefited from the opening up of direct trading links with the newly independent United States after 1783. In 1797, when Spain found itself at war with Britain, Hamburg in addition gained greater direct trade access to Spanish America. Hamburg in this period also served as a staple market for goods imported from Asia, including India, the Sunda Islands, and the Philippines. As for northern Germany more generally, these were also good years for agriculture. British demand for foreign grain in this period was largely met by Prussia and its newly acquired Polish possessions, which together accounted for just over half of Britain's grain imports. Prussia's status as a neutral, and the security umbrella it provided for Germany north of the Main, insured that the region enjoyed the benefits rather than the costs of the French Revolutionary Wars from 1795 onwards.[27]

Southern and western Germany, in contrast, remained war zones in the decade up to 1805. Most of the region to the west of the Rhine came under permanent French occupation from late 1794. The number of French troops stationed in the region at this time – something in the order of 150,000 troops – represented close to 10 percent of the civilian population. This proportion made open resistance to French rule futile, and also imposed great hardship even though in normal times the Rhineland was a net exporter of agricultural produce. Following their earlier experience, the French were now under no illusion that their presence was welcome, or that Germans were enthusiasts for revolution. In consequence, they had fewer compunctions in treating the areas they occupied as conquered territory, ripe for exploitation. French generals like Lazare Hoche, who commanded forces in the Rhineland in 1797, were not interested in sponsoring revolution but rather in insuring the provisioning of their armies. This required a policy of engagement with established German elites rather than native "Jacobins," who were, furthermore, isolated in social terms. Local elites had prior legal and administrative experience, and enjoyed a degree of legitimacy that was needed to extract the resources required by the French army. The consequence of this shift toward pragmatism on the French side was the total marginalization and disillusionment of the local radicals. This, for example, was the experience of the young Joseph Görres, a prominent initial supporter of the French. He soon became disillusioned by their behavior as conquerors and occupiers, and emerged in 1813 as one of the most influential German nationalist agitators against Napoleonic hegemony.[28]

Though southern Germany remained an important theater of military operations for the remainder of the First Revolutionary War, it was in northern Italy that the French broke the stalemate and achieved a decisive victory over the Austrians. This resulted in the Peace of Campo Formio,

---

[27] Katherine Aaslestad, *Place and Politics: Local Identity, Civic Culture, and German Nationalism in North Germany during the Revolutionary Era* (Leiden and Boston: Brill, 2005); Christopher Clark, *Iron Kingdom: The Rise and Downfall of Prussia, 1600–1947* (London: Penguin, 2007).

[28] Monika Fink-Lang, *Joseph Görres: Die Biografie* (Paderborn: Ferdinand Schöningh, 2013).

signed between France and Austria on 18 October 1797. The wider historical significance of the treaty lay in its secret clauses, whereby Austria accepted French annexation of the left bank of the Rhine. This marked a decisive shift in Habsburg policy, in which wider German interests were sacrificed for more narrowly Austrian ones. As part of the treaty, Austria was authorized to annex the Venetian Republic, which meant that its orientation became more Italian and less German. Campo Formio marked an even more decisive step toward the dissolution of the Empire than Prussia's agreement with the French at Basel in 1795: Prussian actions for much of the eighteenth century had challenged the imperial order, so Berlin's disregard for the integrity of the Empire was nothing new. The Habsburgs, in contrast, had for the most part functioned as central European "gamekeepers," so their sacrifice of the smaller German states of the south and west was far more dramatic and damaging. From a narrowly Austrian perspective, however, sacrifice of vulnerable holdings in Belgium and the west of Germany made much sense. A consolidated core of coterminous territories was much easier to defend, govern, reform, and integrate economically than a scattering of disparate holdings bound only loosely together. These practical considerations had already entered the policy mix before the French Revolution, including notably under Joseph II, who during his reign had attempted to swap the Austrian Netherlands for Bavaria. The "creative destruction" of the French Revolutionary Wars allowed German ideas about territorial consolidation and domestic reform, finally, to be put into practice.

Germany's other secular territorial states took note. The three main south German states – Baden, Bavaria, and Württemberg – recognized that French support might allow them to follow the same kind of advantageous territorial rearrangement as had provisionally been achieved by Prussia (in 1795) and Austria (in 1797). Bavaria in particular had always feared Austrian expansion, which it had countered by forging alliances with France throughout the early modern period. Given this, it was quite natural that Bavaria should gravitate increasingly toward France, despite their ostensible ideological differences. This tendency increased with the accession of Maximilian IV as elector in 1799. Within two years, he succeeded in reorientating his state's policy away from Vienna and toward Paris, and so insured that Bavaria emerged as one of the winners from the wholesale territorial reordering in Germany that commenced, formally, with the so-called Reichsdeputationshauptschluß of 1803. This legal act marked the practical end of the Holy Roman Empire, though the old polity staggered on for a further three years before its final demise. Its death was accompanied by a wholesale extinction event that witnessed the disappearance of the hundreds of church states, imperial cities, and *Zwergstaaten* (literally, "dwarf states") that had previously dotted the central European landscape. What emerged from the cull, certainly in the south of Germany, was a map that is recognizable today, in the current delineation of the *Bundesländer*.

Territorial consolidation not only improved a state's position externally, but also facilitated domestic reform that impacted the lives of ordinary people. As noted above, many German territories had already embarked upon enlightened reform programs before the French Revolution. However, under the Old Regime, how far rulers could go was limited by institutional constraints. Most German territories, including the smaller ones, were not absolute monarchies under the old order, but needed to contend with local corporations that had the backing of the imperial courts. However, territorial consolidation made it easier to marginalize representative estates in places like Württemberg. In addition, the extension of French hegemony over Germany at the expense of the Habsburgs, together with the destruction of the church states, imperial cities, and imperial knights, had the effect of neutering the old Reich's institutions, including above all the imperial courts. The legal constraint that had previously prevented far-reaching reform via monarchical fiat was thereby removed. Rulers and the reform-minded bureaucrats who served them were given free rein. Much of Germany now experienced what historians have termed "bureaucratic state absolutism" (*bürokratischer Staatsabsolutismus*). Over the following years, and in southern Germany in particular, this form of rule saw the imposition of top-down reforms. These reforms mirrored those implemented in France under Napoleon after he seized power there in 1799. They included the creation of governmental and administrative structures that were more centralized, uniform, and in many ways professional than had existed previously. They were also authoritarian, in the sense that they marginalized the old representative estates, town councils, and guilds that under the Old Regime had allowed for a modicum of input from the wider populace in public affairs. These intermediate bodies were swept away as states established a direct connection with their subjects, whom, with the further development of cameralist science and statistical methods, they administered with ever greater efficiency. For ordinary Germans, government generally became much more burdensome, as taxes rose, and military conscription was rolled out. For the majority of the poor, there was much to be regretted with the triumph of this brave new world. For a minority, including the professionals who staffed the administrations and the businessmen freed from tiresome guild constraints, there were in contrast tangible benefits.[29]

As for Germany's intellectuals, they were divided in their reaction to the triumph of the bureaucratic state. For some, like Georg Wilhelm Friedrich Hegel (a native of the duchy of Württemberg), this development promised to overcome the selfish narrow-mindedness they associated with the privileged estates-based order of old. Professional officials, so they hoped, were in a position to detach themselves from this world of pettiness, and instead act on the basis of the common good. Other thinkers, including especially those associated with German romanticism and conservatism, rejected the new order as alienating, and argued that the old structures that were in the process of being swept away had been crucial for the reconciliation of competing interests within society. They came to appreciate what they argued was a more organic society, as had supposedly existed in the Middle Ages, a time when the "machine state" had been absent. The plunder of Germany's churches and monasteries, whether it be by the French or by their German allies, encouraged also a new appreciation of medieval art and architecture that fed into gothic revivalism that bloomed more fully in the first half of the nineteenth century. This revivalism was focused especially on the region straddling the Rhine, a river that for the very reason that it was occupied by the French came in this period to assume its character as a symbol of German nationhood.

In conclusion, it is unsurprising that the Revolution in France should greatly disturb the political culture of Germany, given that the two were neighbors. This is not to argue that Germany – or more correctly, the Holy Roman Empire and its constituent members – had been static or devoid of reform before 1789. German princes, influenced by the Enlightenment, strove to introduce important changes in the second half of the eighteenth century. The years immediately before the French Revolution witnessed a dramatic extension of religious tolerance, for example. Other reforms made the criminal justice system in many states more humane, and in places there were impressive improvements in the provision of public education. However, the institutional constraints imposed by the old Empire, an entity geared to preserving laws rather than making new ones, placed limits on what might be achieved. The French Revolution, and above all the

---

[29] Michael Rowe, "Napoleon and the 'Modernization' of Germany," in Philip Dwyer and Alan Forrest, eds., *Napoleon and His Empire: Europe, 1804–1814* (Basingstoke: Palgrave Macmillan, 2007).

Revolutionary Wars to which it gave rise, swept away this barrier to much more fundamental change. Radical reforms, many of which had been on the drawing board before 1789, were ready to be implemented as soon as the French shattered Germany's territorial order. Reform-minded officials now had a free run, and in the space of a few years in the early nineteenth century they built up state institutions. These were designed above all to extract more efficiently the resources necessary to fight the Napoleonic Wars. The problem was that, whilst they achieved this, they at the same time lacked legitimacy, thereby storing up problems that were not resolved until later on in the nineteenth century.

19

Reform and Resistance: Hungary and the Habsburg Monarchy, 1780–1795

ORSOLYA SZAKÁLY

"The revolution taking place here before my eyes appeared important from a distance but is even more interesting when seen at close quarters. It makes a deep impression. I feel that during the last two months I have undergone a complete change," wrote the Hungarian nobleman, Gergely Berzeviczy in a letter to his mother. Young Berzeviczy, just a week shy of his twenty-fourth birthday at the time, was on his way home. He had completed his university studies in Göttingen and now his tour of England and France was drawing to a close. However, the year was not 1789, and neither was the letter penned in France. Instead, Berzeviczy was describing events in Brussels in June 1787. He had this to add:

> The entire Austrian Netherlands are in ferment. The population has firmly decided to do everything necessary to protect its freedom and its constitution. The emperor's edicts have been cast aside and the entire country has taken up arms, just like 200 years ago. . . . The jubilation is extraordinary. Every city is illuminated, the nobility gives free dances and feasts for the people, everyone wears a yellow and red cockade as a sign of their patriotic fervour. It is not known what the emperor has to say to it all. The country is therefore getting ready to resist. . . . It is an uplifting sight to see the courage and determination of a nation to be free.[1]

The emperor in question is, of course, Joseph II (Figure 19.1). What adds piquancy is that he, as king of Hungary, was Berzeviczy's sovereign too. Moreover, Berzeviczy was not the only Hungarian to record his first-hand impressions of the great political upheaval Joseph II's reforms provoked in the Austrian Netherlands. Captain Baron Miklós Vay witnessed even more

---

[1] Quoted in Derek Beales, *Joseph II*, vol. II: *Against the World, 1780–1790* (Cambridge: Cambridge University Press, 2009), 513. This citation originally appeared in Éva H. Balázs, *Berzeviczy Gergely: A reformpolitikus, 1763–1795* (Budapest: Akadémiai Kiadó, 1967), 127.

Figure 19.1 Emperor Joseph II. Getty Images.

dramatic scenes on 22 January 1788. His long travel journal ends abruptly with the uncharacteristically rushed comments about the crowds that "are amassing on the large streets and squares" of Brussels.[2] Later that day, he must have seen General Alton's troops firing on the protesters and killing some of them – or at least he must have seen the aftermath. At the time of writing, both eyewitnesses had been absent from Hungary for several years. Soon they were to experience in person how Joseph II's reforms changed Hungary and affected the political mood. The diary entry of the ever-rational Vay was factual, while Berzeviczy expressed strong sympathy, even admiration for those who resisted the reforms that had been imposed on them.

[2] Baron Miklós Vay's Travel Diaries, 1785–1788, Vay Family Archive, The Collections of the Calvinist College, Sárospatak, Kii.IV.2.J 1, f. 286.

This chapter charts Joseph II's reign and its aftermath in Hungary, focusing on the choices that were available to those in positions of power, men like Berzeviczy and Vay. However, in order to understand their options, it is important to consider Hungary's position within the wider Habsburg realm.

Hungary constituted a problem for the centralizing forces within the Habsburg Monarchy. While the "agglutination" of disparate lands under Habsburg rule tellingly lacked even a distinct name,[3] Hungary had a clear and well-established identity as a political entity. This identity was rooted in and safeguarded by its estates-based political system. The presence of estates in *ancien régime* polities was a given, but their power was increasingly challenged by absolutism. In the Habsburg Monarchy, the estates of the lands of St. Wenceslaw (Bohemia, Moravia, and Silesia; hereafter referred to as Bohemia for brevity) were crushed following an abortive anti-Habsburg rebellion in the early seventeenth century. In the middle of the eighteenth century, the estates of the Habsburgs' Austrian provinces[4] were also effectively defanged by reform and state centralization. (These lands were Lower and Upper Austria, Styria, Carinthia, Carniola, the Tyrol, and Vorarlberg. The last two provinces were geographically more detached and less affected by reform.) These Austrian and Bohemian territories together formed the *Erblande* (hereditary lands) and in this chapter are referred to as the Habsburg core provinces.

The kingdom of Hungary was substantially different. Theoretically, it became a Habsburg domain at the same time as Bohemia in the mid-1520s. However, for a century and a half effective Habsburg control extended only to a third of its territory, so-called Royal Hungary. One-third formed part of the Ottoman Empire and another third was turned into the principality of Transylvania, a semi-independent state ruled by a Protestant prince under the Ottoman Sultan's suzerainty. The Ottomans were driven out at the turn of the seventeenth and eighteenth centuries but remained a credible threat. As for the successive Habsburg sovereigns, this turbulent period left them with three unwelcome legacies in Hungary: an elite that was less integrated into court life than geographic proximity might suggest, a significant and powerful Calvinist and Lutheran minority amounting to a quarter of the population, and confident and assertive estates.

---

[3] See Martyn Rady, *The Habsburg Empire: A Very Short Introduction* (Oxford: Oxford University Press, 2017).

[4] Charles Ingrao, *The Habsburg Monarchy, 1618–1815* (Cambridge: Cambridge University Press, 1994), 7.

At the end of the Ottoman era and following a partially successful revolt (1703–1711),[5] the estates managed to retain Hungary's "constitutional independence," including its system of limited monarchy. This was characterized by a duality between the monarch and the "country" (*regnum*).[6] The latter was interpreted within Hungary as the community of the estates, which in turn equaled the nobility and bodies with noble-like privileges. Royal free cities, for instance, with their own political rights, were treated legally as corporate nobles. Consequently, the defense of noble liberties was seen as the preservation of the kingdom itself. These privileges were extensive and embraced exclusive political rights: the right to hold office, personal immunity from arbitrary arrest, freedom from taxation on grounds of personal military service, and, within Hungary's customary practices, an exclusive right to the ownership of land. In an overwhelmingly agricultural economy, this right of landownship amounted to a monopoly of economic power.[7]

Economic hegemony was coupled with political dominance. Hungary's bicameral parliament, the Diet, was a powerful body since any new legislation by the ruler ultimately had to be subject to its consent. The prelates (of the Roman Catholic Church) and the magnates (aristocrats, titled nobles) attended in person and sat in the Upper House. The Lower House consisted primarily of the delegates of the untitled nobility, representing roughly fifty counties (with two delegates from each), and the representatives of the royal free cities. The cathedral chapters and the associated territories of Slavonia, Croatia, and Dalmatia were also represented and had one vote each. Delegates of absent aristocrats sat in the Lower House, too, but had no right to vote.[8] The roughly fifty cities cast a single collective vote, while each county had its own vote. Additionally, after 1700 practically all prelates were aristocrats. Consequently, out of the four estates, only the representatives of the royal free cities, accounting for around 3.6 percent of the total population, were independent of the nobility. Most royal free cities had lost their

---

[5] István M. Szijártó, "The Rákóczi Revolt as a Successful Rebellion," in László Péter and Martyn Rady, eds., *Resistance, Rebellion and Revolution in Hungary and Central Europe: Commemorating 1956* (London: Hungarian Cultural Centre London, 2008), 67–76.

[6] László Péter, "The Aristocracy, the Gentry and Their Parliamentary Tradition in Nineteenth-Century Hungary," in Miklós Lojkó, ed., *Hungary's Long Nineteenth Century: Constitutional and Democratic Traditions in a European Perspective. Collected Studies* (Leiden: Brill, 2012), 305–42.

[7] R. J. W. Evans, "The Nobility of Hungary in the Eighteenth Century," in H. M. Scott, ed., *The European Nobilities in the Seventeenth and Eighteenth Centuries*, vol. II: *Northern, Central and Eastern Europe*, 2nd edition (Basingstoke: Palgrave Macmillan, 2007), 252.

[8] István M. Szijártó, *A 18. századi Magyarország rendi országgyűlése* (Budapest: Országgyűlés Hivatala, 2016).

economic clout by the end of the eighteenth century, and their population was stagnating. The fastest growing towns, such as Pest, were market towns subject to their noble landlords' jurisdiction and lacking in political representation.[9]

In theory, the Hungarian nobility was "one and undivided," forming a homogeneous elite encompassing the aristocracy as well as the untitled nobility. By European standards, it was very numerous. In 1787, it comprised 4.6 percent of the total population, a political base comparable to that of contemporary Great Britain. The nobility's main career opportunities, apart from being landowners, were the military and the law. Nevertheless, nobles were not legally prevented from practicing any other professions. All legitimate sons were entitled to a share of the father's landed property. Again, this applied to untitled nobles and aristocrats alike. Despite theoretical equality, there was an immense diversity in wealth, opportunities, and lifestyle. The nobility was geographically unevenly spread, amounting to under 1 percent of the population in some counties and up to 16 percent in others. It was also religiously divided. Most nobles were Roman Catholic, but a significant Calvinist block existed in northeastern and eastern Hungary, while the Lutheran nobility was scattered in the northern and western regions. The majority of nobles were ethnic Hungarians (Magyars), but many were Germans, Croatians, Serbians, Slovaks, Romanians, or even Ruthenians. That said, the official language was Latin, smoothing over linguistic differences.[10]

The aristocracy was a Habsburg creation, since inheritable titles originally were a rarity in Hungary. Starting from the early seventeenth century, successive Habsburg monarchs granted titles and land to selected members of the Hungarian nobility for loyalty and military service. By the end of the eighteenth century, there were just over 100 aristocratic families. Around a dozen of the oldest of these had been granted entails to safeguard their landed wealth from fragmentation. From the start, the role of this usually pro-Habsburg top aristocracy was to mediate between crown and "country." In return, they dominated the top secular and ecclesiastical positions. Between 1681 and 1765, the office of the highest secular dignity, the viceroy (palatine), for example, was occupied by a prince Esterházy, two count

---

[9] Éva H. Balázs, *Hungary and the Habsburgs, 1765–1800: An Experiment in Enlightened Absolutism* (Budapest: Central European Press, 1997), 123–33.

[10] A few nobles were Greek Catholic or Orthodox, but as a rule the populations professing these two faiths did not have a nobility. Evans, "The Nobility of Hungary," 251–2.

Pálffys, and a count (later prince) Batthyány.[11] Prince Esterházy was by far the richest of them all, with his over 1,000,000 acres of land and 300,000 peasants. To put his fabulous wealth into context, the next richest aristocrat lorded over around 300,000 acres.[12] At the other end of the spectrum were the untitled nobles who lived at the level of the peasantry. The Habsburg practice of ennobling many without land and the fragmentation of estates due to partible inheritance resulted in the existence of tens of thousands of these noblemen. There were those who cultivated land roughly equal to a single peasant portion (*curialisten*) and those who owned no land at all (*armalisten*). Unlike in Bohemia, however, this situation did not lead to aristocratic hegemony, as a muscular and relatively wealthy segment of the untitled nobility occupied the middle ground.

The power base of this well-to-do untitled nobility was the local administration, the county. The monarch staffed and controlled the two central institutions of the executive branch: the Hungarian Royal Chancellery in Vienna and the Hungarian Royal Lieutenancy in the Hungarian capital, Pressburg (today's Bratislava in Slovakia). At a local level, the county was headed by a royal appointee, the *főispán* (high sheriff), normally an aristocrat. The administration itself, however, was run by his deputy, the *alispán* (deputy sheriff). The holder of the office of *alispán* and all his subordinate officials were elected from among and by the local nobility for three-year periods. The county's political, financial, and judicial competence was extensive. At its monthly assemblies, the very center of the untitled nobility's public life, local nobles selected delegates to the Diets and drew up their instructions when a Diet was convoked, published laws approved by the Diets, put royal decrees into practice, and supervised tax collection and military recruitment. Additionally, the counties had the right to "respectfully put aside" and remonstrate against royal decrees that were deemed "unconstitutional."[13]

This mattered in the post-Ottoman period because of Hungary's sheer size once its total territory had been brought under Habsburg control. Taken as a single unit with its relatively small associated territories (Croatia, Slavonia,

---

[11] Peter Schimert, "The Early Modern Hungarian Nobility," in Scott, *European Nobilities*, 210–48.

[12] Zoltán Fónagy, "Nemesi birtokviszonyok az úrbérrendezés korában," *Századok* 133:6 (1999), 1141–92: 1173.

[13] Orsolya Szakály, "Managing a Composite Monarchy: The Hungarian Diet and the Habsburgs in the Eighteenth Century," in David Hayton, James Kelly, and John Bergin, eds., *The Eighteenth-Century Composite State: Representative Institutions in Ireland and Europe, 1689–1800* (Basingstoke: Palgrave Macmillan, 2010), 205–20: 211.

and Dalmatia) and with Transylvania, it constituted nearly half of the Habsburg Monarchy's territory, and by the end of the eighteenth century, 45 percent of its population. With its over 9 million inhabitants, Hungary was a large European state in its own right. Successive Habsburg sovereigns limited the power of the Hungarian estates by not restoring Hungary's pre-Ottoman integrity. Transylvania, for instance, was incorporated as a separate political entity ruled through its own, much more compliant, estates. A similar strategy of administrative separation was deployed in the cases of the Military Frontier Zone, a buffer on Hungary's southern border with the Ottoman Empire, and the last reconquered piece of Ottoman Hungary, the Banat of Temes (from 1718). This practice did not escape notice, and was one of the many grievances brought up at the start of each Diet. However, it ensured that within the entire "composite" Habsburg Monarchy, Hungary remained a "junior partner," albeit a formidable one.[14]

The political settlement of 1711 that followed the anti-Habsburg revolt of 1703–1711 acknowledged this duality and enabled coexistence between the Habsburg monarch and the estates, and allowed for much-needed economic reconstruction in Hungary. That this arrangement enjoyed the estates' continued backing is illustrated by their actions when Maria Theresa's right to succeed her father on the female line was challenged and the rich province of Silesia was seized by the Prussian king, Frederick II, in 1740. The iconic image of the Hungarian estates offering Maria Theresa (r. 1740–1780) "their lives and blood" at the Diet of 1741 notwithstanding, the tensions generated by Hungary's constitutional autonomy were plain to see. In the Habsburg core provinces, the state's ability to mobilize resources increased considerably thanks to Maria Theresa's reforms. In 1749, these lands were brought under a single central administration in the form of the Austrian–Bohemian Chancellery. The estates of these individual lands were deprived of their power of the purse and, in conformity with a wider European trend, noble land became taxable, albeit at a favorable rate.[15] Even in Hungary, there was some progress on taxation. Since the mid-1710s, the estates granted at regular Diets a considerable tax (*contributio*), to be paid by the peasantry, for the upkeep of the Habsburg standing army. The tax could be collected indefinitely, but not raised without the consent of a Diet. Moreover, in 1723, the tax base was widened when the poorest nobles, the *armalisten* and the *curialisten*, were made liable to pay tax. In reality, noble "taxation" (*subsidia*) in an

---

[14] Evans, "The Nobility of Hungary," 249.
[15] Ingrao, *The Habsburg Monarchy*, 159–72.

emergency and theoretically on a voluntary basis was relatively frequent in wartime. However, the principle of the noble land's tax exemption prevailed.[16]

The ultimate aim of all Maria Theresa's reforms was to safeguard the Habsburg Monarchy's preeminence in Central Europe. The view from the imperial capital of Vienna was that Hungary, which paid only a third of the total running costs of the Habsburg Monarchy, did not pull its weight. Habsburg officials in Vienna attributed this to the selfishness of its nobility. When successive Diets refused to raise the tax considerably, in 1754, Maria Theresa introduced a system of dual tariffs, turning Hungary into a source of primary products (cattle, cereals, wine, and wool) for the Habsburg core provinces and a market for their budding industries. The tariffs ranged between 2 and 60 percent. The logic behind this was to penalize the recalcitrant Hungarian nobility where it hurt most, that is, economically, since they profited most from agricultural exports.[17]

In the wake of the Seven Years' War (1756–1763), and after another refusal of additional taxes at the Diet of 1764–1765, the stage was set for twenty-five years of absolutist rule. It operated through the exploitation of the Hungarian crown's strong executive powers.[18] Hence, it was through royal decrees that key reforms were introduced in the last fifteen years of Maria Theresa's reign. Two stand out as particularly significant. The first was an intervention into what until then was regarded as the estates' competence: the nobles' relationship with their peasants. Nobles owned the land and enjoyed peasant services in return for its use. The *Urbarium* of 1767 set a limit to what could be demanded of the peasants, especially the number of days per year they owed in unpaid labor (*robot*). The second was a comprehensive reform of the education system (*Ratio Educationis*, 1777) that affected all tiers of education and was funded by the confiscated wealth of the disbanded Jesuit order. By making primary education compulsory for boys and girls between the ages of six and twelve, it had a considerable effect. Over time, it produced an ever-growing crop of non-noble officials and independent intellectuals (journalists

---

[16] István M. Szijártó, "A nemesi adómentesség," in István M. Szijártó, ed., *Nemesi társadalom és politika: Tanulmányok a 18. Századi magyar rendiségről* (Budapest: Universitas Könyvkiadó, 2006), 145–61.

[17] Zoltán Fónagy, "A bomló feudalizmus gazdasága," in András Gergely, ed., *19. Századi magyar történelem, 1790–1918* (Budapest: Korona Kiadó, 1998), 27.

[18] Martyn Rady, "Nonnisi in sensu legum? Decree and Rendelet in Hungary, 1790–1914," *Hungarian Historical Review* 5:1 (2016), 5–8.

and writers), but its impact was felt primarily after the period under consideration.[19]

A selected group of Hungarian functionaries, exclusively nobles, skillfully enacted these decrees. This was a complicated and long-drawn-out process. For example, the *Urbarium* was in practice fully implemented only in 1774.[20] Their rewards were dazzling careers, aristocratic titles, and, from 1765 onward, the newly established Order of St. Stephen, tactfully named after the founder king of Hungary. This new "administrative" aristocracy was represented by figures such as György Fekete, Kristóf Niczky, and Pál Festetich. All three were untitled nobles, who became counts in 1760, 1765, and 1770, respectively.[21] These men were no carpetbaggers. They were informed, no doubt, partly by self-interest. Nevertheless, they also epitomized a strong tradition of royalism (centered on the Hungarian monarch) and a recognition that reform was inevitable. They could reconcile their actions with their identity as nobles because they worked within a system that respected constitutional constraints.

In parallel with rewarding close collaborators, Maria Theresa carefully cultivated pro-Habsburg sentiments in the Hungarian nobility. Arguably, it was during her reign that the Hungarian aristocracy came closest to integrating into the Habsburg court aristocracy. This is borne out by a notable rise in intermarriage between the two groups. More unusually, Maria Theresa reached out to the untitled nobility as well. In 1760, she established the Hungarian noble bodyguard. This was made up of 100 untitled nobles from Hungary and 20 from Transylvania. Others, aristocrats and untitled nobles alike, took advantage of the high-quality military and civilian education that was increasingly available in Vienna.[22] There were also gestures that Maria Theresa extended to Hungary as a whole. The most significant amongst these was the reincorporation of the Banat of Temes into Hungary in 1778.

Joseph II (1780–1790) inherited this delicate political operation upon his mother's death on 29 November 1780. His reign was much anticipated.

---

[19] Domokos Kosáry, "Értelmiség és kulturális elit a XVIII. századi Magyarországon," *Valóság* 24:2 (1981), 11–20.
[20] Fónagy, "Nemesi birtokviszonyok," 1145.
[21] Balázs, *Hungary and the Habsburgs*, 108–9.
[22] Orsolya Szakály, "War, Science and Professionalization: Military Engineering in the Habsburg Army in the Eighteenth Century," in András Forgó and Krisztina Kulcsár, eds., *"Die habsburgische Variante des Aufgeklärten Absolutismus": Beiträge zur Mitregentschaft Josephs II., 1765–1780 / "A felvilágosult abszolutizmus Habsburg-variánsa": Tanulmányok II. József társuralkodói időszakáról, 1765–1780* (Vienna: Ungarische Geschichtsforschung in Wien, 2018), 181–200.

Despite having been Holy Roman Emperor for fifteen years, at the age of thirty-nine, he had just stepped out of his mother's shadow. He was a well-traveled man, who made an impression during his various study tours. Enlightened circles at home and abroad watched him with particular interest and expectation. Some even thought, mistakenly, that he was "a disciple of the French *philosophes*."[23] During his journeys, Joseph II was unusually accessible. He engaged willingly with the public with no regard for rank and formality, and was always intent on informing himself with an eye to improvement in every possible field.[24] Indeed, in time his reign became coterminous with "enlightened absolutism": large-scale rationalizing reforms introduced from above without political consultation. Joseph II's goal was to form his disparate lands into a uniform and centralized state that commanded the loyalty of its personally free and useful inhabitants. In his seminal biography, Derek Beales described Joseph II's "fanatical cult of the impersonal, unified state ... under a single absolute sovereign" and talked of his "radical, almost revolutionary, proposals for change."[25] Joseph II's burning desire was informed by fear, the understanding of the Habsburg Monarchy's relative weakness due to its fragmented internal structure, the difficulties posed by its geographic spread and position, and its apparent inability to tap into its considerable resources, especially compared with the much smaller Prussia.

No wonder, then, that Joseph II was in a hurry. This is illustrated by the volume of legislation, which grew fivefold in the course of the first year of his reign. Given the new monarch's intention to unify his various lands, it is important to note that his decrees were in reality enacted at different times and often in slightly different forms in the main administrative divisions, namely in the Austro-Bohemian core provinces, Hungary, Transylvania, the Austrian Netherlands, and Lombardy. According to customary practice, as the new ruler of Hungary, Joseph II should have convoked a coronation Diet in order to be crowned and take an oath on a coronation diploma containing the fundamental laws of the country. Except in the Austrian Netherlands, and, of course, his earlier coronation as Holy Roman Emperor, he avoided taking such oaths. In retrospect, his failure to do so earned him the clumsy

---

[23] Beales, *Joseph II*, vol. II, 14–15. For Joseph II's early life, see Derek Beales, *Joseph II*, vol. I: *In the Shadow of Maria Theresa, 1741–1780* (Cambridge: Cambridge University Press, 1987).
[24] Krisztina Kulcsár, *II. József utazásai Magyarországon, Erdélyben, Szlavóniában és a Temesi Bánságban, 1768–1773* (Budapest: Gondolat és Magyar Országos Levéltár, 2004).
[25] Beales, *Joseph II*, vol. II, 1.

epitaph in Hungary of the "hatted" king, that is, an uncrowned king who wears only a simple hat. At the very beginning of his reign, however, Joseph II's failure to convene the estates could be explained away by invoking his priorities of reform. Moreover, in August 1781, a brief Diet was held in Transylvania, which gave at least the illusion that a Hungarian Diet might follow in due course.

In fact, Joseph II's early reforms were received rather well in Hungary. They signaled a break with Counter-Reformation Catholicism and focused on a fundamental reform of the Catholic Church, which in effect brought with it a raft of related legislation. In June 1781, the first major decree in this regard concerned censorship, earlier a Church competence, which set the tone for public debate in all Habsburg lands. In accord with the new legislation, censors banned only works that were deemed harmful, while previously they had positively needed to approve of their content. This was a huge shift, and enabled a relatively wide public debate via pamphlets and other publications. It must be emphasized, however, that it did not amount to press freedom. Besides, different standards applied to an educated audience and the rest of the population.[26]

The key early Josephist reform, however, was the Edict of Toleration, issued in October 1781, which regulated the rights of Protestant and Greek Orthodox subjects. It has to be remembered that in Hungary, the Catholic Church was much weaker and the Protestant minorities were much stronger than anywhere else in the Habsburg Monarchy, with the single exception of Transylvania. Calvinists and Lutherans alike chafed at the legal restrictions they had been subject to since 1731 when the Carolina Resolutio compelled all office holders to take an oath which, in practice, disqualified all Protestants from government positions. They were also frustrated by the daily vexations meted out by their local Catholic clergy. Thanks to Joseph II's Edict, over 700 new "tolerated" parishes sprang up by 1784 (586 Calvinist, 162 Lutheran, and 10 Greek Orthodox parishes were newly established).[27] A Jewish Edict was issued in March 1783.[28] Moreover, the legislation opened up administrative careers to the influential Protestant component of the Hungarian nobility, which was reempowered politically. The Edict also resonated with

---

[26] The most influential work on Joseph II's reign in Hungary remains Henrik Marczali, *Magyarország története II. József korában*, 3 vols. (Budapest: Pfeifer Ferdinánd, 1885–1888). See also Győző Ember and Gusztáv Heckenast, eds., *Magyarország története, 1686–1790*, vol. II: *Felvilágosult abszolutizmus, 1765–1790* (Budapest: Akadémiai Kiadó, 1989); Balázs, *Hungary and the Habsburgs*.
[27] Beales, *Joseph II*, vol. II, 195.   [28] Ibid., vol. II, 203–8.

large sections of the Catholic nobility. Admittedly, conservative Catholics remonstrated with Joseph II, but their objections were brushed aside. Instead, the new monarch coupled his policy of religious toleration with the more traditional Habsburg practice of granting aristocratic titles, this time to some leading Protestant families. In the course of 1782 and 1783, for instance, members of the Lutheran Podmaniczky and Prónay families as well as of the Calvinist Ráday family gained baronial titles. It was as part of this wave that the above-mentioned Calvinist nobleman Miklós Vay and his brother became barons. Incidentally, the Lutheran Gergely Berzeviczy, the other eyewitness of the events in Brussels, benefited from the Edict too.[29] With his dual approach, Joseph II achieved his aim of removing an important obstacle to mobilizing the resources of all his subjects irrespective of religion and gave an incentive to Protestants to support his agenda.

For those nobles who wanted to get involved, there were plenty of new jobs on offer in the expanding bureaucracy which was to implement Joseph II's blizzard of reforms. For example, the Hungarian Chancellery had sixty-five employees in 1781, and ninety-three the following year.[30] Joseph II wanted these men, just like all his other officials, to be dedicated professionals, chosen and judged on merit. They were kept busy with various reforms and the enormous amount of paperwork they generated. The Hungarian and Transylvanian Chancelleries were merged in 1782, and in 1783 the Lieutenancy was relocated from Pressburg in the vicinity of Vienna to centrally located Buda, which in effect made Buda the new capital. The list could be greatly extended.[31] Despite this flurry of activity, there was relative calm in the country. There was also considerable administrative continuity between Maria Theresa's reign and these initial years of Joseph II's rule. Obviously, there was an awareness in Hungary that, in November 1781, Joseph II had decreed the suppression of all monasteries of the purely contemplative orders in the core provinces and that this decree was already being implemented in some of those lands as early as January 1782. Famously, in November 1781, Joseph II abolished perpetual serfdom in Bohemia through his Emancipation Edict. These two measures and their quick succession reflect the pace and ambition of Joseph II's reform program, but initially neither of these decrees extended to Hungary.

---

[29] Balázs, *Hungary and the Habsburgs*, 110.
[30] István Fazekas, "A Magyar Udvari Kancellária és hivatalnokai a 16–18. században," *Századok* 148:5 (2014), 1131–55.
[31] P. G. M. Dickson, "Monarchy and Bureaucracy in Late Eighteenth-Century Austria," *The English Historical Review* 110 (1995), 323–67.

This changed dramatically in 1784, when Joseph II turned his reforming zeal on that recalcitrant "province." In April, he set the tone with an intentionally provocative act. The Hungarian crown was removed from Pressburg Castle and placed in the Imperial Treasury in Vienna. The message was clear: there would be no coronation, and the country's constitutional autonomy would not be respected. This was followed up by a two-pronged approach: on 1 May a decree ordered a census of Hungary's total population, for the first time including the nobility. This injured noble sensibilities and raised the prospect of the introduction of taxation of nobles. Another piece of legislation indirectly attacked institutional independence. Joseph II decreed that German was to be used as the official language at all levels of government, including the counties. The central institutions went through the motions of objecting, but obliged, dutifully switching from Latin to German in their communications on 1 November. However, there were howls of anger from the counties, despite the fact that they, together with the judiciary, had been given three years to comply. Subsequently, this Language Edict has generally been interpreted by Hungarian historians as a trigger for the resistance to Joseph II on grounds of Hungarian national sentiment. However, it might be closer to the truth if it were regarded as the eruption of pent-up suspicions regarding the monarch's intentions toward the exclusively noble-dominated counties. There was the added problem that many, if not most, county officials, particularly on the lower official rungs, simply did not speak German. In July 1785, even the Hungarian Chancellery could plausibly claim that the statistics it had presented to Joseph II were misleading, "no doubt because of their limited knowledge of German."[32] The decree threatened them with a loss of livelihood and opened up the possibility of German-speaking officials from outside Hungary being employed instead. After all, officials from other parts of the Habsburg Monarchy were regularly deployed in Galicia, the former territory of Poland acquired in 1772.

Direct confrontation first broke out because of the census, which incensed the conservative majority of the nobility. The vast majority of the untitled nobility was firmly wedded to tradition and resisted any change.[33] In autumn 1784, the census was successfully carried out but, in some counties, only with

---

[32] Beales, *Joseph II*, vol. II, 192. For the more general question of national identity, see R. J. W. Evans, "Joseph II and Nationality in the Habsburg Lands," in R. J. W. Evans, *Austria, Hungary, and the Habsburgs: Essays on Central Europe, c. 1683–1867* (Oxford: Oxford University Press, 2006), 134–46.

[33] This point was made most recently and forcefully by Gábor Vermes, *Hungarian Culture and Politics in the Habsburg Monarchy, 1711–1848* (Budapest: CEU Press, 2014).

military assistance. Unsurprisingly, Joseph II's next step was to deprive this type of resistence of its power base. In March 1785, he organized the counties into ten districts and totally subordinated them to handpicked Josephist royal commissioners, who were already in post at the end of April. The office of the once powerful *alispán* became subject to royal nomination, which essentially transformed these men into state bureaucrats. Regular county assemblies, a vital political platform for the local nobility, were simply abolished. This move was accompanied by an equally radical restructuring of the judicial system. Nevertheless, the counties themselves, bar the odd merger, survived, and the overwhelming majority of their officials remained in post. A curiosity of this reform is that the royal free cities lost their former administrative autonomy and found themselves under the authority of the *alispán*.

The commissioners were inundated with work. They wrote detailed yearly reports on various aspects of their district, ranging from religious affairs to the state of the infrastructure. It was also under their close supervision that the Emancipation Edict was enacted. The Edict was issued for Hungary and Transylvania in August 1785, almost four years after its original introduction in Bohemia. It abolished perpetual serfdom, guaranteed the peasants' freedom of movement, and gave them a free choice of career. Its moral impact was enormous, as it signaled the state's intention to improve the condition of the peasantry. Given that the overwhelming majority, over 90 percent of the population, were peasants of various kinds, the significance of this piece of legislation cannot be overstated. However, by the time of the Edict many peasants already enjoyed some or even all of these freedoms in practice. Arguably, the flagship Josephist policy, the suppression of the monasteries, was almost a nonevent in Hungary. In the course of 1786–1787, roughly half of the country's relatively poor and weak monasteries were dissolved. Opening up government posts, including at the county level, to non-nobles was more contentious. Moreover, when a comprehensive land survey was ordered in 1786, it was obvious that a total overhaul of the tax system was imminent and taxation of nobles was just around the corner.[34]

The question that arises is, who actively supported Joseph II's reforms in Hungary? By the time of the commissioners' appointment, it was clear that

---

[34] Gábor Pajkossy, "Az abszolutizmus és a rendiség utolsó küzdelmei, az első reformtörekvések," in András Gergely, ed., *19. századi magyar történelem, 1790–1918* (Budapest: Korona Kiadó, 1998), 127–8.

the reforms were radical and would be implemented by military force. It might be informative, then, to consider briefly the profiles of those individuals who were willing to accept the controversial post of commissioner, one that made them the face of Josephist reform in the locality. During the period of 1785–1790 when the office was in existence, altogether fifteen men held this position. They were all nobles, in fact the majority (ten of them) were aristocrats. Five of them had become aristocrats in their own lifetime, and several others came from the relatively newly minted "administrative" aristocracy. None were members of the oldest top aristocracy. The untitled nobles amongst them were also trusted Habsburg officials. József Ürményi, the brain behind the educational reform of 1777, was and remained an untitled noble all his life despite a distinguished career. Ürményi and the majority were Catholics, but there were also two very prominent Protestants: the Lutheran Baron László Prónay and the Calvinist Count Sámuel Teleki, who had his family roots in Transylvania. Five commissioners stayed in post until 1790, others served for a shorter period. One was dismissed for incompetence due to his inadequate response to a disastrous famine in Máramaros county in 1785–1786. Three were promoted, and one, Count Ferenc Széchényi, resigned after a year, ostensibly for health reasons. In reality, he passionately disagreed with Joseph II's methods, although he identified broadly with his aims. In 1786, before his departure, Széchényi secured the position of deputy sheriff in Szerém county for his former secretary and friend József Hajnóczy. Hajnóczy was a brilliant legal mind, but also a non-noble, the son of a mere Lutheran pastor. In the context of the dominant social attitudes of the time, this was a "revolutionary" development. (The fifteen men in question are Pál Almásy, János Bachó, Count Ferenc Balassa, Count Antal Brunszwik, Count Ferenc Győry, Count József Haller, Count József Majláth, Baron László Prónay, Baron Simon Révay, András Rosenfeld, Baron József Splényi, Ferenc Szentiványi, Count Ferenc Széchényi, Count Sámuel Teleki, and József Ürményi.)[35]

As far as the commissioners are concerned, then, there are broad outlines, with some variety in social standing and religion. There is, however, uniformity when it comes to age. All of the commissioners were roughly the same age as Joseph II. This signals a generational shift, partly the result of the educational opportunities available abroad but also increasingly within the Habsburg Monarchy. What also stands out is the number of freemasons in

---

[35] Antal Szántay, "II. József kerületi biztosai," *Századok* 148:5 (2014), 1171–85.

this group. Éva H. Balázs goes as far as to claim that in the first four years of Joseph II's reign freemasonry can be equated with Josephism in Hungary.[36] In their lodges, aristocrats and untitled nobles freely mingled with some townsmen and a few clergy, which was a thrilling novelty. The lodges of the influential "Draskovich Observance" functioned as veritable workshops for a reformist program. Moderate reforms, especially in the field of the economy, their creators hoped, would defuse social tensions and bring economic prosperity. Along the lines of the British model, they envisioned a nobility that retained its political influence and power of patronage but simultaneously enjoyed the fruits of economic enterprise that brought general prosperity. In the masonic lodges and at the top of the administrative hierarchy we find the most distinguished and powerful aristocratic families too. Count Károly Pálffy, a personal friend of Joseph II and just over five years his senior, was the leading figure in freemasonry in Hungary. He also became Hungarian Royal Chancellor in 1787.[37]

What was true for the commissioners can be more generally applied to the roughly 500–1,000 individuals who flocked to serve Joseph II and increasingly filled posts in the Hungarian Chancellery, the Lieutenancy, and, to a lesser extent, even in the counties. They were usually well-educated, and many were integrated into Europe-wide networks through their study abroad or grand tour as well as new institutions of sociability such as masonic lodges. They identified Joseph II as an ally in the face of traditionalist noble opposition at home. There is just one proviso. Although most commissioners were aristocrats, the untitled nobility predominated in the wider group of Josephists. However, the aristocrats and untitled nobles alike generally hailed from a broad middle stratum of landowners. Their estate sizes ranged from 1,500 to 15,000 acres.[38] All of them faced the challenge of partible inheritance but were in a favorable position to benefit from the market opportunities offered by their relatively large estates. Through his actions, Joseph II initially nurtured this group. It is perhaps no surprise, then, that young Berzeviczy, himself an active freemason, who was so inspired by the events he witnessed in Brussels, had no compunction about seeking employment in the service of Joseph II upon his arrival home in 1787. Captain Vay, another freemason,

---

[36] Balázs, *Hungary and the Habsburgs*, 271–3.
[37] Ludwig [Lajos] Abafi, *Geschichte der Freimaurerei in Oesterreich-Ungarn*, 5 vols. (Budapest: Ludwig Aigner vols. I–IV; Martin Bagó und Sohn vol v, 1890–1899), vol. v, 151–6.
[38] Fónagy, "Nemesi birtokviszonyok," 1174–9.

duly re-joined his regiment in the Habsburg army and fought bravely in the Ottoman War.[39]

All was not well, though. Freemasons were unhappy when Joseph II extended state control over their masonic lodges at the very end of 1785. This undermined the very essence of their movement. It did not help that in the relevant edict, Joseph II dismissed their activities as "hocus-pocus."[40] In general, Joseph II's impatience, shocking lack of tact, inflexibility, inability to listen to advice, and open hostility to the nobility that provided the backbone of his administration gradually eroded the enthusiasm of even his most ardent supporters. The Josephists found it particularly objectionable that Joseph II insisted on strengthening and progressively tilting his mother's dual tariff system of 1754 further and further in favor of the Habsburg core provinces. Later on, they likened Hungary's position within the Habsburg Monarchy to a "colony."[41] In face of these frustrations, they increasingly found common ground with the traditionalist nobles as well as the oldest aristocratic families, whose members were often personally antagonized by Joseph II.[42] All were threatened by the potential fallout of the looming new tax regulation.

In the short run, they faced the Ottoman War (1787–1791) in which the vast Habsburg forces were supplied with food and fodder primarily from Hungary. It was during this war that the administrative reforms were tested and found wanting. The overworked commissioners were short of resources and local county-level experience. Hence, Joseph II was obliged to call the county assemblies back into action in order to raise additional money and recruits. This happened three times: in September 1787, May 1788, and September 1789. Some counties forcefully remonstrated and called for a Diet as early as in 1787. Opposition was loudest and strongest in eastern and northeastern Hungary, mostly along the River Tisza, where the proportion of the noble population was the highest. By autumn 1789, when the counties were requested to raise 900 recruits per month for a four-month period each, more than half the counties strenuously demanded the

---

[39] Orsolya Szakály, *Egy vállalkozó főnemes: Vay Miklós báró, 1756–1824* (Budapest: ELTE Eötvös Kiadó, 2003), 90–7.
[40] Balázs, *Hungary and the Habsburgs*, 274–6.
[41] Orsolya Szakály, "Enlightened Self-Interest: The Development of an Entrepreneurial Culture within the Hungarian Elite," in Richard Butterwick, Simon Davies, and Gabriel Sánchez-Espinosa, eds, *Peripheries of the Enlightenment* (Oxford: Voltaire Foundation, 2008), 105–18: 116.
[42] Evans, "The Nobility of Hungary," 251–2.

convocation of a Diet and a third of them threatened to refuse to raise recruits.[43] To make things worse, the harvest was bad in 1789. When faced with a choice between the well-being of his subjects and the demands of war, Joseph II prioritized the supply of his army, with the military indiscriminately sequestering crops, often without payment. This affected the peasantry and the nobility equally, and allowed nobles to strike a paternalistic pose as the peasants' protectors.

The unfolding events in Hungary were just one, although significant, element of the general breakdown of Joseph II's system in practically all of the Habsburg provinces. The longest and most acute crisis in the Austrian Netherlands ended in Joseph II's local dethronement and the declaration of the United Belgian Estates on 31 January 1790. The Hungarians were on the verge of following suit. From late 1788 onward, the disillusioned Josephists amongst them started to formulate the argument that Joseph II had broken his "social contract" with Hungary. Consequently, they argued, the estates were free to elect a new ruler in defense of their "ancient constitution." This echoed similar arguments deployed in some other Habsburg lands. Some Hungarians established contacts with the Prussian court in autumn 1788, and received cautious encouragement. By the close of 1789, there was a real danger that in spring 1790 Hungary would erupt in revolt and receive Prussian military support.[44] Joseph II was well-informed about these developments. Given the severity of his position, on 18 December 1789, he promised, in a Hungarian-language rescript, a Diet once the war was over. However, this failed to cool tempers. On 28 January 1790, in the face of imminent disaster, Joseph II ungraciously retracted all his decrees relating to Hungary, bar three. The three exceptions were the Edict of Toleration, his reform concerning new Catholic parishes, and the Emancipation Edict. Less than a month later, on 20 February, he died of tuberculosis. This was the end of the Josephist experiment in Hungary. Unlike in his core provinces, where the bulk of Joseph II's reforms remained in force, his legislation in Hungary did not survive him.[45]

The new Habsburg ruler, Leopold II (r. 1790–1792, Figure 19.2) arrived in Vienna only in late March to claim his inheritance, thus subtly distancing himself from his brother's failed system. He immediately let it be known that

---

[43] Horst Haselsteiner, *Joseph II. und die Komitate Ungars: Herrscherrecht und ständischer Konstitutionalismus* (Vienna: Hermann Böhlaus, 1983), 173–92.
[44] Robert Gragger, *Preußen, Weimar und die ungarische Königskrone* (Berlin: Walter de Gruyter & Co., 1923).
[45] János Barta, *A nevezetes tollvonás* (Budapest: Akadémiai Kiadó, 1978).

Figure 19.2 The coronation of Leopold II. Getty Images.

he would call a Diet in Hungary. By this time, Hungary had witnessed extraordinary scenes, rivaling the ones described by Berzeviczy in Brussels in 1787. The counties reclaimed their full authority and started to mobilize militarily under the guise of forming units to escort the Hungarian Crown back from Vienna. Additionally, they reached out to the Hungarian regiments of the Habsburg army. There was also symbolic expression of "patriotism," which took the form of wearing "Hungarian" clothes. Those appearing in "German" attire – a longer coat and shoes instead of boots – were in danger of being beaten up. The brunt of this violent backlash, however, was directed at the physical manifestations of Joseph's reforms. For example, the documents of the nearly completed land survey were systematically destroyed. The disillusioned Hungarian Josephists were in the vanguard of political action, circulating their argument about a broken social contract in March 1790. Most county instructions to the new Diet were drawn up on its basis. Prussian troop mobilization on the Habsburg Monarchy's northern border added further weight to their demand for a new coronation diploma from Leopold II, or else there was a threat of his dethronement in Hungary.[46]

While the bulk of the Hungarian nobility hoped to return to the status quo, former Josephists spotted an opportunity. Riding the tide of general discontent, it was their moment to substantially reform and update the *ancien régime*'s political system on their own terms. One of the leaders was Captain Vay's brother, József Vay. The reformists' economic program was detailed and well-developed. However, their social and political vision was less clear and, given their relatively small numbers, intentionally cautious. József Vay, for instance, proposed to invite village leaders to the county assemblies. The idea of granting increased rights to the free royal cities was also discussed. A few individuals were inspired by events in France. The impecunious nobleman János Batsányi, for instance, hailed the democratic achievements of the French Revolution. The non-noble Károly Koppi, Professor of History at the University of Pest, advocated the abolition of all privileges.[47] While these voices were present, their importance was vanishingly small. More measured, but far too radical for the estates, was József Hajnóczy's proposal that the nobility should be taxed and all landowners should be enfranchised, with non-nobles also enjoying the right to own land.

The Diet finally opened in Buda on 10 June 1790. At the time, Leopold II could count on the support of only a section of the aristocracy and the prelates. On 18 June, inspired by the Tennis Court Oath, the county deputies enthusiastically, and the members of the Upper House more reluctantly, took an oath not to disband before a new coronation diploma had been accepted. This was to restore Hungary's territorial integrity by fully uniting Hungary and Transylvania as well as reincorporating the Military Frontier Zone. It was to reaffirm noble privilege and, adding a new element, make Hungarian the official language. By this time, demanding the use of Hungarian had become an integral part of the estates' wishes. Their hope was to maximize their power by the creation of a new Senate. This permanent body was to oversee financial and military affairs, thus seriously curtailing the Habsburg monarch's rights. Furthermore, the Prussian king was to guarantee the new Hungarian constitution. It is clear from the above that the

---

[46] Pajkossy, "Az abszolutizmus és a rendiség," 128–33.
[47] Sándor Eckhardt, *A francia forradalom eszméi Magyarországon* (Budapest: Kisebbségi Könyvek, 2001).

primary focus was the extension of Hungary's political autonomy and the further expansion of noble influence. There was no sign of progressive steps. In fact, one of the first decisions taken by the Diet was to abolish the right of non-nobles to hold office. József Hajnóczy had already lost his position as deputy sheriff of Szerém county when Joseph II annulled his Hungarian decrees. However, now it was confirmed by law that he and his like had no political future.[48]

The estates' negotiating position, however, was completely undermined when Leopold II came to a surprise agreement with Frederick William II in Reichenbach on 27 July 1790. The Convention of Reichenbach freed up Habsburg troops, and some were marched directly to Buda. Leopold II was also adept at stirring up groups against the nobility in Hungary. He commissioned works that attacked the Hungarian nobility, encouraged loyal royal free cities to petition him for protection, and played on anti-Protestant sentiments in staunchly Catholic Croatia. Additionally, he stirred up ethnic discontent against the Magyars, especially amongst the Serbs. One of his proposals concerned the abolition of the poorest strata of the nobility in a clear attempt to sow division within the ranks of the nobles. Leopold II also played on aristocratic fears of a power grab by the untitled nobility. He even toyed with the idea of enticing the peasantry to act against their landlords.[49] Such tactics were, of course, not unique to Leopold II. It is reminiscent of the recurring threat of American slave liberation as a pressure point on American plantation owners in the South, something that the British on occasion exploited.

Having been deprived of international support, in light of the presence of troops and increasing domestic tensions, the estates had no choice but to compromise. This was clearly illustrated by the fact that, on Leopold II's insistence, the Diet moved back to the old Hungarian capital of Pressburg on 5 November 1790. It was there, a week later, that Leopold II's son, Alexander Leopold, was duly elected viceroy (palatine). For the first time, a Habsburg held the highest secular office in Hungary. Leopold II was crowned on 15 November. He took an oath on Maria Theresa's coronation diploma without any changes in the way that Hungary would be ruled. Latin was reestablished as the official language, but the estates regained their old rights. Article 10:1791 reinstated Hungary's independence (that is, its extensive autonomy within the Habsburg

---

[48] Henrik Marczali, *Az 1790–91, országgyűlés*, 2 vols. (Budapest: Magyar Tudományos Akadémia, 1907).

[49] Elemér Mályusz, *Sándor Lipót főherceg nádor iratai, 1790–1795* (Budapest: Magyar Történelmi Társulat, 1926), 3–37.

Monarchy), and Article 12 reiterated the notion that legislative power was jointly exercised by the monarch and the estates. With the help of the former Josephists, Maria Theresa's *Urbarium*, most of the stipulations of the Emancipation Edict, and the Edict of Toleration were codified. More significantly for those hoping for change, committees were established to work out reform proposals in various fields. This compromise was engineered to a large extent by the highest office holders, amongst them Chancellor Károly Pálffy. Hence, the oldest aristocrac families had reclaimed their function of mediating between the Habsburg sovereign and the "country."[50]

The reform committees started their work in Buda in 1791. At first, they attracted serious attention. The vast majority of the counties, many cities, and trading corporations, as well as around forty private individuals, contributed with their proposals. A considerable proportion of the traditional nobility feared that the committees would act as Trojan horses and smuggle in Joseph II's controversial reforms through the back door. In the end, when they finalized their proposals at the turn of 1792–1793, the committees' suggestions tended to limit themselves to simplifying, rationalizing, and professionalizing the workings of the institutions of *ancien régime* Hungary. Moreover, by that time, the international and domestic scene had gone through a considerable transformation. The new Habsburg ruler, Francis II (Francis I as King of Hungary, r. 1792–1835), and the majority of the Hungarian estates found common ground in opposing French expansionism. In this climate, the committees' recommendations were carefully shelved.[51]

In early 1794, the pressures of a distant war and frustration with an increasingly reactionary climate urged some former Josephists to organize once more against the Habsburg sovereign. Under the charismatic leadership of Ignác Martinovics, a non-noble former monk and erstwhile informant of Leopold II, they formed two parallel organizations. Martinovics claimed the financial support of the French Jacobin government and pointed to the Polish uprising as the beginning of a more general revolutionary movement. The more radical Society of Liberty and Equality called for a democratic republic of equal citizens in Hungary with references to the French Revolution. This inner group was unbeknown to members of the more moderate Society of Reformers, which wanted freedom of religion, freedom of the press, and state support for national cultural institutions. It also aimed to establish an independent Hungarian republic which had a national army and a bicameral

---

[50] Pajkossy, "Az abszolutizmus és a rendiség," 133–5.
[51] Szakály, "Enlightened Self-Interest," 117–18.

parliament, one for the representatives of nobles and one for non-nobles. Elements of the program of early 1790 were clearly present, although, almost in a parody of the economic acumen demonstrated four years previously, the 1794 program claimed that there was no need to pay taxes as the confiscated royal and ecclesiastical lands would provide enough income, together with the benefits derived from free trade.[52]

After around three months of secret activity, this conspiracy was uncovered in the summer of 1794. The first few arrests took place in August 1794, with a larger crackdown following in December. Those implicated had months to dispose of incriminating material. Consequently, the exact number of conspirators, estimated at around 200–300, and their names are largely unknown. In the end, dozens received long prison sentences, and seven death sentences were carried out in early summer 1795. Martinovics was executed, and so was József Hajnóczy. There also followed a systematic purge of the Hungarian administration. Led by Palatine Alexander Leopold, this saw the removal of almost all the key Josephist functionaries from the central Hungarian institutions.[53] Chancellor Count Károly Pálffy was spared from dismissal by Alexander Leopold's accidental death in July 1795. Ironically, the so-called Jacobin conspiracy was the very last in a long line of anti-Habsburg plots. Reform was most definitely off the agenda for a generation, and Hungary dutifully, occasionally enthusiastically, pulled its weight in the Revolutionary and Napoleonic Wars.[54]

What is the balance of Joseph II's reign in Hungary? Turning the disparate Habsburg provinces into a single, unified state on a tight schedule was always an impossible task. However, Joseph II set about it with single-minded determination. Despite provoking considerable resistance in all his lands, his efforts were broadly successful in the Habsburg core provinces.[55] However, they alienated other lands, most importantly the Austrian Netherlands and Hungary. Paradoxically, his reign did not end in complete disaster precisely because his realms were such separate entities, which meant that there was no coordination and cooperation between the various resistance movements. In Hungary, he faced traditional political opposition from the start, but could rely

---

[52] For this so-called Jacobin conspiracy, see Beatrix Boreczky, *A magyar jakobinusok* (Budapest: Gondolat Kiadó, 1977); Orsolya Szakály, "Rebellion or Revolution? The Case of the Hungarian 'Jacobins,'" in Péter and Rady, eds., *Resistance, Rebellion and Revolution in Hungary and Central Europe*, 77–84.
[53] Sándor Mályusz, *Lipót főherceg nádor iratai*, 201–29.
[54] János Poór, *Kényszerpályák nemzedéke, 1795–1815* (Budapest: Gondolat Kiadó, 1988).
[55] This theme is developed in Pieter M. Judson, *The Habsburg Empire: A New History* (Cambridge, MA: The Belknap Press of Harvard University Press, 2016).

on a small but effective group of ambitious, relatively prosperous, well-informed, and internationally connected noblemen who were open to rationalizing reforms in the hope of economic development and increasing the general welfare of society. The formative years of these nobles were during the reign of Maria Theresa. The mid-1770s to early 1790s, in Hungary as elsewhere, was the moment of "enlightened" reformers. In Hungary, after initial enthusiasm for Joseph II, these nobles were set on a collision course with their sovereign due to his meddling and micromanagement, and above all because of his inability to grasp that his Hungarian followers' loyalty was primarily to the kingdom of Hungary. Given a painful choice, they closed ranks with their fellow noblemen, even though the latter were conservative. Reform and resistance cannot be reduced to the antagonism of a reforming emperor and a conservative nobility.

In 1790, Joseph's successor, Leopold II, for his part, skillfully and swiftly reestablished a working relationship with the Hungarian estates, and legally embedded legislation from the previous quarter of a century of absolutist rule in three important fields. First, the Urbarium and the Emancipation Edict improved but, in essence, left unchanged the lot of the peasantry. Second, he continued Joseph II's policy of extending state control over the Catholic Church, which was relatively unproblematic. Third, Leopold incorporated the Edict of Toleration, which was psychologically and practically important in emancipating a significant section of the élite. There was also considerable continuity in personnel between Joseph II's and Leopold II's reigns and beyond. It was only in a moment of panic in the wake of an abortive conspiracy in 1794 that Leopold's son, Francis I, opted to remove the former Josephist elements from his administration. Tellingly, he had to rely on older men to replace this cadre. Nor was this purge permanent. As the demands of warfare increased, these competent and hard-working individuals were recalled into service in the very early 1800s. Their professionalism was vital to Hungary's contribution to the effort during the Napoleonic Wars. In between and even afterwards, many supported "national" causes and channeled their energies into the Hungarian language-reform movement. These contentious but permissible cultural pursuits, such as Ferenc Széchényi's foundation of the Hungarian National Museum and Library in 1802, would eventually develop into full-blown Hungarian nationalism, but that was some way off in the future. What was immediate was an agricultural boom in Hungary thanks to the demands of the Napoleonic Wars. All segments of society benefited from this newly found prosperity, but it was the former Josephists with an eye on economic opportunity who profited the most.

20

Poland–Lithuania in the Age of Atlantic Revolutions: Dilemmas of Liberty

RICHARD BUTTERWICK

On 18 August 1797, a small ship, the *Adriana*, sailed up the Delaware River. Crowds of Philadelphians welcomed General Tadeusz Kościuszko back to the country he had helped to create. The wounded hero had languished in prison until Tsar Paul I freed him soon after succeeding his mother Catherine II. A few months after returning to America, Kościuszko departed again, hoping that the French Republic might help restore Poland to independence. Disappointed, he later rejected Napoleon's blandishments and died in exile in Switzerland in 1817, having never returned to his homeland, which had been partitioned for the third time in 1795.[1] Kościuszko (Figure 20.1), born in 1746 into the impoverished nobility in what is now Belarus, is perhaps the ideal symbol of the Atlantic Revolution. Thomas Jefferson lauded him as "as pure a son of liberty as I have ever known, and of that liberty which is to go to all, and not to the few or the rich alone."[2] Leading the 1794 insurrection against Russian domination of the Polish–Lithuanian Commonwealth,

---

This chapter draws on my book, *The Polish–Lithuanian Commonwealth, 1733–1795: Light and Flame* (New Haven and London: Yale University Press, 2020), with further reading suggestions. Wherever possible, the additional references given here are to works in English. The text was revised during my Leibniz Science Campus Fellowship at the University of Regensburg in July 2022. I thank members of the Leibniz Institute of East and Southeast European Studies for valuable feedback.

[1] Biographies include Mieczyslaus Haiman, *Kościuszko in the American Revolution*, 2nd edition (New York: Kosciuszko Foundation and Polish Institute of Arts and Sciences, 1975); Mieczyslaus Haiman, *Kościuszko: Leader and Exile*, 2nd edition (New York: Kosciuszko Foundation and Polish Institute of Arts and Sciences, 1977); James S. Pula, *Thaddeus Kościuszko: The Purest Son of Liberty* (New York: Hippocrene Books, 1999); Alex Storozynski, *The Peasant Prince: Thaddeus Kosciuszko and the Age of Revolution* (New York: St. Martin's Press, 2009).

[2] Thomas Jefferson to Horatio Gates, 21 February 1798, quoted after James S. Pula, "The American Will of Thaddeus Kosciuszko," *Polish-American Studies* 34:1 (1977), 16–25: 18.

Figure 20.1 Tadeusz Kościuszko. Getty Images.

Kościuszko had tried to transform enserfed peasants into free defenders of a shared fatherland. Unfortunately, Jefferson failed to discharge his duties as executor of Kościuszko's will, and so the estate was not used as intended – to purchase the freedom and education of African-American slaves.

Among the Polish diaspora in the United States, another hero is still more popular. The charismatic Kazimierz Pułaski reformed the Continental Army's cavalry, before dying of his wounds at Savannah in 1779. Earlier, he had been prominent in another republican insurgency. Like Kościuszko's rising, the Confederacy of Bar (1768–1772) fought against Russian domination of Poland–Lithuania, but it was also hostile toward Protestant "heretics" and Orthodox "schismatics." Wishing to reverse the enlightened reforms of King Stanisław August Poniatowski (r. 1764–1795), most confederates looked back nostalgically to the soporific reign of the Saxon elector, King Augustus III (1733–1763). Pułaski was involved in planning the botched abduction of Stanisław August in 1771, and condemned *in absentia* to death as a regicide. He traveled to France, and thence, recommended by Benjamin

Franklin, to America. More than the luminous Kościuszko, this *chiarascuro* figure reveals ambiguities in the "Age of Democratic Revolution." Pułaski inherited and cultivated a hostility toward kings which he transferred to the American cause.[3]

Poland's contribution to the Atlantic Revolution was recognized by the great historians Robert Roswell Palmer, Jacques Godechot, and Franco Venturi.[4] From the 1760s to the 1790s, the country's upheavals were connected to revolutionary changes in ideas and power on both sides of the Atlantic. The twenty-first-century revival of the concept of Atlantic Revolution has foregrounded contests for transatlantic trade – particularly in slaves and commodities dependent on slaves – in the struggles between the maritime powers. Probably because of this shift, the Polish–Lithuanian Commonwealth, which had no colonial empire, has become less prominent in the recent historiography of Atlantic Revolutions. Polish contemporaries, however, had a clear sense that they lived in an age of revolutionary upheaval: in 1789 the *Historical, Political and Economic Recorder* announced that it would cover "great events and revolutions of nations, which change their state, government, laws and their relations with other nations."[5] This chapter will first explain the paralysis of the Commonwealth and then trace the fiery trajectory of its final three decades. The Enlightenment revealed much in the Polish–Lithuanian world in need of renewal, but it also lit up potential for growth. Dilemmas of liberty briefly seemed capable of solution, before the country's neighbors destroyed this felicitous future.[6]

---

[3] Władysław Konopczyński, *Casimir Pulaski* (Chicago: Polish Roman Catholic Union of America, 1947).

[4] R. R. Palmer, *The Age of the Democratic Revolution: A Political History of Europe and America, 1760–1800*, updated edition (Princeton: Princeton University Press, 2014), 307–25, 437–46, 482–90; Jacques Godechot, *France and the Atlantic Revolution of the Eighteenth Century, 1770–1799* (New York: Free Press, 1965), 135–8; Franco Venturi, *The End of the Old Regime in Europe, 1768–1776: The First Crisis* (Princeton: Princeton University Press, 1989), 172–234; Franco Venturi, *The End of the Old Regime in Europe, 1776–1789* (Princeton: Princeton University Press, 1991), 784–7, 907–47.

[5] Piotr Świtkowski, *Pamiętnik Historyczno-Polityczno-Ekonomiczne*, quoted after Anna Grześkowiak-Krwawicz, "Konstytucja 3 Maja. Rewolucja – prawo – dokument," in Anna Grześkowiak-Krwawicz, ed., *Konstytucja 3 Maja 1791 na podstawie tekstu Ustawy Rządowej z Archiwum Sejmu Czteroletniego* (Warsaw: Muzeum Łazienki Królewskie, 2018), 5–52: 5.

[6] For alternative overviews, see Jerzy Lukowski, *Liberty's Folly: The Polish–Lithuanian Commonwealth in the Eighteenth Century* (London: Routledge, 1991); Jerzy Lukowski, *The Partitions of Poland: 1772, 1793, 1795* (Harlow: Routledge, 1999); Józef Andrzej Gierowski, *The Polish–Lithuanian Commonwealth in the XVIIIth Century* (Kraków: PAU, 1996).

Paralysis and Remedies

Before the first partition in 1772, the Polish–Lithuanian Commonwealth covered almost three quarters of a million square kilometers, encompassing most of the current territories of Poland and Lithuania, all of Belarus, and about half of Ukraine and Latvia. The Commonwealth had coalesced from unions contracted and renewed since the fourteenth century. Its principal components were the Polish Crown, the grand duchy of Lithuania, Royal Prussia, Livonia, and the vassal duchy of Courland. These were subdivided into various provinces, palatinates, lands, and districts, whose boundaries often derived from medieval lordships. The Crown encompassed the kingdom of Poland, and took in the southern Ruthenian (Ukrainian) and Podlasian lands transferred from the grand duchy of Lithuania in 1569. Although it functioned as a territorial term, the *Corona Regni Poloniae* originally signified the community of the realm rather than the realm itself.[7] Between 1697 and 1763 the elective king of Poland and grand duke of Lithuania was the hereditary elector of Saxony. Such a combination was not unusual: the elector of Hanover inherited the British and Irish crowns in 1714, while the elector of Brandenburg crowned himself king in Prussia in 1701. However, the Commonwealth was no longer a typical early modern "composite polity."[8] Indeed, the names usually used by historians today, "the Polish–Lithuanian Commonwealth" and "the Commonwealth of the Two Nations," cannot be found in official documents. Eighteenth-century diplomats were accredited to "the king and republic of Poland." The Polish word *Rzeczpospolita* was, like the English "Commonwealth," an early translation of the Latin *res publica*. Here "the Commonwealth," "Poland–Lithuania," and "Poland" will be used as synonyms. Complementary local and national patriotisms, anchored in similar parliamentary and judicial institutions, contributed to a shared political culture.

The Commonwealth was a political community whose principal purpose was the liberty of its citizens, not the martial "reputation" of its kings. That said, the Commonwealth was generally successful against its enemies from the 1560s until the 1640s. The subsequent decline in Polish–Lithuanian fiscal

---

[7] See Robert Frost, *The Oxford History of Poland–Lithuania*, vol. 1: *The Making of the Polish–Lithuanian Union, 1385–1569* (Oxford: Oxford University Press, 2015).

[8] Richard Butterwick, "Lawmaking in a Post-composite State? The Polish–Lithuanian Commonwealth in the Eighteenth Century," in D. W. Hayton, John Bergin, and James Kelly, eds., *The Eighteenth-Century Composite State: Representative Institutions in Ireland and Europe* (Basingstoke: Palgrave Macmillan, 2010), 221–43. Cf. J. H. Elliott, "A Europe of Composite Monarchies," *Past & Present*, 137 (1992), 48–71.

and military performance left the country not only smaller, but also highly vulnerable.⁹ Russian interventions would prove that independence was a necessary condition of both civil and political freedom. Finally, the three partitions – in 1772, 1793, and 1795 – turned free citizens into the subjects of more or less absolute monarchs, who had every interest in caricaturing Polish liberty as license, anarchy, chaos, and oppression. However, even at the zenith of the Commonwealth's prosperity, the quality of its freedom was sometimes questioned by Polish thinkers. At issue were, first, whether liberty could be enjoyed in practice by most of those who possessed it, and second, the persons to whom that possession was denied.¹⁰

Up to three quarters of a million hereditary nobles believed they had a monopoly on citizenship. Polish freedom – an umbrella protecting many individual and collective rights and privileges – was their freedom. They were, in effect, the Polish nation (nobles of the grand duchy of Lithuania came to consider themselves members of the Polish and Lithuanian nations). Nevertheless, many of the Commonwealth's Christian burghers also called themselves citizens. The Jewish population, similar in numbers to the nobility, had autonomous communal institutions. About half of the far less numerous Muslim Tatars enjoyed noble-style civil liberties in return for military service. Even among the 10 million or so peasants – generally considered insensible to liberty – a privileged elite exercised some responsibility for governing rural communities, bringing them freedom from many of the burdens imposed on others. The sense of freedom was particularly strong among the highlanders of the far south, where many enjoyed liberties in return for military service.¹¹

---

⁹ Robert I. Frost, *The Northern Wars: War, State and Society in Northeastern Europe, 1558–1721* (Harlow: Longman, 2000).

¹⁰ Jerzy Lukowski, *Disorderly Liberty: The Political Culture of the Polish–Lithuanian Commonwealth in the Eighteenth Century* (London: Continuum, 2010); Anna Grześkowiak-Krwawicz, *Queen Liberty: The Concept of Freedom in the Polish–Lithuanian Commonwealth* (Leiden: Brill, 2012); Jerzy Lukowski, "Noble Republicanism in the Polish–Lithuanian Commonwealth: An Attempt at Description," *Acta Poloniae Historica*, 103 (2011), 31–65; Karin Friedrich, "Polish–Lithuanian Political Thought, 1450–1700," in Howell Lloyd, Glenn Burgess, and Simon Hodson, eds., *History of European Political Thought, 1450–1700* (New Haven: Yale University Press, 2007), 409–47.

¹¹ This case has been made by Andrzej Sulima Kamiński and his pupils, esp. Karin Friedrich, *The Other Prussia: Royal Prussia, Poland and Liberty, 1569–1772* (Cambridge: Cambridge University Press, 2000); Curtis G. Murphy, *From Citizens to Subjects: City, State and the Enlightenment in Poland, Ukraine, and Belarus* (Pittsburgh: University of Pittsburgh Press, 2018). See also Michał Kopczyński and Wojciech Tygielski, eds., *Under a Common Sky: Ethnic Groups of the Commonwealth of Poland and Lithuania* (Warsaw: Polish History Museum, 2017); Gershon D. Hundert, *Jews in Poland–Lithuania in the*

Since the sixteenth century, Polish writers had quoted the ancient Roman historian Sallust's maxim, "better perilous liberty than tranquil servitude," to justify the disorder thought inevitable in a free state. Abuses of liberty prompted laments at Poles' fall from ancestral virtue. However, under Augustus III, the paralysis of the legislature had led a few thinkers to propose constitutional changes. The greatest of these reformers, Stanisław Konarski (1700–1773), the principal pedagogue of the Piarist order, proposed political institutions for sinful men, rather than paragons of virtue. His *opus magnum*, *On the Means of Efficacious Counsels*, published in four volumes between 1760 and 1763, demolished the case for one of the most notorious features of "Polish anarchy."[12]

The right of an individual to curtail parliamentary proceedings – the *liberum veto* – had emerged in the middle of the seventeenth century from the practice of decision-making by consensus in the Polish–Lithuanian parliament – the sejm (composed of a senate comprising palatines and castellans and a lower house of envoys elected by the nobility at local assemblies called sejmiks). Early instances of the *liberum veto* involved refusals to extend parliamentary sessions beyond the statutory six weeks – most notoriously by a single envoy in 1652. However, in 1669, the sejm was ended by an objection to its continuance before the six-week term had expired. A further precedent was set in 1688, when the sejm was "ruptured" before it was legally constituted. Foreign powers began to use this means of preventing the sejm from taking unwelcome decisions. They did that so effectively that during the thirty-year reign of Augustus III only the sejm of 1736 passed any laws at all.

The *liberum veto* was commonly justified as a last chance for a virtuous citizen to save the Commonwealth from a corrupted majority. Konarski demonstrated that such a majority would not scruple to override opposition, whereas a corrupt individual might prevent the virtuous and law-abiding majority from taking the measures necessary for the public good. Having

---

Eighteenth Century: A Genealogy of Modernity (Berkeley: University of California Press, 2004). On peasant elites, see Józef Rafacz, *Ustrój wsi samorządnej małopolskiej w XVIII wieku* (Lublin: Nakładem Uniwersytetu Lubelskiego, 1922), 189–380; Józef Rafacz, *Dzieje i ustrój Podhala Nowotarskiego za czasów dawnej Rzeczypospolitej Polskiej* (Warsaw: Wydawnictwo Kasy im. Mianowskiego, 1935), 118–234, 258–62. I owe this reference to the kindness of Dr. Wioletta Pawlikowska.

[12] Władysław Konopczyński, *Stanisław Konarski* (Warsaw: Wydawnictwo Kasy im. Mianowskiego, 1926); Jerzy Lukowski, "Stanisław Konarski (1700–1772) [sic]: A Polish Machiavelli?," in Jeffrey D. Burson and Ulrich L. Lehner, eds., *Enlightenment and Catholicism in Europe: A Transnational History* (Notre Dame: University of Notre Dame Press, 2014), 433–53.

surveyed parliamentary institutions elsewhere, Konarski concluded that simple majority voting was best. Given this revitalized sejm, which he compared to a "monarch," he planned an unwieldy council to govern between sejms.

This reduction in royal powers would remove a key justification for the *liberum veto*. However, qualified majority voting would prove a more palatable solution during the next three decades. A more radical step than abolishing the *liberum veto* would be to render the monarchy hereditary, at least when deprived of its prerogatives of distributing Crown estates and nominating senators. The boldest thinkers envisaged extending political rights to property-owning burghers, while restricting those of landless nobles. Civil freedoms, however, would be for all inhabitants, including an emancipated peasantry. Insurrectionary discourse in 1794 left no doubt that both political and civil liberty depended on national independence. Such was the general direction taken by Polish republican thought in the eighteenth century, but it was far from a straight highway to the vision of the future symbolized by Kościuszko.[13]

In contrast to the quickening pace of mid-century intellectual life, the political outlook was dismal. By about 1720, little was left of the resilience with which the Commonwealth had weathered merging storms of revolts, invasions, civil wars, famines, plagues, and icy temperatures. The price of the ensuing period of peace and economic and demographic recovery was a Russian protectorate. This was usually unobtrusive. As long as politics boiled down to magnate factions posturing as guardians of republican liberty while competing for royal patronage, the leash stayed loose. However, the underlying loss of sovereignty was violently demonstrated in 1733. Russian arms denied the throne to Stanisław Leszczyński, the father-in-law of Louis XV of France, and assured it to Augustus III. The Commonwealth was thus suspended in an external equilibrium and paralyzed by an internal impasse.

Currents of Change

Poland's political torpor was shattered by fallout from the Seven Years' War. In 1756 King Frederick II invaded Saxony, forcing its elector to decamp to

---

[13] Jerzy Lukowski, "Political Ideas among the Polish Nobility in the Eighteenth Century (to 1788)," *Slavonic and East European Review* 82:1 (2004), 1–26. Cf. Andrzej Walicki, *The Enlightenment and the Birth of Modern Nationhood: Polish Political Thought from Noble Republicanism to Tadeusz Kościuszko* (Notre Dame: University of Notre Dame Press, 2000).

Warsaw. Augustus III consoled himself with the support of Russia and Austria. This presaged his recovery of his electorate, and his being succeeded in the Commonwealth by one of his sons. However, at the beginning of 1762 Empress Elizabeth was succeeded by her Prussophile nephew Peter III, who after six months was deposed and killed. His wife and successor Catherine II kept Russia out of the last stages of the European war, which ended with the restoration of the territorial *status quo ante bellum*. Augustus III returned to Dresden, where he died on 5 October 1763.

Catherine would not countenance a third Saxon king of Poland. Her armed intervention gifted the election to her former lover Stanisław Poniatowski on 7 September 1764. She concluded an alliance with Frederick II on her own terms, and the courts of Vienna and Versailles lacked the appetite for war. The new king, who reigned as Stanisław August, was a scion of the *Familia*, a magnate faction led by his maternal uncles Michał and August Czartoryski. Although they played the dirty tricks of politics, and had long sought Russian support, they wished to strengthen the Commonwealth. The empress's prioritization of the election, together with the scattering of the Czartoryskis' foes, made possible some long-discussed reforms. Most were passed in the late spring of 1764 by the convocation sejm.[14]

A convocation, whose purpose was to make arrangements for the royal election, was held under a general confederacy. Nobles could confederate themselves as an armed league in order to save the Commonwealth and its liberties from peril. An interregnum triggered such a procedure. The confederacy was thus a kind of state of emergency, involving abbreviated judicial and legislative procedures. A confederacy's highest authority, its general council, could decide by majority vote if necessary. A confederated sejm could therefore circumvent the *liberum veto*. The idea had been floated during the reign of Augustus III, but Russian diplomats had let it be known that it was intolerable to their court.

The *Familia* used this rare opportunity to increase state revenues, ease the logjam in the courts, and establish treasury and military commissions. In return for the sparing of an exceptionally corrupt Crown treasurer, the dying Russian ambassador agreed not to notice a breach in the *liberum veto* – treasury

---

[14] The fundamental work is Zofia Zielińska, *Polska w okowach "system północnego" 1763–1766* (Kraków; Arcana, 2012). On Stanisław August, see Adam Zamoyski, *The Last King of Poland* (London: Jonathan Cape, 1992); Jean Fabre, *Stanislas-Auguste Poniatowski et l'Europe des lumiéres: Étude de cosmopolitisme* (Paris: Les Belles Lettres, 1952).

business would henceforth be decided *forma iudicaria*, in the judicial manner, that is, by the majority. These changes were cemented at the sejm that followed Stanisław August's coronation on 25 November 1764.

The new monarch was a more radical reformer. A convinced Anglophile, he felt a "noble and ardent desire to do what [Montesquieu] had written."[15] The *philosophe* had warned that the concentration of legislative, executive, and judicial power in the same hands would result in arbitrary despotism, whose principle was fear. This was the opposite of the secure tranquillity of spirit he defined as political liberty. Montesquieu had seen the remedy for the aggrandizing French monarchy in the judiciary, but for Poniatowski the main problem was the weakness of the Commonwealth's executive power. He penned his vision privately in 1763 and pursued it for thirty years. It entailed an effective executive headed by the monarch, working in partnership with a revitalized legislature. Properly functioning courts would restore the rule of law, enabling citizens to enjoy their liberty and property. The happy English, he claimed, were the freest of all nations. During his reign, this understanding of liberty, more liberal than republican, was espoused by a small but growing number of Polish writers.[16]

Stanisław August, who was never seen attired and shorn in the traditional Polish fashion, told the sejm of 1766: "We now seem to have a new, or rather a second creation of the Polish world before us. This is the critical moment, [...] when it is necessary to move almost everything at once."[17] He could hardly do that. But among his early initiatives was a military school, attended by Tadeusz Kościuszko. The *Monitor*, an essay-periodical modeled on the *Spectator*, campaigned against superstition, coarseness, ignorance, prejudice, and fanaticism. Similar messages were conveyed by plays staged at the new National Theater. Many nobles thought their traditions were being insulted, but it was Catherine II's intransigence which plunged the Commonwealth into crisis.

The empress had been annoyed by Stanisław August's attempts to establish diplomatic relations with Austria, France, and the Ottoman Empire, as well as having to mediate a customs dispute between Poland and Prussia. She

---

[15] Stanisław August to Joseph and Charles Yorke, 6 October 1764, quoted after Richard Butterwick, *Poland's Last King and English Culture: Stanisław August Poniatowski, 1732–1798* (Oxford: Clarendon Press, 1998), 165.

[16] Ibid., esp. 147–55.

[17] Quoted after Zofia Zielińska, "'Nowe świata polskiego stworzenie.' Stanisław August – reformator 1764–1767," in Angela Sołtys and Zofia Zielińska, eds., *Stanisław August a jego Rzeczpospolita: Dramat państwa, odrodzenie narodu* (Warsaw: Arx Regia, 2013), 9–32: 15.

then crushed the king's hopes for the sejm of 1766. This enshrined the hitherto vaguely defined *liberum veto* in law. Still worse were the reverberations of the "dissident question." Catherine II sought an obedient party composed of Protestant and Orthodox nobles. The latter, few in number, impoverished, and mostly illiterate, were of no use to her. However, among the several hundred noble families that professed Calvinism or Lutheranism were men of education, wealth, and ambition, driven to seek foreign protection by worsening discrimination. The coronation sejm of 1764 and the sejm of 1766 both rejected St. Peterburg's demands, seconded by Berlin, Copenhagen, and London, for the restoration of equal rights to the "dissidents."[18]

Following this rebuff, Catherine instructed her ambassador, Nikolai Repnin, to form confederacies to achieve her aims. An extraordinary, confederated sejm opened in October 1767. After Repnin had had three recalcitrant senators sent off to Russia in captivity, the sejm chose a plenipotentiary delegation from among its members. The delegation worked out a constitutional and religious settlement, including "cardinal laws" formally guaranteed by Russia, which was ratified by the plenary sejm before it concluded on 5 March 1768.[19]

A week earlier, a very different confederacy ignited at Bar, far to the southeast. Initial Russian attempts to suppress the insurgency provoked the Ottoman Porte, which declared war on 25 September 1768. Whenever the stretched Russian forces pacified one area, fighting erupted elsewhere.[20] The Confederacy of Bar sought counsel on the future form of government. Jean-Jacques Rousseau penned paeans to the Poles' love of liberty, while urging caution in reforming "ancient" institutions such as the *liberum veto*, elective monarchy, and serfdom. He hoped that an Ottoman victory would allow Poland a twenty-year breathing space in which his advice could be applied and a new generation of republican patriots educated.[21] However, the confederacy's general council nullified the election of Stanisław August – and all the laws since. The attempt on 3 November 1771 to abduct Poniatowski failed, and the confederate leaders, including Kazimierz Pułaski, were denounced as

---

[18] Jerzy T. Lukowski, "The Papacy, Poland, Russia and Religious Reform, 1764–8," *Journal of Ecclesiastical History* 39:1 (1988), 66–92.
[19] George Tadeusz Lukowski, *The "Szlachta" and the Confederacy of Radom, 1764–1767/68: A Study of the Polish Nobility* (Rome: Institutum Historicum Polonicum Romae, 1977).
[20] Władysław Konopczyński, *Konfederacja barska*, 2 vols., 2nd edition (Warsaw: Volumen, 1991).
[21] Jerzy Michalski, *Rousseau and Polish Republicanism* (Warsaw: IH PAN, 2015).

regicides. During the following months Russian forces, aided by Polish troops loyal to the king, finally pacified the insurgency.

In 1772 Russia, Austria, and Prussia seized about a third of the Commonwealth's territory and population. A combination of factors had persuaded Catherine II to favor Prussian overtures for a partition. First, Russian victories over the Turks alarmed the Austrian court. Second, continuing difficulties in the Commonwealth made the traditional policy of maintaining it intact under Russian hegemony less attractive. A smaller Poland should prove quiescent. Once Russia and Prussia had reached agreement, Austria was faced with the choice of fighting them both or joining in. The three powers signed the treaties in St. Petersburg on 5 August 1772.[22] The Commonwealth then had to ratify these amputations. Threats, bribes, and another plenipotentiary delegation procured the acceptance of the partition treaties by another confederated sejm. This assembly met in September 1773, but was not wound up until March 1775. The changes it made to the form of government were intended to stabilize the Commonwealth's weakness. At its heart was the Permanent Council, comprising eighteen senators and eighteen envoys, organized into five departments, which would exercise supervisory and some executive functions between sejms. The king chaired the Council, with a casting vote. This solution owed something to Konarski's ideas, but more to Swedish models from the "Age of Liberty" which King Gustav III had brought to an end in 1772.[23]

The Commonwealth remained in the political doldrums until 1788.[24] Frontier violations, vexations visited by Russian, Prussian, and Austrian troops, and the arrogance of the Russian Ambassador, Otto von Stackelberg, all reminded the Poles of their impotence, while the Americans set a different example, sympathetically reported in the press. Catherine II did permit Stanisław August one more confederated sejm in 1776, which somewhat strengthened the Permanent Council. Employing a

---

[22] Dorota Dukwicz, "The Internal Situation in the Polish–Lithuanian Commonwealth (1769–1771) and the Origins of the First Partition (in the Light of Russian Sources)," *Acta Poloniae Historica*, 103 (2011), 67–84.

[23] Dorota Dukwicz, "Restricted Sovereignty of the Sejm. The Plenipotentiary Delegation and Ratification of the First Partition Treaty," in Kazimierz Baran, Wacław Uruszczak, and Anna Karabowicz, eds., *Separation of Powers and Parliamentarism: The Past and the Present: Law, Doctrine, Practice* (Warsaw: Sygnatura, 2007), 454–67; Dorota Dukwicz, *Rosja wobec sejmu rozbiorowego warszawskiego (1772–1775)* (Warsaw: IH PAN, 2015); Władysław Konopczyński, *Geneza i ustanowienie Rady Nieustającej*, 2nd edition (Kraków: Ośrodek Myśli Politycznej, 2014).

[24] Daniel Stone, *Polish Politics and National Reform, 1775–1788* (New York: Columbia University Press, 1976).

modest number of officials, it began to accumulate competences and expertise. It helped to bring about improvements in the functioning of the courts, the condition of many royal towns, military administration, and the Crown and Lithuanian treasuries (whose separate commissions it supervised).[25] A low-ranking, but professional, diplomatic corps emerged. Kept separate from this structure was the Commission of National Education, established by the sejm in October 1773, following the suppression of the Jesuits by Pope Clement XIV.[26]

Major political and legal reforms remained out of the question. The "free" sejms of 1778, 1780, 1782, 1784, and 1786 were subject to unanimity in all but carefully defined "economic matters." The royalist majority encountered an opposition led by a clique of aristocrats. The latter proclaimed themselves defenders of Polish liberty, but their strategy was to outbid the king for the empress's favor. The most important of them was Ksawery Branicki. Having been raised to the highest military office, the grand hetmanship of the Crown, and granted a vast Crown estate, he turned against the king. Married from 1781 to the favorite niece of Grigorii Potemkin (Catherine's effective coruler and, in all probability, morganatic husband), he belonged to the extended imperial family.[27] Through Branicki, the opposition lobbied St. Petersburg for a new ambassador with instructions to cooperate with the "first families." However, although their hopes were sometimes encouraged in order to check Stanisław August, the would-be oligarchs were denied power and Stackelberg stayed. The ship of state seemed becalmed, but the depths hid deeper currents.

The king built up a "royalist party." He used the patronage still at his disposal to recruit men of talent. A consensus among historians has pronounced that the royalists were virtually devoid of ideology.[28] However,

---

[25] Ramunė Šmigelskytė-Stukienė, "From Clientage Structure to a New Social Group: The Formation of the Group of Public Servants in the Grand Duchy of Lithuania in the Late Eighteenth Century," in Richard Butterwick and Wioletta Pawlikowska, eds., *Social and Cultural Relations in the Grand Duchy of Lithuania: Microhistories* (New York: Routledge, 2019), 148–65.

[26] Richard Butterwick-Pawlikowski, "Before and after Suppression: Jesuits and Former Jesuits in the Polish–Lithuanian Commonwealth, c. 1750–1795," in Robert A. Maryks and Jonathan Wright, eds., *Jesuit Survival and Restoration: A Global History, 1773–1900* (Leiden: Brill, 2015), 51–66; Ambroise Jobert, *La Commission d'Éducation Nationale en Pologne (1773–1794)* (Paris: Droz, 1941); Kamilla Mrozowska, "Educational Reform in Poland during the Enlightenment," in Samuel Fiszman, ed., *Constitution and Reform in Eighteenth-Century Poland: The Constitution of 3 May 1791* (Bloomington: Indiana University Press, 1997), 113–55.

[27] Simon Sebag Montefiore, *Prince of Princes: The Life of Potemkin* (London: Weidenfeld and Nicolson, 2000).

[28] For example, Lukowski, *Liberty's Folly*, 214–15.

employing a wide range of media, the monarch sought to convey the benefits of the rule of law, stability, trust, education, humanity, and prosperity, emphasizing various forms of patriotism. Confessional tensions were defused in the postpartition settlement (no more than three envoys to each sejm could be "dissidents"), and the Catholic hierarchy proved generally supportive. The alliance between throne and altar was embodied by the king's youngest brother. Michał Poniatowski entered the episcopate in 1773, and ascended to the archbishopric of Gniezno and primacy of Poland in 1785. He became the monarch's closest political partner.

The Commonwealth also saw economic, social, and cultural changes. Rural economic growth was steady rather than spectacular. Abandoned land was brought back into cultivation, and seeding ratios climbed as the climate warmed. Work resumed on canals while new opportunities for export opened via the Black Sea. Experiments in commuting labor services and sharecropping to cash rents remained rare. The threat to serfdom implicit in the project of legal codification commissioned in 1776 led to its vehement rejection by the sejm of 1780.[29]

Rising domestic consumption helped growing cities such as Poznań, Kraków, and Wilno (today Vilnius) to sustain lively cultural scenes. Warsaw's population tripled from about 30,000 to 90,000 between the late 1750s and the late 1780s. The Commonwealth's 1,500 or so towns were of three kinds – royal (with various forms of self-government), ecclesiastical, and privately owned. Some saw dynamic growth, others stagnated. The overall urban population was swelled by high birth rates and low death rates among Jews, immigration from abroad, and noble residents.

The growing number of nobles combined with partible inheritance to aggravate the shortage of viable landed estates. Indebted magnates offered fewer opportunities for service and patronage. Competition grew more intense for employment in the law, the Catholic Church, officialdom, and the army, and of course for heiresses, even burghers' daughters. Many impecunious young nobles sought fortunes in trade or through their pens – herein lay the social origins of the nineteenth-century intelligentsia.

By 1788 a restless spirit was tangible. According to the king, "the ferment of minds continues apace, especially among the youth."[30] Some narratives

---

[29] Lukowski, *Disorderly Liberty*, 109–20.
[30] Stanisław August to Augustyn Deboli, 3 May 1788, quoted after Emanuel Rostworowski, *Sprawa aukcji wojska na tle sytuacji politycznej przed Sejmem Czteroletnim* (Warsaw: PWN, 1957), 224.

credit the schools of the Commission of National Education, but these had yet to produce many graduates taught according to the enlightened new curricula. Indeed, pedagogical novelties irked many parents. Their criticism found its way into sejmik instructions, along with complaints about foreign-style dress and travel abroad. The king's efforts to cultivate the middling nobility ran into the headwinds of cultural nostalgia and national pride. The opposition magnates portrayed themselves as true republican patriots.

Stanisław August had hoped to outmaneuver the aristocrats, respond to nobles' hopes for an expanded army, and capture a little glory through the Commonwealth's participation in the expected war between the Russian and Ottoman Empires. In the spring of 1787, he journeyed to meet Catherine II as she progressed down the River Dnieper. She received him on her galley on 6 May. He submitted his proposals for an alliance, increases in revenue and the army, and a confederated sejm. However, she kept him waiting until September 1788, when she finally approved a watered-down plan. By then Polish–Lithuanian politics were veering out of control.[31]

Parliamentary Revolution

The sejmiks held in August 1788 proved turbulent. The opposition scored significant electoral successes. Several sejmiks opposed war with the Ottoman Empire and criticized the Permanent Council. While there was a consensus for expanding the army, most sejmiks demanded that it should be funded mainly by the clergy and Jews, and through cuts in government expenditure.[32]

Stanisław August still believed he had a slim majority when the sejm opened on 6 October. However, during the negotiation of the parliamentary confederacy, the Russian Ambassador belatedly tried to defuse the ticking bomb. He even denied that his court had any plans to involve the Commonwealth in a war. The decision that even a single envoy would be able to demand a secret vote, following an open one, except in matters of taxation, weakened patrons' ability to control their clients.

---

[31] The standard history of the Four Years' Sejm remains Walerian Kalinka, *Sejm Czteroletni*, 2 vols., 4th edition (Warsaw: Volumen, 1991 [1880–1887]), supplemented by Emanuel Rostworowski, *Ostatni król Rzeczypospolitej: Geneza i upadek Konstytucji 3 maja* (Warsaw: Wiedza Powszechna, 1966). The best study of the international situation between 1788 and 1793 remains Robert Howard Lord, *The Second Partition of Poland: A Study in Diplomatic History* (Cambridge, MA: Harvard University Press, 1915).

[32] Richard Butterwick, *The Polish Revolution and the Catholic Church, 1788–1792: A Political History* (Oxford: Oxford University Press, 2012), 41–6.

In a declaration read out on 13 October, the king of Prussia advised against an alliance with Russia, and offered his own friendship and alliance, safeguarding the Commonwealth's borders while recognizing that it could establish its own form of government. Frederick William II's prestige was already high following Prussia's intervention in the United Provinces in 1787 and consequent alliance with the Dutch Republic and Great Britain. Many envoys who had hitherto reluctantly accepted the Russian "guarantee" were dazzled by the prospect of a sovereign Poland befriended by Prussia. Stanisław August was skeptical; he proposed first to raise more revenue, and then to recruit the number of soldiers that could be afforded (he was planning on about 45,000). However, this cautious position fell woefully short of expectations. On 20 October, the sejm ecstatically acclaimed an army of 100,000 men. Only later would it decide on the command structure; only after that – the necessary taxes.

The monarch became dependent for his shrinking majorities on the votes of lower-ranking castellans, so much so that rhymesters began to use the word "castellan" as an insult. An outburst of pamphlets, verses, riddles, and other political ephemera engaged with the sejm.[33] Warsaw's public gardens played a similar role to the courtyard of the Palais Royal in Paris. Impromptu orators, and their cheering and jeering audiences, mixed with the purveyors and customers of carnal pleasures. Royalists had the worst of these encounters. Even parliamentary sessions increasingly resembled political rallies. The tone was set by the ladies in the packed public galleries. Led by Princess Izabela Czartoryska, they applauded the orators of the opposition, waving their fragrant scarves. A few royalists reprimanded the "prejudiced public," but more were persuaded by the mockery either to remain silent or to change sides. At balls and assemblies, the leading "patriots" were rewarded by the ladies with garlands and kisses. Czartoryska theatrically sheared off the tresses of Kazimierz Sapieha, who then reattired himself in national costume.

The voluble Sapieha was the marshal of the Lithuanian parliamentary confederacy (the Commonwealth's dualist composition was best reflected in its confederacies). His colleague, the marshal of the Crown parliamentary confederacy, Stanisław Małachowski, struggled to direct proceedings. Although popular, he had neither the power nor the personality to curtail

---

[33] Anna Grześkowiak-Krwawicz, "Political and Social Literature during the Four-Year Diet," in Fiszman, *Constitution and Reform*, 175–202; Anna Grześkowiak-Krwawicz, *O formę rządu czy o rząd dusz? Publicystyka polityczna Sejmu Czteroletniego* (Warsaw: IBL, 2000).

perorations; nor could he prevent parliamentarians from straying from the matter under discussion. Moreover, all laws had to be approved clause by clause. The sejm swiftly acclaimed an army of 100,000, but needed most of November and December 1788 to agree the detail of military governance.

The latter task was necessitated by the sejm's decision on 3 November 1788 to abolish the Military Department of the Permanent Council. The king's majority in open voting was reversed in the secret vote. The department would be replaced with a Military Commission subordinated to the sejm. The Russian Ambassador, taking this as a rejection of the empress's "guarantee," demanded that the king and his closest supporters leave Warsaw and form a counter-confederacy. They refused, forestalling an opposition plan to invite in the Prussian army. After Stackelberg's protest was read out on 6 November, the king adjourned sessions for four days, stoking the blaze: "the spirit of opposition has so increased hatred toward Muscovy in all estates and kinds of people that it is almost impossible to believe."[34]

On 15 November the sejm demanded the evacuation of Russian troops from the Commonwealth. In a second note, read out on 20 November, the king of Prussia announced that he had asked the empress to withdraw her forces, and that he respected the Poles' right to change their laws, wishing only to guarantee their independence. Frederick William II was fêted as a disinterested friend, and waverers were won over by his adroit envoy, Girolamo Lucchesini. The sejm's vote on 19 January 1789 to abolish the Permanent Council completed the first stage of the Polish Revolution.

Sovereignty was the key to this revolution. "Patriot" orators often declaimed about the omnipotence of the Commonwealth constituted in its parliamentary Estates. The king of Prussia beckoned the Poles into the unknown, while the Russian protectorate was shattered. Being at war with both the Ottoman Empire and Sweden, Catherine II had to bide her time. The sejm had extended its own term indefinitely and taken control of the government, including diplomacy, the military, and the treasury. Sovereignty was also expressed in raising revenue. In March 1789 the sejm decided that in addition to the existing *subsidium charitativum*, the Catholic clergy of both rites (Latin and Ruthenian) would pay tax at 20 percent – twice the rate volunteered for the lay nobility. On 17 July 1789 the sejm voted to

---

[34] Stanisław August to Augustyn Deboli, 7 November 1788, quoted after Kalinka, *Sejm Czteroletni*, vol. 1, 191.

secularize the estates of the vacant bishopric of Kraków – one of the richest in Europe. The next bishop would be paid an annual salary of 100,000 złotys, leaving almost half a million a year for the army. The principle was then extended to all the bishoprics of both rites, to be implemented as current holders died or were translated to other sees. The measure was calculated to increase the net public revenues, but the promised annual salaries would exceed the existing revenues of more than half of the bishoprics.

This unprecedented act stunned the Holy See: in the Habsburg Monarchy the arch-reformer Joseph II had at least established a religious fund. The principle, although not the scope, of the Polish law bore comparison with the later ecclesiastical secularization and reorganization ordained by the French National Assembly. However, a schism with Rome was averted. During the winter and spring of 1789–1790, the sejm's deputation, the episcopate, and the papal nuncio worked out a compromise which kept boundary changes to a minimum, and crucially, allowed bishops to receive their equalized revenues from landed estates. Many of the Catholic clergy would propagate the Constitution of 3 May 1791.

The debates on revenue overlapped with a rebellion scare. When the peasants of the Polish Ukraine had last risen up – in 1768 – a chiliastic slaughter of nobles, Jews, and Catholic clergy of both rites had been followed by savage repression. Besides ongoing socioeconomic grievances, the confessional situation was still volatile. The Russian Orthodox hierarchy was extending its authority on the right bank of the Dnieper. Rumors of a revolt fomented by Potemkin's agents turned to panic when a noble family was murdered in April 1789. Local nobles executed many peasants for loose talk; more were flogged. In the end nothing comparable to the French "Great Fear" of 1789 occurred, but the scare focused minds on the strategic vulnerability of the Ruthenian lands. Most parliamentarians had little understanding of the region's problems, and without such an alarm, their neglect of Ruthenia might have continued.

The sejm adopted a two-pronged confessional strategy. First, it admitted the metropolitan archbishop of the Ruthenian rite of the Catholic Church to the senate. This was a partial and belated fulfillment of one of the terms of the 1596 Union of Brest, which had sought to bring the Commonwealth's Orthodox Christians into unity with Roman (or Latin-rite) Catholics while retaining the Slavonic liturgy and a separate structure. However, this Union actually split eastern Christendom into rival "Uniate" Catholic and "Non-Uniate" Orthodox Churches. Second, the sejm cut off the Orthodox Church in the Commonwealth from the Holy Synod in St. Petersburg. This necessitated an autonomous Orthodox hierarchy, negotiated in the summer of 1791 and confirmed by the sejm in May 1792.[35]

In April 1791 the sejm decided not to give preference to Catholics regarding municipal office in royal towns. This was part of an urban reform responding to the political movement which had emerged almost two years earlier.[36] Hugo Kołłątaj, a nobly born priest and pamphleteer, helped draft burghers' demands for fuller self-government, extensive civil liberties, and representation in the legislature in December 1789. Following royal pressure, the memorial's language was toned down, emphasizing the restoration of ancient rights, but the references to violent revolution elsewhere roused terrifying specters in the imaginations of the nobles. Besides the obvious events in France, it seemed to evoke the coup earlier that year in Sweden, when the clerical, burgher, and peasant estates had all supported Gustav III. Stanisław August was desperate to avoid such suspicions.

More enlightened members of the sejm argued for giving burghers a stake in Polish liberty, but others insisted on preserving the nobles' monopoly on law-making. The parliamentary deputation's projects became more restrictive the longer it deliberated. In the end, the king and others realized that if an exclusively noble legislature was conceded in theory, a great deal else, of more practical import to burghers, might be achieved. A garrulous traditionalist, Jan Suchorzewski, was persuaded to present a project which restricted the burghers to some "plenipotentiaries" who would advise the sejm in urban and economic matters, but granted them virtually all the civil liberties and self-government they desired. Passed on 18 April 1791, the law on royal towns, henceforth called "free towns," soon afterwards became an integral part of the new Constitution.

For the sejm to agree a new form of government, a major political shift had to occur.[37] The first year or so of the sejm saw the opposition in the

---

[35] Barbara Skinner, "Borderlands of Faith: Reconsidering the Origins of a Ukrainian Tragedy," *Slavic Review*, 64:1 (2005), 88–116; Barbara Skinner, *The Western Front of the Eastern Church: Uniate and Orthodox Conflict in Eighteenth-Century Poland, Ukraine, Belarus, and Russia* (DeKalb: Northern Illinois University Press, 2009); Sofia Senyk, "Religious Conflict in Dnepr Ukraine in the 18th Century," *Orientalia Christiana Periodica*, 73:1 (2007), 5–59; Richard Butterwick, "Deconfessionalization? The Policy of the Polish Revolution towards Ruthenia, 1788–1792," *Central Europe* 6:2 (2008), 91–121.

[36] Krystyna Zienkowska, "Reforms Relating to the Third Estate," in Fiszman, *Constitution and Reform*, 329–55; Krystyna Zienkowska, *Sławetni i urodzeni: Ruch polityczny mieszczaństwa w dobie Sejmu Czteroletniego* (Warsaw: PWN, 1976).

[37] Richard Butterwick, "Political Discourses of the Polish Revolution, 1788–1792," *English Historical Review* 120:487 (2005), 695–731.

ascendant. However, in the second half of 1789 this coalition began to split. The socially inclusive agenda of enlightened republicans led by Ignacy Potocki and cheered on by Kołłątaj clashed with the nobles' republican discourse voiced by partisans of Ksawery Branicki. The hetman stayed close to Potemkin, despite the Russophobic slogans of his faction. The following year brought a royal recovery. Stanisław August defused most remaining suspicion by accepting the Commonwealth's alliance with Prussia signed in March 1790. The task of drafting a 658-clause *Project for the Form of Government* exhausted Ignacy Potocki, who then had to face it being mauled in the sejm. The monarch took advantage when royalist orators, drawn from the middling nobility, launched a devastating, demagogic attack on the "aristocrats" and "lords" during the debates on the royal prerogative in September 1790. Stanisław August recovered most of the prerogatives – including the nomination of senators – he had held before the creation of the Permanent Council in 1775.

Things went from bad to worse for Ignacy Potocki. The two-year term of the sejm was almost up, and the work on a new form of government stalled. The sejm's decision that a new complement of envoys be elected to sit alongside, rather than in place of, the existing ones provoked grumbling in the provinces. The sejmik instructions of November 1790 were even more forthright than those of 1788. Most explicitly defended royal elections. For his part, Stanisław August, although distressed by attacks on the Educational Commission, consoled himself with the election of many envoys well-disposed to himself.

For Potocki the best that could now be hoped for was "limited monarchy." On 4 December 1790 he asked the king to take the initiative in drafting the new Constitution. Stanisław August took up the challenge, while Potocki pushed back in a republican direction. Their negotiations were facilitated by a Tuscan democrat, Scipione Piattoli, who moved into royal service. Stanisław Małachowski was brought in as an honest broker, and Kołłątaj polished the text. After just over 100 supporters had been let in on the secret, the project was sprung on the sejm on 3 May 1791.[38]

The galleries and surrounding streets were packed. When the session opened at ten o'clock, extracts from diplomatic despatches were read out, suggesting terrible threats to the Commonwealth, before the salutary project was announced. Faced with protests amidst the clamor for its acclamation,

---

[38] The drafting of the Constitution is illuminated by Emanuel Rostworowski, *Legendy i fakty XVIII wieku* (Warsaw: PWN, 1963), 265–464.

Małachowski commended it as combining the best features of two "republican governments" – the English and the American.[39] The impassioned debate lasted until the late afternoon. When the monarch once again raised his hand to speak, it looked as if he wished to swear an oath to the new Constitution. Stanisław August seized the moment. Two days later, the sejm unanimously endorsed these revolutionary proceedings.

The text of the Constitution is brief and didactic.[40] It begins with a stirring preamble and an article maintaining the prohibition against "apostasy" from the Roman Catholic "dominant and national religion," while assuring freedom of worship and the protection of government to all creeds. It then deals with the structure first of society (in three articles) and then of government (in four), before sketching arrangements for a regency and the education of royal children. The eleventh article enlists the armed forces in support of the government, before a final declaration addresses questions of enforcement and propaganda.

Much detail remained to be filled out by subsequent laws.[41] Their content and language tended to be more republican than those of the Constitution – which preferred the more flexible terms "Poland" and "nation" to the traditional "Commonwealth." The virtual omission of the grand duchy of Lithuania raised fears for the Polish–Lithuanian union. These were assuaged by a solemn act in October 1791 which set stringent conditions and quotas in return for Lithuanians' agreement to joint government commissions.[42]

The fifth article juxtaposes the principle that "all power in human society derives from the will of the nation"[43] with the division and balance of government between its legislative, executive, and judicial powers – elaborated in Articles 6–8. Here Rousseau, who admired traditional Polish republicanism, met Montesquieu, who was venerated by the king. The subsequent laws on the sejm and the various executive bodies clarified the

---

[39] Zofia Libiszowska, "The Impact of the American Constitution on Polish Political Opinion in the Eighteenth Century," in Fiszman, *Constitution and Reform*, 233–50: 233.
[40] See esp. Jerzy Michalski, "The Meaning of the Constitution of 3 May," in Fiszman, *Constitution and Reform*, 251–86; Zbigniew Szcząska, "The Fundamental Principles Concerning the Political System in the 3 May, 1791 Government Statute," in Fiszman, *Constitution and Reform*, 287–308.
[41] Jerzy Lukowski, "Recasting Utopia: Montesquieu, Rousseau and the Polish Constitution of 3 May 1791," *Historical Journal* 37:1 (1994), 65–87; Lukowski, *Disorderly Liberty*, 223–49.
[42] Juliusz Bardach, "The Constitution of 3 May and the Mutual Guarantee of the Two Nations," in Fiszman, *Constitution and Reform*, 357–78.
[43] Grześkowiak-Krwawicz, *Konstytucja 3 Maja*, 66.

supremacy of the legislature. The key feature of the judicial system was the election of judges by the nation. Regarding the sejm, whereas the Constitution envisaged simple majority voting, solemnly abolishing the *liberum veto*, the later law introduced qualified majorities. Stanisław August's right to nominate senators was later removed from his successors. The king was to choose the ministers who sat on the supreme executive body, the Custodial Council, but the relevant law omitted any provision for him to dismiss them.

Despite the republican brakes, the Constitution of 3 May did approach the king's vision of a stronger executive in partnership with a revitalized sejm. Much was due to the generally harmonious cooperation between Stanisław August, Ignacy Potocki, Stanisław Małachowski, and Hugo Kołłątaj, who became Crown vice-chancellor.[44] A crucial move was from the principle of delegation to representation. Although the reform of the sejmiks passed in March 1791 had maintained mandatory instructions, the Constitution declared envoys "representatives of the entire nation," entrusted with making decisions on behalf of all.[45] Nevertheless, endorsement by the sejmiks was politically essential.

Following months of choreographed celebrations, sermons, pamphlets, and political arm-twisting, this aim was achieved. One reason was the success of the local government reforms, which entrusted real responsibilities to over 1,000 pillars of communities.[46] Of the seventy-eight sejmiks held in February 1792, not one criticized the Constitution, and only eight passed it over in silence. The others either voted thanks, or pledged to maintain it, or – in thirty-seven cases – swore to defend it. Support was strongest in Lithuania. Moreover, the calm proceedings and the resolutions revealed the predominance of a new discourse – that of orderly freedom (*rządna wolność*), sanctified by Divine Providence.

Orderly freedom would be shared by landed and urban citizens. The reform of sejmiks had removed most rights of political participation from landless nobles – the justification being that magnates had often manipulated their impoverished "brethren." On the other hand, the law on towns had accelerated inter-estate fraternization. Many nobles accepted urban

---

[44] Daniel Stone, "The First (and Only) Year of the May 3 Constitution," *Canadian Slavic Papers* 35:1–2 (1993), 69–86: 85.
[45] Grześkowiak-Krwawicz, *Konstytucja 3 Maja*, 69.
[46] Łukasz Kądziela, "Local Government Reform during the Four-Year Diet," in Fiszman, *Constitution and Reform*, 379–96.

citizenship. In Kołłątaj's vision of the Commonwealth, political participation would depend on property – both landed and urban – rather than birth. Even the title of the second article of the Constitution associated nobles with landowners. Nobles' hereditary privileges were flatteringly guaranteed, but this article also declared "the preservation of personal security and property, as by law ascertained, to be a tie of society, and the very essence of civil liberty, which ought to be considered and respected forever."[47]

Kołłątaj was also responsible for the Constitution's fourth article, on "peasants and villagers." This has ever since been faulted for not abolishing serfdom, but it deserves closer reading. It declares the rural population the most useful and numerous part of the nation, under the protection of law and government. Moreover, every newcomer and every returning person would become free the moment they stepped onto Polish soil. They could either enter into legally enforceable contracts with a landowner or settle in a town. The road to the end of serfdom was clear.

The position of Jews remained unresolved. Most Jews wished to preserve their communal and cultural autonomy while being free to live and trade in all towns (they had hitherto been allowed into Warsaw only for the duration of sejms, for example). However, many burghers resented Jewish competitors; if Jews had to be permitted to reside among Christians, they should be subject to municipal jurisdiction and taxes. Enlightened ideologues led by Kołłątaj desired Jews' far-reaching assimilation, with Polish replacing Yiddish, and Hebrew reserved for religious rituals. The king was more sympathetic to Jews' distinctiveness, but he had an interest in their settling his debts. The sejm deputation for the Jews was unable to work out reforms which could satisfy all parties; in the end, the sejm did not consider its project. This left the central Police Commission, established by the Constitution, holding the ring. It often upheld Jewish complaints against municipal authorities, and decided that the medieval nobles' privilege of no incarceration without trial, extended in 1791 to burghers of "free towns," also encompassed their Jewish inhabitants.[48]

An almanac published early in 1792 reviewed "four constitutions: the English, which served others as a model, the American, which was formed

---

[47] *New Constitution of the Government of Poland*, 2nd edition (London, 1791), 8.
[48] Artur Eisenbach, *The Emancipation of the Jews in Poland 1780–1870* (Oxford: Blackwell, 1991), 1–112; Krystyna Zienkowska, "Citizens or Inhabitants? The Attempt to Reform the Status of Jews during the Four Years' Sejm," *Acta Poloniae Historica* 76 (1997), 31–52; Murphy, *From Citizens to Subjects*, 86–117.

from it, the Polish, which made use of both, and in the end the French, which has had these three models together before it."[49] Although the Constitution of 3 May was acclaimed on both sides of the Atlantic, the French Revolution was headed on a different course. Its fiercest critic, Edmund Burke, praised the Polish Constitution for its moderation and British inspiration in his *Appeal from the New to the Old Whigs* (1791). This delighted Stanisław August. He had earlier applauded the French move from absolutism to constitutional monarchy in his letters to his agent in Paris, Filippo Mazzei, a Tuscan veteran of the American Revolution. By 1791 he was anxious to refute claims of rampant "Jacobinism" in Poland. Few of Warsaw's radicals would admit to such a label, but a handful of "malcontent" magnates and their clients used it as they begged Catherine II to restore the Commonwealth's republican liberty.[50]

The Polish Revolution was thus condemned by its domestic and foreign opponents for being "democratical" and "monarchical." (The Polish word used was the unusual and pejorative *demokrackie* as opposed to the standard *demokratyczne*. "Democratical" seems to capture the flavor better than "democratic.") Its least palatable aspect was the Constitution's provision for hereditary succession to the throne: Elector Frederick Augustus III of Saxony would initiate a new dynasty. Although most sejmiks had rejected hereditary succession in November 1790, many had endorsed the elector as the next king. However, the elector had only a young daughter, whom the Constitution designated Poland's "*infantka*." Regarding her future husband, the leadership entertained contradictory hopes, while the interests of the neighboring powers were incompatible. The text of the Constitution eloquently evoked the perils of interregna, but there was nothing to be gained by introducing the principle of hereditary monarchy without establishing it firmly. Worse, the elector's agreement had not been secured in advance. After 3 May 1791 he made his acceptance conditional on the consent of the rulers of Russia, Prussia, and Austria. Catherine II remained silent.

---

[49] *Kalendarzyk polityczny na rok przestępny 1792* (1792), quoted after Grześkowiak-Krwawicz, "Konstytucja 3 Maja," 27.

[50] Jörg K. Hoensch, "Citizen, Nation, Constitution: The Realization and Failure of the Constitution of 3 May in the Light of Mutual Polish–French Influence," in Fiszman, *Constitution and Reform*, 423–51; Samuel Fiszman, "European and American Opinions of the Constitution of 3 May," in Fiszman, *Constitution and Reform*, 453–95; Jerzy Michalski, "La Révolution Française aux yeux d'un roi," *Acta Poloniae Historica* 66 (1992), 75–91.

Immolation

The Treaty of Iaşi concluded Russia's victorious war against the Ottoman Empire in January 1792. Catherine II had resisted British and Prussian pressure, and could now deal with Poland. The question was whether to resubject all of the country or annex much of its territory. The "malcontents" helped her. In the Polish Crown they were led by the Commonwealth's richest magnate, Feliks Potocki, Crown Grand Hetman Ksawery Branicki, and Crown Field Hetman Seweryn Rzewuski, who had appealed to the American example in his campaign against hereditary succession. With their hangers-on they formed a confederacy in St. Petersburg on 27 April, post-dated to 14 May in Potocki's border town of Targowica. The separate confederacy in the grand duchy of Lithuania was led by Szymon Kossakowski, a former Barist who had become a major-general in Russian service, and his brother Józef, bishop of Livonia.

Following the Russian invasion, which began on 18 May, the Polish–Lithuanian armies made a fighting retreat, with Major-General Kościuszko commanding the rearguard. However, on 23 July 1792 Stanisław August, supported by the majority of a ministerial council, decided not to make a final stand before Warsaw. His capitulation on Catherine's terms ended any possibility of negotiating from strength.[51] The counterrevolutionary regime installed by the Russians won at most a reluctant acquiescence among the provincial nobility. Its traditional slogans rang hollow amidst onerous requisitioning, spiteful persecutions, and then, at the start of 1793, the news of a second partition.

Frederick William II had long coveted more Polish land. Given the opportunity to replace Russian influence in the Commonwealth, he had played the long game. Having failed to make war on either Austria or Russia in 1790–1791, the king of Prussia betrayed his Polish ally in May 1792. By that time, he and the future Emperor Francis II were already at war with revolutionary France. Catherine II needed to keep both Austria and Prussia fighting in the west, leaving her free to crush "Jacobinism" in Poland. According to the assumptions of eighteenth-century diplomacy, all expected "indemnity" for their own efforts and "compensation" for their partners'

---

[51] Vadzim Anipiarkou, "Konfederacja targowicka w 1792 r. w świetle korespondencji służbowej rosyjskiego generała Michaiła Kreczetnikowa," *Studia z Dziejów Rosji i Europy Środkowo-Wschodniej* 54:1 (2019), 75–97; Adam Danilczyk, "'Jeśli król przystąpi do konfederacji ...'. Rosja wobec Stanisława Augusta w 1792 r. (kwiecień–sierpień 1792 r.)," *Studia z Dziejów Rosji i Europy Środkowo-Wschodniej* 54:1 (2019), 99–115.

acquisitions. The court of Vienna was fobbed off with agreement to conquests from France, which proved unachievable. Berlin demanded a thick slice of Poland. Catherine agreed, partly because Austria would not expand into the southeast of the Commonwealth, while she could take a vast swathe of strategically vital territory.

Once again, the Poles had to ratify the amputation, this time at a confederated sejm called to Grodno (or Hrodna, now in Belarus) in the summer of 1793. The rump Commonwealth was resubjected to Russia, more explicitly than ever. The stability of this settlement was always doubtful. Catherine II was open to another partition, but not yet; at the start of 1794 she moved troops to the Ottoman frontier.

By the beginning of 1793 émigrés, including Ignacy Potocki and Kołłątaj, had given up hope of a compromise, and began to plan an uprising. In Paris the National Convention honored Kościuszko as a hero, but the Committee of Public Safety refused him military assistance. The rising was triggered in March 1794. A cavalry commander decided not to wait for his brigade to be disbanded, and it fought its way toward Kraków. Kościuszko arrived in the city and was sworn in as the head of the Insurrection. Within a few weeks he had defeated a minor Russian force in battle with the symbolically resonant participation of peasant scythe-men, while Wilno and Warsaw had risen up and bloodily expelled their Russian occupants.

Kościuszko headed an insurrectionary government whose most urgent task was to recruit, train, supply, and deploy an army. He also had to balance rival political constituencies: moderates led by Ignacy Potocki looking to restore the Constitution of 3 May via a negotiated solution; and "Jacobin" radicals around Kołłątaj, who demanded the abolition of serfdom and noble privileges, a French-style mobilization of the entire populace, and the extirpation of "traitors." On the whole, Kościuszko tempered his radical instincts. Needing to recruit peasants to the army, he chose half-measures, rather than abolishing serfdom outright. This limited the impact among peasants, while not overcoming the suspicion of many noble landowners. He was also determined to uphold the rule of law. Except for two occasions when the Warsaw crowd forced the authorities to hang several suspected traitors, including two bishops, after summary trials, the courts worked according to humane and enlightened principles, with concern for due process and evidence. It was a world away from the French Terror.[52]

---

[52] Jerzy Kowecki, "The Kościuszko Insurrection: Continuation and Radicalization of Change," in Fiszman, *Constitution and Reform*, 497–518.

Frederick William II besieged Warsaw, but retreated when a Polish raid caused chaos in his rear. General Aleksandr Suvorov's corps left the Ottoman frontier and marched toward Warsaw. Kościuszko engaged another Russian corps on 10 October 1794, but was wounded and taken prisoner. On 4 November Suvorov's veterans stormed Praga, Warsaw's right-bank suburb, and unleashed a slaughter. The terrified city capitulated the following day, and the remaining insurrectionary forces surrendered on 16 November.

The ultimate outcome of the rising was not in doubt. The hoped-for aid from France never came, but the Insurrection helped the French cause: Prussian and Austrian forces were transferred east, as their commanders scrambled to occupy Polish territory. Catherine adjudicated between the rival claims. The third partition treaty, signed in St. Petersburg on 24 October 1795, assigned Russia territories larger than those which went to Austria and Prussia combined. Stanisław August was pressured into abdicating on the empress's terms on 25 November.[53]

The 1797 treaty dealing with the final dismemberment of the Commonwealth was accompanied by a secret clause to erase the name and memory of Poland. However, in the same year, Polish legions were formed in Italy, fighting alongside the French against the Austrian Monarchy. Their hopes of restoring Poland were disappointed in the short term, but the "Polish Question" became inseparable from revolutionary movements in the Old and the New World during the nineteenth century. Only after 1989 did Poles' Sallustian dilemma – perilous liberty or tranquil servitude – again seem redundant, but for how long?

---

[53] Robert Howard Lord, "The Third Partition of Poland," *Slavonic Review* 3 (1924–1925), 481–98.

21

Transnational Perspectives: The French Revolution, the Sister Republics, and the United States

ANNIE JOURDAN

In the beginning was the Declaration of Independence of 4 July 1776, soon to be followed by the Bills of Rights of six American states, which were known in Europe as early as 1782 and translated into French in 1783. For the first time in history, these texts proclaimed to the world the natural rights of men: "All men are created equal, ... they are endowed by their Creator with certain unalienable Rights, that among these are Life, Liberty, and the Pursuit of Happiness."[1] This declaration was at once a declaration of independence, a declaration of human rights, and a manifesto. (Note that the English Bill of Rights was intended exclusively for English subjects.) Therefore, a revolutionary spirit had already emerged before 1789. In North America for the first time, then in the United Provinces, in the Republic of Geneva, and in Switzerland, the 1770s and 1780s were marked by more or less radical uprisings and revolutions, which resulted in nothing, except in North America.[2] Paradoxically, the French king, Louis XVI, rescued the American Patriots, whereas he helped repress the Geneva Revolution of 1782. Without help from a great power, revolutions in small countries were indeed doomed to failure, since they were immediately put down by old regime potentates and kings, who opposed any change in the status quo. The Dutch Patriot revolution (1781–1787) had been crushed by the Prussians; the Fribourg revolts (1780–1784) by Bern; and that of Geneva (1782) by Piedmont and France. In Italy, revolutionary attempts achieved no more success. Its authors were jailed, tortured, exiled, or executed. However, these unsuccessful uprisings gave birth to many innovative ideas and plans, long

---

[1] David Armitage, *The Declaration of Independence: A Global History* (Cambridge: Cambridge University Press, 2007), 165.
[2] R. R. Palmer, *The World of the French Revolution* (Basingstoke: Taylor & Francis, 2016).

before the French took the Bastille. In the United Provinces, for example, bills of rights, and provincial or local constitutions were drafted as early as 1784–1785. But they were never as influential as the American texts, except perhaps in their impact on Mirabeau, who knew the *Leiden Draft* and published it in his papers.[3]

In contrast to revolutions, eighteenth-century reformism aimed most of the time at rationalizing, simplifying, and standardizing the state in an attempt to increase its financial resources, which were jeopardized by warfare. Its objective was never the people's happiness. American anger of the 1760s and 1770s indeed concerned new taxes forced upon the colonists by Great Britain, hence the American motto: "No taxation without representation."[4] In the United Provinces, it was the defeat of the Dutch navy against England which provoked hostilities against the prince of Orange, who was seen as a traitor, favoring British over Dutch interests. The Austrian Netherlands rose up against Emperor Joseph II's reforms, which challenged the Church and traditions; in Geneva, the people rose up against political inequalities and local oligarchy, as in Switzerland, where the peasants asked for lower taxes while the new elites clamored for political rights and liberation from despotic cantons, such as Bern. Even Ireland looked jealously at America, dreaming of emancipation from Great Britain.

Sister Republics

Would revolutionary France rescue these rebellious nations and liberate them from their tyrants? Several decrees from 1790–1792 suggested France would, particularly the decree of 19 November 1792, which promised to support peoples against their "tyrants."[5] Consequently, and thanks to the war (against Austria, Prussia, England, Spain, and the Netherlands), the French "liberated" the Rhineland and Belgium in 1792–1793. It was only for a short time. In spring 1793, following defeats, the first areas to be "liberated" had fallen back into their old masters' hands. In 1794, conversely, the French

---

[3] Wayne te Brake, *Regents and Rebels: The Revolutionary World of an Eighteenth-Century Dutch City* (Cambridge: Cambridge University Press, 1989); Jeremy Popkin, "Dutch Patriots, French Journalists and Declarations of Rights: The Leidse Ontwerp of 1785 and Its Diffusion in France," *The Historical Journal* 38:3 (1995), 553–65.
[4] Tim Blanning and Peter Wende, eds., *Reform in Great Britain and in Germany, 1750–1850* (Oxford: Oxford University Press, 1999).
[5] Eddie Kolla, *Sovereignty, International Right and the French Revolution* (Cambridge: Cambridge University Press, 2019); Marc Belissa, *Fraternité universelle et intérêt national* (Paris: Kimé, 1998).

armies managed to reconquer Belgium before entering the Dutch Republic. On 20 January 1795, French troops arrived safely in Amsterdam after Dutch Patriots had prepared the revolution in the previous summer and autumn. The outcome shows that they were up to their task. The French representatives in Holland had nothing else to do but proclaim the small republic's independence. At the same time, the Dutch were ingenious enough to resist unreasonable requests from the French government.[6]

A peace treaty with France was signed at The Hague on 16 May, after which the first French "sister" republic was free to organize its new government. From May 1795 until January 1798, it tried to persuade its seven provinces to adopt a new republican constitution. And yet, several provinces opposed the National Assembly and refused to be part of a single convention, since they were afraid of losing their (local) sovereignty. After all, the United Provinces had always been a loose federation. Concurrently, popular societies sought to influence the ongoing discussions on unity and democracy. The provisional government was thus threatened by radicals and by federalists who rejected important changes. The prevailing chaos following the treaty is living proof that the Batavian Republic was really independent, even if French troops and representatives were still on the spot. In the Netherlands, just as elsewhere, the revolution provoked disorder and struggles between political factions that hindered the implementation of steady government. In fact, it took four years and a "coup" before the Dutch finally adopted a constitution. Meanwhile, the Batavian government was still a provisional one and could not fulfill its commitments to France, which explains why the latter decided to intervene by sending a commissioner to the Netherlands. Charles Delacroix chose to ally with radical patriots, who launched a coup on 22 January 1798 and seized power. They lost no time, and enacted a bill of rights and a constitution within three months. In May 1798, the people could vote for or against the constitutional act. It was accepted and implemented during the same month, and would be applied until 1801.[7]

Meanwhile numerous changes had taken place in Europe. The first country to have enacted a written constitution without any outside help was Poland. It was ready before the first French text, in May 1791. But, like

---

[6] Annie Jourdan, *La Révolution batave entre la France et l'Amérique* (Rennes: Presses universitaires de Rennes, 2008); Simon Schama, *Patriots and Liberators. Revolution in the Netherlands, 1780–1813* (New York: Alfred A. Knopf, 1977).

[7] Jourdan, *La Révolution batave*, 151–4, 179–84.

Paoli's transformation of Corsica in the 1750s, this was a top-down revolution, brought about by an individual to strengthen the state against foreign powers. Admittedly, some improvements were made, but the Polish constitution did not turn the social and political order upside down. Quite different was the situation in Geneva, which was at the time a small republic, independent from Switzerland. This "miniature republic," as it was called, had lost no time, and revolutionized itself as early as December 1792, without France's intervention. It implemented a bill of rights at the start of 1793 and a democratic constitution in May 1794. But the situation remained unstable: factions fought one another, trying to seize power. When France's first Italian campaign started, the disorders were still going on and worried neighboring Switzerland, which feared revolutionary contamination.[8] Until 1796, thus, "sister republics" were few in number. To be fair, the expression "sister republic" was seldom used by the French or by her allies. The first to use it were North Americans such as James Monroe and John Quincy Adams, to evoke French or Dutch relations with the United States.[9] When, later on, the French spoke about these "satellite" republics, they called them allied or daughter republics, as a counterpoint to the "mother republic."

By the year 1796, which would change the face of Europe, only two older republics had overthrown their government and set up a new one. The republic of Mainz had been broken up in July 1793 after successive French setbacks. In one case after another, European patriots showed their inability to survive without French troops.[10] When they were defeated, the counter-revolution got the upper hand. This happened in Poland too, when her mighty neighbors invaded the country in 1793 and 1795 and divided it among themselves, reversing the reforms.

At that time, however, France was looking for allies and resources, and not emulators. The diverse peace treaties signed in Basel in 1795 are living proof of this new policy. And yet, all these peaceful expectations were called into question by the Italian campaign of 1796, directed by a young general, Napoleon Bonaparte.

Like the Dutch, the Swiss, and the Irish revolutionaries before them, Italian patriots had been pressuring the French Directory into intervening in their country. Among them were Philippe Buonarotti, a friend of Babeuf,

---

[8] Alfred Rufer, *La Suisse et la Révolution française* (Paris: Société des Études Robespierristes, 1973); Annie Jourdan, *La Révolution: Une exception française?* (Paris: Flammarion, 2004). See also Richard Whatmore's Chapter 12 in this volume.

[9] Annie Jourdan, *Nouvelle histoire de la Révolution* (Paris: Flammarion, 2018), 440–1.

[10] Jean-Louis Harouel, *Les Républiques sœurs* (Paris: Presses universitaires de France, 1997).

who had written a plan of revolution for Italy, and Giuseppe Ceracchi, a Roman sculptor who had visited the United States to make a bust of Washington. These patriots suggested the liberation of Piedmont, Rome, Lombardy, or even the whole peninsula.[11] The Parisian government was not certain whether this was a good idea. Reports submitted by its diplomats and officers warned against a "liberation," pointing out that the Italians were not ripe for liberty, and alleging that they were too religious and too ignorant to appreciate actual freedom.

For the French Directory, the goal of the Italian campaign was to secure an advantageous and quick peace with Austria and Piedmont and to help them keep Belgium, the left bank of the Rhine, Nice, and Savoy. Their goal was to preserve France's "natural frontiers." The official instructions of 2 March 1796 stipulated that Bonaparte's victories would provide compensation that could be offered to the defeated in return for these territories.[12] Although Bonaparte agreed at the time, he would later change his mind, on the basis of the successes he achieved and the challenges he faced.

Italy and Its "Sister" Republics

At the beginning of the campaign, Bonaparte obeyed his instructions. And if he listened to Italian patriots, he did not follow their advice. In Piedmont, he refused to support the republic of Alba, created by local patriots, and preferred negotiating with the king, who promised him troops to protect his army. That was preferable over a revolution which would provoke anarchy and disorder. Indeed, Bonaparte's priorities were strategic and not ideological. However, some weeks later, after conquering Lombardy, he asked himself whether it would not be better to emancipate the Milanese population, because, unlike the Piedmontese, they would be "open to liberty."[13] Accordingly, he promised the Milanese independence on 19 May

---

[11] Archives Nationales, France, AF III-185; Anna Maria Rao, "Conspiration et constitution. Andrea Vitaliani et la République napolitaine de 1799,"*Annales Historiques de la Révolution Française* 313 (1998), 545–73: 547–50; Anna Maria Rao, "L'expérience révolutionnaire italienne," *Annales Historiques de la Révolution Française* 313 (1998), 387–407.

[12] Antonin Debidour, *Recueil des actes du Directoire exécutif*, 4 vols. (Paris: Imprimerie nationale, 1910–1917), vol. I, 717–18.

[13] *Correspondance générale de Napoléon Ier*, publiées par la Fondation Napoléon, 15 vols. (Paris: Fayard, 2004–2018), vol. I, 402–3, 454, 460–1, 480–1. The correspondence between Bonaparte and the members of the Directory can be found in *Correspondance inédite, officielle et confidentielle de Napoléon Bonaparte*, 7 vols. (Paris: Panckoucke, 1819–1820), vol. I, 220–2, 285, 347, 358.

1796. In the meantime, several papal states, liberated from Rome, were occupied by French troops and started their reorganization. Reggio and Modena joined them. Despite the Directory's orders, which advised Bonaparte "not to hurry" and not to do anything definitive, four of the Italian provinces convened in a congress – with the approval of the general-in-chief – and on 27 December 1796 created the first Italian republic, the Cispadane Republic. Its constitution was enacted in March 1797. It enforced the suppression of the feudal system, the sale of church estates, the abolition of cruel customs such as torture, and the introduction of indirect suffrage with three degrees, that was wide open at the first degree. (The three-tiered voting system started democratically at the first degree.) Furthermore, Catholicism was recognized as the prevailing religion.

This move was a first step in the republicanization of Italy, since Bonaparte now played with the idea of creating another republic in Lombardy. Although his government told him that "the fate of Lombardy depends on political events and the success of the other two armies,"[14] he kept doing what he wanted. (Engaged in fighting at the time were the Italian army, the army of the Rhine and Moselle, and the army of the Sambre and Meuse.) He was concerned about protecting his army's rear and desirous of having reliable allies, who would help him in case of setbacks. A new republic would give him this support, but it would have to be a republic without revolution. "You can," he argued, "you must be free, without revolution, without the misfortunes the French people have suffered."[15] By dint of complaints and arguments, Bonaparte had his way on 7 April 1797. Invoking the safety and well-being of the army, the Directory accepted the proposal to organize Lombardy under a provisional government. Bonaparte would introduce a "regulation" instead of a representative constitution and would keep it under strict military supervision. The legislators were not allowed to deliberate or to organize elections, since nothing was definitive. The new entity would be called the Cisalpine Republic. At the same time, director Carnot advised Bonaparte to "steer public opinion toward liberty, while keeping in mind that the future of these states depended on the peace negotiations with Austria," and reminded him in the same letter not to abandon Italian patriots in case of defeat.

Meanwhile Bonaparte and his generals had stimulated uprisings in Terra Ferma "under the guise of strict neutrality": Bergamo, Brescia, Crema, and

---

[14] Bonaparte's letters can be found in *Correspondance générale de Napoléon Ier*.
[15] *Correspondance générale de Napoléon Ier*, vol. 1, 703–4.

Salò had revolutionized their localities and emancipated them from "aristocratic" Venice. One of these generals, André Masséna, would later write that "civil divisions [in Terra Ferma] were beneficial to Bonaparte's views,"[16] as they weakened Venice. It was precisely what the young hero had intended, as can be seen during the peace preliminaries at Leoben of April 1797, when France and Austria shared the Venetian cake between themselves. Bergamo and Crema, then Modena and Massa, would be united with the Cisalpine Republic and the other provinces were allocated to Austria.

Worried about the situation, the oligarchic republic of Genoa decided to change its regime to a democratic republic before being compelled to do so. The Genoese suspected Bonaparte had an eye on one of their ports in order to give the Cisalpine Republic access to the sea. The new constitution of the republic of Genoa was subjected to a popular vote and accepted on 2 December 1797. At the end of 1797, there were thus two new republics in Italy: the Cisalpine Republic, which now encompassed the Cispadane Republic and the Swiss Valteline, *and* the Ligurian Republic. Venetia was broken up and Venice ceded to Austria. From May 1797 on, Bonaparte also thought of building a road through the Swiss Valais and thereby uniting the Italian bailiwicks of Switzerland with "his" Italian republic. Unsurprisingly, therefore, the Directory invited him to its discussions with two Swiss representatives, Frédéric-César de La Harpe and Peter Ochs, about a democratization of their country. For months, these men had tried, like other foreign patriots, to involve France in their plan for revolution. Now that Italian republics had been established under French influence, the idea of revolutionizing this small neutral country became more attractive to the Directory. It would bring the "sister" republics closer and increase their communications and strengths. After all, Switzerland was the natural road to Italy, but it was also a hostile country full of spies and royalists. For these reasons both directors, Merlin de Douai and Reubell, accepted the proposal to work together with Ochs and La Harpe to design an original constitution for William Tell's country. Bonaparte attended one or two sessions.[17] But before the Helvetic Republic was created, another event led to new disruption in Italy.

For some time, the executive Directory had aimed to destroy Rome and the papacy, but it lacked a legitimate reason to do so, since peace with Pius

---

[16] *Mémoires de Masséna publiés par le général Koch*, 7 vols. (Paris: Paulin et Lechevalier, 1848–1850), vol. II, 368.
[17] Harouel, *Les Républiques sœurs*, 50–7.

VI had been signed in February 1797.[18] The popular uprising in Rome of 28 December 1797, and the following murder of General Duphot, provided the opportunity the directors had been waiting for. Immediately a new French general was nominated to take reprisals and to discreetly implement a republican regime. A civil commission was formed for this purpose and sent to Rome. On 15 February 1798, Roman patriots proclaimed the republic and formed a provisional government, while the commission adapted the French constitution to the Roman people. It was ready on 20 March. But no elections were held. Instead, the French general, who enjoyed full power, nominated the legislature and the members of the executive power. The Roman constitution – also adopted in Lombardy in August 1798 – is nevertheless interesting, because it introduced into Italy a number of novelties France would have liked to include in its own constitution: universal suffrage and a uniform poll tax; a ban on popular societies or clubs; limited freedom of the press; no permanent legislature; a procedure against judicial abuses of authority; graduality of political functions; and suppression of annual elections. The national treasury would be entrusted to the executive, which would also have the power to nominate magistrates, civil servants, and generals.[19]

Meanwhile, Switzerland was invaded by French troops under false pretenses, which allowed General Brune, who was in charge of these troops, to overthrow the oligarchy of Bern. La Harpe and Ochs' constitution was brought to a popular vote and accepted by most cantons, so that the Helvetic Republic was implemented on 12 April 1798. This could have brought order and peace to the country, but Inner Switzerland rejected the new constitutional laws and the unitary state. These rural Catholic cantons feared a disturbance of their religion, independence, freedom, and political organization,[20] while the traditional oligarchy refused to give up its powers. However, and in contrast to Rome, a great part of the Swiss population wanted a democratic republic and found common ground by agreeing on a constitution. Since it was largely drafted by Basel-born Ochs, the text reflected Swiss traditions, even though it also revealed a watershed in

[18] Raymond Guyot, *Le Directoire et la paix de l'Europe: Des traités de Bâle à la deuxième coalition* (Paris: Félix Alcan, 1911), 601–65.
[19] See *Le Moniteur Universel* (1798), 1421; *Le Patriote français*, no. 202 (1798), 809; Raymond Guyot, "Du Directoire au Consulat. Les transitions," *Revue historique* 111:1 (1912), 1–31.
[20] Marc Lerner, *A Laboratory of Liberty: The Transformation of Political Culture in Republican Switzerland* (Leiden: Brill, 2012), 124–7.

French politics, as we will see. The framework was reminiscent of the French constitution of 1795, although the Swiss would vote less frequently, since, as in Rome, the legislators would be elected every two years. Furthermore, they had to take at least a three-month recess each year. Only legislators who had previously held office were eligible, and the executive power controlled the treasury and secret funds. It also had the right to initiate laws concerning finances, war and peace, and the right to nominate judges, generals, and public servants. It was the executive power which chose the prefects and underprefects – an institution that would stand out in French history. The judicial proceedings were simplified: there was no jury and no justice of the peace. Insofar as the bill of rights is concerned, it was even shorter than the French one. The bill obviously proclaimed natural liberty and freedom of the press, thought, and religion, the right of property, and proportional taxation, but remained silent about the right to assemble and to resist oppression. No mention was made of equality and social rights either, and the liberty of petition was hidden in Article 12. This may be surprising, considering that Switzerland's closest neighbor, Geneva, had enacted the right of the poor to receive assistance and to be educated, and adopted the social guarantee, that is to say: the protection of citizens against oppression and the right of citizens to assemble and to discuss public matters. Nevertheless, the Swiss bill was original. The bases of public good mentioned in this bill are safety and enlightenment – instead of liberty, equality, and property!

Surprisingly, two articles recalled Robespierre's and Saint-Just's principles: Article 13, which declared that "the exclusive right to property leads to slavery," and Article 14, which invited each citizen to seek "the moral ennoblement of humankind" and to nurture friendship and fraternity.[21] Admittedly, feudality was abolished and tithes could be bought – but at fifteen to twenty times their yearly value. However, this measure would be annulled more than once, being reintroduced before being suppressed again, and consequently did not win over the peasants – who had the impression that the Helvetic revolution had brought them no advantages, but only burdens.[22] Hence their resistance!

Although the Roman and the Helvetic Republics were created by the Parisian Directory, both were a direct consequence of Bonaparte's politics in

---

[21] Ochs' design and the Swiss constitution of 1798 can be found in Alfred Kölz, ed., *Quellenbuch zur neueren schweizerischen Verfassungsgeschichte* (Bern: Stämpfli, 1992), 113–25.

[22] More on Swiss opposition can be found in Lerner, *A Laboratory of Liberty*, 124–33. On tithes, see Rufer, *La Suisse et la Révolution française*.

Italy. While Switzerland formed a shortcut to Lombardy, the creation of the Roman Republic is less understandable, especially since it seemed to suggest that the whole Italian boot would soon be republicanized. However, the Directory excluded the idea of uniting Italy in a single state: "The south of Italy will not be united with the north. But it would be fine if liberty expanded everywhere."[23] In 1798, the French government was actually carrying out an adventurous policy, all the more so since the directors agreed to send Bonaparte to Egypt and did not give up the plan to invade Ireland.

For the great European powers, the inescapable conclusion was that France wanted to democratize the whole continent and establish its hegemony over more countries.[24] After they heard of the new republics and the Egyptian expedition, a wave of panic swept through the allies' states, which explains why the Austrians had no problem convincing Russia to join them in the war against democracy, while the Ottomans, until then a constant ally of France, interpreted Bonaparte's expedition as a violation of their sovereignty, and consequently enlisted in the second coalition.

Europe had more reasons to be worried, since Bonaparte had spawned emulators. In the Rhineland, General Hoche imitated his famous colleague by creating a Cisrhenane Republic. On 14 September 1797, five days before his death and a month before the Campo Formio peace treaty between France and Austria, the Cisrhenane Republic came into existence.[25] Meanwhile, Piedmont was menaced by French troops and the king finally abdicated. General Joubert would have liked to create there a Subalpine Republic, but the Directory disapproved. In autumn 1798, at last, the directors started to worry about the situation and forbade their generals to establish new republics in Italy.[26] Notwithstanding this new turn of events, General Championnet transformed the Neapolitan monarchy into a republic in January 1799, and General Serrurier democratized the Lilliputian republic of Lucca in February. Tuscany itself might have been republicanized in spite of the Treaty of Basel, and Piedmont was almost annexed to France as a result of the January 1799 referendum.[27] (Piedmont would finally be annexed in September 1802.) The dynamic in progress since Bonaparte's first victories

---

[23] Debidour, *Recueil des actes du Directoire exécutif*, vol. I, 349–50.
[24] Alfred Ritter von Vivenot, *Zur Geschichte des Rastadter Congresses* (Vienna: Braumüller, 1871), Part II, 149–52.
[25] Harouel, *Les Républiques sœurs*, 30–4.
[26] Michel Vovelle, *Les Républiques sœurs sous le regard de la Grande Nation* (Paris: L'Harmattan, 2000), 34.
[27] Harouel, *Les Républiques sœurs*, 73.

worried the other great powers so much that a strong reaction was unavoidable. In fact, 1799 signaled their revenge. The Italian republics collapsed before might of the second coalition, while Switzerland split into two fierce factions and a civil war broke out. The Austrians occupied the country and fought the French and the Swiss patriots. The only "sister" republic to stand up to the antirevolutionary wave was the Batavian Republic.[28]

Improvements and Benefits

In view of the political, economic, and social consequences, the so-called sister republics were a flagrant failure. Their alliance with the French Republic brought them continuous disorder, increased taxation, military violence and depredations, and infinite abuses of power. It is true that each new republic did not have to endure the same treatment. The Batavian Republic was more independent and better treated than the later ones. Furthermore, its legislators gave the Dutch a constitution that satisfied the general expectations, and French generals did not behave as badly there as they did in Switzerland, and above all, Italy, where the army and the army's contractors dipped into local and national coffers and their abuses and depredations alienated the populations. From the start, however, the objective of the Italian campaign was surely not to bring about the happiness of the people and the emancipation of local population, but rather to secure both peace with Austria and France's natural borders. It was not that the Directory opposed Italian patriotism, but it contemplated it pragmatically. Its view was that this patriotism should not be encouraged, even though it would be better to have the Italians as allies rather than enemies. This was the official position. As long as peace was not on the agenda, each plan for Italy indeed was fanciful and provisional. The Leoben preliminaries led to a slight shift. The Directory understood that it was better for the army's safety to organize the conquered states by giving them a sham "independent" government, which would also have the advantage of avoiding anarchy and chaos. On 4 May 1797, therefore, the Directory ordered Bonaparte to organize the Milanese – Cisalpine – Republic.

Accordingly, during the following summer the Cisalpine Republic adopted a constitution, replacing the military regulation Bonaparte had imposed. The text derived from the French one of 1795 and was adapted to the

---

[28] Jourdan, *Nouvelle histoire de la Révolution*, 464–7.

"circumstances." To facilitate the transition to a constitutional regime and to avoid "upheavals and anarchy," all political appointments would be made by the general-in-chief. Free elections would take place the following year. In spite of there being a number of common features, some constitutional articles differed from the original. The treasury, for instance, was already put into the hands of the executive power. One year later, however, the Cisalpine Republic would be constrained to modify this constitution and accept that of Rome. Popular clubs were closed, the press muzzled, elections held less frequently, and the number of departments and of legislators was reduced.[29]

Meanwhile, Genoa, which was thus threatened by Bonaparte, worked speedily to complete its constitution. The result was the Ligurian charter, which was highly different from the French one. It proclaimed sovereignty as the result of the general will, vested in the people, and described the law as an expression of the general will based on justice and happiness for all. These expressions had disappeared from the French text of 1795. Furthermore, the aim of society, it was stated, is general happiness, and the government is established solely to maintain the exercise of human rights. This nuance could have been inspired by the United States of America, which mistrusted human laws, in contrast with the French, who trusted them far too much.[30] Individual liberty, civil equality, and liberty of thought and expression are explicitly mentioned. There is also a chapter devoted to the duties of society to its members. "Social safeguarding" is described as the action of all to protect the rights of everyone. Society must give the poor the means to survive and provide state education. The treasury is still in the hands of the legislature, in contrast with the new tendency to bring it under the executive power. Constitutional amendments are requested and made by primary assemblies – not by the legislative power as in France. As the icing on the cake, there would be free societies or clubs, devoted to the sciences and arts, and educational establishments that would obviously be controlled by the authorities. As in France and the other sister republics, feudality, privilege, nobility, and the other social orders would be abolished. Civil and criminal legislation was also enacted, and a codification would standardize the laws through the whole republic. Justice would be free and public, and punishment human and impartial. Justices of the peace and juries would be

---

[29] Raymond Guyot, "Du Directoire au Consulat," *Le Moniteur Universel*, 218 (1797), 871.
[30] Stéphane Rials, *La déclaration des droits de l'homme et du citoyen* (Paris: Hachette, 1989), 364–9.

introduced. The text, which differs from the French example on important points, also shows a will to extend popular participation and to remedy unequal treatment of capital and country. That can be seen as a common feature among the new republics and as an expression of older frustrations. The very fact that Church estates would be nationalized, however, provoked a fierce uprising in September 1797: peasants, members of the lower classes, and priests rose up against the constitution, marching to shouts of *Viva Maria!*[31] The French army had to restore order.

The last sister republic to come into existence was the Neapolitan or Parthenopean Republic. Its constitution, drafted in large part by Italian lawyers such as Mario Pagano, a disciple of Giambattista Vico, is very interesting for the new elements that were introduced. Here too, the people have rights and the politicians duties. The people also have the right to resist oppression, the right to live, and the right to be educated. The text announced a limitation to wealth and a progressive taxation, and the treasury was entrusted to the legislative. There was a clear separation of the three powers, and there were two new institutions: the ephors (an antique Greek institution), who would settle disagreements between the three powers, and the censors (an ancient Roman institution), who would control national mores. Finally, each citizen was considered to be active as long as he paid a contribution.[32]

In short, the frame of the new republics' constitutions was inspired by the French text of 1795. The legislative power was divided into two councils and no longer formed a single body as it had in the French constitutions of 1791 and 1793. The executive power was shared by five members, and there was no elected president. Otherwise, all of the new republics' constitutions displayed more or less distinct features and differed from the original. First of all, the nomenclature was different and inspired by Antiquity, especially in Italy (although later in Bonaparte's Consulate as well – and that can be seen as a French imitation of foreign models). Other differences included the absence of a jury in Holland and Switzerland, and the absence of a justice of the peace in Switzerland. Likewise, the Batavian and Helvetic Republics named their bill of rights "fundamental principles" – as Madison had once called them. Indeed, one must not forget that the US precedent was still

---

[31] Giovanni Assereto, "Gouvernement et administration dans la République ligurienne," in N. C. F. van Sas, W. Frijhoff, C. Santing, and H. de Valk, eds., *Repubbliche sorelle* (Assen: Nederlands Historisch Instituut te Rome, 2002), 107–22: 115.

[32] Anna Maria Rao, *La Repubblica napoletana del 1799* (Naples: Newton, 1999), 36–9.

engraved in contemporary memories. If many European legislators rejected the *imperium in imperio* (sovereignty within sovereignty) they identified in the American constitution and did not understand its "checks and balances," they appreciated part of its federalism, since most of them were not really enthusiastic about French unity and indivisibility, which were far too absolute for them. That was especially the case in Holland and Switzerland, which had always been a (con)federative union. Moreover, the French themselves referred to the balance of powers in the United States when they enforced the 1795 constitution. Boissy d'Anglas, a member of the Committee of the Constitution, quoted Samuel Adams (where he should have quoted John Adams) in this context. The Dutch patriots also had the US example in mind throughout their legislative debates. Owing to the lack of transcripts of Italian parliamentary discussions, it is impossible to ascertain the references made to the American example by Italian legislators. What is clear is that they had a greater choice of models than others thanks to their antique republican tradition. Moreover, the French model was more appropriate here than elsewhere, because most Italian patriots were longing for national unity. But, last but not least, Italians and others were convinced that they had to create their own model and to do better than the Americans or the French. Indeed, precedents provoke emulation rather than imitation![33]

The last constitutions of 1798–1799 revealed above all that the French example was outdated. That is why it would be wrong to speak in this context of an imitation of the French constitution of 1795, as most historians do.[34] By a strange irony of fate, the French themselves started this process. The repetitive "coups" they launched at home persuaded them to change their constitution. They had not done so in 1797 – after 18 Fructidor – and regretted it. These regrets explain why they experimented elsewhere. The "sister" republics thus became a "research laboratory."[35] Henceforth, the executive power was given far more power, gaining control over the treasury, while the legislature was weakened, since it had to go into recess for three or four months each year. Elections were no longer held annually, in order to avoid popular unrest. Popular societies and clubs were prohibited, while juries and justices of the peace were no longer considered necessary.

---

[33] Marcel Gauchet, *La Révolution des droits de l'homme* (Paris: Gallimard, 1989), 56–9; Rao, "L'expérience révolutionnaire italienne," 397.

[34] I fully agree here with Antonino de Francesco, "La constitution de l'an III et les Républiques jacobines italiennes," in Van Sas et al., eds., *Repubbliche sorelle*, 97–106.

[35] Guyot, "Du Directoire au Consulat." Here, I am building on Guyot and my earlier studies.

Likewise, a special control on the judicial power, called the *tribunal de forfaiture*, was introduced in Rome and consequently in the Cisalpine Republic. This institution jeopardized the independence of judges and revealed a deep distrust of them. Finally, as mentioned above, social rights were eliminated from the constitutions drawn up by the French, whereas they were maintained in the freely drafted texts. All these changes indicate that the French had become anxious about the influence of the people and the judges, and that they were displeased by their own organization of powers. Pierre Claude François Daunou, who was to become one of the drafters of the Constitution of Year VIII, argued in this context that "authority had to be rebuilt without lapsing into despotism."[36] Bonaparte had an even more authoritarian view, in due course correcting and betraying Daunou's plan. What survived in 1800 from the democratic years was the near-universal suffrage at the first degree. Bonaparte would add the referendum and maintain meritocratic equality. The bill of rights would vanish, and with it, all liberties and social rights.

The daughter republics had to prove their gratitude to their liberators by supporting a French army on the pretense that these soldiers would reestablish order and put an end to the revolution. To explain this request, the French invoked the example of the Batavian Republic, where French troops intervened several times to crush uprisings against local authorities. Even in the Netherlands, where the population would have needed "more spur than rein," the government was several times threatened by popular uprisings.[37] Revolts threatened time and again the stability of the Cisalpine, Ligurian, and Roman Republics. In Switzerland, regular uprisings took place in the Catholic cantons, where the priests hated a constitution that jeopardized their influence and nullified their resources. In Geneva, the first democratic republic on the continent after France, two successive revolutionary tribunals were active, now judging their old leaders, now sentencing radicals, or eliminating aristocrats.[38] The aggressive actions of the Dutch and the Genevans against their old elites were surprising. The Patriots did indeed want to take revenge on the men who were responsible for their former

---

[36] On authoritarianism as a result of revolutions, see Wim Klooster, *Revolutions in the Atlantic World: A Comparative History* (New York: New York University Press, 2009), 165–70.
[37] Jourdan, *La Révolution batave*.
[38] Jourdan, *Nouvelle histoire de la Révolution*, Part II; Michael Broers, *The Napoleonic Empire in Italy, 1796–1814* (Basingstoke: Palgrave Macmillan 2005), 41–71.

exile. General Soult discovered the same thirst for revenge in Switzerland, where the cantons despised each other. Italy was no exception.[39]

Civil War and Terror

Obviously, each revolution triggers a civil war and terrorizes the protagonists. Inhabitants, neighbors, friends, and families feud with each other, giving rise to terrible hate and taking of revenge. The new republics lived through such a crisis. After France, Geneva was the first to experience factional struggles. In this small republic, 3.45 percent of the population fell victim to a political trial or legal proceedings. Eleven citizens were slaughtered in the town of Geneva – a terrorizing reminder of the Parisian September massacres. However, most of the suspects had left the country and were condemned in absentia. Jacques Necker, a former minister of Louis XVI, for instance, was sentenced to exile for life.[40] In the Batavian Republic, popular uprisings went hand in hand with factional struggles. No figures are available, except that the coup of January 1798 sent about twenty federalist and moderate legislators to jail. After the second coup in June, the moderates took their revenge and prosecuted their enemies even more furiously. In that context, an exceptional law was enacted, which looked, strangely enough, like that of the so-called Jacobin "Terror."[41] In Switzerland, as mentioned above, unrest was endemic and ended up in fatal fights. There too, severely coercive laws were enforced.[42] In 1799, during the Austrian occupation, the country was divided into two camps: the first included patriots and the French; the second, counterrevolutionaries and the Austrians. This second camp was even stronger than the first, which had to flee its capital and could have been slaughtered if General Masséna had not won the war. This intense division reemerged in 1802, when Bonaparte called his troops back. A new civil war broke out. Here too, there are no figures for the number of victims, but two examples give an idea of the intensity of violence: in the village of

---

[39] *Mémoires du maréchal-général Soult*, 3 vols. (Paris: Librairie D'Amyot, 1854), vol. II, 70–1.
[40] Édouard Burnet, *Le premier tribunal révolutionnaire genevois, juillet–août 1794: Études critiques* (Geneva: Julien, 1925).
[41] About those terrors, see Jourdan, *Nouvelle histoire de la Révolution*, 496–512. For the Dutch terror, see *Nieuwe Nederlandsche Jaerboeken* (1798), vol. II, 534–8 and the law's translation in French in Annie Jourdan, "Amsterdam en revolution. Un jacobinisme batave?," *Working Papers European Studies Amsterdam* 5 (2006), 43–4, available at www.uva.nl/en/discipline/european-studies/research/working-papers/working-papers.html.
[42] *Bulletin officiel du Directoire helvétique*, 10 vols. (1799), vol. VI, 221.

Uri, 3.7 percent of the men and 1 percent of the overall population were mortally wounded. In the Nidwald, 386 persons died in the uprising of September 1798.[43] The situation was even worse in Italy. Uprisings followed one another – in Rome, Genoa, Venice, and Naples – claiming many French and Italian victims. At Easter 1797, for instance, 2,000 people were left dead or wounded in Verona. Marching to cries of *Viva Maria!*, peasants and priests were often the first to revolt, but the urban lower classes were also involved. Like the residents of the Inner Swiss cantons, they rejected the new constitutions and assaulted French soldiers and Italian patriots alike. The French army retaliated just as fiercely, as shown by its severe reprisals in Verona or the village of Binasco, which was entirely destroyed by Bonaparte. There were also brutal military lootings in rebel towns such as Pavia. Violence was frequent and rough. The bloody repression of Neapolitan, Piedmontese, Roman, and Milanese patriots by their king or prince proves that the traditional authorities were not milder. To this endemic violence can be added the acrimonious little wars that the new Italian republics were waging with each other for territorial expansion.[44]

Popular, military, or judicial acts of violence, whether they were spontaneous or official, thus did not spare the diverse countries engaged in revolution. They were bloodier and crueler, in a sense, because there was no institution or power to regulate them. Violence meted out by the traditional authorities was even rougher because of old-fashioned judicial laws such as those of torture and corporal punishment. Nevertheless, the French Revolution is the only one which entered history as a regime of "Terror," because of its revolutionary tribunal and its guillotine. And yet, the Revolutionary Tribunal in Paris tried to rationalize and limit revolutionary violence by taking responsibility for it, while the guillotine meant progress in humane execution. The very fact that it was public – and not secret, like the *ancien régime*'s justice had been – might have been interpreted as a form of dissuasive repression or coercion. But, until recently, historians did not interpret it in this way.

Consequently, although each western or Atlantic revolution has accumulated a lot of victims, historians have not tried to count and estimate their

---

[43] Anton von Tillier, *Histoire de la République helvétique depuis sa fondation en 1798 jusqu'à sa dissolution en 1803*, 2 vols. (Geneva and Paris: Cherbulliez et Cie., 1846).

[44] Anna Maria Rao, "Révolution et Contre-Révolution pendant le Triennio italien (1796–1799)," in Jean-Clément Martin, ed., *La Contre-Révolution en Europe* (Rennes: Presses universitaires de Rennes, 2001), 233–40.

number, except for those killed by the French during their so-called "Terror." Nonetheless, some figures are known, especially for the American War of Independence, whose dead amounted to 0.9 to 1.52 percent of the population.[45] In France, the percentage was between 1.15 and 1.9 percent. However, in comparison with England's Glorious Revolution of the seventeenth century, in which 3.7 percent of Englishmen, 6 percent of the Scots, and 40 percent of the Irish were killed, these figures show that the "Terror" period was more dissuasive than deadly – except in the Vendée or in Saint-Domingue, where the civil war reached its peak.[46] Be that as it may, the Parisian tribunal sent about 2,600 persons to the guillotine, which is certainly not insignificant. But when we realize that the total population of France at the time was 26 million, it is not that many. This figure can be compared to the casualties in Verona of April 1797 and is less than Bonaparte's 3,000 victims in Jaffa. One can reasonably argue that revolutionary justice made it possible to avoid the worst: a global civil war between Frenchmen. Think of the civil war in the Vendée (with between 0.8 and 1 percent casualties) and the victims of Saint-Domingue (30 to 33 percent of the overall population), or even the wild massacres of 1795–1799 in which thousands of people were murdered without any form of trial in Lyon, Marseille, Nîmes, Tarascon, and other towns.[47] The same was true for Italy and Switzerland, although not for the Batavian Republic, since a majority there was aligned with the Patriots. In short, and even though the forms and intensities are different, each revolution brings about a lot of violence and casualties. Talleyrand knew it, since it was he who advised that the young republics should be protected with French soldiers against their internal enemies. He was right: the presence of the French army in Holland, Switzerland, and Italy made it possible for the new regimes to establish themselves without too many problems and to be protected from factional strife. While they were feared and hated for their depredations, and although they alienated foreign populations from the French Republic, these troops were the true protectors of European patriots. Once they were gone, domestic revenge occurred on a large scale, as in Milan in 1799, when 3,000 Italian republicans were put in jail, or in Naples

---

[45] Holger Hoock, *Scars of Independence: America's Violent Birth* (New York: Crown, 2017); Jourdan, *Nouvelle histoire de la Révolution*, 475–9, 572–4. See also Klooster, *Revolutions in the Atlantic World*, 162–5.
[46] Jonathan Scott, *England's Troubles: Seventeenth-Century English Political Instability in European Context* (Cambridge: Cambridge University Press, 2000), 47–8.
[47] Thanks to Jeremy Popkin and Bernard Gainot for the figures on Saint-Domingue. On the so-called White Terror, see Jourdan, *Nouvelle histoire de la Révolution*, 308–13.

where all of the patriots were hounded down and executed, despite the earlier promises that they would be amnestied.[48]

Conclusion

Latent or effective civil wars; violence and murder; factional strife and national chaos; military abuses and lootings; exceptional justice ... all this does not mean that revolutions brought only disillusion. In contrast with the historians who think that it would have been better had the French Revolution been avoided, and that successive reforms would have been preferable, we have to admit that in France, at least, the achievements were highly valuable, and the French recipients were attached to the new order.[49] From a political viewpoint, they obtained meritocratic equality instead of heredity and venality, and the right to choose their representatives and vote. Laws were made by an elected body and no longer by a single individual, and above all, laws were now written and accessible to everyone. Liberty of the press, liberty of expression, and freedom of religion were recognized – and from time to time respected. Property was liberated from feudal constraints, and national estates had been redistributed among individuals. More than 30 percent of the peasants received a piece of land of some kind, and the abolition of corporations signified the liberty to work everywhere. From a legal viewpoint, many improvements were introduced, such as the standardization of the legal system – civil code, penal code, criminal code – and the suppression of torture and (in France) corporal punishment. Justice was now public and free. With the secularization of civil laws and civil society, divorce was made possible and civil status became independent from the Church. From a cultural viewpoint, the Revolution encouraged and favored public education for everyone; it spawned the creation of national museums, and of a national art that no longer addressed exclusively an elite, but instead addressed all citizens – French or not French. Admittedly, in contrast with the prior French constitutions, the 1795 text was less generous regarding social rights. But, although it did not discuss the right to work and to live, it still maintained the right to be educated and established elementary schools for children. This was no small feat, certainly compared with the United States, where, despite Jefferson's wishes, the states did not bother to involve

[48] Rao, *La Repubblica napoletana*.
[49] See Palmer, *The World of the French Revolution*, on the myths about the French Revolution.

themselves in public education and did not speak about social rights. Most of the state constitutions did announce that they would seek to bring happiness to their citizens and to respect the natural rights of men, but the financial situation of the young republic provoked unjust expropriations of farmers, while the promise of plots of land made to volunteer soldiers was not fulfilled. These injustices provoked several uprisings and led to the constitution of 1787, which obviously was an American Thermidor, and signified a democratic regression. That regression would become even more perceptible with the enforcement of the Alien and Sedition Acts of 1798.

In the "sister" republics, the improvements were more or less similar, although the sale of national estates was not as egalitarian as in France, and the tithes had to be bought. Both measures favored the wealthy and not the peasants or the lower urban classes. The corporations were suppressed on paper, but they resisted at least until the 1810s or 1820s, as in the Netherlands. In Italy, religious liberty was introduced, but Catholicism was favored. It remained the prevailing religion in various countries, while divorce was not implemented everywhere. Justice, which hitherto had always been secret, became public, torture disappeared, and codification was planned. In Rome, the civil code was ready just before the republic fell into Austrian hands. Public education was also a priority in all these new republics. The most accomplished educational system was the Dutch one, which became a model for other countries. More than Directorial France, the Batavian and Italian republics cared about the duties of society toward its members, and not only about the social duties of citizens. Naples, for instance, planned to control the representatives and the public mores. All new republics had a broad suffrage at the first degree and a written constitution that served as a bastion against arbitrary rule. These great advances had been impossible without revolution. Where the restoration destroyed them, they remained on the agenda, as in Italy, Germany, Portugal, Spain, and Greece, which tried to finally put an end to their Old Regime in the 1820s, and above all in the 1840s during the "Springtime of the Peoples."

To conclude, interactions between revolutions were legion, including the American Revolution, which became a model in the 1780s, even though the French Revolution soon overshadowed this precedent. However, the North American bills of rights and constitutions were well-known in Europe, even in Poland, whose constitution was inspired by them. But American federalism was not really appreciated, and was soon rejected as an *imperium in imperio*. The Europeans – with the obvious exception of Britain – did not appreciate their "checks and balances" either and refused to introduce a president, who reminded them of their prince or king. In fact, while they esteemed the American bills of rights and the Declaration of Independence, they did not understand the federal constitution. It was not that all European patriots desired a French-style centralism. Some of them preferred a "modified" or "decentralized unity."[50] Each republic was also divided about the degree of democracy to introduce. If they had been really free to choose, it seems that the young republics would have been more democratic than France. The legislation of Naples, Holland, Genoa, and Geneva provides ample proof of their predilection for a democratic system. They engaged with the 1793 constitution rather than that of 1795. Switzerland was a different case: La Harpe and Ochs wanted to enforce a constitution as soon as possible to avoid the chaos they had seen in the Batavian Republic. First, they needed a constitutional text, and then the revolution would happen. Like Bonaparte, in a way, they wished for a revolution without revolution, but they accepted the idea that their constitution would be soon modified.[51]

Transnational perspectives make it possible not only to compare the western and Atlantic revolutions with each other, but also to discover the particular features of each of them. By contrasting them, the historian can find out what would otherwise not be discernible. The best example is perhaps the discovery that Directorial France tried out in foreign countries the laws and institutions it wanted to implement at home. Such an approach shows that each revolution had its own priorities and that none of them truly imitated the "mother" republic. Although the constitutional framework was similar to the French text, there were plenty of articles that diverged from the initial model, often explained as stemming from different national characters. A global history of revolutions would be unable to bring out these divergences rooted in national identity. This explains why the Age of Revolutions is still portrayed as partly American and partly French. What this chapter has shown is that in spite of French interventionism, the Dutch, Swiss, and Italian revolutions all thrived with original features of their own.

---

[50] Jourdan, *La Révolution batave*, 157–63.
[51] Frédéric César de La Harpe, *Correspondance*, 4 vols. (Neuchâtel: La Baconnière, 1982–2004), vol. I, 245, 402–3, vol. II, 99–103, 383–5.

PART III

★

HAITI

22

Overview of the Haitian Revolution

ROBERT D. TABER

> The Constituent Assembly itself, overcome by tasks too heavy for it, would allow itself to be unhappily influenced by movements and changes in opinion, now for, now against emancipation. These fluctuations will cast their repercussions on some difficult legislation, which in its turn will provoke both outbursts of enthusiasm and regrettable errors of judgment, but which will nonetheless lead eventually to the triumph of the ideals of Revolution, unfortunately for France, at the expense of her most prosperous colony.[1]

In 1925, Anna Julia Cooper completed her Sorbonne doctoral thesis on French metropolitan debates over the future of slavery during the years of revolution. Cooper's life itself was an indication of the stakes central to the Haitian Revolution. Born with slave status in North Carolina, Cooper had a distinguished career as a writer, organizer, and educator before arriving at the Sorbonne, and is considered a germinal figure in Black feminism.

Cooper's composite of three ideas – triumph of the ideals of the Revolution, unfortunate results for France, and the loss of France's most prosperous colony – drew on ideas popularized by Haitian and African American historians. While many white French and US writers could only see the loss of "prosperity," Cooper recognized that the Haitian Revolution achieved the greatest fulfillment of certain aspects of the Age of Revolutions: colonial representation in the metropole, home rule, "creole" identity, dramatic shifts in landholding, and, most significantly, the end of chattel slavery, achieved through a war of liberation. While at times the French government cooperated with these changes, or ratified them after the fact, the war of liberation from France became essential to preserving the gains of Haiti's revolution.

---

[1] Anna Julia Cooper, *Slavery and the French and Haitian Revolutionists*, trans. Frances Richardson Keller (London: Rowman and Littlefield, 2006), 39–40.

The Haitian Revolution also represents a turning point in the broader Age of Revolutions. White French and US responses to its successes prompted many revolutionaries in those countries to curtail their ideas about the universalism of revolution. Broad-based liberation from chattel slavery, however, increased the number of people free from slavery and served as a continuing reminder of the possibility of emancipation while pressing key questions about the proper structure of reconstruction. Haiti was also the first independent state in the Caribbean and Latin America, and the first in the Western Hemisphere to be led by people of African descent. Haitian approaches to governance also paralleled French, Latin American, and US debates about monarchy and authority, liberty and empire, and popular sovereignty and social order.

The first state to eliminate slavery and maintain that elimination, Haiti has long been a topic of fascination, misreading, and debate. This chapter provides a brief introduction to the colonial order France built, enslaved resistance, the entwined histories of the Haitian and French revolutions, the achievement of liberation, the political order introduced by Toussaint Louverture and Napoleon Bonaparte's perfidy, the victory won by the Haitian Army (Armée Indigène) and Jean-Jacques Dessalines, and foreign responses to the new state. In 1789, chattel slavery was a legal and economic technology that was simultaneously over 2,000 years old and thoroughly modern, hegemonic in its social power. Finding resilience and exercising creativity within it were achievements; overturning it was a world-historical triumph that refashioned the Atlantic system.

In 1789 French Saint-Domingue (colonial Haiti) seemed an unlikely candidate for revolution or liberation. While the Maroons in Jamaica and the Ndyuka in Suriname had forced Great Britain and the Dutch, respectively, to recognize their territorial autonomy earlier in the eighteenth century, those fleeing slavery in Saint-Domingue received no similar recognition and had to be on the lookout for patrols staffed by free men of color.[2] A treaty of extradition between Saint-Domingue and the Spanish colony of Santo Domingo made self-liberation through flight even more difficult. Uprisings were also infrequent, and none on the scale of Tacky's War of 1760, which also occurred in Jamaica. The most notable moment of resistance to slavery, a poisoning scare blamed on the fugitive leader François Mackandal, ended

---

[2] Jean Fouchard, *Les marrons de la liberté* (Port-au-Prince: H. Deschamps, 1988); Crystal Eddins, "'Rejoice! Your Wombs Will Not Beget Slaves!' Marronnage as Reproductive Justice in Colonial Haiti," *Gender & History* 32:3 (2020), 562–80.

with his death by execution in 1758, though some colonists continued to fear poisoning, and the enslaved told stories about Mackandal escaping execution by turning into a mosquito.³ The colonial government worried far more about placating white colonists, particularly enslavers. Historians debate what to call those who held others captive to exploit their labor, whether one should refer to them as slaveowners, slaveholders, enslavers, planters, or, less-favored, masters. I use enslavers throughout to highlight that keeping someone in chattel slavery was a continuing process involving surveillance, violence, coercion, financial capital, and the support of the colonial state.⁴

The name "Haiti" is steeped in history and meaning, drawing on insurgents' ideas about the locale's Taíno past and the ravages of colonialism. At this site of the first Spanish fort in the Americas, with French towns built over, and named for, the Spanish settlements that had replaced Taíno cities, the past was never far away. As the early Haitian national writer, the baron de Vastey described: "Everywhere I step, everywhere I look, I see shards, vases, utensils, figurines, the forms of which bear the imprint and the traces of art's infancy. In more remote and solitary locations, in the caves of inaccessible mountains, I come across skeletons still intact, human bones scattered about and blanched over time, and I tremble."⁵ Or, as Jean-Jacques Dessalines put it, "Yes, I have saved my country – I have avenged America."⁶ For the early leaders, calling their new state Haiti was a restoration of one Taíno name for the island. The battle over memory, of narrative and counternarrative, is central to the history of the colony, the revolution, and the nation.

---

³ Charles Frostin, *Les révoltes blanches à Saint-Domingue aux 17ᵉ et 18ᵉ siècles (Haïti avant 1789)* (Paris: L'École, 1975); John D. Garrigus, *Before Haiti: Race and Citizenship in French Saint-Domingue* (New York: Palgrave Macmillan, 2006), Chapter 4. Mackandal has inspired a large literature because of his salience as a figure of liberation. See Pierre Pluchon, *Vaudou: Sorciers empoisonneurs: De Saint-Domingue à Haiti* (Paris: Karthala, 1987); Trevor Burnard and John Garrigus, *The Plantation Machine: Atlantic Capitalism in French Saint-Domingue and British Jamaica* (Philadelphia: University of Pennsylvania Press, 2016), Chapter 5; Sylviane Diouf, *Servants of Allah: African Muslims Enslaved in the Americas* (New York: New York University Press, 1998); Carolyn E. Fick, *The Making of Haiti: The Saint Domingue Revolution from Below* (Knoxville: The University of Tennessee Press, 2004).

⁴ See P. Gabrielle Foreman et al. (community-sourced document), "Writing about Slavery/Teaching about Slavery: This Might Help," https://docs.google.com/document/d/1A4TEdDgYslX-hlKezLodMIM71My3KTNozxRvoIQTOQs.

⁵ Baron de Vastey, *The Colonial System Unveiled*, trans. Chris Bongie (Liverpool: Liverpool University Press, 2014), 86.

⁶ "Liberty or Death. Proclamation. Jean Jacques Dessalines," in *Connecticut Herald*, New Haven, Connecticut, 12 June 1804, vol. 1, no. 33, p. 2, https://haitidoi.com/2013/08/02/i-have-avenged-america.

The Colonial Order

The Spanish colonizers introduced sugar cultivation and chattel African slavery to the island they alternately called Hispaniola or Santo Domingo (for the largest city and capital) by the early 1500s. In 1521, twenty Wollof captives bent on liberation burned Diego Colón's sugar plantation before taking refuge in the mountains, eventually joining the rebellion then being led by the Taíno cacique Enrique. The various mountain ranges of Hispaniola would be a perpetual site of refuge for people freeing themselves. In addition to raising livestock and growing crops, these fugitives from slavery also destroyed up to two-thirds of Spain's sugar plantations on the island.[7] The Spanish called them *cimarrones*, from the Taíno word *simaran* for animals that returned to the wild – the origin of the English word "maroon."

By the end of the sixteenth century, the Spanish settlements on the western, mountainous side of Hispaniola faced three challenges. Removed from the *flota* system that protected the silver and gold flowing from Peru and Mexico to Europe, they had little legal access to metropolitan markets. Smugglers and pirates from rival powers, including France, filled the commercial gap. And the self-liberated continued to evade the colonial order. Frustrated, the Spanish colonial governor ordered the evacuation of the western third of the island. Refugees soon moved in. Famous for their hunting and rough camps, they took their name from the Taíno style they used to cook meat: *boucaniers* or buccaneers.

The French state arrived after the buccaneers and the freebooters, with the intent of creating a majority-white colony that would focus on tobacco cultivation, absorbing out-migration of poor white men from the eastern Caribbean, and returning profits to the French West India Company. Colonists disagreed. Enslaved Africans provided labor as early as the 1650s, and worked in sugar by the 1680s. Colonists worried about conspiracies led by Hispanicized men of color while enforcing a severe work regimen that kept most enslaved workers ill-fed. Laws required enslavers to provide food, clothing, and religious instruction to the enslaved, but adherence was fitful. By the 1720s, Saint-Domingue was a key part of France's first overseas empire, with workers from one continent brought to labor in a second to produce luxury goods consumed in a third. By 1789, it was the pillar of the Atlantic system, in which 400,000 enslaved workers produced greater coffee

---

[7] Robert C. Schwaller, "Contested Conquests: African Maroons and the Incomplete Conquest of Hispaniola, 1519–1620," *The Americas* 75:4 (2018), 609–38: 620.

and sugar exports than any other place in the world, more valuable than Brazil's gold or Mexico's silver production, underwriting the French navy.[8] The labor regime was brutal: merchants had transported around 800,000 captive women, men, and children to the colony over the course of the eighteenth century, of whom 700,000 survived the voyage.

The French government saw the colony as a significant part of its Caribbean and larger colonial strategy. A military government, headed by a governor-general, oversaw two garrisons, and an intendant supervised tax collection and the creation of irrigation works to enable sugar-growing. Carved by mountains into two large plains, many smaller ones, and the Artibonite plateau, the geography made the interior forbidding to colonists, though some overland trade brought in mules from Spanish Santo Domingo. The port towns boasted segregated theaters with enslaved musicians, gambling halls, and a scientific society. French visitors found the white colonists to be irreligious, vain, sex-obsessed, and consumed with obtaining enough of a fortune to return to France as soon as possible. Landowners in nearby Spanish colonies envied the amount of government investment, particularly in facilitating the slave trade and sugar cultivation. Disease shortened life expectancies for colonists, free residents, and the enslaved.

The enslaved, who primarily came from west or west central Africa, though a growing contingent had grown up in the colony or elsewhere in the Caribbean, experienced different circumstances depending on where in the colony they were held. Captivity in a city could mean greater surveillance and confrontation with the casual brutality of the colonial state, including executions. A few worked in skilled trades, sometimes enabling self-purchase. Workers on sugar plantations had to grow their own food on individual plots, one day a week, sometimes traveling several miles to do so, but were more likely to encounter people who shared their language and culture. Coffee farms, dotting the mountains and beginning the process of deforestation and social erosion, usually had greater availability of food but more social isolation.

Colonial Haiti also had a growing population of people of mixed race, often but not always the children of European men and African or Afro-Haitian women. The circumstances and possibilities for residents of mixed race varied. Some became enslavers and landholders themselves; others

---

[8] David Geggus, "Saint-Domingue on the Eve of the Haitian Revolution," in David Patrick Geggus and Norman Fiering, eds., *The World of the Haitian Revolution* (Bloomington: Indiana University Press, 2009), 3–20: 3.

worked as laundresses and artisans; others remained enslaved; a few, such as Thomas-Alexandre Dumas and André Rigaud, received education in France. Over the course of the eighteenth century, many white colonists shifted their definitions of honor and respectability to lower the salience of traditional French markers and heighten racial barriers, including sumptuary laws, barring free men of color from the professions, and forcing free men of color to bear most of the burdens of militia service and conducting patrols. Some free women of color had economic and familial power in the cities and towns, often earning a living as landladies, while free men of color tended to exert leadership in rural settings and enjoyed greater recognition from the colonial state as heads of household. In the 1780s, free resident of color and enslaver/planter Julien Raimond began a campaign for greater recognition of rights.[9]

The World of the Enslaved

Enslaved people made up the overwhelming majority of the colonial population across the eighteenth century, and did what they could to survive, resist, and create. While opportunities for formal manumission existed, only a few of the enslaved, around 2 percent, would obtain formal liberation at some point in their lifetime, though the planter class pressured the colonial state to limit such availability and that of the informal "liberté de savanne."[10] Enslaved people also pursued self-liberation, seeking refuge in the mountains or passing as free residents in towns. Laws in the 1770s demanded that notaries public and priests ask for documentation from people of color before describing them as "free," and the state-administered newspaper published notices of fugitives and lists of captives held in town jails. While enslaved men new to the colony attempted escape most frequently, enslaved people born in the colony had the greatest chance for success. An extradition treaty

---

[9] For more on free people of color, see Garrigus, *Before Haiti*; Dominique Rogers, "Les libres de couleur dans les capitales de Saint-Domingue: Fortune, mentalités et intégration à la fin de l'Ancien Régime (1776–1789)" (Ph.D. dissertation, Université de Bordeaux III, 2009); Stewart King, *Blue Coat or Powdered Wig: Free People of Color in Pre-Revolutionary Saint-Domingue* (Athens, GA: University of Georgia Press, 2001). For perceptions of free people of color, see Doris Garraway, *The Libertine Colony: Creolization in the Early French Caribbean* (Durham, NC: Duke University Press, 2005); Yvonne Fabella, "Inventing the Creole Citizen: Race, Sexuality, and the Colonial Order in Pre-Revolutionary Saint-Domingue" (Ph.D. dissertation, State University of New York-Stony Brook, 2008).

[10] Garrigus, *Before Haiti*, Chapter 1; Malick Ghachem, *The Old Regime and the Haitian Revolution* (New York: Oxford University Press, 2012), Chapter 2.

signed with Spanish Santo Domingo in 1777 made self-liberation more difficult, but some early leaders of the Saint-Domingue rebellion, most notably Jean-François and Charlotte from the Papillon farm, lived as fugitives before the revolution.

Enslaved men and women did not need exposure to "Enlightenment" ideas to decide to resist their captivity and exploitation. Overt resistance began on slave ships, with rebellions and suicide, as captives preferred death to a lifetime of slavery. Degrading, brutal punishments, including floggings, having to wear muzzles and yokes, sexual violence, and tortures large and small clarified the stakes of evading and subverting the power of enslavers. While some enslaved men sought positions as crew foremen (drivers) to protect their fellow workers and/or enhance their own authority, other men, women, and children pursued other creative ways to protect themselves.

The enslaved found various ways to resist and to undercut the power of their captors. While many colonists dismissed fears about poisoning, others took the threat seriously. In the 1780s, Marie Kingué, a Kongolese woman, convinced her captor that she could detect poisoners, or "Mackandals." While those she accused experienced floggings, being burned alive, or being sold away, Kingué gained wealth and authority before the resulting panic culminated in her arrest.[11] Other enslaved people feigned illness, such as a young adolescent named Telemaque, who had been enslaved to a ship captain before the captain sold him to a sugar planter. After the sale, Telemaque experienced a series of epileptic seizures, so much so that the captain had to take him back from the planter, after which the epilepsy did not reemerge.[12] Work strikes, such as when forty enslaved workers led by the foremen left the Ferronnays plantation outside of Port-au-Prince to protest their treatment by new overseers, also might mitigate the worst circumstances.[13]

Creativity and resilience within slavery took many forms, including the emergence of Vodou as a set or range of spiritual practices and Kreyòl as a lingua franca. The use of provision grounds for growing food, and the ability to sell surplus in markets, enabled some of the enslaved to purchase personal effects. More time for growing food and the abolition of flogging were foci of

---

[11] Burnard and Garrigus, *The Plantation Machine*, 258–9.
[12] Douglas R. Egerton, *He Shall Go Out Free: The Lives of Denmark Vesey*, 2nd edition (Lanham: Rowman and Littlefield, 2004), 20.
[13] Paul Cheney, *Cul de Sac: Patrimony, Capitalism, and Slavery in French Saint-Domingue* (Chicago: University of Chicago Press, 2017), 79–80.

late-eighteenth-century reform efforts. Sunday evenings were times of dances and other gatherings. Vodou, which draws on west African and west central African traditions, including Christian syncretism that began in the kingdom of Kongo, provided community and promises of spiritual power and protection. By connecting certain Vodou *lwa*, or spirits, with Catholic saints, practitioners could evade the colonial gaze. In the 1780s, due to the arrival of many captives from west central Africa, the *Petwo* nation of *lwa*, more connected to ideas of firmness, tenacity, and protection, gained prominence, but even in the eighteenth century, adherents turned to *lwa* for many purposes. Kreyòl, which drew on various European and African dialects and languages for vocabulary, emerged as a common language.

Even as enslaved individuals, families, and groups pursued resistance and creation, and as some Enlightenment writers criticized slavery and colonialism, planters bristled at any attempts to curtail their authority. When a 1780s law enabled the enslaved to denounce cruelties, workers from Nicolas LeJeune's coffee plantation told the colonial judiciary about his tortures. Enslavers intimidated the courts into acquitting LeJeune. Meanwhile, rumors spread through the colony that King Louis XVI wanted to give the enslaved an extra day a week to work their provision grounds and to prohibit the use of the whip, but planters had blocked these laws from taking effect.[14]

A Revolutionary Age

The calling of the Estates-General, the emergence of the National Assembly, and the Declaration of the Rights of Man and Citizen of August 1789 raised the stakes for people living in or connected to colonial Haiti. While some had served in the French military during the US War of Independence, including a contingent of free men of color at the Battle of Savannah, most experienced the American Revolution through rumors and reports brought by North American smugglers, which tended to exaggerate colonists' victories, and dispatches from London and Paris papers. The abolition movement in France was small compared with its equivalent in Britain, and news of a revolt in Martinique, which arrived in Paris in late 1789, set back the cause of reform.[15]

---

[14] Julius Scott, *The Common Wind: Afro-American Currents in the Age of the Haitian Revolution* (London: Verso, 2018), Chapter 3.

[15] David Geggus, *The Haitian Revolution: A Documentary History* (Indianapolis: Hackett, 2014), 36.

The French abolitionist movement did include luminous figures, who found their best chance of success involved allying with free men of color from Saint-Domingue eager to achieve legal equality. In late 1788, white liberals founded the Société des Amis des Noirs (Society of the Friends of the Blacks), led by the journalist Jacques-Pierre Brissot, who would be joined by the priest Henri Grégoire and the nobles Lafayette, Condorcet, and Mirabeau.[16] Mirabeau was one of the most radical members of the National Assembly, denouncing slavery in the session and attacking the idea that Saint-Domingue's elected deputies represented the whole colony when only a few wealthy white colonists had voted for them. Free men of color residing in Paris formed the Society of American Colonists in September 1789 to press for full legal equality and the seating of deputies of color in the National Assembly. Julien Raimond and Vincent Ogé soon joined them in their lobbying. Although the society was founded exclusively by men of mixed-race descent, it soon included free Black men in the membership. Members of the society made demands for equality, though they based many claims on their European ancestry, and called for the immediate manumission of enslaved people of mixed race. (Whether to capitalize "Black" centers on the history of racialization, including racial exclusions from the rights of citizenship. I have opted to capitalize it here because of the aims and name of the Société des Amis des Noirs. This convention has been followed throughout the chapters of this Cambridge History.)[17]

Planters and defenders of slavery formed the Club Massiac to defend the rights of white colonists, including demanding special laws for Saint-Domingue and other plantation colonies. Vincent Ogé, one of Saint-Domingue's wealthiest residents of color, thought he could make common cause with the Club Massiac around key points of colonial autonomy – their shared desire for free trade, their goal of making it easier to discharge debt, and their demand of a greater ability to select colonial officials. After he met with them, Club members seized on Ogé's allusion to slave insurrection as an excuse to reject allying with planters of color. The most notable white support outside of the Amis des Noirs came from provincial Jacobin clubs, in a campaign organized by Claude Miscent, a radical white planter from Saint-Domingue's northern mountains, who sympathized with the plight of free men of color. Legislative support, however, had to wait until the National Assembly became worried about civil strife occurring within the colony.

---

[16] See Chapter 4 by Erica Johnson Edwards in this volume.
[17] See Foreman et al., "Writing about Slavery/Teaching about Slavery."

During the years 1789–1791, the colonial police state broke down. Arbitrary terrorism, including street brawls and acts of violence, occurred, as a royalist government tried to keep the sugar flowing while the rest of the free residents jockeyed for position. White planters and merchants wanted to guarantee colonial representation in the National Assembly that they would control, a greater ability to trade with the United States, and permanent recognition of colonial assemblies. About half of the white men in the colony, however, were not considered planters (*habitants*) or of similar social rank. These "little whites" (*petits blancs*), as the enslaved called them, formed "Patriot" clubs and took to the streets to defend their claims to universal white male suffrage and to attack free people of color. By the end of 1789, white landowners had soured on the idea of forming an alliance with neighbors of color, who, they feared, would soon outvote them.

In West Province, the area around Port-au-Prince, free men of color had to submit an oath of "respect, submission, and devotion to the whites." Many protested, leading to violence in which Vincent Ogé's brother was killed. Around 100 free people of color fled from the mountain parish of Grande-Rivière to the Spanish side of the island to avoid attacks from white neighbors. When Ogé returned from France, he met up with this group, and together they issued demands that the colonial government open up the professions and all administrative positions to men of color. The white-run Assembly of North Province refused, and in response raised an army to disperse Ogé's force. The Spanish authorities captured him and twenty-three of his companions and, despite guaranteeing their safety, sent them back to Cap Français, the capital of North Province, where the royal governor ordered Ogé broken on the wheel. While Ogé's force included no one of slave status, many of those who had evaded capture would link up with the insurgency after it began.

News of Ogé's execution pushed the National Assembly to pass the decree of 15 May 1791. In some ways, the decree did little: it gave the vote only to men of color who owned property and had been born with free status. But the National Assembly (1) established its right to issue legislation regarding race and civil rights in the colonies; (2) drew a line against legislating reforms of slavery; (3) alienated deputies from the colony, who campaigned successfully for its exclusion from the Constitution of 1791; and (4) went beyond what the royal governor of Saint-Domingue was willing to countenance or enforce. In response to the governor refusing to enforce the May Decree, free residents of color rebelled against the colonial government in August 1791. They defeated the white militia and royal troops. While local treaties, forced by the growing insurgency among the enslaved population, would go beyond the May Decree in granting full racial (though not gender) equality, the National Assembly remained reluctant to ratify these agreements. Only after several months of fighting did the decree of 4 April 1792, prohibiting formal systems of racial discrimination, arrive from France. By that time, enslavers, whether white or free people of color, had to confront what was already one of the largest, most successful slave insurgencies in history.

The Saint-Domingue Slave Rebellion

The causes of the start and success of the Saint-Domingue slave revolt that began on the Northern Plain in August 1791 are many and intertwined, including factors internal and external to the colony. Many enslaved people knew about the French government's efforts to curb the worst abuses by prohibiting the use of the whip, allowing them to report cruel enslavers to the judiciary, and allowing them an extra day or two to work provision grounds, efforts local enslavers blocked. The colonial administrator François Barbé-Marbois wrote of these reports and rumors, faulting the metropolitan abolitionists and "barbarous" enslavers for making it harder to preserve slavery as a general economic system. Throughout the autumn of 1789, enslaved people in colonial Haiti told a simple, and powerful, account of the storming of the Bastille, demonstrations against the feudal order, and the initial reforms passed by the French National Assembly: "the white slaves [had] killed their masters and that, now they are free, they govern themselves and have recovered possession of the land." Enslavers and the government did their best to neither confirm nor deny these rumors, for fear of spreading them.[18]

The most prominent internal factors included the divisions within free society detailed above, the availability of self-liberation through flight, and the growing presence of captives from the kingdom of Kongo in west central Africa, including young men with military experience. While many individuals and families pursued self-liberation in the decades prior to the rebellion, those who had succeeded generally avoided participation in the later rebellions.[19] The newspaper lists of caught fugitives tended to be longer than

---

[18] Geggus, *The Haitian Revolution*, 75–6.
[19] Charlton W. Yingling, "The Maroons of Santo Domingo in the Age of Revolutions: Adaptation and Evasion, 1783–1800," *History Workshop Journal* 79:1 (Spring 2015), 25–51.

advertisements for those who had succeeded, an indication that self-liberation had become so difficult that rebellion became a more attractive option. Evidence from ship itineraries, plantation lists, and other period sources also support claims that the people from the kingdom of Kongo and its environs, speakers of Kikongo, formed an plurality of enslaved people in Saint-Domingue, which was unusual compared with other places in the French Caribbean, particularly in the 1770s and 1780s. Kongolese debates about absolute versus limited monarchy, a key factor in civil wars within the kingdom of Kongo, would thus inform insurgents' attitudes about the revolution and resulting forms of governance.[20] Prior military experience would also inform insurgents' tactics and morale.

The rhythm of enslaved life, the privileges enjoyed by a few enslaved individuals, and the unifying element of Vodou all fostered coordination of the rebellion of August 1791. Most enslavers worried little about the gatherings the enslaved enjoyed on Sunday evenings, regarding them as harmless parties. On Sunday, 14 August 1791, two delegates apiece from many of the northern parishes gathered at the Lenormand plantation in Morne Rouge, close to Cap Français. By this point, one of the colony's two garrisons had deserted and tensions between white colonists and free residents of color had been building for over a year. A young delegate read the news and announced (falsely) that King Louis XVI had granted the enslaved three days a week to work their provision grounds and was sending an army to support the enslaved. Shortly thereafter, many of the leaders took part in a Vodou ceremony at Boïs Caiman presided over by Dutty Boukman, a *hougan* (priest), and Cécile Fatiman, a *mambo* (priestess), to ratify the commitment to the rebellion and access spiritual powers of protection. The use of talismans and other items designed to provide invulnerability to the rebels would be a common feature of the army of liberation. Despite some early attacks on plantations leading to interrogations, most enslavers in the area refused to believe the rumors of an imminent, large-scale rebellion.

The rebellion began in earnest on 22 August 1791, as the enslaved burned plantations, attacked enslavers, and marched on smaller port towns, with Cap Français as the ultimate goal. Enslavers and the colonial administration responded by fortifying the capital and launching a propaganda campaign

---

[20] Chris Davis, "Before They Were Haitians: Examining Evidence for Kongolese Influence on the Haitian Revolution," *Journal of Haitian Studies* 22:2 (2016), 4–36; John Thornton, "'I Am the Subject of the King of Congo': African Political Ideology and the Haitian Revolution." *Journal of World History* 4:2 (1993), 181–214.

that downplayed divisions among colonists and dehumanized the rebellion as an expression of inchoate rage, despite, or perhaps because of, its successful planning and coordination. Appealing to the National Assembly for help in putting down the rebellion, the colonial assembly described the rebels as "cannibals," a rhetorical positioning that would show up repeatedly in anti-Black descriptions of the Haitian Revolution and liberation movements in general, and which early Haitian writers would subvert.[21]

When the rebels failed to take Cap Français but strengthened their position in the northern countryside and mountains, the rebel leader Jeannot thought about what to demand of the government. In an unsent letter responding to the governor's demand for surrender, Jeannot likewise told the governor and the colonists to abandon the colony and allow the enslaved their freedom. Refusing to recognize the humanity or capabilities of the rebels, some white colonists spread rumors that white counterrevolutionaries were aiding the rebellion to undercut the National Assembly and the gains of the French Revolution. Meanwhile, Jean-François Papillon, a coach driver who had spent some time as a fugitive from slavery, and Georges Biassou, a crew foreman, displaced Jeannot. Concerned about reports that a French army would soon arrive, Papillon and Biassou tried to negotiate amnesty for the rebels and manumission for their close associates, but they and the civil commissioners the National Assembly sent to broker an end to the fighting failed to reach an agreement, and the rebellion in the north stalled with neither side gaining an advantage.

Rebellions also occurred in places beyond the Northern Plain and involved women. While free people of color in the west armed enslaved fighters they called the "Swiss," as a nod to these mercenaries (fighters they would deport to Central America after reaching a peace agreement),[22] Romaine La Prophétesse led the most notable rebellion outside of the north. A free man of color, a coffee planter and enslaver who had children with the enslaved woman Marie Rose, whom he eventually married and freed, La Prophétesse claimed to be the godson of the Virgin Mary and drew on Kongolese Christianity and Vodou as he and an unidentified woman led an army of several thousand rebels in the mountains between Léogane and

---

[21] Geggus, *The Haitian Revolution*, 81; Grégory Pierrot, *The Black Avenger in Atlantic Culture* (Athens, GA: University of Georgia Press, 2019); Marlene L. Daut, *Baron de Vastey and the Origins of Black Atlantic Humanism* (New York: Palgrave Macmillan, 2017).

[22] David Geggus, *Haitian Revolutionary Studies* (Bloomington: Indiana University Press, 2002), 99–118.

Figure 22.1 Fighting in the hills. Getty Images.

Jacmel outside of Port-au-Prince (Figure 22.1).[23] While many enslaved women took refuge in colonial towns, others joined various armies of rebellion.[24] More study is needed of Black women's experiences and ideas of gender during the revolution, including the role of marriage between enslaved women and free men as a path to emancipation.[25]

The Rise and Rule of Toussaint Louverture

By the beginning of 1792, the enslavers and the rebels in the north had entered a long period of stalemate. While contingents of the French army arrived in Saint-Domingue, soldiers fell victim to disease, ambush, and the determination of the

---

[23] Robert D. Taber, "'The Issue of Their Union': Family, Law, and Politics in Western Saint-Domingue, 1777 to 1789" (Ph.D. dissertation, University of Florida, 2015), 137–44, 309–19; Terry Rey, *The Priest and the Prophetess: Abbé Ouvière, Romaine Rivière, and the Revolutionary Atlantic World* (New York: Oxford University Press, 2017).
[24] Geggus, *The Haitian Revolution*, 91–2.
[25] Elizabeth Colwill, "'Fêtes de l'hymen, fêtes de la liberté: Marriage, Manhood, and Emancipation in Revolutionary Saint-Domingue," in Geggus and Fiering, *The World of the Haitian Revolution*, 125–55.

army of rebellion and liberation. The rebels, however, failed to take any of the major ports. White colonists, faced with the total destruction of plantation slavery, became more willing to recognize the legal equality of free men of color, making common cause to preserve the colonial order. When new Civil Commissioners, sent by the National Assembly with broad powers to enforce racial equality and put down the rebellion, arrived in the colony in September 1792, some colonists feared they planned to introduce general emancipation of the enslaved. While general emancipation, not just in Saint-Domingue but for the whole French colonial world, would be proclaimed in February 1794, it was due to a combination of factors, including the resistance and rebellion of the enslaved, the outbreak of war in Europe and the Caribbean, and the idealism of enough French politicians. Legal emancipation across the colony was not the inevitable result of a successful rebellion, as the treaties colonial powers brokered with individual groups of rebels in Jamaica and Suriname attested, nor would it match the demands of many of the insurgents.

The Civil Commissioners, Étienne Polverel and Léger Félicité Sonthonax, met with initial success after their arrival in September 1792. They supported the free residents of color, shut down colonial assemblies, deported antirevolutionary conservatives and pro-independence Patriots, and coordinated an offensive against the rebellion that forced the surrender of several thousand rebels, the seizure of several mountain camps, and the rolling back of many rebellions in the west and south.

The execution of Louis XVI and the resulting entry of Britain and Spain in the War of the First Coalition against France complicated the situation for the commissioners and provided new opportunities for the rebels. War with Britain meant it would be difficult for the French Republican forces to receive reinforcements; war with Spain meant that rebels could receive direct support as auxiliaries. Spain provided guns, uniforms, cash, and promises of freedom and land grants, building on a long-running Spanish American policy of providing shelter to refugees from slavery and earlier informal ties between Spanish officials and merchants and the insurgents. Spain also offered a king, a potent symbol of good government. As the rebel leader Macaya explained in June 1793, "I am the subject of three kings: of the King of Congo, master of all the blacks; of the King of France who represents my father; of the King of Spain who represents my mother. These three Kings are the descendants of those who, led by a star, came to adore God made man."[26]

---

[26] Thornton, "I am the Subject of the King of Congo."

The possibility of support from Britain or Spain made the white colonists far less patient with the commissioners, their sweeping power, and their support for free residents of color. In June 1793, General François-Thomas Galbaud du Fort, who had arrived in the colony the month before to serve as governor, grew impatient with Polverel and Sonthonax. He decided that the best way to save the colony for the French Republic would be to overthrow the Commissioners and their allies. Supported by a force of white sailors, he stormed Cap Français. In the resulting fighting between white colonists, Cap Français, long the ultimate target of the slave uprising, burned. Galbaud fled to the United States with many of his supporters; this was one of the main waves of refugees from Saint-Domingue to North America.[27]

Sonthonax, who earlier in his career as a journalist had supported abolition, found emancipation and embrace of the idea of freedom – though not all of the rebels' demands – the best path forward. He issued an emancipation proclamation on 29 August 1793 that also outlined a system of forced labor aimed at keeping the plantation system intact, though it prohibited the use of flogging as punishment and granted two hours a day for working provision grounds. The next month, Sonthonax organized the first multiracial elections anywhere in the Caribbean.[28]

Among the elected deputies was Jean-Baptiste Belley. Belley was born in Senegal in the 1740s and was enslaved and transported across the Atlantic while still a toddler. He grew up enslaved in colonial Haiti, eventually purchasing his freedom. During the years of fighting, he had climbed the ranks in the French National Guard, becoming an infantry captain. In Paris, Belley championed universal emancipation, which the National Assembly ratified with the decree of 16 Pluviôse (4 February 1794), which abolished slavery throughout the French colonies and made the formerly enslaved citizens. A few years later, Belley would be the subject of a now-famous

---

[27] The most detailed account of these events is Jeremy Popkin, *You Are All Free: The Haitian Revolution and the Abolition of Slavery* (New York: Cambridge University Press, 2010), particularly Chapter 6. For more on refugees to the United States, see Ashli White, *Encountering Revolution: Haiti and the Making of the Early Republic* (Baltimore: Johns Hopkins University Press, 2010); David P. Geggus, ed., *The Impact of the Haitian Revolution in the Atlantic World* (Columbia, SC: University of South Carolina Press, 2001); Alfred N. Hunt, *Haiti's Influence on Antebellum America: Slumbering Volcano in the Caribbean* (Baton Rouge: Louisiana State University Press, 1988). For the impact of Dominguan refugees and the revolution on Cuba, see Ada Ferrer, *Freedom's Mirror: Cuba and Haiti in the Age of Revolution* (New York: Cambridge University Press, 2014).

[28] For more on the question of integration in revolutionary Saint-Domingue, see Erica R. Johnson, *Philanthropy and Race in the Haitian Revolution* (New York: Palgrave Macmillan, 2018).

portrait by Anne-Louis Girodet de Roussy-Trioson, a student of famed neoclassical painter Jacques-Louis David. Belley, dressed as a deputy and shown in the three-quarters pose reserved for nobility and royalty, leans on the white marble bust of the Enlightenment philosopher and critic of colonialism Guillaume Thomas Raynal, underscoring the universal possibilities of a French–Dominguan revolution centered on liberty, reason, and republicanism.

Reality differed. Local enslavers helped Britain occupy much of the west and south. Spain conquered much of the north, inviting former planters to return. In places under French control, the emancipated resented the new labor regime and the expectation that they would work as "cultivators" on sugar estates, going on strike in retaliation if not decamping entirely to provision grounds and hillside holdings. Georges Biassou and Jean-François Papillon never joined the forces of the Republic, preferring the treatment they received from Spain. But the third-ranking leader in the northern rebellion, a middle-aged man named Toussaint Bréda, had started to build power and would shape the next seven years of the rebellion.

Toussaint had been born in colonial Haiti with slave status to African parents, but had gained his freedom almost twenty years before the revolution.[29] He continued to live on the Bréda estate where he had been enslaved, occasionally renting enslaved workers but also, like Romaine La Prophétesse, having many family members in slavery. He learned to read, and would probably have had the opportunity to meet enslaved coachmen such as Papillon, but not the wealthy white counterrevolutionaries with whom he was later accused of associating. He joined the rebellion a few months after its start, and supported Biassou and Papillon's offers for a brokered end to the fighting. Aware of Sonthonax's impending declaration of emancipation, in August 1793 Toussaint, taking the name Louverture ("the opening"), declared that general liberty was his goal, though he remained loyal to Spain for many more months.

Like other political figures, particularly those who held power for an extended time during great change, historians have debated Louverture's motivations, the mix of pragmatism and idealism in his thinking, and conservative and progressive impulses in his policies. A rash of forged documents and most of the archives of the Haitian Revolution existing in the hands of the defeated powers make these analyses even more fraught, but key themes

---

[29] See also Philippe Girard's Chapter 25 in this volume and Philippe Girard, *Toussaint Louverture: A Revolutionary Life* (New York: Basic Books, 2016).

endured throughout Louverture's public career. Skilled in military tactics and strategy, Louverture was also a savvy politician, using promises of negotiated truces and amnesty to expand the territory under his control and to rise in the ranks. His transition to alliance with the French Republic was a process – not a moment – that included playing off the Spanish and British for months with promises of support. Once aligned with the French, he maneuvered rivals for power, including Sonthonax, out of the colony, even while continuing to reclaim the colony for France.

Louverture sought to preserve the gains of the revolution, including the formal end of slavery, while continuing the plantation system. He also had to contend with a French government that was becoming more conservative, as it sought a way to reassert French rule. For a time, Louverture's approach of pursuing his own governing instincts, marginalizing rivals, and pledging loyalty to France continued to work. He negotiated an end to Britain's occupation. When the French administrative agent General Théodore Hédouville objected to being cut out of the talks, Louverture expelled him from the colony. Louverture also pursued his own foreign policy, arranging trade agreements with Britain, which was still at war with France, and the United States and disallowing French privateers. He warned Britain of French efforts to incite a rebellion among enslaved people in the colony of Jamaica, perhaps believing that the response to such a rebellion would threaten liberation in Saint-Domingue.

Louverture controlled the north and west provinces but had to contend with André Rigaud in the south. In some ways similar – they were both men of color who had held free status before the revolution and had risen to positions of prominence in the French Republic's military – Louverture had lived much closer to the world of the enslaved, while Rigaud's white father had seen to his education in France. In a series of attacks, reprisals, and a struggle between regions known both as the War of the South and the War of the Knives, Louverture triumphed in July 1800, though he lost important support among other *anciens libres*, or individuals who had enjoyed free status prior to 1791. Rigaud, like so many of Louverture's erstwhile rivals, went into exile in France. To further consolidate his power, Louverture invaded the eastern portion of the island, in violation of French orders.

While Louverture had invited white planters back to the colony and had *anciens libres* advising his government, he came to depend most on a small circle of formerly enslaved men who had been born in colonial Haiti. These officers, including Jean-Jacques Dessalines, who had waged a vicious campaign against Rigaud, leased plantations abandoned by those who had fled the colony. For the most part, they supported the increased militarization of the labor regime and Louverture's laws against absenteeism, policies he pursued because the colonial government depended on export taxes on sugar and coffee. In a groundbreaking step for a colonial governor, Louverture promulgated a constitution that enshrined the system of forced labor, Roman Catholicism, loyalty to France, the end of slavery, and his right to be Governor-General for life, including naming his successor. Cultivators in the north rebelled against Louverture's government, for which Louverture blamed his nephew Moyse. Louverture linked what he perceived to be poor morals, particularly of adolescents who had come of age without doing field labor, with the spirit of rebellion, and sought the moral regeneration of the colony. Louverture's 1801 Constitution is a benchmark in African American literature and was the most-read document by a Black author in the United States until the publication of *Narrative of the Life of Frederick Douglass, an American Slave* in 1845.[30]

The War of Independence

Napoleon Bonaparte had grown tired of Louverture's pursuits. Bonaparte had come to power with the support of many who had profited from slavery, and he sought the reassertion of French control over sugar and coffee production, even if it meant the reestablishment of slavery. Preliminary peace negotiations with Britain provided the French government with the opportunity to place a definitive check on Louverture.[31] In late 1801, Bonaparte dispatched his brother-in-law Charles Victor Emmanuel Leclerc and almost 30,000 troops to Saint-Domingue to reclaim control.

Leclerc arrived in Saint-Domingue in February 1802 to discover that General Henry Christophe, on Louverture's orders, refused his initial entry. Leclerc repeated Bonaparte's promise that the people in the colony would remain French and remain free. He also promised Louverture's deputies, including Christophe and Dessalines, that they would retain their ranks in the French army.

---

[30] Michael J. Drexler and Ed White, "The Constitution of Toussaint: Another Origin of African American Literature," in Gene Andrew Jarrett, ed., *A Companion to African American Literature* (Malden, MA: Wiley-Blackwell, 2010), 59–74.

[31] Margaret B. Crosby-Arnold, "A Case of Hidden Genocide? Disintegration and Destruction of People of Color in Napoleonic Europe, 1799–1815," *Atlantic Studies* 14:3 (2017), 354–81.

After a few months of fighting, Louverture stepped aside and went to live with his family. Leclerc, in his reports, alleged that Louverture was sending secret missives to generals in areas still in rebellion. Using that pretext, Leclerc arrested Louverture and deported him to France, where he was placed in prison but never charged. Denied medical care and sufficient food, not to mention privileges due to his military rank, Louverture died a prisoner in October 1803.[32] Louverture's treatment might be compared to that of his fellow French general of color Thomas-Alexandre Dumas, also born with slave status in colonial Haiti. Dumas' ill treatment, which inspired his son's novel *The Man in the Iron Mask*, came at the hands of the kingdom of Naples, then at war with France.[33] Comparisons can also be made with George Washington and Simón Bolívar's retirements or Bonaparte's own exiles.

Leclerc did keep his promise to Christophe and Dessalines that they would be allowed to maintain their rank in the French army, using them to disarm the rural population. Leclerc's fortunes began to reverse in the summer, however, as word arrived in the colony of the French reestablishment of slavery in Guadeloupe, prompting a surge of resistance. At the same time, yellow fever began to take a toll on the European troops, killing two-thirds of the force by the time Leclerc died of the disease in November.

While many of the *anciens libres*' leaders who traveled with the Leclerc expedition were happy to see their rival Louverture gone, and Dessalines and Christophe would not fight an overwhelming army that promised to maintain the emancipation decrees, French policies of reestablishing slavery and racial discrimination clarified the situation and solidified the anti-France coalition. Led by Dessalines, those who formed the coalition took the name Armée Indigène, a nod to the Taíno past and the anticolonial mythos. Continued loyalty to France made little sense in an atmosphere of broken trust.

The French army responded with tactics of mass murder and destruction (Figure 22.2). The memoir of the French soldier Jean-Pierre Béchaud details mass drownings that killed thousands of Haitians at a time, the use of war dogs from Cuba, and summary executions by burning and hanging.[34] With a decade of conventional and guerrilla military experience, and knowledge of the local landscape, the Armée Indigène soon gained the upper hand. After

---

[32] Marlene Daut, "The Wrongful Death of Toussaint Louverture," *History Today* 7:6 (2020), www.historytoday.com/archive/feature/wrongful-death-toussaint-louverture.

[33] Tom Reiss, *The Black Count: Glory, Revolution, Betrayal, and the Real Count of Monte Cristo* (New York: Random House, 2012).

[34] Geggus, *The Haitian Revolution*, 178.

Overview of the Haitian Revolution

Figure 22.2 French reprisals. Getty Images.

victory at Vertières in North Province, Dessalines issued an initial declaration of independence on 29 November 1803.[35] A more formal, and forceful, declaration followed on 1 January 1804.[36]

Dessalines took the title Governor-General for life, and would soon be crowned Emperor Jean-Jacques I. As Deborah Jenson explores, Dessalines crowning himself emperor punctuated and, in his words, consolidated Haiti's declaration of independence and the new state's right to self-determination.[37] Haiti was not the only state to explore monarchism in the nineteenth century, as the careers of Napoleon I and Napoleon III in France, Agustín I in Mexico, and Pedro I and Pedro II in Brazil show. Even the United States saw calls to crown George Washington and the fear of democratic rule that led to the US Constitution of 1787 and the US electoral college. The "myth" of republicanism and the paradox of authoritarian rule is a theme of French political theory.[38] In the decades after Dessalines' death, the southern Republic of Haiti would define itself against the northern Kingdom of Haiti led by Henry Christophe as King Henry I, generating fierce debates about the meaning of liberty, civilization, and postcolonialism.[39]

Responses

Early Haitian leaders crafted citizenship around racial lines, but by inverting the white supremacy that governed politics elsewhere in the Americas, defining all Haitian citizens as "Black." They also granted honorary citizenship to key allies, including a group of Polish soldiers who had defected from Leclerc's army and joined the insurgents. Dessalines ordered the execution of other white colonists who had remained, the context for his proclamation declaring that he had avenged America. These reprisals occurred after over a century of brutal chattel slavery and a decade of French colonists imagining, and French military officers carrying out, the mass killing of Haitians of

---

[35] For more, see Jean-Pierre Le Glaunec, *The Cry of Vertières: Liberation, Memory, and the Beginning of Haiti*, trans. Jonathan Kaplansky (Montreal: McGill-Queen's University Press, 2020).

[36] See the essays in Julia Gaffield, ed., *The Haitian Declaration of Independence: Creation, Context, and Legacy* (Charlottesville: University of Virginia Press, 2016).

[37] Deborah Jenson, *Beyond the Slave Narrative: Politics, Sex, and Manuscripts in the Haitian Revolution* (Liverpool: Liverpool University Press, 2011), 142.

[38] Jean-Clément Martin, *Contre-révolution, revolution et nation en France (1789–1799)* (Paris: Éditions du Seuil, 1998).

[39] Chelsea Stieber, *Haiti's Paper War: Post-Independence Writing, Civil War, and the Making of the Republic, 1804–1954* (New York: New York University Press, 2020).

color, a notion that resurfaced in French schemes to retake the colony in the 1810s.[40]

While many European and North American merchants would visit Haiti, trading for the sugar, coffee, beeswax, and tortoise shells the new nation produced, they were less willing to acknowledge the new state's formal sovereignty.[41] France extracted a humiliating and expensive indemnity in 1825 in exchange for dropping the threat of reinvasion and allowing Haitian merchants to sell goods in France. In the United States, Congressional debates about recognizing Haiti served as a proxy for debating the status of slavery in the United States, and recognition would not be extended until the midpoint of the US Civil War, when the United States was in the midst of its own emancipatory struggles.[42] Haiti, for its part, paid attention to regional politics, with early leader Alexandre Pétion providing key support to Simón Bolívar in the 1810s, and the country formally mourned the abolitionist John Brown in 1859.[43]

Enslaved people throughout the Greater Caribbean showed an awareness of the Haitian Revolution, and individuals from Saint-Domingue or Haiti participated in various conspiracies and rebellions, ranging from Venezuela (Maracaibo, in 1799) and Cuba to Louisiana. The young man Telemaque, who had used epilepsy to evade life on a Dominguan sugar plantation, purchased free status after winning the lottery. Now known as Denmark Vesey, he allegedly promised Haitian military aid to antislavery plotters in his new hometown of Charleston, South Carolina. Toussaint Louverture's life and the achievements of Haiti would be an inspiration to African-Americans and a specter invoked by proslavery propagandists and white supremacists. Haitian achievements inspired writings by William Wordsworth, Georg Wilhelm Friedrich Hegel, and many others.

---

[40] Marlene Daut, "'Genocidal Imaginings' in the Era of the Haitian Revolution," *Age of Revolutions*, January 2016, https://ageofrevolutions.com/2016/01/25/genocidal-imaginings-in-the-era-of-the-haitian-revolution; Marlene Daut, "All the Devils Are Here: How the Visual History of the Haitian Revolution Misrepresents Black Suffering and Death," *Lapham's Quarterly*, October 2020, www.laphamsquarterly.org/roundtable/all-devils-are-here.

[41] Julia Gaffield, *Haitian Connections in the Atlantic World: Recognition after Revolution* (Chapel Hill: University of North Carolina Press, 2015).

[42] Alejandro E. Gómez, *Le spectre de la Révolution noire: L'impact de la Révolution haïtienne dans le monde atlantique, 1790–1886* (Rennes: Presses universitaires de Rennes, 2013); Elizabeth Maddock Dillon and Michael Drexler, eds., *The Haitian Revolution and the Early United States: Histories, Textualities, Geographies* (Philadelphia: University of Pennsylvania Press, 2016).

[43] Matthew J. Clavin, *Toussaint Louverture and the American Civil War: The Promise and Peril of a Second Haitian Revolution* (Philadelphia: University of Pennsylvania Press, 2010), 53–4.

While Haiti's emancipation from slavery helped speed the abolition of Britain's slave trade, the increased market share for sugar and coffee probably helped strengthen slavery and plantation agriculture in Brazil and Cuba. Early Haitian leaders would try to maintain the sugar plantation system, but Haitian farmworkers voted with their feet and settled at the old provision grounds, growing foodstuffs and coffee.[44] The clearest response to the Haitian Revolution occurred in the Dominican Republic, where a strong strain of Dominican nationalism formed around rejecting Haitians as foreign invaders and restoring plantation slavery.[45]

Conclusion

Haiti would face challenges, but the revolution achieved monumental status. Haiti was the second independent state in the Americas, the first in Latin America, the first to be led by people of African descent, the first to prohibit chattel slavery in its borders, and the first postslavery society in the Atlantic. Early leaders worried about preserving the nation's independence amid the threat of reinvasion. The propaganda around Haiti, including flattening perception of the rebellion by reducing it to "violence," "rage," or "retribution," began even before the rebellion itself, but would be repeated following the same pattern many times in many places.[46]

The white supremacist Lothrop Stoddard and the Trinidadian Marxist C. L. R. James, writing just before and just after Anna Julia Cooper at the height of European imperialism, would recognize Haiti as a harbinger of the coming wave of decolonization. Robert Palmer, writing *The Age of Democratic Revolution* as the decolonial wave crested, would dismiss Haiti, preferring to focus on the United States, France, and short-lived European moments.

---

[44] Jean Casimir, *The Haitians: A Decolonial History*, trans. Laurent Dubois (Chapel Hill: University of North Carolina Press, 2020); Johnhenry Gonzalez, *Maroon Nation: A History of Revolutionary Haiti* (New Haven: Yale University Press, 2019).

[45] Anne Eller, *We Dream Together: Dominican Independence, Haiti, and the Fight for Caribbean Freedom* (Durham, NC: Duke University Press, 2016), Chapter 1.

[46] James Alexander Dun, *Dangerous Neighbors: Making the Haitian Revolution in Early America* (Philadelphia: University of Pennsylvania Press, 2016); Matt D. Childs, *The 1812 Aponte Rebellion in Cuba and the Struggle against Atlantic Slavery* (Chapel Hill: University of North Carolina Press, 2006); Cristina Soriano, *Tides of Revolution: Information, Insurgencies, and the Crisis of Colonial Rule in Venezuela* (Albuquerque: University of New Mexico Press, 2018); Michel-Rolph Trouillot, *Silencing the Past: Power and the Production of History* (Boston: Beacon Press, 2015); Alyssa Goldstein Sepinwall, "Still Unthinkable? The Haitian Revolution and the Reception of Michel-Rolph Trouillot's 'Silencing the Past,'" *Journal of Haitian Studies* 19:2 (2013), 75–103.

A wider Atlantic lens, however, shows that Haitians, by taking control of their own destiny and fulfilling revolutionary ideals of self-determination, reshaped the Age of Revolutions in a fundamental way, with lasting questions about postcoloniality and what it means to reconstruct society and the political order after the end of chattel slavery and racial segregation.

23
Saint-Domingue on the Eve of the Revolution

JOHN GARRIGUS

Introduction

As the largest, most profitable slave society in the eighteenth-century Atlantic world, the French Caribbean colony of Saint-Domingue played important roles in the Age of Atlantic Revolutions. Its sugar tempted North Americans to break British colonial trade laws, an important factor in the outbreak of the American Revolution. The expense of defending Saint-Domingue's colonists helped bankrupt the French monarchy, leading to the French Revolution. Most importantly, Saint-Domingue's enslaved people launched and sustained the Haitian Revolution, ending slavery, defeating French colonialism, and creating the second independent nation-state in the Americas.

Saint-Domingue was also critical to the economic transformations that were part of the Age of Atlantic Revolutions. Sugar production created attractive profits for capitalistic planters. As a leading producer of raw cotton and indigo dye, Saint-Domingue fed Europe's emerging textile factories. More than any other Caribbean colony, Saint-Domingue provided Europeans with ever-cheaper luxuries like sugar and coffee, leading to what Jan de Vries has labeled the "Industrious Revolution."[1]

Saint-Domingue's Plantation Economy

Eighteenth-century Caribbean plantations were markedly different from their counterparts on the North American mainland. Island colonists were not "settlers"; they came to the Caribbean to make their fortune and then return to Europe. Saint-Domingue's masters drove their enslaved workers so

---

[1] Jan de Vries, "The Industrial Revolution and the Industrious Revolution," *The Journal of Economic History* 54:2 (1994), 249–70.

hard that, on average, Africans died within eight years of arriving.² Planters clamored for ever more African captives, even in 1789 when enslaved people made up 88 percent of the colony's population.

Sugar in Saint-Domingue

Sugar was at the heart of Saint-Domingue's prominence in the Atlantic world. By 1787 the French colony produced 40 percent of Europe's sugar supply, or about 87,000 tons, compared with 49,000 for Jamaica, its nearest rival. Saint-Domingue's most important advantage as a sugar producer was its size, with an area of 10,714 square miles compared with 4,411 for Jamaica.³

Size was important because eighteenth-century Caribbean plantations combined cane-growing and processing. Saint-Domingue's planters believed a sugar estate needed its own mill, at least 318 acres of land and 150 to 200 slaves. Fourteen to eighteen months after enslaved workers first planted the cane, the mature stalks would stand six to eight feet tall, ready for harvest. Workers had only a few days to cut the canes before they rotted in the field. Then, within forty-eight hours, they had to push the harvested stalks through a grinding mill, again racing the clock to prevent the sweet juice from spoiling. Planters who owned their own mills could control the timing of this work; cane farmers who waited to use someone else's mill might have to watch their crop decay in the field. In practice, there were many factors affecting the profitability of a given estate.⁴

After the mill had pressed the juice from the sugar canes, workers refined it into crystals. They boiled the liquid in six progressively smaller cauldrons, thickening it into a syrup. When the refiner believed the smallest cauldron was ready, he plunged it into a vat of cold water. If all went well, the clear syrup would turn cloudy, as the crystals precipitated from the solution. Then the sugar would sit in clay pots for three weeks as molasses drained off,

---

[2] Gabriel Debien, *Les esclaves aux Antilles françaises, XVII–XVIII siècles* (Basse-Terre: Société d'histoire de la Guadeloupe, 1974), 346.
[3] Robin Blackburn, *The Making of New World Slavery: From the Baroque to the Modern, 1492–1800* (London: Verso, 1998), 433.
[4] See the case study in Paul Cheney, *Cul De Sac: Patrimony, Capitalism, and Slavery in French Saint-Domingue* (Chicago: University of Chicago Press, 2017), 42–70; on the process of planting and refining sugar, see Robert Louis Stein, *The French Sugar Business in the Eighteenth Century* (Baton Rouge: Louisiana State University Press, 1988), 60–5.

leaving brown crystals that could be shipped across the Atlantic, for further refining in France.

After 1763, the French government gradually began allowing its planters to sell so-called "clayed" sugar to foreign countries. "Claying" required three more weeks, but it produced a near-white sugar that brought higher prices and cost less to ship. It also produced more molasses, which planters distilled into rum. Brandy distillers successfully blocked rum from entering France, but Saint-Domingue sold its molasses to British North America, despite London's objections. In 1787, after US independence, Saint-Domingue produced 66 million pounds of molasses and sent 40 million to distilleries in ports such as Boston, New York, and Providence. France gradually relaxed its monopoly over colonial trade after 1763, both by reforming laws and by relaxing enforcements, especially after signing a commercial treaty with the Continental Congress in 1778.[5]

An eighteenth-century Caribbean sugar plantation was more like a nineteenth-century factory than nearly any other business of the time. Saint-Domingue's planters operated on a giant scale, planting tens of thousands of sugar canes to recoup the cost of their grinding mills and the hundreds of enslaved people who toiled in their fields. Captive Africans were expensive to purchase; to buy a single enslaved adult man, a planter paid a slave trader three to four times the annual income of a French worker. This amount, 1,500 to 2,000 colonial livres, was equal to 947 to 1,263 French livres (here I use McCusker's conversion factor, valuing a French livre at 1.5834 colonial livres); contemporaries estimated that a man in France needed to earn 300 livres to survive.[6] To buy 100 people, therefore, a planter needed at least 95,000 French livres tournois, worth over 1 million US dollars in 2015.[7] Planters typically worked slaves so hard that between 4 and 10 percent of them died every year. Even with such losses, sugar plantations often earned

---

[5] See Jean Tarrade, *Le commerce colonial de la France à la fin de l'ancien régime: L'évolution du régime de l'exclusif de 1763 à 1789*, 2 vols. (Paris: Presses universitaires de France, 1972), especially vol.I, 173, 331–2, 452–4, vol. II, 593–8; see vol. I, 173 describing a 1752 French law prohibiting rum reexports. See also Stein, *French Sugar Business*, 66, 72–3.

[6] Gwynne Lewis, *France, 1715–1804: Power and the People* (New York: Pearson Longman, 2004), 101; Daniel Roche, *A History of Everyday Things: The Birth of Consumption in France, 1600–1800*, trans. Brian Pearce (Cambridge: Cambridge University Press, 2000), 63–6; John J. McCusker, *Money and Exchange in Europe and America, 1600–1775: A Handbook* (Chapel Hill: University of North Carolina Press, 1978), 280–1.

[7] Rodney Edvinsson, "What Is the Equivalent of 150000 French Livres Tournois [1663–1795] in Year 1757 in the Currency of US Dollar [1791–2015] in Year 2015?," *Historical Currency Converter (Test Version 1.0)*, January 2016, www.historicalstatistics.org/Currencyconverter.html.

their owners a return on investment somewhere between 5 and 15 percent annually.[8]

Sugar plantations shaped Saint-Domingue in three ways. More than any other commodity, sugar planting killed enslaved Africans, leading to the importation of more captives, and an ever-increasing diversity of African cultures in the colony. Second, sugar manufacturing pushed planters to create proto-industrial institutions; they organized enslaved workers' lives around the time requirements of sugar refining to maximize their own profits. Third, by the 1760s Saint-Domingue's sugar and molasses lured North American merchants to the colony, in violation of British laws. This illegal sugar commerce sharpened North America's resentment of Britain, helping produce the American War of Independence. Similarly, profits from selling to North America made Saint-Domingue's colonists chafe under French trade laws. Versailles limited what Dominguan planters could sell to foreigners and what those planters could buy from North America – lumber and animals, not food or textiles.

Coffee, Indigo, and Cotton

Sugar was just one of four main crops Saint-Domingue exported. The others influenced the Age of Atlantic Revolutions in their own ways.

Coffee was the colony's second-most-important crop. Introduced from Martinique in the 1730s, by 1787 it had almost surpassed sugar in export value, with shipments worth 71 million livres, compared with 75 million livres of sugar. Coffee planting was more affordable than sugar, requiring just twenty to fifty slaves and no expensive mill. Coffee bushes thrived in the mountains, where the land was cheaper. After the Haitian Revolution, French officials valued the land and buildings of an average Saint-Domingue coffee estate at 150,000 francs, compared with 700,000 for a sugar plantation.[9] New coffee

---

[8] Gabriel Debien, *Les esclaves aux Antilles françaises*, 345; David P. Geggus, "Les esclaves de la Plaine du Nord à la veille de la révolution française: Les équipes de travail sur une vingtaine de sucreries. Partie III," *Revue de la société d'histoire de géographie d'Haïti* 42:144 (1984), 8–44: 39; Natacha Bonnet, "L'organisation du travail servile sur la sucrerie domingoise au XVIIIe siècle," in Philippe Hrodĕj, ed., *L'esclave et les plantations: De l'établissement de la servitude à son abolition* (Rennes: Presses universitaires de Rennes, 2008), 150–2; on profits, see Stein, *French Sugar Business*, 85; Pierre Pluchon, "L'économie d'habitation dans les Antilles françaises," *Revue d'histoire maritime* 1 (1997), 197–241: 231.

[9] Pluchon, "L'économie d'habitation," 209; Michel-Rolph Trouillot, "Motion in the System: Coffee, Color, and Slavery in Eighteenth-Century Saint-Domingue," *Review* 5:3 (1982), 331–88: 344–8.

estates, along with the expansion of sugar and other slave-grown crops, pushed Saint-Domingue's transatlantic slave trade to new heights. In 1788, the colony imported 33,830 Africans, nearly sixteen times as many as the 2,151 captives imported in 1730.[10]

Coffee planting changed colonial society in other ways. Thousands of Frenchmen migrated to Saint-Domingue after 1763, believing they could make a fortune in coffee. This influx helped produce a new emphasis on white superiority in Saint-Domingue, described below. Some former slaves and free-born people of color also grew coffee; a few became wealthy, like the family of Vincent Ogé, mentioned below.

Saint-Domingue's coffee and sugar were coveted consumer products in Europe. In the first half of the eighteenth century most French workers could not afford these luxuries. But prices dropped as colonial production increased, so that, in the 1790s, Parisian workers described sugar and coffee as "goods of prime necessity."[11]

Cotton was another luxury product that Saint-Domingue's brutal slavery and abundant land transformed into a common consumer good. In 1700, only 3 to 8 percent of French people owned cotton clothing when they died. By 1789 cotton was in 25 to 40 percent of death inventories. As Sven Beckert explains, Saint-Domingue pioneered slave-grown cotton, which would eventually transform the US economy. In the late 1700s cotton was not an important crop in the British West Indies or North America, yet Britain imported an average of 4.8 million pounds of raw cotton annually from 1770 to 1775, much of it probably smuggled from Saint-Domingue. As British textile makers adopted new industrial technology such as Arkwright's water frame (1775) and Compton's mule (1779), the demand for raw cotton increased dramatically. Saint-Domingue's slave masters profited from this early industrial revolution; in 1791, the colony had over 700 cotton plantations and its cotton exports had increased 80 percent since 1774.[12]

---

[10] "Slaves Disembarked in Saint-Domingue, 1730–1788," *Trans-Atlantic Slave Trade Database*, https://slavevoyages.org/voyages/TuJqVEpV.

[11] Paul R. Sharp and Jacob L. Weisdorf, "French Revolution or Industrial Revolution? A Note on the Contrasting Experiences of England and France up to 1800," *Cliometrica* 6 (2012), 79–88: 80; Roche, *History of Everyday Things*, 245; Colin Jones and Rebecca L. Spang, "Sans-Culottes, sans Café, sans Tabac: Shifting Realms of Necessity and Luxury in Eighteenth-Century France," in Maxine Berg and Helen Clifford, eds., *Consumers and Luxury: Consumer Culture in Europe, 1650–1850* (Manchester: Manchester University Press, 1999), 37–62; Peter N. Stearns, *Consumerism in World History: The Global Transformation of Desire* (London: Routledge, 2001), 20.

[12] These numbers are from Michel Placide Justin, *Histoire politique et statistique de l'île d'Hayti, Saint-Domingue, écrite sur des documents officiels et des notes communiquées par Sir*

Social Groups

The society that developed in Saint-Domingue shaped the Age of Atlantic Revolutions in two ways. First, as enslaved Africans and their descendants created new cultures in the colony, they planted the seeds of the Atlantic world's most successful slave uprising. The colony imported at least 680,000 captive Africans during the eighteenth century and attempted to reduce them to gears in the plantation machine.[13] But Dominguan slavery did not produce cultural homogenization because planters were always buying new African captives. Moreover, people enslaved on sugar, coffee, or cotton plantations had very diverse experiences. In Saint-Domingue there was never one single African group that rose up in revolution. The Haitian Revolution succeeded in part because its leaders were able to forge coalitions among different ethnic and regional groups.

Saint-Domingue also contributed to the Age of Revolution by pushing the ideology of white superiority, or antiblackness, to new levels. By 1700, Europeans had developed deep prejudices that justified the profits they made from enslaving Africans. Their racism did not prevent masters from raping black women, or having children with them in other types of relationships. The legal identity of those children varied from case to case; most biracial people were born and died in slavery, while a few found freedom and even wealth.

Saint-Domingue was different from Brazil, Jamaica, and other Atlantic societies, where elite colonists accepted wealthy biracial people into their ranks, especially if powerful white men acknowledged that these were their children. In the years after 1770, Dominguan courts and colonists began to define wealthy biracial people as nonwhite, even calling them *affranchis*, or former slaves. When members of this group challenged white supremacy in the early years of the French Revolution, they destabilized the slave system,

---

James Barskett, *agent du Gouvernement Britannique dans les Antilles* (Paris: Brière, 1826), 501; see the cumulative numbers in Tarrade, *Commerce colonial*, vol. II, 748; for the number of plantations, see Bryan Edwards, *An Historical Survey of the French Colony in the Island of St Domingo* (London: John Stockdale, 1797), 197–8; for rising French cotton consumption, Madeleine Dobie, *Trading Places: Colonization and Slavery in Eighteenth-Century French Culture* (Ithaca, NY: Cornell University Press, 2010), 90; Sven Beckert, *Empire of Cotton: A Global History* (New York: Alfred A. Knopf, 2014), 89–92; Michel-René Hilliard d'Auberteuil, *Considérations sur l'état présent de la colonie française de Saint-Domingue*, 2 vols. (Paris: Grangé, 1776), vol. I, 281–2; Richard L. Roberts, *Two Worlds of Cotton: Colonialism and the Regional Economy in the French Soudan, 1800–1946* (Stanford: Stanford University Press, 1996), 46–8.

[13] "Slave Voyages," *Trans-Atlantic Slave Trade Database*, https://slavevoyages.org/voyages/fKrLhuZg.

inadvertently helping the 1791 slave uprising that became the Haitian Revolution.

Africans and Their Descendants

Enslaved people outnumbered colonists in Saint-Domingue fourteen to one by 1789. According to David Geggus, the official statistics gathered during the first half of 1789 were as follows: whites 30,831, free coloreds 24,848, and enslaved people 434,429.[14]

In most Caribbean slave colonies, when masters described their fears of slave resistance, they talked about revolts. Saint-Domingue was different. In 1757, colonists became convinced that slaves in northern Saint-Domingue had created a vast poisoning plot, led by an escaped slave or maroon named François Makandal. This episode, described below, illustrates how some people created moments of dignity and self-determination in slavery.[15]

Repression is one likely reason Saint-Domingue's enslaved people did not rise against their masters until political violence between whites and free people of color erupted in 1790 and 1791. The working conditions of plantation life were brutal; those enslaved on sugar plantations worked twelve hours per day, and longer in harvest season. Many enslaved people were malnourished and periodically starving. Masters gave them garden plots, but these could be far from water and vulnerable to droughts and hurricanes.[16]

People enslaved in every other contemporary Caribbean plantation slave system experienced similar levels of brutality, exhaustion, and malnutrition, but Saint-Domingue had some unique repressive institutions. Until the 1780s, for example, the colony had a proportionately larger garrison of

---

[14] See David Geggus, "The Major Port Towns of Saint Domingue in the Later Eighteenth Century," in Franklin Knight and Peggy K. Liss, eds., *Atlantic Port Cities: Economy, Culture, and Society in the Atlantic World, 1650–1850* (Knoxville: University of Tennessee Press, 1991), 87–116: 102.

[15] John D. Garrigus, "'Like an Epidemic One Could Only Stop with the Most Violent Remedies': African Poisons versus Livestock Disease in Saint Domingue, 1750–88," *The William and Mary Quarterly* 78:4 (2021), 617–52; Jean Fouchard, *Les marrons de la liberté* (Port-au-Prince: H. Deschamps, 1988), 361–91. Fouchard intended the list as evidence of the resistance tradition among Saint-Domingue's slaves, but his list is a "dictionary of maroonage."

[16] On working conditions and hours, see Karen Bourdier, "Vie quotidienne et conditions sanitaires sur les grandes habitations sucrières du nord de Saint-Domingue à la veille de l'insurrection d'août 1791" (Ph.D. dissertation, Université de Pau, 2005), 92; M. L. E. Moreau de Saint-Méry, *Loix et constitutions des colonies françoises de l'amérique sous le vent*, 6 vols. (Paris: self-published, 1784), vol. v, 729.

soldiers than neighboring Jamaica, though this only meant there was about one French soldier for every 100 slaves.[17] Two other institutions, the militia and the rural constabulary, were far more active in slaves' lives because they were based in each parish. Naval officers and colonists commanded these forces, but free men of color – both former slaves and free-born biracial men – made up much of the rank and file. They performed the hardest duties, including searching for escapees and potential rebels.

Saint-Domingue's militia was initially composed of all able-bodied free men. Former slaves, freed for bravery in a 1697 raid against the Spanish American port of Cartagena de Indias, created their own free Black militia units a few years later. Sometime after 1724, the administration created "mulatto" militia companies when colonists refused to serve alongside biracial men, who in turn refused to muster with free Blacks. As planters resisted difficult duties such as searching for escaped slaves, the state charged free colored militias with these responsibilities.

To further relieve the militia from slave-hunting, in 1705 Saint-Domingue created a professional police force for rural areas. By 1739 most of its members were free men of color. They hunted maroons weekly, checked slave cabins for weapons, and reported masters who let enslaved people hold disruptive dances. Constables could double their income by collecting a bounty when they captured a maroon or criminal. Starting in 1775, the colonial government rewarded some men of color for years of policing or militia work by giving them official freedom papers.[18] In this way, Saint-Domingue's free Black militia and constabulary not only prevented slave revolts, but also functioned as a "safety valve" for the slavery system.[19]

Marronage was a second safety valve. Throughout the eighteenth century, maroons fled to the mountains or crossed into Spanish Santo Domingo, creating hidden communities or bands that raided plantations for supplies. Historian Jean Fouchard counted at least fifteen maroon leaders active in Saint-Domingue between 1719 and 1787. For Fouchard, maroon raids showed that people were fighting slavery, even if there were no plantation uprisings during this long period. Although colonists feared maroon raids,

---

[17] David P. Geggus, "Saint-Domingue on the Eve of the Haitian Revolution," in David P. Geggus and Norman Fiering, eds., *The World of the Haitian Revolution* (Bloomington: Indiana University Press, 2009), 3–20: 8.

[18] Stewart R. King, *Blue Coat or Powdered Wig: Free People of Color in Pre-Revolutionary Saint Domingue* (Athens, GA: University of Georgia, 2001), 238; John D. Garrigus, *Before Haiti: Race and Citizenship in Saint-Domingue* (New York: Palgrave Macmillan, 2006), 43, 103; Moreau de Saint-Méry, *Loix et constitutions*, vol. II, 25, vol. V, 612.

[19] Geggus, "Saint-Domingue on the Eve of the Haitian Revolution," 5.

these attacks never seriously threatened the colonial order. Maroon activity slowed markedly after the 1740s, as colonists began planting coffee in the interior. By 1789 Saint-Domingue had no permanent maroon settlements. The island's two largest maroon villages, Le Maniel and Bahoruco, across the border in Santo Domingo, had only a few hundred residents, not thousands as planters sometimes claimed. The leaders of the 1791 slave uprising included only one former maroon, Jean François.[20]

Religion may have been a third safety valve for Saint-Domingue's enslaved people. Planters fought Catholic missionaries when they allowed enslaved people to lead their own church services. In 1763 Saint-Domingue evicted the Jesuit order after an enslaved woman named Assam claimed a Jesuit told her not to implicate other slaves when authorities tortured her during the Makandal affair.[21]

The Makandal conspiracy shows how spirituality permeated Saint-Domingue's African-inspired cultures, though colonists often did not understand this. Investigators never found any toxins in Makandal's possession, but they convicted him of leading a poison conspiracy because he had created a community of intensely loyal followers. Those followers came to admire Makandal for his ability to create spiritually powerful charms. The size of a finger, these charms were wrapped carefully in twine, sometimes with a small lead crucifix at the core. Makandal taught that these charms were alive, could protect their owners, and could foretell the future. This description suggests that they were modeled on *nkisi* (plural; singular *minkisi*) from the lower Congo, objects containing the spirits of the dead, who could help the person who carried the charm.[22]

Executing Makandal did not stop the sudden mysterious deaths that colonists ascribed to his poisons. Later, this chapter presents evidence that

---

[20] Fouchard, *Marrons de la liberté*, 385; David P. Geggus, "Marronage, Voodoo and the Saint-Domingue Slave Revolution of 1791," in Patricia Galloway and Philip Boucher, eds., *Proceedings of the Fifteenth Meeting of the French Colonial Historical Society* (Lanham: University Press of America, 1992), 22–35: 27; M. L. E. Moreau de Saint-Méry, *Description topographique, physique, civile, politique et historique de la partie française de l'isle Saint-Domingue*, 2 vols. (Philadelphia: self-published, 1798), vol. II, 501–2.

[21] John D. Garrigus, *A Secret among the Blacks: Slave Resistance before the Haitian Revolution* (Cambridge, MA: Harvard University Press, 2023), 74.

[22] Todd Ramón Ochoa, "Prendas-Ngangas-Equisos: Turbulence and the Influence of the Dead in Cuban-Kongo Material Culture," *Cultural Anthropology* 25: 3 (2010), 387–420: 390–3; Robert Farris Thompson, *Flash of the Spirit: African and Afro-American Art and Philosophy* (New York: Random House, 1983), 117–31; Trevor Burnard and John D. Garrigus, *The Plantation Machine: Atlantic Capitalism in French Saint-Domingue and British Jamaica* (Philadelphia: University of Pennsylvania Press, 2016), 109–11.

a food-borne illness killed these victims. But the mythic image of Makandal as an uncanny African master poisoner – an idea shared by masters and enslaved people alike – shaped master–slave relations down to the Haitian Revolution.

A fourth safety valve for Saint-Domingue's slavery system was the possibility of legal freedom. Besides the military manumissions described above, enslaved people might buy their own freedom if their master was willing. This could require decades of tenacious savings and the ability to negotiate with a master. A colonist could simply free the person he or she had enslaved, but after 1711 the enslaver had to convince the colonial governor to sign the liberty paper. After 1767, the colony imposed a tax of 800 livres on all conferrals of freedom, and in 1775 this rose to 1,000 livres for a man and 2,000 livres for a woman aged under forty. In other words, an enslaved person had to convince her master to free her, and to pay the government a sum equal to her market value. Stereotypically, this type of manumission went to a woman who had been her enslaver's concubine, borne his children, and ensured that he bonded with them.[23] Some writers criticized manumissions for allowing male colonists to reward their enslaved concubines. But others insisted manumission protected the colony. In 1762 the royal attorney of Fort Dauphin claimed that without the promise of manumission, "there would have been among the slaves many open revolts, secret plots, and acts of despair."[24]

Marriage was another way an enslaved person could find freedom. The 1685 Code Noir decreed that a master could free a slave by marrying him or her. Marriage would also free the couple's children. The law was aimed at white men with enslaved concubines, but as manumission grew more expensive, free and enslaved people of color began to marry, which freed the enslaved spouse and the couple's children. By the 1780s over 40 percent of free colored marriages in key districts of Saint-Domingue's South Province involved one enslaved person.[25]

Manumission, be it by self-purchase, gift, marriage, or militia service, was a remote possibility for most enslaved people. Self-purchase made up 10 percent of manumissions near Cap Français and Port-au-Prince, but less than

---

[23] Garrigus, *Before Haiti*, 42, 56–8, 86, 197.
[24] Emilien Petit, *Traité sur le gouvernement des esclaves*, 2 vols. (Paris: Knapen imprimeur de la Cour des aides, 1777), vol. II, 62–78; Marie François L'Huillier de Marigny, "Mémoire sur les poisons qui règnent à Saint-Domingue," 1762, Archives Nationales d'outre-mer (henceforth ANOM), F³88, 260–4.
[25] Garrigus, *Before Haiti*, 198–9.

1 percent in the isolated South Province. David Geggus estimates that in the 1770s and 1780s only 3 out of every 1,000 people enslaved in Saint-Domingue ever attained freedom.[26] Nevertheless, by the 1780s, Saint-Domingue had nearly as many free people of color as whites. The enslaved population dwarfed both groups, but the presence of free Blacks and free people of color shaped the political imagination of enslaved people. In 1757, when Médor, an enslaved servant, confessed to giving his master powders so that the man would free him, he admitted that some enslaved and free Blacks were secretly sharing these medicines. Members of this group believed that the substances would push colonists to free so many Blacks that eventually they could "confront the whites if necessary."[27] The conspiracy Médor described did not aim to drive all whites from the island; it imagined forcing them to respond to free Blacks' demands.

The Refinement of White Superiority Culture

Saint-Domingue did not invent the concept of white superiority, but anti-Black practices there took two important turns. After 1770, the colony adopted laws that segregated even wealthy biracial people from whites. Then, in 1791, biracial colonists in Paris convinced the revolutionary National Assembly that they should have the same civil rights as whites. In Saint-Domingue, when the colonial government refused to accept this change, free people of color began to fight for their rights. This violence over racism was a contributory factor leading to the slave rebellion of 1791.

Saint-Domingue redefined whiteness after 1770 with new laws that restricted the activities of wealthy slave-owning families of color. In Saint-Domingue, as in other slave societies, colonists fathered biracial children by raping, prostituting, or setting up households with enslaved women. A few of them freed these children and left them land, slaves, and livestock. Some newly arrived men jumpstarted their colonial careers by marrying wealthy free women of color. The Augers had at least six children, and educated most of them in France. Marie Begasse, the biracial daughter of an early planter, married Pierre Raymond, who migrated to Saint-Domingue in the 1720s.

---

[26] David P. Geggus, "Slave and Free Colored Women in Saint Domingue," in Darlene Clark Hine and David Barry Gaspar, eds., *More Than Chattel: Black Women and Slavery in the Americas* (Bloomington: Indiana University Press, 1996), 259–78: 268; Garrigus, *Before Haiti*, 55.

[27] Garrigus, *A Secret among the Blacks*, 52.

Begasse had land and slaves, which she and Raymond developed into a valuable estate. They had eight children, and sent them to schools in France. When they returned, these children started their own slave plantations and married other wealthy people of color.[28] There were also marriages between island-born colonists and free women of color, such as the 1750 union between the illiterate Jacques Ogé and the free Black woman Angélique Hossé, who could sign her name and was the child of two free Black parents.[29]

Colonial administrators had long noted the existence of free biracial people. However, it was only in the aftermath of the Seven Years' War that they began to write laws specifically aimed at this group. That story is told below.

How Atlantic Wars Affected Saint-Domingue

Political unrest in west central Africa had a major impact on Saint-Domingue over the course of the eighteenth century. Weakened by eighty years of civil war, the once-powerful kingdom of Kongo could not stop local lords from fighting or from selling their prisoners to Europeans. In the 1740s and 1750s French slave traders began to buy a majority of their captives in west central African ports. By the 1790s, these so-called "Congo" people, many of them military veterans, made up about 60 percent of the enslaved workers in Saint-Domingue's North and South Provinces. Although island-born slaves planned the slave revolt of August 1791, bands of Kongo soldiers were essential to the military success of the Haitian Revolution.[30]

Wars between the French and British empires affected Saint-Domingue too, for by 1730 it was the most valuable possession in the Americas. Naval officials ran the colony, from the governor-general right down to the parish level, and France stationed thousands of men in its port cities. After the

---

[28] Garrigus, *Before Haiti*, 47, 67.
[29] Matthew Gerber, "Race, empiétement de propriété et compétence juridictionnelle dans le monde atlantique français du XVIIIe siècle: L'affaire de la veuve Ogé," *Revue d'histoire moderne et contemporaine* 68:3 (2021), 91–116.
[30] Linda Heywood, "Slavery and Its Transformation in the Kingdom of Kongo: 1491–1800," *The Journal of African History* 50:1 (2009), 1–22: 20–2; John Thornton, "Cannibals, Witches, and Slave Traders in the Atlantic World," *The William and Mary Quarterly* 60:2 (2003), 273–94: 287; David P. Geggus, "The French Slave Trade: An Overview," *The William and Mary Quarterly* 58:1 (2001), 119–38: 122–3; John K. Thornton, "'I Am the Subject of the King of Kongo': African Political Ideology and the Haitian Revolution," *Journal of World History* 4 (1993), 181–214: 185, 201–3.

Seven Years' War, Cap Français and Port-au-Prince had proportionally more resident soldiers than Spain's great Caribbean fortress cities of Havana and Cartagena. These garrisons were expensive because tropical diseases killed at least 20 percent of European soldiers stationed in Saint-Domingue every year. By 1789 Louis XVI was spending one-sixth of his annual naval budget just to maintain 7,408 men in the Caribbean.[31]

Colonists did not like Saint-Domingue's military government, which they described as "tyrannical." They argued that laws, not haughty naval officers, should govern the colony. Saint-Domingue's two highest courts, known as *Conseils supérieurs*, were located in Cap Français and Port-au-Prince. They were courts of appeal that also worked with governors to write local laws. The Conseils could not block royal taxes or legislation, but decrees sent from France had no legal force in Saint-Domingue until the two courts registered them into the local law code. This tradition allowed Conseil judges to delay and debate unpopular changes.

From the 1750s to the French Revolution, Saint-Domingue's political life was whipsawed between the conflicting priorities of naval governors and the two Conseils. The military worked to integrate Saint-Domingue into the empire, increasing the number of troops and administrators, who collected taxes and enforced the French trade monopoly. Naval officials promoted better military, scientific, and cultural communication with France. They expected planters to put their duty to the French monarchy first, even if that meant sacrificing their fortunes to fight the British.

Many colonists disagreed, and the Conseils reflected their viewpoints. After France required that Conseil judges have law degrees, these colonial courts began modeling themselves after the politically active *parlement* of Paris. Colonial judges and writers advocated for civilian, not naval, administrators: they argued for liberty of commerce as opposed to the French commercial monopoly, peace instead of war, and the rule of established laws instead of military decrees.[32] Atlantic wars ensured that conflict

---

[31] David P. Geggus, "Urban Development in Eighteenth-Century Saint-Domingue," *Bulletin du Centre d'histoire des Espaces Atlantiques* 5 (1990), 197–228: 201; Boris Lesueur, "Les troupes coloniales aux Antilles sous l'Ancien Régime," *Histoire, économie & société* 28:4 (2009), 3–19: 13–14, 18.

[32] Laurie M. Wood, "Across Oceans and Revolutions: Law and Slavery in French Saint-Domingue and Beyond," *Law & Social Inquiry* 39:3 (2014), 758–82; Malick W. Ghachem, "Montesquieu in the Caribbean: The Colonial Enlightenment Between Code Noir and Code Civil," *Historical Reflections/Réflexions Historiques* 25:2 (1999), 183–210.

between the military ideal of patriotic sacrifice and the reality of planters' self-interest remained central in colonial affairs.

At the middle of the century, as imperial tensions simmered between France and Britain, Saint-Domingue was growing vigorously. Its plantation system doubled, from 3,550 plantations in 1751 to 7,404 in 1788. During the same period the enslaved population nearly tripled, increasing from 148,514 to 405,528. This increase of 257,014 masked the early deaths of tens of thousands of enslaved people, for during this period slave traders disembarked at least 429,722 Africans into the territory.[33]

The Seven Years' War

The Seven Years' War affected Saint-Domingue in two powerful ways. First, at the beginning of the war, a British blockade created a food crisis in the region around Cap Français that led Saint-Domingue's colonists to imagine the Makandal poison conspiracy of 1757–1758. Second, the threat that the British would invade Saint-Domingue in 1762 brought to the fore deeprooted tensions between military governors and profit-minded planters. Like the mythic figure of Makandal, those administrator–planter tensions hovered over the colony until beginning of the Haitian Revolution in 1791.

At the beginning of the Seven Years' War, London created the tightest blockade French Atlantic commerce had ever known. Cutting shipments from France and smuggling from North America, the British navy created a food crisis in Saint-Domingue's North Province, which was especially reliant on Atlantic trade. To survive, colonists accustomed to wheat bread had to eat the provisions that slaves grew: cassava, yams, plantains, and maize. Colonists complained, but enslaved people were the ones who starved. A drought shriveled their gardens just as whites purchased or confiscated their produce. The blockade ended imports of salted fish that masters distributed when local food was scarce. Enslaved people, especially those whose masters kept them on the edge of malnutrition in the best of times, suffered terribly.[34]

---

[33] "Recensement général de la colonie de Saint-Domingue pour l'année 1751," 1751, ANOM, 5DPPC63, ark:/61561/ca168avyxtr; 1788 data from François Barbé-Marbois, *L'état des finances de Saint-Domingue, contenant le résumé des recettes & dépenses de toutes les caisses publiques, depuis le 1er Janvier 1788, jusqu'au 31 Décembre de la même année* (Paris: Imprimerie Royale, 1790), Table III; "Slaves Disembarked, 1751–1788," *Trans-Atlantic Slave Trade Database*, https://slavevoyages.org/voyages/fKrLhuZg.

[34] Garrigus, *A Secret among the Blacks*, 30; Pierre-François-Xavier de Charlevoix and Jean-Baptiste Le Pers, *Histoire de l'isle espagnole ou de S. Domingue: Écrite particulièrement sur*

There was one more resource: cross-border trade with Santo Domingo. Imports of livestock from the Spanish colony were crucial to Saint-Domingue's economy. By the early 1740s, the French depended so much on Santo Domingo for meat that when livestock populations plummeted in the Spanish colony, for unknown reasons, meat prices skyrocketed in French colonial towns.[35] It seems likely that a disease was killing Spanish animals, for French animals were dying too. In 1750 and 1751 an epidemic that colonists described as anthrax killed 2,000 horses in the French colonial district of Cul-de-Sac, leading the governor to quarantine the district. At about the same time, colonists in Cap Français started dying after eating meat sold in the city's butcher shops. Their dogs died, too, when the colonists threw them meat that looked unfit for humans to eat. They accused local butchers of selling bad meat from Santo Domingo. In 1756, after a ten-month period in which meat killed more people than ever, ninety-eight of Cap Français's leading citizens formally petitioned the Conseil to take action.[36]

This tainted meat complicated Saint-Domingue's wartime food shortage. On plantations close to the Spanish border, healthy-looking animals began to die suddenly. Hungry enslaved people likely feasted on their carcasses, then died quickly. In May 1757, a West African man named Médor, enslaved on a struggling coffee plantation, admitted that Gaou, another West African on a nearby ranch, had sold him mysterious preparations. Médor told his master, Delavaud, a French-trained surgeon, that he had given Gaou's substances to livestock – and to twenty enslaved people – many of whom had died. Surprised by these deaths, Médor concluded that Gaou had betrayed him. He urged Delavaud to tell authorities to arrest Gaou and other Black poisoners. In the course of naming these "pernicious men," Médor admitted that he had been dosing Delavaud and others for decades with similar preparations, which he got from many other Blacks – enslaved and free. Until now, Médor implied, no one had ever died from what he called in French his "poisons," a word choice that reflected how

---

des mémoires manuscrits du P. Jean-Baptiste Le Pers, jésuite, 4 vols. (Amsterdam: François L'Honoré, 1733), vol. IV, 366; Jean-Baptiste Pouppé-Desportes, *Histoire des maladies de S. Domingue*, 3 vols. (Paris: Lejay, 1747), vol. II, 16, 271; Jean-Barthélemy-Maximilien Nicolson, *Essai sur l'histoire naturelle de l'isle de Saint-Domingue avec des figures en taille-douce* (Paris: Gobreau, 1776), 54.

[35] Charles de Brunier (Marquis de Larnage) and Simon-Pierre Maillart, "Lettre des Adrs au ministre sur le commerce des mulets avec la côte d'Espagne; les bateaux achetés de l'étranger etc.," 9 October 1746, ANOM F³79, 178–87.

[36] Moreau de Saint-Méry, *Loix et constitutions*, vol. IV: 37–9, 187–90.

many West African languages used the same word for medicine, poisons, and powders.[37]

Médor had given his master powders he had bought from other slaves to strengthen Delavaud's affection for him and hasten his manumission. He admitted that he and others were using these substances to create more free Blacks, and referred to a day when there would be so many free Blacks that they could "confront the whites if they needed to." The deaths of animals and slaves, Médor's description of this conspiracy, and his use of the word "poison" led Delavaud to conclude that a network of African poisoners was trying to kill Saint-Domingue's masters.[38] As word of Médor's confession spread, whites began to fear for their lives.

Relying on the testimony of poisoners arrested in 1757 and 1758, the governor wrote that poison had killed "a very great number of whites" and at least 6,000 to 7,000 enslaved people. (In the original text, "qu'outre un fort grand nombre de personnes blanches, qu'on a apris par les instructions avois pery par le poison, on compte au moins six à sept mille nègres, qui ont été détruits par cette malheureuse pratique.") No source attaches a more precise figure to the white death toll. Nor did anyone make a connection between the deaths Médor described, the death of 2,000 horses in Cul-de-Sac five years earlier, and the bad meat killing people and dogs in Cap Français.[39]

In 1757 and 1758, on the basis of Médor's confession, the colonial authorities arrested and tortured hundreds of enslaved and free Blacks. They burned dozens of them at the stake, including the maroon Makandal in January 1758. This witch hunt ended in 1759, about the time that North American smugglers learned how to evade the British blockade, making imported food plentiful and cheap again. In October 1759 the commander of Cap Français announced new regulations punishing butchers who sold meat from animals that were sick, dying, or dead, for bad meat was still killing residents of the city.[40] Saint-Domingue's mysterious killer was probably an as-yet-unidentified food-borne disease, not an African poisoner. That disease would strike Saint-Domingue again during the drought-stricken years leading up to the American Revolutionary War.

---

[37] Suzanne Preston Blier, *African Vodun: Art, Psychology, and Power* (Chicago: University of Chicago Press, 1995), 212; B. Segurola and J. Rassinoux, *Dictionnaire fon–français*, corrected edition (Madrid: SMA Société des Missions Africaines, 2009), 76.

[38] Garrigus, *A Secret among the Blacks*, 35.

[39] François Philippe Bart and Laporte Lalanne, "Lettre des Adrs au ministre sur les empoisonnements," 30 June 1758, ANOM, F^{3}88, 231–4: 231.

[40] Garrigus, *A Secret among the Blacks*, 75–97. Moreau de Saint-Méry, *Loix et constitutions*, vol. IV, 287.

In the early 1760s, the Seven Years' War was still going on and Saint-Domingue's government faced a new challenge. The British had captured French Canada in 1759, and in 1760 they took Guadeloupe. Many officials in France believed that Guadeloupe's colonists had surrendered to serve their own interests. In occupied Guadeloupe, planters sold their sugar for high prices on the protected British market and bought enslaved Africans from British slavers. In four years, British ships unloaded over 23,000 captives in Guadeloupe, seven times more Africans than French slavers brought directly to the colony between 1713 and 1755.[41] In 1762, the British conquered Martinique. It seemed that Saint-Domingue was next. Would colonists there sacrifice their plantations to fight the British?

More concerned with the military threat than with politics, Saint-Domingue's governor, the vicomte Belzunce, began constructing a defensive line of linked military camps in the North Province, which bordered the Atlantic Ocean. His engineers mapped the mountainous interior to find the best locations. Belzunce put his camps where troops could control the mountain passes that led inland to the island's high interior plateau. This would pen British invaders on the humid coastal plain, where malaria, yellow fever, and other diseases would kill them. The French defenders and Saint-Domingue's inhabitants would retreat into the interior, where they would be far less vulnerable to disease. Belzunce incorporated Saint-Domingue's free colored militias into his camps to create more defenders.[42]

Colonists opposed Belzunce's projects, for they understood that he planned to force them into the interior with their slaves, abandoning their plantations to the invaders. They argued that the French navy should defend Saint-Domingue from the sea, breaking the blockade and preventing a British landing. Belzunce's critics were doubly relieved when the British attacked Havana instead of Cap Français in 1762 and the governor died of tropical disease. His camps fell into decay.[43]

The next year, as soon as the war ended, Versailles announced that it would abolish Saint-Domingue's unpopular colonial militia. Elected civilian officials would replace the naval officers commanding the colony's parishes. France would station more European soldiers in the colony and, to offset

---

[41] Burnard and Garrigus, *The Plantation Machine*, 87–90.
[42] Bernard Gainot, *La révolution des esclaves: Haïti, 1763–1803* (Paris: Vendémiaire, 2017), 24–7; Burnard and Garrigus, *The Plantation Machine*, 90.
[43] Burnard and Garrigus, *The Plantation Machine*, 157.

their vulnerability to disease, create a permanent unit of free colored soldiers. Versailles also announced that colonists would pay a tax of 4 million livres.[44]

The colonial ministry enacted other "liberalizing" changes after the war. Saint-Domingue's first successful printing press began operation in 1763, turning out administrative forms, but also publishing a commercial broadsheet, the *Affiches Américaines*, starting in 1764. In 1763, the colonial ministry established a Chamber of Agriculture, with the right to advise the ministry about possible reforms. In 1767 the colonial ministry began to allow foreign merchants to buy molasses and sell certain goods out of one of Saint-Domingue's ports, partially opening the unpopular French trade monopoly.[45]

Then, as these reforms took shape, Versailles canceled the elimination of the militia, citing concerns about colonial defense. Saint-Domingue's first postwar governor, Charles d'Estaing, tried to reestablish the old system, and to collect the 4 million livres tax that colonists believed was their payment for the end of the militia.[46] The colony's Conseils blocked d'Estaing's efforts, and Versailles quickly replaced him with the duc de Rohan Montbazon, who took a more forceful approach. Arriving in 1766, he faced Conseils that saw themselves as colonial parlements. From 1765 onward, *parlements* in Paris, Brittany, and Normandy fought a fierce political struggle against the imposition of new taxes. In 1766, inexplicably, the colonial ministry sent eight lawyers from the Paris *parlement* to fill judicial vacancies in Saint-Domingue. One of them, Marcel, became a leader in the Port-au-Prince Conseil's opposition to Rohan. In 1769, with secret support from that Conseil, colonists in the colony's West and South Provinces took up arms to prevent the militia's reestablishment. They planned to march on Port-au-Prince, arrest Rohan, and send him back to France. Royal troops easily broke up the rebellion, but colonial officials were alarmed to learn that its leaders had forged a temporary alliance of white working-class men and free men of color who shared a belief that militia service was "slavery."[47]

This multiracial coalition endangered France's hold over Saint-Domingue. Rohan sent the Port-au-Prince judges back to France and installed new

---

[44] Garrigus, *Before Haiti*, 115–17.
[45] James E. McClellan, *Colonialism and Science: Saint Domingue in the Old Regime* (Baltimore: Johns Hopkins University Press, 1992), 97–9; Pierre Pluchon, *Histoire de la colonisation française* (Paris: Fayard, 1991), 613; Tarrade, *Commerce colonial*, vol. I, 318.
[46] Moreau de Saint-Méry, *Loix et constitutions*, vol. IV, 637, 644–705, 825–31.
[47] Burnard and Garrigus, *The Plantation Machine*, 174–5; Tarrade, *Commerce colonial*, vol. I, 81, note 60; Charles Frostin, *Les révoltes blanches à Saint-Domingue aux XVIIe et XVIIIe siècles (Haïti avant 1789)* (Paris: L'École, 1975), 345–6; Garrigus, *Before Haiti*, 109–37.

personnel in the Conseil. In 1770 the new royal attorney of Port-au-Prince, Guillaume Delamardelle, welcomed Rohan's successor with a speech that urged him "to maintain the necessary superiority of the free and unmixed race over that which still carries on its brow the mark of slavery."[48] In other words, all European colonists, rich and poor, must be elevated above people of African and part-African descent.

Within a decade, colonial courts and officials passed new laws that cut free people of color, including wealthy French-educated slave owners, out of the white population. They prohibited free men of color from practicing "respectable" professions, like goldsmith, apothecary, notary, or doctor. Colonial theaters established separate seating for whites and people of color. A 1773 law forbade free people of color from taking "white" names, requiring them to take names of "African" origin. Some families simply added a letter to the name they shared with their white relatives; others scrambled the letters, so that Fabre became Erbaf, or Pilorge became Golerep. After 1778, free people of color had to show their manumission papers when they drafted legal documents, even if they had been born free. By 1785, some colonists argued that the honorific "Sieur" – equivalent to the eighteenth-century English "Master" – should never be applied to men of color, no matter how wealthy they were. In the dozen years following the Seven Years' War, race replaced class as the primary criterion of social status among free people in Saint-Domingue, even though there were at least a dozen families of color who were wealthier than many French colonists.[49]

The War of American Independence

Drought and disease returned to Saint-Domingue in the 1770s. When France joined the North American rebels in 1779, the British blockaded the colony again, producing a crisis in which enslaved people and animals died by the thousands, as they had in the 1750s. This time doctors understood that disease caused these deaths. Nevertheless, as planters searched for poisoners, enslaved people experienced the War of American Independence as a time of famine, disease, and continuing persecution.

---

[48] Frostin, *Les révoltes blanches*, 345–6; Burnard and Garrigus, *The Plantation Machine*, 182–3.
[49] Garrigus, *Before Haiti*, 141–2, 163–8, 186.

In 1772, during a severe drought, entire herds of mules began to die on sugar plantations outside Cap Français. The deaths continued until 1774. When colonial doctors wrote to the head of a newly established royal veterinary school in France, describing the animals' symptoms, he diagnosed anthrax. French doctors had only begun to accurately describe the fast-acting disease in 1769, noting that it spread from animals to humans and took both dermatological and intestinal forms. People who ate meat from dead animals were especially likely to die.[50]

Planters ignored veterinarians' anthrax warnings and searched for a new Makandal. In 1773 mules began dying on the Haut-de-Cap sugar estate where the future Toussaint Louverture was once enslaved. The manager began torturing enslaved workers to force them to reveal the poisoner. He asked his employers for permission to kill an enslaved person as an example. The head animal keeper attempted suicide, and twenty-five people fled the plantation. They appealed to the owners, who eventually fired the manager.[51]

Because of the drought, famine threatened the slave population and the government accelerated imports of rice, salt meat, and other slave provisions. In a terrible coincidence, the winter of 1775–1776 was one of the harshest western France had ever experienced. Frozen Atlantic ports could not ship enough food to Saint-Domingue. In August 1776 colonial administrators began requiring planters to plant provisions for their slaves, but hungry people were already dying from eating tainted meat. As anthrax struck cattle in Santo Domingo, ranchers there turned their carcasses into sundried jerky, known as *tassau* in French. Peddlers sold this cheap meat to plantation workers, who ate it and died. In June 1776, the Cap Français authorities ordered constables to destroy all the *tassau* they could find.[52]

---

[50] Moreau de Saint-Méry, *Description topographique*, vol. I, 236; Charles Arthaud, ed., *Recherches, mémoires et observations sur les maladies épizootiques de Saint-Domingue* (Cap François: Imprimerie royale, 1788), 8; [Simeon] Worlock, "Mémoire sur la maladie épizootique pestilentielle de l'île Saint-Domingue," in Charles Arthaud, ed., *Recherches, mémoires et observations*, 162–79; David M. Morens, "Characterizing a 'New' Disease: Epizootic and Epidemic Anthrax, 1769–1780," *American Journal of Public Health* 93:6 (2006), 886–93: 888–9.

[51] Philippe R. Girard, *Toussaint Louverture: A Revolutionary Life* (New York: Basic Books, 2016), 39–40.

[52] Moreau de Saint-Méry, *Loix et constitutions*, vol. v, 392, 400, 701; Charles Frostin, "Saint-Domingue et la révolution américaine," *Bulletin de la société d'histoire de la Guadeloupe* 22 (1974), 73–114: 79–80; Moreau de Saint-Méry, *Loix et constitutions*, vol. VI, 3; Moreau de Saint-Méry, *Description topographique*, vol. I, 76.

Then in October, after Saint-Domingue fully opened its ports to North American rebel ships, the British navy began blockading Saint-Domingue.[53] This blockade was not as thorough as in the Seven Years' War, but it caused even more suffering for enslaved people in the North Province. Wartime uncertainties about food imports added to the scarcity caused by the drought and colonists' panic over mysterious slave and livestock deaths. Despite evidence of animal disease, colonists searched for poisoners. In December 1777, the authorities burned an enslaved man known as Jacques at the stake in Cap Français for poisoning 100 animals belonging to his master over a period of eight months. The decree of execution said that Jacques was found carrying a container of arsenic, a poison that many plantations kept for killing rats, but his master's estate was on the Santo Domingo border, which suggests the animals may have been infected by the ongoing anthrax epidemic. This seems likely, for experts by this time had concluded that the disease was endemic in northern Saint-Domingue. In 1779, meat sickened thirty enslaved people on the Galliffet plantation and killed twelve of them. Neighboring estates had similar problems. In January 1780, for a second time, the colonial administration ordered constables to confiscate *tassau* from Santo Domingo.[54]

After the war had ended, colonists who favored free trade used this suffering to illustrate the dangers of the French colonial monopoly. They claimed that anthrax-tainted *tassau* from Santo Domingo had killed 15,000 slaves in border parishes and that hunger had killed another 15,000.[55]

Amid these troubles, in 1779 a French military expedition sailed from Cap Français, bound for the North American mainland. The fleet, commanded by the former governor Charles d'Estaing, included 545 free men of color from the colony. They had answered d'Estaing's call for patriotic service, while colonial elites were creating new racist laws. Their war experience took them far from home. They dug trenches for d'Estaing's siege of the British fort at Savannah. After the siege failed, the navy sent some free men of color to Charleston; others accompanied d'Estaing to France, then returned to the colony in 1780. Between 150 and 200 men were sent to garrison the island of

---

[53] Frostin, "Saint-Domingue et la révolution américaine," 82–4, 86, 98.
[54] Moreau de Saint-Méry, *Loix et constitutions*, vol. v, 805; Karen Bourdier, "Les conditions sanitaires sur les habitations sucrières de Saint-Domingue à la fin du siècle," *Dix-huitième siècle* 43:1 (2011), 349–68: 356.
[55] Pierre Ulric Dubuisson and Laurent François Lenoir (Marquis de Rouvray), *Lettres critiques et politiques sur les colonies & le commerce des villes maritimes de France* (Geneva: n.p., 1785), 122.

Grenada, which d'Estaing had conquered from the British. Most of the volunteers returned home after about twelve months, but the Grenada troops were away for over two years.[56]

They returned to find that Saint-Domingue's interim governor, François Reynaud de Villeverd, was trying to transform their volunteer unit into a permanent part of the colonial military. Repurposing an idea from the Seven Years' War, Reynaud ordered all free men of color to serve in the new company for three months, rotating out of their parish militias. Their new obligation would reduce white militia service. As men of color saw it, the new unit robbed them of the chance to show patriotism by volunteering to serve. It would turn them into "slaves of the state," as colonists sometimes called enlisted soldiers. Men fled into the woods rather than muster in the new company. Their white militia commanders complained to the colonial ministry, which forced Reynaud to dismantle his new unit within a year. The Savannah expedition of 1779 was a turning point for free men of color, for it demonstrated the influence they could exert by appealing to the imperial authorities.[57]

Versailles understood that racism against free people of color was a problem in Saint-Domingue. In 1781 a new governor, Guillaume de Bellecombe, arrived with a list of possible reforms, including improvements to the status of wealthy men of color. On a tour of the colony he met Julien Raimond, a wealthy biracial indigo planter, educated in France. Raimond was one of eight children born to Marie Begasse, a free biracial woman, and her French husband Pierre Raymond. The post-1770 white supremacy laws had been especially humiliating for Raimond, who proposed to Bellecombe that freeborn light-skinned men like himself be counted as white. Bellecombe advised Raimond to send his ideas to the colonial minister at Versailles.[58]

In 1784, Raimond and his family left for France, where his wife had inherited a rural estate from her late white husband. Raimond traveled to Versailles to meet with colonial bureaucrats about his proposals. Another wealthy French-educated biracial man, Vincent Ogé, was also petitioning the colonial ministry at the same time, asking officials to stop a road that was to

---

[56] Burnard and Garrigus, *The Plantation Machine*, 210–12.
[57] John D. Garrigus, "Catalyst or Catastrophe? Saint-Domingue's Free Men of Color and the Savannah Expedition, 1779–1782," *Review/Revista Interamericana* 22 (1992), 109–25: 112; Garrigus, *Before Haiti*, 123.
[58] Jean Tarrade, "L'administration coloniale en France à la fin de l'Ancien Régime: Projets de réforme," *Revue Historique* 229 (March 1963), 103–22: 119; Garrigus, *Before Haiti*, 217–20.

be built right through his family's coffee plantation. The ministry did little for either man, but both would be drawn into revolutionary politics in 1789.[59]

Prerevolutionary Tensions

In 1784, with the American war over, the colonial ministry created a law to solve two problems it believed weakened Saint-Domingue's plantation economy. Plantation owners living in France complained that their colonial employees were cheating them. Some of France's wealthiest investors had purchased their own Dominguan estates, which they entrusted to local managers. At the same time, the ministry worried that colonists were such harsh masters that they would cause a slave revolt, like those that had happened in nearby British Jamaica. Versailles believed that new regulations would prolong slavery and its profits.[60]

Introduced as a single legal package in December 1784, the new plantation laws addressed both problems. They required plantation managers to register with the authorities and maintain multiple account books recording births and deaths of enslaved people, commodity shipments, and other critical information. The law made masters and managers legally liable for mutilating or murdering their enslaved workers and gave the constabulary the right to inspect plantations and to interview enslaved people about their treatment. Royal administrators, not planter-friendly Conseils, would punish cruel masters. The changes, especially those regulating the treatment of enslaved people, alarmed many colonists. Planters argued that their own self-interest prevented flagrant cruelty. One plantation manager wrote that "if the ordinance is maintained, the fate of a good slave will be preferable to that of a manager or an attorney, I would even say of an owner ... the more I see that they want to free the slaves and put the whites in chains."[61] The Crown did not need Saint-Domingue's two Conseils to consent to the new legislation, but the judges refused to register it, meaning that the law could not be enforced.

In December 1785, Versailles responded with a lightly revised version of the original legislation. The law now ordered enslaved people to show "total obedience" to their masters and authorized masters to punish enslaved

---

[59] Garrigus, *Before Haiti*, 171–2, 217–20; Garrigus, "Vincent Ogé Jeune," 47–8.
[60] Malick W. Ghachem, *The Old Regime and the Haitian Revolution* (New York: Cambridge University Press, 2012), 121–7.
[61] Cited in Burnard and Garrigus, *The Plantation Machine*, 254–5; Moreau de Saint-Méry, *Loix et constitutions*, vol. VI, 655–67.

people in cases of "insubordination, absence, lack of discipline, and disobedience." However, it specified that planters could not claim that enslaved people were insubordinate if they had been "unjustly treated or malnourished." Militia officers and constables were still charged with inspecting plantation conditions, with some restrictions. Under severe pressure from France, both Conseils registered the revised law in May 1786, but the Cap Français Conseil waited until March 1787 to register the earlier version, despite being ordered by Versailles to register both immediately.[62]

In January 1787, the Naval Ministry ordered Saint-Domingue's two Conseils to merge into a single body located in Port-au-Prince. The merger occurred in June. Versailles described this change as a question of efficiency, but elite colonists in Cap Français believed France was punishing them for fighting the new plantation regulations.[63]

The following year they had their revenge, in the case of a coffee planter who admitted to torturing his slaves. In March 1788, fourteen Africans enslaved by Nicolas LeJeune left his plantation under cover of darkness, after witnessing the terrible burns he had inflicted on two women. The Africans presented themselves before the criminal court in Cap Français, which sent a royal attorney and a surgeon to LeJeune's estate. They verified the condition of the two victims, recorded their testimony, and removed them to the surgeon's home. Both women died soon after. LeJeune did not deny that he had tortured two women with burning branches, but he claimed it was necessary to force them to reveal the identity of a poisoner. Although he lived in a region where doctors and veterinarians now understood that anthrax was endemic, LeJeune believed that his slaves were killing each other and his mules, too. In a long memorandum to the court, LeJeune's father described a history of mysterious deaths on the family estate. He claimed that fifty-two of his best workers, most of them new arrivals, had died within a six-month period before he turned the property over to his son. He was convinced a poisoner had done this. After the father had turned the plantation over to his son, he wrote, forty-seven slaves and thirty mules died within a two-year period. In that very year, from January to 10 March 1788, twelve of the son's slaves had died mysteriously, with another five becoming seriously ill.[64]

---

[62] Moreau de Saint-Méry, *Loix et constitutions*, vol. VI, 893, 918–29.
[63] Moreau de Saint-Méry, *Description topographique*, vo. I, 1000; Burnard and Garrigus, *The Plantation Machine*, 256.
[64] Jean-Baptiste Suarez d'Almeida, "Remontrance du Procureur du Roi afin de décret de prise de corps contre le Sr Lejeune fils," 15 March 1788, ANOM E 274 bis, ark:/61561/

LeJeune *père* argued that the judicial system could not effectively investigate these deaths; distance and the tropical heat destroyed whatever evidence an official might gather from a corpse. The impossibility of definitively proving the crime and the importance of moving swiftly meant that a slave owner should be free to investigate and punish as Nicolas LeJeune had done.

LeJeune's neighbors supported him. They claimed that even if LeJeune were guilty of cruelty, convicting him would doom Saint-Domingue's slave system. Under this pressure the local court at Cap Français ruled that the state's evidence against LeJeune was inadmissible. When royal administrators appealed to the colonial Conseil at Port-au-Prince – over which they presided – they lost the case by a single vote. Colonists won this battle in their war against the Crown for local sovereignty.[65]

This was the background to the opening of the French Revolution in Saint-Domingue. In November 1787 a group of colonists began to gather in Paris, understanding that Louis XVI was to summon the Estates General to suggest fundamental reforms. By May 1788 they had written to the king, arguing that despotism had overtaken the rule of law in Saint-Domingue. They proposed that he create three permanent provincial assemblies in the colony, to advise the governor and other royal administrators and gradually move to administrative autonomy.[66]

At the same time, in 1788 colonial bureaucrats in Versailles were telling Julien Raimond and Vincent Ogé that they could not consider their requests, given Louis XVI's pending reform of the kingdom. In 1789 the two men would emerge as unofficial spokesmen for colonial free people of color. Raimond in particular would convince Revolutionary deputies to focus on racism against free-born people, not slavery, as they set about reforming France's plantation colonies.

In 1789 enslaved people, the majority of them born in Africa, made up 88 percent of Saint-Domingue's population.[67] Many of them came from monarchical societies that had experienced civil war and foreign invasion. Many had fought in those wars or been stripped of their freedom by political changes. In Saint-Domingue in 1789, those enslaved in colonial port cities or

up424qklnlq; Armand Romaine huissier (bailiff), "Assignation au 14 Nègres et Nsses du Sr LeJeune detenus ez prisons, extrait des Minutes du Greffe de Sénéchaussée Royale du Cap," 9 March 1788, ANOM E 274 bis, ark:/61561/up424qklnlq; Moreau de Saint-Méry, *Loix et constitutions*, vol. VI, 370; Nicolas LeJeune père, "Requête d'intervention," 21 May 1788, ANOM E 274 bis, ark:/61561/up424qklnlq.
[65] See the detailed narrative and analysis in Ghachem, *Old Regime*, 186–206.
[66] Pluchon, *Histoire de la colonisation*, 785.
[67] Geggus, "Port Towns of Saint Domingue," 104.

plantation households understood that change was coming to the colony. No one, enslaved or free, could predict those changes, but enslaved people had their own ideas. In the 1750s the enslaved valet Médor imagined a future in which Saint-Domingue had so many free Blacks that they could "stand up to the whites, if necessary." In 1788 some of the people Nicolas LeJeune enslaved asked a royal court to enforce a new law that prohibited cruel treatment. Their case failed. But their attempt, like Médor's vision of Black power, suggests that many in Saint-Domingue's majority population believed change was possible, whether that came through applying new laws or actively confronting the master class.

24

The Haitian Revolutions

BERNARD GAINOT

Preliminary Considerations

Reducing a galaxy of events to a unified linear account is necessarily a deceit. As a preliminary, I will go over a few principles concerning methodology and writing which have become self-evident over the course of thirty or so years of prolonged contact in the archives with the traces left by what was once the French colony of Saint-Domingue.

One may query whether there was a single Haitian revolution. There were, rather, multiple "Haitian revolutions," at least three in number: the slave revolution on the sugar plains, as typified by the great northern plain; the revolution in the fortified camps and pioneer fronts in the hills, where free people of color fought for partition, typified by the central province, stretching from the gates of Port-au-Prince to the town of Mirebalais; and lastly, the particularly violent revolution in the towns, where militias comprised of people of color clashed with white patriots over control of neighborhoods and institutions. These local contests for power gave rise to shifting political configurations. For reasons of clarity, I have opted for a chronological account. Still, it is important to warn against the pretenses of a linear account which might incline us toward a deterministic reading of this history. The 1804 independence was in no way visible on the horizon of the 1791 slave uprising; and in 1801 nothing prevented Bonaparte from governing with Toussaint Louverture as unified commander of the island, as he belatedly regretted in his memoires. Likewise, Rochambeau's capitulation in November 1803 was not due to bands of insurgent slaves: first, because, from a legal point of view, slavery had been abolished since 1793–1794; and second, because the pro-independence army was a regular army issuing directly from the colonial army recomposed in 1794–1795.

Having stated these caveats and made these transnational and diachronic choices, the flow of men, ideas, cultural models, and techniques clearly invites us to privilege an imperial line of inquiry. The image of a universalist republic and an imperialist nation was primarily built up around the ties between France and Saint-Domingue, and at times in contradiction with them.[1] In what follows, I posit the link between the two revolutions as the structuring factor, though at times I emphasize the importance of other places, in the United States and Spanish Caribbean in particular. Although during this revolutionary decade political events in Paris were key in shaping the conflictual dialogue between colony and metropole, it is essential to factor in other relays such as the great ports, and to point out that the tropical "peripheries," far from being places where decisions taken in the metropole were straightforwardly enacted, could also influence the course of history. From this point of view, periods of conflict and particularly international conflict were crucial.

The Magic Lantern: The Revolution and Its Mirror Image

After the American War of Independence, colonial affairs were no longer the preserve of the closed world of Versailles offices. They were scrutinized in public debate, which was fueled by a wave of memorandums and pamphlets, the establishment of *sociétés de pensée*, and an incipient independent press. Yet the rhetoric used to formulate this debate is misleading once it went beyond general and abstract principles. Colonists speaking of *liberty* were only thinking of *particular liberties* (commercial freedom, administrative autonomy); free landowners of color calling for equality had primarily *equality amongst masters* in mind; and as for *universal fraternity*, it soon shattered on the dubious rock of *identities* in this world of castes and statuses.

The Protagonists

In the metropole, colonial policy was directed by the Versailles offices. From 1780 to 1787, the secretary of state for the navy and colonies was the Marquis de Castries, who wished to open up and modernize the French empire. This was to be implemented through the *Exclusif mitigé* (designating a partial relaxation of the obligation upon colonies to trade solely with their imperial

---

[1] Yves Bénot, *La Révolution française et la fin des colonies* (Paris: La Découverte, 2003 [1987]).

capital),² which accepted some of the colonists' demands: allowing foreign merchants – mainly from the United States, but also from the Dutch Republic and Denmark – to operate in the colony, and granting more extensive colonial representation than in the traditional sovereign councils. But de Castries also included free men of color in his ambit. In 1784, Julien Raimond, a rich southern mixed-race landowner, came to Paris, where he argued that it was iniquitous and absurd to segregate free men of color. The dynamic and enterprising group of people of color living in Paris was seeking to establish itself as a rival to the white colonists, who had a well-organized "lobby" defending large plantations, the slavery system, and color prejudice. Its advocates found a responsive audience among the Caribbean community living in Paris, numbering a little under 2,000 people, who, since they resided on French soil, were legally free, and were actively seeking to establish their autonomy by constituting themselves as a corporation.³

In February 1788, the Société des Amis des Noirs (Society of the Friends of the Blacks), with close links to the Society of the Friends of the Blacks in London,⁴ was founded by the essayists Étienne Clavière and Jacques-Pierre Brissot. Its objective was the very gradual abolition of slavery, starting with a concerted international campaign against the slave trade. Its priority was to convince planters that improving the condition of slaves would provide a lifeline for the entire colonial system. But the planters were far from convinced, and in August 1789 reacted defensively against what they saw as the excessive influence "philanthropists" exerted over the authorities by founding a group, the Club Massiac, at the private townhouse of one of their members.

In Saint-Domingue, "American patriotism" was maturing in the aftermath of the American War of Independence.⁵ The United States agreed fully with the demands by white creoles of Saint-Domingue, who called for free trade, tax reform, and the representation of landowners. In the large towns on the island, an "American" public opinion crystallized around the many Masonic lodges and the *sociétés de pensée*, such as the Cercle des Philadelphes in Le

---

² Jean Tarrade, *Le commerce colonial de la France à la fin de l'Ancien Régime: L'évolution du régime de l'"Exclusif" de 1763 à 1789* (Paris: Presses universitaires de France, 1972).
³ Erick Noël, *Être noir en France au XVIIIᵉ siècle* (Paris: Tallandier, 2006).
⁴ Marcel Dorigny and Bernard Gainot, *La Société des Amis des Noirs (1788–1799): Contribution à une histoire de l'abolition de l'esclavage* (Paris: Éditions de l'UNESCO, 1998). See also Erica Johnson Edwards' Chapter 4 in this volume.
⁵ Charles Frostin, *Les révoltes blanches à Saint-Domingue aux XVIIᵉ et XVIIIᵉ siècles* (Rennes: Presses universitaires de Rennes, 2008).

Cap, which imitated the typical forms of sociability of the Enlightenment and acted as the crucible for an "American" identity.[6]

At the same time, the group of free men of color was expanding and becoming individualized.[7] It consisted mainly of, first, mixed-race large landowners in the south (the Fond des Cayes Plain and the countryside around Jérémie and Jacmel) and west (the Cul-de-Sac Plain and the upper valley of the Artibonite); and, second, emancipated traders and merchants in the main cities of Le Cap and Port-au-Prince.[8] These "free blacks" were the intermediaries between plantation society and urban society. They assiduously served the militia and constabulary, and generally managed to make themselves indispensable to the colonial authorities. They ran a cluster of brotherhoods and associations, which were the driving spirit in the process of creolization. Some rose to the status of small landowner and owned a few slaves. Such was the case of Toussaint, not yet known as Toussaint Louverture.[9]

Color prejudice drastically separated the 30,000 whites, who alone were entitled to hold public employment, the rank of officer, or any honorific status, from the 27,000 free people of color, who were denied the recompense to which they would have logically been entitled by their ascent and position in creole society.

Facing this elite of plantation masters (about 5,000 individuals in all, said to be the real "inhabitants") was the servile mass of some 550,000 individuals who had arrived on slave ships. The term "African" covered great diversity in origin, with the label functioning as a negative assignation at this period. It was Creole culture which largely redefined their codes and representations, but also fashioned new identities after the great crossing. The colonial authorities, which were largely external to vertical and horizontal sociabilities, were less involved in transmitting this culture than were the various intermediaries such as the slave drivers, militia sergeants, coachmen, peddlers, traditional healers, and deacons, who structured plantation society in the broad sense. The smaller urban milieu served as its extension.[10]

---

[6] James MacClellan and Francois Regourd, "The Colonial Machine: French Science and Colonization in the Ancien Régime," *Osiris* 15 (2000), 31–50.

[7] Stuart King, *Blue Coat or Powered Wig: Free People of Color in Revolutionary Saint-Domingue* (Athens, GA: University of Georgia Press, 2001).

[8] John Garrigus, *Before Haiti: Race and Citizenship in French Saint-Domingue* (New York and Basingstoke: Palgrave Macmillan, 2006).

[9] Jacques De Cauna, *Toussaint-Louverture, le grand précurseur* (Bordeaux: Éditions Sud-ouest, 2012).

[10] Anne Pérotin-Dumon, *La ville aux îles, la ville dans l'île: Basse-Terre et Pointe-à-Pitre, Guadeloupe 1650–1820* (Paris: Karthala, 2000).

Political Representation of an "Exotic" Territory

Issues concerning the link between representation and taxation had been a root cause of the American Revolution. They also lay behind the troubles in Saint-Domingue. On 26 December 1788, a Royal Ordinance proposed consulting the Inhabitants (that is to say, the 5,000 or so white planters) about creating a delegation from the colonies to the Estates General. A secret committee seized on this proposal to hold clandestine elections for a delegation to Versailles.[11] Eighteen colonists were "elected," but the Third Estate granted consultative rights to only eight of them.

Discussions about admitting them to the Constituent Assembly took place in early July 1789. Mirabeau was against it, contesting the white colonists' claim to be the sole ones entitled to speak in the name of the landowners. He indirectly raised the issue of slavery in denouncing the fact that the colonists claimed to represent the entire population of the colony: "in making the number of parliamentarians proportional to the population of France, we did not take into consideration the number of our horses and our mules; and if the blacks are, as said, the agents of colonial wealth, our cattle and our horses are also the agents of our wealth." The great landowners residing in Paris were also opposed to representation for the colonies, wishing to preserve the authority of the king, the keystone holding up the colonial status quo.[12] Eventually six parliamentarians were accepted for the Saint-Domingue colony in July 1789.

Saint-Domingue's governor, De Peynier, organized the loyalist colonists, who took the name *Pompons blancs*. The radicals, with the strong backing of the white urban lower-class population, and sporting the tricolor rosette, adopted revolutionary rhetoric, wishing to see an end to "ministerial despotism" and the introduction of administrative autonomy (strictly regulated by the whites, but that was left unsaid). These *Pompons rouges* exhorted the regular troops in their barracks to switch camp, in which they were victorious. This revolutionary fervor then spread to the navy in the ports.

Behind the question of representation lies that of the political rights of free men of color, a matter which came increasingly to dominate public debate. The Société des Amis des Noirs now prioritized this issue, privileging action to end the colonial status quo over their previous desire to persuade white

---

[11] Blanche Maurel, "La campagne pour la représentation de Saint-Domingue aux États-Généraux," in *Cahiers de doléances de la colonie de Saint-Domingue pour les États généraux de 1789* (Paris: CTHS, Publications de la Commission de recherche des documents relatifs à la vie économique de la Révolution, 1933), 15–27.

[12] Jules Saintoyant, *La colonisation française pendant la Révolution (1789–1799)*, 2 vols. (Paris: La Renaissance du livre, 1930), vol. 1.

colonists of the need for gradual reform to the system of slavery. Additionally, the Constituent Assembly was faced with urgent questions. Was colonial territory an integral part of the Empire? Were the populations of such territories subject to the same laws?

In November 1789 proposals were put forward to recognize the rights of free men of color, hence to admit them to elective assemblies. Acting in the name of the colonial committee, dominated by planters, Antoine Barnave referred the decision to the colonial assemblies, thus handing the legislative initiative on the citizenship of men of color to their most determined enemies. At the same time, the colonial assembly of Saint-Domingue convened in the town of Saint-Marc. It made the slave regime harsher and segregationist legislation more discriminatory, and drafted a constitution placing Saint-Domingue on the path to secession. With the support of the white urban lower-class population and the line regiments, the pro-independence *Pompons rouges* party clashed with the authority of the governor, who unleashed the *Pompons blancs* against them. When the Saint-Marc assembly was dissolved in July 1790, Barnave wished to reassure the planters about the intentions of the metropole. To this end, another decree, dated 12 October 1790, confirmed the status quo: "no law about the status of people shall be voted except at the formal and precise request of the colonial assemblies." Harsh police measures were taken against people of color, forbidding them from traveling across the Atlantic. It was at this stage that the legislative debate leading to the decree of 15 May 1791 started. Men of color were granted the status of active citizens, if both their parents had been born free – in the vast majority of cases the mother was of servile status – and if they additionally fulfilled the general requirements concerning residency and fiscal matters.[13] Thus, very few acquired citizenship, about 400 individuals in all. Nevertheless, symbolically, this decree opened an initial breach which, in the volcanic circumstances of Saint-Domingue, was the prelude to a violent and widespread eruption (Map 24.1).

Various Forms of Violence

Violence habitually marks social relations in colonial societies suffering from scarcity and fear.[14] There is a permanent fear of shortages should supplies fail

---

[13] Jean-Daniel Piquet, *L'émancipation des Noirs dans la Révolution française (1789–1795)* (Paris: Karthala, 2002).

[14] Caroline Oudin-Bastide, *L'effroi et la Terreur: Esclavage, poison et sorcellerie aux Antilles* (Paris: La Découverte, 2013).

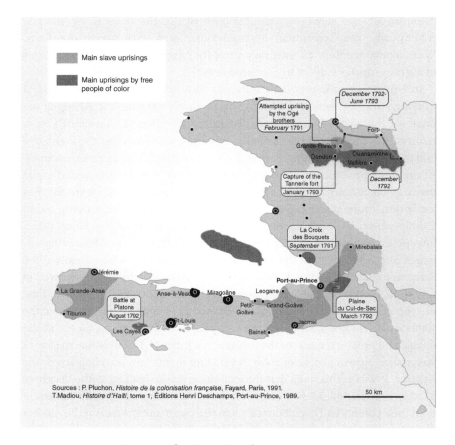

Map 24.1 The Haitian Revolution, 1791–1793.

to arrive, and of death by illness, assassination, or natural cataclysm. To stave off a state of permanent anxiety, there is a pronounced tendency to eliminate the supposed malevolent threats, even more feared for being large in number.[15] Political assassinations, which were akin to lynchings, constituted one form of violence. The murder of a judge, Ferrand des Baudières, at the town of Petit-Goave in November 1789 triggered a cycle of violence. He had been gathering signatures for a petition to send a colored representative to the Port-au-Prince provincial assembly. A rampant crowd decapitated him

[15] Pierre Pluchon, *Vaudou, sorciers, empoisonneurs: De Saint-Domingue à Haïti* (Paris: Karthala, 1987).

with an axe before then setting about attacking homes belonging to free people of color.

Mutiny spread, in ships and barracks. The troops made common cause with the *sans-culottes* in the towns, regrouped into *gardes nationales*. The colonel of the Port-au-Prince regiment, Thomas-Antoine Mauduit, was hated by lower-class whites, for he was one of the staunchest supporters of the party of order, the *Pompons blancs*. It was he who had conducted the dissolution of the Saint-Marc assembly. On 21 March 1791, during a riot in Port-au-Prince, his throat was slit by soldiers from his own regiment.

Lynching and mutiny are not specific to colonies. These bloody scenes are familiar "tableaus of the French Revolution." But while the avowed motives of "patriots" in the metropole were associated with matters of egalitarianism, the "patriots" in Saint-Domingue – behind a shared rhetoric of natural rights, antiaristocratism, and the legitimacy of self-defense – were driven by a violent rejection of equal rights.

The Vincent Ogé affair shows that colonial justice was not wholly in step with the humanitarian tendencies of the metropole. Vincent Ogé came from an important mixed-race family from northern Saint-Domingue, and had become a key figure among Caribbean people of color in Paris.[16] Intent on drawing attention to the texts which, to his mind, guaranteed the political participation of people such as he, and determined to defy the colonists' illegal bans on the circulation of men of color and of official revolutionary texts, he returned in secret to his homeland in October 1790, and, together with a handful of accomplices, organized an armed uprising to oblige the colonial assembly of Cap Français to promulgate the decree of 15 May. The expedition was a fiasco, and Ogé and his accomplices took refuge in the Spanish part of the island, whose authorities handed them over to the assembly of Cap Français in December 1790. Its Conseil Supérieur subjected them to torture and, in February 1791, sentenced Ogé and his lieutenant Chavannes to execution by being broken on the wheel.

The colonial mental universe was fundamentally rooted in drama and torment. It was a reciprocal terror in which constant fear at the extreme violence of masters was a response to the terror unleashed by the terrorized during slave revolts. It may be detected in the self-righteous records of atrocities left by witnesses of the period emphasizing transgressions (rapes, torturing executioners with their own implements, and the murder of

---

[16] Florence Gauthier, *L'aristocratie de l'épiderme: Le combat de la Société des Citoyens de couleur, 1789–1791* (Paris: CNRS Éditions, 2007).

children). These transgressions explain why public opinion was stupefied on hearing of the uprising of slave gangs in the great northern sugar plain, in the hinterland of Le Cap, during the night of 22–23 August 1791 and the following days. This is evidenced by the fact that the few direct images we have of the colonies for this period relate to this event.

The event itself remains shrouded in mystery for that matter. Its intensity is attributable to the context and organization. The atmosphere in the colony suggested civil war was imminent, with counterrevolutionary whites and free men of color in turn fomenting revolt among slaves in the opposing camp, thereby indicating just how brutal the political climate had become. But who were the instigators? Was it the *Pompons blancs* party seeking to avenge Mauduit by triggering the ruin and massacre of the *Pompons rouges*, who enjoyed widespread support among planters? Or, more plausibly, the survivors of Ogé's expedition wishing to avenge their martyred victim for the oppression wrought by the Le Cap assembly? The fact that the revolt became an insurrection is attributable to its meticulous organization, with the middle-ranking members of plantation society (the slave drivers, taskmasters, and craftsmen) playing a key role. Even though the revolt was in no way a brief spontaneous outburst, it largely escaped its instigators' control. It continued over time, transforming the heart of the colonial economy into a field of smoking ruins strewn with corpses.[17]

But however profound, striking, and symbolic it was, this great revolt of the northern plain was but one of the localized slave revolts of this period. The Cul-de-Sac plain inland of Port-au-Prince became a fortified camp. Further south, a troop of insurgent slaves transformed the Les Platons uplands into a fortress, repelling attempts by the colonial authorities to reconquer the area. These insurgent zones took the revolution to another level, with the collapse of established powers and dissolution of authority.

The Revolution of the Free People of Color

The group of free men of color lay at the heart of this devolution of power. They form the axis around which the revolutionary chaos acquires a form of intelligibility. The National Assembly was hard put to stake out a clear position, and incomprehension between the metropole and its colony fueled radicalization.

---

[17] Laënnec Hurbon, ed., *L'insurrection des esclaves de Saint-Domingue (22–23 août 1791)* (Paris: Karthala, 2000).

For several months, the position of free men of color had been the center of everyone's attention. They were rightly considered as "the boulevard running through the colony,"[18] but how should one interpret this strategic line, given the insurrectional context? For the most farsighted of those upholding the colonial order, they were the "faithful dogs guarding the entrance to the sheepfold."[19] Priority was given to the security aspect, for the colonial authorities had always relied on militias of color to maintain order. For the advocates of humanitarian universalism, and most of their group's mouthpieces (such as Julien Raimond and Pierre Pinchinat), men of color were the natural intermediaries between their racial brethren and the white landowners, and the spearhead of a movement that called slavery into question. They were the "true inhabitants" of the colony, the "natives" whose citizenship was legitimized by the right of first settler.

The leaders (Grégoire, Clavière, and Brissot) of the Society of the Friends of the Blacks argued that free men of color were the most naturally placed to defend the colony in the event of aggression by the neighboring imperial powers of Spain and Britain. Since they were well acclimatized, attached to their land, and of proven military capability, all that remained was to procure their loyalty by granting them political rights. Strategically, however, the Society relied on the free men of color to subvert the slave society's status quo. This was no timorous withdrawal in the face of increasingly widespread slave uprisings, but a deliberate strategic choice: white colonists ought to share their power with their compatriots of color, a stance from which the more moderate among them subsequently took their distance.[20]

The full ambiguity in the metropole's standpoint transpired in reactions to the new flare-up of violence on the northern plain in August 1791, news of which reached Paris in early November of the same year. Prior to this, the National Assembly had taken an initiative which ultimately upset the institutional equilibrium. It had sent out a civilian commission (composed of three commissioners) tasked with restoring order and enforcing new laws (including the decree of 15 May on the citizenship of free men of color), a step to counterbalance the power of the governors. As in revolutionary

---

[18] Bernard Gainot, "La presse métropolitaine et la violence coloniale en novembre 1791," in Michel Biard, ed., *Combattre, tolérer ou justifier? Ecrivains et journalistes face à la violence d'État (XVIe–XXe siècles)* (Mont-Saint-Aignan: Publications de l'Université de Rouen et du Havre, 2009), 73–94.
[19] J.-P. Brissot de Warville, *Discours sur la nécessité de maintenir le décret rendu le 15 mai 1791 en faveur des hommes de couleur libres, prononcé le 12 septembre 1791* (Paris: n.p., 1791).
[20] Piquet, *L'émancipation des Noirs*.

France, the legislature was encroaching on the powers of the executive. Nevertheless, the governors (the representatives of the executive) still had armed forces at their disposal, considerably hampering the means available to the commissioners.

Locally, the governors lost their monopoly over armed force in the course of 1791. The white colonists formed a new colonial assembly in Léogane, in total disregard of the decree of 15 May. They considered breaking away from the metropole and placing themselves under British protection. They could rely on the units of national guards. In the past, free men of color had set up confederations backed by militias. Their headquarters was Le Mirebalais, in the mountains above the Cul-de-Sac Plain. They offered to share power with the white landowners, no longer on the basis of elections but according to the balance of respective force. This approach was intended as an alternative response to the increasing number of slave uprisings, which were coalescing to become a "Black uprising." In the north, the insurgent zone now reached the Spanish border, across which arms and supplies were smuggled. In the south, the rebel stronghold at Platons, sheltered in the mountains above the Les Cayes Plain, continued to exist.

It was this dilution of authority and multifaceted menace, not just a slave revolt, that revolutionary France had to confront. The Legislative Assembly, where the former Amis des Noirs held influence, passed the law of 4 April 1792 granting free men of color full civilian equality, together with political rights under identical conditions to those in metropolitan departments. To see to the enforcement of this law (which, given the circumstances, meant respecting order and property), a second civilian commission was dispatched. Brissot in person appointed its two dominant figures, Léger-Félicité Sonthonax and Étienne Polverel, both of whom were determined abolitionists. A return to order implied a two-pronged combat against white separatists and against Black insurgents. To this end, the civilian commission was accompanied by an expeditionary force. The position of the governor, the incarnation of colonial power, was increasingly an empty shell.

Militarization of the Territory

The state of widespread civil war altered the landscape, which became militarized. Certain buildings on plantations were fortified, thus becoming armed camps. Fighting, with the purpose of seizing enemy positions, resulted in an increasing number of ruins. Some enslaved people ran away, while others – at a subaltern rank – joined the garrisoned troops camping on the plantations and overseeing the few remaining slave gangs. The production of cash crops plummeted, while the relative share of staple crops increased. Coffee, being less labor- and energy-intensive than sugar, became the main speculative crop.

Each party had its own militia, transforming community networks into armed factions. In the main towns, there were bloody conflicts in which white soldiers fought men of color for control over the companies of national guards. The regiments of regular troops were dissolved on 29 September 1791, and many soldiers deserted and joined the white national guard.[21] Control of barracks and especially of ammunition depots was an additional factor in this ubiquitous conflagration.

In 1792, the second civilian commission arrived in Le Cap, backed by an expeditionary force of 6,000 men, partly patriot soldiers and partly national volunteer battalions. This strike force transformed the entire situation, and it formed an alliance with the companies of men of color. The colonial assembly was dissolved, and after three days of fighting in October 1792, the pockets of armed white resistance in Le Cap – officially assimilated by the commissioners to the "royalists" – were annihilated. In this struggle against "royalism," henceforth synonymous with "counterrevolution," the commissioners and their allies, the "citizens of 4 April," wished to strike at white power throughout the colony. In December 1792, they got rid of the agitators in the clubs at Cap Français who conflated patriotism with white exclusivism. The key figures, such as Page and Brulley, were sent back to the metropole, where they presented themselves as victims of the commissioners' tyranny.

Militarization Leading to General Freedom

The armed forces loyal to the commissioners then sought to stamp out Black uprisings. General Étienne Laveaux, the commander of the northern province, took most of the positions held by the insurgents. The latter were former slaves who had become soldiers in a permanent army led by Jean-François and Toussaint Bréda. They were pushed back to the border with the Spanish colony, where they took refuge when Spain joined the war against France in February 1793, and obtained ranks in the Spanish army. At the same time, the Platons' resistance in the south was broken. These military

---

[21] Boris Lesueur, *Les Troupes coloniales d'Ancien Régime: Fidelitate per Mare et Terras* (Paris: SPM, 2014).

successes in the north and south were achieved only thanks to the free men of color's support for the commissioners, who turned their militias into regular troops headed by former volunteers in the American War of Independence, with Jean-Baptiste Belley taking command in Le Cap and André Rigaud in Les Cayes.

The pockets of white resistance were eliminated in turn. With the help of free men of color, who had formed a Legion of Equality, Polverel crushed the royalists at Les Cayès. In April 1793 Sonthonax bombarded the town of Port-au-Prince, which was ruled by white independentists. On 20 June 1793, in Cap Français, the governor, François-Thomas Galbaud, wishing to overthrow the commissioners, had navy troops attack their positions held by Laveaux's dragoons and Belley's companies. Street combats raged and Le Cap went up in flames. From their fortified camp, the commissioners called on the bands of maroons, who had been roaming the countryside since the plantations had become fortresses, promising them freedom in exchange for their support.[22] Galbaud and his troops left the island, as did many colonist families.

During the summer of 1793, general freedom, as established by a decree drawn up in French and in Creole, was progressively extended to the entire colony. The state of general insecurity, the proliferation of the phenomenon of bands of maroons, and the increasing number of petitions from slaves calling for an end to slavery made any attempt to return to the status quo ante illusory. Edmond Genet, the plenipotentiary minister for the French Republic in Philadelphia, noting the subversion of the former colonial order, observed: "Saint-Domingue can no longer be governed by whites, the people of color's revolution must be allowed to run its course."[23]

From Isolation to Insularity: Local Contexts and International Conflict

Between 1791 and 1803, the Haitian Revolution ejected thousands of refugees across the Caribbean in successive waves, triggering one of the largest population transfers in the early modern period. In 1791, the first mass departures, mainly of independentist and Anglophile colonist families,

---

[22] Jeremy Popkin, *You Are All Free: The Haitian Revolution and the Abolition of Slavery* (New York: Cambridge University Press, 2010).
[23] Manuel Covo, "Commerce et révolutions dans l'espace atlantique. États-Unis/Saint-Domingue, 1784–1806" (Ph.D. dissertation, EHESS, 2013).

headed for Kingston in Jamaica.[24] The overthrow of white power in the summer of 1793 led to spectacular mass departures northwards, toward Louisiana and the United States.[25] Cities on the eastern seaboard such as Savannah, Baltimore, and Charleston had long-standing business ties with Saint-Domingue families, but it was especially Philadelphia which saw its demography suddenly and profoundly altered with the influx of 4,000 whites and 20,000 Blacks.[26] In 1798, the end of the war caused colonists who had taken up arms against republicans to depart. The main destination this time was Cuba, particularly the east of that island.[27] Others spread out and settled in various places in the Spanish Empire throughout the period, including Puerto Rico in the early nineteenth century[28] and Venezuela.[29]

It is hard to establish any overall figures, especially as each "family" emigrated with their servants and slaves, and not all heads of emigrant families were white. Still, if it seems implausible to place the figure as high as 30,000 individuals, which would amount to all of the whites disappearing from the colony, it may be reckoned that two-thirds (17,000) of the whites were no longer present in the colony as of 1798. Though no longer in the colony, they were neither inactive nor silent, quite the contrary. They introduced their production and production techniques in their new countries of adoption: sugar and coffee in Cuba, cotton in Mississippi and Georgia. They produced numerous newspapers, sometimes with opposing political views, as in Philadelphia, and helped shape public opinion which host governments needed to take into account.

Nor should we forget the singular role played by the metropole for this diaspora. Paris, in particular, received incomers from all the waves of migration, acting as the sounding board for virulent debates being conducted in the press on either side of the Atlantic. There was a constant flow of

[24] Jacques De Cauna, "La Diaspora des colons de Saint-Domingue et le Monde Créole: Le cas de la Jamaïque," *Revue Française d'histoire de l'outre-mer* 304 (1994), 333–59.

[25] Nathalie Dessens. *From Saint-Domingue to New Orleans: Migration and Influences* (Gainesville: University of Florida Press, 2007).

[26] Ashli White, "'A Flood of Impure Lava': Saint-Domingue Refugees in the United States, 1791–1820" (Ph.D. dissertation, Columbia University, 2003).

[27] Agnès Renault, *D'une île rebelle à une île fidèle: Les Français de Santiago de Cuba (1791–1825)* (Mont-Saint-Aignan: Publications des universités de Rouen et du Havre, 2012).

[28] Anne Pérotin-Dumon and Paul Estrade, "Les Antilles espagnoles (1770–1855)," in Christian Hermann, ed., *Les révolutions dans le monde ibérique (1766–1834)*, 2 vols. (Bordeaux: Presses universitaires de Bordeaux, 1991), vol. II, 47–111.

[29] Alejandro E. Gómez, *Le spectre de la Révolution Noire: L'impact de la Révolution Haïtienne dans le monde atlantique, 1790–1886* (Rennes: Presses universitaires de Rennes, 2013).

people and ideas between Paris and Philadelphia, with the latter even becoming a place to print pamphlets and opinions that could no longer be disseminated in the metropole.

Separate yet United

When Spain and especially Britain joined the war in February 1793, the effects were not felt immediately. However, the two new belligerents turned out to have a decisive influence on the course of the revolution. The colonial delegations in London sent by the separatist minority of the colonial assembly of Saint-Marc and by some groups of French émigrés had been involved in lengthy preparations for a British intervention – the crucial figures being Venault de Charmilly and Malouet – a step increasingly called for by the colonists who had stayed in Saint-Domingue, especially after they had all lost their positions in the state apparatus to men of color in the wake of the decree abolishing slavery.

In September, Jérémie went over to the British side, followed by Môle Saint-Nicolas, giving the British navy a solid foothold. Saint-Marc fell in December, where the British met up with the Spanish forces who had come down the Artibonite Valley. The colony was cut in two. Throughout the western province, some of the former free men of color also called upon the British, such as Jean-Baptiste Lapointe, who was fiercely opposed to Pinchinat and the commissioners.[30] The British expeditionary force was fairly slight, and its leader, John Whitelock, rather than intervening rapidly and dispersing his forces, prudently took advantage of the civil strife ravaging the colony. Reinforcements arrived from Europe in May 1794, and on 3 June the British captured Port-au-Prince. By now they controlled one-third of the colony, and their ships were able to impose a strict blockade, on which they counted to trigger the collapse of the positions held by the republicans: the redoubt in Le Cap and that in Port-de-Paix in the northwest, opposite Tortuga Island, an important supply base.[31] In the south, the mixed-race republican Rigaud controlled the town of Les Cayes, which was fortified to act as a center of resistance.

---

[30] Bernard Gainot, "Les libres de couleur et les révolutions de Saint-Domingue," in Association Les Anneaux de la mémoire, ed., *Couleur et Liberté dans l'espace colonial français (début XVIIIe–début XIXe siècle): Cahiers des Anneaux de la mémoire* n° 17 (Paris: Karthala, 2017), 93–109.

[31] David Geggus, *Slavery, War, and Revolution: The British Occupation of Saint-Domingue (1793–1798)* (Oxford: Clarendon Press, 1982).

Elections were held in the northern province in September 1793. They were carefully controlled and had a triple purpose: exhibiting the continuity of republican law on both sides of the Atlantic; making the proclamation of the abolition of slavery irreversible; and displaying the new balance of power in the colony, symbolically embodied by the "union of colors." Two Blacks were elected (Jean-Baptiste Belley, the hero of the fighting in June 1793, and Joseph Boisson, who had enjoyed a similar military career to that of Belley), as were two mixed-race candidates (Pierre Garnot and Jean-Baptiste Mills), along with two whites, Étienne Laforest and Louis-Pierre Dufaÿ,[32] officials who had remained loyal to the commissioners. Three representatives of this three-colored deputation (Belley, Dufaÿ, and Mills) were sent to the metropole. The British blockade meant they were obliged to sail via the United States, where there were hostile protests by refugee colonists waiting to lynch them. Page and Brulley, the emissaries of the colonial assemblies, denounced them in terms evoking the radical rhetoric of the Jacobin club, and on arriving in mainland France the three were arrested. They were finally released and given a triumphal welcome by the Convention, which had just discovered that part of Saint-Domingue was still republican, and went on to play a key role in the adoption of the decree of 4 February 1794 (16 Pluviôse Year II) on general freedom, which universalized the commissioners' partial decision to abolish slavery.[33] Though separated by distance and isolated by the enemy blockade, the metropolitan and colonial territories were united under a single law – a state of republican isonomy – which recognized the sole status of citizen. The foreign war, which had looked like an insurmountable obstacle for the civic bond, turned out on the contrary to accelerate the course of history. Without (either civil or foreign) war, general freedom would never have come about.

This simple reminder of the circumstances in no way diminishes the role of the commissioners as key protagonists in this tropical revolution. Sonthonax and Polverel were pragmatists, not opportunists. Without their firmly anchored belief in abolition, the immediate abolition of slavery would no doubt not have taken place either. But, at the time, any reminder of a militant abolitionist past in the metropole was highly dangerous, for it linked the two commissioners to the Brissotin group, whose high-profile leaders

---

[32] Jean-Charles Benzaquen, *Louis-Pierre Dufaÿ, conventionnel abolitionniste et colon de Saint-Domingue (1752–1804)* (Paris: Éditions SPM, 2015).
[33] Yves Bénot, "Comment la Convention a-t-elle voté l'abolition de l'esclavage en l'an II?," *Annales Historiques de la Révolution française* no. 293–294 (1993), 349–61.

were guillotined in October 1793. The revolutionary tribunal did not omit charging them with having incited the Blacks to rise up, thus causing the ruin of the finest jewel in the colonial empire – a plot carried out to the great advantage of the British.

The colonial assemblies' envoys to Paris viewed these executions as a great victory and a reward for their very active lobbying of Jacobins, with whom they adopted the rhetoric of the *Pompons rouges* and passed themselves off as the *sans-culottes* of the tropics, and of government committees, some of whose members they managed to win over. Presenting themselves as the persecuted victims of the commissioners, they managed to get an arrest order issued against the latter. In June 1794, Sonthonax and Polverel fled from the British, who had just captured Port-au-Prince, and went to Jacmel along the well-named "commissioners' hill," where they were placed under arrest aboard a corvette which set sail for France.

Resistance and Victory

Republican resistance regrouped around figures of military power. General Laveaux, the commander of the northern province, was named head of the provisional government in the colony. Entrenched in the redoubt at Port-de-Paix, he managed to hold out by fusing regular troops with local militias of color, and thanks to supplies of food and gunpowder brought by American privateers, who used Tortuga as their rear base. He also managed to maintain contact with mixed-race General Jean-Louis Villatte, who was organizing resistance in Cap Français and in the northern province. It was far harder to communicate with the two other mixed-race generals, Louis-Jacques Beauvais, who was maintaining the pressure on Port-au-Prince in the western province, and André Rigaud, who was slowly recapturing positions in the south.

Once again, the standpoint adopted by former free men of color is crucial for understanding the reversal in the balance of power which took place in summer 1794. Mixed-race individuals bridled at the status imposed on them in regions occupied by the British and their colonial allies, who were eager to take revenge for the revolutionary egalitarian legislation. Jean Delair, who had called for the British to capture the town of Jean-Rabel, went over to General Laveaux, who by now was on the offensive throughout the northern peninsula.

This advantageous position was a prelude to another even more significant switch of sides, by the Black officer Toussaint, who had by now adopted the surname Louverture. His troops turned against the Spanish garrison in the town of Gonaïves, massacring the white counterrevolutionaries and hoisting the French tricolor. Several factors explain this change of sides. The decree on general freedom consolidated the revolution by people of color, which Black officers in the Spanish army had hitherto viewed with suspicion. But it was above all the longstanding reciprocal trust between Louverture and Laveaux which guided the political transition and paved the way for future military successes. Toussaint's 4,000 highly disciplined and battle-hardened soldiers, trained in the same manner as professionals in European armies, joined forces with the 10,000 or so men under Laveaux's command.

Departmentalization in July 1795

The positions held by the British were recaptured foot by foot, one place at a time, sometimes plantation by plantation. The colonial war was a war of positions rather than a guerrilla war. Laveaux and Louverture's objective was to recapture the upper valley of the Artibonite, which would enable them to unite the republican camps in the north with those in the southern and western provinces. The British were progressively confined to the coastal garrison towns (Le Môle, Saint-Marc, Port-au-Prince, and Jérémie), thronging with refugees and on the verge of famine.

Reinforcements sent from Europe were rapidly decimated by yellow fever, to the considerable advantage of the republican troops, who were acclimatized, resilient, and motivated. The latter had to rely wholly on their own forces, given that they were completely isolated from the metropole. Many of the small vessels they used to get round the British blockade had been fitted out by merchants in Charleston, who negotiated with the agents of the republican French government which played a central role in administering the colony.[34]

Back in Paris, the members of the Convention thought that Saint-Domingue was lost. Therefore, when they received the first dispatches from Laveaux announcing military successes it was like manna from the Supreme Being. It was at this stage that the decree of 4 February 1794 was issued, lending the August 1793 decision force of law. Sonthonax saved his head, but his colleague Polverel had died of exhaustion during a lengthy trial, at the

---

[34] Covo, "Commerce et révolutions."

end of which the commissioners were acquitted. Laveaux was confirmed as governor-general, and his aides Louverture, Beauvais, Rigaud, and Villatte were promoted to the rank of major general.

It was now a matter of embedding general freedom once and for all. The 1795 constitution established territorial continuity, dividing the island into five departments, throughout which the French republic recognized the sole status of citizen with equal rights. The metropolitan and colonial territories – including the Spanish part of the island acquired by France under the Peace of Basel – were now in a state of symbiosis. Exoticism was no more. But, for the moment, this republican isonomy was achieved in bellicose circumstances. For as long as parts of the territory were occupied by the British, the military government remained in place, and the republic slipped into an imperial mold.

The War between Colors

The very equilibrium which had given rise to victory contained destabilizing factors. It was a double victory: on the one hand, against the proslavery imperialist powers (with the British holding onto just a few strategic coastal positions until 1798, and Spain having withdrawn from the conflict in 1795); and, on the other, against the supporters of white colonial rule. But the mass emigration of former masters created a formidable vacuum.

General Laveaux was among those particularly alert to the fact that a balance had to be maintained between the whites, Blacks, "reds," and "yellows," that is to say, those of mixed-race, if Saint-Domingue were to remain part of the republic. This policy of balance is hard to interpret today, for we tend to impose categories and vocabulary from the nineteenth century on the very different realities and representations of the late-eighteenth-century world. One instance of this is the term "race," which underwent major semantic shifts over the course of the eighteenth century, when it was not universally linked to a hierarchy of human groups based on supposedly immutable physical and moral characteristics.

For Laveaux and the republicans, using such a category was a fundamentally political step. The mass emigration of masters had created a dangerous vacuum, so it was essential to attract a white population who would be patriotic and metropolitan. But the source of greatest concern was the appetite for power of mixed-race individuals who might confiscate the revolution of people of color and turn it to their own advantage. On the one hand, the republic could not do without mixed-race individuals, who were the spearhead in the struggle against internal and external counter-revolution. On the other hand, mixed-race people's condescending attitude toward Blacks, many of whom (about one-third) were the slaves of masters of color, provided solid grounds for mistrusting them.

Mixed-race officers viewed the problem very differently, reckoning they had been poorly rewarded for their unflagging commitment to the republic. The fact that before leaving the colony Sonthonax had entrusted the fate of the republic to the gang leader and former slave Dieudonné rather than to the mixed-race General Beauvais had already been perceived as a humiliation by the powerful camarilla of officers of color. And then the matter of blank officer commissions liberally dispensed to Toussaint Louverture's army as a mark of trust, and to ensure that mixed-race officers were flanked by Black officers, was a source of irritation for the military commander of the northern province, General Villatte.

Drawing on a strategy used in the revolution by people of color, Pierre Pinchinat and Jean-Louis Villatte tried to take Cap Français by force, since it was a town where mixed-race people had great influence. They had General Laveaux arrested and imprisoned for a few days.

After initially hesitating, Louverture launched his troops against the town of Cap Français. Laveaux was delivered and, during a grandiose ceremony marking the failure of the coup, rewarded Toussaint Louverture by naming him his lieutenant as governor of the colony. He even described Louverture as the "black Spartacus" prophesized by Abbé Raynal.

Sonthonax's return to Saint-Domingue, on being appointed by the Directory to head a third civilian commission after his acquittal in the "colonies affair," provided a way to legitimize a republican policy of uniting colors, which had been jeopardized by hostility from mixed-race officers. Sonthonax sent a delegation to the south, with the main task of arresting Pinchinat. The two key figures in the delegation, Leborgne and General Desfourneaux, heaped provocations and humiliations on Rigaud and his entourage. A great insurrection by black plantation slaves gathered pace on the Les Cayes plain in August 1796 (Fructidor of Year IV), led by mixed-race individuals. Many whites were butchered, in a "massacre policy" which became a recurrent feature in the war between colors.[35] The delegates had to abandon the south, but they produced numerous reports discrediting Rigaud in the eyes of the Directory.

---

[35] David El Kenz, ed., *Le massacre, objet d'histoire* (Paris: Gallimard, 2005).

The Exploitation of Divisions by Politicians in the Metropole

Indeed, as the troubles persisted, the Directory acquired a key role arbitrating between positions, but without any means of action or any relays. The colonial party, which had never accepted general freedom, turned these divisions to its own advantage. Led by a former planter from Saint-Domingue, Viénot-Vaublanc, this party joined forces with the right, which had just won the elections of spring 1797. It conducted intensive lobbying through the newspapers it controlled and in speeches before the Council of Five Hundred. It was wholly impossible to come out publicly in favor of reintroducing slavery, which would have placed the party in breach of the constitution. It therefore sought to widen divisions by supporting the cause of mixed-race people. Although there was nothing new about factions in the metropole using colonial protagonists to further their own aims, it placed the proslavery lobby at the center of the political contest, whose issue determined the subsequent course taken by the revolutionary process in Saint-Domingue.

The Problem of Independence: Louverture's Double Game

At any given stage in the struggle between factions, it was not rare for a protagonist to stand accused by his adversaries of wanting to secede. The reference was always negative, for it pointed back to the bugbear of white Creole autonomism in the early phase of the revolution. Louverture in turn now used a stratagem to compromise Sonthonax in the eyes of those in power in Paris. Was this a matter of indiscreet confidences? Sonthonax had reportedly sought to convince Louverture to make the colony independent to guard against the possibility of a royalist restoration in Paris which would throw into doubt the decree of 4 February 1794. Was Louverture so torturous in his calculations as to publicly denounce the colonial lobby and its leader Vincent de Vaublanc while pledging to the latter that he would offer him the head of Sonthonax, viewed by the colonists as their bitterest enemy?[36] Be that as it may, once Sonthonax was forced to leave the colony in August 1797 (Fructidor Year V), Louverture governed alone.

---

[36] Pierre Pluchon, *Toussaint-Louverture, un révolutionnaire noir d'Ancien Régime* (Paris: Fayard, 1989).

At the same time, there was a reversal of situation in Paris. The Directory conducted a military purge of the right, including the leaders of the colonial lobby. The election of Sonthonax to the legislature, along with other figures from Saint-Domingue who were not favorably inclined toward Louverture (with the exception of Laveaux), was approved. Such a situation necessarily fueled Louverture's instinctive distrust of interference by the metropole, which he saw as the work of his adversaries.

Conclusion

Despite the rivalry raging at the highest level of government, a form of republican acculturation slowly took place around the representations of power in festivals, education, and newspapers. Sonthonax embodied the promise of emancipation for the "newly free" working people, who adulated him and referred to him affectionately as "Papa Sonthonax." But he could also count on a solid loyalist party of Black generals and newly elected administrators. The final step awaited from the legislature was an organic law of republican isonomy consecrating equality for all parts of the French republic, and hence full and immediate citizenship for all of its inhabitants.[37]

Toussaint Louverture had no choice but to go along with these republican forms. But he feared the moment when the end of the war would lead to the end of the emergency measures, in which event his powers as governor would no longer be appropriate.

He consolidated his power by placing loyal followers in positions of responsibility. He sketched an alternative project of two-tier citizenship, with officers of color being the only true citizens. To relaunch the economy, planters – the "new citizens" – had to return to the plantations, where they would be overseen by officers. The republican commissioners accepted the need for such "harsh agrarian authoritarianism." What Louverture added was his conviction that the economy would start functioning and society be stabilized once again only if former landowners and white managers returned. This project diverged very significantly from republican isonomy. Was it thereby a separatist project? No, Louverture was wholly sincere in applauding the article in the 1799 constitution stipulating that the colonies were to be ruled by specific laws. He embedded these laws under a form of associate sovereignty, which is not at all the same thing as independence.

---

[37] Bernard Gainot, *La révolution des esclaves, Haïti 1763–1803* (Paris: Vendémiaire, 2017).

That leaves the southern bastion. The postrevolutionary economic and social structures there differed little from those elsewhere (forced assignment to plantations, profit-sharing for planters, leases to officers of color). Republican acculturation was evident, further accentuated by the fact that mixed-race officers, wanting to be viewed by the metropolitan authorities as the "best republicans," denounced Louverture for having orchestrated the restoration of the *ancien régime* in encouraging white colonists to return from overseas, and in the all but official status of the Catholic Church and refractory priests – foreshadowing, to a certain extent, the policies of the Consulate.

25

Toussaint Louverture, the Cultivator System, and Haiti's Independence (1798–1804)

PHILIPPE GIRARD

In October 1798, the last British troops evacuated Môle Saint-Nicolas in the French colony of Saint-Domingue, ending a British invasion that had begun in 1793 (a Spanish invasion had ended in 1795). For free people of color, who represented 95 percent of Saint-Domingue's population, the defeat of these two openly proslavery powers indicated that the Haitian slave revolt, which had begun in 1791, might succeed after all. For the French government, the withdrawal of foreign troops indicated that France, which had been on the verge of losing control of its Caribbean holdings in 1793–1794, might retain its colonial empire. Toussaint Louverture, a former slave who was now the general in chief of the army of Saint-Domingue, underscored these two points when he took over Môle Saint-Nicolas in France's name. After planting a tree of liberty, he told planters and Black laborers that now was the time to prove to the "detractors of liberty" that plantations and free labor could coexist. He also urged those who had collaborated with the British invaders to show their "inviolable attachment to the mother country."[1]

The British evacuation still left some unanswered questions, starting with the nature of freedom in post-emancipation Saint-Domingue. Should fully free labor become the norm, former slaves would be able to leave their former plantations and set out on their own as subsistence farmers. This option, popular with Black field hands, would entail substantial land reform, the breakup of large sugar estates, and a radical reorganization of the colonial economic model. Alternatively, colonial authorities could force field hands to remain on their former plantations, albeit as paid laborers who would no

---

[1] Toussaint Louverture, "Discours," 5 October 1798, CC9B/9, Archives Nationales d'outre-mer (henceforth ANOM).

longer be subjected to cruel punishments such as the whip. This intermediate labor status, known as the cultivator system, had first been defined in the 1793 decree abolishing slavery in Saint-Domingue, but it had not been fully enforced due to the ongoing war with Spain and Great Britain. A last option was the outright restoration of slavery. Britain and Spain were unlikely to intervene again, but some planters hoped that the current French regime, known as the Directory, would renege on the principle of abolition or that a new regime might replace the Directory – both distinct possibilities in the unsteady days of the French Revolution.

The nature of the colonial bond was the second unsettled question. With the end of foreign occupation, Saint-Domingue could be fully reintegrated into a centralized French empire in which the metropole's laws applied de facto and French-appointed administrators ruled the colony. Alternatively, colonial representatives in the Caribbean could remain nominally subservient to France while achieving substantial autonomy over their day-to-day affairs, while France satisfied itself with the façade of imperial authority. Last on the list was full independence, following the precedent set by the United States in 1776. The strategic context was favorable: France had a powerful army in Europe but limited control of Atlantic sea lanes, while Britain, the dominant naval power, had learned the hard way that its military could not occupy Saint-Domingue.

The subject of emancipation has been the focus of most scholarly attention. Most historians no longer describe the Haitian Revolution as a one-sided struggle for universal liberty, but instead describe it as a protracted and messy process in which leaders of the slave revolt were divided over their political goals and partisans of slavery remained active long after abolition was proclaimed.[2] The issue of independence has received comparatively less attention, as if the creation of Haiti were the logical closing point of the Revolution. In keeping with the heroic scholarly tradition, Yves Bénot argued that the rebels of 1791 fought for both emancipation and independence from the outset.[3] Aimé Césaire cited the 1798 British evacuation of Môle as the moment when Toussaint Louverture effectively declared Haiti's

---

[2] For the traditional view, see Nick Nesbitt, *Universal Emancipation: The Haitian Revolution and the Radical Enlightenment* (Charlottesville: University of Virginia Press, 2008). For the revisionist view, see Jeremy Popkin, *You Are All Free: The Haitian Revolution and the Abolition of Slavery* (New York: Cambridge University Press, 2010).

[3] Yves Bénot, "La parole des esclaves insurgés de 1791–1792: Indépendance immédiate!," in Franklin Midy, ed., *Mémoire de révolution d'esclaves à Saint-Domingue* (Montreal: CIDIHCA, 2006), 95–112.

independence (Sabine Manigat used his 1801 constitution instead).[4] Julia Gaffield and David Armitage more accurately dated the transition to "the period after 1802," but that question warranted only a few lines in an entire book on the Haitian Declaration of Independence.[5]

The rebels of Saint-Domingue were actually still debating independence as late as 1803 because that issue was intertwined with the equally contested issue of emancipation. Traditionally, proslavery planters were the main advocates of colonial autonomy in Saint-Domingue. Prior to the Haitian Revolution, they hoped to rid themselves of the French colonial hierarchy (which they described as a "ministerial dictatorship") to escape French restrictions on how they exploited their workforce, and the French trade restrictions known as the *exclusif*. At the outset of the French Revolution, planters in the Saint-Marc Assembly toyed with independence to prevent revolutionary France from abolishing slavery and race discrimination in its colonies. The white planters of Saint-Domingue were accused (with limited evidence) of organizing the 1791 slave revolt in a misguided attempt to wrest control of the colony away from revolutionary France. They were also accused (with far more convincing evidence) of encouraging Spain and Britain to invade in 1793 to prevent abolition from taking hold.

Conversely, free people in Saint-Domingue initially preferred to retain a political bond with France, even if perfunctory, because Versailles had backed measures to limit the worst labor abuses prior to the Haitian Revolution. As a result, it was ostensibly to protect Louis XVI that slaves revolted in 1791; they then shifted their support to the Bourbon monarchs of Spain after Louis XVI's execution in 1793. When revolutionary France finally embraced universal abolition in 1794, many people of color switched their allegiance from the French king to the French Republic, which they now saw as their main protector. Convinced that independence would put them at the mercy of white planters and their British and Spanish allies, people of color in Saint-Domingue viewed the colonial bond as the main guarantor of their individual freedom, though they kept a close eye on political developments

---

[4] Aimé Césaire, *Toussaint Louverture: La révolution française et le problème colonial* (Paris: Présence Africaine, 1981), 257–9; Sabine Manigat, "Le régime de Toussaint Louverture en 1801: Un modèle, une exception," in Yves Bénot and Marcel Dorigny, eds., *Rétablissement de l'esclavage dans les colonies françaises 1802: Ruptures et continuités de la politique coloniale française (1800–1830): Aux origines d'Haïti* (Paris: Maisonneuve-Larose, 2003), 109.

[5] Julia Gaffield, ed., *The Haitian Declaration of Independence: Creation, Context, and Legacy* (Charlottesville: University of Virginia Press, 2016), 4.

in France, where the proslavery camp was never fully vanquished, to assess whether to maintain their allegiance to France.

In this complex situation, the moderate camp was initially dominant. When Toussaint Louverture seized power in Saint-Domingue in 1798–1800, he imposed the cultivator system and sought autonomy (but not independence) from France. A free but firm labor system, by his reckoning, was the only way to reconcile the interests of Black laborers and the French economy and thus to preserve political ties between France and Saint-Domingue (Map 25.1), however tenuous. Political changes in France upset this delicate balance in ensuing years. After Napoleon Bonaparte seized power in 1799, he became convinced that Louverture was preparing to leave the French empire, so in 1802 he sent a massive expedition to restore direct French control of the colony, white rule, and possibly slavery. Refusing to be reenslaved, most free people of color forsook their allegiance to France, though after much soul-searching. Jean-Jacques Dessalines, who served in the French army until October 1802, finally declared Haiti's independence in January 1804. France, he explained, had lied to Haitians about "the phantom of liberty," so independence had become necessary "to seize from [France] all hope of re-enslaving us."[6]

Who Will Rule Saint-Domingue? (1798–1800)

The 1798 British evacuation from Saint-Domingue sparked a three-way power struggle in Saint-Domingue between French civilian agents, northern Black generals led by Toussaint Louverture, and the southern mixed-race general André Rigaud (a fourth faction, the independent groups known as Maroons, will be discussed later). Emancipation and independence were an important subtext to that struggle: Louverture often accused his rivals of betraying France and favoring slavery in an effort to secure the support of the Black population in Saint-Domingue and the French government in Paris.

Officially, French colonial representatives in Saint-Domingue ruled the colony at the behest of the French minister of the navy and colonies in Paris. In practice, their authority was limited by the fact that they had few white troops at their disposal, the large reinforcements sent by France after the initial slave revolt having been ravaged by war and yellow fever. Léger-

---

[6] "Appendix: The Haitian Declaration of Independence," in Gaffield, ed., *The Haitian Declaration of Independence*, 241.

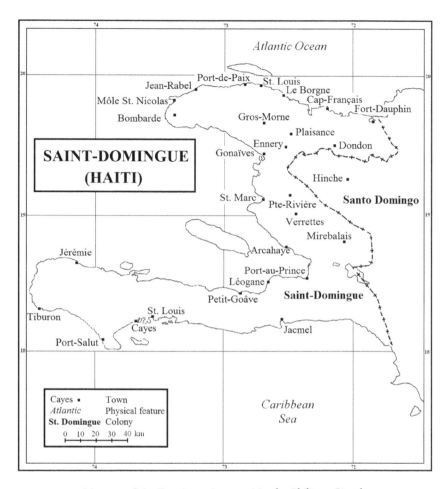

Map 25.1 Saint-Domingue in 1791. Map by Philippe Girard.

Félicité Sonthonax, the commissioner who had issued the 1793 decree of abolition, was the only French representative with broad support among the Black population. But Louverture had expelled him in 1797, alleging that Sonthonax had offered to "declare our independence from France" in order to sap his popularity.[7]

---

[7] Toussaint Louverture, *Extrait du rapport adressé au Directoire Exécutif* (Cap Français: Roux, 1797), 2, https://gallica.bnf.fr/ark:/12148/bpt6k9788606r.

To replace Sonthonax, the Directory appointed Gabriel de Hédouville as France's agent. Centralization and abolition were the order of the day. Hédouville's instructions indicated that he alone had the right to appoint, dismiss, and deport colonial officials in Saint-Domingue. "Blacks should have no doubt as to the abolition of slavery in Saint-Domingue," the instructions also noted: the constitution of the Directory had incorporated colonies into the French legal system, thus guaranteeing that citizens overseas would have the same individual liberties as citizens in France (early in the Revolution, proslavery planters had insisted on placing colonies under distinct laws to preserve racial discrimination). Still, Hédouville was informed, a "well-regulated liberty" entailed "rights" as well as "duties," so as to promote the "restoration of the prosperity of cultivation."[8]

After reaching Saint-Domingue in March 1798, Hédouville did his best to reassert direct control over the colonial bureaucracy and army. This put him at odds with Toussaint Louverture. Though Louverture was nominally junior to civilian officials appointed in Paris, Hédouville was an outsider who came with a mere three frigates, 100 administrators and officers, and 180 troops. Louverture did not seek the agent's approval before appointing officials, disbursing funds, judging civilians, welcoming émigrés back from exile, pardoning prisoners, and negotiating with British envoys. Hédouville quickly suspected Louverture of being a tool of the British and conservative émigrés, whose loyalty to France and abolition was suspect.

In keeping with his instructions, Hédouville published in July 1798 a new code of cultivation whose preamble assured cultivators that freedom was an inalienable right while warning that "laziness" would be punished.[9] Louverture agreed with this basic premise, but he sensed that Black Dominguans' concerns about France's ultimate intentions could be used to discredit the French agent. Rumors soon convinced "cultivators that there was a plot against their liberty,"[10] Hédouville reported, and some Black generals threatened to declare "independence" if he ever tried to restore slavery.[11] Hédouville asked Louverture to put an end to these rumors;

---

[8] "Instructions pour le général Hédouville," 29 December 1797, doc. 250, B277, FM, ANOM.

[9] Gabriel de Hédouville, "Arrêté concernant la police des habitations et les obligations réciproques des propriétaires ou fermiers et des cultivateurs," 24 July 1798, Box 1/47, Rochambeau Papers, University of Florida (henceforth RP-UF). For a Kreyòl version, see Agence du directoire exécutif, "Arrêté concernant la police des habitations," 24 July 1798, CC9A/19, ANOM.

[10] Hédouville to Louverture, 17 September 1798, CC9B/6, ANOM.

[11] Hédouville to Directoire Exécutif, c. 1798, CC9A/19, ANOM.

Louverture did no such thing. In October 1798, Black troops in Fort Liberté rebelled and Hédouville fled the colony.

Unwilling to sever all links to France, Louverture followed the same playbook he had used after Sonthonax's ouster: he explained that cultivators had insisted on Hédouville's departure because the agent was preparing "the reestablishment of slavery."[12] Far from mistreating a French official, Louverture had saved the colony for France and liberty by acting to prevent a general uprising. He merely held the reins of power "provisionally," he explained, and promptly asked France's agent in Santo Domingo (today's Dominican Republic), Philippe Roume, to come to take Hédouville's place.[13]

As Roume traveled from Santo Domingo to Port-au-Prince to take up his post, Louverture organized threatening popular demonstrations along his route to remind the new agent that the Black population was questioning its allegiance to France. Suitably chastened, Roume embraced a nonconfrontational strategy: he would reaffirm his commitment to abolition and gently channel Louverture's energies in a direction favorable to France because "men who just emerged from slavery are naturally suspicious when it comes to their liberty."[14]

Roume did his best to nurture the bonds between France and the colony by emphasizing his commitment to racial equality. Following the adage that the personal is political, he explained that he had married his mixed-race mistress and was "the son-in-law of a negress" (Sonthonax had also married a mixed-race woman).[15] Roume also led public commemorations of the 1794 law of abolition, which he described as the "festival of French liberty."[16] Unwilling to confront a symbol of French republicanism, Louverture did not attack Roume head-on at first, using him instead as a figurehead who gave legitimacy to his policies by signing his decrees in France's name.

As French representatives became ever more ineffectual in the North and West of Saint-Domingue in 1798–1799, Louverture's main rival became General André Rigaud, who had also established a quasi-autonomous regime in the southern province. The rift did not stem from profound ideological differences: both men were landowners who favored a free but firm labor system; both wished to retain official ties to France while ruling the colony as

---

[12] [Louverture], "Suite et copie des pièces relatives à l'événement du Fort Liberté ...," c. 1 November 1798, Pièce 49, AF/III, 210, Archives Nationales, Paris (henceforth AN).
[13] Louverture, "Ordonnance," 17 November 1798, fr. 12104, Bibliothèque Nationale, Paris (henceforth BNF).
[14] Roume to Eustache Bruix, 22 November 1798, Papers of Philippe Roume, Manuscript Division, Library of Congress.
[15] Roume, "Discours," 18 July 1799, CC9B/9, ANOM.
[16] Roume, "Discours," 9 February 1800, CC9B/1, ANOM.

they pleased. In an effort to reconcile Louverture and Rigaud, Roume invited them to Port-au-Prince in February 1799 for the fifth anniversary of the abolition of slavery. "True friends of liberty" should strive to maintain the "constitutional order" and "attachment to France," Roume insisted.[17] But the two generals ignored his pleas, and a civil war known as the War of the South began in June 1799.

After suffering initial military setbacks, Louverture reframed his personal feud with Rigaud as an ideological and racial war, hoping to rally the Black majority to his side by associating his mixed-race adversary with an elite group that had often owned slaves prior to the Haitian Revolution (Louverture had actually been free prior to the Revolution and had owned slaves, but he kept such facts hidden from the general public). "Was it not a negress who gave birth to me?," Rigaud countered. "Did I not have a black older brother?" Rigaud was no enemy of Black liberty, he emphasized; in fact, Louverture was suspiciously close to the British and to white colonists, who had "a project to exterminate the defenders of liberty and restore slavery."[18] Louverture replied that he was actually "the first who dared to break the irons" of the slaves back in 1791.[19] The propaganda war unfolded in a series of public proclamations. Louverture won the argument and established his credentials as the champion of Black liberty and Republican France. With the majority of the Black population behind him, Louverture summoned superior resources and defeated Rigaud by August 1800.

With the exception of inland areas controlled by Maroon groups, Louverture ruled Saint-Domingue unchallenged by 1800. He now had three important decisions to make: whether to export the slave revolt overseas; how to revive the plantation economy at home; and whether to seek political autonomy from France. All three had important implications for the future of abolition and Saint-Domingue's status as a French colony.

Exporting the Revolution? (1799)

With the end of the British invasion of Saint-Domingue, the French government began making plans for offensive operations. France's agent in

---

[17] Pélage-Marie Duboys, *Précis historique des Annales de la Révolution à Saint Domingue*, vol. II, 49, NAF 14879 (MF 5384), BNF.
[18] André Rigaud, "Réponse ... à l'écrit calomnieux du général Toussaint Louverture," 8 May 1799, doc. 253, B277, FM, ANOM.
[19] Louverture, "Réponse ... aux Calomnies et aux Écrits mensongers du général de brigade Rigaud," 19 May 1799, Bibliothèque Haïtienne des Pères du Saint-Esprit.

Guadeloupe, Victor Hugues, used freedmen to invade Saint Lucia, support revolts in Grenada and Saint Vincent, and outfit privateers.[20] In the Greater Antilles, French plans targeted traditional objectives such as British Jamaica, but they were reframed in Republican terms: they were now a crusade for abolition, not just an imperial land grab. "Let's toss liberty at the colonies; today, the English are dead" was how Georges Danton welcomed the 1794 law of abolition.[21] Emphasizing abolition was a way to secure the support of Black freedmen, who formed the vast bulk of the forces at France's disposal in Saint-Domingue, as well as the enslaved majority in Jamaica, and who could be convinced to fight for France if France stood for racial equality. The surest way to seize Jamaica, Agent Roume explained, was to "set all African hearts ablaze with the sacred fire of liberty."[22]

Patriotism and idealism intersected in a unique way for the man most associated with the efforts to export the Haitian Revolution to Jamaica: Isaac Sasportas. As a member of the Sephardic Diaspora, he had once been considered a foreigner in the island of his birth because Jews were merely tolerated in prerevolutionary Saint-Domingue. The French Revolution, by incorporating Jews as well as people of color into the French nation, had made him a convert to radical abolitionism and French patriotism. Emancipating the slaves of Jamaica, Sasportas explained, would be a "fight for liberty and the French."[23] In 1799, Sasportas was expelled from Curaçao for allegedly plotting a slave revolt there; he then headed to Jamaica to finalize the preparations for a French invasion.[24]

The invasion of Jamaica, which was scheduled for December 1799, was the closest that the Caribbean ever got to a second Haitian Revolution. But it failed because Louverture leaked the plans to the British, after which

---

[20] Laurent Dubois, *A Colony of Citizens: Revolution and Slave Emancipation in the French Caribbean, 1787–1804* (Chapel Hill: University of North Carolina Press, 2004), 222; Myriam Alamkan, *Vous irez porter le fer et la flamme: Les corsaires français de la Révolution française et du Premier Empire en Caraïbe (1793–1810)* (Matoury: Ibis Rouge, 2015), 24.

[21] *Gazette Nationale, ou le Moniteur Universel*, 5 February 1794.

[22] Philippe Roume, "Instructions ... aux citoyens Sasportas ... et Devaux," 19 July 1799, Crawford Muniments, Acc. 9769, Personal Papers, 23/10/1176–88, National Library of Scotland.

[23] "At a Council Held in Santiago de la Vega," 5 December 1799, CO 137/103, British National Archives (henceforth BNA).

[24] Hans Jordaan, "Patriots, Privateers and International Politics: The Myth of the Conspiracy of Jean Baptiste Tierce Cadet," in Wim Klooster and Gert Oostindie, eds., *Curaçao in the Age of Revolutions, 1795–1800* (Leiden: KITLV Press, 2011), 143.

Sasportas was captured and executed.[25] Louverture's opposition to a French-inspired slave revolt in Jamaica may be seen, as his enemies did, as an indication of his lukewarm embrace of universal liberty and his treacherous closeness to émigrés and the British. Louverture saw it in a different light: attacking Jamaica was a "chimerical project" that had no chance of succeeding. It would needlessly antagonize the British navy and risk the "annihilation of the colony" of Saint-Domingue.[26] Abolition would survive in Saint-Domingue only if he appeased powerful neighbors. Accordingly, in 1799, Louverture signed treaties of nonaggression with Jamaica and the United States in which he pledged not to interfere with their internal social order, in exchange for which he could import the guns needed to defend Saint-Domingue from reenslavement. Louverture's policy, narrowly focused on preserving freedom within Saint-Domingue, would form the basis for the foreign policy of Haiti after 1804, which also prioritized the preservation of national sovereignty at the expense of universal abolitionism.

Which Economic Model? (1800–1801)

Having defeated Rigaud and made peace with regional powers, Louverture could focus on the revival of the colonial economy, which had sharply contracted after a decade of war. By one estimate, the colony produced only 4 million colonial livres worth of tropical crops in 1796, a 98 percent decline since 1789.[27]

Reviving the plantation sector would be personally beneficial to Louverture, who acquired dozens of plantations during the Haitian Revolution, but it also had important implications for the future of emancipation and colonialism. Conservative critics lambasted emancipation as impractical: no Black laborer worked without duress, they claimed, so free labor would lead to the ruin of French colonies. Harrowing accounts of Saint-Domingue's economic downfall were a staple of the proslavery lobby, which published extensively in France. "One must either renounce having colonies," wrote one such author, "or consent to governing them under the discipline of forced labor," by which he meant slavery.[28]

---

[25] Philippe Girard, "Isaac Sasportas, the 1799 Slave Conspiracy in Jamaica, and Sephardic Ties to the Haitian Revolution, *Jewish History* 33 (2020), 403–35.
[26] Louverture to Roume. 4 February 1800, CC/9A/26, ANOM.
[27] Barré de Saint-Venant, *Des colonies modernes sous la zone torride, et particulièrement de celle de Saint-Domingue* (Paris: Brochot, 1802), 51.
[28] Félix Carteau, *Soirées bermudiennes, ou entretiens sur les événemens qui ont opéré la ruine de la partie française de l'isle Saint-Domingue* (Bordeaux: Pellier-Lavalle, 1802), 306.

Accordingly, for Louverture, convincing cultivators to work was a way to prove "to the whole universe that Saint-Domingue can become rich again with free laborers."[29] Taxes on tropical crops would also finance purchases of weapons and gunpowder, and so protect Saint-Domingue from any plot to invade and reenslave its people. Establishing himself as a successful administrator would endear him to the French government and silence his critics in Paris. If this failed, imported weapons could also be used to repulse a French invasion and chart a path to independence.

With this in mind, Louverture maintained the cultivator system established by previous French agents. He had occasionally criticized their regulations as a new form of slavery to score political points with Black laborers, but his own regulations proved even stricter. Under his October 1800 labor code, he tasked the army with enforcing discipline on plantations. His July 1801 constitution (Figure 25.1) tied cultivators to their plantation for life (Sonthonax had imposed one-year contracts, extended to three years under Hédouville). Most controversially, he sought the assistance of the British governor "for the importation of negroes (from the coast of Africa) into Saint-Domingue: cultivators as he termed them."[30] Though cultivators were legally free, moral suasion failed to convince many of them to go back to the fields, and Louverture's generals, notably Dessalines, employed violence and even the death penalty to enforce compliance. By 1801, ten years into the Haitian Revolution, whether free labor would prevail in Saint-Domingue was still an open question.

The main opponents of the cultivator system were the Maroons, whose social agenda differed markedly from that of elite figures like Roume and Louverture. These independent groups were often referred to as "Africans" and "Bossales" by their contemporaries, reflecting the fact that, unlike Louverture and Rigaud, they were not Creoles but survivors of the Middle Passage. Many had been field hands before the Haitian Revolution, whereas Creoles had been more likely to be free or to occupy skilled positions on plantations (Louverture had been a coachman and Rigaud a goldsmith).

Though the Maroons represented a large segment of the colonial population, the documentary record about them is sparse because they were often illiterate and lived in voluntary seclusion from the colonial authorities. Historians have not been kind to them either: Beaubrun Ardouin dismissed them as "ignorant groups," and C. L. R. James referred to their armies as

---

[29] Louverture, report to Étienne Laveaux, 14–20 February 1796, fr. 12104, BNF.
[30] George Nugent to William Cavendish Duke of Portland, 5 September 1801, CO 137/106, BNA.

Figure 25.1 Louverture's constitution. Courtesy of Library of Congress.

mere "bands."[31] Haitian historiography long criticized the Maroons for delaying the coming of independence by refusing to follow the lead of

[31] Beaubrun Ardouin, *Études sur l'histoire d'Haïti, suivies de la vie du général J.-M. Borgella*, 11 vols. (Paris: Dezobry et Magdeleine, 1853–1860), vol. v, 273; C. L. R. James, *The*

founding fathers like Louverture and Dessalines. It was not until the works of Jean Fouchard, Carolyn Fick, and Michel-Rolph Trouillot that historians began to take them seriously.[32]

For lack of adequate documentation and research, assessing the Maroons' political agenda on matters such as plantation work and national autonomy is difficult; but it is not impossible. The fact that many contemporaries referred to them as "maroons" (meaning "runaways") hints at their visceral opposition to plantation work. Refusing to submit to slavery or the cultivator system, they retreated to Saint-Domingue's interior to set up subsistence farms in a manner reminiscent of their Jamaican namesakes. In its instructions to Hédouville, the Directory had left open the possibility that some laboring families might set up "small estates set apart from the rest," but generally colonial elites were opposed to individual land ownership because sugarcane grew best on large estates.[33] Louverture banned sales of estates smaller than 50 carreaux (about 160 acres) to prevent "one, two, three cultivators" leaving their plantation and choosing to "settle on new, uncultivated land."[34]

Elite proponents and opponents of Saint-Domingue's independence framed the issue in Enlightenment terms: whether the people of Saint-Domingue should define themselves as part of the French nation or form their own social compact. The Maroons' cultural frame of reference was different. They spoke Kreyòl or African languages rather than Parisian French and they practiced Vodou rather than Roman Catholicism or Deism. Their main loyalty was not to the French nation but to their immediate group. That group could be defined by a shared ethnolinguistic identity inherited from Africa, hence the labels of "Congos," "Dokos," and "Mandinko" ascribed to some Maroon groups (French authors often describe such ethnic markers as "nations"). Allegiance to a leader was another unifying factor, so contemporaries wrote of the group of Lubin Golard (near Jean-Rabel), Sans Souci (near Dondon), and Lamour Derance (near Jacmel). Territory also mattered: rather than try to control the whole colony, the

---

Black Jacobins: Toussaint L'Ouverture and the San Domingo Revolution (New York: Vintage Books, 1989 [1938]), 149.

[32] Jean Fouchard, *The Haitian Maroons: Liberty or Death* (New York: Edward Blyden Press, 1981 [1972]); Carolyn E. Fick, *The Making of Haiti: The Saint Domingue Revolution from Below* (Knoxville: University of Tennessee Press, 1990); Michel-Rolph Trouillot, *Silencing the Past: Power and the Production of History* (Boston: Beacon Press, 1995).

[33] Directory, "Instructions pour le général Hédouville," 29 December 1797, doc. 250, B277, FM, ANOM.

[34] Ardouin, *Études sur l'histoire d'Haïti*, vol. IV, 318.

Maroons sought autonomy in a mountainous region in the interior. The Maroons of Maniel (or Bahoruco), for example, were located along the southern border between Saint-Domingue and Santo Domingo, where a community had existed since the days of the Taíno Amerindians in the 1500s. Dessalines described the Maniel Maroons as "Blacks who have been free for a long time, who were maroons until the Spanish gave them their liberty and conceded this country to them. This very large people, completely independent, is known as *Doco*."[35]

The elite factions vying for control of Saint-Domingue sought the Maroons' military support, but the Maroons distrusted them all. They opposed whichever side was dominant, in order to preserve their freedom and autonomy. During the War of the South, "bands of black bossales" supported Rigaud and harassed Louverture's forces.[36] Louverture defeated Rigaud, but not his Maroon allies: as late as 1802, he was still railing against Lubin Golard, "this dangerous rebel, who would arrange for owners to be assassinated on their plantations," and Lamour Derance, "who incited all the cultivators to rise up."[37]

The future of abolition was accordingly uncertain as of 1801. In France, some members of the planter lobby called for the restoration of slavery, while in Saint-Domingue the Creole elite was trying to impose a strict labor system that was deeply unpopular with the Black laboring force, particularly the Maroons, who remained undefeated. Which labor system would prevail would depend on who would rule the colony, which itself was still an open question.

Autonomy or Independence? (1801)

Two issues preoccupied Louverture in 1801, the year that marked the peak of his powers: whether to annex Santo Domingo (today's Dominican Republic) and whether to promulgate a formal constitution. He and his contemporaries approached both questions through the prism of independence and slavery.

Spain had agreed to cede Santo Domingo to France under the 1795 Peace of Basel, a territorial swap that smacked of old-fashioned colonialism but had

---

[35] Jean-Jacques Dessalines to Victoire Leclerc, 26 August 1802, Ms. Hait. 71-4, Boston Public Library (henceforth BPL).

[36] François Périchou de Kerversau to Bruix, 23 September 1799, CC9/B23, ANOM.

[37] Philippe Girard, ed., *The Memoir of General Toussaint Louverture* (New York: Oxford University Press, 2014), 99, 101.

important ideological implications. Should Santo Domingo become a French colony, the 1794 French law abolishing slavery in all French colonies would become applicable there. The Directory, insisting that all colonies "are an integral part of France itself," initially made plans to take over Santo Domingo and to declare "the abolition of slavery, liberty, and the equality of men of all colors."[38] But the Spanish governor of Santo Domingo, who remained in office until France formally took over the colony, delayed the abolition process so that local planters would not have to free their slaves. The delay stretched into years, and France eventually concluded that it would be best not to add to Louverture's growing power. Keeping Hispaniola divided would make it easier to send troops should France ever feel the need to restore direct control and possibly slavery.

Louverture decided in 1800 to take over Santo Domingo for related reasons: to preserve political autonomy and abolition in Saint-Domingue. Rumors reached him regularly that France was about to send an expedition to overthrow him, so he needed to control all landing spots in eastern Hispaniola. He also wished to deny a base of operations to Rigaud, many of whose supporters found refuge in Santo Domingo after the War of the South. Louverture complained that, due to the delayed transition from Spanish to French authority, Black Dominguans were still held as slaves in Santo Domingo, where their masters had taken them during the course of the Revolution. He also accused Spanish traders of crossing the border to kidnap Black laborers and sell them in Santo Domingo.

In April 1800, Louverture announced that he would take over Santo Domingo to end such cross-border kidnappings. Roume refused to issue the necessary order, but Louverture sent thousands of cultivators to threaten the agent and his family until he recanted. This was a tactic Louverture had employed before. By hiding behind a mob, he could claim that he was not challenging French authority but merely bowing to public concerns about reenslavement. After Roume had reluctantly consented to the takeover, Louverture sent an envoy to seize Santo Domingo in France's name. To silence Spanish critics, Louverture asked his envoy "to change nothing to the system that exists among the Spanish who have become French," that is to say slavery.[39] As he had done when opposing the invasion of Jamaica,

---

[38] Laurent Truguet, "Instructions données par le Directoire Exécutif à ses agens," 12 February 1796, doc. 212, B277, FM, ANOM.

[39] Louverture to Pierre Agé, 27 April 1800, in "Procès-verbal de la prise de possession de la partie espagnole," 27 January 1801, CO 137/106, BNA.

Louverture framed the defense of abolition as a purely local concern tied to the territorial integrity of Saint-Domingue, not as a Messianic campaign to spread liberty everywhere. But Spanish colonists refused to be ruled by a *negro francés*, even one willing to compromise on the issue of slavery, and the Spanish governor again delayed the takeover.

Louverture put his plans on hold until the end of 1800, when one of his spies in France informed him that an expedition bound for Santo Domingo was about to set sail from the French port of Brest. He invaded Santo Domingo at once. The invasion was the opportunity to finally emancipate Santo Domingo's enslaved population, but Louverture negotiated an intermediate approach with the Spanish governor: Spaniards who wished to leave could take their enslaved domestics with them but had to leave behind their field hands to allow plantations to function. These field slaves would receive their "liberty," Louverture explained, albeit under the strict cultivator system, so they should expect to "work, even more than before" and to "remain obedient."[40]

The unification of Hispaniola put Louverture one step closer to full autonomy. Bypassing the normal chain of command, he wrote directly to Napoleon Bonaparte to warn him that Black troops had fought so well during the invasion of Santo Domingo that "soon, they will be as good as those from Europe."[41] Then, after hinting that he would fight any incoming French force, he took a step back. In a printed account, he insisted that the Spanish had committed an "insult against the French Republic" by refusing to implement the Peace of Basel, which he had to avenge "in my quality of general in chief of the army of the French Republic in Saint-Domingue." "Preventing the kidnapping of French cultivators" was also on his mind.[42]

Leaving his brother Paul in charge of defending Santo Domingo, Louverture then returned to Saint-Domingue to oversee the deliberations of a new assembly summoned at his request. This was merely a "central assembly of the colony," he insisted, not a constitutional assembly establishing a separatist regime.[43] But several deputies had previously served in the Assembly of Saint-Marc, which had come close to declaring independence in

---

[40] Louverture, "Proclamación," 8 February 1801, Estado, 60, N.3, Archivo General de Indias (henceforth AGI). See also Philippe Girard, "Did Dessalines Plan to Export the Haitian Revolution?," in Gaffield, *The Haitian Declaration of Independence*, 136–57: 144.
[41] Louverture to Napoleon Bonaparte, 12 February 1801, dossier 1, EE1734, ANOM.
[42] Louverture, "Procès-verbal de la prise de possession de la partie espagnole."
[43] Louverture, "Proclamation," 5 February 1801, Estado, 60, N.3, AGI.

1790 when they had set up "the constitutional bases of Saint-Domingue" to avoid implementing the Declaration of the Rights of Man.[44] Louverture's decision to summon a "central assembly of the colony" in 1801 thus built upon a conservative tradition of colonial autonomy that harked back to the early days of the Haitian Revolution.

In France as well, the legal status of the colonies was being redefined in a way that had profound implications for Saint-Domingue's Black population. Under the Directory's 1795 constitution, colonies were an integral part of France, so laws pertaining to the rights of man (including, crucially, individual freedom and citizenship) were de facto applicable in the colonies. But, as Bonaparte's Consulate replaced the Directory in 1799, a new constitution specified that colonies would be governed by "special laws" (Article 91). This left open the possibility that slavery could be restored in colonies at a future date and that Black inhabitants in the colonies could lose their French citizenship. By legislating first, Louverture hoped to preempt any future attempt by Bonaparte to restore slavery in Saint-Domingue.

The text of Louverture's constitution was finalized in June 1801. He immediately sent it off to the printer so that it could be put into effect at once. The 7 July 1801 ceremony in which Louverture presented the constitution to the public, modeled self-consciously after the ceremonials employed by governors of the *ancien régime*, was another indication that Louverture wished to break with revolutionary-era centralization – though ostensibly to protect the Revolution's greatest achievement, emancipation, from French meddling.

The actual text of the constitution was an exercise in contradictions. Article 1 emphatically stated that Saint-Domingue remained a "colony" that was "part of the French empire." French sovereignty, however, was curtailed by Louverture's unilateral decision to make himself governor general for life (Article 28) with the authority to name his successor (Article 30). Article 3 banned slavery forever and guaranteed that everyone in Saint-Domingue "is born, lives, and dies free and French." But oblique references to forced labor on plantations (Article 14) and importations of African laborers (Article 17) were hints that slavery and the slave trade were not completely dead in Saint-Domingue.

As was his wont, Louverture took two steps after promulgating his constitution, one forward and one back. He finally dismissed Roume, who had

---

[44] "Décret de l'Assemblée Générale de la partie française de Saint-Domingue," 28 May 1790, Kurt Fisher Collection, Folder 1A, Howard University.

spent nine months under house arrest for opposing the invasion of Santo Domingo, and sent the agent off to the United States, thus doing away with even the pretense of operating under a French representative. Meanwhile, concerned that Bonaparte might regard his constitution as a declaration of independence, Louverture sent a special envoy to France with a manuscript copy of the constitution (as if it were still a work in progress) and insisted that he would "provisionally" implement it while awaiting the "approval" of the government.[45]

When the text of the constitution became public in the summer of 1801, many contemporary observers assumed that Louverture had effectively declared independence or would soon do so formally. "You will observe by the [attached account] that the island is declared INDEPENDENT," one Philadelphia paper commented.[46] The constitution, "if it does not render that island absolutely independent, leaves to France scarcely anything but the name of authority," another US paper noted more accurately.[47] The governor of Jamaica began referring to the colony as "the late French part of Saint-Domingue."[48]

Whether to break from France altogether was actually still a matter of debate within the upper echelons of Louverture's regime. According to Roume, a Black general under Louverture's command, Henry Christophe, was opposed to independence, while another, Moïse, spoke overtly of "projects of independence."[49] After the War of the South, Dessalines told his troops that there were two more wars to wage, "one with the Spanish to chase them from the island, and one with France, which, when peace [with Britain] arrives, will come to ravish their liberty."[50]

Moïse's views are intriguing because, as Louverture's nephew, he was rumored to be next in the line of succession for the governorship. He had grown up on the Bréda plantation, where Louverture had been a close associate of the white manager, but he had not made the same impression: "the whole family is very lazy" was the manager's assessment of Moïse and his siblings.[51] Moïse had been promoted to general during the Haitian Revolution at Louverture's insistence, but Sonthonax, Hédouville, and

---

[45] Louverture to Bonaparte, 16 July 1801, Dossier 1, AF/IV/1213, AN.
[46] "St. Domingo," *Aurora* no. 3228, 6 August 1801, p. 2.
[47] "St. Domingo," *Herald of Liberty* no. 187, 7 September 1801, p. 2.
[48] Nugent to Duke of Portland, 11 October 1801, CO 137/106, BNA.
[49] "Projets d'indépendance," from Roume to Pierre-Alexandre Forfait, 2 December 1801, BN08270/lot 132, RP-UF.
[50] Capt. Baptiste, "Notes sur la colonie de Saint-Domingue," c. 1801, CC9C/1, ANOM.
[51] François Bayon de Libertat to Pantaléon II de Breda, 3 November 1776, Dossier 12 (Pantaléon II de Breda), 18AP/3, AN.

Roume all described him as rebellious and hostile to white Frenchmen. Moïse had his reasons: he had lost an eye during the slave revolt and a brother during the 1798 Fort Liberté affair; then, in 1801, he learned that his son had died while studying in France.

In Moïse's worldview, independence would entail substantial labor reforms. He showed markedly less enthusiasm for enforcing the cultivator system in his area of command, northern Saint-Domingue, than Dessalines did in the West and South. By 1801, a rift had developed between Moïse and his uncle. In a rare handwritten letter, Moïse complained that "all I tell you, you do not take into consideration" and that he stood ready "to fight and not have my throat cut by the enemies of our liberty."[52]

Assessing the intentions of a secretive and complex figure like Louverture is more difficult. He was certainly willing to threaten independence when France wavered in its commitment to abolition. In 1797, when a French deputy in Paris called for the restoration of slavery, Louverture warned that "there exists in the heart of Jamaica, in the Blue Mountains, a small number of men quite jealous of their liberty, who have forced to this day the pride and power of Britain to respect the rights they derive from nature, and which the French constitution guarantees."[53] "Hédouville thinks he can scare me?," Louverture asked a year later in the midst of his feud with the French agent. "I waged war against three nations and vanquished them all. I am tranquil. My soldiers will always be firm when defending their liberty."[54] Each time, the French government sent new reassurances and Louverture backtracked, insisting that "I am French ... I love liberty, and the French are free."[55] But he also appointed Moïse and Dessalines, two of his most Francophobic generals, as his seconds-in-command in the North and West/South Provinces. In violation of Bonaparte's orders, he also refused to place the inscription "brave Blacks, remember that France alone recognizes your liberty" on regimental flags.[56] Louverture hoped to keep the Black population unsure of Bonaparte's intentions, and thus more likely to follow him if he ever chose independence.

The fate of Louverture's sons Placide and Isaac, whom he had sent to France to study in 1796, pulled him in another direction. As his relations with

---

[52] Moyse to Louverture (4 September [1801]), Ms. Hait. 66-182, BPL.
[53] Toussaint Louverture, *Réfutations de quelques assertions d'un discours prononcé au Corps Législatif le 10 Prairial, an 5, par Viénot-Vaublanc* (Cap Français: Roux, 1797), 11, https://gallica.bnf.fr/ark:/12148/bpt6k97886075.
[54] Kerversau, "Rapport sur la partie française de SD," 22 March 1801, Box 2/66, RP-UF.
[55] Louverture to Roume, 29 October 1799, CC/9A/26, ANOM.
[56] Roume to Forfait, 25 September 1801, BN08270/lot 132, RP-UF.

the metropole deteriorated, Louverture asked repeatedly for their return, but Bonaparte consistently refused in order to keep some means of leverage. In February 1801, when Louverture informed the French minister of the navy that he had taken over Santo Domingo and summoned a constitutional assembly, two decisions that brought him close to full independence, he took this opportunity to yet again ask for the return of his sons, officially "for the consolation of their mother who greatly wishes to see them again."[57] Louverture went as far as sending a special envoy to France to kidnap his sons and bring them back to Saint-Domingue, to no avail.

Louverture's conflicted views on independence and forced labor were on full display when General Moïse, angry that his uncle had offered to purchase Africans from British slave traders and "sold Blacks to the whites," backed a major cultivator uprising in October 1801.[58] The uprising quickly spread in the plain of Cap Français and a copycat revolt broke out near Jacmel at the behest of the Maroon leader Lamour Derance. Eager to portray himself as a friend of France and white planters, Louverture crushed the revolt and insisted that Moïse be shot.

As the repression was in full swing, however, Louverture received news that France and Britain had signed a provisional peace agreement in London, which sharply increased the likelihood that Bonaparte would send a fleet to overthrow him. In a speech that was remarkable for its emotional tone (even though it was printed and distributed), a distraught Louverture dismissed rumors that "France will send thousands of men to annihilate the Colony and Liberty." France had been the main guarantor of Black freedom for almost eight years and would not pay back with "ingratitude" those who had fought for her. And yet, he could not shake off that thought. Half-way through the speech, he warned that he would stand firm in the event of a French invasion. "I am a soldier, I am not afraid of men, I fear only God."[59]

Restoring Slavery? (1801–1802)

For the Black population of Saint-Domingue, individual freedom was the main goal: allegiance to France derived from it and could be revisited if France ever reneged on the law of abolition. The process was reversed

---

[57] Louverture to Forfait, 12 February 1801, 61J18, Archives départementales de la Gironde.
[58] Louverture, "Récit des événements qui se sont passés dans la partie du nord," 7 November 1801, CO 137/106, BNA.
[59] Louverture, "Proclamation," 20 December 1801, CO 137/106, BNA.

among French governmental elites: the primary goal was to keep Saint-Domingue within the French orbit for strategic and economic reasons. If supporting abolition was the way to retain the loyalty of the Black colonial population, so be it, but many officials (with the exception of true abolitionists such as Henri Grégoire) saw abolition as a means to an end.

This pragmatic approach was particularly evident with Bonaparte, who took over as First Consul when he overthrew the Directory in 1799. Scholars such as Yves Bénot have accused him of plotting to restore slavery as soon as he seized power, but the historical record is muddier.[60] In 1800, Bonaparte explained that Saint-Domingue "would go for England if the Blacks were not attached to us by their interest in liberty" and that he would continue espousing abolition to keep Black soldiers on France's side.[61] His views changed only in 1801, when various critics of Louverture reached France and informed Bonaparte of his controversial policies, including his betrayal of Sasportas, the invasion of Santo Domingo, and the 1801 constitution. In October 1801, as soon as peace with Britain reopened Atlantic sea lanes, Bonaparte decided to send an expedition to overthrow Louverture. Even then, he reexpressed his support for the cultivator system because he hoped to turn the Black population against Louverture. His policies were purely pragmatic: in colonies where France could regain control without the support of Black soldiers, such as Martinique and Guadeloupe, he chose to preserve or restore slavery.[62]

Accordingly, when the general in charge of restoring French rule, Bonaparte's brother-in-law Victoire Leclerc, landed in Saint-Domingue in February 1802, he distributed a proclamation in French and Kreyòl in which Bonaparte promised the Black population that he would never restore slavery. If Blacks were told that "the forces [of Leclerc] are destined to seize liberty," they should answer "the Republic gave us liberty, the Republic will not suffer that it be taken away."[63] Meanwhile, Louverture accused Leclerc of planning to restore slavery, leaving Black cultivators unsure whom to support: the white army sent by Bonaparte, supposedly to keep Saint-Domingue free and French, or their own Black governor, whose labor

---

[60] Yves Bénot, *La démence coloniale sous Napoléon* (Paris: La Découverte, 1992), 49.
[61] Pierre-Louis Roederer, *Mémoires sur la Révolution, le Consulat, et l'Empire* (Paris: Plon, 1942 [1840]), 131.
[62] On Bonaparte's views, see Philippe Girard, "Napoléon Bonaparte and the Emancipation Issue in Saint-Domingue, 1799–1803," *French Historical Studies* 32:4 (2009), 587–618.
[63] Bonaparte, "Proclamation du Consul à tous les habitants de Saint-Domingue," 8 November 1801, FM/F/3/202, ANOM.

regime had been so strict? Many cultivators in the North rejected the entreaties of Louverture's envoys. "When we took up arms with General Moïse, against the whites, did the governor not exterminate us?," they asked. "Why does he not resuscitate Moïse to combat the whites!"[64] Abandoned by many of his countrymen, Louverture embraced the radical agenda of his deceased nephew in a last-ditch effort to recruit partisans. He made overtures to Maroon groups and encouraged his subordinates, notably Dessalines, to kill white planters. This was not enough to rally the Black population. In May 1802, an isolated Louverture signed a ceasefire with Leclerc and retired from public life.

The military campaign of the spring of 1802 did not fundamentally alter the ongoing debate over abolition and independence. Louverture never publicly renounced France, not even after Leclerc deported him to France, where he died in captivity in April 1803. Most of his generals, including Dessalines and Christophe, were reintegrated into the French colonial army after the ceasefire. When Leclerc issued a new labor code in May 1802, he purposely modeled it after Louverture's. The basis for this code "will be liberty and equality, and all Blacks will be free," Leclerc promised Christophe.[65]

The political equilibrium shifted only in the summer of 1802, when news reached Saint-Domingue that the French were in the process of restoring slavery in Guadeloupe. Though Leclerc continued to insist that liberty would remain the norm in Saint-Domingue, the Maroon groups, many of which had sat out the spring 1802 campaign or even supported the French because they resented Louverture's labor record, rebelled when they concluded that the French were no better. Sylla (near Plaisance), Sans Souci (in the North), Makaya (near Marmelade), Lamour Derance (near Port-au-Prince), and Lafortune (near Bahoruco) joined the revolt. Louverture's former subordinates Dessalines and Christophe remained in French employ for now, even helping Leclerc contain the uprising by the Maroon groups with which they had battled in the past.

Most Black and mixed-race members of the colonial army finally defected in the fall of 1802 when Leclerc began advocating a "war of extermination" because "a large part of the cultivators, accustomed to banditry for ten years,

---

[64] Thomas Madiou, *Histoire d'Haïti*, 3 vols. (Port-au-Prince: Courtois, 1847), vol. II, 222.
[65] Victoire Leclerc to Henry Christophe, 24 April 1802, in Christophe, "Manifeste du roi," 18 September 1814, 25, Publications on the independence of Haiti, RG 59/MLR A1632, National Archives, College Park.

will never subject themselves to work."⁶⁶ The racial undertones of his new policy meant that soldiers and officers of color no longer felt welcome as French citizens. The law of 20 May 1802, in which Bonaparte left open the possibility of restoring slavery in Saint-Domingue, convinced many people of color, even those who had been free prior to the Haitian Revolution (the so-called *anciens libres*), that slavery would soon be restored. "I am an *ancien libre*," General Augustin Clervaux told Bonaparte's sister Pauline, who had followed her husband Leclerc to Saint-Domingue. "But should there be any plan to restore slavery, I would immediately join the ranks of the rebels."⁶⁷ He joined the rebellion a day later.

Declaring Independence? (1803–1804)

Even after most officers of color had defected from the colonial army in October 1802, they did not yet embrace independence as a goal. "I am French, a friend of my country and liberty" was how Dessalines explained his decision to defect.⁶⁸ Many Frenchmen of all colors, in France as well as Saint-Domingue, remained committed to abolition, so there remained the hope that French policies might change yet again if Bonaparte's reactionary party was defeated. "Onward, army of Moreau, onward!," the rebels chanted in reference to General Jean Moreau, a liberal rival of Bonaparte.⁶⁹ Donatien de Rochambeau, who replaced Leclerc as captain-general of the expeditionary army when Leclerc died of yellow fever in November 1802, privately favored a restoration of slavery, but he was so disliked by liberal white officers that some tried to oust him. Many of Rochambeau's white troops, especially Polish units sent by Bonaparte, joined the rebel army of Dessalines rather than help restore slavery. This was not yet a war of independence, but rather it was a civil war waged along ideological lines, in which Rochambeau and other holdovers from the *ancien régime* battled partisans of France's revolutionary legacy. The rebels do not "consider themselves rebels at all," explained a Polish officer. "They fight under the French colors and in the name of the French Republic."⁷⁰

---

⁶⁶ Leclerc to Denis Decrès, 17 September 1802, B7/26, Service Historique de la Défense (Département de l'Armée de Terre), Vincennes.
⁶⁷ Madiou, *Histoire d'Haïti*, vol. II, 341.
⁶⁸ Jean-Jacques Dessalines to Pierre Quantin, 24 October 1802, Box 13/1238, RP-UF.
⁶⁹ Jean-Baptiste Brunet to Donatien de Rochambeau, 17 February 1803, Box 16/1625a, RP-UF.
⁷⁰ Jan Pachoński and Reuel K. Wilson, *Poland's Caribbean Tragedy: A Study of Polish Legions in the Haitian War of Independence, 1802–1803* (Boulder: East European Monographs, 1986), 203.

Dessalines and other advocates of the cultivator system remained at odds with the Maroons, with whom they fought a separate civil war in the winter of 1802–1803 that Trouillot has described as "the war within the war."[71] Dessalines lured, betrayed, and then killed Lamour Derance, the main Maroon leader in the West, after which various rebel leaders gathered in Arcahaye in May 1803 and recognized Dessalines as commander-in-chief of the rebel army. Even then, many Maroon leaders still refused to accept his command and reverted to their usual policy of supporting the weaker side, particularly near Cap Français, where Maroons continued to provision the French army and fight by its side until the French evacuation.

Haitian traditions hold that Dessalines created the modern Haitian flag at the Arcahaye conference when he tore the white strip from the French tricolor, thus signifying his support for the independence of a Black state. The archival record is not so categorical. Early versions of the Haitian flag symbolized one's attachment to French revolutionary principles, not nationhood per se. According to a sailor who attended the Arcahaye conference, Dessalines had not yet made up his mind on Saint-Domingue's future as of May 1803: he was still "willing to make arrangements" with the French, while Christophe "was opposed," having lost his trust in French promises.[72] Dessalines began to list independence as his goal only in August 1803, when he explained to a British admiral that he would rather die than "bear the odious name of Frenchman."[73] The Haitian Revolution, having finally become a war of independence, ended three months later, in November 1803, when Rochambeau evacuated the city of Cap Français. Rebel leaders declared independence shortly thereafter, invoking Bonaparte's proslavery agenda as the main impetus for their decision to break from France: "We shall be inexorable, perhaps even cruel, towards all the troops who ... forgetting the object for which they have not ceased fighting since 1789, should come yet from Europe, to carry among us death and servitude."[74]

A more formal declaration of independence followed on 1 January 1804. In it, Dessalines again presented national sovereignty as a decision he had

---

[71] Trouillot, *Silencing the Past*, 40.
[72] Louis-René de Latouche Tréville to Decrès, 20 May 1803, CC9/B20, ANOM.
[73] Dessalines to John T. Duckworth, 13 August 1803, ADM 1/253, BNA.
[74] Dessalines, Christophe, Augustin Clerveaux, "Proclamation," 29 November 1803, in *National Intelligencer and Washington Advertiser* no. 504 (13 January 1804).

reached when France had forsaken its revolutionary principles. "We must seize from the inhumane government that has for a long time kept us in the most humiliating torpor, all hope of re-enslaving us."[75] Though the Declaration was notable for its Francophobic tone, in many ways the new Haitian state built upon a tradition of French Republicanism. The text, drafted by a French-educated secretary, was written in formal French and peppered with references to "liberty." Dessalines even adopted the French colonial title of Governor General. Haiti's first national anthem, culminating with the verse "free and independent," was based on the Marseillaise.[76] Attachment to French Enlightenment principles, which had underpinned allegiance to France during the Revolution, became the foundation for Haiti's independence now that France had betrayed its legacy.

An alternate narrative of nationhood, derived from the French colonial era, also endured. It embraced theories of race and geographic determinism popular in some sectors of French and Caribbean thought. A mixed-race Creole explained to a white colonist that "you whites, France is your fatherland, just like Africa is for the Blacks. As for us, Saint-Domingue is our fatherland, the land belongs solely to us."[77] That notion occasionally surfaced in Louverture's rhetoric, such as a speech in which he referred to "foreigners, more specifically those from the metropole."[78] It came back in full force during the last year of the Haitian Revolution, when fighting took on genocidal overtones. "What do we have in common with these executioners?," Dessalines erupted in his Declaration of Independence in reference to the massacres of the Leclerc and Rochambeau era. "Their color [contrasts] with ours, the vast expanse of the seas that separate us, our avenging climate, all tell us that they are not our brothers, that they will never be."[79] Within a few months, Dessalines ordered the execution of most white Frenchmen remaining in Haiti. In May 1805, he further associated race with citizenship when his new constitution stated that "Haitians shall hence be known only by the generic appellation of Blacks" (Article 14).

---

[75] "Appendix: The Haitian Declaration of Independence," 241.
[76] "Hymne haytiène" (c. late January 1804), in Dessalines, "Journal de la campagne du Nord" (2 December 1802), CO 137/111, BNA.
[77] M. J. La Neuville, *Le dernier cri de Saint-Domingue et des colonies* (Philadelphia: Bradford, 1800), 9.
[78] Louverture, "Au nom de la colonie française de Saint-Domingue," 25 November 1801, West Indian Collection, Sc Micro R1527, Schomburg Center, New York Public Library.
[79] "Appendix: The Haitian Declaration of Independence," 242.

Conclusion

The numerous references to "liberty" in the Haitian Declaration of Independence are ambiguous as the term can refer to at least three concepts: political freedom (as opposed to dictatorship), individual freedom (as opposed to enslavement), and national freedom (as opposed to colonialism). Political rights were probably not on Dessalines' mind, as his regime was notoriously top-down and militaristic. Liberty, in his mind, meant national sovereignty and the abolition of slavery (though he went on to enforce a cultivator system that fell far short of the more expansive labor freedom favored by Maroons).

Those two freedoms – from bondage and from colonialism – imposed themselves remarkably late in the history of the Haitian Revolution; they were also intractably linked. Slavery was not legally abolished until 1793 in Saint-Domingue and 1794 in France. Even then, that principle remained in dispute as landholders and field hands battled over whether to restore slavery, dismantle large plantations, or adopt some intermediate labor system. The labor debate was not completely over in 1804, and groups of Maroons continued to battle the cultivator system throughout Dessalines' regime and beyond.

Independence also took a long time to impose itself, in sharp contrast with the American Revolution, which began, rather than ended, with a declaration of independence. The difference between the two revolutions stemmed from their diverging approaches to slavery. The United States' Founding Fathers supported self-determination for white planters, a goal that did not conflict with their economic interests: some British policies, such as Virginia Governor Lord Dunmore's promises of emancipation to rebel-owned slaves, only reinforced the white Patriots' eagerness to break with Britain. In Saint-Domingue, some conservative planters toyed with the idea of independence as early as 1790, hoping, like their US counterparts, to distance themselves from an abolitionist metropole. But the purpose of the Haitian Revolution shifted when Black slaves, who represented a much larger proportion of the population in Saint-Domingue than in the thirteen American colonies, revolted in 1791. The Haitian Revolution became a conflict over Black freedom, which tightened, rather than weakened, the ties between France and its colony – until 1802, when Bonaparte's renunciation of the French revolutionary heritage created an unbridgeable chasm with France's Black citizens and convinced them to redefine themselves as a new nation.

26

Establishing a New Nation: Haiti after Independence, 1804–1843

ERIN ZAVITZ

On 1 January 1804 General Jean-Jacques Dessalines officially declared the independence of Haiti, the former French colony of Saint-Domingue. As he gazed out on an audience of formerly enslaved men, women, and children and free(d) people of color, Dessalines embarked on a political, economic, and social experiment in the Americas: to establish the first Black state and fulfill the radical Age of Revolution promises of freedom and equality. In the country's first constitution he upheld the abolition of slavery and proclaimed racial equality. Dessalines also initiated a policy of land redistribution by nationalizing former plantations. Nevertheless, to keep the cash crop export economy running, he set up a system that tied agricultural workers (*cultivateurs*) to a plantation and provided minimum payment for their labor. The rhetoric of abolitionism and racial equality clashed with the demands of the capitalist global economy and left Dessalines with a fractured populace that did not share his national vision. In October 1806, military officers and top government officials led a coup and assassinated the first head of state. After Dessalines' death, the Haitian state divided, and competing leaders jostled to define the country's direction. By 1820, the president of the central state based in Port-au-Prince, Jean-Pierre Boyer, emerged, thanks to military assistance, as the leader of a newly unified Haiti. Boyer proceeded to extend his rule to the eastern part of the island and brought the former Spanish colony of Santo Domingo under Haitian control. Furthermore, he agreed to French recognition of Haiti, though not without controversy, and continued to develop Haitian diplomacy. The longest-serving Haitian president, Boyer's rule came to a close with a revolution in 1843 as Haitians of all classes vied to define the political and economic direction of the country.

As the brief historical survey above suggests, the decades following independence were critical for Haiti's development and were a period of dynamic change as well as colonial continuities. Nevertheless, the nineteenth century is frequently skipped over as scholarship jumps from the revolution to the twentieth century. Yet, as this chapter will explore, the struggles and debates of the early decades illustrate the contentious postcolonial process of building a Black nation-state in a world dominated by racialized slavery. As Haitians sought to interpret their revolution's ideals, in particular the meaning of liberty, they developed competing definitions that shaped the country's political, social, cultural, and economic development.

This chapter will explore these competing meanings and the development of the Haitian nation-state from 1804 to 1843. I have divided the forty years up by head of state. I will begin with an extended discussion of the rule of Jean-Jacques Dessalines, Haiti's first head of state. Although Dessalines ruled for under three years, these first years of independence were critical because they established the contours of nation-building. Between 1804 and 1806, we see how various groups in the new country sought to define its economic and political direction as well as create a new culture. Integral to this work were questions of landownership, the organization of labor, and systems of government. These questions continued to define Haiti's development after 1806 and will be the focus of the subsequent sections on Dessalines' successors: Alexandre Pétion, Henry Christophe, and Jean-Pierre Boyer.

Haiti's Founding: Jean-Jacques Dessalines and the First Haitian Empire

After fifteen years of revolution, though not all directed toward the goal of independence, people gathered in the town of Gonaïves on 1 January 1804 to celebrate the defeat of the French and the creation of a new country, Haiti. The name and day were symbolic of the people's break with slavery and colonialism. First, Haiti was the Taíno name for the island. It represented an era before European colonialism.[1] Second, while the victorious indigenous generals issued a preliminary declaration on 29 November 1803 in the northern port city of Fort-Liberté, Dessalines selected 1 January 1804 for a second, more accusatory and passionate, declaration and national fête. There is some debate on the 29 November proclamation. The nineteenth-century Haitian historian Thomas Madiou quotes the text but contends that it was an invention of foreign writers. More recently, Leslie Manigat has proven its validity by demonstrating its existence in contemporary foreign newspapers. The second text is the accepted founding document of Haiti, and 1 January became the first national

---

[1] David Geggus, *Haitian Revolutionary Studies* (Bloomington: Indiana University Press, 2002).

holiday, Independence Day.[2] The first day of a new year, 1 January represented the past and the future. A holiday on plantations, Dessalines refashioned the day to denote the birth of a new nation, the first to be born from a slave revolt and the second in the hemisphere to defeat a colonial power.

The crowd in Gonaïves welcomed their revolutionary hero, Dessalines, and his secretary Louis Félix Boisrond-Tonnerre. Together the two men declared Haiti's independence through Dessalines' speech in Kreyòl and Boisrond-Tonnerre's reading in French of the Declaration of Independence. The bilingualism of the fête represented the diverse crowd that included recently freed men and women, many of whom had been born in West Africa, and a handful of free people of color who had been educated in France. The range of cultural backgrounds posed a nation-building challenge as the various sectors of the new Haitian society interpreted their identities and their new liberty differently. In addition, they had competing ideas about the organization of the new state and its economy.

The accounts of Haiti's founding ceremony, penned decades after independence, are celebratory and capture neither these social and cultural tensions nor the reality of a war-torn country and people.[3] The Pearl of the Antilles resembled an apocalyptic landscape. Plantations, fields, and towns were ash and rubble, and exports had dropped to a quarter of the island's former output. In addition, war, disease, and migration had dramatically reduced the population. Notably a literate minority, a crucial group for state and nation building, was almost nonexistent.[4]

---

[2] Thomas Madiou, *Histoire d'Haïti*, 3 vols. (Port-au-Prince: Henri Deschamps, 1988–1991 [1847–1848]), vol. III, 125 note 1; Leslie Manigat, "Une brève analyse-commentaire critique d'un document historique," *Revue de la Société haïtienne d'histoire et de géographie* 221 (2005), 44–56. An English translation of the proclamation appeared in *The Times*, 6 February 1804, 3. For more discussion of the two declarations, see David Geggus, "Haiti's Declaration of Independence," in Julia Gaffield, ed., *The Haitian Declaration of Independence: Creation, Context, and Legacy* (Charlottesville: University of Virginia Press, 2015), 25–41; Patrick Tardieu, "The Debate Surrounding the Printing of the Haitian Declaration of Independence: A Review of the Literature," in Gaffield, ed., *The Haitian Declaration of Independence*, 58–71.

[3] For more on the history of Haitian Independence Day, see Erin Zavitz, "Revolutionary Commemorations: Jean-Jacques Dessalines and Haitian Independence Day, 1804–1904," in Gaffield, ed., *The Haitian Declaration of Independence*, 219–37; Erin Zavitz, "Revolutionary Memories: Celebrating and Commemorating the Haitian Revolution" (Ph.D. dissertation, University of Florida, 2015). The accounts of the day come from later nineteenth-century historians: Madiou, *Histoire d'Haïti*; Beaubrun Ardouin, *Études sur l'histoire d'Haïti, suivies de la vie du général J.-M. Borgella*, 11 vols. (Port-au-Prince: F. Dalencour, 1958 [1853–1860]).

[4] On the Revolution's aftermath, see Gaffield, ed., *The Haitian Declaration of Independence*; David Geggus, *The Haitian Revolution: A Documentary History* (Indianapolis: Hackett, 2014); Johnhenry Gonzales, *Maroon Nation* (New Haven: Yale University Press, 2019).

As Independence Day festivities concluded, Jean-Jacques Dessalines and his advisors turned to the challenges of turning the war-torn country and populace into the first independent Black nation-state. The initial step was establishing Dessalines' position. Included in the three-part Declaration of Independence is a decree that named Dessalines governor-general for life.[5] There is little information about the creation and signing of the proclamation. Nevertheless, Dessalines' title, suggesting authoritarian rule, raises questions about the new state's governing style. Both in the declaration and in later proclamations, Dessalines fashioned himself as a strong executive who was the "protector of liberty" and owed obedience from the Haitian people.[6] He would go on to accept nomination as emperor and create the first Haitian empire, momentarily, at least, further limiting the chances for a democratic form of government.[7] Although Dessalines and later heads of state attempted to create a strong central state, factors including the country's topography limited their ability to fully integrate Haiti's provinces. Port-au-Prince, the eventual capital, became a political and economic center, but regional port cities and their respective economic, political, and military leaders maintained a degree of independence from the state.

The early state had no singular governing document; instead, Dessalines and his ministers issued proclamations and decrees to establish his rule. A year in, Dessalines codified his empire in the first national constitution and collected the various decrees in the *Code penal militaire*.[8] The 1805 constitution included a number of articles that reinterpreted the Eurocentric focus of the Age of Revolution ideals. It formally extended the bounds of sovereignty to include people of African descent and established the state's commitment to abolitionism. Articles 2, 12, and 14 abolished slavery, limited

---

[5] "Haitian Declaration of Independence," The National Archives of the United Kingdom, CO 137/111/1, ff. 113–17.

[6] On Dessalines the protector of Haitian liberty, see "Haitian Declaration of Independence"; Laurent Dubois, *Haiti: The Aftershocks of History* (New York: Metropolitan Books, 2012); Claude Moïse, *Constitution et luttes de pouvoir en Haïti: La faillite des classes dirigeantes, 1804–1915*, 2nd edition (Port-au-Prince: Éditions de l'Univérsité d'État d'Haïti, 2009); Mimi Sheller, *Democracy after Slavery: Black Publics and Peasant Radicalism in Haiti and Jamaica* (Gainesville: University Press of Florida, 2000).

[7] The date of Dessalines' imperial nomination and acceptance is subject to some debate. See Deborah Jenson, *Beyond the Slave Narrative: Politics, Sex, and Manuscripts in the Haitian Revolution* (Liverpool: Liverpool University Press, 2012) for more on the possible dates as well as the postcolonial identity politics at play.

[8] Jean-Jacques Dessalines, "Codes of Hayti," 26 May 1805, Reserve 4275.68 no. 1, Boston Public Library.

property ownership to Haitians, and proclaimed all Haitians to be Black.[9] Subsequent constitutions upheld these commitments and definitions of belonging and even adjusted as the Haitian state incorporated new territory. For example, when Jean-Pierre Boyer incorporated the eastern half of the island, he even extended citizenship and property rights to Spaniards who had been living there before 1822.[10] In the case of property ownership, this article remained until the US occupation, when US officials demanded a revision, although by the late nineteenth century, foreigners had found a loophole by marrying Haitian women. Dessalines and other early heads of state were quite adamant about who had the right to own property. The British consul, Thomas Ussher, noted in 1842 that Boyer was unwilling to give British residents burial land because this could be interpreted as foreign landownership.[11] An additional article stated that there was no state religion, a tacit acknowledgement of early Haitian Vodou's legitimacy. These legal documents performed a Black sovereignty that challenged the Enlightenment's Eurocentrism and incorporated Africans and their descendants into the category of the civilized. Black men and women could establish a state, write a constitution, and create a body of laws.

These performances were key for Haiti's international audience that watched with bated breath as formerly enslaved people established an independent country. Unlike its northern neighbor, Haiti had to wait decades for formal international recognition. The absence of a diplomatic treaty did not mean that Haiti remained isolated. Beginning in 1804, Haitian merchants kept up an active trade with the British, Americans, Danish, and Dutch. Haitian officials also corresponded with their Atlantic World counterparts in the hope of achieving diplomatic gains for the new country.[12] Nonetheless,

---

[9] On the 1805 constitution, see Joan [Colin] Dayan, *Haiti, History, and the Gods* (University of California Press, 1998); Sibylle Fischer, *Modernity Disavowed: Haiti and the Cultures of Slavery in the Age of Revolution* (Durham, NC: Duke University Press, 2004); Julia Gaffield, "Complexities of Imagining Haiti: A Study of National Constitutions, 1801–1807," *Journal of Social History* 41:1 (2007), 81–103; Anne Gulick, "We Are Not the People: The 1805 Haitian Constitution's Challenge to Political Legibility in the Age of Revolution," *American Literature* 78:4 (2006), 799–820; Moïse, *Constitution et Luttes*; Karen Salt, *The Unfinished Revolution: Haiti, Black Sovereignty, and Power in the Nineteenth-Century Atlantic World* (Liverpool: Liverpool University Press, 2019).

[10] Jean-Pierre Boyer to Council of Santo Domingo, 7 February 1823, quoted in Madiou, *Histoire d'Haïti*, vol. VI, 371.

[11] Thomas Ussher, "Notebook, Letterbook and Diary, 1841–1856," WMS/Amer. 105, Wellcome Collection.

[12] For more discussion of early trade and diplomacy, see Julia Gaffield, *Haitian Connections in the Atlantic World: Recognition after Revolution* (Chapel Hill: University of North Carolina Press, 2015).

the lack of a formal treaty acknowledging Haiti's independence left the country in a precarious position that fueled a gendered militarization of society.[13] Motivated by a fear of French reinvasion, Dessalines and his generals invested heavily in building forts, most notably La Citadelle in the northern mountains, which is the largest fort in the western hemisphere. Dessalines also maintained a large standing army of approximately 20,000 men to garrison these forts and provide protection. With a French agent still in Santo Domingo, the fears of invasion and reenslavement felt quite real and led Dessalines one step beyond fortifying his country. In late 1804 and early 1805, he led these troops on several failed campaigns against Jean-Louis Ferrand, the French agent in Santo Domingo.[14]

As Dessalines and his officials defined the geographic and political bounds of the new nation-state and sought to uphold trade agreements, they grappled with postcolonial economic challenges. Dessalines' military strategy of *koupe tèt boule kay* (cut off heads, burn houses) left thousands of acres of agricultural land in ashes. Nevertheless, in 1804 coffee and sugar plantations remained in production, and Haitians found American and British merchants interested in purchasing their goods. Haiti's new military and political elite sought to maintain the plantation economy and profit from abandoned or seized French properties. The elite were divided on how to distribute this land and organize the labor needed to maintain sugar plantations.

Dessalines offered his vision to nationalize properties and set up a labor system that tied recently freed men and women to plantations. To further emphasize the importance of agricultural production for the state, he created a national holiday, Agricultural Day. The fête would continue under later leaders and became one of the most regularly celebrated holidays, along with Independence Day, in the early nineteenth century.[15] Beginning in February 1804, he annulled any property transfers to current Haitians and during the following two years initiated a country-wide campaign to verify land titles. These policies angered Haiti's emerging elite, particularly in the south and

---

[13] Mimi Sheller, "Sword-Bearing Citizens: Militarism and Manhood in Nineteenth-Century Haiti," *Plantation Society in the Americas* 4:2–3 (1997), 233–78.

[14] Graham Nessler, *An Islandwide Struggle for Freedom: Revolution, Emancipation, and Reenslavement in Hispaniola, 1789–1809* (Chapel Hill: University of North Carolina Press, 2016), 159.

[15] "Haiti, Imperial Constitution (1805)," *Haiti and the Atlantic World* (blog), https://haitidoi.com/constitutions/1805-2. For continued state support of the holiday, see the subsequent constitutions, all compiled at https://haitidoi.com/constitutions by Julia Gaffield, and see for reports on the celebrations the longest-running newspaper of the day, *Le Télégraphe* (1813–1843), which contained articles each May about events in Port-au-Prince and other cities.

west, who had hoped the land would fall to private owners, not the state. As Dessalines' state amassed land, it faced a growing labor problem. Who would work on all these plantations? While the constitution abolished slavery, the state's dire need for laborers to continue producing Haiti's exports created new systems of forced labor that foreshadowed post-emancipation labor challenges other Atlantic World societies would face. Dessalines established a system that tied laborers to specific plantations in exchange for a quarter of the profits. Moreover, the government required workers to carry an identity card.[16] To Haiti's recently freed men and women, Dessalines' labor policy infringed on their new freedom and stood in contradiction to their ideal of liberty: landownership and production rights.[17] This contradiction led to the creation of an alternative export economy, including foodstuffs to neighboring islands, run by smallholders and the state-supported/controlled cash crop economy of coffee and to a lesser extent sugar.[18] In the nineteenth century, logwood, cotton, and cacao were also exported, but coffee remained the main source of revenue.[19] In addition, just as enslaved Saint-Dominguans had fled to the mountains to escape slavery, so Haitians ran to avoid plantation labor. These Maroons, as well as small landowners, developed a network of family farms in the nineteenth century.

The questions of labor and land illustrate that Haiti in 1804 was a demographically different place from 1789 Saint-Domingue. The revolution and the 1804 massacres reduced the population by at least a third and eliminated much of the literate minority. The few remaining Europeans faced two contrasting fates. Most were massacred on Dessalines' orders between February and April 1804.[20] Others, notably the Polish mercenaries who had deserted the Napoleonic expedition, became integrated into the

---

[16] For more details on the identity card, see Gonzales, *Maroon Nation*, 114–20.
[17] On this idea of liberty, see Chelsea Stieber, *Haiti's Paper War: Post-Independence Writing and the Making of the Republic (1804–1954)* (New York: New York University Press, 2020); Gonzales, *Maroon Nation*; Robert LaCerte, "The Evolution of Land and Labour in the Haitian Revolution, 1791–1820," in Hilary Beckles and Verene Sheperd, eds., *Caribbean Freedom: Economy and Society from Emancipation to the Present* (Princeton: Markus Wiener Publications, 1993), 42–7; Michel-Rolph Trouillot, *Haiti, State against Nation: The Origins and Legacy of Duvalierism* (New York: Monthly Review Press, 1990).
[18] Gonzales, *Maroon Nation*.
[19] See Victor Bulmer-Thomas, *Economic History of the Caribbean since the Napoleonic Wars* (Cambridge: Cambridge University Press, 2012).
[20] On the massacres, see Geggus, "Haiti's Declaration of Independence"; Jeremy Popkin, "Jean-Jacques Dessalines, Norbert Thoret, and the Violent Aftermath of the Haitian Declaration of Independence," in Gaffield, *The Haitian Declaration of Independence*, 115–35; Philippe Girard, "Did Dessalines Plan to Export the Haitian Revolution?," in Gaffield, *The Haitian Declaration of Independence*, 136–57.

Haitian nation; the first state constitution even defined them as Black.[21] A few whites escaped death thanks to mixed-race neighbors or family members, or because they could offer a service to the new Haitian state, as doctors or priests. In the end, the small colonial white population almost vanished. The demographic loss left postrevolutionary Haiti in need of people, and Dessalines and subsequent heads of state sought to encourage immigration to repopulate the new nation.

The remaining population that would become Haitian was overwhelmingly either African-born or of African descent. This shared African ancestry became the cornerstone of Haitian identity, and, along with the alliance of former slaves and free people of color in the War of Independence, inspired the national motto: "L'Union fait la force" (unity is strength).[22] Nevertheless, the ideological emphasis on unity did little to prevent the creation of new social divisions based on revolutionary and colonial categories.

The majority of Haiti's population were *nouveaux libres* (formerly enslaved people). Born on the island or in west or west central Africa, they spoke Kreyòl and/or their native languages, practiced Vodou, and maintained an African-oriented culture. Emancipation and independence held mixed promises for the masses. Some remained on state-run plantations either by choice or because they were forced to remain and received payment for their labor. Others turned to the hills, as slaves had done during the colonial era, and formed squatter communities, the foundation for what Haitian sociologist Jean Casimir terms "the counter plantation model."[23] The idea originates from the work of the anthropologist Sidney Mintz on Caribbean peasantries.[24] A small number of peasants would, like the Black revolutionary heroes, achieve limited social mobility through the military. Mimi Sheller notes that, by 1840, "there were approximately 25,000 men in the army and another 40,000 in the national guard . . . perhaps close to one fifth of the adult male population."[25] Alain Turnier's biographical study of Mérisier Jeannis illustrates the opportunity for social mobility the military provided in nineteenth-century Haiti.[26] In all three cases, the peasants would create an

---

[21] "Haiti, Imperial Constitution (1805)."
[22] For a discussion of the motto and other Haitian founding myths, see Maximilien Laroche, "The Founding Myths of the Haitian Nation," trans. Martin Munro, *Small Axe* 9:2 (2005), 1–15.
[23] Jean Casimir, *La cultura oprimida* (Mexico City: Nueva Imagen, 1981).
[24] Sidney Mintz, *Caribbean Transformations* (Chicago: Aldine Publishing Company, 1974).
[25] Sheller, "Sword-Bearing Citizens," 250.
[26] Alain Turnier, *Avec Mérisier Jeannis: Une tranche de vie jacmélienne et nationale* (Port-au-Prince: Imprimerie Le Natal, 1982).

identity that incorporated their African heritage and New World experiences that seldom matched the elite's Eurocentric national vision and rarely entered the written archive.

Alongside the nascent peasantry, there emerged a new ruling class consisting of *anciens libres* (individuals who had been free before 1789) and former revolutionary army officers. This class, referred to in Kreyòl as "milat," included Black and mixed-race individuals. Here, I follow the historian Matthew J. Smith in the use of the term *milat*. In Kreyòl, it signifies more than skin color (mulatto); it also references one's social class and culture, specifically the use of French and practice of Catholicism. The term highlights the complex interplay of class, color, and culture in Haitian identity politics.[27] In 1804, educated and battle-wise *anciens libres* who had stayed in Haiti (or returned) quickly filled positions in the new independent government and formed a portion of the new Haitian elite.[28] The majority of these men were mixed-race and a select few had received an education in France. Regardless of their education level, many of them embraced European culture, spoke French, and practiced Catholicism. They lived primarily in the new country's southern and western port cities. This new elite also included in its ranks men of full African descent who had ascended the social ladder via the military. Their military prowess had enabled them to rise from slavery and receive abandoned French plantations as a reward for their victories. Black officers became property owners and had their own laborers. Though of full African descent, these men were more often than not born on the island, spoke Kreyòl but used French-educated scribes, and had an ambivalent attitude toward African traditions. They resided predominantly in the north.

United in support of general abolition, Haiti's nascent ruling class disagreed on understandings of liberty. As literary scholar Chelsea Stieber eloquently illustrates, they divided along ideological lines into two groups, Dessalineans and republicans. Republicans valued "individual rights, political equality, and the active contestation of any arbitrary government." In contrast, Dessalineans privileged "independence from colonial rule" over individual liberties or rights.[29] Despite their different notions of liberty, both the

---

[27] See Matthew J. Smith, *Red and Black in Haiti: Radicalism, Conflict, and Political Change, 1934–57* (Chapel Hill: University of North Carolina Press, 2009), 198, note 6.
[28] For a discussion of individuals who returned to Haiti, see Vanessa Mongey, "Going Home: The Back-to-Haiti Movement in the Early Nineteenth Century," *Atlantic Studies* 16:2 (2018), 184–202.
[29] Stieber, *Haiti's Paper War*, 4.

anciens libres and military officers "sought access to an exploitable labour force, and were thereby opposed to the transformation of the former slave producing masses into an independent, self-subsistent, land-owning peasantry."[30] The ruling class was unable to achieve this economic model due to internal divisions, which shaped the development of post-1804 Haiti.

The French-literate elite became Haiti's intellectuals and had the privilege and power to record the country's founding and narrate its history.[31] Early Haitian literature has often been overlooked on account of its being considered imitative and not Haitian enough; however, recent publications are correcting this.[32] As Dessalines and his generals repurposed captured French cannons in the newly built forts, government secretaries and printers used formerly French printing presses to create Haitian newspapers, publish decrees, and narrate the new nation's history. Engaged in an anticolonial and antislavery battle of words, Haiti's first national writers employed their pens and printing presses as weapons against the dominant colonial and racial ideologies of the Euro-American authors. The Haitian anthropologist Michel-Rolph Trouillot contends that even the most radical European and American authors lacked a "conceptual frame of reference" within which to explain the revolution and creation of a postslavery state run by men of African descent.[33] In so doing, Haiti's first national writers built upon the revolutionary traditions of educated free men of color, who had earlier taken up their pens to fight racial inequality before and during the revolution.[34] It was to this

[30] Alex Dupuy, "Class Formation and Underdevelopment in Nineteenth-Century Haiti," *Race & Class* 24:17 (1982), 19.
[31] For a more detailed biography of these men, see Délide Joseph, *L'État haïtien et ses intellectuels: Socio-histoire d'un engagement politique (1801–1860)* (Port-au-Prince: Imprimerie Le Natal, 2017).
[32] See, for example, Baron de Vastey, *The Colonial System Unveiled*, ed. and trans. Chris Bongie (Liverpool: University of Liverpool Press, 2014); Chris Bongie, "The Cry of History: Juste Chanlatte and the Unsettling (Presence) of Race in Early Haitian Literature," *MLN* 130:4 (2015), 807–35; Marlene Daut, *Tropics of Haiti: Race and the Literary History of the Haitian Revolution in the Atlantic World, 1789–1865* (Liverpool: Liverpool University Press, 2015); Marlene Daut, *Baron de Vastey and the Origins of Black Atlantic Humanism* (New York: Palgrave Macmillian, 2017); Doris Garraway, "Empire of Freedom, Kingdom of Civilization: Henry Christophe, the Baron de Vastey, and the Paradoxes of Universalism in Postrevolutionary Haiti," *Small Axe* 16:3 (2012), 1–21; Gregory Pierrot, "Juste Chanlatte: A Haitian Life," *Journal of Haitian Studies* 25:1 (2019), 39–65; Stieber, *Haiti's Paper War*; Erin Zavitz, "Revolutionary Narrations: Early Haitian Historiography and the Challenge of Writing Counter-history," *Atlantic Studies* 14:3 (2016), 336–53.
[33] Michel-Rolph Trouillot, *Silencing the Past: Power and the Production of History* (Boston: Beacon Press, 1995), 82.
[34] For more on the efforts of educated free men of color in Saint-Domingue, see John Garrigus, *Before Haiti: Race and Citizenship in French Saint-Domingue* (New York: Palgrave Macmillan, 2006); Daut, *Baron de Vastey*.

group that most of Haiti's first authors belonged. Their publications served to reconstruct state and society after fifteen years of warfare and to glorify Haiti's existence in a white colonial world. Their publications also demonstrated Haiti's civilization. Novels, histories, even legal codes served as proof that Haitians could "progress" just like white Euro-Americans.[35] Authors hoped these literary performances would help Haiti garner diplomatic recognition by combating misinformation circulating in white publications.[36] Moreover, postindependence Haitian writing became "performative speech acts by which formerly colonial subjects and the enslaved seized the means to (re)define themselves as human, independent, postcolonial, black writing and publishing subjects."[37] Haiti and Haitians became subjects with a past, present, and future. Thus, across literary genres, authors celebrated the achievements of Africans and their descendants in the Americas, legitimated the new country, and "unsilenced" its origins.

Two early texts demonstrate Haitian intellectuals' immediate attempts to "unsilence" the new country's history and illuminate cultural work during Dessalines' short reign. Boisrond-Tonnerre, after writing the Declaration of Independence, published the first history of the revolution, *Mémoires pour servir à l'histoire d'Hayti*.[38] Boisrond-Tonnerre concentrated on his personal experience of the final years of the revolution, 1802–1803. His text testifies to the horrors of the French expedition and validates Haiti as an independent country whose citizens fought for its existence.[39] While Boisrond-Tonnerre turned to prose to preserve the history of Haiti's founding, a fellow young intellectual, Pierre Flignau, chose to perform the origin story. One of Haiti's earliest playwrights, Flignau composed and produced *L'Haïtien expatrié*:

---

[35] For more on writing as a symbol of white Euro-American notions of civilization and progress, see Ramsey, *Vodou and Power in Haiti*; Daut, *Tropics of Haiti*; Joseph, *L'État haïtien et ses intellectuels*; Stieber, *Haiti's Paper Wars*.

[36] See Count of Limonade (Prévost) to Thomas Clarkson, 24 March 1819, in Earl Leslie Griggs and Clifford H. Prator, eds., *Henry Christophe and Thomas Clarkson: A Correspondence* (Berkeley: University of California Press, 1952), 153; Baron de Vastey to Thomas Clarkson, 29 November 1819, in Griggs and Prator, *Henry Christophe and Thomas Clarkson*, 178–9.

[37] Stieber, *Haiti's Paper War*, 15.

[38] Louis Félix Boisrond-Tonnerre, *Mémoires pour server à l'histoire d'Hayti* (Dessalines: Imprimerie Centrale du Gouvernement, 1804).

[39] For more on Boisrond-Tonnerre's life and writing, see John Garrigus, "'Victims of Our Own Credulity and Indulgence': The Life of Louis Félix Boisrond-Tonnerre," in Gaffield, ed., *The Haitian Declaration of Independence*, 42–57; Daut, *Tropics of Haiti*.

Comédie en trois actes et en prose in 1804.[40] Flignau's play recounts the story of two Saint-Dominguan refugees who fled to the Danish island of St. Thomas during the final years of the revolution. While there, they experience racial prejudice and ultimately decide to return home upon hearing of Dessalines' victory over the French. Both texts use the cruelties of colonialism and racism to justify Haiti's existence and call for the united efforts of Haitians to build a new country.

The project of building the first Black and postslavery nation-state in the Americas turned out to be far more difficult than Flignau's main characters imagined. While crowds applauded readings of the declaration, unrest was building. The elite and peasantry were growing weary of the new regime and its policies. The alliances that had helped to secure independence crumbled, and the first head of state faced a rebellion launched from the south and supported by his own generals. To bring an end to the "yoke of Dessalines," military leaders marched on Port-au-Prince.[41] On 17 October 1806, Dessalines rode to Port-au-Prince to meet the insurgents and, caught in an ambush, died at Pont Rouge on the city's outskirts. His assassination led to a power struggle that primarily divided Haiti between two main rulers: Alexandre Pétion and Henry Christophe. Nonetheless, for a short period of time (1810–1812) four different states existed: a republic under Alexandre Pétion based in Port-au-Prince, a breakaway Republic of the Department of the South under André Rigaud, an insurgent state led by Goman (Jean-Baptiste Perrier) in Grande Anse (the tip of Haiti's southern peninsula), and a northern kingdom under Henry Christophe. The next section will focus on the first and last of these states.

Although Dessalines ruled for under three years, I have focused more on this period because it established a series of trends that would come to define postcolonial Haiti. First, the Haitian state was and would continue to be nondemocratic. Second, the Haitian elite followed their French colonial predecessors and continued to support an agro-export economy that relied upon systems of coerced labor. Third, the Haitian peasantry cultivated an alternative economic vision that allowed them to control their own labor and land. Fourth, while formal diplomatic recognition remained elusive, Haitians turned to other avenues (trade agreements, publications) to legitimate their country's existence.

---

[40] Pierre Flignau, *L'Haïtien expatrié: Comédie en trois actes et en prose* (Port-au-Prince: T. Bouchereau, 1840).
[41] Madiou, *Histoire d'Haïti*, vol. III, 370.

Henry Christophe and Alexandre Pétion: Civil War and Division

In the aftermath of Dessalines' assassination, both of his top generals, Henry Christophe and Alexandre Pétion, were possible successors. Pétion stepped aside and invited Christophe to be the next head of state. However, the invitation came with the caveat that Christophe had to accept a revised constitution. Pétion and his supporters wanted to move away from Dessalines' autocracy and favored creating a legislative body that could check the power of the executive. They drafted a new constitution in 1806 that dissolved the empire and created a Haitian republic. Christophe did not agree to the revisions and refused his appointment as president. He rallied supporters in the north and marched on Port-au-Prince, the new capital. Pétion responded with his own regional army and civil war ensued. Neither general achieved victory; they withdrew to their respective regions and established competing states.

After refusing the 1806 constitution, Henry Christophe established himself in the northern port city of Cap-Haïtien and wrote a new constitution in 1807. Although the constitution used the title of president, Christophe followed Dessalines' authoritarian model. Christophe as president had extensive powers, such as to make treaties, propose laws, and designate his successor, and had an advisory Council of the State that had no authority to check the power of the executive.[42] In Port-au-Prince, Pétion accepted the position of president in the spring of 1807. While he entered office under the constitution of 1806, which he had helped write, he quickly moved to reduce the power of the Senate and increase the power of the executive. Three years later, he was reelected with a Senate of five members that functioned similarly to Christophe's advisory council. Thus, the disagreement over executive power that had prompted the civil war and division of the Haitian state seemed a moot point as both heads of state fashioned themselves as autocratic rulers.

In 1811, as a response to the civil war and Haiti's precarious international position, Christophe and his advisors revised the constitution again and established a monarchy.[43] Haiti's first and only king, Christophe embraced

---

[42] "Haiti, Constitution de l'État d'Haïti (1807)," *Haiti and the Atlantic World* (blog), https://haitidoi.com/constitutions/1807-2.

[43] "Haiti, Constitution Royale d'Haïti (1811)," *Haiti and the Atlantic World* (blog), https://haitidoi.com/constitutions/1811-2.

Figure 26.1 Parade ground at Sans-Souci. Alamy.

all the trappings of monarchy. He created a nobility with heraldry[44] and constructed a palace, Sans-Souci, filled with the luxuries of the day. Recent archaeological work has revealed the splendor of Sans-Souci (Figure 26.1).[45]

Christophe was also a patron of the arts and Haitian literature flourished during his rule.[46] The most prolific writer was Baron de Vastey who, along with Juste Chanlatte and Julien Prévost, wrote "to produce black people as subjects rather than objects."[47] In over half a dozen pamphlets and

---

[44] See Clive Cheesman, ed., *Armorial of Haiti: Symbols of Nobility in the Reign of Henry Christophe* (London: College of Arms, 2007).

[45] See James Cameron Monroe, "New Light from Haiti's Royal Past: Recent Archaeological Excavations in the Palace of Sans-Souci, Milot," *The Journal of Haitian Studies* 23:2 (2017), 5–31; Daniel Weiss, "Haiti's Royal Past," *Archaeology* 71:4 (2018), 36–41.

[46] On literature, see, for example, Baron de Vastey, *The Colonial System Unveiled*; Daut, *Tropics of Haiti*; Daut, *Baron de Vastey*; Garraway, "Empire of Freedom." On art, see Tabitha McIntosh and Grégory Pierrot, "Capturing the Likeness of Henry I of Haiti (1805–1822)," *Atlantic Studies* 14:2 (2017), 127–51.

[47] Daut, *Baron de Vastey*, xxxviii.

monograph-length works, Vastey appealed to Haitian and foreign readers and sought to legitimate the Haitian revolution and Christophe's monarchy. British abolitionists were an important group of Vastey's readers. Vastey and Prévost (Count de Limonade) sent Vastey's work to Thomas Clarkson to inform the British abolitionist of Haiti's current events and correct French authors' racialized interpretations of its history.[48] Moreover, Clarkson's correspondence put Christophe in contact with a wider network of Atlantic abolitionists, including the American Quaker Evan Lewis, who sent Christophe Clarkson's book *The Abolition of the African Slave Trade*.[49]

Exchanging texts was just one facet of Christophe's relationship with Great Britain. He had a representative in London, Jean-Gabriel Peltier, who advocated for British recognition, corresponded with Thomas Clarkson, and, through Atlantic abolitionists' networks, welcomed African American intellectuals like Prince Saunders to his kingdom.[50] Born in New England, Saunders was an experienced teacher and proponent of African American emigration who traveled to Haiti in February 1816 on the recommendation of Clarkson. Christophe embraced Saunders and sent him to England to be his adviser and work to recruit British teachers to help develop the Haitian kingdom's schools.[51] Saunders returned that fall with teachers, and more followed, leading to the creation of thirteen schools and instruction of as many as 72,000 students.[52] In cultivating these relationships, Christophe and his advisors hoped for eventual diplomatic recognition. Unfortunately, the Haitian monarch, like Dessalines before him, gained only informal recognition, through limited trade and the exchange of people and ideas. Neither Christophe nor contemporary heads of state signed an official trade agreement with Great Britain and, aside from

---

[48] Vastey enclosed his 1817 publication *Réflexions politiques sur quelques ouvrages et journaux français concernant Hayti* in Baron de Vastey to Thomas Clarkson, 24 March 1819, in Griggs and Prator, *Henry Christophe and Thomas Clarkson*, 136. Several months later, Julien Prévost (Count Limonade) sent Vastey's newest publication, *Essai sur les causes de la révolution et des guerres civiles d'Hayti* (1819), in Count of Limonade to Thomas Clarkson, 3 September 1819, in Griggs and Prator, *Henry Christophe and Thomas Clarkson*, 153; Vastey sent a second copy of *Essai sur les causes*, in Baron de Vastey to Thomas Clarkson, 29 November 1819, in Griggs and Prator, *Henry Christophe and Thomas Clarkson*, 178.

[49] Christophe mentioned to Clarkson that Lewis gave the king Clarkson's book, King Henry to Thomas Clarkson, 20 November 1819, in Griggs and Prator, *Henry Christophe and Thomas Clarkson*, 165.

[50] For more on Peltier, see Gaffield, *Haitian Connections*.

[51] Henry Christophe to Thomas Clarkson, 5 February 1816, in Griggs and Prator, *Henry Christophe and Thomas Clarkson*, 91–3.

[52] Henry Christophe to Thomas Clarkson, 18 November 1816, in Griggs and Prator, *Henry Christophe and Thomas Clarkson*, 97–8; Dubois, *Haiti*, 73.

exceptions during the War of 1812, Haitian merchants faced obstacles trading with Caribbean British colonies. In 1843, the British Parliament lifted all obstructions to trade between Haiti and its colonies.[53] The two countries also signed an agreement to suppress the slave trade.[54]

While Christophe sought British support and recognition, his approach to negotiations with France contrasted greatly. With the end of the Napoleonic Wars, Louis XVIII turned his attention back to the Americas and schemed to retake Haiti.[55] French envoys traveled to the island in 1814 to meet with both Pétion and Christophe. They had secret instructions from Pierre-Victor Malouet, the Minister of the Colonies and Navy, to recolonize Haiti and, as Thomas Madiou explains, were little better than spies.[56] To give their mission more legitimacy, Dauxion Lavaysse presented himself as an agent of France and initiated contact with Pétion, who invited him to land at Port-au-Prince.[57] After securing his entry, Lavaysse sent a letter to Henry Christophe which threatened use of force "if he did not submit to the French government" ("s'il ne se soumettait pas à le gouvernement français").[58] Christophe and his advisors responded with outrage, published a pamphlet refuting Lavaysse's claims, and waited for Agostino Franco de Medina, the envoy France had sent to the northern portion of the island.[59] Shortly after Medina's arrival, Christophe ordered his arrest and, upon finding inflammatory secret instructions from Malouet, his execution.[60] Although Christophe later tempered his view toward the French and asked Clarkson to open negotiations with the former colonial power, his directions for Clarkson echoed his actions in 1814 and demonstrated his commitment to Haiti's independence and abolitionism. He explained that the "most important items from our point of view are *that Haiti be recognized as a free, sovereign, and independent nation; that her commerce be free; and that the demands of the ex-colonists be abandoned* [italics in original]."[61]

---

[53] See Matthew Smith, *Liberty, Fraternity, Exile: Haiti and Jamaica after Emancipation* (Chapel Hill: University of North Carolina Press, 2014), 82.

[54] See "Convention for the Suppression of the Slave Trade," 23 December 1839, National Archives of the United Kingdom, F.O. 84/330.

[55] For a complete discussion of Franco-Haitian relations, see Jean-François Brière, *Haïti et la France, 1804–1848: Le rêve brisé* (Paris: Karthala, 2008).

[56] Madiou, *Histoire d'Haïti*, vol. v, 245.   [57] Madiou, *Histoire d'Haïti*, vol. v, 249.

[58] Madiou, *Histoire d'Haïti*, vol. v, 249.

[59] Madiou, *Histoire d'Haïti*, vol. v, 257–9. For the pamphlet, see Chevalier de Prézeau, *Réfutation de la letter du general français Dauxion Lavaysse* (Cap-Henry: P. Roux, 1814).

[60] For a contemporary account, see Baron de Vastey, *Notes à M. le Baron V. P. de Malouet* (Cap-Henry: P. Roux, 1814).

[61] Henry Christophe to Thomas Clarkson, 20 November 1819, in Griggs and Prator, eds., *Henry Christophe and Thomas Clarkson*, 169.

As Christophe and his advisors navigated diplomacy in a white, slaveholding Atlantic world, they faced the challenging question of how to fund the monarchy and attract British merchants. Just as Dessalines had done, Christophe turned to Haiti's cash crops and a system of forced labor to fund and protect his kingdom. In the *Code Henry*, published one year after his crowning, Christophe laid out in over 800 pages a detailed corpus of laws that regulated the actions of his subjects, both *cultivateurs* and plantation owners.[62] Laborers were tied to plantations, just as they had been under Dessalines. Access to land was tightly held by Christophe and his nobles. Only as his kingdom was crumbling from internal strife did Christophe turn to appeasing the populace through landownership and labor policies. Late in 1819, he began to distribute land to the military, though in smaller parcels than Pétion.[63] Christophe's late attempt to acknowledge the peasantry's definition of liberty was not enough to ensure the continuation of his kingdom. Facing invasion from the south, internal unrest, and poor health, Christophe committed suicide in October 1820. With his death, the dream of a Black kingdom that could rival European courts vanished as troops from Port-au-Prince entered Cap-Haïtien and reunified the country.

While Christophe's kingdom flourished momentarily but failed to reconcile competing economic visions and understandings of liberty, Pétion's state – though far from democratic and inclusive – offered an alternative that ultimately triumphed. Pétion's success was a product of the economic reality of his war-torn republic. He did not enjoy the profits of Christophe's sugar-exporting kingdom. Madiou claimed that Christophe had a reserve of 11 million Spanish pesos in silver and 6 million in gold.[64] Pétion turned to what his state had available: land.

After an attempt to maintain Dessalines' land and labor policies, Pétion designed a system of land distribution that provided the Haitian majority with an opportunity to fulfill their vision of liberty. At the same time, Pétion ensured that his elite supporters also profited and amassed private estates. In 1809, his government rolled out a series of land grants according to one's military rank and service during the revolution. While the highest-ranking officers received the largest plots, even a soldier could obtain a distribution of five *carreaux* (not quite sixteen acres).[65] These grants helped to create new

---

[62] *Code Henry* (Cap-Haïtien: P. Roux, 1812). [63] Gonzales, *Maroon Nation*, 177.
[64] Madiou, *Histoire d'Haïti*, vol. v, 238, 319.
[65] Gonzales, *Maroon Nation*, 175–6. For more discussion of the land grants, see also Alex Dupuy, *Haiti: From Revolutionary Slaves to Powerless Citizen: Essays on the Politics and Economics of Underdevelopment, 1804–2013* (New York: Routledge, 2014).

social classes in which one's status was defined by one's relationship to land. There were peasants who owned land with a legal title, peasants who possessed land without a title, peasants who rented land from larger landowners, and day laborers who had no land.[66] Within these new divisions came new systems of labor, such as *métayage* or sharecropping. Moreover, access to land provided the peasantry with means to produce an alternative economy. They grew foodstuffs to sustain themselves and even to export.[67] The peasants used their acres to cultivate coffee and brought their beans to market on their own terms. They also participated in the hardwood and dyewood trade, which, as with the coffee trade, could be carried out with nonhierarchical and decentralized labor.[68]

Pétion's wartime decision ended up shaping the development of Haiti as the majority embraced their access to land and control of the means of production. The decision also ensured Pétion's political position and garnered him popular support. Confident in his power, in 1816, he wrote a new constitution that created separate legislative and executive branches of the government and male suffrage.[69] Nonetheless, he named himself president for life and stipulated that future presidents would be elected by the Senate, not by popular vote. Pétion's state was an oligarchy with a democratic veneer.

Similarly to Christophe, Pétion and his advisers courted international support as Haiti lacked formal diplomatic recognition. Foreign merchants, particularly British subjects residing in Haiti, such as Robert Sutherland, had the president's ear.[70] Pétion's foreign relations contrasted vastly with Christophe's and tested his commitment to the republican project, Haitian independence, and abolitionism. As mentioned earlier, Pétion invited Dauxion Lavaysse, the French envoy, to land at Port-au-Prince and opened negotiations with him. Lavaysse arrived in the southern capital on 24 October and remained there for over a month.[71] He never revealed the full extent of his mission, but through letters with Pétion sought to persuade the president to rejoin Haiti with France because "we are all French" ("nous

---

[66] Dupuy, *Haiti*, 5.   [67] Gonzales, *Maroon Nation*, 4.
[68] For more discussion of this alternative economy, see Gonzales, *Maroon Nation*; Bulmer-Thomas, *Economic History of the Caribbean*.
[69] "Haiti, Révision de la Constitution Haïtienne de 1806 (1816)," *Haiti and the Atlantic World* (blog), https://haitidoi.com/constitutions/1816-2.
[70] Ernesto Bassi, *An Aqueous Territory: Sailor Geographies and New Granada's Transimperial Greater Caribbean World* (Durham, NC: Duke University Press, 2017), 160.
[71] Madiou, *Histoire d'Haïti*, vol. v, 249–57.

sommes tous français").[72] Pétion gathered the generals and magistrates to hear Lavaysse's proposition. They unanimously rejected it, as did Pétion in a private conversation with his top advisors. Nevertheless, they were open to paying an indemnity and saw it as a way to ensure that former colonists would not return and try to reconquer Haiti.[73] In his closing letter to Lavaysse, Pétion proposed three conditions for negotiations: recognition of Haitian independence, commercial agreements, and the establishment of the basis for an indemnity.[74] In contrast to Christophe's retributive justice, Pétion's performance suggests his desire to demonstrate Haiti's treaty-worthiness through his ability to engage in white Euro-American diplomatic norms. Recognition never came during his lifetime, though.

Pétion continued a nuanced approach to foreign relations in the Atlantic. As independence movements developed in the Greater Caribbean, the historian Ernesto Bassi argues (Volume III, Chapter 8), Pétion saw a chance to spread republicanism and support abolitionism.[75] Moreover, as the literary scholar Chelsea Stieber contends, Pétion and his fellow republicans envisioned Haiti as the "radical instantiation of Enlightenment liberalism."[76] They believed that the republic based in Port-au-Prince offered to the Greater Caribbean and Spanish America an example of how to reconcile republicanism and antislavery.[77] Nevertheless, Pétion had to act discreetly, given contemporary fears of Haitians exporting slave insurrection. Beginning with the Declaration of Independence, Haitian heads of state proclaimed a policy of nonintervention to assuage white Euro-American fears of the Black state's ability to incite revolution among other enslaved communities: "Let's take care, however, so that the spirit of proselytism doesn't destroy our work; let's let our neighbors breathe in peace ..." ("Gardons-nous cependant que l'esprit de prosélitisme ne détruise notre ouvrage; laissons en paix respire nos voisins ...").[78] While Christophe maintained the Haitian tradition of nonintervention in regard to Spanish American revolutionaries, Pétion welcomed Spanish American insurgents and, in the case of Simón Bolívar, provided financial and military aid.[79]

---

[72] Dauxion Lavaysse to Alexandre Pétion, 19 November 1814, quoted in Madiou, *Histoire d'Haïti*, vol. v, 253.
[73] Madiou, *Histoire d'Haïti*, vol. v, 255–6; Jean-François Brière, "L'Emprunt de 1825 dans la dette de l'indépendance haïtienne envers la France," *Journal of Haitian Studies* 12:2 (2006), 126–34: 126.
[74] Madiou, *Histoire d'Haïti*, vol. v, 257.   [75] Bassi, *Aqueous Territory*, 162.
[76] Stieber, *Haiti's Paper War*, 96.   [77] Stieber, *Haiti's Paper War*, 95.
[78] "Haitian Declaration of Independence," CO 137/111/1.
[79] On Christophe's views, see Henry Christophe to Thomas Clarkson, 18 November 1816, in Griggs and Prator, eds., *Henry Christophe and Thomas Clarkson*, 99.

For example, in the late 1810s, there were upwards of 200 Spanish Americans who sojourned in Les Cayes or Port-au-Prince.[80] In exchange for support, Pétion asked Bolívar to follow Haiti's example and abolish slavery. Bolívar was grateful for the aid, yet he had hoped to receive support from "a 'civilized' and powerful nation" and was ambivalent about complete emancipation.[81] He issued an initial decree on 2 June 1816 offering freedom to enslaved men who joined him within twenty-four hours of the decree's publication.[82] Pétion's risk did not lead to the immediate emancipation of enslaved men, women, and children across Spanish America; however, it did contribute to the process. Moreover, it demonstrated his commitment to anticolonial struggles in the hemisphere and the spread of republicanism which could support his Haitian republic both in its internal civil war and in its desire for international recognition.

If Bolívar and other Spanish American revolutionaries were hesitant to end slavery, Pétion found alternate ways to spread abolitionism in the Atlantic. In the 1816 constitution, Pétion extended citizenship after a year of residence to anyone of African or Indian descent who arrived in Haiti.[83] The historian Ada Ferrer contends that "Article 44 thus made freedom and citizenship more widely attainable, and gave the promise of Haiti's radical antislavery a more robust life and international project in an age and place where neighboring states remained very much invested in the regime of slavery."[84] People of color, including former Saint-Dominguans, risked their lives to travel to Haiti's shores from Jamaica, Cuba, Santo Domingo, and the United States.[85] Although Dessalines had also welcomed Saint-Dominguans of color back in early 1804, Pétion's article opened Haiti as a refuge for all people of color. (Jean-Jacques Dessalines issued a proclamation to American ship captains to transport any "Native Blacks and Men of Colour" who were in the United States and unable to return to Haiti "for want of the means." Dessalines backed up this request with money; he would pay captains "Forty

---

[80] Bassi, *Aqueous Territory*, 159. [81] Bassi, *Aqueous Territory*, 167–9.
[82] Bassi, *Aqueous Territory*, 168.
[83] "Haiti, Révision de la Constitution Haïtienne de 1806 (1816)," *Haiti and the Atlantic World* (blog), https://haitidoi.com/constitutions/1816-2.
[84] Ada Ferrer, "Haiti, Free Soil, and Antislavery in the Revolutionary Atlantic," *American Historical Review* 117:1 (2012), 40–66: 50.
[85] See Ada Ferrer, *Freedom's Mirror: Cuba and Haiti in the Age of Revolution* (Cambridge: Cambridge University Press, 2014); Ferrer, "Haiti, Free Soil, and Antislavery in the Revolutionary Atlantic"; Johnhenry Gonzales, "Defiant Haiti: Free-Soil Runaways, Ship Seizures and the Politics of Diplomatic Non-recognition in the Early Nineteenth Century," *Slavery & Abolition* 36:1 (2015), 124–35.

Establishing a New Nation: Haiti after Independence

Dollars" for each person brought home.)[86] The 1816 Constitution would pave the way for later waves of African American emigration under Jean-Pierre Boyer; in the 1820s, approximately 6,000 African Americans traveled to Haiti.[87] Similarly to his support of Bolívar, Pétion's offer bordered on violating Haiti's tradition of nonintervention, as Christophe and his advisers, specifically Baron de Vastey, were quick to point out.[88] Nevertheless, Christophe too sought to combat slavery, by seizing slavers who entered northern Haiti's waters.[89] This could be seen as intervening in the commerce of Haiti's Caribbean neighbors because only Britain and the United States had abolished the slave trade at the time of these seizures. Therefore, even though Pétion and Christophe differed in their interpretations of nonintervention, both of them sought to uphold antislavery and offer alternative notions of freedom and citizenship.

Pétion oversaw less than two years of the new constitution and its free-soil policy. In contrast to Christophe, who took his own life in the midst of a possible coup, Pétion died in office of natural causes, Haiti's only early nineteenth-century head of state to do so. He had demonstrated an ability to navigate between the elite and the masses and to establish policies that found a middle ground. His lessons, unfortunately, were not heeded by his successor Jean-Pierre Boyer.

Jean-Pierre Boyer and Reunification

Upon Pétion's death in March 1818, senators in Port-au-Prince quickly assembled to elect Pétion's successor, fearful of an invasion from Christophe. Jean-Pierre Boyer, a veteran of the revolution and top general under Pétion, emerged as the top choice and had the backing of the military, which was willing to make him president by force. Within a day of Pétion's death, Boyer became president.[90] Just like his predecessor, Boyer ruled as a president only in name, illustrating the limits and paradoxes of Haiti's republicanism. His term from 1818 to 1843, the longest of Haiti's nineteenth-century heads of state, provided the country with a period of

---

[86] See Marcus Rainsford, *An Historical Account of the Black Empire of Hayti* (London: Albion Press, 1805), 350.
[87] See Dubois, *Haiti*, 94.
[88] Baron de Vastey, *Essai sur les causes de la révolution et guerres civiles* (Sans Souci: Imprimerie Royale, 1819), 320–1.
[89] Marlene Daut, "The King of Haiti's Dream," *Aeon*, 14 July 2020, https://aeon.co/essays/the-king-of-haiti-and-the-dilemmas-of-freedom-in-a-colonised-world.
[90] Madiou, *Histoire d'Haïti*, vol. v, 484–6.

stability and unity, though not without contestation.[91] And, like his predecessors, his inability to reconcile the country's divisions ultimately led to his downfall.

Following his assumption of power in the spring of 1818, Boyer continued Pétion's commitment to republicanism and turned to unifying Haiti under his rule in Port-au-Prince. The first step was to subdue the peasant state in southwestern Haiti. Led by Goman, the state represented the largest critique of the neocolonial agro-export economy supported by Pétion, Boyer, and Christophe.[92] Boyer equipped a large force to surround the region, and then sent divisions in to root out Goman and his community based in Grand Doco.[93] While Goman evaded capture, Boyer entered Grand'Anse in August 1819 and proclaimed victory and the reintegration of the region into the Haitian republic.[94]

A year later, Boyer and his troops marched in the opposite direction to pacify northern Haiti and reunite the country. With Christophe's death on 8 October 1820 formerly loyal generals attempted to create a new state in Cap-Haïtien (Figure 26.2). In response, Boyer issued an order proclaiming reunification of the country and authorizing the use of force to accomplish this.[95] As Boyer's forces moved northward, generals and magistrates gathered in Cap-Haïtien and voted to join the republic, allowing the president to enter the city peacefully.[96] Nevertheless, in under a month, Boyer would face plots and uprisings from northern factions that continued throughout his presidency.[97] In reunifying the southwest and north, Boyer brought these regions under the nominal control of his government in Port-au-Prince; however, regionalism continued to be a significant obstacle.

With the country united under one head of state after fourteen years of division, Boyer turned his attention to the eastern section of the island. The Spanish colony of Santo Domingo had not participated in the independence movements of the hemisphere; however, by the early 1820s, factions arose in support of joining Haiti or Gran Colombia.[98] Prompted by fears of French

---

[91] For a discussion of the creation of the Haitian myth of unity and the republic under Boyer, see Stieber, *Haiti's Paper Wars*, 128–62.

[92] For more on Goman, see Crystal Eddins, "African Diaspora Collective Action: Rituals, Runaways, and the Haitian Revolution" (Ph.D. dissertation, Michigan State University, 2017), 282–4.

[93] For details on the expedition, see Madiou, *Histoire d'Haïti*, vol. VI, 9–14.

[94] Madiou, *Histoire d'Haïti*, vol. VI, 14.   [95] Madiou, *Histoire d'Haïti*, vol. VI, 131.

[96] Madiou, *Histoire d'Haïti*, vol. VI, 143.   [97] Stieber, *Haiti's Paper War*, 131.

[98] Anne Eller, *We Dream Together: Dominican Independence, Haiti, and the Fight for Caribbean Freedom* (Durham, NC: Duke University Press, 2016), 5.

Establishing a New Nation: Haiti after Independence

Figure 26.2 Cap-Haïtien. Alamy.

invasion and dreams of spreading republican universalism, Boyer organized troops to "liberate" Santo Domingo and unite the whole island under his rule.[99] Residents of the Spanish colony also took to flying the Haitian flag, a sign of their willingness to join Boyer's republic.[100] Thus, by the middle of January 1822, Boyer had accomplished what previous heads of state had only dreamed of: an island-wide rule. Although, as the historian Anne Eller notes, the reach of the Haitian state was limited, Boyer would oversee a period of stability on both sides of the island and craft a narrative of unity and concord to cover up divisions and unrest.[101]

A stable, unified state that purported to be republican was integral in portraying Haiti as a civilized country worthy of diplomatic recognition. Boyer returned to negotiations with the French with the hopes of resolving Haiti's precarious international standing and furthering the republican value of economic liberalism. Even without official recognition, in the early 1820s,

[99] Stieber, *Haiti's Paper War*, 129–30.
[100] Madiou, *Histoire d'Haïti*, vol. vi, 268–70, 276–83.
[101] Eller, *We Dream Together*, 5–6; Stieber, *Haiti's Paper War*, 131.

Haiti carried on a lively trade with Great Britain, the United States, and France as well as other European nations. For example, in 1823, 664 ships from those three countries visited Haitian ports and purchased over 33 million pounds of coffee, 884,370 pounds of cotton, 3.7 million pounds of Campeche, 224,134 pounds of cacao, and 652,291 pounds of sugar.[102] For Boyer and other Haitian republicans, foreign trade needed to be further developed, and official international recognition was critical to support this growth.[103] Moreover, Boyer, like Pétion, was not averse to paying an indemnity. Nonetheless, the royal ordinance from the French King Charles X recognizing Haiti's independence that the baron de Mackau carried to Port-au-Prince in the summer of 1825 was not quite what the president expected.[104] The ordinance recognized the independence of the former French colony, not the whole island, required a payment of 150 million francs indemnity, and gave France preferential trade duties.[105] There were no negotiations and Mackau backed up his word with a threat of force.[106] After a series of exchanges, Boyer agreed, and the Haitian state became indebted to France for 150 million francs. While the sum would be reduced in 1838, it took most of the nineteenth century to repay the indemnity and loans the Haitian government borrowed to pay the first debt. The "double debt" was paid off by 1893.[107]

Boyer had achieved formal recognition, though at a great cost. The historian Julia Gaffield contends that "Agreeing to this massive debt at least opened the door for other forms of recognition, which might then have helped the state mitigate the significance of this concession."[108] European consuls flocked to Haiti beginning in 1826, and diplomatic negotiations increased. At the same time, internal unrest grew, and the Haitian people became the bearers of a huge economic burden.

To fund indemnity payments, Boyer sought to revitalize Haiti's agricultural exports. He codified "the relationship between citizen and land" in the 1826 Code Rural that forced rural residents to labor as agricultural workers, restricted their movement and that of their children, and established a

---

[102] "Haiti," Archives Nationales de France, AE/B/III/380.
[103] Stieber, *Haiti's Paper War*, 133.   [104] Madiou, *Histoire d'Haïti*, vol. VI, 452.
[105] Madiou, *Histoire d'Haïti*, vol. VI, 448.
[106] Madiou, *Histoire d'Haïti*, vol. VI, 454, 460.
[107] See Brière, "L'Emprunt de 1825," 133.
[108] Julia Gaffield, "The Racialization of International Law after the Haitian Revolution: The Holy See and National Sovereignty," *American Historical Review* 125:3 (2020), 841–68: 848.

separate rural police force to enforce the Code.[109] This was the antithesis of life for Haitian peasants who up to this point had cultivated an alternative economic vision. On paper Boyer's Code Rural sent a clear message about labor and liberty; on the ground, little changed. Peasants continued their system of *métayage* (sharecropping) and organizing their lives around the *lakou* (extended family compound). By 1839, there were 46,000 small farms that provided sustenance to families, goods for local markets, and cash crops for export.[110] Moreover, regional État Civil records, Winter Schneider argues, demonstrate how rural inhabitants, specifically women, "strategically connected themselves and their children to more legally visible and privileged men, and sometimes women ... to alleviat[e] obstacles of access and mobility."[111] The Haitian peasantry found ways to circumvent the strict labor regulations and continue to define liberty on their own terms.

Rural inhabitants were not the only Haitians pushing back against Boyer's rule. Even before French recognition, Haiti's literate minority were critiquing Boyer's preferential treatment of foreign merchants and limited expansion of individual freedoms.[112] Following 1825, intellectuals reflected on the internal divisions and sought a solution from within. Often referred to as the School of 1836, these writers "attempted to theorize an inclusive, capacious national culture that resonated with the various societal fractions across the 'unified' island territory."[113] They articulated the first Haitian cultural nationalism or an early *indigénisme*. In the columns of the newspaper *Le Républicain*, later *L'Union*, authors penned historical essays and short stories that nuanced the narrative of the revolution proclaimed by the republic's proponents in the capital. (Alternatives to *Le Télégraphe*, the state-sponsored paper, *Le Républicain* and *L'Union* were printed during the years 1836–1837 and 1837–1839, respectively.) Influenced by French Romanticism, Haitian authors turned to the "folk" or Haitian peasant for inspiration. The literary scholar Michael Dash states that the interest in Haiti's majority was "based on protest against Boyer's inability to arrest the fragmentation taking place in Haitian society."[114] Romantic works incorporated Vodou and Black

---

[109] Smith, *Liberty, Fraternity, Exile*, 40; *Code Rural de Boyer 1826* (Port-au-Prince: H. Deschamps, 1992 [1826]).
[110] Smith, *Liberty, Fraternity, Exile*, 41.
[111] Winter Rae Schneider, "Between Sovereignty and Belonging: Women's Legal Testimonies in Nineteenth-Century Haiti," *Journal of Caribbean History* 52:2 (2018), 117–34: 128.
[112] Stieber, *Haiti's Paper War*, 132. [113] Stieber, *Haiti's Paper War*, 140.
[114] J. Michael Dash, *Literature and Ideology in Haiti, 1915–1961* (Totowa: Barnes & Noble, 1981), 7.

peasant characters.[115] To further their "folk" characterization, authors, particularly Ignace Nau, incorporated proverbs and terms in Haitian Creole. In his stories, the reader encountered a vision of Haitian popular culture replete with local vocabulary. The inclusion of local expressions and peasant characters constituted an attempt to construct a more inclusive national vision. And, for many of the intellectuals associated with these newspapers, it provided a space to oppose Boyer and highlight the paradoxes of his rule. Nonetheless, the stories and editorials did little to resolve the divide in Haitian society or enfranchise the rural population.

Jean-Pierre Boyer, the longest ruling nineteenth-century Haitian head of state, encountered increasing criticism by the early 1840s. While plots had been exposed throughout his twenty-five-year rule, the legislative elections in 1842 were a decisive symbol of the growing resistance. The editors of the opposition paper *Le Manifeste* exclaimed that the elections had "ushered in a glorious era of regeneration."[116] In addition to these domestic power struggles, Haiti had to deal with the criticism of foreigners, consuls, merchants, and statesmen. The final straw was a series of catastrophic events: an earthquake in Cap-Haïtien and fire in Port-au-Prince.[117] Days after the fire, a revolt in the southern peninsula on 27 January 1843 furthered this regeneration and led to the Liberal Revolution and Boyer's overthrow. The end of Boyer's rule demonstrates the continual struggle over definitions of liberty as the peasantry as well as members of the ruling class sought to reshape the state in the Revolution of 1843. While democratic change was not achieved and autocracy remained the governing style of Haitian heads of state, the peasantry's alternative economy of small farms ensured the success of the rural Haitian masses' definition of liberty for years to come.

---

[115] Vévé Clark, "Fieldhands to Stagehands in Haiti: The Measure of Tradition in Haitian Popular Theater" (Ph.D. dissertation, University of California, Berkeley, 1983), v.
[116] *Le Manifeste*, 6 February 1842, 1.   [117] Smith, *Liberty, Fraternity, Exile*, 52.

27

Aspirations and Actions of Free People of Color across the Caribbean

JESSICA PIERRE-LOUIS

Introduction

Composed largely of societies which were colonial plantocracies, the Caribbean was particularly sensitive to the revolutionary messages of the eighteenth and nineteenth centuries. The principles of popular sovereignty, human rights, democracy, and, of course, freedom and equality were reappropriated in different ways, depending on the social status of the people engaging with them. It mattered whether they were officially recognized or considered themselves as whites, free people of color, or enslaved Africans. The existence of legal and social prejudice was the main preoccupation of free people of color; it deprived them of the full enjoyment of their freedom. That explains why free people of color were major, and perhaps inevitable, actors during the age of Atlantic revolutions.

Although most often a numerical minority in the middle of the eighteenth century, with the exception of Trinidad, Puerto Rico, and Santo Domingo, where their number exceeded that of whites,[1] free people of color, particularly mixed-race people, served as an intermediary class between whites and enslaved people.

The free people of color had their roots in enslaved African people who had been freed. From the very beginning of colonization in the Caribbean, in the face of the constant increase in the number of freed people, colonial authorities tried to control, centralize, and block the routes to emancipation. Although expressed differently from place to place, the accumulation of regulatory texts contributed, throughout the eighteenth century, to the development of a legal and social color-based prejudice directed at the free people of color.

[1] Stanley L. Engerman and B. W. Higman, "The Demographic Structure of the Caribbean Slave Societies in the Eighteenth and Nineteenth Centuries," in Franklin W. Knight, ed., *General History of the Caribbean*, vol. III: *The Slave Societies of the Caribbean* (London: UNESCO, 1997), 45–104: 48.

The terminology denoting free people of color is complex.² In this chapter, I will use "free people of color" to refer to people who were Black or *métissés* (mixed-race), whether manumitted or born free. These people officially enjoyed freedom, but constantly faced discrimination because they had enslaved ancestors and/or as a result of their physical features (especially skin color), whether their own or of one or more of their ancestors. I will also employ *métissés* to describe people who were considered as mixed-race people rather than the taxa used in the archives of the period, because their use varies between colonies both in the choice of words and in their precise definition.³

In order to better understand the sometimes-divergent aspirations and actions of free people of color in the Revolutionary era, it is useful to focus on *métissés* free people, especially those whom the phenotype brought closer to whites than to Blacks. Historically *métissés* free people were borne of sexual relationships between masters and their enslaved concubines. On occasion, enslaved women were manumitted along with the master's *métissés* children. There was a direct and strong correlation between being classed as *métissés* and the ability to access emancipation. White parentage, even when illegitimate, could offer even more than precious freedom. There was unambiguous reciprocity between the degree of mixedness – how much European ancestry a free person of color could claim – and social status.⁴

The majority of free people of color were thus *métissés* free people. That was certainly true during the revolutionary period (1775–1825) for the elites of the communities of free people of color across the Caribbean. They tended to come from families which had been free for several generations, and were well-educated and wealthy. In French Saint-Domingue, this "aristocracy of the epidermis," as Florence Gauthier described it,⁵ was particularly politically active. Further removed from the environment of enslavement than from that of free high colonial society, their egalitarian aspiration was

---

² Jay Kinsbruner, *Not of Pure Blood: The Free People of Color and Racial Prejudice in Nineteenth-Century Puerto Rico* (Durham, NC: Duke University Press, 1996), 1; Melanie J. Newton, *The Children of Africa in the Colonies: Free People of Color in Barbados in the Age of Emancipation* (Baton Rouge: Louisiana State University Press, 2008), 17–19.

³ Jessica Pierre-Louis, "La couleur de l'autre: L'altérité au travers des mots dans les sociétés coloniales françaises du Nouveau Monde (XVII–XVIIIᵉ siècle)," in Karine Bénac-Giroux, ed., *Poétique et Politique de l'altérité: Colonialisme, esclavagisme, exotisme (XVIIIᵉ–XXIᵉ siècles)* (Paris: Classiques Garnier, 2019), 143–54.

⁴ Frédéric Régent, "Couleur, statut juridique et niveau social à Basse-Terre (Guadeloupe) à la fin de l'Ancien Régime (1789–1792)," in Jean-Luc Bonniol, ed., *Paradoxes du métissage* (Paris: CTHS, 2001), 41–50.

⁵ Florence Gauthier, *L'aristocratie de l'épiderme: Le combat de la Société des citoyens de couleur* (Paris: CNRS, 2007).

Figure 27.1 Marius-Pierre Le Masurier, *Famille métisse*. Mixed-race family in Martinique, 1775. Bridgeman Images.

not to abolish slavery, but, as Julien Raimond's memoirs show,[6] to abolish color prejudice, that is, the existence of various legal and social

---

[6] Mémoires de Julien Raimond. Archives Nationales outre-mer, Aix-en-Provence, Fonds Moreau de Saint-Mery, COL F3 91 ff. 177, 185, 190, 193.

discriminations and limitations that affected free people of color. *Métissés* free people were opposed to the arbitrary socioracial stratification of colonial societies that affected their political participation and civil rights, and limited their social and economic power.

The American War of Independence (1775–1783), the French Revolution (1789–1799), and the Haitian Revolution (1791–1804) profoundly disrupted the organization of the New World and the aspirations and actions of the Caribbean free people of color. During the American War of Independence, which ushered in the age of the Atlantic Revolutions, contingents of free people of color fought alongside American insurgents. This military experience led to an eruption of political engagement amongst Caribbean free people of color, who had become aware of their communal strength, and observed a growing awareness of a shared political identity. The French Revolution and the Declaration of the Rights of Man promulgated in 1789 created an opportunity to test the concept for the universality of the principles advocated. Throughout the Age of Revolutions, the Caribbean experienced multiple insurrections, the most resounding of which was undoubtedly the Haitian Revolution, which began with the uprising of the enslaved in 1791. But the Caribbean was also rocked by many other rebellions, some initiated by free people of color, some inspired by them.[7]

Like in the archives covering the political events and struggles of the revolutionary period, free women of color are barely visible in this study. The notion of citizenship in the Caribbean was mainly built around the right to vote and armed service, from which women were excluded, and studies have been more focused on formerly enslaved people defending their right to freedom in the context of republican emancipations.[8] Even if their active participation is less documented, free women of color were nevertheless involved in the revolts, whether at the front of the fighting or in the

---

[7] David P. Geggus, ed., *The Impact of the Haitian Revolution in the Atlantic world* (Columbia, SC: University of South Carolina Press, 2001).

[8] Judith Kafka, "Action, Reaction and Interaction: Slave Women in Resistance in the South of Saint Domingue, 1793–94," *Slavery & Abolition* 18:2 (1997), 48–72; Laurent Dubois, "Gendered Freedom: Citoyennes and War in the Revolutionary French Caribbean," in Karen Hagemann, Gisela Mettele, and Jane Rendall, eds., *Gender, War and Politics: Transatlantic Perspectives, 1775–1830* (London: Palgrave Macmillan, 2010), 58–70; Sue Peabody, "Négresse, Mulâtresse, Citoyenne: Gender and Emancipation in the French Caribbean, 1650–1848," in Pamela Scully and Diana Paton, eds., *Gender and Slave Emancipation in the Atlantic World* (Durham, NC: Duke University Press, 2005), 56–78.

background;[9] they were also active in the economic sphere, and participated in specific forms of sociability to support each other.[10]

On the basis particularly of the French experience, this chapter will seek to illustrate the evolution of the aspirations and actions of free people of color of the Caribbean islands. It will also consider the consequences for colonial institutions in the most important stages of the Atlantic revolutions.

Free People of Color in the Age of the American Independence War

Free People of Color in the Military Sphere

The second half of the eighteenth century in the Caribbean was profoundly shaped by the Treaty of Paris signed at the end of the Seven Years' War in 1763. The colonies of the Caribbean and, more broadly, the New World experienced a redistribution of imperial rule. Like Spain, France strengthened its colonial defense policy, and consequently discussed the place of the free people of color in military as well as social terms.

The use of free people of color for military purposes was therefore well-established when the American War of Independence broke out. This war marked a turning point for free men of color. In the islands, defensive needs had very early on led to the military use of whites and free people of color who lived in the colonies. They were grouped in the form of militia companies, to defend the territories in anticipation of or in support of units of regular army soldiers. In peacetime, free men of color were employed to police the enslaved, participating in the hunt for runaways and in the repression of rebellions. If the army had sometimes offered an opportunity for egalitarian experiences in the seventeenth century,[11] color prejudice was nevertheless expressed in the military sphere in the eighteenth century. Military regiments of free people of color were usually separated from white

---

[9] Philippe Girard, "Rebelles with a Cause: Women in the Haitian War of Independence, 1802–04," *Gender & History* 21:1 (2009), 60–85.
[10] Kit Candlin, *Enterprising Women: Gender, Race, and Power in the Revolutionary Atlantic* (London: University of Georgia Press, 2015); Dominique Rogers and Stewart King, "Housekeepers, Merchants, Rentières: Free Women of Color in the Port Cities of Colonial Saint-Domingue, 1750–1790," in Douglas Catterall and Jodi Campbell, eds., *Women in Port: Gendering Communities, Economies, and Social Networks in Atlantic Port Cities, 1500–1800* (Leiden: Brill, 2012), 357–97.
[11] Boris Lesueur, "Les paradoxes de la liberté par les armes (Antilles, XVIIIe siècle)," in Dominique Rogers and Boris Lesueur, eds., *Sortir de l'esclavage. Europe du Sud et Amériques (XIVe–XIXe siècle)* (Paris: Karthala CIRESC, 2018), 199–220: 201.

units of English, French, and Spanish colonies.[12] In addition, the highest military ranks were in some cases inaccessible to soldiers of color, as their regiments were led exclusively by senior white officers,[13] although there were some counterexamples.[14] Nevertheless, military service was a path to freedom for enlisted enslaved males, which would over time increase the number of free people of color.[15] Above all, military service conferred on free people of color a certain mobility, social status, and access to some privileges, including carrying arms, which was refused to other free people of color.[16]

The growing role given to free people of color in the military sphere, both in local militias and as regular troops, helped to boost the egalitarian aspirations of free people of color during the Atlantic revolutions.[17] Indeed, all the European imperial nations had massive recourse to free people of color in this conflict. Although initially only Britain opposed the thirteen colonies, the war quickly engulfed other colonial powers. France joined the American insurgents in February 1778, as did Spain in June 1779. In these power struggles, free people of color were solicited for battles on the North American mainland, but also in the Caribbean.

The impact of this war on the free people of color was particularly noteworthy in Saint-Domingue, whose geographic position and financial power to fund the war made it an important base in the Caribbean. Some

---

[12] Frédéric Régent, "Armement des hommes de couleur et liberté aux Antilles: Le cas de la Guadeloupe pendant l'Ancien régime et la Révolution," *Annales historiques de la Révolution française* 348 (2007), 41–56: 41; Herbert S. Klein, "The Colored Militia of Cuba: 1568–1868," *Caribbean Studies* 6:2 (1966), 17–27: 17; Bernard Marshall, "Social Stratification and the Free Coloured in the Slave Society of the British Windward Islands," *Social and Economic Studies* 31:1 (1982), 1–39: 15–16.

[13] Lesueur, "Les paradoxes de la liberté"; Gad J. Heuman, *Between Black and White: Race, Politics, and the Free Coloreds in Jamaica, 1792–1865* (Westport, CN: Greenwood Press, 1981), 27.

[14] See Baptiste Bonnefoy, "Les langages de l'appartenance. Miliciens de couleur et changements de souveraineté dans les îles du Vent (1763–1803)," *L'Atelier du Centre de recherches historiques* 20 (2019), https://journals.openedition.org/acrh/9607; Andrew J. O'Shaughnessy, *An Empire Divided: The American Revolution and the British Caribbean* (Philadelphia: University of Pennsylvania Press, 2000), 180.

[15] Anne Pérotin-Dumon, *La ville aux îles, la ville dans l'île: Basse-Terre et Pointe-à-Pitre, Guadeloupe, 1650–1820* (Paris: Karthala, 2001), 674.

[16] María del Carmen Barcia Zequeira, "Les Bataillons de pardos et de morenos à Cuba (1600–1868)," in Carmen Bernand and Alessandro Stella, eds., *D'esclaves à soldats: Miliciens et soldats d'origine servile, XIIIe–XXIe siècles* (Paris: L'Harmattan, 2006), 245–62: 245.

[17] For more on the three broad rubrics (rural police, militia, and regular armed forces), see Stewart R. King, *Blue Coat or Powdered Wig: Free People of Color in Pre-Revolutionary Saint Domingue* (Athens, GA: University of Georgia Press, 2001), 55–77.

1,500 free men of color were recruited by Admiral d'Estaing, then sent to fight with the insurgents in Georgia, where they distinguished themselves at the Battle of Savannah.[18] Following France's entry into the war, the British were forced to reinforce their troops by mobilizing free people of color as soldiers, but also enslaved people from Jamaica, Barbados, Antigua, and Saint Lucia.[19] Cuban battalions of *pardos* and *morenos* also conducted various campaigns abroad.[20] This development of the military force through the use of free people of color was also visible, for example, through the creation in August 1782 of a corps of "free volunteers from Guadeloupe" which aimed to make it possible to hold off invading forces in the event of a siege, while awaiting reinforcements from Europe: 527 men of color served there.[21] The American War of Independence certainly contributed to an awareness among the free people of color of their numerical strength, their ability to fight for a cause, and their weight as a group. As John Garrigus and David Geggus explain, these men could then have hoped that military service would improve their civic and social status, especially since they had been given increasing responsibilities.[22]

The 1780s: The *Métissés* of Saint-Domingue in Politics

The 1780s were characterized by attempts by the elite of the free people of color, particularly in Saint-Domingue, to gain civil rights both in their own island and from the royal government in Versailles. In Saint-Domingue, their situation differed from that of the other colonies, which could explain their earlier mobilization. There, the free people of color already formed nearly half of the colony's entire free population, and while the free people of color were usually characterized by their predominance in urban areas, those of Saint-Domingue were also present and economically active in the rural world.[23] Both David Geggus and Bernard Gainot have outlined the *métissés*

---

[18] John D. Garrigus, "Catalyst or Catastrophe? Saint-Domingue's Free Men of Color and the Battle of Savannah, 1779–1782," *Revista/Review Interamericana* 22:1–2 (1992), 109–25: 119.
[19] O'Shaughnessy, *An Empire Divided*, 174–81.
[20] Barcia Zequeira, "Les Bataillons de pardos et de morenos," 247.
[21] Régent, "Armement des hommes de couleur," 3.
[22] John D. Garrigus, "Redrawing the Colour Line: Gender and the Social Construction of Race in Pre-Revolutionary Haiti," *Journal of Caribbean History* 30:1 (1996), 29–50: 42.
[23] Geggus, "The Haitian Revolution," 13.

free people as a group which formed the elite of the free people of color.[24] It was composed primarily of sons or grandsons of white settlers, married to rich daughters or granddaughters of white settlers. They had possessions that were far larger than those found in other French colonies, even if overvalued.[25] These men gained social status through military service, and many were involved in the American War of Independence. They had left to study in France, so they had a network of acquaintances based in Paris and were familiar with French political culture. As their subsequent designation as "American settlers" in revolutionary debates testifies,[26] they had built an awareness of their own American identity, with a mythical connection to the Amerindians.[27] It was in the middle of this decade that the figure of Julien Raimond emerged,[28] emblematic of Saint-Domingue's elite. He refused to accept the accumulation of discriminatory regulations that contributed to the reinforcement of color prejudice and prevented assimilation of free people of color into the white class. In 1784, after having toured the western districts of Saint-Domingue, he went to France to plead his cause and that of men in his class. He then circulated several memoirs aimed at abolishing color prejudice, and met with Charles de la Croix, marquis de Castries, Minister of the Navy, in the hope of raising awareness of his cause. This resulted in a circular from 1787 inviting the colonial authorities to discuss whether it would not be appropriate to reduce the prejudice against those of free people of color who were closest to whites.[29] At the dawn of the revolution, as Geggus reminds us, a dangerous situation had been created.[30] A social group whose size, wealth, and self-awareness were growing rapidly was repressed. Free people of color had become indispensable both for the slave police service and for military battles between colonial powers. The elites of free people of color

---

[24] Bernard Gainot, "Les Libres de couleur et les révolutions de Saint-Domingue," in Association Les Anneaux de la mémoire, ed., *Couleur et Liberté dans l'espace colonial français (début XVIIIe–début XIXe siècle): Cahiers des Anneaux de la mémoire n° 17* (Paris: Karthala, 2017), 93–109.

[25] John D. Garrigus, "Saint-Domingue's Free People of Color and the Tools of Revolution," in David Patrick Geggus and Norman Fiering, eds., *The World of the Haitian Revolution* (Bloomington: Indiana University Press, 2009), 49–64: 50.

[26] Gauthier, *L'aristocratie de l'épiderme*, 32.   [27] Gainot, "Les Libres de couleur," 100.

[28] John D. Garrigus, "Opportunist or Patriot? Julien Raimond (1744–1801) and the Haitian Revolution," *Slavery and Abolition* 28:1 (2007), 1–21. See also John Garrigus' Chapter 23 in this volume.

[29] Jessica Pierre-Louis, "Les Libres de couleur face au préjugé. Franchir la barrière à la Martinique aux XVIIe–XVIIIe siècles" (Ph.D. dissertation, Université des Antilles et de la Guyane, 2015), 184.

[30] David P. Geggus, *Slavery, War and Revolution: The British Occupation of Saint Domingue 1793–1798* (Oxford: Clarendon Press, 1982), 22.

no longer hesitated to let the highest authorities know that they were looking for some recognition and a form of equality by eliminating color prejudice. The French Revolution would provide a favorable environment to express their demands.

The Years 1789–1793: From the Start of the French Revolution to the Abolition of Slavery in Saint-Domingue

On the eve of the French Revolution, power in France was based on the model of divine right of an absolute monarchy. Without being fundamentally challenged, this model was, however, confronted with a popular desire for profound political reform. The opening of the Estates General on 5 May 1789 gave further hope for change to many segments of society with few or no privileges. In the Caribbean colonies, whites, free people of color, and enslaved people all saw in the events in Paris an opportunity to express their demands and to improve their situation. But the interests of all were not necessarily compatible.

The French Elite People of Color's Quest for Equality in Paris

In Paris, the elite of Saint-Domingue weighed in heavily in the debates in the National Assembly. As early as July 1789, the elite of the free people of color demanded the suppression of color prejudice, and therefore equality with whites in terms of political rights.[31] Within weeks, a group of free people of color established a Société des Amis de Couleur (Society of Friends of Color).[32] On 26 August, Julien Raimond approached the lobbying group of white planters, known as the Massiac Club, in Paris. On 8 September, Vincent Ogé, a landowner from the North Province, who, like Raimond, belonged to the elite of color, did the same.[33] They proposed an alliance of common interests, advocating equality before the law for the people of their class. On 22 October 1789, representatives of *métissés* free people were heard at the National Assembly, and their demands received a very favorable reception. But, as Laurent Dubois points out, "At the heart of the colonial

---

[31] Dominique Rogers, "On the Road to Citizenship: The Complex Route to Integration of the Free People of Color in the Two Capitals of Saint-Domingue," in Geggus and Fiering, *The World of the Haitian Revolution*, 65–78.
[32] Gauthier, *L'aristocratie de l'épiderme*, 32–40.
[33] Pierre Pluchon, *Toussaint Louverture: Un révolutionnaire noir d'Ancien régime* (Paris: Fayard, 1989), 30.

question lay a contradiction: The Declaration of the Rights of Man and Citizen had been declared universally applicable, and yet its application in the colonies seemed unimaginable."[34] The whites of the islands had no intention of allying themselves with the free people of color, nor with their elite. The *métissés* free people were forced to change strategy.

Julien Raimond reported that the Société des Amis de Couleur was welcomed by representatives of the Société des Amis des Noirs (Society of Friends of the Blacks), the French abolitionist association opposing slavery, which had been created in 1788.[35] From that point on, the Société des Amis des Noirs decided to defend both causes simultaneously, but distinctly: the antislavery cause and the egalitarian cause for the free people of color. The debates in the National Assembly in March 1790 on the right to vote and the colonial situation constituted two important moments for the free people of color. The first decree allowed any active citizen to vote: "All persons over twenty-five years of age, owners of buildings domiciled in the parish for two years, paying taxes ... will enjoy the right to vote."[36] The elite of color met these conditions and therefore felt entitled to obtain this right to vote. But the implementing decree of 8 March 1790 led to the adoption of a law granting almost autonomous decision-making to the colonial assemblies. The question of the right of the free people of color to vote was therefore temporarily left to the goodwill of the whites of the colonies, who were not in favor of extending that right. Nevertheless, the free people of color and their allies in the Société des Amis des Noirs continued their struggle. The incidents and clashes in the colonies between whites and freemen of color and the slave revolts contributed to raising the question of the situation of the free people of color on several occasions. The law of 15 May 1791 – which was canceled shortly afterwards – granted the right to vote only to the small group of free men of color who had been born to free fathers and mothers. Finally, after several years of political struggle, the free people of color obtained on 4 April 1792 the right to vote and to be represented in assemblies. The assemblies previously elected without the participation of free people of color in the colonies were now considered null and void by the

---

[34] Laurent Dubois, *A Colony of Citizens: Revolution and Slave Emancipation in the French Caribbean, 1787–1804* (Chapel Hill: University of North Carolina Press, 2004), 99.

[35] Marcel Dorigny, Bernard Gainot, and Doucou Diène, *La société des amis des noirs, 1788–1799: Contribution à l'histoire de l'abolition de l'esclavage* (Paris: Unesco, 1998), 21. See also Erica Johnson Edwards' Chapter 4 in this volume.

[36] Jacques Adélaïde-Merlande, *La Caraïbe et la Guyane au temps de la Révolution et de l'Empire: 1789–1804* (Paris: Karthala, 1992), 37.

Constituent Assembly in France. However, the application in the islands of the measure adopted in Paris was not without difficulty.

The Struggles in the French Colonies

In addition to the political struggle in France, the three main French colonies in the Caribbean (Martinique, Guadeloupe, and Saint-Domingue) were also the scene of confrontations. In the French islands, the beginnings of the French Revolution were immediately accompanied by "turbulence," as Geggus has called it.[37] For example, in October 1789, a company of militia of color refused to stand guard as long as the whites evaded this chore.[38]

In both Martinique and Guadeloupe, free people of color wanted to take part in the celebrations of revolutionary events, starting with the wearing of the cockade, the revolutionary insignia. But their claim to be involved in the process of obtaining civil and political rights, especially the right to vote and to be elected, and the desire to see the principle of equality applied to their class were not to the liking of all whites.

The historian Frédéric Régent has highlighted the ways in which free people of color and enslaved people were involved in the revolutionary unrest at the heart of division between the population of rich rural white planters, seeking greater autonomy in the affairs of the colonies, and the white people of the city.[39]

In Martinique, the poor urban white people (united in the patriotic party of Saint-Pierre), fearing the loss of their only privilege, that of whiteness, were strongly opposed to any evolution of the colonial order in favor of the free people of color. Tensions between the two groups led to the tragic *massacre de la Fête Dieu* on 3 June 1790, when white urban people hunted down, killed, and imprisoned dozens of free people of color in the city of Saint-Pierre.[40] This massacre may explain why the free people of color

---

[37] David B. Gaspar and David P. Geggus, eds., *A Turbulent Time: The French Revolution and the Greater Caribbean* (Bloomington: Indiana University Press, 1997).

[38] Léo Élisabeth, *La société martiniquaise aux XVIIe et XVIIIe siècles, 1664–1789* (Paris: Karthala, 2003), 444.

[39] Frédéric Régent, "Révoltes, factions, catégories juridiques et sociales en Guadeloupe (1789–1794)," *Cahiers d'histoire* 94–95 (2005), 87–99. For more about Patriots and Royalists, see also William S. Cormack, *Patriots, Royalists, and Terrorists in the West Indies: The French Revolution in Martinique and Guadeloupe, 1789–1802* (Toronto: University of Toronto Press, 2019).

[40] Adélaïde-Merlande, *La Caraïbe et la Guyane*, 55.

initially joined forces with the white planters in the countryside to stand up to the urban white people.

However, two years later, in December 1792, when Raymond Lacrosse, appointed commander of the Windward Islands, proclaimed throughout the French colonies republican principles and the implementation of the decree that gave voting rights to free people of color, the white planters declared themselves royalists and opposed a republic that challenged the established order; then some free people of color, understanding that they would not make progress, rallied the patriots and their republican troops. They then experienced around one year of full citizenship before the British conquest of 1794 restored the old system.[41]

In Guadeloupe, the free people of color also became citizens in accordance with decisions made by the Legislative Assembly. However, most of them could not be active citizens; that is, they could not vote or be eligible. The censitary vote prevented the participation of these generally poor citizens. Thus, on 18 December 1792, the citizens of color, white sailors, and city dwellers of Pointe-à-Pitre found themselves on the same side in a rebellion against the royalists, followed on 4 January by those of Basse-Terre. The insurrection allowed General Lacrosse to proclaim the Republic in Guadeloupe on 5 January 1793.

From 1793, the free people of color and enslaved people of Guadeloupe revolted more for their own causes. The enslaved people emphasized the claim to freedom and the free people of color advocated for social equality. On August 1793, in the town of Sainte-Anne, 1,000 to 1,200 free people of color and enslaved people revolted, demanding the right to inherit property, but also, and this explains the rallying of enslaved people, the liberation of those fighting for the Republic.[42]

The most intense revolts took place in Saint-Domingue.[43] In 1790, the whites who defended autonomy and the perpetuation of racial prejudice created a general assembly, called the Saint-Marc Assembly, in which any participation of the free people of color was refused.

The resistance of most whites to the evolution of the rights of free people of color prompted Vincent Ogé to leave Paris for Saint-Domingue. On

---

[41] David P. Geggus, "Esclaves et gens de couleur libres de la Martinique pendant l'époque révolutionnaire et napoléonienne: Les moments de résistance," *Revue historique* 295 (1996), 105–32: 118.

[42] Régent, "Révoltes, factions, catégories juridiques et sociales," 32.

[43] Laurent Dubois, *Avengers of the New World: The Story of the Haitian Revolution* (Cambridge, MA: Harvard University Press, 2005).

16 October 1790, he went to Cap Français, issuing an ultimatum for the implementation of the decree of 28 March that allowed the vote of the active citizens, including him. Faced with the lack of results, he recruited a small army of 300 men of color with the help of another free man of color, Jean-Baptiste Chavannes, and launched the "mulattoes' revolt" in North Province. The intervention of armed troops forced them to take refuge on the Spanish side of the island, but the Spanish authorities delivered the rebels at the end of 1790. The members of Cap Français' town council judged and executed Ogé and Chavannes on 25 February 1791.[44]

A few months later, on the night of 22–23 August, the great slave revolt led by Boukman, Georges Biassou, and Jean-François broke out. The great insurrection of the north very ephemerally united whites and free people of color against insurgents whom they thought were the common enemy at the moment that they signed a Concordat at Croix-des-Bouquets in West Province on 7 September 1791. But the recurrent inability of some whites in the colonial assembly to consider a real alliance, and in particular the systematic refusal to grant political rights, quickly contributed to the resurgence of conflicts between the two groups. Thus, in November 1791, Port-au-Prince burned in a battle between radical whites and *métissés* free people of color.

In September 1792, the civilian commissioners Sonthonax, Polverel, and Aillaud, accompanied by 6,000 soldiers, were sent from France to Saint-Domingue; one of their tasks was to impose on white residents the badly received decree of the Legislative Assembly of Paris of 4 April 1792, that gave the free people of color the right to vote and to be represented in the assemblies. Until December 1792, the three officials adopted a moderate attitude toward free people of color; Sonthonax even sought to make allies of them in order to restore the republican authority of France and end the insurrection of enslaved people in North Province. He relied on the military strength of André Rigaud and the political power of Pinchinat, both *métissés*, to take care of the south after the death of Civil Commissioner Aillaud.[45] But when Sonthonax proclaimed the general freedom of all enslaved people in August 1793, in order to face the resistance of white planters and the risks of a Spanish invasion, his attitude toward free people of color changed considerably.

---

[44] John D. Garrigus, "Vincent Ogé Jeune (1757–91): Social Class and Free Colored Mobilization on the Eve of the Haitian Revolution," *The Americas* 68:1 (2011), 33–62.
[45] Pluchon, *Toussaint Louverture*, 80.

Some Effects in the Rest of the Caribbean

The effects of the events of this first stage of the French Revolution (1789–1793) were not limited to the free people of the French islands. The voluntary or forced movement of French colonial inhabitants (whether white, free colored, or enslaved) led to the spread of their ideas and aspirations throughout the Caribbean and North and South America.[46] We often think of the threatened white owners of Saint-Domingue who fled the island, but enslaved and free people of color left too.[47] From the early days of the French Revolution, the free people of color of Saint-Domingue went to Cuba in successive waves.[48] They were among the more than 1,000 creoles from the French islands who settled in Trinidad in December 1792 and January 1793,[49] and also increased the number of craftsmen in Jamaica.[50] These population movements were probably not unrelated to actions that imitated the political activities of French free people of color. In Jamaica, a *métissé* named Dickson, who had studied law, initiated a petition process in 1792 against legal incapacity in court and restrictions to inheritance by free people of color. Thus, the actions of the free people of color under French domination could have reactivated the petitioning processes of Jamaicans aimed at improving their condition as a group.[51] Dickson died before he could complete the process, but the collective claims process continued.[52] The French Revolution thus carried its ideals of equality beyond the French territories alone. Informed by armed contacts and the migration of refugees from the French colonies, free people of color from the British and Spanish colonies saw new opportunities for their class. In 1794, the proclamation of the abolition of slavery in all French colonies was to constitute a new stage in

---

[46] Alejandro E. Gómez, *Le spectre de la révolution noire: L'impact de la révolution haïtienne dans le monde atlantique, 1790–1886* (Rennes: Presses universitaires de Rennes, 2013), 121–36.

[47] About the exile of the leaders of the insurrection of enslaved people of Saint-Domingue following the Treaty of Basel of 12 July 1795 to various territories under Spanish rule, see Barcia Zequeira, "Les Bataillons de pardos et de morenos," 250.

[48] Alain Yacou, "Esclaves et libres français à Cuba au lendemain de la Révolution de Saint-Domingue," *Jahrbuch für Geschichte Lateinamerikas* 28:1 (1991), 163–98.

[49] Frédéric Spillemaeker, "Quand les cocardes étaient marronnes: La Trinité espagnole en révolution," *Monde(s)* 12:2 (2017), 221–37: 229.

[50] Heuman, *Between Black and White*, 10.

[51] Samuel J. Hurwitz and Edith F. Hurwitz, "A Token of Freedom: Private Bill Legislation for Free Negroes in Eighteenth-Century Jamaica," *The William and Mary Quarterly* 24:3 (1967), 423–31.

[52] Heuman, *Between Black and White*, 23.

the actions undertaken by the free people of color and help generate a firestorm throughout the entire Caribbean.

The Years 1794–1802: The French Republic, Abolition, and the Burning of the Caribbean

The execution of Louis XVI on 21 January 1793 led France and its colonies into war against England on 1 February and against Spain on 1 March. In Saint-Domingue, Léger-Félicité Sonthonax saw in the liberation of enslaved people the only possible solution to both fight against the white planters, who rejected a revolution that was too radical for them, and simultaneously face the threats of invasion from Britain and Spain. Thus, the abolition of slavery was decreed locally in August 1793, cementing an alliance between a Republican official and insurgent slaves. The deputies sent to France at the beginning of 1794 called for the universality of the principle of freedom advocated by the Republic. On 4 February 1794, or 16 Pluviôse Year II, the abolition of slavery was then proclaimed throughout the French territories.

The Republic of Victor Hugues in the Lesser Antilles

One of the immediate consequences of the proclamation of slavery's abolition throughout the French territories was the sending of Republican commissioners to the colonies to enforce the decision. At the beginning of June 1794, Victor Hugues arrived in Guadeloupe.[53] Once abolition had been decreed, Hugues founded a large part of the military forces he directed against the English on the mass mobilization of formerly enslaved people, who constituted the main part of the revolutionary troops until the restoration of slavery in 1802. The preservation of general freedom became an argument for mobilizing troops from the French Caribbean. That created a unique situation in these colonies and changed the nature of the fighting in the Caribbean. In addition, the massive armed force thus created by Hugues forced the British to recruit and emancipate more enslaved conscripted soldiers to cope with the increase in French troops. Thus, general French freedom also generated, albeit to a lesser extent, emancipation in the British

[53] Michel Rodigneaux, *Victor Hugues: L'ambition d'entrer dans l'histoire, 1762–1826* (Paris: Éditions SPM, 2017), 195–296.

Figure 27.2 Nicolas André Monsiau, The National Convention abolishes slavery in the French colonies, 1794. Getty Images.

colonies. But above all, the armies of the French Republic became the place where enslaved and free people of color experienced equality. All strata of colonial society were now fighting side by side and were amalgamated by Hugues into the ranks without distinction of origin. For the first time, some men of color commanded whites.[54]

Another important aspect of Hugues' policy for Caribbean free people of color was his propaganda campaign intended for the French colonies taken by the British in 1763 (Saint Vincent, Dominica, and Grenada) and 1794 (Saint Lucia and Martinique) to incite enslaved and free people of color living there to rise up against the British enemy in the hope of seeing the ideals of the Republic applied.[55] By inciting uprisings in the new English colonies in the Lesser Antilles, Hugues was behind the slave uprising on the island of

---

[54] Frédéric Régent, *Esclavage, métissage, liberté: La Révolution française en Guadeloupe, 1789–1802* (Paris: B. Grasset, 2004), 355.

[55] Régent, "Armement des hommes de couleur," 227.

Saint Lucia, in April 1795, and the major uprising of the free people of color on the island of Grenada, known as the Fédon Rebellion. Free people of color *métissés*, such as Julien Fédon, were sensitive to the ideas of equality and citizenship conveyed by the French revolutionary battles, as they belonged to the elite of the free people of color on their island and were affected by the return in 1783 of English occupation in Grenada, which had previously been dominated by France. Thus, in March 1795, after the transmission to the ruling council of Grenada of an ultimatum from Julien Fédon, who signed as "Officer of the Republic, appointed at Guadeloupe," the island fell prey to a one-year-long bloody insurrection. Hugues did not send the military reinforcements hoped for by the insurgents, and by June 1796, after more than a year of ravages, the British were able to overcome the revolt.[56]

Hugues also relied on the Republic's privateers to fight against Britain on the seas. Privateering allowed the formerly enslaved and free people of color who participated in it to be enriched, and also enabled them to have contact with other free people of color from all over the Caribbean.[57] Not only did French sailors and soldiers spread the aspirations and stories of the free people of color, which had already been relayed by the circulation of merchant ships and the many refugee movements, but also simply the sight of these crew members of color carrying arms or wearing uniforms made quite an impression on other free people of color. Sometimes, the presence of French ships in foreign ports may also have led to insurrectional movements of enslaved and free people of color, as on the Dutch island of Curaçao in August 1795 or in Spanish-ruled Trinidad in 1796.[58]

Thus, in many ways, Hugues' propaganda and policy encouraged the free people of color to think of themselves as active citizens defending the nation and its ideals and to propagate them directly or indirectly.

The Ascent of Toussaint in Saint-Domingue

In Saint-Domingue, Sonthonax had allied himself since December 1792 with the free people of color – who aspired to the introduction of civic and

---

[56] For more about the major peoples of color implicated in this rebellion, see Candlin, *Enterprising Women*, 15–31, 57–79; Kit Candlin, *The Last Caribbean Frontier, 1795–1815* (London: Palgrave Macmillan, 2012), 1–23.
[57] Dubois, *A Colony of Citizens*, 244.
[58] Gert J. Oostindie, "Slave Resistance, Colour Lines, and the Impact of the French and Haitian Revolutions in Curaçao," in Wim Klooster and Gert J Oostindie, eds., *Curaçao in the Age of Revolutions, 1795–1800* (Leiden, KITLV Press, 2011), 1–22: 9.

political equality – in order to restore France's republican authority and end the slave uprising in the Northern Province. André Rigaud had been a supporter of Sonthonax since 1792; he was thus promoted to colonel in July 1793 and brigadier general in July 1795. He successfully defended South Province against the British invaders, whereas Port-au-Prince fell to Britain on 1 June 1794. But after the proclamation of the general freedom of all slaves in August 1793, the main figures representing the party of free people of color, such as André Rigaud, were confronted with the rise of Toussaint Louverture, which symbolized the struggle of enslaved people.

A Creole black man who could read and write, Toussaint was born enslaved around 1743 and was freed around the 1770s. He was noticed during the revolts of 1791 for his ability to lead an organized insurgent troop. After joining the camp of Republican France in 1794, he established his military dominance in North Province, which earned him promotion to Brigadier General; he then became Lieutenant Governor in 1796 and Commander-in-Chief of the army in 1797. His military ascension was accompanied by a broad political ambition that pushed him to confront, or move away from the island, all those he saw as rivals on his way to a very personal power. The complex character of Toussaint Louverture gave rise to an abundance of literature and varied interpretations of his unusual journey that it is impossible to summarize here.[59]

In June 1799, Louverture – supported by Jean-Jacques Dessalines – and Rigaud – supported by Alexandre Pétion – clashed in the "War of the South" or "War of the Knives," a power struggle that ended in March 1800 following the takeover of Jacmel by Louverture's troops. The human losses were heavy – some 10,000 dead among free people of color alone. André Rigaud left the island, while Louverture continued his ascent.

Between Conspiracies and Petitions in the Spanish and English Greater Antilles

Between 1795 and 1802, free people of color in the neighboring islands of Cuba, Puerto Rico and Jamaica, informed about revolutionary events and

---

[59] Among the best-known works, see Pluchon, *Toussaint Louverture*; Jacques de Cauna, ed., *Toussaint Louverture et l'indépendance d'Haïti* (Paris: Karthala – SFHOM, 2004); C. L. R. James, *The Black Jacobins: Toussaint Louverture and the San Domingo Revolution* (New York: Dial Press, 1938); Philippe Girard, *Toussaint Louverture: A Revolutionary Life* (New York: Basic Books, 2016). See also Philippe Girard's Chapter 25 in this volume.

struggles for freedom and equality, also sought to advance their rights in various ways.

The aspirations of the free people of color sometimes took the form of conspiracies. They justified their expectations by relying on (more or less accurate) knowledge of the events taking place in other territories, and justified their plots by reference to rumors or by misinterpreting metropolitan decisions that they thought were not being carried out by local officials.

Cuba's officials had to deal not only with some slave uprisings inspired by the events in Saint-Domingue, but also with plots by free people. Alejandro Gómez thus refers to the case, in August 1795, in the town of Bayamo, of a free man of color named Nicolás Morales, who was captured and executed as the leader of a conspiracy that aimed in particular at obtaining the introduction of a decree that would have made free people of color equal to whites.[60]

In other cases, the free people of color were not the conspirators or initiators of the insurrections, but on the contrary the force of repression; they sought to obtain rights in recognition of this role. In Jamaica, several plots and slave revolts were reported by the authorities, who had to fight hard against the Maroon community of Trelawny in August 1795. It was with the help of the militia of color in particular that they were able to quell the revolt. Also, when the free people of color resumed the petition processes (which had not been followed up in 1792) and in 1796 obtained the opportunity to testify in court, it was as a reward for the loyalty of the militia during the campaign against the Maroons of the previous year. On this island, the free people of color therefore tried to prove their eligibility for equality with whites through their "loyalty" to the colonial system by distinguishing themselves from the aspirations of enslaved people and Maroons.[61]

The actions of free peoples of color did not achieve the expected results. At best, fears of insurrections and possible collusion of free people of color with enslaved people had led to some concessions in limited areas for some Caribbean islands. In any case, the process of challenging slavery and the colonial order was definitely under way, even if whites who were opposed to full equality and general freedom were challenging these aspirations every step along the way.

---

[60] Alejandro E. Gómez, "Le syndrome de Saint-Domingue. Perceptions et représentations de la révolution haïtienne dans le monde atlantique, 1790–1886" (Ph. D. dissertation, École doctorale de l'École des hautes études en sciences sociales, 2010), 128.

[61] Heuman, *Between Black and White*, 24.

The Years 1802–1830: Abolitions and Political Struggles for Civic Equality

The end of the French Revolution in 1799 and the restoration of the old colonial system in 1802 by Bonaparte put an end to Caribbean movements supported by French politics. In the nineteenth century, as Saint-Domingue slid toward independence, Caribbean free people of color had to face increased repression by whites, who were concerned about their numerical growth and their possible collusion with enslaved people, and therefore anxious to maintain a balance of power that would prevent the collapse of a system that had made their fortunes possible. Nevertheless, the free people of color continued their actions to improve their situation and obtain rights during what is usually called the century of abolition.

From Repression to the Abrogation of Prejudice in the French Colonies

In Saint-Domingue, following his victory over André Rigaud, Toussaint Louverture made himself governor for life in 1801. The Leclerc expedition, sent by Bonaparte in February 1802 to prevent this seizure of power by a former slave, obtained the arrest and deportation of the Black general to France in June 1802. Some former free people of color, who saw Louverture's deportation as a way to eliminate a rival, supported and participated in the French action. But when they became aware of the consul's true intentions and realized that their right to social equality was as much threatened as the freedom acquired by the formerly enslaved people, they united with them in the rebellion against France. What remained of the French army left Saint-Domingue, defeated in clashes and by disease, in November 1803. On 1 January 1804, independence was proclaimed by Dessalines as Saint-Domingue became Haiti. For the former free elite of color as well as for the representatives of the formerly enslaved people, what was at stake was no longer the obtaining of rights, but a power struggle between old free and new free, symbolized by the division between Pétion and Christophe.

The destiny of Guadeloupe, on the other hand, was quite different. General Antoine Richepanse was sent to Guadeloupe with armed troops to carry out Bonaparte's directives. Following the arrests of some personalities of color and the disarmament of some companies of color, the announced intention to install the legal authorities of the Republic of Richepanse was quickly questioned; the soldiers of color found themselves caught between their loyalty toward the nation and the universal application of republican principles

Figure 27.3 G. Thompson, The British capture of Martinique in 1809. Bridgeman Images.

abandoned by France. Of those who fought against the French army, history has remembered the name of the commander of color Louis Delgrès, who, faithful to his motto "Live free or die," took the decision to blow himself up with powder barrels on 28 May 1802, killing himself, his troops, and Richepanse's vanguard.[62] The defeat of the formerly enslaved and free people of color of Guadeloupe resulted in a violent restoration of the old system.

The restoration of the old colonial system in Guadeloupe and its continuation for Martinique did not prevent free people of color from trying to improve their situation and obtain rights, but changed their methods.

Cyrille Bissette in Martinique offers an interesting portrait of the aspirations of free people of color in the first half of the nineteenth century. A merchant of color in Fort-de-France, he belonged to the elite of his group. In 1822, when a slave revolt broke out, he helped to subdue it, which

---

[62] Jacques Adélaïde-Merlande, *Delgrès ou la Guadeloupe en 1802* (Paris: Karthala, 1986), 135–49.

suggests that, like other men in his class (and like the Haitian elite in the past), he felt distant from the enslaved class. However, his opinion seems to have changed rapidly afterwards. In December 1823, Bissette's house was raided following a denunciation; a brochure was found entitled "De la situation des gens de couleur libres aux Antilles Françaises" ("The Situation of Free People of Color in the French Antilles"), which defended the extension of civil rights to free people of color and denounced the slave system. Condemned, he went into exile in Paris in 1824. In the early 1830s, when those in his class officially obtained the repeal of all discriminatory rules in force until then, Bissette's position became more radical as he focused on the abolition of slavery, probably under the influence of the antislavery movements of Parisian intellectuals, as evidenced by the creation of a journal and a society, and his involvement in politics after abolition.[63]

Of course, some free people of color were still involved in revolts alongside enslaved people, but their struggle continued, relying more on the struggle of ideas until the end of legal discrimination by various laws. Thus, on 14 September 1830 a ministerial order instructed the colonial authorities to repeal all discriminatory local regulations. It was followed by a ministerial reminder of 11 January 1831. Then, in April 1833, full citizenship for free people of color was decreed. During these years, several measures, such as *patronage*, were used to facilitate the emancipation of enslaved people, which contributed to the numerical increase of free people of color. The informal and precarious freedom of *de facto free* enslaved persons was legalized by an order of the governor simply upon the declaration of a patron, who could be the former master or another free person.[64]

The Petitions Process of Free People of Color in the British Colonies

In the British territories, the achievements of the abolitionist movement, particularly the advances made in 1823 to improve the condition of enslaved

---

[63] Nicolas Armand, *Histoire de la Martinique, des Arawaks à 1848* (Paris: L'Harmattan, 1997), 320.

[64] Jean-François Niort, "Les libres de couleur dans la société coloniale, ou la ségrégation à l'œuvre (XVIIe–XIXe siècles)," *Bulletin de la Société d'histoire de la Guadeloupe* 131 (2002), 61–112; Frédéric Régent, *La France et ses esclaves: De la colonisation aux abolitions, 1620–1848* (Paris: B. Grasset, 2007), 281–8. On *patronage*, see Chapter 4 of Leticia G. Canelas, "Escravidão e liberdade no Caribe Francês: A alforria na Martinica sob uma perspectiva de gênero, raça e classe (1830–1848)" (Ph.D. dissertation, Universidade Estadual de Campinas, Instituto de Filosofia e Ciências Humanas, 2017).

people, seem to have led the free people of color to pursue their political struggles with significant recourse to petitions, to obtain civil rights or more broadly to put an end to color prejudice. Their intended audiences were their islands' ruling councils as well as Britain's Parliament. The petitions of free people of color were successful as early as 1823 in Grenada.

In the same year, Trinidad, which had fallen under English rule in 1797, saw a campaign for civil rights led by the Philips family, free people of color who called for complete equality and the abolition of all of the discriminatory laws which had been in force since 1797. In January 1826, the free people of color obtained the withdrawal of certain vexatious measures.[65]

In Jamaica, after the petition drives of 1792 and 1796, a new petition was signed in 1813 by 2,400 free people of color for the abolition of discrimination on inheritance and for equality before the court. It was followed in 1816 by another petition for the extension of the rights obtained (in particular the ability to testify and to receive inheritances of any value). This second petition revealed differences of opinion among the free people of color about the tactics to be adopted to advance their cause; but, as before, they invoked their role as a barrier against enslaved people and their loyalty to whites to justify the legitimacy of demands for equality.[66]

An identical process took place in Barbados.[67] A slave revolt in 1816 had been controlled with the help of the free militia of color. In the following year, this "loyalty" toward whites justified some limited progress in court in the free people of color's struggle to attain equality.[68]

It was only in 1830 in Jamaica and in 1831 in Dominica and Barbados that the free people of color of the islands under English domination obtained what was popularly called the brown privilege bill, a law that granted them full legal equality.[69] As in the contemporaneous French (1833), Swedish (1831),[70] and Danish (1834) cases (considering the dates, Fredrick Thomasson suggests that a comparison of the lists of petition signatories could show links between the

---

[65] Bridget Brereton, *A History of Modern Trinidad, 1783–1962* (London: Heinemann, 1981), 63.
[66] Heuman, *Between Black and White*, 28–31.
[67] See Newton, *The Children of Africa*, 65.
[68] Jerome S. Handler, *The Unappropriated People: Freedmen in the Slave Society of Barbados* (Baltimore: Johns Hopkins University Press, 1974), 86.
[69] Ibid., 102.
[70] Ale Pålsson, "Smugglers before the Swedish Throne: Political Activity of Free People of Color in Early Nineteenth-Century St Barthélemy," in Robert D. Taber and Charlton W. Yingling, eds., *Free Communities of Color and the Revolutionary Caribbean: Overturning, or Turning Back?* (London: Routledge, 2018), 56–73.

free people of color of the different islands),[71] this civic equality law was part of a broader framework of measures also supported by antislavery intellectuals to facilitate emancipation and remove various restrictions applied to the enslaved and free people of color.

The Situation of the Free People of Color of the Spanish Territories

In the first half of the nineteenth century, as abolitionist movements expanded in the English and French colonies, Spain faced the wave of wars of independence (1810–1825) ending its domination on the American continent. However, the movement did not spread to the Spanish islands of the Caribbean, where racial exclusions remained in effect in Cuba and Puerto Rico until the 1880s, the period of their own revolutions.[72] On the contrary, these islands strengthened their economic model by importing more and more slaves. The Cuban and Puerto Rican white creole elites, who had witnessed the major revolts in the neighboring colonies of Saint-Domingue and Jamaica at the end of the eighteenth century, feared a similar process, especially in Cuba, which had become the leading sugar colony after Haiti's economic collapse.[73]

But, for the free people of color, whose numbers had been increased by the influx of refugees, the example of the Haitian revolution did not instill fear, but on the contrary inspired them, as shown by Aponte's conspiracy in Cuba in 1812. The conspiracy involved free people of color, enslaved people, and some English abolitionists, and seems to have had ramifications in the neighboring islands and even on the American continent. Taking as a model the Haitian case and well aware of the abolitionist debates, its initiators aimed at the liberation of slaves and Black sovereignty.[74]

The case caused an increase in white people's fear about arming free people of color.[75] But, despite oppressive measures against the actual or

---

[71] Fredrick Thomasson, "'Vous-même, ôtez votre chapeau!' Les Libres de couleur dans la colonie suédoise de Saint-Barthélémy (1785–1831)," *Cahiers des Anneaux de la Mémoire* 17 (2017), 111–27.

[72] Ada Ferrer, *La guerre d'indépendance cubaine: Insurrection et émancipation à Cuba 1868–1898* (Bécherel: Les Perséides, 2010).

[73] Juan R. Gonzalez Mendoza, "Puerto Rico's Creole Patriots and the Slave Trade after the Haitian Revolution," in Geggus, *Impact of the Haitian Revolution*, 58–71.

[74] Matt D. Childs, *1812 Aponte Rebellion in Cuba and the Struggle against Atlantic Slavery* (Chapel Hill: The University of North Carolina Press, 2006); Ada Ferrer, *Freedom's Mirror: Cuba and Haiti in the Age of Revolution* (New York: Cambridge University Press, 2014).

[75] Michele Reid-Vazquez, *The Year of the Lash: Free People of Color in Cuba and the Nineteenth-century Atlantic World* (Athens, GA: University of Georgia Press, 2011), 129.

supposed conspiracies of that period, the Cuban free people of color continued to assert their rights, at least individually.

By contrast, in Trinidad, which had been Spanish until 1797, the proximity of the American mainland and the change in sovereignty over the island allowed the use of this territory as a strategic space for the independence revolutions of Spanish America in the nineteenth century. In addition to the men from the mainland who had come to take refuge on this now British island, there was the free man of color Jean Baptist Bideau, a privateer from Saint Lucia who worked for Victor Hugues as he spread his revolutionary ideas in Trinidad in 1796. In 1813, alongside the *Libertador* Simón Bolívar, he was at the head of troops formed partly by free people of color recruited in Trinidad, who contributed to spreading the principles of the French Caribbean Revolution to the American continent. Bideau's example shows the links inherited from the eighteenth century between the French and Spanish colonies along the Puerto Rico–Guadeloupe–Trinidad–Venezuela axis, as highlighted by the historian Anne Pérotin Dumon. But it also exemplifies those free individuals of color from the Caribbean islands who shared revolutionary ideals of equality and freedom both in space and in time, thus contributing to a form of internationalization of the struggle of free people of color.

Conclusion

Britain, France, and Spain developed in the Caribbean islands a colonial model based on the massive exploitation of slaves of African origin. Doing so meant that the islands required significant defenses, whether to guarantee the safety of white minorities by the slave police or to have local militias and armed troops defend the territories coveted during conflicts between colonist powers. The ever-increasing importance given to free people of color to provide for these needs led them to become aware of their numerical strength and fighting ability and to aspire to a certain recognition of their role, particularly following their participation in the American War of Independence.

The elites of color in particular became less and less accepting of a color prejudice that limited their economic and social advancement and made them unable to assimilate into the white class, and thus engaged in political denunciation and revolt against the color prejudice of which they were victims. But at the beginning of the French Revolution, they did not fundamentally question the system of slavery, as they themselves owned slaves and their wealth depended on that system.

The egalitarian ambitions of free people of color spread from the beginning of the French Revolution to the other islands of the Caribbean, but it was especially after the abolition of slavery was proclaimed in 1794 throughout the French territories that the actions of free people of color in the islands under non-French rule intensified.

During the Atlantic revolutions, the strong movement of people, further increased by the migration of refugees during conflicts, and the multiplication of contacts – through the army, privateers' campaigns, or the movement of merchant ships – increasingly contributed to the spread of the aspirations and actions of free people of color, who became interconnected in a network of multiple and complex relationships contributing to a kind of international movement.

Historians note the resurgence in 1795 of conspiracies and insurrections in the Caribbean, largely inspired by the French and Haitian revolutions. But, whereas the last five years of the eighteenth century were marked by revolts, the nineteenth century was a time of petitions in the Caribbean islands.

With the restoration of the old regime in the French colonies, the free people of color of the Caribbean had to campaign on their own for equality, which France had abandoned for the colonies. In the absence of this support, they took political action. Parallel with the antislavery movements that were spreading in the major cities and gradually leading to the abolition of the slave trade and then slavery, the free people of color demanded specific rights or the more global repeal of color prejudice. Thus, after nearly sixty years of striving for equality, free people of color in the British and French colonies obtained the repeal of the discriminatory rules that related to them. Those on the Spanish islands had to wait until the end of the century. But, in both cases, the historical legacy of the structures would survive these legal advances for a long time to come.

28

The Unruly Caribbean: Reverberations of Saint-Domingue's Rebellions on the Caribbean Coast of New Granada and Venezuela, 1790–1800

CRISTINA SORIANO

On 24 April 1804, the captain-general of Venezuela, Manuel Guevara y Vasconcelos, sent a written communication to the king of Spain in which he lamented not having detailed information about the "unhappy disgraces" that had recently taken place in Saint-Domingue, "an island [sic] that was under the monstrous domination of the blacks."[1] He added, however, that he had been able to acquire a paper that a person in Caracas had brought to his attention. According to Guevara y Vasconcelos, the manuscript offered evidence of the strong union that existed among different Black generals in Saint-Domingue and it also included "discourses directed to attract and get positive opinions and enthusiasm among the crowds." "This paper," he added, "shows that they [the Black generals] will continue with the same artifices, acts, and concepts" that "the evil Tousaint" sought to promote in the past, but this time their actions might have "a more lasting success" because they have perfected "the operations designed to maintain this miserable island independent and in a state of anarchy."[2] Imploring the king to share with him his wise advice, Guevara y Vasconcelos attached a manuscript copy of the mentioned document to his letter.

"*Liberty or Death*" were the two words with which the document began, to be followed by the date it was proclaimed: 1 January 1804. The paper that Guevara y Vasconcelos was holding in his hands was, in fact, a complete

---

[1] "No. 158. Guevara Vasconcelos to the King of Spain. Noticia con copia de papel adquirido de un particular sobre el estado infeliz de la Ysla de Santo Domingo. Caracas, 24 de abril 1804," Archivo General de Indias, Seville (AGI), Estado, 68, no. 12, 1 and 3.
[2] Ibid.

manuscript copy of the Declaration of Independence of Haiti, translated into Spanish. Proclaimed by the Haitian leader, Jean-Jacques Dessalines, in the town of Gonaïves and signed by thirty-seven military officers who swore to renounce France, the Declaration of Independence of Haiti not only marked the end of fifteen years of revolution, but signified the beginning of the birth of the first Black nation in the Americas, one whose Black leaders firmly declared equality among the races and the definitive abolition of slavery.[3] Guevara y Vasconcelos was not able, or perhaps not willing, to recognize the tremendous relevance of this document, but he was aware of the danger its circulation in the Spanish American territories represented.

As Julia Gaffield argues, this Haitian proclamation was destined to announce to the nations and empires of the Atlantic world that Saint-Domingue, now renamed Haiti, was no longer under French authority and that the Haitian Black leaders were deeply committed to defending their liberty and independence. The document surely sparked mixed and contrasting feelings of either sympathy or horror in the international community; Guevara y Vasconcelos, however, seemed unaware of the significance and implication of this document that he repeatedly characterized as a simple "paper." For him it seemed to be one more example of those seditious written texts originating in the turbulent Caribbean intended to convince mixed-race and Black (free and enslaved) people to join the revolutionary cause, and that in the previous ten years had circulated intensely and frequently throughout Venezuela. After receiving Guevara y Vasconcelos' written communication, the king of Spain did not hesitate to offer his opinion, it was clear to him that Haiti was "a terrible example for all the blacks that lived in the European colonies and Islands of the Continent." Therefore, the colonial authorities must do their best to control the "spread of these doctrines and the potential increase of followers."[4]

Guevara y Vasconcelos knew that what the king of Spain was asking for was not an easy task. The open and vast Caribbean coast of Venezuela made official efforts of control futile and useless. In fact, between 1789 and 1808, hundreds of political papers – pamphlets, broadsides, manuscripts – from the Caribbean were smuggled into the Spanish Main (a name commonly used

---

[3] Only two copies of the original printed version of the Declaration of Independence of Haiti survive today. Historian Julia Gaffield found both surviving copies in TNA, CO, 137/III/1. See Julia Gaffield, ed., *The Haitian Declaration of Independence: Creation, Context, and Legacy* (Charlottesville: University of Virginia Press, 2016).

[4] King Charles IV to the Captain General of Venezuela, Aranjuez, 16 June 1804, AGI, Estado, 68, No. 12, 4.

among British traders to refer to the Spanish mainland in northern South America, usually denoting Venezuela and the northern coast of New Granada), arousing the curiosity of different social groups and the concerns of colonial officials who desperately tried to collect them. Printed broadsides and manuscript texts, however, were not the only media available for the coastal residents; oral information spread by travelers, foreign soldiers, refugees, fugitive former slaves, smugglers, and Black corsairs, who temporarily visited the coastal towns of Venezuela and New Granada, also caused waves of rumors that created a vibrant, yet very tense, political environment in which white fears of a racial war intersected with hopes for the elimination of unfair taxes, racial equality, and the abolition of slavery.

During the last decade of the eighteenth century, the revolutionary narratives that arrived on the coast of the Spanish Main challenged the already tense relations that existed among different socioracial groups. The majority of the white population interpreted news on the revolutions as a violent torrent that sought to destroy their political system and social order, while many free and enslaved people of African descent saw this flow of ideas as their opportunity to reactivate narratives to fight for social justice and emancipation from the system of slavery, or to at least renegotiate their labor conditions and political roles. Information about the Caribbean turmoil represented a real menace to local authorities and elites, who unsuccessfully tried to isolate enslaved and free Black workers from the tumultuous world outside. Subordinated groups such as *pardos*, free Black people, and captive laborers used multiple webs of circulation of information to pursue diverse political agendas, organizing rebellions against local governments, questioning the system of slavery, the colonial social order, and even the nature of monarchical rule.

In colonial Venezuela and New Granada, the term *pardo* was used to refer to mixed-race people. It broadly included free people of African descent in all kind of variants: *mulatos*, *zambos*, *terceroures*, *cuarterones*, *quinterones*, and so on. Generally, they were considered of a higher social status than free Blacks. Some educated *pardos* became savvy merchants and businessmen and possessed sizeable fortunes that allowed them to maintain ostentatious lifestyles, but they were never perceived as equals of white individuals, because they lacked the necessary purity of blood.[5]

---

[5] Marixa Lasso, *Myths of Harmony: Race and Republicanism during the Age of Revolution, Colombia 1795–1831* (Pittsburgh: University of Pittsburgh Press, 2007), 14; Cristina

In fact, between 1791 and 1799 *pardos*, free Blacks, and enslaved people in different regions of coastal Venezuela and New Granada organized and joined local rebellions and conspiracies, using the revolutionary language to confront both the colonial government and the white elites. The most striking examples are the rebellion of Coro in 1795, the mixed-race conspiracy of La Guaira of 1799, and the conspiracies of Cartagena and Maracaibo of 1799.[6]

By paying attention to the presence and impact of the Caribbean revolutionary media and texts in the coastal towns of Venezuela and New Granada, this chapter contributes to the large body of scholarship on the impact of the Haitian Revolution in the Atlantic World that has emerged in the wake of its bicentennial commemoration in 2004. This scholarship has analyzed how the Haitian Revolution reshaped politics in different regions of the Atlantic world, especially the French, British, Spanish, and Dutch Caribbean zones, but also within European nations and in the United States.[7] By following this path, this work intends to shed more light on the impact of the turbulent events of the French Caribbean in the Spanish territories, and argues that during the last decade of the eighteenth century the Saint-Domingue rebellions, as well as different movements in the French colonies, became a much closer and more familiar reality for the residents of the northern coast of the South American continent than the American or the French Revolutions.

Soriano, *Tides of Revolution: Information, Insurgencies, and the Crisis of Colonial Rule in Venezuela* (Albuquerque: University of New Mexico Press, 2018), 24–5.

[6] Pedro A. Gil Rivas, Luis Dovale Prado, and Lidia Luzmila Bello, *La insurrección de los negros de la Sierra Coriana: 10 de mayo de 1795* (Caracas: Universidad Central de Venezuela, 1996); Eleazar Córdova Bello, *La independencia de Haití y su influencia en Hispanoamérica* (Caracas: Instituto Panamericano de Geografía e Historia, 1967); Pedro Grases, *La conspiración de Gual y España y el ideario de la independencia* (Caracas: Academia Nacional de la Historia, 1997); Soriano, *Tides of Revolution*, Chapters 4–6.

[7] Michel-Rolph Trouillot, *Silencing the Past: Power and the Production of History* (Boston: Beacon Press, 1997); David P. Geggus, *Haitian Revolutionary Studies* (Bloomington: Indiana University Press, 2002); David Geggus, ed., *The Impact of the Haitian Revolution in the Atlantic World* (Columbia, SC: University of South Carolina Press, 2001); David Geggus and Norman Fiering, eds., *The World of the Haitian Revolution* (Bloomington: Indiana University Press, 2009); Ada Ferrer, *Freedom's Mirror: Cuba and Haiti in the Age of Revolution* (Cambridge: Cambridge University Press, 2014); Nick Nesbitt, *Universal Emancipation: The Haitian Revolution and the Radical Enlightenment* (Charlottesville: University of Virginia Press, 2008); Sibylle Fischer, *Modernity Disavowed: Haiti and the Cultures of Slavery in the Age of Revolution* (Durham, NC: Duke University Press, 2004); Ashli White, *Encountering Revolution: Haiti and the Making of the Early Republic* (Baltimore: Johns Hopkins University Press, 2010); Alejandro E. Gómez, *Le spectre de la Révolution noire: L'impact de la révolution Haïtienne dans le monde Atlantique, 1790–1886* (Rennes: Presses universitaires de Rennes, 2013); Julia Gaffield, *Haitian Connections in the Atlantic World: Recognition after Revolution* (Chapel Hill: University of North Carolina Press, 2015).

The Unruly Caribbean

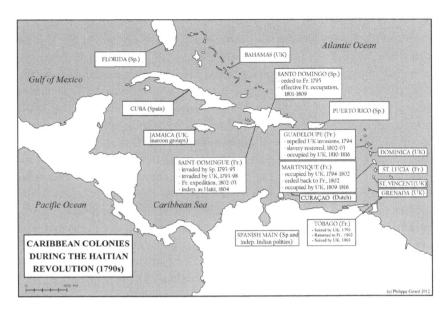

Map 28.1 The Caribbean in the 1790s. Map by Philippe Girard.

In this chapter I will analyze how revolutionary pamphlets, anonymous broadsides, and manuscripts, and also rumors from the Caribbean that circulated on the northern coasts of Venezuela and New Granada opened new spaces for political reflection and social mobilization, in the form of rebellion and conspiracies, that challenged colonial rule and forced local authorities to contemplate new strategies of negotiation and appeasement. By looking into common experiences shared by communities living on the Caribbean coasts of South America (Map 28.1), this chapter seeks to challenge traditional historiographical approaches that have separated the national histories of Venezuela and Colombia, and offers a more integrated analysis that compiles the visions and reactions of imperial agents and colonialized subjects in the Spanish Main. Here, I follow the proposal that the historian Miguel Izard presented in his book *Tierra Firme*, where he offers a history that transcends national frontiers, looking into the common experiences that indigenous groups, African enslaved people, and creoles shared during Spanish colonial rule.[8] Official authorities throughout the coast

---

[8] Miguel Izard, *Tierra Firme: Historia de Venezuela y Colombia* (Madrid: Alianza Editorial, 1986).

reacted in similar ways and developed a myriad of strategies in order to preempt Black insurrections and movements in the region. In 1800, New Granada's Viceroy, Pedro Mendinueta, expressed deep concerns about the potential emergence of a "revolution inspired by Saint-Domingue" in the coastal cities of the domain; a year later, in 1801, Guevara y Vasconcelos issued several orders requiring greater vigilance and control of the Black population by white masters and local authorities in the plantations and rural towns of Venezuela.[9] Colonial authorities, however, not only demanded more local control, but also encouraged masters to moderate their punishments and discipline strategies, encouraging them to even negotiate with their enslaved laborers some of their demands in order to "restore" the quietude and submission of the region. The Haitian Revolution, then, became a form of shared knowledge, a common reference point that was used by rebels during negotiations with the colonial elites, and by powerful groups to justify repression or, on the contrary, accommodate demands in order to preserve the fragile stability of the colonial order.[10]

Communication Networks: The Caribbean and the Spanish Main

In an official letter written in December of 1794, the War Office magistrate of Spanish Trinidad, Josef Damián de Cuenca, explained that the close connections and intense trade between the island of Trinidad and Venezuela represented a serious threat to the South American continent. "The island," he wrote, "is close to those French islands of Martinique, Guadeloupe, St. Lucia, and its inhabitants are mostly French; the island does not have forts, nor enough troops; the number of foreign slaves is excessive; Trinidad is clearly exposed to the fire of the revolutionaries." In addition, he argued that if French insurgents were to take control of the island, they would also assume de facto control of the eastern coast of Venezuela – in particular the Gulf of Paria. It is not completely clear what Cuenca meant by "French insurgents," but he was probably referring to the Republican troops that Victor Hugues led to take the island of Guadeloupe from the British earlier that year. Between 1794 and 1798, Hugues turned Guadeloupe into a Republican stronghold of the eastern

---

[9] Aline Helg, *Liberty and Equality in Caribbean Colombia, 1770–1835* (Chapel Hill: University of North Carolina Press, 2004), 80; Soriano, *Tides of Revolution*, 211.

[10] See Cristina Soriano, "'Avoiding the Fate of Haiti': Negotiating Peace in Late-Colonial Venezuela," in Michael Goode and John Smolenski, eds., *The Specter of Peace: Rethinking Violence and Power in the Colonial Atlantic* (Leiden: Brill, 2018), 187–215.

Caribbean, raising the concern of Spanish and British colonial officials in the nearby region.[11] French republican ideas would thus spread along "the huge rivers of Orinoco, Guarapiche, and El Tigre and the infinite numbers of streams"; the "contagion" would soon spread to "the Provinces of Cumaná, Guayana, Barinas ... and as far as the Kingdom of Nueva Granada."[12] In this letter, Cuenca expressed the idea – quite popular among colonial officials – that Venezuela and New Granada were turning into particularly vulnerable colonial spaces because they represented the gateway that connected the turbulent Caribbean with the vast continent of South America. Therefore, it became imperative to control and guard the northern coast, especially the multiple rivers that could easily serve as channels for news and ideas about the turbulent state of the French colonies to flow to the rest of the Spanish mainland. In Europeans' imagination, rivers could also play a symbolic role that marked actions of possession and occupation in the competition among various powers in the Atlantic world.[13] Although, by the end of the eighteenth century, the Caribbean coast of New Granada and Venezuela was ruled by two different entities – the viceroyalty of New Granada, and the general captaincy of Venezuela, respectively – their geographic location and close proximity to the Caribbean, and the comparable demographic and socioracial structures of their communities created similar scenarios of social tension fueled by revolutionary ideological influences.[14]

During the eighteenth century, gold mining, cattle raising, and the cultivation of export crops were the most important economic activities on the northern coast of the Spanish Main. Small haciendas located along the coast and in the fertile nearby valleys produced crops such as tobacco, indigo, sugar, coffee, and cacao that supplied both the small internal market of Venezuela and northern New Granada and other nearby Spanish American markets such as those of Santo Domingo, Cuba, and New Spain. Illegal trade also allowed the export of these products to Kingston in Jamaica, Curaçao, and Saint Thomas.[15] In Venezuelan port cities such as La Guaira, Puerto

---

[11] See Laurent Dubois, "'The Price of Liberty': Victor Hugues and the Administration of Freedom in Guadeloupe, 1794–1798," *The William and Mary Quarterly* 56:2 (1999), 363–92.
[12] Report by Josef Damian Cuenca, War Office magistrate of Trinidad to the Captain General of Venezuela, December 1794, AGI, Estado 66, n. 26.
[13] Lauren Benton, *A Search for Sovereignty: Law and Geography in European Empires, 1400–1900* (Cambridge: Cambridge University Press, 2010), 41.
[14] Lasso, *Myths of Harmony*, Chapter 2.
[15] Ernesto Bassi, *An Aqueous Territory: Sailor Geographies and New Granada's Transimperial Greater Caribbean World* (Durham, NC: Duke University Press, 2016), Chapter 1.

Cabello, and Maracaibo, cash crops such as cacao, indigo, and sugar, mules, and leather products were exchanged for European goods. In New Granada, Cartagena and other minor, but very busy, ports such as Riohacha, Santa Marta, and Portobelo dominated the viceroyalty's trade. Historically, the city of Cartagena had always been central to the Spanish American commercial system. As the historian Aline Helg notes, "Cartagena was the most important not only for the coast, but for the Andean interior as far as Quito. Through its port, manufactured goods, cloth, and wheat entered New Granada, and precious metals, tropical agricultural products, brazilwood, and emeralds were sent overseas."[16]

Socially, the coastal towns and ports of Venezuela and New Granada were diverse, dynamic, and heterogeneous: *pardo* artisans and merchants, poor white peasant tenants, white planters and traders, free Black workers, enslaved Africans, and a few Indigenous cultivators were all involved in complex relations of production.[17] In important port cities such as La Guaira, Maracaibo, Cartagena, and Santa Marta, there was a large number of enslaved Black people who did not perform agricultural tasks but instead worked as domestic servants, fishermen, sailors, muleteers, or skilled artisans, but there was an even larger number of free people of color dedicated to a variety of economic activities from trade to artisanal activities. The economy of these coastal regions did not rely heavily on enslaved people, but their presence was particularly noticeable in the adjacent rural regions, where cacao and sugar plantations played more important roles. Demographically, La Guaira's and Cartagena's societies were very similar. In late 1770, Cartagena had a population of 13,396 inhabitants, 56.8 percent of whom were free persons of color and 15.7 percent enslaved, while whites amounted to 27 percent.[18] By the 1780s, La Guaira had a population of approximately 7,000 people. Free people of African descent accounted for approximately 50 percent of the population, a little more than 20 percent were enslaved people, around 10 percent were Indians, and some 15 percent were whites (Spanish and creoles).[19] By the end of the eighteenth century, frictions frequently emerged among these diverse social groups, usually emanating from their contrasting ability to influence political decision-making, status inequalities, and everyday forms of social exclusion. Local

---

[16] Helg, *Liberty and Equality*, 82.
[17] José María Aizpurua, *Relaciones de trabajo en la sociedad colonial venezolana* (Caracas: Centro Nacional de la Historia, 2009), 14–15.
[18] Helg, *Liberty and Equality*, 82.   [19] Soriano, *Tides of Revolution*, 156.

tensions surfaced increasingly as ideas of equality, freedom, and fraternity became more familiar to the residents of these coastal towns. Thanks to the vast and exposed coast of Venezuela and New Granada, their port cities and towns became multicultural and multilingual hubs for encounter and exchange, where locals frequently met with foreign traders and visitors with whom they shared news and their impressions about the Atlantic Revolutions.

In his groundbreaking book *The Common Wind*, Julius Scott encourages historians to pay close attention to the flow of bodies, goods, and information that connected different port cities of the Greater Caribbean region.[20] By virtue of their geography, New Granada's and Venezuela's Atlantic coasts were at the center of the Atlantic Revolutions: information and rumors about the French Revolution and the Caribbean revolts and upheavals arrived with relative frequency and intensity. Between 1789 and 1808, hundreds of political pamphlets and broadsides from the Caribbean were smuggled into the Spanish Main. Waves of French-speaking refugees shared news and subversive ideas with locals, and everyday conversations transformed the "turbulent" French Caribbean into a familiar reference point for a complex set of political ideas and aspirations.[21]

The open nature of these Spanish American port societies thus facilitated an intense flow of information about the Atlantic Revolutions, but especially about Saint-Domingue. In the coastal regions of Venezuela and New Granada, the flow of written and oral information about the first events of the Saint-Domingue rebellion was frequent and varied. From 1791 to 1799, the anxiety of colonial authorities in these regions increased as more news about the insurrection in Saint-Domingue arrived on the mainland through various written and oral channels.[22]

Revolutionary written materials such as pamphlets, broadsides, and newspapers circulated throughout these coastal towns, promoting discomfort among the white elites, and threatening the political tranquility of the towns. People of different socioracial groups and with diverse educational

---

[20] Julius Scott, *The Common Wind: Afro-American Currents in the Age of the Haitian Revolution* (New York: Verso, 2018).

[21] For works that analyze the interimperial character of the Caribbean region, see David Barry Gaspar and David Patrick Geggus, eds., *A Turbulent Time: The French Revolution and the Greater Caribbean, 1789–1815* (Bloomington: Indiana University Press, 1997); Bassi, *An Aqueous Territory*.

[22] See William J. Callahan, "La propaganda, la sedición y la Revolución Francesa en la capitanía general de Venezuela, 1780–1796," *Boletín histórico* 14 (May 1967), 177–205; Soriano, *Tides of Revolution*, Chapter 2.

backgrounds had different levels of access to these foreign or locally produced written materials. In these communities, which lacked a printing press and in which the proportion of literate people was small, people lived on the fringes of the literate world, one in which the boundaries established between the written and oral worlds were not clearly defined. For example, the oral reading of brief written materials such as pamphlets and newspapers was a common practice, which provided a way for nonliterate people to access the written word. In La Guaira, Puerto Cabello, and Maracaibo there were literate artisans (barbers, tailors, carpenters, musicians, pharmacists, and shoemakers) who read newspapers and pamphlets to others in public places, such as markets and barbershops. See the cases of the hairdresser André Renoir, the *pardo* pharmacist Tomás Cardozo, the *pardo* musician Juan Bautista Olivares, the *pardo* barber Narciso del Valle, and the *pardo* tailor Francisco Pirela, who read texts to curious listeners in La Guaira, Maracaibo, and Caracas.[23]

The lack of printing presses and the scarcity of books and newspapers in the coastal towns of Cartagena, La Guaira, and Maracaibo did not prevent these communities from exchanging ideas and participating in an emerging public sphere during the intellectually agitated period of the Age of Revolutions. The geographic location of these towns made relatively easy the entrance of foreign written texts that were either smuggled in by visitors, merchants, and sailors, or brought from urban centers such as Bogotá, where the residents could avail themselves of the operation of the printing press. For example, The Declaration of the Rights of Man and Citizen, illegally translated by the *bogotano* Antonio Nariño in 1793, circulated in Mompox and Cartagena.[24] As Aline Helg points out, "Momposinos and cartageneros had more access than residents of other cities to revolutionary news from Bogotá, the Caribbean, and Europe, reported by free and slaves, sailors, and merchants ..."[25]

Several written texts from France, Saint-Domingue, and Trinidad – in printed or in manuscript form – were collected by officials in different coastal towns of Venezuela. From 1793 until 1808, officials continuously reported the ease with which these papers circulated in the region. Among the texts that circulated in the coastal towns, there were political proclamations and letters, such as a translation of the "Réponse de la Convention nationale aux

---

[23] Soriano, *Tides of Revolution*, Chapter 2.
[24] For Antonio Nariño, see Clément Thibaud's Chapter 6 in this volume.
[25] Helg, *Liberty and Equality*, 89.

manifestes des tyrans ligués contre la republique, proposé par Robespierre au nom du comité de salut public, et décrété par la Convention dans la séance du 15 frimaire (an II, 5 décembre 1793)" (summarizing the arguments that members of the National Convention in revolutionary France used against the monarchical system),[26] which was locally distributed in the town of La Guaira by a navy captain and the port merchant Juan Xavier Arrambide, who translated it into Spanish, or the "Instrucciones que debe servir de regla al Agente Interino Francés destinado a la Parte Española de Santo Domingo" ("Instructions that shall serve as rules for the French interim agent stationed on the Spanish side of of Santo Domingo"), a text written by Phillipe-Rose Roume de St. Laurent, the French agent appointed, after the Treaty of Basel in 1795, to Spanish Santo Domingo in order to organize the local civil administration. Crucial political texts such as the Declaration of Independence of the United States (1776), the Rights of Man and Citizen (1790), and the Declaration of Independence of Haiti (1804) found their way to the Spanish Main, where they even underwent discursive and narrative adaptations that made them more comprehensible to the population at large.[27]

The initial attention to the French Revolution and its propaganda was quickly superseded by a serious preoccupation with the eruption of violence in the French Caribbean colonies. In a December 1790 letter to Floridablanca, Captain-General Carbonell underlined the direct connection that he believed existed between the Revolution in France and the nascent instability in the French colonies, especially in the French Windward Islands. In Guadeloupe, Carbonell recounted, struggles between the Monarchists – who refused to obey equal rights for free Black people – and the Republicans had recently led to a conflagration that destroyed one-third of Pointe-à-Pitre.[28] An intense epistolary relation between Carbonell and the governors in Margarita and Trinidad, but also with the governors of Santo Domingo, Puerto Rico, and Cuba, provided him with information about the developments in different French colonies and increased his concern that more news and seditious ideas would spread on the mainland.[29] The governor of

---

[26] Clément Thibaud, *Un Nouveau Monde républicain: Les premiers États sans roi dans l'Atlantique hispanique* (Bécherel: Les Perséides, 2017), Chapter 2.

[27] "Instrucciones que debe servir de regla al Agente Interino Francés destinado a la Parte Española de Santo Domingo," AGI, Estado 58, no. 8, and AGI, Caracas, 169, no. 86.

[28] "Orden del Presidente de la Real Audiencia de Caracas," Archivo General de la Nación (Caracas) (AGN), Gobernación y Capitanía General, XLIII, 96–7. See also Dubois, *A Colony of Citizens*, 23–124.

[29] "Orden del Presidente de la Real Audiencia de Caracas," AGN, Gobernación y Capitanía General, XLIII, 96–7.

Trinidad, in particular, maintained a frequent correspondence with Carbonell, offering him information about the quality and character of the French families coming from Grenada, about the presence of foreign ships along the coasts, about the situation of Martinique and Guadeloupe, and, later, about the development of events in Saint-Domingue.[30] Chacón usually collected this information from merchants who stopped in Port-of-Spain, but also from French residents who received letters from family members and acquaintances still living in Grenada, Martinique, and Guadeloupe.[31]

Written texts, however, were not the only sources of information about the Atlantic Revolutions to which coastal Venezuelans and New Granadans had access during the tumultuous decade of the 1790s. Waves of refugees, soldiers and prisoners, Black corsairs, and maritime Maroons visited coastal towns and shared their experiences of revolution with curious locals. Regardless of the different mechanisms of control that the Spanish colonial state had put in place during this last decade in order to prevent communication between locals and foreigners, rebellions and war in the French colonies produced an important movement of people of diverse social status, races, and political tendencies across the Atlantic world. This mobilization altered, in turn, the social compositions and dynamics, the geopolitical perceptions, and even the economies of those regions impacted by the increasing entry of people and information.

In 1792, for example, the captain-general of Venezuela ordered local governors and regional lieutenants to investigate foreigners living in their jurisdictions. These officials were told to find out "who they are, the lifestyle and customs of each one of them, their occupation or profession, and the reasons for their presence in the Province."[32] Likewise, lieutenants were instructed to determine whether these foreigners, especially Frenchmen, had made suspicious verbal statements.[33] Immediately, information about the presence of suspicious Frenchmen began to circulate throughout official channels. Several French individuals living in towns in Venezuela were interrogated by colonial agents about their presence and occupation in the region and were put at the center of paranoid suspicions of revolutionary

---

[30] See diverse communications from Governor of Trinidad José María Chacón to the captain-general of Venezuela, in AGN, Gobernación y Capitanía General, XLIII, 48; XLVII, 14; XLVIII, 218, 297, 307, 348; XLVII, 14.

[31] "Sobre los eventos rebeldes que surgieron en St. Pierre, Martinique, junio 1790, reportados por el mercader Jean-Baptiste Floreusa," AGI, Estado, 58, no. 1.

[32] "Orden a los Tenientes Justicias Mayores de Coro," AGN, Gobernación y Capitanía General, XLVII, 68.

[33] Ibid., 69.

contagion. These methods employed by the colonial state fueled a counter-revolutionary animosity toward all French people in the Spanish territories – a collective anxiety that, by the end of the eighteenth century, had devolved into outright "Francophobia." Encouraged by colonial officials, the local population began to pay closer attention to the actions and words of their French neighbors and shared this intelligence among themselves and with the authorities. On different occasions, colonial authorities arrested some of these French suspects and sent them to Spain. They often depicted them as persons who challenged both colonial authorities and the Church, the pillars of social order and harmony.

In 1794, for example, Francisco Combret, a Frenchman who worked as a tobacconist in the city of Maracay, was accused by his workmates of expressing subversive ideas in public. Combret was arrested "along with all his books and papers," and sent to Cádiz in 1795. Accompanying Combret in the same ship was a Basque merchant, Santiago Albi, who was accused by his neighbors of celebrating the fall of the port of San Sebastián to the French during the War of the Pyrenees with fireworks and joyful cries. In an official report, Albi was described as "an insolent, vain, and atheistic young man, capable of inspiring others with the project that the National Assembly of Paris has spread."[34]

But French visitors and temporary residents did not monopolize the attention of colonial agents. Maritime Maroons were also an important source of concern. Throughout the eighteenth century, enslaved people had fled from the Antilles to the vast and unpatrolled coasts of Venezuela and New Granada. A royal decree of 1750 manumitted all slaves fleeing foreign colonies who agreed to convert to Roman Catholicism. From that point on, hundreds of maritime Maroons from the Caribbean felt driven to flee to Venezuela and New Granada to gain their freedom.[35] The policy changed abruptly in May 1790 when the king issued a royal order forbidding the entry of foreign slaves into his American domains.[36]

---

[34] "El Gobernador a Juan N. Pedroza, noviembre de 1794," AGN, Gobernación y Capitanía General, LIII, 30.
[35] Ramón Aizpurúa, "Coro y Curazao en el siglo XVIII," *Tierra Firme* 4:14 (1986), 229–40; Ramón Aizpurúa, "En busca de la libertad: Los esclavos fugados de Curazao a Coro en el siglo XVIII," in *II Encuentro para la promoción y difusión del patrimonio folclórico de los países andinos: Influencias Africanas en las culturas tradicionales de los países andinos* (Bogotá: Fundación Bigott, 2002), 69–102. See also "Real Cédula de Su Majestad sobre declarar por libres a los negros que viniesen de los ingleses u holandeses a los reinos de España buscando el agua del bautismo," Buen Retiro, 24 September 1750, AGN, Caracas, Reales Cédulas, X, 332.
[36] "Real Orden reservada del 21 de mayo de 1790," AGI, Caracas, 115.

Although the viceroy of New Granada, the captain-general of Venezuela, and provincial governors restricted the entry of fugitive slaves, the clandestine immigration of Black self-emancipated people from the Caribbean on the northern coast of South America continued. According to the historian Ramón Aizpurúa, there were three different regions through which foreign maritime Maroons could enter Venezuela in the eighteenth century: the southeast, where slaves from Dutch Essequibo entered the Spanish province of Guayana; the east, where slaves from British and French colonies, such as Grenada and Trinidad, entered the region of Cumaná; and the west, where slaves from Curaçao came ashore, mostly in the Province of Coro. In a report written to the Spanish king in 1794, the captain of Venezuela warned about the danger the proximity between Curaçao an Coro posed for the province: "the closeness of that province [Coro] to the island of Curaçao is such that one might estimate that it is almost a Dutch possession on the coast."[37] In the case of New Granada, most of these maritime slaves arrived on the northern coast and established themselves in ports and towns such as Riohacha, Barranquilla, and Cartagena.[38] In the region of Coro in Venezuela, the presence of escaped slaves from Curaçao was so relevant that they formed their own communities, commonly known as *luangos*, *minas*, or *curazaos*. These communities contributed to the economic development of the region as their presence helped to mitigate the region's labor shortage. Therefore, Coro's local authorities showed no particular interest in returning these former slaves to Curaçao. However, after the 1790s the frequent travel and communication between these communities and Curaçao and other islands created significant anxiety among local authorities, who took drastic steps to restrict their mobility and suspended permission for them to settle in the region.[39] The fear of revolutionary contagion triumphed over the region's labor needs.

This fear might have also influenced Venezuelan white planters to limit their purchase of enslaved workers. The historian Alex Borucki shows that the arrival of slaves in Venezuela decreased drastically during the period 1795–1811. In the previous decade, 1784–1794, approximately 1,551 slaves arrived per year in the province, whereas in the roughly fifteen-year period

---

[37] See Captain General of Venezuela to King Charles IV, 13 March 1794, AGI, Caracas, 95. See also Aizpurúa, "En busca de la libertad"; Linda Rupert, *Creolization and Contraband: Curaçao in the Early Modern Atlantic World* (Athens, GA: Georgia University Press, 2012), in particular the chapter "Curaçao and Tierra Firme."

[38] Lasso, *Myths of Harmony*, Chapter 2.

[39] Soriano, *Tides of Revolution*, Chapters 3 and 4.

1795–1811, on average only 120 slaves annually were introduced. Borucki explains that economic factors (lack of capital and credit, rising slave prices in the British Caribbean, and lack of long-distance commercial networks) are just one set of possible explanations for this sudden decrease. He believes that the Atlantic warfare and the eruption of slave revolts in the Caribbean may have played a more significant role in this decrease. Venezuelan masters seemed mortified by the eruption of violence in the Caribbean, and these uprisings may have discouraged them from importing more slaves.[40] José María Aizpurua agrees with this interpretation. He argues that "warfare among the different European powers and the social upheaval in the Caribbean region completely disrupted the importation of slaves to the region."[41] Although Venezuela's slave trade decreased drastically after the Saint-Domingue rebellion, the extension in 1791 of free trade in slaves for another six years, and the inclusion of New Granada (along with Cuba, Venezuela, Santo Domingo, and Puerto Rico) in the free trade zone, are clear evidence that the Madrid authorities were willing to promote the slave trade in the Spanish Caribbean.[42] In New Granada, colonial authorities had contrasting opinions about the need to increase the slave trade during turbulent times. While the governors of Santa Marta and Cartagena supported the importation of slaves to promote agriculture in the coastal region, Viceroy Josef de Ezpeleta argued that this would expose the coastal provinces either to a potential Black uprising or to "the pernicious maxims of the French National Assembly" if the slaves arrived with refugees from the French islands.[43] In 1796, when war broke out between Spain and Great Britain, the Spanish authorities renewed restrictions on the importation of slaves into New Granada, and Cartagena's and Santa Marta's governors complained that this measure was affecting the agricultural development of the region.

As the military conflict in the French colonies of Guadeloupe and Saint-Domingue escalated in 1792 and 1793, the Spanish governor of Santo Domingo sent an increasing number of French prisoners of war, soldiers, and slaves to other Spanish American destinations. In Venezuela, more than

---

[40] Alex Borucki, "Trans-imperial History in the Making of the Slave Trade to Venezuela, 1526–1811," *Itinerario* 36:2 (2012), 29–54: 43.
[41] Aizpurua, *Relaciones de trabajo*, 78.
[42] Borucki, "Trans-imperial History in the Making of the Slave Trade." See also John V. Lombardi, *The Decline and Abolition of Negro Slavery in Venezuela, 1820–1854* (Westport, CN: Greenwood Press, 1971).
[43] Helg, *Liberty and Equality*, 53–6.

3,000 French militiamen, prisoners, and slaves from Saint-Domingue, Martinique, and Guadeloupe reached the towns of Puerto Cabello, La Guaira, and Cumaná, and also came to Port of Spain in Trinidad.[44] New Granada did not receive a comparable number of officially captured prisoners, but its coastal towns were subjected to frequent visits by Black corsairs. In fact, between 1797 and 1800, military commanders and governors of Venezuela's western provinces (mainly Puerto Cabello, Coro, and Maracaibo) and New Granada frequently reported the presence of corsairs from the French Antilles near the coast and asked for military reinforcements. In some cases, they even provided the exact number of ships captained by "Black Frenchmen" that had been seen "visiting" their communities and detailed their suspicious practices; others reported wholesale attacks on coastal towns. For the Spanish colonial authorities it seemed evident that these Black corsairs, imbued with revolutionary ideas, sought to incite sedition and destabilize the region. The list of denunciations of the presence of French corsairs on the coasts of Venezuela and New Granada between 1798 and 1801 is extensive.[45]

All these Franco-Caribbean temporary visitors brought contrasting stories of republicanism, Black insurrection, the abolition of slavery, and equality, which spread rapidly among the local population. People in Venezuela and New Granada responded differently to this new wave of oral information. Having absorbed the profound Francophobia of colonial elites, some white

---

[44] See Jesse A. Noel, *Trinidad, Provincia de Venezuela: Historia de la Administración Española de Trinidad* (Caracas: Academia Nacional de la Historia, 1972); Carl Campbell, "The Rise of a Free Coloured Plantocracy in Trinidad, 1783–1813," *Boletín de Estudios Latinoamericanos y del Caribe* 29 (1980), 33–54; Ángel Sanz Tapia, "Refugiados de la Revolución Francesa en Venezuela (1793–1795)," *Revista de Indias* 47:181 (1987), 833–67; Rosario Sevilla Soler, *Inmigración y cambio socio-económico en Trinidad (1783–1797)* (Seville: Escuela de Estudios Hispanoamericanos, CSIC, 1988); Alejandro Gómez Pernía, *Fidelidad bajo el viento: Revolución y contrarrevolución en las Antillas Francesas (1790–1795)* (Mexico City: Siglo XXI, 2004); Soriano, *Tides of Revolution*, Chapter 3.

[45] See "Expediente sobre negros y mulatos franceses dejados en la Península Goajira, 1799," AGI, Estado, no. 60; "Comunicación del gobernador de Maracaibo sobre presencia de corsarios franceses en Río de Hacha, mayo 1799," AGN, Gobernación y Capitanía General, LXXVII, 76; "Comunicación de Fernando Mijares al Capitán General, sobre presencia de Corsarios franceses, junio 1799," AGN, Gobernación y Capitanía General, LXXIX, 223–7; "Comunicación del Capitán General de Venezuela al Virrey de Santa Fé sobre presencia de corsarios franceses en las costas, octubre 1799," AGN, Gobernación y Capitanía General, LXXXI, 287; "Comunicación del Gobernador de Maracaibo para el Capitán General sobre presencia de corsarios con 120 franceses de color, julio 1800," AGN, Gobernación y Capitanía General, LXXXVIII, 7; "Informe del Comandante de Coro, Andrés Boggiero al Capitán General, enero 1801," AGI, Estado, no. 60.

and *pardo* locals avoided the new arrivals and questioned their presence in their towns. They were concerned because the news and information they carried with them, whether true or fabricated, might incite rebellions. Others responded by opening spaces for discussion of these new ideas. Overall, colonial authorities were convinced that this influx of written texts and unwelcome visitors from the turbulent Caribbean could represent a true danger for the tranquility and proper order of the Spanish American domains.

Black and *Pardo* Movements on the Caribbean Coast of Venezuela and New Granada

During the entire eighteenth century, diverse mixed-race, Black, and slave rebellions and conspiracies took place in different towns of Venezuela and New Granada. These episodes not only revealed the vulnerability and unstable character of the colonial system and its sociracial order, but also provided evidence of the impact that the Atlantic Revolutions, especially that of Saint-Domingue, had in the northern coastal region of South America. The colonial societies of Venezuela and New Granada had complex relations with the metropole that shaped their political and economic developments, while the unique social composition, the hybrid nature of the labor force, and increasing administrative pressures complicated political and social stability.

In the year 1795, about 300 slaves, free Black people, and some Indigenous people revolted in the Serranía of Coro, an area mainly dedicated to the production of sugar in the northeastern region of Venezuela. The rebellion not only aimed to exonerate the inhabitants from sales taxes (*alcabala*) and to reduce Indian taxes (*tributos*), but also sought the freedom of the slaves and the creation of a "Republic," while applying what rebels themselves denominated the "Law of the French." In order to reach one or other of their goals, or all of them, people of African descent – enslaved and free – who participated in the rebellion expressed their hatred for white people by sacking and burning their houses, beating and killing white males, setting fields on fire, and assaulting travelers while remaining in the outskirts of the city of Coro. The Coro uprising, like many other slave revolts throughout the Caribbean, was met with overwhelming force by the colonial state: white colonial authorities and elites captured, tortured, and summarily executed most of the participants. In 1796, José Leonardo Chirino, the zambo leader of the rebellion, was finally arrested and sentenced to death. (In Venezuela and New Granada, the word *zambo* referred to the children of unions between

Amerindians and Black people, and zambos were despised as a "bad race" because they supposedly distilled the worst aspects of these groups of color, and completely lacked the desirable characteristics of whites.) After Chirino had been hanged, his body was mutilated and decapitated; his remains were displayed publicly as a warning against insurrection.

The rebellion of Coro has mesmerized and intrigued scholars of Venezuelan slavery, anticolonial insurgency, and Afro-Venezuelan resistance. Historical sources show that Coro's rebels not only called for the end of sales taxes and the elimination of Indian tribute, but also invoked the "Law of the French" to denote profound changes they sought in the colonial system, such as the abolition of slavery and Black people's political autonomy. While traditional historiography considered this rebellion a direct result of the effective circulation of "French-Caribbean" revolutionary ideas in the province and Black people's willingness to produce a "second Saint-Domingue" in Venezuela,[46] more recently historians have paid closer attention to the rebels' demands and interpreted these as a direct response to the local exploitative system and unpopular administrative adjustments.[47]

The available sources on the rebellion reveal, however, a complex reality: in Coro the demands of the Black rebels, such as the elimination of taxes and Indigenous tributes responded mainly to local economic and administrative circumstances, but these demands were also accompanied by revolutionary calls for the abolition of slavery and, in some cases, the reversal of colonial socioracial hierarchies. These more radical demands allowed colonial officials to imagine connections between Coro and Saint-Domingue and, as a result, to justify violent and illegal measures to eradicate the movement. While it is important not to diminish how local circumstances of oppression and economic pressures shaped rebel demands, it is clear that Saint-Domingue remained a powerful narrative for the people of Coro, a very familiar point of reference that allowed them to imagine different political scenarios for themselves. The rebellion deepened feelings of mutual mistrust while increasing frictions among white elites and the Black population in Coro. For years, the white elite of Coro silently remembered its effects and remained wary of any sign that could evoke an insurgent movement, while

---

[46] See Pedro Manuel Arcaya, *La insurrección de los negros de la serranía de Coro* (Caracas: Instituto Panamericano de Geografía e Historia, 1949); Federico Brito Figueroa, *Las insurrecciones de los esclavos negros en la sociedad colonial venezolana* (Caracas: Editorial Cantaclaro, 1961); Federico Brito Figueroa, *El problema tierra y esclavos en la historia de Venezuela* (Caracas: Ediciones Teoría y Praxis, 1973).

[47] Aizpurua, "La insurrección de los negros de la serranía de Coro."

the Black population remained traumatized by the disproportionate violence of the colonial state.

Two years later, in 1797, the captain-general of Venezuela heard rumors about a republican conspiracy organized in the town of La Guaira, the most important port on the Caracas coast. The colonial authorities soon discovered that the movement had two leaders, Manuel Gual and José María España, and therefore named it "the conspiracy of Gual and España." Historians agree that the main goals of the movement were various: the establishment of a republican government, the imposition of free trade, the abolition of slavery with compensation to masters, the elimination of Indian tributes, and the abolition of taxes were among the most important ones. The movement also argued in favor of social harmony between whites, *pardos*, Amerindians, and Black people, because all these racial groups were seen as "brothers in Christ." Gual and España, both white creoles, obtained support from a group of *pardos*, white laborers, small merchants, royal officials, soldiers, and some free Black people from La Guaira and Caracas, with whom they shared a rich network of information related to the ideas of revolution, equality, and republican principles.

The enormous quantity of documents produced by the colonial state during the inquiry revealed that the co-conspirators produced and shared a considerable number of texts designed to instruct their followers in the republican principles of the movement. Among these documents were proclamations of insurrection, poems, stories, songs, and the Declaration of the Rights of Man, as well as other revolutionary documents from France, Spain, Saint-Domingue, Trinidad, and Guadeloupe that are essential for an understanding of the political roots of the movement, but also provide a favorable vantage point for understanding the diverse communicational strategies used to impart political knowledge to the "common people" and prompt their mobilization.[48]

Historical records also show that the colonial authorities believed the conspiracy was a consequence of the significant presence of French prisoners and refugees from the Caribbean in La Guaira in the years 1793–1794. A government report, written a week after the discovery of the movement,

---

[48] See Alí Enrique López Bohorquez, ed., *Manuel Gual y José María España: Valoración múltiple de la conspiración de La Guaira de 1797* (Caracas: Comisión Presidencial del Bicentenario de Gual y España, 1997); Grases, *La conspiración de Gual y España*; Juan Carlos Rey, Rogelio Pérez Perdomo, Ramón Aizpurua Aguirre, and Adriana Hernández, eds., *Gual y España: La independencia frustrada* (Caracas: Fundación Polar, 2007).

explains that the presence of many foreigners who openly expressed ideas of "liberty and equality" generated a permissive and liberal environment that allowed revolutionary voices to be frequently heard on the streets and in public spaces of the port. They also believed that numerous written texts from France and Saint-Domingue spread the "false seeds of equality and liberty," "introducing an anarchy presented as the source of an imaginary happiness that seemed real to all simple people."[49] For the colonial authorities, it was clear from the beginning that the liberal atmosphere of La Guaira was fertile ground for the emergence of a movement that followed the French Caribbean revolutionary republican model: opposing the monarchical system, slavery, and a system of social privileges that was perceived as unfair and obsolete by the majority of the mixed-race population.

With the label "Conspiracy of Gual and España," traditional historical narratives have emphasized the leadership of white creoles in the planning of the conspiracy, leaving aside the important participation of lower-rank officials and people of African descent.[50] Only recently have historians recognized that the social groups involved in the conspiracy were connected thanks to the activities of seven ringleaders of different sociocial backgrounds: the *pardos* Narciso del Valle and José Cordero, the white creoles José María España and Manuel Gual, and foreign residents José Rusiñol, Patricio Ronán, and Juan Picornell.[51] All of them wrote pamphlets and songs, encouraged people to read and circulate revolutionary texts, recruited people to attend their meetings in La Guaira, and sought to communicate with each other with the purpose of elaborating a political plan.

The La Guaira movement ultimately failed, but this case shows that revolutionary ideas and experiences from the Caribbean traveled to the mainland, where individual actors received, interpreted, and reproduced words, ideas, and practices through particular social networks, elevating their local struggles into an Atlantic political struggle. In La Guaira, people of diverse sociocial backgrounds dealt with the ambiguity that the example of Saint-Domingue represented. They tried to offer the promise of a "multiethnic" political movement to the population of African descent while

---

[49] "Informe de la Real Audiencia de Caracas sobre la sublevación que se ha descubierto en aquella Capital, 18/7/1797," AGI, Caracas, 434, no. 232.

[50] Pedro Grases, *Derechos del hombre y del ciudadano* (Caracas: Academia Nacional de la Historia, 1959); Grases, *La conspiración de Gual y España*; López Bohorquez, *Manuel Gual y José María España*.

[51] See Ramón Aizpurua, "La conspiración por dentro: Un análisis de las declaraciones de la conspiración de La Guaira de 1797," in Aizpurua, *Gual y España*, 213–44.

guaranteeing political control and social order to white elites. Local people of different socioracial groups, status, and occupations sought to create a new political movement, but their divergent agendas ultimately complicated the unity of the plan.

A year later, in 1798, another slave conspiracy was discovered by colonial officials in the town of Cariaco, in the Gulf of Paria, in the Venezuelan east. Enslaved people from different plantations had planned to rise up on the morning of 10 January, when most of the whites would be attending mass. A free mulatto man, Francisco Villaviciosa, heard that slaves had been holding suspicious meetings and revealed the plans of the revolt to a local hacendado. According to Villaviciosa, the Black insurgents intended to "take control of the city, declare war and kill all the whites, and announce their freedom."[52] Venezuela's captain-general appointed Captain Luis Mejía and his troops to control the situation in Cariaco. Within a short time, Mejía successfully apprehended the alleged ringleaders and defused the rebellion. In the opinion of the captain-general, this conspiracy was inspired by Black men who traveled back and forth between Trinidad, now controlled by the British, and the coast west of Cumaná.[53]

The contagion was allegedly widespread, penetrating nearby districts. During Holy Week 1799, the *pardo* Corporal Manuel Yturén denounced a slave conspiracy in the heavily fortified port city of Cartagena in New Granada. Apparently, a group of French slaves, recently bought by naval officers, had allied with Black local residents and conspired to rebel against their masters. The main goals of the movement were to kill all the whites, including the governor, to seize the town's fortresses, and to plunder the city. The French slaves supposedly had convinced a local Black militiaman to join their movement. The group had also tried to recruit Yturén, along with his *pardo* militia unit, though he promptly reported the conspiracy to the governor of Cartagena, Don Anastasio Zejudo.[54] Zejudo acted immediately, arresting six French slaves and securing the port. Two conspirators, however,

---

[52] Manuel Vicente Magallanes, *Luchas e insurrecciones en la Venezuela colonial* (Caracas: Academia Nacional de la Historia, 1982), 203–4.

[53] "Vicente Emparan al Gob. Y Cap. Gral. Anuncia regreso de los hombres que fueron a Cariaco a dominar una sublevación de negros. Cumaná, 2 de marzo de 1798," AGN, Gobernación y Cap. General, LXVIII, 351–2.

[54] Ermila Troconis de Veracochea, *Documentos para el estudio de los esclavos negros de Venezuela* (Caracas: Academia Nacional de La Historia, 1969), 325–8; Aline Helg, "A Fragmented Majority: Free 'of All Colors,' Indians, and Slaves in Caribbean Colombia during the Haitian Revolution," in David P. Geggus, ed., *The Impact of the Haitian Revolution in the Atlantic World* (Columbia, SC: University of South Carolina Press, 2001), 157–75.

managed to escape and set fire to a hacienda near the city. A week after the discovery of the plot, Cartagena's governor announced that he had arrested all those who had been implicated. At the same time, he asked for additional military support from Spain to reinforce the Cartagena coast guard, which remained, in his opinion, extremely vulnerable to attacks by French Black corsairs.[55]

A month later, in May 1799, a similar movement was uncovered in the Venezuelan port of Maracaibo. This movement was denounced by the *pardo* militiaman Francisco Pirela, who reported that French Black corsairs, the leaders of the conspiracy, had encouraged local *pardos*, mulattoes, and slaves to "introduce into the city the same system of freedom and equality that has reduced to total ruin ... the French ports of the island of Saint-Domingue."[56] The movement was named "The Pirela Conspiracy." The colonial authorities in Maracaibo acted quickly, arresting the main suspects and securing the region. Inevitably, colonial officials – in Cartagena and Maracaibo but also in the inland capital cities of Bogotá and Caracas – linked the two alleged conspiracies. They expressed great concern about the influence of French Black corsairs in these coastal communities, which were populated mostly by people of African descent and Indigenous communities.

This movement was supposedly planned by some local *pardos* or free men of color, in conjunction with the captains and crewmembers of two visiting ships from Port-au-Prince in Saint-Domingue. After months of investigation, however, the colonial authorities were not able to identify more than two suspects among the local population; most of the accused conspirators were Black corsairs who were stationed for two months in Maracaibo. The conspiracy languished because its leaders had failed to secure sufficient popular support. On the one hand, Maracaibo, like Cartagena and other coastal cities on the mainland, was divided along stark socioracial lines that hindered any effort at collaboration between *pardos* and Black people. Many *pardos* in Maracaibo were slaveowners and probably would not have been interested in joining a revolutionary movement organized by Black insurgents, or one that advocated the abolition of slavery. On the other hand, it is clear that the leaders of the movement lacked the time and strategic methods to promulgate their ideas and coordinate common actions among different

---

[55] Helg, "A Fragmented Majority," 160–2.
[56] "Comunicación del Gobernador de Maracaibo, Don Juan Ignacio de la Armada, al Capitán General de Venezuela, Guevara Vasconcelos, May 1799," AGI, Estado 71, no. 3.

social groups. Local participation was minimal: the locals who did hear of the movement may well have perceived it as a foreign plan with little connection to the daily social reality of the city. The foreign conspirators' ultimate failure to win broad support from the local population reveals that local people of African descent were not interested in following foreign leaders who seemed unaware of their complex local realities.[57]

Conclusions

During the final years of the eighteenth century, Spanish colonial officials became convinced that news and images of the Haitian Revolution and associated ideological forces had reached the Caribbean coasts of Venezuela and New Granada. The quick and thorough expansion of revolutionary ideas, the example of Haiti, the development of local rebellions and conspiracies, and the fear of foreign invasion all left strong impressions on the coastal populations, who wanted to see change and improvements in their lives. By the end of the eighteenth century, the concepts of liberty, equality, emancipation, and racial fraternity had become more familiar and tangible for these populations that sought to challenge the status quo. Colonial officials and white elites, for their part, began to reconsider their relationship with mixed-race, free Black, and enslaved groups. Rumors of revolution, especially those carrying news and ideas from the French colonies, made them particularly suspicious of people of African descent, undermining a fragile sense of unity and loyalty that they imagined had existed before the development of the Atlantic Revolutions. In fact, those people most dedicated to preventing the outbreak of conflict and war were enslavers and colonial authorities – two groups of people who benefited immensely from a colonial system based on the brutal system of slavery. For them, the instinctive response to rebellion and conspiracies was fear and repression, but the very sense of mistrust and fear, surprisingly, encouraged them to also open new spaces of negotiation with local Black people, both enslaved and free.

In 1801, the captain-general of Venezuela confessed that when he arrived in Venezuela he was deeply committed to accomplishing the important assignment that the king of Spain had given him: "to introduce and keep peace among his [the king's] vassals, and to eradicate, if possible, the deepest

---

[57] Soriano, *Tides of Revolution*, Chapter 6.

root of disagreement."[58] He also recognized that his mission was not an easy one, since he needed to achieve calmness in the middle of the tempest: on the one hand, he must control the external incendiary news and narratives of revolution that flooded the province; and on the other, he needed to find agreement and harmony among different socioracial groups which had engaged in tense and conflictual relationships fed by mutual mistrust, fear, and desire for revenge.

The vast and open coast of the province of Venezuela made the first goal particularly difficult, but the captain-general was aware that socioracial frictions and injustices created important tensions and that it was the colonial state's responsibility to keep social order while maintaining justice. Therefore, he needed to set new boundaries: limiting the abuses by the white elites and controlling the challenges of subordinated groups of color. During the years Guevara Vasconcelos was captain-general, he issued several orders requiring greater vigilance and control of people of African descent and the Indigenous populations by white masters and local authorities, but also encouraged masters and colonial authorities to moderate their punishments and use rational methods to discipline slaves and control free workers of color. The royal authorities demanded that local rulers soften their disciplinary techniques and try out new strategies to please the increasingly discontented population of color in order to restore the quietude of the region. Slaves and free people of African descent, for their part, perceived this shift in colonial authorities' dispositions and demanded more attention, made accusations of abuses, and were more diligent and decisive in presenting their petitions to the colonial authorities. This new wave of adjustments and negotiation made clear that the tangible realities of the Caribbean revolutions had exposed the fragility of Spanish colonial rule, awakening a new political awareness among colonial agents and subjects living on the northern coasts of Venezuela and New Granada. The opening of new spaces for negotiation kept this region in a tense and fragile calmness that would be interrupted later, in 1808, when Napoleon's invasion of Spain created a new and decisive crisis in the Spanish American territories.

---

[58] "El Capitán General de Venezuela, Manuel Guevara Vasconcelos, informa el estado político de las Provincias de su mando, medida que há tomado y toma para ello, y las buenas consequencias que de todo espera en obsequio del mejor servicio al Rey. Caracas, 28 de enero de 1801." AGI, Caracas, 98.

29

The Impact of the Haitian Revolution on the United States

ASHLI WHITE

As histories of the Haitian Revolution have become at once more nuanced and more wide-ranging, so, too, has our understanding of its impact on numerous sites throughout the Atlantic world. The United States is an especially significant place to consider this influence. Its position as the first independent republic in the Americas raises fascinating questions about its relationship with Haiti, the second New World nation. In recent decades, scholars have located signs of the revolution's effects on the United States everywhere from the president's cabinet to the theater, from the burgeoning press to the whisperings of the enslaved, and from the counting house to plantation quarters. This pervasiveness meant that all sectors of society – high, middling, and low; enslaved and free; men and women – felt the reverberations of the Haitian Revolution. In the early US republic, it seems that no segment of the population and no arena of activity remained untouched by this seminal event.[1]

This chapter brings together several of these crucial influences around a central contradiction that plagued the early United States and revolutionary Saint-Domingue, namely the realization of republican ideals in an Atlantic world driven by plantation economies. Elites in both places struggled with the problem of how to establish societies built on new formulations of freedom and equality and, at the same time, maintain an economic base of plantation commodities. As protests by the enslaved made clear, the economic project, with its dependence on coerced labor, conflicted baldly with

---

[1] My book *Encountering Revolution: Haiti and the Making of the Early Republic* (Baltimore: Johns Hopkins University Press, 2010) undergirds this interpretation, and I encourage readers to consult it for more in-depth coverage of the issues explored in this chapter (and of some issues that, given space considerations, are not). To avoid tedious, self-referential footnotes, this chapter's citations include only primary sources and the works of colleagues whose scholarship I have found insightful for the specific themes covered in this selective appraisal of the Haitian Revolution's impact.

the ideological one. In the United States and revolutionary Saint-Domingue, however, rulers felt compelled to preserve plantation economies, in part because of racism and personal economic interests. Their commitment also resulted from the structural constraints of Atlantic mercantilism, which had shaped the economies of Saint-Domingue and North America around plantation commodities – either cultivating them directly or supporting those regions that did. Under pressure to revive their economies as quickly as possible in the aftermath of revolution, leaders in both sites relied on prerevolutionary economic roots.

US and Saint-Dominguan approaches to this key problem of the age of revolutions developed not in isolation but in tandem. To follow the waves of action and reaction, this chapter organizes their relationship into four major phases – ones that track chronologically with the revolution and that highlight major aspects of the clash between republican ideals and oppressive economic systems. The first considers the development of economic, social, and intellectual ties between the French colony and the United States during the American Revolution and the 1780s, demonstrating the ways that these connections, while new, became fundamental to the profitability of both regions. This context helps to explain why, as soon as disruption rippled through the French colony in 1789, Americans took such a keen and active interest. The second section examines the years from 1789 to 1792, when white and Black Americans tried to make sense of the various forms of unrest in Saint-Domingue: political discord among whites, protest by *gens de couleur* (free people of African descent), and slave insurrection. Observers struggled to determine whether these challenges might result in changes beneficial for or detrimental to the United States and its republican project.

The third section appraises the longest stage of the Haitian Revolution (1793–1802) – its republican phase during which the aims of the French revolutionaries and former slaves formally aligned. The landmark policies of abolition and citizenship to freedmen challenged US slaveowners and abolitionists alike, and inspired Black Americans, even if their abilities to act on that inspiration were circumscribed. Although slavery was outlawed on the island, republican Saint-Domingue remained wedded to plantation agriculture, and this commitment shaped its relationship with the United States in unexpected ways. Finally, the chapter assesses the consequences of the transformation of the Haitian Revolution into a war for independence (1802–1804). The last stage of the war and the rise of the second nation in the Americas had material and ideological effects for the United States that would resonate throughout the nineteenth century and beyond.

Taken together, these sections show us the dynamic process of Americans responding to this landmark event as it transpired – their almost constant engagement with and attempts to use the revolution to their own benefit. The Haitian Revolution exposed the tensions that lay at the heart of a republic still attached to plantation economies. As the French republican approach to this problem unfolded in Saint-Domingue, Americans were forced to confront the feasibility of their slaveholding republic.

Foundations

In 1776, the French colony of Saint-Domingue was one of the most lucrative places in the Americas. In that year, it produced more wealth than the entirety of Spanish America, or, in another estimate, more than the British Caribbean colonies combined. By either measure, its affluence was extraordinary, and made it an economic pillar of the French colonial system.[2] The recently declared independent states in North America hoped that Saint-Domingue might serve as one of their economic cornerstones, too. Officially cut off from British trade circuits, Americans needed outlets to buy and sell commodities – in the short term, to back the war effort, and in the long term, to ensure the economic viability of their nation. While US diplomats pursued treaties with several European powers for these ends, a deal with France was seen as crucial, partially because of the wealth and proximity of Saint-Domingue. Americans reasoned that the French colony could help to fill the gap left by the British Caribbean, providing the United States with sugar and its various by-products as well as indigo, coffee, cotton, and enslaved people, in return for the provisions harvested from American farms, forests, and oceans. What's more, decades of illegal trading with Saint-Domingue had given merchants a sample of the profitable possibilities.[3]

With the Treaty of Amity and Commerce of 1778, North Americans gained formal access to Saint-Domingue, and this was a tactical advantage during the war. The patriots received concrete military and material support via the French colony. The island funneled supplies and sent soldiers, including some of African descent, to North America to fight on the

---

[2] James E. McClellan III, *Colonialism and Science: Saint-Domingue in the Old Regime* (Baltimore: Johns Hopkins University Press, 1992), 2.
[3] Cathy Matson, "A Port in the Storm: Philadelphia's Commerce during the Atlantic Revolutionary Era," in Thomas Bender, Laurent Dubois, and Richard Rabinowitz, eds., *Revolution! The Atlantic World Reborn* (New York: D. Giles, 2011), 65–90: 68.

Franco-American side. It was also a key waystation for the French navy, which proved decisive in, most famously, the Battle of Yorktown. Viewed from the French perspective, the agreement with the Americans appeased Saint-Dominguan planters who, chafing under the mercantilist policies of the *exclusif*, had agitated for more liberal trade relations. The treaty gave them some of the new, legitimate commercial outlets they desired and, for the moment, cemented their loyalty to the metropole that had widened their economic field.[4]

In the immediate aftermath of war, the inevitable depression dampened volume and yields. So, too, did French doubts about the wisdom of open traffic with the North Americans. By the end of the decade, however, merchants in Saint-Domingue and the United States witnessed plenty of profits and potential – so much so that they understood their commercial relationship as one of boundless opportunity. Mercantile firms established offices at both sites. Stephen Girard, after clerking in Cap Français and Port-au-Prince, made his way to New York and then eventually to Philadelphia to set up his own house, specializing in Francophone commerce. Samuel Perkins went in the other direction, moving from Boston to Cap Français in 1785 and staying for the next nine years.[5]

Mercantile connections facilitated other ties. As ships ferried goods between Saint-Dominguan and US seaports, they promoted the flow of news, carrying letters, pamphlets, and newspapers, and when docked, sailors – white and Black – disseminated stories, too. Passengers traveled on those same vessels – some, like Girard and Perkins, migrating for long periods, and others, usually wealthy planter families with retinues of enslaved persons, looking for a temporary respite from the sultry Caribbean summer. Emerging scientific communities in Philadelphia (the American Philosophical Society) and in Cap Français (the Cercle des

---

[4] Paul Cheney, "A False Dawn for Enlightenment Cosmopolitanism? Franco-American Trade during the American War of Independence," *The William and Mary Quarterly* 63:3 (2006), 463–88; Manuel Covo, *Entrepôt of Revolutions: Saint-Domingue, Commercial Sovereignty, and the French–American Alliance* (New York: Oxford University Press, 2022); John D. Garrigus, *Before Haiti: Race and Citizenship in French Saint-Domingue* (New York: Palgrave Macmillan, 2006), 209–10.

[5] Covo, *Entrepôt of Revolutions*; James Alexander Dun, "'What Avenues of Commerce, Will You, Americans, Not Explore!': Commercial Philadelphia's Vantage onto the Early Haitian Revolution," *The William and Mary Quarterly* 64:3 (2005), 473–504: 481–2; Matson, "A Port in the Storm," 71–6; Samuel Perkins, "Sketches of St. Domingo from January 1785 to December 1794, written by a Resident Merchant at the Request of a Friend, December 1835," *Proceedings of the Massachusetts Historical Society* 2 (1886), 305–90.

Philadelphes) maintained correspondence with and extended membership to one another.[6]

Although separated (at least officially) by rival imperial systems for centuries, Saint-Domingue and the United States soon discovered that they were, in the words of one observer, "congenially suited to each other."[7] By the end of the 1780s, US trade with Saint-Domingue ranked second (behind trade with Great Britain) in terms of its volume and value to the national economy. Not surprisingly, then, elites in both places nurtured the notion that their relationship was crucial to future economic interests. This outlook helps to explain why, as Saint-Domingue began to experience revolutionary tremors, Americans were not distant observers, but felt the effects acutely.

First Ruptures

Word of political turmoil in Saint-Domingue arrived in the United States in the fall of 1789. The French Revolution had, it seemed, reached its most prized Caribbean colony and instigated a rapid series of disturbances that shook the social order. Americans learned how discontented and politically marginalized white men (known as *petits blancs*) turned to the National Assembly in Paris to agitate for greater political voice in Saint-Domingue. The colony's ruling elite (referred to as *grands blancs*) countered, using their leverage in the capital to attempt to expand their control in Saint-Domingue. The two groups came to blows in St. Marc, in the western province, and soon discord – political and physical – spread throughout the colony. The pressing demands of free people of African descent further complicated the factionalism among the master class. Although they were economically powerful, especially in the southern province, they were denied political and civil rights, and they lobbied Paris to ensure that the 1789 Declaration of the Rights of Man and Citizen applied to them as well. Frustrated with white colonial resistance to any concession on this front (including very limited ones made by the National Assembly in 1790), Vincent Ogé led his fellow *gens de couleur* to take up arms and assert their rights. As the master class fought among itself, enslaved people on the northern plain saw an opportunity to make their bid for liberty and rebelled in the summer of 1791.

---

[6] McClellan, *Colonialism and Science*; Julius S. Scott, *The Common Wind: Afro-American Currents in the Age of the Haitian Revolution* (London: Verso, 2018).
[7] Quoted in Matson, "A Port in the Storm," 74.

Between 1789 and 1792, the news from Saint-Domingue came fast and furious to the United States. Reports sometimes conflicted, or quickly became outdated, and Americans had to parse accounts in order to make sense of what was happening in the colony and what it meant for them. Initially, white observers in the United States, particularly merchants, were concerned about the impact of political developments on trade with the island. On the one hand, the disruptions could adversely affect commerce, but on the other, they could prove a boon, increasing demand for all kinds of goods. Merchants tried to secure reliable information about the market for provisions, the availability of colonial commodities, and the attitudes of port officials, and they speculated about whether the unrest signaled a possible loosening of restrictive trade regulations. Despite contradictory reports on all fronts, American merchants were undeterred, and in the case of Philadelphia alone, vessels from Saint-Domingue comprised anywhere between one-fifth and one-quarter of the total number of foreign ships entering the city between 1789 and 1792.[8] Discord offered other economic advantages, too. US slavers surpassed Spanish and French competitors to become, by 1793, the leading reexporters of enslaved people from Saint-Domingue to Cuba.[9]

Merchants were not the only Americans interested in events in Saint-Domingue. The persistent traffic between Saint-Domingue and the United States abetted the dissemination of news to diverse sectors of the population, including to Black Americans. Black sailors were a common sight on the high seas, even on vessels sailing between the Caribbean and the United States, and wherever they moored, they circulated information among people of African descent. Enslaved and freed people also learned about events in Saint-Domingue from the press, albeit indirectly. Caught up in tracking the latest news from the island, the white population discussed it, without discretion, and as a result, reports about the slaves' fight for liberty and about *gens de couleur* demanding equality circulated openly. Some state legislatures tried to clamp down on this flow of information, wary of what it might stir up among enslaved inhabitants. In December 1792 the Virginia assembly, attempting to

---

[8] Dun, "What Avenues," 477. On parsing, see James Alexander Dun, *Dangerous Neighbors: Making the Haitian Revolution in Early America* (Philadelphia: University of Pennsylvania Press, 2016), Chapter 1.

[9] Scott, *Common Wind*, 139. On transshipment, see Gregory O'Malley, *Final Passages: The Intercolonial Slave Trade of British North America, 1619–1807* (Chapel Hill: University of North Carolina Press, 2014), Chapter 8; Elena Schneider, *The Occupation of Havana: War, Trade, and Slavery in the Atlantic World* (Chapel Hill: University of North Carolina Press, 2018), Chapter 6.

check "idle & busyheaded people ... [who] forge & divulge false rumors & reports," passed an "Act against divulgers of false news."[10]

As the concerns of the Virginia legislature suggest, there was some recognition – among both white and Black residents – that the political uproar in Saint-Domingue had dimensions that distinguished it from its metropolitan counterpart. While Americans almost uniformly celebrated the early moments of the French Revolution, seeing them (in a self-congratulatory manner) as a continuation of the US revolution, the racial dimensions of its colonial repercussions gave white Americans pause and Black Americans cause for hope. In the late summer of 1791, the federal government and the state of South Carolina responded to white Saint-Dominguan planters' pleas for aid to quell the slave rebellion. The governor of South Carolina expressed his state's support in terms of racial solidarity, explaining that the insurrection in the French colony threw into stark relief the parity between the slaveholders in Saint-Domingue and those in his state.[11]

At the same time, some white commentators on the island and throughout the Atlantic world contended that "philanthropists," namely the Société des Amis des Noirs (Society of Friends of the Blacks) and other antislavery groups, were responsible for the slave rebellion in Saint-Domingue. They accused abolitionists of distributing pamphlets, medallions, and other inflammatory items to the enslaved, encouraging them to take up arms.[12] There is some evidence that French officials were worried about antislavery iconography reaching the West Indies. In October 1789, the intendant of the colony, François Barbé-Marbois, and its governor, Louis-Antoine Thomassin, comte de Peynier, had written to the Minister of the Navy in France because they had heard a rumor about the arrival of some earthenware plates, painted with "a kneeling black man stretching his chained hands toward a white man; underneath is this inscription: *am I not also your brother*" ("un negre à genoux élevant ses mains chargées de chaînes vers un blanc; on lit au dessous cette inscription: *ne suis je pas aussi ton frère*"). The administrators admitted that although the sentiment was "humane," it was perhaps "too humane" to

---

[10] Quoted in Scott, *Common Wind*, 142; Dun, *Dangerous Neighbors*, Chapter 2.
[11] Dun, *Dangerous Neighbors*, 69.
[12] On the activities of the small minority of white philanthropists during the Haitian Revolution, see Erica R. Johnson, *Philanthropy and Race in the Haitian Revolution* (London: Palgrave Macmillan, 2018) and Erica Johnson Edwards' Chapter 4 in this volume.

travel on naval vessels, especially those cruising the Caribbean.[13] The possibility of such objects circulating among enslaved people in Saint-Domingue is fascinating, yet difficult to verify. Nevertheless, by attributing the inspiration for the slave insurrection to the distribution of antislavery items, white observers insinuated that the enslaved would not have rebelled without such a prompt. The implication was that they lacked the motive and capacity to devise the scheme on their own.

For the emerging US abolition movement, these accusations about the early phase of the Haitian Revolution had the potential to threaten their endeavors. As of 1791, every northern state, except New York and New Jersey, had passed legislation to enact an achingly gradual end of slavery, and by 1804, the two northern holdouts had joined the cause. State manumission laws projected freedom into the future, liberating children born after a certain date, but requiring that they serve periods of indenture, sometimes for as long as twenty-eight years, to masters. It was a cautious and paternalistic approach to emancipation, one controlled by white men with little input from people of African descent, and one designed, in the patronizing view of the times, to accustom slaveholders and the enslaved to freedom. The insurrection in Saint-Domingue was a form of liberation that manumission societies wanted to avoid, so they disassociated their activities from it.

Their response was a source of frustration to a few white men in the ideological vanguard, such as Abraham Bishop. In 1791, he published "Rights of Black Men," a series of articles that appeared in several northern newspapers. Bishop argued that the slave insurrection in Saint-Domingue was a just movement, fought in the name of liberty and equality, and he defended enslaved people's decision to seize their rights through violence. On this premise, he chastised American abolitionist societies for their lack of support for rebelling slaves in Saint-Domingue, mocking how white Americans, including abolitionists, recoiled at any word of the enslaved striking out against oppressors. In one passage, he describes a weekly news cycle about slavery, in which on Wednesday, "we" (the abolitionists) find "distressing" the report of "insurgents" in the West Indies killing forty-three white people and taking twelve prisoners. On Thursday, however, it is "comforting" that a group of slaves "sallying out upon the whites" was repulsed and that "20 were taken and hung on a gallows, after some exemplary tortures." He goes

---

[13] Many thanks to Jeremy Popkin for generously sharing this document. Letter from Intendant Barbé-Marbois and Governor de Peynier, 10 October 1789, Archives Nationales, Paris, Series C 9 A 162.

on to ridicule the form and stance of manumission societies: "On Friday evening, the society for the abolition of slavery is convened, where the President, Vice-President, the honourable and esquirated Members of the corresponding Committee, the Secretary, Vice-Secretary, Treasurer and Vice-Treasurer, and honourable Members, are unanimously of opinion, that though the blacks are entitled to freedom, they ought to *have petitioned for it*, and not to have taken up arms."[14] Weighed down by its hierarchical bureaucracy and love of procedure, the abolitionists scuttle the very ideals they purport to defend.

Bishop, however, was one of the few willing to call publicly for rights for Black men, but no doubt hundreds of thousands of Black Americans wanted the same, as evidenced by the writings of Black abolitionists during the American Revolution.[15] That said, there was a moment in this early phase of the Haitian Revolution when white Americans debated the extension of rights to free men of color, or *gens de couleur*. After months of campaigning in Paris in 1789–1790, free men of African descent won a limited concession, namely a law that recognized the rights of men born of free grandparents (a circumstance which applied to few individuals). Further lobbying of the republican legislature, combined with metropolitan shock at the brutal execution of Ogé in Saint-Domingue, resulted in more ambitious legislation pertaining to *gens de couleur*. The law of 4 April 1792 granted all men of color the rights of citizens – a measure at which *grands* and *petits blancs* recoiled. Although white Americans were against this legislation because of its challenge to racism, reports in the US press mused that the acceptance of the law might be the only way to save the colony. By consenting to the law, the white population would prevent *gens de couleur* from finding common cause with the enslaved, and with the master class – white and *de couleur* – no longer at loggerheads, they could work together to bring the slave rebellion under control.[16] This line of reasoning was a strain of realpolitik that sidestepped racism, in this specific instance only, to uphold slavery.

---

[14] Tim Mathewson, "Abraham Bishop, 'The Rights of Black Men,' and the American Reaction to the Haitian Revolution," *Journal of Negro History* 67:2 (1982), 151–2. See also Manisha Sinha, *The Slave's Cause: A History of Abolition* (New Haven: Yale University Press, 2016), 59–60.
[15] Sinha, *The Slave's Cause*, 41–7.
[16] James Alexander Dun, "(Mis)reading the Revolution: Philadelphia and 'St. Domingo,' 1789–1792," in Elizabeth Maddock Dixon and Michael J. Drexler, eds., *The Haitian Revolution and the Early United States: Histories, Textualities, Geographies* (Philadelphia: University of Pennsylvania Press, 2016), 42–57.

For white Americans, considerations on this front were short-lived and eclipsed by events the following year. Yet, their toying with this possibility was in keeping with their general view of the early years of the Haitian Revolution as a set of disturbances. To be sure, they recognized that some of these disruptions – the battles between white factions, and between free people of African descent and white inhabitants – had political content. But they thought these controversies would eventually be adjudicated by the metropole. As for the slave rebellion, although lone voices went on record to cast it as a sweeping call for freedom, white Americans classified it among revolts that had punctuated the Atlantic world for centuries. They consistently refused to acknowledge the political agenda of the enslaved. Meanwhile, Black Americans held their breath, waiting to see whether rebellion would become revolution. In 1793, they got their answer.

Republican Promises and Problems

The year 1793 was a major turning point in the war on Saint-Domingue and in its impact on the United States. The slave insurrection united with the French Revolution when, in the summer of that year, the republican commissioners, Léger-Félicité Sonthonax and Étienne Polverel, faced losing control of the colony to counterrevolutionary forces, and so they offered emancipation to any Black rebel willing to fight on the republican side. Thousands made the switch, turning the tide in the critical battle of Le Cap in June 1793 (Figure 29.1), and forcing many Saint-Dominguans into exile in the United States. While the commissioners' measure was a tactic made necessary by the nature of the war in Saint-Domingue, the Jacobin-controlled National Convention embraced their decision, and in February 1794 expanded it: slavery was abolished in the French West Indies, and all men were granted the rights of citizens.

The implementation of this legislation, however, was fraught. For the next eight years, the war in Saint-Domingue worked to translate the laws of freedom and citizenship into a lived reality on the ground. As part of this undertaking, republican forces had to fend off a British invasion (1794–1798) as well as quell counterrevolutionary elements within the colony. Moreover, the metropole missed the financial windfall of prerevolutionary Saint-Domingue and pressed its colonial officials to find ways to resume plantation agriculture. Central to both endeavors was Toussaint Louverture. His meteoric rise and increasing power captured the attention of people of African descent throughout the Atlantic world and of elites in the United States, Britain, and France.

The Impact of the Haitian Revolution

Figure 29.1 Pillaging of Cap Français, 1793. Courtesy of the John Carter Brown Library.

Under his rule, the French experiment with a plantation economy and freed laborers reached its fullest, if vexed, realization.

Audiences in the United States could barely keep up with the pace of events in Saint-Domingue during this republican phase, and the volume and effect of the news were amplified by the arrival of exiles from the French colony. Although some Saint-Dominguans had left the colony in preceding years, the battle of Le Cap sent thousands of whites, Blacks, and free people of African descent to cities along the eastern seaboard, and waves of refugees continued to migrate over the next ten years, with a final surge to New Orleans (via Cuba) in 1809.[17] The very presence of Saint-Dominguans made

---

[17] Recent studies of the refugees include Susan Branson and Leslie Patrick, "Étrangers dans un pays étrange: Saint-Domingan Refugees of Color in Philadelphia," in David P. Geggus, ed., *The Impact of the Haitian Revolution in the Atlantic World* (Columbia, SC: University of South Carolina Press, 2001); Carl A. Brasseaux and Glenn R. Conrad, eds., *The Road to Louisiana: The Saint-Domingue Refugees, 1792–1809* (Lafayette: University of Southwest Louisiana Press, 1992); Emily Clark, *The Strange History of the American Quadroon: Free Women of Color in the Revolutionary Atlantic World* (Chapel

manifest the consequences of republican policies in the colony, and, in the United States, the most controversial (or, seen from the perspective of Black Americans, the most promising) policies were the abolition of slavery and the granting of rights of citizens to freedmen.

Prior to 1793, both antislavery and proslavery observers categorized the uprising of the enslaved in Saint-Domingue as a slave rebellion, one with unique facets to be sure, but still akin to others that had been experienced across the Atlantic world for centuries. Yet, with the emancipation decrees, the rebel slaves became republican revolutionaries, and this legitimacy added a new urgency to the conversation over abolition. The explanatory fiction promoted in 1791 – that the antislavery movement was to blame for the insurrection – took on greater proportions after 1793–1794, which seemed to affirm, in some minds, that the rebellion had been an abolitionist plot from the start. They blamed the continuation of war on the island not on the British invasion or on resistance from counterrevolutionary forces but on the "false philanthropy" of misguided activists who liberated men and made them citizens well before they were prepared for either. Claiming the privileged knowledge of eyewitnesses, white refugees in the United States perpetuated this explanation in the press. They complained that abolitionists had "let loose on the white race 500,000 black and yellow tigers" who wanted "to drink the blood" of their former masters.[18] In this reading, the war was fought not to secure liberty and equality, but for revenge.

Hill: University of North Carolina Press, 2013), Chapters 1 and 2; John Davies, "Class, Culture, and Color: Black Saint-Dominguan Refugees and African-American Communities in the Early Republic" (Ph.D. dissertation, University of Delaware, 2008); Nathalie Dessens, *From Saint-Domingue to New Orleans: Migration and Influences* (Gainsville: University Press of Florida, 2007); Paul Lachance, "The Formation of a Three-Caste Society," *Social Science History* 18:2 (1994), 211–42; Paul Lachance, "The Politics of Fear: French Louisianans and the Slave Trade, 1786–1809," *Plantation Society in the Americas* 1:22 (1979), 162–97; R. Darrell Meadows, "Engineering Exile: Social Networks and the French Atlantic Community, 1789–1809," *French Historical Studies* 23:1 (2000), 67–102; R. Darrell Meadows, "The Planters of Saint-Domingue, 1750–1804" (Ph.D. dissertation, Carnegie Mellon University, 2004); José Morales, "The Hispaniola Diaspora, 1791–1850: Puerto Rico, Cuba, Louisiana, and Other Host Societies" (Ph.D. dissertation, University of Connecticut, 1986); Gary Nash, "Reverberations of Haiti in the American North," *Explorations in Early American Culture: A Special Supplemental Issue of Pennsylvania History* 65 (1998), 44–73; Jennifer J. Pierce, "Discourses of the Dispossessed: Saint-Domingue Colonists on Race, Revolution and Empire, 1789–1825" (Ph.D. dissertation, Binghamton University, 2005); Jeremy D. Popkin, *You Are All Free: The Haitian Revolution and the Abolition of Slavery* (New York: Cambridge University Press, 2010), Chapter 9; Bertrand Van Ruymbeke, "*Refugiés* or *Émigrés*? Early Modern French Migrations to British North America and the United States (1680–1820)," *Itinerario* 30:2 (2006), 1–17.

[18] *Gazette française* (New York), 23 March 1796.

The turmoil in the colony was cast as the result of emancipation (rather than of slavery and racism), and this interpretation fell on receptive ears among slavery's adherents. As the war in Saint-Domingue dragged on in the mid-1790s, US slaveowners brooded over the possibilities of such "bloody scenes" coming to North America. That said, they also looked for ways to, as Thomas Jefferson put it, "try to avert" those scenes.[19] To this end, white Americans took measures both rhetorical and concrete throughout the 1790s. First, they worked to distinguish between North American and French Caribbean slavery, characterizing the latter as more brutal and horrific than its US counterpart. This distinction helped to explain (along with those misguided abolitionists) the explosion of violence on Saint-Domingue: slave masters there, through their sadism, had created an enslaved population bent on retribution. The theory was that better treatment of the enslaved (or, in the slaveowners' self-serving view, continued better treatment) would protect US masters from a similar fate. Second, since these "French negroes," as white Americans called Black Saint-Dominguans, were so dangerous, the United States should bar their entry into North America. A ban would prevent them from importing their rebellion to the United States – either through their own actions or by goading American slaves to take up arms, and during the 1790s individual states passed laws that limited or prohibited altogether the migration of the enslaved and free people of African descent from the West Indies.

This approach to the threat of "French negroes" ran into a practical problem: the waves of refugees from Saint-Domingue. Throughout the republican phase of the war, white exiles showed up in Charleston, Norfolk, Baltimore, Philadelphia, New York, Boston, and elsewhere – often with people whom they defined as slaves in tow. To circumvent the exclusionary laws, white Saint-Dominguans argued that these enslaved people were essential to their livelihoods in the United States and insisted that they were not firebrands. Perhaps persuaded by these claims, white Americans found themselves, from "motives of humanity," evading their own laws and letting in thousands of Black refugees.[20] More practically, enforcing the law would have been logistically impossible. The bureaucratic resources available were insufficient to handle the number of exiles and the sudden nature of their migration.

---

[19] Thomas Jefferson to James Monroe, 14 July 1793, in John Catanzariti, ed., *The Papers of Thomas Jefferson* (Princeton: Princeton University Press, 1995), vol. XXVI, 503.
[20] Tommy L. Bogger, *Free Blacks in Norfolk, Virginia, 1790–1860: The Darker Side of Freedom* (Charlottesville: University Press of Virginia, 1997), 27.

White residents may, on occasion, have set aside concerns over their safety by admitting Black refugees, but their entry also raised the question of their legal status. After February 1794, all Saint-Dominguans were free, but it remained to be seen whether US cities would acknowledge French law in their jurisdictions. Dozens of brave Black refugees pressed this issue into consideration by bringing freedom suits to state courts. Both in "free" and in slaveholding states, the courts avoided engaging with French law and instead came to decisions based on state ones.[21]

The legal gymnastics are most apparent in cases where local manumission societies acted. When it came to applying American state laws related to the migration of enslaved or free Black people, abolition societies were, for the most part, motivated to intercede. In the 1780s and 1790s, manumission groups spent a good deal of energy trying to check the illegal movement of slaves and former slaves into and out of their states, and they met with some success in the enforcement of such laws – so much so that individuals in Saint-Domingue were aware of these efforts. Before migrating to Philadelphia, Mr. Aubert, a merchant in Le Cap, wrote to Stephen Girard to inquire whether he would be allowed to bring enslaved people with him. Girard warned that Aubert could take them to Pennsylvania, but if he stayed in the state longer than six months, then the law required their manumission. As a result of such laws, hundreds of Black Saint-Dominguans were manumitted, and often then indentured to their former owners, much like their Black American counterparts. This version of freedom mattered to the lives of Black refugees: it was, after all, freedom of a sort.[22] It paled, however, in comparison with the much more radical and immediate form of liberation taking shape in Saint-Domingue.

Manumission societies faltered in their attempts to advocate for "French negroes" on the grounds of French law, though. Consider the case of the widow Volunbrun, who migrated to New York City in 1797, with twenty people of African descent. They were technically free, but she claimed them as her slaves. Abolitionists did not challenge Volunbrun when she first arrived, perhaps since New York's manumission laws were not yet in effect. After New York's process of manumission began in 1799, city abolitionists defended the "French negroes" in Volunbrun's household when, in 1801, she

[21] Sue Peabody, "'Free upon Higher Ground': Saint-Domingue Slaves' Suits for Freedom in U.S. Courts, 1792–1830," in David Patrick Geggus and Norman Fiering, eds., *The World of the Haitian Revolution* (Bloomington: Indiana University Press, 2009), 261–83.
[22] Branson and Patrick, "Étrangers dans un pays étrange"; Davies, "Class, Culture, and Color"; Nash, "Reverberations of Haiti"; Sinha, *The Slave's Cause*, 61.

attempted to transport them out of the state. Word spread of her plans to move, and protestors, many of whom were Black Saint-Dominguans and Americans, gathered in front of Volunbrun's home, drawing attention to the situation. At first, the society's lawyers contested the status of the Black members of the household, citing both American and French laws. But, in the face of stiff competition in court and in the (white) public sphere, they retreated from the effort to secure US acknowledgment of the French abolition law. The widow and her entire household eventually moved – without contest – to Baltimore.[23]

Members of the US antislavery movement were, in this era, wary of being associated with the more immediate and radical version of abolition being tried in Saint-Domingue. In every American city, including the migration to New Orleans in the early nineteenth century, arguments for freedom based on French law failed – usually before they got out of the gate.[24] Equally troubling from the perspective of white Americans was that the men freed by the 1794 French law were citizens. State manumission societies in these years advocated for eventual freedom but not for immediate political or civil rights for freed people.

Although most white Americans turned away from the more capacious and direct form of freedom and citizenship evolving in Saint-Domingue, the Volunbrun case – with the scores of Black Americans and Saint-Dominguans demonstrating outside her door – reminds us that people of African descent in the United States understood the full political potential of the Haitian Revolution. Some saw events on the island as an opportunity to effect change in the United States. The most ambitious were homegrown rebellions. Throughout the 1790s, white Americans identified conspiracies in which "the negroes and mulattoes intended to serve [them] as the inhabitants of Cape-Francois were served."[25] Rumors about slave plots are interpretatively tricky – in this instance and in others across the Atlantic world. Clearly, enslaved people did conspire, repeatedly, to overthrow the master class. But slaveholders often invoked the threat of a conspiracy and rooted out its organizers for their own political and social ends, finding it a powerful and

---

[23] Peabody, "Free upon Higher Ground," 272–5; Martha S. Jones, "Time, Space, and Jurisdiction in Atlantic World Slavery: The Volunbrun Household in Gradual Emancipation New York," *Law and History Review* 29:4 (2011), 1031–60.

[24] For a discussion of similar legal issues with refugees in New Orleans, see Rebecca J. Scott, "Paper Thin: Freedom and Re-enslavement in the Diaspora of the Haitian Revolution," *Law and History Review* 29:4 (2011), 1061–87.

[25] *Virginia Chronicle* (Norfolk), 19 October 1793.

public way to reassert mastery and instill fear among the enslaved.²⁶ In the case of plots in the 1790s, white Americans attributed them to the influence of "French negroes," in keeping with the self-serving fiction that US slavery was "better" than that in Saint-Domingue, and hence only outside agitators could possibly be responsible for such schemes.²⁷

Even as masters tried to twist slave conspiracies to serve racist agendas, their explanations included the concession that there was, as poet William Wordsworth observed at the time (and historian Julius S. Scott has so brilliantly analyzed), "the common wind" that bound together different sites across the Black Atlantic and facilitated the movement of information among people of African descent.²⁸ Black people used these networks to learn about and react to the republican phase of the Haitian Revolution. In light of trenchant racism and the powerful violence that accompanied it, they faced extraordinarily constrained options when it came to embracing the revolution openly. Nevertheless, glimpses of their active support surface. They donned tricolored cockades – the symbol of revolutionary France and, in these years, of republican Saint-Domingue as well – to express their support for revolution; and they turned up at parades and other public events designed to celebrate the French Revolution, much to the consternation of some white observers.²⁹ Prince Hall, in his address to the Boston African Masonic Lodge in 1797, reviewed the "insults" that Black Americans endured "daily ... in the streets." Then, he encouraged them to persevere, invoking the example of "our African brethren ... in the French West Indies" as a sign that change was on the way.³⁰ But, for some individuals, this change took too long to reach the United States. Crispin, a young man from Malabar, indentured to Stephen Girard, fled Philadelphia for republican Saint-Domingue, hoping to find a more secure liberty and citizenship there.³¹

According to Wordsworth, Toussaint Louverture was a part of every "breathing of the common wind," which animated people of African descent

---

²⁶ On the fear that "French negroes" experienced, see Sara E. Johnson, *The Fear of French Negroes: Transcolonial Collaboration in the Revolutionary Americas* (Berkeley: University of California Press, 2012).
²⁷ James Sidbury, "Saint-Domingue in Virginia: Ideology, Local Meanings, and Resistance to Slavery, 1790–1800," *Journal of Southern History* 63:3 (1997), 531–52.
²⁸ Scott, *Common Wind*.
²⁹ Simon P. Newman, *Parades and the Politics of the Street: Festive Culture in the Early American Republic* (Philadelphia: University of Pennsylvania Press, 1997), 120–51.
³⁰ Prince Hall, *A Charge, Delivered to the African Lodge, June 24, 1797, at Menotomy* (Boston: Ben Edes, 1797), 10–11.
³¹ Stephen Girard Papers, American Philosophical Society, Philadelphia, Pennsylvania.

in this era.[32] He was also central to how white Americans understood the republican phase of the revolution. In fact, no individual personified the remarkable new possibilities and challenges of the republican phase of the Haitian Revolution more than Toussaint Louverture. Reports of his campaigns, translations of his pronouncements, and reflections on his growing influence filled the US press. In general, the tenor of these accounts was moderate, and at times, even positive. Louverture avoided the racist typecasting heaped on other Black leaders of the revolution, perhaps because of his sympathy for American merchants and his actions to reestablish the plantation economy in Saint-Domingue.[33]

Yet Louverture was not simply a subject of American scrutiny; he was an active participant in exchanges with Americans, especially when it came to commerce. The republican phase of the revolution was a tricky time for US trade with Saint-Domingue. In the early years of the British invasion of the colony, British privateers went after American ships by the hundreds, until the Jay Treaty, brokered in 1795, established terms of trade between Britain and the United States. Consequently, US vessels entered British-held ports in western Saint-Domingue and provided material support to the occupying army there. This development sparked the ire of the French government, which exacted its revenge by seizing American ships in the Caribbean whenever possible. By 1798, the United States was engaged in a "Quasi-War" with France: an embargo was passed, and some hawks in the Federalist-held Congress were calling for all-out war.

As the head of the French republican army in Saint-Domingue, Louverture was aware of the tense situation and looked for a solution. He needed trade in order to accomplish the twin goals of sustaining the war on the island and resuscitating the plantation economy. In 1798, Louverture took a bold step: in a letter to President John Adams, he offered to facilitate and protect trade between Saint-Domingue and the United States. With this proposal, Louverture was essentially circumventing the metropole in an effort to acquire essential goods, and, some speculated, to consolidate his control over the island.[34]

---

[32] William Wordsworth, "To Toussaint L'Ouverture," *Morning Post* (London), 2 February 1803, https://thelouvertureproject.org/index.php?title=To_Toussaint_Louverture_-_poem_by_Wordsworth.

[33] Matthew J. Clavin, *Toussaint Louverture and the American Civil War: The Promise and Peril of a Second Haitian Revolution* (Philadelphia: University of Pennsylvania Press, 2010), Chapter 1.

[34] Gordon S. Brown, *Toussaint's Clause: The Founding Fathers and the Haitian Revolution* (Jackson: University Press of Mississippi, 2005); Ronald Angelo Johnson, *Diplomacy in Black and White: John Adams, Toussaint Louverture, and Their Atlantic World Alliance*

The proposition became a point of political contention in the United States for several reasons, but at the heart of the issue was whether the agreement with the Black leader would challenge US slavery and hence, in the view of some observers, imperil the republic. Congress debated the measure in its February 1799 session, in the context of a renewal of the previous year's embargo of France. Arguments both for and against what became known as "Toussaint's clause" split along party (rather than sectional) lines. Democratic Republicans maintained that Louverture's interests would be "wholly black," and therefore, trade would not only bolster this "black" regime, but also provide him with the financial wherewithal and practical opportunities to export his agenda to the United States.[35] Federalists argued that trade with Louverture would, on the contrary, prevent that possibility. They contended that commerce would keep the United States better informed about events on the island, encourage Louverture's good will, and provide the United States with the economic and political means to check the leader's potential ambitions to spread abolition.

Unable to reach a decision, Congress voted to renew the embargo, but left "Toussaint's clause" to President Adams' discretion. Adams was desperate to ameliorate the economic hardship wrought by the embargo, and, after further negotiations with Louverture, he decided to reopen trade with the colony – for a year and on certain terms, which included extracting a promise from Louverture to thwart all attempts to foment rebellion in the United States. Merchants were ecstatic about their access to this "mine of gold," and the desire to cultivate a profitable relationship with Louverture soon pushed US support beyond trade to military aid.[36] In October 1800, the US frigate *General Greene* aided Louverture's final triumphant attack on his rival to the south, General André Rigaud, leading to Louverture's ascendancy over the entire island.

At the beginning of 1801, it looked as if Toussaint Louverture had secured the republican project in Saint-Domingue. Yet a central tension persisted, namely the commitment to a plantation-based economy and the promise of freedom and citizenship. It troubled the revolution in the French colony after

---

(Athens, GA: University of Georgia Press, 2014); Tim Matthewson, *A Proslavery Foreign Policy: Haitian–American Relations during the Early Republic* (Westport, CN: Praeger, 2003).

[35] Thomas Hart Benton, *Abridgment of the Debates of Congress, from 1789 to 1856* (New York: AMS Press, 1970), vol. II, 339.

[36] Ibid., vol. II, 340.

emancipation, and especially during Louverture's rule. Like his metropolitan contemporaries, he could not imagine the economic and political survival of the island in the Atlantic system on any other terms, and so he implemented policies to compel freed people to work on plantations and enforced those policies with violence. Throughout the republican phase, he and his army quelled several revolts among laborers, who resisted the circumscription of their freedom in service to the plantation regime. From the vantage point of US merchants, however, these policies – and the commodities they produced – made trade with Louverture's Saint-Domingue appealing. They also attracted the attention of Napoleon Bonaparte, who would drive the issue to its breaking point, with repercussions that resonated throughout the Atlantic world.

Independence and Its Aftershocks

Napoleon Bonaparte, First Consul of the French Republic, was none too happy with the situation in Saint-Domingue. He wanted to reinvigorate the French Atlantic empire and to reassert metropolitan control in the colony, mainly by purging the Black military leadership, particularly Louverture. To that end, in 1801, he sent his brother-in-law, General Charles-Victor-Emmanuel Leclerc, along with tens of thousands of troops, to Saint-Domingue. Initially, Bonaparte managed to hide his aims from the Black republican army in the colony. It was also unclear – to the Black revolutionaries and even to those within Bonaparte's government – what the expedition meant for emancipation.[37] The seizure, deportation, and incarceration of Louverture in the summer of 1802 raised questions about the French commitment to abolition, and the violent reinstatement of slavery in Guadeloupe confirmed the Black leadership's worst suspicions. That fall, generals Jean-Jacques Dessalines and Henry Christophe, among others, led their armies in a war against Leclerc's forces to safeguard liberty, and, within two years, they defeated the French. In January 1804, Jean-Jacques Dessalines issued the new nation's declaration of independence and gave it the name of Haiti, an indigenous term for the island.

Haiti's war of independence occurred during Thomas Jefferson's first term as president. Throughout the 1790s, Jefferson had been horrified by the

---

[37] David Geggus, "The Louisiana Purchase and the Haitian Revolution," in Dillon and Drexler, *Haitian Revolution*, 120–1.

republican phase of the revolution in Saint-Domingue and by its consequences for his vision for the United States.[38] Given his longstanding opposition to the republican project in the French colony, Jefferson was sympathetic to Bonaparte's goals – at least, at first. Approached by French officials about providing supplies for the Leclerc campaign, Jefferson pledged US support, seeing the French attack on the island as a way to remove a threat to North America. As the enormous scale of the expedition became clear, however, Jefferson saw a new danger possibly taking hold in Saint-Domingue – that of an aggressive French empire with designs not just in the Caribbean, but perhaps in North America as well, maybe even Jefferson's pet project of Louisiana. There was a good deal of speculation about what form these imperial ambitions might take – a stricter mercantilism, territorial expansion, and so forth, but whatever the details, they were all, for Jefferson, cause for alarm.[39]

Consequently, the president turned a deaf ear to French officials' calls for provisions and left it to the discretion of merchants to determine with whom they traded. Leclerc continually complained that US merchants sold to Black armies rather than French ones. Month by month the situation of the French army became more precarious, as yellow fever ravaged its ranks and as a complex web of geopolitics forced Bonaparte to reconsider his strategies. Sometime in 1803, he abandoned his western campaign and offered to sell Louisiana to the United States. Jefferson regarded the purchase as one of the greatest legacies of his presidencies – doubling the size of the country and, in the process, providing the material basis for securing his idealized "empire for liberty." Although the war for independence in Saint-Domingue may not have been the only reason for the Louisiana Purchase, the Black army's military victories certainly influenced the process. As Alexander Hamilton relished pointing out at the time, "To the deadly climate of St. Domingo, and the courage and obstinate resistance made by its black inhabitants, we are indebted for ... Louisiana."[40]

In subsequent decades, enormous swathes of Jefferson's empire for liberty became an empire for slavery, as the plantation complex pressed

---

[38] Tim Matthewson, "Jefferson and Haiti," *Journal of Southern History* 61:2 (1995), 209–48; Michael Zuckerman, *Almost Chosen People: Oblique Biographies in the American Grain* (Berkeley: University of California Press, 1993).
[39] Geggus, "Louisiana Purchase," 121.
[40] Quoted in Anon., "Hamilton on the Louisiana Purchase: A Newly-Identified Editorial from the New York Evening Post," *The William and Mary Quarterly* 12:4 (1955), 268–81: 274.

further and further west. Southern planters found a new cash crop in cotton, and its expansion throughout the southwest resulted in the dislocation and enslavement of millions of people of African descent. Slavery took on even greater centrality in the South, and the master class was brazen in the ways that it continued to build the political and economic freedom of white men on the backs of the enslaved. Yet, the specter of the Haitian Revolution still loomed large for the master class. Its members invoked the so-called "horrors of St. Domingo" to argue against emancipation, to make claims for the "benign" character of US slavery, and to undergird racist ideologies.

Although the second quarter of the nineteenth century witnessed – finally – the end of slavery in Northern states, their economies remained, in many ways, entwined with the plantation regime of the South. And while northern Black Americans were free, they endured the consequences of endemic racism, as they were judged unworthy of the full rights of citizens. During subsequent decades, though, the US abolitionist movement radicalized, demanding the immediate end of slavery, and eventually, individuals – Black and white – were willing to take up arms to achieve it. As part of this process of radicalization, abolitionists became bolder in their defenses of Haiti and its revolution.

For enslaved people in the United States who were trapped within the tyrannical plantation regime, and for free Black Americans who continued to feel its racist aftershocks, the Haitian Revolution and the independent nation of Haiti were beacons of possibility and hope. Early national Haiti suffered from political and economic woes because of ostracism from other Atlantic nations as well as domestic turmoil among its leaders. Nevertheless, for people of African descent throughout the Atlantic world, much about the new nation was inspiring. In an attempt to secure liberty, Haiti turned away from plantation agriculture toward an economy dominated by individual cultivators. It offered freedom and citizenship to any Black man who arrived at its shores. To a certain extent, these decisions cost Haiti dearly in broader political and economic spheres. But for all the young nation's difficulties, the story of its revolution and its tenacious, independent presence in the Atlantic world served as constant reminders to those in the United States – free and enslaved, white and Black – that their slaveholding republic fell well short of its celebrated Enlightenment ideals. As Frederick Douglass pointed out in his "Lecture on Haiti," the Haitian Revolution, not that of the United States, "has grandly served the cause of universal human liberty …

When they struck for freedom, they builded better than they knew ... and striking for their freedom, they struck for the freedom of every black man in the world."[41] Well after the Civil War, the United States still reckoned with the consequences of the fullness of this strike – a reckoning which continues to our present.[42]

[41] Frederick Douglass, "Lecture on Haiti" (1893), www.loc.gov/item/02012340, 34.
[42] Michel-Rolph Trouillot, *Silencing the Past: Power and the Production of History* (Boston: Beacon Press, 1995).

Index

Aachen, 479–80
Aargau, 304
Aberdam, Serge, 280
abolitionism, 44
  American, 740, 746–7, 752–3, 759
    blamed for the uprising in Saint-Domingue, 750–1
  British, 49, 396–8, 570, 586, 683
    1787–1792, 399–402
    1793–1804, 402–5
    adaptation to other forms of abusive inequality, 419–20
    call for end to apprenticeships, 415–16
    following emancipation, 414–17
    global influence, 405–9, 416–17
    steps toward emancipation, 409–14
    working-class objection to and the descent of, 417–19
  French. *See* Gallo-American Society; Society of the Friends of the Blacks; Society of the Friends of the Blacks and the Colonies
Aboukir Bay, Battle of, 453
absolutism, 53–4, 143–4
  bureaucratic state, 487
Act of Mediation (1803), 304
Adams, Christine, 285
Adams, John, 20, 161, 265, 364, 755–6
Adams, John Quincy, 543
Adams, Samuel, 553
Affiches Américaines, 605
Africa, 35–6
  British intervention in the slave trade, 408
  free labor farms, 417
African Americans, influence of the Haitian Revolution, 740, 744, 748, 750, 752–4, 759–60
African Free School, 118
Agency Committee, 413–14

Agustín I, emperor of Mexico, 33, 584
Aix-en-Provence, 93
Aizpurúa, Ramón, 728
Alba, republic of, 544
Albert, duke of Teschen, 378, 381
Albi, Santiago, 727
Alembert, Jean d', 106, 336–7, 338, 339, 340
Alexander Leopold, Palatine of Hungary, 510, 512
Alien and Sedition Acts (1798), 160
allodiality, 82
Almelo, 369
Alsace, 7, 108, 479
Alton, General, 381–2, 491
Amar, André, 281
American Patriots, 16, 540
American Revolution, 3, 334, 540–1, 591
  as a model for European revolutions, 559
  casualties, 557
  desertion, 40
  impact on Saint-Domingue, 606–10, 616
  influence on Louis XVI, 57
  international dimension, 40
  involvement of enslaved population, 40
  involvement of free people of color, 570, 713
  Italian interest in, 449
  military experience of free people of color, 693–5
  role of women, 21
  violence, 30
American Society of United Irishmen, 161
Ami des Lois, L', 314
Amsterdam, 362, 366, 367, 371, 542
Analyse des papiers anglais, 125, 128
Angers, 253
Anglo-Spanish War (1796), 729
Annecy, Jean Louis, 137, 138–9
Anspach, Isaac Salomon, 344

Index

Anstey, Roger, 403
anti-abolitionism, 401, 416, 418
Anti-Corn Law League, 418
Antigua, 695
anti-Jacobinism, 216–17, 218
  punishment of, 224
antiseigneurialism, 107–11, 195, 199–201
antislavery movement, 120, 745–6, 753
Anti-slavery Reporter, 418
Antoine, Pierre, 137, 139
Antonini, Santiago, 187
Antwerp, 221, 377, 394
Aosta, 447
Aponte's conspiracy, 712
Appenzell, 325
apprenticeship, 414, 417
  calls for an end to, 415–16
Arcahaye, 660
Argenson, Louis de Voyer de Paulmy d', Marquis, 332
Argentina, 35. *See also* Buenos Aires
Armitage, David, 396, 639
Army of the Holy Faith (*Santa Fede*), 459
Arrambide, Juan Xavier, 725
Artibonite, valley of the, 617
Artigas, José, 26
Assam, enslaved woman, 596
Assembly of Notables, 59, 121
Aubagne, 217
Aubremez, Antoine d', 384
Auger, Jacques, 598
Augereau, Pierre, 270
Augustus III, king of Poland, 515, 519–21
Austria, 47, 231, 471. *See also* Habsburgs; Austro-Turkish War
  reforms of Joseph II, 474–7
Austrian Netherlands, 209, 490, 499, 507, 512, 541. *See also* Belgian provinces; Brabant Revolution
  Flemish and French populations, 471
Austrian-Bohemian Chancellery, 496
Austro-Turkish War, 477–8, 506
Avignon, 203

Baartman, Sara (the Venus Hottentot), 298
Babeuf, Gracchus, 160, 219, 253–5, 445, 458
Baden, 484, 486
Balázs, Éva H., 505
Ballinamuck, 432
Baltimore, 627
banalités (seigneural privileges or rights), 105
Banat of Temes, 496, 498
Banda Oriental, 41

banditry, 38–40, 74, 222–3
Baptist War, 412–13
Barbados, 695
  slave uprising, 410
  struggle for equality, 711
Barbarin, 187
Barbé-Marbois, François, 573, 745
Barère, Bertrand, 48, 236
Barnave, Antoine Pierre Joseph, 133, 198–9, 229, 619
Barranquilla, 728
Barras, Paul, 270, 317
Barthélemy, François, 270
Basel, 304, 319–22, 325–6
Basel National Assembly, 304, 319, 322, 325–6
Bassal, Jean, 248
Bassi, Ernesto, 681
Bastille, 18, 62, 69, 120, 197–8, 200, 385, 573
Batavian Commonwealth, 354
Batavian Republic, 15, 180, 185, 352–4, 358–60, 542, 550, 552, 554, 555, 557, 559–60
  guild system, 358
  national institutuions, 359
  power structures, 370–2
Batsányi, János, 509
Baudières, Ferrand des, 620
Baudot, Marc-Antoine, 238
Bavaria, 479, 484, 486
Bayamo, 707
Bayly, C. A., 2
Bazin, Rigomer, 256
Beales, Derek, 499
Béarn, 180
Beauvais, Louis-Jacques, 630, 632, 633
Beauvaisis, 105
Beccaria, Cesare, 449, 450
Beckert, Sven, 592
Begasse, Marie, 598
Bélair, Suzanne (Sanité), 289
Belarus, 514, 517
Belgian provinces, 375–6
  Habsburg rule, 376–8
  pamphleteers, 380–1, 382
  resistance to reforms of Joseph II, 378–81
  revolutionary war, 381–91
  trade and industry, 377
Belgium, French liberation of, 46, 541
Belgrano, Manuel, 177
Bellecombe, Guillaume de, 609
Bellem, Jeanne de, 375, 381, 382
Belley, Jean-Baptiste Mars, 135, 138–9, 578, 626, 629

Belzunce, vicomte, 604
Benezet, Anthony, 118, 125
Bénot, Yves, 638, 657
Bergama, 545
Bergasse, Nicolas, 121, 122, 124
Bergzabern, 479
Berlin, 470, 484, 486, 523, 538
Bern, 41, 268, 306, 312–19, 322, 323, 330, 333, 342–4, 540, 541, 547
Berthier, French official, 62
Berthier, Louis Alexandre, 268, 453
Berzeviczy, Gergely, 490–2, 501, 505, 508
Biagini, Eugenio, 462
Biassou, Georges, 575, 579, 701
Bideau, Jean Baptist, 713
biens nationaux, 27
Bignon Commission, 213
Bilād al-Sūdān, 36
Billaud-Varenne, Jacques Nicolas, 25
Binasco, 556
Bishop, Abraham, 746–7
Bissette, Cyrille, 709–10
Black corsairs, 188, 717, 726, 730, 736
Boca de Nigua hacienda, 187
Bodin, Jean, 82
  Six livres de la République, 330
Bogotá, 19, 176, 183–4, 724, 736
  elite of, 182, 183
Bohemia, 475, 480, 492, 495
  abolition of serfdom, 501, 503
Boisrond, Louis-François, 137, 138–9
Boisrond-Tonnerre, Louis Félix, 665
  Mémoires pour servir à l'histoire d'Hayti, 665
Boisson, Joseph Georges, 135, 138–9, 629
Boissy d'Anglas, François Antoine de, 19, 247, 553
Bolívar, Simón, 18, 175, 408, 582, 585, 681, 713
  land policy, 26
  monarchism, 33
Bolivian Constitution (1826), 15
Bologna, 268, 452–3, 455, 456
Bonaparte, Joseph, 464
Bonaparte, Napoleon, 143, 270–1, 440, 487, 554, 564, 584, 614
  absolutism, 165
  approach to internal dissent, 168–9
  as a role model for Pepe, 465
  attack on Jaffa, 557
  attempt to blow up, 24 December 1800, 223
  casts blame on the Swiss for failures of the Helvetic Republic, 304

  closure of the Panthéon Club, 270
  communications with Louverture, 652–4
  destruction of Binasco, 556
  Egyptian expedition, 76, 264–6
  establishment of the Sister Republics, 268, 550
  invasion of Portugal and Spain, 172
  invasion of Saint-Domingue, 141, 581–2, 640, 657–9, 708, 757–8
  Italian campaign, 264, 443, 452–3, 543–6, 548–50
  liberation of Milan, 47, 455
  Life Consulate, 224
  measures to end the civil war, 222
  mobilization of troops on the Channel opposite England, 404
  patriarchalism, 167–8
  plan to reinstate slavery in Haiti, 290
  popular support, 165–7
  reaction to the violence of the Tuileries massacre, 205
  refusal to negotiate abolitionism, 403, 406
  refusal to return Louverture's sons, 656
  suppression of the 13 Vendémiaire insurrection, 218, 270
  travels through Switzerland, 315
  withdrawal of troops from Switzerland, 555
Bonaparte, Pauline, 659
Bonnot de Mably, Gabriel, 48
Bordeaux, 210, 280
Bordereau, Renée (the Angevin), 288
Borucki, Alex, 728
Bouches-du-Rhône, 251
Boukman, Dutty, 574, 701
Bourbon Restoration, 465
Bourbon, Charles of, 448
Bourbons, 150, 177, 184, 288, 447–8, 451, 454, 639
Bourmont, Count of, 222
Bourrit, Marc-Théodore, 339
Boves, José Tomás, 39
Boyer, Jean-Pierre, 663, 667, 683–8
Brabant Revolution, 375–6, 381–91
  divisions and factionalism, 392–5
  suppression, 395
Brabant, Estates of, 379, 382–3
  endurance of the Joyeuse Entrée, 376
Branciforte, Marquis de, 182
Branicki, Ksawery, 525, 532, 537
Brazil, 41, 586
  censorship, 48
  constitution (1824), 16

Brazil (cont.)
  effect of the Haitian Revolution, 586
  religion, 9
  royalism, 33
Breda, 383, 386–8
Breda Committee, 386–8
Brescia, 545
Breton Club, 228
Brienne, Loménie de, 59–60
Brissot, Jacques-Pierre, 68, 121–41, 204, 402
  and the Gallo-American Society, 121–5
  and the Jacobin Club, 231
  and the Society of the Friends of the Blacks, 125–6, 133, 134–6, 571, 616, 623
  appointment of Sonthonax and Polverel to the civilian commission in Saint-Domingue, 624
  dream of seizing Spanish America, 178
  Examen critique des Voyages dans l'Amérique, 123
  execution, 136
  Le patriote français, 129
  on the relocation of enslaved Africans, 130
Brissotins, 68–70, 136, 190, 231–2, 629
Britain, 16, 28, 41, 47
  abolition movement. *See* abolitionism, British
  acquisition of empire, 436–7
  and Geneva, 333
  blockades of Saint-Domingue, 601, 606–8
  capture of Port-au-Prince, 628, 706
  Catholic relief bills, 7
  conflicts with Hugues, 704–5
  demands for Irish reform, 424
  development of commerce, 331
  Dutch peace treaty, 351
  enlistment of Irish Catholics to the military, 437–8, 441
  entry to the War of the First Coalition, 577
  Haitian relations, 677–8, 686
  negotiations with Louverture, 580
  North American resentment of, 591
  occupation of Saint-Domingue, 579
  peace agreement with France, 656
  recruitment of troops from the Caribbean, 695
  relations with Haiti, 407–8
  textile technology and demand for cotton, 592
  threat of war with France, 425
  threat to Saint-Domingue, 604
  trade deal with France, 58, 265
  trade deal with the United States, 755
  war against the Dutch, 350
  war with France, 48, 57, 703
British America, 10, 144
  counterrevolution, 37
  popular sovereignty, 9–10
  royalism, 34
British and Foreign Antislavery Society, 416
British East India Company, 416, 419
Brittany, 103, 105, 117, 202
Brothier, Martin-Noël, 137
Brown Privilege Bill (1831), 711
Brown, John, 585
Bruges, 377
Brulley, Augustin-Jean, 135, 136, 625, 629
Brune, General, 264, 304, 315, 320, 322, 325–7, 547
Brunswick, duke of, 350, 351
Brussels, 375, 381–3, 386, 387, 388, 389, 490–1, 501, 505, 508
  Joseph II's visit to, 377–8
Buda, 501, 509, 511
Buenos Aires, 32, 41, 176, 190
  repression of the *peninsulares*, 48
Buonarroti, Filippo, 254, 445, 458, 543
Burke, Edmund, 424–5
  Appeal from the New to the Old Whigs, 536
  Reflections on the Revolution in France, 80
Burrows, Simon, 292
Buxton, Fowell, 414
Bwa Kayiman (Bois Caïman), 289
Byrne, Miles, 441

Cabanis, Pierre, 298
Cádiz, 178, 193
Cádiz, Cortes of, 14, 16, 173, 191
  constitution (1812), 7, 16, 43, 174, 189, 193, 465
Caen, 210, 280
Caesar, Julius, 240
Calabria, 451, 459
Calonne, Charles Alexandre de, 59
Calvinism, 335
  Dutch Republic, 370
  Geneva, 329, 330, 336, 337, 339–40, 346
  Hungary, 492, 494, 500–1
  Poland–Lithuania, 523
Cambacérès, Jean-Jacques Régis de, 233, 236
Cambrésis, 108
Camden, Lord, 428, 429, 430–1, 434
Camp Grenelle, 251
Campomanes, Pedro Rodríguez de, 177

Cap Français (Le Cap), 604, 624
  anthrax outbreak, 607–8
  arrival of the second civilian commission, 625
  Battle of, 626, 748–9
  Conseils supérieur, 600
  cultivator uprising, 656
  European garrisons, 600
  food crisis, 601–2
  free Black community, 617
  Galbaud's attack on, 578
  implementation of revised legislation, 611–12
  Louverture's attack on, 633
  Ogé's retreat to and execution, 572, 701
  rebel march to, 574–5
  republican resistance, 630
  Rochambeau's evacuation of, 660
  scientific community, 616, 742–3
  slave uprising, 622
Capellen, Joan Derk van der, 354–6, 358, 368–9
  Aan het volk van Nederland (To the People of the Netherlands), 355, 368
Cap-Haïtien, 675, 679, 684, 688
Capper, Mary, 120
Caquetío Indians, 186
Caracas, 733, 736
Carbonell, Captain-General, 725
Cariaco conspiracy, 735
Carlos III, king of Spain, 176, 177
Carlos IV, king of Spain, 47, 176
Carnot, Lazare, 236, 545
Carolina Resolution (1731), 500
Cartagena, 176, 183, 595, 600
  circulation of ideas, 724
  conspiracy, 187, 718, 735–6
  demographics, 722
  import of slaves, 729
  settlement of fugitive slaves, 728
  trade, 722
Caseneuve, Pierre de, 82
Casimir, Jean, 670
Castaing, Charles Guillaume, 134
Castelnau, Jean-Baptiste, 342
Castlereagh, Lord, 435
Castries, Charles-Eugène-Gabriel, Marquis de, 130, 615–16, 696
Catherine the Great (Catherine II, empress of Russia), 471, 514, 521, 522–5, 527, 529, 539
Catholic Church, Catholics, Catholicism, 257
  and natural law, 191
  and the Batavian Revolution, 352, 358, 373
  and the government of the Belgian provinces, 376
  and the Irish Rebellion, 423–6, 441
  and the Polish Revolution, 529–31
  exclusivity and tolerance, 6–9
  French Revolution
    decree of 4 August 1789 and curtailment of financial autonomy, 85
    encouragement of marriage, 294
    expropriation of, 85–90
    impact of, 115–16
    influence on rural culture, 103–4
    resistance to, 201–2
  Germany, 476
  persecuted by the Dutch Patriots, 370
  recognition of in the Cispadane Republic, 545
  reforms of Joseph II, 500–1, 513
    Austria, 475–7
    Belgian resistance to, 378–9
  slaughter of clergy in Polish Ukraine, 530
  spread of in Spanish America, 181
censorship, 7, 36–7
  Brazil, 48
  France, 56, 60, 72–3, 169, 292, 448
  Germany, 477
  in Habsburg lands, 500
Censorship Edict (Prussia, 1788), 477
Ceracchi, Giuseppe, 544
Cercle des Philadelphes, 616
Cercle Social, 134
Césaire, Aimé, 638
Cévennes mountains, mass peasant gatherings, 201
Chacón, José María, 726
Chalier, 210
Championnet, Jean-Antoine-Étienne, 264, 268, 454, 458, 549
Chanlatte, Antoine, 137
Chanlatte, Juste, 676
Charette, 220
Charlemont, earl of, 432
Charles IV, king of Spain, 185
Charles X, king of France, 686
Charleston, 608, 627, 631
Charlotte, a leader of the Saint-Domingue rebellion, 569
Charmilly, Venault de, 628
Chartism, 418
Chastellux, François-Jean de Beauvoir, Marquis de, 24, 122–3
Chaumette, Pierre Gaspard, 284

Chavannes, Jean-Baptiste, 134, 621, 701
Chemin, Jean-Baptiste, 257
Cherokees, 49
Chile, 14, 41, 191
　banditry, 39
　independence, 189
Chirino, José Leonardo, 731
Chirinos, Juan José, 185
chouans, chouannerie (royalist rebels, uprising), 218, 220–3, 251, 253, 264
Choudieu, Jacobin deputy, 232
Christophe, Henry, 32, 404, 584, 664, 683–4, 708, 757
　death, 679
　economic and labor policies, 679
　established as head of state, 674–6
　interpretation of nonintervention, 683
　negotiations with France, 581–2, 660, 678–9
　opposition to independence, 654
　patronage of arts and literature, 676–7
　reintegrated into the French army, 658
　relationship with Britain, 407, 677–8
Church of Ireland, 439
Cilento, 461
Cisalpine Republic, 268, 270, 453, 454, 463, 545–6, 554
　constitution, 550
Cispadane Republic, 268, 453, 454–5, 545, 546
Cisrhenian Republic, 268
Citadelle (Haiti), 668
Civil Constitution of the Clergy, 7, 287
Clare, Lord, 434
Clarkson, Thomas, 118, 124, 129, 132, 134, 400, 401, 407, 677–8
　The Abolition of the African Slave Trade, 677
Clavière, Étienne, 335, 339, 340, 343, 344, 346–8, 616, 623
　and the Gallo-American Society, 121, 123–5
　and the Society of the Friends of the Blacks, 125–6, 134
　arrest and death, 136
　participation in the Kornmann group, 122
Clement XIV, Pope, 525
Clervaux, Augustin, 659
Clichyens, 137, 256
Club des Patriotes, 253
Club Helvétique, 311
Club Massiac, 131–3, 142, 571, 616, 697
Code Henry, 679

Code Noir (1658), 597
Código negro, 186
coffee production, 591–2
Colombia, 33, 190, 684, 719
　religious toleration campaign, 9
Colón, Diego, 566
Colonial Committee, 127–8
Combret, Francisco, 727
commerce, development of, 331
Committee of Public Safety (France), 209, 538
Compagnoni, Giuesppe, *Elementi di diritto costituzionale democratico*, 456
Comte, Auguste, 193
Condorcet, Marie-Jean-Antoine-Nicolas de Caritat, Marquis de, 123, 126, 130, 134, 571
　Chronique de Paris, 129
　correspondence with Stanhope, 402
　Esquisse d'un tableau historique des progrès de l'esprit humain, 266
　Réflexions sur l'esclavage des Nègres, 128
　support for rights for free people of color, 288
　support for women's rights, 273
Confederacy of Bar, 515, 523
Confederation of the Friends of the Truth, 134
Congress of Reichenbach, 395
Congress of Vienna, 32, 406, 409
Conspiracy of Equals, 157, 158, 219, 253–5, 458
Constant, Benjamin, 193, 372
constitutionnaires, 344
constitutions
　Bolivia (1826), 15
　Brazil (1824), 16
　Cisalpine Republic (1797), 550
　Cispadane Republic (1797), 545
　France
　　1791, 15, 68
　　Constitution of Year I (1793), 254, 256
　　Constitution of Year III (1795), 15, 72, 136, 137, 184, 192, 219, 247–51, 256, 548, 553, 632
　　Constitution of Year VIII (1799), 653
　Geneva (1794), 543
　Genoa (1797), 546
　Haiti
　　1805, 661, 666–7, 669
　　1806, 675
　　1807, 675
　　1811, 675
　　1816, 680, 682–3
　Helvetic Republic, 303–5, 319–22, 547–8

766

Neapolitan Republic, 552
Poland–Lithuania (1791), 9, 542
Rome (1798), 547
Saint-Domingue (1801), 294, 581, 647, 650, 652–4, 657
Spain (1812), 7, 16, 43, 174, 189, 194, 465
United States (1787–89), 25, 449, 553, 584
Zurich, 310
Convention of Reichenbach (1790), 478, 510
Cook, James, 436, 481
Cooke, Edward, 434, 435
Cooper, Anna Julia, 563–4, 586
Copenhagen, 523
Coram, Robert, 25
Corday, Charlotte, 273, 280
Cordeliers Club, 66, 209
Cordero, José, 734
Cornwallis, Lord, 431
Coro
  rebellion, 186, 718, 731–3
  settlement of fugitive slaves, 728
Correspondent Society, 131
Corsica, 102, 452, 543
cotton production, 592
counterrevolution, 36–40
  elastic nature of, 214
  France, 65–71, 201–2
    measures taken against, 233–5
  Italy, 452, 459–62
  women, 286–8
County Antrim, 430
County Down, 430
coup d'état of 18 Fructidor, 137, 160, 161, 220, 256, 260, 268, 270, 553
coup d'état of 18–19 Brumaire, 222, 270–1
coup d'état of 22 Floréal, 252, 270
coup d'état of 30 Prairial, 161, 252
Craeybeckx, Jan, 391
Crema, 545
Crèvecœur, Michel-Guillaume-Saint-Jean de, 121, 123–4, 127
Croix-des-Bouquets, 701
Cromwell, Oliver, 240
Cuatro Compañeros hacienda, uprising, 187
Cuba, 179, 187, 585, 627, 712–13
  effect of the Haitian Revolution, 586
  migration to from Saint-Domingue, 702
  Morales conspiracy, 706–7
Cuenca, 183
Cuenca, Josef Damián de, 720–1
Cul-de-Sac Plain, 617
cultural practices, 13
Cumaná, 179, 728

Cuoco, Vincenzo, *Historical Essay on the Neapolitan Republic*, 443–5, 459, 462–3
Curaçao, 180, 185, 705, 721, 728
  Sasportas expelled from, 645
  slave rebellion, 186, 188
Curry, John, 439
Cuvier, Georges, 299
Cuzco, 177
Czartoryska, Izabela, 528
Czartoryski, Michał and August, 521
Czechs of Bohemia, 471

Dadizeele, 385
Daendels, Herman, 354
Dagverhaal, 363
Dames des Halles, 277, 281–2, 293
Danton, Georges, 202, 204, 232, 234, 645
Dantonists, 214, 238
Darnton, Robert, 122, 335
Dash, Michael, 687
Daunou, Pierre Claude François, 193, 554
Dauphiné, 108
David, Jacques-Louis, 267, 579
Davis, David Brion, 397
De Coster, 386
De Nicola, Carlo, 460, 462
Debien, Gabriel, 131
Décade philosophique, La, 138, 257, 266
Declaration of Independence of Haiti (1804)
  circulation of, 725
Declaration of Independence of the United States (1776), 5, 311, 725
Declaration of the Rights of Man and Citizen (1789), 8, 42, 64, 113, 201
  and the rights of free people of color, 131–2, 743
  compared with the Stäfa Memorial, 309, 311
  criticisms, 5
  exclusion of references to slavery or slave trade, 399
  influence in Spanish America, 183–4, 725
  influence in the Caribbean, 570, 692, 698
Declaration of the Rights of Woman and Citizen (1791), 273, 283
Defenders (Irish secret society), 426–8
del Valle, Narciso, 734
Delacroix, Charles, 542
Delacroix, Jacques-Vincent, 127
Delair, Jean, 630
Delamardelle, Guillaume, 606
Delgrès, Louis, 709

Demerara, slave uprising, 411
democracy, 15–21, 143, 224
  direct, 326, 455
  exclusion of women from, 281
  Franco-American comparisons, 151, 156–7, 164, 167
  French Revolution and the birth of, 112–13
  French system of, 251–3
  in the Sister Republics, 560
  relationship between monarchy and, 31
  representative, 303, 351, 354, 356, 358, 359, 363, 369
Democraten, De, 363
democratic absolutism, 143, 168, 170
Democratic Society of New York, 161
Denmark, 343, 405, 467, 478, 616
Dentand, Julien, 342
Derance, Lamour, 649, 650, 656, 658, 660
Derechos del Hombre, 186
Desan, Suzanne, 285, 292, 295
Description of Egypt, 266
Desfourneaux, Edme Étienne Borne, 633
Desmoulins, Camille, 232
Dessalineans, 671
Dessalines, Jean-Jacques, 404, 564, 565, 649, 654, 677, 679, 682
  appointed Louverture's second in command, 655
  assassination, 663, 674
  campaign against Rigaud, 580, 706
  constitution, 9, 666–7
  crowned Emperor Jean-Jacques I, 32, 584
  declaration of independence, 584, 640, 659–62, 663, 664–6, 708, 716, 757
  description of the Maniel Maroons, 650
  economic and labor policies, 663, 668–9
  encouragement of immigration, 670
  enforcement of the cultivator system, 647, 655, 658
  established as head of state, 666
  fortifications, 668, 672
  massacre of white European colonists, 584, 669
  rebellion against French attempt to reinstate slavery, 582–3, 659–60, 757
  service in the French army, 581–2, 658
Destutt, Antoine, 193
Deventer, 354, 368
Deville, Jean-Baptiste, 139
Diamond Necklace Affair, 292
Diario de Madrid, 181
Dickson (a *métissé*), 702

Dickson, William Steele, 439
Diderot, Denis, 18, 56, 106, 335
Dieudonné, slave gang leader, 633
Diplomatic Revolution (1756), 54, 480
divorce, 73, 269, 274, 277, 279, 284, 288, 294–5, 299, 558
Doctrina et Amicitia (Dutch cultural society), 362
Dohm, Christian Wilhelm von, 480
Dom João (John IV of Portugal), 33
Dom Pedro I, emperor of Brazil, 33
Dom Pedro II, emperor of Brazil, 33
dominial inalienability, 88–90
Dominica, 704, 711
Dominican Republic, nationalism, 586
Douglass, Frederick, 414, 759
Draskovich Observance, 505
Drennen, William, 438
Drenthe, 368, 371
Dresden, 470, 521
Du Roveray, Jacques-Antoine, 334–5, 340, 341, 348
Dublin, 440
Dublin Castle, 429, 440
Dubois, Laurent, 697
Dufay, Louis-Pierre, 135–6, 138–9, 629
Duff, General Sir James, 431
Dumas, Thomas-Alexandre, 568, 582
Dumon, Anne Pérotin, 713
Dumont, Étienne, 11, 335
Dumoulin, Charles, 82
Dumouriez, General, 209, 233–4
Duphot, General, 268, 547
Dupont, Félicité, 121
Duport, Adrien, 229
Dupuch, Louis Elias, 138
Durrey, Jean, 182
Dutch East India Company, 359
Dutch Republic, 267, 306, 616
  Batavian Revolution, 349, 352–4, 358, 362–6, 372
  cultural objects, 13
  development of commerce, 331
  Patriot Revolt, 349, 350–1, 540, 542
  peace with Great Britain, 351
  power structures, 367–70
  public opinion, 11
  religion, 358
  repertoire of contention, 360–7
  stadtholderian system, 350–2
  theory and practice of revolutionary ideas, 354–60
  war with Britain, 350

East India Company Act V (1843), 419
economic equality, 23–7
Edict of Moulins (1566), 88, 89
Edict of Toleration (1781), 500–1, 507, 511, 513
Edict on Reunion (1607), 88
education policy, 18–19, 74, 257–9
Églantine, Fabre d', 281
Egypt, French Enlightenment campaign, 75, 264–6
Elburg, 351
Elizabeth, empress of Austria, 521
Emancipation Act (1833), 415
Emancipation Day (1834), 414
Emancipation Edict (of Joseph II), 501, 503, 507, 511, 513
Encyclopédie (Diderot and d'Alembert), 106, 335–6
engagements (revocable grant of domanial property), 94–6
Enlightenment, 176
   Belgian provinces, 376, 380
   debates, 307–8, 445–6
   Egypt, French campaign of, 264–6
   French, 4
   Geneva, 336
   Germany, 476–7, 488
   Italy, 449–51
   Poland–Lithuania, 516
   Spanish America, 175–7
Enragés, 17
Enrique, Taíno cacique, 566
Erblande (hereditary lands), 492
Erthal, Franz Ludwig von, Prince-Bishop of Würzburg and Bamberg, 472, 476
Erthal, Friedrich Karl Joseph von, 476
España, José María, 733–4
Estaing, Charles d', 605, 608, 695
Estates-General of France, 12, 60–2, 105, 107, 128, 199, 570, 612, 697
Este, d' family, 447
Étampes, 1792 riot, 203–4
Ezpeleta, Josef de, 729

Fatiman, Cécile, 289
Fatio, Pierre, 330
Faubourg Saint-Antoine, 216
Fayettists, 68–9
Federalist Revolt, 210, 216, 280–1
Federalists, 10
   American, 145–6, 157–61, 169–70, 756
   Dutch, 10, 542, 555
Fédon Rebellion, 705

Fédon, Julien, 188, 705
Feller, Abbé François Xavier de, 379
Ferdinand, king of Naples, 453, 465
Fernando VII, king of Spain, 32, 33, 47
Ferney, 337
Ferrand, Jean-Louis, 668
Ferrara, 268, 452
Ferrer, Ada, 682
Festival of the Supreme Being, 287
feudalism
   Italy, 448, 451
   revolutionary understanding of, 79–80
feudalism, abolition of, 20
   Bohemia, 501
   France, 27, 78–81, 167, 200–1
      benefits of, 116
      emptying of the national domain, 94–7
      expropriation of the Church and creation of the National Domain, 85–90
      Great Demarcation, 4 August decree, 64, 81–5, 109
      put into practice, 90–4
   Hungary, 503
   Italy, 460, 463
Feuillant Club, 68, 203, 230
"Festival of the Law," 204
Feuille du cultivateur, 261
Fick, Carolyn, 649
Filangieri, Gaetano, 177, 449
   Scienza della Legislazione, 449
Fisco, Claude, 384
FitzGerald, Lord Edward, 430
Flanders, 267, 382, 388, 394
Flesselles, Jacques de, 62, 198
Fletcher, Andrew, 354
Fleurus, battle of, 240
Flignau, Pierre, 673–4
Florence, 459
   collapse of (1537), 331
   intellectual hubs, 448
Floridablanca, Count of, 36, 179, 181, 725
Fond des Cayes Plain, 617
Forster, Georg, 25, 476, 481
Fort-Liberté, 643, 655, 664
Foscolo, Ugo, 458, 465
Foster, John, 434
Fouchard, Jean, 595, 649
Foulon, Joseph, 62
Fox, Charles James, 474
France
   abolition of slavery in Saint-Domingue, 703

France (cont.)
　abolitionist movement. *See* Gallo-American Society; Society of the Friends of the Blacks: Society of the Friends of the Blacks and the Colonies
　agricultural systems, 102–3
　anti-abolitionism, 416
　banditry, 38
　colonial order in Saint-Domingue, 566–8
　declaration of war against Britain, 402
　development of commerce, 331
　diplomatic relations with Haiti, 678–9
　economic equality, 24
　entry to the American War of Independence, 695
　geographic and administrative diversity, 102
　influence in Geneva, 332–4
　influence of the Catholic Church on rural culture, 103–4
　intervention in Switzerland, 268
　invasion of Geneva, 341–5
　invasion of Switzerland, 547
　invasion of the Austrian Netherlands, 209
　national domain, 27, 85–90
　　emptying of, 94–7
　peasant grievances (*cahiers*), 105–7
　popular sovereignty. *See* sovereignty, popular: Franco-American analogues
　reaction to British slave emancipation, 414–15
　relations with Haiti, 685–6
　religious intolerance, 7
　royal domain, 27, 87–9, 95
　　expropriation of, 91, 92
　rural demographics, 101–2
　seigneurial privileges and the culture of heirarchy, 104–5
　support for the American Revolution, 41
　women's rights, 22
Franche-Comté, 108
Francis II, Holy Roman Emperor (Francis I, king of Hungary), 511, 513
Francis Stephen, Duke of Lorraine, 447
Franklin, Benjamin, 118, 123, 426, 449
Frederick Augustus III, king of Saxony, 536
Frederick the Great (Frederick II, king of Prussia), 54, 342, 473, 477, 496, 520–1
Frederick William II, king of Prussia, 477, 510, 528, 529, 537, 539

free people of color, 120, 689–93
　advocacy for the rights of, 130–6, 568, 571–2, 612, 618–20, 697–9, 747
　conflict with white landowners, 572, 574, 594, 701
　conspiracies and petitions in the Spanish and English Greater Antilles, 706–8
　discrimination against in Saint-Domingue, 568, 598, 606, 617
　from repression to the abrogation of prejudice in the French colonies, 708–10
　in the military sphere, 608–9, 693–5
　in the Saint-Dominguan police force, 595
　involvement in revolutionary unrest
　　Guadeloupe, 700
　　Martinique, 699–700
　　Saint-Domingue, 700–1
　involvement in the Coro rebellion, 186
　involvement in the politics of Saint-Domingue, 695–7
　petitions process in the British colonies, 710–12
　population in Saint-Domingue, 598
　population movements in the Caribbean, 702
　power and recognition, 568
　rebellion against the colonial government over rights, 572–3, 700–1, 743–4
　revolution of, 622–4
　situation of in the Spanish colonies, 712–13
Free Society of Sciences, Arts, and Humanities, 140
freemasonry, 163, 450, 464, 504–6
Freiburg, 268
French Canada, British capture of, 604
French Conspiracy movement, 187
French Consulate, 175, 192, 222–3, 240, 267, 552, 636
French Directory, 31, 175, 192, 240, 247, 353, 635, 638, 657
　and Spain, 185
　and the Sister Republics, 458–9, 544–50
　and the success of the *nouveaux riches*, 263–4
　arts, architecture and decor, 263–4
　Babeuf and the Conspiracy of Equals, 253–5
　Bonaparte's expedition to Egypt, 264–6
　censorship, 72
　comparative American policy, 161–2

Index

Constitution of Year III, 247–51
democratic system, 251–3
dispatch of third civil commission to Saint-Domingue, 139
economy and finance, 260–1
festivals and exhibitions, 257, 261
influence on the Helvetic constitution, 304, 319–20, 326–7
intervention in Switzerland, 303, 313–15, 317–18
investment in the arts, 259–60
Italian campaign, 452–5
laws pertaining to the rights of man in the colonies, 653
laws relating to mortgages and sale of national goods, 262
plan to assist in the Irish Rebellion, 428
plans to take over Santo Domingo, 651
policing and punishment of provincial violence, 218–22
policy on land ownership in Saint-Domingue, 649
politics and policy, 74–6
replacement of Sonthonax with Hédouville in Saint-Domingue, 642
rise of the royalists and the coup of 18 Fructidor, 256
schools and education, 257–9
Second Directory, 221, 224
social problems, 262–3
Sonthonax and the third commission to Saint-Domingue, 633–4
war and diplomacy, 264–71
withdrawal of paper money, 96
French Guards, 197. *See also* French National Guards
French Guiana, 130
French Legislative Assembly, 68, 135, 204
elections, 200
extention of the 1791 amnesty, 203
law granting equal rights to free men of color, 624, 700, 701
poor relief decrees, 24
promotion of Simonneau as a national martyr, 203
French National Assembly, 62, 128, 145, 146, 199, 201
abolition of feudalism, 81, 109, 200
abolition of primogeniture, 276
abolition of slavery in the colonies, 578
and the rights of free people of color, 131–5, 571–3, 598, 622, 697–8
anmesty of 1791, 203

appeals for assistance with the slave rebellion in Saint-Domingue, 575
changing attitudes to the French colonies, 129
collection of national rents, 96
Committee on the Colonies, 133–4
compared with the Basel National Assembly, 320
concealment of the king's dissent, 67
Jacobin deputies, 228, 229
legalization of divorce, 294
murder of royal officials in, 198
offer of honorary citizenship to Wilberforce and Clarkson, 401
opposition from the United Provinces, 542
reactions to the Great Fear, 82
recognition of male Protestants and Jews, 274
refusal to allow popular ratification of the 1791 constitution, 147
restructuring and expropriation of the Catholic Church, 86–8, 202, 530
taxation, 110–11
women's invasion of, 285
French National Convention, 69, 72, 96, 135, 206, 232, 295
abolition of slavery, 141, 748
address from the British Club, 425
closure of women's clubs, 281
Committee of General Security, 135, 212, 235
Committee of Public Safety, 136, 212, 214, 235–6, 239–40, 313
economic controls, 282
elections, 201, 207
expulsion of women from the military, 278
insurrection of 13 Vendémiaire, 218
invasions of following food shortages, 216
Legislative Committee, 236
refusal of military assisance to Kościuszko, 538
responses to revolutionary violence, 209–12, 214
ruling on feudal arrangement, 94
Terror legislation, 210, 226
French National Guard, 46, 68, 70, 113, 200–2, 205, 209, 210, 222, 578
French Patriot, 62
French Revolution, 3, 477
agency and lived experience of, 244
amnesty of 1791, 203–4
and Italy, 451–4
anti-Jacobist violence, 216–17

771

French Revolution (cont.)
  Catholic resistance, 201–2
  Champ de Mars massacre, 68, 202
  chouannerie, 218, 220–3
  citizenship of women. *See* women: citizenship during the French Revolution
  consequences of the king's capture at Varennes, 202–3
  counterrevolutionary violence, 201–2
  effects of in the Caribbean colonies, 702–3
  Federalist Revolt, 210
  governance. *See* French Consulate; French Directory; French Legislative Assembly; French National Assembly; French National Convention
  in the countryside, 100–1
    brigandage, 222–3
    peasant revolts, 30, 107–12, 199–200
    social, administrative, and religious changes, 112
    violence, 199–200
  influence on German affairs, 479–89
  influence on the Haitain Revolution, 573
  influence on the Irish Rebellion, 422, 424, 441
  insurrection of 13 Vendémiaire, 218, 251, 270
  justification for popular violence, 206–8
  overthrow of the monarchy, 204–6
  Pepe's critique of, 465
  personal freedoms, 72–4
  political crisis and the fall of the Girondins, 208–10
  politicized unrest, 201
  precursors, 53–62
  principles and politics, 62–72
  prison massacres of 1792, 207–8
  propaganda, 725
  reappropriation of the symbols of, 182–4
  reign of terror. *See* French Revolutionary terror
  sexual scandal, 292–3
  Swiss support for, 311
  urban violence in the early revolution, 1788–1792, 197–9
  victims and survivors, 74–7
  violence, 29, 195–7
French Revolutionary terror, 70, 74, 225–8, 251
  comparative casualties, 556–8
  definitions and ideology, 226–7
  emotional dimensions, 227–8, 238, 243–4
  enactment of, 238–9
  fallacies and misconceptions, 225
  implementation, 241
  incidences of, 237–9, 242–3
  legislation, 226, 233–7, 241–2
  Loi Prairial legislation, 239–40
  origins, 227
  redefinition of, 244
  revolutionaries' understanding of, 234–5
  Robespierre's objection to the militarization of, excessive violence and his execution, 239–41
  turning points on the pathway to, 230–3
  violence of, 210–15, 310
  women's involvement, 282–5
French Revolutionary Wars, 154, 231, 480–6
French Society for the Abolition of Slavery, 415
French West India Company, 566
Fribourg, 313, 317, 319, 540
Friedland, Paul, 145
Friesland, 15
Frisians, 366
Frölich, Carl Wilhelm, 25
Fruci, Gian Luca, 445

Gaceta de Lima, 181
Gaffield, Julia, 639, 686
Gainot, Bernard, 695
Galbaud du Fort, François-Thomas, 578, 626
Galiani, Fernandino, 177
Galicia, 502
Gallatin, Albert, 335
Gallo-American Society, 121–5
Gálvez, 177
Gandhi, Mahatma, 420
Garnot, Pierre Nicolas, 135, 629
Garrigus, John, 695
Garrison, William Lloyd, 414
Gauthier, Florence, 690
Geggus, David, 45, 420, 598, 695
Genet, Edmond (Citizen), 157, 158, 626
Geneva, 41, 221, 305, 543, 548, 554, 555, 560
  and Rousseau, 335–8
  civil unrest, 330
  events of 1782, 341–5
  legacies of the revolution, 345–8
  political turbulence, 329–32
  représentants movement, 338–41
  revolution of 1792, 540–1
  revolutionary era, 332–5
  sovereignty and government, 330

Index

Genoa, 331, 449, 453, 546, 551, 556, 560
Genovesi, Antonio, 177, 449
George III, king of Great Britain and Ireland, 31, 346, 350, 385
Georgia, 627, 695
Gerbey, Joseph Servan de, 138
German Customs Union (Zollverein), 473
German Enlightenment, 476
German Jacobins, 481–4
Germany, 46, 559
   Catholicism, 476
   censorship, 477
   domestic reform, 487–8
   economic equality, 25
   effects of the French Revolution, 479–80
   impact of the French Revolutionary Wars, 480–5
   imperial institutions, 467
   intellectual reaction to the triumph of the bureaucratic state, 485–7
   judicial system, 473–4
   legalism, 472
   localism, 472
   rule of Duke Karl Eugen, 474
   territorial rearrangement, 485–7
Germinal uprising (1795), 157–8
Ghent, 221, 382, 388
Gioia, Melchiorre, 455
Girard, Stephen, 742, 752, 754
Girodet, Anne-Louis, 267
Girondins, 69–70, 136, 231–5, 257
   confrontation with the Montagnards, 209, 279
   expulsion of, 209
   reinstated by the National Convention, 216
   show trials, 214, 238
   women's association with, 277, 279, 284, 293
Giroud, Alexandre-Benjamin, 140
Glacière massacre, Avignon, 203
Glarus, 325
Glorious Revolution, casualties, 557
Godechot, Jacques, 446, 516
Godineau, Dominique, 283
Godoy, Manuel de, 185
Goethe, Johann Wolfgang von, 477
Golard, Lubin, 649
Goman (Jean-Baptiste Perrier), 674, 684
Gómez, Alejandro, 707
Gonaïves, 631, 664, 716
Gordon Riots, 7
Görres, Joseph, 50, 485
Gosse, Étienne, *Political Women*, 285
Gosse, Henri-Albert, 344

Gouges, Olympe de, 22, 273, 283, 288
Gouy d'Arsy, Louis-Marthe, Marquis de, 127
Gramsci, Antonio, 444–5
Grand Doco, 684
Grand'Anse, 674, 684
Graubünden, 270
Great Demarcation, 81–5, 87, 90, 91, 98–9
Great Fear, 63, 82, 108, 200
Great Terror, 214, 239
Greater Antilles, 645
Greece, 559
Green, Jacob, 25
Grégoire, Henri, 118, 126, 132, 133, 134, 136, 140, 571, 623, 657
Grenada, 179, 728
   French troops in, 609
   information from, 726
   petitions of free people of color, 711
   uprising, 188, 645, 705
Grenoble, uprising, 197, 224
Grenus, Jacques, 341
Grisons, 331
Grodno (Hrodna), 538
Grondwettige herstelling (Constitutional Restoration, 1784–86), 356
Guadeloupe, 45, 136, 187, 645, 699, 703, 705, 720, 725–6, 729, 733
   British capture of, 604
   rebellion, 290, 295, 700
   restoration of slavery, 141, 167, 290, 582, 657, 658, 708–9, 757
Gual and España conspiracy, 185–6, 191
Gual, Manuel, 733–4
Guelphs, 470
Guerra, François-Xavier, 173
Guevara y Vasconcelos, Manuel, 715–16, 720, 738
Guiana, 141, 167
Guillotin, Joseph-Ignace, 154
guillotine, 153–4, 193, 225, 233, 238, 243
   number of casualties, 557
   presence outside major cities, 212
   symbolism of the, 181
Gulf of Paria, 720, 735
Gustav III, king of Sweden, 524, 531
Gusti, Francesco, 461
Guyomar, Pierre, 273, 278

Habsburgs, 447, 450, 467–70, 471, 478, 480–1.
   See also Joseph II, Holy Roman Emperor; Leopold II, Holy Roman Emperor; Maria Theresa, Holy Roman Empress

Hahn, Jacob, 372
Hainaut, 108, 382, 389
Haiti, 141, 404, 564
  Christophe and Pétion's interpretations of nonintervention, 681–3
  civil war and division, 675–6
  Code penal militaire, 666
  constitutions, 663, 666–7, 675, 680
  Declaration of Independence, 662
  First Empire under Dessalines, 664–74
    demographics, 669–71
    divisions over the understanding of liberty, 671
    economic and labor policies, 668–9
    founding ceremony, 664–6
    international trade relations, 667
    literary culture, 672–4
  Kingdom of Haiti under Christophe
    diplomatic relations, 407–8, 677–9
    economic and labor policies, 679
    literary culture, 676–7
  Liberal Revolution, 688
  rule of Boyer
    diplomatic relations with Britain and France, 685–6
    economic and labor policies, 686–7
    end of, 688
    literary criticism of Boyer, 687–8
    reunification, 683–5
  State of Haiti under Pétion
    diplomatic relations, 407, 680–1
    economic and labor policies, 679–80
Haitian Army (Armée Indigène), 564, 582
Haitian Revolution, 28, 39, 42, 180, 396
  attempts to export to other colonies, 645–6
  British and Spanish involvement, 628–30
  British withdrawal and questions relating to independence, 637–41
  departmentalization, July 1795, 631–2
  exploitation of divisions by politicians in the metropole, 634
  French invasion and threat to restore slavery, 141, 657–9, 708
  influence on Venezuela and New Granada, 715–19
  international responses to, 584–6
    French, 563–4
    United States, 563–4, 739–41, 743–8
  militarization leading to general freedom, 625–6
  militarization of the territory, 624–5
  mixed-race war, 632–4

  Ogé's uprising, 621
  power struggle 1798–1801, 640–4
  prerevolutionary unrest, 621–2
  protagonists, 615–18
  refugees from, 626–8
  resistance and victory, 630–1
  revolution of the free people of color, 622–4
  rise and rule of Toussaint Louverture, 576–81
  role of women in, 288–91
  slave rebellion, 573–6, 621–2, 701–2
  violence, 622
  War of Independence, 581–4, 659–62
    impact on the United States, 757–60
Hajnóczy, József, 504, 509, 512
Hall, Prince, 754
Hamburg, 470, 477, 484
Hamilton, Alexander, 147, 758
Hardenberg, 369
Hassan al'Attâr, sheikh, 266
Hasselt, 386, 387
Hattem, 351
Haut-de-Cap sugar estate, 607
Haüy, Valentin, 257
Havana, 600, 604
Hébertists, 214, 238, 254
Hédouville, Gabriel de, 222, 580, 642–3, 647, 649, 654
Hegel, Georg Wilhelm Friedrich, 488, 585
Helg, Aline, 722, 724
Helvetic Republic, 6, 46, 305, 319–20, 327, 552
  constitution, 303–5, 319–22, 547–8
Henri Goffin, 382
Henri IV, king of France, 58
Hesse, Carla, 286
Hidalgo's revolt, 8, 29, 38
Historical, Political and Economic Recorder, 516
Hobbes, Thomas, 224, 449
Hoche, Lazare, 218, 220, 222, 264, 452, 485, 549
Hohenzollerns, 470, 471
Holbach, baron d', 18, 388
  Éthocratie, 184
Holland, 264, 351, 352, 354, 368, 371, 542, 552–3, 557, 560
Holy Roman Empire. *See also* Austria; Germany; Prussia
  end of, 486
  geopolitics, 471–3
  structure, 467–71
homosexuality, decriminalization of, 273, 295–6

Houdetot d', Elisabeth Françoise Sophie Lalive de Bellegrade, comtesse, 123
Howick, Lord, 405
Hugues, Victor, 44, 178, 186, 645, 703–5, 713
Humbert, Jean, 430, 432, 440
Humboldt, Alexander von, 179
Hume, David, 331
Hungarian Chancellery, 501, 505
Hungarian National Museum and Library, 513
Hungarian Royal Chancellery, 495
Hungary, 42, 467
  extent of Habsburg control, 492
  freemasonry, 504–6
  German population, 471
  Habsburg rule, 470
  Jacobin conspiracy, 511–12
  Military Frontier Zone, 496
  nobility, 493–5
  Ottoman era, 492
  plot to overthrow Habsburg rule, 478
  political settlement following the anti-Habsburg revolt of 1703–1711, 496
  reforms of Joseph II, 498–506, 512–13
    opposition to, 478, 506–7
  reign and reforms of Maria Theresa, 496–8
  reign of Francis II and I, 511, 513
  reign of Leopold II, 507–11, 513
  structure, 492–4
Hutchinson, Thomas, 28

Ideologues, 266
Incroyables, 263
indigenous populations, royal tribute, 34–5
Insurrectionary Commune's Surveillance Committee, 207
international connections, 40–50
Ireland, 6, 49, 541
  plan to set up New Geneva, 333, 346–7
Irish Rebellion, 29, 242, 347
  aftermath, 432
  Atlantic context, 436–7
  atrocities, 28, 430–2
  attempted French invasion, 264, 426–9, 549
  counterinsurgency and repression, 427–8
  demands for political reform, 422–4, 433
  enlistment of Catholic support, 423–6
  formation of the Society of United Irishmen, 422

French intervention, 452
French opinion of the Irish, 435
motivations of the rebels, 440–1
proscription of the Society of United Irishmen, 426
spread of the rebellion, 430–1
Irish Volunteers, 423, 432
Islam, 6
Italian Legion, 463
Italy, 264, 557, 559
  Austro-Russian offensive, 454, 459
  counterrevolution, 459–62
  economic equality, 26
  French Revolution and the "Passive Revolution" in, 443–6
  influence of the French Revolution, 451–4
  legacies of the republican experiments, 462–6
  prerevolutionary Enlightenment, reform, and the crisis of the *Ancien Régime*, 446–51
  religious policies, 456
  Sister Republics, 268, 453, 454–9, 544–50
  uprisings and violence, 556
Iturbide, Agustín de, 33
Ivernois, François d', 340, 346, 348

Jacmel, 617, 630, 656, 706
Jacobin Club, 66, 202, 233, 254, 401, 629
  closure, 216, 240
  influence of Robespierre, 236
  joined by Sonthonax, 135
  Mirabeau's speech on Africa, 129
  origins and membership, 228–9
  split and formation of the Feuillant club, 230
  split with the Brissotins, 231
Jacobin clubs
  campaign for free men of color to join, 134
  provincial, 229, 571
  women's
    closure of, 282
    defense of the Civil Constitution, 287
    foundation of, 276
Jacobinism, 219, 229–30
  Hungary, 511–12
  in creole revolutionaries, 190–1
  Irish, 439–40, 442
  Italy, 444, 445, 461
  Lafayette's attempted coup against, 69
  Poland, 536, 537, 538

Jacobins, 19, 25, 68, 195, 630
   alliance with the Irish revolutionaries, 428
   alliance with the *sans-culottes* movement, 210
   altercation in Sète, 224
   and the trial of Louis XVI, 232–3
   attainment of power in the regions of Marseille and Toulon, 206
   attitudes to women, 275, 285, 291
   conflict with the Girondins, 234
   divisions between the Girondins and Montagnards, 209, 232
   exclusion from office in the Italian Republics, 458
   exclusion of foreigners, 48
   German, 481–4
   ideology, 229–30, 511–12
   involvement with the terror legislation, 234–7
   "law of hostages," 222
   massacre of in the Bouche-du-Rhône, 251
   neo-Jacobins, 161, 252, 253, 256
   plot to bring down Robespierre, 240
   protests relating to punishment of Nancy mutineers, 204
   regrouping of and the Conspiracy of the Equals, 253–5
   reprisals against, 216–17, 240
   response to the September massacres, 231
   revolutionary terror, 210–13, 225–6
Jacques, slave, 608
Jaffa, 557
Jamaica, 404, 564, 577, 627
   attempts to export Haitian Revolution to, 645–6
   British recruitment of troops from, 695
   petitions by free people of color, 711
   plots and slave revolts, 707
   settlement of free people of color, 702
   slave uprising (1831), 412
James, C. L. R., 586, 647
Jansenists, 80, 379, 450
Jarnac, Louis Charles de Rohan-Chabot, comte, 131
Jarvis, Katie, 277, 282
Jaucourt, Marquis de, 345
Jay Treaty (1795), 755
   protests against, 157–8
Jay, John, 28
Jeannot, 575
Jean-Rabel, 630

Jefferson, Thomas, 127, 143, 158, 161, 163, 558, 751
   and the Gallo-American Society, 121, 122–4
   and the Haitian Revolution, 757–8
   approach to political opposition, 169–70
   Notes on Virginia, 123
   on Tadeusz Kościuszko, 514
   on the Genevan Academy, 329
   patriarchalism, 167–8
   popular support, 165–7
Jemappes, Battle of, 481
Jérémie, 617, 628, 631
Jesuits, 176, 379, 497, 525
   evicted from Saint-Domingue, 596
Jews
   and the Batavian Revolution, 358, 372, 373
   France, 7, 8, 116, 274
   Germany, 472, 476, 480
   Holland, 352
   in the Caribbean, 645
   Poland–Lithuania, 518, 526, 527, 535
   slaughter of in Polish Ukraine, 530
   targeted for suspected hoarding in Tuscany, 461
Joly, Étienne Louis Hector de, 132–4
Joseph II, Holy Roman Emperor, 450, 473
   and the resettlement of Genevans in Brussels, 346
   attempt to swap the Austrian Netherlands for Bavaria, 486
   death, 394, 478
   lack of interest in Geneva, 343
   reforms, 530
      Austria, 474–7
      Austrian Netherlands, 376–81
         resistance to, 381–91, 478, 490, 541
      Bohemia, 475, 480
      Hungary, 491, 498–506, 511
         resistance to, 478, 512–13
   visit to Brussels, 377–8
Josephists, 503, 505–9
Joubert, General, 264, 269, 549
Jourdan, Mathieu Jouve ("Head-Chopper"), 203
Journal de Paris, 125, 128
Journal des Défenseurs de la Patrie, 256
Jovellanos, Gaspar Melchor de, 177
Joyce, James, *Ulysses*, 347
Joyeuse Entrée, 376, 379–80, 383
Judaism, 6
Jullien, Marc-Antoine, 269

Karl Eugen, duke of Württemberg, 474
Karl II August, duke, 479

Kattenburg, 366
Kemp, François Adriaan van der, 361, 368
Killala, 430, 432, 435, 440
Kingston, 721
Kingué, Marie, 569
Knox, General Thomas, 429
Kołłątaj, Hugo, 531–2, 534–5, 538
Kollum, 366
Konarski, Stanisław, 519–20
Kongo, Kingdom of, 35, 574, 599
Koppi, Károly, 509
Kornmann Group, 122
Kornmann, Guillaume, 122, 127
Kościuszko, Tadeusz, 514–15, 520, 522, 537–9
Kossakowski, Szymon, 537
Kraków, bishopric of, 530
Kwass, Michael, 12

La Ferme Générale, 110
La Guaira, 730
  conspiracy, 182–4, 186, 718, 733–5
  literacy and exchange of ideas, 724
  population, 722
  trade, 721
La Guajira, 188
La Harpe, Fréderic-César de (Philanthropus), 311–17, 326, 546, 560
La Paz, 177
La Prophétesse, Romaine, 297, 575, 579
Laclos, Choderlos de, *Dangerous Liaisons*, 294
Lacrosse, Raymond, 700
Lafarge, Madame, 283
Lafayette, Gilbert du Motier, Marquis de, 60, 65, 233
  as a role model for Pepe, 465
  attempt to launch a military coup against Jacobinism, 69
  attempt to turn his Northern Army against Paris, 207
  command of the National Guard, 201, 202
  involvement with the Gallo-American Society, 122–3
  involvement with the Society of the Friends of the Blacks, 127, 130, 132, 571
Laforest, Étienne, 629
Lafortune, 658
Lamartinière, Marie-Jeanne, 290
Lameth, Alexandre de, 229
Lamiral, Dominique, 129
Lancaster, Joseph, 19

Landes, Joan, 281, 293
Landschaft March, 306
Lanjuinais, Jean-Denis, 278
Lanthenas, François Xavier, 129
Lapointe, Jean-Baptiste, 628
Laqueur, Thomas, 298
Larose, Jean-Louis, 139
Latin America, monarchism, 32
Latvia, 517
Lauberg, Carlo, 269
Launay, Marquis de, 197
Launey, Bernard René Jourdan de, 62
Lausanne, 303, 318
Lavater, Johann Caspar, 311
Lavaysse, Dauxion, 678, 680
Laveaux, Étienne, 137, 139, 625–6, 630–3, 635
Law of Suspects (1793), 236, 283
Le Mans, 213, 222
Le Môle, 631
Leborgne de Boigne, Claude Pierre Joseph, 137, 139, 633
Lecarlier, Marie Jean François Philibert, 268
Lechi brothers, 464
Lechi, Teodoro, 463
Leclerc, Charles Victor Emmanuel, 290, 581–2, 584, 657–9, 708, 757–8
Leiden, 354, 361, 364
Leids Ontwerp (Leiden Draft, 1785), 311, 356, 541
LeJeune, Nicolas, 570, 611–13
Lemanic Republic, 303
Leoben preliminaries, 268, 546, 550
Léogane, 624
Leopold II, Holy Roman Emperor, 537
  and Hungary, 507–11, 513
  campaign to win back the Belgians, 394
  invasion of Belgium, 395
  measures to restore international relations and re-establishment of Habsburg authority, 478
  rule in Tuscany, 447, 478
  support for the Jansenists, 450
Les Cayes, 626, 628, 682
Les Cayes Plain, 624
  insurrection, 633
Les Vans, 223
Lescallier, Daniel, 130
Lesegesellschaft am See (reading society), 308
Lesser Antillies, Victor Hugues' Republic, 703–5
Leszczyński, Stanisław, 520

Lewis, Evan, 677
Liège, 386, 471
Liestal, 321
Ligurian charter, 551
Ligurian Republic, 268, 453, 454, 460, 546, 551–2, 554
Lima, 176
Limousin, 105
Locke, John, 86, 449
Lodi, 452
Lombardy, 268, 447, 448, 450, 453, 459, 461, 499, 544–5, 547
London, 453, 523, 590
  abolitionism. *See* Society for Effecting the Abolition of the Slave Trade
  World Anti-Slavery Conference (1840), 417
London Chronicle, The, 311
Longaunay, Mme. the Marquise de, 108
Louis Philippe Joseph, duc d'Orléans, 53, 65
  support for the Gallo-Amerian Society, 121
Louis XIV, king of France, 53–4, 58, 67–9
Louis XV, king of France, 55, 520
Louis XVI, king of France, 53, 62, 101, 128, 148–9, 181, 199, 385, 451, 577, 703
  attempt to regulate slavery in the colonies, 570, 574
  attempted reforms in Saint-Domingue, 612
  attempts to increase his popularity, 57
  deposition and imprisonment, 231
  flight to Varennes, 202, 230
  forced to accept the August decrees and the Declaration of the Rights of Man and Citizen, 201
  forced to settle in Paris, 11
  impotence, 292
  maintenance of the naval fleet in the Caribbean, 600
  rescue of the American Patriots and repression of the Geneva Revolution, 540
  response to the invasion of the Tuileries Palace, 204
  support from the enslaved rebels of Saint-Domingue, 32, 639
  trial, conviction and execution, 209, 232–3
Louis XVIII, king of France, 406
  plan to retake Haiti, 678
Louisiana, 180, 585, 627
Louisiana Purchase, 758
Louvain University, 382

Louverture, Isaac, 655
Louverture, Paul, 652
Louverture, Placide, 655
Louverture, Toussaint, 179, 564, 579–81, 607, 614, 617, 625, 635, 637, 661
  alliance with the French, 630–2, 633
  arrest and deportation, 708
  as an inspiration for African-Americans, 585, 748, 754
  ascent, 703–6
  attack on Cap Français, 633
  conflicted views of independence, 634–5, 654–6
  confrontation with the French and surrender, 581–2, 657–8
  constitution (1801), 9, 294, 581, 652–4
  dismissal of Sonthonax, 265
  forced recruitment of African laborers, 141, 403
  imposition of the cultivator system, 640
  opposition to a Jamaican slave revolt, 645–6
  power struggle, 1798–1800, 640–4
  relations with the United States, 754–7
  revival of the colonial economy and the cultivator system, 646–50
Lovejoy, Paul, 35
Lower Normandy, 108
Loyseau, Charles, 82
Lucca, 331, 454, 549
Lucchesini, Girolamo, 529
Lucioni, Branda da, 461
Lutherans, Lutheranism, 492, 494, 500–1, 504, 523
Luxembourg, 375, 382
Luzern, 268, 319, 322, 325
Lyon, 70, 210, 212, 221, 280, 557
  massacres, 217
  women's protests, 289

Macaya, 577
Machecoul, 209
Machiavelli, Niccolo, 449
Mackau, Baron de, 686
Mâconnais, 108
Madiou, Thomas, 678
Madison, James, 158, 161, 165, 552
Mainz, 470, 543
  siege of, 481–4
Mainz, University of, 476, 481
Makandal, François, Makandal conspiracy, 564, 594, 596–7, 601, 603, 607
Makaya, 658
Małachowski, Stanisław, 528, 532–3, 534

Malone, Caroll (William B. McBurneh), 347
Malouet, Pierre-Victor, 128, 628, 678
Mamluks, 266
Manchester, abolitionist movement, 399, 405
Manifeste, Le, 688
Mansfield, Lord, 419
Mantua, fortress of, 453
Maracaibo, 730
  conspiracy, 188, 585, 718, 736–7
  economy and trade, 722
  literacy and exchange of ideas, 724
Máramaros county, famine, 504
Marat Company, 213
Marat, Jean-Paul, 66, 202, 232, 253, 273, 280, 341
Marche, 460
Marck, comte de la, 394
Margarita, 725
Maria Carolina, queen of Naples, 452
Maria Christine, duchess of Teschen, 378, 381
Maria Theresa, Holy Roman Empress, 376, 447, 475, 496–8, 501, 510, 513
Marie Antoinette, queen of France, 451, 474, 481
  accuastions of sexual misconduct, 292
Markoff, John, 106
maroons
  Haiti, 669
  Jamaica, 188, 564, 707
  maritime, 726, 727
  Saint Vincent, 188
  Saint-Domingue, 39, 595–6, 626, 644, 658, 660, 662
    opposition to the cultivator system, 647–50
marriage
  compared with slavery, 288
  freedom through, 290
  revolutionary reform, 278–9, 293–5
Marseille, 70, 93, 210, 221, 280, 557
  Jacobin attack on, 217
Martinique, 136, 141, 167, 187, 570, 657, 699–700, 704, 720, 730
  aspirations of free people of color, 709–10
  British capture of, 604
  information from, 726
  role in the American Revolution, 40
Martinovics, Ignác, 511–12
Marx, Karl, 97
mass drownings (*noyades*), 213–14
Massa, 546

Massachusetts, 158
  charter of, 192
  religious legislation, 6
Masséna, André, 546, 555
Massif Central, 102, 103, 105
material culture, 12–13
Mauduit, Thomas-Antoine, 621
Maupeou coup, 55, 57
Maximilian Francis, elector of Cologne, 476
Maximilian IV, elector of Bavaria, 486
Mazzei, Philip (Filippo), 123, 127, 449, 536
Mazzini, Giuseppe, 444
McConville, Brenda, 144
McCracken, Henry Joy, 439
McTier, Samuel, 422
Mechelen, archbishop of, 383
Medina, Agostino Franco de, 678
Médor, enslaved servant, 598, 602–3, 613
Meekle, M., 122
Mejía, Luis, 735
Ménard, General Philippe-Romain, 303, 304, 318
Mendinueta, Pedro, 720
Mennonites, 358
Mentor, Étienne Victor, 137, 139
Mercier, Louis-Sébastien, 127
Méricourt, Théroigne de, 292–3
Merlin de Douai, Philippe-Antoine, 236, 313, 315, 316, 327, 546
mesmerism, 122
métissés (mixed-race), 690–2, 695–7
Metternich, Mathias, 476
Mexico, 48
  royalism, 33
  violence, 28
Mexico City, 16, 176
  seditious graffiti, 181
Mey, Claude, 80
Milan, 46–7, 268, 443, 448, 452–3, 463
  "What Form of Representative Government Is Best Suited to Bring Happiness to Italy" competition, 455
  Bonaparte's promise of independence, 544
  jailing of republicans, 557
  Society for Public Education, 458
  welcoming of Bonaparte, 455
  military revolution, 331
Miller Arnold affair, 473
Mills, Jean-Baptiste, 135, 629
Mirabeau, Honoré-Gabriel Riqueti, comte de, 87, 125, 127–9, 134, 335, 347, 426, 541, 571, 618
  Analyse des papiers anglais, 128

Miranda, Francisco de, 190
Miscent, Claude, 571
Mississippi, 627
Modena, 268, 447, 452, 545, 546
Moïse, 581, 654–6, 658
Môle Saint-Nicolas, 628, 637
Mompox, 724
Monitor, 522
Monod, Henri, 315
Monroe, James, 165, 543
Montagnard Convention, 185, 190–1
Montagnards, 69, 136, 209–10
Montauban, 201
Montesinos y Rico, Manuel, 185
Montesquieu, 79, 175, 348, 380, 449, 522, 533
Montgomery, Reverend Alexander, 435
Montmartin, 108
Mora, José María Luis, 35
Morales, Nicolás, 707
Moreau, Jacob-Nicolas, 80
Morelos, José María, 175
Moreno, Mariano, 190
Morley, Vincent, 439
Morris, Gouverneur, 3
Moser, Johann Jakob, 474
Mounier, Jean-Joseph, 174
Munich, 470
Murat, Joachim, 464–5
Murray, William, First Earl of Mansfield, 120
Muscadins, 263
Musgrave, Sir Richard, 439
Mussolini, Benito, 444

Namur, 379, 382
Nancy, repression of the 1792 riot, 204
Nantes, 213
Naples, Kingdom of, 268, 448–9, 455, 582
  adoption of the Spanish Constitution of 1812, 465
  and the War of the First Coalition, 451–2
  founding of royalist clubs, 461
  revolution of 1820, 465
  uprising (1797), 556
  war with France (1798), 454
Napoleon I, emperor of France. *See* Bonaparte, Napoleon
Napoleon III, emperor of France, 584
Napoleonic Code, 285
Napoleonic Wars, 480
Nariño, Antonio, 182, 183–4, 185, 724
natifs (Genevan inhabitants), 341–2, 344
National Institute of Sciences and Arts (Paris), 140

Nationale Vergadering, 352
Native Americans, dispossession, 49
Native Americans, patriarchal attitude to, 168
natural law, 43, 87, 184, 191, 307, 313, 316
Nau, Ignace, 688
Ndyuka, 564
Neapolitan (Parthenopean) Republic, 268–9, 443, 454, 464
  abolition of feudalism, 460
  constitution, 552
  counterrevolution, 270, 459, 461
  democracy, 559–60
  reprisals following the collapse of, 462, 557
Necker, Jacques, 60, 61–2, 197, 555
Neerwinden, Battle of, 233
négatifs, 344
negros franceses (French Blacks), 185, 186–9
Nehracher, Heinrich, 308
Neilson, Samuel, 422
Nelson, Horatio, 404, 407, 453, 461
Nemours, Pierre Samuel Dupont de, 79
Netherlands, 405
Neuchâtel, 345
Neufchâteau, François de, 259, 261
New Geneva, 346–7
New Geneva Barracks, 347
New Granada, 10, 32, 41, 177, 179, 191. *See also* Venezuela and New Granada, coastal regions
  independence, 189
New Spain, 4, 33, 176, 179, 180, 181
Nice, 221, 447, 451–2, 457, 460, 544
Nicolai, Friedrich, 477
Nidwald, 269, 556
Nîmes, 201, 557
Noailles, Adrienne de, 130
North, Lord, 346
Northern Star, The, 426
Novgorod, 331

Ó Longáin, Micheál Óg, 440
O'Connor, Charles, 439
O'Higgins, Bernardo, 175
Ochs, Peter, 304, 311, 319–20, 322, 326–7, 546–8, 560
October Days March, 201, 273, 291
Ogé, Vincent, 592, 606
  advocacy for the rights of free people of color, 131–4, 571, 612, 697
  conspiracy against the colonial government, 572, 621, 700–1, 743

execution, 572, 701, 747
petition to prevent road building through his plantation, 609
Oldenzaal, 369
Ootmarsum, 369
Orange, 214
Orange Order, 429
Orangists, 37, 350–2, 361–2, 366, 369–71, 373
Orthodox Church, 530–1
Ossé, Angélique, 598
Ottoman Empire. *See also* Austro-Turkish War; Russo-Turkish War
  diplomatic relations with France, 265, 549
  diplomatic relations with Poland–Lithuania, 522
  Hungary, 492, 495
Oulart Hill, Battle of, 430, 440
Outrepont, Charles Lambert d', 380–1
Overijssel, 354, 368–9

Paape, Gerrit, 22
Pagano, Mario, 456
Page, Pierre François, 135, 136, 625, 629
Paine, Thomas, 18, 24, 362, 425
  Agrarian Justice, 160
  Common Sense, 31
  The Rights of Man, 80, 356
Palatinate, 479
Palermo, 448, 452, 454
Pálffy, Károly, count, 505, 511, 512
Palmer, R. R., 446, 447, 516
  The Age of the Democratic Revolution, 396, 586
Panthéon Club, 253, 270
Paoli, Pasquale, 452, 542
Papacy, 444, 448, 546
Papillon, Jean-François, 569, 575, 579, 625, 701
Paraguay, 16
pardos, 188, 717–18, 733–7
Paris
  "Festival of Liberty," 204
  migration of refugees to, 627
  revolutionary violence, 197–8
  women's protests, 289
Paris Commune, 209, 210, 242, 284
  women barred from, 282
Parmentier, Antoine-Augustin, 261
patriarchalism, 165, 167–8
Patriota de Venezuela, El, 190
Pau, uprising, 197, 224
Paul I, tsar of Russia, 514

Paulus, Peter, Verhandeling over de vrage: In welken zin kunnen de menschen gezegd worden gelyk te zyn? (Treatise on the Question: In What Sense Can People Be Said to Be Alike?, 1793), 362
Pavia, 269, 556
Pays de Vaud, 303–4, 306, 311–19, 322
Peace of Basel (1795), 185, 484, 486, 543, 549, 632, 650, 652, 725
Peasants' War (1798), 221
Pedro I, emperor of Brazil, 584
Pedro II, emperor of Brazil, 584
Peep of Day Boys, 429
Pelham, Thomas, 434
Peltier, Jean-Gabriel, 677
Peninsular War, 28
Pennsylvania
  opposition to religious leniency, 6
  violence, 30
Pennsylvania Society for the Abolition of Slavery, 140
Pepe, Guglielmo, 464
Perkins, Samuel, 742
Perrinet Des Franches, Horace Bénédict, 342
Peru, 35, 37, 40, 41, 48
Peter III, emperor of Russia, 521
Peterloo Massacre, 410
Pétiniaud, Jean-François, 137
Pétion de Villeneuve, Jérôme, 127, 204
Pétion, Alexandre, 32, 45, 407, 585, 675, 678–84, 686, 706, 708
Petty, William, 346
Peynier, Louis-Antoine Thomassin, comte de, 618, 745
Pfalz-Zweibrücken, 479
Pfenninger, Johann Caspar, 308
Philadelphia, 628
  abolitionist society, 140
Philanthropic Institute, 256
Philip II, king of Spain, 377
Philip V, king of Spain, 178
Philippines, 484
Philips family of Trinidad, 711
Phillips, James, 120, 122, 124
physiocrats, 79, 83, 261
Piarist order, 519
Piattoli, Scipione, 532
Pichegru, Jean-Charles, 270
Picornell, Juan, 186, 734
Piedmont, 269, 447–54, 458, 459, 465, 540, 544, 549
Pigott, Robert, 120

781

Pimentel, Eleonora Fonseca, 457, 462
Pinchinat, Pierre, 623, 628, 633, 701
Pirela Conspiracy, 736
Pirela, Francisco, 736
Pisa, 331
Pistoia, bishop of, 450
Pitt, William, 346, 383, 424–5, 430, 435, 436
Pius VI, Pope, 453, 547
Plan of Iguala, 33
Platons, 622, 624, 625
Plumauzille, Clyde, 296
Po valley, 454
Podmaniczky family, 501
Polish–Lithuanian Commonwealth
  alliance with Prussia, 532
  citizenship, 518–19
  civil and political freedom, 517–18
  Constitution of 3 May, 9, 532–7, 538, 542
  economic, social, and cultural changes, 526–7
  Kościuszko uprising, 514, 538–9
  liberum veto, 519–23, 534
  paralysis and remedies, 519–20
  parliamentary revolution, 527–37
  partitions, 518, 524, 543
  Russian intervention and reforms, 520–7
  Russian invasion, 537
  structure, 517
Politieke Blixem, De, 363
Politieke Kruyer, De, 361
Polverel, Étienne, 135–6, 577–8, 624, 626, 629–30, 631, 701, 748
Pompons blancs party, 618, 619, 621, 622
Pompons rouges party, 618–19, 622, 630
Poniatowski, Michał, 526
Poniatowski, Stanisław August. *See* Stanisław II August, king of Poland
Popiel, Jennifer, 275
Port of Spain, 187, 730
Port-au-Prince, 569, 576, 621, 630, 631, 663, 678, 680, 681
  as political and economic center, 666
  attack on Dessalines, 674
  battle between radical whites and *métissés*, 701
  Boyer's government, 684
  British capture of, 628, 706
  Christophe's attack on, 675
  Conseils supérieur, 600, 605–6, 611, 612
  European garrisons, 600
  fire in, 688
  free Black community, 617
  Pétion accepts presidency, 675
  protests by free men of color over oath of submission to the whites, 572
  Sonthonax and Polverel's flight from, 630
  Sonthonax's attack on, 626
Port-de-Paix, 628
Portobelo, 722
Port-of-Spain, 726
Portugal, 405, 465, 559
  Napoleon's invasion of, 172
  women's rights, 23
Post van den Neder-Rhijn, De, 361
Potemkin, Grigorii, 525, 530, 532
Potocki, Feliks, 537
Potocki, Ignacy, 532, 534, 538
Prairial uprising (1795), 157–8
Presbyterians, Irish, 430, 438, 439, 441, 442
Pressburg, 501, 510
Prévost, Julien, 676–7
Price, Richard, 354–5
Priestley, Joseph, 354
Pro Aris et Focis (Belgian secret committee), 384–8, 389, 392, 394
Pro Patria, 394
Prónay family, 501
Prónay, László, 504
prostitution, decriminalization of, 273, 296
Protestant Ascendancy, 441
Protestants, Protestantism
  enlistment to the British military, 437
  Geneva, 329
  Irish, 6, 423–4, 426, 429–31, 434, 438, 439
  pathways to power offered during the French Revolution, 201
  reforms of Joseph II, 500–1
  religious intolerance, 6–7
Provence, 108
Prussia, 54, 69, 345, 452, 471, 484, 522
  and Poland–Lithuania, 524, 528–39
  entry into the War of the First Coalition, 481
  relations with Austria, 477–9
  religious reforms, 477
  signing of the Peace of Basel, 484, 486
public opinion, 11–15
Puerto Cabello, 722, 724, 730
Puerto Rico, 179, 627, 706, 712
Pufendorf, Samuel von, 467
Pułaski, Kazimierz, 515–16, 523

Quakers, 118, 120, 124, 126, 418
Quesnay, François, 176
Quiberon, 219
Quito, 183

Ragan, Bryant, 296
Ragusa, 331
Raimond, Julien, 131–6, 139–40, 568, 571, 609, 612, 616, 623, 691, 696, 697–8
Raymond, Pierre, 598
Raynal, abbé Guillaume Thomas François, 48, 175, 579
  Histoire des deux Indes, 123
Réchin, 135
Rédacteur, Le, 256
Régent, Frédéric, 699
Reggio, 268, 447, 452, 545
Règlement (domestic peace treaty of 1738), 343
Reichsdeputationshauptschluß (1803), 486
Reichstag, 467, 471
Religion Edict (Prussia, 1788), 477
religious riots, women's participation, 287
religious tolerance, 6–9
Remonstrants, 358
Rennes, uprising, 197, 224
Repnin, Nikolai, 523
"Réponse de la Convention nationale aux manifestes des tyrans ligués contre la republique, proposé par Robespierre au nom du comité de salut public, et décrété par la Convention dans la séance du 15 frimaire (an II, 5 décembre 1793)," 725
représentants movement, 338–41
  aftermath of the revolution, 345–6
  and the Genevan Revolution of 1782, 341–5
Republic of Letters, 265
Républicain, Le (later *L'Union*), 687
Republican Monitor, 457
republicanism, 151, 170, 206
  Boyer's committment to in Haiti, 684
  Dutch Republic, 367
  Geneva, 331, 333–4, 340
  Irish, 433, 439
  Italy, 449, 455
  Pétion's committment to the spread of in Haiti, 682
  Polish, 533
  Swiss, 307–8, 311
Republikein, De, 363
Reubell, Jean-François, 267, 314, 546
Réveillon riot, 181, 197
Révellière-Lépeaux, Louis Marie, 259, 317
Revolutionary Tribunal (Paris), 209, 214–15, 234, 242–3, 284, 556

Reynaud de Villeverd, François, 609
Rhenish-German National Convention, 482
Rhineland, 452, 480–5, 541, 549
Richepanse, Antoine, 708
Richeprey, Henri de, 130
Richmond, duke of, 423
Rigaud, André, 568, 580–1, 626, 628, 630, 633, 640, 646, 647, 674, 701, 708
  feud with Louverture, 643–4, 650, 651, 706, 756
  promoted to rank of major general, 632
rights, 4–9
Río de la Plata, 191
  independence, 189
Riohacha, 722, 728
Risorgimento, 444
Robespierre, Maximilien, 48, 69, 136, 181, 205, 225, 237, 247, 257, 282, 285, 286, 482, 548
  alliance with the *sans-culottes*, 210
  antimonarchical pamphlet of, 185
  argument for the admission of women to royal academies, 275
  condemned in *El Patriota de Venezuela*, 190
  defense of terror, 210
  leadership of the Jacobin Club, 202
  membership of the Committee of Public Safety, 236
  narratives of his "Reign of Terror," 244–6
  offensive against Brissot and the Girondins, 136
  overthrow and execution, 71, 157, 215
  turning points on the path to terror, 230–3, 239–41
Robespierrists, 216, 238, 254
Rochambeau, Donatien de, 614, 659–61
Rochefoucauld-Liancourt, François Alexandre Frédéric, duc de la, 123, 127
Rodríguez O., Jaime, 173
Roget, Jean, 343
Rohan Montbazon, duc de, 605–6
Roland de la Platière, Jean-Marie, 344, 348
Roland de la Platière, Madame, 277, 345
Romagna, 460
Rome, 268–9, 337, 448, 449, 453, 455, 460–1, 475, 530, 544, 545
  civil code, 559
  constitution, 547, 551
  Protestantism, 329
  tribunal de forfaiture, 554
  uprising (1797), 269, 547, 556

Romilly, Samuel, 343
Romme, Gilbert, 273
Ronán, Patricio, 734
Roume, Philippe, 643–4, 645, 647, 651, 653–5, 725
Rousseau, Jean-Jacques, 48, 56, 86, 175, 195, 334, 346, 357, 380
  admiration for Polish republicanism, 523, 533
  and Geneva, 329, 335–8
  and the Genevan *représentants*, 338–40
  cited by Vonck, 385
  concept of the "general will," 226
  Contrat social, 339
  critique of Christianity, 191
  Émile, 275, 339
  Lettres écrites de la montagne, 340
  model of gender roles, 274–6
  on economic inequality, 24
  on sovereignty, 17
Roussy-Trioson, Anne-Louis Girodet de, 579
royalism, 31–6
Ruffo, Cardinal Fabrizio, 270, 459, 461
Rush, Benjamin, 118
Rusiñol, José, 734
Russell, Thomas, 422–3
Russell, Thomas, *A Letter to the People of Ireland*, 49
Russia, 97, 549. *See also* Russo-Turkish War
  German population, 471
  intervention in Poland–Lithuania, 518, 520–5, 537
  insurrection against, 514–15, 538–9
Russian Orthodoxy, 530
Russo, Vincenzio, 18
Russo-Turkish War, 478, 523, 527, 529
  Polish–Lithuanian opposition to, 527
  Treaty of Iași, 537

Saavedra, Cornelio, 190
Saegermans, Jean Joseph, 382, 386
Saint Lucia, 187, 695, 720
  Hugues' invasion of, 645
  slave uprising, 704
Saint Marc, Henriette, 289
Saint Thomas, 721
Saint Vincent, 188, 645, 704
Saint-Domingue, 76, 134–7, 179, 403–4, 422, 588, 730
  British campaign against, 402
  casualties, 557
  Catholic exclusivity, 7
  conflict between the *petits blancs* and the *grand blancs*, 743
  cultivator system, 638, 640, 646–50
  culture of white superiority, 598–9
  development of economic, social, and intellectual ties with the United States, 741–3
  drought, famine, and disease, 606–8
  economics of slavery, 590–1
  enslaved population, 612
  experience of slavery in, 566–7, 594–8
    marronage, 595–6
    mechanisms for freedom, 597
    religion and spirituality, 596–7
    repression, 594–5
    self-liberation, 568, 573
    survival, creativity, and resistance, 568–70
  female protests, 22
  flow of information to the coastal regions of Venezuela and New Granada, 723
  free people of color and politics, 695–7
  French colonial order, 566–8
  French violence in, 31
  impact of Atlantic wars, 599–601
  impact of the American War of Independence, 606–10, 616
  impact of the Seven Years' War
    creation of a food crisis, 601–4
    French reforms following, 604–6
    threat of British invasion, 604
  issues concerning the link between representation and taxation, 618–20
  migration from, 626–8
  militia and constabulary, 595
  mulattoes' revolt, 701
  plantation economy
    coffee, 591–2
    cotton, 592
    laws addressing problems in, 610–11
    sugar, 589–91
  prerevolutionary tensions, 610–13
  role in the American Revolution, 41, 743–8
  royalism, 32
  rule of Toussaint Louverture, 703–6
  slave rebellion, 573–6, 622, 701–2
  social groups, 593–4
  translation of the policies of abolition and citizenship and their influence in the United States, 748–57
Saint-Just, Louis-Antoine, 232, 236, 239, 548

Saint-Marc Assembly, 619, 621, 628, 639, 652, 700
Saint-Pierre, 699
Salerno, 461
Saliceti, Christophe, 458
Sallust, 519
Salò, 546
Salvador, 45
Samaná Bay, 187
San Marino, 331
San Martín, José de, 33, 175
Sanfedists, 270, 459, 461, 462
sans-culottes, 25, 69–71, 181, 204, 209–10, 213–14, 216, 218, 231–2, 234–5, 236, 281, 621
Sans-Souci palace, 676
Sans-Souci, Jean Baptiste, 649, 658
Santa Marta, 722, 729
Santo Domingo, 134, 566, 729
  anthrax epidemic, 607–8
  attempted rebellion in Samaná Bay, 187
  Boyer's invasion and reunification, 684–5
  Dessalines' campaigns against, 668
  extradition treaty with Saint-Domingue, 564, 569
  maroon population, 595, 650
  overtaken by Louverture, 179, 650–2
  trade with Saint-Domingue, 567, 602
Sapieha, Kazimierz, 528
Sardinia, 447, 452, 454
Sarthe, Moreau de la, 298
Sasportas, Isaac, 645, 657
Saunders, Prince, 677
Savannah, 608, 627
Savannah, Battle of, 570, 695
Savenay, 213
Savoy, 41, 329, 333, 336, 447, 451–2, 460, 544
Savoy, dukes of, 447
Saxe-Weimar, 477
Saxony, 47, 480, 520
Say, Jean-Baptiste, 138
Schaffhausen, 322
Schiller, Friedrich, 474
Schimmelpenninck, Rutger Jan, 354, 357
Schneider, Winter, 687
Schubart, Friedrich Daniel, 474
Schwyz, 269, 306
  Landsgemeinde, 322–5
Scott, Joan, 274
Scott, Julius S., 754
  The Common Wind: Afro-American Currents in the Age of the Haitian Revolution, 723

Secrétan, Philippe, 387
seigneurialism
  Dutch Republic, 367–8
  France, 58–9, 61, 64, 79–85, 104–7, 116–17
Selim III, sultan, 265
Sepinwall, Alyssa, 275
September Massacres, 207, 231, 234, 555
Sérurier, Jean-Mathieu-Philibert, 549
Sète, 224, 253
Seven Years' War, 54, 436, 441, 476, 481, 497, 520, 599, 693
  impact on Saint-Domingue, 600, 601–6
Sewell, William, 276
sexuality, during the French Revolutionary period, 272
  changes effected by military service, 297–8
  changes in the expressions of, 297
  decriminalization of sodomy and prostitution, 295–6
  marriage reforms, 293–5
  medical notions of "natural" differences between men and women, 298–9
  sexual scandal and political struggles, 292–3
Shapiro, Gilbert, 106
Sharp, Granville, 118, 124
Sheller, Mimi, 290
Short, William, 127
Sicily, 448, 451, 454
Sienna, 331
Sierra Leone, 129
Sieyès, Emmanuel Joseph (abbé), 17, 60, 62, 84, 127, 270, 393
Silesia, 496
Simonneau, Jacques Guillaume, 203
Sint-Niklaas, 388
Sister Republics, 46, 180, 247, 268–70, 541–4
  civil war and terror, 555–8
  improvements and benefits, 268–70, 550–5
  Italian, 544–50
  political, economic, and social consequences, 550
Slave Trade Act (British, 1807), 404
Smart, Annie, 275
Smith, Adam, 177, 347
  Lectures on Jurisprudence, 332
social contract theory, 316
Société des Amis de Couleur (Society of Friends of Color), 697
Société des Amis des Noirs. *See* Society of the Friends of the Blacks

Société Patriotique, 392–4
Society for Effecting the Abolition of the Slave Trade, 124, 399, 400, 403, 406
Society for Promoting the Manumission of Slaves, 126
Society for Relief of Free Negroes Unlawfully Held in Bondage, 118
Society of American Colonists, 132, 571
Society of Liberty and Equality (Hungary), 511
Society of Literature and Games, 253
Society of Reformers (Hungary), 511
Society of Revolutionary Republican Women, 281–2
Society of the Friends of the Blacks (Société des Amis des Noirs), 44, 118–21, 125–38, 399, 402, 570–1, 616, 618, 623, 698, 745
  advocacy for free people of color, 130–6
  challenges to the activities of, 127–8
  constitution, 126
  end of, 136–8
  experiments in gradual emancipation, 130
  journal, 128
  membership, 126–7
  plans for free colonies in Africa, 129–30
  successful campaigns, 128
Society of the Friends of the Blacks and the Colonies, 44, 120, 138
  goals, 138
  membership, 138–40
Society of United Irishmen, 347, 422, 423, 426–8, 430, 432, 433, 439–41
Socinians, 336
Sokoto, 408
Solitude (Guadeloupe), 290
Solothurn, 268, 319
Somerset v. Stewart case, 120
Sonthonax, Léger-Félicité, 135–7, 631, 705, 748
  and the cultivator system, 647
  and the Society of the Friends of the Blacks and the Colonies, 139–40
  appointed to the civilian commission to Saint-Domingue, 624
  attack on Port-au-Prince, 626
  declaration of emancipation in Saint-Domingue, 578, 579, 703
  dismissed by Louverture, 265, 580, 634, 641
  elected to the legislature of the Directory, 635
  imposition of the rights of free people of color, 701–2

  initial successes in Saint-Domingue, 577
  marriage to a mixed-race woman, 643
  opinion of Moïse, 654
  organization of the first multiracial elections, 578
  replaced by Hédouville, 640
  return to Saint-Domingue, 633
  role in the Haitian Revolution and arrest, 629–30
Sorgdrager. Cornelis, 372
Soufflot, Jacques-Germain, 267
Soult, General, 555
South America, 29
South Carolina, 745
sovereignty, 81, 82–3, 85, 91
  and the Polish revolution, 529
  Belgian, 376, 379, 385, 391–2
  royal claim to, 79
sovereignty, popular, 10–11, 17, 117, 172, 210, 217, 229–30, 564
  Belgian, 393, 394
  Dutch Republic, 355, 356, 363
  France, 206–7
  Franco-American analogues, 143–4
  c. 1791–1794, 144–50
  c. 1792–1795, 150–6
  c. 1794–1800, 156–64
  c. 1799–1820s, 164–71
  Geneva, 330, 332
  link with popular justice, 224
  Swiss debates on, 307
  women's embodiment of, 285
Spain, 405, 465, 559, 577–8
  entry into the War of the First Coalition, 577
  Napoleon's invasion of, 172
  occupation of Saint-Domingue, 579
  peace treaty with France, 452
  role in American Revolution, 41
Spanish America, 26, 27, 41–3
  British involvment in the revolutionary wars, 408
  fear of the underground activities of the *negros franceses* (French Blacks), 186–9
  palimpsests of the French and Haitian Revolutions in, 189
  revolutionary influences on, 175–80
  Rights of Man in, 183–4
  sovereignty, 10
  suppression of seditious texts, 185–6
Spanish Inquisition, 36
Sparta, 337

Index

St. Baaf's Cathedral, Ghent, 378
St. Eustatius, 41
St. Gallen, 322
St. Gudule Cathedral, Brussels, 390
St. Mark, Republic of, 447, 453
St. Petersburg, 453, 537
Stackelberg, Otto von, 524, 525, 529
Staël, Madame de, 193
Stäfa, 306, 321–2, 323
Stäfa *Memorial*, 307–11
Stanhope, Earl, 402
Stanisław II August, king of Poland, 515, 521–8, 531–4, 536, 537, 539
Starke, Mariana, 457, 460–1
States-Brabant, 367, 370, 371
Steffens, Henrik, 4
Steinberg, Ronen, 286
Stieber, Chelsea, 671
Stoddard, Lothrop, 586
Stofflet, 220
Stuttgart, state library of Württemberg, 474
Suchorzewski, Jan, 531
sugar production, 589–91
Sunda Islands, 484
Suriname, 564, 577
Sutherland, Robert, 680
Suvorov, General Aleksandr, 539
Swabia, 471
Sweden, 343, 405, 478, 529, 531
Swiss cantons, 268, 269, 303–4, 307, 319–26, 331, 336
Swiss Confederation (*Eidgenossenschaft*), 303–6, 311–12, 316–17, 319–22, 326
Swiss Directory, 320
Swiss *Freiheit* (inherited freedom), 308–10
Swiss liberty, 306–7, 311–16, 319, 320–1
Switzerland, 264, 268, 331, 540, 541, 543, 547–50, 557, 560. *See also* Geneva; Helvetic Republic
  Bonaparte's plan to build a road through the Valais, 546
  civil unrest, 555–6
  human rights, 6
  religious tolerance, 8
  uprisings, 554
Sylla, 658
Széchényi, Ferenc, 504, 513

't Kint, Jacques Dominique, 384
Tacky's War (1760), 564
Talamante, Laura, 280
Talleyrand, 557
Tallien, Madame de, 285
Tammany Society, 163
Tarascon, 557
Teeling, Bartholomew, 435
Teleki, Sámuel, 504
Telemaque (Denmark Vesey), enslaved youth, 569, 585
Tellgau, 326
Tennis Court Oath, 509
Terra Ferma, 545
Terror. *See* French Revolutionary terror
theophilanthropy, 257
Thermidorian Reaction, 71, 240
Thermidorians, Thermidorian Convention, 71, 210, 215, 218, 240, 247, 287
Thibaud, Clément, 10
Thibaudeau, Antoine-Claire, 238
Third Estate, 62, 128, 198, 392–3, 618
Thomany, Pierre, 137, 139
Thornton, John, 35
Thurgau, 322
Times, The, 418
Tobago, 187
Tocqueville, Alexis de, 271, 415
Toggenburg, 322
Tone, Theobald Wolfe, 422–3, 424, 428, 436–7, 438
  An Argument on Behalf of the Catholics of Ireland, 424
Tonnelier, Jacques, 137, 139
Torfs, J. J., 384
Toulon, 206, 210, 213, 217, 221, 223, 253, 452
Toulouse, 222, 253, 264
Tours, 93
Trafalgar, Battle of, 404, 407
Transylvania, 492, 496, 498, 499–500, 504, 509
  Chancellery, 501
  Emancipation Edict (1785), 503
  German population, 471
Treaty of Amiens (1802), 180
Treaty of Amity and Commerce (1778), 741
Treaty of Basel (1795). *See* Peace of Basel
Treaty of Campo Formio (1797), 265, 268, 269, 453, 458, 485, 549
Treaty of Iași (1792), 537
Treaty of Lausanne (1564), 313
Treaty of Lunéville (1792), 480
Treaty of Sistova (1791), 478
Treaty of the Hague (1795), 267, 542
Trelawny, 707
Tréville, Latouche, 451
Trinidad, 705, 728, 730
  campaign for civil rights, 711

Trinidad (cont.)
  clashes between royalists and republicans, 187
  settlement of free people of color, 702
  settlement of French migrants, 179
  spread of revolutionary ideas, 713, 724, 725, 733, 735
  threat of the close relationship with Venezuela, 720
Tronchin, Jean-Robert, *Lettres écrites de la campagne*, 340, 341
Trouillot, Michel-Rolph, 649
Tuileries Palace, attacks and massacre, 204–6
Tunja, 183
Túpac Amaru's revolt, 35
Turgot, Anne-Robert-Joseph, 57, 86, 176
Turin, 448, 452
Turnhout, Battle of, 388
Turreau, General, 214
Tuscan Penal Code, 450
Tuscany, 346, 447–8, 450, 453, 454, 459, 461, 478, 549
  counterrevolution, 269–70

US Electoral College, 584
Ukraine, 517, 530
Ulster, 427–9, 441
Union of Brest (1596), 530
Union of Utrecht (1579), 355, 357
United Provinces, 269, 270, 331, 540–1, 542
United States
  abolition of slavery, 683
  abolitionism, 399, 414
  Bills of Rights, 540
  conflict with Britain over antislavery measures, 416
  Constitution, 25, 449, 553, 584
  debates on the recognition of Haiti, 585
  Declaration of Independence, 42, 540
  development of economic, social, and intellectual ties with Saint-Domingue, 741–3
  end of the alliance with France, 265
  German migration to, 471
  impact of the Haitian Revolution, 563–4, 739–41, 743–8
  on policies of abolition and citizenship, 748–57
  impact of the Haitian War of Independence, 757–60
  migration to following Haitian Revolution, 627

popular sovereignty. *See* sovereignty, popular: Franco-American analogues
  relations with France and the abolitionist movement, 121–5, 140–1, 164–71
  trade with Haiti, 686
United States of Belgium, 375, 391, 507
universal male suffrage, 32, 206
Unterwalden, 325
Urbarium (1767), 497, 511, 513
Uri, 325
Ürményi, József, 504
Ursel, duc d', 393–4
Ursel, duchesse d', 387
Ussher, Thomas, 667
Utrecht, 354

Valais, 269, 319
Valmy, Battle of, 425, 481
Valteline Republic, 546
Van der Mersch, Jean-André, 376, 385, 387–9, 394
Van der Noot, Henri, 375, 379, 381–4, 386–9, 391, 392–4
Van Eupen, Pierre, 375, 391, 392, 395
Van Eyck, Jan, Adam and Eve triptych, 378
Van Schaack, Peter, 28
Vastey, baron de, 565, 676–7, 683
Vatry, Marc-Antoine Bourdon, 141
Vaublanc, Vincent de, 634
Vaud, 268
Vay, baron Miklós, 490, 501, 505
Vay, József, 509
Vendée, civil war in, 36, 38, 47, 70, 77, 264, *See also* chouans, chouannerie
  casualties, 214, 242, 557
  mass conscription as a cause of, 233
  suppression of, 220
  violence, 28, 31, 213–14, 431
Venetia, 546
Veneto, 458
Venezuela, 191, 585, 627. *See also* Venezuela and New Granada, coastal regions
  Gual and España conspiracy, 8, 185–6
  independence, 189
  influence of the French Revolution, 175, 179–80, 190
  proposal to move seat of Congress away from Caracas, 11
Venezuela and New Granada, coastal regions, 737–8
  black and *pardo* movements, 731–7

circulation of revolutionary information
  communication between locals and foreigners, 726–31
  written texts, 723–6
communication networks, 723–31
demographic and socioracial structures, 722–3
economy and trade, 721–2
effect of the arrival of republican prisoners, 182–3
influence of the Haitian Revolution, 715–19
Venice, 268, 269, 331, 344, 449, 453, 456, 546, 556
Venturi, Franco, 446, 516
Vergennes, Charles Gravier, comte de, 341, 342–3
Vergniaud, Guillaume-Henri, 137
Verjus, Anne, 273
Verlooy, Jan Baptist, 384, 386, 395
Verona, 269, 452, 556, 557
  "Easter Revolt", 460
Verri, Pietro, 450, 456
Versailles, 521
  meeting of the Estates-General, 61
  revolutionary violence, 207
  women's march to, 201, 273, 291
Vienna, 375, 453, 470, 472, 475, 484, 486, 497, 521, 538
  arrival of Leopold II, 507
  Hungarian crown placed in the Imperial Treasury, 502
  Hungarian Royal Chancellery, 495
  Joseph II's threat to centralize Belgian judicial institutions in, 379
  military and civilian education, 498
Vienna Settlement, 466
Viénot-Vaublanc, 634
Villatte, Jean-Louis, 630, 632, 633
Villaviciosa, Francisco, 735
Villoteau, Guillaume André, 266
Vilmorin, Philippe-Victoire Lévêque de, 261
Vinegar Hill, Battle of, 430
violence, 27–31, 555–8
  French Revolution, 195–7, 246
    1788–1792, 197–204
    1792–1795, 204–18
    1795–1802, 218–24
  Haitian Revolution, 619–22
  Haitian War of Independence, 582
  Irish Rebellion, 430–2
  Italian counterrevolutionary, 459, 462
Virginia Declaration of Rights, 6

Virginia, religious tolerance, 6
Viva Maria! movement, 270, 459, 461, 552, 556
Vodou, 289, 570, 574, 575, 649, 667, 670, 687
Volney, comte de, 193
Voltaire, 48, 340, 380, 423
Volunbrun, widow, 752–3
von Haller, Karl Ludwig, 316
Vonck, Jan, 384, 385–6, 392, 394–5
Vreede, Pieter, 361
Vries, Simon de, 354

Wadström, Charles-Bernard, 141
Walckiers, Edouard, 393
War of the Austrian Succession, 54
War of the First Coalition, 452, 577
War of the Polish Succession, 54
War of the Second Coalition, 221, 270
Ward, Bernardo, 177
Warsaw, 46, 521, 526, 528–9, 536, 537, 538–9
Washington, George, 49, 130, 146, 148–9, 157–9, 161, 166, 582, 584
Waterford, 346
Waterloo, Battle of, 409
Weemaels, J. B., 384, 386
Wettins, 470
Wetzlar, 472
Wexford, 347, 430–1, 440
What Is the Third Estate? (pamphlet), 60
Whiskey Rebellion, 157, 159
White Terror, 251
Whitelock, John, 628
Whyte, General Richard, 426
Wilberforce, William, 124, 401, 403, 406
William I, king of Orange, 354
William IV, king of Great Britain and Ireland, 415
William IV, prince of Orange-Nassau and stadtholder of the Dutch Republic, 350
William V, prince of Orange-Nassau and stadtholder of the Dutch Republic, 350–1
Williams, Helen Maria, 138
Willot, Amédée, 270
Wittelsbachs, 470
Wollstonecraft, Mary, 22
women, 21–3
  citizenship during the French Revolution, 272, 291
  activity following Thermidor, 285–6
  arguments for suffrage, 273
  closure of political clubs, 281–2
  counterrevolution, 286–8

women (cont.)
    economic controls, 282
    expulsion from the military, 278–9
    involvement in the Terror, 282–5
    legal autonomy, 274, 276–7
    political activity, 273, 276–81
    political exclusion, 273–4
    religious activism, 287
    Rousseau's model of gender roles, 274–6
    citizenship in the Caribbean, 288–91
    experience of the Haitian Revolution, 576
    in the British abolitionist movement, 401, 411
    involvement in the campaign to terminate apprenticeships, 415
    march to Versailles, 201, 273, 291
    medical opinions on the anatomy of, 298–9
    role in the Brabant Revolution, 388

women's rights, 5, 22–3, 273–4, 282, 283, 288
Wordsworth, William, 585, 754
Württemberg, 474, 484

Ya'qûb, 266
Yorktown, Battle of, 742
Yturén, Manuel, 735
Yves, Comtesse Anne Thérèse Philippine d', 386, 393

Zeeland, 370
Zejudo, Don Anastasio, 735
Ziegenhagen, Heinrich, 26
Zug, 325
Zurich, 14, 268, 307–11, 321, 322, 330, 333, 342
Zwolle, 354, 368